For a Kate Bush fan there was nothing more satisfying, other than perhaps Kate herself dropping around for a quick cup of tea, than the arrival of a much awaited issue of HomeGround*... Never giving in to celebrity gossip,* HomeGround *has always been like 'arriving' home. A home for news, information, analysis and discovery. A place to indulge in the wondrous world of Kate and her beautiful music.*

Guy Pearce

The first issue of *HomeGround* appeared in 1982, four years after Kate's dramatic début with 'Wuthering Heights'. Starting with an ancient manual typewriter, and a pot of genuine paste, the editors mounted articles on recycled backing sheets and added hand-drawn 'artwork' to fill the gaps. The first issue was photocopied, the pages hand-stapled together and twenty-five copies were given away to fans they knew. Only later did they discover the magic of word processing, and desktop publishing.

From those beginnings *HomeGround* became a cornerstone of the 'Kate-speaking world', the editors going on to organise four official fan events at which Kate Bush and members of her family and band appeared, arrange at Kate's request a team of fans to be extras in two of her videos and organise informal fan gatherings at Glastonbury and Top Withens, the storm-blown ruin on Haworth Moor. Years before the internet, *HomeGround* became a place where fans could discuss Kate's music, and a place where they could publish creative writing and artwork that music inspired.

This anthology includes material inspired by all periods of Kate's musical progression. It is not a definitive authorised book about Kate Bush, her life and music. It is a book about the reaction to her work and how her unique music has touched the lives of so many people.

Katebushnews.com – the website of *HomeGround,* the international Kate Bush magazine.

I0585744

HomeGround
THE KATE BUSH ANTHOLOGY

VOLUME ONE
Wuthering Heights to Sensual World

About *HomeGround* • The Readers, the Editors, the Magazine • Before *Wuthering Heights* • *Wuthering Heights* • *The Kick Inside* • *Wow* and the *Tour of Life* • On Stage and at the Albert Hall • *Never For Ever* • *The Dreaming* • *Hounds of Love* and the 1985 Convention • *The Big Sky* and Comic Relief • *The Whole Story* and the Video Party • *The Sensual World*, the 1990 Convention, and *This Woman's Work*

VOLUME TWO
The Red Shoes to 50 Words For Snow

The Nineties, Noughties, and Beyond • *The Red Shoes* and the 1994 Convention • *Aerial* • *Director's Cut* and *50 Words for Snow* • Afterwords

HomeGround

The Kate Bush Magazine

ANTHOLOGY TWO • *The Red Shoes to 50 Words For Snow*

Edited by Krystyna FitzGerald-Morris,
Peter FitzGerald-Morris & Dave Cross

CRESCENT MOON

CRESCENT MOON PUBLISHING
P.O. Box 1312, Maidstone
Kent, ME14 5XU
Great Britain, www.crmoon.com

Printed and bound in the U.S.A.
Set in Baskerville, Gill Sans and Hafnium.

British Library Cataloguing in Publication data available for this title.

ISBN-13 9781861714817 (Pbk)
ISBN-13 9781861714824 (Hbk)

ACKNOWLEDGEMENT

Thank you to Kelly Hosford for her help with this book.
And to Krystyna FitzGerald-Morris and Peter FitzGerald-Morris
for their collaboration.

Contents

Volume 1

Volume 2

Introduction

by the HomeGround Editors

This is a book about the reaction of Kate's fans to her work, from those who felt the urge to chronicle her career, to those who were inspired by it to be creative themselves. We need to make it clear what this book is not: it is *not* a definitive book about Kate Bush her life and music. As yet there is no such thing and no prospect of any such thing.

It is principally an anthology of what appeared in 30 years of issues of *HomeGround* "The International Kate Bush Fanzine" as we grandly called our magazine. The first *HomeGround* issue appeared in 1982, four years after Kate's dramatic début with *Wuthering Heights*. The question for us in structuring this anthology was whether we followed a *HomeGround* chronology or something rather more logical. So we followed a Kate chronology, dividing the material from the magazine into three parts covering the first thirty-five years of Kate's career.

Though *HomeGround* was not around in the very early years, we wrote up *The Kick Inside*, *Lionheart*, the Tour of Life and *Never For Ever*, in later issues. All of that material is pulled together in the first part of the book, 'Before HomeGround'.

The second part of the book 'The Eighties' covers a high point of Kate's public career from *The Dreaming*, through *Hounds of Love*, to *The Whole Story* and *The Sensual World*.

The third part of the book 'The Nineties, Noughties and Beyond' covers Kate's removal of her symbolic *Red Shoes* and the end of her illusory career as a public rock star, though not of course of her real career as a creator of beautiful songs and music, as the hugely successful 2005 album *Aerial* indicated. It brings the story up to date with the material from issue 79 about *Director's Cut* and *50 Words For Snow*.

Whilst sifting the articles for this book we noted with some surprise the now professional artists, musicians, singers and performers we first knew as fellow Kate fans. Also the now doctors, and academics we first met at Kate conventions, and the now parents and grandparents we first met up on Haworth Moor or on Glastonbury Tor. We thought it would be a good idea to invite some of our long term readers to write down what being a Kate fan and *HomeGround* had meant to them over the years, and their recollections appear with ours in the "About HomeGround" section which follows this introduction.

We have included the work of many graphic artists who contributed to the magazine. What has surprised us in the making of this book was actually how much good artwork we had. Two of our principal contributors Steven Brown and Paulina Stuckey, who made their first contributions to *HomeGround* over twenty years ago, have gone on to become professional artists and illustrators, their work used in numerous books and magazines. We thank them for their permission to use their work in this book.

In putting this project together we organised for the first time many hundreds of photographs taken by the *HomeGround* team and sent in by readers. We had used some of these in the magazine, and have now taken the opportunity to use many others. We should mention and thank three photographic contributors, our good friends Rob Assenberg, Jules R. Angel and Paul Camilleri, who had the gift of being on the spot when Kate appeared and who gave us open permission to use as much of their work as we wanted.

Was there a *HomeGround* "editorial policy"? We struggled over more political articles in early issues. One particular aspect we found difficult was expressed in two articles 'Gurus and Glass Onions'. Although we loved Kate and her work, we always thought a sense of proportion was good for fans and for Kate. Less the revelations of the Grail than postcards from the front.

Dave, Krys and Peter
HomeGround Towers, Spring, 2014

Some Moments...

...... A Kate Bush time line and discography 1958-2013

Peter, who wrote this time line used some of the material he wrote for the chronology in *Kate Bush Complete* (EMI Music Publishing 1987)

1958 July: Kate is born in Bexleyheath.

1970 Kate's brother Paddy needs someone on piano to accompany his violin playing. Kate's father Dr. Bush shows her the C major chord and she begins to play.

1971 Kate begins to set her poems to her own chord formations. Embryonic versions of songs such as *The Man with the Child in his Eyes* and *Saxophone Song* begin to emerge.

1972 A family friend, Ricky Hopper, tries to place Kate's earliest demo recordings with a record company. None are interested. Hopper makes contact with old old friend Dave Gilmour, who is persuaded to hear Kate perform. He is impressed.

1973 Amongst the songs recorded at Gilmour's home studio is *Passing Through Air*. The resulting recordings are circulated to the record companies with no result.

1975 Gilmour decides that the only way to interest the record companies in Kate's talent is to make a short demo to full professional standards. **June:** three-track full demo recorded by Gilmour at AIR studios includes *The Man with the Child in his Eyes*. **July:** whilst Pink Floyd are at Abbey Road recording *Wish You Were Here*, Gilmour plays the demo to Bob Mercer of EMI, who is immediately interested. **August:** Kate leaves school, buys an old piano, and begins to take dance training with Lindsay Kemp.

1976 July: Kate secures a publishing and subsequently a recording contract with EMI and receives a small advance.

1977 March: *Wuthering Heights* is written at the full moon. **April:** Kate's brother Paddy forms a band with his friends Del Palmer, Brian Bath and Vic King. Kate is asked to be the vocalist. The first performance of the 'KT Bush Band' is at the Rose of Lee (now The Dirty South) in Lewisham. **August:** *The Kick Inside* recorded, Andrew Powell producing, and halves of Pilot and Cockney Rebel backing. **September:** EMI want to release *James and the Cold Gun* as the first single. Kate is set on *Wuthering Heights*, and gets her way, not for the last time. **November:** The original release date for the single, but Kate wants a change from the original album artwork to Del Palmer's photo concept of *Kite*. By the time the new campaign materials are ready, Christmas is approaching and EMI puts the release date back into the new year. But Eddie Puma and Tony Myatt at London's Capital Radio were issued with a demo of *Wuthering Heights* and play it.

1978 January: *Wuthering Heights* fi nally released and builds further substantial airplay **February:** Kate's first album *The Kick Inside* is released (no.3). **March:** *Wuthering Heights* is no.1 in the UK for four weeks. **May:** Kate's choice for the second single is *The Man with the Child in his Eyes* (no.6) "a song-writing song". **June:** Kate begins to assemble material for a second album in her own demo studio in Welling. **July-September:** Kate's second album *Lionheart* is recorded by Andrew Powell at Superbear in Nice. *Wuthering Heights* is released in the USA but Kate is considered "too bizarre" for the US popular tastes. **October:** *Hammer Horror* (no.44) released in the UK and is not a success. **November:** Kate's second album *Lionheart* released (no.6). **December:** Eric Idle invites Kate to perform on NBC's 'Saturday Night Live'. Paul Simon drops by to watch.

1979 January: Preparations begin for Kate's first and only live tour. **February:** Kate records the theme for *The Magician of Lublin* by Maurice Jarre and Paul Webster. **March:** *Wow* is released to trail the tour (no.14). **April:** Kate is "Best Female Artist" in the British Rock and Pop Awards. She is nominated for three Ivor Novello Awards and wins "Best Lyric" for *The Man with the Child in his Eyes*. **April and May:** Kate tours the UK and Europe. Her own music; her own band, in her own way. **June-August:** Kate prepares material for her third album, and mixes live tapes with Jon Kelly. She decides to make her third album this way. **September:** *On Stage* EP released featuring *Them Heavy People* (no.10). **November:** Kate appears at The Royal Albert Hall to sing live with the London Symphony Orchestra on their 75th Anniversary. The first version of *December Will Be Magic Again* is recorded but not released. **December:** 'Kate', a 45 minute BBC TV special includes previews of *Violin*, *Egypt* and *Ran Tan Waltz*.

1980 January: Kate records backing vocals for *Games Without Frontiers* and *No Self Control* for Peter Gabriel. **February:** Kate records *You*, a duet with Roy Harper for his *Unknown Soldier* album. Kate continues to receive awards including *Music Week* and British Rock and Pop for Best Female Artist. **April:** release of *Breathing /The Empty Bullring* (no.16) and Kate is interviewed about her "protest" song. Kate performs *Babooshka* and *Delius* on a BBC2 Dr.

Wuthering Heights

The Kick Inside

The Man with the Child in his Eyes

Wuthering Heights

Hammer Horror

Lionheart

Wow

Kate BushOn Stage

Breathing

Babooshka

Never For Ever

Army Dreamers

December Will be Magic Again

Sat In Your Lap

The Dreaming (single)

Hook TV special. **May:** Her third album completed. Kate attends the Kate Bush Club Convention at London's Empire Leicester Square. **June:** release of *Babooska /Ran Tan Waltz* (no.5). **September:** Kate attends Stevie Wonder gig and thereafter creates first demo of *Sat In Your Lap.* Release of *Never For Ever.* Kate is the first British female artist to top the album chart, let alone enter it at no.1. Release of *Army Dreamers /Passing Through Air* (no.16). Kate continues to work on her fourth album. **November:** Release of *December Will Be Magic Again /Warm and Soothing* (no.29)

1981 April: a poll in the *Daily Telegraph* finds Kate is both the most liked and the least liked British singer. **May:** Kate goes into Townhouse studios with Hugh Padgham to commence recording of her fourth album. **June:** release of *Sat In Your Lap*, the first and successful single from Kate's fourth album (no.11). **July:** Kate moves to Abbey Road studios with Haydn Bendall to continue recording. **August:** Kate moves to Odyssey Studios with Paul Hardiman. **October:** release of *Kate Bush Live at Hammersmith Odeon* on VHS/Beta video cassette.

1982 January: Kate moves to Advision Studios with Paul Hardiman. **May:** the album is completed and named *The Dreaming.* **July:** at 48 hours notice Kate replaces David Bowie in the Prince's Trust Royal Rock Gala before the Prince and Princess of Wales. *The Dreaming* single is released to critical acclaim and radio indifference (no.4). **September:** release of *The Dreaming* album. British reviewers are mystified, but the album peaks at no.3. **November:** release of *There Goes a Tenner /Ne T'en Fui Pas* in the UK and *Suspended in Gaffa* elsewhere. *There Goes a Tenner* does not chart but *Suspended in Gaffa* is the second successful single from Kate's fourth album. *The Dreaming* album is released in the US to excellent reviews and enters the *Billboard* 200. US 'progressive' radio stations put the album in their top ten of 1982.

1983 June: release in the US of a five-track mini-album *Kate Bush* which enters the *Billboard* 200. Kate decides that the way forward is to build her own full standard studio. **July:** release of *Ne T'en Fui Pas /Un Baiser D'Enfant* in France and Canada. **September:** Kate begins writing and demoing for her fifth album. **November:** release of *Night of the Swallow* in Ireland. **December:** release of *The Single File,* a collection of Kate's videos on VHS cassette. In 1984 *The Single File* will be a best selling video.

1984 January: Kate begins work in her own studio on her fifth album. She opens inaugural broadcast of Sky Channel (the precursor of Sky TV) at a cable station in Wiltshire.

1985 January: Terry Gilliam's film *Brazil* is completed. Kate had recorded a version of the theme but it is not used. **June:** Kate's fifth album is completed and named *Hounds of Love.* **August:** Kate performs *Running Up That Hill* on BBC TV's 'Wogan'. Release of *Running Up That Hill /Under the Ivy* (no.3). It gathers much airplay and critical acclaim. The single enters the US *Billboard* 100 (to peak at no.30); the 12" (including *Running Up That Hill (Instrumental Version)* also enters the *Billboard* dance/club chart. **September:** release of *Hounds of Love* which enters the UK album chart at no.1. **October:** release of *Cloudbusting /Burning Bridge* (no.20). The promotional video features Donald Sutherland as Dr. Wilhelm Reich. The 12" (*The Orgonon Mix*) includes cover cover the traditional Irish folk tune *My Lagan Love.* The album enters the US *Billboard* 200 at no.74 (it will peak at no.30). **November:** Kate attends the Kate Bush Club/*HomeGround* Convention at The Dolphin in Romford.

1986 February: Kate is nominated for, but does not win, three BPI Awards (best female artist, single, and album). Release of *Hounds of Love/Handsome Cabin Boy* (no.18). The 12" *Alternative Hounds of Love*, also includes *Jig of Life.* Kate performs *Hounds* at the 1986 Brit Awards. Kate records *Don't Give Up,* a duet with Peter Gabriel for his fifth solo album. **March:** Kate and *HomeGround* assemble over 100 fans at Elstree for the video for *The Big Sky.* **April:** Kate performs *Breathing* and a comic duet *Do Bears* with Rowan Atkinson at Comic Relief. **May:** release of *The Big Sky /Not This Time* (no.37). The 12" also includes *The Morning Fog.* Kate records *The Seer* with Big Country. **June:** release of *Hair of the Hound* video EP which enters the video chart at no.1. **October:** *Don't Give Up* is the second single from Peter Gabriel's *So* album. Kate performs *Experiment IV* on BBC TV's 'Wogan'. Release of *Experiment IV / Wuthering Heights (new vocal)* (no.23). The 12" includes *December Will Be Magic Again.* **November:** the video for *Experiment IV* features Hugh Laurie, Dawn French and Richard Vernon. Release of *The Whole Story.* It will be no.1 in January 1987 selling over a million copies in the UK. Kate attends the Kate Bush Club/*HomeGround* Video Party at the Video Cafe in London's Argyll Street. **December:** release of the *The Whole Story* video, a no.1 in video charts for most of first quarter of 1987.

1987 February: Nicholas Roeg's film *Castaway* released featuring *Be Kind to My Mistakes.* Kate is nominated in the MTV video awards for *The Big Sky* but the award goes to Whitney Houston. Kate wins the BPI Award for Best Female Artist, and the US College Music Award for Best Female Singer. *Running Up That Hill* is placed at no.13 in an *NME* journalists' poll of the best singles of all time. Kate is the highest placed UK artist in that poll and shared 13th place with Bob Dylan. **March:** Kate records a line in the

Ferry Aid charity single; performs *Running Up That Hill* and *Let It Be* for The Secret Policeman's Third Ball organised by Amnesty International; records backing vocals for *The King is Dead* on Go West's *Dancing on the Couch* album and records the original version of *This Woman's Work* for John Hughes' film *She's Having a Baby.* **May:** Kate begins work in her own studio on her sixth studio album. **June:** Kate appears with Peter Gabriel at Earl's Court to perform *Don't Give Up.*

1988 January: *The Whole Story* video is nominated for, but does not win a Grammy. In the US Kate changes labels from Manhattan to CBS/Columbia soon to be known as Sony. **April:** Kate records a duet with Midge Ure *Sister and Brother* for his *Answers to Nothing* solo album. Ken Russell's 'South Bank Show' special 'The ABC of British Music' includes Kate. **July:** Kate appears in Blazer, a menswear shop, for Shop Assistance organised by the Terrence Higgins Trust. **September:** Kate is in Bulgaria recording demos with the Trio Bulgarka. **October:** the Trio Bulgarka come to Kate's studio to record material for her next album. This effectively finished the recording of that album and mixing begins.

1989 May: Kate's sixth album is completed and named *The Sensual World.* **June:** Kate records *Rocket Man* and *Candle in the Wind* for the Elton John tribute album *Two Rooms.* **September:** release of *The Sensual World /Walk Straight Down the Middle* (no.12). The 12" had a double groove which either played the original version or an instrumental version. **October:** release of *The Sensual World* album which entered the chart at no.2. **November:** release of *This Woman's Work /Be Kind to My Mistakes* (no.25). The 12" and the CD single included *I'm Still Waiting.* **December:** Kate performs *This Woman's Work* on BBC TV's 'Wogan'.

1990 *The Sensual World* is at no.1 in the *Rolling Stone* US College Album chart in the early months of 1990. **February:** broadcast of the 'Comic Strip' episode 'GLC' with theme *Ken* and incidental music by Kate. Release of *Love and Anger /Ken /One Last Look Around the House Before We Go /The Confrontation* (no.38). The track earlier released in the US, reached no.1 in the *Billboard* Modern Rock Tracks chart. **March:** Kate's acting début in the 'Comic Strip' episode 'Les Dogs'. **April:** Kate records backing vocals in Paris for Alan Stivell's *Kimead* for his *Again* album. Roy Harper releases *Once* with backing vocals from Kate. In the US the VHS release *The Sensual World - the Videos* is followed by the EP *Aspects of the Sensual World.* **October:** release of the box set *This Woman's Work Anthology 1978-1990.* Kate begins writing and demoing for her seventh studio album. **November:** Kate is nominated in the *Billboard* Video awards for *This Woman's Work.* At the 1990 Kate Bush Club/*HomeGround* Convention Kate takes questions for 45 minutes and sings a short tribute to the fans. Release in the UK of *The Sensual World - The Videos* on VHS cassette. **December:** Kate appears in two TV appeals for Amnesty International's 'Prisoners of Conscience'.

1991 January: Kate is nominated in the US for a Grammy in the 'alternative: best alternative music performance (vocal or instrumental)' category for *The Sensual World.* **February:** Kate is invited to a luncheon held by Prime Minister John Major for the President of Bulgaria. Throughout the rest of the year Kate is working on the album with the intention that it could be toured. **November:** release of *Rocket Man /Candle in the Wind* (no.12) from the Elton John tribute album *Two Rooms.* **December:** Kate performs *Rocket Man* on BBC TV's 'Wogan'.

1992 February: Kate's mother Hannah passes away. **December:** the 'Comic Strip' episode 'Wild Turkey' includes Kate's *Home for Christmas.*

1993 January: release of *Brazil* soundtrack album including Kate's rendering of the main theme. **April:** Kate's seventh studio album is completed and named *The Red Shoes.* **June:** Kate performs *Moments of Pleasure* on the ITV programme 'Aspel & Company'. **July:** in place of a live tour, Kate begins working on a film that will be known as *The Line, the Cross & the Curve.* The film will feature Miranda Richardson, Lindsay Kemp, and Lily Cornford. **September:** release of *Rubberband Girl /Big Stripey Lie* in the UK (no.12). In the US Sony releases *Eat the Music /Big Stripey Lie /Candle in the Wind.* **November:** release of *The Red Shoes.* It enters the Network chart at no.1, and the Gallup chart at no.2. In the UK the album soon goes Gold and then Platinum. In the US the album enters the *Billboard* chart at no.28, two places higher than *Hounds of Love. The Line, the Cross & the Curve* is completed and premièred at the 37th London Film Festival. Release of *Moments of Pleasure* (no.26). This release includes variously, depending on format, *Moments* instrumental, *Home for Christmas, Show a Little Devotion, December Will Be Magic Again,* or *Experiment IV* making the latter tracks available on CD for the first time.

1994 April: release of *The Red Shoes* single (no.21). This release included variously, depending on format *You Want Alchemy, Cloudbusting (Video Mix), This Woman's Work, Shoedance, The Big Sky (Single Mix),* or *Running Up That Hill (12" mix)* making these tracks available on CD. Release of *The Whole Story '94* on CD-ROM. **May:** release of *The Line, the Cross & the Curve* on VHS cassette. The film is promoted

The Dreaming (album)

There Goes a Tenner

Suspended in Gaffa

Ne T'enfuis Pas

Night of the Swallow

The Single File

Running Up That Hill

Hounds of Love (album)

Cloudbusting

Hounds of Love (single)

The Big Sky

Experiment IV

The Whole Story

The Sensual World (single)

The Sensual World (album)

through a cinema programme which includes seven other videos. Alan Stivell releases *Again* which includes the track *Kimead* on which Kate recorded backing vocals. Kate records a version of Marvin Gaye's *Sexual Healing* for Davy Spillane's album *A Place Among the Stars.* The track is not used on that album and not released until 2005. Kate attends the Kate Busg Club/*HomeGround* Convention at the London Hippodrome. **July:** release of *The Man I Love* (no.27) from Larry Adler's *The Glory of Gershwin* album. Kate scores a number of advertisements for Coca-Cola's new product Fruitopia. **August:** release of *Kate Bush Live at Hammersmith Odeon* CD and video double pack. **October:** Kate contributes a work of art for the War Child exhibition in aid of Bosnian refugees. **November:** release of *And So Is Love /Rubberband Girl (US mix) /Eat the Music (US mix)*(no.26). To promote the single Kate appears for the last time on BBC's 'Top of the Pops'.

1996 February: Kate is nominated for, but does not receive, a Grammy for *The Line, the Cross & the Curve.* **May:** release of Donal Lunny's album project *Common Ground – Voices of Modern Irish Music.* This included Kate's version of *Mná na hÉireann* an Irish traditional melody with Irish lyrics by Sean O'Riada. **November:** release of Prince's album *Emancipation* which included Kate's backing vocals on *My Computer.*

1997 Kate does some preliminary work for the next album. **February:** Kate contributes a sculpture to the Milestones Gallery in aid of War Child. **June:** release of EMI Centenary edition of *Hounds of Love* with additional tracks. **November:** Kate attends The Banquet at Buckingham Palace for the Queen's 50th Wedding Anniversary

1998 March: Michael Kamen's album *Opus* includes a different version of Kate's take on *Brazil.* **May:** Kate's son Albert ("Bertie") is born.

1999 October: Kate's new studio is ready. She records the theme for Disney's *Dinosaur.* After many misadventures the track is not used. Kate continues writing and making demos for her next album.

2001 October: Kate appears at the Q Awards to accept 'Classic Songwriter'. She is greeted by a standing ovation and is praised by John Lydon.

2002 January: Kate performs live, joining Dave Gilmour on vocals for *Comfortably Numb.* **May:** Kate attends the Royal Academy for a special ceremony to celebrate the Queen's Golden Jubilee. Kate attends the Ivor Novello Awards to accept the PRS Award for Outstanding Contribution to British Music.

2003 October: a poll conducted by Sunday heavy *The Observer,* names Kate no.1 'Greatest Eccentric in Music'. Kate goes into Abbey Road studios to complete her eighth studio album.

2004 December: Kate's announcement of the forthcoming album becomes an internet and media sensation.

2005 March: Kate is invited to a reception at Buckingham Palace to honour the British Music Industry. **October:** release of *King of the Mountain /Sexual Healing,* Kate's first download single (no.4). **November:** release of Kate's eighth studio album *Aerial* to an avalanche of media coverage (no.3). The album is a substantial international triumph, and Platinum in the UK within four weeks.

2006 November: the BBC 'Culture Show' lists Kate as one of Ten 'Living Icons'.

2007 Kate starts re-recording some of her older tracks, and working on new material. **October:** Kate short-listed for BBC Radio2's 'Ultimate Icons of the last 40 Years'. Kate composes a closing credits track, *Lyra,* for the major fantasy film *The Golden Compass.*

2008 July: Kate's father Dr. Bush, passes away.

2009 Kate records a version of traditional folk song *She Moves Through the Fair* with Rolf Harris.

2011 April: release of *Deeper Understanding* Kate's first download-only single (no.87). **May:** release of *Director's Cut* (no.2) a re-imagining of tracks from *The Sensual World* and *The Red Shoes.* These are the first releases on Kate's own record label, Fish People. **October:** release of *Wild Man* as a download single (no.73). **November:** release of Kate's tenth studio album *50 Words For Snow* (no.5).

2012 May: *50 Words For Snow* wins the South Bank Sky Arts Award for Best Pop Album of 2011. **August:** release of *Running Up That Hill 2012* the track used in the London Olympics closing ceremony. **December:** HM Queen Elizabeth II creates Kate CBE in the 2013 New Years Honours.

2013 April: invested with her CBE, Kate dedicates the award to her family, musical collaborators, and also to her fans to whom she says: "Thank you so very much for all your fantastic support and encouragement. I feel extremely privileged to still have an audience. It's you that have made my work, which would otherwise have just been creative projects, into a success. Many, many thanks to the best fans ever.".

They Made Me Look at Myself ...

... ...people involved in the story

Kate's Collaborators: ***John Carder Bush*** and ***Paddy Bush***: Kate's older brothers, poets and musicians. ***Bertie (Albert) McIntosh***: Kate's son and vocalist. ***Danny McIntosh:*** guitarist and Kate's partner. ***Del Palmer***: original member of the KT Bush Band, bass player, and long since Kate's engineer. ***Brian Bath:*** another KT Bush Band original, guitarist. ***Lisa Bradley***: school-friend of Kate, ran the official fan club, organised conventions. ***Geoff Jukes***: Kate's current business manager. ***Dave Gilmour***: guitarist with Pink Floyd, produced Kate's early demos. Instrumental in obtaining contract with EMI. ***Andrew Powell***: produced Kate's first two albums. ***Jon Kelly***: engineer on Kate's first two albums, co-produced with Kate her third album. ***Hugh Padgham***, ***Nick Launay***, ***Haydn Bendall***, and ***Paul Hardiman***: engineered *The Dreaming*. ***Kevin Killen***: mixer, engineer and producer used by Peter Gabriel and Elvis Costello ***Joe Boyd***: producer and writer who has worked with Pink Floyd, Fairport Convention, and Nick Drake. ***Stephen W. Taylor***: engineer on some of *Director's Cut* and *50 Words For Snow*. ***Jim Jones***: engineer at Abbey Road who maintained Kate's own studios ***Gary Hurst*** and ***Stuart Avon Arnold***: dancers who appeared in the 1979 live dates and many of Kate's early videos. ***Anthony Van Laast***: dance teacher and choreographer. ***Simon Drake***: magician and illusionist. ***Bill Duffield***: lighting director in preparation for the tour. ***Dwayne Grey-Gullert:*** Kate's dance teacher in the '80s. ***Gered Mankowitz***: photographer responsible for much of Kate's early photographic image. ***Guido Harari***: photographer and music journalist. ***Roy Harper***: singer, songwriter, and friend. ***Peter Gabriel***: Former Genesis frontman, solo artist, founder of WOMAD. ***Eric Clapton***: blues guitarist and singer-songwriter, member of the Yardbirds and Cream. ***Midge Ure***: guitarist, singer, songwriter, member of Visage and Ultravox, co-organiser of Band Aid. ***Alan Stivell***: Breton Master Harpist. ***Susanna Pell***: exponent of the viol who has played with the Dufay Collective and Fretwork. ***Peter Erskine***: jazz drummer and composer who has played with Steely Dan and Weather Report. ***Emma Murphy***: exponent of the recorder who has played with the Gabrieli Consort, and Ex Cathedra. ***Jeff Beck***: rock guitarist, member of The Yardbirds and founder of The Jeff Beck Group. ***Stuart Adamson***: guitarist singer songwriter, founder of The Skids and Big Country. ***Youth (Martin Glover)***: guitarist producer, founding member of Killing Joke. ***Larry Adler***: legendary harmonica player. ***Rolf Harris***: legendary Australian, painter, and player of the wobble board and digeridoo. ***Stoyanka Boneva***, ***Yanka Rupkina*** and ***Eva Georgieva***: the Trio Bulgarka. ***Donald Sutherland***: actor, played Dr Reich in the *Cloudbusting* video. ***Miranda Richardson***: film, TV and stage actress most memorably in 'Blackadder', *The Crying Game* and *Enchanted April*. ***Lenny Henry***: actor, writer and Comic Strip comedian. ***Dawn French***: actress writer and Comic Strip comedienne. ***Hugh Laurie***: actor, musician, director, noted for portraying Dr. Gregory House. ***Tim McInnerny***: actor, best known as Captain Darling. ***Robbie Coltrane***: actor, comedian and author, noted for performances in 'Cracker' and as Hagrid in the 'Harry Potter' films. ***Stephen Fry***: actor, writer, journalist best known for 'Blackadder' and 'QI'. ***Frances Barber***: actress with long stage, film and TV career, most recently in 'Dr. Who'. ***Noel Fielding***: comedian, artist musician known for 'The Mighty Boosh'. ***Nigel Kennedy:*** third generation musician, classical and jazz violinist, friend. ***Prince***: singer, songwriter, actor, originator of the Minneapolis Sound. ***Michael Kamen***: composer, arranger, conductor who also worked with Pink Floyd, David Bowie. ***Jonathan Tunick***: orchestrator and composer who worked with Stephen Sondheim. ***Steve Gadd***: session drummer who has played with Paul Simon, and Eric Clapton ***Gary Brooker***: songwriter, keyboard player, founder of Procul Harem. ***Mick Karn***: songwriter and bassist with Japan. ***Al Murphy***: guitarist with Go West and Level 42. ***Preston Hayman:*** drummer with Tom Robinson and Atomic Rooster. ***Charlie Morgan:*** drummer with Roy Harper and Elton John. ***Danny Thompson***: exponent of the double bass. Played with Blues Incorporated and Pentangle, and John Martyn. ***Eberhard Weber:*** bass player and composer. Standard of ECM label. ***Donal Lunny***: Irish folk musician and producer who has played with Planxty and Moving Hearts. ***Morris Pert***: drummer, composer, pianist who played with Brand X, and Elvis Costello. ***Davy Spillane***: songwriter, exponent of the uilleann pipes, producer, founder of Moving Hearts. ***David Paton:*** bass player with Pilot, and Elton John. ***Stuart Elliot:*** drummer in Cockney Rebel and the Alan Parsons Project. ***John Giblin:*** bass player with Brand X, and Simple Minds. ***Mica Paris***: soul singer who has worked with Prince, and Dave Gilmour. ***Andy Fairweather-Low***: guitarist songwriter and singer who played with Amen Corner, and Roger Waters. ***Keith MacMillan***: director of Kate's videos from *Wuthering Heights* to

Over the years Kate has worked with a huge number of people This is by no means a definitive list but is a rough guide to some people who have been mentioned in *HomeGround* over the years.

This Woman's Work

Love and Anger

Rocket Man

Rubberband Girl

The Red Shoes (album)

Moments of Pleasure

The Red Shoes (single)

The Man I Love

And So is Love

King of the Mountain

Aerial

Deeper Understanding

Directors Cut

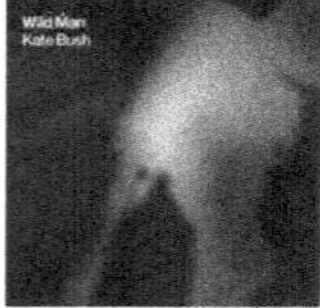

Wild Man

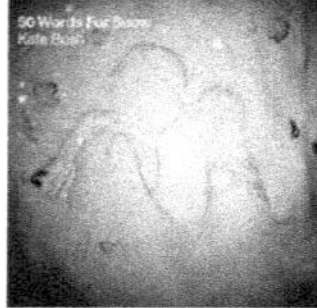

50 Words for Snow

Army Dreamers. ***Peter Richardson***: actor and director. Founder of the Comic Strip. ***Julian Doyle***: film maker who worked on *Life of Brian* and *Time Bandits*. ***Roger Pratt***: cinematographer who worked on *Brazil* and *Harry Potter*. ***John Hughes***: film director, producer and writer noted for *The Breakfast Club*, and *She's Having a Baby*. ***Michael Solinger***: film editor and producer on *The Curse of the Were-Rabbit*, and *Quantum of Solace*. ***Finn Brandt***: animator who worked on *The Gruffalo* and *The Imaginarium of Doctor Parnassus*.

The Guys from the Company: some of the people who have worked on Kate's music over the years at EMI, people who have been mentioned by Kate, or in the press or TV or *HomeGround* have met. Some of them started at EMI and then went on to work with Kate: ***Brian Southall***: press, promotions and marketing in '80s. ***David Munns***: director of A&R during the *Hounds of Love* period and still a friend and advisor. ***Bob Mercer***: MD when Kate was signed and great supporter throughout her career. ***Hilary Walker***: international executive, later Kate's business advisor during '80s and '90s and liaison with the company. ***Paul Baines***: marketing *Aerial*, *Director's Cut* and *50 Words For Snow*. ***Malcolm Hill***: Promotions. ***Jill Wall***: marketing for *Hounds of Love*. ***Dwayne Welch***: marketing for *The Whole Story*. ***Tony Wadsworth***: CEO during the big gap and *Aerial*. ***Steve Davis***: marketing for *The Sensual World* and the *This Woman's Work* box set. ***Ian Ramage***: marketing for *The Red Shoes*. ***Brian Munns***: Head of press for a large part of Kate's career in the '80s and '90s. ***Dave Cross*** (yes that one): marketing on the *Hounds of Love* re-issue. ***Murray Chalmers***: formerly Parlophone head of press now with Kate as Press Officer.

The Media: some we noted for their enthusiasm for Kate's music or lack of it: ***Tony Myatt***: DJ at London's Capital Radio in the '70s and '80s. Probably the first to play *Wuthering Heights*. ***Tommy Vance***: Radio Heavy Rock DJ and ***David "Kid" Jensen***: Radio 1 DJ, both supportive of Kate's music as were later ***Simon Mayo, Chris Moyles***, ***Ken Bruce***, ***Mark Radcliffe*** and ***Rob da Bank***. ***Laurie Brown***: VJ on Canadian music channel Much Music. Maker of appreciative interviews and programme segments. ***Simon Bates***: Radio 1 DJ in the '80s who appeared not to like Kate's music very much or at all. Sorry Simon – we caricatured you as "Cybates". ***Harry Doherty***: "the Dragonfly" - supportive music journalist, at the *Melody Maker* in the 70s and 80s. ***Kris Needs***: editor of *ZigZag* and early punk enthusiast for Kate. ***Mick Wall***: heavy rock journalist in Kerrang! and elsewhere, enthusiast for Kate and her music. ***Dermot Stokes***: journalist and editor of *Hot Press* Ireland's premier music weekly who showed Irish enthusiasm for genuine music. ***Paul Kerton***: author of 1980 instant biography of Kate, most importantly a source of Kate's early poems. ***Kerry Juby***: DJ and producer, author of 80s bio of Kate at the time of the *Whole Story* project. ***Sean Mayes***: pianist and co-author of *A Visual Documentary*, another '80s bio. ***Kevin Cann***: artist designer, the other co-author of *A Visual Documentary*. ***Gillian Gaar***: journalist, respected author of music books, and former producer of a Kate fanzine. ***Julie Burchill***: former punk-era young lioness of the *NME*, now author and journalist. Originally scathing, later respectful of Kate's integrity. ***Deborah M. Withers***: academic, feminist, author of philosophical studies of Kate's music. ***Graeme Thompson***: music journalist, author of 2010 biography of Kate.

Inspiration... ***Lily Cornford***: founder of the Maitreya School of Healing. Inspired Kate's song *Lily*. ***G.I. Gurdjieff***: a spiritual teacher who wanted us to wake up and "remember ourselves". ***Emily Brontë***: author of *Wuthering Heights*, thanked by Kate on the 7inch single of *Wow*. ***Lindsay Kemp***: dancer and choreographer. Early teacher of Kate's who appeared in *The Line, The Cross and The Curve*. ***Terry Gilliam***: film maker, inspiration and friend. ***Elton John***: singer, songwriter, piano player. Kate was a great fan and sent an early fan letter. ***David Bowie***: singer and songwriter, exponent of mime and dance. ***Fee Waybill***: lead singer and songwriter of The Tubes whose theatrical presentation inspired Kate. ***John Lydon***: former Sex Pistol, enthusiastic fan of Kate's music. ***Stevie Wonder***: singer and song writer. His 1980 live show inspired Kate to write *Sat In Your Lap*. ***John Lennon***: musical hero of Kate's. She bought and later donated to charity the Two Virgins statuette. ***Billie Holiday***: legendary jazz singer and song-writer. ***Bert Lloyd***: folk song collector and performer. Inspired Kate's early folk music interest. ***Captain Beefheart***: his integrity and originality inspired Kate. ***Werner Herzog, Sergei Eisenstein, François Truffaut, Alfred Hitchcock, Nicholas Roeg*** and ***Michael Powell***: film directors whose visual style fascinated and inspired. ***Peter Reich***: son of Dr. Wilheim Reich, author of *A Book of Dreams*, inspiration for *Cloudbusting*.

And ... ***Zoodle, Pyewacket, Rocket***: cats who lived with Kate. ***Pamela Stephenson***: psychologist. Former 'Not the Nine O'Clock News' comedienne who performed remembered parody of Kate. ***Faith Brown***: the media's in-house Kate impressionist in the 1980s.

The Nineties, Noughties, and Beyond

The Red Shoes and the 1994 Convention
Aerial
Director's Cut and *50 Words for Snow*

Retracing the Scenes

Somewhere in between (3): 1991-93

From Spring to Autumn 1991, a number of rumours emerged as to what was happening with Kate's new album, or who was working with her. The most interesting was the Prince (he was still 'Prince' at this stage) story. As it emerged in Spring 1991, we did not know the full truth of this. As stated rather unflatteringly in the press, Prince was hoping to "boost his flagging music career" (the words are those of the *Eastern Daily Press,* 10th May) by bringing in big names to direct the videos for his new album, provisionally entitled *Pearls and Diamonds,* and due in August of that year. There were other versions of the rumour: that Kate was actually doing a duet with Prince on either his or her new album, and the other was that Kate was actually to open for Prince on his next tour.

Diamonds and Pearls appeared in Autumn 1991, without any duet, although interestingly, Kate did get a name check in the sleeve notes for 'inspiration'. Variants on the 'Kate working with Prince' story were, however, still circulating in the British and US media. One such had them writing a soundtrack together, "Prince having met Kate a couple of years ago when he was last touring in London… and they have kept in touch by fax constantly..."

The way we see the Kate and Prince story is as follows. Prince had long been aware of Kate, and Kate of Prince. Interviewed later at the release of *The Red Shoes,* Kate said "I'm so glad he agreed to work with me, I've been a big fan of his for a long time..." and "I listen to a lot of his work. I'm into dancing and I put it on in our dance classes. It's great to dance to."

Michael Koppelman, a musician and studio engineer who worked with Prince in 1991 and before, told the story like this to rec.music.gaffa: "It's funny because Prince knew I was a huge KB fan. He was too, but not like me. The first time I asked him if he liked Kate Bush he said, 'she's my favourite woman'. I also made him a tape of all the KB b-sides... When *The Sensual World* came out he had someone go get it and we listened to it in the studio. He didn't dig it that much."

Another analysis from rec.music.gaffa by Michael Koppelman is interesting: "In 1985 Prince released an album called *Around The World In A Day*. On this album was a song called *The Ladder*. The song is about seeking some sort of spirituality, and included the line "Everybody is looking for the ladder". Kate '93 (from *Top of the City*): "Keep looking for the ladder", Kate '93 (from *Constellation of the Heart*): "Ohh... find me the man with the ladder". By the way – the type format of the heart symbol used on *Constellation of the Heart* is the exact – EXACT – as used on Prince's *Sign of the Times* album. So – Kate and Prince, and both talking about looking for the ladder. It goes deeper than that however. Prince (from *7*): "And I saw an angel come down unto me/ In her hand she holds the very key..." Kate (from *Constellation of the Heart*): "Ohhh, and if you see the woman with the key/ I hear she's opening up the doors to heaven". I think it is either pretty obvious that Prince and Kate are (1) completely and utterly on the same wavelength or (2) they are working together. There is a Prince biography (not really a bio but it is hard to classify) written by Pers Nilssen. A revised copy just came out which places Kate at being at Prince's Paisley Park in either late '91 or early '92. The symbol that Prince is now named for does not stand for a name – rather it is indeed the shape of the key to heaven being talked about in these songs.

The story was then that Kate went to see Prince at a gig and was flattered to be asked to meet him after the show, when they discussed a collaboration. Which gig? The likely one is the *Nude* tour in 1990 (London dates June and August 1990). The *Diamonds and Pearls* tour itself in 1992 is surely too late.

Prince.

The following extract is from an interview by Chris Heath with Prince published in November 1991: "He talks some more about his new projects. I mention the possible video with Kate Bush. Frequent transatlantic phone conversations with the fbaty Ms. Bush have been openly alluded to during my tenure at Paisley Park, but Prince denies any knowledge. Strange".

This is what Del Palmer said in his November 1993 interview in *Future Music*: "Kate went to see him at a gig and was flattered to be asked to meet him after the show, when they discussed a collaboration. Unable to physically get together in the same room, they swapped multi-track tapes, with a slave reel returning from Prince's Paisley Park studio covered in vocals, guitar solos and keyboards. The problem then was to put the track back together into something resembling its original form while retaining the best of what Prince had done. He hadn't added one of the vocal parts which would have been particularly good for him, so it basically took two years to put it back together. What's left is his lead guitar, some digital synths and some chorus vocals. Then Lenny Henry came in to do a vocal on the end – he's really got a great voice and ought to be doing a serious record of his own."

Prince.

Lenny Henry (below).

If it took the best part of two years to sort out the track after Prince had laid his hands on it, and as the album was released in 1993, the action took place in 1991.

Michael Koppelman continues his story: "One day Prince's assistant, Therese, told me that Kate

Bush had called. Therese also knew I was a big Kate fan. Then, in the studio that day, Prince said, "Guess who I talked to today". Me, being stupid and unable to keep my mouth shut, said, "Kate Bush?" So, Prince tells me that he and Kate are going to work on a tune together. He also told me that while they were talking he told her that his engineer would rather work with her than him! I was at home and the phone rang. My answering machine picked it up and I heard Julie, from Paisley Park, saying "Mike, I got Kate Bush on the phone and she has some questions about what format they should send things over on, and I thought it would be best if she talked to you". I, being an admitted Kate Bush fan, freaked, but picked up the phone and talked to Julie. She says, "Kate, I have Prince's engineer Michael Koppelman on the phone and he can answer your questions". The conversation consisted only of her asking me if they could send 24-track tapes and what series SSL computer disks. I also asked her if she was going to come to Minneapolis, and she said "I don't think I'm wanted out there right now". Then we basically said good-bye and hung up.

"Eventually the tapes arrived and I put them up and got a rough mix up. I still have a cassette of it. It is 1 million times better than the lame disco Prince put on it. There was, of course, no disco on it before Prince got his hands on it. So Prince comes in and listens to it. And the brutality began. First we sampled the drum thing and synced it up to my Powerbook so we could do MIDI. At that point, we essentially created a new song on a new piece of tape and then flew all of Kate's tracks back on top of it. So now we could run the sequencer and add all the keyboards that Prince put on. So Prince stacked a bunch of keys, guitars, basses, etc, on it and then went to sing background vocals. It took him a few hours and then he called me back in and played me the thick, multi-tracked background vocals he had put on.

"Now, as we all know, the song in question goes "Of all the people in the world why should I love you". When Prince called me back in and played me what he had done, he had sung "All of the people in the world", instead of "Of All". I said, "Isn't it of all the people in the world? Not all of?" He said, "No, we had a little talk about that", in his cocky way, as if to say he had talked with Kate about changing the words. The next day, I was waiting at my hotel room for the call to go to the studio when the assistant engineer, Sylvia Massy, called and said Prince was in the studio doing vocals. I was surprised; I was always called well in advance of Prince going into the studio. When I got there he was changing all the vocals to "Of All", and was sampling them in himself, which is something he would normally never do himself. My interpretation? He made a mistake, as humans do, and didn't have the guts to admit it. That's weird. So I sorta poked my head in at one point and asked him if he needed any help, and we went on with the day.

"Eventually he had me do a rough mix, and when he had approved it, we sent it to Kate. I got a call from Therese a few days (or weeks, I forget) later. She said, "Kate Bush said to destroy all copies of that mix". I said, "Huh? Did she not like it or something?" (my heart rejoiced, because I hated what Prince did to it). She said, "I don't know, she just said to destroy them". Later on Prince told me Kate Bush liked what we did. She said it sounded very American. So at that point I wasn't sure if she was even going to use it. We sent the tapes back and she sort of split the difference with what he sent and what's on the record. Kate, if you read this, stick the pre-Prince version of *Why Should I Love You* out on something. And let me do a remix of *Not This Time*!"

In the Christmas 1991 *HomeGround*, we reported that Kate was very pleased with the progress on the new album, though release dates very sketchy, being pencilled in for around about Spring 1992. Ah, optimism!

At this stage of course there seems to have been a rather more than half-formed intention to tour this album. Lindsay Kemp, who prompted Kate's interest in dance and bodily expression some fifteen years earlier, appeared on BBC Radio 4 in early May 1991 and amongst other things said that he was at the moment working with Kate "in preparation for her next tour". During her interview with Johnny Walker on the BBC Radio 1 Saturday Show on 14th December 1991, Kate said in reply to Walker's inevitable question about when the album was due: "Well, er... I... next year! I would like it next year. I can't say when because it depends sort of on what else we want to do next year". She would not be drawn on the album save to say that she felt it was: "very different".

Meanwhile Kate's influences were turning up in all sorts of places. In a scene in Terry Gilliam's recently released film *The Fisher King* the lead characters lay down in the middle of New York's Central Park "cloud-busting"! It seems that Kate may have been approached by the film production company that made *Robin Hood – Prince of Thieves* to complete and sing the title song that Bryan Adams made such a huge world-wide hit. The link is of course that the song was basically put together by Michael Kamen who was involved as arranger on *The Sensual World*. Variants on that story had Kate being offered the chance to duet with Adams on the track, an opportunity also apparently offered to Liz Fraser. In any event Kate appears to have turned down any such offer because either she felt the song wasn't right for her or she couldn't spare the time off from the new album.

Somebody else who was wanting Kate for a

part was the director of a new musical about Charles Manson and his lunatic 'family'. Apparently he wanted either Kate or Lene Lovich for the part of 'Squeaky'.

Alek Kershishian, the director of *Madonna: Truth or Dare*, revealed in an interview in the May 1991 *Rolling Stone* how as a Harvard senior in 1986 he spent $2,000 producing *Wuthering Heights* as a rock opera featuring music by Kate, Billy Idol, and Madonna, the first time a theatrical piece had ever been approved as a senior thesis at the famous US university. The show was staged at the American Repertory Theatre and led to a run on Kate's albums in Boston. One of the contributors to rec.music.gaffa, Greg Bossert, actually saw the performance and reported as follows: "The production told the Brontë story in mime and dance with loud and glorious music in the original recorded versions. Heathcliff was represented by Sting, and Cathy by Kate of course. The middle of the story drifted a bit as H. and C. left the moors for the big city and turned into Billy Idol and Madonna. The set was magnificent, the lighting was beautiful, and the dancing was pretty good (some of the dancers were clearly inspired by *Running Up That Hill*. Many people were confused by the show since there was no live music or speech. Of course what I liked was hearing Kate at 100+ db. The ending was *Hello Earth*, followed by *Wuthering Heights* and was pretty much devastating".

Graphic: Paulina Stuckey

KITS San Francisco on its Labor Day countdown of the 105 Greatest Modern Rock Artists of All Time included Kate at no.44, four places down from a similar countdown two years previously, and towards the end of May the station had its annual Memorial Weekend countdown of the 'Top 300 Modern Rock Songs of All Time' (as voted by listeners). Kate appeared at no.36 with *Running Up That Hill* (it was no.200 in 1990) and at no.20 with *Wuthering Heights* (the new one), the best she had ever done on this particular countdown. In Italy Kate was

As Dinger on the KB News board pointed out from a rec.music.gaffa post by Scott Telford, the publication concerned was actually the 1991 edition of the *Oxford Companion to Popular Music* and not *The Oxford Encyclopedia of Popular Music*. The accuracy of this particular 'companion' may be judged from the fact that it has Kate born in Plumstead, Surrey. Dinger concluded that a full manuscript of *Leaving My Tracks* is still elusive and likely non-existent.

voted no.2 'Best Foreign Female Singer' by the readers of *Ciao 2001* in the 19th March issue. In the June *Vox* the results of the readers poll for the top 100 albums and singles of all time showed *Wuthering Heights* at no.44 single, and three entries in the album chart: *The Kick Inside* at no.60, *Hounds of Love* at no.75 and *The Dreaming* at no.95.

The US record collecting magazine *Goldmine* finally created a separate 'Kate Bush' category in its May 91 issue, and in the August issue ran a comprehensive article by Gillian Gaar (formerly editor of the *For the Love of Kate* fanzine). The UK record collecting bible *Record Collector* ran its annual list of the top 500 collectible artists in its May 91 issue. Kate came in at no.11, down from no.7 in 1990.

Amongst the odds and sods that we reported in *HomeGround* in this period were – Germany: New compilation *Rock'n'Ride – Dream Songs* includes *Wuthering Heights*; France: Kate's music used in advertisements, *Wuthering Heights* for 'O' perfume by Lancôme, *Running Up That Hill* for a building firm called La Maison Bouyges; Italy: Guido Harari's new book of photos featuring Kate and Peter Gabriel on the cover launched at Milan's mega-store on 22nd October, with introduction also written by Kate; Czechoslovakia (as was): the company Popron released *The Sensual World* under licence; Kate has a track on the recent compilation put together by the music magazine *Q*, an instrumental version of *Wuthering Heights* is included on the recent album by the Sonny Sharrack Band entitled *High Life*; *Vox* May '91; *The Vox Encyclopaedia of Rock* reaches Kate, with a short appreciative article and photo, *Q* June '91 includes free give-away sleeve notes for *Hounds of Love*, *Goldmine* (US) 31st May reviews the box set, and *Daily Mirror* 10th April had a pic of Kate and Betty Boo at the *Silly Cow* bash.

In late Spring 1991 EMI video finally released *Live at Hammersmith* in the US, at last putting a halt to the lucrative trade in Japanese imports. We saw these reviews:

"It's very easy to appreciate her bewitching countenance, fluid body English and bold dramatic strikingly imaginative conceptual skills... highly recommended". Barry Gulman, *Pulse* May '91

"Those who don't appreciate the talents of Kate Bush haven't seen this video… it could convert anyone… Each song is a mini-musical". Anon, *Chicago Tribune* 28th May

The packaging had some peculiarities in that one track was entitled: *Don't Put Your Foot on the Heartache*, and the tape was said to be in PAL, though of course it was actually in the US NTSC system!

The famous book by Kate that never was, also showed up again. *The Oxford Encyclopaedia of Popular Music* cited *Leaving My Tracks* as a reference. We think this establishes beyond doubt that a completed text, if not a full proof copy must exist. The editors at the Oxford University Press do not cite texts that do not exist.

A plethora of new bootleg albums appeared in 1991 probably as a reflection of Kate's 'collectible' status. It was, however, just the same old material, either the early demos or 1979 live material, presented in a variety of forms and formats under a variety of titles: *Alone At My Piano* was a CD containing 28 of the early demos; *Piano Demos No.1* was another CD containing much of the above; *Backsides* was a vinyl LP of B-sides, non-album tracks, odds and 12" mixes; *Burning Desire* was another CD, this time with our old friend the soundtrack from the *Live at Hammersmith* laser disc; *If You Could See Me Fly* was yet another CD with the 16 demo tracks from the bootleg *Cathy's Album* plus two demo versions of *Babooshka*; *Cathy's Album Too* was an album proclaiming itself to be "Kate Bush home demos".

As if to underline Kate's status in the record collecting market, *The Illustrated Collector's Guide to Kate Bush* by Robert Goodwin appeared, a 142 page round-up of Kate's work in all media (vinyl, CD, Video – as well as TV appearances and bootlegs), on a worldwide basis.

It seems Kate was approached before Christmas '91 to record a cover version of a song called *Nature's Way* for a new album by the British Electric Foundation entitled *Music of Quality and Distinction Vol 2*. The producer apparently wanted Kate to sing it in a soul style. Kate it appears, declined, again the excuse being that she was too busy with the work on her own album.

The big event of Autumn 1991 was the *Two Rooms* Elton John/Bernie Taupin tribute album with Kate's contribution *Rocket Man*. In the Summer *HomeGround* we reported that Phonogram Records UK had told us that the album was to be released on 30th September 1991.

Kate's contribution to *Two Rooms* was noticed instantly by UK pop radio, and we think the first playing of the track was on the Simon Bates show on BBC Radio 1 on 11th October. It was discussed as an obvious single from an early stage and was finally released by Mercury/Phonogram on 25th November in four formats: 7" with Kate's beautiful version of *Candle in the Wind* (like the A-side actually recorded in 1989, but put to one side when Phonogram preferred *Rocket Man* for the album) as the B-side (and a limited edition poster bag – one of the photos from the *This Woman's Work* session), 12" with a *Candle in the Wind* instrumental as the extra track, cassette (as 7") and CD (as 12").

The track garnered radio play straight away,

the first play of the single we think being on the Dave Lee Travis show on Radio 1 on 17th November. The track was in any event placed on the Radio 1 C-list the week of release. Phonogram press releases earned mentions and photos in most of the music press, and this was followed up in the week of release by prominent adverts. Phonogram were urging Kate to do 'Top of the Pops' and 'Wogan', but it seems that at this stage Kate was preferring to keep these tricks up her sleeve for her own new material.

The video (directed by Julian Doyle in tasteful monochrome, with Kate and the musicians who appeared on the track playing as a band) was an event in itself, and had several interesting features. Firstly we should remember that *Rocket Man* included guitar work by the late Al Murphy, and rather poignantly on the stage there was a guitar stood up on a chair with a single candle burning in remembrance, featured in close up in one shot. Then there are the female backing vocalists: a first in any Kate video (and we wondered if there was any tour significance), and then there was Kate miming ukulele! The video was first played as an exclusive on 'The Chart Show' on 30th November, and made an instant impact. A short clip was shown on 'Top of the Pops' on 5th December.

The reviews were er... mixed:

"her ill-advised decision to croon breathily over an abysmal 'reggae' arrangement causes widespread vomiting within a five-mile radius".St Etienne, *NME* 30/11/91

"a real curio, La Bush's ickle-girl quaver is applied as liberally as Elt's cod-space-epic is unexpectedly white-reggaed up behind her. Kate's husky vocal even makes a minor silk purse out of the flipside sow's ear of Reg's Monroe tribute dirge... if only Kate had tackled Crocodile Rock". Ian Gittins, *Melody Maker* 30/11/91

On Radio 1's review programme 'Roundtable' on 22nd November the response was entirely positive. DJ Paul Gambaccini: "great artist, great song... this single will chart even higher than the album". Zoe Ball: "I love Kate Bush, she's my favourite artist... fab". Gary Glitter: "She's one of the best singers in Britain... this is my tip for no.1, and my single at no.2... brilliant!"

The single entered the official chart at no.13 on 30th November 1991. The chart figures were as follows: 7th December no.13, 14th no.12, 21st no.18, 28th no.19. The track was listed as the no.1 breaker in *Music Week* 30th November, and the airplay chart figures were as follows: 7th December no.47, 14th no.29, 21st no.15, 28th no.29.

The single was placed fifth in a list of the ten best singles of 1991 by *The Independent*'s rock music critic Ben Thompson, who commented: "you may acquire an abiding fondness for something from an unexpected source, like Kate Bush's delightfully loopy reading of Elton John's *Rocket Man* complete with mandolins, bagpipes and reggae chorus, when you would rather not own the album it came from". The track was also listed in the *Q* December play-list.

Kate cancelled her earlier decision not to do 'Wogan' when it appeared that the programme would not air for much longer. Kate's presentation of the song in December, was without Davy Spillane, but included the candle that bore witness to Al Murphy. In the Johnny Walker interview Kate explained her early attachment to Elton John, and her sadness at Al Murphy not being able to enjoy the success of the track.

The album *Two Rooms: A Celebration of the Songs of Elton John and Bernie Taupin* was released on 14th October 1991 with a full-sized publicity campaign by Phonogram behind it. It entered the official compilation album chart at no.1, and remained in the top ten until the end of November.

From the release of *Two Rooms* in the US, Kate's track was lined up for special attention, being the track presented to the alternative rock radio stations. *Billboard* reported that the album was largely conceived and produced in the UK and that PolyGram US became involved relatively late. However, the company were firmly behind the project and planned various promotional activities throughout 1992. US reviews of the album picked out Kate's contribution:

"Kate Bush certainly renders the most imaginative contribution, blending a reggae beat, touches of harp, and uillean pipes... her inimitable siren's voice arching up like a missile every time she approaches the title". Ted Drozdowski, *Boston Phoenix* 25/10/91

"Of the album's four gems, three are by women... Kate Bush brings... eloquence to *Rocket Man* with surprise touches of concertina and uillean pipes". Steve Morse, *Boston Globe* 22/10/91

Kate's track was presented to alternative radio programmers (with a promo CD that quickly became a collectors' item) and reviewed by the 9th November *Billboard*: "Bush's high-pitched, chirping performance is a bit off-putting at first, but her gentle, heartfelt treatment of this Elton John classic does update it for alternative radio formats. Reggae vibed beats and folky stringed instrumentation definitely add a new twist to an old favourite".

Kate's ukulele work in the *Rocket Man* video was plainly intended to recall the Marilyn Monroe ukulele scene in *Some Like It Hot*, and thereby linked to the B-side, *Candle in the Wind*.

Rocket Man Charts	Nov 30	Dec 7	14	21	Jan 4	Jan 11
Modern Rock Tracks	no.14	**no.11**	no.15	no.23	no.24	no.30

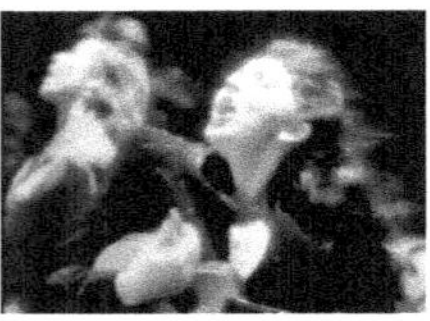

Rocket Man entered the *Billboard* Modern Rock Tracks chart at no.24 on 9th November, then moving to no.15 and no.14, showing as one of the tracks with greatest airplay gains on the alternative stations each week.

The album had been launched at a dinner hosted by PolyGram in New York on 16th October, with various celebrities including Elton and Bernie, but not Kate. It entered the *Billboard* chart at no.28 on 9th November, then going to numbers 19 and 23. The Associated Press news agency report on the album (syndicated in many US newspapers and magazines) contained the following: "Eric Clapton's... *Border Song* and Kate Bush's lightly reggae treatment of *Rocket Man* are arguably the best performances".

Other reviews which mentioned Kate included the *San Francisco Chronicle*: "the only originality brought to the ambitious project comes from Kate Bush who gives a vaguely reggae-ized treatment to *Rocket Man* and refuses to change the lyrics gender; and Sinéad O'Connor", and the *New York Times*: "nearly everything on this album is a pale imitation of Elton John's original versions with the exception of... Sting... Kate Bush's *Rocket Man*, a pop-reggae version that is worth hearing... and Sinéad O'Connor".

Harry LeBlanc, the Canadian correspondent of *Billboard* put *Two Rooms* as no.2 in his best albums of 1991, and cited Kate's "passionate performance". Finally the San Francisco radio station KITS ("Live 105") had *Rocket Man* at no.85 on its annual countdown of the top 105 tracks, the record having been on its play-list for November and December.

Somewhat unexpectedly *Rocket Man* became the biggest hit Kate had had in Australia for some little time. From release in December 1991 the track earned instant radio and TV attention, the video being seen on the popular 'Today' programme on 11th December. It would show very good chart positions in the new year.

When Led Zeppelin weren't actually touring the US and UK in the '60s and '70s the promoters desperately tried to fill the gap with any heavy rock band they could find, and would often bill them as "the new Zeppelin". Many heavy rock bands earned their bread this way. So it is with Kate; her prolonged absences inclined and incline record companies to do much the same. Throughout much of 1991 it was Beverly Craven, who couldn't do an interview without mentioning Kate. At the end of the year, however, it was the arrival of Tori Amos.

Tori, whose first incarnation in the US as a heavy rock Lee Aaron look-alike was a complete failure, was relocated by her record company in the UK and relaunched as a sensitive singer-songwriter. In retrospect now we know how successful that re-launch was. Typical of the phrases in her new record company hand-outs was: "Like Kate Bush when she was HOT!"

As 1992 opened *Rocket Man*, was still in the UK singles chart, although on its slow slide out: 4th January no.23, 11th 43, 18th 74, then curiously up the following week 25th to no.70, before disappearing for good. Airplay remained good and was clearly responsible for the upward blip. On the *Music Week* airplay chart the figures were 4th January no.29, 11th up to no.15, then down on the 18th to no.44 and out. *Two Rooms* remained in the top twenty of the Gallup compilation album chart well into the Spring.

Rocket Man had also performed well in the US. *Two Rooms* went platinum in the US at the end of January and reviews were still coming in: "The album... in several cases makes the material come alive in a new way. Kate Bush's version of *Rocket Man*... uses her ethereal, otherworldly whisper to bring out the loneliness and fear an astronaut in space might readily experience". *Stereo Review* February 1992.

In France, *Rocket Man* entered the top 50 at the end of January and peaked at no.45. The track was well-received on RTL, the first national radio station by the premier DJ Francis Zegut, who said that: "Kate's version of *Rocket Man* is in my opinion the most original... because of the reggae rhythm, because of Davy Spillane, and because of Kate's voice". About *Candle in the Wind* he said: "Beautiful! We wonder why this version wasn't on the *Two Rooms* LP! With Kate Bush we can expect a beautiful version!"

The DJ on RFM commented that: "the best cover by far is that done by Kate Bush". The video was seen on the TV channel M6, and the advert for the album including snippets of Kate's track was seen on all the channels. The Australian success also continued. The single appeared in the top 20 on 1st March at no.14, and then rose to no.12 on 8th March, to 5 on 15th, and peaked at no.2 on 22nd. The single remained in the Australian top 20 until May. *Two Rooms* remained on the compilation chart for 19 weeks peaking at no.1 on 9th February.

On 25th January BBC Radio 1 broadcast the interview with Kate which had been recorded some months for the 'Classic Album' programme. The album was, of course, *Hounds of Love*. It was a good interview, and one of only three where Kate went through the album track by track. Some interesting bits: "I think it was probably the most difficult stage I've been at so far. Because *The Dreaming*, the album before... I'd never produced an album before that one. And because it had a lot of unfavourable attention from some people, I think it was felt that me producing *Hounds of Love* wasn't such a good idea. And for the first time I felt I was actually meeting resistance artistically. I felt the album had done very well to reach number three, but I felt under a lot of pressure and I wanted to stay as close to my work as possible. And everyone was saying 'Oh, she's really gone mad now'. You know, 'hey, listen to this, it's a really weird record'. But it was very important that it happened to me because it made me think, 'Right. Do I really want to produce my own stuff?' You know, 'Do I really care about being famous?' And I was very pleased with myself that, no, it didn't matter as much as making a good album".

"So we started *Hounds of Love* in our own studio, and I started to find out an awful lot of things that I wouldn't have realised otherwise. I relaxed tremendously within my own environment, for a start. And also, on *The Dreaming*, because I was working in such an experimental way, the studio costs were becoming absolutely phenomenal, and I really don't think I could have afforded to have made *Hounds of Love* in a commercial set-up. So, here I was in a situation of having as much creative control, really, as I could ever ask for. And at the time I was writing this album, we were living in the country and my keyboards and stuff were in this room overlooking a valley and I'd sit and watch the clouds rolling up the hill towards me. And there is a lot of weather on this album. The countryside was a big inspiration at this time, and it's always changing, it's a very different perspective from living in the city, sometimes you hardly see the sky above the buildings at all".

"But I did love it, I did enjoy it and everyone that worked on the album was wonderful. And it was really, in some ways, I think, the happiest I've been when I'd been writing and making an album. And I know there's a big theory that goes 'round that you must suffer for your art, you know, 'it's not real art unless you suffer'. And I don't believe this, because I think in some ways this is the most complete work that I've done, in some ways it is the best and I was the happiest that I'd been compared to making other albums".

Graphic: Paulina Stuckey

It was with the greatest possible regret that we announced the death of Kate's mother, Mrs. Hannah Bush on 14th February 1992. Mrs. Bush was always a friend to us – as fans even before we started this magazine. We still miss her very much. We are sure that the effect on Kate was profound. Our thoughts were with Dr. Bush, and Kate and her brothers Paddy and John.

At the beginning of 1992 there was some optimism that the album that was to be named

Eric Clapton.

The Red Shoes would appear before the end of the year. In March, despite the news about Kate's mother, the word was that the recording was more or less finished, with a few bits and pieces to be done. At the same time it appeared that Eric Clapton had contributed to at least four songs on the album. There was some discussion at EMI Towers of releasing the odds'n'sods from the box set together with one or two other sweeteners. Our views were sought and we indicated that we felt the fans would not welcome such a release – even with the sweeteners, having forked out for the box set usually, if not exclusively, to get the odds'n'sods. Whether or not they listened to us we do not know. The release never happened.

By Summer it was clear that Kate was still adding to some tracks, and that part of the mixing had still to be done. Because of the famous 'lead times' (the space required by the record company from the delivery of the master tapes to the release of the album – when things like videos, artwork, and marketing are sorted out) it was *HomeGround*'s feeling that the album would not appear until 1993. Our famous crystal ball (known for its eccentric calibration) suggested Spring 1993 at the earliest. We'll be right one day!

Fred Vermorel

The last known Kate-related sighting of Fred Vermorel occurred on 5th March. It was a lecture at the Royal College of Art in London, part of a series entitled 'Musicians and Music'. This lecture was actually called 'What I Did To Kate Bush'. As you may remember, Vermorel along with his wife Judy were responsible in the early '80's for two rather peculiar books about Kate. These were *Kate Bush: Princess of Suburbia* and *The Secret History of Kate Bush*. Since that time there had been one or two rather strange press articles, an attempt to gatecrash the BPI Awards, but so far as we in the Kate-speaking world were concerned, nothing. So we were a little surprised when a few days before the lecture we received a handbill advertising it. We assume it was actually sent to us by Vermorel. Dave went along.

The lecture started with a copy of Kate's birth certificate projected on the screen. The lecture consisted of Vermorel explaining why and how he came to write the two books. He began by explaining that his real subject was not Kate, or her music, but fans – and by that he meant people who are obsessed by another person they don't know personally. His aim was to build a picture of the fan mentality. The best way to do this, he thought, was to become a fan himself and indulge in obsessive behaviour. Kate was merely in the right place at the right time. She was an attractive intellectual type of whom Vermorel felt he could be a fan. He asked the students if they knew who Kate was – "only she's not very current now". Laughter from the students, some of whom must have been aware of *Rocket Man*.

Vermorel then played *Under the Ivy* and showed slides of Kate's parents' house. He talked about his first book *Princess of Suburbia*. He said it was a deliberate attempt to parody the tabloid press and EMI press releases. To his great surprise he actually received many letters from Kate fans saying how much they liked the book. He then showed slides of some of the pictures in John Carder Bush's book *Cathy*. When one of the students asked about JCB's motives, Vermorel said he felt sure that there was no financial reason for the book and disputed that her family were "cashing in" on Kate's success.

The subject then turned to *The Secret History of Kate Bush (& the Strange Art of Pop)*. Vermorel said it was a deliberate over-the-top attempt to push out the boundaries of pop books. He could not understand why it was still selling. He saw the research into Kate's family history as the ultimate act of a true fan. The students laughed out loud when he talked about the famous ditch, and putting himself in it, although whether they were laughing with him or at him it was difficult to say. When asked if he was concerned that Kate might have been upset by the book, he said that he regretted that she had been upset, but that: "it was vital to avoid thinking of her as a person rather than as an object".

He then played *Oh England My Lionheart* and showed a slide of a letter written by this author in the early '80's apparently to one of our readers. It turned out that 'Fernandez Butterworth' was actually Vermorel's alias for *HomeGround* subscription purposes. He had others! Talking of *HomeGround*, Vermorel said it was well-informed and useful to him, and then told a story which must illustrate the state of the man's mind. It seems that inspired by the Woody Allen film *Stardust Memories* he had gone to Kate's house and climbed the drain pipe. Before anyone within discovered him he fell off and ran away.

When asked if he liked her music his answer was blunt: "I like the piano stuff, but the rock stuff is a bit naff". His closing assertion was that you choose to be a fan and you rededicate yourself everyday: "the music is unimportant". This last point caused a great deal of dissent in the hall, and a number of the students tried to convince Vermorel that surely the music and the lyrics were the whole point. Vermorel was not impressed by that argument.

Peter: It should of course be pointed out that Krys and many other Kate fans are also huge fans of Tori, who has subsequently had a very successful live and recorded career.

These were my views then, and really haven't changed an awful lot since.

The launch marketing of Tori Amos continued in the UK with the release of the first single *China* on 25th January and the album *Little Earthquakes* in April. Look, this whole argument has been done to death in the fanzines and newsgroups. This author's views (which are not necessarily shared by the *HomeGround* collective ("a sort of anarcho-syndicalist commune") are that Tori clearly has a great musical talent, but at the end of the day is too contrived to fully cut it in comparison to Kate. She quite clearly was the subject of a massively successful niche marketing campaign. The market research clearly analysed Kate's audience. What would you like? Kate touring (a lot) please. Kate not being quite so distant, Kate being a little more explicit in her songs, putting herself more clearly in the confessional frame. That'll get the girls. What would the lads like?

Tori's label encouraged her to write songs and perform live in a way which addressed all these matters. And of course the cover of *Little Earthquakes* bore some resemblance to the US cover of *The Kick Inside*. Oh yes, I've read all the denials, and the suggestions that it was just a coincidence. I'm sorry, I don't believe it. The clearly identified target marketing by Tori's label (which could teach Peter Mandelson a lesson or two) belied any other explanation.

It was all famously successful as *Vox* (April 1992) found in interviewing some of the punters at the first Tori gigs: "she's like Kate Bush, but we'll never get to see Kate Bush live, so this is compensation".

It was clear that the strategy was to relaunch Tori in the UK as a sensitive female singer-songwriter, comparable to Kate, then take the results of that campaign and re-launch her on her home territory as the same kind of artist. In an article posted to rec.music.gaffa by Donna Henderson (to whom thanks) she recorded how she was on the receiving end of the initial US push: "I was working for a pre-recorded music distributor when Tori was being promoted. I got this item right before *Little Earthquakes* was released. I saw the bold Kate Bush comparisons and demanded a promo from our buyer. So, I can testify that the marketing worked. I also remember flyers being passed around at the first show she did in Minneapolis... In talking with others at the second show I found a large percentage who viewed Tori as a Kate stand in, 'since she wouldn't tour'".

Henderson then gives the details of what she calls a 'pseudo-magazine' put together by Tori's label for the US release of *Little Earthquakes*. This collected together much of the coverage Tori had obtained in the UK, and highlighted in bold type every mention of Kate's name. Additionally on pages 22 to 24 of the hand-out were 19 short clips collecting together virtually every other mention of Kate in the Tori context, including this from *Entertainment Weekly* January 31st 1992, which gives the game away: "Amos, 28, last year took refuge in Britain, where critics regularly compare her to Laura Nyro, Kate Bush and even Patti Smith".

Oh well. Does it matter, especially at this point? Not a lot. Tori has her own niche now, and new artists are being promoted as "the new Tori Amos" and so it goes. Those of us with long memories remember Kate in 1978 being compared to Joni Mitchell and Karla Bonoff. At least Kate could say she made her own audience.

Kate's music featured prominently in the mega-TV programme 'The Last Show on Earth', shown on 27th April, an attempt to raise environmental consciousness ahead of the Earth Summit in Rio. Various excerpts from *Hello Earth* were used during the stunning title sequence and elsewhere in the three-hour programme. In the same vein PolyGram released a UN sponsored compilation entitled *Earthrise – The Rain Forest Album*. Released on 1st June, the album was masterminded by the Earth Love Fund with all the royalties going to environmental charities. Kate's contribution was the duet with Peter Gabriel on *Don't Give Up*.

The *HomeGround* tenth birthday took place on Sunday 24th May at the Wag Club in London's Soho, for the Editors an event which was alternatively happy and emotional.

On 20th April, top dance act Utah Saints released a track called *Something Good* which sampled that very line from Kate's *Cloudbusting*. Most people including EMI had put their chances of getting Kate to agree to the sampling at nil. But she had listened sympathetically. Interviewed in their local newspaper, singer Jezz Willis said: "We hadn't a clue how Kate would react when we sent her a tape of the track, especially since we'd nicked the strings and drums of *Cloudbusting* as well as the vocals. We didn't want people to think we were taking the piss. We wanted it to sound cool rather than quirky. Kate even agreed to sell us a 30 second clip of the video. The only trouble was that we had to edit Donald Sutherland out. If we'd kept him in it would have cost us an arm and a leg".

The club play reviewers were interested: "Kate Bush's ravishing *Cloudbursting* (sic) sampled to good effect and transformed into a whirligig electro swirl that is packed with the kind of lecherous tics that are always guaranteed to separate this kind of stuff from the massed ranks of the frighteningly ordinary": Jon Wilde *Melody Maker* 30/5/92.

In early June the track broke into the Gallup singles chart. The band appeared on 'Top of the Pops' twice performing the track, with the picture discs featured on the scratch console courtesy of *HomeGround*.

Kate did not at any time give any undertaking to become involved in the 28th June shambles on Clapham Common inspired by Mick Jagger and attended by Government Minister David Mellor and somewhat grandly entitled 'National Music Day'. It is not known why the BBC programme weekly the *Radio Times* announced her involvement, but we can guess that this was on the strength only of her being asked!

In the Summer of 1992 we were waiting for news of a new album. The Spring deadline had

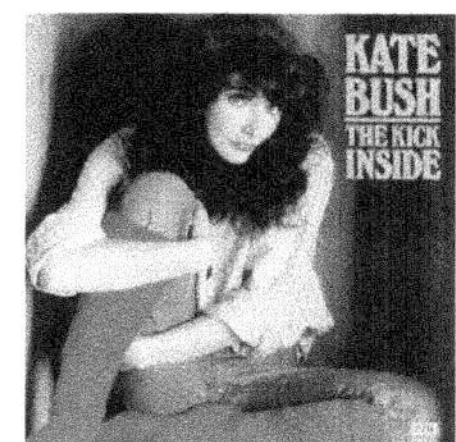

Peter Mandelson with Gordon Brown and Tony Blair were the "Troika" of Labour Party "modernisers" who invented "New Labour" which led to three General Election victories.

For the remix and reissue of *Something Good* in 2008 the Saints did not use a Kate sample but rerecorded the vocal with a session singer.

passed, and there was no firm news, but we thought that Kate's seventh album proper was finished to all intents and purposes, and that a September 1992 release date was realistic. So much for our predictions!

In the Autumn the talk was again of Kate and Prince; Kate seen talking to Prince backstage at his gigs, telephone conversations, and even that they might be recording together. Now, as told above, we know that they did not record together, but swapped multi-track tapes, even so ending up without the vocal part which Del Palmer later noted would have been particularly good for him. Actually, the next new material we got from Kate was *Home for Christmas*, written for the Comic Strip's 24th December Christmas show 'Wild Turkey'.

Opposite: the page from issue 48 on which we reproduced the letter from Revoloutionary Comics, together with some of the art work from the comic and our further comments.

The first sighting of Kate in 1993 was her attendance at a Roy Harper gig at London's Bloomsbury Theatre on 9th January. Then there was the Brits palaver. That year the awards committee nominated Kate for "best female artist" on the basis that she had a hit in October 1991 with *Rocket Man*. In the 23rd January *NME* issue, journalists Terry Staunton and Keith Cameron interviewed the chairman of the awards committee who explained rather unhelpfully: "Someone like Kate Bush, for instance, she only has to breathe and she gets voted for, because the British record industry loves Kate Bush". Jonathan King, a former producer of the awards, defended the nomination: "the prolific Kate Bush is a fine contemporary artist". Others were not so kind. Richard Roberts, partner in Too Pure Records, the home of PJ Harvey, spat: "It's a load of crap... Who are the nominees? As for Kate Bush, well I think if they actually checked they'd find these people are all dead".

The famous lost soundtrack (including Kate's rendering of the main theme) to Terry Gilliam's 1985 cult classic film *Brazil* appeared in record shops in late January, released not by MCA, but by the French record company Milan. The company blurb raved: "Michael Kamen conducts the London Philharmonic Orchestra through a score as rich in imagery as the film it accompanies. Kamen fuses a stunning variety of forms, ranging from jazz to symphonic to '30s pop, and includes allusions to everything from Ravel to Woody Woodpecker. Woven around well-known conversational pieces from the movie and ethereal vocals by Kate Bush, the soundtrack is by turns haunting, melodic, and powerful."

The sleeve notes contain much about Michael Kamen (he says it was his finest hour), and there was Terry Gilliam's quote: "When I'm being interviewed I always lie in case I'm being misquoted!" Kate was the top of his list of credits.

In early 1993 Revolutionary Comics of San Diego, California published a comic-book style graphic biography of Kate, and they described it thus:

"The fairy princess of rock and an enduring cult favourite. Little seemed to be known about the ethereal singer's life until Revolutionary got on the case. Six months in the making, meticulously researched and beautifully illustrated, this one promises to be a perennial seller. Lots of insider info and rare pics, with guest appearances by Peter Gabriel, Pink Floyd, and others. Our biographies are written in a dramatic, cinematic style rather than being presented as a encyclopaedic recitation of facts and dates. So you can look forward to this issue reading, and looking, like Kate's life story as dramatised for motion pictures: romantic, sweeping, and full of stunning imagery"

We wanted the sick-bag. Although we had not seen the comic in its full glory at that stage, in *HomeGround* 47 we ran some comments from a Love-Hounds correspondent who had actually "read" it:

"In this comic Kate is drawn inconsistently at best and completely unrecognisable the rest of the time... The other thing that drove me absolutely crazy was the repeated reference to Kate's breasts! Get a life guys! They make it sound like she's about to explode any minute! Geez! As for the actual story... well I am definitely not an expert but it seems to follow the basic history so far, though the dramatisation probably blows a lot of things out of proportion. *Sigh* Oh well, it's cute, it's fun, if not very well-done. And it's nice that Kate was remembered for a change instead of being ignored by the main stream here in North America like she usually is. It's also probably one of the least expensive bits of memorabilia available."

Revolutionary Comics weren't about to let us get away with this, however, and we reproduced their letter in issue 48. That told us! We still thought it was crap. Entertaining crap, but still crap.

In early 1993 the first solid information about Kate's new album started coming through. By February EMI had heard half the album and they then believed they had some of the biggest hits ever written by Kate, an album far more accessible than *The Sensual World*. They were then hoping for a single in May and the album out in June. However, problems in the US meant the release date was put back first to September. The album was actually finished on 21st April. Del went to the USA in mid-May to present the album to Sony and it was first presented complete by Kate and Del to the top EMI staffers at Abbey Road on 20th May, together with its title, *The Red Shoes*.

Comic Kate

Ouch! And that was just for our comments on the press release!

Actually, despite Mr Allen's assertions, we did not review his comic unseen, we used the comments of a LoveHound who had read the thing. In the event our warnings seem amply justified.

It's easy to demolish this thing - but is it worth it? On its own level as a comic it works. It will be read, on the whole, by people who know very little about Kate, not even what she and her family look like. It will not matter that reading this comic makes them little the wiser. For them Kate will continue to be a fantasy character that lives in the comic book world with Superman, Terminator vs Aliens, and Judge Dredd.

Having said that, the audience **HOMEGROUND** addresses represent the hardcore of Kate's fans, and hopefully they want to know what we think before parting with their money.

The crucial thing about a comic book is the artwork, and the artwork in this comic is scarcely adequate. I assume the artist worked from photographs. He did not succeed in capturing the likeness most importantly, of Kate, in any of the frames, although he does seem to have concentrated in catching her in her underwear. He does not catch any of the other characters including Kate's brothers, parents, Dave Gilmour or Rowan Atkinson - and the Trio Bulgarka look like the three Kings from the *Life of Brian*.

Much of the information that informs this comic seems to have been taken from the chronology in the official EMI publication *The Complete Kate Bush*, but even so, it is not always accurate, and its representation is often, but unintentionally, quite funny: East Wickham farm does not actually have Greek columns, and there are few four masted sailing ships on Loch Ness. The characterisations of the principal characters are also very funny. Many of them seem to live in a world drawn from *This is Spinal Tap* and too much watching of MTV. The intimate scenes between Kate and Del are especially funny.

Look, you know the sort of thing this is. If only for entertainment purposes you ought to have it. Not to be taken seriously.

9528 Miramar Rd., #213
San Diego, CA 92126

1 (800) 765-2669
FAX (619) 530-4808

Homeground Magazine
Attn. Krystyna, Peter & David
PO Box 176
Orpington Kent
BR5 3NA
England UK

Dear Homeground,

Enclosed is a copy of our Kate Comic. I would have hoped that you'd wait to actually SEE a copy before "warning" readers about it in your issue #47, as I thought you had more journalistic integrity than that (though the constant typographical errors in your magazine should perhaps have tipped me off).

Your Lovehounds correspondent who DID see the comic gave a rather accurate review, I thought, though I think you'll find that very little was blown "out of proportion" and that the "breast" references (of which there are only a couple) come from actual quotes from participants in the story. I do feel that our characterization rings very true to life, and that there are some genuinely charming and moving moments in the story.

The art is a bit more problematic. It's quite unfair to compare what our artists do with the still portraits which appear in Homeground. It's fairly easy to get a good likeness when rendering a single drawing (and many of the Homeground illos are directly based on photographs), but it's much harder to maintain that consistent likeness when the subject is moving around from panel to panel in different motions and scenes. The artist on our comic, Marshall Ross, did indeed have problems with this, but all in all I think that it's still a beautifully illustrated comic. Since I'm tooting our own horn, I'll add that I've gotten dozens of letters, from both casual and hardcore Kate fans, who love the way we've worked in so many interesting tidbits and in-references. A couple of readers who collect all our comics, regardless of the subjects, wrote to say that they were so interested in Kate (whose music they'd never heard) because of our comic that they went out and bought some of her records.

So in our own way, we're really helping to spread the word about Kate in America, something very few publishers of our caliber and size are doing. Many thousands of people will see this comic, in grocery stores, bookshops, record stores and newsstands (in other countries as well).

One would think that our effort would earn some sort of POSITIVE note from the small press fanzines like yourself. Our one issue presents more information about Kate, to more people all at once, than probably any other North American publication ever has. And we've sold even more copies in Europe!

You're welcome.

Jay Allen Sanford, Managing Editor

PS: I fail to see why our press release earned the "Ugh! Pass me the sick bag" note. Advertisements like this are traditionally full of hyperbole, and ours was not nearly so cloying and fawning as many of the things I've read in Homeground! This insult mystifies me - could it be that you folks are so possessive of Kate that you don't want anybody but yourselves writing about her?! A left field guess, to be sure, but that's how confused I am by your commentary. Hopefully, now that you've seen the real comic, you can give a more informed opinion to your readers. I don't even mind if you hate it, but at least this way you'll know what you're talking about.

Scenes from a life: Some of that artwork!

Issue 44: March 1992

The sadness with which we received the news of the death of Kate's mother echoes even now some twenty years later.

Hannah Bush
1919 - 1992
"Ma"

Everyone who met Kate's mum will have their own special memory of her very special warmth and kindness. Quite frankly it was as if Hannah was a mother to us all. She was always interested in everything we did, and always supported us.

It was she who on seeing the first and rather humble issues of HomeGround encouraged us to stay with it and keep going. All the fans who ever went to East Wickham Farm were greeted by Hannah just as if they were Kate's friends. She made time for us, though goodness knows we must have been quite a nuisance at times.

It was Hannah who enquired after our lives and jobs and health - we will always remember when on one visit Peter had something of a head cold and Hannah promptly served up coffee laced with brandy (or was it brandy laced with coffee?) She was concerned with us and for us, in all that we did, whether it related to Kate or to HomeGround or to our personal lives. She was a true friend.

On many occasions it was Hannah who persuaded and gave Kate the courage to go on and do those things she might not otherwise have done.

This is a grievous loss to Dr. Bush, and to Kate and her brothers, and to Lisa. We share in the grief. We were in tears when we heard. We shall miss her dreadfully. Goodbye Hannah. May your inspiration of love and friendship long be a shining example to us all.

Peter, Krys & Dave

Issue 46: October 1992

HomeGround has received many moving letters in response to the very sad news of the death of Hannah Bush, Kate's mother. Here are just a few of those, expressing the emotions felt by us all.

Lisa Matriccino: My deepest sympathy to Kate and her family on the passing on of Hannah. I know how I feel about my Mum.

Jeff Clarke: Even though I'm many miles away, I'm with you in my heart; I'm deeply shocked to know of Hannah's death.

I can't begin to express in words the sorrow and loss I've been feeling since I received the news in *HomeGround*. I've been crying and needing so much to be close to my friends, to say I love you, and I'm hurting too. I would like to express my sincerest sympathy and love to Dr. Bush and family and their friends at a time of such great loss. I am so deeply sorry. Goodbye dear Hannah, I'll miss you and I will always remember you.

Thank you also Krys, Sharon, Peter and Dave for being here for me; you know what it really feels like. Thank you for sharing with me your friendship with Hannah. I love when you mentioned the way she would ruffle Peter's beard when you said your goodbyes. I know Hannah was a wonderful and warm lady and I'm really going to miss her. I don't think the Kate-speaking world will ever be the same.

I love you guys very much. I wish I could hug you all. With All My Love.

Nello Russo: Our hearts are full of sadness because of the death of Kate's mother.

Jacqui Fox: I was saddened to read of the passing away of Kate's Mother, Hannah. Many are unaware of the integral part a family is to artists such as Kate. I know she is very much a family person and so my sympathies go to her and her family.

Seán Twomey: I cannot say how deeply I've felt the loss of Hannah Bush. I'll never forget that day, excitedly opening my beloved *HomeGround*, only to be heart-broken by the news. I sat in my room and listened to *Mother Stands for Comfort* over and over. My family thought I was being silly crying for someone I'd never met. Yet somehow through Kate's music I think I did meet 'Ma'.

Len Bullard: It is very sad to hear about Kate's mom. She was Kate's shelter and your own for many years and her loss is dear. There are few harbors for our hearts. When one closes for ever, the ways of our emotions are lost. All of the maps become relics, memories still fresh but painful and joyful, irreconcilable... it is sad to be deprived of the harbor of your heart. Hold on to the love and protect the hearts of those that remain. Kate must be the strong center now. Your hearts are deep enough to harbor her grief, I think.

Jaakko: I was most saddened when reading the sorrowful news... Even though I did not know Mrs. Bush, I somehow feel that somebody very important has now gone away. A woman who has given birth and raised such precious children as she has, must be somebody very precious herself too.

The Clarity of Loss

Collin Kelley

This year I did not mark
The day of your death.
I let it slip by in an afternoon
filled with music you'll never hear,
words you'll never read,
a chorus of voices raised in protest
at the unwavering passage of time.
I don't need a number
to know that you are gone.

Since you went away, other tragedies
have left their toll, the media
mining the fragile, the exhaustion,
the relentless sorrow of things we cannot change.
We have made high art out of twisted cars,
planes crashing, buildings falling.

I have dissected my past into little pieces
and put them in their proper places.
I have begun the process of growing up
and older, of stripping down memories
to their essence and casting off the extraneous.

Even without a calendar, we will be born
and die, clock work beyond our control.
And there is a clarity in loss because
it reveals the true path, the one common
experience, the thing we all share.
You have died and I will join you, and time,
which we have enslaved ourselves to, will snap,
and in whatever an instant is,
it will be as if we never parted.

Rockets and Candles

Kate's Elton John Covers

Issue 44: March 1992

Keith Pitches: A fall or a push?

My heart soars with delight every time I think of *Candle in the Wind*. It's a stunningly powerful B-side, so familiar a trademark of all Kate releases. The voice thrills me to the core as it pitches itself headlong into a river of emotion. The music synchronizes with telling phrases such as "loneliness was the toughest role you played" tugging at the heartstrings.

I'm not a huge fan of Elton John, but this track of his and Bernie Taupin's really asks questions! For example, did Marylin Monroe commit suicide or was she murdered because she knew too much? *Candle in the Wind* is similar in this way to many Kate tracks. On 'Top of the Pops' many of her tracks have had controversial bits removed. *Breathing* (official reasons – too frightening), *Cloudbusting* (too long) and *Experiment IV* (also too frightening) come to mind. Are we drifting towards censorship in this country?

The way Kate's voice almost laments for Norma Jean is touching. Both of their backgrounds couldn't be more different. Kate has her family. It is my fervent wish that when she faces her first live audience for years she will realise that she has another "family".

Graphic: Paulina Stuckey

Opposite: issues 44 to 48: two more covers by Debi Bowes, and one by Neil Loughran

As the love and emotion contained within Kate's music and poetry pours out of hi-fi and transistor radios nationwide, so we reciprocate. May the energy generated by her fans worldwide be channelled via the ether, through her close associates, friends and family for Kate to draw on as a source of strength.

From Remember Yourself issue 58 October 1996

Eddie Holland: I never knew Marilyn either

At last something from the vocal chords of our beloved Kate. It's hard to say something about both *Rocket Man* and *Candle in the Wind*. Just the fact that the latter made me cry, even though I never knew Marilyn either, should be enough.

Letters from issue 44

Michael Booker: An Older Reader Writes

The reason I subscribe to *HomeGround* is mainly for any up-to-date news of Kate, and photographs, and any bits of information on her records. I am afraid the articles are above my head! However, they are obviously of interest to your younger readers who, no doubt, are more intelligent than I and can understand their meaning!

It is quite amazing that I have had an interest in Kate for almost ten years now. I can still remember driving with my wife and turning on the radio to hear possibly the first airing of *Wuthering Heights*. I told my wife it would be a hit, and then did something I had not done since I was a teenager. I went out and purchased a pop record. Unfortunately my wife, my son (who is 30 years old) and daughter (who is 32 years old) do not understand my liking. I'm afraid that the playing of Kate's records is restricted to the times when my wife and family are not present, or whilst I am in my "den".

Although I feel like an early Christian, hiding my beliefs, I was very pleased to have a shot in the arm with the release of *Rocket Man* and the performance on 'Wogan' has been added to my collection. I was with my wife when I remembered that I hadn't put a tape in the video. I had to stop at a telephone box and ring my daughter at home. She had a good laugh at my expense, but she taped it!

Krys: People who will use and abuse

The classic icon, Marilyn Monroe, was exploited by most of the people around her and she wasn't in control of her personal life or career. I wonder whether Kate held this in mind when she decided to record *Candle in the Wind*, and whether in her own way was saying something about herself. For many famous people such as Kate, it must get very difficult to discern people's true motives for wanting to know you, whether it is for yourself, or whether it is for your fame so they can impress people at parties with the odd name-drop here and there, or maybe they want your money. Hangers-on are everywhere, and there are people who will use and abuse. Even friends. There are always people ready to jump on the bandwagon.

HOMEGROUND 44

The HOMEGROUND 46

47 nzine Summer 93

The KATE BUSH Fanzine Winter 92

The KATE BUSH Fanzine Spring 93

HOMEGROUND

Hello All,

Another issue, another typeface: Do you like this one better? We do. We think we'll stick with this one.

Now to something more interesting. You'll see the album news opposite. Have patience all ye believers. It will be worth it.

I'm sure our British readers will agree with us that the furore over Kate's nomination for a Brit was indicative of two things: the irrelevance of the awards themselves and the ignorance and stupidity of most British so-called 'music journalists'. Within, Dave (again) considers what might be done with the Brits (ugh!)

Isn't it wonderful to have a proper copy of Kate's beautiful rendition of the main theme from *Brazil*. What a shame it wasn't actually used in that brilliant film.

If you wait long enough...So a clip of Kate on an early 1978 *Top of the Pops* gets aired on BBC-TV. Now all we want is the very first *TOTP*, *Saturday Night at the Mill*, and the 'barefoot in the snow' version of *Wuthering Heights*, filmed in March 1979 in Leysin, and...oh well, some day perhaps.

We've had some contrary reactions to our story in the last issue about the separate release of the odds and sods CDs. Some said "How did we know the fans didn't want such a release?" The answer is that we got a heap of mail on the box set, much of it from those who paid out about £100 essentially to get the odds and sods. We don't seek to represent the great plurality of record buyers, but we do seek to represent that hard core of Kate fans who are our readers. Quite clearly EMI are a massive commercial company. I doubt if our views were crucial in the matter. In the end it was down to Kate, and we suspect Kate is more concerned about creating new material than going over old stuff, however good those old tracks are.

It is a while since **HOMEGROUND** last increased its prices. Nearly two years in fact. We're afraid we have to bow to the inevitable. The prices of paper, printing, and weird bits of computer equipment wait for no man, and certainly not for us. We hope it will put no-one off. We shall continue to try to deliver the service we set out to do now some eleven years ago, to tell you all the news in the Kate-speaking world, and give you the chance to have your say.

Next time, at last, we hope to have some real information on the album and single. Honest!

See you then,

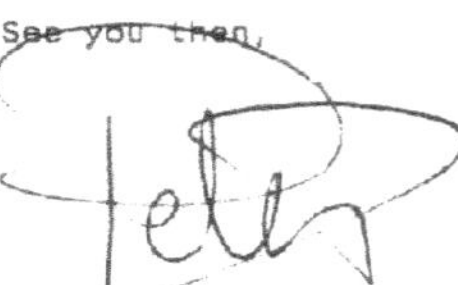

The Wag

Dave, Krys and Peter on the HomeGround 10th Birthday Party

After talking about our tenth birthday for what seems like years, on Sunday 24th May 1992 the event finally took place. Kicking around many different ideas, we decided on an informal event at which Kate fans could let down their collective hair and have a really good time. Once we had found the venue (and we wanted to be fairly imaginative) the actual organisation was fairly straightforward. Peter and Krys handled the ticket sales, and Dave concentrated on the event itself.

We arrived at the club (in the wonderfully seedy and cosmopolitan area of Soho – all erotic review-bars and exquisite delicatessens) at about 2 o'clock along with our team of 'willing' helpers. The Wag, although being a very 'happening' place is quite sparse inside, and the first task was to create a rather more 'Katey' atmosphere, whilst Dave talked serious stuff with the management. To this end Peter had welded himself to the photocopier during the week before and had produced A3-sized copies of all the *HomeGround* covers, as well as about fifty copies of the cartoon by Paulina Stuckey we were using as the party logo. By the time these were all up, the Wag looked rather more like an explosion in a paper factory. By the end of the party the posters had all mysteriously vanished!

As we worked, we watched with some relief (on the TV monitor) the little crowd gathering, and finally opened the doors at 4 o'clock. Whilst everyone came in we played videos and did our best to remember the faces ("It's erm er – XXX – isn't it?" "No, she's over there, I'm YYY!").

We started formally about an hour later with Dave welcoming everyone to our celebration and kicking off with (by popular demand) another showing of the compilation video *This Woman's Work* originally put together for the 1990 Convention, and added the video for *Rocket Man*.

To the astonishment of the club staff, everyone sat in almost reverent silence throughout the film which lasted over two hours, and we began to wonder whether the disco was going to come off! Will they wake up? Will we have to drag them onto the floor? At about seven Dave entered the DJ box and we were about to find out.

Of course we started with Kate tracks. No response apart from some twitching toes and two partygoers who hit the floor from the off. Three records in, Dave put on *Sledgehammer*, and whoosh, the dance floor was full – and stayed that way all night (well apart from a Stranglers track or two). Most of the music played was Kate's, but we also included U2, Peter Gabriel, Shakespeare's Sister, Bowie, Bob Marley, Madonna, The Smiths, and even Kylie! (we're not sure what was more non-reportable – the fact that you lot asked for Kylie, or the fact that Dave actually had an album with him!)

For us the party was alternatively happy and emotional. We threw ourselves around the floor, and watched others having a good time whilst we reflected on ten years of *HomeGround*.

The party was an event for one reader who lives in what *was* (how great it is to be able to say that!) East Germany, on his very first expedition beyond the frontier that used to hold him in (with razor wire, starving dogs, automatic machine guns, and guards with orders to shoot to kill). He told us about taking the channel ferry and how he'd wept on seeing for the first time the white cliffs he had before only read about, and never imagined he would ever see in reality.

All of us who took a stint on the door enjoyed talking to the club door staff, and hearing their stories. We suspect they are not very often treated like human beings. They in turn were very complimentary about the party-goers, and they and the management invited us all back sometime.

We knew from the start that Kate would not be attending, but she donated signed albums, CDs, photographs and six signed *This Woman's Work* vinyl box sets for us to give away and raffle. Jon Bishop and Nev Williams from *Never Forever* fanzine won one of the box sets, and very kindly gave their prize back, which was auctioned and raised £100 for the Terrence Higgins Trust from one generous reader.

The hot weather and the stifling atmosphere of the club had a startling effect on Kate fans fashion-wise. Most were down to the basics, and all that exposed flesh did have an effect on the other party goers, resulting in some interesting and unlikely liaisons! As we were packing up, a catwalk for the next day's event – a fashion show – was being laid on the floor of the club, and to our amusement the very friendly Jamaican bouncer, who Krys had taken quite a shine to, started to shake his little tush on the catwalk. He paraded up and down a few times, and really looked the part. It was so funny.

The important thing was that everyone had a really good time. I rather think we'll do it again when we feel like it. Any excuse for a piss up!

Issue 46: October 1992

This was the *Locomotion* era before Kylie became cool!

Photo: At The Wag Club - The *HomeGround* Editors drink a glass of bubbly to the first 10 years!

Photo: *HomeGround*

Opposite: editorial issue 47 "another issue another typeface".

Graphic by Paulina Stuckey

Overleaf: The 10th Anniversary Editorial from issue 45 and the announcement for the *HomeGround* tenth birthday Party.

The next *HomeGround* Party as such was actually held in 2012 for our 30th Anniversary!

Homeground

"Where does the time go, does anybody know?"

HomeGround has been such an important part of my life that it is impossible for me to untangle it from any part of the last ten years. Looking through the old issues to put this 'best of' together has been like looking through a diary I didn't realise I was keeping. 'Did I really think that, then?' 'What the hell does that personal message mean?' For me, some of the best moments have been the events: the Brew-Up in 1983 (cringe!), the Romford Convention in 1985 – a real turning point for us, the 1986 Video Party, and of course the 1990 Convention, still my proudest moment. There are also so many little moments to treasure, most of which are unprintable, unthinkable, and insane, and lose a lot in translation! On the negative side there was all that stupid stuff with the cretins from Under the Ivy, and the odd row and minor upset (No, Krys, we can't do your latest article in scratch and sniff!) For me though, the best thing has been the friends that I have made along the way. I would like to say a personal thanks to Jay for the trust and friendship, to Elaine for all your support and help, the lunches, the laughs, and everything, to Kate for putting up with us, and most of all to dear Peter and Krys, the best bastards a boy could have. **Dave**

It's 3 in the morning on and I've just about stopped tearing my hair out after trying to piece this issue together for the past couple of weeks. Out of all the issues, this has been the hardest to create. I hope you like the result. Well, it's been ten years and in that time so much has happened. They have been the best years of my life (so far!) *HomeGround* has brought us many friends and a lot of love. I cannot add much more to what Peter and Dave have said. I'll let the pages speak for themselves. I would like to thank Kate for her love and support, and for bringing us all together in the first place (lots of love and hugs to you, Kate), her family for everything; Peter for all his love these past ten years (I love you so much, you big hairy bastard!); Dave for the choccy, hugs and all the fun (I love you too, you BAAASTAAARD you!); Pami and Pauli for all the love and stuff...! Sharon for her love, friendship and hard work; Helen for being a wonderful human being, and being there; Debi for her friendship and all her hard work over the years, Peter's Mum for her endless work at the general admin end; and Amber who has done his damnedest to create even more havoc than me in the process of making this mag. This issue is dedicated to the memory of Hannah, our very dear friend who was there at the beginning, and whose encouragement helped us go from strength to strength. Hannah, this is for you... with Love. **Krys**

As I stood over the photocopier reducing the stuff for this issue, I saw the last ten years of my life flash before me. Being connected with *HomeGround* has probably been the single most important factor of my life in that period. Through it I first contacted Krys, my darling lady, and through it I came to meet many people who are more dear to me than I can know, or can say. *HomeGround* has meant the thrill and elation of the Conventions and the pressures, strains and tensions of meeting print deadlines – and many times of not meeting them. It has been the story of the warmth of the trust and friendship with Kate and her family, and the responsibilities that went with that. It has been the difficulties of dealing with reflected glory, and the jealousy and sniping that sometimes brings, but also the privileges. I thank Krys and Dave for putting up with this moody bastard, and everyone who has ever written in in appreciation of our efforts. I wonder where we will all be in ten years time? **Peter**

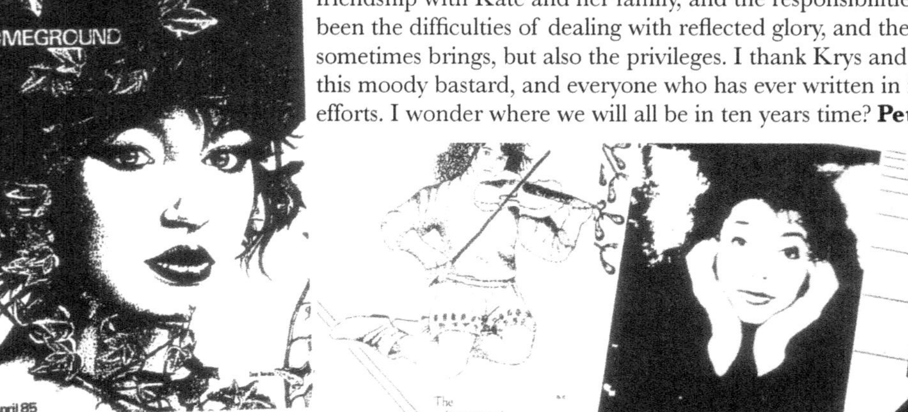

HOMEGROUND

HOMEGROUND

The International KATE BUSH Fanzine
Christmas 85 No. 21

HOMEGROUND

KATE BUSH
Issue 10 Christmas 1983

HOMEGROUND

April 85

HOMEGROUND

The Tenth Birthday Party!

24th May 1992

THE WAG CLUB
WARDOUR STREET, LONDON W1
FROM 4PM UNTIL 11PM.

Have you ever wished you could go to a club and hear Kate's music?
Dance to *The Dreaming*?
Slam to The Sensual World?
Boogie to *The Big Sky*?
Vogue to...Whatever?

In May 1992 the oldest continuing Kate Bush fanzine celebrates its first ten years.

To celebrate we are holding a party.

No set events. This is not a convention.

Just a chance to have a bloody good time with other Kate fans.

The tickets are £6.00 each.

Available from the HOMEGROUND address, and please send an SAE.
(Cheques and POs made payable to HOMEGROUND)

Be there, or miss the fan event of 1992!

Where Does the Time Go?

A Chronology of the First Ten Years of HomeGround

Issue 45: July 1992

HOMEGROUND (4-issue subscription £4.70 U.K. & Europe/£9.30 USA & Canada/£9.70 Australasia & Japan, from Homeground Fanzine, P.O. Box 176, Orpington, Kent): As ever, this Kate Bush fanzine has a very comprehensive news section, plus a fascinating collection of features and photos. Collectors should be particularly interested in the expose of the origins of the Kate Bush interview picture disc currently in circulation, one of a number of extremely unofficial interview records available in the shops at the moment.

Review in *Record Collector* January 1987

HOMEGROUND (12-issue sub. £5.20 U.K., £6 Eire/Europe, £9.20 U.S.A./Canada, £9.80 Australasia/Japan, payable to Homeground Fanzine, PO Box 176, Orpington, Kent BR5 3NA) Issue 29 of this glossy fanzine takes a look at Kate Bush's activities five years ago and lists bootleg recordings. Issue 30 includes a bibliography, and both are packed with the latest news plus articles about or inspired by the singer.

Review *Record Collector* May 1988

HOMEGROUND (4-issue sub. £5.20 U.K., £6 EEC, £7.10 Europe (non EEC), £9.20 U.S./Canada/S. America, £9.80 Australia/New Zealand/Japan, elsewhere write to P.O. Box 176, Orpington, Kent BR5 3NA): Plenty here for Kate Bush fans, from gushing prose to hard collector's info, with lots in between!

Review Record Collector September 1989

Every issue of *HomeGround* from January 1984 onward has now gone into the British and Irish Deposit Libraries, the British Library, the National Libraries of Scotland and Wales, the Bodlian in Oxford and the University Library in Cambridge, and the Library of Trinity College Dublin.

In the future all this material will be available to scholars researching the history of popular music and Kate in particular.

1982 MAY: *HomeGround* is conceived in Dave's flat at Tarnwood Park, Mottingham. The first issue (25 copies run off on the office photocopier) is born a couple of weeks later to the proud editors: Dave, Peter and Mandy. The aim is to give it away to the fans we know. Our first scoop is Kate's new single – a track to be called *The Abo Song* (the working title of *The Dreaming* single). **JUNE**: The first issue is revamped to include Peter's missing article and 150 copies are printed. *HomeGround* announces its existence to the world in its first music press adverts. We accept that it's going to be an ongoing project and begin on the 2nd issue. **JULY**: *HomeGround* attends the Prince's Trust Rock Gala at London's Dominion Theatre, proudly wearing our home-made badges! We are noticed! The 2nd issue is printed. *HomeGround* adopts the format it has had ever since. We begin to seek subscriptions and right away begin to get enquiries from Europe and the USA. **SEPTEMBER:** *HomeGround* gets to as many events relating to the release of *The Dreaming* as it can. The three editors run into Kate at Capital Radio's Euston Tower. Later that month we relax on the first great *HomeGround* camping trip at Sandling in Kent. We discover the infamous invisible giant bunnies! **OCTOBER:** The editors attend the Gabriel and Genesis gig at Milton Keynes. The open air concert becomes a morass as the rain pours torrentially. It takes us nearly four hours to get out of the car park. The event becomes a *HomeGround* legend. Issue 3 reviews *The Dreaming* and berates BBC Radio 1 for its lack of support of the single. Issue 3 also contains Krys' first contribution. **DECEMBER:** The first *HomeGround* Yuletide issue complains about the lack of support for *There Goes a Tenner* and Dave's dad gets his say.

1983 FEBRUARY: Issue 5 is an artistic triumph and a financial disaster. It is our largest yet at 38 pages, contains our first interview (with Roy Harper), the first installment of *Five Years Ago* (originally to be just a one-off!), and the results of our first readers poll of Kate's tracks (narrowly won, after some adjustment, by *Breathing*). **APRIL**: Issue 6 contains a review of Fred Vermorel's *Secret History* and a letter from the man himself putting himself up as the Devil in the religion constructed by Kate's fans. **JULY**: *HomeGround* attends the first known fan gathering in the UK in Birmingham organised by Donna Clifton and Dawn Wilbraham. In the Summer months the editors receive a trickle of visitors from foreign parts, including the USA. There is much controversy both within and without the editorial team over the political content of some articles in issues 6, 7, and 8. **AUGUST**: Issue 8 sees the departure of Mandy to pursue her own star, and Krys becomes the new Editor. She has been involved for some time in keeping our manual subs records up to date, and in the general production of the magazine. **SEPTEMBER**: *HomeGround* first hears from Dale Somerville in Canada. He has spent a fortune trying to persuade Kate to appear live in Canada, and is now channelling his energies into a new fanzine to be called *Breakthrough*. **NOVEMBER**: *HomeGround*'s first event, the famous 'Brew-up'. You name it, and it went wrong! The hall was double booked, and we had to make do with a smaller room with no catering facilities, and so there was no tea! We remember Debi Bowes making the huge sandwiches that were our main form of subsistence.

1984 JANUARY: In the great *HomeGround* tradition of being late, the Yuletide issue is a new year issue. We receive a letter from the agent for the Copyright libraries demanding free deposit copies. **FEBRUARY** Dale Somerville makes his UK trip and spends a lot of his time with us. We all go to the Kate Bush Evening at Fagin's Night Club in Manchester organised by John Brent. Issue 11 rounds up on the other fanzines which have now appeared including *Breakthrough*, *For the Love of Kate* and *Dreamtime*. **APRIL**: Issue 12 has the first *Gurus and Glass Onions* article aimed at those fans who we felt were taking things rather too seriously, and the hysterically funny *1984* by Rob Reaney. Another run-in with Fred Vermorel! Channel 4 broadcasts the *Earsay* programme inspired by his forthcoming book on fans, and questions the sanity of two of Kate's fans. *HomeGround* takes up the challenge in pressing for, and partially receiving an apology. **JUNE**: The results of the first *HomeGround* census are revealed in issue 13. We have readers all over the world, even behind the then Iron Curtain. Their ages range from 17 to 59, with the average being 22. The 'most preferred' tracks were *Breathing* and *Night of the Swallow*, the most preferred album being *The Dreaming*. 13 also contained our very first letter of complaint and cancelled subscription. We're pleased to say that the person concerned was disappointed by the presentation of the magazine – and rejoined at a later stage. **JULY:** The very first Wuthering Hike. This apparently crazy idea that the readers should come and meet the editors up at Top Withens on Haworth Moor was actually a success. We wondered if anyone was crazy enough to take us up on it! **AUGUST**: Issue 14 announced the event that didn't happen – the 'Afternoon for Kate Bush Fans' at Hornchurch in Essex. Conceived as a follow-up to the 'Brew-up' this was abandoned after we realised we could do something much, much, better. **OCTOBER**:

The second *Gurus and Glass Onions* article appeared in issue 15, this one aimed at a group of fans who were attempting to promote Kate by means of a chain letter. **NOVEMBER**: Krys and Peter get married and go to live in deepest Kent.

1985 A wonderful year for both Kate and *HomeGround*! **APRIL**: Issue 18 contained an article entitled *My Least Favourite Album*. This was about *Never for Ever*, and the nature of the contents is obvious. Had we known then what we know now about what happened, we probably wouldn't have bothered. Following issues contained a response, and so started the train of events that led to the anti-fanzine *Under The Ivy*. **JULY**: The awful saga of issue 19. For our sins we decide to change our printer to the Youth Kick outfit set up by Paul Weller for the precise purpose of printing fanzines. Again, if we had known etc. and etc. The printer promised us 14 days and took seven weeks to print the issue, and then it got lost in the post back to us, together with the originals. Arrgghhh!!! We then had to put the issue together again! The only good thing was that we were able to include a stop-press sheet with the cover of the new album *Hounds of Love*. **AUGUST**: Kate's mum puts us on the guest list for 'Wogan' when Kate makes her stunning comeback. **SEPTEMBER**: Dave attends the Laserium launch party for the album. Peter and Krys don't realise there are invites waiting on the door, and that Kate's mum had been trying to get hold of us to let us know. **NOVEMBER**: A pivotal moment in *HomeGround*'s history. The 1985 Kate Bush Convention, principally organised by Dave and attended by Kate. For us an almost astonishing success that cemented our confidence and our relationship with Kate. Issue 21 (and 22) were also watersheds. We used our new electronic typewriter on 21 and for the first time got the layout to look something like we wanted. The printing quality still left something to be desired, and so we sacked Youth Kick.

For 10 years

you have produced

the perfect chronicle

of

This Woman's Work.

Congratulations

from

everyone at EMI

EMI

We were extremely pleased that EMI took a full page advert in issue 45 to congratulate *HomeGround* on it's first ten years!

1986 MARCH Issue 22 is the first to be printed by our current printers, and the first all glossy issue. We were so proud of this we almost glowed! We use photos successfully for the first time, having had them properly screened. Issue 22 also included the first part of the interview Kate had recorded especially for the Convention. This was to run over the next 3 issues. At Kate's request, *HomeGround* organises the fans for the *Big Sky* video shoot, and Dave and Peter play airmen in a number of the shots. **SEPTEMBER**: Issue 24 is not one of our greatest moments. Put together in a wild hurry the end result is deeply unsatisfactory. Not the contents you understand, the layout, a mish-mash of typefaces. We take on some help as Sharon becomes the *HomeGround* secretary. **NOVEMBER**: *HomeGround* is asked by Kate to organise some bodies to take part in the video for *Experiment IV*, and we spend some very enjoyable days being made up in green death make-up. The Video Party is principally organised by Dave, and enjoyed by all who attended (over 400) but does not live fully up to our expectations as Kate is mobbed by the fans. Valuable lessons are learned.

1987 MARCH: In issue 26 Dave's Dad celebrates the fact that Dave has finally left home! In fact Dave's progress through the record

Next Wednesday (20th) is the 10th anniversary of the release of one of the most significant debut singles in rock history — **Kate Bush**'s 'Wuthering Heights'.

Kate's output since then speaks for itself, but how do her more fervent supporters rank the 70 songs she's committed to vinyl in the last decade?

The current edition of **Homeground**, the Kate Bush fanzine, provides the answer, as established from the individual top 10 of over 340 committed Kateophiles.

It's not surprising that 'Wuthering Heights' takes top place, or that's it's followed by 'Running Up That Hill', 'The Man With The Child In His Eyes' and 'Cloudbusting', but few would expect 'Night Of The Swallow', a track off the album 'The Dreaming' to complete the top five.

Another track from 'The Dreaming' — 'Suspended In Gaffa' — ranks ninth. Both are therefore judged to be superior to the three singles lifted from 'The Dreaming' — the title track, which is ranked twelfth, 'Sat In Your Lap' (13th) and 'There Goes A Tenner', the least loved of all Kate's singles in 40th place. Another surprise is 'Under The Ivy', issued only as the B-side of 'Running Up That Hill', taking 10th place.

I regularly receive a number of fanzines, and Homeground is perhaps the best. Professionally printed on glossy A4 paper it runs to 32 pages, and provides exclusive news, reviews and essays directly or indirectly pertaining to the charismatic Kate at quarterly intervals.

Review in *Record Mirror* January 1988

business is no end of help to *HomeGround*. **JULY**: Issue 27 celebrates 5 years of *HomeGround*. There could scarcely be greater contrast between this glossy issue full of photos and artwork, and the crude scissors and paste job of issue 1. This is almost wholly due to Krys who is in effect by now the *HomeGround* layout editor. Kate disappears into another 'gap' and *HomeGround* gets on with doing what it does well, seeking to fill that gap for its readers. *HomeGround* guesses right and attends the Gabriel concert at Earl's Court at which Kate appears to duet with Peter Gabriel on *Don't Give Up*. Meanwhile Peter has been working with EMI Music Publications on their book *The Complete Kate*. He writes the introduction, the chronology (since much copied), and the discographies. His only disappointment is that they don't let him correct the proof before the book goes to the printer. **SEPTEMBER**: Debi Bowes has been contributing much to *HomeGround* over the years, but only since issue 22 have we been able to do her artwork justice. Issue 28 contains the first of her full scale A3 centres, a representation of *The Dreaming*. **DECEMBER**: The Yuletide issue has the results of the 1987 *HomeGround* census. The age range of readers has widened and is now 15 to 65 years, with the majority between 18 and 24 years. The most favourite track was *Wuthering Heights*, closely followed by *Running Up That Hill*.

Graphic: Paulina Stuckey – the Official *HomeGround* 10th Anniversary logo!

1988 MARCH: Issue 30 celebrates Kate's ten years in the record business and announces that 1988 will be a Kate-filled year with the release of Kate's 6th album. Well, you can't get 'em all right! Issue 30 also warns *HomeGround* readers against the fake gold discs fbating around, and starts the bibliography project (as yet unfinished). The letters page contains missives from Finland, Netherlands, Argentina, Italy, USA, Iceland, and the Channel Islands. **MAY**: Some readers take objection to the explicit nature of some articles and artwork in recent issues. A petition is got up. We try not to worry. **JULY**: On Kate's birthday the editors attend the 'Shop Assistance' AIDS fund raiser in Covent Garden and run into Kate in Blazer's. **NOVEMBER**: Wuthering Hike II comes and goes, and four times as many people turn up to meet us at Top Withens. **DECEMBER**: Issue 33 slates Kerry Juby's book *The Whole Story*.

1989 MARCH: *HomeGround* never had much luck with competitions. In issue 34 we hit the nadir. We run a competition that nobody enters. Do you all hate Hue and Cry? Issue 34 also sees the Judie Tzuke interview. Kerry Juby's publishers write to us expressing their sadness at our review, and admitting that they sent uncorrected proofs to the printer. **JULY**: On Kate's birthday Peter and Krys and a number of readers assemble on Glastonbury Tor to play *The Morning Fog*. **SEPTEMBER**: *HomeGround* at last correctly predicts the release date of Kate's 6th album, and reviews it at the same time.

1990 We get a little worried this year about the increasing trend in the USA toward censorship of explicit song lyrics and the implication of that trend for Kate. Some people misunderstand that concern. **JULY**: We try to retain our sense of humour and in issue 39 run the infamous *Sinful Music* article. We find out that some of Kate's fans don't have a sense of humour. Meanwhile, *HomeGround* is full of articles by people (including editors) still trying to get a handle on *The Sensual World*. **SEPTEMBER**: Wuthering Hike III came, and ended in the Golden Fleece at Haworth. A marvellous day. **NOVEMBER**: Perhaps the most moving moment in *HomeGround*'s history to date occurs when Kate is on stage at the 1990 Convention. Held at the Hammersmith Palais and again principally organised by Dave over 1,200 of Kate's fans get their fondest wish – to hear Kate sing live. And then to hear her announce her intention to do live dates!

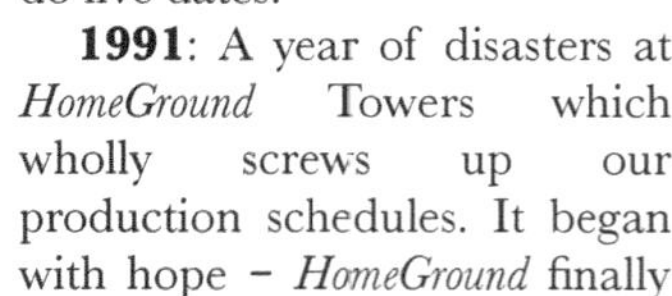

1991: A year of disasters at *HomeGround* Towers which wholly screws up our production schedules. It began with hope – *HomeGround* finally went computerised. Subs first (database) then partially the production (word processor). Presentation was still hampered by our equipment however (bog standard 9-pin matrix printer). Roll on the DTP and the ink-jet! The pen-pals database should be large enough before too long to enable us to start releasing information to enable fans to get together locally.

1992 FEBRUARY: *HomeGround* loses one of its greatest friends and supporters with the death of Kate's mother. Hannah will be dearly missed. **MAY**: *HomeGround* is 10 years old, and celebrates with a party at the Wag Club. We look forward to Kate's seventh studio album, her second tour, Wuthering Hike IV, and the 1993 Convention, whenever it is.

Opposite: Weren't we even more pleased when we received this note from Kate for the 10th Anniversary issue!

KATE BUSH

Many Congratulations
on
your 10th anniversary
with thanks
and
with love,

Kate x

Wuthering Hike IV

Krys and HomeGround Readers on the 1992 Return to Top Withens

Issue 48: May 1993

For weeks before the Fourth Wuthering Hike, to the by now infamous Top Withens, we prayed that it wouldn't rain. Dave had bottled out at the last minute – I'm beginning to think he may be some kind of mollusc type creature – no legs.

The morning of the Hike we made our way through torrential rain. For a moment I thought I could see the word DOOM written in large black clouds across the sky above the M62. "Oh my God, no-one's going to turn up in this!" thought I. This was just one more verification that we are quite, quite mad. Kate's right, you know!

After a brief stop at the same small chippy from Wuthering Hike III, for some 'orrible chips but a very nice fish, we drove the last few miles to Haworth. When we reached our usual car park about half a mile from Top Withens, the sun came out and we were nicely surprised by the number of cars already there.

Out we struggled, after Pami and I furtively did a bit of chocolate first. It took ages to put my wellies on, and sort out all those stupid bits and pieces (like umbrellas, jumpers, Winnie-The-Pooh bag, Arctic survival kit, more chocolate, Moggy, cloudbuster (sorry, wrong venue) we were taking with us. Peter gave up on me and strode boldly ahead with Pauli and Jason and Steve, two *HomeGround* readers we met in the car park. Pami and I were left struggling like a couple of pack horses. Debi, Rod and Teena caught us up, and a young girl called Kirsten. Rod was eating grass, Teena was full of energy and had Stinky Bear with her (no not Peter, he's a cuddly toy). And Debi, Kirsten, Pami and I talked about films we'd seen recently, *Dracula, Lady Chatterley's Lover*, and other girlie things.

HomeGround editors up on the heights

Photo: Sarah Mackenzie

When we arrived, hot, sweaty and knackered, we found about thirty people sitting outside the ruins – and a few sheep who were on the scrounge for butties, bottoms and anything else they could nibble. Peter was talking to long-time reader Jan-Erik Svensson who had come from Sweden, and had included the Wuthering Hike on things to do whilst in this country for a few days.

I went round everyone with the usual thing to sign for Kate, and recognised quite a few faces from Conventions and parties in the past. I talked Roy Harper with a fellow fan, Trevor Wilson – he looked remarkably like Roy during his *Lifemask* period. Our old buddy Ian Park and his wife Julie were there – he's such a great guy, so much fun and it's always a pleasure to be with him and Julie – they had been on another journey to some obscure part of the Planet. Chris Chamberlain arrived but could only stay for about twenty minutes, having a steam train to catch. But we did have an very enjoyable conversation. At one point I heard Debi taking the piss out of Pauli's amazing technicolour dream shirt, which he bought for £9.99 from a little shop in Chester. A shirt once seen, never forgotten.

I was sitting next to Liz Pamment, who had travelled from Okehampton in Devon, having a chat, when I felt something stroke my arm. I turned around to find Stinky Bear trying to attract my attention, and Teena too. The last time I saw Teena was about three years ago, so we had a little catching up to do – she's eight now. I was telling her about Amber our cat, when I realised that everyone had stopped talking and was listening to what Amber had been up to lately!

Pami was doing her Gerald impressions (you just wouldn't want to know – but I'll tell you anyway. Pami runs a local Laurel and Hardy mag and one of the leading members of their group is a rather precocious fifty-two year old bachelor called Gerald, who lives with his ancient mother... anyway, he has some pretty strange little ways and our Pami is always taking the piss out of him, in fact she's got her impersonation almost perfect, (I'm waiting for her to develop a bald patch and start knocking back seven pints a night) and she's been driving me mad with her Geraldisms, she's even recorded his quite obscure laugh on tape and made a fifteen minute mix from hell called *The Gerald Rap*, which could drive anyone insane.

So after doing one of her impressions specifically to annoy me, I ran after her, tripped, did a pretty spectacular head-dive and landed inches away from some sheep poo.

Unlike Pami's alter ego, Moggy, a deranged, smelly, moth-eaten, too-many-times-repaired, crusty-mooned, cock-eyed, occasionally one-eyed, almost ancient soft toy who was once a cute little lion cub, and is now a perverted, sheep mad, sex mad monster with a Mona Lisa smile, who to everyone's delight (including his own) landed face first into sheep poo when we were throwing him about (which is what you do with Moggy) to see just how far we could hurl him. Oh, I forgot he talks and swears a lot, and all his words begin with the letter 'R'. He wanted to do the write-up of the Hike, but seeing as he was in Pami's rucksack for half of the time, and falling into sheep poo the rest of the time, we didn't think there was much point.

An editor (Peter), two readers (Steve Nobes and Jason Cuss) and a sheep's bum (name unknown).

Photo: *HomeGround*

At about four-ish we decided collectively that it was time to hit The Fleece, the cosy unpretentious pub in Haworth High Street. I thought Peter and I should stay a little longer in case anyone else turned up. So a few of us did, whilst the rest made their way to the pub.

The remaining few wondered what to do whilst waiting, so we got Moggy out and played rounders, using him as the ball and our big umbrella as the bat. Needless to say, no-one turned up. But the rounders was fun. And the readers who waited with us are by now convinced that Peter and I are insane.

At The Fleece, we managed to grab one room for the Hikers. It was really cosy. And after a few beers everyone mellowed out even further. There was much Kate talk, and stuff like that, and then another area of common ground emerged (it was only a matter of time) – Monty Python. And it all started with 'The Four Yorkshiremen' sketch – what else could it be? There was Pauli, Glyn and Ian reciting the said sketch, in very loud voice and in full accent. This was followed by The Bruces' Song, and lots of others joined in including Pami (yes, I saw you!)... "I drink therefore I am!"

Jan-Erik and Glyn swapped tales of valves and amplifiers. Peter talked with Kirsten, Jason, Steve, Jan-Erik and anyone who would listen. Pami and Shelley both did more Gerald impressions at me. Pauli cadged the rest of Peter's cash out of him for another pint. And Moggy had his tail pulled off.

People were mingling and swapping tables. The atmosphere was really warm and everyone seemed to be having a good time. At one point Jason leaned across to me and said that his mate Steve (who had got up to get another beer) was dead keen to know what I looked like after all that stuff I'd written in *HomeGround*! Which I thought was so funny.

Whilst this was going on, Moggy drank himself under the table, and threw up all the way home.

And I've just realised that all of this is on video!

Amit Gandhi: Having just recovered from the rigours of Wuthering Hike IV I wanted to thank you for arranging it. It's the first event I've ever been to although I've been a lover of Kate's music for years. The one thing that really struck me was the range of people who came, and the range of people who are somehow touched by Kate's music generally. Everyone couldn't have been more friendly and outgoing. I can't wait until the next event, whatever it is.

Trevor Wilson: Thank you for organising the Wuthering Hike. It's very rare for me to meet so many great people. I didn't get round to speaking to everyone. I liked talking to Krys about Roy. I would have liked to have said more... I'm glad I met you all. P.S. I hope Moggy gets his appendage sewn back on.

Liz Pamment: The Wuthering Hike was a soul-busting experience and I wouldn't have missed it for the world. I've got five new friends – Ian, Julie and Rob have sent a postcard, and Mel from Totnes will be visiting. We went to a record fair in Exeter on Saturday.

After this article appeared in *HomeGround* we received a letter from a highly distressed reader in France horrified that we were forcing alcohol down a cat's throat and then pulling his tail off. Krys had to explain that Moggy was Pami's now legendary childhood cuddly toy lion cub who over the years had got got somewhat the worse for wear.

Going up!

Dave looks at the performance of Kate's singles

Issue 44: March 1992

Over the past few years you may have noticed that Kate's UK singles have tended to follow a similar pattern in the charts: a high entry in the first week followed by a small climb, and then a quick exit. Why does this happen? What effect does it have? Can it be prevented?

Before I attempt to answer these questions it is worth grasping how the charts actually work. The main chart – the one used by the BBC and most magazines in the UK – is that compiled by the Gallup market research company. This is the only chart that is recognised by the British Phonographic Industry, and the only chart of which anyone in the record business takes any notice. Despite the periodic bad publicity, and despite the nasty suspicions of many people, Gallup do go to incredible lengths to ensure the accuracy of the chart, which is based purely on sales across the counter from Monday morning to Saturday afternoon.

Singles are allowed in four formats and these are usually 7-inch, 12-inch, cassette, and CD. Sales on all four formats are combined to reach the panel sales total. On Thursday afternoon Gallup issue a midweek chart which shows where the singles are as of Wednesday afternoon. This chart is purely for the use of the business, and is meant as an aid to manufacture and promotion. The information is only released to the relevant company – information on Kate's records is only given to EMI – although by Friday afternoon most companies have exchanged data.

Using the midweek chart it is possible to see how a single performs at various stages during the week, and perhaps with the aid of this information we can answer the questions I asked above. Let's look at the release of a typical Kate single (yes I know Kate doesn't release "typical" singles, but you know what I mean!).

Kate, as you may have noticed, doesn't release records all that often, so when she does it is something of an event. Her record company, EMI, obviously want to sell as many albums as possible, and there is still no better way of achieving that than by having a hit single. Accordingly a lot of effort is put into the first single from one of Kate's albums. The press will usually be told 'unofficially' about the album and single sometime before the release, and they will publish this information.

About three weeks before the release the EMI press office will send out a press release with a photo, and the music papers will usually carry a story about the new record stating release date and details. At this time the single is pre-sold into the record shops via EMI tele-sales who try and make sure that every important store has ordered it. The chains – Woolworths, WH Smiths etc. will make their decision at head office as to how much stock each shop will carry.

At two weeks from release radio promotion will begin, and airplay will start any time thereafter. If the response is good, then people will hear the record for well over a week before they can buy it. EMI will also be seeking to get the video shown, and reviews in the music press. The actual week of release will usually see full page advertisements in the music press as well as an increase in other promotion. Kate may well be persuaded to do a live TV show such as 'Wogan'.

The effect of all this activity, together with the information given out by the Kate Bush Club and *HomeGround* means that a lot of people will know that Kate has released a single, and they will have heard it. Kate has a lot of very dedicated fans, and many general music fans will also buy most of her records. The result is a large number of people buying the record in week one, and the single charts at a reasonable high place.

The problem is the following week. Either the panel sales remains about the same, or slightly fewer, and the single either stalls or drops in the chart. The midweek figures are illustrative. Let's take *This Woman's Work*. The first midweek on the Thursday after release was a new entry at no.22, but by the week-end chart it was a new entry at no.30. This had happened because a lot of dedicated fans had rushed out and bought the record on Monday giving the high midweek placing. That momentum of sales is simply not maintained throughout the week, and especially not on Saturday, the biggest day for selling records.

In the case of *This Woman's Work*, the following week EMI released the picture disc and Kate did 'Wogan' on Wednesday. The midweek was no.15, but as the fans had snapped up all the pic discs early in the week the week-end chart position was a drop to no.25.

Kate, of course, is a very adult artist, and her singles do sell albums. She makes her songs and puts them into the world. She is not the only artist whose singles behave like this. U2, Simple Minds and Depeche Mode singles tend to suffer the same fate. Of course Kate could do more promotion in the form of TVs and press interviews – everyone else is doing these things frantically. Kate is, however, Kate, her own person and we love her for it, and because she is different.

This article really doesn't have a conclusion, but I hope I have explained why things happen the way they do.

Ash Wednesday

Collin Kelley

Beth's porcelain forehead is smudged
with a priest's fading fingerprint,
as if she were a page being turned,
the sins of Tuesday flipped to penitence.
So she reads a poem about Madonna,
who lost her religion years ago,
dabbles in others for the perfect fit,
some organization to contain her
oversized soul.

It's 4702 by the Chinese calendar,
so happy new year.
I'm no spring chicken, not even a rooster,
but I've been called a cock a time or two.

I died in a dream this morning,
my car skidding on ice, going over
a guardrail, my arms spread wide,
my mouth an O in the rear-view mirror,
my chest tight, heart in spasm,
then de-fibrillated by waking.

They've painted over the red walls
in Tina's old fifth floor apartment,
a flat white, taking the blood out.
Careers and tears came and went,
along with a line of dancing girls
who had no rhythm.
No good memories linger here,
save me, and I'm moving soon.

As I'm putting up a poetry flyer
on the lobby bulletin board,
deciding what to give up for Lent,
the pushpin sticks my thumb,
white lines smeary with ink,
almost breaks the skin, almost bleeds.

After the Rain

Paul Holland

After the rain has fallen
When the flower's hair is wet
I'll sit in my personal hell
And wait for you.

After the ground is dry
When the clouds are smiling
I'll sit and ask why
I wait for you.

After the sky is clear
When the birds fly in new formations
I'll sit and ask
Do we wait for each other?

After imaginary lands awake
When nature begins burning life's energy
I'll sit and ask
Will you wait for me?

After fierce winds have blown
When grassy field and proud trees rustle whispers
I'll sit and dream
You will wait for me.

After the moon has smiled
When shadows dance and deceive the senses
I'll sit and know
You did not wait for me.

Lyrically Speaking ...

Paul Thomas looks at the Words

Issue 46: October 1992

How important are lyrics in today's pop songs? It does seem that most of the Top 40 is dominated by club/dance records, where the emphasis is on a certain sound or beat, rather than the lyrical content. Many of the non-dance pop songs and the more down tempo ones are often about love – be it unrequited, lost love, mutual love or no love at all. This is not by far a criticism; a lot of good, classic pop songs are very simple and speak about subjects that most people can relate to, and that is why they sell so well; it is a bit like soap opera on TV – people like to see themselves in the characters of the programme, or in the situation portrayed in a song.

Occasionally, a record will come out that says more than the average pop/love song; songs that work on more than one level. Examples can be found in songs such as Soul II Soul's *Get A Life* – this worked as an excellent club/rap record as well as delivering a strong lyric about self respect and growth. Jimmy Somerville's *Read My Lips* spoke about the lack of financial support for education and research into AIDS, yet was a dance floor and radio hit, and probably many of the people bopping away to it were unaware of its message. I could list others: Massive Attack's *Safe From Harm*, Pet Shop Boys *Being Boring* and U2's *One*.

However, there are not many artists who have had continued chart success with so-called 'pop songs' and maintained strong and original lyrics, lyrics that deal with more than 'boy meets girl' themes. Kate Bush has managed to do this over her fourteen years of chart success. She has had at least one major hit single from every album she has released, and always her lyrics have provoked thoughts and ideas uncommon in most of the songs that shared a chart placing with her at the time.

Wuthering Heights, which portrayed the tormented spirit of Catherine Earnshaw, emerged from the grey fog of punk in the late Seventies. Subject matter on Kate's first two albums ranged from incest and homosexuality to the supernatural and love of country. Even her songs about love and relationships are far from straightforward. *Running Up That Hill* focused on the insecurities in relationships; it is a desperate plea to God to ask to change places with a lover so they can see how the other feels. *Hounds of Love*, on a similar theme, sees love metaphorically as baying hounds on the trail of your scent and the reluctance to be caught. *This Woman's Work* tells of a man reflecting upon his relationship with his wife in a time of crisis. Even *Babooshka*, a fairly light song initially, tells a story of a woman who plans to catch out her husband by disguising herself as another woman, the crockery smashing at the end of the record representing the wife revealing her true identity and her anger! Each one of these songs was a hit and nestled down in the charts beside songs like Baltimora's *Tarzan Boy*, Joyce Sims' *One Dance Won't Do*, and Sonia's *Can't Forget You* – what a contrast! Yet all are considered to be 'pop', but in varying degrees.

Other Kate singles have covered subjects such as the plight of an unborn child during a nuclear war (*Breathing*); a secret experiment in sound and weaponry (*Experiment IV*); and the endless search for wisdom and knowledge (*Sat In Your Lap*). Kate has also focussed on family relationships in songs like *Army Dreamers*, where a mother grieves over her son, and *Cloudbusting*, about the beauty of a relationship between father and son.

Graphic: Krys

Some would consider a lot of Kate's subject matter 'depressing', however, her originality cannot be denied; she always manages to bring a refreshing breath of clean air into the sometimes stale world of pop. She has been described in the past as 'thinking man's pop', which I guess sums up what I have been saying. But even if you are the sort of person who doesn't really want 'heavy' lyric subject matter in your songs, Kate's blend of music and arrangement creates certain moods in her work which makes her material pleasing to the ears of those who do not necessarily want to think about post-holocaust birth or the plight of the Aborigines. Her music works well on many different levels, for as many different reasons.

Pop music is still an important culture in Britain, and we should be proud of artists like Kate who give us music to think about – if we want to – as well as giving us good tunes to bop to, drive to, and hum along with... music for every occasion and every mood... "Music made for pleasure, music made to thrill..."

Castles in the Air

Seán Twomey

Issue 46: October 1992

Staring through the steam covered panes of the kitchen window she guided her finger-tip over its moist surface creating a landscape of droplets in the sheen. Alone, she could at least let her mind wander, just wander, the same as the trickle of moisture which made its way slowly to the sill. Beyond the glass the garden ran its length of greenery to where shrubbery gave way to the stark slate roof of a neighbour's garage. Over the roof, the clouds, like wisps of hair decorated the evening sky. "There are castles in those clouds," her father had said, but try as she might she could not see them.

She had had the kind of father read about in books and fairy tales. A kind yet weathered face, always creating fantasies, always suggesting adventures. One morning – and she remembered it well – she had trotted downstairs into the spacious kitchen to be greeted by silence. This was strange, her father was usually busy preparing breakfast, whistling one of the many tunes which he would play to death on the gramophone on long winter evenings.

Silence, and with it came an immediate dread, her fear of being alone. This sensation was not new to her and she hoped it would not last long. She found him sitting on the steps leading down to the rockery. He was reading aloud from a book he was holding in his hands. On seeing her he left down the volume and she ran into his outstretched arms. As she stared at the face she worshipped she could see the shimmer of tears in his eyes. Even at four years of age she was moved by this experience so much that it would seem significant years later.

"Catherine love, when will the meal be ready? The ladies are waiting, you know."

It was her aunt, authoritative as ever and the question had broken her day-dreams. Later, after serving up the meal to the guests, she reported – as was the unwritten law in the household – that she was going out for a walk. She left the house and stepped into the world. The sky was a dome of wonder to her as she crossed the road and opened the wooden gate which led to the old house.

The others disliked visiting the place, but for her it was comforting and every inch was filled with the magic of secrets and stories untold. She felt it in the way the sun filtered through the rafters of the bare roof of the barn. She felt it in the whispering of the branches, the smell of the autumn debris underneath her boots. And in the shrill cry of an evening bird that she could not name.

All was calm, all was deserted and serene. Yet she knew she was not alone here. She could hear his voice as clear as the day in her head, and for an instant, through the branches of the Oaks, she could see little turrets in the autumn sky.

They Have Returned!

Krys sees Spinal Tap – the Majesties of Rock

Issue 46: October 1992

No-one knows who they were or what they were doing,
But their legacy remains...

8th July, The Albert Hall, and my pilgrimage to see in the flesh three of my long-time heroes. Three men who have over the long years inspired many on the way – it is a little known fact/myth that they were a huge influence on Kate after seeing them perform in the South East London pubs in the early Seventies *Cups and Cakes* era – did Kate wonder something like "If *they* can do it, so can I!" (and it was good to see they had returned the compliment for in their gig at the Albert Hall, Nigel was indeed sporting the very latest in leotards – a bright little number with spiders webs design).

Three men – more *gods* than men – no longer to reside in the "where are they now?" file.

The tension, the excitement, the nervous breakdown, was building, the Albert Hall packed with adoring fans. I was waiting for one of my greatest dreams to come true, for tonight it was going to happen. After years of longing, I was to see Spinal Tap – the guys who go to eleven – play live. I'll let you into a secret; before I got into Tap, my life was cosmically a shambles. Bits of this, bits of that...

Tap were supported by the crazy talented Hornchurch Morris men clad in leathers and denims, who belted bloody hell out of each other with big scaffolding bars in a style even more violent and truly heartfelt than the Witchmen of Northampton (a brilliant Morris dancing team – see them if you can!) and singing the dirtiest of folk songs with a few new and naughtier verses thrown in... for example, "tra, la, la,la, la, OH! willies and bums and fannies and tits!" I loved it! They were so funny.

Then *that* moment... that wonderful moment...

The audience were still booing the Hornchurch Morris when Tap came on stage. Only kidding!

The show opened with a large black screen onto which Tap's faces were projected. It was very 'Doctor Who'. They spoke in unison, their voices eerily echoing around the Hall. Words of deep, deep wisdom penetrating the air, the ears, the very soul. I can't really remember what they said... the poem ended with the immortal words "WE HAVE RETURNED!" The faces faded, the screen disappeared, and the curtains beyond opened. An experience akin to seeing God, as the three were lowered from the heavens – well, somewhere up near the lighting thingy – David St. Hubbins, his blond hair cascading all around him like an angel; Derek Smalls, as gently menacing as ever; both lowered on the stage to the tones of *Hell Hole*, whilst Nigel Tufnel, wearing the above mentioned leotard, dangled halfway between the two, and valiantly got on with playing his guitar as attempts were made to free him by the end of the song. What a hero. And so obviously used to dealing with such cock-ups.

Peter and I were about thirty feet away from the majesties of rock themselves. Sheer Heaven. Or should that be hell? From the first number to the last everyone was standing, out of the utmost respect, or so they could boogie, or just so they could see the stage. It was like we, the audience, were at one with the guys in the band. David did most of the talking between songs. The show was segmented into themes – rock material (*Rock and Roll Creation*, *Sex Farm* – a serious look at sex on a farm; and *Heavy Duty*); new songs from their album *Break like the Wind*, (*Diva Fever*, *Bitch School*, *Christmas with The Devil* – which features some pretty heavy lyrics: "The elves are dressed in leather, And the angels are in chains (this sounds more like Madonna's *Sex*)... There's someone up the chimney hole, And Satan is his name" – and the title track); early stuff (*All The Way Home* – the very first song that David and Nigel ever made together – (*Listen To The*) *Flower People*, and *Rainy Day Sun* – a sheer masterpiece); there were also Irish folk influenced songs, and more. There was an interval, where not a lot happened, other than gathering my head together at the shock and disbelief that this was real.

Tap played for around two and a half hours. It was wonderful. The costume changes were great too. David arrived on stage with crown and gown to do *The Majesty of Rock*. The stage set and props were also really good, and included a small painted cloud for extra effect during *Break like the Wind* (which is incidentally Peter's favourite track, and on the album version features guest guitarists, Jeff Beck and Slash). The big question was, would they be doing *Stonehenge*? Of course they would. But there was a problem; they couldn't actually fit the mock-up of Stonehenge through the doors this time, as the audience witnessed on the aforementioned screen the roadies attempts to push and shove the megalith but to no avail. The song itself was incredible – how could it be anything else – and is now hewn into the living rock of my memory.

Tap ended the last of several encores with *Big Bottom*, a classic of our time. What lyric writing, who else but Tap could create a line like "Talk about mud flaps, my gal's got 'em..." About ten or more dancers from one of the major London Ballets joined them on stage and wriggled and gyrated about a bit to emphasise the strong lyrical content of this song.

Sadly, Tap didn't do *Gimme Some Money*, and it would have been nice to have heard a complete raga-cum-barbershop rendition of Elvis' *Heartbreak Hotel*. I have a vague impression that they did inject *Lick My Love Pump* somewhere.

Thankfully, the drummer managed to survive, and not once exploded as had two of his predecessors before him. At least six have died under bizarre circumstances. Remember for a moment if you will poor Eric 'Stumpy Joe' Childs, who choked to death on someone else's vomit. The authorities couldn't prove whose it was because as Nigel wiseley says, "You can't really dust for vomit". Unless *you* know different.

Graphic: Spinal Tap

I hope I have managed to capture just a little of the sights, the sounds, the smells of this hard-working rock band. And remember those immortal words "Have a good time, all the time" – a motto that we at *HomeGround* hold dear to our hearts, together with the one that goes "It's a fine line between stupid and clever". How true, how very true. But hey, enough of my yakking. Let's boogie!

In all seriousness Spinal Tap are excellent musicians, very versatile indeed. David, Nigel and Derek, thank you for making one of my dreams come true – I didn't think it ever would. Thank you for a great night! I'm a fan for life. I love you! And I really hope you get to read this. How about an interview?? Pleeease?

The Marathon Beat Poet

The HomeGround 1993 Roy Harper Interview

Issue 47: January 1993

HomeGround interviewed Roy in March 1993 at the Wedgewood Rooms in Southsea, and at The Pavillion Theatre in Worthing.

HG: Are you working on new material at the moment?

Roy: No. I am in my head. I can't do it at the moment, it's not feasible. Things are coming, things are there you know. I want to write songs, there are songs to be written but it would be a very sad album. I'm writing the ideas down and it can maybe be the album after next after next or whatever, to get rid of it quietly.

HG: I thought *Death or Glory* was absolutely brilliant. What was the response like?

Roy: The response from people who bought it has been absolutely fantastic. They all love it, but with the record company going broke it's not sold that many. There's no way to put it out on the market and it's a very strange state of affairs really because Our Price wanted four thousand quid for putting it in their chart. You know which is like "yeah, 'scuse me boys, but don't things happen naturally sometimes". We don't even have the distributor to do that, so forget it.

HG: So what's happening to your material?

Roy: It's all reverted to me. I own everything now.

HG: What was your real problem with EMI?

Roy: It's just that the problem is a huge one. It's the individual versus the corporation, and the problem is that the original label Harvest was set up for a group of us who are like we are and half the people on that label became superstars. The other half dropped out altogether. People like Barclay James Harvest, for instance, became huge in Europe and still managed to sell millions of records. So they had a history of dealing with me. EMI had this history of dealing with me, and I was the odd one because I was the one that might have dropped out or made it to the top. So I was an anomaly. Enigmatic Roy again. Let's see if we can have another go with him but they were in an even worse position. This country isn't able to handle someone like me I don't think.

HG: Was it that they couldn't imagine the audience to present you to?

Roy: I think what I need in this country is to dispel the myth, to create some kind of a reality about what I do instead of the usual remark which is like "clapped out hippy" or whatever. I need to be rehabilitated. The only way is going to cost a lot of money.

HG: In effect you're suffering from a bad image, which obscures the reality which is underneath?

Roy: Yes. The only way of getting over that is to go public with it but none of the relevant chat shows or arts programmes or media slots that you could fit me in want to know at all. They've all got that image.

HG: And you've got the same sort of problem with the music press...

Roy: Yes, it's the same. It's the same throughout...

HG: Their preconceptions stand smack in the way, it doesn't even allow them to listen?

Roy: Yes. The reputation goes a long way before me and it's very unfair. There's nothing I can do about it really. The only thing I can do about it is to go to the USA and start again.

HG: How seriously are you thinking about that?

Roy: Not very. I need to recover first from my recent trauma. It's something that I've got to do. I think I've got to go to the USA and plant myself in the middle of 280 million people – which is six times the number of people here – and say 'here am I, this is what I've got'. If I can exist on the same level as I do here then it'll be a break.

HG: And it could be something much bigger..?

Roy: Yeah... people could actually hear me in a totally different light. I should have done it fifteen years ago.

HG: That's interesting because Kate has the same kind of image problem. People would say "oh, Kate Bush, poppy songs, don't want to know"...

Roy: I don't know what to do really except just carry on. It's all I can do.

HG: It seems you've reached some kind of position of equilibrium at the moment where you can make your way, preserve your niche by touring like you have been.

Roy: Yes I can. Its kind of a bit much here. Its kind of very wearing but I like doing it. It's very good.

HG: Our experience is that the people are there. They do turn up.

Roy: Yeah. When somebody gets to know you then that's fine. It's nearly always the people who can't really move public opinion. It's nearly always people who are themselves in a way suffering from the same thing.

HG: What do you think of the current music scene. Do you see anything to enthuse about?

Roy: Can I raise my eyebrows here? Well it's not a question of whether you enthuse or not, I think you have to. I think what is here is the end of an era, a genre. A genre that was started in 1953 or 54 and its coming to an end now, it's like forty years from the rockabilly beginnings to stadium rock...

HG: Do you see something being born?

Roy: It's very hard to tell. I think we're only going to see that in the next couple of years. I think it would be nonsense to say rock and roll is dead because it's not. Like jazz – with only huge people coming through, like Springsteen, all those, but I think its days are numbered as roots music for kids to come through with.

HG: What are your opinions of Kate's work as a fellow singer songwriter?

Roy: Well she's the best Brit female writer by a long way. It's very difficult to know and say anything else because I really feel close to her as a friend so it's very difficult to separate that from a really objective look at what she's done, but some of the albums are really tremendous. Some of the songs, you know, I mean *Hello Earth* always brings a tear to my eye. Always. It never fails. I leave it a month or two or three, and then listen to it again. But you see the problem is I'm listening to a friend. I can be objective enough to know that there's nobody in these isles to touch her. No-one, anywhere.

HG: What did you think of the version of *Another Day* that Kate and Peter Gabriel did?

Roy: I really liked it. But you see that was a treat because you don't often – ever – see people of that rank singing your songs. Kate did 'phone me up and ask me what the song was, where Peter could sing, where she could sing and we discussed where we could open the song up, and sing different lines. It was obvious that it was her idea to do that, to involve Peter in something together, and it was a task really, thinking about it being sung by two people rather than one.

HG: What happened to *Commercial Break*? I know there are bootlegs of it around.

Roy: Yeah I know that but I stopped it. The record company said, after *Bullinamingvase*, "Right we want another record now, straight away." I said "Okay, when's the release date?" and they said February. So I've got to get everything ready for November 1st so they can process it and so that it can actually come out on February 1st. So I worked like a slave, and I got it to them on about the 2nd or 3rd November and apologised, and they said "Oh, what record? What studio tape... oh, you've got a record?" They were completely unprepared, absolutely unprepared.

I know exactly what had happened in the meantime – it was the period where they signed Jagger and Bowie and they were all sort of pleased as Punch and chuffed with themselves and had ignored everything else that was happening. But anyway, that's not that important. What happened to the record is that I pulled it. They said "Okay, well we'll put it out then. It'll be March or April." And I said "Look, we've organised a tour. We've got the whole thing happening. The dates, three-quarters of the dates are booked. What are you going to do, you've got to do something about it now."

And I had a listen to the record again and I thought I've rushed this record, I've rushed it for them and it's not as good as it should be and I shouldn't put it out. And I just pulled it, and the way I pulled it was by not signing the publishing rights, so the publisher couldn't make the songs public. So that pulled the rug from under them and they were furious with me. They were really furious with me, and it went on for like two or three years, and it was the end of one saga really. I kind of signed my own death warrant.

HG: What is the biggest inspiration for a song, what spurs you to write something new?

Roy: Something new. That's exactly what it is.

HG: Obviously there are personal things but what about bigger things, political things?

Roy: Well yeah, there's a cognition there, a recognition of things in your society that you're not quite *au fait* with and okay they provide a kind of mental knowledge of your society – those things never inspire me at all. I'm inspired by a moment, in a moment – something like that [*Roy snaps his fingers*] and I've said this before, but it always happens, I always get a tear with it, I think "Aah yes". I've got a crystal, I've held a crystal, I've got a crystal in here of something I can work on and a tear comes with it, then it's either down to ten minutes' work which is a blessing. *Old Cricketer* was written in ten minutes and I didn't realise it. And *Another Day* was another one that was done in a quarter of an hour-ish. And then some of them that you have inspirations for – "I must do that."

You see *Another Day* was an inspiration I had when I saw this girl – I had been her boyfriend when she was fifteen, when I was eighteen, nineteen – in Copenhagen, and there she was stood in front of me at the Cambridge Folk Festival, twelve, or thirteen, maybe fourteen, fifteen years later and she had four children and she had a lot of her teeth missing and she'd lived for those fifteen years in India. And we went back and we looked at each other, and we looked and there was a fifteen year gap and there was an inspiration there straight away. It was like, why don't I do that? Because it was a reality, it was a reality, it is...

So they come and you have the tear with them, you know, this beautiful thought – this is all crap, this is absolute fucking crap – then you work your way towards getting to that tear again and then you get to the tear, and you've written the song and you play it and it makes you get back there, it brings back the emotion then you realise you've actually done that – got there.

HG: What is your favourite album or song of your own?

Roy: I think *Stormcock*, *HQ* and various bits of various others.

HG: What are your influences in music and literature?

Roy Harper at the Bloomsbury Theatre January 1993

Credit: The Guardian

Roy: Oh Jesus, too many to remember. Where do you start from? Lenny Bruce? Leon Tolstoy...

HG: What influenced you to make music when you were ... however early you started? How early did you start?

Lenny Bruce.

Roy: That's a good question. Well, my Dad used to listen to classical music on the radio and his taste was rather heavier than his Mother's – his mother used to go to St. Anne's Pier with her sister-in-law, Lily Harper, and they went to see a man called Lionel Jeffries who was a rather good-looking 65 year old who had a sort of palm court orchestra, which she liked – she liked classical. Anything like Wagner was a row, it was just a row, but she was Victorian, she was 30 when Victoria died so she was absolutely Victorian.

And so I listened to my father's taste I guess but then what happened was Frank Sinatra came along and that was totally different from Victor Sylvester and the choice on the radio. My Dad used to listen to tennis on the radio, you know, he used to listen to Wimbledon on the radio. That's what he used to do. And then my tastes got rather more catholic with Frank and when I was a very young person Frank was there as a young man, with all the girls in bobby socks, white socks, the fashion, the initial start of screaming, and then after Frank there was the whole traditional jazz thing, and then Skiffle, and then the Beatles, and then... we all know the rest. And we all know that Mick Jagger and Robert Plant are just reiterating what Chester Burnett did 30 years previously.

Frank Sinatra.

HG: What made you pick up the guitar?

Roy: Because I suddenly realised I could sing the poems.

HG: The poems came first?

Roy: Yeah. I was the 'marathon jazz poet'. That was my first ever title. I walked from Lytham to Fleetwood for 48 hours. There and back and there and back and there and back and there and back. And had a reading on Central Pier at the end of it. Anyway, such is life.

Chico Mendes

HG: How did you become involved with the film *Made?*

Roy: Well it was a process. The studios, EMI films I suppose, went through a whole list of candidates and the final three under consideration were me, Ray Davies and Ian Anderson from Jethro Tull.

HG: They were looking for the singer-songwriter type?

Roy: Yeah, it was that kind of thing. We all did screen-tests with Carol [White] and I think Carol had a big say in who was chosen, and that's how I got involved.

HG: Did you enjoy it?

Roy: Yeah, but it was a very strange experience. Now that Carol has departed it's not difficult for me to say this. On the first day of shooting down in Brighton on the beach, stones and all – I was looking from the Pier and the producer and the director were walking together, and I get called into the conversation, and they iffed and butted and aahed and erred and maybeed for a quarter of an hour, twenty minutes, and they couldn't finally get it out. The producer walked away and left me with the director who was a Scotsman and he said [*Cue Roy's Glaswegian impression*] "Roy, she won't come out of her-er dressing room until you've given her one". So I had to do this thing, I had to spend six or seven weeks with Carol, and then when I'd agreed to do that, that night we had a dinner with all of the crew, and all of the actors and everything, with Carol at the head of the table and me next to her, it was Roman. And she drank like a fish, and she was obsessive... very very very obsessive. And that is a long story but that's what happened, it was a deal.

HG: What did you think of the finished film?

Roy: Not very much because it was an argument. It was an argument between the producer whose son was flunking art at university, the director whose daughter had run away from home aged fifteen, Carol who had run away from every home she'd ever been in, and me who'd never had a home. So it was a four-way tug, it was ridiculous and everybody wanted something else. And I saw that the film could be much better than it was, than it actually turned out. It's easy to see, it's easy to watch that film and pick it up on anything... the end is ridiculous.

HG: When did you first hear Kate?

Roy: At about the time she released *Wuthering Heights*. That's the first thing I heard. I can remember hearing *Wuthering Heights* in a clothes shop in Bristol or Manchester and that's when I first heard her.

HG: Do you have any plans to release any of the recent live material?

Roy: No. It's not good enough. It's too involved with what's just happened to me in my life. It's too personal to really think about. I mean I've not been like that in the past, nothing's been that personal but I think, I feel now as if I need to get rid of something that's poisoned an atmosphere for me and the only way of doing that is to actually shut it out, and part and parcel of shutting that out is not really to listen to what I've done over the last year, including *Death or Glory?* I think that I've got to stop gigging, I know that I've got to stop gigging, I know that it's a necessity now. For a while. I think, I think that I can go away to the fountain and refresh myself, renew myself, but I need to actually go away... But no, there are certainly no plans.

HG: Did you know that David Puttnam was making a film about Chico Mendes?

Roy: Yes, I did. I wrote the song because of what he said to me. That song is also the song that I lost my last relationship to. It's quite a

Graphic: Krys

As I walked over North Botley copse...

funny thing that. Whilst I was writing that song, she was doing something else. That's beside the point. That song was written because David Puttnam and I had a conversation and I said to him "What are you doing now?" and he said "Oh I'm making a film about Chico Mendes" and I said, "I must write the song". It's two or three years now since I've been aware of this thing and I've wanted to write this song for a while. He said "Write it. It could earn you a lot of money". I said "What are looking for?", and he said "Well something like Enya, something ethereal..." The conversation was longer than that – we were on a TV thing together – and I went away and I thought "Can I do that?" And I thought "No, I can't do it, I can't do it." What I want to do is write a song the way I want to write it and turn it into the celebration that I wanted it to be – nothing ethereal, nothing ephemeral in that for me. I didn't see it as being anything ephemeral. Maybe the script in the film lends itself to that but I've not seen the script, but I know what script I'd have, I know which film that I'd want. And it would be a celebration of that man's life. So I went away and wrote the song and it exists because of our conversation really. Whether he uses it or not is another thing.

HG: What happened with Watford Gap – are you allowed to talk about it?

Roy: Of course, yeah. What am I not allowed to talk about? They took it to court. I was saying to them, "When's it due to be in court then?" and they were saying things like "Next week." I was saying "When next week?" And they were saying "Sorry it's been postponed now, it's next month..." Then one day I went to Peter Jenner and said "When is this thing gonna happen?" and he said "It's happened". Cos I wanted to go to court and say at the time "I think that you're serving shit in your motorway cafés and your motorway service stations". And it was, it was crap. It was a reflection of the rest of Great British society at the time and I wanted to stand up and I wanted to get Egon Ronay to give me a few words, I tried to enlist people, but it wasn't really *au fait*. And I found out why later. One of the people who owned the Blue Boar was also on the board at EMI so they did it from the inside from start to finish and everything I've ever known has been like that, it's been a fixed job from the inside. There's nothing you can do. That is wholesale in this society, that is total. Forget anything else.

HG: So it had to be deleted from the album...

Roy: Yeah, we changed the album, you know, took the song off it. By then most of the copies of the album had been sold, so the rare one that's changed... But that's all irrelevant. It's an age ago.

HG: Well we like it! We sing it every time we go past!

Roy: It's different from that now, it's more cynical. That's the problem that everybody's got now, the words aren't there for you to write the song that's cynical enough to mean what it should mean and the problem is that if you do that you're up against your own audience so you've got to strike a kind of mean. I'm even tired of doing that, so I'm going to head off out there. See what happens.

HG: You were there making music in the sixties and there was great optimism about what could be done and we headed into the Eighties, when it came back and hit us in the face with people like Roger Waters making almost cynical albums...

Roy: We're all disappointed with the times. I think the problem, the best way round it is with humour, and I think that's why comedy is so popular in depressed times because it's the only thing people really want to relate to. I think the market place speaks. The market place does speak. Suddenly there's a lot of young guys who are influenced by blues music and stuff that has never been heard in this country before at all, and suddenly it's available to a lot of young thirteen year olds, they go out and buy it and get influenced by it and it's Muddy Waters and it's Chester Burnett, Howlin' Wolf, it's things that nobody ever heard.

Muddy Waters

Howlin' Wolf

Forget Mantovani, forget Victor Sylvester and the Palm Court Orchestra – it never occurred. Suddenly truth, suddenly – "I'm fucked up man, I'm really fucked up... my baby's just gone and pissed all over me" – it was incredible, it was incredible stuff, and suddenly everybody who was that age bought it and it was a rage, it was an absolute rage, and everybody who could played, we all played, we all got hold of guitars and played something.

I was more interested in writing from the Percy Shelley part of my personae, my collection of personas, but I still picked up the guitar and was still in there with the rest of the human beings doing it, you know, we were all doing it. Then what happened was that it went worldwide, it re-exported itself back to the USA, totally Anglicised by the Rolling Stones and The Beatles and The Kinks. Just wham! Right round the world. It was huge, it was just huge and there were loads of people who rode on the bandwagon, and loads of side issues, like Paul Simon had a hit – another guy, the same as all of us, his timing's better than mine, Paul's timing has always been better than mine – he did tell the joke at twenty minutes past eight, and twenty seconds every night, and it was the same joke and it was precise, he was absolutely precise.

I'm totally a different animal, so is Billy Connolly. Everybody's different. It was re-exported to the world, it was worldwide, it was huge and then suddenly there was a youth culture to speak of and it kind of looked as though it was going out of control just for a while. There were two deaths and four births or something at Woodstock, it was a city, it was a city out of control, and if you went to Stonehenge in the seventies and eighties you realised it was the same place and that the law didn't actually go in there, that it didn't exist, it was like seeing the ozone layer disappear over the pole, it was a no-go zone in the middle and then it shrank back again as leisure activities began to be more profound.

From the youth culture, from that freeing up of spirit from the whole of the revolution that was, what you've got now is computer software, fitness, you name it. There are so many things you can now do that you couldn't. When I was young the one thing you did was own a record player. Now you can own a world, it's virtual reality, that's the difference. So the market has shrunk, it's not there any more, it's shrunk, it's gone, and there are no young people coming up doing what we did because its not there any more. The force for them to do it isn't there any more... It's an ebb, a natural ebb and I'm glad I was part of it, the side issues. Bob Dylan came over here, and Paul Simon, came over here to learn British folk music so they could take that over there and give that to the world, and it would have been much better for me on a commercial level if I'd have behaved properly and taken another culture and Anglicised it a lot more. What I did was just Anglicised my own image.

Reader's Letters

… …we receive them with a strange delight

William Johnson: Two years ago I took an apartment with some friends. One evening I found myself in the still empty apartment sanding and painting before the furniture arrived, with no company save a cassette player and someone else's tapes. Of all the selections, only a tape by the Police and *Hounds of Love* were even vaguely familiar. I had 'discovered' Kate Bush.

I played that tape thirty-odd times by the time all the work was done, and found myself more and more drawn to this woman ever more so with each playing! I hunted down all the other albums during the next several months – not an easy task in this town – and was thrilled to find an unauthorised biography. I hear so little of her music on the radio and about her in print that I despaired that I was the only fan of Kate's this side of the pond!

Mark Binmore: Can it really be ten years since issue 1? Was I really eleven years old then, bopping away to the likes of Dollar and Bucks Fizz (I still like them!). Times have changed, and so has *HomeGround.* The best things being the stories and the drawings. Sadly the only bad comment is that it isn't in colour. Here's to the new year of '92 and ten more years of *HomeGround*!

Marc Laurent: I send you this little letter just to tell you that I find *HomeGround* always interesting. I don't always understand all what you say in it, because my English isn't very good, but it is for me the only way to get information about Kate and her work, so you're very important to me. Now I have to wait for the next album, it's going to be so long until the release! I also hope that there will be a tour and that Kate will come to France where we have all been waiting for her for such a long time!

Jason Anthrope: Yesterday I got mag number 47 and read it, but I must complain: why do cats chew the biggest letters that come through the door? My cat sniffed around at the four letters that had been delivered that morning and he had a choice. He could have nibbled on a nice bill or dug his teeth into a juicy Severn Trent Water letter. But no, he and his palate agreed on the big one. When I trotted down the stairs, and opened that particular letter and saw that my *HomeGround* was nibbled, I could have fainted. Just for that, I won't let the cat see Paulina Stuckey's great picture 'Cats Of Comfort' on page 13. Ha! The mag was a great read. All the stuff about sex made me blush a bit, though!

Fabian in Argentina: Hi! We can't ignore the terrible fact – the war of 1982, but I believe wars are made by the governing class, not by us, and I'm sure none of us would have wanted that to happen. A minute's silence for those who died for that stupidity... Let's change the mood. I am writing to you because of the passion of my dreams, of my inner child! I listened to Kate's music for the first time in 1980, the track was *Babooshka,* included in an album called *17 Top Hits.* I discovered her again six years later, in 1985 when someone lent me a copy of *The Whole Story* – and was there something in there! That voice! Those arrangements! Those melodies! That atmosphere! All of these elements create moments of magic! I felt as though these songs were calling to me, and I answered and got on the crystal cloud. I was someone who liked solitude, there seemed to be nothing I could do about it. Now after breaking through some painful barriers I can enjoy the wonderful feeling of friendship – although I still do need sometimes, just a little time for myself. I used to go walking around the city centre, or by the railway, or by the river bank – alone with my walkman and I fly! All of these things make me happy, as well as stroking an ally cat, buying chocolate, and looking at the moon – but those songs – *Egypt, Breathing, Violin, Under Ice* – I find it hard to explain the sensations they cause, the emotions – gentleness, softness, aggression, crying, sex... but always company, always protection, always unique. The magic of song made by someone who leaves something of herself in every note of every song. Because of that magic I am writing to say thanks, for the hope, for the helping hand symbolised in Kate (and in her musicians, and technicians). In writing this I feel I am alive, and I can face all that comes!

Sally Jackson: Just to let you know that I really enjoy receiving and reading *HomeGround* and am amazed at the time and effort you all put into it. When I've got my two children off to sleep it's so relaxing and enjoyable to put my feet up and read the mag with a cup of tea and some choccy biccies. I find *HomeGround* very informative, interesting, and entertaining. I must congratulate Krys on her beautiful and imaginative pieces – they bring tears to my eyes when I read them – even if I don't always understand them. The artwork is also very beautiful. Maybe one day I'll pick up the courage to write an article for *HomeGround.* In the meantime I have no worthwhile suggestions to make as I think you are doing Kate proud.

Donna: Well, it looks like things are starting to happen! After the stunning performance of

Letters from issues 44 and 48 which included missives from the USA, Finland, Canada, France, and Argentina (especially pleasing to us), as well as Blighty.

Graphic: Steven Brown

Moments of Pleasure, we know that Kate is back with a bloody vengeance! One quibble – I do wish Michael Aspel had opened out the questions to all the guests. I for one like to know what '70s music Kate enjoyed.

Mo Maclean: It was great to see Kate on Michael Aspel's programme last night. What a moving song! Her voice is lovelier than ever. I can't wait to hear *The Red Shoes*! Regarding *Moments of Pleasure*, a song about love and loss. My favourite parts are: "this sense of humour of mine, it isn't funny at all", "The buildings of New York, they look like mountains through the snow", and of course, "every old sock meets an old shoe". As to the closing lines, is that Gary Hurst "dancing down the isle of a plane", Alan Murphy "playing his guitar refrain", and is Bill the guy from the tour? But who is "Teddy, spinning in the chair at Abbey Road"?

Jan Millington: What can I say? 'Moments of Pleasure' indeed. Katy may take her time to make her music – but when she does, it hits home! What a jewel, the way it builds up and then eases off; a melancholy minor chord, but not depressing – about happiness and life and pleasure – and pain and loss. Saying "hello" to past friends, not "goodbye" in death. I sat with tears dripping down my face. Kate has an assuredness, a maturity in her music now that is worth waiting for.

Phoebe Coombs: I got your address through the publication *Kate Bush Complete*. I wish that there was some kind of machine that I could be tested on to show how much of a big fan I am of Kate Bush. If this machine existed I am sure it would show that I am her biggest fan in all the United States. She is pure inspiration!

Retracing the Scenes

The Red Shoes and the Hippodrome: 1993-94

Why *The Red Shoes*? Clearly the principle influence was Michael Powell and his classic film, but there was clearly a deeper resonance for Kate in the older European folk tale that inspired the film. It seems to me that when "it really happened" to Kate in 1978 she was first mesmerised, then some way down the road, determined to wrest back control. She would not join the record industry dance, as many record industry execs have constantly noted half in admiration, half in complaint. After all, record companies are there to sell records and make profits. Kate had no care for the latter, and was often indifferent about the former, especially in so far as it involved promotion, which she saw at times as akin to prostitution. If people wanted the music they would buy it, if they didn't, well that was just too bad. To my way of thinking the whole *Red Shoes* project, both album and film were Kate's clearest declaration that she wished to end her involvement in the record business. The red shoes, seen now for what they were would be taken off. She would take back her own smile, her own heart, and would tread her own path.

Kate had already accepted an invitation to appear on the British commercial TV programme 'Aspel and Company' on Sunday 20th June. It was her first TV appearance for some considerable time. She had known Michael Aspel from the very beginning of her career – in 1978 he was a DJ at London's Capital Radio where Kate's public career effectively began, and he had interviewed her a number of times since. It was therefore something of a disappointment to see the way he handled the "chat" section of the show, with stale and shallow questions that did not really engage Kate's interest. The 20th June was also Hannah Bush's birthday. It was an ideal day to present the first performance of *Moments of Pleasure*, a song full of precious memories of those no longer with us.

On 2nd July Kate began working on "the film". First conceived, apparently, as a TV special, the plan was to include approximately 40 minutes of music footage incorporating six tracks from the album, and 20 minutes of dramatic footage to "explain all". Lindsay Kemp was taking care of the choreography and Miranda Richardson had agreed to take a leading acting role. Kate's plan was to have the film completed by 16th August, with the sequences that would constitute the promos for the singles a particular priority. But what, we thought, about live dates? This was, after all, an album that had been conceived and recorded around the concept that it could be performed live.

In *HomeGround* 48 (Summer 1993) we were able to run the banner headline: "Kate's seventh album is named *THE RED SHOES* and is set for world wide release on 13th SEPTEMBER 1993", with at last some assurance of being more or less right. There was a little confusion about the first single. The original plan was to go with *Eat the Music* on 16th August with a 10 minute extended version (engineered by Del Palmer) entitled *The Madagascan Mix*, and *Big Stripey Lie* on the B-side, although EMI had considered interview material, and when asked for ideas we had suggested *Brazil*, or some of the rarities missing from the box set. Whatever; one week later there was to be a picture 12" disc. In fact Kate's US label Sony, although extremely enthusiastic about the album, considered very carefully both *Rubberband Girl* and *Eat the Music* for the first US single before falling into line with EMI on the latter.

It was Kate who decided, however, at the end of July, after hearing some feedback from people to whom she had played the album, that she would like *Rubberband Girl* as the first UK single instead. EMI agreed, although their already prepared promotional material for *Eat the Music* had to be junked. In the first week of August, EMI sent out teaser CDs to radio stations and the music press. This CD appeared to be an actual promo CD for *Rubberband Girl* but actually featured an EMI staffer reading the lyrics in a ham actor voice. The national commercial radio station Virgin 1215 actually played this on air on 10th August! The first play of the real single was on the BBC Radio 1 breakfast show, hosted by Simon Mayo, on August 16th, where Kate talked for about 30 minutes about the single, the album, and the film to follow, and the tour not to follow! The track did not become 'single of the week' because Kate could not fit in time for a further interview appearance. A taped interview just wouldn't do.

Virgin 1215 started playing the single on the same day, and it was the start of very strong airplay support by UK commercial and BBC radio. In the first week of release the single was promoted to the A list on Radio 1, and Virgin broadcast an instant "special" (i.e. playing a number of older tracks). It was *HomeGround*'s impression that airplay at this early stage was greater than that for *Running Up That Hill* in 1985, and probably stronger at this stage than any of Kate's singles since the first. The track entered the *Music Week* airplay chart as a breaker at no.8 on 28th August, and the figures in the main chart thereafter were: 9, 29, 31, 12, 12, 10, and 10. EMI took adverts in the music press on September 4th and 11th for the single which was released on Monday 7th September in three

formats. The cover photograph by Guido Harari featured a shot from the video. The few reviews were welcoming, if not actually wild about the track:

"this is Bush at her most direct... rhythmic, almost raunchy workout with the occasional outburst of rock guitar, strange lyrics – and a wired vocal impression of said office accessory being stretched. It is also a very commercial rejoinder..." Alan Jones, *Music Week* 28/8/93

"perhaps a little too up tempo for my tastes – I prefer my Bush all dreamy and mysterious. A minus the drums... but it still has enough kookiness to draw me under. And she's still the only artist for whom the word 'kooky' isn't an insult." Everett True, *Melody Maker* 11/9/93

"an upbeat charmer. Solid dance floor beat, slithery lead guitar and a lively horn section..." David Sinclair, *Sunday Times* 6/9/93

The video was a problem. In fact all the videos for the *Red Shoes* singles were to be a problem. It had seemed a good idea to make promotional clips for those songs the sequences from the film which would tie them all together. The visual media did not agree. Their almost uniform complaints were due to what they saw as lack of action or glamour content: "nothing happens". Kate was asked to re-shoot or at least re-edit the clips, and as most of the noise was coming from the US where she wanted to make an impact with this album, she was to some extent willing to comply.

Regardless, Kate Bush was still Kate Bush and a name to conjure with, at least in the UK. The world première of the *Rubberband Girl* video was on the ITV 'Chart Show' on Saturday 11th September as a "new release exclusive". The following day MTV Europe played 48 seconds of the clip on Paul King's 'First Look' feature.

In the following week MTV made up for a tardy start with at least nine Kate video-plays in less than 96 hours. Five plays of (48 seconds of) *Rubberband Girl* and segments of *Running Up That Hill* (twice) and *Babooshka* (twice) on 'MTV Greatest Hits'. Occasional plays continued. BBC TV's 'Top of the Pops' only showed short clips in the breakers and charts section of the programme. The official chart figures were as follows: début on Sunday 12th September at no.12, thence 14, 36, 50, and 60. On the network chart used by the commercial radio stations, the figures were: 22, 15, 19, and 30. Finally on the MRIB chart used in the music press, the figures were 7, 7, and 25.

Kate did not promote in Europe. In Germany the single entered the official chart at no.68 twelve weeks after release. In France airplay was patchy, but major stations like Radio France-Inter and Europe 1 and 2 did give it some support in September and October. The single did not chart in the Netherlands, though it did "bubble under" for a few weeks. In Israel the track was first played on 22nd August, and had achieved 13 airplays (considered a lot!) by the end of the day. Consequently on the daily phone-in chart of Reshet Gimmel (one of the biggest radio networks) the track entered at no.3. The senior DJ on the station, Ofer Nashon, the first to play the track, described Kate as "Britain's most original artist, and one of the world's best musicians, unique, talented, bizarre, and gifted". As a result plans were made by two of the biggest radio stations in Israel for a "Kate Bush Marathon", a five-hour programme dedicated to Kate featuring album tracks, singles, rarities and interview material. Sales of the single were brisk enough in Eire to put the single at no.1 in the Gallup chart in Dublin's branch of Tower Records. It gained a certain amount of airplay, but DJs tended to welcome Kate's "return" and then play older tracks! *Hot Press* said:

"what first appears like one-pacedness actually succeeds, with the help of an almost traditionally British dose of eccentricity... insinuating under your skin and wrapping it around your aesthetic earlobes..."

Having been persuaded out of *Rubberband Girl*, the US single was finally *Eat the Music*, released on 7th September. Some programmers (and US fans) were sceptical about Kate releasing such a commercial sounding track, but many were overcome by the infectiousness of the music. The reviews were enthusiastic.

The Hard Report, a well known tip-sheet, classified the track in their 10th September issue as AAA, Adult Alternative Airplay/Albums and as a hot new release: "Let's face it, if Kate Bush isn't a staple artist on your station, you're in the wrong format. Kate Bush is always at her best, and this release is no exception". WXPN's Mike Morrison agrees, "Kate Bush is an automatic for this format. From what I've heard from this record, it could be her best yet. She is a core artist for my station". WMMM's Sybil McGuire is convinced "We all like Kate. The lyrics are incredible. Talk about sexy! And all that fruit on the cover! It's got a nice techno beat, but it's not so techno that it's too much for Triple A."

The Gavin Report 17th September (also under AAA) agreed: "Anyone remember the scene from the film *Women in Love*, where Rupert (Alan Bates) equates the eating of a raw fig to the sexual act? Kate Bush, always one to analyse the tumultuous roles of men and women, draws a similar analogy... I like the modern Celtic bounce."

The single entered the Gavin alternative chart at no.42 – the most added, on 24 radio stations. The full review reflected the optimism: "Although the calendar says Summer is just about over, this breezy number inspires vivid memories of those

Graphic: Steven Brown

warm, relaxing days on the beach, and is the perfect antidote to the back-to-the-grind-blues many of us experience this time of year." (Linda Ryan).

Billboard reviewed the track on September 25th, categorising it as a "pick": "a kooky blend of delicate Celtic melodies and breezy Caribbean rhythms. Fleshed out by swooping support vocals and a glistening horn section, track shows Bush at her most vocally relaxed. She has, gratefully, put her brooding poetry on temporary hold, in favour of more playful verbiage..."

At the beginning of October *Eat the Music* entered the *Radio & Records* New Rock chart at no.15, rising to no.10 on 11th October. It had briefly appeared in the *Billboard* Hot Dance maxi-singles chart at no.31 on 25th September. The video was shown on MTV's '120 Minutes' on 19th October, but was, ominously, not listed for rotation on MTV or VH-1.

After further delays from September to October, and some grief between EMI in the

From top above: Eric Clapton, Jeff Beck, Trio Bulgarka, Prince and Gary Brooker.

UK and Sony in the US, Kate's seventh studio album was finally released world-wide on 1st November 1993. Featuring guests Eric Clapton, Jeff Beck, The Trio Bulgarka, Prince, Gary Brooker, and Lenny Henry, as well as the many talents of Kate's brother Paddy, the album was recorded at Kate's home studio in Kent, with additional overdubs done at Abbey Road.

In advance of the album, and indeed whilst she was still busily engaged in editing the film, Kate was interviewed by Chrissey Iley of the *Sunday Times*. The result was a less than enthusiastic feature in the colour supplement on 12th September. The remainder of the interview material was used by *Vox* in their November issue. Kate speaks of her work, and its emotional input.

Iley asks: "If something traumatic occurs in your life, do you find it easy to express, or does it come out in some other form?" Kate: "Usually, I can pull myself through things like feeling low or having problems by working that through. But I have been at points where I just couldn't work. I couldn't possibly sing – it was beyond me, it just hurt too much... I think the biggest thing on this album is that I lost my mother. I haven't been able to write about any of it – nevertheless, the experience is in there. It's something I couldn't possibly express in music, and yet it is being expressed through very subliminal things, like the quality of some of the performances. I couldn't work for months, I couldn't go near the whole process. I had no desire to start, no desire to work at all...

"There's a song called *The Red Shoes*. It's not really to do with his film but rather the story from which he took his film... the story that I'm aware of is that there's this girl who goes to sleep in the fairy story and they can't work out why she's so tired. Every morning, she's more pale and tired, so they follow her one night and what's happening is these shoes... she's putting these shoes on at night before she goes to bed and they whisk her off to dance with the fairies."

Vox (Stephen Dalton) also reviewed the album: "Think of the most unlikely pop collaborators you can imagine. Now double them. Forget it, because Ms Bush got there before you... Kate's musical vision is reassuringly bonkers and ambitious as ever... but this time Kate dances dangerously close to the tranquil cul-de-sac inhabited by Peter Gabriel and Annie Lennox... rigid and sterile... only saved by odd flashes of that distinctively finty, heart stopping warble. While previous outings harnessed studio technology to Kate's maverick whims, much of *The Red Shoes* sounds imprisoned by it... any Grand Plan is conspicuously absent. Considering Kate may just be our last remaining pop genius, *The Red Shoes* ultimately adds up to less than the sum of its unorthodox parts."

The feature by Colin Irwin, which appeared in the November issue of *Rock World,* was more friendly – and included an article by Paddy Bush. "It's an event. A major, MAJOR event when Kate Bush releases a new album these days... The new album... has been threatened for three years, but even by Kate's own tortuous standards, it's been a painful one. Personal problems, including the death of her mother, permeated the recording... and it shows... complex emotional puzzles dwelling on farewells and traumatic affairs. If we can ever read any personal outpourings in Bush's music, traditionally based on literature and wild, offbeat scenarios, then she's had a shattering of the heart in these lost years, too. Of course you can never be sure. She's always used her passion for fiction and escapism through drama and theatre as a way of camouflaging any reference to her own personal life in her music. The single – and opening track – *Rubberband Girl* is a red herring, deceptively bouncy and dance-oriented. Whatever anyone throws at her, she zings right back, she sings brightly over a thunderous backing. She lies. The rest of the album is a firmament of distress that leaves you fbored, even when Prince joins the throng for an excellent bout of light relief. It makes you worry about exactly what she has been through in the lost years. Oh them heavy people."

Paddy's article *My Brilliant Sister* was about the way that Kate works. He explained why there actually weren't going to be any live dates: "We even had a few rehearsals earlier in the year so it's definitely something in the head, but then Kate got involved in the idea of a film to go with the album and she's been so busy on that all plans for live shows have gone out of the window for the time being".

Q was anxious for Kate to give them a feature interview, and even offered her the November cover. However, Kate was still very busy, especially on the post-production work on the film. The magazine was given an upfront copy of the album to review. That review (Andy Gill) scarcely seems to get to grips with Kate's work: "Initially somewhat shrill and unimpressive, *The Red Shoes* improves immeasurably after repeated plays over a long period of time, gaining solidity at odds with disparate musical strategies... it soon finds its natural centre with *And So Is Love*, the first of several tracks dealing, in an unfocussed, woolly-mystical manner, with the connections between love and the abstract, spiritual nature of creativity... As a whole, *The Red Shoes* is more musically varied than thematically, as Bush's constant returning to the links between love, spirituality and creativity become wearing. In compensation, there's a rich pan-global tapestry woven here in which the textures and designs from distant cultures are being used not for effect, but for the way they express an emotional truth beyond mere words."

Inevitably, and at this point with a certain rewriting of history going on in some circles, worth remembering, *The Red Shoes* was a huge success in the UK, gold on release, and soon enough platinum. Other reviews were very good, even if sometimes a little confused. Some could understand the emotions being expressed, others heard what they expected to hear, and wrote the clichés they were expected to write:

"an utter masterpiece... if you only buy one album this year, you're probably very smart. And it'll be this... Kate Bush is on form like the Bible is well-known... clearly anyone, male or female, who is not desperately and devotedly in awe of Kate Bush, is either sick or retarded. *The Red Shoes* dances so far ahead of the rest, it's embarrassing. Apparently the contest for second place is to be allowed to continue, out of magnanimity." Chris Roberts, *Melody Maker* 30/10/93

"How many of us could stand the self-imposed exile that has been the adult life of Kate Bush. She's elevated privacy to an art-form... it's her most personal album to date, yet it is her most accessible, in which the listener can identify directly with the pain she's trying to pull herself through... There's nothing any of us can do to help Kate Bush through this difficult time in her life but if by telling us about it on this exceptional album she is able to see the light at the end of the tunnel herself, then we can at least listen and wish her well... a truly exceptional album." Terry Staunton, *NME* 6/11/93

"Kate Bush exudes Englishness of a different kind. Croquet and gingham and scones on the dainty patio. She is our dottiest dame since Margaret Rutherford and she is, to use an overworked and undervalued word, unique... Her new LP... does not disappoint. There is nothing here that quite compares with her most splendid songs – 1980's *Breathing* and 1986's *The Big Sky*... but *The Red Shoes* is a triumph nonetheless... She still sings like the slightly crazy girl on the lacrosse team alarming the opposing Vicarage XII... Her music is exotic and clever – not clever-clever, you understand, just imaginative... And, most important of all, her lyrics are still utterly potty... Kate Bush's only mistake, the first of her glittering career, is to invite the fiddling goon Nigel Kennedy to scrape his Strad on the LP." Tom Hibbert, *The Independent on Sunday's Night & Day* supplement 14/11/93

"*Red Shoes* is Bush's most pensive album yet... its mood of wistful mystery maintained by elaborate arrangements... the occasional number is overwrought, but the best confirm Bush as an artist of substance." Neil Spencer, *The Observer* 7/11/93

"Kate... applies herself to hymning the links between the creative, religious and sexual impulses... as luxuriant and richly textured as Bush's previous work, but with a few harder centres than usual." Andy Gill, *The Times* 28/10/93

There were a number of good magazine features and interviews. The *Q* feature finally showed up in the November issue, improbably titled 'Booze, fags, blokes and me'. It is an important interview: "Later, we shall enquire what she does for fun. But already it's obvious what she doesn't do. Interviews. Right down at the foot of the list with slam dancing, casual abattoir work and unanaesthetized surgery we would wager. It's not that Kate Bush is anything less than charm, elegance and fragrance during interviews. Rather that behind the winsome smile and girlish laugh, there's the seasoned reluctance of a woman who decided at 21 that spending twice as much time talking about her records as she did making them was a pretty preposterous state of affairs."

There are some telling answers from Kate: Do you worry about getting old? "I don't actually worry about ageing, but I am at a point when I'm older than I was and there's a few things I'd like to be doing with my life. I've spent a lot of time working and I'd like to catch up. Over the next few years I'd like to take some time off."

...And, finally, are you a recluse and a publicity-shy enigma? "That does amuse me. Well, the reclusive thing is because I don't go clubbing and I don't do a lot of publicity. I'm a quiet, private person who has managed to hang around for a few years. Ridiculous, really. I didn't think it would be like this. All I wanted to do was make an album. That was the dream. I'd been writing songs since I was little and I just wanted to see them on an album. This was my purpose in life – to just look at the grooves and think, 'I did that'. And then from my first record my life was very dramatically changed. My music was popular instantly. It's a pressure. You can't quietly get on with it. But it was so exciting. My life was turned upside down very fast when I was very young. I was quite a way down the road before I got a chance to look back."

The interviews in *Q*, *Rolling Stone*, and *Details* should be required reading every morning for every Kate fan who feels like saying "she owes me a new album – and a tour".

The *Rolling Stone* feature was not published until 24th February 1994: "It's very moving that a lot of people that I don't know are so supportive of what I do. I don't tour, I don't give them that much, really. Obviously I try to make the best music that I can, but after about two years of making an album you start to worry: 'Is it going to come out all right? Is it all going to sound churned out?' And then you get odd little letters from fans here and there encouraging you, and that's a fantastic boost. I suppose I hope that if I keep an integrity in my work, then they'll

Let no-one say we weren't warned!

always feel that."

Details did not appear until March 1994: You say in one of your lyrics that life and love are sad. When did you decide that? "It was a line from Joseph Campbell, and I'm not saying it's something I believe – quite often there are things said in a song that I don't believe at all, but they are beliefs of other people, and sometimes that's very relevant." Hmm. Have you found joy in romantic love? "Yeah, I think so. But there's also a great deal of joy in love that isn't necessarily romantic." Do you still improvise? "Not like I did, and there was a big attempt on this album to get back to that. With the last three albums, I've been writing straight onto tape, but actually sitting and playing the piano without the technology all around me was really good. *Top of the City* was written like that."

That's us apparently.

So do members of your cult scare the shit out of you? "My cult!? What cult?" You have a cult. C'mon, don't be coy. "What kind of cult? There is a figure that is adored, but I'd question very strongly that it's me. My work speaks far more eloquently than I do, and if people get anything at all out of the tracks, whether it's what I intended or not, then that's great. But I don't care if people like me or not – I am what I am, I do the best I can, and that's what matters."

A friend of mine said he got the feeling from your music that you don't feel accountable to anyone else. "Well, we are slaves to ourselves, but it could be worse." Is that why you've never had kids? "Huh? That's very personal." Well, would you? "I would like to have kids, yeah." More so since your mum died? "It's certainly loss that heightens the realisation that life is short."

Del Palmer expounded upon the technical issues in the muso press. In *Future Music* he explained that there had been a complete changeover in the set-up at Kate's personal recording studio. She actually started work on *The Red Shoes* using 48-track analogue techniques, but changed midway to digital recording – along with all the advanced editing possibilities that implies: "Oddly enough, the idea of this album was to get it recorded quickly and get out on to the road with it. It didn't work out that way, but the idea did influence the way the album was put together. Because I wanted to concentrate on engineering and didn't want to be in the live band, I didn't play much bass on the album, and we used the same drummer and bassist – Stuart Elliott and John Giblin – almost throughout. A lot of the time we got them to play together live to create a consistent backing for a song, even if we had to go back and change that as the song developed."

Electronic Musician also set out the technical background: "*The Red Shoes* was recorded and mixed by Del in Kate's state-of-the-art facility housed in two adjacent barns in Kent County, near London. The studio is equipped with an SSL4048E console (with a G-series computer), a Fairlight, and AMS, Eventide, and luantec signal processors. After the project began, Bush purchased two Sony 3324A24-track digital recorders making *The Red Shoes* her first 48 track digital production. Del explains: "We used to be dyed-in-the-wool analogue lovers, but after day one of going digital, we were totally convinced that it was the best thing since sliced bread. Everything sounded so great direct from the microphones, that I barely touched the EQ during recording. And the absence of tape hiss is a boon for Kate's music, where arrangements sometimes break down to literally nothing.

"Bush developed keyboard and vocal ideas over simple, 4-bar drum loops programmed by Palmer on the Fairlight. When a song was adequately fleshed out, drummer Stuart Elliott was called in to replace the Fairlight loop. "All the drum sounds on the record are Akai S1000 samples played by Stuart on Simmons pads," says Palmer, "The only live sounds are the cymbals. We used samples because our studio is relatively small, and if we miked acoustic drums we'd always get the same room sound, which is not very exciting." Bush's lush vocal orchestrations were recorded on a Neumann U87, usually by herself. "She didn't want to bore me while she worked things out," explains Palmer. "So I'd set up a vocal sound, hand her the remote, and leave. When she felt she had enough good performances on tape, we'd select the best complete performance and fix little things by punching in lines from other tracks.

"According to Palmer, the album practically mixed itself. The sounds on tape were good, so he just added reverb and made sure each had enough space. 'Kate really doesn't like to use samples or sequences,' reveals Palmer. 'Everything on the record except a few drum loops is played real-time. We definitely wanted a band feel, so we didn't get obsessed with technology. I just twisted knobs until things sounded good.'"

The Red Shoes entered the Network album chart at no.1! However, in the industry standard Gallup album chart it entered at no.2, pipped by the ubiquitous MeatLoaf. In many in-store charts, the album was placed (by guesswork and anticipation) at no.1. In the Gallup chart it slid to no.18 by early December. The strangest thing to happen was that as a result of the three-track demo sent out by EMI in late October, *Eat the Music* actually became an airplay hit over the first few weeks of the album's release. In early November it was actually getting daily airplay on BBC Radio 1, Virgin 1215, and commercial radio stations, and showed on the *Music Week* airplay chart in the breakers section. TV advertised in the run up to Christmas, *The Red Shoes* went platinum in the UK (300,000 sales) in mid-December. EMI commented that the album was selling faster than *The Sensual World*. In the *Music Week* end of year chart the album came in at no.32. The album chart numbers from 4th December were 16, 17, 19, 21, 1st January 1984 – 19, 23, 20, 22, 22, 5th February 33, 42, 63, and out of the top 75 on the 26th.

In the US, Sony sent out promotional copies of the album to press and radio in mid-September. The press release accompanying was exultant: "Ordinary words cannot describe the artistry of Kate Bush. Ever since her breakthrough in 1978 with the huge international hit *Wuthering Heights* Kate has done nothing short of dazzle and amaze, and reinvent what we might call rock music, especially rock music so daringly created by a woman. With every release, Kate has nurtured her sound, her talents, making music so astonishingly refreshing and new that it simply overwhelms the listener."

The flyer also referred to Kate's American fans: "her recordings sped through an amazingly sophisticated network of fan clubs, fanzines and computer on-line networks. The legion of Kate's incredibly loyal and dedicated fans – the 'Love Hounds' – will purchase any and all material on her, from books to photographs to overseas releases. They also celebrate Katemas parties – yearly celebrations that take place on Kate's birthday – to talk about their favourite artist – Kate!"

Billboard's Melinda Newman previewed the album in her *The Beat* column on 11th September: "With a voice that could make angels cry, Bush plays the role of willing but woeful supplicant on the bouncy *Rubberband Girl* and the hopeful romantic on the dreamy *Top of the City*. Her girlish voice, heavy with passion, drips all over *And So Is Love* while the organ – drenched, throbbing ballad *You're the One* sounds like the kind of song Prince would die for..."

Sony made a significant promotional effort spearheaded by in-shop promotional parties. Timed for anything from midnight on the day before release, to anything up to a few days later, these had varying success. The general approach was to hand out T-shirts, video singles and lapel pins to the first customers and raffle a lithograph of the album cover. Stores added their own refinements – the San Francisco branch of Tower Records gave door prizes to customers wearing red shoes!

The quality of these events was patchy. Some fans reported lively parties with significant numbers enjoying themselves, but another fan reported from a branch of Rough Trade as follows: "Other than sort of hearing the album at too low a volume this event was a disappointment. The litho was not on display. The employees kept moaning about having to play Kate all day when they wanted to be playing Nirvana. The one Kate fan who works there was obviously excited, but a bit embarrassed that they did not receive any give-away items other than buttons depicting the album cover. They did get one copy of the video singles for *Eat the Music* and *Rubberband Girl* but did not have a monitor to play them on."

Sony directed much the same promotional effort at the radio stations, who responded quite well in the places one would expect (those with the looser modern rock formats) with album and promo item give-aways. There was noticeable airplay of a selection of tracks, and at least one station played the whole album! Sony took space on the front page of the 4th November *Billboard* for a small but prominent strip advertisement announcing the new album and the film. In the same issue was a full page advert for the next US single.

It was a measure of the importance of the album for Kate in the US, that it was actually reviewed by *Rolling Stone* (Richard C. Walls), which had not noticed *The Sensual World* at all. In their 25th November issue they reviewed *The Red Shoes* together with Jane Siberry's latest: "On her first album since *The Sensual World* in 1989, Kate Bush continues in the manner of that album's verbal directness while displaying a melodic sense that's in peak form... Bush seems content now to dress her songs in simpler – though still occasionally antic – colours. The result is offbeat pop that refines but doesn't sacrifice her signal eccentricity... It's not all fainting hearts on *Shoes*, though. The mood ranges from the pure pop of *Rubberband Girl* to the exuberant reel of the title cut, from the wistful verse and funky chorus of the Prince collaboration *Why Should I Love You?* to the West Indies-flavoured *Eat the Music*. *The Red Shoes* is a solid collection of well-crafted and seductively melodic showcases for Bush's hypercaberet style".

Entertainment Weekly (Ken Tucker) said: "In this country, Bush's fbrid vocal eccentricity – undulating gulps and shrieks of meandering melody – have consigned her to the rank of 'oddball, English Division'. *The Red Shoes*, with its tightened tunes and catchy choruses, is designed to break Bush State-side, but it's no sell-out. Filled with lovely, if loopy, pop songs, *Shoes* makes sense of Bush's excesses without squelching her beguiling silliness. B+".

The album made its début at no.28 in the *Billboard* chart, the highest ever chart position Kate had achieved in the US, and two places higher than the peak position achieved by *Hounds of Love*. However, as Ed Suranyi explained on Love-Hounds, *Billboard* had changed the method it uses to determine the charts in 1991. Before then, these were determined by surveying a representative sample of record stores. After 1991 they actually tracked album sales as they were purchased, by electronic links to stores' cash registers. After this system was introduced, the chart changed substantially. In the old system, an album of moderate popularity such as a Kate album, would start in the middle of the chart, then slowly move up the chart to peak some time later. *Hounds of Love*, *The Sensual World*, and (to a

lesser extent) *The Whole Story* all followed this pattern. But with the new system of tracking album sales instantly many albums débuted at what turned out to be their peak positions. And so it was for Kate. The next week the album slid to 55, thence 83 and 117.

Sony pursued their album campaign with advertisements in the January 1994 issues of *Première*, *Mondo*, and *Wired*, and to the surprise of some US fans the company also managed in the run-up to Christmas, to place record shop co-operative advertising on TV, at least in those areas where Kate fans congregate – the East and West coast. In the local in-store charts, especially in those areas where Kate fans concentrated, the album did especially well, in some California stores actually being no.1, driven by a further crop of mostly good reviews:

"Bush is a genius. Geniuses do overreach. Some of her stuff is awful, paint-peeling noise... Bush has used Bulgarian women's choirs and African drummers and David Gilmour's guitar to magnificent effect... Her malleable and expansively ranging voice pairs with her studio wizardry to give her the most astonishing vocal control of any recording artist extant. *The Red Shoes*... adds to her stature and could add to the size of her American audience... It's accessible... Kate Bush has produced her most gleeful album in a decade... From the most serene bliss to the most desperate urgency, no singer locates as many spots on the emotional spectrum as Bush does." Paul Gambaccini, *New York Press* 24/11/93

"Alternative rock icon throws a sumptuous feast of sounds that is destined to take a high place in her body of work." *Billboard* 27/11/93

"For the past 16 years, record companies have been trying to figure out how to break Kate Bush in America. That they haven't given up after the mega-hyped failure of 1989's *Sensual World* is fortunate because the often-challenging songstress has delivered another strong effort… Some songs are still tough going for the casual listener, but Bush's work has a lyrical and musical richness that demands repeated listening." Dan Le Roy, *Graffiti*, December 1993

"Ms. Bush is... a musical philosopher... divining meaning from her experience and giving it universal scope... Ms. Bush was seeking increasingly complex ways to express the landscape of consciousness and the soul's connection to God and the supernatural world. On *The Red Shoes* Ms. Bush, is in a wiser, less breathlessly romantic mode. Gone is the grandiose mysticism... Instead, Ms. Bush's quest for meaning is more earthbound, concentrating on the pangs of the heart and the joys of the flesh." Peter Galvin, *New York Times*, 2/6/94

"She breathlessly dives into dance-club beats, Celtic instrumentation, bluesey guitar-vocal dialogues, grunge guitar, Bulgarian chorales, sunny world-music tangents, art song, Princely funk, and incantatory trance music...Vocally, she's got more stretch in her than a slingshot, reaching for the top of her range with no loss of power... Musically inventive, emotionally audacious, and entrancing in an all too rare way, *The Red Shoes* will set your feet dancing and your head spinning." Parke Puterbaugh, *Stereo Review*, March 1994.

In *Billboard*'s review of the year, Fred Bronson, the editor of the 'Chartbeat' column, chose Kate's album as his no.2 record of the year, commenting that "Kate was always worth the wait".

Kate was putting some significance on the promotion of this album in the US. In the original promotional plans she intended to visit the US for 10 days in November 1993 with appearances on the prime time David Letterman and Arsinio Hall shows pencilled in. As planned, Kate went to the US on Sunday 28th November 1993. The schedule was kept tightly under wraps by Sony, but finally amounted to only a handful of radio and local TV interviews. Despite earlier hopes and plans, appearances on the peak time TV programmes did not materialise. Other appointments were fixed and unfixed rapidly. An appointment at radio station Z-100 (New York) was advertised and then cancelled, as was apparently an interview on MTV's '120 Minutes'. However, that show did finally show a brief interview clip on 13th March. Kate did TV interviews for JBTV in Chicago and RAGE TV in Boston and World Café, APR. Some interviews appeared long after Kate had returned to Britain: on 8th February 1994 NPR's 'Weekend Edition' had a review of the album together with short interview clips.

On 9th December Kate went to down-town Tower Records in New York to sign copies of the new album. The following reports were compiled from material by Andrew Marvick, Doug Alan, Sam Warren, Mike, Jason Pascucci and Debra Wentorf:

"I arrived at the 4th and Broadway intersection slightly before 6am. By twenty past six there were already two more people in line: Illana had flown all the way from San Francisco! She spent all her money getting to New York and had to sleep on the NYC subway. She was going to ask Kate to autograph her arm and then go have the autograph tattooed in! By 7am there were about ten people standing in line. The line continued to grow until at some point before noon a few guys working at Tower Records brought out police barricades to define the line a bit more formally. By noon, there were about a hundred people in line.

"At about 3pm things started going into a

Graphic: Paulina Stuckey

higher gear. The line grew until it went nearly all the way around the city block. Tower Records workers rearranged the barricades again to keep us better fenced in and also put numbered wrist bands on everyone in line; apparently a precaution against people sneaking into the autograph area inside the store. A reporter from Tower Records and a camera crew from CBS came and talked to us. They were making a news clip that would be sent off to CNN and other news broadcasters.

"Kate arrived in a white limo about 20 minutes before 4pm. Film crews from MTV and Entertainment Tonight were there. People were literally standing on garbage bins and even on the side of the building in hopes of getting a glimpse of her and taking pictures. Finally, the folks in Tower Records caught on and put cardboard up over the windows.

"Andrew went first, carrying the white roses he had brought for Kate. Once we were inside the store however, Andrew was no longer first, because a couple of VIP's had been allowed in without paying the dues of the long, cold wait. They let us in, in groups of ten. Rules were one item only to sign, and no cameras. The two first groups averaged about a minute a person, but it went more quickly thereafter.

"Kate wore all black, with high-heeled boots, opaque black tights, a long black dress and a black leather biker's jacket. Her hair really is that long! Illana tried to get her arm autographed, but when she explained that she was going to get it tattooed in, Kate refused saying "You'll be off me in a couple of years!" Del was keeping track of time for Kate. She signed some of the bootlegs without comment. However, one guy came up with one which was obviously one she hadn't

seen before. She showed it to Del and to a couple other guys, and was amiable enough to the guy, but looked over at Del and was visibly upset for a moment. I saw her sign about three of the halter top pictures, each with obvious distaste but directed at the picture, never at the person.

"She was scheduled to stay until 6pm, but ended up staying until gone 7pm. When I got there the line went from the entrance to 4th Street, 4th to Lafayette, down to 3rd and back to Broadway. There was no way all of those people were going to get in. It was like her birthday all over again! At the end of the night, she had three and a half full large shopping bags of stuff given to her, and when Kate and Del finally left at about 7.20pm it took two people to carry them all away."

In Canada *Rubberband Girl* was released on 17th September. By the end of the month, at least in Toronto, the single was figuring in the chart of the local radio station CFNY at no.12, and the charts of local record stores at nos. 13 and 29. The video was seen as part of a special two-part 'Spotlight' on Kate aired on 3rd October on the video channel Much Music. The programme included eight of Kate's videos and interview material from the years 1985-89. CFNY FM in Toronto held an album preview party on 26th October 1993, with admission determined by a phone-in ballot. They gave away advance copies of the album and for the first time they served a sit down dinner. The station explained this saying: "we decided to do it with class this time 'coz Kate herself exudes class".

The album was released on lst November, and the premier rock monthly (Jon Young) reviewed it as follows: "If you've pegged Kate Bush as a dreamy cosmic spirit, don't miss the climax of *The Red Shoes*, where the stunning *You're the One* renews the tradition of brazenly pitiful love songs... The rest of this fevered meditation on the meaning of it all isn't as wonderfully raw or direct, but desperate impulses abound. Exploring the terrain of the heart in her hyper-dramatic way, Bush argues that romance is all we have, even if life stinks... Bush has clearly laboured to do justice to the soul's storms. Mostly, she succeeds. Thus, let us hail this woman who stops at nothing in pursuit of inner truths, even to the point of imitating the sound of a stretching rubberband in *Rubberband Girl*. And, above all, unleashes that dreadful howl at the end of *You're the One*. Awesome!".

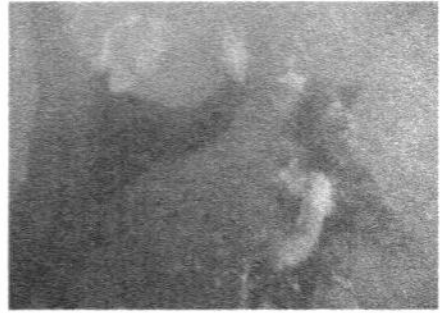

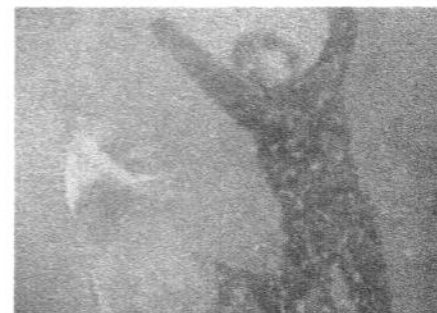

The second single in the UK was the emotional *Moments of Pleasure*, the track Kate had performed on 'Aspel'. The package included a 12" poster bag (*Moments of Pleasure* c/w *Moments of Pleasure instrumental* and *Home for Christmas*), and a special limited edition CD box (*Moments of Pleasure* c/w *December Will Be Magic Again* and *Experiment IV*) including four 5"x5" prints and two pictures of Kate, the single sleeve and a lyric sheet.

In the second week of release a further CD was released which included a new track *Show a Little Devotion*. Ah, the arts of selling records (the same record over and over again to the same people and then pretending the "chart" means anything). Whatever happened to two sided vinyl pressings in a sleeve made out of chip paper! Gone for good it seems – for the first time there was no 7" vinyl format.

Although the track was very well received, and got a great deal of air play, *Moments of Pleasure* went the way of *Rubberband Girl*. It was bought by the fans, but did not make a huge commercial breakout. It entered the Gallup chart at no.26 on 21st November, and fell back to no.32 the following week. There were few reviews:

"Beautiful and traditional Bush fare with expansive orchestrations, poignant vocals and off-her-trolly lyrics." Alan Jones, *Music Week*, 20/11/93

"Well, where are they then?" Ian McCann, *NME*, 20/11/93.

The video (another segment from the film) appeared on the ITV 'Chart Show' and on BBC TV's 'Top of the Pops', in the breakers section. Kate recorded a live performance of the track for the 22nd December 'Des O'Connor Show' on ITV. It was, however, never used by the programme, the only explanation having filtered through being "they didn't like it".

UK radio decided to prompt the choice of the next single itself. It plumped for *Why Should I Love You*, and for a few weeks in January and February turned it into a minor airplay hit, actually registering on the bubbling under section of the *Music Week* airplay chart.

The follow-up single in the US was the track they had wanted in the first place, *Rubberband Girl*. It was, as they thought it would be, immediately popular. In the 11th November *Billboard* it was the single reviewers critic's choice: "Fun, funky, and full of appropriately flexible sounds, including the subtle vocal tricks Bush has made her calling card. Toe-tapping and head-bopping, this one would be a cool, ear-catching addition to any play-list, but perceptive pop/rock programmers may hear drive-time potential here."

Having heard the almost unanimous opinion of the US visual media on the clipped-from-the-film videos, Kate made another video for this single for US use, in which she boogied around a bit and pretended to be a rock star. This went down well, and was featured on MTV's '120 Minutes' on 31st October. The JBTV music channel was behind *Rubberband Girl* from the start, the single appearing in their playlist from 28th November to 21st January. Despite having the second version of the video, MTV were a little late in their support, only adding the single to the play-list on 18th December when it was already showing in the bubbling under section of the *Billboard* singles chart. It remained on the MTV list until 5th February and US fans were of the opinion that it was seen more times than any other Kate track. After disappearing from the main MTV list, the clip then turned up on the MTV Latino list for two weeks! The single entered the *Billboard* modern rock chart at 21 on 20th November. It was Kate's most successful in the US since *Running Up That Hill*, actually appearing on the *Billboard* Hot 100 for six weeks.

From the US, Kate travelled to Toronto where on 13th December 1993 she attended the Canadian première of *The Line, the Cross & the Curve* at the Royal Ontario Museum. The FM radio station CFNY ran yet another phone-in competition to give away 102 pairs of passes to the film. On air they said that their phone lines were "melting from all the calls begging for passes". The going rate from the ticket touts outside the museum was apparently $100. Inside, the head of EMI-Canada welcomed the fans and introduced Kate. As she walked down the aisle from the back row the fans cheered, whistled, and gave a standing ovation. Kate welcomed the audience and introduced the film. Then she walked back up the aisle, to renewed and thunderous applause. After the film she left whilst the credits were rolling and went directly to the CFNY radio studios.

This special interview was broadcast world-wide by satellite, and Kate took questions from anyone who could reach her on the phone. The show was heard on all radio stations in North America which carried the syndicated show 'Modern Rock Live'. The host of that show had a direct connection with Kate at CFNY. It seemed that contrary to EMI-Canada's intentions, listeners were invited to drop by and ogle through the glass front of the studio, but as the fans arrived they found that the glass had been covered with brown paper. As a senior CFNY staffer later explained on air, EMI was worried that Kate would be put off by the crowd. The crowd gathered nonetheless, and peacefully listened to the interview through the speakers the radio station had rigged up. Someone then thought it would be a good idea to send in a petition, and so it was done, and going through what was estimated at 40 pairs of hands, it reached Kate. About 15 minutes before the end of the show, Kate herself got up and removed the centre strip of paper from the studio window, much to the surprise of the fans immediately on the other side. To their cheers she then removed the rest, and then carried on with the interview!

Kate gave a further conference phone interview to five journalists across Canada on 13th December. The journalists were restricted to three questions each and the resulting reports giving diametrically opposed versions of what she said about touring showed exactly why Kate does not like doing such things.

In the new year, MuchMusic put together another 50 minute special on Kate in their 'Egos and Icons' series. Entitled 'Kate Bush: This Woman's Work', it aired first on 20th January, and was then repeated over the next week. The programme included excerpts from past MuchMusic interviews, bits from a recent programme on City-TV called 'The New Music', and a new interview recorded whilst Kate was in Toronto in December 1993, and which included a short interview with Del. Interspersed between the interview footage were clips from virtually every video Kate has ever made.

Picking up in a non-linear way another thread of this frantic time, "the film" which Kate had started shooting on 2nd July, finished shooting toward the end of July, edited between all else that was going on from July to early November working at the end 15 hour days to get it done, was first presented to EMI executives on 10th November.

EMI had originally thought of staging a special "film première" for *The Line, the Cross & the Curve*, but as its completion was delayed and the cinema they had chosen was closed down, this idea was scrubbed and the film was actually premièred at the 37th London Film Festival at the Odeon West End 2 on Saturday 13th November. The festival programme commented: "We are delighted to welcome acclaimed singer-songwriter Kate Bush to the world of images with this, her directorial début. Although the inspirational source is the music contained in her new album, her visual energy, flair and use of colours is simply great."

The film début had a rapturous reception from an audience of fans and members of the British Film Institute. Kate attended with Del and Dr. Bush, and Miranda Richardson was also in the audience. Before the film began, Kate was invited onto the stage to make a few introductory comments, in which she said she was honoured that the British Film Institute had accepted her work for inclusion in the Festival. She thanked all the people who had helped her, said she was a bit nervous as it was her first film, and said that the previous film (the Nick Park animation *The Wrong Trousers*) was a hard act to follow! As the final credits faded however, the audience rose in a spontaneous and lengthy standing ovation, which Kate was finally persuaded to rise and accept. The press reaction was not so enthusiastic:

"mixed artistic results... a music promo flick high on whimsy and low on content... Richardson... steals the acting stakes as a kind of

The sequence for *And So is Love*, a meditation on love and liberty

wicked witch. When not warbling, Bush is colourless. Mime artist Lindsay Kemp... is reliable. Pic's visual style is relatively conservative, far from the usual music vid fare." *Variety*, 6/12/93

"not so much a movie as the sort of linked sequence of promo vids that pop stars are wont to hang themselves with, given a feature length rope... While the metaphor may well refer to the fiendishly obsessive nature of artistic creativity... the effect suggests a peculiarly daft corner of the '70s... Still, if the viewer approaches it as opera or ballet – sod the plot and soak in the sound and vision – it's more lively. The six songs come across at stunning big-concert power and Kate dances with a wild passion which will make devotees ache for her to take to the boards again." Derek Elley, *Q*, December 93

After the London Film Festival, the film was featured in a number of other festivals around the world, including the Irish Film Festival (26th February 1994) in Dublin, and the Tromsoe Festival in Norway. In the US at the end of 1993 Sony were actively seeking opportunities to show the film. These were all cancelled before Kate arrived in the US, though at the time it seemed like only a delay. Kate took the film to the USA with her and it was shown to the press and promoters on the 10th December. After Kate went back to the UK, it seemed that Sony showed little interest in pursuing further showings, and weren't even sure that it would be released on video.

The lack of enthusiasm by Sony was amply demonstrated at the showing in the new year at the Berkeley UC theatre on 25th February as part of the Berkeley Women's Film Festival. Sony provided little promotional support, and the festival did not sell out even half of the available seats in the theatre. The only evidence on the day of any promotional intent was a copy of the album poster that was pinned up in the preview area at about 7:30 pm to go with the small black and white picture of Kate that had been put there earlier. Kate did appear to promote the film at its showing at the 12th Brussels International Festival of Fantasy, Thriller, and Science Fiction Films on 23rd March 1994.

In the *NME* 1993 year-end poll, Kate was no.9 'best solo artist', and *The Red Shoes* was voted at no.45 in their journalists' lists of albums of 1993, with the comment: "An LP so comprehensively downcast, it ought to be accompanied by a sick note... some of the bleakest music of her life... when the blues really burn she'll tear your heart".

In the *Melody Maker* poll Kate was voted no.7 'woman of the year' and no.4 'female artist'. In *Music Week*'s survey of the year, Steve Gallant, brand development manager at Our Price Retail, nominated *The Red Shoes* as his 'album of 1993'. In the 1993 *Musik Express* Sounds poll Kate was voted 'darling of the year' by the German magazine, with 22½% of the vote – from Madonna with 14½% of the vote. Kate also did quite well in the 1993 polls in the Italian music press. In *TuttiFrutti* she was no.4 'Best Female Artist', (and incidentally no.2 'worst return'), and *The Red Shoes* was no.5 'best sleeve'. In *Rockstar*, Kate was no.3 'best female artist', *The Red Shoes* was no.3 'best album', *Moments of Pleasure* was no.3 'best song' and no.2 'best video'. In the record collector's magazine *Raro* Kate was no.9 'foreign female artist most collected'.

As if to compound the irrelevance of the whole Brits (ugh!) nonsense, despite having an album that was clearly released in 1993, Kate missed the 31st October (eh?) qualification deadline for the 1994 Brits by one day. Ironically, it was the fuss over Kate's nomination last year which led to a change in the rules!

In the Spring/Summer 1994 issue of *CD Plus*, Kate gave a short interview: "It is not that I don't like touring, but I think touring takes the artist away from the process of writing music. And I always worry that if I spend too long away from writing I will never get better at it. It's one of those things you need to spend a lot of time and effort on. Besides, there was never the time; by the time I'd finished an album, did promotion and videos, I was very tired. So you take a break and you start another album. After two or three circles like that I found myself getting more and more removed from performing, feeling very nervous about getting up on the stage... I think it is a shame for me as well as my fans that I am not in closer contact with them by touring, but I suppose I feel I have a responsibility to them and myself to do the best I can musically, and that means concentrating on writing."

In the early part of 1994 as Kate decided that she needed to pay some attention to the US market, and having departed on her promotional trip, EMI tried to get on with promotion of *The Red Shoes* in the UK. Without Kate's personal participation they encountered resistance from the media. They previously had problems caused by last minute changes to the lead single, disagreements with Sony in the US over album release date, and media resistance to the promotional videos for the singles being more or less the relevant sequences edited out of *The Line, the Cross & the Curve*. Altogether the promotion and sales of the album and its singles were not regarded by EMI or Kate with satisfaction. From Kate's point of view she had worked all hours to complete the film, and she was determined more than ever to take a break, after the promotion of this album was done with. The temptation to take off those red shoes was overwhelming.

And So Is Love was released early March as the third US single, and the video was picked up (for a couple of weeks) by JBTV and PowerPlay music video TV. The third UK single was *The Red Shoes*, released on 5th April 1994 on a million formats: 7" vinyl – contrary to reports that *Moments of Pleasure* would be Kate's last 7" single – tape cassette and two CDs. The 7" and cassette featured *The Red Shoes*, and a new track entitled *You Want Alchemy*. The first CD featured those tracks together with *Cloudbusting (Video Mix)* and *This Woman's Work*. The second CD featured the basic tracks plus *Shoedance* (the 10 minute remix of the title track), *The Big Sky* (the single mix), and *Running Up That Hill* (12" mix). The versions of *Cloudbusting* and *The Big Sky* not previously available on CD were included partly at *HomeGround*'s suggestion. The release was moderately successful. The reviews, as ever, were mixed:

"Only as a grown-up will I be able to fully apprehend the texture and allegorical resonance of the themes that are dealt with in *The Red Shoes*. Until then I'll content myself with Tori Amos... they don't call me superficial Pete for nothing." Peter Paphides, *Melody Maker*, 9/4/94

"Amos' spiritual grandmother hangs up the folk clogs and puts on her dancing pumps... a crap drum loop and tinpot synth arrangement... Bjork has easily overtaken Ms. Bush in the enigmatic scale jumping stakes... nobody dances to beepy new romantic excesses... Cobblers!" *NME*, 16/4/94

"Although rhythmic and literate, it's not the stuff of which top ten singles are made." *Music Week*, 9/4/94

"Over the last 15 years or so Kate has beaten off all challengers to her title of 'the barmiest bird in pop'... if only her taste in music was as good... a very weird single, but not a very good one." Mark Sutherland, *Smash Hits* 16/4/94

"Another... spooky dance obsessed legend... rhythmically compelling with a dose of her own identifiable ethnicity, but the dance mix seems to bury the 'real Kate.'" Dave Hunter, *Grooves* (Channel 4 text).

Initial radio play on the single was quite good. It entered the *Music Week* airplay chart at no.28 on 23rd April, rising to no.26 the next week. It entered the breakers section of the UK official chart at no.15 on 9th April, rising to no.2 the following week, and then into the top 40 proper at no.28 on 11th April. The following week with the release of the second part of the two CD package, it went up (not a common occurrence for Kate's singles these days) to no.21. Despite good radio support, and showings of the video on the ITV 'Chart Show' and on MTV Europe, on 30th April it fell to no.53.

The computer age was at last upon us. In Spring EMI/PMI released an update of Kate's video compilation, on CD-ROM entitled *Kate Bush The Whole Story '94*. A number of *HomeGround* readers noted problems such as sound hiss at high volume, defective pixelisation, jerky slow-motion, defective synchronisation, and over active centring. Time was when all we worried about was fluff on the needle!

The April/May 1994 issue of *CD-ROM Today* magazine described these releases as "a 5" disk capable of holding up to 65 minutes of video using MPEG1 compression". However: "there is also a limited number of machines that you can play Video CD disks on. A Philips CDi player fitted with their Digital Video Cartridge is one option; the Commodore Amiga CD32 games console fitted with their Digital Video Cartridge is another; and a PC fitted with the ReelMagic digital video board is the only other choice."

We spotted one review:

"When a soft focus Kate Bush and her doppelgänger rise from an exotic pool of liquid passion to begin a high-pitched and hysterical tale of scorched jealousy based on the Brontë pot-boiler, you can suddenly recall why Katie was such an overnight sensation. *Wuthering Heights* is still an extraordinary song and Bush's astonishing warble combined with her Home Counties Gothic princess persona was a heady audio-visual cocktail... The superbly encoded VideoCD underlines just how attuned Bush was to the then embryonic medium of rock videos... the simplest videos in which a soft-focus Kate whirls and wuthers in a lovingly lit room are invariably the best to watch. Less successful are the plot heavy videos for... *Cloudbusting* and *Experiment IV*... Overall this is a reasonable testament to one of the most original artists to emerge in the late 1970s, and is proof that there is no substitute for good song writing... One gripe, though. The whole package was woefully short on any background information, even omitting to tell you in what year each track was recorded or the album from which it was taken. For twenty quid a throw, consumers have every right to expect a little more effort on the presentation front." Paul Nesbit, *CDROM*, October 1994.

In the last week of April 1994 the Kate Bush Club sent out the list of cinemas that were to show *The Line the Cross & the Curve* in the UK in a programme that also included seven videos: *Cloudbusting*, *This Woman's Work*, *Experiment IV*, *Love and Anger*, *The Sensual World*, *Hounds of Love*, and *Running Up That Hill*: the full list was: May 6 Lee Valley, Edinburgh, Gateshead; May 13 Solihull, East Kilbride, Telford; May 20 Hatfield, Sheffield, Clyde; May 27 Tamworth, Warrington, Hull; June 3 Portsmouth, High Wycombe, Dudley; June 10 Derby, Preston, Bracknell; June

The Red Shoes sequence. An essay on the seduction of celebrity.

17 Milton Keynes, Poole, Swansea; June 24 West Thurrock, Sutton, Plaza Piccadilly. The attendances at the showings of the film were variable. Some of the early North London showings garnered audiences not in excess of half a dozen. In other places the local Kate fans made a day of it and turned the occasion into a mini-convention.

Much to EMI's relief, Kate also set out on a short round of promotional interviews, doing stints with Radio 1 FM, the commercial breakfast station GMTV, and the BBC's children's news programme 'Newsround'. During Kate's interview with Tania Bryer (the "Showbizz" correspondent of 'Good Morning With Anne and Nick' which was broadcast on BBC1 on Friday 29th April, several clips from the film were shown. Amongst Kate's comments were: "I have a very great curiosity for words; I think there is a word for everything. It's a great gift to be very eloquent but the only dialogue that I've ever been involved in is in this film... There are areas where there should have been more dialogue; I would have liked that but we just didn't have the time to develop the story any more but really one of the scenes that I think I'm the most proud of in the film is Miranda's entrance into the room and the dialogue that in a way sets up the whole story... In this particular film I took on the role as the singer and I think in some ways by doing that I took on a bit too much. If I was to make a film, I wouldn't want to be in it so much, just maybe a tiny bit."

The film was also mentioned on The ITV 'Chart Show', and on Barry Norman's 'Film '94' on BBC TV, which also showed a clip.

In the US the film was shown later on 22nd and 23rd April at the University Theatre in Berkeley, California, at the Brattle Theatre as part of the Boston International Women's Film Festival, on 29th April and at the NUART Theatre in West Los Angeles on 1st and 2nd July, and also at Florida Film Festival in June. Kate's film was exhibited in Finland at the Espoo Cine Festival, Finland on 25th and 28th August. Rather strangely, in view of the great care being taken to prevent any bootleg copies of the film from getting into circulation, it was shown in full on Swedish television in mid-July, and on satellite channel JSB on 18th October.

As part of their promotional effort for *The Red Shoes*, Toshiba EMI in Japan prepared a 2xCD compilation of Kate's work entitled *Moments of Pleasure The Best Works 1978 to 1993*. This 32 track compilation had the picture of Kate that was used as the *Pulse* cover (film costume with bird on head) and the few copies produced were soon changing hands for over $500! The Shinko Music Publishing company of Japan brought out in March a new official music and lyric book, which was essentially a superior remix of *Kate Bush Complete*. The title was *Moving: A Collection of Poems* (ISBN4401613295). The 256 page book contained the lyrics of 79 songs side by side with Japanese translations by Anri Kitazawa, and an album discography up to the box set. For some obscure reason Toshiba EMI also finally released *The Sensual World* video on 27th July 1994, but not also on LaserDisc.

On 8th August PMI released the first in a batch of CD and video double packs. This included *Kate Bush: Live at Hammersmith Odeon* (cat no. SAV 4913063) The release was part of a new series called 'Sound and Vision'. It came in a slightly larger than usual video box with the CD inserted on one side and the video on the other. The tracks on both video and CD are those on the previous release. There were no special booklets or anything else with the package.

The Line the Cross & the Curve was intended to be released in the UK on video by PMI on 10th October 1994 along with a LaserDisc version. In the USA there was some confusion over the release date for the film, both VHS cassette and laser disc. It was first said to be 25th October, and then moved to 1st November. The film was shown in Seattle (Varsity Hall) on 1st and 2nd October, and in New York (Quad cinemas), Chicago (Facets Multimedia), and Madison (Orpheus Theatre) as part of the Sony publicity effort. These usually double showings were either wholly free or free to the first 150 or so people admitted.

Sony also seemed to have persuaded some local radio stations to sponsor showings of the film, and to give away goodies. WXPN sponsored such an event in Philadelphia, where the film was shown at the International House on 8th October. Free CDs and an autographed lithograph were on offer. As part of their promotional effort Sony aimed advertising precisely at those who knew of or read the rec.music.gaffa internet group, or took advertising in computer oriented magazines. Unfortunately they seemed to have regarded internet users as a captive group, and do not seem to have gone after a wider audience. US fans commented on the lack of poster campaigns and adverts in general magazines and the press.

The 1994 Kate Bush Club/*HomeGround* Kate Bush Convention took place on 8th May at the London Hippodrome. A very enjoyable day which ended with a brief appearance from Kate, and then some serious dancing to Kate's music at deafening volume!

On 13th July 1994 MTV's Beavis and Butthead watched *Love and Anger*. Naturally "it sucked". They thought that the opening scene looked like one of those Christmas glass snowballs, the kind they liked to smash.

The Brazilian heavy metal band Angra released their début album *Angels Cry* that same

Graphic: Neil Sherrif

month, containing a cover version of *Wuthering Heights* which owed more to Pat Benatar than to Kate. In a number of interviews the band emphasised that they were great fans of Kate, and dedicated their version with the greatest respect.

To celebrate his 80th birthday, the world renowned harmonica player Larry Adler organised a tribute album to the US composer George Gershwin. Entitled *The Glory of Gershwin*, the album was produced by George Martin, and featured many top rock singers and musicians. Kate's contribution, a cover of the classic Gershwin track *The Man I Love* produced by George Martin, was released as a single on 18th July 1994. The track got a fair amount of airplay amidst the expensive promotional effort for the album, and the tasteful 1940s style monochrome video was aired on the ITV 'Chart Show'. The single went into the official chart at no.22, but fell out of the top 40 the following week. The album

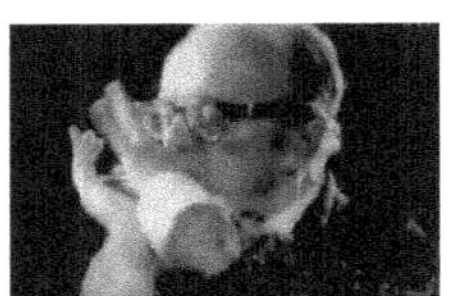

entered the chart at no.2 and garnered much further promotion including a number of TV appearances by Larry Adler.

Ice Newsletter, which specialises in new release info, box set info, bootlegs, imports and collectibles, reported in its October 1994 Collector's Corner as follows: "UK: This month's most elaborate promo only item comes from England, where Mercury produced an especially classy sampler to plug *The Glory of Gershwin*. A silk-screened, four-track disc with songs from Kate Bush, Cher, Sting and Peter Gabriel comes in a six-by-nine inch hard-bound book featuring comments on Gershwin from the four superstar contributors, plus additional background information on the project. English dealers claim only a few hundred copies of the promo were pressed".

The Man I Love garnered significant airplay in Israel (more than any of the singles from *The Red Shoes*), but failed to enter the chart. A radio special, inspired by the album, aired on 5th August, amidst much other promotional activity. Kate's track was prominent. A daily newspaper *Yediot Ahronot* went so far as to run a review of the album headed "Kate saves Gershwin", in which the reviewer found only three tracks of any merit, Kate's receiving special mention.

Kate's work with Alan Stivell, the Breton who was among the leaders of the revival of traditional music in Celtic France, saw the light of day in his new album *Again*. This was a collection of re-recorded versions of some of his older material. Kate provided backing vocals and keyboards on a track called *Kimiad*.

Kate had never shown much enthusiasm for her music to be used in advertisements, but one offer finally came along which tempted her, a substantial advertising campaign, for the $30 million US launch of Coca-Cola's fruit drink 'Fruitopia'. The campaign was criticised by some for attempting to jump on an environmental bandwagon. However, to quote one contributor to rec.music.gaffa: "Yes, it is obnoxious. Yes, the bottles are covered with silly pseudo environmentalist verbiage, faux peace'n'love crap and a pretty poor imitation of Peter Max artwork. People will vote with their pocketbooks... What do any of us care what the sort of fools who would be persuaded to drink one fruit drink over another based on a TV ad, drink? The simple fact is an ad agency with a track record for producing innovative adverts had the insight to approach Kate Bush. They had the good taste to not ask her to do anything overtly 'commercial'. And it was for a giant client which ensured that her music would be heard by almost every US TV viewer. And that last made sure that Kate will get a large chunk of change. Two things are almost certain; more people will hear the Fruitopia spots than have ever heard a single song from any of Kate's albums – Kate may well make more money from these mini-songs than she has from almost all of her albums. Kate acquitted herself well. She produced nine really intriguing short pieces of music that even friends who aren't into Kate like. Nobody has to drink the stuff."

The Fruitopia *Fighting Fruit* spot made it into the Siggraph (Special Interest Group on Graphics Association for Computing Machinery) Electronic Theatre in August 1994. This is the yearly conference for everyone involved in any area of computer graphics, and the Electronic Theatre is a 2 hour show of the best of the year.

An article by Michael Clark entitled *A Bushel of Fruitopia* appeared in the 29th July issue of the US magazine *Shoot*: "When Kate Bush took the assignment to do the music for Coca-Cola's new Fruitopia spots, it was indeed free rein for the British singer/songwriter... Creative director Marty Cooke and executive producer Andrew Chinich were overjoyed when Bush agreed to do not only one, but all nine of the spots in the Fruitopia campaign. Perhaps the fact that they told her she could do anything she wanted with the scores had something to do with it. 'In early tests, we played different music against the visuals, and Kate Bush music felt intuitive and right,' Cooke says. 'It gave the campaign a lot more consistency than it would have otherwise'... Bush... was told only to provide a 'variety' of styles and moods for the Fruitopia spots directed by Greg Ramsey out of bicoastal Fahrenheit Films. The spots... feature intense kaleidoscope-style manipulations of brightly colored fruit. Serendipitous text appears in the center of the psychedelic frame, with the soundtracks by Bush giving the spot an almost dizzying pace. 'We're very pleased... all the indications are that the music is one of the strongest parts of the campaign,' says Chiat/Day's Cooke. Bush supplied a variety of soundtracks, from a version that is heavy on percussion, to a poppy 'lounge' guitar/keyboard combination, to one Cooke describes as sounding 'like a bunch of Japanese schoolchildren.' For the cinema: 60 *What If*, which is number one on the most recent *Shoot* Top 10 Spot Tracks chart, Bush put down a track of very tribal percussion with layers of rhythmic chants that blend with the changing fields of rotating fruit. 'She said she was interested in providing a lot of variety, from Japanese drummers to Moroccan music... and she came through in spades.' The other four go under the titles of *Nice*, *Fighting Fruit*, *Summer Solstice*, and *Soul*'.

Just running ahead for a moment, the 13th August 1995 issue of *Entertainment Weekly* listed a few TV commercials that they like and a couple that they really dislike. The Kate-scored Fruitopia ads fell into the latter category, mostly due, they said, to the irony of a massive global corporation like Coca-cola positioning repackaged fruit juice in such a 'love the planet' kind of way. Of Kate's music, referred to as 'quasi new age', there was only a passing reference, neither flattering nor incendiary.

Sadly the music for the Fruitopia adverts in the UK was not provided by Kate. The advertising agency concerned told a *HomeGround* reader that they were unable to reach agreement with Kate for her to provide the music for the campaign in this country. As an alternative the Cocteau Twins were approached, and were quite willing to provide a somewhat similar sound to that provided by Kate for virtually identical ads.

The Davy Spillane album *A Place Among the Stars* was released in the UK in mid August but the cover of Marvin Gaye's *Sexual Healing* with Kate on lead vocals, was not included. No official reason has ever been given, but Davy Spillane's own explanation was given to Dr. Parks, a contributor to rec.music.gaffa. The track was left off because it didn't fit in with the feel of the rest of the album, so he had given the rights to release it to Kate and he thought she might do so at some point.

In Washington DC over the period 9th to 11th September 1994 the collectors' record shop The Intergalactic Garage (in co-operation with Sony) organised a special series of screenings of *The Line, the Cross & the Curve*, including a matinee and a late show. The main performance was on September 10th, with a DJ and door prizes. The films were shown at the Shepherdstown Opera House which has a state-of-the-art JBL sound system. Coca-Cola joined in sending over prints of the Fruitopia commercials and also provided free drinks. Oh the slippery slope!

Kate contributed a work of art for the October 1994 'War Child' exhibition in London in aid of Bosnian refugees. Kate was also reported to have been at the Pink Floyd apres-gig do in late October, and was also spotted in November at the Leicester Square premières of both Disney's *The Lion King* and Kenneth Brannagh's *Frankenstein*.

And So Is Love was the last *Red Shoes* single in the UK, released on 7th November 1994, with many gimmicks – the 'deluxe' CD contained the 'A' side, together with the US remix of *Rubberband Girl* and the 12" mix of *Eat the Music* and featured three postcard stills from the film. The 7" vinyl version was contained in a plastic wallet that also contained a full size copy of the flyposter for the single. The release included no new tracks other than *Rubberband Girl (American Dance Mix)*.

This time Kate accepted the invitation to appear on 'Top of the Pops' (for the first time since 1986). It was obviously quite a big thing for the programme, and Kate was introduced with due reverence! We are told that Kate enjoyed the occasion immensely. She did not sing live however, 'TOTP' being a little flexible on this occasion.

The single entered the charts at no.26 on 13th November and slid straight out the following week. It was almost an unexpected release, and a victim of Kate's general low key approach to promotion of *The Red Shoes* album. It may be that the media had finally got the message that Kate would like to be left alone. Certainly there was very little airplay of the single, which did not even make it as a breaker on the *Music Week* airplay chart. It was single of the week on Simon Mayo's breakfast show, but other Radio 1 support amounted to zilch, although airplay on commercial radio stations was better.

Kate's interview on Simon Mayo's show on 13th November was quite interesting with Kate giving Simon a message from the dolphins she had been out with the night before. Kate did however comment that she had learnt a lot in making *The Line, the Cross & the Curve* although it had perhaps been a rushed, and perhaps she had now got film-making out of her system for the moment, as she realised that any new film project would take a lot of work. Her comments about live work were tantalising: "if I do get a chance to move away from records again, it would be nice to do some live shows".

At the beginning of 1995, the Israeli artist Mazi Cohen re-released her début album on CD. This included a Hebrew cover version of *Army Dreamers* entitled *Shem Baeven* (literally 'A Name on the Tombstone'). The Hebrew words were written by lyricist Roni Eran. We were told by a reader in Israel that Kate's original track was a favourite on IDF, the official Israeli Army radio station.

Having missed the nomination period for the 1994 awards by just one day, Kate was reasonably enough, nominated for the 1995 Brit awards. Quite frankly we thought she was going to get the 'Best Female Artist' gong this time. You only have to look at the other nominees to see why. Nothing against them, but with the possible exception of Lisa Stansfield, Des'ree, Michelle Gayle, and Eddi Reader are not in the same class. In the nomination period (for the 1995 gongs it was 1st November 1993 to 31st October 1994, remember!) Kate had had a platinum album and three top 40 singles. Sadly it wasn't EMI's turn for this award and the gong actually went to Eddi Reader. The voting system had been changed again after last year's complaints by the Electoral Reform Society about "organised voting", but the results, again, were somewhat odd. *The Red Shoes* is on the usual compilation album.

In the early part of 1995 Kate returned to her private life. For Kate's fans, patient as they are, the next wait for new material was to be a long one.

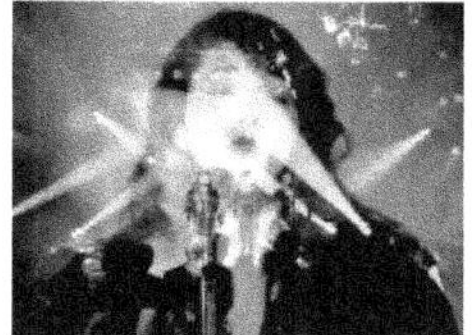

Kate's version of *Sexual Healing* was first played in public at the 1994 Convention

A Moment of Pleasure

HomeGround sees Kate perform on 'Aspel' 20th June 1993

Issue 48: July 1993

Peter: Swept away by the emotion

We heard that Kate had been invited to appear on 'Aspel & Company' a few weeks before. How were we going to get tickets as the programme was the last in the series and subject to special allocation?

Luckily, after twelve years in the business Dave has contacts strategically placed in most important entertainment companies and three tickets soon came falling out of a plain brown wrapper. We arrived outside the London Weekend TV studios on the South Bank at about half past eight, and were soon accosted by Kate fans desperate for tickets to see Kate's first public appearance since well... whenever it was!

After what seemed like an age, the security guards opened up the studio audience gate, and we were admitted via a circuitous route (that had me at least murmuring "Hello Cleveland!") to the 'Aspel & Company' studio.

The wait continued; an hour to kill sitting in the most uncomfortable bench seats I've ever had the misfortune to plonk my bum on. There were some funny moments. We stopped whispering amongst ourselves at one point to listen to the woman behind who was holding forth to her friend about Kate and why had they bothered to ask her on the show "She's only ever had one song hasn't she? What was it called...?"

LWT Nº 169
WELCOMES YOU TO
"ASPEL & COMPANY"
"LIVE"
Hosted by Michael Aspel
SUNDAY 20th JUNE 1993
FROM 10.00 p.m. - 10.45 p.m.
DOORS OPEN 9.00 p.m. - 9.40 p.m.
NO ADMITTANCE AFTER 9.40 p.m.
Please dress smartly as audience members are likely to be seen on camera during the programme.
TICKET NOT FOR SALE
CHILDREN UNDER 15 ARE NOT ADMITTED
AT THE LONDON TELEVISION CENTRE
UPPER GROUND LONDON SE1
ADMIT ONE

First on was Victoria Wood. I love her work, but I do think she was in a snide mood that evening. I felt her answers had claws out.

We were slightly surprised when Kate came on second. We were expecting her toward the end of the show. She came bouncing down the gangway looking fabulous. Michael Aspel could have asked her about many things from many phases of her career. He could have reminisced about the early days at Capital Radio. Instead he asked a number of inane questions, including the oldest of all, and one I had thought I would never hear again – yep! The 'sex symbol' one. I squirmed on Kate's behalf.

The situation was saved when Lenny Henry came on, a true man of many parts – comic, actor, and now soul singer? Will he appear on the Prince track? We shall see.

After an age Kate was disappearing from the sofa set to prepare for the song. The studio lights found the piano placed at the centre of a circle of candle-stands. Placed on the piano was a pair of red ballet shoes. The opening chords...

Some moments that I've had,
Some moments of pleasure...

Kate sang of all those special people...

Until ...

Hey there Bill,
Would you turn the lights up?

And we were gone; swept away by the tangible emotion. It took us all very powerfully. I remember first hearing *This Woman's Work*, I remember being present when other fans first heard it. The effect of this song was likewise electrifying. I had a sense of those special people present. The energy of all that they were bound up in this musical matrix.

Then it was over, and we were again in the TV studio whilst the official photographer recorded the occasion. It took days for the energy of the song to work through, as Dave and Krys set out. I had the pleasure of playing the track over the phone to Vickie and Chris in Chicago and hearing their response.

We're now on edge, waiting for the new album, and all those other wonderful new songs.

Dave: A profound effect

In the last few weeks since I first heard *Moments of Pleasure* it has had a profound effect on me. Above and beyond the sheer beauty of the song it has made me think about my own life and my own moments of pleasure.

"I'm listening to Rain Dogs
And thinking of another moment.

Stolen kisses in the street,
While Charlie Chaplin waits.

Because we know something of Kate's life we can understand some of her references, but actual historical details are not as important as the sharing of those moments – that is where the heart of this song is for me, the sharing with us.

The journey of the fried egg
How it still makes me laugh.

Or the water ski-ing story,
I thought that I would burst.

Kate sings about people in her life who have died. She uses these moments to remember them.

And I can see my mother smiling,
Kissing me goodbye.

When we lose people, they leave us these moments, these little pictures. Like sitting on the floor going through old photographs.

Hey there Stephen, screaming fit to burst,
So full of life.

Kate's song has made me want to share these moments of mine, and focus on them and on the people they represent to me. Thank you.

Krys: My eyes fill with tears

Moments of Pleasure is wonderful! Peter, Dave and myself went to the recording of the 'Aspel' show on 20th June. It was a strange experience. We were three rows from the front, about twelve feet or so away from Kate. When she sat at the piano and sang her song, it made me feel very weird. It was so moving. I clutched tightly to Peter. It felt like a wound had been opened, and it bled. My heart hurt, for Kate and for her sorrow, and for her many losses of the ones she loved and still loves.

This song is a tribute to those people, and to the marks they made on Kate's life, and a tribute to her strength too – to be so open, have her wounds exposed to the public, because those wounds are human, and common to us all. *Moments* made me hurt inside, really hurt, especially the part about Hannah. I still miss her terribly. I know I always will.

I have been told once or twice that we shouldn't continue to mention Hannah in the pages of *HomeGround* for fear of hurting Kate and her family. Is that so wrong? She was our friend too. We never got to say goodbye. Lots of you out there miss her too. As I write my eyes fill with tears, yet again. I loved her very much. It was Hannah's birthday the day of the Aspel show, and I feel that Kate was singing the song for her. This I feel is the real reason she chose to do that show.

Moments touched me very deeply. It was like a rushing in of all the emotions that get caught in the heart and throat, and they hurt. I couldn't cry that night, though I wanted and needed to. I felt as though I was in shock. Does that make sense? I felt as though I had been caught on the impact of a stomach punch. Right inside. I couldn't cry.

The following day I went to the White Horse of Uffington with a friend of mine, and we sat at his head, our toes just touching the white chalk of his eye. I still felt the impact of the song, the same as the night before. We watched the Solstice sun setting to the left of Dragon Hill (the hill Kate used in *Cloudbusting*). A few other people had gathered at the Horse, probably to celebrate the Solstice. I was writing to a friend up there on that hill, when all of a sudden I came to a part in my letter, and I broke into huge sobs. It felt like a block of emotion trying to escape from deep within.

Moments of Pleasure is a song of healing, because of the depths it reaches into. The power of the healer to reach inside someone's heart, and to show the world her own heart, and to show at the same time how human she is. It has to be one of Kate's most honest and personal songs ever, if not the most personal. She hasn't disguised her feelings. Is Kate aware (I'm sure she is) of the power she has released into the world with a song such as this. She unleashed a great wave of emotion to an audience of millions, and I'm sure she must have touched even the coldest of hearts.

I have only heard the song twice. The other day I read the lyrics that someone had transcribed. I can't remember the tune. It was like reading a poem. The tears poured down my face... "Here come the hills of time..." I cannot bring myself to listen to it just yet, much as I want to, because I know that when I do I'll cry and cry and won't be able to stop. Such is the power of this very beautiful song.

Vickie Mapes: Lots and lots of Kates

How I'm moved, how you move me,
with your beauty's potency...

Having heard *Moments of Pleasure* at Aspel, we had to play it over the phone to Vickie in Chicago.

This song... is beautiful, simple, and moving. *Moments of Pleasure* will take its place alongside *This Woman's Work* and *Reaching Out* in my heart.

This song is from one of the many, many, 'Kates' I know and love: from the beauty and power of *Reaching Out*, to the awesome magnificence of *Breathing*, to the simple vulnerability of *In Search of Peter Pan*, to the terrible anger of *Get Out of My House* to the sly comedy of *Coffee Homeground*, to the passionate sexuality of *Feel It*, to the passionate sensuality of *The Sensual World*, to the cinematic brilliance of

Night of the Swallow, to the spooky terror of *Hammer Horror*, to the confusion and yearning of *Running Up That Hill*, to the powerful strength of *Not This Time*, to the pure love of homeland in *Oh England My Lionheart*, to the tension of *Pull Out the Pin*, to the comical frustration of *Ran-Tan Waltz*, to the unaffected cheerfulness of *The Big Sky*, to the searching chaos of *Sat In Your Lap*, to the carefree silliness of *Kite*, to the intrigue and larceny of *There Goes a Tenner*, to the genuine gift of *Under the Ivy*, to the frightful horror of *Waking the Witch*, to the lazy vacation of *Warm and Soothing*, to the ghostly pining of *Wuthering Heights*, to the exotic eccentricity of *Egypt*, to the vengeful violence of *The Wedding List*, to the sardonic sanctuary of *Leave It Open*, to the reluctant curiosity of *Rocket's Tail*, to the worldly seduction of *In the Warm Room*, to the graceful elegance of *Delius*, to the cool deception of *Babooshka*, to the puzzling labyrinth of *Suspended in Gaffa*, to the serene trust of *The Fog*, to the precarious honesty of *Love and Anger*, to the extraordinary and alien *The Dreaming*, and on and on and on and on.

All these songs and more came from the Kate I know and love. The pensive Kate. The private Kate. The bizarre Kate. The insecure Kate. The bold Kate. The flashy Kate. The sexy Kate. The motherly Kate. The loyal Kate. The loving Kate. The sad Kate. The happy Kate. The serious Kate. The lazy Kate. The hard-working Kate. The smart Kate. The brilliant Kate. The human Kate. The how-did-she-do-that Kate. The peaceful Kate. The overwhelmed Kate. The creative Kate. The morbid Kate. The fibbing Kate. The Cathy Kate. The public Kate. The Kate nobody knows. The Kate everybody knows. Kate the artist. Kate the musician. Kate the lyricist. Kate the poet. Kate the experimenter. Kate the story teller. Kate the trouper. Kate the survivor. The innocent Kate. The cynical Kate. The beautiful Kate. The bad-hair-day Kate. The Kate who introduced a song of hers by saying "yeah, here it is" and the Kate who presented her songs as a 3-act play and the Kate who thinks we're all mad, and the Kate who repeats herself endlessly and the Kate who would really rather not say anything at all about her songs, and the Kate who loves her family and friends and Del and unusual musical instruments and her garden and her cats and her privacy. Lots and lots of Kates. The Kate who gave us 6 albums and a bunch of b-sides and remixes and who is about to give us another album.

So many Kates. So little time...

I already love *Moments of Pleasure* and it has been floating through my brain all day long.

I'm Not Dreaming!

Katelyn Shusas sees Kate in New York

Issue 51: February 1994

Graphic opposite: Alex Lake

December 9th, 1993. For us hundreds of fans lined up around Tower Records in New York City, this was the day we had all been living for. Kate Bush was here. In America. Signing autographs at Tower Records. OH MY GOD! Somebody wake me up and tell me I'm not dreaming! I arrived at noon, not knowing that people had been there since 6am I was lucky to be there – I live in Massachusetts and my mother had agreed to bring me to see Kate as a Christmas gift. Little did she know it would turn out to be the gift of a lifetime...

I took my place in line and smiled at the guy next to me. Then I took out my Walkman and popped in *The Red Shoes*. I only had it on for about a minute when I heard the people beside me talking about Kate. I was only too happy to join in their conversation. This was so great. I had never been with so many Kate fans at the same time, and the feeling was just overwhelming. It was like we had known each other for years and were remembering all the good times. Here I was, sixteen years old, talking to people who were twice my age as if we were best friends. There were middle-aged men in business suits talking to teenage girls in bell-bottoms. There were absolutely no barriers. It was wonderful and all because of one unbelievable person who had brought us together. Kate.

It was one o'clock. Three more hours until our dreams came true. Someone went into the store and came out with the *Moments of Pleasure* CD box. We looked at the cover and smiled at Kate's sense of humour. A woman came over and asked what we were waiting for. We told her Kate was making an in-store appearance. "She is?! Oh my God!!" she screamed, grabbing a place in line.

Two o'clock. Two more hours. Everyone was excited. "What do you think she'll look like?"

"I heard she's even prettier in person than she is in photographs."

Then it hit me. What was I going to say to KATE BUSH? What does one say to a person who is the biggest influence in her life? I asked if anyone else knew what they were going to say.

"I'll probably faint before I even get to her."

"You're God and I worship the ground you walk on."

"This is the best day of my life."

"Kate, I love you so much."

The man with the wristbands came around. I was no.72. Oh God, it was really happening. I'm the luckiest girl alive. What else could I ask for? A beautiful day, tons of Kate fans, and Kate herself! Isn't life great?

Three o'clock. Kate would be arriving soon. A man came walking down the side walk, yelling to

Opposite: issues 49 to 54 including another two beautiful covers by Debi Bowes

all of us, "One item each. No photographs." Oh man! A once in a lifetime chance to see Kate and they wouldn't even let us get a picture of her. We held on to our cameras anyway. Then a woman came running around the corner telling us "Kate just got out of the limo!"

"What did she look like?" we asked.

"I couldn't believe how tiny she was! Just a little peanut of a thing. Her hair had a lot of red in it."

This was it. The line began to move. The greatest moment of my life was taking place and I was in a total daze. Someone jumped up onto the window ledge and looked inside: "There she is! Oh my God, she is so beautiful!" People were taking turns looking in at the window and snapping pictures. It was awesome. Only a piece of glass separating us and Kate. I wasn't going to miss my moment at the window. Someone boosted me up and I grabbed onto their shoulder. And there she was. Sitting at the table talking to a fan, smiling. I could not contain myself, and exclaimed, "Oh my God, Mom! There she is! I can't believe it's actually her! I really am going to meet Kate Bush!"

I jumped down. We were all laughing together. A man with a video camera and a microphone came up to me, probably because I was screaming like a lunatic. He asked what the record in my hand was. I said, "It's Kate Bush's *Running Up That Hill* 12" single." "Why Kate Bush?" he asked. What kind of a stupid question was this? "Because Kate Bush is the best singer in the world, she's totally awesome, absolutely brilliant, she's in America now and we wouldn't miss it for the world!" The crowd cheered me on. The reporter asked if we could sing a Kate Bush song for the camera. We told him that we could never sing as good as Kate and we wouldn't even attempt it. He kept nagging us, and we kept refusing. As he walked off someone suggested that we should have sung "Don't want your bullshit!"

The line kept moving and before we knew what was happening, we were in the doorway. Everyone who had already met Kate had a smile on their face. People kept telling us "She is so nice!"

"The next ten people please." We were ushered in and taken behind a wall of *Red Shoes* CDs. I looked down the middle of the aisle, hoping for a glimpse of Kate. There she was in the flesh. And it finally hit me that Kate was REAL. Not some Goddess, just a regular, wonderful, giving, intelligent woman with the talent to help people through her extraordinary music. Before I knew it, it was my turn to meet Kate. "Oh God, please don't let me say anything stupid," I thought. I walked up to her and smiled.

"Hi!" she greeted me.

"Hi!" I replied, placing my *Running Up That Hill* single on the table. She looked at it and smiled. She looked totally flawless. Absolutely stunning.

"My name is Kate, too!" I told her.

She picked up her pen. "Sign it to Kate, then?" she asked. What a sweet, soft voice. And that accent! "Yes!" I told her. I had written a poem for her, and I decided it was now or never.

"I wrote you a little poem," I said to Kate, slipping the card on the table.

"Oh, thank you very much! That was so nice of you." She looked up at me. "Are you a poet?" Kate was asking me if I was a poet?

"Yeah, well I hope I am!"

Kate smiled at me and I thought I would melt. "It was great to meet you!" she said.

"It was great to meet YOU!" I replied. We smiled at each other, and I extended my arm. She took my hand and shook it. I couldn't believe I was actually touching Kate Bush! She held my hand for what seemed like forever, and we just smiled at each other, recognition pouring out of us both. Kate wasn't a fake – she really cared. It was the best moment of my life. In a total daze, I walked up the stairs to find the other fans. There they were waving me over to them.

"What did you guys say to her?" I asked.

"I don't remember!"

"My voice was shaking so bad!"

"I told her that everything I had planned to say had absolutely escaped my mind!"

"I told her how great she was."

"I probably said something ridiculous!" But we really didn't care what we had said. We had met Kate, and that's all that mattered. The smile was locked on my face. I left the building and it finally hit me, all at once. I had met Kate and had got her autograph, and I had held her hand.

I couldn't hold it in any longer. I started to cry and there was no stopping me. Kate is the nicest person you could ever want to meet. I cried for hours. It was more than I ever expected, a day I will never forget. Thank you so much Kate, for giving us these moments of pleasure.

Photo: *HomeGround* Reader

The queue at New York's Tower Records December 1993

HOMEGROUND 49
KATE BUSH Fanzine Autumn 93
HOMEGROUND 50
HOMEGROUND 54
HOMEGROUND 51
The KATE BUSH Fanzine Spring 94
HOMEGROUND 53
KATE BUSH Fanzine Autumn 94
HOMEGROUND 52
The KATE BUSH Fanzine Summer 94

HOMEGROUND

Dear Friends,

All being well, this issue should reach you in time for Christmas. Whilst I was in the throws of putting this issue together (you wouldn't believe the mess - paper all over the floor, Amber the cat skidding on HG pages as I'm trying to stick them down...) I had the TV mumbling in the background. *The Sooty Show* came on and Matthew Corbett (the man who has his hand up Sooty's bottom - Sooty is a bear glove puppet) was waving around a copy of *The Red Shoes* CD!

Don't miss *The Nightmare Before Christmas*. We were sent the video by our dear American friends, Vickie and Chris. One of the animators, Paul Berry, was at art college with a close friend of ours. Small world.

Thanks to everyone who came on Wuthering Hike V. There were 35 of us altogether, and it was lots of fun. We will try to hold a Hike to Top Withens every year if possible. We're thinking of having gatherings at other places - perhaps Uffington White Horse, Glastonbury again (I have fond memories from Kate's birthday 1989), and Avebury. We'll keep you posted, though any hikes will be in the warmer months me thinks!

We have some great artwork in this issue from Paulina, and new artist, Alex Law who also did the great drawings on pages 7 and 23 in **HOMEGROUND** 53. Debi will be back again in the Spring issue.

Now to something which is bothering us here. In the Season of Good will, it is sad that not everyone feels understanding or compassion towards their fellow fan. It is only a few who seem to behave in this way, but nevertheless it is not very pleasant. Back in the early 1980s there seemed to be a family atmosphere amongst fans. It is still there, but things have changed as all things do and should. Is it that many of us have grown up, we have our own problems and demands that this world makes of us? I don't know.

One thing I do know is that the Kate-speaking world has not been the same since the death of Hannah, Kate's mum. I had a feeling this would happen. This change was almost tangible. Hannah's death has touched us all. In many ways she was the mother figure of Kate's fans. She loved all of us. She was one of the kindest, most compassionate people I ever knew. An example to us all. This arguing between some fans makes me wonder what Hannah would say. I think I know what she would say and I feel she would be saddened that people are so vehement towards each other. And we wonder why there are wars. Everyone wants to be right.

One or two letters and complaints about Kate's appearance at the Convention are still coming in, some of which we have included in this issue. It makes me sad that something that was supposed to be a fun day for everyone has become a little tainted by this kind of response. We have said it before, but people don't seem to realise that it is entirely up to Kate as to her contribution on the day. The thing that strikes me is whether people still want Conventions in the future. Many attend to have fun and meet other fans, whilst others attend soley to see Kate. Because of the complaints I wonder whether Kate will now be discouraged from attending any future events. I'm not saying that people are not entitled to their opinions - far from it, we have printed many letters about many subjects over the years - but I feel a little compassion and understanding towards *Kate* would not go amiss. I would be interested to know how Kate feels when she reads the letters of complaint that she didn't give some people what they demanded. Perhaps she should do a Right To Reply slot. What would people think if she never appeared again, or if there was never another Convention?

Please note that our e-mail address has changed (see renewals page). Also, articles can be sent to us on disc, which would be helpful to me.

Have a very Happy Christmas, play all those Christmas songs very loud, have lots of fun, (Christmas most definitely isn't just for kids in these quarters!), eat lots of Christmas Pudding and be happy.

The Red Shoes

The HomeGround Editors Review Kate's Seventh Album

Issue 49: August 1993

Peter: The Devil's Dancing Shoes OR Is This the Right Thing To Do?

It goes without saying that what follows is my humble opinion. It might change. I couldn't say I have come to grips fully with the richness of experience on this album.

First some basics. Kate is a human being who writes music. That's her job. She resigned from being a famous personality at the end of 1978. She does her stuff and presents it to those who are interested. If you're not interested, that's cool, you are not required to be. Although she would like you to be interested, Kate isn't going to change her work that much to make you interested, any more than she's going to make glam videos so that MTV will fall over itself to show them.

This is the most emotionally raw album Kate has ever made. It is another volume of her emotional diary, and here I think we are dealing with the great simplicities. These songs tell you everything.

Do you have graphic memories of the years 1991-92? Many of us still bear the personal scars. The world is still working out the consequences. On the global scale apparently impregnable dictatorships collapsed, and the world order changed irrevocably. At the personal level apparently secure relationships and patterns of life were challenged dramatically. Some were found wanting and simply eliminated; others were fundamentally transformed.

The theme of this album appears to be 'death' in its full sense, as in the 'death' tarot card, or the symbolic meaning of the planet Pluto in astrology. The reference is not only to physical death – although it includes that – but to the complete transformation of congealed or redundant structures.

Everything that has form (from Governments to personal relationships) must change – form must be a conduit for energy. If change is resisted it will happen anyway – but explosively. Your choice is to work with change or have it run over you. What do you think *Rubberband Girl* is about?

Energy trapped in stale and lifeless structures will attempt to burst free and return to a primitive, wild state. The danger, trouble, and injury caused in trying to burst free from artificial constraint is the inner meaning of the ancient story of 'the red shoes', known in many forms in many different folk traditions. It is always a story of stagnation, temptation, and the awful consequences.

As *The Sensual World* was released in 1989, Kate was brushed by the wings of the Angel of Death. Close friends and colleagues, and people she knew and respected suddenly weren't there. She faced the irrevocable nature of death. There is no appeal.

But the mist cleared temporarily and toward the end of 1990 things seemed to come together. At the Convention Kate talked of live dates, and shortly after was said to be working very fast on a new album.

As Winter died in early 1991 however, the world went awry. Talk of an early album release disappeared. Kate faded again from public view.

In the year that followed Kate experienced the searing experience of her mother's translation from this life, (which was concluded on the day of St Valentine in 1992. Love and death) and other deeply personal difficulties. Suddenly the emotional certainties of life weren't.

"*The minute I put them on*
I knew I'd done something wrong...."

I'll start with the exquisite ethnic swirl of the title track, *The Red Shoes*, since it is the essence of the story. This is the nature of the deal – "put them on and your dreams will come true" – but it is a deal with the devil and the price is your soul. You are offered all you ever wanted, and compared to what you've got – well when looked at in a certain way – it's very tempting. But you want it all, you want the security of what you've known and the excitement of something new. You don't understand you can't have it all, and your attempt to have it all may destroy what you already have.

And So Is Love is the most beautiful song Kate has ever written. It is also the most heartbreaking. I use the word advisedly. It is also perhaps the simplest song Kate has ever written. Poignant simplicity grips the heart with chilling efficiency. Only those who have seen the relationships they steer their life by change, dissolve, and even at times apparently cease to be there at all will understand:

"*You let it slip, I let it slip*"

If you haven't gone through it you will one day. Don't worry. It will pass. The relationship has changed, and you have to return to your loved one the freedom that was never really yours. If your relationship retains any value this leap into the unknown will strengthen it. If it doesn't then perhaps it is time to part:

"*You set me free; I set you free*"

There is an invisible, inaudible song on this album, it is about the death of a loved one, and

Opposite: editorial issue 54

Graphic opposite: Steven Brown

though it does not quite materialise, it is certainly there.

"*Life has blown a great big hole in me*"

When the ceiling falls in, the walls collapse, and the floor isn't quite as solid as you think it ought to be, you close in on yourself. You don't trust any one, or their motives, and you despise their demands on you. Especially if they only want one thing. *The Song of Solomon* is a puzzle to me. The chorus sounds like it could be a fan letter, something Fred Vermorel might have retrieved from an EMI dustbin. We all know this sort of fan. He (not always) looks at Kate and sees only one thing – a female body. The music and the emotion are not really of consequence, "I want it... just for me... you owe it to me... I bought your record."

Loneliness and isolation lead to thoughts of the ultimate desperation. There is a brittleness, and almost somnambulist feel to *Top of the City*. Why do you go alone to a high place? Sure you can review your life. You can see that person who was special to you – with the new person who is special to them. You can look down on the world, and it does look like hell. You can look up to heaven, and that special peace which passeth all misunderstanding:

"*I don't think we should ever suffer;*
There's just one thing we can do about it"

Madness. Paranoia. Hopeless, unquenchable grief. *Big Stripey Lie* is a glimpse of emotional desolation, as effective in its way as *Get Out of My House*. It might very well be at home on *The Dreaming*. What is the lie? Perhaps it was the offer of The Red Shoes, remember – "*put them on and your dreams will come true*". You survey the wreckage in wild desperation. You feel under attack from people and from things unseen. You desperately need protection.

"*You can protect yourself;*
I'll show you how, with Fire"

If Lily is who I think she is, she is a figure long established in the Golden Dawn school of hermetic magic. She teaches Kate a basic ritual of psychic self-defence. You can check the original in Israel Regardie's *Teachings, Rites and Ceremonies of the Golden Dawn*, there set out in its full version and called 'the lesser ritual of the pentagram'. Regardie says the rite is "a protection against impure magnetism. The... ritual can be used to get rid of obsessing or disturbing thoughts" Lily's version is more familiar from Dion Fortune's book *Psychic Self-Defence*. There are strange sounds in the background of this track, wailings and distorted voices, that carry over from the previous track. This suggests psychic attack to me. Fortune says:

"The physical phenomena are of several types. They may take the form of noises, usually creakings, thuds, or more rarely bell like notes or wailing sounds."

Fortune prescribes the drawing of a circle of pale gold fire, and calling upon the names of the four archangels who command the four elements.

The circle of fire creates a place of safety. A place of peace and respite. In such a space healing can begin, love and trust can be re-kindled. *Why Should I Love You* is a song of great comfort. It is about love, and it uses images from Kate's Roman Catholic upbringing. In times of crises, you return to your roots. There is the image of Jesus, hand upheld in that gesture of unquestioning forgiveness and unqualified love. Despite all, there is love in the world.

You can begin to understand what a strange thing is man. He spends most of his life trying to pretend that he does not have emotions, and periodically being bowled over by them. He develops defences against his better nature. Like the seeds inside fruit, those emotions are hidden. *Eat the Music* is a jolly Madagascan influenced jape, completely infectious. But there is a point to the lyrics:

"*Does he conceal what he really feels?*
I split him open...
All is revealed...
Not only Women bleed"

There is no cure for death, just as there is no cure for life. Both can cause equal pain and joy. In *Constellation of the Heart* the starship faces something the crew and captain have never seen before. It has to be faced and dealt with, but the captain "can't do that" for fear of the pain:

"*the pain of being on earth;*
The pain that never heals...
Just being alive, it can really hurt"

But it is life, in all its power and glory, the heart of emotions is the place of heaven and hell. Yes life can hurt, but it is also the place of paradise.

"*A rubberband bouncin' back to life...*
A rubberband girl Me!"

The lesson is simple but hellishly difficult. You can't resist the changes, you have to ride them. *Rubberband Girl* is a wonderfully funky and crazy ride, a hymn to survival. All things are possible. Relationships that meet apparent dead ends can suddenly find new avenues. It's not the same street, and the method of travel might be unfamiliar, but perhaps the destination is still the same – if we ever knew what it was!

You're the One sums up all that that

transformation means. There is so much of value that can not and should not be lost – "*there's a little piece of you... in whatever... we're best friends*".

The only possible conclusion to this album is *Moments of Pleasure.* It is a huge track, full of the emotion of life and the experience of death. It is the summary and conclusion of all the moods of this album, and if you haven't shed a tear at some point when listening to it, you aren't alive. Here at last is Hannah Bush, and with her are Gary Hurst and Alan Murphy and Michael Powell and Bill Duffield and John Barrett, and others, those precious people whose lives gave such special moments.

It takes a lot to make me cry. This album has made me cry several times.

Dave: A Naked Work of Art

Honestly, it's like waiting for a bus. You wait years for a new song, then twelve come along at once! As always there is so much to take in and so little time to try and make sense of it.

Musically *The Red Shoes* is more diverse than *The Sensual World*, and it shows Kate's continuing development as a producer. Although more varied the album is less 'dense' than its predecessor and contains some of Kate's finest productions to date. As you will realise from our reviews and from your own ears the real differences here is the subject matter of the lyrics. Whereas in the past Kate has given us a whole range of subjects on each album, here, with one obvious exception, all the songs seem to deal with personal relationships or coping with life itself. More than any of her other albums this does seem to be a report from the front, an update on the life of Kate.

The album opens with *Rubberband Girl*, a slammin' pop tune if ever there was one. A strident pounding workout, complete with brass section, tooting sax and OTT guitar solo. Kate has often said in interviews that she wishes she could be more flexible, go with the flow more, perhaps she is trying to explain why the albums take so long? Frustration at her own limitations has cropped up before, most obviously on *Sat In Your Lap* and *Suspended in Gaffa*, where she sings about the frustrations of the creative process. That seems to be a part of this song too. She wants to be able to "Twang like a rubberband" and obviously admires people who are more flexible than she. In the past she has spoken of her admiration for artists who play the game, even if she doesn't herself. It is ironic that the track here which sounds most like a live band is probably an explanation of why she won't tour.

And So Is Love is a sad, hesitant song about the grief that can arise from love. Is there any point in loving when it always ends in tears? "We let it in, we give it out" – she could almost be talking about AIDS. The danger of youthful enthusiasm and unprotected sex – "We used to say 'Ah hell, we're young'". I may be wrong about the AIDS theme but Kate is definitely saying that we all get hurt, one way or another, in the end. Kate's vocal is quiet, almost spoken until halfway through she lets go and her voice soars in a true show of emotion. The effect is startling, like someone who just can't put on a brave face any more. The guitar contribution of Clapton is also quite moving, little flashes like Summer lightning. I'm sure that this track will be among most people's favourites.

Eat the Music is all bananas and mangoes, very Carmen Miranda Kate! "Rip me open" she demands, "Put your hands in" ooh er, steady on missus! I'm not sure whether this is about one man in particular or men in general. Certainly a lot of men "Conceal what they really feel" but how many are "a woman at heart"? Is this about a gay man or the feminine side of all men? It is a sexy and sensual song about someone Kate clearly admires? He shows "Emotion and such devotion". The fruit imagery is very erotic. She sings of putting the stone of a mango in your mouth, and of sticky fingers. The track has a really authentic Soca/Calypso sound, more Notting Hill Carnival than Gloria Estefan. Great guitar and wonderful brass section. Outrageous and camp, it is easy to see this as a single.

For many people, the stand out track on this album will be *Moments of Pleasure.* A really 'big' song that is both moving and uplifting. Strings that are almost outrageous in their beauty and one of Kate's finest vocals ever. "Just being alive can really hurt" takes us back to *And So Is Love*, but here Kate is almost proud of her grief, proud to have had these memories and proud to be sharing them with us. For me the sharing of her memories is the very core not only of this song but of the whole album. For the first time Kate sings about Kate Bush the famous person, she hides nothing; New York, Abbey Road and the names of her friends and family. She knows that we will all know who she means and that is incredible in itself. This is one of the best songs she has ever given us and seems to strike a chord with all those who have heard it, regardless of what they think of Kate. I really hope that this is a big hit when released as a single.

Of all the songs, *The Song of Solomon* has me the most confused. A delicate, moody song with a vaguely Eastern feel. Kate's voice is high, trembling, and almost bitter. She tells us that this is a song for "Everyone who walks the path of a solitary heart". The chorus is a woman saying "Don't want your bullshit, just want your sexuality". Is this the bullshit of the flowers and chocolates type or the macho 'real men don't eat quiche' type? Is the sexuality a physical need or a desire for the man to be a male rather than a 'man'? Solomon himself had hundreds of wives and concubines, and the song is full of biblical references and imagery. Is this a song about casual sex? The woman's need for sex being ignored by her partner perhaps? I don't know, but it is a lovely song, beautifully sung. Please put us straight Kate.

Lily begins with a woman (presumably Lily) reciting a spiritual verse asking God to reveal His true Son, who is hidden by a disc of golden light. I'm not sure if this is actually relevant or if it is just Kate setting the scene, making sure that we know that Lily is a spiritualist of some kind. Kate is seeking help. "Life has blown a great big hole through me" she tells Lily. The answer she receives appears to be a technique called visualisation – picture yourself full of white light pulled down from above, picture a circle of fire, usually blue, around you and ask the angels to protect you. It is a form of meditation that works for many people. Perhaps this song is an indication of how Kate had coped with the last couple of years. If so, then this is yet another example of just how open this collection of songs is. It also contains biblical images. Musically, *Lily* has a hard, hasty edge, with almost grunge back beats, a great big chorus and a fantastic little growl in the middle eight.

The Red Shoes is the one exception I mentioned earlier, inspired as we all know, on the film of the same name. This is a whirling Dervish of a song, all Irish fiddles and pounding drums. Our heroine wishes she could "Move like the diva do" and she gets her wish when she puts on the shoes. Straight away she knows that she's done something wrong but it's too late, "The shoes do, their voodoo" and she cannot control them. As she gets more frantic, so does the music. More instruments, more layers. The effect is terrific. "Really happening to ya!" screams Kate. "It's the shoes, they won't stop... dancin'". The final ingredient to the musical mix is a great big chorus of backing vocals, a little like the end of *The Big Sky*. I could also see this as a single. My only criticism is that the faded ending is a bit of an anti-climax. A definite ending would have been more fitting.

If the title track reminds me of *The Big Sky* musically, *Top of the City* reminds me of it lyrically. A song of escape, she needs to get away from real life. If she could only get up to the roof, away from the "Hell down there" she would be alright. Once again the root of the song is a relationship gone wrong. "I can see you with her... she's no good for you". She is begging to be taken up, she wants to be on the "angel's shoulders". Could this be a more final solution to her problems, a suicide note? The bare verse with just Kate and the piano is in stark contrast to the big sweeping chorus, all crashing drums and soaring voice. Despite the dark hint to the lyric this is an uplifting song, which also reminds me of *I'm Still Waiting*.

With every album to date Kate has introduced new musical influences, and *The Red Shoes* is no exception. Nowhere is this clearer than on *Constellation of the Heart*. Dance, soul, whatever you want to call it, has rarely shown itself within Kate's music, but here the elegant dance of Nile Rodgers and Bernard Edwards (better known as Chic – also responsible for Sister Sledge, Bowie's *Let's Dance* and loads more) seems to be the main influence. In particular I would cite the Chic produced Carly Simon track *Why* as a starting point. Yet again *The Big Sky* has its place here. We are told to turn our telescopes away from the big sky and point them towards our own hearts. In contrast to *Lily*, Kate is saying to outside 'things': "listen to your heart". We even have what I can only take as a 'Star Trek' reference (Kate and *Trek* together – joy of joys. Get a life, Dave!) "There's something up ahead Captain". The backing vocal chorus urging Captain Kate that she has to face it, that it will be wonderful. Kate quotes from *Moments of Pleasure* – "Sometimes just being alive..." The thrust here seems to be, yes sometimes life is bloody horrible but if you are really going to cope you have to face it head on, like Kirk or Picard heading into the unknown. Not only do I love this song but I think, like *Moments of Pleasure* it is a key part of the album, both musically and lyrically. What price a dance remix for the clubs, Kate, if not as a single in its own right, maybe as an extra track on a future 12"?

In the past Kate has recorded a number of songs that one can only describe as unpleasant and that is meant as a compliment. *Get Out of My House* and *Mother Stands for Comfort* are the two that spring to mind. *Big Stripey Lie* is this album's little monster and scary it is too. A dirty, almost grungy sound over which Kate sings in a 'tuneless' way. "Young gentle dreams drowning in life's grief". Yet another song about the down side of life. For some reason there is something about this song which reminds me of the feel David Lynch gets in his films. Don't ask me what or why, it just does!

The last two tracks on the album further show the influence of American music. *Why Should I Love You* is, of course, one of the most talked about and anticipated pieces Kate has ever recorded – her collaboration with Prince. The presence of the small purple one is all over the track, from the jittery funk backing track to his distinctive guitar. Kate sings of many colours; purple, the grey of the ghost and of purest gold (a brooch of purest green... sorry I keep thinking of Percy in *Blackadder II*, okay, as you were!) and asks "Of all the people in the world, why should I love you?" A beautiful and happy song that brings us back to things of a spiritual, even biblical nature. "Have you ever seen a picture of Jesus smiling... a smile that healed". Kate is rejoicing in the things that makes this loved one so special. After all the speculation regarding Prince this song does not disappoint.

You're the One seems to carry on where *Why Should I Love You* leaves off. Kate once again marvels at what it is that makes that one person special, but this time she is singing about a lost love. Once again we return to the unfairness of love and the hardship of facing reality. "I know where I'm going but I don't want to leave". This is more than just the physical need of the woman in *The Song of Solomon*, she tells us of another male 'friend' and the fact that "He is very good looking" doesn't make up for the fact that he isn't her lost love. This track is the closest Kate has ever come to a 'rock ballad', and with its haunting Hammond organ sound has the feel of *A Whiter Shade of Pale*. She seems to pour everything into this song – "Sugar, honey" she sings with desperation. In the hands of lesser folk this song would undoubtedly end up over the top, but Kate fills it with dignity and an understated power.

As an album *The Red Shoes* is an extraordinary piece of work, not just for its music but for the subject matter Kate tackles. Never before has she been so open about her own feelings, her own life. On past albums we have tried to second guess the meanings and motives behind songs, but here there seems to be no disguise at all. On *Moments of Pleasure* I think Kate is saying "I'm Kate Bush and these are the people I know who have died and this is a private memory that I'd like to share with you". *Lily*, *Top of the City* and *Constellation of the Heart* talk about dealing with all the shit life throws at you. *And So Is Love* and *You're the One* deal with the end of a major love affair. Kate's private life has always been something that we have avoided talking about in *HomeGround*, but in light of the comments made in at least two recent interviews it is impossible not to think that these songs are about Kate herself. She has often said that making music is a kind of therapy for her and this whole album has a therapeutic feel about it. The constant spiritual references and the theme of lost love suggest that this was all better out than in.

Kate has always done what we didn't expect. Who would have predicted what a startling effect three middle-aged Bulgarian women would have had on *The Sensual World*, and who would have predicted that this album would show the influence of Chic and Prince? Kate has poured her heart and soul into *The Red Shoes*.

It is a naked work of art.

Thank you for these moments, Kate.

Krys: Ladders, Angels, Hearts and Paths

For the moment I will feel my way through this new album, and not think. I cannot think. I will feel it through emotion and intuition, and write from the safety of those things. These are my feelings...

The Red Shoes strikes me as being Kate's most personal album to date. It seems to be made up of her own experiences, there seem to be few disguises here. *The Red Shoes* appears to be the only song inspired by the Andersen story or the Michael Powell film, but paralleled to her own career. There is the Biblical reference in *The Song of Solomon*, but these songs aside, the album appears to be biographical. This is Kate. This is Life. There is no illusion. An album of moods and human suffering. The highs and lows, the questions, the need to understand the reasons why. Much of the material feels so sad to me, like Kate has had some crises in her life over the past few years. It feels like birth, death, and re-birth. Another chapter in her life. And perhaps the most difficult to close.

Against the funereal black background, and the symbolic cycle of life, birth death, we see the ballet shoes, those red shoes that stand in a pool of ribbon blood. Have they been chopped off? Is she awaiting the axeman to release her from this eternal dance? She stands in the limbo of land or water. Life or death. She stands in the pose (right way up) of the Hanged One, the sacrifice of the self for a cause or for the soul to evolve higher up the spiritual ladder. The Initiate – the Fool – as she was in *Sat In Your Lap*, now wears the bloodied shoes of experience; she must discard them, sacrifice her desires, ambitions, human traits, for the sake of her immortal soul, that it will be easier next time. She is once again the Fool, the Seeker of the Grail; she is also the Wounded King, the Hanged One. It is the Fool who is the most important card in the deck. She represents all who journey on the spiritual quest; through trust will learn how to heal and balance. She must make the journey alone to discover "Whom does the Grail serve?"

The significance of the colour Red – the initiate, the sacrifice, the chosen one. Red – the colour of passion, sex, love, jealousy, anger, blood, pain, birth, menstruation, the Empress.

Kate uses a lot of symbolism, religious imagery, colours, fruits, wheels and cycles of emotions, words and sounds. Sometimes we understand things from our own experiences. We recognise the symbols, the signs, for they are now beginning to make sense. *The Line, the Cross & the Curve*... "Where on your palm is my little line?" Perhaps the key lies in the archetypes within the Tarot. Is she telling her stories through these particular symbols? Perhaps she is using these symbols, singing symbols that we will all recognise.

It is an organic album, it seems to have grown from the deepest roots, pushed its way up from the darkest depths, from the womb, the house of the emotions, from the darkness of ancestral ground, like West Kennet burial chamber, from the darkest night of the soul... in to the darkness, that terrifies, but turn around and see the Light, and when you're ready walk into it... climb, climb out of it, look to the light and let the darkness go, disperse it with love and with light, let the Angels take it away...

The burial chamber of our ancestors runs deep, of stone and earth and bone. The dark

Graphic opposite: Alex Lake

night of the soul, where we venture deep into the earth to gain insight, wisdom, solace. A place to think and feel, and learn to trust your own intuition. It will never fail you. Released in the death-time of the year, the album may exorcise some things, it may go with the flow of things natural rather than against it. It is easier that way. The Autumn and Winter is the natural culling time for land, animal and human alike. The time when each is called home. The burial chamber of the heart, where all is still and dark and deep, where she must retreat to the soul's darkest night before the sun returns to warm. It will be released on All Saints Day, the morning after the night of the dead, Samhain, or Halloween, when the veil is very thin between the two worlds of the earthly and the spirit, the living and those who have passed through. The Celtic New Year. Nothing happens by accident, all things are meant to be, and each have their purpose.

This is Kate's walk through the valley of death, having lost so many friends and loved ones over the recent years. It is a grieving process. An album to help her heal herself, to face fear and pain, the fear of death and the fear of living without those loved ones, to exorcise some of the ghosts. Death has shadowed her for a few years. I now know what it feels like to be shaken to the very core when someone you love dies. The foundations of your life shake and fall with it. A hole blown through us, and something inside you dies too. To have that happen time and again must be soul destroying. That is the price of love. As they say, it is better to have loved and lost...

This album is Kate's bravest and most honest. This is Kate, this is what she has been through, this is Kate the human being, this is her pain, her tears, her losses, her fear, her healing, her love, her life, her playfulness, this is Kate, the woman and the child. This is Kate behind closed doors. And this is Kate opening those doors. She has put more of the real Kate into this than any other album.

The Red Shoes is full of paths, ladders, Angels, death, life, fear, fire, sex, sorrow, and Love. There are many levels and many gateways in. The tangible pain of its birth, the blood and tears. This album is Kate's dark night of the soul. A trip into the pit, collapse. She let her defences down, rendering her fearful, insecure and unsure of her own strength. Into the pit, the downward spiral, brought on by her losses. Shaken to her core. There are battles between good and evil, choices between life and death, divine love versus human love, ambition versus human need. At the end the soul must be true to herself. Sacrifices are made, blood is shed, that the soul may move on.

Above all *The Red Shoes* is about letting go. Kate's release of the pain, that she may hold close to her heart those *Moments of Pleasure*.

It is beautiful and sad and emotional.

Now to the songs.

Rubberband Girl, the opening song on the album, is about being flexible. She has been stretched beyond the limit, by external and internal sources, demands from herself, and others and situations over which she has no control. She keeps bouncing back, that is the strength from within, the spirit that rekindles regardless of whatever tortures life throws at her – the coming up after the dark depression? She has done so many times before, *The Ninth Wave* especially.

This idea of flexibility reminds me of the trees in the great storm of 1987 – those which could bend still stand, those who were rigid and wouldn't bow to the winds of change, broke and fell to earth. We are like trees. Those who can be flexible will hurt the least; those who resist change are in for trouble. All things change; that is the way of Nature. Nothing stands still. If it does it becomes like stagnant water, and is of no use to anyone or anything. It just pollutes. In being flexible we accept the things we cannot change or have control over.

In the video, not only is Kate wearing a Garth jumper around her waist (very *Foxy Lady*!), but she is ushered into yet another straitjacket. First in *Suspended in Gaffa*, then poor Paddy was jacketed-up in *Experiment IV*. We all have our own madnesses. And who wants to be normal anyway?!

This is the song of the Seeker, the Fool.

And So Is Love is a lament about giving up the ones we love. "Life is sad and so is Love". It makes my heart ache. This song hurts. We all have to set each other free at some time or another, either we split and go our separate ways, or through (more drastically) death. We have to set each other free from our parents too. We have to let go of many people we love. It doesn't mean we won't ever see them again, it's simply not living in each others' pockets, which isn't really very healthy anyway. "You let it slip" – complacency sets in, it's easily done, we all do it. We flog the dead horse. Which is futile, it makes people unhappy, frustrated, angry. People change, move in opposite directions, and instead of growing closer together, drift further apart until they become strangers. It is easily done, sometimes the realisation happens when it is just too late. Even trying again to make the relationship work, fails to reconcile the differences, or break down the barriers. What happens when you still love him? What happens when you love him but can no longer live with him? This is the problem. People change. It happens to us all. The relationships change too. We have to move with Change, and try not to fight it. It is easy that way. The saddest part is the last line "I set you free..."

Letting love go, releasing it, is never easy, in fact it can be the hardest thing to do. It means change, and many humans are resistant to change. It can shake our lives into turmoil, but it has to be. We have to all let go of many things in

Sugar? ...
honey?! ...

our lives, sometimes they are hopes and dreams, sometimes they are the ones we love the most, either through the finality of death, or because as we grow we change and sometimes move apart from each other. No-one is really to blame, it is just the way people and relationships change. But it hurts so much. The reality of life and the problems we encounter as individuals and in our relationships, take their toll on us all, can grind us down, and the once beautiful relationship begins to lose its original spark. Sometimes too much damage has been done and the only way is out. There is no other choice. A letting go of love song. And it hurts.

Eric Clapton plays on this track, which he agreed to do only because it was Kate – his little son had died a few weeks before the recording, something that makes this song all the more poignant and heartbreaking.

This is the song of Grail Five.

Eat the Music is a very sensual song, with the totally tropical taste! It makes you just want to plunge into the fruit section at Safeways! A lively song with a serious message; peel back the layers to see what is hidden, the stone, the heart. Humans like fruit, hiding what is inside, hiding deep inside their emotions, soft and raw and dripping... What you find is not what you would expect. Turning people inside out to see what they really feel, "when all is revealed". Some skins are tougher to peel than others. Some need a bloody big mallet to break that wall down.

It could be about men hiding their emotions, with references to fruits containing seeds, or it could be directed to us all. We all hide our true feelings at some stage or other. We cannot always be honest about how we feel, and it is not always safe to be open; we can get hurt. Sometimes our hearts ache and bleed, and we are the only ones who will ever know. Because those emotions are so deep inside.

Of course, the other side of this argument is that some people do not want their emotions exposed, even to their nearest and dearest. Do you force them out? Do you get that mallet out? Do you tear your hair out in frustration because you can't seem to get through that fruit wall? And if you're the one holding back, do you retreat further, you don't want to be ripped open, have your emotions extracted from deep within?

The fertile, sensual imagery of fruits and seeds goes without saying. Fruit has always had erotic symbolism and connotations, and who can ever forget that naughty food eating bit in the film *Tom Jones*, based on the Henry Fielding classic novel? The eroticism of fruit – the eating of fruit, all that juice as it trickles down your fingers and forearms, down your face... How often the genitals are likened to fruit. Especially the fig, which when opened resembles the female genitals.

It is a bouncy, uplifting song, with the most sensual lyrics. I have to be honest and say I love the lyrics, but musically is not one of my favourites. That is my only criticism. But if you're in the right mood, it's a great song. The lyrics are its strength. They are very clever, and full of amazing imagery.

This is the song of King Arthur, the Emperor.

Moments of Pleasure is such a wonderful tribute to those Kate has loved, and lost. It is perhaps the most honest and moving song Kate has ever written. A song of dealing with loss and death, a song to heal herself and others. It still makes me cry, it still hurts to listen to it. Kate has lost so many loved ones through death, that she must have seemed surrounded by it. This is bound to have had a profound effect on her and has perhaps forced her to face death again and again. This song is a part of Kate coming to terms with her losses, and letting go. Instead of making the song morbid, plays on her love for all those who have died, turning it into a very positive song, which no doubt many people out there will gain great comfort in their own losses. I have gained comfort from this song myself; my beloved Grandma, who's name was Hannah, died two weeks ago. For the first time I am experiencing the death of someone I was close to. I now know what it feels like to have your whole life shaken to its very foundations. All my memories of her are happy, and I have my own precious moments.

There are hints of *The Morning Fog* at the end when she calls the Roll of Honour, naming her loved ones. This song is a wonderful celebration of their lives. They will be remembered by millions of people forever more. But the most moving line in the song relates to Hannah – "And I can hear my Mother saying every old sock meets an old shoe". In my own small way I know the lady she is talking about. I miss her terribly. I wrote some of my feelings in my Ed's letter in *HomeGround* 48, so I will not repeat them, other than to say this song tears me apart.

This is the song of Death, the Washer at the Ford.

The Song of Solomon is the strangest song, if not the most difficult to grasp the meaning of. It is sad, the perfect picture in the original text of the Old Testament, and the reality of life. A lament of the heart, as though she is on the outside, sadly looking in. It has a lulling, seductive, Middle Eastern feel musically. But the lyrics tell another story. She quotes directly from the original Old Testament *Song of Solomon*, but has twisted its meaning. In the Bible it reads "For I am faint with love..." where she substitutes "I am sick of love", changing the meaning from being faint in the peak of passion or orgasm, to being disillusioned with the whole thing.

There are sexual images of "His left arm is under my head and his right hand it doth embrace me" probably refers to the act of foreplay and lovemaking. Trying to please, satisfy, giving it all but it is never enough. "I'd come in a hurricane for you" because probably early in the relationship, when the passion was new and exciting, she did; now familiarity and change only brings contempt. She gives him what he wants – but is it reciprocated? She gives him everything she thinks he wants. He only wants her sexuality (or she his?) not the whole emotional package, the problems or everything else she is. Perhaps she needs to be alone, perhaps he is the wrong one for her. His demands she cannot meet, or hers he cannot fulfil. The perfection is an illusion and they are fooling each other in the bedroom and the whole relationship. The sex isn't fulfilling, for either or both. She is something to boost his ego. What about what she needs? Perhaps she is the one making demands of him. Perhaps he is making demands that she cannot meet. People change, and grow apart.

Another interpretation could be that it is the lonely cry of the "solitary heart", in a world were the 'norm' is to be a couple. Perhaps it is Kate's shout at the world who sees her as something purely sexual, not the emotional being, just a poster on the wall, or public property because of her fame. There is something here which reminds me of *Candle in the Wind.* Maybe it is that Kate simply is fed up of being seen by some as nothing more that a sex symbol, and that her creativity is not taken seriously. People – the media, the company, the fans – want a piece of her soul. The demands of fame. Demands which cannot be met. She will not play the game.

The Song of Solomon is ambiguous, leaving a bitter-sweet taste. It is difficult to grasp exactly what she's saying here. Perhaps it is the loss of Paradise and the loss of innocence.

This is the song of the Lovers, the White Hart (inverted?).

Between *The Song of Solomon* and *Lily* there sounds like some kind of psychic interference, a weirdness, the Seens and the Unseens trying to tune in; the background to the song literally.

Lily – as the music started I physically felt a swirling spiral of energy spinning gently around my body. I felt something similar on first stepping inside The Sanctuary, at Avebury. This physical sensation is not surprising since this is the Golden Dawn protection ritual set to music, a very powerful ritual not to be undertaken lightly. By singing this she is placing each of us "In the circle of fire". All over the world thousands of protection rituals will be performed by the playing of this song, invoking the archangels to protect us all from harm. Powerful indeed. It'll be interesting to see what effect this will have on our planet. And it will have an effect.

Is this Kate's Quest for the Grail? Is the whole Album just that – Kate's Path-working towards the Grail? Her sufferings bring insight into her self and to us. Kate is the Fisher King, the Wounded King (she refers to another wounded King in *Why Should I Love You*). She seeks advice and sanctuary from the Lady of the Lake – 'Lily', one of the few she can trust. Heal Thyself oh mighty King, heal thyself. "With a pinch of salt and protect yourself with fire". Cast a circle of salt, and ask the angels to protect you.

The pressures Kate must be under being famous – also being a sensitive and all that involves – must be enormous. People turn to her for help, but who heals the healer, and what happens when she needs help? Who can she trust, especially if she has lost the ones she would normally turn to for advice and wise words. She cries "Life has blown a great big hole through me"; this is what happens when someone you love dies. Grief can leave us weak, open to other external influences, be they people, or things unseen, which can enter our lives and make us weaker and very unhappy. It is a very honest song. There is real fear here about feeling defenceless against all the shit that comes in. Soaking it all up like a sponge, unable to get rid of the things which harm. There are very few people to trust in the field of occult; I have had experience of this kind of person. It is wise to know who your friends are, who you can trust, and who is only your friend for their own selfish purposes.

This is the song of the Lady of the Lake, the High Priestess, the Grail Hermit.

The Red Shoes reminds me of *Jig of Life*. It is full of symbols – "This curve is your smile, This cross is your heart, This line is your Path". All mapped out in her hand. Is it about her career, is it the demands of fans and co to tour, the constant demands of life versus career, relationships versus career. Ambition and dreams. The dream and reality. Sacrifices have to be made, you can't have it all. This is the suppression or repression of the spirit that longs to fly, be free. The woman who started a path and cannot leave it; she chooses her career at the sacrifice of other things. A recurring dilemma for women. You've got to dance... Everything is running out of control. She danced her dream, 'til her dream came true. She has danced so hard, that she bleeds, she is weary, resigned to her destiny mapped out in the palm of the hand, as in *Jig of Life*. It is all written. Line, Cross and Curve.

We don't always know where ideas come from. Can ideas be channelled through us from Higher sources? We are not always in control of what we create. We just do it, we keep on dancing... The woman who has forged her own chains from youth's dreams and hopes and ambitions, they are the shoes she willingly put on and they are the same red shoes which carry her on and on in a frenzied dance, a life from she cannot escape. The fame from which she cannot unmake, even if she wanted to, which I'm sure she must have wanted many times. She must long for anonymity, she must long to walk down the street without anyone pointing at her. How does she cope with her fame?

This is the song of the Hanged One, the Wounded King.

Top of the City feels so sad to me, another lament for lost love. A plea or a prayer. Resignation, submission, weary of life, she would rather place herself in someone else's hands – "take me up to the top of the city". Jealousy eats away, she can't cope "I see you walking down the street with her... she's no good for you baby" It is all too much. She wants to be lifted from this life, the mud of depression perhaps. "Put me up on the angels shoulders".

The need to escape. The lost dreams. Disillusioned, she has lost her way. In an ideal vision the city would be Atlantis. But this city is alien, frightening, she is scared. She asks for help, someone to lift her up, lift her spirits because she cannot do it alone. Sadness, loneliness when the blackness has gone and some time has passed. Perhaps it is a song of death, about dying and being lifted. The stillness and hollowness that remains after the shock of losing someone through death. She is alone. Maybe watching from above like the dead watching the living.

"Feels like hell down there" – the city can be soul destroying, it is alien down there on the ground where no-one cares, where people are destitute. The dehumanisation, the concrete, the pollution of lungs and hearts and souls. Where are the trees? She's almost there, with only "One more step to the top of the city" Is she assessing her life? Is she looking at her options? "I don't think we should ever suffer". Perhaps it is the choice between life and death. One more step to death. Should she jump?

This is the song of Death, Sword Ten.

Constellation of the Heart – is it about death and dying – the experience of actually dying? The journey of death? She is the captain of her spaceship, her destiny. Sleeping at the controls, she is awakened, this is it. She has to complete this stage of the journey – death – alone. She "can't run away from it". "Can't face it" – but she has to face it, she has no choice. In facing death she can let her fears go. She has reached the end of her earthly life – "What do you mean that's it?" She is scared, angry, fighting it. She is frightened of the place where she has never gone before – "Is it gonna hurt, is it gonna hurt real bad?" Her guides and companions tell her "It's gonna be beautiful, it's gonna be wonderful, it's gonna be paradise". Her loved ones will be waiting to meet her at the end of her journey; "The man with the ladder" (Bill Duffield?); "The woman with the keys" (Hannah?); "The man with the stick" (Michael Powell?).

It is a serious message about fear – of life and death. Yes, you can do it! Be brave. It is about looking inside ourselves, "put your eye to the glass and here we'll find the Constellation of the heart". Look within, it is all there. We are forever looking for external things to give us the answers. I feel we are a small version of what happens in the universe. Perhaps in death she becomes a part of this Universe that from the earth seems so far away.

This is the song of Death, the Moon, the Star.

Big Stripey Lie is madness, psychic attack even, confusion, similar kind of fear that was in *Get Out of My House*. The Nigel Kennedy violin reminds me of *Experiment IV*. There are strange, otherworldly sounds that frighten. A song to warn. It can only be from a real experience, and if so she is brave to write of such a thing... "coming up behind" I feel her fear shoot through my back as the song progresses, like being stabbed in the back. It is an excellent song reminiscent of much of *The Dreaming*, but I do not like listening to it. It makes me feel sick; it reminds me of some very weird experiences I had in 1991.

"Your name is being called by sacred things which are not addressed or listened to, sometimes they blow trumpets" – this makes me feel weird, makes my spine chill; it sounds like a quote to me, possibly Crowley. Trumpets could be angels or elementals, posing as something they are not. Feeding on her, hurting her, having prised through the doorway. Has Kate been under some sort of psychic attack? Under attack from things seen and unseen. Is it a result of some very strange and frightening things many of us experienced in 1991? Common amongst the sensitives. A lot of people have been through it over the past couple of years. Kate too, by the sound of it. Was her trust abused by a fraud, a la Rosabel? There are sexual and psychic vampires everywhere who mess with peoples lives, and use forces they cannot understand or control. Unseens are always looking for doorways through which they can enter and cause havoc, that is why ouji boards are so dangerous. All sorts of shit comes through via those things, which can seriously screw people up.

She must cast away the bad vibes, the little waves, the stripey lies, depression, blackness, the negative thought-waves of interference on the psychic wavelength. The power of thought – good and bad – is released into the universe. The cold hand on the crown, the cold hand on the back, pushing, or protecting. It is not clear.

There seems a lot of paranoia and fear, and almost every time I hear this I get a headache or weird sensation at my forehead. Weird things were happening to a lot of people about two years ago and I feel Kate may have had similar experiences. There is real fear here, is it like facing the fear, looking the demon in the eyes in order to cast it away, like in Gilliam's *The Fisher King*. The fears come back again and again until they are dealt with and dissolved with the power of Light and Love. Emotionally weakened, there was a doorway for the shit – the cosmic and psychic interference – to come in.

People lash out when they are hurting and are unhappy and afraid. Paranoia and fear, helplessness, not knowing what to do, too much coming in, too much remaining behind, to go bad and prey on the mind, to gnaw at the soul. The cosmic battle between good and evil, God and the Devil, within the person. This song is an exorcism of her demons.

This is the song of the Spiral Tower, the Devil, Sword Nine.

Why Should I Love You? is like a prayer, like she has found comfort. It is a very positive song. "This chapter says put it out of your mind and give it time" – put the past behind you and move on. Time out to heal and recuperate. This song makes me want to cry, it is like being born out of the pit of despair. The calm after the big stripey lies. Rebirth. Like coming out the other side of a really bad time. The healing waters, coming up out of the spiral of despair. The peace of being after so much suffering.

It is brimming with religious imagery and colour. "Have you ever seen a picture of Jesus laughing, do you think he had a beautiful smile?" Kate presents the image of Jesus as a human being; laughing, not as he usually portrayed, suffering and bloodied upon the cross. An image of comfort, without the guilt trips, but the joy. As was intended, not as portrayed in man made religion. The real message of comfort and joy, not guilt and pain. She gains solace from the familiarity of her childhood. A song of healing, a love song, platonic love. This song spells LOVE.

This is the song of the Sun, the Star.

You're the One made me cry straight away, and as much as *Moments of Pleasure*. This is perhaps the saddest song on the album, another ballad of lost love. When love changes from what it once was, and things move on leaving others behind. It is too real. We all know the story. When I first heard this I held onto Peter, and cried into him... can it ever be the same, can it?? When so much happens in between the beginning and the now? A song about the break-up of a relationship, running out, escaping, when you don't really want to. Feeling like you have to go, that you don't really have the choice. It's just got so bad, there's no other way. This is sometimes what happens when we danger it up. We take risks. Sometimes we lose more than we gain. You can never go back. You can never forget "He's not you, he can't do what you do".

One of the saddest lines is "I just have one problem, We're best friends". That's a great big problem too. Often in a relationship we lose half of ourselves to someone else, and when he or she leaves, half of ourselves leave too. Love never dies, it just changes. The problems arise if we don't change with it, go with the flow. We need to bend like the trees then we won't be broken. This happens to so many people. It's just not easy to be in a long term relationship and expect things to stay the same as they were in the beginning. The things that happen along the way take their toll. They test the relationship, but sometimes it can be just too much, and it is better to split. Most people probably go through the turmoil of whether to try to continue or not.

It reminds me of June 1991. My eyes fill with tears thinking about it. You picked me up and just phoned. 1991 was a very bad year for many people – lots of couples split up, there was turmoil on the planet, old outworn systems were overthrown. Those things which wouldn't bend to the changes – broke, were destroyed, not strong enough to withstand the force of change.

1991 was a very difficult year. Our house was partly wrecked by a flood, we couldn't have a baby. I was scared, I hurt, I got ill. It was a trying and terrible year. But I love him more, maybe more than ever before. He makes me angry at times, when he seems not really care or be aware of how I feel. I make too many demands. *You're the One* says so much to me. I need him in my life. I love him. We recognise the Symbols.

This is the song of Guinevere (inverted?), Grail Five, Sword Three.

This is probably all a load of crap! I may be totally wrong and I stress that these are only my feelings.

Graphic; Paulina Stuckey

The Red Shoes Myth

Peter Manchester looks at What Lies Beneath...

Issue 50: October 1993

This article was edited from rec.music.gaffa with grateful thanks to the authors

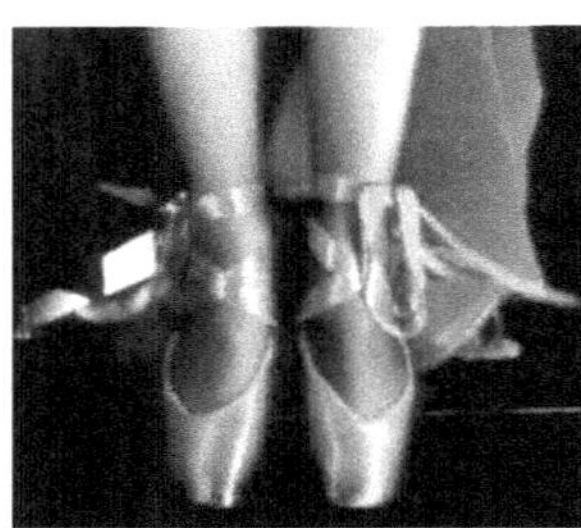

I was not left lonely when I volunteered to organise research into the mythical aspects of 'The Red Shoes' story. Brian Gallagher advised me to look into a book entitled *Women Who Run With the Wolves* by Clarissa Pinkola Estes. Chapter Eight reproduces an ancient version of the story and interprets it in the light of the author's over twenty years as a storyteller and practising Jungian psychologist.

The version Estes presents is "a Magyar-Germanic version my Aunt Tereza used to tell us when we were children" (p. 215). Her knowledge about the story and about its traditions means that she has probably very accurately portrayed a version current in early mediaeval times. However, she also talks about the roots of the 'red shoes' motif in very ancient Persian, Indian, and Egyptian threshold rites for young women at the time they enter into their roles with respect to the passage of blood, in which they paint their feet red. There are a lot of layers between that stratum and the early European story!

Estes really doesn't need to reconstruct all that history in order to get at the archetypal dimension of the story we know from Hans Christian Andersen. Her family's version makes loud and clear the way Andersen has moralised the story.

First you need to know this much about Estes' interpretation: she is clear that the brutal ending is truthful about the nature of the red shoes. Her theme is that the girl has had the Wild Woman in her captured and injured in instinct by the dry and near-blind rich woman who 'domesticated' her, so that when she later tries to let the Wild Woman out, she is vulnerable to "Leg Traps, Cages, and Poisoned Bait" (the title of the chapter). The specific hazards that Estes discusses, are:

The Gilded Carriage, the Devalued Life

The Dry Old Woman, the Senescent Force

Burning the Treasure, Alma, Soul Famine

Injury to Basic Instinct, the Consequences of Capture

Trying to Sneak a Secret Life, Split in Two

Cringing Before the Collective, Shadow Rebellion

Faking it, Trying to be Good, Normalising the Abnormal

Dancing Out of Control, Obsession and Addiction

This last, the most drastic, is the one dramatised by the story. It ends in disaster, with the girl quite abject. The last line is: "And now the girl was a poor cripple, and had to find her own way in the world as a servant to others, and she never, ever again wished for red shoes". Several times in the chapter, Estes talks about Janis Joplin, as an illustration of how it can go if the 'dancing-out-of-control' Wild Woman gets an audience who egg her on for vicarious excitement.

Andersen's major changes can be set out thus:

MAGYAR-GERMANIC:

Karen, a little girl, poor, whose mother dies.

Taken to "old mother shoe-maker" for her childhood red shoes; given to her, first worn when mother dies.

Wealthy old woman in gilded carriage takes her in, cleans her up, burns her shoes.

Finds red shoes in shop of old crippled cobbler. He winks at her as the old woman, colour-blind, buys them for her. Shoes said to "glow".

Confirmation on the "Day of The Innocents".

Details on red shoes in church emphasise lusciousness "like burnished apples, red-washed plums... bright like crimson, bright like raspberries, bright like pomegranates".

Old soldier with red beard taps the soles of her shoes with a little song that made the soles of her feet itch.

Old lady hides the red shoes.

She becomes bed-ridden, and so Karen is free to search them out, obsessively.

When she finds them and puts them on, they dance her out the door.

A Spirit of Dread prevents her from entering the churchyard; he pronounces her curse.

Executioner cuts off her feet,

The shoes dance them off into the forest,

She becomes a cripple and a servant.

End.

ANDERSEN:

A motherless poor girl.

Makes her own red shoes, sewn from cloth straps, crude, but she loved them and they help her accommodate her hard life.

Big old lady portrayed as kind and feeling sorry for her, asks the parson if she can take care of her.

Shoes burned.

[Spurious sub-plot involving Queen and Princess, tempting Karen to vanity and envy]

Goes to rich shoemaker;

Thinks of the Princess' shoes;

Is told these were made for an earl's daughter;

Shoes are said to be "shiny".

Merely said to be old enough to be confirmed.

Karen "thought only of the red shoes",

The story details not how she thought about them, but all the pious activities going on that she was ignoring.

Old soldier with red beard simply "struck the soles with his hand".

Old lady becomes very ill. Has to be nursed

and tended, but Karen is invited to a grand ball.

Looks at lady "who after all could not live", and at the shoes, goes to the ball, and there the dancing shoes take over.

Gets in among the gravestones, but is accosted by an angel at the church door.

Curse toned down, and a moralising note on "proud, vain children" is added.

Asks that feet be chopped off so she can "repent of my sins".

He makes her wooden feet and crutches, teaches her a penitent's psalm.

She keeps trying to go to church, but is blocked by the dancing shoes.

Frightened, and seeking "real repentance in her heart", begs the parson to be taken into service.

The rest of the 'redemption' theme from there on is totally spurious preachment: "She proved to be very industrious and thoughtful. She sat very still and listened most attentively in the evening when the parson read the Bible". It gets progressively more ghastly, until finally, "Her heart was so overfilled with the sunshine, with peace, and with joy, that it broke. Her soul flew with the sunshine to heaven, and no one there asked about the red shoes".

What I expected to find as the 'magic' in this, as a children's story, is actually some pretty drastic and violent action (an authenticating aspect, as Estes makes clear) some pretty powerful 'voodoo' as Kate Bush's lyric has it.

So far as I can tell at this point, in Kate's song only the shoes themselves and the frenzied dancing come from the folk story. The dramatic situation ("She," dancing like the Diva ('Goddess': Sanskrit) in red shoes, dancing like "I" would love to, but can't, because "all her gifts for the dance had gone") seems quite different. Also, it is not clear that for Kate the shoes are the devil's only: is the stanza with "your eyes are lifted to God" supposed to be redemptive?

It Really Hurts

Jan Millington Deals with Death

Issue 55: April 1995

Jan Millington MA, a *HomeGround* subscriber since the 1980s, is now an artist, teacher and lecturer.

"whilst I do not describe myself as a 'landscape painter', the land is where I go for my creativity to be fed. I'm particularly drawn to those places which have had long relationships with people. places where ancient people lived, celebrated, worshipped, and died. Stone circles: standing stones: liminal sites. these are the places I feel a connection to."

We have many rites of passage throughout our lives. Some we mark with festivals, parties, celebrations: christenings/namings, weddings, coming of age. In this culture we're very good at the joyous celebrations. We're less successful at the last; dealing with Death.

Death is tucked away, hidden. People don't die of 'old age', the ending of their time; they have diagnosed illnesses written on death certificates. It's almost as if the medical profession regards death as some kind of failure. We keep people attached to drips and pipes and machines ignoring the quality of life this gives the 'patient'. Old people die in hospitals surrounded by strangers and the dying. We fear the emotional and psychical fall-out that comes with the last journey. We are not prepared for it. Death passing close to us is a sobering, frightening experience. And the death of a parent is especially deep with meaning. Parents are the portals we come through into this life. Losing one of those guardians leaves a big hole, it brings the grave a step closer, one less person between ourselves and eternity. A landmark gone, a safety-net gaping. We have reason to stop and consider our own mortality. Any parent's death is difficult; we have to consider our relationship in a different light. Unresolved problems can cause us panic and distress "All the things I should have said that I never did" memories can cause us 'moments of pleasure', and pain.

For the rest of our lives we will have to live without that person; they will never see our future successes, never give us a band-aid to heal our future hurts. It doesn't matter if the relationship has been good or bad, or whether the parent has been 'good' or 'bad'. Death brings many confusing emotions churning up to the surface, sometimes ones we least expect: relief after a long illness; hysteria with the suddenness of death; anger at being left; guilt for being the one left behind. Time can help, but sometimes others' conversations can cause sudden emotions. Everyone thinks it's in the past, 'we're over the worst', 'we've put it behind us', but words and feelings tug at us and bring it all back. I need to learn to be a rubberband girl. Learn not to resist; to bend in the wind; to learn to give.

The Red Shoes came out at the end of 1993; my dad was in and out of hospital. I knew he was dying. They kept patching him up and sending him home. He'd wear out again ("snap like a rubberband") and return to the clinical wards of the terminally ill. I'd drive to the hospital with *The Red Shoes* on the cassette. Sometimes it would lift me up ("three rubberbands won't keep you up"). Sometimes I'd smack down to the bottom. I could hardly bear to listen to *Moments of Pleasure*; driving became dangerous as my eyes would fill up. I'd shout out the words alongside Kate; catharsis of sorts. Watching the video... "He isn't well at all"... I was alive and it hurt. After he died he gave me back all those moments he'd taken from me. He could become 'my dad' again in a more real way than when he was alive. I could hear him laughing, something I'd not had since before his stroke twenty years earlier.

My best friend from childhood came up in March. We went to see Kristen Hersh (from Throwing Muses) play an acoustic set in Leeds.

That night my dad died. Lesley being there was a gift. She knew dad from our time as troublesome teenagers. We had a shared past, have a shared present. She was there for me, my extended family, my chosen family. She knew my problems with my family, we'd been there. I put *The Red Shoes* in the car, and kept it there for months. It went round and round the spools. "Live your life for love"... but sometimes it's a hard love you find, not the one you want or need. His death set me free. I'm free to find bond in our relationship now, not bondage.

Eat the Music is the piece which would always set my feet tapping; a slice of sunshine and rhythm drumming through those dreary winter drives to and fro, home to hospital to mum's to home. It would bring me to my here and now, my present state of love instead of the sticky fingers of the past. I'd eat it and eat it as sustenance through the dark, imagining the colours of the fruit. "May you never hunger" Kate was telling me. *Song of Solomon* touched me with the yearning in Kates's voice. I was sick of 'love'. The love of duty and 'should' and obedience. I couldn't do it for you, dad. I had to do it on my own terms, walking my own path. My love needed to be unconditional and he'd put strings on it. Death cut the strings: I could have love freely given as a gift.

Lily is my protection: the goddess watching out for me in the fog. I wasn't safe. As a driver I was a danger to myself and others with eyes full of tears. Death had blown a great big hole through my life. I drove along casting a circle of fire around me. She protected me from accident and protected others from my mistakes. We all survived. I went accident-free throughout that Winter.

The Red Shoes is dancing with Death. Being out of control of the emotions spilling around. "Gonna dance, gotta dance"... no choice but to dance to the tune Death plays. No escape, just have to keep going. Let the feelings whirl, dervishing through and out. The rhythm keeping going, no pause, dancing, dancing. *Top of the City* is protection again; angels. It's an aural version of Wim Wenders film, *Wings Of Desire*. I see it in black and white, the city at night, the lights, lost love. But I'm safe away from the cold night in the soft feathers of the carved angels wings. Here I am looking down: climbing the ladder to heaven.

Constellation of the Heart... out in the stars of Heaven we can steer our course. Find a way back through the cold void to the warmth of love. Find our way with the 'Map of The Human Heart' (a wondrous film!). Having to face up to what I've lost, face up to the hurt of my rocky relationship with my dad. Recognise we can never reconcile now he's dead. The final shutting of heaven's doors. No chance now to heal each other. Lots of things to face, but I want to run away from it! "Without the pain there'd be no learning, without the hurting we'd never change".

Big Stripey Lie... it's a jungle in here. I'm drowning in grief. Hanging on to a sense of the sacred. Have I lost it? Scary feelings. Realising I don't want him back. Glad he's dead. Guilt. A sense of release; of his release, of my own. Him tossing and turning on the hospital bed the last time I saw him. Agonised. Nigel Kennedy's violin so sweet, poignant. Then, the end. *Why Should I Love You*... Recognition of my ambiguous feelings towards my dad. I can speak of loving him now in a way I never could when he was alive. A breakthrough, a healing. And another rite of passage. When me and Pete marry that summer we devised our own ceremony. No hymns, music on tape. We walk from the chapel to the strains of the Beatles' *All You Need Is Love* and Kate singing this – "Of all the people in the world why should I love you?"

You're the One... A coda. My dad wasn't the only one. The howling vocals at the end, the way Kate screams "sugar, honey" with such loss. It reminds me of primal screaming. John Lennon used it on his harrowing LP *John Lennon, Plastic Ono Band*. *Listen to Mother* and *Well Well Well* and hear the pain in his voice. *JLPOB* has a lot of pain about his mother, the loss of her. "Mother you left me, but I never left you"... how she left him, and then was killed. The album reeks of pain and desolation. His love song to his mother, *Julia*, is on the Beatles' *White Album*. It's very poignant. On *JLPOB* he's angry with his mother; he shouts, screams, wails. All his grief for her pours out. Kate sounds as if she's doing something similar on *You're the One*. The ending of a significant relationship. Did we all think it was about a partner? Could it be about her mother? Let's not forget how close Kate was – is – to her mother. She dedicates *The Red Shoes* to Hannah. Because of my own circumstances when the album came out, it's very connected to my dad's last few months and his death. Because I associate it so closely with death (and catharsis I might add) that doesn't mean that's 'what it's about'. Only how it fits to my life.

In the time of *The Red Shoes* Kate's mother died, and for me, that loss howls through the music. I had death close by too, but my father's death was very different from that of Kate's mother. My relationship was very different, based on a sense of escape, on estrangement. Kate's was based on closeness, embracing, "I don't want to leave". The death of a parent is deep with meaning, whatever the relationship. We stand in the presence of death and are changed by it. If we can face death and learn from it, it can transform our lives... though I'm not sure I've got there yet! If we ignore it and don't deal with it, it can destroy us. Death is our last taboo. We shut Her out and try to deny Her power. But that only makes Her laugh. We must all face the Morrigan; we all die and have loved ones who will die. Life is hard, and so is Death. But there's always love.

Graphic: Paulina Stuckey

And just as Death transforms, so does love. It is up to us how we try to work it through. And we always have Kate, helping us through, with love.

Thinking of what Krys wrote in the editorial of HomeGround 54, let's play *The Red Shoes* and think of Hannah, and our other loved and lost ones. Let's try and take into account that Kate lost her mother only very recently, it must still be very new to her. And from now on Kate will be left with one less star to guide her. I know I don't spend my days grieving for my dad, yet every so often it creeps up. I don't miss him, for many reasons, but I sense a gap. For Kate this must be even stronger.

Death changes us. The death of a parent changes us in ways we don't expect. Let's give Kate space and time to heal and remember her loss. It will have touched her in ways even she hardly knows yet. The death of a parent is the end – childhood's end.

Kate: It's Okay

Martin Carolan on those Red Shoes

Issue 54October 1994

Many people seem not to like *Rubberband Girl.* To me it is one of those 'nothing' songs, not meaning to be harsh because I like it. The beat made me bounce around the kitchen. The lyrics have a sense of humour about them. It's great to be able to take a simple item and sing about how you wish you could be more flexible in life. I don't think it's meant to be too serious, just a song to enjoy.

And So Is Love is beautiful. "You do huh?" – so human, as if Kate is just sitting talking to someone. A very personal song all of us can relate to. A sad song but not without hope – "You set me free, I set you free". Even before I saw the première of *The Line, the Cross & the Curve*, I could see and feel the emotion in the music, the guitar and Kate's voice. "Life is sad and so is love" but we must go on alone.

I'm still in the middle of a Brazilian rain forest surrounded by luscious fruit, as butterflies dance to the valihas and drums of *Eat the Music.* "He's a woman at heart and I love him for that" – how so many times close female friends have said this to me because they felt I could understand where they were coming from. I like this song a lot. It's so happy. The brass section is excellent, makes you want to get up and dance.

Graphic: "Lily" Paulina Stuckey

Moments of Pleasure is an amazing and emotional song. A very personal song and one that has to touch even the coldest heart. I just want to put my arms around Kate and say "hey, it's okay" and hold her. Maybe it's me that wants to be held? Yeah, it can really hurt but we have to give these moments back to those we love cos it's too late when our friends die. This is so powerful, Kate's voice is so strong. If she made no more records for the next ten years (God forbid!) this would keep me going. It makes you place yourself outside past experiences and observe them as who you are, yet somehow detached from those moments.

The Song of Solomon touches me personally. Being gay and walking the solitary path, and like Kate not wanting any male sexual ego, just someone who is honest and himself, without the male ego crap so many men have – "don't want your bullshit". The Trio sing beautifully.

Lily and *The Red Shoes* are my two favourites. When I first heard Lily's narration, I felt so safe and protected by her. A real protective figure, almost like the Virgin Mary. My faith again, and the narration is like a prayer to me. A great way to bind faith and music. I wish Lily was my granny. "Gabriel before me" reminds me of our prayer St Patrick's Breastplate. There is a sense of evil here but we are being protected. Surround ourselves with fire or a circle of friends for protection.

When I hear *The Red Shoes* I'm immediately at home in Ireland, running crazily through fields with the wind in my face and my hair blowing. There is a magical feel to this song that tunes into the magical eeriness of Eire. There is a ritualistic feel – not negative, but positive – here of spirits that are the essence of the place. What it is. It's hard to explain, you would have to have visited to know what I mean.

In *Top of the City*, I like the contrast between the chorus and the quiet intro. I listened to this when I was in Paris, by the Sacre Coeur overlooking the city. I felt as though I was at the top of the city. If we are here, above it all, with someone we love, we are safe, everything is okay again.

Constellation of the Heart is brilliant. I'd love this at a concert so we could all sing "We think you'd better wake up Cap'n"! I hope this is a reference to 'Star Trek' cos I'm a bit of a fan. Almost afraid to face up to life, reality, but as long as we have a good crew of friends we'll make it. It'll be tough, but it will also be paradise.

I love the confusion of sounds on *Big Stripey Lie.* A real crazy feeling like you are about to explode. Trumpets blowing and wild animals freaking out.

Why Should I Love You? is not my favourite track, nor am I sure why. I think it's the Prince bit, I like him but I'm not too sure here. Again the Trio are amazing, and Lenny Henry is great here too. I love the lyrics and the Biblical references make me feel very safe. I love the way Kate makes Jesus human. "A smile that healed" – what a beautiful observation of Christ.

You're the One – You know, I've always thought about how hard it is to devote so much of your life to one person and then say, that's it, all over. Life is not that simple. If a relationship ends, why should the friendship? This is a situation I don't want to get into, but if you never love someone to this extent you are missing out – which I am. Is it better to never have loved? We should be best friends, yeah? You can't ignore years of love like that.

Life is sad and so is love. Kate, it's okay. We love you. Never stop, never.

Shooting Through The Veil

John Carder Bush

Tinged with orange from the tungsten bulbs
The mato blend and blur across the snow
And I know the deep grief moves again.

Tears for my mother, and for my friend,
Gone and the going, and for all the others
Death is moving along and away from us
Until they are like faces on the targets,
Still there but growing fainter,
Harder and harder to reach.
The images of her hand and wrist making the cross
As they lay, so neatly, across the elbow and arm,
Of the desperate fighter gone beyond his tears
Standing above us all in a mist of will.
All still there but growing fainter,
The warmth going out of them
Until there is no doubt
And no longer any life,
Just the urine and the blood,
The room getting colder,
The electric presence
of once familiar darkness
Gone crazy now that
The beloved patterns in the air
Are no longer there.

These arrows of natural grief do not hit -
The heart is the source of the shot,
And the heart is the source of the sparkle
That turns the mato into rainbows
And the azuchi in the falling snow
To an angel of dancing lights.

From a collection of poems relating to the Japanese art of Kyudo.

Mato = target
Azuchi = target house
Yumi = the longbow

Lavender

Beck Siàn

I plant lavender
wherever I go
As if my spirit
depends on these
Seeds I sow
I need to keep
Kathleen alive
It's in these
lavender plants
That her spirit thrives
And memory survives

The Red Shoes...

HomeGround Readers react - and not everyone liked it!

Issue 50: October 1993

Issue 51: February 1994

Graham Cowan

It's been days since I first played the album, and in that time I have played it constantly. It is such a relief to find that it is a masterpiece after all the "average" reviews it got in so many magazines.

Rubberband Girl always makes me smile, it's just so exuberant, and although the actual subject matter of the song is despairing up to a point; when Kate declares "Here I go!" and proceeds to "bend like a rubberband" it just shows to everyone that we can all give a little more, not just in relationships, but also in our everyday existence. Maybe we shouldn't be so self-occupied all the time. *And So Is Love* moves me as much as anything Kate has ever done. The vocals are stunning, and the whole song has a feeling of warmth which seems typical of this album, and which was perhaps missing on *The Sensual World*. The melody must be one of the most beautiful Kate has ever written.

Eat the Music is bizarre, but I wonder if this would make a good single and so I was glad to hear that *Moments of Pleasure* would be the next. I don't know what to say about this song except that it hurts to listen to it; it is achingly beautiful I suppose, if you want to be really clichéd about it.

The Song of Solomon and *Lily* go so well together that one seems almost to be a continuation of the other, and once again Kate proves that lyrics are not necessary to move people, just three simple sounds "wap bam boom". I'm not sure why that moves me so much, but I suppose it's the way Kate delivers them.

The Red Shoes is great. Kate has really used the Celtic instrumentation to advantage and in such a subtle way. She is such a great story teller! However, to me, *Top of the City* is the weakest track on the album, though in saying that I must admit that it is growing on me. Maybe it's one of those songs which is less immediate, but eventually wriggles its way into your consciousness. *Constellation of the Heart* and *Why Should I Love You* are blasts of joy - both make me feel so good, and seem to dispel that strange myth that "you can't dance to Kate's music"! *You're the One* has become an instant favourite, and along with *This Woman's Work*, *Breathing* and *Hello Earth*, it has made me cry - and it brings back so many memories of sadder times...

The Red Shoes as an album is stunning. It already feels and sounds like an old friend. I can't fully convey my feelings about these songs as I simply don't have the words. However, to Kate I would say "thank you for being you". Your work brings so much to us. How can we imagine an existence without you?

Keith Pitches

For my first impressions of this, Kate's seventh album, I have after much consideration chosen to cover *The Red Shoes* as a whole rather than track by track because such is the artistic brilliance of each one that a proper comprehensive review would take a week to write and reams and reams of paper. The richness and diversity of musical styles expressed on the different tracks is a source of endless enjoyment.

I cannot pinpoint a weak composition on the album. Of course, I could begin at *Rubberband Girl* and review KB VII until I fall off the edge of the final track only, unusually (for Kate), *You're the One* has a "commercial" fade out! Or I could pick up on the funkiness of *Constellation of the Heart*, noting how vividly it contrasts with *Big Stripey Lie*, which for me is rather like The Art Of Noise performing a storyline by H.P. Lovecraft and dramatised by Simon Drake!

When I first played the album I'd been cheered by the first track, had my heart gently squeezed (nice chords, Mr Clapton!) by the second, and gorged myself silly on the third, I was already closer to Heaven, and then to hear *Moments of Pleasure* after that lot - well, I think I'd almost stopped breathing. There were tears in my eyes for Kate and her epitaph song for Hannah. Too bad the record buying public didn't share the same opinion. One possible explanation for its relative lack of chart success as a single could be the obscure (to non-Kate fans) references to people - Murph and Bill for instance. The piano riff reminds me of *I'm Still Waiting*, but that aside like almost all of Kate's songs is startlingly original. *Moments of Pleasure* could be my favourite Kate track of all time.

Although a beautifully compiled album, *The Red Shoes* contains within its wholeness songs which are self-sufficient works of art in their own right. Loosely conceptualised around the title track - a little like *The Ninth Wave* - Kate's latest reminds more of *Never For Ever* in the way it entertains; the diversity of images as I settle into the chair, close my eyes and breathe in genius. Mmmmmm - know the feeling? Yeah!

One thing that doesn't change - and hasn't since *Wuthering Heights* - is the spiritual completeness of Kate's music. *The Red Shoes* is no exception. Kate's songs have always been women's songs, sung from the female viewpoint, yet Kate has never hesitated to use masculine energy to instill the wholeness which can be found in all great pieces of music. This is why you can trace Kate's musical masterpieces back from *You're The One*, past *Rubberband Girl*, even including songs on the early 'Cathy demos' from her teenage years, and you'll find pure Yin and Yang – the music of life! That's what fills my heart – it's probably why I so love Kate's music and why I love this album.

Neil Roberts

So here it is. It's 3rd November. I dimmed the lights, grabbed a glass of port, and settled down with a CD of *The Red Shoes*. Fifty minutes later I'm a happy man. Here are what I considered to be the highlights:

Rubberband Girl – joyful and fun. Already a classic.

And So Is Love – moving and emotional. The instantly recognisable Clapton chords send shivers down my back.

Eat the Music – Kate does modern romance! "Split me open... put your hands in... bananas... sticky fingers..." Kate!!! Shocking, erotic and extremely funny. Can't wait for the video!

Moments of Pleasure – shivers time again. Pure emotional beauty. Number One if there's any justice.

The Red Shoes – light, frothy and great fun.

Big Stripey Lie – okay, so every album has it's dud, and I'm afraid this is it. Deservedly a B-side. Noisy.

You're the One – after a slightly weaker second half (but how could such a stunning A-side be topped?), the album finished with one of the best tracks. Very moving, sad, and heartfelt. I was a wreck at the end of it. Beautiful.

A word has to be said about the wonderful packaging. The fold-out poster/lyric sheet being far, far better than most albums. And that beautifully erotic cover photo! There's something about ladders in stockings – or is it just me?!

So all in all a stunner. Who gives a damn if Kate takes four years to produce an album if she comes up with brilliance like this. Beautiful.

Robert Brown

Rubberband Girl – an ideal opener, being both lively and direct. Perhaps the least interesting track on the album, *Rubberband Girl* nevertheless boasts the best sound. *And So Is Love* – a classic Bush ballad if ever there was one! From the beautiful 'pan-pipe' synth sound to Kate's lovely hesitant vocal performance, this is sheer class from beginning to end. Best track on the album by a good mile! *Eat the Music* – well, it starts, it continues, and it eventually ends. It is certainly different, but not my cup of tea I'm afraid. Reminds me a little of Ginger Baker's *Airforce*.

Moments of Pleasure – what at heart is a very pretty ballad is all but swamped by an overblown orchestral arrangement. Never mind a mix minus the vocals, how about a mix minus the orchestra? *The Song of Solomon* – musically a belated follow-up to *Kashka From Baghdad*, Kate has created here a beautiful, evocative keyboard based soundscape, onto which the Trio Bulgarka have added some wonderful harmonics. My second favourite track on the album. One problem though, I keep thinking that someone has rung my doorbell when I play this track. *Lily* – the album's only real 'rocker' despite its deceptive start. All the musicians excel themselves here, particularly John Giblin, whose bass playing is a dream.

The Red Shoes – from the electrification of *Lily*, we go into acoustic mode for another up-tempo number. The valiha and mandola drives the song along, but it is Paddy's whistle that really stands out. Nah, I don't think I'll bother to re-phrase that! *Top of the City* – an odd song in many ways, which never really makes up its mind as to what it wants to be, namely a ballad or a rocker. The piano laden chorus is quite lovely though, and saves the song. *Constellation of the Heart* – *The Big Sky* revisited, but more radio-friendly. Personally, I would like to have heard the backing vocals given more prominence in the mix, but overall, it's a pleasant enough track.

Big Stripey Lie – Kate slips into Laurie Anderson mode, on a track that doesn't sound too far removed from *Leave It Open*. Nigel Kennedy's string work is the instrumental performance of the album, whilst Kate creates a rather impressive guitar sound. *Why Should I Love You* – despite a messy chorus, this is another excellent track, blessed with a memorable keyboard riff that once heard is never forgotten. Along with *And So Is Love*, *Why Should I Love You* would be a great single. *You're the One* – another excellent performance by everyone involved, let down by what is in effect a fairly weak song. Vocally, Kate gives it her all, but at the end of the day it proves not enough.

Overall, *The Red Shoes* is another very good album by Kate. Track by track, I find it more consistent than *The Sensual World*, and musically a lot more interesting. The autobiographical nature of the lyrics makes me care a lot more about what Kate is saying than perhaps on past albums. Most artists create their best work whilst under stress; Kate is no exception.

Adrian Durrant

Being twelve days younger than Kate, I consider that I've grown up with her. Since *Wuthering Heights*, I've shared all the moments, from magical empathy to alienation. Fifteen years later, we have another new album, and I'm ploughing through it wondering why she matters, why she winds me up, and why I'm writing to *HomeGround*.

The Red Shoes contains all the usual dark and light elements, but for me, the overall quality of this album is disappointing. Of course, Kate has had a difficult time personally, but it's unfortunate that this is reflected negatively in her song writing. She's obviously found difficulty in writing, and gone for simplicity. It is a difficult thing to bring off, and the result here is the sort of insipid lines that would incur the scorn of any competent English teacher; "Life is sad and so is love". The bottom line is that however sympathetic we are, the work has to stand up on it's own – you can't have a footnote saying "she was having a bad day".

For me, the term "moments of pleasure" with it's gratifying inference, is not appropriate as a reference to precious personal memories. The combination of naively expressed emotions and saccharin, clichéd music is an alarming symptom of creative bankruptcy. Even dear Mrs. Bush's baffling sayings can't save the day. Elsewhere, we have the dreary *Song of Solomon*, and the terrible imitation dance track with childish lyrics (is this really a woman of thirty five?) *Constellation of the Heart*, for cold comfort.

But there is hope! There's the delicious and infectious *Eat the Music*, the exhausting Morris dance title track, and the universally resonant *Lily* with it's satisfying funk-factor. But for me there's one really cool track. *Top of the City* stands above the rest; it is all there, she's got it together; it is an inspired and uplifting song about putting yourself at the top with style. It's what I expect from Kate and it proves she can do it. The next album is the one I'm waiting for.

P.S. You'll probably be flabbergasted by this review, but I mean every word. For me it's a shame when Kate doesn't do her best, or isn't able to. My problem is the lack of thinking. It is incredibly naive, as if she has taken refuge in a second childhood. Even *Moments of Pleasure* itself starts with the sort of underlined heading (the first line) that could grace a school composition. Take away those ghastly violins and the song may have stood a chance, with just Kate at the piano it would have worked better. Sorry!

Mel Cansell

What can I say? Another masterpiece from Katie. On an emotional level *And So Is Love* grabs hold of my heart and gives it a vicious tug. The lines "life is sad and so is love" sums up how I felt at the time I first heard this song. For reasons beyond my control I thought I may have to part with my girlfriend. Thankfully that won't have to happen now. On a similar vein *You're the One* gives my heart yet another twist, and *Moments of Pleasure* makes me feel happy and sad at the same time. Maybe it's just because I'd been down for a while; my personal life had more peaks and troughs than the Swiss Alps. The rest of the album is very good, but the tracks mentioned have lodged with me.

One final thing, why does the audio quality of Kate's albums vary so much? *The Sensual World* and *Hounds of Love* were spot on in the vocals, but much of the instruments, especially the bass and drums, were muffled. With *The Red Shoes*, the bass is about right, but the vocals and cymbals are very over-emphasised. This makes it very hard to listen to at a reasonable volume. This is most noticeable on *Constellation of the Heart*; played quietly it is a good song, but turn up the volume and the percussion starts to spit at you like a bus load of skinheads. Perhaps Kate believes in Safe Sound, or in other words, don't destroy your hearing with loud music.

Arto Polvikoski

The most important thing about *The Red Shoes* is the fact that despite all the sad things in her life, Kate has produced an album of great joy. There are enough examples of artists drowning in their grief, without any hint of hope, making music that is good but just wearing to listen to. With Kate sadness and happiness walk hand in hand, just like it does in real life.

I've heard *Rubberband Girl* sooo many times and I'm still not sure if it is any good. Nevertheless, I love the positiveness, and Kate's catchy words are like a nursery rhyme. John Giblin's bass line is very important – and not just in this song. The dialogue between Kate and Clapton's guitar on *And So Is Love* is simply beautiful. It appears to be a very simple song, and perhaps that's why the atmosphere is so thick and strong, and Kate's wailing cry in the middle is truly one of the greatest moments on this album. I don't know if I should cry or smile. "Life is sad and so is love" sounds so pathetic when read, but when Kate sings it, suddenly there's this magical sense of hope.

I first thought that *Eat the Music* should have had something more to it, a pause in the middle or something. Then I took it as it was and now I'm beginning to enjoy it. I'm repeating myself but I can't help it; it's simply great that Kate's joy for life is still there.

For me, the next three tracks are the peak of the album. *Moments of Pleasure* is one of Kate's best songs: beautiful, moving, with mighty strings that flow in and out like waves, and with probably the best lyrics of the whole album. *The Song of Solomon* is the song that wipes away the four years. This was well worth the wait! Okay, I don't know about the words; hopefully Kate will give us some clues as to what it's all about, but the atmosphere of the song, the way she sings... and that "a wop bam boom" at the end... I LOVE it! *Lily* moves with irresistible pulse and is a song that Peter Gabriel would have been proud of.

After this, Kate never reaches that level of intensity, although there are no fillers. The title track grows beautifully; I especially like Kate's backing vocals and the guitar reverbs. The pipes have a nice South American flavour. *Top of the City* took some time to get used to; it just wasn't going anywhere. Now I find I am humming that tune quite often, and I like the visual imagery it evokes. The full meaning of the lyrics, however, still escapes me.

Constellation of the Heart is probably the album's least impressive track. Someone remarked that in the early '80s this would have filled the discos. It does sound a bit stagnant. But anyway, I can't be too harsh; at least it leaves me with a good mood.

I still find it hard to believe that Kate herself plays that marvellous, distorted guitar on *Big Stripey Lie*! I love everything in it and reminds me of *The Dreaming*, and that can't be bad! It feels like watching a horror film. On the other extreme, *Why Should I Love You* is so happy and positive that it's almost ridiculous. Where she finds that strength?! Prince is all over the track and I find it exciting. I can imagine some people don't.

You're the One ends the album and I'm not sure if that is such a good idea. The song is really so painful, so real, it leaves you numb. *Moments of Pleasure* would have been a perfect choice to end the album with, but that's just my opinion. *You're the One* seems like a very personal song, a wound torn open. I wonder if Kate can even talk about it's content if asked. A tough song. What a brave lady she is.

The Red Shoes feels like a compilation album. Each song is a marvellous achievement, but it is hard to draw any patterns between this and other albums, except for the lyrics perhaps. But that's okay, we can't have another *Ninth Wave*. *The Red Shoes* grows, I can see that now, and already I'm just overwhelmed by the fact that *The Red Shoes* is such a happy album. THAT is important.

Sarah-Jane Mackenzie

A review of Kate's album? Well, I don't think I could write a review as the 'critics' do, I mean who the hell do they think they are anyway? A bunch of unimaginative pretentious failers of art. They drool at those they accept and condemn those they don't. Surely after a while their criticisms must become totally formalised and automatic. Automated criticism. Chop it up, put it into a box, state what that box represents and give it a label, add them together for a "wop-bam-boom" review. Couldn't we have occasional critics, not vocational critics. We might find that reviewing then becomes more of an art form in its own right, rather than the anti-art form I believe it is.

Rubberband Girl. Out of all the things that have happened to me, I'm still here. I've hurt and been hurt, yet I have learned from the experiences. But to be a rubber band would mean I'd bounce back, with these experiences having little effect on me. Is that really a good thing? To be a rubber band would be unchangeable, set, stable. No matter which way I were plucked, pulled, ping-ed, I'd still be the same thing. None the wiser.

And So Is Love. Everything must be love. Revolving, turning, spinning round the circuits of repetition. The love, the love, the love, "Oh baby live your life for love". Have we the choice? Youth, it gives all, with little regard or consideration for rejection, failure, although they'll be waiting. Hurt; watch it unfold like some Thames Great Barrier stopping floods, of tears, of emotion, of heartache. Not to have loved is not to have lived. To love is to live. To find unconditional love is a gateway from the life we love, to move on... "You set me free, I set you free" and so it goes on, the cycles, the circuits, the spinning, the revolving around and around, find the unconditional. Everything must be love, love is life, life is sad. Therefore love is sad too. I accept that.

Eat the Music. Is Kate still after that elusive glimpse into the male soul? Like *Running Up That Hill* II. It has a playfully cruel flavour to it. "Does he conceal, what he really feels... let's split him open" and inside the man is he like woman, like ripe fruit? I picture a woman making love to a man. She's in control, grabbing at him, ripping him open, trying to find his inner depth, or as some would say, his inner weakness. Finding him out, exposing him. And once she's captured this frightened bird, she carefully caresses it, lulling him into a safe area where his exposed soul is safe, so both can share the sacred bird, to tame it, observe it... Eat the music, digest the soul, taste the essence of the "woman at heart".

Moments of Pleasure. Thoughts of death. Why am I alive? Life looks upon her. It has her within its realms. Everything was alright for a while, and then she stopped trusting. Life wants a reconciliation with her. She now feels caught, trapped, frightened, as timid as a captured bird. In its concern, life gives her some gifts from time. He hopes to soothe her, to bring her moments of pleasure. She accepts them, but what was once pleasure has now changed. She tells Life "these gifts are moments of sadness to me now. I feel your grip pinching. How can I trust you?" The Beast of Life, always with claws, withdrawn now, but the potential for hurting is still there. Held within the realms of Life. "Just being alive can really hurt".

The Song of Solomon. I'm not prepared to show my soul. I'm pleading with you, cut the bullshit. I have my own insecurities, why should I have to deal with yours? My soul just needs reviving, revitalise it, feed it. It's deflated, I'm deflated, pump me up. I need life, energy, fill me up, reach the insides of me. Just us two, man and woman, creating energy, our own power station. I'll come and bring energy to you; you'll come and bring energy to me. So just clear the way, forget the past, the future, get it out of the way. I'm hurting, but I need you, your contact, your sexuality. Just give me you, I'll give you me. "Don't want no bullshit, yeah".

Lily. Life, where's the direction? Where's my viewpoint? I admit it, I need help, I can no

Graphic opposite:
Paulina Stuckey

"RED VOODOO"
PAULINA STUCKEY '97

longer help myself. "Life has blown a great big hole through me", I lay myself open. Bringing in the light, bringing down to earth the universal power, the sun coming in. Protection. Lily, white Lily of the Valley, pure white light. Such purity evoking the power of an element associated with the devil, but cure fire with fire? Like with like? (See the film!) The sun, the fire, messenger of the "True spiritual self". This is your space, your energies concentrated, the disc of light hiding your true spiritual self. No entity can harm you. This will bring light to the veil of darkness.

The Red Shoes. I love the stickiness of the sounds on this track. It sounds like feet crushing through fruit, which I know is more the imagery of *Eat the Music*. When I close my eyes and enter into the song and the images it brings, I feel like I'm entering chaos, where the body is taken over. I can just imagine Kate being possessed by the red shoes. Like entering into your own dreams, into a world you have created within yourself, but now it has a separate existence to your power. Now see what power your thoughts, wishes and dreams have. A casualty of your own imagination.

Top of the City. What is it like being not of this world? Can I feel it up here, up high? I really don't know about this track. It's just a great track, as simple as that. It just hasn't created any ripples within the pools of my mind or soul that would relate it to anything I've felt, done, experienced. It is refreshing to find something like that.

Constellation of the Heart. I love it, love it, love it! It's a recipe for recovery, a recipe for life. Look inside for the truth, face the truth, follow your heart. I guess it could be the next chapter in a "you can heal your life" type book. This song is so truthful, so beautiful, and bloody good advice.

Big Stripey Lie. Square boxes, cutting crosses, enclosed as four walls enclose a house. And she falls and she falls, past the realms of sanity, Cutting the crosses that drew the boxes of her life, slashing slashing out. Pain oozed from self-inflicted wounds, cutting the bondage of her only securities. She wants out, the hard way always hurts the most. She knifes, and knifes back towards sanity, a sanity of her own. And for all the ties she cuts, so many more appear to replace them. It's a jungle out there, with wild animals out there. But is it better out there? No longer to be controlled by these square boxes, with the cutting crosses that held her in with straining edges, she's trembling between worlds, holding onto the past, only grasping at the future. An exorcism.

Why Should I Love You? You said "I can't wait for you to go". I said "I'll be gone by Saturday". The anger fell from your face, and was replaced by sad defeat. And in a way it made me feel good, the fatal bullet had been aimed well. The argument was over, both wanting to hold each other, but no. Later in the evening. You said "Can I come in? I want to talk to you". I said "Come in". I was lying, my head on my pillow. We talked and cried and forgave. You stood up, moving closer to me. And I knew just what you were going to do, yet neither moved towards or moved away. We kissed for one moment, both remembered what we'd had. But never again.

"This chapter says put it out of your mind, mmm give it time... Of all the people in the world, why should I (have) love(ed) you?"

You're the One. "It's alright I'll come round when you're not in, and I'll pick up my things". The next evening, after the argument, Sarah didn't come home. She had left a note by the back door saying "If you're wondering where I am, I'm staying with friends. I'll be back on Friday to finish packing, I might see you then".

Friday. With her hand trembling, Sarah put the key in the lock and opened the door. No-one was in. She felt as if she were breaking in. She didn't belong here any more. Walking up the stairs she thought of all the evenings she had spent stripping, scraping and sanding the banisters and skirting boards, in preparation for Laura to decorate, and what was it all for? She couldn't believe how she'd got herself in this destructive relationship that was bound for failure from the beginning. The packing finished, Sarah was on the landing ready to leave, when she heard Laura come in. She didn't venture any further, instead quietly crept back to the bedroom and sat down on the bed. She was shaking at the thought of seeing Laura again within these four walls. At work it was just about bearable, but here...

She heard her clutter about the kitchen making a cup of coffee, then heard her move into the lounge. Heard her playing back messages on the answer-phone; they drifted up through the floorboards into the un-carpeted room, and then she heard his voice. She got up and made her way downstairs. By this time Laura was talking to someone on the phone. Not wanting to confront her, Sarah scrawled a note and quickly left. "Didn't want to disturb you, I'll be picking up my things tomorrow between 9 and 12, I know you'll be working, so 'GOODBYE!' See you around at work. Take good care of yourself. Love Sarah".

The next morning she found Laura had left a list of things to complete before leaving. It ended "Please post the keys through the letter box". Two car loads later, Sarah entered the house that was no longer her home, for the last time. She took a last look around, just for the pain of it. She walked out of the front door, turned around, pulled the door shut and posted the keys back through the letter box...

"I know where I'm going, but I don't want to leave. I just have one problem, we're best friends yeah? We tied ourselves in knots, doing cartwheels 'cross the floor. Just forget it alright... You're the only one I want, you're the only one I want".

Capt'n Flare (Chris Schalkwijk)

It was such a strange feeling. Four years of slow waiting, the agony of all those release dates being postponed over and over again... Finally, somehow I believed that the album would never ever arrive. But what can you do, what other artist can you buy? Looking at all those trays full of CDs, leafing through all those albums... Oh yes, there's a lot of music out there waiting to be sold. But there's always that little problem: no-one sings quite like her. No-one ever does those little things to you... It's just never the same, it's not what you need, not what you're searching for.

Thus, 2nd November, I was standing in the record shop again. With a very strange feeling indeed. There on the shelves high at the back of the counter, there all along the new releases corner... CDs with a big black hole. Astonished, you stare at the picture of those Red Shoes. You blink your eyes, pinch your arms. Blink again... still there!

I slowly walk home. After all those years, I just can't believe it. Jeez, she's made such beautiful albums, giving it all she's got. She's given us so much, everything that really matters. What more could you possibly want? What more could she give and share with us? How could this album contain anything new? I feel the CD in my hand, yet I do not fully comprehend.

First the music looks more straightforward, almost more conventional. There seem to be less weird sound effects, the music seems less outspoken.

But listen carefully. It is as though the musicians have more freedom, more of their own ideas come flowing in. Soon the new disc seems more and more beautiful. The more you play it, the more you feel that this music is made just right. Like a can-opener for the heart. Gently it pushes you towards that voice singing and dancing everywhere between the instruments. And that is where the album is really happening. Slowly that voice grabs you, and begins to tell you a long, long story. Like news from a friend, someone you haven't heard from in years. She tells you about the good and the bad, she shares all with you. Your tears flow before you know it. There's so much to be found. She tells you everything. Four years of life are in there. She opens the door to her heart. All the feelings flow out. Open a little plastic CD box and a real human being steps out. This album will become a very good friend of mine. This one I am going to play many, many times.

Rubberband Girl – Rubberdebubberdebub! For a moment a star can be seen glittering, then she waltzes down to earth, descending on a long white stairway. She's wearing sunglasses, and looks very en vogue. With a big smile and a firm grab on her microphone stand, she struts through her dance hall.

And So Is Love is a very sad song, and yet is so very beautiful. Such a paradox, but so is life. This is the song of those beautiful memories of lost love, of the wanting, of the longing for those arms that slipped away. Clapton's guitar blends perfectly with the moody organ. As the song proceeds, the guitar grows stronger, adding to all those feelings flowing out. Thanks, Eric. Live your life for love, she says. It is all we've got, it's all we need.

Eat the Music is full of vitamins! Papaya, sultanas A, D, bananas are everywhere. A tropical beach sound from the almost frantic twanging on the valiha or similar instruments. A nice slippery bass beneath on the long-necker to rip it up. You like it. But it does sound a bit weird, because the lyrics say otherwise – put your hands in, and rip her heart out. The sound of the choir is harsh, at first it is difficult to understand what they sing. Grab the lyric sheet, fold it out, then follow those lines, and split her open. All is revealed. Maybe she wants to ask "Why do you want to know everything? Why analyse every song, why do you want to find a logical explanation in every line? You rip it to pieces and lose the real emotions". But it all belongs together. Kate is a human being at heart, and we love her for that.

The soothing strings of *Moments of Pleasure* are very beautiful. Those violins act like a time machine, and carry your memories back to you. The warmth in Kate's voice makes you drift into another moment. You were not there when her memories took place, but she conjures up your own thoughts. There is much to look back to on those hills of time. So many faces, so many hearts. So much sunshine, so much rain.

The Song of Solomon is another sad song. Her painful voice is lamenting a lack of understanding: you give me your body, but not your soul. She also sings about her love for him. If only they could share their hearts, she'd come running and would do anything for him. Roomy reverberating sounds weave like a spacey breeze through the background. Maybe she has sampled Paddy's singing bowls from *Lily*, and uses them here for healing the relationship. A-wop-bam-boom – Red Suede Shoes, I guess.

Lily is a poem on life's journey, and then it all takes off. Powerful music kicks you into the second part of the album. She needs protection from the pressures from the outside world. Her Sun is a fire sign, and thus she uses the fire element to draw her pentacle. She kindles the candles in their corners. Flames are burning steadily all around you. Their lights reveal shuddering shadows, flickering fleetingly past the trees surrounding the little open space. Her supple voice recites the names of the Archangels. The circle of fire seems unbreakable. But one of the wavering shadows looms closer. There's a huff and a puff, and suddenly a small black creature is with her in the smokey circle of light. Rrrr!

The Red Shoes is a powerful, steamy Irish tune, complete with tin whistles to chase your blues away. Together with *Constellation of the Heart*, this must be her revenge for *Sledgehammer* at The Wag Club! Well you see, you can't get rid of those red shoes, only by giving them to someone who really wants them. So what do you think is going to happen at the next Kate party/gathering? She's gonna dance you with these songs, she's gonna whirl you up until your legs fall off. You'd better turn the volume up and start practising!

Top of the City might be anywhere... maybe New York, L.A. or Paris... maybe Lebanon or Yugoslavia... That big city is no good. The streets are loveless. A crazy battle for survival rages on. So they grab each other's hands, and run to the top of the city. To hell with the rain. Look at the wisdom of the pigeons – why suffer? One more step... Upon the angels shoulders they fly away.

Constellation of the Heart – Aahh! Now here, here we have real good music! Real good sea-faring brew, serious captain's food. It feels so dancey; the funky guitar reminds me of that old *Le Freak* maxi – I still have it around somewhere. According to *HomeGround*, there are one or two reminders of 'Star Trek'... Thus, imagine an old wooden sailing ship at sea by night. The sails show their age with a multitude of discoloured patches, and many a stain from the salty sea spray. Upon the creaky stern, the flaking name "Enterprise" can just be deciphered. The ship is protected by a small wooden figure at the helm, a fragile woman clad in blue, her arms outstretched to guard the ship as it speeds over the deep dark waters...

In *Big Stripey Lie* I hear a strange, regular creaking sound. And it is coming closer, something is approaching me. I try to wipe the salty water from my eyes, and peer through the cold dark night. On the heaving waves I can make out a wavy white line coming up behind. Slowly an old rowing boat appears from the murky darkness. I see a small person standing at the bow. There comes the woman with the cooking utensils... There goes my arm and leg. Aahhrgg!

Why Should I Love You? – Prince is pretty way out and damned good! I remember when I saw his *Batman* video, with all the bad jokers and funky meanies having a ball. I was instantly impressed. Sort of 'Blackadder' appeal... With this song you immediately rejoice – serious, good, very edible stuff, not the usual immature commercial junk that just makes you throw up. He can be emotional – he's all right. I knew that when he and Kate joined forces to make music, the result would be nothing less than phenomenal.

The music is powerful and sunny, a celebration of new found love. "Why should I love you?" she asks. She marvels at the colours, she feels something is there, something you can't capture in words. The music grows, the organ kicks up the power, the guitar jumps up and dances. Listen, and you'll feel how the music breaks free from the sadness in some of the previous songs. This is beautiful. And would make a great single.

I was not prepared for *You're the One*. You should have warned me. I had to turn it off. Then I cried more than I ever had. Life has not been easy on me, and your song hit me right in the one wound I cannot heal... But you're right I guess, for not hiding the pain. There's wisdom in sharing the good and the bad. Life is about sharing everything, and then you can only gain... So thank you anyway for this song. I can play it now, and yes, it's worth it. There can be beauty even in pain.

Dave Grogan

Rubberband Girl is quite a jolly little number, isn't it? Great for cleaning and doing press-ups to! My first impression was that it just went on and on without really getting there, but that's what the song is really about. It works because Kate uses the repetitiveness to emphasise the meaning of the lyrics. The limitations of being stuck in the mud. You know, nothing ventured, nothing gained.

It's strange, you know, sometimes as soon as you hear a track, there's an automatic connection and you know it will be a favourite. I knew this even before Kate sang a note on *And So Is Love*. I love the melody, lyrics and vocals, and the way Clapton's guitar flashes like a bolt of Summer lightning. When you're young you never think about getting older; a day seems to last forever and naturally you grow up relating your whole life to this philosophy. You think that love lasts forever too, but when you're older you learn about life and realise that it doesn't. "Life is sad and so is love". Life doesn't last forever, nor does love. No matter how much you love someone, there is no guarantee they will always be with you. As in a relationship breakdown. As in Death.

I love the laid back lyrics of *Eat the Music*. I like listening to this really loud (stuff the neighbours!) A celebration of life. I like the comparisons between people and fruit; both have skin and mushy insides. I'd never seen myself as a pomegranate before! It reminds me that "There's a woman in every man and a man in every woman"! Kate looks at it from a woman's viewpoint. Being gay, people have told me that I'm a woman at heart. I think this applies to a lot of men, though I think gay men have different egos to many straight men. One of the main points about coming to terms with being gay is honesty. Gays are not afraid to show the feminine aspects of their nature, at least not as much as most straight men, who are expected to stand rigid (forgive the pun) in society's norms.

Vocally and musically *Moments of Pleasure* is

second to none. I'm not surprised that it wasn't a massive hit. I think the problem lies in the meaning of the song. I have nothing but admiration for Kate in baring herself to the world, but I feel that in doing so she lets the song down a little. I just wish I knew the joke about George the wipe!

I love *The Song of Solomon*. The Trio Bulgarka are excellent and Kate's little squeals at the beginning of every "I'll do it for you" make my hair stand on end. I love the idea of having someone's sexuality but none of the crap that comes with it. A lover arrives as a package deal! You love the person you see, you love what you have learned about them since you met, but you don't know everything about their past. I think everyone has got at least one shadow in their past, one regret (I know I have!) So you get the love, sex and closeness of that person but you also get the hidden problems. Is there any such thing as true love?

It is uncanny how much *Lily* relates to my own life. It's almost as if Kate wrote this for me! Scoff if you like. I won't go into detail here but between 29th September and last Christmas I had terrible experiences with a ghost. The narration on this song sounds as near to her voice as anyone's going to get. To start with I recorded my CD to tape cutting it out. It is hard to talk about this without sounding melodramatic, but when I think back to this time last year I think myself luck not to be in a mental home. When your doctor is prescribing sedatives that aren't working, you're in tears at work and you're finding yourself armed with duvet and alarm clock heading for your parents' house in the middle of the night, you know there's something wrong! Anyway, I reluctantly called up a medium who taught me how to protect myself with a dome shaped bubble. It sounds strange, but this worked better than anything from the doc! This song is very special to me.

Ooh! What it would be to see and hear Kate perform *The Red Shoes* live! She manages to somehow reproduce her own unique version of Irish folk music in the instrumentation and arrangements of some songs. The same applies here. I love the way this track builds into a kind of frenzy, akin to *The Big Sky*. I wish it finished properly rather than faded; it would have been more dramatic.

I was unsure of *Top of the City* at first. I found the arrangement a little bland, but after several plays I now really like it. I love the strength in Kate's voice – "I don't know if you'll love me for it" I can't help but wonder that with Hannah's death, does Kate see the top of the city as the closest place to Heaven – to be with her?

After initially thinking that *Constellation of the Heart* stuck out like a sore thumb, it has now become one of my favourites. Life is a journey through time and space, your body is your spaceship, your mind is your captain. Instead of looking out for answers, look inside yourself. Face your own destiny instead of letting someone else face it for you. Be in charge of yourself, be positive and you'll get there. "It's gonna be beautiful".

Big Stripey Lie – what a confused, frightening nightmare. My Mum always says "Even a good liar needs a good memory!" I wonder if Kate refers to something similar when she sings "Oh big stripey lie, like a wavy line, coming up behind". Is this a liar being caught out because they've not remembered what they've lied about and changed the story? This track wouldn't have sounded out of place on *The Ninth Wave*. There's so much atmosphere.

I love the Trio on *Why Should I Love You?* and the way it starts whimsically. I find the chorus a little mundane, but it is quite a commercial sound – a possible single perhaps? I admire and respect Prince as an artist but I don't connect with his style. Someone with Kate's talent doesn't need to collaborate with anyone to achieve first class results. It does lend a different musical perspective to the album. Perhaps if Lenny Henry had spoken the lyrics (in a similar way to John Carder Bush on *Jig of Life*) to the backing harmonies of Kate and the Trio, it may have been more effective. Despite pulling the song to bits, I do like it!

You're the One is a definite favourite. No introduction, Kate just gets straight in there doesn't she. Honest and straightforward. I love the Hammond organ, it blends perfectly with the Trio. Love can be so difficult to find. Sometimes we're in love with the idea of being in love. Sometimes we think we're in love but a better looking, sexier model comes on the scene. Sometimes we do perhaps fall 100% in love but does your partner feel the same? If he or she loves you 100% back would the relationship not suffocate through jealousy and possessiveness? This song deals so sensitively with the devastation of the typical relationship breakdown, and the picking up the pieces of your life. This has never happened to me, but then I can't say I have ever found true love. Am I lucky or should I be sad?

I love the album. Kate's voice has matured so much, it is just stunning on some of the songs, BUT – I wish she had used it more as a vocal instrument, as on *Hounds of Love*. I think this is one of the reasons why *Hounds of Love* was such a huge success, with those wonderful howls through *Mother Stands for Comfort*, and the mocking barks on *Hounds of Love*, not to mention the way she converted her voice to something similar to a drum machine on *The Big Sky*. In this respect *The Red Shoes* isn't as inventive, but Kate still keeps the originality and genius we know her for, and that wonderful imagery – "Feel your hair come tumbling down, Feel your feet start kissing the ground, Feel your arms are opening out, And see your eyes are lifted to God" – what a great way to describe someone possessed.

I have no doubt that the album will keep us all more than happy until the next one and beyond. God, I still play *The Kick Inside* to death! Kate really is a friend for life isn't she? Did Leonardo De Vinci know what a great artist he was? Do you think that Kate truly realises what a genius she is?

Jayne in Australia

The circle opens and the dance begins. Hands-on, sticky, juicy and REAL – to me, this is Kate as never before. She's left that "leafy vacuum and shares with heart"; the music has stepped right off the page and into living, breathing, sensual life.

From reading others' thoughts on *The Red Shoes*, I've felt that some people are perhaps looking with half-open eyes, or eyes cast backwards to some other old, well-worn patterns, and therefore are looking through this album rather than at it. I was guilty of this myself when I heard the first single, but now, more than ever, as it has wrapped itself around my body and into my consciousness, I see how wrong I was.

Hiding on the mid-tempo dance floor of *Rubberband Girl*, among the incredible bouncy-string keyboards, addictive bass and spaghetti-wriggly guitar solos, is an incredible metaphor for bravery and conviction. Spring back! Snap right into your real shape! Bend for trouble like a sapling! If you can yell loud enough you'll convince yourself – and everyone who's hurt you. This is funked-up hero(ine)ism, a true song of courage. And those Rubberband vocals are magnificent.

And So Is Love couldn't be more different – another brilliant aspect of this album: complete diversity. Clapton's weeping guitar shedding petals like a dying rose over the desert of the windy keyboards. And the vocals – the wail of "And so is LOVE" – a voice crying in the wilderness, calling to the other angels and demons and hells and heavens on the album. Heartbreaking.

A Celtic jig dressed up in Carribean sunshine, all juice and fruit and flesh. How can anyone call this a 'filler'?! *Eat the Music* may sound like a tropical frolic, but those lyrics tell all; erotic, intimate, joyous, edible words, taking in all those sexual allusions – the fruit of our loins; the way to a man's heart is through his stomach. MMMmm, delicious!

Musically, *Moments of Pleasure* sounds like classic Kate – sweeping strings filling out the gentle piano. The vocals reach emotional heights beyond most singers' wildest dreams. Even "reaching out for Mama" and "all the things I should have done but I didn't" pale beside that unbelievable "look just like mountains through the snow". The lyrics have changed though: airy metaphors have gone, and this is a real life Kate who's seen New York, and Michael Powell, air-plane aisles and felt the loss of friends. It's delicacy belies the emotional, devastating, heart-wrenching feelings it contains.

And then... hmmm. Mystery. But what more beautiful puzzle than *The Song of Solomon*, smoking like incense among the biblical harp and the Trio's voices, would be possible to find. Maybe it is appropriate, considering the strange romantic nature of the original book. That beautiful pause before "And I'll do it for you", then those beautiful (cheeky!) biblical references, all the way through to that quintessential rock'n'roll nonsense "a-wop-bam-boom", sounding almost sacred. I wonder how many people went to look at the Old Testament after hearing this?..."Come away, my lover, and be like a gazelle or like a young stag on the spice-laden mountains" (8:14) Mmmmh, yes.

Is *Lily* any relation to Clarissa Pinkola Estes La Que Sabe, the wise grandmother who knows everything and speaks to every woman? I love the way her solemn voice comes out of the humming, fire-whip sounds, as though she is speaking from the heart of the universe. And the grungey, loop-drum sound of the rest of the song is magnificent – a slow walk through a fiery heaven with God's archangels. The circle of protection, spiritual bodyguards. *Lily* is a companion piece to *Rubberband Girl* when it comes to celebrating strength in the face of fear. Listen to Kate growl in the bridge if you don't believe me!

The title track, amid the classic fairy story, might as well be subtitled "Why I love to dance". Everything about this song – the jiggling mandola and the whipping rhythms – tells a story of uncontrollable dance, both in words and music. Anybody who has ever loved dancing will immediately understand this song, even if they had never heard the folk tale. It speaks so simply, so magically and so Irish-ly. Dance the dream. At last – "It's really happening to ya!" Enchanting, dangerous, musical magic.

Top of the City is almost a return to classic Kate mode of her late '80s sound. Emotional, almost filmic. Doesn't everybody have a secret place to look down from? But to be deserted by someone with whom you'd shared that place could break your heart. If only I could take him back there again, maybe everything would turn out right. The soft, yearning piano steps of the chorus give way to the hectic cityscape of the verse. If only I could escape...

So she turns back the clock and escapes to the stars. Intergalactic Cruiser Bush Seven is headed for a *Constellation of the Heart*, and Captain Kate is asleep at the controls. The funky disco rhythms, the groovy guitar and those wonderful shiny keyboards make this song so much fun, and the crew-to-captain/heart-to-brain dialogues are amazing. Love has appeared up ahead, and it is scary-looking, but we've gotta go through – it might hurt, but it could be paradise. Beam me

Graphic: Alex Lake

up!

Suddenly those grungey drums and distorted guitar are back. *Big Stripey Lie* is like a small but powerful demon, just waiting to catch you before you think you're safe. It sounds like an electronic nightmare, a hand reaching out for help, drowning in computerised lies or lost in a maze of scary virtual reality. Short, compact, frightening, electrifying.

The door from this hell leads straight to heaven, and heavenly is the perfect way to describe *Why Should I Love You?* It is a dance party in a cathedral, a wonderful fresh feeling of starting over and allowing somebody new into your heart. The choral voices of the Trio, as Kate serenely reads words of wisdom – then the sudden snap of the snare drum that brings that wonderfully fizzy Prince sound – pop heaven. The sparkly keyboard meets the tranquil church organ head on, the guitars groove, and the whole congregation is celebrating. Mmm – Hallelujah.

You're the One bored me until I realised I was looking at the song, and not through it, to the clever way Kate has used the bluesy form. *You're the One* reaches new dimensions of heartbreak, a devastating soul wail that could drive you crazy. Soft chords and humming organ connect with that lazy drumbeat like sighs of misery, and despair so deep it is almost surreal. I imagine what it would be like to cry until you drowned in your own tears. "We're best friends, yeah?" is possibly the most agonising lyric I have ever heard. Keep away from sharp objects at all times when listening to this one.

The Red Shoes is not an album of lightness or delicacy, it's not even a safe album. You can't let it wash over your mind like *The Kick Inside* or even *The Sensual World*. It is REAL, to stick your hands in, roll around in, a wonderful gift of pain and recovery that we can all use. Eat me, drink me – see how it transforms you. This is an album to use, to feel. It's delicious, sticky, juicy, sensual, divine and earthy all at once. Eat this music! Thank you, Kate.

Ruth Steadman

Issue 53: August 1994

A confusion of colour spins before me as I watch Indian women perform their traditional folk dances to the music of their lives. When I first heard *The Red Shoes*, I wanted to write about it, yet I couldn't. It was not the right time or something, despite how much I loved it. But now so much has changed, and the experience of the album has become unique and on a parallel to my life of today. It seems bizarre that half way round the world I have discovered a new understanding and inspiration, but perhaps that is just so.

For several weeks before I came away, all I could think of was the life I would be leaving behind, and just how long six months really was. I was numb to the voices of friends telling me how wonderful it would all be and how brave I was. Yet at the same time I felt extremely positive. Everyone was watching me. For generations, members of my family have wished to travel to India, and here I was, the first to succeed. I felt proud, and yes, perhaps brave. I remember turning to my mother and father the night before I left, quoting:

> "*Just put your feet down, child*
> *The water is only waist high...*"

It was a shared moment. I saw it in my parents eyes. We were all thinking "Yes it is time. This little child has grown and we must all let go". This is the only way in which I can be free to return. And the love that I feel now only proves how true this is. So what has this got to do with Kate's *Red Shoes* album?

Rubberband Girl – I feel this elastic within me, the one that pulls with emotion, and hell, it's been wrenched! And now it has its biggest test so far... will it snap? No, this rubberband reaches thousands of miles round the world, connecting me with my loved ones and bearing all the pressure of separation. And each day experienced is like a new mark accepted; we learn and we grow. When the time is right I shall return home with my rubberband (a little stretched as rubberbands get) and I shall read them the stories of my piece of elastic – "Back on my feet".

How much emotion can one person bear in one lifetime? "Life is sad and so is love" Yes it is. Nothing else in all the world causes so much pain. Pain in all its guises can eventually be rooted back to love. I have met a lovely Indian gentleman who studied (amongst other things) Astrology, and from knowing my date of birth, read me the tales of my life. He told me that I loved my family so very dearly, and that I do, and now I am realising it is just that love which has caused me so much anguish. Yet love is so wonderful – I see lepers and beggars everyday here and their very existence depends on the love they have for one another. Life is sad but there is love. "It's all we've got, isn't that enough?"

To *Eat the* (people's) *Music* of such a beautiful land, to fall asleep to the exotic sound of pan pipes and the snake charmer's flute. Here men walk the streets hand in hand with no inhibitions or fear, everyone is respected for who they are (and there are negligible incidents of rape). Someone said to me the other day, "We see each other's feelings" and they do, as visibly as the opened coconuts on the street stalls... This isn't really what I wanted to say, but I love this song, and it reminds me of the day my father unashamedly cried in front of me... "Not only women bleed".

Is it the *Moments of Pleasure* that hurt the most or those of pain? I remember standing on the beach one winter's night with a friend, silently letting tears fall to the sand, so beautiful that it hurt. And then sitting on some mountain path watching the Himalayan peaks rise above the mist. A small beggar child kisses my friend's hand in New Delhi. And we laugh as a monkey attacks my shirt. When I first heard *Moments of Pleasure*, I could never have known the times it would take me back to, nor those people in my life now to which this song is so closely linked. And then there is the line "Just being alive, it can really hurt" – I'm sitting here in this place so very far from home and I remember times spent with my family before I came away; sitting with my father in our beautiful garden, playing (and trying to explain) *The Red Shoes* in the car to my mother (she actually quite liked it!) and our "last cigarette" that lasted so long, all of us sitting in the kitchen before driving down from Carlisle to Heathrow for my flight... These moments are so very special to me now, so much so that they do hurt when I see the distance between myself and their roots. This is a song anyone can identify with, and for me it has become my Song of India, of the whole experience – before, during and no doubt, after.

The *Song of Solomon* I shall probably never understand. All I know is that right from the start it has been my favourite track on the album. Something about that line "And I'll do it for you" just makes me weep. Now as I look at that same line, and those that follow, I find myself once again thinking of my family and that relationship. Once upon a time I felt I had to hold them all together and felt only exhaustion in doing that, but now as I picture my little home I so badly want to sacrifice all as proof of my love, and with the power in Kate's voice here – the urgency, the need to have my loved ones next to me, is almost unbearable. Yes, perhaps even India – I'm doing that for you, and see now how I recognise the love? I can't say any more than that.

Although I have no idea who *Lily* is, I feel that these words at the beginning of this song are those of the path of self-discovery "That we may know the Truth". Origen, in Leviticum Homiliae states "You yourself are even another little world and have within you the Sun and the Moon and the Stars" and that path ultimately leads to the Point of Total Return, as in the words of Jung "The Life of Man is a journey... how in the beginning man at his best is outward bound only in order to return from across the seven oceans the inward way from where he started and to see the place for the first time".

To me *Lily* is so similar to *Constellation of the Heart* and in both songs we can see the tremendous element of fear, embarking on such a journey, of truly experiencing and understanding our lives. And how that can hurt – "Life has blown a great big hole in me" but through that hole we can see ourselves and learn how to build, protected by that "circle of fire". I see now this is my quest for knowledge and how scary that is in this strange and foreign land, but oh, how wonderful!

It is very difficult for me to disassociate *The Red Shoes* from the 1994 Convention (and wasn't it fantastic!). But personally speaking this is the song of one morning in July when I woke up and suddenly realised "Shit! Life is fantastic!!" It was as though overnight someone had placed these Red Shoes on my feet, and now after all the pain, the tears of watching others enjoying living, after all that darkness, I was waking to "Dance the dream". I thought of these lines:

"It's gonna be the way you always thought it would be
But it's gonna be no illusion,
Oh it's gonna be the way you always dreamt about it
But it's gonna be really happening to ya..."

And oh my God, I'd left school and all those petty rules that had tied me down, and I was going to India... life now was like I never dared believe it could be. And I was happy. So yes, maybe it is a little dangerous, but what is life without risk? Yes "You can dance... having the time of your life!" (where did Abba suddenly spring up from?)

Top of the City was the song that first made me want to write something about the album, as it seems to be my position here in India. I am sitting on a veranda watching such a beautiful sunset... a haven of Westerners, smoking, drinking, talking... I look down. Small squalid 'buildings' cling like cardboard boxes to the hillside. The noise of traffic on the too-worn roads is so bloody noisy, and oh how many buses have lost control on those steep corners and been sent crashing over the edge. Death. Smells of the piles of rotting afternoon rubbish, and too much spice, makes my nostrils curl. As Westerners we walk these streets "on the angels shoulders", the stares we receive are laced with awe, we feel famous... "closer to Heaven"... Take a rest from emotion, climb away from my heart and soul, from the mess of feeling, "Take me up to the top of the city" to my head. I can only think here, I can't be touched, I won't feel a thing. "And I don't mind if it's dangerous". Yes, I probably have become callous, cold. My brain teaches me the logic – if you give to one beggar you must give to all – you just can't. I need to escape from what I see and what I feel, looking up for the ladder... "It looks like hell down there".

Constellation of the Heart came bouncing into my head while I was in the plane flying over the Middle East somewhere. Looking out of the window, the clouds were as far below me as they usually are above, and somehow everything seemed reversed. It all became very introspective, looking at myself, my journey. In my mind the pilots had become like some obscure mix of the pilots out of some naff aeroplane disaster movie and the 'Muppets'! I felt drunk with jet-lag, but every so often I would twitch and wake up thinking "What the fuck am I doing? What's going on? I wanna go home. I can't bear the thought of being away for all that time". Needless to say, the flight continued (for fifteen and a half hours!) and now I see that as a kind of doorway through which I can explore the memorabilia of my eighteen year long life, the good and the bad. Although it is a difficult process, I know "It's gonna be wonderful!"

When contemplating writing about *The Red Shoes* in context with my feelings here in India, I realised that *Big Stripey Lie* would create a problem – that was then. Now I shall never hear this song without remembering the experience of today; I came up to my room this morning only to find it completely overturned with many obscure items missing. The lines "Oh my God, it's a jungle in here, You've got wild animals loose in here" could refer to the mass of complexities in someone's subconscious, but in this case they took on their literal meaning! Four bastard monkeys had got in through the window and were now thoroughly enjoying themselves on the roof outside with much of the small amount of stuff I had with me. I should give them credit for taste, since among their 'choices' were Anais Nin's *Henry and June* (although on closer inspection they obviously weren't too keen as it ended up in shreds) and the *Hounds of Love* tape (which thankfully I managed to retrieve). So there I stood, utterly helpless as batteries and papers and things flew from the hands of one evil beast to another. My only consolation (or perhaps it was revenge) came when I thought of the lethal cocktail of medication that the animals had consumed, but it did little for my shock and later despair when I realised what I had lost (not to mention anger at myself for having left the window open).

But to bring this all back to the song, I couldn't help but realise that if you do leave your mental crap around the place, and visibly so, eventually those vultures, those "wild animals", those demons will descend and make you their prey.

There are sadly, people in this world, manipulators, tricksters who make their move when you're at your weakest – full of charm, just as the monkeys appeared so cute. "Big stripey lies... coming up behind"... it is only then that you realise the strength and power of true concern (thank you, my family and friends).

Why Should I Love You? – God this is difficult. How much bloody pain has there been. I can't even acknowledge the number of times I've cried 'cos of you, there have been that many. And how those scars have hurt and bled. You caused my work to suffer, you made me so very ill, you tore me apart. So why do I think of you now, see your faces in the photographs on my wall, and feel the tears stinging my eyes? And once again I'm thinking of my arrival at Heathrow, walking through the gates to you and your open arms – it makes me cry so very hard, I so badly want to be with you all again... I know that you'll be waiting – "The 'I' that loves you". And that's just it – our love that's twisted and pierced and screwed us into anguish. Can we all be friends now. Please? "This chapter says..."

You're the One... I want to dedicate this review to my family, and oh how precious you all are. Can you see now this love of ours that we held in all the wrong places. So much wasted energy. The day that you let me go, look how important it was. It's true what they say about absence, yet it is bizarre that it's taken me thousands of miles to understand. Now let us build.

This is also for a very special friend without whom I doubt I would have ever got this far, let alone braved coming to India (you didn't have to push me onto the plane though, did you?!) I owe you so much. Thank you. I love you all better now.

Some people may resent what I have written here, perhaps I wouldn't blame them. *The Red Shoes* is such a beautiful piece of work and I'd hate for it to appear that I'd used it purely as a means of expressing myself. This album is the product of sheer genius in craftsmanship, in every little element. Above all I want to stress how much I appreciate that. It just felt right to express it as I have.

Doug Alan

For this momentous work, in addition to reviewing each song, I also assign a letter grade to each song on a scale from A+ to F. The grades are B/C centred on Kate's average song quality. A grade of C for a track by Kate might be a grade of A+ for some other artist. For your convenience and correlation I will mention that I would give songs such as *Get Out of My House*, *Night of the Swallow*, *Under the Ivy*, and *Jig of Life* grades of A+. *Don't Push Your Foot on the Heart Brake* and *Army Dreamers* would get grades of C+ and B-, respectively. *Reaching Out* would get an F.

The album opens with *Rubberband Girl*, a song that reminds me a bit of *The Big Sky*, both musically and thematically. Like *The Big Sky* it is a seemingly fun, silly song that is really about a serious topic: the ways in which we cope with hurdles in life. Both songs also feature sections where Kate goes wild with her vocals. *Rubberband Girl* also features some cool ersatz Bulgarian singing by Kate, "rub a dub a dub". Unfortunately, when I listen to this track, it mostly makes me want to put on *The Big Sky*. Grade: B-

Eric Clapton does not disappoint us on *And So Is Love*. His guitar adds significantly to the profoundly melancholy feel of this song. Most of the lyrics are rather trite, but the music is not at all. It is very heartfelt. This is classic mellow Kate, *Symphony in Blue* for the '90s, featuring exquisite emotive Kate sounds and a perfect Kate ending. Grade: A (95)

Despite Kate's assertions that she feels only love and gratitude towards her fans, in *Eat the Music* she again comes up with the kind of imagery ("split me open with devotion") you would expect from someone who is quite nervous about being idolised. A previous example of this is the song *Hounds of Love* ("the hounds of love are hunting"). Just as in the song *Hounds of Love*, a fear of fans is not what the song is really about, however. Both songs are about the intensity of feelings, both positive and negative that arise when two people are in love. In *Eat the Music*, the two lovers are willing to open themselves up completely to each other, but the imagery of splitting open and tearing guts out accurately conveys the scariness of making oneself vulnerable. The song portrays more of the positive aspects of relationships than *Hounds of Love* does, and alludes to the joyous messy stickiness of sex with compelling metaphor.

Despite sophisticated, rich lyrics, the song fails because of the music. The background vocals in *Eat the Music* are interesting, but the horn section is annoying. The song is repetitive, and strives to be hypnotic, in the way that tribal drumming often is. Unfortunately, there is no tribal drumming to be heard, and the music just bores. Grade: C-

Moments of Pleasure is a gentler translation of

that song that goes "These are friends of mine who died, died!" The imagery is very personal, but specific and resonant. It would be better without the schmaltzy orchestral backing. Despite its heartfeltness, it makes me want to listen to *Under the Ivy*. Grade: B

From the strange soft sounds at the beginning, to the muted, distorted "a wop-bam-boom" at the end, *The Song of Solomon* is nearly perfect. Musically, it starts out as a sexual lullaby and builds to a torrent of passion - just like a good time in bed. Wonderfully emotive Kate sounds are the whipped cream.

The story is of a woman paraphrasing part of the biblical *Song of Solomon*; she doesn't want the complications that come along with a relationship, she just wants the spiritual and sexual pleasure of making love. The end of the song, however, finds her turning about and pledging her eternal fealty to her lover. It turns out that the heart won't allow the sexuality without the emotional bullshit. Stunning! This is the only song on the album where satisfactory use of The Trio Bulgarka is made. Grade: A (98.5)

Lily has more great emotive Kate sounds. An army of Kate's singing in harmony with different voices. Awesome! This is Kate doing her own unique brand of funk. It's Katefunk! The story isn't quite self-contained, however. The movie, I am sure will make things clearer, but as it is we can tell that the song describes a magical spell of protection: "This is my space". Grade: A (97)

The Red Shoes tells of the tragic fairy tale of The Red Shoes sung as a jolly Irish ditty. It has some charm, but it just doesn't work for me. There's no emotional resonance. Grade: B-

Top of the City starts and stops in fits. The arrangement and Kate's voice change abruptly. I think that Kate's been listening to too much '70s Progressive Rock (e.g. ELP, Genesis, Yes). I didn't think it was all that great the first time around, and it's not all that great this time around either. The story: Kate's beau is apparently out with another woman. Kate wants to go to the tallest building in town and hope that he will see her up there and climb the ladder she offers him. The plot, which is stolen from an archetype of cheesy fifties movies, is not without its charm, but this song won't get him to climb that ladder. Grade: B-

Kate gets real funky on *Constellation of the Heart*. Has she been listening to Funkadelic? Or maybe it was just Paula Abdul. Well, who cares? This silly pop ditty is trés catchy and funks home its message with classic clever-Kate imagery. Travel with Kate, Captain Kirk, and Jean-Luc Picard on an ongoing mission to where all of us fear to trek... inner space. Your conclusion, Spock? One doesn't need to read the horoscope to figure out her love life - she has to do the dirty work herself, by looking inside her heart, but "just being alive, it can really hurt". Kate slips in two self-references: *The Big Sky* and "the woman with the key" (alluding to the cover of *The Dreaming*). These two references prove that the constellation of the heart orbits around *The Dreaming* and *Hounds of Love*. Grade: A-

Big Stripey Lie is all rusty swing, crunching guitar, feedback, and shit-loads of passion. It is everything music should be. Kate sings a devastating combination of patient, reasoned discussion, and unrestrained wailing. Nigel Kennedy's violin is the final touch that makes this track a true masterpiece. *Big Stripey Lie* is about someone who is depressed and scared of love. The narrator offers herself as a buoy in the ocean of life's grief. The lie is that all of one's youthful dreams must drown in this ocean. We can keep our heads above the waves with some help.

Big Stripey Lie is the kind of song that seems to come around only once every several years. You hear it and for a few minutes it's as if you had forgotten how to see colours, you had been living so long in a monochrome world that you had forgotten how to see them, and now the smoky film has momentarily been removed from your eyes, and you can see beautiful colours in all their glory again. The colours are so beautiful and bright that they hurt and it makes you cry, but you wouldn't trade this moment for anything. Then the song ends and the colours fade again to monochrome. Over the next few weeks, you listen to the song again and again, and each time it is another wonderful experience, but each time, as the song becomes more familiar, the colours get less intense, until eventually all you are left with is a joyful memory of the colours. Then you begin the long wait for another song, which may come in a few years, or may never come at all, that will bring the colours back. And, ironically, you are not sure whether or not you would be happier with or without the memory and knowledge of those beautiful colours. But this is what life is all about. Grade: A+ (100)

The first time I heard *Why Should I Love You?*, I thought that [insert bisexuality symbol here] had ruined what might have otherwise been a good song. Well, after listening to it some more, I've concluded that it's still a good song, but I'd still prefer to have heard what Kate might have done by herself. Then again, a failed experiment might be better than none at all. Unfortunately, the Trio are wasted here. Has Kate gone Christian on us? There's a lot of Christian references on this album. I'm not sure what purple, red, and grey have to with anything. Or why it's the "O" of the Host. But it sounds nice. Grade: B-

You're the One is boring! You'd think if Kate went through something really bad, she'd write something intense and powerful. Well, not this time, baby. The Trio are wasted again, unlike on *The Sensual World*, where they were used to perfection. *You're the One* is slow and plodding, completely predictable. There are some musical references to Pink Floyd and The Beatles, which is a laudable goal, but they just don't save this stinker. Send Jeff Beck and his clichéd '70s sounding guitar from whence they came. What a bad way to end an album. Real bad. Grade: F

So... Overall it's a very good album. (The GPA for this album is 85, a solid B). Would you expect anything less from Kate? But if you were expecting something approaching the dazzling heights Kate set on *The Dreaming* and *Hounds of Love*, you will be disappointed. Yes, there are glimpses of that stunning perfection, but there are also moments of mediocrity. Kate, I guess, is following the path of most great musicians: (1) Early, flawed material filled with promise and hints of brilliance. (2) A golden period, while the musician is still young, where she wants to blaze her own unique path in the world. During this period a musician will create her best, most stunning works. (3) A plateaued period that remains for the rest of the artist's life. During this period, the artist has grown weary of the emotional drain of always striving for something daring, something new, and settles down into a comfortable niche, creating works of excellence, but missing some of the passion and magic of the golden period. I think that Kate is in stage (3), and who can really complain about that, since it happens to all musicians and still can yield wonderful music. Secretly, however, I hope that Kate at some point will make an unprecedented swoop back to stage (2). *Big Stripey Lie* proves that the embers of stage (2) are still there, glowing quietly inside.

Issue 55: April 1995

Eike Brunhober

"You must love in order to be able to play."
Louis Armstrong.

It is always useful to begin an essay with a quote from a wise man. But considering that I shall write about Kate's album *The Red Shoes*, it occurs to me that the quotation above should be supplemented: "You must also love to be able to listen".

"If music be the food of love, play on". Not only *Eat the Music* and the album cover refer to Shakespeare, so does the whole album in a way. And even before *The Red Shoes* with its emotional, sensitive songs and lively grooves, we already know that Kate Bush is one of the 'loving musicians', as Louis Armstrong would call them.

I really like this album. But I must admit that I don't like it as much as *The Dreaming*, an album I use to compare nearly every other album I listen to, especially Kate's own creations. I can't help doing so because *The Dreaming* is by far one of the most fascinating and stunning albums I have ever heard and will ever hear.

At the age of about eight, I was forced to play the recorder and to learn about music. Like most of the guys at that age, I didn't get a buzz out of the recorder and at the age of ten I refused to continue my musical career. It was Peter Gabriel's fourth album and *The Dreaming* that made me learn the piano at the age of sixteen, and bass at twenty. I felt that the chords I had detested in my early days, were some of the most exciting things in life, and today at the age of twenty three, it repels me to have started to play music at the late age of sixteen.

"This album was made to be played loud" it proclaims on the inner cover of *The Dreaming*. Play it loud, 'loving', passionate and wilful listener, play it loud as a means of shouting out all your frustrations, fears and disappointments in a world where financial success has reached even a religious status, in a world where adjustment and assiduity are praised as a sensible and steady life, in a world whose people mainly care about scratches on their cars and talk about how many miles they get to a gallon. *The Dreaming* is an album that I can only hear whilst standing. The adrenaline spins and the hands start to sweat.

Perhaps *The Red Shoes* ought not be compared to Kate's earlier masterpiece because it is probably meant to be more playful and less of a mystery. But despite the fact that Kate's voice on the new album is as fascinating as ever and the lyrics are really great (as ever), I do think that *The Dreaming* has more passion and intensity. It's more complex song structures and instrumentation show even more love for the detail and experiments with sound. The music interprets the lyrics to a higher degree than on *The Red Shoes*. The compositions are full of tone painting (*The Dreaming*, *Pull Out the Pin*); the bass is used as an instrument of melody that creates moods and atmosphere (*All the Love*, *Houdini*); the keyboards and piano reflect the mood of the lyrics (the dissonant keyboard playing at the end of *Pull Out the Pin* referring to the horrors of the Vietnam war).

On *The Red Shoes* most of the song structures are similar and there are more repetitions. The bass is often restricting itself to just give the harmonic foundation, the guitars are often just to play repeated patterns and the keyboards to give a sound foundation of chords. The best moments of the album are where Kate presents her best composing qualities: expressive instrumentation to reflect and interpret the moods and themes of her even more expressive voice and lyrics. There is the depressive keyboard playing and reserved instrumental activities of *Song of Solomon*; the restless and heart-stirring guitar in *And So Is Love*; the sudden dynamic changes in *Top of the City* alluding to the sudden emotional changes of the character in the song.

Maybe Kate was worried that her original composing style of *Never For Ever*, *The Dreaming* and *Hounds of Love* with their expression of human voice, eccentric laughter, screaming, and the variety of different sounds would become outworn after a while. I think that while developing her song-writing style, Kate ought not to neglect that love of hers for experimenting that gives us such wonderful albums as the three mentioned above, and song like *Big Stripey Lie* and films like *The Line, the Cross & the Curve*. Let us look forward to the next Kate album. Music is the food of love. Play on, Kate.

Anthony Ingram

I thought the album cover very sweet until I saw the blood the next time I looked. My wife noticed the blood straight away, and woke up one morning and told me out of the blue that the album cover was disturbing her. As with all Kate's albums, we see and hear a little bit of magic. This album reminds me of Pandora's Box in a way that is hard to explain. *The Red Shoes* itself conjures up images of magic and spells that seem unapparent in my life now. I'm getting older you see, like you. It is nice to be sent back in time just a little now and then.

I had been working all day so was not in the best mental state. My wife passed me the cassette and we went up the long mountain, turned off the car engine and listened. As with the preceding albums another triumph of glowing warmth and harmony, nothing misplaced, nothing wasted. Seemingly as perfect as the view from our steamy windowed car.

I love the simplicity of *Rubberband Girl* and the amazing vocal trick which I stupidly thought was a harmonica. I heard *And So Is Love* on the radio before the album was released. Simon Bates had played it by mistake (instead of *Eat the Music*). I can still remember the place where I first heard it. It is a very erotic song for me. I really like that windy pipe sound and the ending.

Eat the Music comes from a sunshine state and is very uplifting and colourful. I could certainly live there surrounded by all that fruit! *Moments of Pleasure* is very melodic and unique. I love the deep string sound and the piano. Mrs. Bush would have liked this. In fact I'm sure she does.

I love the backing harmonies of *The Song of Solomon*, and the tired perplexed sound of Kate's vocals. *Lily* is my wife's favourite. *The Red Shoes* is folky and very catchy. I love the vocals on this.

There is so much space in *Top of the City*. She had to be somewhere up high. *Constellation of the Heart* sounds great in the car. Very bouncy. As a contrast *Big Stripey Lie* is a mind-blowing, multi-layered collage of mental agony.

I love those Bulgarians so much on *Why Should I Love You?* A very clever song. *You're the One* is sweet and sour, with many hidden depths. I try hard now not to delve too deeply into the content of Kate's music. It can become distorted and misinterpreted.

Tarsam Singh-Khela

A sufficient length of time has passed from the first listening to *The Red Shoes* for me to have formed a 'constant' opinion of the album. I stress 'constant' because over the past few weeks my views have ranged from utter love to complete loathing and back again. Suffice to say, it has been a difficult album to come to terms with, but now I feel I 'know' the album well enough to offer a review. I should start by saying I profoundly dislike (I hate to say hate!) both *Eat the Music* and *Rubberband Girl*. *Eat the Music* is clichéd and overblown. The blend of instrumentation just doesn't work for me. The lyrics, are beautiful and evocative but the song would have been vastly improved if it had been realised in a simpler manner. Maybe with just a piano, accompanied by Celtic strings.

Graphic: Paulina Stuckey

Rubberband Girl is my least favourite track. It took me ages to be able to just listen to it without flinching. The music is sterile and boring, and is in complete contradiction to its dynamic message. The track's poppy obviousness is its greatest weakness, as the music lacks Kate's characteristic depth and sophistication. I apologise for starting this review on such a low note, but I feel it is imperative that Kate's fans introduce an element of objective criticism in their appraisal of her music. We all in the past have been guilty of blind adoration.

The rest of the album has not been a disappointment. *And So Is Love* is a moody classic. Kate's voice, drenched with melancholy, is perfectly matched to Clapton's weeping guitar. The song's hypnotic dark centres are very reminiscent of *Running Up That Hill.*

Moments of Pleasure is a very adult and moving song. The lyrics (surely Kate's finest vocal), the ambient piano and the soaring strings combine to produce a breath-takingly sad piece. The song is even sadder because it illustrates Kate's loss of innocence, which is the quality that illuminated her earlier works. However, the overall mood is joyous as Kate overcomes outrageous fortune by turning the pain of her loss into the joy of her memories. I salute her genius.

Issue 56: October 1995

The Song of Solomon is a revelation, and is my personal favourite from the album. I realise that many have found its meaning ambiguous and I share that confusion, but to me it speaks volumes about desire and the falsehoods of love. The closing chorus where Kate voices her desperation is the most beautiful music she has composed since *The Kick Inside*. In the chorus where she sings, "I'll do it for you... I'll be Isolde or Marion for you" is she offering bribes for his love? Is she begging to him? Are her offers sincere, carnal or cynical?

Lily is a short piece of magic. Its jaunty, poppy vibe reminds me for some reason of *Babooshka.* Indeed the whole album is reminiscent of *Never For Ever* in its blend of pop and ballads. Kate's invocation of the four Angels on *Lily* is beautifully realised. From reading the last issue of *HomeGround* I understand that this song is some kind of protection ritual taught to Kate by her guru, Lily. Although I am far from being an adept, I too can appreciate its healing qualities.

The title track should in all honesty have been the first single. The song's hypnotic backing track, Kate's narrative and Paddy's haunting pipes create a powerful mantra which carries the listener into a Pagan land of devilish divas. This very immediate song perfectly evokes the fairy-tale.

Top of the City is Kate's saddest song and is glorious in its despair and solitude. I must say that I agree with Dave in that it is possibly a suicide note to the world. All her fears and jealousies have broken through her wall of 'Positivism' and she seeks refuge in oblivion. She seeks the ladder. This particular symbol pops up time and time again on the album and indeed in her previous work. I believe *Sat In Your Lap* was the first song to mention ladders. I'm not completely sure of the meaning of this symbol but I imagine that it represents 'going up'... ascending... maybe into Heaven. Most of Kate's symbols, like all good symbolism, have simple meanings.

The remaining three songs are all fine but don't quite fly as high as the earlier ones. However, the final song, *You're the One* is the perfect way to end the album and so to close this painful chapter of her life. Throughout the album Kate shows us that she has faced her sorrows and accepted them. Although her positive attitude has evaporated in the face of these losses, she is an adult. She will survive, and yet... he's the one she wants! Kate's weaknesses shine through like a beacon of mortality.

Graphic opposite: Alex Lake

To end, let me say that this isn't Kate's finest work to date (*Hounds of Love* has that particular honour) but it is her most honest. I remember reading somewhere that Kate believed all art was artifice. *The Red Shoes* must be the exception to the rule.

Tim Edwards

It is now over a year since *The Red Shoes* was released and all that was likely to be released has been released, including *The Line, the Cross & the Curve* video. During that time I have played the album and all the added tracks attendant with it, watched the film and then the video, and read all the response to it in *HomeGround* as well as Kate's own words via the Kate Bush Club – and 'the problem' remains.

The problem is that after literally dozens and dozens of listens and watchings, I still come to the conclusion that this latest set of Kate offerings isn't what it should be, could be, or ought to be. I do not want to simply 'blame' Kate (or anyone else) for this or descend into a detailed review of everything that is 'wrong' with either the music or the film. I will, however, summarise some of the main sticking points and then go on to look at some of the potential reasons why we have the results we have. This is, I think, more positive than another Kate 'postmortem'.

The main problems with *The Red Shoes* and what accompanies it, are I think, threefold. The first issue is that the record lacks an overall theme, underlying message, call it what you will, that holds it all together. This seems partly intentional on Kate's part, yet this doesn't explain why the album is quite so inconsistent or uneven. Part of this depends on the sheer diversity of musical (rather than lyrical) styles involved, yet Kate is a past master at pulling everything together and marrying together many different styles and ideas – *The Dreaming* and *The Sensual World*, or even *Never For Ever*, let alone *Hounds of Love*, are good examples of apparently unthematic records that still end up sounding and hanging together. The reason is that the quality of the material is also uneven: *And So Is Love* and *Moments of Pleasure* and the title track are good, strong (if not necessarily great) songs whilst others such as *Rubberband Girl*, *Constellation of the Heart*, *Eat the Music*, or worst of all, *Why Should I Love You*, sound like strained attempts at 'poppiness'.

This then takes me on to the second sticking point, which is the sheer commercialisation of much of *The Red Shoes*. If the record itself is insufficient evidence of this, then one only has to take the extended remixes of singles to realise

THE
RUBBERBAND
GIRL!

just how far some of this material is pushed towards the mainstream world of pop and disco (one cannot say the same of previous remixes).

The third and most difficult area of all is that *The Red Shoes* at the end of the day doesn't really seem to say anything other than 'life is a series of ups and downs', which isn't saying anything much. I could go on at great length on all of these points and say that I never thought Kate would write a line so clichéd as "There's just something 'bout you", produce something as repetitive as *Eat the Music*, or 4:4 bump'n'grind-ish as *Rubberband Girl*, or sing as many "Ooh baby's" and the like on one album – but this is both rather hurtful and pointless. There's rather more point to asking why this is so and for this one has to start to wind back the clock to 1989 and 1990...

The Sensual World was a very good, if not great, album (and frankly I thought it was great). It did, however, nearly finish Kate off trying to do it. When *Q* magazine interviewed Kate, it was quite clear that she had found this album the hardest to produce yet, and was starting at least to realise that she could not go on working in that way. She therefore set out on a new, simpler, and hopefully easier direction.

I suspect factors such as recording costs, falling sales and her contract with EMI formed a material aspect to a personal decision. Kate, as we all know, also made the famous announcement at the Convention in 1990 that she would tour once again, for only the second time in more than eleven years. These two factors I think explain in part some of the more commercial-cum-simplistic aspects of the album and also some of the added rock band and disco feel. In other words, Kate was gearing herself up to produce something quicker, easier and which she could use on tour.

As Kate has said, most of the writing went quite quickly and easily and most of the album was done before the great tragedy of the loss of her mother, which forms the third factor. As we all know, Kate was very close to her mother and her death affected her greatly even relative to anyone else's standards. Kate also said a very long time ago that she tends not to thrive on the artist's angst and works most successfully when she is happiest.

The net result of this was that completion of *The Red Shoes* was suspended for at least a year as Kate could not work and that the tour was postponed indefinitely once again. At the same time, I strongly suspect that Kate was under pressure from EMI to complete *The Red Shoes* at least within the same kind of time as it took her to do *The Sensual World* and ended up rushing it with the effect of leaving it unfinished and under-polished in some senses.

Whether the film was purely an idea of Kate's or whether she was pressured into producing some kind of alternative to the tour, we will never know. What is clear is that through factors of personal decisions concerning her career, personal loss and a difficult to estimate, yet nonetheless significant degree of economic and commercial consideration, *The Red Shoes* and Kate herself, were compromised. We can only hope she has conditions more conducive to artistic creation for the next album.

Album Shorts

Stephen Thomas: I think I was one of the last people to hear *Rubberband Girl* on the radio. I actually managed (finally!) to catch it yesterday, on the day of it's release. Anyway, I've just been listening to the single. I think it is excellent – it sticks in the mind and is as individual as we have come to expect of Kate. However, I personally prefer *Big Stripey Lie*. I don't know why, but there is something compelling about it. If these two tracks, and *Moments of Pleasure* are representative of the album, then we are in for a real treat. Something alive, intense, that grasps you around the throat and won't let go! I can hardly wait!

Kate Elliott: I don't want to write screeds and screeds because I'll probably end up not saying what I want to say ('cos I already had two attempts and it didn't) so here in simple terms are my thoughts and feelings – *The Red Shoes* is fucking brilliant. In my very own opinion this is Kate's best ever work, which is a huge statement for me to make because I adored her and her music since I was eleven (I'm twenty) and didn't realise it could just get better and better and BETTER! Not only that, it proved extremely cathartic listening because I have been recovering from a bone marrow transplant which I had in January to cure my Leukaemia, and this masterpiece has finally helped me release a lot of ignored and pent up emotions. Now I can't wait to return to my studies at college in London where I will be impatiently awaiting the next Kate Bush Convention/Bash/Get Together/Get Up/Get On! So thanks Kate, *HomeGround* and Kate fans. P.S. Who is Maureen? (re: *Moments of Pleasure*).

Steve Jones: Well, I can only endorse all of the good things that have been said by everybody else. It may in time take over from *Hounds of Love* as my all time favourite. I particularly like the title track and *The Song Of Solomon*. Both *Lily* and the Prince collaboration are also favourites and I would love to see either as a single. To me, the album represents a very painful experience, although there is always hope *Rubberband Girl* shows that life can be upbeat as well as difficult. After the initial excitement of getting the album home and listening to it for the first time, it became an emotional insight into the past few years of Kate's life. For this I am grateful.

You Gotta Dance!

Dave feels the beat

Issue 51 February 1994

The dance never stops; the rhythm of life beats in all of us. The Whirling Dervishes whipping themselves into a mad frenzy, for a glimpse of God. The Native Americans beating out a rhythm that would last for days, inflicting terrible pain on themselves so they would keep dancing.

"Living in the gap between past and future"

Your blood pumping, head spinning. All that matters is the dance, the music, the rhythm.

"Close my eyes, I am rhythm"

Those beautiful shoes, those dazzling shoes, creep onto your feet like an afternoon nap, warm and friendly.

"Put them on and your dream will come true"

You were warned; Hans told us that the girl had to plead for her feet to be cut off. Michael told you; they took over a young life. But you want the dream, you want to feel that thrill, the thrill of the dance.

"You can dance the dream..."

Even when there is no music you have to dance.

"With no words, with no song.."

Pick up the beat from the Earth, the Sky, the sea, the city, from yourself.

"With your body on"

But the best times are with the music, when you are really with the music. You can dance to the radio, TV, someone whistling a ditty, but the real thing is when its LOUD. So loud that the beat goes right through you, becomes part of you. The rhythm is not something you hear, it is something you feel, something you become. The beat is everything. It is you.

"A kind of voodoo"

You're on the dance floor. It is dark and hot. Around you shapes move, caught for a second in the moving light. The shapes are other people, other people wearing the shoes. You are still for a second, taking it in, letting the rhythm in. Then you start to move. At first you are awkward, self-conscious, hesitant, then the music begins to work it's pagan spell. Freedom beckons.

"Only when I'm dancing can I feel this free"

Blood pumps, adrenalin flows. The room hot, dark; the air thick with life. You're moving towards that place.

"Feel your hair come tumbling down"

There is no escape now, you are wearing the shoes.

"Feel your feet start kissing the ground"

The spirit soars, the energy rush.

"Feel your arms are opening out"

The rest of your life falls away, you're in the gap, the place.

"And see your eyes are lifted to God"

You are the Whirling Dervish, the Native American. All that matters is the here and now, the gap. The past and the future no longer exist. All that matters is the frenzy of the music and the dance.

"Having the time of your life"

The dance is easy. Your feet, your legs, your body, your arms know what to do. The spirit moves them. Even when it's the first time, you know you've been here before, here in the gap, wearing the shoes. A half remembered dream, like deja vu, but this is real.

"It's really happening to ya"

The rush of life, of really living, of escape. The place, the gap is escape, the dream we all have. The past and the future exert their pressure on us all the time, filling the here and now with their regrets and worries. The dance can purge the present.

"Take away the love and the anger"

Once the red shoes are on your feet they can never come off. Once you have danced into the light, you never want to take them off. We have come full circle, we have reawakened the pagan in us. The dance becomes the trance of the Dervishes and we find ourselves.

"Do you want to dance?"

Graphic: Paulina Stuckey

Selling the Shoes

Dave and others consider the market place

Issue 50: October 1993

Dave: How does Kate get into Woolworths?

For all of us, buying a copy of *The Red Shoes* was a foregone conclusion. We would all, quite happily have spent hours hunting for it in the dark recesses of some obscure little record shop. Of course, it wasn't like that on 1st November. We just walked into Our Price and picked up one of the copies racked there. How does this happen? How does an album get from Kate's tender hands to the shelf of your local Woolworths?

About 80% of all records sold in the UK are sold through eight major chain stores, various supermarkets, petrol stations, and smaller chains. Only 20% are sold through independent record shops.

Once the artist has delivered the finished tapes to the record company, the Product Manager will begin to work out the marketing campaign for the album and the singles, and the sales department will begin selling the album in. Most of the big chains make their buying decisions at head office level. The buyer looks at the track record of the artist, the proposed marketing and promotion, the likely competition, and of course, will also actually listen to the album. The buyer will decide how many copies each of his stores will need. This varies a great deal from chain to chain. This is for the simple reason that i.e. Barry Manilow will sell better in WH Smith than in HMV, and Suede will sell better in Virgin than in John Menzies.

It is likely that the record company will take part in some kind of co-op campaign with most of the big chains. This can range from point of sale in store, to TV advertising. Most of the chains have their own 'charts' that they work out on Thursday or Friday. These are normally based on a mixture of the weeks' actual sales and guessing where new releases will chart - which is why *The Red Shoes* was no.1 in Our Price, Woolworths, and HMV the week of release!

Record company representatives pre-sell direct to the independent shops. Singles are pre-sold via telephone sales staff. Back at the record company, all is coordinated by the Product Manager; sales, marketing, promotions, press, and also liaising with the artist and management.

When Kate's career began in 1978, record companies only made an effort for the first couple of weeks after release, relying on subsequent singles to keep the album sales bubbling along nicely. Singles are still used as a marketing tool, but the marketing campaign is now continuous and can last up to a year.

The Red Shoes got off to a good start, charting at no.2 and so far (November 26th) selling over 150,000 copies. It will continue to sell, but the task for EMI is to get the 800,000 people that bought *Hounds of Love* to go out and buy this album. The obvious answer is to capitalise on further singles. The problem with the obvious answer is the level of success anticipated. If *Rubberband Girl* couldn't make the top ten of the singles chart, it is difficult to imagine what else on the album could.

Why do Kate's singles seem to have a very short chart life? The answer is the lack of exposure. Radio was fantastic with *Rubberband Girl* and for *Moments of Pleasure*, but, and it is the biggest 'but', the TV exposure has been minimal. A couple of plays on 'The Chart Show' is not enough. Live TV is the only thing that makes a real impact, and, love it or hate it, 'Top of the Pops' is still the key show along with prime time shows like 'Des O'Connor'. None of this is rocket science stuff. Kate knows all this and it is her decision as to what she does, or does not do.

What should be the next single? The logical choice is *Eat the Music*, and radio have already shown good support. A lot of people seem to go for *And So Is Love* and *The Red Shoes*. Me? I'd like to see *Constellation of the Heart*; but what do I know?

Phil Anstee: Rethink the singles

Issue 51: February 1994

I read with interest Dave's article in *HomeGround* 50 and felt I had to put pen to paper regarding this subject. As fans we all know that *The Red Shoes* is a fantastic album. The problem, however, is how to get people to buy the album who have shown interest in Kate's music in the past by buying *The Whole Story* or *Hounds of Love*.

I believe *The Red Shoes* is Kate's most commercial album to date. There are so many tracks which are *so* radio playable that it is hard to decide which should be chosen as singles. Singles are the best way of giving the record buying public some idea of the musical content of an album. If singles flop then the album's success is put in jeopardy and so it is imperative that correct decisions are made regarding singles.

Rubberband Girl was a pure pop song that gained major radio play and *Moments of Pleasure* was just one of the most beautiful songs ever written. However, it has already been established that both these songs were bought by Kate's loyal fans and failed to cross over to the record buying public at large. Why?

As a devoted fan I would find it very difficult to answer the question. My wife, Jill, however, has no difficulty in proving the answers. I would class Jill as a true representative of the British record buying public. She likes some of Kate's songs, but not all. She thought that *Rubberband Girl* didn't have enough about it, couldn't sing along with it easily and after a time there was a tendency to get fed up with it. The video was poor. *Moments of Pleasure* was a lovely song but too personal. What is Kate singing about? It just appears nonsensical. The part about socks and shoes could be laughed at if the real reason was not known by the listener. If *Eat the Music* was released as the third single, Jill believes this would follow the fate of the previous two. Although cheerful, its lyrical content would not make anyone rush out and buy it.

You may ask yourself, is there anything the woman does like? The answer is yes, and here are her thoughts: *You're the One* is top 5 material, distinctive and will cross over to the general record buying public who wish to say to their loved one "you're the only one I want". *Why Should I Love You* is a beautiful catchy song that has a greater appeal especially when it is known that Prince and Lenny Henry are both involved.

Once these two songs have proved themselves in the singles chart Kate should be able to release songs such as *The Red Shoes*, *Constellation of the Heart*, *And So Is Love* and even *Eat the Music*. All these songs will do reasonably well based on the success of the above two suggested singles and hopefully by then the strong album sales.

As for the album itself, Jill thinks it is good, but would not have heard it if she had not been married to me. If, however, *You're the One* and *Why Should I Love You* had been released as singles it is almost certain she would have purchased the album. I appreciate that my wife's views are not gospel, but I do think she has hit a nail firmly on the head. All I want is for as many people as possible to enjoy Kate's music as I do. Surely that isn't such a tall order?

Linda Jones: The heart is disappearing

Issue 52: June 1994

Although I agree with Phil Anstee's comments (*HomeGround* 51) about the choice of singles, I believe the problem with the poor chart positions goes deeper than that.

Unfortunately, these days, a brilliant song is not enough - it has to be promoted and I believe this has been inadequate by both EMI and Kate herself. For me, part of the excitement over a long-awaited release is the chance to see or hear

Kate in the media. With *The Red Shoes*, there was little of this that I know of - apart from 'Aspel'. Even the interviews in the press have been repetitive.

Although I sympathise with Kate in her wish to remain private and realise that most journalists would focus on her personal life rather than music, I do believe she came across as patronising and hostile in some articles. The press (especially the music papers) seem to be taking their revenge by writing Kate off now she has some 'real competition' - i.e. Tori and Björk. If radio phone-ins and in-stores signings can happen in other countries, why not here?

I've always thought that some of the attraction to Kate has been that it did seem that she really cared about us, her fans, but the whole business is becoming increasingly exploitative. Various different formats may get a single into the charts, but it won't stay there unless 'non-fans' get to hear it. Maybe EMI have given up and just hold the attitude of 'take the money and run', and that Kate herself has lost some of her interest after so long. I DO feel the 'heart' is disappearing.

It's Really Happening To Ya!

The Line, The Cross & the Curve has a mixed reception

Issue 50: October 1993

The short film that Kate made to accompany *The Red Shoes* , and, as it appears in place of the anticipated live performances, was controversial with the fans from the start.

In recent years Kate herself has regretted lost opportunities in the making of *The Line, the Cross & the Curve*

Graphic opposite: Alex Lake

Dave: Who cares if it's flawed?

Kate has made it clear that this film is something she has wanted to do for a long time. The subject of a long form visual piece first appeared with *The Ninth Wave*, but it never happened, which I always thought was a shame. Since the times of *Hounds of Love* all of Kate's videos have been cinematic in their feel and look. She has always favoured the narrative style rather than the typical 'MTV style' of fast cuts and multiple images. A short film is the natural progression for Kate. It is difficult to imagine any other artist who would suit the format better.

It seems to me that there are three main reasons why Kate made this film. Firstly – she wanted to – and a damn good reason that is. Secondly, as a tour substitute. Thirdly, as a source of promo videos.

The film opens with the *Rubberband Girl* sequence that you've all seen, with Kate and Stuart Avon-Arnold throwing themselves around a rehearsal studio. Kate seems unhappy with her performance and we see her make a wish in the dance mirror. The power goes out in the studio and Kate is left alone to sing *And So Is Love*, a beautifully lit and shot sequence with Kate giving her most convincing performance of the whole film. I particularly liked the shots from the point of view of the trapped blackbird.

The mood is shattered with the sudden arrival of Miranda Richardson, who appears from the other side of the mirror. There is a nice little double take when the two are face to face. The sequence for *The Red Shoes* is terrific, with Kate and Miranda dancing around the studio before Kate explodes through the mirror. The timing here is spot on; the visuals exactly compliment the music.

Once through the mirror we meet a wonderfully over-the-top and somehow sinister Lindsay Kemp, who takes Kate to meet Lily. The sequence for *Lily* is the most visually spectacular of the film, with the four archangels rising out of the mist, and the demon being expelled. Lily advises that Kate should call upon her loved ones for help, and the sequence for *Moments of Pleasure* that you have seen in the video begins. Despite the sheer beauty of the song, I don't think this sequence works. The idea of flying above the city landscape is a good one, but I think it has been poorly executed. The buildings of New York look like models, and the people at the end of the sequence look all too self-conscious. I am not a fan of the *Eat the Music* that follows; it is dark and disjointed and difficult to follow.

It is great to have so much visual Kate in one go, and in that sense it will please an awful lot of fans, including me. But do we really need a substitute for live shows? I think the plot is a little thin and some of the acting a little self-conscious, but despite what I've said above I really like the whole film. Kate's use of colour and her sense of composition are extraordinary. It is a fine directorial début, and it is refreshing to see something that gets away from the main stream concept of music video - and if it's flawed - who cares!

Peter: Kate did not seem at ease

This film is visually stunning. Kate wears her influences well. Michael Powell's films of the Forties are synonymous with the rich use of the then new technicolour. Her directorial début uses rich full blooded colour in such a way as to reinforce the emotional strength. Directorially the film is beautiful. There is no doubt that behind the camera she has a talent that should be encouraged.

I do not think that Kate was at home in front of the camera in a dramatic role. However much the dance and musical sections were wonderful, Kate simply did not seem at ease with dialogue, and wisely, I think, limited her involvement in such scenes. Miranda Richardson and Lindsay Kemp in the main acting roles provided the strength that with Kate's music and direction

made the film work.

The story is this – Kate is rehearsing *Rubberband Girl* with the band, possibly for live appearances. A storm breaks out, the power goes down. The rehearsal is interrupted and Kate says goodnight to the band and is left alone in the studio block. Alone in a room with a piano, lit only by a candle, and with a table with overripe fruit on it she sings *And So Is Love.* A blackbird has been trapped in the room, and Kate attempts to catch it. She does, but then releases it, and in a frenzy trying to escape it dashes itself against the window and is killed. The veil becomes thin. Miranda Richardson crashes through Kate's rehearsal mirror from another world, and she cannot keep still. Her hands are bandaged and she is wearing the red ballet shoes. Kate asks how she can help her.

Richardson says that Kate must draw a line, a cross, and a curve. The slip of paper Kate draws the symbols on instantly reminded me of the paper with the runes on it in one of Kate's (and mine) favourite films *Night of the Demon.* When the paper leapt from Kate's hand to Miranda's, I knew I was not wrong!

In repayment for her kindness, Miranda offers Kate the shoes. It is too late – Miranda is released from the spell of the shoes, and Kate is trapped. The shoes magically fix themselves onto Kate's feet, and she is trapped in the wild, frenzied dance. The sequence for *The Red Shoes* begins, and Kate dances into the mouth of hell. Lindsay Kemp comes to explain that something is really happening, and that Kate must sing back the symbols. He takes Kate to Lily. Lily explains what must be done, and in one of the most powerful sequences in the film the four archangels rise up out of the mist to form the protective phalanx, and Lily draws a circle of fire with her walking stick.

Lily explains that Kate must call upon the spirits of her dear departed, and in *Moments of Pleasure* Kate does exactly that. Miranda becomes aware that Kate's power is growing, and in *Eat the Music* the power of rhythm and dance is called, and Miranda crashes back into the mirror and the spell of the shoes is broken.

Krys: An exorcism, a dream, and a nightmare

The Line, the Cross & the Curve is a film of emotions, and that I feel is perhaps the most important aspect of the film, and its strength. I laughed, cried, felt joy and fear. I loved the rich, luscious colours, the turning of the seasons. I found it quite an overwhelming experience and was haunted by the imagery and atmosphere for the following few days. It will take several more viewings to begin to take it all in. An exorcism. A dream. A nightmare. A delight.

Kate creates the most moving scenes. In *And So Is Love,* she takes the dead blackbird in her hands, lays it down, and bends to kiss it's breast. It was so moving, and that kiss reminded me of Feeps, my little Robin friend. I found *Lily* the most emotional piece of the film, even more than *Moments of Pleasure.* I can't remember much of *Lily* because I was shaking, and the tears were uncontrollably pouring down my face. Lily reminded me of my Grandma. I just wanted to go over to Kate and say "Look – this is how you affect people, this is how you move me – and look at what you've done to my make-up!" Kate's soliloquy, where we see only her eyes, was also very emotional, her words delivered through sobs. Again I cried. She has one hell of an impact on people.

I liked Kate's use of humour; Kate and Miranda's little dance holding the red shoes was fun; the devils made me really laugh; the frenzied back-to-front legs (which I hope was supposed to be funny!), and Kate dancing on them bones (though they should have been more worn and earthy-looking). There is much play with the senses, a bittersweet feast for the eyes, ears and imagination. Kate has directed very well, and it will be interesting to see if she ventures further into this area. I hope so.

It is a gift to be able to move people, to make them laugh, cry, feel in a world that is too often cruel and callous. Kate has that gift.

Ernie Heramia: The Shadow

When I first heard *Army Dreamers,* it conjured up images from the Vietnam war. Huge transport planes off-loading coffins on conveyor belts whilst immaculately uniformed military pallbearers waited in crisp straight lines to carry the coffins to a seemingly endless procession of glinting hearses. I imagined a video for the song, with Kate in a black dress carrying 'a bunch of purple flowers', awaiting her son's return. As each coffin descended from the transport plane she imagined her son descending the stairs of an airliner - as a rock star, a politician, as a father - but always the scene faded to the harsh reality of the coffins.

When I saw the video for *Army Dreamers* I was disappointed. Instead of the sombre indictment of a senseless waste of life, it was a video of Kate and the boys playing soldiers. My friend Notaine, who had trained as an army ranger, found the video amusingly stupid. Soldiers who got bunched up like that could be easily machine-gunned. My sister however found the video very sad. I asked why.

She explained to me that it was actually the mother's dream. The soldiers were bunched-up because it was a mother's idea of how soldiers would fight, huddled together so that they could protect each other. The dream expressed her wish that she could have been there to protect her son, and if necessary die in his place. Kate was actually able to portray the terrible grief the mother was feeling with masterful subtlety.

After that I decided it would be wise in future

to give careful thought to Kate's works before I commented on them, lest I dismiss a very large diamond as a hunk of glass.

When I saw *The Line, the Cross & the Curve* I was disappointed. This was probably inevitable – for the same reasons that Paris would be a disappointment to me. I have dreamed of Paris for most of my life; from my childhood after seeing the cartoon feature 'Gay Pur-ee', through movies set in The City of Lights, to my adult love for impressionism, French jazz, sensual women, and the romance of the La Boheme life style. The real Paris could not possibly live up to the 'Paris' of my dreams. Remembering *Army Dreamers* though, I gave the new film time and thought, and came up with what follows.

The opening dance number seems to me to represent Kate's career up to *The Red Shoes*. It recalls the routines of 'The Tour of Life'; but here she is being manipulated in a way that seems symbolic of the way the record company manipulated the teenage Kate. When she is not dancing she is tired. Ultimately the male dancer puts her in a strait-jacket, and she then dances on her own, not manipulated but maniacal, perhaps representing the 'she's gone mad' period of *The Dreaming*.

The frenzy is interrupted by the wind machine, which brings to mind songs like *Cloudbusting* and *The Big Sky*, and seems to symbolise the *Hounds of Love* period. The struggle with the wind machine seems to represent the chaos of that period as she struggled to get her professional and personal life under control. Order is restored when someone simply turns the machine off. Her helplessness is illustrated by the fact that someone other than her actually turns it off. This is in direct contrast to the fact that Kate had a great deal of control over her work schedule and production. The things manipulating her are no longer the record company execs, but some inner 'demon'. During the dialogue section we get a hint at what this inner demon is, perhaps her disappointment at not being a better dancer. It is possible that Kate's departure from the world of dance following the *Running Up That Hill* video was prompted by frustrations at not being able to dance up to her self-imposed high standards; and of course the dance may represent other, hidden, sources of frustration.

Kate is then plunged into a world of darkness. Literally. Against this she lights a candle, and then enters *And So Is Love*. Note that she covers the candle, a symbol of hope, with a sooty glass chimney, a symbol of her present 'burnt-out' state of mind. The candle casts a harsh light that exposes every line in her face. She is a young girl grown old, and time is working against her. There are fewer tomorrows in which to achieve her goal of becoming a great dancer, of finding that one great love. 'Life is sad, and so is love'.

Kate's acting has been generally panned. Given past examples of her acting skills, I am inclined to think that the stilted acting in this film is by design, to establish an audio surrealism. Note for example the change in acting styles that takes place when the lights go out. Before that Kate is acting in a very natural manner, but after that she begins acting more strangely and melodramatic. This continues until she successfully passes back through the mirror. Note too that Miranda Richardson, an accomplished actress, likewise acts in a very surrealistic manner.

An element of symbolism that hits very close to home for me is when Kate frees the blackbird, only for it to break its neck when it mistakes a glass pane for an open window - and of course this foreshadows her mistake of thinking that being a great dancer will bring her worth as a person, and it will later take a tangible form in Miranda Richardson's birdlike character.

The Richardson character is actually the dancer's Shadow, the ruthlessly ambitious individual deep inside of her, that had already sold her smile, heart, and path in exchange for the Red Shoes. The dancer has been reluctant to give in to her ambitions, but in the despair of the introspective darkness she has become vulnerable to her Shadow's temptation.

She is initially shocked by the appearance of the Shadow (as are most people when they first see their 'evil' side) but quickly recognises her as her Shadow self, believes her ridiculous story about a fire and follows her lead. There is a wonderful predatory tension between the two women. A mutual seduction is going on, the Shadow trying to get the dancer's smile, heart and path, and the dancer trying to get the Shadow's feral power, all beneath a farce of need and helpfulness.

The dancer quickly learns that she has gotten more than she bargained for, and at the urging of the Kemp character, jumps through the mirror into an infernal realm. She has started on an Inannaque journey of self-discovery from which there is no turning back. Note that Kate is now wearing make-up, has adapted a youthful persona, and is dressed similarly to the Richardson character. She is no longer the tired burnt-out woman in black, but a flaming youth so full of energy ambition and talent that she is self-destructing. It is the elderly Kemp character that calms her down and stops the rapid self-destruction by the application of the wisdom of age.

It is at this point that the theme of the film emerges. What are the important things in life? Are they youth, fame and power? Or are they destiny, love and joy? The dancer has sold the latter for the former and now regrets the deal.

The first thing the dancer must face is her fear of growing old and not achieving the goals she set herself. She faces these fears in Lily, the old lame priestess. There is a wonderful Hecatean/ Persephonean symbolism in this meeting. True to type the dancer kneels at Lily's feet and rests her head in her lap in the classic position of a maiden seeking comfort from a crone. Thus out of love for Lily, and ultimately love for her future self, she accepts her unavoidable fate of one day being also old and lame. It is this acceptance of an undesirable future that enables her to begin recovery of her lost path. You may remember that Kate has often written on this theme of 'letting the weirdness in' in such songs as *Symphony in Blue*, *Rocket's Tail*, and *Leave It Open*.

Once the dancer has accepted her path, Lily teaches her to invoke the Higher Power and protect herself with fire (one of the things that have, like the dance, previously tormented her). Note that to cast the protective fire spell and invoke the angels she has to dance. The path gives her direction to use her power constructively rather than self-destructively. Unlike the power of the Red Shoes this power is hers, and will always be hers regardless of age and physical infirmity. I get a kick out of Lily growling, thus showing she is a far fiercer being than the Shadow.

The test of the dancer's commitment to her path comes when she suffers a psychotic break, in which she realises that she is descending into madness and becoming possessed. As one lets more of the weirdness in, one gains insight into one's own and mankind's collective insanity. This insight gives you the ability to rid yourself of your insanity; but in an insane world the sane people are seen as insane. To put it another way, the only difference between a sane man and an insane man is that the sane man knows the extent of his insanity.

The dancer overcomes her fear of insanity by turning her attention from her lack of conformity to the commonly accepted standard of normality, to thoughts of her loved ones. This is another product of 'letting the weirdness in'; your sense of existence shifts from a self-centred one of fear to a cosmos-centred one of love. The dancer continues her descent into madness and possession, but with her loved ones firmly in mind the fall is controlled and is made in Love rather than in fear. The dancer is allowing herself to become possessed by love and ultimately broken by love. And so she is able to recover her heart.

It is after she has learned the value of love that she is able to confront her 'evil' self. Her Shadow wants this confrontation too, because she actually stays in the mirror-land and seeks out the dancer instead of leaving the mirror-land for the real world.

The Shadow knows that a certain order of things needs to be established, and she must play her role in helping the dancer do this. She taunts the dancer with her lack of a path, a heart, and especially a smile. The Shadow incites her to a chase. It is in the chase that the dancer recovers her smile. As it turns into a prancing romp, the Winter snow changes into Summer fruit and the whole pursuit is lost in a mass of smiling dancing people and tropical excess. Gone is the tired grey clad girl being manipulated and driven to madness. Gone is the black clad woman mourning her perceived failures. Gone is the red clad woman possessed by the Red Shoes. In their places is a fruit clad woman at peace with her destiny, loving and smiling. The presence of the African Animist shaman and the 'spirit horses' sets up a nice contrast between the dancer's previous state of bondage and her present state of freedom. Previously she was being manipulated by her circumstances and obsessed by her failures, then possessed and manipulated by the Red Shoes, but now she is free to give herself completely over to possession by Joy and Life.

When the dancer awakens after being 'ridden', the three pieces of paper that are the tokens of her destiny, heart, and smile, fly to her hand and the Red Shoes have returned to her Shadow. She makes a run for the mirror but the Shadow intercedes. They fight and the Shadow appears to have the upper hand until the dancer remembers the power of her destiny, heart, and smile. Drawing on their power she is able to find superhuman strength to throw her Shadow self against the mirror, which shatters bringing down the ceiling and unleashing a flood of water and fruit (symbols of birth and death). The dancer walks through the mirror and the waterfall which the flood had become, and is reborn into the real world. The Shadow remains in the infernal realm of the subconscious, buried in a warding monument to the dancer's victory over her and the Red Shoes.

Patrick Routen: No pleasing some people!

Kate's film is very good, full of evocative images and contrasts. I am delighted to see her experimenting with this medium. I personally can't see her as an actress, but as a director (and artist) in films like *The Line, the Cross & the Curve*, she is given the freedom to experiment and let her creative juices flow, and this is where I feel she will excel. I don't know what all the fuss is about as to people wanting her to tour again. Her pursuit of perfection and her dabblings with film are more than ample compensation. Don't people realise that she doesn't have the time? There isn't pleasing some people!

Tiny Twinkling Lights

John Stedman attends an art exhibition

"The show includes an intriguing piece by Kate Bush". My ears sprang to attention. Surely the radio interview was about an art exhibition? Had Kate decided to go for the Turner Prize? Confusion reigned until the next day when a news release from the Kate Bush Club and an item in *The Independent* confirmed that Kate had indeed created a work of art for an exhibition and auction called 'Little Pieces From Big Stars'. The event was to benefit War Child, a charity striving to get food, clothing and medical supplies to Bosnia. Their latest ambition was to refurbish a kindergarten in Sarajevo and set up a music therapy centre in Mostar.

Brian Eno had invited top artists from the music world to each donate a small piece of art to the cause. There had been a strong response from many well known names including David Bowie, Paul McCartney, Bryan Ferry and Kate. They had all been asked to make or find a small artwork, photograph or sculpture which they had signed and could offer for exhibition and public auction.

The exhibition was being staged for just a few days at the Flowers East Gallery in London Fields. Cancelling all appointments, I was off to Hackney like a heat-seeking missile. A phone call had given a hint of what to expect. Apparently, Kate had prepared a pair of exhibits entitled *Someone Lost At Sea Hoping Someone In A Plane Will Find Them* and *Someone In A Plane Hoping To Find Someone Lost At Sea.* The titles seemed to be bigger than the works!

On the journey I tried to fit mental images to the titles. I first thought I might be about to see pieces derived from *The Ninth Wave* project, which I vaguely remembered was once to be translated into a film. But that was some years ago, and just as Kate's song writing ambitions had moved on, so it was likely had her visualisation of ideas. Remembering the sleeve artworks over her career, I decided one thing was certain - the works of art would definitely not be of an abstract nature.

My arrival at Flowers East was an uneasy experience in itself. Having been dragged round a few Mayfair emporia in my youth, I was quite intimidated by the word "Gallery". Would they let me in? After all, my Gucci shoes were at the cobblers, my only Bentley had 'Dinky' stamped underneath and I don't talk loudly in restaurants. But Flowers is nothing like that, situated in a converted industrial building and on this occasion staffed by a friendly bunch of people from the War Child charity and Brian Eno's office.

The place was crowded, and little pictures dotted every available space on the walls. I bought a catalogue and sought out Kate's exhibit, Lot 80. I found it. Her work was hanging in the centre of a large white free-standing screen. I waited for a gap in the crowd and moved in.

There were two tiny black frames, each smaller than this page. Very dark, very solid and very heavy looking, almost ominous in their initial impact. The frames each had a large engraved brass title plate along their lower edge and a thin gold line all around. Strangely, within the frames there seemed to be nothing but inky blackness. Was there no image at all? I got closer. Closer to the first piece, *Someone Lost at Sea*... And then I saw it.

Caught within a field of nothingness was a tiny twinkling light. On and off it blinked, a tiny red pinpoint in the void. In the context of the title the pinpoint evoked ideas of isolation, distress and hope. By eliminating extraneous detail and focussing on this pinpoint, the work seemed to achieve a real intensity of purpose. Its impact was entirely in the mind's eye, in a different but complimentary way to the effect of fine music. Even taken at face value, the idea of being lost in a featureless, scale-less void must rank highly in the list of primal fears. The metaphorical allusions of 'loss' are limitless. But by its title the piece suggests that the human condition finds hope even in the most desperate of circumstances. Powerful stuff.

After a while, I moved across just a few inches to look at the other work, *Someone In A Plane*... I was expecting something similar to the first piece, but I was curious to find out how the reversal implied by the title had been visualised. From a distance the pieces had superficially looked similar, but how subtle would the differences be? I should have realised that this was a day for surprises, because however hard I looked, the second piece was, in all practical terms, identical to the first. Another black void. Another blinking pinpoint of red light. Just the title panel was different, challenging the viewer to place a different set of values against ostensibly identical visuals.

Considering the ideas of the two pieces together, I began to think that what first appeared to be a forbidding concept was in fact founded in optimism, even more so now that I realised the perception of the two identical yet opposite situations seemed to evoke the complimentary ambitions of seeking and being sought.

Standing back a few feet, I tried to contemplate both pieces in the same gaze. It wasn't possible. Once I had moved far enough away to focus on the two works as one, the tiny

Issue 54: October 1994

The two pieces were secured by a huge fan of Kate, Neville Judd

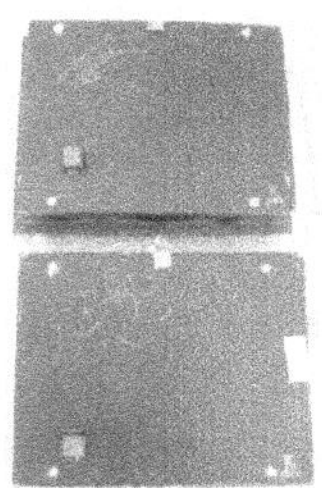

Neville told his story on Kate BushNews in July 2012, when as he explains, he needed, reluctantly, to sell them:

"I have always been a fan, and like most of us, collected everything. I have to sell this because I need to help someone pay a bill, it's as simple as that. I never thought I'd need to sell them (duh!) hence me having sat on them for almost twenty years. They have never been exhibited. There are no other photos of them and no one knew where they were, except for Brian Eno and Anthea Norman-Taylor from the Warchild Charity.

"I am also a David Bowie fan and over the years have been involved in many Bowie related projects, including the official Bowie biography Strange Fascination which I helped with. In 1994 I went to the Private View for 'Little Pieces by Big Stars' at the Flowers East Gallery in Hackney. I didn't have an invite to it but spoke to Kate on her way in and asked her about her contribution. "It is about the Sea and about me too, I guess" was all she would say and I decided there and then to try to buy it.

"My friends left when Bowie came out but I hung around and eventually David's Art dealer, Kate Chertavian, let me in. Nick Roeg was looking at 'Someone Lost at Sea Hoping Someone In A Plane Will Find Them' when I walked in to the small room. I told him what Kate had said to me. "In that case one of us needs to buy them", he said and tapped me on the shoulder. I looked at the blinking red light in each picture. I thought about what Kate had said, and I made up my mind to bid for them at The Royal College of Art the following week. And I got them. I later discovered that David Bowie had spoken at the time in both the press and on television about Kate's two pieces and had suggested that he was going to bid on them himself, and I later asked him about this. He said "I thought they were the most fabulous things and I intended to send in bid but something happened and I never did. Anyway, they should hang in a fans home I reckon." And that is exactly where they have hung, in secret, for eighteen years."

lights disappeared. This suggested another perspective on the theme of emptiness and vastness in the subject. Sometimes it is very difficult to see things from both points of view. Especially if these viewpoints are diametrically opposite, even more so if to consider another viewpoint means that the viewer has to challenge their own.

The scale of the pieces had worked to their benefit, because by insisting on close encounter and inviting considered personal interpretation, they demanded engagement with ideas beyond the obvious. Perhaps it was just good luck that the terms of the exhibition demanded that the works be small, because at a larger size their impact would have been dissipated. These were not things to be experienced and discussed simultaneously. In this, they reminded me of the works of the artist James Turrell, whose installations are also about transcending the ordinary and challenging the everyday preconceptions involved in the process of 'looking'. Turrell's works too promote silent contemplation, reflection and later maybe discussion.

I wondered if the themes and concerns shown in the works paralleled Kate's recent music, but perhaps that is too obvious. Unlike many of the contributors to the exhibition, it was clear that she had attempted to do something special and was not simply relying on her name to attract interest. As a counterpoint to the mass-produced output of the music industry, her individual one-off artworks invited speculation and raised many more questions than answers. This seemed to have real value, and although she is perhaps unlikely to forsake the music world for a career in art, Kate should be confidant that, by any standards, the were superb pieces of work.

Although a folio of exhibition works was published, it unfortunately did not include Kate's piece since the photography deadline came too soon. Fuzzy photographs did eventually appear in the December issue of Q magazine, but these showed nothing of the qualities of the real thing. Quite how one would secure a still photograph which captured the essence of these works is an interesting question.

Other visitors at the Gallery were enthusiastic about Kate's work, notably David Bowie who mentioned the pieces when interviewed on GMTV.

The auction was due in a few days, and I thought about developing a strategy for raising a bid. Unfortunately my experience in this field extends only to watching a few episodes of 'Lovejoy'. This explains why I thought the first stage should involve robbing a bank, selling sundry relatives into slavery and maybe becoming an MP and asking questions. One thing I was sure of after witnessing the auction at the Convention was that the two pieces would fetch much more than the estimate of £200 – £300.

War Child had secured a wonderful venue for the auction, the major gallery space at the Royal College of Art, beside the Albert Hall. On the evening of 4th October there were many hopeful, enthusiastic fans and media people queuing to register for the opportunity to bid for the works of their idols. Events began with a very civilised meal followed by live music and video reports of the latest situation in Bosnia. The artworks had been brought over from Flowers East and were now arranged on the long white walls of the Henry Moore Gallery. Under the glare of spotlights, Kate's pieces twinkled away through the evening.

At 9pm, Ted Owens, the Rock Pop and Entertainment Consultant from Bonhams of Chelsea took the rostrum and began taking bids. As the level of excitement rose, various well-heeled bidders began playing the psychological games that make all auctions so fascinating. But this was a special evening, and among the faces I spotted Malcolm McLaren, Marie Helvin and Brian Eno. All tastes and pockets were indulged, from a drawing of a cat by Adam Ant (a snip at £170 to you, sir) to a strange woodcarving by Paul McCartney (sold for an astonishing £12,500 to the quivering chap sitting next to me).

Then Lot 80 came up. After amazingly reciting the title of the pieces word perfectly, Ted led a spirited round of bidding with offers coming from all corners of the room. The estimated selling price was soon left for dust as offers went into four figures. The eventual sale for £1,150 was to an exuberant lady who beamed from ear to ear for the remainder of the evening.

At the end of the day all the lots had been sold, raising over £58,000 for the charity. The sale of catalogues and dinner tickets added a healthy amount to this total, and the officers from War Child were overjoyed – and exhausted. There was a party atmosphere to the whole proceedings, even those who had been unlucky in the bidding seemed happy to have taken part in what had been a remarkable initiative.

And that was that, or so I thought. But there was an extraordinary coda. Later, in the small hours, I spooled back the video to check out the news. The lead item was the sinking of the Estonia ferry. The stories were of heroism, of tragedy and of hope. The aural images were unforgettable: through the gloom and the enveloping blackness came muffled shouts, desperate cries and the thudding of helicopter blades in the storm. But you couldn't see anything of the survivors or the rescuers. Unless you looked really closely at the screen. Then you could just make out traces of the life-rafts and aircraft. You could just see lights. Tiny twinkling lights.

Fans

Eleanor Johnson considers why we do this

Issue 54: October 1994

On the day Freddie Mercury died, I rang a cousin of mine who was a great Freddie Fan. Naturally she was devastated by the news and in a total state of disbelief. Everybody who knew her was aware of how big a part of her life Freddie had been. It therefore astounded me that in the week after his death, out of all her friends and family she received only two telephone calls to check if she was okay. No-one seemed to consider that she would be experiencing very real feelings of bereavement and grief. When I spoke to my cousin it started me thinking, what if this was me? What if Kate had died and it was me experiencing these feelings?

I am sure many of you felt the same as I did when I saw the media treatment of the fans who had come to pay their respects at Freddie's house in London. I started to wonder why I was so angry. I came to the conclusion that I was angry at the total misunderstanding by the world of what a "fan" is and what a fan feels for the person they follow. It was obvious that none of my cousin's friends perceived Freddie to be a real person in her life. It was obvious the TV people wanted to make the fans at his house appear weird when they cried.

Yet Kate is a real person in my life. Someone who is able, through her music, to pick me up when I'm down – just like 'phoning my best friend. Someone who exists with a real personality in my mind – like a friend. Someone who appears to understand (if I pick the right track) how I'm feeling without saying anything – just like a life-long friend. I can agree with her, or disagree, just like a friend. Does this make me weird? Or mean that I'm missing something and using Kate to replace it? I don't think so. Surely it is natural when someone is placed in the public eye for some of the public to find an affinity with that person. In fact, if you think about it, the media thrives on it. Why then do they find us so disturbing that they have to depict us as "unhinged", "not quite right" or something to protect themselves from? What do they think we're going to do?

Of course I have fantasies about meeting Kate, being able to sit down with a cup of tea and find out what goes on in that incredible mind, but that is no different from imaginary conversations we all have with people we know when we can't get in touch with them. We just know these people so well, we know what they will say to us, or we seek comfort in imagining them saying what we want to hear. Of course, I don't believe I know Kate this well, but the person who has spoken to me through her music is in my head, and I know her well. Moreover, just because I would like to have a conversation with Kate does not mean that if I see her driving along in her car, I'm going to force her over and insist that she sits down with a cup of tea and tells me her innermost secrets! I'm sure if she dragged out the thermos and said let's have a chat, I'd be such a gibbering wreck, I wouldn't even be able to discuss the weather.

I would be interested to hear the other side of the story. How does it feel to have fans? Few people, to my knowledge, have discussed this publicly. Madonna says that she feels a great responsibility towards the people that follow her. She says she knows she has a large gay following and that is why she makes safe sex such an issue in and around her work. Kate said on 'Rapido' in 1989 that she thinks we're all completely mad – but she said it with a smile.

So why do I do it? Why do I rush out and pester the life out of my local record shop on the day of a Kate album or single release? Why do I treasure the signatures? Why do I continue to think of all those sensible questions I'd ask her over that cup of tea? Why? Because I have a great friendship that I want to last. Isn't that worth putting yourself out for?

Photo: Paul Camilleri

Kate with fans at the première of *The Line, the Cross & the Curve.*

You are under the spell of the Red Shoes!

London 8th May 1994: The Hippodrome Kate Bush Convention

Dave: A true moment of pleasure

The plans for this Convention were actually started some months before *The Red Shoes* was released. I went and saw The Hippodrome a full year before the event took place. As we all know, Kate was incredibly busy with making the film and she was unable to give us the go-ahead until the week before Christmas. This meant that the real work couldn't begin until the new year. Because of circumstances beyond my control, I had a rather "eventful" January and didn't have my first proper planning meeting with Lisa Bradley of the Kate Bush Club until the end of that month, which effectively pushed the Convention date back to April, which eventually became May.

Most of the main plans and ideas were in place at this point. Kate was keen for the film to be screened and we were hoping that we would have access to some behind the scenes footage, but this failed to materialise. What appeared, however, was the excellent Canadian interview that we did end up showing. The main organisation of the Convention followed the same method as the last one – i.e. Lisa and myself did most of the planning, with me liaising with the Hippodrome. Elaine Davis once again provided the excellent merchandise, and our technical people, Chris Stone on video, and Lorne Hamilton on sound. Lisa reported back to Kate.

When I think now that the original date for the Convention was two weeks before the actual one, I go cold all over because there is no way we could have made that date. Everything seemed to take longer than I anticipated, and then two weeks before the date, I go and get a new full time job (I'd been working freelance prior to this). So all the time I had allotted for editing videos had to be moved to the evenings and was consequently rushed. The end results were okay but could have been better. While all this was going on, Peter and Krys were sorting out the ticket sales (with the help of Peter's Mum, Olive) and putting together the Top 100 Kate Chart, as well as the quiz questions. I must confess that we were sorely tempted to hype *Moments of Pleasure* to No. 1, but Kate was adamant that if *Wuthering Heights* was No.1, then so be it!

The day before the event Lisa and I went to the Hippodrome to deliver merchandise, and so that Lisa could have a look around the venue. This resulted in the two of us getting trapped in the labyrinth of passages under the stage. We both had visions of being trapped there forever. Luckily we found the kitchen, so we wouldn't have to eat each other! And then we spotted an exit! We burst out only to find that Lisa's husband hadn't even noticed that we were missing!

The day dawned and we had a very early start. The meeting point for many of the helpers was my house at 7am. And what a wide awake, happy bunch we were – NOT! By 8am were we all at the Hippodrome and ready for action. The first action was a scouting party to MacDonalds for breakfast for thirty people. Once we had fed the troops and had a pep talk, we started getting everything ready. Elaine and Lisa got the merchandise stall into shape; Krys sorted out the box office and my friend Pam supervised putting up posters and decorating the place. My main task was to run the sound-checks for the performers. All too soon it was time to open the doors.

As always the day seems a blur to me. I seemed to be on edge all the time. On top of worrying about what I was supposed to be saying on stage we had a nightmare with the Hippodrome not catering for anywhere near enough people and not being able to find any management when we wanted them. Aaaargghhh! But the day also holds so many special memories for me. All the brave performers who each deserve a meddle (er, medal!), especially Mike Winter and his dancers who worked so hard to produce their routine for *Ken*, or Kate Forbes-Pitt and Krys Thomas (Rare Flowers) having their DAT begin while they were still coming up through the floor. By the way, coming up onto the stage via that lift was very weird; it would have been even more weird if Lisa had had her way!

I remember all the hard work the helpers put in, especially Rob and Alison on the merchandise stand; my friend Ian who acted as stage manager, bodyguard for Kate and emotional prop for me. All the helpers were great but special thanks must go as always to Elaine Davis and Chris Stone.

I was really thrilled that Paddy agreed to perform and that Del wanted to do the auction, which went better than we ever could have hoped – that man is completely mad as if you didn't know! We knew that Del would bring the new dance mix for *Rubberband Girl*, but *The Man I Love* and *Sexual Healing* were a surprise to us.

Kate arrived about half an hour before she was due on stage and needed some persuading that she should use the stage lift. I think she just said yes to shut me up in the end! Of course the elusive Hippodrome manager suddenly became very visible when he knew that Kate was in the building. We finished the auction, showed the interview, then Kate came on stage, did her bit, drew the winning raffle ticket (what is it when

Del and I try to draw a raffle ticket – something always goes wrong!) then introduced her film. Then we were into the disco. I think everyone enjoyed the disco, though it was a shame more people didn't stay. We finally finished at midnight with *Moments of Pleasure*. We cleared up, and were home by 1.30am.

Looking back now it wasn't a perfect day. There were things I would do differently, and will do differently next time, but it was a good day and I hope everyone had a good time. But my favourite memory is of American fan Vickie Mapes coming up and giving me a big hug and saying it was worth coming over for and thanking me. A true moment of pleasure.

Krys: The sights, sounds, & smells ..

At 1.15am, Sunday 8th May, I woke up with a sudden start at the terrifying realisation that the day had arrived. The day we had been looking forward to and dreading with equal passion. Three sleepless hours later I thought, "Sod this!", so got up and lay comatose in the bath for half an hour, trying not to wake the others in the house, with my huffing and puffing and sneezing and swearing and splashing about. It turned out they were all awake anyway, too excited to sleep, and could hear every huff and puff and sigh... so much for trying to be quiet.

As with most *HomeGround* adventures, it began on the boring A2 (there's only one way out of here you see). I turned the radio on. The Beatles song *It's All Too Much* was being played, whilst great stomping blue cats danced in my stomach. I regressed to the 1985 Romford Convention, and the 1990 Convention at the Hammersmith Palais. The fear was the same. After sixteen weeks of preparation it was really happening to us!

We descended on Dave on time for a change, and made primeval "Ugh" grunting noises at each other – it was too early to speak – then packed the cars with crates of CDs and records to be played at the disco that night, and all sorts of Kate goodies. We took a Dave-short-cut (with five carloads of us in convoy) to the West End, via East London's Limehouse area, which would always be *Experiment IV* country to us. Past the still derelict field that had been so lovingly saturated for the unsuspecting 'dead bodies' to occupy. Past the site of the Music For Pleasure shop where Dave and I had been laid to rest on an icy pavement in that November chill air – reliving our very fond and treasured memories and funny moments. We arrived *en masse* at 7.50 am at the Hippodrome and were greeted by the foul smell of rubbish bags festering in the Soho street from the night before. These are the sights, sounds, smells of the 1994 Kate Bush Convention... and did I need a sick bag!

I had gone down with a 'flu bug the night before (oh what timing!) and dosed myself up with cold capsules and tried my best to wake up. God, I felt yukky! Much of the day was, as a consequence, a blur to me – and I was probably more spaced out than most people there! The whole thing was like a dream. The Hippodrome was dark, quiet, like the morning after the night before, as everyone gathered for what was to be the longest day. Voices echoed around the place

Photo: *HomeGround* Readers

which seemed so small with so few of us in occupation.

The 'Eat First' *HomeGround* motto applied, as always, and there was a mass order taken to Macdonalds. So all the helpers stuffed their faces with McMuffins, Big Macs, milkshakes, doughnuts, gallons of coffee, and Peter I seem to remember had TWO breakfasts. It was then time to start getting this show on the road. Dave went into organisation overdrive and was unapproachable, unless you wanted some kind of Alien-esque attack (believe me, he's quite capable!) Our helpers stuck posters on every available surface, the merchandise shop was set up, the live acts arrived and sound checks and final rehearsals began. I set the box office up and hoped to God it would run smoothly.

It is always really exciting and a bit scary the last few minutes before we open the doors. Those last moments to check and double check before

Photos: *HomeGround* Readers

it's too late. At just after midday we opened the doors. It was great to see people happy and excited about the day. And it is always a good feeling to see the familiar faces of old friends, as well as meeting new people, and being able to put faces to names. There were people from all over the world gathered together in one place to have a day with like-minded souls. There to enjoy themselves, have fun and share that love of Kate and her music in an atmosphere where no-one would disapprove or ridicule.

Sharon, Mick, Pauli and Pami were my box office companions, who were threatened with a week with Dave if they dared cock up my closely guarded ticket system! As people were coming through the main doors, I was sure I heard Peter mutter "Line on the left, one cross each!" a la

Python's *Life of Brian*. It was great to see Vickie, Chris, Andrew, Doug and the rest of the Love-Hounds crew who had travelled from America especially for the Convention. People had flown from Japan, Australia, Brazil, Italy, Germany, Finland, Switzerland, Sweden, Holland, France, Ireland, Scotland, Wales, England, London... That is the kind of dedicated following Kate has.

Then it was time for the event to begin. Dave grabbed Lisa, Peter and myself and lead us into the lower recesses of the Hippodrome. Down steps, tunnels, corridors (it was almost as long a trek as Beryl Reid takes in the opening titles of *The Killing of Sister George*!) The place resembled a stage set from 'Dr. Who' or *Aliens*, and I half expected the slavering Mother alien to suddenly appear in front of us, baring her slavering jaws. It was also like that scene in *Spinal Tap* where the band get lost trying to find their way to the stage. In fact, the situation was just a little too close to the film for my liking.

In keeping with the occasion, we attempted a repeat of the *Spinal Tap* "Hello Cleveland!" and "Rock and Roll!" bits from the last Convention. However, as we were clanking noisily down the heavy metal staircase, it was virtually impossible to hear what the person in front or behind was saying. I said "Hello Cleveland!". There was no response. Then Dave said "Hello Cleveland!". Everyone looked puzzled and asked "What?" Followed by the usual satellite delay, Peter, thinking he was being really clever and full of sharp wit, loudly proclaimed "Hello Cleveland!", to which Dave and I responded flatly and in unison, "We've already done that one!". (Peter sometimes suffers from serious satellite delay,

Photo: *HomeGround* Reader

mainly 'cos he's not listening or has his head wedged in the pages of *MS-DOS 6.2*, or *What To Do When Your Modem Is Fucked*, or a large plate of food!)

If Lisa had actually heard any of these pathetic ramblings above the deafening racket of shoes on steel, she would probably have clobbered us all. She is probably sick to death of bleedin' *Spinal Tap*-isms by now!

Our *Tap* attempts had lost most of their impact after the third consecutive repeat. So we shut up and followed Sigourney Dave on this endless expedition through grey walled corridors until the destination was found. A rather miserable, and humourless stage guy from the Hippo met us and told us where to stand. We all attempted a little joke or two with him, but gave up. We were wasted on him.

The stage was like a lift without walls. The said miserable guy told us to stand on the rectangular shape, and stay there until we reached the top. We were going to stand with our backs to everyone but that was a bit silly, so we didn't, and Lisa suggested we stood on our heads! That would have meant our feet came out first in some weird kind of breech re-birth experience! Now that would have been very *Stonehenge*! Unfortunately, Dave wasn't up for the idea of dressing up as the four Archangels for the intro bit. I tried my hardest to persuade him but he wasn't having any of it. Peter would have made an excellent Muriel! We were even going to dye his beard white and everything.

We had a quick hug all round, our knees quaked, and I could feel Lisa shaking like a leaf when I hugged her. Then the stage began to move upwards. Oh God, this was it! My stomach was churning with a lethal cocktail of utter nerves and excitement, as *The Red Shoes* pounded and stampeded above us. The music grunged its way through me, until it was all I could physically feel. That unforgettable sensation as the stage rose from the bowels of the Hippodrome – where incidentally we found one of our most valuable missing displays which the Hippodrome people had kindly lost on us. I guess we could have held it up as we came out of the pit! That was the longest and shortest journey of my life. *The Red Shoes* will never be the same! We all felt really silly as the music stopped, and the stage reached the top with a clunk, like the sound of a coffin lid sliding into place. I'm not comfortable with this side of things and I could feel myself squirming like never before, wishing that I had even a fragment of Dave's incredible confidence to do what he does so well.

Dave is such a showman, as anyone who has been to previous Conventions will know. Again, this is where that other *HomeGround* motto of "Stick to what you're good at!" is enforced. (He began his stage début some years ago with an interesting interpretation of Shirley Bassey's *Big Spender*... [on reading this divulgence, my fellow editor has just threatened me with some very serious revenge if I don't censor!] And somehow Dave managed not to say "Fuck" for the whole time he was on stage! (Though Lisa remembers otherwise!) Now, that is some feat I can tell you.

Incidentally, for Dave to say in his Convention article that January was "eventful" is somewhat an understatement. He was stabbed in the stomach by some deranged bastard on the

Photo: Mark Semic

Photo: Keith Woodhouse

London Underground, and was seriously ill in hospital for a week. He had to undergo some pretty nasty surgery. It was heartbreaking seeing him so ill. It was also quite funny (my sick sense of humour!) seeing him doped up to the eyeballs on morphine – (Peter and I kept asking "Can we have some?") He was away with the fairies, and saying very rude things about the "old gits" in the beds nearby! I doubt if he remembers any of it!

Seriously, it was not a pleasant time for Dave, or for any of his friends who were worried sick about him. These things really do make us aware of how precious our loved ones are, and cast a very clear perspective on the important things in life. Being the brave bunny that he is, Dave told me not to mention this episode in the Spring issue of *HomeGround*, so I didn't, but... He was just so brave, so undeterred, and even had the Convention plans by his side in his hospital bed. He wasn't bitter about the incident, and he wasn't going to let it drag him down. He was determined that he would get on with the Convention no matter what...

The day was interwoven with several live performances – the first being Markus from Germany who danced beautifully to *Moments of Pleasure*. Conny Ely performed *Oh England My Lionheart* and *Another Day* on guitar. Glen Vickers gave a folky acoustic version of *Running Up That Hill* and an ode to Joseph Bush, Kate's grandfather. Lonely Planet did *Be Kind to My Mistakes* and *The Big Sky*. Rare Flowers performed *The Red Shoes* and *Wuthering Heights*. Mike Winters' dancers, who performed last time, did an excellent routine to *Ken*. A pat on the back to all those who were brave enough to go out there and do their stuff. It takes a hell of a lot of courage to stand in front of all those people – they were all incredibly brave to perform those much-loved Kate tracks to probably the harshest critics in the world.

Peter conducted the quiz with a smile as welcoming as the brass plate on a coffin. Yes, it is he and I who had bastardly put the questions together, working into the small, dark hours, with the rubbing of hands and an evil glint in the eye. Ha! Ha! Ha! Ha! Ha! (insert evil Dracula or Dick Dastardly laugh here). Those who wanted to join in formed teams of four or thereabouts (there were only four *Red Shoes* boxes which were the much coveted prizes). The Norfolk Alchemists won – when they came on stage it turned out that they were the same team as last time, headed by Amanda Greenway. The team modestly accepted their prizes.

Kate had generously given us heaps of signed stuff for the spot prizes and runners-up in the raffle. In contrast to our evil quiz, the spot prize questions were easy. But that is because it is quite frightening being called up on stage and having to answer in front of a thousand or so people. Faced with that, most people go completely blank!

Later that afternoon, I was passing the back door to find that Paddy had just arrived and was heavily laden with bags and instruments, including his tree trunk. We said our hello-how-are-yous? "Would you like me to help you carry something?" I asked. There were about five or six flights of stairs to the dressing rooms, so I led the way. By the time we reached the rather unimpressive dressing room, we both needed oxygen!

A little later Paddy was due on stage. He emerged, tree-trunk first, out of the pit, which looked very effective, and also quite funny! He was later joined by Colin Lloyd Tucker and the two of them – known as Bushtucker – performed a couple of songs from their excellent new album *Skyscraping*. It was great that Paddy had agreed to perform his music at the Convention. I talked with Colin afterwards for some time – he's such a

Photo: *HomeGround* Reader

Photo: Leigh Norwood

lovely guy and one of the nicest people I have ever met, the sort of person who restores your faith in humanity. And he makes the most amazing music!

The Pink Mules, an affectionate spoof of *The Line, the Cross & The Curve*, was a definite hit. We wondered whether we should show it, but after having done the Peter test (he thought it was hilarious!) we knew we could actually screen it. I just love that bit when Potty Pam says "Ooh it's all too runes, very Stonehenge", (which has become a slogan amongst Kate fans now!) I also love the *And So Is Love* bit with the bird glove puppet, and of course, the scene where the mules magic themselves onto his feet! The audience was almost dying with laughter. Well done Paul Thomas, Kevin Hall and Gary Boulton for this triumphant piece of screen history. How much lipstick did you get through, guys?

One of the highlights was the Auction. Del brought many rare Kate items with him, perhaps the most valuable being his Tour programme which had been signed by everyone involved. The original white cover CD of *The Red Shoes* went for £600! About £2000 was raised for Kate's chosen charity, Great Ormond Street Hospital for children, by the auction alone. (Did anyone else spot the Peter Pan connection?) Del and Dave make a great team – will they one day be the new Laurel and Hardy, Morecambe and Wise, Tom and Jerry? Or will they ever remain The Dangerous Brothers. Who knows. Del is a wonderful guy. He's so friendly and funny and a pleasure to chat with.

Almost everyone who submitted their Kate Top Tens complained that this was one of the hardest tasks they had been asked to perform! When *Wuthering Heights* was announced as No.1, there was a very audible groan and grumble from the audience. This reaction was a complete surprise to us because you had voted it into that position! Dave had wanted to rig the poll so that *Moments of Pleasure* was No.1 instead, but that would have been a waste of everyone's time and

Photo: *HomeGround* Reader

Photo: Peter Chow

would have been dishonest. But *Wuthering Heights* it was and *Wuthering Heights* it stayed. From the very beginning it was way ahead of the rest.

There were so many people we just didn't get a chance to say hello to. There just wasn't time. I seemed to be running everywhere, and kept seeing Lisa doing the same. And those mirrors meant that we all kept running into ourselves. Oooh, it was all too Stonehenge for me! And the number of times I got lost and ended up in completely the wrong place!

Peter and I were to meet Kate outside the building. We were waiting for the signal that she was on her way, and waited for the limo to arrive. Well, just as her car turned into the narrow back street, a large bin lorry turned into the same street, and was trying to squeeze through the gaps between the parked cars. We thought this was quite amusing, because we could see Kate sitting in the back of the car, waiting patiently for the bin men to get past.

After about five minutes, the lorry disappeared, and Kate's car pulled up. We had a quick hug and ushered her safely into the Hippo and to her room, at the top (or so it seemed) of the city. There were five flights of stairs which I had become so familiar with that day, up and down, up and down, past the beer stains, past the cigarette butts, and past Dave's friend, Ian, who seemed to get more and more inebriated (and happy!) each time I passed him!

As Kate began coming up from the gaping hole in the ground Dave was looking somewhere other than at the stage. I could see the top of her head from where I was standing. It seemed to me that he wasn't aware that Kate was on her way up. So to get Dave's attention I grabbed hold of his bottom – it was all I could think of to attract his wandering mind. He had a mad panic 'cos he thought he was going to fall down the hole, right onto Kate. He was absolutely nowhere near the stage hole, but I guess it was about time he had a major outburst, and I was the victim of that demon tongue. Dave, Darling, Sweetie, you really are like Eddie, you know... Panic attack! Panic attack!... "I can't believe the way you treat me! After all I have done for you! I try so bloody hard to make your life wonderful... I could get you all T-shirts made...Video screens, catering... Tell me what you need... You are not to organise a surprise unless I know about it ..." Darling, it's no use denying it!

Kate arrived safely on stage and the audience gave her a huge welcome. Kate said that it was great to see everyone. She chose the winning raffle ticket, belonging to Bill Atmore. Kate then introduced the film and said she hoped to see everyone again in the not too distant future. She left the stage and disappeared to the top of the building.

We went to see Kate for a few minutes. I collapsed in a messy heap beside her (having accidentally kicked over her beer – how embarrassing!) I was so tired and spaced out that I didn't manage to say anything of any sense or worth to Kate and the only thing I remember saying was that my beloved Grandma, who died last September, looked so uncannily like Lily. That was the first time we'd stopped all day, and all I wanted to do was sleep! But we couldn't stop; jobs needed doing, missing cases had to be found and packed with the remaining merchandise. So off Peter and I went, and Kate made a quiet exit with Lisa and Dave.

The disco gave everyone the rare chance to dance to Kate's music – which was played loud, in fact too loud. Dave, who was the DJ (as well as MC, all round yummy man in charge, slave-driver and tea-maker – are there no ends to his talents?), was asked to turn the volume down! In a spare moment, Dave and I on passing, vaguely recognised each other ("Aren't you Whatsisname?"). I grabbed Dave, Dave grabbed me and we improvised to *Rubberband Girl* at the

Photo: Mark Semic

back of the music desk. That was great fun as we galloped and Tangoed down the aisle. Dave decided to schwing me around, and nearly broke his back.

Just before midnight, Dave played what was to be the last song – *Moments of Pleasure*.

One of my favourite memories of the whole day was the vision of Markus (who had danced in the circle of candles) and another guy (wearing dreadlocks), both dancing their own interpretations of the song, both inseparable from the music; the only two people left on the dance floor. Everyone stood around the edge and watched in silence. I was sitting right at the top looking down at these moving strangers. They both looked so beautiful. I turned to my friend and cried... Then the clock struck midnight, and we all turned into pumpkins. It was time to gather our chattels, bags, socks, knickers, friends, and go. I have never ever felt so knackered!

This was the most informal event, complete with one or two technical hitches, but these things happen. Dave is right when he says it wasn't perfect, but it was more cozy than other events and we all agreed that the atmosphere was the most friendly and relaxed ever. Here's to the next Convention, and maybe then we'll have Dave's performance of *The Sensual World* in the same vein as Peter Sellers' *A Hard Days Night*! Titter ye not – Dave is currently rehearsing as I write! And despite all the teasing, I do love you enormously, Dave.

Photo: Leigh Norwood

KATE BUSH
CONVENTION
SUNDAY 8TH MAY
1994

KBC/HOMEGROUND
8TH MAY 1994

Welcome to the 1994 Kate Bush Convention, especially to those of you who have travelled so far to get here.

Today we will be celebrating the release of Kate's seventh album, "The Red Shoes" and her debut film project, "The Line, The Cross & The Curve". We will of course be showing the film today, plus an interview in which Kate talks at length about both the film and the album. We will also be remembering the past by showing a selection of rare TV and video clips, including the BBC 2 "Kate" special from 1979. Thanks are due to everyone who sent us their Kate Top Ten (we know it was a tough job!) we will reveal the results later.

Other things happening today include the brain stretching quiz, with some very special prizes for the winning team, some great live music and dance from other fans, a raffle and some surprises. The day will end with the largest ever Kate inspired Disco/Party, a chance to hear Kate's music really loud and go completely mad!

Many thanks to everyone who has been involved in the organisation of the Convention and to our brave team of helpers.

Have fun !

Lisa, Dave, Peter and Krys.

Dear Friends

Really looking forward to seeing you all, hope you enjoy the film. Have a great time. Many thanks, as always, for your continued support

with lots of love

Kate x

You are under the smell of the Pink Mules!

That alternative classic ...

Issue 53: August 1994

Jasper Sorbet: Muffin' the Mules

The celluloid classic I am reviewing today is *The Pink Mules*, a star in the night sky that is set to hit the visionary world by storm now it is available in its unedited Director's Cut on video – with all the essences of love, sorrow, deception and greed that epitomise life itself.

Reeling into the depths of one's innermost self, this film explores the very core of our nature, an illuminating classic guaranteed to hit the hearts of the humble coal merchant and the polo-playing prince alike. It is an emotional truth beyond mere words.

The story is introduced by the Jacques-esque character of Ms Daisy Bosche (aka Fiona Cross), broaching the world with an entanglement of raw sex and feminine sensitivity that only dares to glimpse the imminent awakening and truths held within the pink mules' glittering and cavernous depths.

The central character manoeuvring the sable nuances of the film is Post-Modern mime and orange juggling artiste, Kevin Hall, the '70s Diva of Boscombe Gardens, presently recovering from rickets at Guy's Hospital with Una's daughter, Sybil. Kevin, recreating his role of Potty Pam The Palmist (first seen in the video *The Melamine Cupboards*) descends gracefully back into the role, remoulding admirably into the new and abstract concepts he struggled to perceive.

The other leading character is Matilda Bagette (aka Gary Boulton), whose charismatic charm and brow line earned him the part in this lavish costume drama, even beating hunky ex-'Doctor Who' star, Jon Pertwee, to this sought after and ground-breaking role of the evil temptress who tricks poor Pam into accepting the hallucinogenic powers of those mystic mules. Gary, who shot to fame as a table on 'Noel's House Party', is currently touring with the late Terry Scott in *Oh No, I'm Wearing The Au Pair's Underwear* at various seaside resorts.

The only male role in the film belongs to Roly Bolokortu (aka Paul Thomas), an escaped Russian Cypriot oil-tanker navigator who was exiled from his native lands due to a frustration with hats, and who, on landing on British shores was guided by the queen of tap dancing, chiffon cravatted Lionel Blair, who remodelled Roly's frost ridden legs, made them dance and become the inspiration to countless 1970s starlets, including Bonnie Langford and Leo Sayer.

...And so the fairy tale begins in a storm-plagued dance studio inhabited by a lost and forlorn palm reader, Potty Pam, who struggles with reality and her inner depraved personality. After a particularly traumatic stretch in a rehabilitation unit she takes up dancing again, but is soon spooked and shaken, when after she is left alone in the studio she has an important vision of her past and future experiences, portrayed here metaphorically in all its beauty and sensitivity by a misguided crow who dies in Pam's hands.

In an attempt to capture her elusive alter-ego and escape from the mundane world of Our Price adverts and Pop Tart binges, Pam destroys that very free and whimsical spirit that she aspired to keep.

Racked by grief and fifty Marlborough Lights, Pam is seduced by the Delilah-esque charms and demonic forces of Matilda Bagette, who in an attempt to draw Pam from her bottomless pit of despair, tricks her into slipping on the incredibly beautiful fluffy pink mules. In putting on the mules, Pam is transported into the twilight world of pleasure, pain, 'The Block', and Jim Davison Pier Shows. Revelling in her alter-self and losing control of time, space and her coil, Pam is suddenly aware that she is losing all aspects of her former sad, paltry life as she grasps at that grey world of Jimmy Jewell, Slim-Fast and The Krankies.

The pink mules drag her further in, tripping away into the multi-coloured kaleidoscope world and finally through the mirror of eternal youth. Pam realises that reality wasn't so bad after all, in her technicolour trip of nasty wigs and badly applied make-up, and so attempts to return to the real world via *The Wizard of Oz* routine of clicking heels and crack addiction. We see Pam returning to her familiar studio and all seems well, or does it? Is that the satanic cackle of Matilda? Or Ernie's ghostly Gold Tops a-rattling in their crate?

Paul Thomas: The Director's dossier

Issue 59: July 1997

This is the real story behind the making of the blockbuster.

9am: Early morning calls to Gary, Kevin and Fiona, nursing severe hangovers following the Crème De Menthe promotion night at the Pansy Gush Tearooms, and incapable of stringing runner beans let alone syllables together. Ushered into waiting sedan chairs (tastefully decorated with purple damask and tassels) and despatched to Pokesdown Community Church Hall for rehearsals.

10.30am: Tea break. Four heavily sweating bodies lumber into canteen to be revived with chipped mugs of fennel twig tea, All Butter Shorties and twenty Rothmans.

Opposite: The 1994 Convention programme

11am: Barely revived, the cast slope off across the grease stained lino with a pack of king-size

Rizlas, rolling tobacco and what appeared to be an Oxo cube, to be ushered into their awaiting garments.

11.15am: In costume and barely conscious, the cast embark on the first scene. Primadonna-esque heroine Potty Pam (Kevin Hall) throws neurotic tantrums over minor script changes and the line "Has anyone fed the Shite-Hawk?" is hacked from the original script.

11.20am: Matilda Baguette slips into drug induced coma: filming temporarily suspended.

11.22am: Matilda revived by insertion of very high fibre herbal pessary. Filming further delayed when Matilda's bandages became soaked in Amyl Nitrite and ignited on a frayed electrical camera cable.

11.29am: Filming delayed (again!) during surreal bandage scene when Matilda's now charcoal stained bandages became entangled in the wind machine.

11.40am: Crow dies on set. Anthrax suspected; Public Health Inspector alerted causing further delays in filming.

1.30pm: Giles decides to keep "Crow death scene" in the film. Potty Pam concerned over virulence of anthrax in Crow-kissing sub-scene.

1.35pm: Mules dance unaided through mirror causing great distress to all assembled. The words "I think there's some on the piano" retrieved them with great haste.

1.40pm: Lunch break at the Salvation Army soup kitchen. Concrete hard stale rolls and watery leek and potato concoction served by scaly elbowed Sally "Army" Earnshaw, (who smelled of stale urine and moth balls).

1.50pm: Cast forcefully ejected onto pavement following "incident" involving spoon, tin foil and icing sugar. Crew informed in no uncertain terms never to darken doors of the Sally Army again due to garish costumes and drug abuse.

2.55pm: Cast bailed from police station following G & T smash and grab. Potty Pam triumphantly waving an economy toilet roll stated, "I was under the spell of the Pink Mules".

3.05pm: Filming commences on return to studio.

3.06pm: Filming completed: inspired, and heart-rending performance.

3.07pm: After film party at Working Men's Railway Club. Pam overwhelmed by flowers and particularly smelly pair of grey pants.

5.00pm: Sedan chairs hailed for return to cast members' Boscombe bed-sits, but were undergoing fumigation. Cast members decide to hijack the Boscombe Beach Noddy train

7.00pm: Giles shovels together butchered extracts from the day's fiming, breaking all copyright laws with the soundtrack.

7.15pm: All cast members in drying-out clinic at Cemetery Junction. Day fades to a frail voice muttering "What a trip!"

It Really Happened to Us!

HomeGround readers react to the 1994 Convention

Letters from issue 52 June 1994 to issue 55 April 1995

Whilst the press and media were already propagating the myth of Kate's "reclusiveness" most fans were of course pleased to see her at the convention at all.

But It is of course impossible to please everyone.

Gordon Beadle: I just had to write and tell you what a wonderful time I had at the Convention. I'm sure I speak for all the other Kate fans present when I say that it was a magical occasion completed by the appearance of the lady herself. Just to have her there talking to us made the trip to London worth it a thousand times!

Everything about the Convention was superb. The live acts all did incredibly well, especially the dancers who took the technical hitch in their stride! I was amazed by how much money some of the items in the auction raised, but I'm so pleased because the charity that will benefit is very important.

I thought it was good to see Paddy step into the limelight for once. His talent has been hiding for far too long. Hopefully his album will do very well and expose his music to a wider audience.

The film was very interesting. Although Kate has said in the past she is not an actress or indeed does not have any aspirations in that direction, I felt she carried the spoken parts with conviction. The film also reinforced what a versatile actress the lovely Miranda Richardson is.

Although Kate's appearance was short, it was lovely to see her. She did appear to be overwhelmed by the amount of people who had turned up. I just wanted to tell her how much she inspires me and what an important part of my life she is. I'm sure the reaction Kate received when she appeared on the stage conveyed to her what she means to us all. It was the moment of the day we had all been waiting for.

Finally, after two hours or so of serious dancing it was all over and time to go home. My friend, Keith and I agreed that the day was over far too soon. But what a brilliant day it had been!

What can I say? Thanks Dave, Krys, Peter, and the tireless Lisa, for another superb Convention. Thanks to the live acts for some great entertainment, Paddy for revealing his talent, Del for being a great all round entertainer. Finally, thank you Kate for just being there. Here's to the next one!

Bill Atmore: Well, how to start? By saying thank you to all those involved in organising yet another excellent Convention, I suppose! It was wonderful to see so many people, even more than last time, gathered in the same place, all with one thing in common – to enjoy themselves with Kate's music (and presence) providing the ideal catalyst! I hope that the party continued in the same vein. Well done to you all (even if I did only know four or five answers to Peter's questions!)

It was great to see Kate again (just a tiny understatement there!) and I thought Del almost stole the show (somebody ought to tell him that he should be in show business!) My only gripe is that there was no repeat of the 'Question and Answer' session with Kate, which worked so well last time. But there was so much else to enjoy that it really didn't seem to matter.

The Line, the Cross & the Curve was excellent – will this woman ever cease to amaze? Miranda Richardson was a perfect choice. Am I the only one to detect a trace of *Twin Peaks*-isms? Lily's boudoir had major White Lodge overtones and Kate's 'Protector' displayed distinct dancing dwarf tendencies! Or am I going mad?

But as far as I am concerned, the perfect end to a perfect day was being the owner of ticket 391 (and I almost threw it away!) I am only just beginning to recover – I seemed to lose all control of mind and body when Kate drew the number. I couldn't even manage a hoarse "Over here!" I have never ever felt so speechless! If anyone has photos of those 15 seconds please let me know. There's a space on the wall just below the disc that is crying out for a 4x6"!

Photo Hannes Punkenhoffer

The Lucky raffle winner

So, what else can I say, but thanks again and see you at the next Convention! I've already started to swot, determined to reach double figures in Peter's next quiz!

Ian Park: Thank you, thank you, thank you for the Convention! We had a really fab time and my mind boggles at the amount of work that must have gone into it. There were so many excellent moments, especially the opportunity to finally see *The Line, the Cross & the Curve* – surely it must come out on video in the near future? And naturally, to see Kate herself introduce it. I just wish there was some way she could have stayed a bit longer. I have a theory that the longer she stays the more relaxed and comfortable she becomes, as borne out by her delightful Question and Answer session at the last Convention, but of course, balanced against that I realise the rather negative experience of the Video Café crush (which I didn't attend, but have the *HomeGround* reports to go by) has to be taken into account. My friend Dave McArdle reckons that if everybody knows Kate will be there, and for some time, then people could get used to this idea and problems of, er, "over enthusiasm" could be bypassed, but this has the fatal flaw of believing that everyone will be as calm and reasonable as Dave, and myself!

The other highlight, which obviously had you all concerned as regards the reactions of those in attendance, was *The Pink Mules*, which reduced me and those around me to tears of helpless laughter! Already passed into our everyday parlance between my wife Julie and myself is the phrase "It's all a bit Stonehenge!" for anything vaguely mysterious, and I'm wondering if I can come up with a Pink Mules T-shirt for the next get together! The bit where the mules mysteriously put themselves on, echoing the self-lacing Red Shoes, was priceless!

I also thought the American dance mix of *Rubberband Girl* as played at the disco was terrific – how about a mini-album of re-mixes? I know that to put it mildly, opinion appears to be divided over re-mixes, and at the Convention, the version of *The Red Shoes* particularly came in for some disapproval, although I think it's fine, but not really a close relation to the original, and probably better for it. The version of *Sexual Healing* was rather odd at first hearing. I'd like to hear it several times before I make my mind up, but it certainly was different. *The Man I Love* is a beautiful song by any standards and Kate's rendering of it was splendidly and tastefully done, as you would expect.

Wasn't Del excellent? I thought he handled the auction with Dave brilliantly, although this was the part of the Convention where (for obvious reasons) I sat on my hands and maintained a strict silence, apart from (along with everyone else) a few startled gasps!

I look forward to the next issue of *HomeGround*, not least for the answers to the fiendishly difficult quiz! And of course, memories of the 1994 Kate Bush Convention will come flooding back! Doesn't it seem a long time ago? I think I'll go fondle my *Red Shoes* T-shirt! Once again, huge thanks, darlings, you were terrific. Mwah, mwah etc!

Procolo Tortorelli: I dislike that the first time I write to you is a criticism – to you and to the Kate Bush Convention 1994, but I must do it because I just think that it was not good at all!

At first, I criticise Kate. In fact, once again she showed that she doesn't care very much about her fans – coming on the stage and staying for only two or three minutes is to say the least very shameful.

Yes, there were videos, quizzes, lots of music, but above all, people came to see Kate. Whereas, she – she just appears and immediately disappears. Now, didn't Kate think that there were people coming from abroad to see her? Didn't she think that they would have preferred to stay at home if she had not come to the Convention (it was almost the same)? And didn't she think that there were people who came only to see her (me!!) or that they had gone to the toilets just at the moment she was on stage, they would have come to London for no reason? If at least you'd have announced that she was coming I'd have tried to restrain my need. But no, she had to surprise us... and what a surprise! Three minutes on stage. Fantastic!??? I'm sorry, but I think Kate was really wrong this time. This is not the way to swindle people.

Photo: Keith Woodhouse

Of course, the criticism is addressed to you too because there was not a reason to have a Convention if there was not Kate... or almost. But that is very likely not your fault. But I have to say that I think your organisation was not good enough: many things improvised, the finishing of the Convention without an official end, and keeping hidden that Kate would not appear again after her brief appearance!

Also, your distribution of posters, badges and so on was very shameful. I wonder is that the way to do it? Did you know that there are people who went back home with few things? Did you know there were also those who got so much that after they could sell them on and be allowed to make money for themselves, as has already happened with items from previous Conventions? Well, perhaps it is not concern of yours, maybe you think you are superior to us, just throwing things from the stage to people under it, maybe enjoying to see all those people taking pains in trying to collect as many things as possible, finding all that very amusing!? Was it not better if you prepared a parcel to give to everyone entering the Hippodrome? At least you could make sure that everyone had everything, but no – what does it matter to you about that? The most important thing for you was to get as many people to the Convention as possible, coming from everywhere for the greater glory of yourselves, so you could take pleasure yourselves in being able to draw the attention of so many people!

To finish I would like to mention the posters and similar things on the walls at the Hippodrome. I don't understand. They are not for sale, and if you ask for them the answer is that you can't take them, but at the end these items always finish in the hands or bags of fans!

So, which is their function? Is it to see who can resist without plundering them? Is it the important thing to "don't ask, steal"? Please tell us so next time I won't waste time, but as soon as I enter I will start to take them off!

Well, *HomeGround*, I don't say that the Convention was completely wrong (Paddy was wonderful!) but I think it was not a good one. Surely the 1990 Convention was much better than this one! For the future I hope that you (and also Kate) try to be a little more respectful of Kate fans. I think we deserve something more!

Editors' response: *Well, we can't please everyone! The Conventions are about Kate and her music and bringing people together to have a good time. That is what most people want. It is after all the music that has brought everyone together. These events also take a lot of time and energy to arrange (especially for Dave and Lisa). They are also for charity.*

Kate is one of the few artists to actually attend her

own Conventions – most of the big names don't – so we are lucky that she should attend at all. It is entirely up to Kate as to whether she comes along, and how much she wants to do on stage. We feel that everyone should consider Kate, rather than themselves. After all, she doesn't owe anyone, anything. We've said this many times before, but just because people buy her albums, that doesn't mean they are buying her.

We all appreciate that everyone would like to spend a minute or two talking with Kate or getting stuff signed, but imagine how much time and energy that would take for a thousand people or so. This kind of thing would be more of a PA than a Convention.

The Video Party in 1986 is a classic example of some fans not only ruining it for themselves, but also for Kate and her family, and other fans. She was totally mobbed. Some people were selfish and very demanding of Kate, who incidentally was in the middle of filming Experiment IV, *and was tired and had 'flu. I should think that the way those fans behaved then has put her off for life. It simply didn't work having Kate at the same floor level as everyone else.*

We often don't know for definite whether Kate will attend an event until a few days before, therefore, we cannot announce in advance that she will be there, in case she is unable to attend at the last minute.

We feel it is very unfair and rather rude for anyone to say that Kate doesn't care about her fans. Perhaps some of her fans don't care very much about her, and make too many demands from her – the majority don't, but Kate is a human being like the rest of us and deserves the same consideration.

We are sorry if one or two were disappointed with the Convention, but the event, like life, is also what you make it. The majority of people did have a good day.

Leigh Norwood: Thanks for a wonderful day. It was such a good feeling for us to be in such a large friendly group of people all gathered together from all points of the globe – for the one reason; all sharing a deep affection for the music and talent of one magic person – Kate.

The Convention was a great event, even better I think than the last one (I didn't ever think that would be possible). The live acts were tremendous, the rare video footage was a treat (especially the welcome re-run of the 1979 BBC Special), the Top 40 was interesting to say the least, the quiz was infuriating, the flm was captivating and Kate was just gorgeous (there just wasn't enough of her, but I guess we were a bit spoiled at the last Convention!)

I hope the disco went well. Unfortunately, we had to leave before it started, and wend our happy way back to Gloucestershire with great memories of a great Convention.

Bryan Simcott: Firstly, THANK YOU for one of the best days of 1994. The event was so good and it was great to see everyone enjoy themselves so much. How many things I have to say! The value at the shop – how there could still be a profit at those prices I do not know. The free give-away madness, the loyalty, and love from everybody there making sure everyone got something from the free items was a beautiful memory. I'm sure Kate is proud to have such a loving and friendly fan following as this. The fun, the film, the videos, the time taken to organise, edit and get prepared, the live acts (who deserve a huge round of applause for their guts and sheer imagination – to sing *The Red Shoes* in front of other Kate fans, and *Wuthering Heights*; *The Big Sky* was really different – a brilliant interpretation.

The videos and exclusive tracks were a dream. And then we get to the cream of the day – Kate so close, so real, so human. And so to the disco – brilliant. To hear Kate loud and proud was a dream and to dance in a real night club to Kate – Wow! I'm sending this letter to both you and the Kate Bush Club, so thanks to all your hard work as a team. And isn't Dave yummy in the flesh?

Photo: Keith Woodhouse

Graham Cowan: I just wanted to thank you all and everyone involved for the Convention. It was a great day, worth all the saving for flights, hotels etc. I've just read the letters in issue 52 and was very interested in the opinions expressed on the amount of time Kate actually spent on stage. I must admit I was a bit disappointed she didn't spend more time with us – it is after all the only occasion most people ever get a chance to see her in the flesh. But I do agree with your own views; it was great of Kate to appear at all, she didn't have to do it and as such I do believe she really does care about the people who listen to her music. I think most Kate fans would like to see more of her in general. She doesn't tour, doesn't do TV appearances and as a result when she does appear we tend to expect more of her, to make up for all the absences in some way.

Darren Brown: Kate Bush. That name stands out from a page like the word "sex". Yet the two cannot be equated in literal terms. Ask a non-Kate fan for a definition of Kate Bush and you will get a stereotypical answer that has direct links with 1978 and *Wuthering Heights*. Ask a Kate fan for a definition and most probably wouldn't be able to answer – at least not straight away. To most of us, Kate defies definition, purely because she is Kate Bush. She is "amazing" and "genius",

Photo: *HomeGround* Reader

but those are descriptions, personal opinions, not definitions.

One thing that Kate fans do agree on is that she is someone special, capable of affecting people's lives on many different levels. I would even go so far as to suggest that each of her songs has a different meaning for each person who listens to them. Do I feel the same things when I hear *Night of the Swallow* as the next person? Do I see the same images and movements in my mind? Probably not, but then I'll never know. That one person has the gift of being able to do this is something special. Kate gives us these songs, gives them a little push and then leaves the rest to us. Isn't that why her music is so special? She lets us take it on board, to inspire or excite, even sadden. We can sing along, dance to it, draw pictures suggested by it, make friends through it. We are lucky. I would even go so far as to say we are a privileged bunch. And this is where I get saddened.

In May 1994, *HomeGround* and the Kate Bush Club organised a Kate Bush Convention in honour of all things red, ballet shoe-shaped and Kate-related. It gave my pen-friend (whom I met through *HomeGround*) the perfect excuse to come over to England for the first time, meet me and go to the Convention. We both had a fantastic day. The music was the best, the footage was magical and the entertainment was terrific. What more could anyone ask for? Nothing. Just perfect. Yet there were loads of freebies given away – which they didn't have to do – and most people got something. Still perfect. Then Kate came on stage and said some words about the film, pulled out a raffle ticket and presented that disc to an incredibly lucky chappie. Then Kate left the stage and we all watched the film. Still perfect.

So I was completely gob-smacked when I read the latest issue of *HomeGround*. OK, so people are entitled to their opinions. I'm all for that – I'm voicing mine now and that is what the mag is about!

What I really couldn't understand was that some people were not only unhappy with the Convention, but were extremely bitter, almost to the point of hatred. Why? So Kate didn't stay on stage for long enough. How long is long enough? What was she supposed to do? The set-up was such that she couldn't talk with us, only to us. She didn't have to come at all. Why should she? I wonder if people would have had a better time is she hadn't been there. At least that way they would have had one less thing to moan about. If I were in Kate's position and I was aware of the bad feelings that some people were experiencing, I would be upset. I may even think twice about appearing at a Convention ever again.

There is no law or contract anywhere that says Kate is obliged to appear at a Convention. It is her choice. She decides if she appears, when she appears and for how long. Simple as that. To take it out on the *HomeGround* team or the KBC is just ridiculous. The Convention is not a concert. Kate comes on, says hello, then leaves. "Hello" is better than not seeing her at all, surely? It is very sad that on a day such as this, when people are supposed to enjoy themselves, there are still those who bring greed and dissatisfaction with them. People for whom there could never be enough: freebies or Kate in the flesh.

To end this sombre piece, I would suggest three things to those who were unhappy with the event. Firstly, don't go with any preconceptions as to how the day will run – they will always be different. Secondly, organising a Convention is no mean feat. It takes a lot of hard work and a lot of people's time. Thirdly, go back and really listen to your Kate music. You'll realise that you've got everything you need there in your hands. I'm all for healthy criticism, but bitterness and jealousy – no thanks. What's the point?

Some words from a song by an English lady which I think are quite apt – "Just being alive, it can really hurt" and "these moments given, are a gift from time".

Gary Campbell: As a relatively new subscriber (and I consider *HomeGround* to be my second Bible), it gives me displeasure to be writing this letter of complaint concerning a letter which appeared in issue 52. An Italian gentleman wrote a letter telling of his disappointment with Kate

and the Convention, with a poignant criticism of Kate only devoting a few minutes to her fans, many of whom had travelled the globe.

We all share the love of Kate and her art, which could never be faulted. But she is like us – a human being with an equal share of faults. I agree with the gentleman and others who feel that Kate could have given more time and energy to her fans at the Convention, considering the lengths that many people went to in order to be there.

We know that Kate has always said she never wanted to achieve fame and fortune from her work, but it has been her fans loyal support that has enabled her to become even more successful and to continue in the music world to far greater depths.

My issue is I felt Kate was wrong and individuals will start to question if she does care about her fans with such actions, namely her brief appearance at the Convention. I understand that the gentleman's letter aired strong views, but I feel that we should be allowed to have our opinions published without an editor's note criticising the content of our letters, so we, the readers can decide as to who we agree or disagree with and draw our own conclusions. We all share a love for Kate and her work, but she is a person not a God.

Ola Stensson: There was no chance of me attending the Convention. I didn't see what happened (or what didn't happen). I've only read the letters from some of the visitors. I'm sorry to say so, but your answer to Procolo Tortorelli of Italy, was written in a very arrogant manner. A person who has travelled so long for his own (I guess) self-earned money, has a right to be disappointed if Kate appeared on stage for only a couple of minutes.

It is not true, as you say, that she doesn't owe anything to anyone. She does indeed owe something to her fans who are buying her records and videos and by this is making it possible for her to live on her music and having, I hope, a good life. Every artist owes something to her/his fans and you know it, and I'm sure Kate knows it too. The fans, on the other hand, owe Kate gratefulness, respect and letting her have her integrity. I am sure everyone who loves Kate Bush as a singer and song-writer is aware of that.

I don't know what relations you have with Kate, but I find it amazing that you can't tell until a few days before whether she will turn up to her own Convention or not. That makes it very risky for "ordinary" people to attend such a thing in the future. Ordinary people have to ask their employer for vacation, they have to make travel arrangements and they have to pay lots of hard-earned money if they are travelling from, for example, Italy. Ordinary people, therefore, can't afford to be disappointed.

If Kate was feeling ill this particular day, everyone would of course have excused her and then we have nothing to argue about. But no person in the world lives without obligations and

Photos: Hannes Punkenhoffer

I don't think anyone wants to. Kate is of course fully aware of that, as are most of us.

Helen Creighton: I would like to take the opportunity to join the debate regarding Kate's appearance at the 1994 Convention. Concerning Kate's brief appearance, surely anyone with eyes can see that Kate does care about her fans.

In 1990 whilst still a relative newcomer to Kate's music, I attended that year's Convention having no idea that she would be involved at all. I had a thoroughly good time, and when Kate turned up and spent that wonderful half hour or more chatting away like an old friend, I was stunned, then honoured. In her manner there was no hint of a 'star' making a carefully managed PA in order to stir up publicity for herself and sell more records. I was touched by her genuine warmth and interest in the goings-on of the day, and left with the impression of having 'met' a truly special human being. That impression remains to this day.

I was blown away yet again by her attendance at the 1994 event. For myself, however wonderful it is to see Kate, I feel that it is ultimately the music that counts. I was, therefore, surprised and saddened to read that some people regard the music as merely a commodity to be traded for the 'price' of Kate's time and presence. I was surprised to discover there are actually people who have the arrogance to define Kate's 'commitments' and then proceed to 'excuse' her from them, (or not) as they wish.

I have the deepest respect for you all at *HomeGround*, and for Kate for putting up with this abject stupidity. I'm sure most readers are aware of the great deal of time and commitment involved in the production of a magazine of the scale and quality of *HomeGround*. I've only been a subscriber since issue 42 and in that time have been amused, touched, upset (by the terrible life experiences of some readers), intrigued, informed and inspired.

HomeGround is so obviously a work of love and as such is a testament to the generosity of spirit that infects the Kate-speaking world. Let's not allow a tiny minority of rather mean-spirited and greedy individuals to spoil it. Don't let us stop having Conventions. These events are a chance to communicate with those who feel the same way as we do about Kate's music, to have fun and indulge in masses of music and video. Those who attend purely to gawk at Kate have, somewhere along the road, missed the point. Kate's music – beautiful, intelligent, passionate music – touches the hearts and minds of so many people, and serves as an inspiration in ways I won't attempt to describe here. It brings us together at events and in publications like *HomeGround*. We have perfect, life-enhancing music created by an exceptional human being. We have each other. What the hell is there to complain about?

Sophie Hayat: After reading the letters in *HomeGround* 54 I thought I should write. First of all, I would like to tell you how much I enjoyed myself at last year's Convention. Everything seemed too good to be true; I saw videos I had never seen before; I saw Paddy Bush and Colin Lloyd Tucker perform; I admired the talent of the other performers (especially the dancers); I won some items signed by Kate; I watched Kate's film *The Line, the Cross & the Curve*, heard incredible music, and as if that was not enough, I saw Kate. She was so charming, so human, so close. I still can't believe I saw her! It was almost like she was talking to me.

Photo: Hannes Punkenhoffer

Protect Yourself With Fire!

Peter and The Love Hounds investigate a Magick Prayer

Issue 53 August 1994

Peter was quite interested in Kate's apparent use in *Lily*, of a ritual taken from the Western mystery tradition. I say 'apparent' because Kate herself has said of the song that it is not a ritual, it is a prayer. Perhaps that's a distinction without a difference. To pray is to use words of power. What we have here are words of power.

Those who know more than I do about such matters on the internet group alt.magick have discussed various aspects of *Lily*, and I thought it would be interesting for *HomeGround* readers to see two of the contributions that were copied to rec.music.gaffa.

From Rob Henderson: First of all, let me clear up a misconception that the lesser banishing ritual is an "Aleister Crowley ritual". This ritual was used by the Hermetic Order of the Golden Dawn in London in the 1890's, and Crowley was a member or the Order, so if you see it attributed to him, he got it from the Golden Dawn. The origins of the ritual may go further back than that, I honestly don't know. Here is the ritual, as taken from *The Middle Pillar*. (pp. 94-95):

1.Perform the Qabalistic Cross.
2.Face East. Stretch out right hand holding a ceremonial dagger. Trace a Banishing Earth Pentagram. Vibrate the word YHVH (pronounced Yod-heh-vav-heh).
3.Still holding out hand and dagger, turn to the South. Trace another Pentagram in precisely the same way and vibrate the word ADNI (Ah-doh-nai).
4.Then turn to the West and trace Pentagram. Vibrate AHIH (Eh-he-yeh).
5.Turn North. Trace Pentagram and vibrate AGLA (Ah-ge-lah).
6.Return to the East. Extend arms in the form of Cross.
7.Say: "Before me Raphael".
8. "Behind me Gabriel"
9. "On my right hand Michael"
10. "On my left hand Auriel"
11. "For before me flames the Pentagram"
12. "And behind me shines the Six-rayed Star"
13.Repeat the Qabalistic Cross.

The Qabalistic Cross is a simple step, similar to crossing oneself in the Christian traditions. It's a way of getting into the mood of the rituals, for 'getting your energies aligned', as it were.

The tracing of the pentagrams is usually accompanied by visualising blue flames in the air where you've traced. The pentagrams form a circle around you, protecting you from whatever it is you want to banish. "Vibrate" means to intone the words in such a way that your whole body vibrates as you say them.

When the pentagrams have all been traced, the Archangels of the four elements are called to watch over you and the circle. You're not 'summoning' them, you're just asking for their help. Steps 11 and 12 finish things up, finalising the banishing effect. Personally, I visualise a circle of blue flame joining the pentagrams together as I say this. The final Qabalistic Cross, like the first one, is to change your mindset, in this case returning you to the 'ordinary' world.

This is considered a very basic ritual, and is often used as an introduction to more powerful rituals. According to Regardie, "The function of this ritual... is pre-eminently one of banishment. Its aim is to eliminate from the sphere of the mind those qualities or sensations which the critical ego deems unnecessary". (pp. 95-96) The ritual won't cure your psychosis, but if you're feeling angry, sad, depressed, etc., this can help get you out of it and make you feel better. Ideally, you should use it every day, at about the same time of day.

So what the Hecate does this all have to do with Kate?

Oh thou, who givest sustenance to the universe
From whom all things proceed
To whom all things return
Unveil to us the face of the true spiritual sun
Hidden by a disc of golden light
That we may know the truth
And do our whole duty
To journey to thy sacred feet...

This is a beautiful passage, and I have no idea what its source is. It sounds like something a Western mysteries group would use, the same type of group which would use the Lesser Banishing Ritual of the Pentagram.

Well I said "Lily, Oh Lily I don't feel safe
I feel that life has blown a great big hole through me"
And she said "Child, you must protect yourself
I'll show you how with fire..."

Pretty basic stuff here. Kate (or Kate's character in the song) feels unsafe, and asks for protection. Lily will show her how she can do this for herself. The fire obviously refers to the flames of the Pentagrams.

Gabriel before me
Raphael behind me...

Oops! In Regardie's version, the angels were evoked in the other order! One person has pointed out that if Kate is facing West and standing upside down, then everything works out the same. There's another explanation, though. Each of those four angels is attributed to one of

Michael: "Who is like God?" Dan. 10:13; 12:1; Jude v. 9; Rev. 12:7-8.

In Islam called Mikhail

Michael is the Angel of Judgment

Gabriel: "The Power or Strength of God" Dan. 8:16; 9:21; Luke 1:19-26.

In Islam called Djibril or Jibril.

Gabriel is the Angel of Mercy

Raphael: "The Healing of God" Tobit 3:17; 12:15.

In Islam called Israfel.

Raphael is the Angel of Healing

Uriel: "The Light or Fire of God" A.V. II Esdras 4:1. Also called Sariel, Suriel, or Muriel.

In Islam called Azrael

Uriel is the Angel of Creation.

To get things into proportion, it was Dr. Bush who one day talking to us compared "Lily" to the well known prayer St. Patrick's Breatplate.

"Who's on the right?

Who's on the left?"

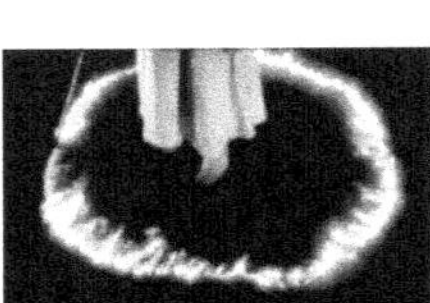

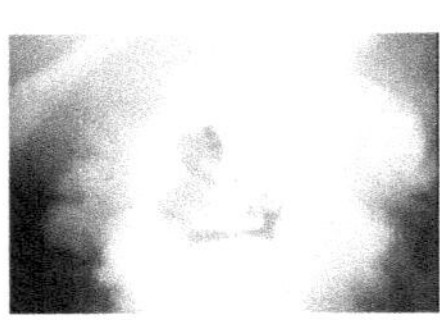

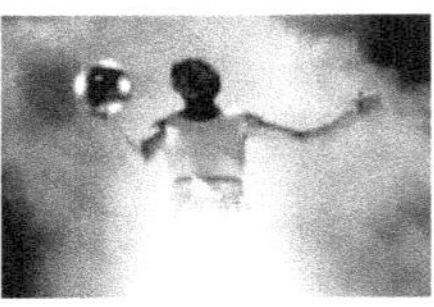

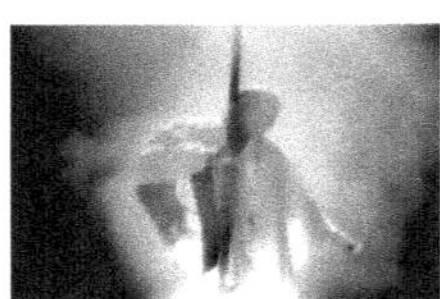

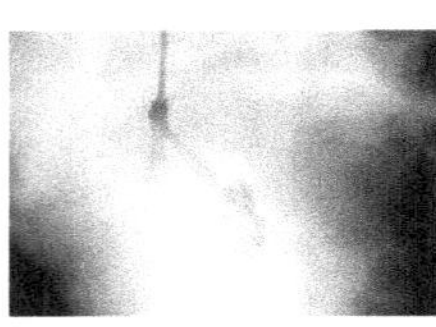

Graphic opposite: Alex Lake

the four elements: Raphael with Air; Michael with Fire; Gabriel with Water; and Auriel (or Uriel) with Earth. The elements are attributed to the directions, similarly: Air with East; Fire with South; Water with West; and Earth with North.

Not all occult groups put the elements in those directions, though. Local geography is the main consideration, so if you have an ocean or lake to your East, and the wind usually comes from the West, why not attribute Water to East and Air to West?

Michael on my right
Uriel on my left side
In the circle of fire

I said "Lily, Oh Lily I'm so afraid
I fear I am walking in the Veil of Darkness"...

This "Veil of Darkness" could mean anything. I don't know of any special significance here.

And she said "Child, take what I say
With a pinch of salt..."

Aha! In my pagan tradition, and many others, salt is considered a symbol of Earth, and is used for purification, of the self or of the temple or circle or sacred space. It's worth noting that the lesser banishing ritual is considered an Earth-oriented ritual - note that you're supposed to trace "Banishing Earth Pentagrams". So the mention of salt here is consistent with the rest of the ritual. (And of course, when studying any kind of occultism, it's always best to take everything with a pinch of salt!)

"And protect yourself with fire..."

So in conclusion, the song is about someone who wants protection from something, and Lily shows her how to use the ritual to do what she wants, to protect herself and banish whatever nastiness she's afraid of.

The Scholarly Stuff: All of the quotes are taken from *The Middle Pillar* by Israel Regardie. (Llewellyn Publications, original copyright 1938.)

From Jean Devitt Kirwin: When Kate references the four angels, she is actually performing an invocation of the four guardians of the corners of the earth, East, West, North and South.

This is commonly one of the first things done when casting a magick circle. The circle is cast and the four guardians are called to protect it from all directions.

Granted, there is some debate on whether Kate actually believes in this or not. Personally, being very well read on the subject, there isn't a doubt in my mind that Kate has most certainly dabbled in the arts of the white witch or the 'wiccan' as many prefer to say, in avoidance of malicious retribution.

When I heard the song, I was thrilled! There isn't a doubt in my mind. It's really not such a bad thing. Wiccans are very good hearted people, and they are very educated, spiritual and enlightened. They spend their lives trying to help others through the use of their spirit, and many succeed.

It is evident that Kate casts a circle in this song, and the introduction by Lily sets the stage. She uses salt, calls the angels, and uses fire. A CIRCLE of fire!

The song is a very powerful statement by Kate of her struggle; perhaps with the death of her mother, and her solution for the protection of her spirit.

Kate has such a powerful essence about her, I'm sure that if she was indeed a fully practising wiccan, much of what she 'willed' would come to be. But then again this all may be just too far out for most of the group readers to accept, so I apologise if I have offended anyone's beliefs or pre-conceptions about Kate and what she REALLY believes in.

Scott: The following article is extracted from the Wiccan magazine *Pagan Express*:

Since mentioning Kate Bush in issue two I have got her latest album, *The Red Shoes*. It's just as good as any of her previous albums. One song which I thought was very interesting is *Lily*. This song starts with the spoken lyrics:

Oh thou, who givest sustenance to the universe
From whom all things proceed
To whom all things return
Unveil to us the face of the true spiritual sun...

Now listen to the words of the Star Goddess from the Wiccan Charge:

I am the soul of Nature
who gives life to the universe.
From me all things proceed,
And unto me all things must return.
Let thine innermost divine self
be enfolded in the rapture of the infinite...

This is obviously not just a coincidence.

There is a gentleman in London who has done some research into the origins of the Wiccan Charge. Gareth J. Medway suggests that the section quoted above is from a Hindu sacred text. His theory is that a member of the Theosophical Society who knew these Hindu scriptures was also a member of the New Forest Coven which initiated Gerald Gardner.

Gardner, (and we must not forget Doreen Valiente also), then unleashed modern Witchcraft on the world.

Make of this what you will.

PROTECT
YOURSELF
WITH FIRE
Alex '94 x

She Will Come

Extracts from the HomeGround/Ecto Happy Rhodes Interview

Issues 48 and 49: May and August 1993

Happy Rhodes (a distant relative of Cecil Rhodes), is an American singer and songwriter of ethereal, strange and intriguing songs, who has often been compared to Kate, and who shares many fans with Kate.

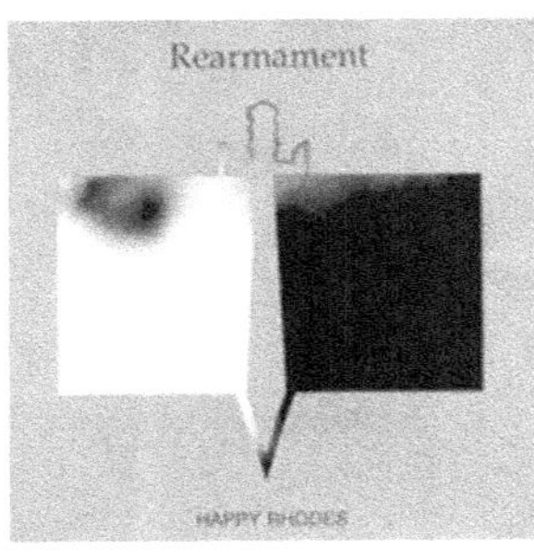

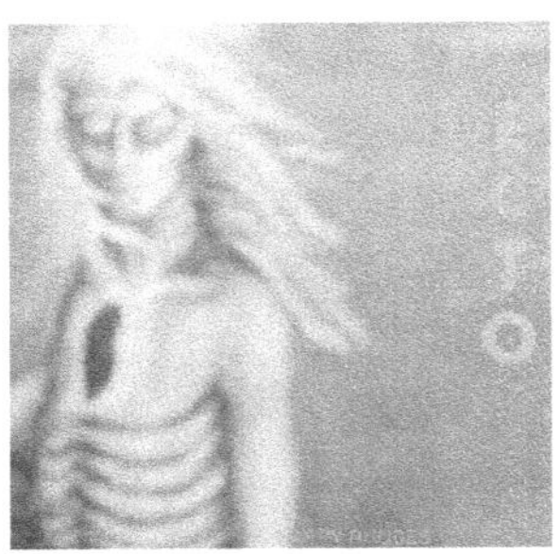

Jeff Abbott: Is Happy your real name?

Happy: I was named Kimberley Tyler Rhodes. However, the first time my brothers saw me, was when I was a day or two old, my brother Mark could not pronounce the name "Kimberley", and I was an especially happy baby, so he decided it would be easier to call me "Happy". From that moment on, my family members never used the name Kimberley. As soon as I turned sixteen, my name was legally changed to Happy Tyler Rhodes. As far as I'm concerned, it's the only name I've ever had.

David N. Blank: What are your influences and favourite artists?

Happy: The biggest influence in my life was my father. Unfortunately, I had to grow up without my mother, but she had a good deal of influence on me when I got older. My father was a painter. He taught me what creativity was. He also had an intense love of music. He showed me respect for *all* life forms and he inspired me to dream big. My favourite artists are, in no particular order, Jon Anderson and Yes, Queen, Sting, Peter Gabriel, Kate Bush, Bryan Ferry, and more recently, Martin Swan of Mouth Music.

Jorn Barger: Do you hear music in your head all the time? How do you keep from losing your best ideas, if you don't read music? Have you gotten any of your melodies from dreams?

Happy: I heard the violin line from *Lay Me Down* in my head days before I wrote the song, but usually the music comes precisely at the time when I'm ready for it (when I'm sitting at the keyboard or with the guitar). I like to think that if an idea is lost, then it wasn't destined to be my best. I don't *recall* getting any of my melodies from dreams, but then, 'recall' is the operative word here.

Kirstin Hargie : Do you write your songs as a kind of catharsis of the past so as to say 'hey this is where I've been, look at me now!' Or do you write them to maybe let people that didn't go through the same types of experiences know what another persons world is like?

Happy: I don't think an artist ever creates anything with an ulterior motive. The point is usually to filter whatever you're feeling through your craft. It is,then, a catharsis, but not necessarily intended for anyone but yourself... at least initially.

Kirstin: Do your songs hold any personal statements against society besides being against the constrictions of the societal norm, do you blame society for the inherent evil (if you believe in that kind of evil) in the world.

Happy: I'm sure I'll always be writing songs dealing with my distaste for the standards society has set. Truly, the only judgement I have is for people who don't *think* things through on their own. As long as we're all willing to take at face value everything our government officials and advertisers have to say, then there's going to be injustice, insecurity, greed and 'evil'. I'll always have faith, that one day, people will give up their places in the comfort zone of apathy and go out and make change. I admire the folks who are already out there.

Gregory Bossert: What instruments do you play? Have you had any formal training on any of them? What instruments would you like to learn how to play?

Happy: The instrument I'm most proficient on, is acoustic guitar, but I will also play keyboards, bass, percussion and anything else, if there isn't someone else available to do it. I've had no formal musical training to speak of. I'm sure eventually I'll try out a wind instrument and maybe cello. No small challenge.

Gregory: How long have you been singing (professionally and otherwise...)? What is your 'range'? Many of your songs feature complex overdubbed vocal parts; how do you come up with these arrangements? If you could sing with anyone, who would it be?

Happy: I probably started singing because of Bach. When I was little, my father used to play a particular J.S. Bach album quite often. It was a challenge for me to try to sing along with all of the notes I was hearing. Later on, at around thirteen or so, I started experimenting with vibrato. My professional singing career began with my first album. I honestly don't know what my range is. If I had been formally trained in music, I'm sure that would be different. I treat all of my backing vocals as I would instruments. If an arrangement needs something, more often than not, I'll use my voice to fill the void. Given my admiration for certain vocalists, I'd probably feel inadequately equipped to sing *with* anyone of stature, but my choices would be Sting, David Bowie, Peter Gabriel, Jon Anderson or maybe Roger Taylor.

Gregory: How do you write songs? Do you sit down with a guitar, or at a keyboard, or just walk around humming?

Happy: Sometimes I have a 'feel' in my head. Just as *The Rhythm of the Heat*, by Gabriel has a 'feel". That's what I try to capture when I sit down at the keyboard, (rarely guitar anymore). Other than that, I usually don't have any idea what a song is destined to be. It just happens. I write the music first most of the time, and get it on to tape. Then I listen. More often than not, the subject matter and subsequent lyrics just pop into my head. I guess whatever the music makes me feel, dictates what the song will be about. It's effortless for me to write music, but not always so to actualise it.

Gregory: Your arrangement tend to mix elements from many musical styles. How do you decide which instruments and sounds to use for a particular song?

Happy: I don't spend hours looking for just the right sound. My main goal initially, is to get the parts down and worry about the sounds later. I usually can just tell what instrument will be most complimentary in a certain part, and get as close to it as I can. Later, when co-producer Kevin Bartlett and I get together to polish the songs, we take more time getting the perfect sounds. He's more meticulous when it comes to sounds and instrumentation, so I'm lucky to be working with him. Kevin and I both like to develop our own sounds. We have keyboards that have incredible factory presets and we like to take advantage of them, but a lot of them have been over-used in recordings, so it benefits us to make our own. When I was recording the material for my first four albums, it wasn't apparent that other people would be hearing them. I cared more about the performance aspect. On *Warpaint* however, Kevin and I took great care in selecting sounds and effects. I personally spent hours getting the right effects for all of my different voices. This is rather new for me and it's a continual learning process.

Gregory: How do you go about recording your music? How much work do you do at home? When you work with other musicians, do you write out parts for them, or is it more of a collaborative effort?

Happy: The bulk of the work is done at home. I write and structure the song, and get it as close to completion as I can. Then Kevin steps in and together, we go over the song with a fine-toothed comb. He adds whatever he thinks is missing and polishes up the tracks I've already laid down. We then take the computer and keyboards to the other studio and lay the tracks down onto tape, straight from the computer. Next, we do any live overdubs that are necessary. No-one ever knows what the vocals will be like until I do them... including myself sometimes. They're the last thing to go down on tape before we mix. My experience with other musicians is limited thus far. If I have specific lines for someone to play, I'll put it on tape for them to learn. Usually, however, a person has a lot of room to play whatever they feel. If I confine a player to a specific part, it's usually just one particular melody line that only happens occasionally in the song.

This 1993 interview was organised for HomeGround by Vickie Mapes and the internet mailing list Ecto.

Gregory: The production on *Warpaint* is much more complex than on your past albums. Did the extra resources (musicians, or better equipment or editing) change the way you wrote and arranged songs? will your future albums continue to grow more elaborate, production-wise? Do you enjoy playing with musical gadgets and technology?

Photo: Happy Rhodes

Happy: I think having access to better equipment allowed me to do the things I'd always wanted to do on the previous four albums. My writing didn't necessarily change, though. When I did the earlier albums, I only owned one key-board and a guitar. That meant that I'd be forced to stop at a certain point in the orchestration, whether I wanted to or not. My songs never turned out the way I knew they *could* sound. This was an endless source of frustration for me. I was being categorised as 'folk' because of the acoustic guitar and overall sparse arrangements. I always knew that I was as far from 'folk' as a person could be. I suppose more elaborately produced albums will be a natural progression for me, but certainly not a goal. The musical content is still the most important factor. I don't get all goofy over new and upcoming technical gadgets. If you put one in my hands, chances are I'll enjoy using it. I'm not afraid of modern technology, and seem to have adequate user-skills, but you won't hear me talking about the latest equipment at parties, and you won't see me in the music store every week, looking for 'new' stuff to trade my week-old keyboards in for.

Klaus Kluge: Do you like to read, and what are you reading now? Favourite authors? Books?

Phobos and *Wrong Century* gave me the impression that you're into reading SF.

Happy: I do like to read science fiction. In fact, I read little else. I'm currently reading two books *Journeys Out of the Body*, by Robert Monroe, (not SF, but as close to it as you can get) and the other is *My Father Immortal*, by Michael Weaver. I don't think I'm well enough read to actually have favourite authors yet, although Frank Herbert never disappointed me. My favourite books are not science fiction, but most people would consider them to be.

Klaus: If everything works out, you should soon be painting your first book cover, a science fiction novel. How did that come about and what are your thoughts about getting into this new venture?

Happy: This came about when Michael Weaver asked me if I'd be interested in doing the cover for his next book. He liked what he had seen of my work. I was flattered and not altogether sure if I could do it. I don't actually think I have any place doing the cover art of a published SF novel. There are so many brilliant artists out there, who are more capable of the task than I am. I had considered it as a career, at one point in my life, but music seems to be the dominant force at play here. If the Art Department at Avon Publishing House approves me, it will be an exciting challenge and I'll do my best, but it probably won't become a habit.

Photo: Vickie Mapes.

Happy with long term supporter and HomeGround Reader/Lovehound Vickie Mapes.

Vickie is the founder of the Ecto mailing list focusing on Happy and similar artists.

Klaus: Are there more monster paintings? When did you start painting? What is your favourite medium to work in? Do you like painting and drawing as much as writing music?

Happy: There are other gruesome looking critters lurking around the premises here. I started painting when I was about fourteen. My father was the catalyst. The reason I started painting monsters was because I didn't have to follow any rules, such as anatomical proportion. I always hated 'rules' in art. I don't exclusively paint monsters anymore, but I'll never do a landscape. I prefer to use oils, but acrylics have their advantages sometimes. I love to create with a canvas, but honestly, a painting has never evoked the kind of feelings in me, that music can.

Klaus: Were you inspired by the paintings of H.R. Giger?

Happy: Indeed. Not only that, but two of my favourite movies are *Alien* and *Aliens.*

David N. Blank: What were your SAT scores? Tell us about your schooling.

Happy: I left school when I was 16, at the start of eleventh grade. I never took my SATs. I left because it was the right thing for me to do at the time. I was very unpopular in school, and I had my sights set on music. I got my G.E.D. the following year, in case I ever decided to torture myself with those kinds of social pressures again, and go to college. I'm not ashamed of my limited education, and I don't think it afekted my abilaty too cumunikayt at al.

Gregory Bossert: What kind of equipment do you and Kevin use?

Happy: A tech question? O.K. In our home studio, we use a Korg M1, Korg T3, Korg DW-8000, (no, Korg isn't paying us), Juno 106, (analog lives still!), a Roland Octapad 2, occasionally we dust off the sequential Circuits Six-Traks and Tom Drum machine and the Oberheim Cyclone. We have an Amiga computer and the sequencer we use is Dr. T's KCS V3.5. We have two Alesis Quadraverbs for effects, and a Soundcraft 200SR mixer. I didn't include the noise reduction units or tape decks... that might get boring. When we go to the other studio to do the actual recording, there's more equipment involved.

Klaus Kluge: Which of your own albums do you like best? Try to answer it not from the artists view, but through the eyes and ears of Happy, the music lover. Which of your albums would you like most if they were by somebody else (a strange question, I know)? Can you take that remote viewpoint?

Happy: I've always said that if I were hearing Happy Rhodes for the first time, and the album was *Rhodes Vol.1* or *II*, I wouldn't pay much attention to it. The same really goes for *Rearmament* and *Ecto.* There are qualities that I would appreciate, but none of those albums would ever be enough to capture me. I don't mean that to be self-effacing. I just know that the qualities I look for in other artists, are not present in my first four albums. *Warpaint,* on the other hand, harbours a few of those qualities, so it's the obvious choice to date. Being *too* aware of other people's opinions of one's music, *could* have an effect on how one writes in the future. However, I'd like to think I'm smart enough to know that I'll never please everyone. The only logical thing to do is please myself, and hope for the best.

Well, that's all folks... It's been great fun and I thank you all for your support. It's meant the world to me.

I Found a Fox

A Story by 'The Lewis Collins Fan Club'

Issue 52: June 1994

Once there was a young woman who belonged to no-one but herself.

Ah, what a beautiful way to begin a story, a parable. Beautiful in its simplicity, and the way it leads you on and inwards. Opening doors inside the soul. For, as we all know, all good parables should open doors.

So what of this young woman? This woman whom, from the very start we feel a little afraid of. Was she tall, was she small? What was her name? Well, I shall tell you later, perhaps; but this I will say – she knew something about miracles.

"Oh, miracles," you say and...

Yes, I see the light in your eyes grow dim. Your imagination, your power (just beginning to emerge from behind the mask which shrouds your spirit) has suddenly been cut off, dead! You manage those shutters with such skill. Now, inside I watch you, closing up, giving your mind to other matters. Matters of importance! Your credit card bill, overdue this month. Whether to drive into town with 'the wife' this weekend. No, you never did tell me her name. Dreaming up some sarcastic retort to annoy old John at the office. Oh a thousand and one things. Those important things which make up life. Ordinary, real things, none of this 'miracle' nonsense. "So was this girl religious?" you ask stifling a yawn.

No, she was a young woman, a person, like you. She carried nothing with her and sometimes she wore a long, dark coat. But if miracles bore you, then let me simply tell you of the sad day I met her.

I was watching them bulldoze the blossom trees that edged the car park. Ugly machines to build a soulless warehouse and for this they destroyed the only touch of beauty in that bleak place. Someone stopped by me, as I stood amongst a handful of observers. I could sense the rough woolishness of her coat.

"What are they doing?" she asked, her voice calm, soothing and so low that I had to draw near to catch her words.

"Tearing down the trees."

"Ah."

Something in her quietness touched me and I added, "I wrote poetry for them last spring, they were so lovely."

She smiled and we watched together, at once united in the memory of sweet cherry blossom. Quietly gazing. The engines laboured noisily, grinding metal and stone and I sighed.

"Don't be sad," she said. "Of course it is sad to see the foolishness of these men who are digging in their loud and terrible trucks. Stupidity is a very sad thing. But, you see, we can be happy, because there are always other trees that will be beautiful to us."

I turned then and looked her full in the face. Pale, girlish, open, yet eyes so full of power and warmth, so honest they unsettled me. I quickly looked down at my feet and she continued in a gentle, melodic tone.

"Remember you cannot grieve forever, nor even for long, because if you do, you invest too much in pain and sadness, and life takes on those colours. Life is sadness, but it is joy too, and we need to understand both to be complete and full."

She paused for a moment and then went on, "But yes, it is easy I know, to see the dark side of life. Because of the loneliness, the busy confusion, the exhausting need. Because we are taught by a world which is itself afraid and lost. How many people miss the door to freedom by investing all their happiness in the future – something that will never happen? They wait for the future. 'I will be happy *when*' they say. 'It would all be OK *if only*'. Yes, the future will save them, but right now they are too busy being worried and responsible to bother with such things. They forget that the future only comes to them in the guise of the present. Moments, moments, so precious...

"If only these people simply waited with a quiet heart and looked, why they would find heaven all about them. They would find more happiness in a wild flower, fragile in the spring breeze, than they could in all their frantic race for life. You see, happiness cannot be pursued. It is no poor fox, chased by hounds. Happiness just is. It is a fox playing in the moonlight, or held close in one's arms. The secret, you know, is to open up your eyes and see!"

Of course, she may not have said all of this in her very first breath. But later, it seemed she had. I remember feeling terror and wonder all in a moment, because she refused to let me escape from those darkly gold, lionish eyes. Fire (a child on Guy Fawkes Night, dreaming into some brilliant volcano of sparks).

I remember half-heartedly hiding behind my defences. Flimsy protection! When I was really thinking in amazement, 'My God! How real this person is. Dangerous, but real! She's not talking about, you know, those mundane things. She has cut straight through to the heart of the matter. The essence of being!'

So this was how I found myself suddenly sharing lunch and a delicious cup of tea with her in some poet's retreat. A down-beat pizza café with a smiling face behind the counter and real bottled tomato sauce on the table.

"So what do you do then?" she asked with a crafty smile and...

Well, I told her – but of course explained that

I was a writer by instinct. In fact, a veritable artist, a student of life. My creed – "To Live Poetically". To see each moment as a fresh and beautiful creation, teeming with opportunities, with life, with love.

"Of course I am afraid too. Weak, fallible, but oh I so much want to work on these things, I mean I am working on them... but..."

"But?" Her eyes were gentle, smiling. I felt so awkward, making myself vulnerable to this strangest of strangers.

"But... well, you know, life can be hard."

Still smiling, she said, "We are all weak and fallible in some way. It is part of being human. Don't worry, there is a good deal of strength to be gained in understanding and accepting our weaknesses. Anyone who claims perfection, or to know all the answers, well, my advice... avoid them like the plague!"

She laughed, a rich wonderful laugh and then, still laughing, we talked. And as I sit here, with her – Oh God! I can't believe that she exists, that someone so full and free should be sitting HERE sipping her hot, fragrant tea... and what's more, I am here, sharing this moment with her. If this feels so good, what must heaven be like? And if so happy, why did I suddenly, desperately want to cry? With male pride I struggled to hold back the tears, but she smiled, reaching across to touch my face.

"Let go," she said, "Let go for me."

"Why for you, if not for myself?" I asked, voice thick with tears and shame.

"Because it is always easier to do things for others."

Then the tears and how they came! There I was sobbing my heart out in a faded backwater of culinary delights. The Greek man behind the till in a checkered apron, peering in concern between the flaky pastries and the tandoori chicken browning on the hotplate.

The young woman held my hand (limp with sweat) in her hand (warm, strong). Working her healing on me. A miracle worker's hand. This woman's work. And what a beautiful gift! This miracle. This vision she gives to me. Being woken up to the essential life. Becoming part of the sensual world. Relaxing into every moment. Making every now a full and lucid experience. Precious, precious moments.

Thinking... one day I am going to die. This is real, no "the film is over and back to reality" escapism. NO! My death is as real (and natural) as this leaf in my hand, the touch of my skin, this cup of tea. And that is what makes life so incredible, so wonderful! *Because of death we see how limitless life is!*

We said goodbye on the doorstep of the café. She had a train to catch and I, well I had everything to do. She hugged me and even then I blushed because I was still a little shy of her lionheart. But she laughed, kissed my cheek and then was off. The strangest thing though, glancing back over my shoulder, in the crowd she looked no different from those around her. Less conspicuous if anything, in old worn grey. And I laughed, full to the brim with warmth and love. Yes, look at them all! Such a crowd of angels... and... there... what was that running raggedly across the street? Dodging car wheels and legs – heading boldly for the open fields.

Yes, I swear it - a golden brown fox!

Combat Ducks

Me Ears are alight!

Issue 49: August 1993

I guess you're wondering how this very silly feature came about? The idea has been brewing for years, and even though Krys' Dad has begged us not to print it, we thought what the hell, and did! And the title?

In *Hounds of Love* a friend of ours was convinced that Kate was singing "Combat ducks" when what she was really singing was "caught by dogs"! Here are a few Combat Ducks we've received. Not many people offer their surname for some strange reason! Keep sending them in.

"Asshead from Baghdad lives in Simasai" – from *Kashka from Baghdad*. ***Tina***.

At one point in *The Big Sky* I'm sure Kate sings "My toast is cold". Presumably this is an insight into what happens when you spend too much time slaving away over a hot mixing desk, and not enough time finishing breakfast. ***Kevin Gomm***

My Mum always thought the strange bit in *Watching You Without Me* was: "Don't eat more, don't eat more knees, let me in, on the door-knee knock. We're greasy, we're greasy". I didn't have any better ideas though! Now this is what I always sing. ***Terry***.

Krys' Dad's most popular misheard lyrics: "Riding down on by bicycle, hot cheese and custard", from *December Will Be Magic Again*. In the chorus of *Hammer Horror* he used to sing "Have a holdall". He also did some of the dance routine! Once he even did a rendition of *James and the Cold Gun* wearing a white technicians coat and my tennis racket. If he reads this he'll kill me! ***Krys***

"You can dance a dream with your bunnies on" – *The Red Shoes*. ***Krys and Peter***.

A Remarkable Man

Colin Lloyd Tucker (sometimes with Paddy)

Issue 53: August 1994

Photo: Colin Lloyd Tucker

Colin's Own Bit

It was 1976 or thereabouts, and I was working for a Music Publishers in London's Wardour Street. There was a small studio on the premises and my days were spent recording music for the "Test Card" and radio jingles. My nights, however, were spent performing at the nearby Marquee Club and anywhere else that would put up with the various "experimental" bands I found myself in. From time to time the studio would be booked by major record companies for their new acts to 'demo' material. I remember a spotty guitar band on RCA and a rock group called Tonight who had a hit with a song called *Drummerman*. One such demo session was booked by EMI for The Kate Bush Band.

The session took place at night and three or four songs were committed to eight-track tape. The haze of time has blurred my memory of which songs were actually recorded, although I know *Them Heavy People* was among them. What I do remember is the astonishment felt around the building the following morning as we made tape copies of the previous night's work: "What a weird sound", "Is it running at the right speed?" "Does she really sing like that or have you done something technical?"

I remember a young Kate in purple vest being fascinated by the flm-sound machines, and I remember Paddy.

In fact Paddy returned to the studio soon afterwards to sing vocals on a song called *Fingerprint City*, a track from the début album of a band I was in at the time called Plain Characters. The album's title, *Invisible Yearnings*, proved profound and the band split soon after its release.

Eating People

Kate, meanwhile, was enjoying great success and soon the tour and recording commitments piled up. It would be some time before I would see Paddy or Kate again.

I recorded a solo LP called *Toybox* on which I played all the instruments as well as engineering and producing the record. The experience was indeed an education, but it was also exhausting, compounded by the fact that a release was not immediately forthcoming and the tapes were placed frmly "on the shelf". *Toybox* was eventually released a couple of years later. In the meantime I got together with fellow studio employee, Matt Johnson and ex-Plain Character, John Hyde, and formed an experimental "recording" band, The Gadgets. Three pretty awful LPs followed before myself and Matt left to concentrate on the embryonic The The. John Hyde, however, continued to release material under the name The Gadgets. At this point The The consisted of Matt, myself and Simon Turner, an ex-actor who is now better known for his film soundtracks. When we weren't working with Matt, Simon and I released our own records under the name, Jeremy's Secret. Also, encouraged by the belated release of *Toybox*, I recorded a second solo LP, *Mindbox*, and formed my own band to go out and promote it, but not until I completed a chaotic string of gigs at the Marquee Club with The The, which marked the end of my involvement with Matt Johnson. These gigs were notoriously disorganised and the pull of my own band gave me the confidence to leave. I signed to Glass Records for whom I recorded a mini LP called *Head*. One of the songs planned for this record was called *Eating People* and it was decided a digeridoo was what was needed – "Pad plays the digeridoo – I'll call him".

By now it was 1985. *Hounds of Love* had just been released. When I discussed *Eating People* with him, Pad also made suggestions for backing vocals we could try, and so for the first time we sung together – well, shouted actually. Whatever, we enjoyed it and liked the result.

I was invited to take part in the video for *The Big Sky* at Elstree Studios a couple of weeks later. As with all things cinematic there was a lot of hanging around involved. Pad and I chatted and found we had much in common, although at this time the idea of writing together had not evolved. Over the ensuing years I would never cease to be amazed at his musical scope and adaptability, helping to bridge the gap between our own very individual styles. Anyway, after a long two days on *The Big Sky* set, it seemed we were really getting to know each other. From now on we would talk on the 'phone more often, sometimes for hours.

Remarkable

Then... Crash – Bang – Wallop! – I fell madly in love with Yvonne (a remarkable girl) and after an extended holiday in Mexico with Simon Turner, I returned to London and moved in with her. We were married within six months. We lived in Regina Road in the Finsbury Park area of North London.

It was some time before I was able to articulate my feelings for Yvonne in song, but eventually I wrote the *Remarkable* album as a kind of snap shot of the emotional tidal wave newly weds and lovers ride. A local studio was booked and the songs were recorded. Paddy was ever present at these sessions, along with my regular band. Both Tim Broughton (drums) and Neil Huckstepp (guitar) would contribute greatly to the *Skyscraping* album.

But what of *Remarkable*? Well, it was recorded in a couple of weeks in a room the size of a cupboard that we shared with man-eating gnats. We worked at night and had a lot of fun. Yvonne was working as production manager for The Pet Shop Boys gig/film at the time, but would look in on us at the studio in the middle of the night only to find me and Paddy in uncontrollable hysterics around the microphone – we were discovering weird vocal harmonies and a shared fascination for the ambiguity of lyrics. We were also becoming friends.

As the sun came up at the start of another hot summer day, we would return to Regina Road for breakfast and a listen. Soon it was finished, the entire *Remarkable* project had cost less than £800 (is this a record!?!) Yet Glass Records, who had been in financial trouble before they put us in the studio, finally went bankrupt and like *Toybox* before, *Remarkable* would not be immediately released.

John Porter, who had produced Brian Ferry's *These Foolish Things*, and more recently The Smiths and my own *Head* LP, called to invite me to dinner (now there's an offer I couldn't refuse). When I arrived, I found John and Johnny Marr (guitarist) pouring over my LP sleeves and listening to *Head*.

It emerged that Johnny had become quite a fan and was keen for me to spend some time with him at his Manchester home, writing and recording new material together. The Smiths had broken up and he had been in the USA playing guitar on Talking Heads' *Naked* album. He had also begun working with Matt Johnson who had enjoyed some success of his own with the *Infected* album. In fact, Johnny would soon become a full-time member of The The. I enjoyed my time with Johnny in Manchester. We worked incessantly, Johnny with his head full of guitar riffs, me with my bits of paper containing snippets of lyrics. We talked of forming a band around these new songs, called Heat, but the relationship was doomed – we never seemed to finish anything; perhaps our musical tastes were too similar and we lacked the friction necessary to spark off a successful writing partnership. We did some songs but decided not to issue them.

I returned to London and my problems with *Remarkable*. Winter was upon us and an on-coming depression made it difficult to muster the enthusiasm necessary to go out and get a new deal with a new record company.

A fever of great intensity

Watching TV one night I saw an amazing documentary about Voodoo music. I called Paddy and he knew what I was talking about. We spoke of creating a contemporary piece of music incorporating trance-inducing rhythms. I wanted to do something away from rock'n'roll and Paddy wanted to do something unique – we opened a department store of ideas: some outrageous and unobtainable, some funny, some musical, others atmospheric – *SKYSCRAPING* was conceived.

At the time Paddy had an eight-track recording set-up at his home and it was there we worked. Like *Remarkable*, we found everything had "humorous connotations" and so really enjoyed creating the music. The only rule was that there were no rules. Then, just before Christmas – it happened – we both caught the 'flu from hell – "that'll teach you to mess with Voodoo". All work on our new project was suspended while we sweated with a fever of great intensity. In fact, illness and mental insecurity would return intermittently throughout the *Skyscraping* sessions, right up to the final forty eight track remixes some years later. In retrospect we now realise that our own depressive states of mind at times during the making of the album meant that we constantly lost momentum and months would go by with the project on ice. There will never be another recording like *Skyscraping*. I am sure our next collaboration will be as different from *Skyscraping* as that record is different from any other; it is indeed unique – an unrepeatable meeting of minds in turmoil... it's not easy having a good time.

Having secured a release for *Remarkable* on the newly formed Humbug label, I reformed my band and began playing a few gigs in London. Humbug would soon release *Skyscraping*. In the meantime, Paddy and I were recruited by Kate to sing backing vocals of *The Red Shoes*, a track that already contained some of Paddy's instrumental work and Justin Valli's valiha playing.

Kate remarked that when we sung together it was hard to distinguish which voice belonged to Paddy and which to me. The two had become one, a product of our previous all-night singing sessions.

On a later date we were again in Kate's studio together, putting vocals on *Constellation Of The Heart*, a slice of funk on which we enjoyed the question/answer nature of the arrangement. Earlier in the session, Kate had played us an embryonic version of a new song, *Rubberband Girl*, and there was much delight and talk of all things rubber.

For the record

Most people who are aware of my small contribution to these sessions ask the same question: "What is Kate like to work with?" This is easy to answer. She is encouraging, patient, perceptive and charming. She knows what she is looking for and how to go about finding it, but she is not an egomaniac, or worse, a cold professional. We once shared the same ambition (we are roughly the same age) to make a record. Music is a gift and once recorded the gift is given and received time and time again. Pad and I were also recruited to be devils in *The Red Shoes* section of the movie (a fantasy we had often discussed – I mean, people expect weird and naughty things from someone sporting horns and a tail). Kate was as genial on the film set as she had been at the studio and we made her laugh with our over-the-top dancing, which thankfully she got us to tone down for the later takes.

Meanwhile back at the ranch

Yvonne and I finally moved out of London in 1993 and now reside on and three hundred and fifty acre island a couple of miles off the English coast. Here I have been busy recording a new album. Now completed, *Songs of Life, Love and Liquid* is set for a January release on Humbug Records. Paddy, as I write, is in France producing an album with Justin Valli, the Madagascan valiha master. He also continues his involvement with the excellent Spondo. Also available now is *Paskaal Japhet Razana* (*Night And Day* – ND 214), an album produced by Paddy Bush. We are both happier now than for some time. Our lives continue to evolve and we enjoy the changes.

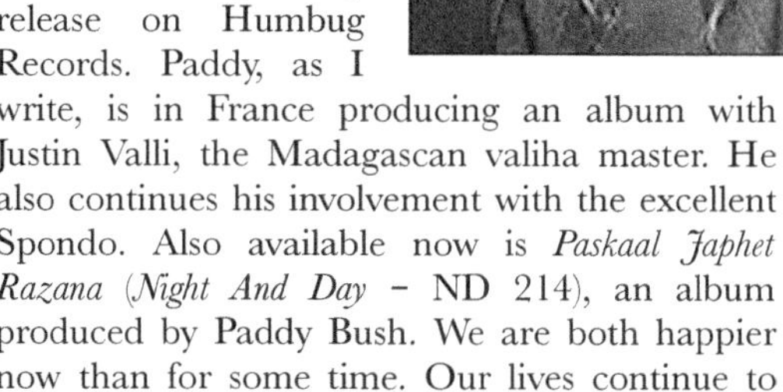

Colin and Paddy

Photo: Colin Lloyd Tucker

Colin: Old Father Time

Issue 57: May 1996

Time has been playing tricks on me. That's the conclusion I came to yesterday, or was it the day before?

There was the time ten months ago when Yvonne realised she was pregnant and I started thinking about being a dad. Things I thought long forgotten began to resurface. Childhood memories jumped out of my subconscious... feeding the ducks, lying in a pram looking up at a hooded sky, the agonies of nappy rash.

The mind's capacity for information storage is indeed a wonder but can it also project forward, anticipate a future event and prepare us for it. We've all had the feeling that we have previously experienced something that is happening in the present.

In 1992 I wrote a song called *Moving World* and at the time I thought I was writing about a kind of spiritual rebirth, about "feeling good again". In the song I (the singer) would be the courier, reintroducing the mind to the wonder of it all – "Let me introduce you to a moving world" "You're volunteered for voodoo in the moving world".

When it came to recording the song I decided I wanted to add the sound of a woman giving birth and after watching lots of videos of women in labour, selected a suitably gut wrenching scream. Then when recording the vocals I ad-libbed a refrain at the end of the song, "I'm very much alive... it feels like I'm aware... and I open my eyes... I see the sky blue sky and I say 'It's a beautiful thing'". (We're back in that pram again).

Was I subconsciously telling my sperm to go forth and multiply? Was this the voice of a lone sperm that just wanted to be someone? Or was it my unborn daughter announcing her imminent conception? It could have been coincidence, but then again I also wrote *Song of Life* around this time, a song I thought was about a love of life but is probably about new life. "Here we go... I know together we can grow".

There was something in the air all lright (I think of Thunderclap Newman, we all should). I wrote a song about my father (*The Last Time I Saw My Dad*), something previously I would have found too embarrassing, articulating feelings that in the past I had denied yet in the future I would embrace.

All of these songs are contained on my new album, *Songs of Life, Love and Liquid*. There are others about the sea. Unsurprising you may think when you learn that I live on a tiny island a couple of miles off the English mainland, but the fact is I wrote the lyrics to *Ocean Blue* and *Glue Man* long before I had any idea I would be moving to such a place. I was living in London at the time.

In some ways I hope my premonition theory turns out to be hog wash as I am currently writing a song about being run down by a bus! Is that the time? Must go, hope you enjoy the album.

P.S. Go on, buy a copy and make an old man very happy.

Your Name

Antonello Saeli

I've got your name on my jeans
Like an indelible tattoo
It hurts me when I touch it
It's like a flame on my skin
I've got your name on my hand
You carefully ironed it
While I was fast asleep
By your side on the bed
I've got your name on my chest
It is written in black
And ink is slowly passing through
To get to my beating heart
I've got your name in my mind
I know it's there,
hidden somewhere
And I can't get rid of it
Since I still think of you
And I don't know why
Why I should think of you
Now that so many names
Have been written on me.

Readers' Letters

...We receive them with a strange delight

Letters held over from issue 48 and from issues 49 to 54, August 1993 to October 1994

Amit Gandhi: Having just recovered from the rigours of Wuthering Hike IV, I wanted to thank you for arranging it. It's the first event I've ever been to although I've been a lover of Kate's music for years. The one thing that really struck me was the range of people who came, and the range of people who are somehow touched by Kate's music generally. Everyone couldn't have been more friendly and outgoing. I can't wait until the next event, whatever it is.

Liz Pamment: The Wuthering Hike was a soul-busting experience and I wouldn't have missed it for the world. I was disappointed with 'Aspel' on Sunday. Of course Kate's song was really beautiful and very touching, but Aspel's interview was tragic. I think he embarrassed Kate and insulted her (re her dress, which was far from simple, and dragging up the old chestnut about being a male sex symbol). It's no wonder she doesn't give many interviews if she gets treated like that. Did I see Dave at the back of the audience?

Tania Malone: A new album! Yes, we've reached that wondrous moment once again when an entire feast is about to be laid before us. Hungering souls we wait in delicious anticipation for those sweet sensations to feed us. To colour our hearts and imaginations with the salt and honey of life and creativity. Once again we are about to embark on a voyage into unknown territory, unexplored wilds with breathtaking sights, dangerous waters, deepest forests. We may turn a corner and find in the midst of all that is unearthly and strange, something familiar. Cornfields, cottage, hemlock, May blossom, red-cloaked child, wolf-like glittering eyes.

Or shall we watch the celluloid un-reel, flickering before the dazzling beam and find that we are spectators of our own life's journey? A man in a doorway lighting a Galoise, clocks ticking with sinister intent, eyes and doorways opening, the vagina, rose petals unfurling at the warm touch of blood and milky whiteness. The dancers, bullish and hoary, their stiff wet arching bridges of life, leaping and laughing before us.

Each album, each gift from the heart, has opened up pathways of new experience for me. I have wanted solitude for this most personal, intimate of moments. Solitude and a bottle of good, red wine. I welcome each album like a friend. Settle down in my secret place of privacy, my warm room and place the record on the turntable. Oh, it brings back memories. The before times, when *Lionheart*, so golden and English, yet spiced with the exotic, warmed and strengthened me. When that story book of theatre and drama, *Never For Ever* charmed me with its magical energy. When the dark, mature psychology of *The Dreaming* broke and healed my heart, and the sheer power and depth of *Hounds of Love* shook me to my very core and flooded me with beautiful inspiration. Then when *The Sensual World* reaffirmed the sense and strength of my Womanhood, yet touched me with loss and pain... "Ooh the thrill and the hurting". And of course, the first time, as *The Kick Inside* spoke to me, I listened through the night, in stillness, hardly daring to believe the beauty of what I was hearing. A thirteen year old waking up to the "punctual blues" of puberty and "the sticky love inside". And, though the metaphors are not subtle, I am sure that this incredible music really helped me to understand the nature of sexuality and love "making". For the music itself caresses, whispers, yearns, excites, arouses, penetrates, fulfils. Wakes my soul and soothes her to sleep... like poppies. I await, arms open for this precious, precious album. What more can I say but "I know that something good is going to happen!"

Tarsam Singh Khela: AAAaaaaarghhhh! *BIG STRIPEY LIE* should have been the first single Not *Rubberband Girl.* It moved me. It made me cry. I never cry over songs. "All you little waves, run away!".

Christopher H. Hoppe: I have a personal thank-you to send to the Utah Saints. I bought their techno album *Something Good,* and was fascinated by the sampled voice on the title track. There it was on the lyric sheet... "Kate Bush". Who??? I went out and bought *The Whole Story* (the only Kate album anyone seems to have around here) and you know how it goes from there. CDs, LPs, videos, posters, books fanzines... My point is that I came across Kate Bush solely by coincidence! I could have lived out the rest of my life in oblivion, just because most people where I'm from blindly accept whatever is forced down their throats by record companies and radio stations whose primary concern is profit. Drivel makes money here. Kate does have fans in the US though, and those I have met are always completely hardcore. To be one of Kate's fans here is to have the frustration of knowing how many people could appreciate her music, but have never even heard her name uttered..

Martin: I have to write to tell you that the past few issues of *HomeGround* have been very important to me. I always felt different, even when I was young, and then throughout my teens it really became evident to me that I knew I was gay. I had doubts due to my Catholic upbringing and especially in Ireland you can imagine how hard it was to admit to yourself that you are gay. I've never had a problem with it, I was just unsure because you read articles saying everyone experiences some doubts about their sexuality. I never dated girls, yes the odd one night stand but no more. Deep down I knew this wasn't for me.

It was only really through Kate's music and, believe it or not, my faith, that kept me going. Even with my Catholic upbringing I knew that my wanting to love another man could not be wrong because in love there is no wrong. The hard part is meeting people. I haven't met many other gay guys. The only way is to go to gay clubs, a lot of which are quite seedy, not my scene. Or you can place adverts in magazines, which is a risk since you don't know who you are going to meet. This is why I'm placing a Pen-Pal ad in *HomeGround*.

I only came out as such over the past few months, but only to a few chosen friends, who have all been fine about it. My parents will never be told. They would only doubt the way they brought me up and they don't need that at this stage in their lives. But I am happy. Being gay is not a problem for me. It's not easy, but what is these days..

Jayne: It's going to be wonderful having Kate – new Kate – on our stereos again. I have seen *Moments of Pleasure* from 'Aspel & Co'. I was in hospital, having had my second nervous breakdown, in July (I'm going for a record to see how many I can have before I turn 21!) when Eugene first sent me the tape. Sitting there, listening with headphones, hearing a new Kate song for the first time in ages. When Kate sang "The buildings of New York look just like mountains through the snow" I knew – felt – that everything would be alright again. It was a really beautiful thing. I don't think I'll ever forget the fact that I should be able to hear Kate's song at that particular stage in my life!

Thomas Roach: I have admired Kate Bush's work since the first album. I saw her tour and was really impressed with her show. Subsequently I bought all of her albums, videos and books (even the dreaded Vermorel). I remember when *The Dreaming* was released I was eagerly anticipating another tour which never happened. When the *Hounds of Love* album was released I couldn't wait to hear it and again like many other fans was desperate for her to tour.

I was into her music so much I had put her up on a pedestal. However, during the long period between *Hounds of Love* and *The Sensual World* I began to change. Prior to this I used to wait for her albums like my life depended on it, but I began to look at her more objectively.

I have listened to her views about interviews and her complaints about the questions she is asked. I saw her on 'Aspel' and I found her answers rather terse. Okay, Aspel did ask her the same old questions but I think she could easily have turned the questions around and elaborated on her answers into something more interesting. It was good to see the early interview with Aspel, she seemed much more enthusiastic. Now, however, she seems to have a rather snobby attitude about her own music and career. I don't think there is anything wrong in interviewers referring to her early work, after all, that is where her present work has evolved. On the 'Aspel' show she should have talked in more detail about the ideas and influences behind *The Red Shoes* album to enliven the interview (for our sake at least).

I still listen to Kate's earlier work from *The Kick Inside* to *Hounds of Love* and these albums still move me. However, I hardly ever listen to *The Sensual World*; indeed I find it very unpleasant to listen to, Kate admits that she went through a period during the making of that album where she couldn't see the point. Well I think that vibe comes through on that album. On certain tracks such as *Love and Anger*, I think her voice sounds rather croaky and throughout the album is sometimes not audible at all.

I think Kate has lost something from her earlier works. Those earlier ballads and songs are haunting and full of unexpected twists and turns both lyrically and musically. However, I think she has lost her lightness of touch and her recent work such as *The Sensual World* album and *Moments of Pleasure* sound heavy and orthodox. Compare, for instance, *Warm and Soothing* to *Moments of Pleasure*; the purity and perfection in Kate's voice which was apparent in the early songs has in my opinion gone. Her voice on the earlier albums was like crystal and would reach right down inside. In terms of production without a doubt her albums have improved greatly, but I think she sacrificed a lot in terms of her music by trying to change her style from her early works.

The reason for writing this letter is really to say that I've changed in that I've stopped putting Kate up on a pedestal; that the image in the posters, album covers and such, bears little or no resemblance to the reality, except perhaps the single covers for *This Woman's Work* and *Rocket Man*, and that it's not going to kill me if she never tours again.

I know there are a lot of people who won't agree with what I've written. I've had this argument with tons of fans and they all think I'm talking out of my arse, which is probably what you at *HomeGround* are thinking too. I'm just glad that I'm free from the burden of being a "completely mad" Kate Bush fan.

Leslie Gardner: I am writing because I want to share a very happy Happening with Kate and all my friends at *HomeGround*! I know we've never physically met, but emotionally Kate has been

Photo: Paul Camilleri

Kate at the première of Disney's *Lion King*

my friend for a long time now – and *HomeGround* too!

Well, this is my happy news: my cancer is gone! And I am done with chemotherapy after one year and four months! Just in time for the new album!

Every time I hear Kate singing I feel as if I've been given a most wondrous gift, like a hug from Kate herself. Some think it silly to write to musicians and artists, but I know that everyone at *HomeGround* knows how wonderful Kate is and won't think me silly. I wish I could let her know what a comfort she was during such a difficult time! I wasn't sure I'd survive this ailment, but I just turned twenty five on July 20th! I'm here and I won't give in to the tumour I had!! I find strength in the things I love, Kate and her music being one!

I am sad for Kate's losses and I wish her strength to carry on and thank her generosity. Even though she's hurting she is still giving inspiring, beautiful, emotional music. I wish there was something I could give her in exchange. I feel so disadvantaged living in the States. I miss seeing the once in a while TV appearances and if she ever were to play live again I would be heart-broken that I'd miss that too. I'm sad that she will probably never know how many lives she touched but I'm happy there are all you guys at *HomeGround* who I'm sure tell her how wonderful we all think she is. Thank you, Miss Kate Bush! Thank you! Thank you! Thank you!

Trevor: It was really great to see you all again at Kate's film première. I was amazed when I realised that Kate, Del and Dr. Bush were sitting not too far away from us, and why not? After that excellent and hilarious animated film by Nick Park it was time for Kate to come on stage to introduce the film. It was great to see her again. We all went a bit mad because we hadn't seen her in three years. I hope she was alright what with all the noise and bulb flashing that seemed to go on and on. It did look like it was a bit much for her.

Thanks to Dave for letting his house be invaded by hordes of marauding Kate fans afterwards. The party was full of Python fans and rebel freaks, and many people I recognised and had met before. Special thanks to Krys for being the nicest person I've ever met and for that great big hug at the end.

Uwe-Lutz Gunzler: I live in the East part of Berlin. For many years I've been a big fan of Kate Bush. I love her music, her voice. For me, she is much more than an ordinary singer-songwriter. Her way of writing songs, singing, dancing, and how she expresses herself I think is extraordinary. But it is a long time between one album and another and in addition I would really like to know more about Kate.

Jeremy Birchington: Congratulations, me old maties on reaching Fifty issues! It's a sad, sad world where Mr Blobby gets to Number 1 in the UK charts. There's much to be said for listening to the shipping forecast "*Baily, Rockall, Shannon...*", more melodious to the ear.

Charles Collins: It's 1st November and I've just arrived home with a copy of *The Red Shoes* in my hot sticky paws, to find a second delight – a double whammy – *HomeGround* 49. As one of your undoubtedly older readers (over 40!) I'd like to reply to Thomas Roach's "Soapbox" item before the deluge, if only for the fact that I AM that much older, and more distanced from the "completely mad" era. Yes, I went through something similar many years ago, although I seem to recall that Dusty Springfield and Diana Ross were the source of certain moments of pleasure. Whatever happened to them?

Over the last twenty five years I've collected thousands of records and been enthusiastic over hundreds of artists. For a number of reasons I was never an ecstatic fan of Kate in the early days – this has grown over the years until now I find that she is, by a huge degree, easily my favourite artist. And why? Not the image, the album covers, the face, the hype, the mystery – purely and simply the music. There was a real moment of pleasure this lunchtime walking into the record store and hearing the album playing, especially as the shop is a small independent in Soho which normally plays only indie/grunge.

From reading Thomas Roach's letter it would seem that Kate's main offence has been to mature. No, she isn't that precocious nineteen year old singing *Wuthering Heights*, but a woman who has lived, perceived and written about her experiences. I found *The Sensual World* the most complete album to date and played it daily in the car for almost two years. There is a depth and range in Kate's music, an intelligence, a sensuality which I've never found in any other artist. As for comparing *Warm and Soothing* with *Moments of Pleasure* (which incidentally made me cry the first time I heard it, and still produces a strong emotional reaction,) well, compare Jane Austin's *Pride and Prejudice* with the later *Sense and Sensibility*; a more substantial work from a mature writer.

An artist must develop, or die, artistically. There are sufficient examples strewn along the path of popular music to illustrate this point. No, of course Kate Bush isn't a Goddess, someone to Deify; she never asked for that. She is surely the antithesis of the archetypal rock star. She's never gone in for what Joni Mitchell referred to as "stoking the star-maker machinery" despite overwhelming pressure to conform to stereotype. And of course she can respond enthusiastically to a sympathetic interviewer, as the recording with the late Roger Scott illustrated. But Aspel's questions were just inane. So Kate Bush doesn't suffer fools gladly? Well, doing the PR and Marketing bit is an unfortunate side-product of making the music; a compromise. And we all know how much Kate enjoys compromise!

Yes, people who worship at the Bush altar are "completely mad" but none the worse for that. Ultimately it's the music that counts and the music certainly is worth waiting for. You experience this equally with your mind and your emotions. And now I'm off to experience some more of This Woman's Work. To listen, enjoy, but above all, to Feel It!

Doron Vidavski in Israel: Have you ever thought about the misery that fans often go through due to their status of "being a fan"? I tell you, it can be HELL! I'm sure there are many fans who feel like me – that being a fan is no picnic! First comes the issue of getting hold of anything that Kate has ever released (or never released, when it comes to bootlegs!) Whatever the cost is, we pay, only to get our hands on that coveted record or poster or magazine. The frustration comes when we only hear about a rarity, that only two fans in the world seem to own. Then come the thoughts of "what I wouldn't give to have that" BUT, you know you'll probably never get that item and you'll never feel complete (and neither will your Kate collection) until you do get it! The ultimate put-down is when you are given the chance to buy it at the cost of about $100 and you don't have enough money.

The second problem is the charts. Unfortunately, we live in an era in which sexy lads and Meat Loaves are the only ones who get to the Top Ten. It's so exasperating to wait for the charts only to find that 25 crappy songs are placed ahead of what should have been Number One (i.e. *Moments of Pleasure*) or to find that the fantastic *Rubberband Girl* fails to even visit the Top Ten. What is going on here? Where are all the fans when you need them? Is nobody interested in listening to the new songs *Show a Little Devotion*, *Home for Christmas* or the instrumental of Kate's finest Moments?

I still can't understand how 2 Unlimited succeed in selling, when Kate's offerings hardly make any chart impact. I'm very bitter about all of this. And, of course, chart success is one of the standards for MTV airplays. I sat for hours, for days, watching MTV, seeing Bryan Adams, Take That and Culture Beat, waiting for a Kate video to show... and, nothing! It is so frustrating.

And last but not least, one of the biggest problems (for me) is not living in England. Apart from being an amazing country, let's face it England is the capital of pop! Everything happens in England. TV shows, single releases, the odd live date, and of course, conventions. I feel so distant from it all and it's depressing. Maybe I'm over-reacting. Maybe I should get a pet, or maybe, just maybe I'm right. But, if only for Kate's music and contribution to my life – it's worth it!

Steve: Before I received my first copy, I thought it would be a simple, gushy "isn't Kate brilliant" sort of magazine. I originally bought a copy so that I might get in early for tickets for Kate's next concert. I feel ashamed for thinking like that. I have been moved, upset, uplifted and entertained by what I've read, gained new insights into Kate's music, seen the beautiful artwork by Debi Bowes, Steven Brown and Paulina Stuckey. I've touched the hearts of other lovers of Kate's music – a common bond of warmth with people I've never met, people who have bowled me over with the open sharing of their feelings. The idea of the Tenth Anniversary issue was wonderful. As a latecomer it let me share the good times you've had – shaping the future times I look forward to sharing.

As a final point, one of the (many) excellent things about *HomeGround* is it's openness of emotional expression. In this country with it's repression of individuality and honesty, the articles and letters are genuine pleasure. You mentioned that some people found some articles too explicit. For me, the sensuality in Kate's songs has always been a delight and it is only natural that her fans appreciate that and use it as a springboard for exploring their own sensuality and sexuality. Also articles such as that in issue 40 (which I did not see, but saw the correspondence regarding it in the following issue) were particularly moving, especially as my partner was sexually abused as a child. It was when I read this in my first issue that I realised *HomeGround* no ordinary fanzine. Let's all keep it that way.

Lone P. Hansen in Denmark: What a choker for me to hear the song *Lily*. I've worked a lot with the ritual of the pentagram (and it really is an effective protection!) so I immediately felt irritated when I hear Kate sing "Gabriel before me, Raphael behind me" – traditionally it is "Raphael before me, Gabriel behind me". But then, Gabriel is the archangel of Water, which relates to emotions, whereas, Raphael is the archangel of Air, which is intellect and "Cutting through", so to speak. And is Kate not in her work putting emotions first and leaving the thinking faculty with its "tearing apart" in the background? It is only natural that she should swap the positions of the two angels. It is interesting to find Kate threading the grounds of Golden Dawn magic. I always saw it as a very masculine part of the spiritual kaleidoscope. I can't help wondering whether Kate has read *The Holy Books of The Lema*? Now, that's the ultimate spiritual and ecstatic book of this century!

The Devil Rides Out (1968).

Emma Rose: Some moments that I've had... It seems such a long time ago now. I was nine years old, sitting at home and bored, when I noticed a pretty face staring at me. I watched *Wuthering Heights*, *Cloudbusting* – that was it. I entered a world, a magical world of music. I'd never bought my own records before, and I'd only ever really listened to the music of my parents, so Kate was special – she was mine.

Kate gave me something, something I'd never had before. Words and music that I could relate to, that I could understand. She gave me hope, made me feel safe, she was there for me while I was growing up. She's still with me and always will be. And now *The Red Shoes* is with us, and my God, wasn't it worth waiting for. I think this is her best album yet. I can't quite describe how it moves me.

Lastly, I want to thank you Kate for everything you've given me. "How I'm moved, How you move me".

Rukhsana Ali: I'm not a subscriber but my boyfriend is and I always read *HomeGround*. I must confess I never took Kate seriously and never listened until I heard *Breathing*. Since then I've been an avid "fan". I love *The Red Shoes*. Kate's music has developed so much and goes from strength to strength. The only thing that annoys me is that Kate does not do more TV appearances. In fact, it frustrates me and makes me downright fuckin' angry.

Some of Kate's lyrics are really subversive and revolutionary yet she seems to have undeservedly got an "airy fairy" label which does not reflect her or her music at all. Her lyrics combined with the imaginative musical arrangements and complex productions undoubtedly make her my favourite singer-songwriter/composer.

The point I'm trying to make is that Kate should go out there and perform so that people can hear and see what her music is all about. I don't mean that she should be the "Saleswoman of the Hour" but a few performances on creditable programmes such as 'The Late Show' rather than 'Aspel' would open many people's ears and eyes.

Gil Alonso-Mier: Kate means "Quest" when you pronounce it in French. More than a songwriter, Kate is a sweet fairy who gives us Love, Light, Magic... She acts like a mirror that reveals who we are and this is the greatest of gifts. Blessed Be Kate!!! Blessed be all the *HomeGround* staff who help many people communicate, for the Universal feeling behind the texts and illustrations. This is great work. I love you.

Raymond: I am writing firstly to congratulate you on a first-rate magazine. The first issues I received were 42, 50 and 51. One letter from issue 42 from Ruth, really touched me. The reason being I know how she feels.

I have been a Kate fan for six years now, but with the long absences between albums I am not always listening to her music. This was especially so at work in Woolworths. However, last year when Kate began to resurface, I began to play her music in-store, much to the ridicule of my colleagues. They couldn't understand how I liked Kate, writing off her music as crap and even pointless.

It is this respect that I feel I can associate with Ruth because she felt the same ridicule. At work there is one person dislikes Kate's music so much that she can get very abusive towards me even when I talk about Kate. Although she is the only one who is abusive towards me, many others make fun of me and even at the nightclub where I socialise, I am known as "the Kate Bush fan". At first I took this well but it eventually angered me as I couldn't understand what they had against Kate.

Unfortunately, I found the answer. It wasn't Kate, but the fact that I liked her. This was extremely hurtful and made me feel very lonely. To add salt to the wound, when I went to see *The Line, the Cross & the Curve* at my local UCI cinema, I discovered that I was the only person there. Granted, it was a midday showing on a Sunday, but at the time I felt no-one liked Kate but me. This was also being reflected in her performances in the singles chart.

So I felt at my lowest ebb, until my sister introduced me to *HomeGround*. She had seen a copy in the library where she worked. Little did she know that she was opening a new chapter in my life. I found there was a whole world of Kate Bush fans out there and I was lifted out of my depression. Whilst reading through all of the many touching letters in the issues I had, I was touched most by Ruth's letter. I could sympathise with her, knowing how she felt. For that, Ruth, thank you!

A Reader: I have felt very dismayed on reading some of the letters in the past two issues of *HomeGround*, primarily over the demands which many 'fans' seem to make of Kate. Criticisms have been made regarding the fact that she keeps a low public profile, and that she cares little about her fans – supposedly conveyed by the fact that she made only a brief appearance at the recent Convention. Other similar criticisms have been levelled at Kate recently. My despair arises from the fact that many fans seem to be too demanding, and unfortunately, in my opinion, this is a reflection of society in general.

Many people expect much of others, or make demands in order to satisfy their own self-centred desires, and not to benefit those they make the demands of. Sadly I see this as humanity becoming empty and individuals diminishing in Spirit. All too often we look to others to carry out our desires, sometimes expecting and demanding the impossible, and certainly imposing our own views where we shouldn't. In doing this we are turning away from our inner-selves, finding it easier for others to try to fulfil us, rather than nurturing and balancing ourselves from within.

Okay, maybe I'm going off on a tangent here. In relation to Kate, the point is, what right does any 'fan', journalist or anyone else have to make demands of her? She owes us nothing. True, she has made a living from people buying her records and in that way 'survives' on fans, but that does not entitle us to expect a share in her very being. If anything we 'fans' owe much to Kate. From the time *Wuthering Heights* emerged, we have been blessed with a collection of beautiful songs which have moved so many people in a variety of ways.

Photo: Paul Camileri

Kate at the premiere of *The Line the Cross and the Curve*

As long as I have copies of Kate's songs, I will be more than happy. And if a time should come when my albums are too worn or scratched to play, I shall remain happy and grateful for all the feelings, thoughts and experiences that Kate's music has evoked. Isn't it time that people appreciated and accepted the good and true things that exist rather than demanding more and more to fuel insatiable desires?

I'm aware this letter is going on and on, and I didn't realise the extent of my despair until I sat down to write. The truth is there's another much more personal dimension behind what I'm writing but in some ways relates to my distress over the demands of others.

I was recently raped and am now trying to come to terms with the hurt I've been through. Such an attack seems to me to stem from the need for one person to satisfy their own greed, regardless of whether it is at the expense of another. Sure, this may seem an extreme analogy, but both stem from greed. I can't bear to think of people criticising Kate because she may not meet with their expectations. Kate has feelings and emotions and shouldn't have to sacrifice or jeopardise her creativity and its expression, just so she can put her energy into pleasing those who want more from her, and so become some superficial public figure. Please be happy with whatever gifts anyone is kind enough to offer. Save yourself from destructive greed which can drive you to take that which doesn't belong to you. Don't crush the lily in the soul.

Dorothy A. Keveny: It is with pleasure that I write to you. I've recently become an enthusiastic listener to Kate Bush's music and am now a serious collector. I have been profoundly affected by her music, melodies, lyrics, gorgeous production and of course her intriguing personae. I'm from the Boston area and have been teaching for over 20 years. I try to incorporate my love for music into the classroom. I'll often have song quotes from favourite tracks up around the room in an effort to inspire and motivate my students.

I have a huge Stevie Nicks and Fleetwood Mac collection and have been fortunate to have seen them in concert over thirty times, including five of Stevie's shows to promote her current *Street Angel* album. It hurts to realise that Kate doesn't tour but I respect the feelings she has expressed on this matter. I was thrilled when I finally was able to procure Kate's *Hammersmith Odeon* video. There is no doubt that this video confirmed in my mind that Kate is indeed a genius to have conceived, choreographed and executed such a production. I was lucky to find out about your excellent publication. I'm quite impressed with your devotion to Kate and how faithful you have been in putting out *HomeGround* for so many years. I can only imagine the work involved in such an undertaking. I've seen at least four Stevie Nicks fanzines come and go. The most amazing thing I learned in *HomeGround* was that Kate actually goes to the Conventions held in her honour. I find that to be incredibly generous of her. I've been to several Stevie Conventions and there was of course no Stevie.

Jennie: I had a great day at Elstree studios yesterday watching the recording of 'Top of the Pops'. Kate was excellent. I couldn't believe I saw her, then spoke to her and gave her a quick kiss on the cheek. I was so excited. My sister and I didn't have tickets and we stood outside for seven hours. It was freezing. Then another Kate fan gave us a ticket. I'd just like to say thank you to the two guys, I think one was called Paul. It was really kind of them, we really appreciated it. Another girl was so taken aback at how desperate we were to see Kate that she gave us another ticket.

Andy Graham: Our Wedding Day started with your letter, which was a great omen. All Friday 29th July we had busied ourselves working like crazy to get everything prepared. How you manage to organise a Convention I will never know. Sara's friends showed early to do her hair and make-up while I went to my parents house as I wasn't to see Sara's dress until we got to the Registry Office (a stone's throw from the principal filming location of *The Pink Mules!*) I hadn't felt nervous until we arrived and saw all of our posse standing outside in their best kit. All of a sudden, there they were – the stomping blue cats I'd read so much about. Fifteen minutes later it was all done and the partying began. I wore a suit for the day, but it was so hot and humid that for the evening I dug out the shorts and *Red Shoes* T-shirt (though I kept the buttonhole and waistcoat as I felt it was the done thing).

We felt it totally necessary to send Kate an honorary wedding invitation in recognition of all the joy her music and her life force have given us. She sent us a card. A very good work friend of mine wrote to EMI. Kate sent him the card to pass on to us.

Tracey Marshall: I found out I was pregnant in November 1993 and the baby was due on 17th July 1994. As with most women I never for a minute imagined that the baby would be late. In the event the baby was thirteen days late and when I went into labour on 29th July I realised that if I could hold onto him for another few hours he would be born on a very important date. Twenty four hours (!) later I gave birth to our little boy, Eric and was thrilled that he had been born on Kate's birthday. I have been a manic fan of Kate since her first single and to have a child share her birthday really made my day. I hope Kate had a good birthday.

Photo: Paul Camileri

Kate leaving Elstree after recording her appearance for 'Top of the Pops'.

Retracing the Scenes

Somewhere in between (4): 1995-98

By the Spring of 1995, Kate considered that the promotional effort for *The Red Shoes* had run its course. She returned to her very private life. There were directions and matters other than music to consider. What we weren't to know at that stage was that it would be more than ten years before she returned with another album.

Later, in her interview in the December 2001 issue of *Q*, Kate would say of the death of her mother, and her decision to make the film, and the aftermath: *"I shouldn't have done it. I was so tired. I'm very pleased with four minutes of it, but I'm very disappointed with the rest. I let down people like Miranda Richardson who worked so hard on it. I had the opportunity to do something really interesting and I completely blew it… I was actually viewed in quite a negative light at that point, more so than after 'The Dreaming' where I was viewed as some kind of nutter. It dissipated my energy severely and threw me into a state of severe exhaustion. You just get worn down… There had been a period, a very big period, where I hadn't been able to work, but I hadn't grieved properly, then work became my way of coping.. I needed to stop working because there were a lot of things I wanted to look at in my life... It was as if I was testing myself to see if I could write, but I didn't like what I was writing. I thought, No, if you don't want to do it, it will be rubbish. Basically, the batteries were completely run out and I needed to re-stimulate again."*

Kate moved from Kent back into a flat in London, though she had now acquired a new house in the country in Berkshire, though there was much work to be done on it before it was ready. She had actually been writing and demoing songs, but as she later indicated, nothing would come of these except later garbled stories that she had junked the album and gone off to write plays.

Actually, as *Q* later indicated, she *"stopped working, slept a lot, and watched a lot of bad TV"*. Kate refused the pressure to write new material, and considered spending time in Africa to work up some ideas. Of that year, Kate said in the December 1995 Kate Bush Club mailout: *"I've been taking time off work this year and it's been really good for me. I've still kept busy but I've also had lots of time to rest and catch up things."*. She *had* made music that year: *"I've just done a song for Donal Lunny who's putting an album together of traditional Irish music. It was fun and very challenging. The lyrics are in Gaelic so I will eagerly await comments from all Irish-speaking listeners in particular. I'm sure Ma gave me a helping hand!"*

This was of course *Mná na hÉireann*. The difficulty for Kate was that she did not speak Gaelic. She assembled some books and tapes on the language and practised the pronunciation. After she'd made some demo recordings and practised the lyrics, Donal Lunny came over from Ireland to help her perfect the lyrics. After he went back she completed the work and sent him a DAT. Apparently he only had to correct her on four items before approving the track.

It is difficult for someone who has been a household name to entirely disappear. Celebrities, willing or not, are the alphabet of the media, who seek to fill the spaces between the adverts with names and faces the public recognise and don't have to think too much about. So it was that excerpts from Kate's videos appeared on 'Top of the Pops' on BBC1 and ' Top of the Pops 2' on BBC2 three times in March/April. Kate appeared (with many others) in a *Sergeant Pepper* pastiche on the front cover of the September *Mojo*, to celebrate their feature on the 'greatest 100 albums ever made', as selected by a cross section of the cream of British rock journalism. No.1 was the Beach Boys' *Pet Sounds*, from Van Morrison's *Astral Weeks* and the Beatles' *Revolver*. Kate came in at no.60 with *Hounds of Love*. *Mojo* commented: "It was almost three years since... *The Dreaming* - barmy, brilliant, and only briefly in the charts... Kate emerged with her most ambitious work yet."

Certain of its target demographics, *Q* continued to make its almost obligatory monthly mention of Kate. Attached to the cover of October's issue was a tape cassette of "driving tracks". *Running Up That Hill* was featured, and *Q* said of it: "Aside from her breakthrough effort, *Wuthering Heights*, this intoxicatingly rhythmic beauty from August 1985 was Bush's most successful single, as well as her most significant, signalling a new complexity and maturity for the already prodigious talent... A wizardette, a true star."

Kate was not spared the traditional press-cuttings job, although apparently in a good cause. *Courses* magazine (for adult and evening education) put a full colour close-up of Kate on the cover of their Autumn '95 issue, and inside a one-page interview, most of which we had seen before. Kate's vocal on *Don't Give Up* was included in a new TV advert for the Victim Support scheme.

On 10th September the very popular Greek TV programme 'Ciao Antenna' featured a danced version of *Big Stripey Lie*. This followed a similar version of *Oh England My Lionheart* in December 1994. In the October '95 *Record Collector* somebody was wanting £150 for a Duffield tour programme. Those who went will remember the Kate Bush Club gave away hundreds of these at the 1994 Convention.

After *The Red Shoes* and in Kate's continuing absence, musicians began noticeably to parade

1995 and 1996 are the last of the original 'Five Years Ago' material.

From 1997 onwards, these chronological articles are compiled from the news items which appeared in *HomeGround*, and (as the 'Five Years Ago' articles would have been compiled) also from our press cuttings files and other sources of information.

their Kate influences, and writers began trying to assess what that influence was. The second *Mojo Music Guide*, issued free with the magazine, listed '100 great voices', and had Kate at no.15: "Apart from being one of the most extraordinary records ever made, *Running Up That Hill* is all the evidence one needs to argue that Bush is a major-league chanteuse. Precisely because she's prepared to sing in that ditsy English convent girl voice, she produces a sound that's nakedly, uninhibitedly, close to the bone". *The Sex Revolts: Gender, Rebellion & Rock'n'Roll* was, however, one of those sociological treatises on rock music that you'd usually avoid other than as a cure for lack of sleep. This one also had a psychoanalytical perspective and mentions Kate and her early habit of saying that when she was creating, she could only imagine herself as a man. Well, until *The Sensual World* that was, but that detail seems to escape the authors Simon Reynolds and Joy Press.

She Bop by Lucy O'Brien, described itself as "the definitive history of women in rock, pop, and soul". It may be something like that and was certainly a good read. The coverage of Kate in the chapter on female singer/songwriters was respectful (in the *NME* post *Hounds of Love* category) although not very well focused. O'Brien fell into familiar *Guardian* clichés describing Kate's work: "like Innocent Art – childlike rather than childish – painted in bright colours and deeply felt emotional hues." In Hampstead sitting rooms this probably passed as perceptive comment, and was not helped by the comment in the chapter on Madonna, manipulation and TV: "Anna and Frida cultivated the slick "girl next door" pop image that ushered in the new video age, while Kate Bush took that polish one step further by turning herself into an erotic fantasy." To be fair the author was making a valid point about the use of woman's sexuality to sell records, and pointed out that Kate may well have been exploited in this way in her very early career before, as she puts it, "the penny dropped".

Christmas 1995 brought charitable matters, and together with Sir Cliff Richard, Lisa Stansfield, Sting, Elton John, Pet Shop Boys and Seal, Kate signed a leather-bound edition of *The Guinness Book of Hit Singles* which was auctioned by Sotheby's on 13th and 14th September, celebrating the publication's 10th edition. The proceeds of the special volume went to go the Terrence Higgins Trust, the Lord's Taverners and Roy Castle Cancer Appeal. Kate was also involved with Brian Eno's "Greeting Stars" Christmas card set sold in aid of the War Child charity. Her involvement with this charity would deepen over the next year. There were twelve cards in the pack, and Kate's card featured the *Red Shoes* image of a dancer's two crossed feet but with ice skate blades on the ballet shoes and the supporting foot resting on a snow covered chimney with glacial scenery in the background. Kate's signature appeared in the lower right hand corner and inside the single word "Peace".

In mid-February 1996 the British band China Drum released a new single *Can't Stop These Things* (Beggars Banquet MNT 8CD) with a cover version of *Wuthering Heights* as the b-side. It was a very fast guitar version elsewhere described as "punk". The band's *Goosefair* album released in April 1996 also included the track, though curiously, it did not appear in the track listing. This cover version was first released in April 1995 in an 800 copy limited edition. It was included on the B-side of the single, and on the album because of the reception it had at the band's gigs!

Valen Hsu was a very popular Taiwanese singer who covered two of Kate's tracks, *The Man with the Child in his Eyes* and *Moving* on her first two albums, 1995's *Appease* and 1996's *Tear Sea*. These are both sung in Mandarin.

Also in February, Kate was nominated in the US Grammy Awards for the second time, in the 'Long Form Video' category for *The Line, the Cross & the Curve*, along with Peter Gabriel's *Secret World Live* which actually won at the ceremony at the end of the month. This nomination came as something of a surprise to many American fans, as the video release of Kate's film had gone practically unnoticed in the American media, and the few critics who did bother to review it, were not enthusiastic, some even labelling Kate as a "has-been". Kate had previously been nominated for a Grammy in 1989 for *The Sensual World*, in the "Best Alternative Album" category.

Australia has a government-funded alternative radio station called JJJ FM (aka 'Triple-J'). At the end of March 1996 a DJ from the station contacted Australian Kate fan Richard Frost seeking help with a 'J-File' programme on Kate. On 31st May this was broadcast as a three hour radio special "including lots of Kate music, snippets of interviews over the years and a quiz. Fans and *HomeGround* readers Graham Dombkin and Richard talked live for a few minutes about their Kate experiences and they even played *Mná na hÉireann*. There was also an interesting story from a guy called Jules about Kate shopping in Harrods with Enya "for Joanna Lumley's OBE party".

Whilst Kate was going about her life doing things other than making music, EMI considered it might be time for another compilation album, perhaps in the form of a double CD box. Luckily Dave of *HomeGround* was now head of Marketing at EMI Dance with responsibility for marketing on other EMI acts including Kate, and was able to assist in considering which tracks ought to be in this new collection. Kate's cover version of *Sexual Healing* was certainly a lost classic which was being considered.

Common Ground, the album of cover versions of

Irish folk songs including Kate's version of *Mná na hÉireann* was released by Premier Records (an EMI label) on 20th May 1996. *Mná na hÉireann* is a popular Irish Gaelic poem written by Peadar Ó Doirnín in the 18th Century, and had been put to music by several artists including The Chieftains and Sinéad O'Connor. The tune used by Kate was composed by Seán Ó Riada, one of the greatest influences on the current popularity of traditional music in Ireland and around the world. *Mná na hÉireann* was first performed at a memorable concert at Dublin's Gaiety Theatre in March 1969, on the occasion of Peadar Ó Doirnín's bicentenary. Seán Ó Sé sang the song but it is today more commonly recognised in Ireland as an instrumental.

The album was a big event in Ireland. TV advertising included a clip from Kate's contribution. The biggest music paper *Hot Press* had a three-page feature in their 29th May 1996 edition. Liam Fay commented that the album was "arguably... a strenuous contender for Irish album of the year". In the interview with Donal Lunny there was much mention of Kate: "For Lunny, the agreement of Kate Bush to come aboard was crucial to the realisation of the whole undertaking. 'When I rang her up about this, her interest was immediate. That was very gratifying. She had taken a year off from work of any kind and this was bang in the middle of it. She opened herself to several weeks' work by taking it on. I knew she'd be good and she didn't give up until it was right. She's a real joy to work with.' Ms. Bush's contribution – a fiery interpretation of *Mná na hÉireann* – as gaeilge – may well prove to be among the most controversial cuts on *Common Ground*. 'She was very excited with the idea of singing the Irish in a way that Irish speakers would understand,' explains Lunny. 'She had Seán Ó Sé's recording of *Mná na hÉireann* as reference. She was as faithful to the pronunciations as she could possibly be. It was with characteristic care and attention that she approached it. She did not stint one bit. Of course you'll get people saying, "Oh, you'd know she doesn't talk Irish straight off". You wouldn't know it straight off. I would defend her efforts as being totally sincere. No matter how perfect she gets it, she's not an Irish speaker. This may rankle with some people.'

Indeed in another review by Joe Jackson in the *Irish Times*, Kate was criticised by the Gaelic purists for exactly the reasons which Lunny suspected she might, but this review seems to be a reactionary piece to the *Hot Press* feature: "There is too much hype surrounding this album, in which I probably originally participated, interviewing its producer Donal Lunny, for this newspaper. As a musical mix of artists who allegedly are equally at home in the "common ground" of rock and Irish music, it is, at best, richly resonant along those lines, at worst, mediocre. Bono and Adam Clayton setting *Tomorrow* in a more acoustic setting than their previous recording of the song is the former and Kate Bush fumbling her way through *Mná na hÉireann*, is the latter. Máire Brennan, Sharon Shannon, Christy Moore and Paul Brady occasionally rescue a project that was obviously full of good intentions but finally falls far more often than it soars."

Somewhat after the event Kate's Gaelic contribution was lifted onto a compilation album partly sponsored by the official Gaelic Language Board *Éist: Songs in their Native Language* (Dara Records/ Bord na Gaeilge). This was reviewed by Mick Moroney in the *Irish Times* on 19th March 1999: "The biggest chuckle is Kate Bush's Darby O'Gill-accented *Mná na hÉireann*, histrionically dragging swathes of Ó Riada orchestration along behind her, but with a whipping knife edge of emotion which makes it all worthwhile. Quality muzak, what more can I say?"

Dónal Lunny

Hot Press officially reviewed the album two issues after their main feature and while it had some reservations about the project, described Kate's track as "impressive". DJs in Ireland especially seemed to comment on Kate's track on the week of release, intrigued that she sang in Irish and remarking after playing the track "and that would you believe was Kate Bush". *Common Ground* entered the Irish album charts at No.6, and peaked at No.5.

So what happened to the enhanced CD, which was to include a video of Kate's version of *Mná na hÉireann*? Pencilled in for September or October it didn't get released. We hear that the project was killed off for some unknown reason when many contributions, including Kate's, were already complete.

On 4th July 1996 Don Black, the songwriter more recently known for *Sunset Boulevard*, began a short series of programmes on BBC Radio 2 on singer/songwriters. "Tonight I'm going to look at the career of a unique talent; a very private person, her albums are so infrequent that when they are finally released they become more of an unveiling. She sings, she writes and she produces her own records. She has only toured once in 18 years. When asked why, she said 'I just don't like all that attention'". He played *The Man with the Child in his Eyes*, *Babooshka*, *Wuthering Heights*, *Moments of Pleasure*, *The Man I Love*, and *Running Up That Hill*. "There is a strong poetic element in Kate's work; she usually constructs the music and writes a general idea of the lyric, and then goes away and spends ages polishing the words. She's passionate about getting those words right, and a lot of her ideas come from real-life scenarios... Her most famous record shows just how brilliant she is. She takes an enormous book, and in a few minutes condenses the story in such a concise and mysterious way... I met Kate just a few weeks ago – she told me that she had only seen one

Don Black

musical in her life, that was *Godspell* some twenty years ago, so I arranged for her to see *Sunset Boulevard*; the reason I mention this is because I was amazed that she was so amazed by it – not just the show but the orchestra, the lights, the costumes... We automatically assume that stars are used to opening nights, fancy parties and hobnobbing with sophisticated friends. I think I can say that Kate is one of the most normal, ordinary megastars I have ever met. There is no "side" to her at all – no show business veneer... I said that Kate is very normal, but there is nothing normal about her creativity. She seems to have her own signature on all her songs; no one else writes like her or sings like her; maybe that's why her songs aren't covered by other artists – her versions are the definitive ones... I asked Kate if she had a favourite singer, and she said her favourite is the blackbird, and her second favourite is the thrush – well I told you she was different! I also asked her which one of her records she particularly liked, and she said *Running Up That Hill*'.

Interesting to note that the birdsong which would feature so prominently in the album released nine years later was already a thread in Kate's consciousness.

Graphic opposite: Neil Sherrif

Gaffaweb, the most important Kate site on the World Wide Web became operational on 3rd August 1996. Designed with love by various members of rec.music.gaffa with most HTML programming by Vickie Mapes, this site includes many fascinating features, a discography, a videography, a dictionary of Kate Bush terms, and many beautiful pages treating of varied subjects dear to Kate Bush fans. Gaffaweb will be a work in continual growth, although it is already the definitive resource for Kate fans.

The world-famous Stev0 reviewed the new site as follows: "First there's the FAQ. While it has always been a group effort, extra congratulations have to go out for Vickie here. Most HTML FAQs I've seen are all the same – links at the top which link to where in the FAQ the question is answered, and the only off-site links go to places specifically mentioned in the FAQ. Vickie did those things, of course, but added an extra great bonus of putting little random (but appropriate) links everywhere hidden in the FAQ. Try it! Next, comes a section about Early Kate (the demo tapes, and everything leading up to *The Kick Inside*). I've only briefly scanned this section, but I do intend to go back soon – it does look fascinating! Then comes a couple of sections which truly makes this a Lovehounds/ rec.music.gaffa Web site: A couple of 'Best of Lovehounds' sections compiled by Wieland Willker. Last year he did a remarkable effort similar to this – here, it's even more comprehensive and nicely HTML-ized. Next up is *The Garden* – a copy of the version HTMLized by Woj previously. One cannot consider oneself a true KateFan(tm) without studying IED's obsessive thesis here. After that is a a videography noting every single appearance Kate has done anywhere on TV. If that doesn't sound interesting, obviously you don't know KateFan(tm) Obsessive Attention to Detail. Then comes a collection of interviews, articles, and reviews. That should be self-explanatory. The next section is my personal favourite. I mean, the FAQ and *The Garden* are definite must-see stops if you've never seen them, but I have so that takes some of the novelty away. This section is a wonderful dictionary compiled by Richard Bensam. A search engine is promised for it, but even without it you WILL spend hours here, and enjoy every minute of it. Every section has a cute little name (for example, the above-mentioned dictionary is called 'Them Heavy People'). The next section is one that lives up to its name: 'Wow!' – dozens and dozens of wonderful pictures of Kate. As of this writing, there's no order to them, but you will not mind flipping through page after page after page of these. Finally comes a Discography, which is still pretty much under construction and looks mostly taken from the FAQ anyway. However, it's not really a bug; it's just not a feature (yet).

"Almost any one of the above sections I would have given at least an 8 or 9 out of 10. The content is amazing, the pages are simple yet very well laid-out, it loads nice and fast. Combine all these elements, and only one synopsis is possible: This is not only the best Kate site on the Web – it's one of best sites on the Web PERIOD. A+ all around, folks. Not only 10-out-of-10: This site goes to 11!"

In autumn 1996 Alan Parsons made a guest appearance on the Viva channel show 'Geschmacksache'. Among the videos he played was *Wuthering Heights*: His introduction: "Back in the early days of the Alan Parsons Project I remember David Gilmour from Pink Floyd walking in with a young lass who can't have been more than about 16 or 17 years old at that time. Her name was Katie Bush, as she was referred to then, and she was about to make an album with another colleague of mine, Andrew Powell, who over the years has done the orchestral arrangements for the Alan Parsons Project albums. And he played me her first album when it was finished, back at my house, must have been the late '70s I suppose. And I heard this next song and said, 'you've got a smash on your hands', and of course it was true. And it launched the career of Kate Bush". Nigel Kennedy also appeared on the same show in September 1996 . His playlist included: "another musician who I really admire and was lucky to meet quite a long time ago is Kate Bush. I've played a bit of violin on a few other songs. And what I love about her is that, you know, she's just like a normal person, she doesn't behave like a

DEC 1998

huge star, she doesn't have monster limos and doesn't tell everyone to piss off all the time like what most rock stars have to do to be taken seriously. She's a cool person, and like – I don't know what track we're gonna play of hers – but, yeah, she's an inspirational musician. I go in there, put down some music and just suddenly it seems when we're making music that the vibe comes right in, but when we stop playing she's just like 'do you wanna cup of tea, mate?', that type of thing, which is a very profound statement to hear and something which always goes to my heart, well, she goes to my digestive system and plays havoc probably. Anyway, here's something from *Hounds of Love*, by Kate Bush."

Prince

And then there was *My Computer* on the latest album from The Artist then known as The Artist Formerly Known As Prince (who for reasons of simplicity, and because this writer is not employed by EMI, we will call simply 'Prince'). Kate contributed backing vocals to the track on the to 3-CD set called *Emancipation* which was released worldwide on 18th November 1996. The song is apparently about Prince's hobby of surfing the net on AOL. The song opens with AOL's greeting "You've got mail" and closes with AOL's "Goodbye". Kate is credited with "additional vox" and Prince states "Thanx Kate". The song was completed (again!) by swapping tapes. EMI was planning on a two year publicity campaign with the release of 10 singles. However, *My Computer* was not one of them.

The January 1997 issue of *Q*, improbably published in the last week of November 1996, reviewed *Emancipation*: "Waiting quietly near the end of this bumper package is maybe the finest moment of the whole 180-odd minutes, the beautiful *My Computer*. Perhaps the most heartfelt hymn to technology since Kraftwerk's *Computer World*, it features both Kate Bush and the computerised voice prompts of the America On-Line computer network and is a career highlight".

Although we saw many reviews of *Emancipation* in the US newspapers, few mentioned Kate's collaboration. The exception was Michael Saunders in the *Boston Globe*, 20th November: "*My Computer* is a timely reflection of a person who burrows in the electronic comfort zone of his computer, looking for someone to talk to 'to make believe it's a better world, a better life...' Kate Bush does a guest vocal that floats above the layers of overdubbed tracks."

Of course, we were all interested in one issue: when would the next album appear? In fact at the end of 1996 there were the first indications that Kate seemed to be getting on with new work, writing and assembling musicians. A rumour from the internet had Kate collaborating once again with David Gilmour, and Stuart Elliott had recently told a group of fans who went backstage after an Alan Parsons Project gig that just before that tour had commenced, he had received a call from Kate regarding working on a new album. We weren't to know at that stage that Kate was about to embark on quite another sort of creative project.

At the beginning of 1997 the stories in the increasingly ridiculous tabloid press said Kate had gone bonkers (again), had become hugely overweight (again!), had turned into a paranoid recluse behind huge security gates, video cameras, and god knows what else and that she had taken to calling herself Catherine Earnshaw. Our response in *HomeGround* 59 was that: "As usual you can discount this garbage. Kate is working on another album. Far from being behind security gates, Kate has been recording at her own studio at the Farm and latterly at Abbey Road". *The Times* reported on 3rd January 1997 that "EMI confidently expects 1997 to be a Kate Bush year, which come only slightly more often than total eclipses". We thought this was being a little optimistic: "Our feelings are that the album won't see the light of day until next year, Spring earliest, but who knows. We've all been here before". There's real optimism! Other stories emanating from the Channel 4 teletext music news on 21st January had Kate working on 'a fun project' and also working with Rolf Harris. This particular piece of 'news' was flogged to death (boomerangs, digerdoos etc – see Simon Bates and Radio 1 in 1982) by Virgin Radio!

'Another World' is the NBC long distance soap, which (it says here) "With its début on May 4, 1964, began a rich tradition of dynamic storytelling that it continues to this day, while honing its dramatic edge against the issues and concerns of today's society". Ok, you get the drift. In an episode screened in January 1997 *This Woman's Work* was used as a backdrop to a romantic dream sequence. This led to questions on internet newsgroups and much publicity for the song and for Kate. This particular song was being noticed in the US. It would pop up again and again during this year, and was on its way to being perhaps the most well known of all Kate's songs in the US due to repeated soundtrack use, and a very special cover version which assumed almost a life of its own.

Kate's next project with the War Child charity was the Milestones Gallery. Contributors were asked to create three-dimensional artworks celebrating the people who were of special significance to them in their musical career. Kate's tribute to Billie Holiday was an elegant bronze of the flower she always wore in her hair. All the pieces were sold at an auction during a charity dinner at the Saatchi Gallery in north London on Tuesday 4th February 1997 and Kate's piece raised £600.

1997 was the year of the EMI Centenary. As part of the celebrations, the company authorised a special audiophile re-release "EMI Centenary Vinyl". This series included *The Kick Inside* released in February and *Hounds of Love* in November. All the albums in the series were direct metal mastered, cut from analogue tapes for much improved sound quality and were pressed on thick (180GM) virgin vinyl.

'Party of Five' was another popular American TV soap, which (it also says here) explored "the lives of the Salingers, five brothers and sisters determined to stay together following the tragic loss of their parents.". Okay. On 26th February 1997 they used the whole of *This Woman's Work* in an emotional scene at the end of that day's episode. It received a massive response from the show's audience who wanted to know what the track was, and who was the artist. This internet posting was typical: "Does anyone know the name of the song that was playing when the drunk brother walked into the Hewitt girl's hospital room and started crying? A girl was singing and her voice was haunting. I really want to get that song." The Sony (ah ha!) Corp's web site in response offered the whole song as a download.

In *HomeGround* 56 we said this: "As to what is going on, we have no cleared official information. Read that again. Perhaps the best clue comes from an encounter that friends of the Editors of the German Fanzine had with Dave Gilmour on March, 21st 1997 at Covent Garden Records, an instruments shop in London's Charing Cross Road. Gilmour said that Kate is very much in control, and certainly is not using a producer. She is in excellent shape. The album at this stage seems to have a whole different feel from the material on which he worked in 1992. There are new sounds and one track is divided (at the moment) into three parts. That may change! Kate is using the talents of a new bass player, Stuart Elliott of the old gang, and the African drummer Manu Katche, who has worked with Gabriel (and can be seen on the *Secret World* video). Gilmour quotes Kate as saying that she knew of Katche because of his work with Gabriel, but until now had not had the right track to use him on. She says that he is brilliant, and that it was important to use his work the best way she could. Gilmour mentions the working titles of some tracks: *Round in my Mirror*, originally set up with Elliott on drums and Kate's voice mixing with Celtic instrumentation. Katche was later used on this track, introducing a huge change. Gilmour himself worked on "a long solo" for *Open Your Sight*. He had some doubts as to whether he fitted exactly into the scheme that Kate wanted, although he was reassured by Del that his work did. According to this information, which we stress again is not official, the present target for the completion of basic recording is July. That leaves the mixing of course".

Although Kate was recording and mixing at the home studio at East Wickham Farm (and we did hear that she had also been recording in Los Angeles) in the May 1997 Kate Bush Club newsletter she said:

"*Hi everyone, thanks for all your letters. Just thought I'd let you know I've had a lovely break away from work – I feel energized and I'm just starting to write again (early days yet so please don't hold your breath). I thought I should dispel a few press rumours – I have not gone mad. I have not changed my name, if Rolf Harris is going to be on the next album – I haven't thought of it yet. I am well and happy and yes, the artist formerly known as Kate Bush is still Kate Bush and is alive and kicking! I hope you're all well and thanks yet again for your continued warmth and support.*

With lots of love,

Kate Bush"

On 15th June 1997 the American soul artist Maxwell recorded an episode of the MTV programme 'Unplugged' in which among other songs, he performed a cover version of *This Women's Work*. In an interview headlined by Gary Graff which appeared on the Reuter Newsline on 22nd July it was said: "Maxwell agreed to do the MTV Unplugged session as a chance to re-arrange some of the *Urban Hang Suite* songs... and to cover *This Woman's Work*, a song by British songstress Kate Bush. 'I was trying to put together a song that represented my understanding, in some way, of what women represent and what they go through,' explains Maxwell, who has received praise for his rendition from Bush. 'I think that's what *This Woman's Work* represented. I couldn't have written a song like that because I'm not a woman, and an exceptional woman wrote it already. I just kind of took it'". The only question is, although Sony had already made it available as a download – why didn't the label have the nous to release *This Woman's Work* as a single on the strength of this kind of publicity? We shall never know.

This cover version by Maxwell became very popular, and many would come to believe that Maxwell was the writer of the song.

As a further part of their centenary celebrations EMI released a number of specially remastered CD editions of classic albums from artists on the label. For Kate, they originally wanted to go with *The Kick Inside*, but were persuaded that the correct choice was *Hounds of Love*. Released on 30th June 1997, just as Dave (who had put in so much work on the project) was getting caught in the crossfire of an EMI boardroom battle, we thought it was quite a nice package. Kate herself did not want to write a retrospective on the album, and instead suggested that this author should draft a sleeve note, which he was pleased and honoured to do.

This re-release of *Hounds of Love* was properly remastered at Abbey Road in a process overseen by Kate.

Within the CD case of the special release was therefore a 16-page booklet including the sleeve note, the complete lyrics, and various photos.

As ever the titles given to these demo tracks are not necessarily the titles even given to them by Kate.

Due to Dave's assiduous work, the album had as additional tracks the B-sides and 12" mixes from that period: *The Big Sky (Meteorological mix)*, *Running Up That Hill* (12" mix), *Be Kind to My Mistakes*, *Under the Ivy*, *Burning Bridge* and *My Lagan Love*. There was some consideration given to the re-release of *Running Up That Hill* as a single, or possibly a CD-EP of remixes of that great track by prominent mixers. Sadly neither idea came to pass.

Despite the multiplicity of bootleg releases of other collections of Kate's early demos, it was only in mid-1997 that tapes of *The Early Years*, the semi-mythical original collection of Kate's early tracks suddenly surfaced in Europe. The tracks in this collection *not* previously available included *Davy* (the prototype of *Maybe*, and also known as *Humming*), *You Were the Star*, *Cussi Cussi*, *Atlantis*, and *Sunsi*.

Other odd bits of Kate news at this time (we were already reduced to finding whatever scraps we could) included: Kate appearing at no.995 in the *Sunday Times* 'Rich List' for 1997. Andy McNab formerly of the SAS, described in *Immediate Action* his autobiography, an evening in the cook-house of an Army camp in Northern Ireland: "At the time, just after Christmas 1978, Debbie Harry and Kate Bush were on the same 'Top of the Pops'. Debbie Harry was singing *Denis* and Kate Bush was doing *Wuthering Heights*. When Kate Bush came on the whole rifle company used to shout "Burn the witch!" Rosalyn Sumners the former US World Champion figure skater used *This Woman's Work* in an ice skating programme. "Kate Bush & Felicity Kendal were the Sodom & Gommorah of '70s British culture" (BBC Radio 4). "There's a slight plus in that Kate Bush, Annie Lennox and Eric Clapton haven't been offered their annual nominations (for the Brit Awards) for existing" ... and a credit to Kate with *The Greenwood Tarot* by Mark Ryan and Chesca Potter? Study those cards carefully, especially 'The Archer'.

Kate *was* invited to the "People's Banquet", the government's tribute to the Queen on her 50th wedding anniversary in November 1997, at the Banqueting Hall on Whitehall. She sat on the table with John Major, the former Prime Minister, Mike Atherton the cricketer, and Darcy Bussell the Ballerina, and was served her food by *HomeGround* reader Thander Easton!

In November 1997 we heard that some friends of the editors of the Italian Kate fanzine had run into Del. Over a cup of coffee he spoke about the work taking shape, and said that they saw it like a concept album constructed in the manner of a film, "a continuity" is what Del called it. Del apparently also spoke of a recent trip Kate had made to a number of the major cities of Europe inspecting venues.

In issue 60 February 1998 we reported: "As ever there is no confirmed news. Kate is still working on an album, and possibly on another project. Whatever she's doing, Kate's keeping this one close. Various stories are flying about, though at least one rumour, that the album had "heavy industrial sounds" appears to have been a deliberate falsification by persons unknown. Another story has Kate filming in a disused part of the London Underground, though that may be a garbled rehash of the work Kate did for *The Line, the Cross & the Curve*".

What we didn't know was that by the beginning of 1998, although Kate was continuing to work as far as possible, she was now pregnant with Bertie.

In the January 1998 *Q*, *Hounds of Love* was voted 48th best album ever; "Despite her earlier success, Bush's previous album, *The Dreaming*, proved too wilfully self-indulgent to attract a mass audience. Three years in the making, *Hounds of Love* was no less ambitious or experimental, but its creator took pains to ensure that stand-out tracks like *Cloudbusting*, *The Big Sky* and *Running Up That Hill* boasted glossy production values and irresistible melodic hooks... Magic Moment... The Huge Drum and chant climax to *Cloudbusting*, falling away to the sound of a train stopping".

New 'releases' included a bootleg called *Organic Acid*. This claimed to be "rare unreleased recordings of Kate Bush recorded throughout her career", but in fact was a collection of the demos that had been around for some time, some songs from *The Early Years*, and a string together of the music from the Fruitopia ads. However, the bootlegger added touches of his own – snippets of Kate interviews to the Fruitopia music, casio keyboards and other studio touches such as sampled Kate voices to the other demos. We advised "Save your money". *XTC Dance*, a Dutch techno compilation featured a cover of *Running Up That Hill* by a group called Distance which included a digeridoo, and a new album of Irish music released in March 1998 on the Celtic Heartbeat/Universal label, *Celtic Heartbeat* Collection 2 featured Kate's version of *Mná na hÉireann.*

We had mentioned Kate's absence from the *Rolling Stone 'Women in Rock'* issue. In a subsequent issue they compiled a list of the artists whose absence had led to most complaints. The Indigo Girls headed this list followed by Kate. Curiously, Kate did appear in *The Rolling Stone 'Women In Rock' Collection,* a 3-CD set released on 15th September by BMG in the US. *The Billboard Guide to Progressive Music* by Bradley Smith was also newly out and widely available (though much criticised) and included extensive and enthusiastic coverage of Kate.

Heard at this time on the internet: "Kate Bush, who is a famous New York city, United States of America singer songwriter with many recordings out". The *NME* gossip column in May reported that Kate "popped along to squint at

BJÖRK at London Shepherd's Bush Empire" and in February reported Goldie saying "There are a lot of people I want to work with, too, which is a matter of timing. I've got a lot of idols that I really love, that I really want to work with. Kate Bush for one. Fuckin' hell, what is she like?" When receiving her Grammy on 25th February, Paula Cole thanked Kate amongst others for inspiration, and later on MTV said that Kate's "visionary" album, *Hounds of Love*, had been very inspirational to her. In *Rolling Stone*, Paula said that she was inspired by *Hounds of Love* because Kate showed it was alright to be "audacious, bizarre and passionate" in music.

Kate's version of *Brazil*, which was recorded for the 1985 Terry Gilliam film, resurfaced in a different version on Michael Kamen's *Opus* album. John Heislman reported: "The original version of this song, released on the *Brazil* soundtrack CD in 1993, featured Kate on vocals, backed by Michael Kamen conducting the National Philharmonic Orchestra of London. The orchestration is light and string-dominated; Kate's phrasing and delivery are quite soft. There's a striking trumpet passage in the middle that plays the lead melody line along with Kate's vocal. The "new" *Brazil* that appears on *Opus* is significantly different. Kate's on vocals, but this time she's backed by Kamen conducting the Seattle Symphony Orchestra. This version is a much heavier, brass-dominated arrangement. Kate's phrasing is real similar to the first version in the beginning, but she becomes much more deliberate towards the end. She also throws in quite a bit of vibrato on one of the sustained notes. The trumpet passage in the first version shows up as a string accompaniment here."

The April 1998 issue of German music mag *Musikexpress* featured Tori Amos in their Mein Plattenschrank ('My Record Cabinet') section. She picked ten favourites from her own collection including *Hounds of Love* and says "I love the second side of this album. I was in Los Angeles when I heard this record for the first time. I had encountered nothing but rejection for months, nobody liked my piano stuff. And I was in a band that did something completely different. Then I found this record, and put it on, listened to side one, liked it OK, listened to side two, listened to side two again, and again, and again and again. This turned me inside out. It changed my life. I decided to leave the man with whom I shared an apartment; I left the man I was living with because of this record."

And Björk (from a recent Swedish magazine): "I often mimic people's voices subconsciously. During a period of my life I was heavily influenced by Kate Bush. She was enormously important for me. Most people just know her special voice but mainly she was a pioneer as a female producer. Her arrangements on the first albums are so brave and original. I got an urge to work more by the mixing table when I listened to them. This very song lulled me to sleep for many years. During the nights I would crawl under the cover in my bed and listen to Kate Bush. When I lay there in the darkness it felt like she was singing to only me."

On the 22nd July BBC Radio 4 'Stereo Nation' broadcast an excellent spoof documentary by Graham Duff about 'Greg', a Kate fan who wrote a Kate fanzine called Bushwacker and had a web site at www.wowwowwow.com. Strangely, although anyone hearing it could have no doubt it was clearly a spoof, shortly afterwards a Press Association reporter contacted *HomeGround* hoping to be able to speak to the fictitious Greg.

In the interview Kate gave to *Q* three and a half years later she indicated that after *The Red Shoes*, after an interval, she did start writing again, and then along came Bertie: "Although I hadn't always wanted children, I had for a long time. People say that magic doesn't exist but I look at him, think I gave birth to him and I know magic does exist ...

"What I have found very difficult since I've had my child is finding time to talk to people, because he comes first. He doesn't care whether the album comes out, so it comes second. I don't want to miss a minute of him. It's so much fun, by far the best thing I've ever done."

Michael Kamen's *Opus*

Q observed "in the face of the absurdities of the trashy popular press and the rumour mongers, Kate's weight is normal, she is in both robust mental health and sharing her life with Danny McIntosh, the rock guitarist, former member of Bandit, and prominent musician on *The Red Shoes*, and working on motherhood first, and a new album second".

On the BBC Radio 2 programme 'Inside Track' on 25th June 1998, Paul Gambaccini answered a question which had been sent in by a few listeners. He said: "We have spoken to her P.A. and the good news is there will be something, sometime. The bad news is it won't be in the immediate future. Work is still at the ideas stage of recording. If you're a website browser and have come across stories about certain musicians like Dave Gilmour being involved, we have it from the most reliable source of all that these stories are completely unfounded and mere speculation". In effect work on a new album more or less stopped for 18 months or more whilst Kate did other, more important, things.

It was, of course, Kate's fortieth birthday that year. The 12th June *Guardian* noted that "Plenty of big names are about to cross the threshold every pop star dreads. Madonna and Michael Jackson hit the big four-oh this year... come on down, 1958 babies Liz Fraser, Kate Bush, Ian Broudie, Ice-T, Jools Holland, Mark E Smith...". *The Glasgow Evening Times* also noted the rite of

Opposite: issues 55 to 62, including another beautiful cover piece by Debi Bowes.

Issue 59 was a huge breakthrough. The first issue produced on a desk top publishing programme.

That programme was Wordstar for Windows 2.0 which had a very effective DTP mode.

The site can now be found at www.katebushnews.com

Or even find it on YouTube

passage: *Pop Stars Finding They're Forty* "The next one to reach the milestone is Kate Bush... You can't imagine Kate Bush, Suzanne Vega, or Joni Mitchell being that bothered about it. But if your career has been based on image rather than ability it might be a different matter". Forty-odd Kate fans came to Glastonbury Tor on Lammas Sunday to celebrate Kate's birthday.

In September 1998 Thomas Dunning, contributor to rec.music.gaffa and *HomeGround* subscriber, released *I Wanna Be Kate: The Songs Of Kate Bush*. This was a rather good album of cover versions of Kate songs. Probably one of the more important milestones in Kate fandom was the establishment by Seán Twomey, a long time *HomeGround* reader, of a new web site to maintain the current news stories from the Kate speaking world. He invited *HomeGround*'s cooperation, and this was gladly given. Seán said: "This is basically a page I hope to keep updated with Kate news, as I feel most non-love-hounds surfers on the web would have to search a lot to get the latest stuff". From these beginnings, Seán's "News and Information" website has grown to be the centrepiece of Kate Bush information on the web.

The Irish Post had been running a series of feature articles about artists of Irish descent working in the UK, and on 29th August 1998 reached Kate: "In many ways, Kate Bush is the antithesis of the other songwriters in this series. Female, middle class, secure in adolescence with a notably placid temperament, she is seemingly free from the warring sense of cultural dislocation experienced by many of her Anglo Irish peers"

How Rumours begin Part xxccvvi: As the culmination of his stage show 'The Man Who Thinks He's It' seen by over 350,000 people, Steve Coogan in his Alan Partridge character, sang a medley of Kate's songs with sections from *Wow*, *Babooshka*, *Running Up That Hill*, *The Man with the Child in his Eyes*, *Don't Give Up*, *Them Heavy People* and *Wuthering Heights* (those of you who missed it can chase it up in the *Steve Coogan Live* video released in December 1998). The Guardian reviewed this. *Time Out* mentions it and thus a rumour begins that Kate is doing a Christmas medley with said Alan Partridge... Milla Jovovich (*The Fifth Element* etc) turned out to be another artist inspired by Kate. Vickie Mapes who met her backstage during her first tour posted that "we had a wonderful discussion about Kate. She adores Kate and respects her tremendously. Her love for Kate prompted her to pursue her musical career (which is her first love and main talent, no matter how many movies she makes or photo shoots she does.)"

Though the music press were now saying "Kate who...?" (a contributor to love-hounds heard the DJ in a shopping mall play *Wuthering Heights* and then comment of Kate "not heard a lot from her for the past couple of years. Wonder if she's split up") various charts and polls were still saying otherwise. The Channel 4 nationwide poll of "the top albums of all time" placed *Hounds of Love* at no.78... May's *Record Collector* showed that Kate was still in strong demand amongst the British if not international collecting cognoscenti. She appeared at no.32 in the 'Top 500 Collectable Artists' list. This was down from no.27 the previous year, but meant that in 1998 she was still the second most collectable solo female artist. Only Madonna was above her at no.16.

In the August 98 *Q*, *Hounds of Love* made it into a list of the 'essential dozen British albums of the '80s': "In the wake of the commercial hiccup of the underrated *The Dreaming*, Kate Bush retired to her 350-year-old studio and tinkered for four years on her masterpiece". Kate also appeared in the '100 Richest Stars in Rock' feature at joint 53rd with Sade, Dave Stewart, Steve Winwood and The Spice Girls.

The *Independent on Sunday* had been conducting a survey to find 'the top 1000 albums of all time', and the results appeared in the 6th September issue. Based on 200,000 votes, which probably made it the largest popular poll on music ever conducted, the poll placed *Hounds of Love* at number 59. The October *Mojo* listed 'The 100 Greatest Singers Of All Time' voted by a panel of vocalists. This had Kate at 81: Paul Du Noyer commented: "the pre-Raphaelite nymph with Minnie Mouse's soprano" who "gained an unsuspected depth and richness... bares her longings and her pain with unparalleled frankness... a gawky lyricist at times, but in her singing she achieves an emotional truth that words alone can rarely locate... The sparseness of her output and the guarded privacy of her life have conspired against her reputation: it's too easily forgotten what a quietly influential presence Kate has been. Sublime moment: Heart-rending emotional gear change, as post romance bravery gives way to grief at 0:54, *You're the One*."

The December *Record Collector* listed the top 100 rarities and placed the abandoned UK 7" vinyl pressing of *Eat the Music* at no.17. According to RC only 17 copies exist and the value of each is placed at £1,500.

Despite all that, it was a matter of debate in the ITV CEEFAX music pages in December 1998 as to whether Kate still had any fans.

At the end of 1998 *HomeGround* issue 62 reported: "The general picture seems to be that the earliest release date for Kate's next album will be well in to 1999 if not beyond. There is no album related activity at EMI". Of course not. Kate was full time occupied with her new son Bertie in his first year of life.

HOMEGROUND 55
ATE BUSH Fanzine Spring 95
HOMEGROUND 56
MEGROUND 57
Homeground 59
H Fanzine Summer 97
HOMEGROUND 58
The KATE BUS
HomeGround
H Fanzine No. 60 Spring 98
HomeGround
The KATE BUSH Fanzine No.61 Summer 98
HomeGround
Number 62 The Kate Bush Fanzine Winter 98

HOMEGROUND

Hello all,

Five years ago (see within) we were first hearing about a rumoured collaboration between Kate and Prince (as he then was), and probably discounting it. We shouldn't have been so hasty. In this issue we also carry news of the latest fruit of that collaboration. The two artists have many things in common, not least their determination to run their careers the way they want. They are both very creative artists secure in their own recording studios, both regarded by some as bizarre, and funnily enough both also written off recently in some circles as 'spent forces'.

From the first reactions to Prince's new album, including the collaboration with Kate, it would seem he has dealt adequately with the scoffers. Kate? It seems that having taken a period largely out of creative work she is back to writing and thinking about the music and who will help her translate her ideas and emotions into amazing music.

At the same time we hear from some parts of the Kate-speaking world the word 'disillusionment'. We at HOMEGROUND don't and never have understood this. Kate's music exists - it's there in the CD rack! Take it out and put it in the player. Where's the disillusionment? You want Kate to stand on a stage and play it? Yes, it would be a wonderful thing. The atmosphere of the hall, the emotions of the musicians and the fans. But it isn't *necessary*.

In early issues of HG, we ran a couple of articles entitled *Gurus and Glass Onions*. The reference was to a Beatles track. We were then concerned at those who had the tendency to turn a group of friends who liked Kate's music into something approaching a religious cult. It is precisely those people who made Kate their God who now shout 'disillusioned' when they find out she isn't. Kate is not God; she is a highly creative, but sometimes vulnerable human being who makes music that moves the heart. For the final word on this see Krys's article within.

ALSO five years ago for the first time we prepared an issue of HOMEGROUND on a word processor. The machine was a Commodore 8088, the word processor was a very basic one made by Psion, and was soon replaced by WordStar 6. This is the last issue to be prepared in that way. The next issue, hopefully out around the end of March, will be prepared on our new Pentium 100 using WordStar for Windows, a cracking WP/DTP programme that sadly seems to have been orphaned by its manufacturer. So this is by way of saying that the next issue may look a little different.

It is always difficult to say that we have had to increase the prices. The occasion of this increase is a large increase in postage costs. However we have taken the opportunity to realistically reassess the costs of producing the magazine. In 1982 the first HOMEGROUNDs were produced on an old 1900s typewriter with scavenged paper, scissors and paste. Up to 1985 we did six issues a year and the UK cost of those six issues in 1985 was £7.50. An issue in those days was about 20 pages and in a year you got 120 pages for £7.50, i.e. just over 6p per page. Our current issues contain 32 double-columned pages, the equivalent of 64 old-style pages. After the increase you'll get 256 column for £10, i.e less than 6p per column. (Unless of course we screw up all the calculations by having three columns of course - but you see what we mean!) I hope no-one will be put off by the price increase. We shall still be here, gathering the news and views about Kate, and still we think an indispensable guide to the Kate-speaking world.

Some of you have asked what has happened to Dave recently. I can now report that he has a new job - he has joined the ranks of the dreaded record company execs, and the company requires him to work 23½ hours a day to justify their faith in him. In the other half hour he has to go to gigs. Terrible but someone has to do it! We are hoping that in the near future (in his lunch break or in the loo or something) he'll have the time to write again. Meanwhile he sends his regards and asks you all to go out and buy the (AFKA) Prince album. Go on, you'll enjoy it!

I hope you all enjoy this issue. Our problem, as usual, was what to leave out. *Them Heavy People* and *The Technical Bit* will be held over until the next issue.

As usual we are soliciting articles and letters on matters Katy. Let's have your opinion on the Prince track, and what else they might do together. Please send any articles by e-mail if you can (the address is at the foot of the Renewals page), or on disc - it does save us a lot of work (and we haven't invested in the dreaded scanner yet!)

Thank you to everyone who has sent us good wishes regarding our IVF attempts. It means a lot to Krys and myself. We are now in the middle of our third go. Special thanks to Jan Willington.

Happy Christmas to all of you and see you sometime in the new year! We hope to hold a few Hikes and the like when the weather is warmer.

Peter

Hello I'm still alive!
Dave
(Honest!)

War Child

HomeGround looks at a favourite charity

Issue 59: July 1997

By 1996 Kate had been associated with the War Child charity for some time. To raise further funds for this work, Fusion Interactive, a leading European interactive communications agency, donated their time to develop the Milestones Gallery, an exhibition and auction of artwork celebrating 'Milestones in Music'.

The artists were asked to create three-dimensional artworks celebrating the people who were of a special significance to them in their musical career. The work received included Lou Reed on Ornette Coleman; Paul McCartney on Buddy Holly, Gary Barlow on Elton John; Brian Eno on The Velvet Underground; Tim Booth of James on Patti Smith and Dave Stewart on Bob Dylan.

There was an amazing diversity among the pieces: Kate's tribute to Billie Holiday was an elegant bronze of the flower she always wore in her hair. Yoko Ono donated a sculpture of John Lennon's trademark spectacles and Gary Barlow put together items of Elton John memorabilia. One of the most dramatic pieces was by Blur's Graham Coxon who created, 'Scream Thy Last Scream', a giant lightening bolt, his tribute to early Pink Floyd member, Syd Barrett.

The work was sold at an auction during a sparkling charity dinner at the Saatchi Gallery in north London on Tuesday 4th February and Kate's piece raised £600. All money collected went to War Child for their two most immediate projects: a landmine clearance programme in Bosnia, Angola and elsewhere and to continue work on the music therapy centre for children in the Bosnian city of Mostar. Music therapy is widely recognised as an effective healer in the traumatic aftermath of war.

Following the auction, the work was exhibited to the general public in the ground floor gallery of the Economist Plaza in St. James's Street London, from 6th to 16th February, 1997.

Kate's contribution was Lot No.2, 'Strange Fruit', a bronze mounted on stone, the base measuring 15" x 13", the height 7½". It was signed 'Kate Bush 1996'.

Kate's short description ran as follows: "Billie Holiday is one of my favourite singers. She is still a great inspiration. I sang with a band when I was eighteen and always wore a flower behind my ear to be like her. I felt it brought me luck. This sculpture shares its name with one of her favourite songs. I've tried to depict her mouth in mid-song growing among the flowers."

The following long description of the piece by Kate, appeared in the catalogue:

Kate Bush – Billie Holiday 'Strange Fruit' – Bronze sculpture of lips and flowers.

"Billie Holiday was a very big influence on me in my late teens. I loved the sound of her voice and I loved the quality of her songs, the sound of the recordings. And I suppose what I found most striking was the way she was able to convey such incredible feeling. When I was in a band years ago, I used to wear a flower behind my ear as a kind of good luck memento (sic), that was something that she always used to do when she performed. So I suppose whenever I think of Billie, I think of her beautiful voice and the flower she used to wear. When the image came up of the mouth and the flower, it just felt for some reason that bronze was a really good medium. I had been wanting to try for six months to do sculpture and to try bronze.

"It was really fun for me. I've not done anything like his before, to work with something that's a solid, three-dimensional object, as opposed to music which is so completely untouchable physically. It was thrilling to have something which was just a lump of metal, which you can turn around but you can no longer change or fiddle with. The Royal College of Art very kindly let me use their facilities and cast the piece for me. I modelled it in wax. I'd never really appreciated how lovely it is to be working with something so tactile. It really does take shapes, it takes your fingerprints into it. I found it very therapeutic, I'd recommend it to anyone. And I'd never appreciated how wonderful bronze is, when it's molten it looks like liquid fire."

What is War Child? The charity was founded in 1993 by film-makers Bill Leeson and David Wilson after witnessing the plight of children caught up in the war sweeping through the former Yugoslavia. Initially raising money through entertainment events and public appeals, War Child set out to bring immediate material help to children of all ages and ethnic backgrounds. They started by organising aid convoys of food and clothing, providing medical equipment to hospitals in Croatia and Bosnia, supplying musical instruments and CDs to young people and radio stations, and initiating a diabetic programme, taking insulin and testing equipment to Sarajevo, Maglaj, Tesanj, Bihac and Mostar. Music was part of the charity from the off. The first album *Help!* was released in 1995 featuring the likes of Blur, Oasis, Radiohead, Paul McCartney, Stone Roses, and Massive Attack – it was recorded, mixed and on sale within seven days.

Opposite: editorial for issue 58, the last issue using Wordstar 6 for DOS.

Dave certifies he is still alive and well and still with us.

Photo: Edwin Pauptit Brussels Film Festival 1994

"I Wanna Be Kate"

The Making of Thomas Dunning's tribute album

From issues 61 (July 1998) to 64 (November 1999)

Thomas: How it happened

I bought my first issue of *HomeGround* back in 1987. It was issue 26 (Spring '87). I was 19 years old. It was wonderful! A connection to Kate fans and to a far-away place called England where everyone was super-cool and dressed like Kate and Depeche Mode. I knew I had something special in my hands because it was an imported fanzine and in 1987 that was beyond cool.

Yep – that sounds like us.

This is the first time I've ever written anything for *HomeGround*. Last summer I was listening to the b-sides from *This Woman's Work*. *Not This Time* came on and I was grabbed by the swells of the chorus and the dramatic crescendo at the end of the song. An idea came to me from out of the blue to make a Kate Bush tribute album which would include a new recording of this song. This has always been one of my favorite Kate songs, although not many people seem to be familiar with it.

This might not come as much of a surprise to the die-hard Kate Bush fan. Perhaps I'm crazy, but I wouldn't be the first Kate Bush fan to be called so. I've spent the last twelve months fulfilling a dream that I never thought possible. I produced a tribute album to honor the music of Kate Bush. I've always been frustrated by people's resistance to hear new music by someone as daring and gifted as Kate. I decided to invite my favorite Chicago musicians to record my favorite Kate Bush songs.

It basically snowballed from there. I talked to producers, engineers, designers, musicians, lawyers, manufacturing plants, and so on. In all 71 musicians and 19 engineers worked together to complete the project. To complicate things even further, the artists recorded and mixed their tracks at 13 different studios.

Many people feel that Kate hasn't gotten proper recognition from the music industry. I also found the general public has neglected our Kate. When I told people about the Kate Bush tribute album, more than one person asked me if she had died. I'd be like "NO. She's not dead. Isn't it great that we aren't waiting until it's too late to let her know how much we love her music?"

This has been a labor of love for me. I hope you will enjoy listening to it as much as I have enjoyed making it.

Peter: How HomeGround Reported it

There have been a few albums of cover versions of Kate's songs over the years. There was *My Life in the Bush of Kate* by the Big City Orchestra, more recently *Kate Covered* put together by Marcel Rijs. *I Wanna Be Kate*, put together by Thomas Dunning of Chicago is an attempt to do the job professionally.

Released on 22nd September this is an excellent collection of very diverse cover versions of songs from all stages of Kate's career by artists and bands from the Chicago indie scene. The title, as Thomas explains, "was inspired by the song *Kate* by a band called Ben Folds Five. It's about a guy who is so in love with his girlfriend, because she is SO freakin' cool, that he sings he wants to be her. The chorus of the song is 'I WANNA BE KATE!' It's not about Ms. Bush. It's a joke, and I think she'll get a huge laugh out of it."

Thomas goes on to explain that "The idea came one morning last June. I realized that even though many people know some of the more popular songs by Kate, there are so many songs that are absolutely phenomenal in their composition and performance that I started thinking to myself – I want my friends to know about this music, its too beautiful not to share this.

The song that started everything was *Not This Time*. So while listening to these rare Kate Bush songs, and thinking about how I wanted to help get them some more attention, the idea came to make a Kate Bush tribute record."

Photo: Thomas Dunning

As to whether EMI Publishing have given their full support Thomas says: "Ha ha, I hope so! No-one has called telling me to scrap the last year of my life yet, so I'll call that support. Someone at EMI is aware of the project, I know I left a voice mail for someone."

Some of the covers are somewhat different to the originals: "Three in particular stand out; *Home for Christmas*, *There Goes a Tenner*, and *Running Up That Hill* performed by legendary bluesman Diamond Jim Greene. He took the soft-shoe jazzy feel of the song and transformed it into an old time jook-joint blues number that is wondrously beyond description."

It was Thomas' first attempt at a project like this: "As the executive producer I had the task of coordinating many aspects of the project, but not all of them. First, I had to find out how to make a CD like this, as I've never attempted anything this massive before. The making of *I Wanna Be Kate* has taken the combined efforts of 13 studios, 19 engineers, and 71 musicians. It's also important to note that many of the artists and engineers worked on more than one track."

Thomas was worried that the musicians would get sick of listening to Kate's songs: "I would have these really strong emotional reactions during the recording sessions, just from hearing the music and Victoria Storm would always say 'It's her writing, it's her damn writing. It's so good that it just goes inside of you and stirs stuff up.' Some people told me that they knew every song from *The Kick Inside* on piano because they grew up with those songs and learned them all as part of their piano homework."

The reviewers have been kind (mostly): "At her best, British composer, dancer, and diva Kate Bush is a visionary who creates elegant and detailed missives from a better parallel universe; at her worst she's a thinking man's Stevie Nicks. The new tribute album... is a mixed bag, displaying both Bush's best and worst tendencies, as well as those of the mostly local performers who render them... The most successful tracks are those by artists who find their own path into a song and then work their way back, turning it inside out in the process." Monica Kendrick *Chicago Reader* 2nd October.

"With all the Kate wannabe singers in the public eye of late, one could easily fill a tribute to the great songstress with crap. Happily, fan Thomas Dunning has assembled an eclectic collection of interesting interpretations... All in all, a solid compilation that shows how Kate Bush's influence extends beyond her most obvious followers." Liisa Ladouceur, *Chart* October 1998

"From an independent Chicago label comes an inspired and long-overdue tribute to the Great Ms. Bush, arguably one of the most influential female rock artists ever... The disc features no artists you've heard of... Still, Bush is done justice here... The star here is The J Davis Trio's acid

Album Cover: Thomas Dunning

jazz reworking of *There Goes a Tenner*, from Bush's masterful and highly experimental 1982 album *The Dreaming*." Mark Lowry, *Dallas/Fort Worth Star-Telegram* 14th September.

"The artists not only capture Bush's majestic and melodramatic sounds but her sense of humor... None of these cuts will make you a convert, but if you're already a Bush fan, you won't be disappointed." Jim DeRogatis, *Chicago Sun-Times* 20th September.

Thomas: I Wanna Party!

On October 8, 1998, the artists who interpreted Kate's songs on the CD committed themselves to performing the songs live at a one-time only release party.

The show was video-taped for a local cable television show. As there were 71 musicians who worked on the album, not everyone was able to make it, but we still had over 40 musicians turn up. The event was promoted in all the major Chicago newspapers and *The Chicago Tribune* and *The Daily Herald* even ran photos of Kate. *New City* (a very popular weekly arts magazine) declared the show to be the 'Rock Pick of the Week!' Just under 300 people showed up and the show was considered a huge success by folks in the local indie rock scene. The only leading performers missing in action were Syd Straw and Diamond Jim Greene who were both unfortunately out of town. Syd called to wish us luck. Even though she couldn't be there, a true highlight of the evening was an unexpected performance of *The Man with the Child in his Eyes* by Catherine Smitko. This was the song that Syd performed on *I Wanna Be Kate*. Catherine was accompanied by Nora O'Connor on harmony vocals and Victoria Storm on piano. It was gorgeous and the audience loved it.

The real highlight for me, other than watching all these amazing performances of Kate Bush songs, was performing *Not This Time* live. I really didn't think it could happen, but we managed to fit 9 of us on the stage and divided up the musical tasks quite nicely. The J Davis Trio's Aimi stepped in to play drums and Victoria Storm covered piano. Liam Davis, along with the phenomenal Jackson Wilson of Mouse, helped out John Ridenour with the 4 guitar parts. The 'gospel choir', consisting of Catherine, Liam, Victoria and Nora O'Connor, was nothing less than mind-blowing. I was delirious standing in the middle of them trying to sing my lead vocal part. The applause was intense and seemed to go on and on... It was one of the best moments of my entire life, to sing my favorite Kate Bush song with great musicians to an audience who really appreciated it. Although it was a kick-off party for the CD, it felt a bit like the end of a cycle for me in the creative realm, having worked with all theses artists for over a year on this project that has been an incredible process.

Thanks to *HomeGround* and all the other Kate fans for their support during this journey. And of course, thanks to Kate for all the great music... Chicago loves you! Come visit!

Peter: Kate wants to be Thomas

Thomas Dunning, the producer and main man of the *I Wanna Be Kate* tribute album has heard from Kate that she is "so flattered to hear such different and interesting versions" of her songs.

The album has received many further reviews: "Last issue *Lexicon* named Kate Bush as the most influential woman of the '80s, so you know that people around here looked forward to a 'tribute' album to her about as much as we do to our next Visa bill. Well, I'm here to tell ya, quit your worrying and head down to your local record shoppe and pick up a copy of this top-notch collection. The first thing this collection does right is to not treat the songs as the word of Allah. I personally think that the original versions of these songs are some of the best 'pop' music ever made, but that doesn't mean I want to hear virtual reproductions. This set's only misfires are the songs that do just that, try to recreate the songs note for note. It simply doesn't work. Luckily that happens on only a couple of the songs. The rest use Kate's songs as a road map, pulling off on interesting side streets and alleys, finding new richness and depth in the material... highly recommended. If fans of Kate Bush approach with an open mind, they will be amply rewarded" David Richards, *Lexicon* Fall 1998.

"A few too many of the covers here simply duplicate Ethereal Kate... But the good stuff toys with Offbeat Kate: the J. Davis Trio turns *There Goes a Tenner* into a rap, Mouse ratchets up the guitars in *Coffee Homeground*, and the Baltimores deconstruct and wackily reassemble *Running Up That Hill*". Ken Richardson, *Stereo Review* February/March 1999.

"Kate Bush has grown from an obscure singer in the Eighties with an intense cult following to a minor icon whose song-writing and vocals have had a far-reaching impact on today's music. It only stands to reason that musicians pay tribute to her. The most common form of tribute is to cover someone's song. So now we have *I Wanna Be Kate*, a rather odd tribute album in that most of the bands covering her music are ones no one has ever heard of... The problem is that since the listener probably does not know the music of the bands performing and that makes it difficult to distinguish what they are bringing to the table to make the song theirs. What the album manages to do is make me appreciate Kate Bush a little more and to want to listen to her sing her songs, instead of listening to covers that sound too much like imitation than tribute." Phil Bailey, *Ink19* November 1998.

"Better than it has a right to be, perhaps. The best tracks here emphasize the strengths of Bush's writing – compelling melodies and personal lyrics – while bringing distinctive and different arrangements to the material... Less successful versions either run the originals through a scanner and hit print... make poor arrangement decisions... or simply choose weak material... Still others emphasize the least appealing aspects of Kate Bush's music: her tendencies toward preciousness, new-agey mythic imagery, and over-dramatic presentation... As a tribute album, though, this is reasonably successful in that it causes us to reassess and rediscover the strengths of the artist in question while giving us a pretty good percentage of successful remakes." J. Norman, *The Architectural Dance Society* 4th January 1999.

The album has been seized on by the Head of Music at Radio Gdansk in Poland for a running feature on the 7 pm Thursday programme 'Run It On'. From April to June the station was playing one of the cover versions together with Kate's original.

We'll leave it with the envelope in which the card and photo from Kate to Thomas arrived. On the flap, she wrote in very small letters – "I WANNA BE THOMAS".

Kate's letter to Thomas

Kat Devlin

"As close as I'm going to get to seeing Kate live"

Issue 62 December 1998

Kat Devlin is an American cabaret artist who had been performing a show based on Kate's songs for some five years previously. Leonard Jacobs of *The New York Insider* reviewed her October 2nd 1998 show as follows: "a breath of fresh air, it's that inhaling of delirium that one experiences every blue moon or so".

Cynthia Conrad: Not just a Kate fan

A frequent performer at New York City's West Village cabaret club, 'Eighty Eights', Ms. Devlin won the prestigious Bistro Award in 1995 for her all-Kate show.

While she is best known for her Kate-related work, Kat also performs jazz and pop standards on a more regular basis, i.e. she's not just a Kate fan, she's a recognized professional singer by her own merits. Her voice has a beautiful controlled quality and her style is non-imitative; Kat really makes Kate her own. Ross Patterson's keyboard arrangements of the more musically complex Kate songs are quite effective – picture 'Kate Unplugged'. I was really surprised that so many Kate songs could even be adapted to a cabaret-style performance!

"The show that I saw culled material from every album of Kate's Korpus and included over 15 songs, including *In Search of Peter Pan*, *Under the Ivy*, *You're the One*, *Feel It*, and a rousing *Coffee Homeground* I'll never forget!"

In her publicity materials Kat says that she was first exposed to Kate while working in a record store and has been an avid fan ever since.

Of the show she saw Cynthia says: "In contrast to the first time I saw this show, a couple summers ago in New York City, this time Kat Devlin was accompanied by drums and upright bass, in addition to piano. The rearrangements and reconstructions of the songs in a jazzy style for the most part worked really well – and Devlin's definitely got the vocal chops to handle everything from *Wuthering Heights* to *Night of the Swallow* without much apparent effort. Hell – she even looks like Kate! She's a bit taller, but she's got the hair and the facial structure, and in each song she acts out the character portrayed within with only a bit too much over the top melodrama – which in itself is quite Kate like, so hey!

Meredith Tapp: Every nuance

The rearrangements that worked the best for me were *Symphony in Blue*, *Feel It*, *Houdini*, *Moving*, and *Night of the Swallow*. The songs from *The Kick Inside* and *Lionheart* lend themselves nicely to more swinging jazz arrangements. *Running Up That Hill* was done way too fast, and I think something went wrong with *Wuthering Heights* because it seemed like a train wreck by the end of it! My favorite performance was *Coffee Homeground*, in which Devlin played up the paranoia for all it was worth, and the result was a funny, dead-on, portrayal of what the song is about. And *Under the Ivy* slew me, but that song could do that no matter the setting.

"Devlin is a true fan, who has obviously let Kate's music into her soul. She understands every nuance of every song, and if this is as close as I'm going to get to seeing a Kate Bush concert in my lifetime, I'll gladly take it!"

Graphic: Michelle Ann

Abstraction and Introspection

Peter reviews Bradley Smith's *Billboard Guide to Progressive Music*

Issue 62:
December 1998

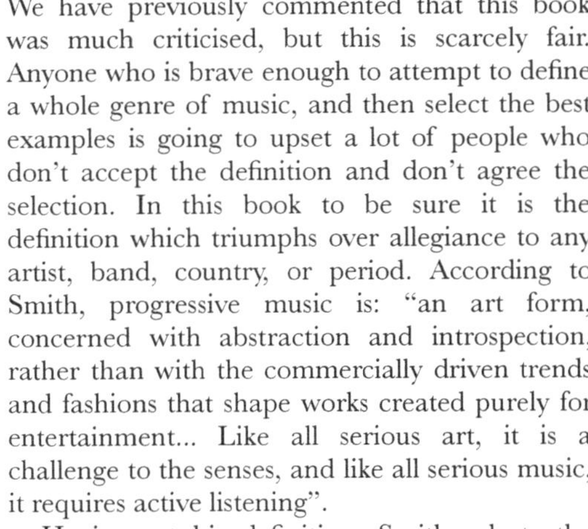

We have previously commented that this book was much criticised, but this is scarcely fair. Anyone who is brave enough to attempt to define a whole genre of music, and then select the best examples is going to upset a lot of people who don't accept the definition and don't agree the selection. In this book to be sure it is the definition which triumphs over allegiance to any artist, band, country, or period. According to Smith, progressive music is: "an art form, concerned with abstraction and introspection, rather than with the commercially driven trends and fashions that shape works created purely for entertainment... Like all serious art, it is a challenge to the senses, and like all serious music, it requires active listening".

Having set his definition, Smith selects the work, and the work is the centre of attention, not who did it. He amply demonstrates that progressive music is not, in the slack assumption of many rock writers, the possession of the '70s, but still lives and breaths in many fine contemporary artists and bands. Bradley notes that "Progressive musicians tend to be minimally concerned with trends, fashions, images, hype, ego, and celebrity. They have a strong desire to experiment, to evolve, to challenge themselves and their audiences, and to take the necessary risks in order to do so. Because of this, they generally operate with autonomy, not allowing interference from those who are concerned with market-driven decisions involving trends and greater profit schemes." Interestingly though, he spots one of the traps the progressive musician may fall in to. Modern music, he notes, is one area where art directly challenges the power of religion. Rebellious youth is hungry for more than the current structures can offer, and progressive musicians have become "a sort of priest, the musical concert a sort of religious gathering for worship or prayer, and the recordings themselves sacred objects, or relics." Here we are in the area of Pink and the Rock Concert as Nuremberg rally as in Roger Waters' concept of *The Wall* where progressive music far from celebrating individuality and emotional and spiritual liberation simply becomes another cult of personality.

Interestingly, I would say Kate is Pink's nemesis. Whether she has a "cult" following depends on your definitions. It is, however, clear that Kate is the priestess who refuses to officiate, the goddess who refuses worship, if only for her own sanity. She is 'Brian' desperately telling the crowd that they're all individuals, and they don't need leaders, and they've "got to work it out for themselves". Bradley cautions against simply seeing progressive music as a type of music done by certain artists: "There have been few artists who have consistently made successful contributions to the overall canon of progressive music. Most of the artists discussed in this book have at one point or another operated in other genres and have not solely concentrated on creating ground breaking compositions with each release." Of his selection, Bradley says: "I have deliberately created a specific canon of progressive recordings, based on an aggressively high standard for quality rather than sales, trends, or overtly technical analysis."

So it is that Bradley only includes part of Kate's work, 1979 to 1986 as truly progressive; the Tour of Life, *Never For Ever*, *The Dreaming* and *Hounds of Love*. He excludes *The Sensual World* and *The Red Shoes*.

He says of Kate: "A well-respected singer/songwriter in the pop realm" who "had a definite progressive phase in her career which has been quite influential" The Hammersmith live recording is "a historic moment of high drama for modern music... it is with this tour that she began the progressive phase of her career... this approach had been utilised before and it has been since by other artists, but never so comprehensively and so successfully." *Never For Ever* has "unusual arrangements and mix, not the usual calculating sound that most popular recordings have... the stereo separation is odd... an uncommon mixture of modern synths and samples with traditional folk instruments"... Throughout these tracks... are incorporated sound effects as if Bush was performing a live storytelling presentation" *The Dreaming* "is one of the finest examples of a meeting point between pop invention and progressive elements... this album was positively risky... slowly built an enormous international reputation over the years. It was on the basis of *The Dreaming* that Bush's devoted, fervent fan movement began". Well yes, in America, but some of us had been fervent fans since 1978! "Bush puts the vocal soundscapes front and centre... the odd production techniques and unique and tight arrangements set *The Dreaming* apart from the conventional in 1982... Musically *The Dreaming* is a wonder". *Hounds of Love* is a "legendary classic of progressive pop... *The Ninth Wave* is her most acclaimed accomplishment... a cathartic voyage of self-discovery... masterful".

In summary Bradley says: "It is these off-the-wall elements, in combination with her increasingly conceptual songs, that put Kate at the center of 1980s progressive music." This is High praise, but he continues: "later Bush releases... had none of the more progressive elements in her earlier music leaving her as little more than a mainstream rock/pop chronicler".

I think here Bradley falls into his own trap. The suggestion is that *The Sensual World* and *The Red Shoes* are not "progressive", and therefore "mainstream" for which read commercial, and therefore not genuine. I refute this. Music is genuine not when it fits any particular criteria of form, but when it accurately conveys emotion. I consider that *The Red Shoes* is the most emotional album Kate has made. Its power is such that I cannot listen to it when I am in a delicate mood. In many ways it is stripped down, less experimental, and uses more conventional musical forms. However, folk music always followed its own very conventional forms, but it could be and is very profoundly moving. It is a credit to Kate's talent that apart from *Big Stripey Lie* on that album she used familiar musical forms to convey profound emotion.

These criticisms apart, this is a good and interesting book. You may not agree with the definitions or the selections, but you will find detailed within the pages a vast amount of excellent and interesting music.

The Technical Bits

Eleanor Johnson looks at how that studio technology works

Part 1: Drum Sounds

I was asked to write an article about the technical side of music for *HomeGround.* I thought it would be relatively easy – wrong! I wanted to look at my favourite Kate album, *The Dreaming,* and to place it in context of the recording technology breakthroughs of the early Eighties. Listening to other albums which I had hoped to use to illustrate the article, I came across what I felt was a development of one particular sound as well as a person responsible. I have always known *The Dreaming* to be an enormously influential album among musicians, well ahead of its time, but it suddenly didn't appear so isolated. I soon realised that I would have to take things one at a time if the article was not to become massively daunting and totally incomprehensible. So – here's Part One. Here I shall look at drum sounds using three tracks to illustrate what I'm talking about. Interestingly these three tracks fit neatly into date order:

No Self Control, Peter Gabriel (III), 1980.
In The Air Tonight, Face Value, Phil Collins, 1981.
Leave It Open, The Dreaming, Kate, 1982.

No Self Control was written by Peter Gabriel and features Phil Collins on drums, Kate on backing vocals and is engineered by Hugh Padgham. *In the Air Tonight* is co-produced by Padgham and he also engineered *Leave It Open.* He has now moved on from engineering to 'top class' production and consistently produces Genesis.

What we are really interested in is not the superficial coincidences, but the sounds. If you have all three tracks, then put them on in the above order and listen carefully to the drum sounds. You will notice how similar they all sound. If you are not used to listening in to a piece and aurally dissecting it then you might want to listen a few times before you hear what I am talking about. The drum sounds, not parts, are very similar.

Important marginal note: Eleanor makes it clear that these articles were written in the context of the recording technology breakthroughs of the early Eighties

I knew I had read about Hugh Padgham and his drum sounds, so I searched through all my magazines and found an article about him in *Recording Musician,* from 1992. He explains how he achieved the drum sound for *In the Air Tonight.* When talking about how he achieved the drum sound for the real drums in the track he says that he first hit on (excuse the pun) the sound when working with Peter Gabriel. He says that it was achieved by "miking from a long distance to pick up the room sound, gating the natural reverb, maximising the compression ratio – and pushing part of the sound into a warm distortion courtesy of valve pre-amps and EQ". And you thought Collins just hit them hard. Anyway I'm sure that means as much to most people as Aramaic, so I'll do my best to shed some light on the jargon.

The first thing to do when trying to make sense of how the recording process works is to picture the studio. Out in the room where the instrumentalists play we have a drum kit. There are two basic types of room for recording – 'live' and 'dead'. A **live room** is where sound bounces around. You can try it for yourself. Ever wondered why everyone loves to sing in the bath? Well, apart from being a place where you can be on your own and pretend no-one can hear you, it is a 'live' room. It has a lot of echo, or **reverberation**, and that is very flattering to a voice. If you go into the bathroom and clap your hands just once, and listen, you will hear that the sound takes a long time to die. This is caused by the sound bouncing off all the hard surfaces – sink, bath, lavatory, mirrors and tiles. If you do the same in the living room the sound will not hang about for so long. This is much nearer to a 'dead' room as many of the surfaces will absorb sound quite effectively – sofas, chairs, carpet.

So, back to our drum kit. It will be set up in a live room or the live end of a room if only one is available. (A friend of mine who is a drummer was recently recorded in a stone room and the sound was terrific!). Hugh Padgham placed four

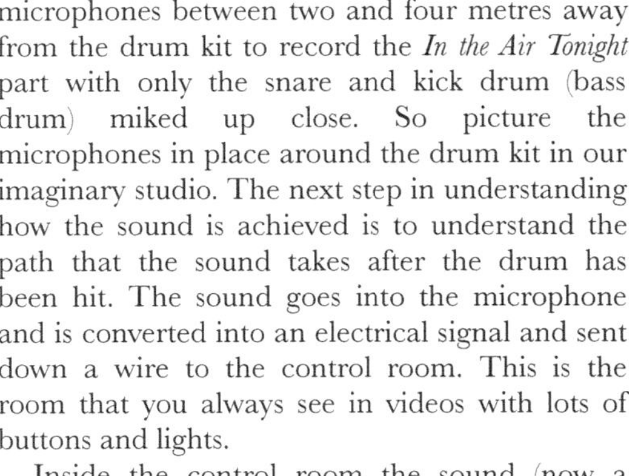

microphones between two and four metres away from the drum kit to record the *In the Air Tonight* part with only the snare and kick drum (bass drum) miked up close. So picture the microphones in place around the drum kit in our imaginary studio. The next step in understanding how the sound is achieved is to understand the path that the sound takes after the drum has been hit. The sound goes into the microphone and is converted into an electrical signal and sent down a wire to the control room. This is the room that you always see in videos with lots of buttons and lights.

Inside the control room the sound (now a signal) takes a more complex route. There are loads of machines in the control room but they come into four main categories. There is the desk. This is the means by which the signal finds its way to tape, and through which the tape plays it back. There is outboard. This is all the boxes that manipulate the sound, before and after it goes through the desk. There is the multi-track tape recorder which is self-explanatory. There is the amplification and monitors (speakers) and usually a fairly hefty computer or two.

Our signal has reached the control room and now must be manipulated to achieve the end sound that is required. This signal was sent through a **noise gate** ('gating the natural reverb'). A noise gate is exactly what it says it is, a gate which either lets through noise or not. It is a very useful tool as it can be set up to let through all or nothing or any amount in between and it can be set to allow a certain timed part of the noise through. Either the beginning, the end or the middle bit. So you can use it to enhance or 'repair' a sound if it has a noise over a section of it. In this case, we are recording the sound of the room which is reverberation, so it is the natural reverb that is being gated. Listening to the track it is most likely that this gate is being used to achieve two ends. Firstly that the reverb doesn't sound like what it actually is. The sound is cut off too quickly for your ear to suss, so you think that what you're hearing is just an enormous drum sound from a very hard hitting drummer. Secondly, if the reverb was allowed to run its natural course for each hit, it would sound like a mess as every hit carries over into the next two. So the gate adds illusion and clarity.

Next, we use a **compressor** ('maximising the compression, while still retaining a fairly low compression ratio'). A compressor is a unit which reduces the dynamic range of a signal. Any signal, ours included, has a dynamic range. This is the difference between the sound at its loudest point and at its quietest. You can imagine that this is huge for a drum hit. Initially the sound is very loud, but even in our live room, it will go very quickly into a noise which will be difficult to hear. So the function of the compressor is to keep all of the sound within a range where it is possible to record it without distortion when it is loud or losing it altogether when it is quiet. If you like, it means there is less of a need to compromise in order to get the sound to tape. The compressor senses these changes in sound automatically and adjusts very quickly to compensate. The **ratio** adjusts the amount of compression, so by retaining a low ratio the signal is not altered a great deal. It is more manageable because of the compression but is not made unnatural.

Hugh Padgham says he pushes part of the sound into warm distortion courtesy of valve pre-amps and EQ. This must have been almost revolutionary in 1980. There is argument about distortion, but I go with the school of 'it's alright if the producer meant it to be there'. The other side of the argument is that it is bad recording technique full-stop and should never be tolerated. I'll leave you to judge for yourself. I doubt if anyone has really heard this drum sound and said "Ooh that's distorted, what a terrible recording technique that engineer must have!"

There has recently been something of a **valve** revival, but this wasn't happening in 1980. It is widely thought that valves provide a warmer sound than transistors in amplifiers and microphones. There is no right or wrong here, just personal preference; if that's what you hear, then that is true for you. The heavy metal guys never abandoned them with Marshall staying true to valves, so maybe they all knew something early on. I'm sure there is an appreciable difference, and I'll go for valves every time, but then I've always enjoyed a good bit of nostalgia, not to mention heavy metal! Anyway, Padgham obviously goes for valves and that is what is important here. **Distortion** occurs when the sound is too loud, basically. It is possible to make so many fine adjustments on the desk that you can push a particular sound so that at its loudest it will be just too much, and this is what they have done here.

EQ or equalisation can be achieved in two ways. There is an equaliser in each part of the desk. So in a 56 channel desk there are 56 equalisers. There are also external equalisers which are available either for a different sound (warm, cold, etc.) or for finer control, 30 or 40 controls within a spectrum of something like 25 Herz to 20 Kiloherz. If you have an equaliser on your hi-fi, check how many points of adjustment you have between these frequencies and which frequencies they are. It is unlikely that you will have more than 12, which gives some idea of the fine tuning that 30 or 40 will give you. If you're interested, try boosting and cutting them while listening to a track you know well and listen to what is at these frequencies – it will be easy to hear where in the spectrum the voice occurs and bass, guitar etc. The adult human ear in good health can hear from about 30 Herz (bass) to about 17 Kiloherz. Bats squeal at about 18-19 Kiloherz. Very low frequency sounds which we can't hear (subsonic) can make us very ill, causing nausea in the first instance and much nastier stuff after that (refer to Hawkwind's *Sonic Attack* on *Space Ritual* for a full description!) So Padgham can now boost and cut to finally achieve the Phil Collins drum sound. And yes, all this can be done live as well, apart from such careful miking.

This sound was first achieved on *Peter Gabriel (III)* and is shown off best on *No Self Control.* I remember hearing it for the first time when it was released as a single, and being blown away by the drum sound. I'm sure some people will be sitting there saying "Well, this is just the Phil Collins drum sound". It is true that he is now identified with this sound, it suits his playing style very well. I thought that I should listen to some of his work pre *PG*III. He plays on the whole of John Martyn's *Grace and Danger* album which was also released in 1980. On the title track, which is fast and contains some classic Phil Collins playing, the drum sound is entirely different. It just sounds like any other kit. Hugh Padgham had nothing whatsoever to do with this album.

I can imagine Phil Collins' face when he heard the playback of his part for *No Self Control.* I have a friend (a drummer) who recently recorded an album in the Maison Rouge studio. He had only ever played live before and had never recorded in a large facility. His drums were recorded in a stone room (imagine how live that is) and he was astounded at the sound achieved. Phil Collins went on to utilise this sound to great effect on his own album, drafting in Hugh Padgham to work on it. He had an enormous hit with *In the Air Tonight* and launched an immensely successful solo career. I'm sure I'm not the only one to pretend to play drum at this point almost every time I hear the song, and I've seen all those drivers beating hell out of the steering wheel to it! Kate brought Hugh Padgham onto *The Dreaming* because of his growing fame for percussive sounds, and she used a similar drum sound to equally great effect on *Leave It Open.*

The saddest part of writing this has been the acknowledgement that Peter Gabriel had a great single with *No Self Control*, Phil Collins had a huge hit with *In The Air Tonight*, and EMI didn't know what the hell to make of *The Dreaming* when they heard it. They had two previous examples of a similarly unusual hit together with a great album, but they couldn't hear it. *The Dreaming* must represent one of the largest failures to date of the music industry in spotting something which represented enormous talent, revolutionary experimentation and which was a superb and virtually faultless album. The sad thing is I don't think they regret this.

I hope what I have written here has interested you and served to throw some light on just one sound as well as the recording process.

Next time I will look at what other brave experimentation on *The Dreaming* EMI failed to spot.

Part 2: The Microphone Never Lies – Not!

I wanted to do a piece about vocals because I think that many people have got the wrong end of the stick when it comes to singers, and singing techniques in the studio. I was nervous of writing it, however, as I know that some people may be very sensitive and I want to make it clear that when I am discussing studio techniques they are in general terms unless I am specifically talking about Kate, and I am not inferring any criticism of Kate's vocals. Most people are not aware of how much difference a good microphone makes to a vocal sound and what happens to the vocal in terms of effects. Last issue I discussed how a particular drum sound is achieved, and sometimes a vocal sound is not that different. It can bear very little resemblance to what was sung in the first place. Also, when recording demos at home, the vocal sound is usually the single biggest give away that it has been recorded in a non-professional set up. I don't pretend to have solved this problem but I have tried to include a few helpful hints.

Have you ever recorded yourself singing? Would you want to? Have you ever got up in front of a crowd to sing when you were sober? Most people would love to do it but don't have the courage. I can't talk, I don't sing in public either. The truth is that we usually have a very false idea of what we sound like. This is because our ears are not capable of hearing ourselves without the embellishments of the bone resonance of our bodies. The bones of the inner ear pick up resonance from the skull and we hear it as an integral part of our own voice. That is why people usually hate to hear their speaking voice played back to them from a tape recorder. Unfortunately, that is what you sound like to other people. Interestingly though, our teeth formation and the height of our palette makes a difference to how we're heard. Changing your teeth by cosmetic dental surgery can seriously disrupt your voice. If you try getting a (good) friend to talk while you jam your ear to the top of their head, you might hear something of how they hear their own voice. At the end of the day we do have to accept what we sound like, however, because there is nothing we can do to change the basic timbre of our voice.

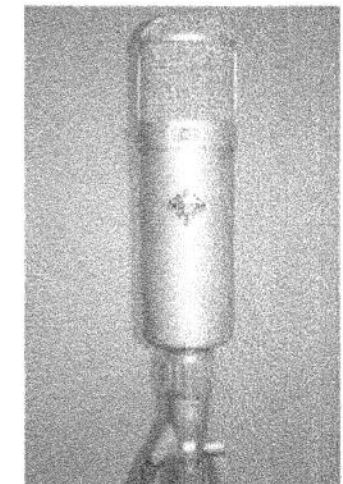

Believe it or not, most vocalists don't like their voices. So the engineer/producer usually starts with a request to make the voice sound more like the sound the vocalist wants to hear. The first point of consideration is **where to record** the vocal. At home you don't have much choice, but as I mentioned last time the room in which the recording takes place can make a vast difference to the sound. Conventional wisdom says that vocals should be recorded in a dead room, to achieve a pure sound which can be worked on later. Kate records her vocals in a stone room, which is very live and more normally associated with drum recording. It sounds corny, but this will help give the vocal a harder sound – I shall go into this in more detail later.

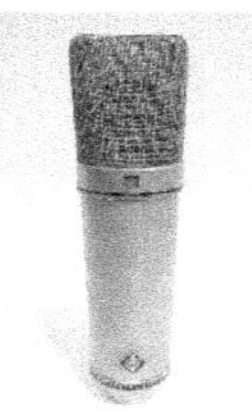

The next thing to consider is which microphone to use, and it is crucial to get it right. To some extent you must consider the experience and technique of the singer and, a too often ignored point, the sex of the singer and the overall range of their voice. As I am consistently recording a female fairly high voice, I get really fed up with microphone reviews that only ever consider male vocals. The needs are entirely different. In the search for the purest sound, some microphone manufacturers have tried to go for an **absolutely flat response**. This means that whatever frequency you put through them, their response to it will be exactly the same. It is interesting that the most widely used range of mics for vocals are Neumanns (pronounced noi-man) and they have ignored this quest to some extent, sticking with a range of mics that have a **natural boost** around10kHz and a small cut between 2kHz and 7kHz. This characteristic remains popular because the boost adds both presence and warmth to a vocal, which can make it sound more pleasing and more natural and more like it does in your head. Many people stick with **valve mics** for vocals, because of the added warmth. This has been particularly popular since the advent of digital recording which some would argue is inherently 'cold'.

Home recordists tend not to spend enough on microphones. There always seems to be something else that you need to buy at the microphone's expense, doesn't there? I would guess that most people recording at home will be using something like the Shure SM58, which is really a **live mic**, or the AKG CS1000. The SM58 is an excellent mic for live work, truly an industry standard, but it leaves an awful lot to be desired for recording. The CS1000 is a better recording mic, in my opinion, but it still leaves out the detail that makes all the difference. Listen to the vocal on the Tori Amos track *Yes Anastasia* and you'll see what I mean about **detail**. The breaths and other noises really do make a tremendous difference to that vocal, they make it come alive. There are also extremely quiet passages and a lesser mic would have missed much of the atmosphere in that. Neither of the microphones I have named would set you back more than £200 – a fifth of what you would expect to pay for a mic at entry level to 'serious' recording and less than a tenth of the cost of Kate's mic. It really is an area where you get what you pay for. The main difference between the cheap and expensive microphones is the size of the diaphragm used to pick up the sound, and the internal circuitry. In a Neumann you would expect the diaphragm to be about an inch in diameter, and gold plated for better conductivity across it. This enables it to pick up much greater detail. The construction of the microphone is another area where you really notice the difference for the money. For example, the capsule in a Neumann is elastically suspended to prevent shock damage when it is being carried.

Interestingly, the argument for and against **valves**, rages in this area. Neumann abandoned valves until about three years ago when they felt there was enough of a demand for them to bring out a limited edition U67 (a valve version of the U87). Their sister company, however, continued to manufacture valve mics throughout their less fashionable period. Before the second world war, Neumann Gefell manufactured microphones in Germany. When the split came between West and East Germany, Neumann continued as a separate company in the West and Gefell did the same in the East. When Reunification happened, Gefell microphones became available on the market in the west, and it became obvious that they were making products that didn't differ a great deal from the ones Neumann Gefell had been producing. They are still making very good quality valve (or tube) mics, and they are selling like hot cakes (well, hot cakes priced at £2,700 anyway). Kate uses a Neumann U47 for her vocals. Neumann made two versions of this mic, but it is reasonably safe to assume that she uses the valve version for vocals, especially since she went digital. It is a very sought after microphone, particularly as Neumann no longer manufacture them, so it must have a fairly good vintage.

The next point to think about is the **polar setting** for the mic. Most small studios won't bother to change this from the usual cardioid setting. Make them think about the alternatives if they are available. **Cardioid** is what it says, a heart shaped pick up pattern picking up mostly to the front of the mic but a little to the side and virtually nothing to the rear. This is great for a dead room, as there is nothing to pick up from anything other than the vocalist, and to keep the pure sound we only want the voice as it comes out from the mouth. There is an 'omni' setting for most professional mics, but this would be inappropriate for vocals, too much extraneous noise. This setting is used for round the table radio discussions. The other setting is **hypercardioid**, and this is worth considering. This is a tight setting to the front and rear of the microphone, and is the setting Kate uses. I'll try and illustrate its advantages and disadvantages by comparing it to cardioid. A vocalist singing into a cardioid mic has nowhere to go to take a breath where it won't be heard. This isn't really a problem, if you don't mind hearing the breaths. Listen to the vocals on any Tori Amos track and you will get all the breath and mouth noises. This is a good indicator that her engineer is using the cardioid setting for her vocals. The other advantage (if you consider noise an advantage) of cardioid is that the vocal will be picked up fairly consistently if the vocalist moves around a bit, at least within the confines of the pick up area, and this is why most studios will use this setting. People who aren't used to putting expression into a vocal while standing still will require to be able to move and for the recording not to suffer. Also, once people close their eyes they will move anyway as they lose some spatial awareness, and people tend to sing with their eyes closed. So, when dealing with an inexperienced singer, cardioid is a good bet. Hypercardioid does not pick up from the sides at all, and so allows the singer to breathe unheard if they move to the side to do it. It will not tolerate much movement without losing sound, and requires someone with a really good sense of what they are doing to get a good result from it (and for the engineer not to have a breakdown!)

Whatever mic is chosen it will have to have a **pop-shield**. This is to stop the explosive sounds ('p' 'b' 'd' 't') sounding a really low bass boom. You can make one out of an old coat hanger and the foot of an old stocking, but this will not be as acoustically transparent as a bought one. (Tip: make sure you wash the stocking first - good results are not achieved when the vocalist has a bad smell under his/her nose!!!) A good example of what you don't want is on Tori Amos' *Flying Dutchman* where just about every 'p' and 'b' is accompanied by a bang in the bass. There is nothing you can do to get rid of them once they're there, and this really is poor. An engineer's job is to record everything that goes on in a session to a good standard so that when a performance happens that is just right, and in all likelihood won't be reproduced, it has been captured. I was reminded of this recently when I recorded a guitarist's rehearsal, just in case. The performance was blinding and whenever I listen to the track I thank the powers that be that I pressed 'record' in time. The piano break in Madonna's *Into the Groove* was also a rehearsal taped almost by accident. One of the tasks of a producer is to decide when a performance has happened that is just right. It is not Tori's fault that a superb vocal performance was not recorded to a good enough standard by the engineer. Obviously the vocal needed to go out as it stood because it is so good, but it is not a good advert for the skills of the engineer involved.

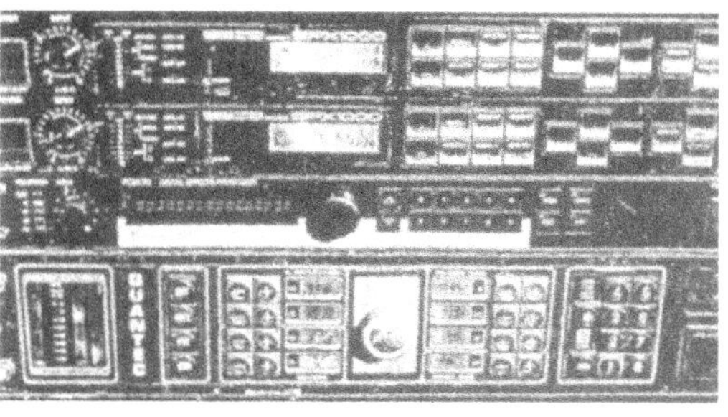

The mic should be in a **cradle**. This is the strange UFO type thing around the base of the mic in all of the pictures of Kate singing in the studio. This isolates the mic so that any vibration from the stand etc. is not passed on to the microphone, and of course, none of the vibration caused by sound is lost.

So, we have the microphone, the singer, a signal and now it has reached the control room. We want to record it. Usually it will be compressed. I discussed compressors last time in the drum sound signal path. They are a great help with setting tape levels, as mentioned before, but they can cause problems with vocals. Compressors can be used to change the characteristics of a vocal to some extent. The more compression you use, the harder the voice will sound. They can take the breathiness off the sound and they can be used as **de-essers** (to remove sibilance). They can also cause lots of problems with breathing. If you are using loads of compression and making the voice sound much harder than it actually is, the breaths will come out sounding much louder than the voice, although it will only be the compressor performing its usual function of keeping all the levels the same. This is really an aural illusion, we don't want to hear the breaths, and our ears usually disregard them, but when they are at the same volume as the voice, we will hear them as louder. If you are going to use a lot of compression, it is a very good reason for using the hypercardioid setting on your microphone. If you use a medium compression ratio then the breaths will probably make the voice sound more natural, and can be quite atmospheric, but they can be unbearable if you are using hard compression. You may also be advised to have an extra pair of monitors lying around, as the hard compression produces a very high frequency biased sound, re: the squeaky introductions to some of the vocals in the latter parts of *The Song of Solomon*. The other problem with loads of compression is **feedback**. The slightest headphone spillage can cause feedback enough to deafen you for weeks! The AR18s, which Kate and Del Palmer use for monitoring a mix, don't last very long by all accounts. Kate's vocal is also gated (see noise gates in the last issue) before and after the voice: before so that any breath you do get is cut off and after so that you get just enough of the sound of the room, "A bit like the Phil Collins' drum sound" according to Del, so I'll refer you to the last issue yet again I'm afraid.

After you've recorded the vocal, you'll want to add some reverb or it will sound very unnatural, and we're back to the bathroom effect here. **Reverb** is always flattering, but don't think you can make a bad vocal sound good with tons of reverb, because it will just sound like a bad vocal with tons of reverb! Reasonable multi-effects units like the ART range aren't that expensive for what they will do, but again, expect to get what you pay for. Cheap effects units will be noisy,

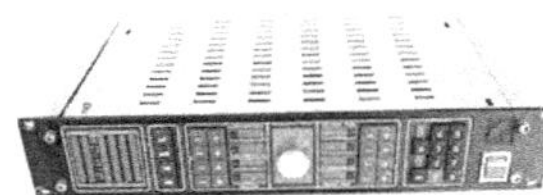

though you may be willing to sacrifice some noise for the effects at a reasonable price. Lexicon, who make very expensive and wonderful reverb units, are now producing a cheaper option – alex – which is well worth checking out. Kate has 3 (non-budget) Lexicons, and an Eventide H3000 and H3000E (to die for) harmonisers but, more often than not, the vocal is treated with a **Quantec Room Simulator**. I believe that this piece of equipment was first mentioned in connection with *The Dreaming*, but I may be suffering short term memory loss! If so, it would put it contemporary with a strange multi effects unit called 'That Infernal Machine' – yes, really. Kate doesn't have one, unfortunately. I was always intrigued by it not least because all its LED communication was in German. I don't know if anyone ever successfully used one. Anyway, if anyone knows when the Quantec came into being, I would like to know.

The clarity given to the top end of *The Red Shoes* by the digital recording makes some of the vocal effects quite easy to pick out. I can hear some subtle phasing on some of them, listen to the long 'S's in *Top of the City*. This is also the best track to listen to if you want to hear the gate, as when the vocal comes in after the quiet passages you can quite clearly hear it cutting in, it is most noticeable on the vowel sounds. Also as the vocals fade out into the silence, you can hear the gate cut off the room sound, and all the effects going quiet. 'S's are also the best letter to hear reverb coming off. You'll have to play it loud, and get the best separation you can from your system. I heard all the vocal stuff best by boosting 0.6 kHz and not much other top boost with my usual bass settings (deep and loud!)

Once the vocal has been recorded, the track must be **mixed** and this is usually when the majority of vocal effects will be added. As I mentioned before, Kate and Del use AR18s to monitor the mix. Kate has always maintained that it is pointless mixing on enormous powerful **monitors** when most people will be listening to the album on a small stack hi-fi. This is perhaps why we can hear so much of the detail she puts in to the recording. Placing vocals in the mix is all a matter of taste, and the techniques for doing it right vary. Conventional wisdom says that you should get the instrument mix largely finished and then mix the vocals in. Peter Gabriel mixes the vocals in after the drums but before the rest of the instrumentation so that the music works around the vocal rather than leaving it isolated on top of the mix. Kate seems to mix the vocal last, but Del says that after the vocal treatment, particularly the SSL compression, the vocal can be placed quite low and still cut through because of the high frequency bias. This negates to some extent the temptation to place the vocal too up front. When mixing a vocal try and visualise the set up of the band. The band are usually around the vocalist, and if you try and reproduce this feel aurally, you'll be alright.

So, all that's fine, but what if you've got a reasonable vocal apart from one note that wavers? You can try '**dropping in**'. This is where you get someone to sing along to the vocal they've already done and hit record at the crucial moment, coming out again just after that note. A kind of patching up job if you like. If you are lucky enough to have **MIDI automation** on your desk and your tape controlled by your computer, you can automate this procedure leaving out that oh-so-fun chance element that you might just screw up the rest of the vocal. What if 'dropping in' doesn't work either? Well, it doesn't matter. You can sample the wobbly note, and use pitch bend to bend the sampled note so that it is in tune, and then 'fly it in' to the mix and no-one will ever know the difference. Again you can have the fun of doing this live or you could sequence the note and bend and not leave it to chance. You can get machines that **pitch correct** automatically and a friend of mine set up a system for someone where this went in to the signal path before the tape, so the singer never knew that they sang out of tune. You can **compile vocals**, i.e. sing several, and odds are that the same mistakes won't come up twice, so you can switch between them in the mix so that you get a near perfect vocal. You need a good singer for this though, because all the vocals will have to have the same sound so that you can't hear the switches. You couldn't do this with someone inexperienced. If all else fails – do it yourself. That's sussed ya!!!

I'm just trying to make the point that when you listen to an album, you're not always hearing what you think you are. The recording process is very complex. If you bought an album where the vocals were recorded with just a voice and a microphone you would probably hate it and think it sounded 'unnatural'.

If you are recording vocals at home, don't expect it to sound like any record in your collection, it won't. Be realistic about what you can achieve with the equipment you have, if you are you can do more than you may think. If you're not a singer and you're trying to get the best out of someone in a home situation, be patient. Putting down a vocal is not an easy thing to do and people without much experience can get very microphone and tape shy. Remember that for all the time that the vocal is going down, the singer is the most important person in the world, and they must have everything as they want it so far as is humanly possible. The mix must suit them at that moment and not you. If they want to rest, let them. If they want guidance, give it to them. If they need to get angry (which they may not know), wind them up! Don't stifle or cajole, just let them get on with it. You want a good performance and it is not an easy thing to do standing cold in front of a microphone with none of the feedback that an audience would give. If you are running the session it is down to you to give them the circumstances in which they can give of their best. Most importantly, tape everything. Often people get more self conscious as the session goes on, not less, and the first or second take will be the best. Act casual, and try to let them think that at least the first time is a run through with no tape running, but tape it anyway. You can put mistakes right in the mix, but it makes life easier if you don't have to. Best of luck!

To change the subject slightly, I have really enjoyed writing the two pieces I have done so far, and thanks for all the feedback. I received one letter asking for a definition of '**warm distortion**', and what is the difference between that and '**cold distortion**'. This is an interesting question because it highlights the difficulty anyone working with music has in expressing the sound that you want to achieve. I am always trying to 'make something rounder/fatter/squarer' when it is a nonsense really as I can't see or touch the sound and really have no idea what shape it is. It is just a means of trying to get your ideas over to someone else. But, as for 'warm' and 'cold', this is more subjective than most. Does the distortion itself give the impression of warmth or not, or is it what you do with it? Distortion is really the result of putting too much sound through a circuit. A valve circuit will generally give you a 'warm' sound. Marshall know this and only replaced bulky valves in some of their equipment when they were sure that they could replicate their famous distorted guitar sounds with more modern technology ('valvestate' for anyone that's interested). Valves operate at high temperatures, so maybe there's something of a practical answer. I'm not sure if anyone would want to use 'cold distortion'. Personally, I think that digital recording makes for cold, and analogue for warm, generally. Perhaps we perceive 'cold' as a sound that makes us shiver, and that can be anything from eerie to unattractive or 'unnatural'. Perhaps we associate cold with sad and warm with happy and so a minor (generally sad) key will feel colder than a major one, although I'm not convinced about this. Have you ever known a bell to sound warm? A standard shaped bell tone always goes into minor harmonics, so that's quite an interesting question. Does this help? Really as musicians we use inappropriate adjectives all the time because we operate in an environment where we constantly deal with an intangible medium and we have to describe it somehow.

I have also been asked what a '**riff**' is. The easiest example is perhaps the old 'TOTP' theme, (in the Jimmy Saville and Dave Lee Travis days), you know - da der da der da d'd'd'da d'd'd'da - from Led Zeppelin's (brilliant) *Whole Lotta Love*. It is a short, catchy sequence of notes or chords which repeats, sometimes, as in this case, throughout the song, or just once or twice. It can be a '**hook**', or not, but it will be short and it will repeat. There are guitar riffs on the end of *Breathing*.

I'm not really an expert, but I have been struggling to get professional sounds out of ailing home equipment for some time. I am interested in the debate for and against **digital recording equipment** in studios. I am aware of it in the recording world, but I am interested to have a forum for the consumers' attitude. I know that many readers are hi-fi buffs like me, so what do you think of *The Red Shoes*? Does it sound clearer to you, or two dimensional? Has the overall sound improved from analogue albums like *Hounds of Love*? Does analogue hiss drive you mad when you hear it coming off a CD or do you like it? No-one has yet asked the consumer what they think of digital recording quality (as opposed to digital mastering quality, which has been generally accepted as a good thing), and the argument continues to be heated in the top echelons of the industry, so why shouldn't we have a say? After all, we pay their salaries.

A debate which came to fruition with Kate's work on the *Director's Cut* album in which the digital sounds of the original *Red Shoes* release were reverted to "warmer" analogue sounds.

Part 3: The Computer as an Instrument

Well, hello again. I hope you enjoyed the last article about vocals, thank you for the letters, by the way. This time I've decided to address what is a controversial subject at least in some quarters, the use of computers in music. I've mentioned it briefly before, but I felt it was an immense subject, and needed to be gone into in some detail. I should begin by saying that I'm not talking about 'chips', which exist in just about everything, or computers incorporated into instruments (like the Fairlight which has a dedicated Central Processing Unit (CPU)), but simply a computer, like the one I'm typing this on, with just a CPU, monitor and keyboard, and no particularly sophisticated ability to make sound. They have become the mainstay of many recording studios, and I'm sure that if you're not working with them to make music their function may be unclear.

It all started with **MIDI** (Musical Instrument Digital Interface). This, as I think I've mentioned before, is a protocol which was first released onto the market in 1981 and which allows musical instruments to exchange data, so that one instrument can send to another details about what note is being played, how hard the note is being hit (velocity), how long it is being held (note on and off), pitch bend etc., which program is required (for synthesisers) and loads of other stuff such as aftertouch and system exclusive data which is only understood by instruments of the same make (for instance, Yamaha will have different system exclusive messages to Roland).

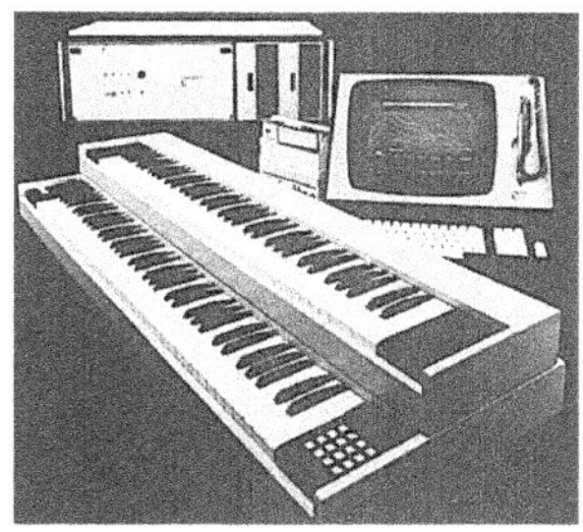

The first notable thing to happen after the introduction of MIDI was that some synthesisers lost their keyboards. Suddenly only one keyboard was needed to send information to all instruments, and so synthesisers became '**modules**'. Modules don't look very exciting as essentially they are just boxes full of different sounds with panels on the front to tell you what sound is being played. It is, however, very exciting the first time you hear a sound coming out of them while playing a remote keyboard. This was the first experience that got me fired up about MIDI.

After modules came boxes which made no sound at all called '**sequencers**'. These just simply stored the MIDI information and played it back on command, essentially acting as 'tape recorders' for digital information, but there are four main differences between sequencers and tape. The first is that instead of listening to a tape of what has been previously played, you are listening to the instrument actually playing. It is just the information and not the actual notes that is stored, so it's like listening to a musician who plays exactly what you played every time. The second difference is that the information is more readily edited and altered than when it is on tape. For instance, you can '**quantize**' the information, which means that you can pull what has been played exactly into time to a specified variable. So, a drum part could be pulled into time by requiring the sequencer to move the note information from when it was actually played to anything from one note every quarter of a bar to another note every one hundred and twenty eighth of a bar. So, human error went out of the window and the early Eighties moved towards very precise and exact electronic music, like Ultravox, to pick a very talented example. The third difference is that the number of tracks with which you are able to work is only limited by your program and the amount of digital storage available to you. So, even on an Atari you could be working with 128 'virtual' tracks. The fourth difference is that the information is not vulnerable to the same kind of unreliability as it is on tape, (dropout, stretching etc.), though there are other problems with corruption which anyone who has ever used a computer will be aware of.

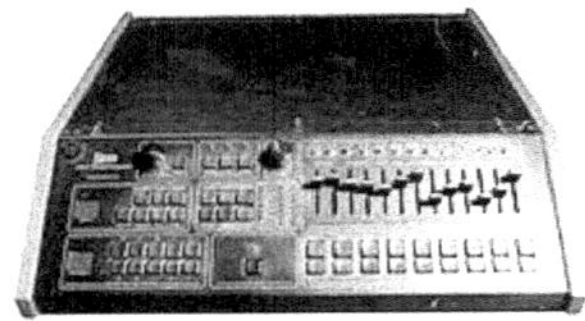

The main problem with sequencers was that they weren't very easy to communicate with. On the whole, they only had a small LCD screen to deal with what was becoming ever more complex editing, and then someone had the brilliant idea of putting a sequencer into a computer program. Two makes of computer became popular with musicians. The Atari, I believe, was the first computer to incorporate a MIDI interface as standard, so, while you all thought it was a games machine, we were all thanking the directors at Atari and buying horrendously expensive programs to make music with! The other was the Apple Macintosh. I think that this was because it was (and still is) the main machine to be used in the media and was therefore available. Apple ended up in an obscure legal wrangle with Paul McCartney's Apple Corporation, about being used for music, and therefore were unable to incorporate a MIDI interface into their machines, but in some ways this was a blessing because specialised external units were developed by music companies for the purpose. More recently very good programs have been developed and adapted for PCs and many people swear by the abilities of the Amiga. Computer programs for the editing of synthesiser programs are now widely used as well, and I think that the ability of the Apple Mac to enable easy movement between programs on the screen has helped its domination of the sector.

The Musician's Union had a problem with all this development in the early days, and drummers, particularly, feared for their jobs. No-one could foresee that what would actually happen would be that all this development would give the average musician greater access to composition and arrangement. The single biggest change in music, in my opinion over the last 15 years has to be that the home musician can now produce music to a good standard. This has largely been due to the availability and drop in price of the technology. This has allowed movements like grunge and jungle to begin underground – essentially in people's bedrooms – and find their place in the market, which has to be a good thing. The industry has to watch underground movements, and these two have been particularly successful. These are realised possibilities that the 'professionals' didn't always see, and while they were worrying about their jobs (on the whole unnecessarily), new work was being created for a generation of very smart, talented programmers and engineers. The truth is, sequenced music will never replace musicians. After all, who is the best person to program a drum part? You got it – a drummer!

When I changed my own system over from Atari, after my machine finally broke down through over-use, I was astounded by my new Macintosh and the program for it. The program really has become another instrument in the studio, in fact I found I was spending more time at the computer and much less at the keyboard. This is not because I am lazy, but the possibilities for dealing with the sound have become almost boundless. As I am writing this I am listening to an excellent mix of *Itchycoo Park* by M-People – which is fab, by the way – and this mix could never have been achieved without the use of a very sophisticated computer system. You can almost hear it working. Björk is another artist whose work, I don't think, could really exist in the form it does without extensive programming ability. So, in my view at least, the use of computers for music is creative. Of course, it needn't be, it can just allow people to buy pre-programmed cover versions of their favourite songs and just plug in and have them play, but anything has a number of uses, and used 'properly' computers can open the doors to tremendous creativity.

So, what happens – how do they work? Well, the MIDI signal is sent to the computer from whichever instrument is being used to send MIDI 'out'. This could be almost anything – not just a keyboard. Yamaha have a MIDI compatible grand piano which works by the hammers cutting light beams, MIDI guitars are available in abundance, MIDI wind controllers for wind players which measure breath control as well as notes, MIDI drum pads, MIDI Marimbas – the list goes on. So you can play the piano over MIDI by playing a guitar, which sounds weird as the natural progressions on a guitar fret board are very different from the natural progressions on a piano keyboard. This information is sent to the computer, which stores it. You have a full sized monitor to cope with the information given back to you, so this makes life much easier than working with an old-style sequencer. You can then do just about anything with that information. You can move it about within the song, change sound or instrument by moving it on the screen, bring it into or out of time, you can copy it or transpose it (move the notes up or down by any amount at all). So, for example, if you have written a double bass part that sounds wrong, you can change it to a violin part through transposition and have it sound natural. You can play with any individual note, extend its length, shorten it, change the note, move it, make it sound as if its been hit (or plucked or bowed or blown) harder or softer, and all that is just within the MIDI information itself.

Then you have the MIDI '**controllers**'. Using these you can 'pitch bend' (this sounds like the bending of a guitar string); you can modulate the note (this sounds like vibrato); you can control the sustain pedal of a piano by switching it on and off, so you can move the end of a sustain period to exactly where you want the sound to stop. You can play with the stereo image (pan) just from the computer, you can turn an instrument's volume up or down, and any of this information can be stored so that it does it every time and it can be edited in much the same way as note information so that it is perfect. You can send program changes to the instrument from the song, so that you could use any amount of different drum kits in one song from one drum machine and have the changes sent automatically. That's all through MIDI.

Then you come to the computer program itself. It is not too fussy about tempo, as you can change it at any point, so, if you want to record a piece slower than it will actually play, this is not a problem. You can 'step edit' which is putting the notes in from the computer itself one at a time. Because you are dealing with digital and not analogue information, the speed with which the computer sends the information is entirely governed by the tempo you set on the screen, and pitch will not be affected. So, you have all this information on the computer, you then have to get it back out to play the piece back so that you can hear what you've done, and how you might want to change it.

MIDI operates on 16 channels. This is so that all the information doesn't get picked up by all the instruments which would then play it all and it would sound like a right bloody mess!! So, let's have a virtual reality studio. You have a piece of music which is piano based, but you have a drum machine playing the drum kit for you and some percussion, a module playing the orchestra, a sampler adding a 'pad' (this is usually a sound with low 'attack' and a long 'decay' which goes underneath everything to give the track body), and another module playing guitar and bass. Each instrument will receive a different channel, and you set the channels to which the computer will transmit from the screen, and the channels the instruments will receive on the instruments. For argument's sake let's put the piano on channel 1, the standard channel for drums is 10, so let's stick with the protocol; the orchestra will go on channel 2, the sampler on channel 3, guitar on channel 4 and bass on channel 5. It probably sounds like a lot of instruments until you realise that you've still got 10 channels free with no information going down them at all.

There are two ways to send information back to the instruments and that is to do with wiring. The first way is to '**daisy chain**' them. Each MIDI instrument will have an 'In', an 'Out' and a 'Thru' (sic) port on the back. 'In' is self explanatory, 'Out' will send out only information which has been generated from that instrument and 'Thru' will send out both the 'In' and 'Out' information merged. Daisy chaining involved linking the instruments via the 'In', 'Out' and 'Thru' ports. The other way is to use a MIDI **patchbay**, which is itself programmable either as a stand alone item or via the computer. The newer patchbays are programmable through the computer, and serve almost as a virtual studio environment with all the instruments plugged into them and then you can 're-wire' your studio on the computer screen. This is one of the most convenient developments of the last 10 years, forget the proliferation of microwaves – believe me!!! So, the computer sends the information either down the daisy chained cables or to the patchbay and the instruments pick up their relevant channels and play them. You can have cables up to 40 feet long before you get any significant time delays in transmission.

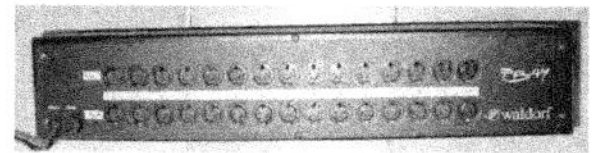

The next problem is how do you run your analogue sounds (live guitar, voices, etc.) exactly in time with what is being generated 'live' from the computer? Well, this is where the mysterious **SMPTE** comes in. SMPTE is a time code. It is put onto the tape you are running, usually on the highest numbered track, and this process is called 'striping the tape'. SMPTE was developed for film and was hijacked, to some extent, by musicians so consequently it works in frame rates, i.e. frames per second. The usual rate for the UK is 25 frames per second – as anyone familiar with animation will know. You take the tape, stripe it, decide where you want the song to start in hours, minutes and seconds, and then you tell the computer the song starting point. Once the computer can 'hear' the **timecode** it will then calculate where it is in the song if the tape is started at any point, and play 'in sync' with the analogue signals on the track. There can be problems with this as tapes stretch or experience drop-out, but the computer can 'jam' with the timecode, which basically means it guesses, and it is usually right!

So, is the computer an instrument? Not strictly, I suppose, but when you start using one you realise that you do play it like an instrument. You use it to hone your instrumentation and, in many cases, to generate notes which you then specify in all the ways I have already mentioned. So, if your definition is that an instrument creates notes, then it is. If your definition is that an instrument is something you can play and express yourself with, then I would say it definitely is.

Computers in studios don't stop there though. The tapeless studio is now a reality. **Hard disk recording** is very exciting, as the analogue signal goes straight to the computer and is converted to a digital signal, and then you can do almost as much with it as a MIDI signal. It is currently being used mostly for mastering, but multi-track hard disk recording is upon us and anyone can do it providing their hard disk is big enough to cope with the storage. Non-destructive editing is available for both these uses. This is really wonderful as this means that the computer doesn't alter the original signal, but gets told how to interpret the signal. So, if after all the editing you don't like what you've done, you can then go back to the original signal and start again, never having lost what was there in the first place. Of course, because the signal is digital, you lose no quality through this process at all. Most mixing desks are now automated via a computer, so mixes can be saved and reproduced. You can play games on it, if you get fed up with making music!!!

I hope this has given you some insight into

Deeper Understanding

HomeGround looks at Kate On-Line

Issue 57: May 1996

"What is a web-site?" How long ago it seems now to have to put the question!

For those readers just getting into the computer world, you may be surprised to learn how much Kate-related material there is 'on-line'. Not only is there the internet discussion group rec.music.gaffa, whose proceedings are distributed via the internet email mailing list 'love-hounds' but there are now an increasing number of sites on the world-wide-web. What is a web site? *HomeGround* asked Garrick Twinney, a reader and web site builder to explain. There are many Kate related web sites. The best guide to them was compiled by Steve0, a regular contributor to rec.music.gaffa. There are even more mysterious things out there with the advent of virtual reality. Len Bullard explains about his Kate VRL.

Garrick Twinney: Building a Kate website

So how did this project come into being? Well, being a member of Termisoc (The University of Plymouth Computing Society) automatically entitled me to some space and facilities on which to store and make available my own pages on the World Wide Web. I wanted to make my mark if you like and Kate and her music is so important to me that it seemed the obvious thing to concentrate on.

One memory relating to this article is that Garrick threatened us with violence if we used the contemporary media phrase "information super-highway"!

If I was going to do this properly, I would have planned it all out on paper first, but no! I wanted to get straight on with it, so jumping in at the deep end I located, downloaded and read (some of) a basic introduction to writing documents in HTML and started toying with the bare bones of my pages.

At this point I'll inject a brief diversion and point out that HTML is the much needed acronym for Hyper-Text Mark-up Language, the language used to describe, in a form understandable by both humans and the computer programs used to browse the World Wide Web, the layout and contents of a page which may contain text, pictures and sounds.

And so it began. I had decided fairly early on that *HomeGround* was going to have big mentions on my pages as there seems to be quite a lack of information on our favourite fanzine available on the World Wide Web. Also I wanted it as the information centre for UK gatherings that have happened in the past and those that are still to come.

Contacting Peter, via e-mail, produced a few words: subscription information and contact details, these I converted to HTML and added to my pages. I added the complete version of my write-up of the '95 Katemas (*HomeGround* 56), and a brief write up of the gathering at White Horse Hill last Easter and the Wuthering Hike-Not, also of last year. More gathering write-ups will be added as they happen. A few links to other peoples' Kate pages, (one of the wonders of HTML is that it allows documents spread across the world to be linked) a few images, some tidying and things are beginning to take shape.

At the time of writing this is roughly how my Kate page stands. I intend to scan some of the wonderful artwork from *HomeGround*, add some of the other articles from past issues and anything else I think of at the time including an interactive Kate world where you may vote on your favourite tracks and see how it ties in with, and effects, the national average!

SteveO: What's out there

When I first got on the World Wide Web, a little over a year ago or so, the first thing I naturally did was look at all the Kate sites I could. The second thing I did was review them all. A lot has happened since then – I've become a Major Web Deity, and a few major and several minor Kate pages have been added. So, it's high time for an update of the reviews. For those wondering, "Major" pages have significant content, while "Minor" pages are specifically about one topic, usually on just one page. That is not to say the Minor pages are in any way inferior to the Major pages – some of the best Kate pages are the minor ones – it's just that they aren't as big.

The Ultimate Band List Kate Card. This should be your first stop on the Web in looking for Kate Resources. The Ultimate Band List (Or UBL by those "in the know") itself is the best source of band resources on the net. That URL should be in your hotlist, your bookmark file, and tattooed on your forehead. The Yahoo 'Music Artists Section' probably has more bands, but only lists "Major" pages and, unlike the UBL, does not include mailing lists, and often doesn't list just the FAQs, or where to ftp lyrics from. Still, you die-hard Yahoo fans, have fun there!

Me? I'll stick with the Ultimate Band List

This was Steve0's review of what was out there on the Kate related internet in the early 1990s.

Some of these sites survive, some did not. Some did not survive the first bizarre attempt by EMI Music Publishing to enforce copyrights.

Url = uniform resource locator, a website address

ftp = file transfer protocol, a method of transferring computer files across the internet

FAQ = frequently asked questions, a component of many websites

html = hypertext markup language, used to construct web pages

ascii = American standard code for information exchange, a method of creating text pages

MIDI = musical instrument digital interface, which allows electronic instruments to talk to computers

Compuserve = one of the pre-web online information services

jpeg = Joint Photographic Experts Group compression standard for computer graphic files

Graphic: Paulina Stuckey

Kate Card, with its (as of this writing) six major pages, seven minor pages, and FAQ, digitized songs links, and lyrics links. Summary: Rating: (on a scale of 1 to 5 stars) Ultimate Band List Kate Card: ★★★★★ Ultimate Band List: ★★★★★ Yahoo Kate Section: ★★★ Yahoo Music Artists Section: ★★★★

Experiment IV: This used to be the best Kate page by far. WordStar also used to be the best word processor. This is what's known in the biz as a "cobweb site". It hasn't been updated since late July, and it looks like it's going to be updated next, right around the same time Kate tours again. It has a nice HTML FAQ – going back to May of '94. It has a couple of out-of-date links, and a rather unintentionally funny page about an aborted Lovehounds T-shirt project (before one was actually made). And, quite frankly, it doesn't have much else. God knows, its heart is in the right place, and if it were updated, it would still be THE source for the Serious Web-Browsing KateFan, but as of now, it's more of a curiosity for people interested in Lovehounds' history. Rating: ★★

Stuart Wilsdon's *Lionheart* is one of the first Kate web pages, and one of the best "major" pages. It started out as just a handful of scanned images, but has grown into a beautiful resource. All of the album covers are wonderfully scanned, plus some digitized songs, and lyrics. This is a must-see stop for all KateFans. Also it has lotsa links to other Kate resources, including one I didn't know about! To top it all off, there is a LARGE number of jpegs ftp-able directly from here (thumbnails or an image index file would be nice, but it's still top-notch without it). Warning: This site's in Australia, so it's often very slow. Grade: ★★★★★

David Benson's *A Lovehounds Page*. There are pages out there that have more info, and there are pages (most notably *Lionheart*, with its stills from the *Rocket Man* video, among other things) that have images this one doesn't. But in terms of sheer aesthetics, this page cannot be beaten. Dozens of beautiful images. Normally, I am one who likes female vocalists for their voice; whether or not they are physically attractive is entirely irrelevant. But even I have to admit some of these pictures are quite stunning. If you look hard enough, you can find a very-recently started under construction page where he's adding lyrics (including the demos!), and another HTMLized version of Andrew Marvick's massive work of Kate reference, *The Garden*. This is already the best looking Kate Site on The Web; once everything is in place, this very well could be the Best Site on The Web. Rating: ★★★★★

Sean Gillhooley's *Kate Bush Page*: I only heard of this page when I saw a link on *Lionheart*. I assume, judging by the lack of content, that the page is "under construction". However, what there is, is very well done. Each album has the lyrics and production notes for each song, and it has one of the more clever "links to other pages" sections I've seen. That's all that's there, but it's so well done, that if other things get added, this will be a serious site. Rating: ★★★

Garrick Twinney's *Under the Ivy:* Since it's a new page, there's not much there, but what is there can be found nowhere else. There are some wonderful stories of gatherings of UK KateFans, information about *HomeGround*, and photos taken from the telly which look surprisingly good. A example of quality being more important than quantity. Rating: ★★★

If someone were to ask me the single best Kate site on the web as of this writing, I would say it's Richard Caley's HTMLized version of Ron Hill's text 'Cloudbusting'. One problem I've always had with Ron's original version, another massive Kate reference, was that it was almost entirely just a bunch of interviews. Nothing can make a Kate Fan wince like reading an interview. What Richard did was cleverly make links to key words, so if you wanted to know everything Kate said about, say, 'Pickles', it would do a search on that. Sure, you could do that with a flat ascii file and any half decent text editor, but that's not as neat now, is it? Plus, common things (such as individual songs) are highlighted, making it an easy task for the Kateologist to find what they want. Now, all this alone would make 'Cloudbusting: The Web Site' an invaluable resource. But Richard went those extra steps, and added other great resources (such as one of the better link pages) not available in the original 'Cloudbusting'. This 'Cloudbusting' is definitely something good! Rating: ★★★★★

Brian Wentz's *The Kate Bush Musical Extravaganza*. This has one of the nicer sets of links to other pages. However, its main claim to fame is that it has lots of digitized Kate songs. However, it struck me as being odd. If you're already a Katefan, you will have most of this, and if you're not, you probably won't bother waiting the 10 minutes it takes to download an average file. What would be cool is if BrianWentz, digitized rarities that several Katefans don't have (such as, say the 'Cathy Demos', maybe some B-sides, especially those pre-*Red Shoes* B-sides not in the boxed set). He already started going in this direction, with recent additions of *Home for Christmas* and *The Man I Love*. Also, there are a few MIDI files here. It's just a snippet from the infamous 'Diner' interview. If you've never heard it, I highly recommend downloading this puppy, but if you have heard it, then, well, you've heard it already. I recommend this page, if only for its novelty value (and, as a lover of novelty, that's supposed to be a compliment). Rating: ★★★

Most of the web pages I've reviewed thus far, with just a minimal amount of work could easily become 'The best' Kate web resource. I realise they each have different aims, but folks love to compare things, I have no idea why. Anyway, of all of these, none has more potential to be 'the best' than *The Garden.* The reason for this is that long before there was The Web, *The Garden* was the on-line source (besides rec.music.gaffa) for Kate Information. What Woj has so far HTMLized, he's done an excellent job. Unfortunately, he never got around to HTMLizing the most important part – the lyrics! There are now other pages that have them, or you can just ftp them (even directly from Woj's page), so it's not THAT big a deal, but still... Another favourite part of *The Garden* is Peter FitzGerald-Morris' chronology of Kate (heavily annotated by Andrew Marvick 'IED'), and an amazingly complete discography. Unfortunately, Woj was a bit too literal in his webbifying it, and didn't do even a brief update, so Kate's career is shown as mysteriously ending early 1990. Still, there is more than enough here to keep the rabid KateFan busy for hours: Kate's early poems, her contributions to the Kate Bush Club Newsletter, as well as those of her brothers, and lots of amazing and wonderful stuff you have to see. However, out in this 'Garden', it's only half of a heaven. Rating: ★★★

I've saved the worst for last. The page you think should be the best is clearly the most pathetic; and that's Kate's 'Official' Sony Website. While it's pretty impossible to make a bad Kate site, this one comes pretty damn close. Just a very brief FAQ (which is a year out of date), some info on the film, and three pictures. Rather interesting pictures, I have to say (the same type as on the cover of the second *Red Shoes* single), but that's it! All of the sites I've reviewed so far have been pretty uniformly great (with Cloudbusting and David Benson's site, standing clearly above the rest), but this one? Ew-weee! It's a stinker! Rating:★ (and of that, one star is for the photos)

Now to the 'Minor' Kate Pages. I'm not going to rate them since they don't pretend to be comprehensive Kate Pages, but still should be seen by the Web-travelling KateFan, if just once or twice. *The Illustrated Collector's Guide to Kate Bush* is an ad for the book of the same name. Actually, it is a great (if no-frills) resource for the Student of Kateology, it's also a simple and no-frills page.

The *Lovehound/rec.music.gaffa Shirt.* Yes, folks, there are still a few of these left; if I remember correctly only in large (no XL). But enough gratuitous advertising – like the rest of these, another no-frills page, run by yours truly. All it has is a description of said shirt and how to order it, and some photos of it. The highlight is seeing me with an incredibly dweebish expression.

The Red Shoes Discography picks up where the discography in *The Garden* left off. A simple text file, but with everything and more you could possibly want to know about the dozens of discs this album produced.

Fruitopia Commercials Kate did the Music For. Both pages have must-get Quicktime films of the one-minute theatre trailer, containing Kate music not available anywhere else. The first one, for some reason, does not credit Kate for the music.

archive.uwp.edu is just a webbified version of their ftp server. For those who never visited the FTP site, this is perhaps the most important Kate Resource out there. Tons of Kate pictures, the complete text of *The Garden*, and Ron Hill's Cloudbusting, lyrics, archives of every single post ever made to Lovehounds, and much more. Looks wise, this site won't win any prizes – it's just a fancy ftp directory, for God's sake! But content-wise, if you could only visit one site, this would be the site to visit.

Marcel's compuserve page is an advertisement for his upcoming *Kate Covered* project, with Lovehounds and other KateFans doing covers of Kate Songs.

Len Bullard: Building the Kate VR Worlds

The secret is, I have been moving government committees, Federal projects, and international standards for about a decade to get to do this. I've known for a long time what the technology would someday make possible, and now, in the last six months, it has come to pass.

I wanted to make a Kate Bush Virtual Reality World. Proof it can be done, and a hint to those who could do it better, how. After ten years in Hell (Department of Defence contracting is odd work for a rock musician. I wake up in meetings in Washington DC with the distinct feeling – where the hell am I?) it can be done.

So, what is VRML? Virtual Reality Modelling Language. It is the animatable 3D analog to HTML, the Hypertext Markup Language used on the World Wide Web. HTML is an application of SGML (Standard Generalized Markup Language) of which I am sorta kinda one of the CheechWizards.

Anyhow, we can use HTML and VRML to build World Wide Web sites that include not only text, but virtual reality graphics as well. While not the stuff of sci-fi yet, the results are still impressive. While I am an expert at SGML, I am an amateur at 3D graphics. What I have built so far is simply an apprentice effort, but it enables me to learn the language and apply it.

For this, many of the Lovehounds sent me links, photos of East Wickham, that sort of thing. I've incorporated these into two animated cubes (slide show thingies... quite tedious to do), and a main world that uses the *Ninth Wave* photo and the KateInKerchief along with the Kate Bush Club symbols that I redrew. It is a Russian Doll construction. In other words, you have to navigate around to find things and click on the worlds to get the animations.

I am hoping to put one more in to represent HomeGround Towers, and have to make up a vision of the Towers – you are in the hands of my imagination... which is loose.

Firefly

Krys

Beautiful Samurai,
amber firefly
your arrows aimed at the sun.
Now my little Warrior,
once my Little Friend,
I watch you fly away
leaving the ghost
of your perfect after-image
on my soul.
Mother, child,
sister, lover.
No more.
I will dream you sometimes
And I will bleed for you sometimes.
I am the arrow in your bow –
released from your heart
I fly away too.

With Cider in Hand

HomeGround Glastonbury in the late 1990s

1995: by Garrick Twinney

Issue 56: October 1995

The celebration of Kate's birthday, for me, actually started the day before. That it was a morning was unusual as I have always been under the impression that mornings are something that other people do. I loaded up my trusty velocipede with all that would be needed, and many things that wouldn't, for a weekend's camping expedition, and set off for Glastonbury.

The journey in my beautiful 2-CV passed without event, so I'll jump, metaphorically, and land in a pleasant little camp site below the Tor in the early afternoon on a gorgeous sunny day. After the erection of my humble nylon and carbon-fibre abode I relaxed in the sun, and awaited the imminent arrival of the other happy campers. At this point I should warn against my inability to recall names so apologies are due to anyone I forget or misrepresent in any way. Maybe I should change names to protect the guilty! Ian, Julie, Rob and Kirsten duly arrived, and after the raising of the canvas commune we decided unanimously that eating was the best plan on offer.

Then Mike arrived, and I found myself sitting in The Rifleman's Arms with fine cider in hand and fine conversation in the air, which flowed as freely as the drink, then Pami, Pauli, Peter, Krys, Glyn, Kate, the other Krys and Moggy arrived. Diverse conversation on such delights as valve amplifiers followed and ponderings on the whys and hows of existence but no definite answers were reached, surprising huh?

Leaving the pub where we had happily spent the evening, the campers arriving back at the site to stare in wonder at the crystal clear night sky. It was so beautiful; living in a city I rarely see the stars without neon street lights spoiling the view. I saw the glow of our galaxy for the first time in years, felt the magic of being alive in this infinite (okay that's questionable) universe. Something I hadn't felt for a very long time.

The next day was *Katemas*! The gathering upon the Tor grew until it reached unimaginable proportions, well 45 people. Everyone signed a card for Kate and there was much socialising, meeting with old friends and making new ones, which is what these events are really all about.

A great big "Hello" to everyone who was there at Glastonbury on that sunny Sunday in July. We all ended up back in The Rifleman's Arms, in the garden and time passed too quickly with such a good time being had by all. The air was filled with warmth and love like a big pink fluffy thing and friends who had to leave went with a hug and many happy memories.

After the pub had closed, (it's funny how our movements seem to be guided by the opening hours of local public houses; maybe *HomeGround* should start printing alco-logical baroscopes by Mishtic Keg or something (Peter?)) and like most things that seem a good idea at the time, the precise reasons are now foggy, and a handful of us headed back up the Tor.

Upon arrival we discovered that the tranquillity we had hoped for and expected was not to be ours. The atmosphere wasn't so good (we had abuse hurled at us by some unfriendly characters inside the tower) and we didn't stay for very long. The air temperature also had an influence on our premature departure, so after a quick peak through Glyn's telescope at Jupiter's moons (Moggy's moon had been publicly exhibited earlier) we descended the Tor in the dark.

Graphic: Krys

At the foot of the Tor, aware that this may be the last time we'd be together for some time as a group, a huge hugfest took place, goodbyes were said and small groups drifted off into the night.

The next morning we headed back into town and mooched, bumping at irregular intervals into assorted Kate people. Soon it was time for goodbyes so after the farewell ceremony I too headed out of town only to bump into Krys and Pauli who directed me to the Chalice Well Gardens where I came upon a small gaggle of HomeGrounders resting themselves by the well and being cured by the waters within. Ever eager for a quick heal I placed my delicate feet into the magical fluids only to discover that the water was at a temperature only marginally above freezing. Quickly realising that nothing this painful could be even slightly beneficial I

At this point we didn't always do Glastonbury every year. There had been a gap when we when we didn't do it at all. But we remember from this period long almost fearsomely hot July days and checking off the passing of time with these special friends we met at this place.

removed my blue feet from the chamber. The others having more hardy souls, or soles, calmly remained and had a complete cure. I skipped the healing, it was probably too late anyway. The ambiance of the surroundings was only disturbed by a delightful little child who insisted on splashing in the water and soaking everyone. No name was discovered for this demon-child but Damian seems like a fair bet.

The remaining small convoy of Peter, Krys, Pami, Pauli, Glyn and myself, headed off in the direction of Avebury. We stopped to walk within a crop-circle just near Silbury Hill, and being an intrepid bunch, solved the long standing mystery of the disturbed crops phenomena. Yes, they are actually caused by Moggy's propelling appendage! Next stop was The Red Lion pub in Avebury for dinner and after a short walk around the standing stones we headed our separate ways. After much hugging I found myself alone in my car elated from the love of the people I'd met.

1998: by Peter (and Jon)

Forty-odd Kate fans came to Glastonbury Tor on Lammas Sunday to celebrate Kate's birthday. We gave thanks to Jon Partridge for the refreshment offered to all who survived the climb. Jon says: "Next time there will be more than whiskey on the Tor, I mean not everyone likes their drink that strong."

Jan-Erik Svenson came all the way from Sweden, and Albert Lust from Holland but living in Dover at the moment, took this opportunity to see the fabulous view of the Somerset levels from the heart centre of England. Jake Gill was the youngest present, at 10 months, and John Beaumont from Leeds, who has attended virtually every Kate do we've ever organised, the oldest at ... (well, gone 60!). The Westbrook film crew and actors (makers of *The Pink Mules*) puffed their way to the top of the Tor, and made a late but large entrance. Thanks to them for the press release and the video-ing (which will be later used as evidence). This place is magic – we had fabulous weather – an interval between torrential rain on Saturday and Monday.

Mike Wade a long lost reader from the early days when Dave was still in nappies (and who was the winner of the Kate Quiz at our first Brew-Up in 1984), managed to find the Tor as per Peter's directions – "just look for a bloody great hill with a tower on it!" – and under the influence of the holy water took out another sub!

Later we went down to the Rifleman's Arms and occupied most of the front of the bar. Whilst quite startling quantities of firewater were consumed, friendships were renewed, and created. The great questions of the day were debated – when will Kate's next album arrive? And the enduring mystery was... why was Jon not smashed after the whisky, beer, red wine, scrumpy (and we can't remember the other exotic fluids) he downed? Has he got hollow legs?

Jon says: "In answer to the mystery: I have been raising my tolerance levels recently and also the starchy lunch helped reduce the effectiveness of the alcohol. The other exotic fluids included Kahlúa and Vodka and Drambuie but I think I need to learn how to spell the names of these drinks that I order!"

Apologies to those whose names we haven't mentioned, and again thanks to everyone for coming along. We did have apologies for absence from a number of people, but it was just as well they all didn't turn up or we would have to have taken over two pubs!

Graphic: Krys

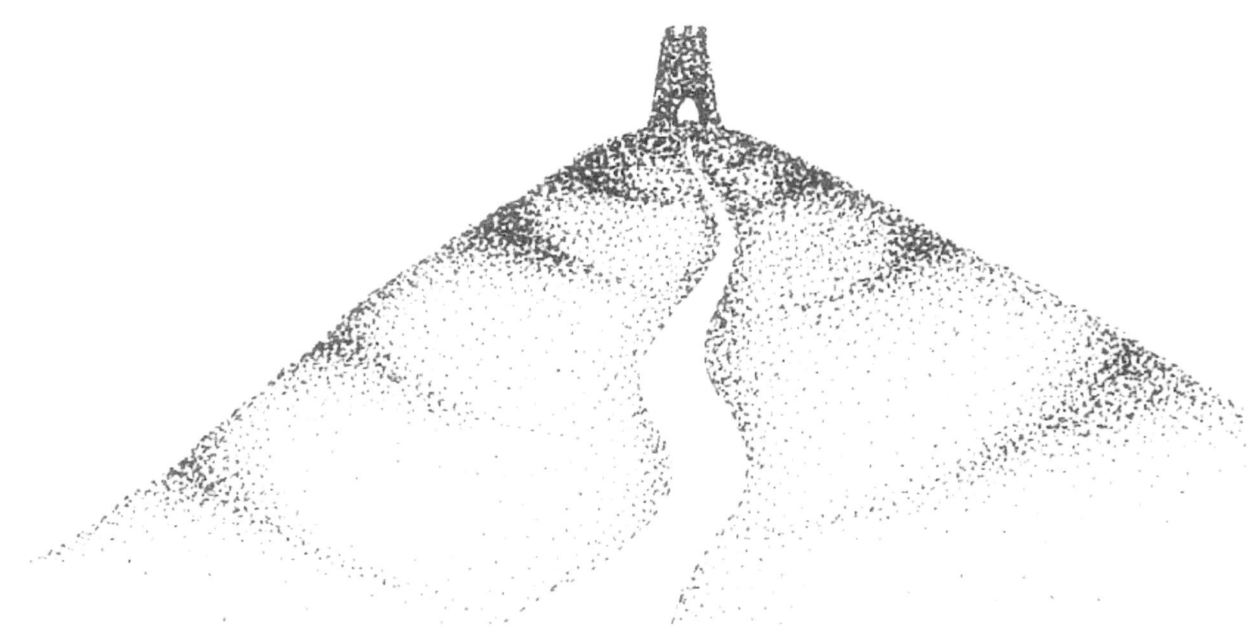

Eye of Awakening

How Bill Sinnking discovered Kate's music

Issue 58: October 1996

San Clemente, California: I have always held a strong love for any modern music written and performed in the progressive and/or theatrical style, a la Jethro Tull, Yes, early Genesis, BeBop Deluxe, Greenslade, Camel and Gong – to name a few. I have also been a firm believer that musicianship from Europe, especially the UK, far outshines anything offered from here in the States, or elsewhere in the world. UK artists have always been one or two steps ahead of the pack since the Beatles.

So it is no wonder that I completely melted upon hearing Kate Bush for the first time.

I remember it well for it touched my life, which hasn't been quite the same since. It was a few years back, around 1988 as I looked for new releases at the local CD store. The owner was changing the tunes on the CD player and cued up *Cloudbusting*. I was stopped in my tracks from the first few notes, and unable to continue my search through the CDs in the bins in front of me. All I wanted at this moment was to listen to the entrancing song that played throughout the store speakers. I was immediately taken by the most beautiful, alluring voice I'd ever heard, the fresh and interesting music, and the excellent production.

Before the song had ended I was at the front counter questioning the owner about it. When he told me it was Kate Bush my mind made a quick connection to a certain album cover I'd become attached to over the years. The photo on that cover was of a girl with a small key in her open mouth, about to embrace her chained lover in a garden somewhere, and the whole thing just hit me like a ton of bricks. She was quite simply the most attractive woman I'd ever encountered in all of my record buying years, and the image of that cover was so powerful that I found myself drawn to it like a magnet with every visit to every record store. The album was *The Dreaming*, and Kate Bush's name from that moment stayed in my mind.

Standing at the front counter I was euphoric with the realisation of this sudden discovery. "So this is Kate Bush..." I kept repeating to myself in a slight daze. "Wow... incredible!" How one woman could possess so much talent and beauty just boggled my mind. The store owner went on to explain that she wrote all her own material, plays the piano and handles the production work as well. That did it – I was hooked.

Needless to say, I left the store that day with an assortment of Kate's music in the form of *The Whole Story*, which was to open a door to a whole new world of magical music, something I hadn't experienced since the days of the '70s progressive art-rock movement. Every song on that collection was so deep and full of emotion, that I was pulled into the centre of her world and held captive 'til the last note.

Since then I have bought as many of her recordings, videos and biographies as I can possibly find here in California, and enjoy them every day. *Hounds of Love* is now added to my stranded-on-a-deserted-island can't-live-without list of must have albums, which also includes *Trilogy* (ELP), *Fragile* (Yes), *Moving Waves* (Focus), *Foxtrot* (Genesis), *Red* (King Crimson), *Aqualung* (Tull), *You* (Gong), *Moonmadness* (Camel), *Time and Tide* (Greenslade), *One of a Kind* (Bill Bruford), *Dark Side of the Moon* (Floyd), *Free Hand* (Gentle Giant), *Led Zeppelin* III, *Revolver* (Beatles), *Nuclear Nightclub* (Wigwam), *Sunburst Finish* (Be Bop Deluxe)... the list goes on.

Graphc: Krys

My only regret in all this Kate Bush madness is that I wasn't exposed to her music at the beginning of her career. If only I had heard *Wuthering Heights* or anything else from that first album back then, I could have enjoyed the whole experience so much sooner. I'm just thankful to be aware of Kate's music now – better late than never.

In closing, I'd like to thank Kate for all the inspiration I receive through the power of communication. She has grown from a beautiful and talented girl, to an even more beautiful and more talented woman. Being an accomplished and natural musician, I highly respect her work and all that it offers. Some of my friends think I'm crazy – they don't see what it's all about, they don't 'feel it', which is a loss on their part, but then Kate's music is not for everyone and those willing to open their ears will be greatly rewarded in return.

Thank you, Kate, and thank you David Gilmour, for knowing a good thing when you heard it.

Remember Yourself

Krys considers the eternal dilemma of the Kate Bush fan

Issue 58: October 1996

Graphic: Paulina Stuckey

Tori or Kate or ...

"This past Sunday, after eighteen years of being a long-suffering Kate Bush fan and waiting in vain for a world tour that will probably never happen, I've done something that I never thought I'd do: I've taken all of Kate's tapes, CDs, videos, poster books, buttons and t-shirts, put them in a large plastic bag and threw them in the garbage.

I won't be renewing my subscription as, like Su G, I've lost the faith. I've come to the conclusion that Kate Bush and her music have nothing to do with me as a fan or as a woman. Lately, I haven't been listening to The Red Shoes *or any of her past albums because Kate represents the way things used to be, when I thought she had musical potential. I find Kate's music too painful to listen to. In all my eighteen years of fanship with Kate, I think* The Line, the Cross & the Curve *was the last straw. I feel personally betrayed and insulted that Kate had sold out of her principles just to make a buck. I felt that the film was a total waste of time and money as far as Kate using it as a substitute for a tour. Another thing that I have a serious problem with is that Kate records and releases deeply personal songs like* Moments of Pleasure *and* You're the One, *but she never talks about these songs in the few interviews she does give. It seems to me that after eighteen years in the business, Kate Bush has a serious attitude problem and isn't doing anything about it. No wonder her fan-ship is deteriorating rapidly and 90% of her fans are flocking to Tori Amos.*

I'm beginning to side with an increasing number of people who now feel that Kate Bush doesn't care about her fans. My biggest disappointment is her too short Convention appearance and her perfunctory appearance on 'Top of the Pops'. I also feel that the Fruitopia commercials in the US were a way of Kate selling her principles to revive her flagging career. It seems to me that Kate Bush had peaked too fast and became a star too late. Like a great many people, I've grown impatient with Kate not making personal appearances in the US. I feel that I could no longer share in Kate's point of view. What is the point of defending an artist's work if she doesn't even care? I'm not going to stand idly by and watch a brilliant artist like Kate drown in her own self-pity. I feel disgusted, disappointed and disillusioned, so I'm out of here. Kate Bush has been everybody else's girl, maybe one day she'll be her own".

Inspired by the disillusionment of some fans, as seen in the letter above, this is an attempt to take a view of fandom from where we stand here at *HomeGround.*

The Background

There was a lot of good, original music around in the post Punk late '70s, a welcome antidote to the dreariness of the early part of the decade. Kate was a major contributor to this, her face and image was everywhere you looked. At that time there didn't seem to be socially (and politically) the kind of negativity and problems that are increasingly obvious today. Thatcher was yet to be voted in as Prime Minister. Those days, were to my memory a more positive time and place to be generally. I look back with affection and a sense of sweet nostalgia.

Back in 1978-79, Kate seemed to exude a happy, positive vibe. It came through her music to a large extent, and she seemed to be thoroughly enjoying making that music. In the beginning it must have been exciting and fresh for Kate, she had achieved what must have once only ever been a dream – she had made an album. There was an innocence and trust about her, and a great energy, that came through the tracks on *The Kick Inside.* Many of us grew up with those first three or four albums as the soundtrack to our young lives. And Kate grew too. Each album could be seen as a kind of diary, a record of change and development, musically, emotionally and personally – a record of change in our own lives as well as Kate's.

This was to be her chosen career, and the success of that first album was to be much more than she (or EMI) had envisaged – or been prepared for. Initially Kate fulfilled her ambition to make an album, but with its enormous success, the pressure must have been put on her from various sources to make another to follow as soon as possible, and more after that. She felt that *Lionheart* was rushed. The 'Tour of Life' took up most of 1979, and took a lot out of Kate. The first 'gap' arrived and two years later *Never For Ever* was released. Inside the sleeve was the powerful image of the bleeding rose, to me a reminder of how much blood, toil and tears went into making that album. After another two year gap, *The Dreaming* was released, one of her strongest albums ever. The songs were more painful, there was a sense of something lost, yet a strength and maturity as Kate emerged as an adult woman, with a musicianship that surpassed her previous works. The British critics slammed and scorned *The Dreaming* mercilessly, though the Americans loved it – it made a remarkable impression over there. But here, the harsh criticisms and the label "weird" must have hurt Kate terribly, and may have encouraged her to retreat further from the public eye – an eye that will not let her shake off the *Wuthering Heights* image.

A three year gap and *Hounds of Love* was born, a far more commercial (the A-side at least) album, where Kate had reached a compromise between writing commercial hits and doing what she really wanted in the form of *The Ninth Wave* concept, her most ambitious creation ever. She went along with the promotional side of things, though she has never enjoyed this part of the process, and still doesn't. She travelled to the US and Europe, and gave countless TV and radio appearances and interviews. We have seen some corkers from US television! One stands out in my mind – we have the complete filmed session of a horrendous, long-winded interview with an American chat show host; virtually no research had been done and Kate's facial expression is one of utter bemusement. You can almost see her thoughts forming in her head; this woman was obviously driving her mad. She asked yet another ludicrous question and Kate's tongue slipped in reply: "Well, that particular prat." What she meant was "that particular track". I think Kate's original answer was more sincere, and very funny. The screened version was heavily edited. You can see how Kate must have got fed up of giving mindlessly boring interviews to people who weren't really interested in her music.

The Sensual World came four years later, and for me was the first album to have weak tracks, and seemed to send out a message of not having all her heart in it. The majority were great tracks, but not all worked. Kate did the usual interviews for the music press, but for the first time personal appearances were not on the agenda. Up to this point in her career, in terms of the promotional side of things, Kate had given the fans and EMI what they wanted – appearances, radio and television interviews, and record signings on a worldwide basis. In cynical terms it helped sell more records, not that she really needed help. But promotion may have seemed to Kate to be superfluous, that she was somehow prostituting herself to sell her work, when she thought it should and could speak for itself. She probably began to feel like she was a commodity for the public and the record company. By Kate not doing promotion, it could be perceived that she was shooting herself through the foot, that she wasn't helping herself or her work. With *The Sensual World* Kate clearly did not want to do personal promotion any longer and considered her work to be finished once the master tapes were handed over to EMI. Since *Hounds of Love* Kate hasn't played this record industry game, and in those terms she must be a company executive's nightmare. She has for most part had hold of the reigns, and final decisions on albums and singles have always been down to her. Many fans have wrongly blamed EMI for not doing this or that, when in fact the choice has been Kate's. She doesn't get pushed around; her side of the bargain is to fulfil her contract for X number of albums.

The following year, 1990, saw the release of the *This Woman's Work* collection. Its funereal black box seemed as though Kate was saying some kind of farewell, wrapping up and laying to rest what she had done to that point. There was a finality about it. This didn't please all the fans, especially the CD format which was retailing at a figure higher than the cost of mid and full price CDs when bought without the box. It is interesting that at this time Kate changed the KT symbol from that of the Knights Templars, to the sign of Chiron, the wounded healer.

The November of that year saw Kate's wonderful appearance at the 1990 Convention. She was happy and cheerful. The atmosphere was comfortable, even cosy despite a gathering of more than 1,200 people. She clearly enjoyed herself and was in good spirits. Her little thank you song at the end was really special as those who were there will remember. To us this Convention was a great success and we all thoroughly enjoyed it. The preparation and organisation had been fun. That day was the highlight of a particularly hard year for us personally.

On Valentines Day 1992, Kate's dear Mum, Hannah, died.

This was a great loss to all who knew her. I can't imagine how Kate and her family coped. Hannah had always been a great support to Kate in her career, and gave her encouragement to go out and do things, and she was vital where fans were concerned. Those of us who visited the Farm were made very welcome by Hannah and Dr Bush. Hannah always spoke kindly and fondly about Kate's fans, she was interested in all our lives and what we were doing. She was the Kate world's Mother figure and she genuinely cared about everyone.

On a personal level, Hannah and Dr. Bush have both been very supportive to Peter and me, particularly in our ten year (so far) struggle to have a baby. I remember the July of 1987, as we were leaving the Farm, Hannah put her arm around my waist and said "There's no sign of that baby yet, Krys?" She *knew* although we hadn't told anyone we were trying. She gave me a big hug and held my hand, and there was a look in her eyes that pierced my soul. She just knew things. I have so many memories of Hannah and luckily at that time I kept a diary, and all those visits to the Farm are in there. In *HomeGround*'s early days, Hannah was so encouraging and told us many times over the years she thought we were doing "a great job" with the magazine. We continue to visit Dr. Bush and I still feel her there. I see the empty chair where she used to sit, but somehow its not really empty. To me the Farm was Hannah, and I think it still is. I don't know if she ever knew how much we loved her. I miss her terribly. We all do.

Moments of Pleasure was a brave statement for Kate to make. The most moving part in the song being the words about her Mum. Kate had experienced the deaths of a number of her friends and loved ones, and *Moments of Pleasure* was a good, positive way to pay them tribute, turning sorrow into a celebration of love and the good times that were had, and probably helped to heal her own grief.

The Red Shoes was released in 1993, 18 months after Hannah died, and Kate's great sadness and loss was there for everyone to see. I feel the loss of Hannah coloured *The Red Shoes* more than anything. Some fans simply couldn't deal with Kate being so open about such personal experiences – some people can't cope with emotional matters, and found it uncomfortable being confronted up close with such personal things; some thought she was wallowing in her emotions. Others simply lost interest at that point and drifted away. Kate lost a number of fans with this album.

The Red Shoes is for many the hardest to listen to, because of the emotion in there and because it shattered some people's illusions about Kate; she too could be raw. Maybe it felt that the crutch had been kicked away, and she could not be leaned on. Nor did she have the answers or strength seen earlier, though her quest for both is there. There were only three light tracks, the rest bleak, tormented, unhappy. *And So Is Love* and *You're the One* spoke loudest. The older we grow, the more experiences we go through. We have to face problems and challenges; relationships can change, and often we have to face the deaths of loved ones. Some people go to pieces and can't cope, others get hard and cynical, most get through as best as they can. Perhaps for some fans there was no reassurance or comfort to be found, perhaps Kate appeared too weak and vulnerable, not the strong woman seen in her earlier work. There was fear and self-doubt too in the form of *Big Stripey Lie* which to me heavily suggested psychic attack (I believe there is such a thing). *Lily* was very telling and honest.

The Red Shoes was probably a turning point in Kate's career; the struggle of its creation comes through, and the strain and exhaustion can be seen in those *Q* magazine photos that appeared alongside the interview that coincided with the album's release. Again Kate did not promote her album, other than a few personal signing sessions that took place in Tower Records in America.

The Line, the Cross & the Curve, was finished to meet the deadline of the 1994 London Film Festival, and was a matter of much discussion between the fans – some loved it, others loathed it – as the letters pages over several issues of *HomeGround* illustrated. In retrospect it may not have been the best thing for Kate to have embarked on at that time, she may have been better waiting a few years, or even having done it earlier as she had originally planned for *The Ninth Wave*. I once thought she would venture further into film-making, but it looks as though she had enough of that particular area, which proved to be extremely time consuming, and probably frustrating and tiring. I now wonder if Kate may follow Peter Gabriel into the world of the CD-rom, should this be an area of interest to her. There could be great adventures with endless creative possibilities, though not all fans would have access to a CD-rom – even more debates.

Kate's '94 Convention appearance lasted only minutes, and caused a great conflict in opinions amongst the fans. The letters flooded in for the best part of 18 months after the event. Many thought she should have stayed longer, others were quite happy that Kate showed up at all. Some were quite bitter about her brief appearance, and took it as a personal insult. This brings us back to the recurring view some fans have that Kate owes them something. The decision to appear at events has always been down to Kate, and almost always she has agreed to come along at the last minute. That day, I was later told, she had a really bad headache; she may not have turned up at all. Those who were disappointed had probably expected Kate to stay as long as she had last time, and felt let down that she didn't do a repeat performance of last time.

Kate is currently at the beginning of the creative process which will become the next album. The years between album releases have never been a problem for us, though in terms of the magazine we do have a problem with the lack of new photographs, which concerns me in that we are portraying images of Kate as she was, not as she is now. Of course it is great when a new album is imminent and when we have new tracks, but to us it has always seemed just a little melodramatic when some fans have taken the waiting time as a personal injury, that Kate is somehow making them suffer by forcing them to wait. Once an album is released into the world, there is no going back and changing any imperfections, so Kate works to the point of exhaustion in pursuit of perfecting her work before handing it over to EMI.

The Fans

Through *HomeGround* we encounter many different fans, from those only mildly interested in Kate's music, to the very serious, obsessive fan. Most of us find a great deal of pleasure and comfort – not to mention friends – in Kate's music, which is what it's all about.

So what exactly is the role of fans? There is a definite need for an artist to be given support and encouragement, especially at the beginning of their career, but perhaps more importantly in quieter times, like Kate at the moment, for instance. She is out of the public eye, most people think she has disappeared and isn't doing anything any more. Many fans write to her to let her know they are thinking of her, and that means a lot to her. The patient fans write and tell her to take her time with her album-making, and not to let anyone hassle her. Kate must feel a kind of security in knowing that we like what she creates, that we understand (mostly) what her music is saying, that we can take that music and use it as inspiration for our own creative abilities.

Many fans feel a genuine love for Kate, not just her music, but for the person. Even if they have never met her, the love is there. She has reached many people through her lyrics, which are more often than not about love, and has struck them at a deep level. Many people have problems in their lives and the music can provide answers, gives them courage to believe in themselves, and is of comfort. Every one of us has felt that I'm sure. Like if you're out somewhere, feeling a bit down, and then out of the blue a Kate track gets played in a shop or a pub or on the radio.

Collecting rarities is something most people do, money permitting. It is enjoyable and many of the items are nice to have. This can get out of control, though I doubt if it causes much harm other than financial.

The friendships we have all made through our love of Kate are one of the most important parts of the picture. Peter and I met through our mutual love of Kate's music, and many of the friends we have made are through *HomeGround.* Many people have made new friends at conventions and smaller gatherings. The common bond is Kate's music, and relationships develop from there, the starting point. Kate is a catalyst in many people's lives; wheels are set in motion, and things happen. However, not all of Kate's fans are angels – we have encountered one or two utter bastards.

Kate has always had some contact with her fans from the very beginning. Back in March 1986, she asked us to get around a hundred fans together to take part in the video for *The Big Sky,* which was a very enjoyable day. She didn't have to choose fans for the job, she could have got people from the record company or an agency. I think it was a kind and trusting gesture on Kate's part. She continues to send cards, gifts, letters and signed photos to many people. She is very supportive of many fans, including Peter and myself, and has been a great comfort to us through our on-going IVF attempts. She has been there for us and little cards to say she's thinking of us have dropped through the letterbox when they're needed the most. Kate doesn't have to do any of these things, and I get very angry when some fans accuse her of not caring. We know that she genuinely does care.

There is the question of whether fans need to see Kate in the flesh. Is there a need to have such contact in order to enjoy the music? I don't think there is, though of course it is great to get to see people we admire. Those moments tend to be special. But it isn't anyone's right to demand an appearance or a tour, just because they want it. Kate may never want to tour again, and that is her choice. She doesn't owe any of us a tour. If she had wanted to do another tour she would have done it well before now, and I'm sure she has given it much serious thought. I don't think she feels the need to do it, she has already made the music and put it out into the world.

It is always really good when everyone gets to see Kate at events, but no-one should get complacent about it. Those who were at the Video Party will remember how she was mobbed at the dinner table, and no amount of asking people to sit down, or reassurance that Kate would get round to see everyone in turn, was listened to. Dr Bush stood up and asked everyone to sit down, Dave, and I think Paddy and Del too, but no-one listened. The lack of respect towards Kate, her parents, brothers, Del, Lisa and for the quiet fans who stayed put, was really quite unpleasant. Those who did the mobbing were in a state of panic, pushing and shoving people who were sitting at Kate's table, including her parents. It was disastrous, and embarrassing for us. That put an end to us ever having an event where Kate was on ground level. She simply wasn't safe from being mobbed by a frantic crowd who are supposed to like and love her. I'm surprised after that Kate ever attended any other convention.

Graphic: Chris Chamberlain

Some fans aren't very nice to Kate; at the end of the '94 Convention, a few guys threw CDs into her car demanding that she sign them. There are others who criticise Kate for her success, craving the fame that she no longer wants for themselves, and getting insanely jealous of her. And there was of course the infamous anti-fanzine, 'Under The Ivy'.

Meeting heroes in the flesh can shatter the illusions people often foist upon them, that pedestal on which the fan has put his hero, can crumble and he or she crashes to the ground. This is the fan's fault. We know of someone who once met Kate, and was seriously disappointed that she was an ordinary person, wearing jeans, boots and woolly jumper. Was he expecting her to drift in on a cloud, wearing the *Babooshka* costume? Had he hoped she would fall at his feet, that he could take her off into the sunset? He 'lost the faith' after that, and became a born-again Christian.

The realisation that Kate is a human being with imperfections comes as a shock to some fans. This plays a major part in the fan becoming disillusioned and placing the blame on her for their own disappointment. Their expectations and demands are too high. The role Kate's music has had in their lives has been of vital importance, and to many this has been the most important thing in their life. Most fans will go through something like this at some point, the majority keep things in perspective, but others may go far beyond. Extreme cases of the obsessive fan have been around for years, the most recent case being the Björk fan who sent a sulphuric acid bomb intended to explode in her face. This made the national television news, with the revelation that he had videoed himself assembling the device and kept the camera running to film him shooting himself in the head. The video was intended for Bjork to see, and to make her feel responsible for his death. She was interviewed and clearly upset by what had happened. There was a similar story with Sarah McLachlan, who wrote a song about an obsessive fan who was stalking her. He too committed suicide. And everyone is aware of what happened to John Lennon. This is the extreme side of obsession, where it seems the 'fan' wants more than some small degree of contact with their idol, he or she wants friendship, or even exclusive rights over that person; the situation can become dangerous, even life-threatening to the idol. These so-called 'fans' do, however, give the genuine caring fans a bad image, and attaches the 'weirdo' label to everyone.

Some fans are satisfied enough with simply having the music, they don't need to meet Kate personally. For others, meeting Kate is their ultimate goal, some even dream of marrying her, and some really believe that one day they will. This is slightly disturbing because it seems that they would like to add the real person to their collection. It is true to say that some more extreme fans live in a fantasy world, and do have a serious problem in getting a grip on reality; there is usually some major problem in their lives at the root of this obsession, and Kate is a convenient and happy escape. It can, however, have a detrimental effect on them finding a partner who can meet the high standards they have woven around their perception of Kate as the ideal. They want Kate; anyone else is second best.

We have to look at ourselves here at *HomeGround* too. Some would deem us as obsessive for producing a magazine about Kate, and some think we're mad (it certainly helps). I wonder if Kate cringes at yet another photograph or drawing of herself, or whether she feels embarrassed or touched when she reads how her music has affected someone's life, or whether she gets upset by an angry fan's letter or a critical article. Does she enjoy the attention, the dedication, the time and energy fans put in to creating work inspired by her own creations? Kate plays the Muse to many. The thing is, she probably can't appreciate or enjoy her own work like we can. She is on the blood sweat and tears end of it, whilst we are at the listening end of the finished result of years' worth of work, time, energy and everything else that goes into its creation. It would be nice to think she does get some enjoyment out of the work she has inspired in others.

To Owe or Not to Owe

This is the on-going debate. Some fans firmly believe that Kate owes them something: personal appearances, tours, endless supplies of albums, preferably one a year, body and soul. They believe that they have put her in the position of acclaim and recognition, that her fame and fortune is down to them buying the records. To a degree this is true. If no-one bought the albums the story would be different. Kate must be the UK's top female artist of all time. There are thousands of aspiring artists out there who work hard, and most will not get wide recognition, money or fame. Many stars have disappeared into obscurity. The music business with its designer bands is different now than when Kate began. What would happen if she was trying to break through now, when talent and originality is not always enough?

Kate owes nothing for her success, fame, wealth. She worked hard for it. The same old argument that "well, we bought her albums, we put her where she is today, without us she wouldn't enjoy the kind of lifestyle she does" comes up again and again. These are often the same fans who grow impatient with her for taking the time she does over making an album, who whinge on and on because they feel hard done by and let down by Kate and EMI. Even if Kate churned out an album a year, that still wouldn't be enough, because they would demand her to tour. These kind of fans freely offer endless criticism, though I doubt if they could make music like she does.

People make such big demands: the record company, completion deadlines, the fans, and demands from Kate herself, being a perfectionist. Everyone should remember Kate is a human being with feelings, her own life, her own joys and problems. She is not a commodity. You pay for the music, the agreement stops there. No-one buys Kate the person. The music is what you buy, the music is what you get. I wonder if people think Mr Heinz owes them something just because they bought a tin of baked beans. I hold firmly with the opinion that Kate owes us nothing. Not even another album. So the next time you have a moan, stop. Could you do what Kate does?

Conventions and the Religious Experience

There is another way of looking at Kate's appearances at conventions or gatherings – perhaps the idolatry gets too much for her; she is up there on a stage with a crowd surrounding her, almost worshipping at her feet, which some artists would feed to their ravenous egos. But for Kate this must be quite daunting, if not terrifying, to have all that attention. Kate is not like the majority of stars. We joked to Kate that we should have ended the 1990 Convention with Python's *Always Look on the Bright Side of Life* (from *The Life of Brian*); maybe it wasn't such a joke when you look at it in this light... "It is her shoe..."

Last night whilst writing this piece, Peter showed me an article in issue 35 of 'Watching Storms' called 'Kate, Her Fans, and Disillusionment' by Ernest Heramia. I think Ernie sums this up perfectly: "Look at us from where Kate stands, on the stage. Out there in the darkness, a thousand-plus faces, a vast, amorphous, amorous monster cheering for her. A monster that could crush her or tear her apart, if frenzied. A monster notorious for its fickle affection; shouting 'Hosanna!' on Palm Sunday, only to scream 'Crucify him!' on Good Friday. Could you return the love of such a monster, or would you want to hide yourself away on a little farm in the English countryside?"

Some of our Wiccan friends visualise Kate as the Goddess aspect, being the perfection of womanhood in their eyes. Some fans have made their love of Kate and her music into a 'religion' or cult, where Kate becomes their God and Guru, the living messiah, for them to follow. People copy her ideas, take things too literally, even to the point of losing their own identity and individuality. Kate becomes the pivot around which their lives revolve. She is put upon that pedestal (not of her making – she just makes the music), and when she falls because she is human and imperfect, the fan becomes disappointed and disillusioned with her, to the point of turning into the anti-fan. It is interesting when a disillusioned fan says that he or she has "lost the faith". Those words, and their allusions to religion, are invariably used. Most people celebrate Kate's birthday, though I do not like the religious overtones of the term 'Katemas', that the US fans have adopted.

Over recent years, we have seen this disillusionment happen quite a few times. The hardest of hard-core fans, have suddenly lost interest in Kate. Maybe it is a part of growing up and developing as individuals, and the realisation that there is more to life than sitting in their bedroom listening to Kate all day. There seemed to be so much seriousness in the devout fan, to the point that they would not find humour in things like those terrible 'Top of the Pops' musak recordings of Kate's songs, or some of the impressionists doing their 'Kate'. In all things there has to be some degree of perspective, and a sense of humour helps. The music and the whole fan thing is meant to be enjoyed. I'm sure Kate would want people to be happy and have fun, not make her the core of their very existence to the exclusion of other things and people.

There will always be a division between Kate and her fans. Fans are generally not able to get close because of the fan-idol thing. I believe this is the usual state of affairs; the fan can be quite intimidating to the idol, and that is the barrier to there ever being a true equally balanced friendship. The idol puts the divide in place just as much as the fan, knowing that the fan will almost certainly put him or her on that pedestal, and that he or she cannot meet the fan's expectations. I think fear on the idol's part is a key reason, he or she has much to lose should things go wrong if they took the risk of letting the fan get close – blackmail in extreme cases or the fan running off to the newspapers to tell what they know to fatten their own wallet. The fan-idol 'relationship' is what stands in the way of friendship. It rarely happens.

The classic icon, Marilyn Monroe, was exploited by many of the people around her and she wasn't in control of her personal life or career. I wonder whether Kate held this in mind when she decided to record *Candle In the Wind*, and whether in her own way was saying something about herself.

For many famous people such as Kate, it must get very difficult to discern people's true motives for wanting to know you, whether it is for yourself, or whether it is for your fame so they can impress people at parties with the odd name-drop here and there, or maybe they want your money. Hangers-on are everywhere, and there are people who will use and abuse. Even friends. There are always people ready to jump on the bandwagon. But I think Kate is a strong person who will not suffer fools gladly. We all know that she is a very private person, and probably draws that close around her for her own protection. I should imagine she has to be very careful about who she trusts and takes into her circle. Her loving family have always been a strong, protective wall around her, and this more than anything has probably saved her from the clutches of a callous, exploitative record industry and the hangers-on who would try to use her.

Kate is unlike so many pop stars who have an appalling attitude, which is made very public – the Oasis bunch for a start – their attitude really stinks and encourages the younger fans to follow suit, because it's cool and trendy. A teacher friend of ours, experiences this snide attitude from teenagers each day at school. These bands do have an effect on those too young and impressionable to know better, and should take seriously the responsibility for their very public actions. This world is hard enough without producing a generation of arrogant, cynical people who think they can do as they please, regardless of others.

Kate must be very conscious of the effect her songs and subjects have on people. Some will cling to her every word and she must feel responsibility regarding this, to the point that she may well have second thoughts about her lyrics or may even discard songs. No doubt she has questioned making public some of her songs, and I wonder if she has ever felt that she has left herself exposed.

The Future

Kate's personal development and the areas she is interested in are her own private business. Everyone should respect her need for and right to privacy. People change and Kate has changed. If we don't have change in our lives and indeed go with the flow, stagnation sets in. The struggle to oppose change causes problems. It is a vital part of our lives, though it can be hard to deal with. We should all appreciate that Kate is not the same woman she was when she was nineteen, she has grown as everyone does and should. How could anyone expect her to stay the same as she was then? Over the years she, like us all, will have had many experiences and encountered many people. These things take their toll and change us.

I feel that Kate has reached a point where she needs to have her own space and time for what she wants to do with her life. There must be times when she wonders what the hell she is doing, what is her direction, how can she better the work she has done before. She must sometimes feel like packing the whole thing in.

She may benefit from having a break from making music for a while, even years, to return refreshed with new inspiration. There is always the possibility that one day Kate will say enough is enough, and that she has nothing more to say in music. If that happens we should all respect that it is her choice. She owes us nothing. I would rather see her happy than torturing herself just to churn out music that her heart isn't in. Who knows what the future will hold.

My only wish for Kate is that she is healthy and happy, and she pursues her life the way she wants to. She will not be dictated to by anyone, be they associates, fans or EMI.

Most of us will still be with Kate for years to come, whatever she does or doesn't do.

All the Voices

Readers Respond to 'Remember Yourself'

Issue 59: July 1997

Martin Wykes: It is likely that there's been a lot of reaction to Krys' article 'Remember Yourself' featured in *HomeGround* 58. The subject of disillusionment has dominated recent discussion in *HomeGround* and it feels like things have reached some sort of crisis. The anger and bitterness in the reader's letter quoted at the beginning of the article summed up a mood that has been increasingly expressed by some. The reader's collection of Kate items could have been left forgotten in a cupboard or sold to one of the eager collectors who advertise in the classifieds. Instead, it was thrown in the garbage. The reader clearly wanted to make a point and wrote to *HomeGround* in order to express the intensity of their feelings.

The *HomeGround* line that Kate simply owes us nothing does little to placate an anger that is felt as a kind of betrayal. There must be two sides to this argument but there is precious little common ground or mutual understanding.

The writer of the letter said they had been a Kate fan for eighteen years, almost as long as I have. They said that 90% of Kate fans are flocking to Tori Amos. I must admit that in recent years I have been far more excited by Tori's work than by Kate's. This is partly to do with the type of music Tori has been recording. I love her vocal and piano styles, her fascinating lyrics and her Irish-reel based melodies. But there have also been developments in Kate's music. She has changed her vocal style and records less piano-and-vocal tracks than she once did. In both of these aspects I preferred some of her earlier work. However, I'm a fan of both Tori and Kate.

It is implicit in a lot of criticism of Kate that she or her music has changed in some dramatic way, and people's expectations have been disappointed. But how major are the changes? Kate continues to record albums at her usual rate, with the traditional mix of radical, excellent and inferior tracks. Her music and lyrics have the same influences they have always had. Her public appearances remain rare and her public image remains 'weird'. There is hardly a criticism you might make today that couldn't have been made ten years ago. Yet some people feel she's no longer giving them what she used to, or more importantly, what they want. When we say we're dissatisfied or disillusioned with Kate, perhaps we should think about what we would like to change. What would we have in an ideal word?

* Do we want her more famous and successful? That would equal even more distance, with the press railing at her like they do Michael

Jackson.

* Do we want her less famous and successful? Then Kate would be a forgotten artist producing records on a shoestring for a handful of remaining fans, which would make it even harder to find friends with whom to share her work.

* Do we want more frequent albums? We know that the quality can suffer under time pressure.

* Do we want more public appearances? That would slow down her recording schedule further and few of us would actually get to see her.

* Do we want more media appearances? Kate would just end up with unsympathetic and disinterested interviewers.

* Do we want a tour? We wouldn't be satisfied if she didn't include songs we wanted or choreography to match the Tour of Life.

I think what a lot of disillusioned people want is to return to 1980 or 1985. They want to experience now the music she made then with the ears they had then and in the circumstances they were in then. Perhaps that is where the anger stems from. I was a lonely teenager when I first heard Kate sing. Now I'm 34 and married. If I'd never heard *The Kick Inside*, hearing it now for the first time wouldn't give me the overwhelming feelings it did in the late 1970s. If Kate were to pastiche her earlier styles for us, it wouldn't bring back our experiences. We've all changed over the past two decades. Undeniably Kate's writing style has developed and become more mature. Hopefully so have we. For some of us her work will speak even louder and more strongly to us. For some of us it will have less relevance as we grow apart from her. For others the connection will dissolve completely. We will find nothing to identify with or be inspired by in what she says or does.

None of this should be a surprise to us. All relationships have the possibility of growing apart, especially that between the fan and the pop star. Kate is unusual in that she has inspired stronger and more durable loyalty in her fans than many artists have, but that only makes the end more traumatic when it happens. Kate has meant a lot to many people over the past two decades, and when it comes to an end there is no formal way, no forum for expressing those feelings. Except *HomeGround.*

Maybe we shouldn't be telling people to accept Kate's idiosyncrasies and remain fans whatever happens. Maybe we shouldn't be telling them that we can't understand how they could possibly feel disillusioned. Maybe we should say that it is okay to feel these things and that they are a sign to move on and look for the things you need in other artists or new areas. Perhaps if after 18 years Kate's new work no longer moves you, then it's a good idea to listen to Tori Amos. Not that she sounds anything like Kate did in the '70s and '80s. Any similarities are superficial. The rhythms and production are totally different; the lyrics and attitudes are miles apart. Twenty years ago Kate wrote about love and sex in a romanticised way. Now Tori writes about them in a confrontational way. Times have changed. Maybe we should accept that we can no longer expect to feel the same about anything, including Kate's music. Maybe this would help us avoid the arguments and acrimony.

Paul Gardener: I just want to say how much I appreciate Krys' article in *HomeGround* 58. It's more than time that someone put down on paper why we should not expect Kate to act the 'star'.

Perhaps I can add something by telling you about how my love of Kate and her music has developed. I got into Kate after hearing *Hounds of Love* and very quickly got obsessed and began collecting everything I could. This was at a time when I was just discovering spirituality and the raw emotion, honesty and spirituality in Kate's music struck a chord. Coupled with this was a personal aspect. I have always been attracted to women who had Kate's looks and this combination saw me at various times being convinced that Kate was my 'other half', my spiritual 'sister' and various other relationships just as unreal. Krys' mention of most fans expecting to meet her or even marry her struck a chord. I'm not sure that I expected to marry her but I knew 'it was only a matter of time' before I met her and in some way we would find that we had always 'known' each other.

Of course, this was all an arrogance on my part and, when I look back, most of my spiritual views then were based on arrogance. The search for spirituality that I was on was valid but I hadn't let go of enough of my ego and still saw my search as revolving about me. No wonder then that Kate had to be 'meaningful' to me in a 'real' way.

I made many connections with other Kate fans, specially those who also saw Kate as part of their 'spiritual quest' and there was often a feeling of belonging, almost like being a member of a religion, that supported and strengthened me.

In 1990 I was in plaster for 3 months and unable to walk properly for 3 months after that. I managed to get to the Convention and even then felt that Kate somehow 'knew I was there'. A side-effect of my injury was that collecting became very difficult and then stopped. I slowly began to realise that what I had seen as almost spiritual was an obsessive need to 'belong', to Kate and the group of fans. Over time I felt the need to identify with her fall away and what took its place was a real appreciation for Kate as a person.

I began to see her as someone who made music because that is who she is and what she does. She was not a guru, guide, leader or any other label that I could attach to her and therefore have expectations of. In other words,

Kate was doing what she does and didn't owe me anything. At the same time, my concept of spirituality changed as well. I started seeing the truth in many Sufi sayings, perhaps the most important to me being 'be in the world not of it or out of it'. I had been 'of it' by expecting Kate to tour, to treat us dedicated fans as special and I had been 'out of it' by seeing Kate as some goddess who gave 'lessons' through her music.

Now I hopefully see her more 'in the world'. At the moment I am a counsellor and psychotherapist and am training as a teacher. I feel that if I suddenly became famous I would love it for a while. However, I am also essentially a private person and I know that I would find fame, once the 'glamour' had worn off, to be frightening and intrusive. I know too that there would be people who touched me and to whom I would want to respond, but that generally I would shun the kind of attention and examination that seems to go with fame. I get the feeling from Krys' article that Kate may well suffer similar feelings.

So now I don't take part in any *HomeGround* or Kate events, though that might change, and I don't collect. I have sold most of my collection. Yet what is left is far more important. Kate herself, through her music allowed me to search for myself and discover that being 'real' is what (my) spirituality is about. She helped me recognise and respect other artists who strive to be real in their music will reflect other parts of myself that, through listening to their music, I can begin to discover. And she helped me touch a part of myself that I didn't know was there. The important part of this is that she doesn't, nor ever need to know that she has done it, because the reality is that she hasn't. She was 'just' herself, and my being who I was and am, allowed me to begin to discover myself.

The bottom line for all of us is that we owe Kate nothing other than our respect and, what is more important, she owes us nothing. We are all being who we are. If we choose to find meaning and significance in what Kate does – fine. But keep it as what she does, not what we want her to do.

Jaakko Nousiainen: I've just read Krys' article in the latest issue, and I agree with her completely. It is important to see Kate as another human being, with her own struggles and complexities. And that is where the true understanding of all art begins.

We all change and grow as humans, and I think it's important to maintain a certain curiosity, a will to try to communicate. It's like saying "Hey, I've changed, you've changed, but can we still find something in common?"

There have been times when I've been less attached to music. They've been periods when other areas of life have needed my main attention. Often I've come back to music, as I've found it is ultimately the strongest of all arts because of its direct emotional effect.

And there I find Kate, a woman trying to fight her own demons, live her own life as she best can. Trying to deal with all the difficulties we all have to face in life. And trying to share the joy and happiness that life has in store for us. And trying to understand the changes. All emotions are universal, they don't depend on age, race, sex, or sexual orientation. An artist's work is a mirror to see yourself in – "Yeah, I know what you're saying, I've been there too."

Karen Newcombe: Thanks Krys for an intelligent and thoughtful answer to recent comments about Kate's career. I think one of the most revealing personal comments Kate has made in an interview (I believe it was in a print interview) was that she couldn't wait until the album promotion was over and she could get back to work on the herbaceous border in her garden. Go Kate!

I hope you folks in England don't think too badly of us for 'Katemas' – and I really hope you don't think we take it as an actual pseudo-religious holiday. Having attended many of these parties and having met a fair number of fans, I have to say Katemas is an excuse to get together and eat a bunch of food and see people we can trade collectibles with. In America the religious connotation of the word 'mass' has long since given way to that of consumerism! Therefore we get together and consume chocolate (which some would contend is a religious experience), toast Kate's health and enjoy her wonderful work. Maybe you'll make it to San Francisco some July and join us?

Marcel Rijs: I joined the Internet in 1993, through an email-only connection at the University where I was studying at the time. This was brought on by things I'd heard about mailing lists and newsgroups. One of the first groups I joined was Love-Hounds, which was a friendly community of fellow Kate Bush fans. The new CD *The Red Shoes* was about to be released – I still remember all the excitement, all the reviews and the many days I played the newly born disc on my walkman on the train from my hometown to Amsterdam, where the University was. I loved the new album, I was thrilled with this very personal, deeply emotional album and amazed at the fact that not everyone shared my opinion.

Obviously I didn't realise that, like all humans, even Kate fans are not alike. We all have our own thoughts and opinions, we can be critical, even cynical when something new is presented – especially when we'd waited for something so long.

I have become less vocal on the Internet since then. I do read some digests, but a lot also goes right into the trash can in my mail program, simply because reading from screen is too much a

Graphic: Paulina Stuckey

strain on my eyes to justify doing it all evening. But I always feel I'm missing something, and this is why I was glad to be reading Krys' piece.

The extremes are more extreme than I thought. Apparently there are people so disappointed with their idols that they throw them away. And apparently there are people who want to marry or try to kill their idols just to add them to their collection. I am just so surprised at these extremes. And I realise, while I'm writing this, that there's no real conclusion. I am just surprised.

Another thing I'd like to point out. The last Convention was one I missed. Still, I have a story. I knew this woman. She came to know me through a mutual friend, and I spent a few weeks with her. She was calling me virtually every day, and talking for hours, mostly about Kate. Too obsessive for me, anyway. But I was touched by one of the things she told me. She'd been to that Convention, and had managed – at least, that's what she told me – to get to Kate while she was on stage, and give her a letter (perhaps someone can confirm this). I wouldn't have had the nerve to do this. A few weeks later, she received a signed photograph from Kate with a letter saying she was touched by what had been written to her. This doesn't sound like someone who doesn't care for her fans. I don't know what happened on that Convention, but to have someone come up to you and give you a letter out of the blue and to answer it... amazing.

I have always considered artists to be normal people and have always treated them like that when I met them. Well, okay, the usual autograph-question aside... but most artists really appreciate that. I think it's important to remind yourself that she could be you. How would you feel to read things about yourself? How would you feel to have to release music every few years and to do all the stupid things most artists are sometimes obligated to do? I imagine that it's just a job for them, and since I hate my job, I must assume they do too.

Perhaps this is all too black and white, but nearer to the truth than some things I hear at times in mailing lists. I just hope Kate will release one or two more albums. If not, well then I hope she can find a good man and marry him and perhaps have kids. She deserves all the happiness she can get after all the BS she's been through these past 20 years. I feel for her, and if I believed, I would pray for her.

Alberto Di Costanzo: I read the article from Krys with great interest and appreciation. I think all the points she makes about things like touring, press relationship and personal contacts with fans are all valid. There is one thing I want to add some comments to, and that's the communication between Kate and us (the fans). In the beginning of her career there was the Kate Bush Club Newsletter, which appeared quite regularly. After a while the periods between these started getting bigger and bigger until they got almost as big as the periods between the albums. In these modern times there are many forms of communication. Kate is described by people who know her well as a person who loves her privacy. I think this sort of letter to the fans is one of the things – apart from the music itself of course – that holds almost no threat to that privacy. So what if she feels she has nothing of any interest to say to us? I tend to think that does not really matter. For example, if some day when opening the mail from this list we see that one of the messages was sent by KATE BUSH, I suppose all our hearts would skip at least one beat. If the message read nothing but "Hello Everybody" most of us would still feel very happy. To make it quite clear, I do not think Kate owes us anything at all; but I do feel that a very small effort from her side could take away a lot of this "She doesn't care anymore" crap. I am sure, knowing her only through her music, that Kate is a truly kind person – the more she shows it, the better.

Lane: Thanks Krys! You said many of the things that I had been thinking while reading recent postings. I was lucky enough to be watching 'Saturday Night Live' those many years ago, and old enough to realise that I had just witnessed something special. Being on the wrong side of the Atlantic to hear Kate on the radio and see her on television again, I thought that I possessed this wonderful secret that no one else could quite understand. Maybe being President and sole member of this Club of One helped build up Kate in my mind to something more than just a wonderfully talented yet shy artist. Over the years I have gone from fanatic, to fan, person with a full life who still really enjoys Kate's music. Am I the same person that I was 18 years ago? No. Is Kate? I doubt it.

She has given me (and the world) around 100 pieces of music and 20 or so videos, many of which I use to identify and remember key points in my life. Music has always been important to me, and I am constantly looking for something new and interesting. I sing along with the Prodigy, The Verve Pipe and Garbage, while others I grew up with cling to The Eagles and other bands that have not put out new music since the Reagan administration. Only one artist from my youth still holds a very special place in my heart – Kate. I listened to *The Dreaming* a few days ago, and it still sounds as fresh as the day it came out. I would be hard pressed to name more than a handful of pop musicians I grew up with that are still putting out anything interesting, and fewer still that had any impact on my life. Does it make Kate special? Yeah – I really think it does.

Finally, if Kate were to decide today that she has said everything that she has to say musically or otherwise, I would offer up a thousand thanks for all she has given, and cherish each note that she has produced. Whether her next album takes another two years, or disappears into oblivion like the book she was supposedly writing a few years back, it will have no effect on my admiration of Kate and her music. She has paid me anything she 'owes' me many times over.

Len Bullard: Thanks for that perspective. I confess, that hurt. In summary, Kate is a normal person wanting a normal life. In some measure, I do know what a disappointed fan looks like. It's scary as hell. At my level where the audience is still three feet in front of us, it is very personal. At her level where the frenzy can kill, it must be devastating.

Impatience is one aspect of desire. If one understands that, it is ecstasy. If one thinks all desires must be satisfied, it is spiritual poison. So we balance that with the list, with 'Katemas' (I also don't care for deification: don't rob someone of their humanity), with the pages and art. This is the good side of fandom. Art spawning art. That is the kiss. If our letters give comfort, and in comfort she makes more music which we buy, that is the rose. Have we hurt her that deeply? If we have, then shut down the list, close GaffaWeb, take down the KateWorlds, and wait for a record. Fair dinkum.

Over My Shoulder

Krys and Peter and Dave look back...

Issue 62:
December 1998

Krys

"The smell of burning fields will now mean you and here..." My first memories of Kate are the 1978 'Top of the Pops' performances of *Wuthering Heights*. She totally fascinated me.

1979 – I remember ice-skating at Deeside ice rink every Sunday morning to *Wow* – it's great to skate to. I didn't get to see the Tour of Life. I remember the tour posters in Liverpool but at the age of 14 my parents thought I was too young to go. I was told I could go next time Kate toured. My Grandma loved *Them Heavy People*. She was such an amazing lady. She looked so much like Lily, as I later told Kate.

1980 – October – I bought *Never For Ever*, my first Kate album, and played it endlessly. My parents gave me *The Kick Inside* and *Lionheart* on vinyl for Christmas. I remember the first time I played *Lionheart* on the stereo downstairs with my Mum and Dad sitting there listening too. *In the Warm Room*... imagine it. I grew up with Kate, her music guiding me through my teens, taking me to places, situations, people of all kinds. It was the most wonderful adventure. And that was just the beginning.

1981 – *Sat In Your Lap* reminds me of the summer I passed my O-Levels. I adored the video. I played Kate's albums to death. *Lionheart* got me through my exams. I based my Art O-Level on *Breathing*. I had to illustrate a poem of my choice and my drawing caused quite a stir. It was a summer of crushes and daydreams. I started Sixth Form and loved it. I escaped into the Art Department every spare minute and immersed myself in my own creative world largely inspired by Kate's music. I had a crush on my art teacher who looked like Oliver Reed in his *Women in Love* era! He tolerated my Kate-inspired artwork and it lined the corridor outside the Headmaster's office. I remember playing *December Will Be Magic Again* in the blue lights of my bedroom, and it started to snow. Perfect.

1982 – March – *The Empty Bullring* is such a beautiful song, but takes me back to a memory I wish I could forget. *The Dreaming* single and my first pair of contact lenses. I can *see*! Through Spring and a hazy Summer I wrote Kate-inspired poetry, and sent the illustrated booklet to a fanzine called *HomeGround*, thinking "I've got nothing to lose" as I pushed the package into the post-box. *The Dreaming* would be released the following week. The first time I heard it was through a splitting headache. A storm raged outside, the sky was black. It remains one of my very favourite albums and sounds as fresh now as it did during that storm. Peter wrote back immediately, his handwriting more a hieroglyphic artform, and over the weeks and months I fell in love with a man I'd never met, but he wooed me with his words. He sent me the single of *The Man with the Child in his Eyes*... "He's here..." On 26th November Peter and I arranged to meet and we just clicked. It was magical as we drove across London in the Winter sun to his home in Kent. I met Peter's Mum, Olive, and she made me very welcome. We watched Kate videos and it was a wonderful day. I met Mandy too. A few days later Peter sent me a card, which I must have read a thousand times and each time there was a strange leap in my heart. *The Dreaming* was the soundtrack for the Autumn of that year. I turned 18 in the December. My first letter from Kate arrived on my birthday. Mum and Dad gave me the Hammersmith video for Christmas – Kate looked like a little Samurai in trilby and trench coat. I stayed with Peter for a few days at Christmas, and I met Dave, his room at his parents home covered from wall to ceiling in Kate, Debbie Harry and Abba stuff. The songs of *The Unknown Soldier* haunted me as memories of candlelight and Christmas trees carried me through my mock A-level art exam. I was in love and there was no going back.

1983 – train journeys between Liverpool and London every weekend. Peter and I got engaged on 30th July on Glastonbury Tor. I started a foundation course at Art College in Southport. Peter and Dave bestowed editorship upon me. Kate played on the Walkman Peter gave me to help me through the unbearable days at college. Covering the entire studio with newspaper and drawing the result wasn't my idea of art. I tried to keep enthusiasm alight by incorporating Kate's music into my work, but the tutors didn't like this at all.

1984 – "She's leaving home..." In February I left college and home and found myself a job in London at an old fashioned print gallery near the British Museum. I twice met Vincent Price, a kind, quiet man who had a keen interest in the Old Masters. My boss was a wonderful gentleman of 82 who loved Winnie the Pooh and had many original E.H. Shepherd drawings. He was a leading expert on Rembrandt and bought original etchings decades ago for around £3. He died in 1985 and his collection was almost certainly dispersed throughout the art collectors' world. I was still there when Chagall died – the prices tripled overnight. It was an honour to handle so many original works – 13th Century woodcuts, Goya, Millais, Blake, Sickert, Picasso... A highlight was doing restoration on a £4000 (1985 value) Dürer.

At 2 pm on 30th November Peter and I would be married. At around 12.40 pm the phone rings whilst I'm getting ready. Dad calls up the stairs, "There's a woman on the phone for you." I pick it up and I hear "Hello Krys, this is Kate Bush here..." It was a huge surprise. She wished us luck for our wedding day and future together. It was a special day and Kate helped to make it extra special. I floated down the aisle to *Moving*. Dave and friends made a strange brew of shaving foam, beer and flour and painted a big heart on the bonnet of the car. We travelled around Somerset with the 'Just Married' stuff all over the car – and I touched up a few areas with spray snow! We later discovered the concoction had baked on and until that poor old car met its maker a couple of years later, bore a big heart with a K & P! We spent our honeymoon in a Jacobean manor in Somerset. We moved into our empty house on 8th December. Well we had our bed, two floor cushions and a radio! Were we all growed up now? Just before Christmas we went to the Farm. I'd had an idea about doing a joint convention with the KBC to raise money for Band Aid and we put it to Hannah and Dr. Bush.

1985 – The evening of 23rd January we had a meeting at the Farm to put forward our ideas for a Convention. That night I met Kate for the very first time. It was a wish granted. She gave us hugs and kisses. She was so lovely. I remember her sitting in her Mum's chair drinking tea and taking a keen interest in our ideas for the convention. Kate stayed with us for about an hour and asked to borrow Peter's log book that detailed her TV and radio appearances. Peter had a bad cold and Hannah gave him brandy with coffee in it. Two weeks later the log book was returned with a letter from Kate to say they would be in touch. April – we went for a Chinese meal with some old school friends of Peter's. One was a guy called Chris who was a roadie for lots of big names. He was a friend of Captain Beefheart. Chris recalled how Beefheart had turned to him and said, "My ears are wobbling – hey, man, someone really heavy just hit the dust." Half an hour later he heard of John Lennon's murder.

May – we get a phone call and the plotting and planning begins. We have further meetings throughout the year as the Convention takes shape. A mutual friend had seen the album cover and told us it was something to do with "dog". The original *HomeGround* 19 got lost on it's way back from the printer in Birmingham. We had to start the issue again. August – Hannah put us on Kate's guest list for the 'Wogan' show to see her perform *Running Up That Hill*. 9th September saw the *Hounds of Love* launch party at the London Planetarium. Dave went along, being in the music industry. Hannah grabbed Dave, then grabbed Kate and said to her "Look who's here to see you!" Kate asked where we were. Hannah told Dave that she'd been trying to ring Peter at work but couldn't get through to tell him that our invitations were waiting for us at the Planetarium. We felt as if we'd missed Christmas. Del sent us a *Hounds of Love* release package back with Dave. We still haven't got over it!

30th November – the first Kate Bush Club/*HomeGround* Convention at Romford and also our first wedding anniversary. A very foggy day. It was a friendly, relaxed affair. Dr Bush, Hannah, John, Paddy, Del were all there. £4000 was raised for Band Aid. We took turns waiting in the drizzly car park for Kate to arrive. She had just returned from promoting *Hounds of Love* in North America. I remember Kate in her moccies. She gave us white roses for our anniversary. I still have them. A few days later we were sorting out the Convention items and at the bottom of a box we found Kate's lyrics to *Breathing*, hand-written in green ink and returned them to her.

1986 – March – a 'phone call from John Carder Bush to ask if we could gather a hundred fans for the *Big Sky* video shoot. It was great to see Kate again and to see her creativity in action. Everyone had a truly memorable day. July – we went to the Farm and Hannah showed us her copy of *Cathy*. I remember looking at that wonderful book for the first time. It was like holding something delicate and precious. Beautifully captured moments of Kate's childhood. Hannah told us how she loved the photograph of Kate dancing in the garden... *Don't Give Up* – the song of that year. We decided to end the misery of working in London and we'd try to have a baby.

In early November Kate invited us to be scientists in the *Experiment IV* video – three of the best ever days in my life. I bumped into Kate in the ladies portaloo and ended up telling her about the horrendous work situation I was in. She was really kind and sympathetic and gave me a big hug and very good advice. Then the Video Party. Unfortunately, Kate and her family were swamped by some fans, who were desperate to see her. The idea was that Kate could have her meal then mingle, but the best laid plans... Kate had 'flu, probably triggered by the long hours she had been working on the *Experiment IV* video.

1987 – February – Kate won the BPI award. Dave was there and she tapped him on the shoulder to say hello. 28th June – the Peter Gabriel gig – we had a 'phone call to say that Kate was appearing at Earl's Court that night. Mad panic! No-one could confirm this. So we took a chance and our mutual friend was right. The intro of *Don't Give Up* was a couple of bars longer than at the previous night's gig and huge blue cats stomped in my stomach. Gabriel started singing, then from out of the darkness Kate emerged, her voice arriving before she did as she stepped into the light. A magical moment. We were told that Kate couldn't hear herself singing because of a problem with the sound system, and she had agreed to Gabriel's request to do the song only at the very last minute.

1988 - On 29th July we went to the Farm. Hannah told us she had thought of the title, *This Woman's Work* because she said to Kate that giving birth was woman's work. Just before we left, Hannah put her arm around my waist and I put mine around hers and we held on to each other for a while. She was "reading" me all evening. As we left she pulled me back and asked what was happening regarding trying for our baby. She said everything would be okay. I always dreamed that she would hold our baby in her arms...

Kate spent her 30th Birthday taking part in the 'Shop Assistance' charity event in Covent Garden, at Blazer, the men's clothing shop. The shop was bursting with people eager to see Kate. She signed a t-shirt for me. It is still in pristine condition. Unworn, unwashed. Sue, Ian, Pami and Pauli came back to HomeGround Towers and we toasted Kate with champagne.

Graphic: Jonothan Coram

1989 - March - the demos appeared from a mystery man in America. *The Sensual World* played in the car as we drove through Somerset. We sent fireworks into the sky to *Rocket's Tail*. Debs and her invisible guitar. Dave, me and a Trio of Bunnies on our heads.

1990 - a cruel Summer where our hopes were crushed. The specialist smiled as he told us there would be no children. We both went into shock...

We immersed ourselves in plans for the forthcoming second Kate Bush Club/*HomeGround* Convention to be held on 17th November. It was a wonderful day. Kate was happy and relaxed and had agreed just a few days before to do the 'audience with...' bit. Remember when she sang her thank you song to the tune of *My Lagan Love*? She fumbled down her sock and brought out the lyrics. That Convention is one of my very favourite moments It was such a happy day and so much fun. I wish I could re-live it. Afterwards, backstage, I flaked out in the corner with my bunny slippers on - Kate liked them so much that we bought her some as part of her Christmas present. She gave me a beautiful bouquet - I still have every flower and leaf. Apart from one which I gave to my dear friend Sean, who loves Kate with all his heart. I am terribly sentimental. I even have two unopened cans of Heineken from the *Experiment IV* shoot! I have a box of sentimental Kate things... the bronze *Lionheart* badge Lisa gave me at the 1990 Convention... ribbons and wrapping paper from presents and flowers from Kate... I still have the foil wrappers and gold wings from the chocolate angels Kate had given Dave for Christmas that year - he gave us each an angel.

1991- "Here comes the flood"... a hard Winter, the water pipes burst and flooded our house. Our signed Kate albums were damaged, including our *This Woman's Work* box set that Kate had given us at the Convention. We were distraught. The house was freezing for weeks. One evening we were waiting for various people to give us quotes for the repairs. There was a knock at the door. Peter was just about to ask the tall guy at the door for a quote when he handed him a brown paper package. Peter thanked him, said goodbye and we opened the mysterious parcel. It was from Kate. Another signed box set with a card inside telling us she's thinking of us. Two little birds had told her about the damage from the flood. Peter then remembered the guy as Andrew, Kate's driver. Peter had trodden on his foot at the *Big Sky* shoot - Andrew was Superman and only had his red socks on, whilst Peter was wearing heavy flying boots. He was very good about it!

July - we went to the Farm. It was to be the last time we saw Hannah. Kate was there and we gave her her birthday present. We said goodbye, then, unable to resist opening the gift, she came back to say thank you and that it was "very appropriate".

In Autumn I had Glandular Fever with serious

complications. It looked scary at one point. 1991 was to be the hardest year. Kate performed *Rocket Man* on the 'Wogan' show and he mentioned that Hannah was ill. We sent her some flowers and Kate phoned to thank us on her Mum's behalf. *Rocket Man* will always remind me of Hannah. We were due to go to the Farm just before Christmas, but Dr. Bush called to say Hannah wasn't well enough to see us. Peter and I weren't the only ones to have a hard year.

1992 – Valentine's Day. Our dear friend Hannah Bush died. I still miss her very much. I still love her very much. The Kate world would never be the same again. Our first Christmas visit to the Farm without her... I cried all the way home.

1993 – 20th June would have been Hannah's birthday. We were in the audience of 'Aspel' where Kate sang *Moments of Pleasure* for the first time. I have a feeling she did this just for her Mum... Sharon (writer of letters) and Mick were married on 25th September. My beloved Grandma died the same day. Her name was Hannah too. It takes four years before I can think about her and not cry. *The Red Shoes* dance a bloody dance. The album makes us cry; we see some familiar scenes. "You set me free..."

1994 – In response to something I wrote in the 'Feel It' series, a letter and poetry book arrived from John Carder Bush who is to become my favourite novelist of all time, whose words will take me on great adventures and give me an avenue of escape from the hard smacking reality that grabs me by the throat. I admire him enormously. He introduces me to Nicholas, Marc-Ange, Nathalie, Jean-Jerome... I fall in love with a Snapdragon... "Snick, snack..."

Plans for the third joint Kate Bush Club/*HomeGround* Convention were under way. I remember Dave modelling the prototype *Red Shoes* long-sleeved t-shirt at Lisa's... "Quick, Dave get your clothes on!" 8th May saw the third Convention. I caught 'flu the night before, and my throat felt like I'd swallowed broken bottles. I felt so dreadful and couldn't enjoy the day, though there were great moments... Some of us were still reeling from our bereavement... I was told that Kate had a really bad headache, so it is understandable that she didn't stay on stage for very long. The following day Peter and I had our first IVF appointment at a leading London hospital and the ball started rolling again. Sharon and Mick's son, Michael, was born on 15th August.

1995 – Summertime and our first IVF attempt begins. It takes months of nasal sprays, daily injections and cancelled cycles to reach the operation in October. Kate sends a card – the first of many – to wish us luck. It's a hard journey into the unknown but also exciting – it is the first real chance of having our baby. Since then I have discovered that each subsequent attempt gets harder... The day of the operation arrives; I need the comfort of familiar things, so I take Little Brown Ted to hold and *The Ninth Wave* on a cassette. As I lie on the operating table, trying to make magic happen, the Pethidine cocktail slithers through my veins and Kate lullabies me and brings me some solace in a very scary and painful situation. I think of Hannah and my Grandma, and ask them to watch over me, help me through this, as a long needle pierces me deep inside, again and again. I think beyond the physical pain to the future... The magic of conscious conception as two tiny embryos are transferred inside me. Pregnant for a few days maybe. Maybe next Christmas we'll have our child.

1996 – I spent eight days in hospital and my Snapdragon friend sent another book of short stories to get me through the long days. I miss my cats. Two more IVF attempts, again I take *The Ninth Wave* for comfort. Maybe next Christmas...

1997 is coloured in dark shades as two more attempts to bring our children through, fail. A very bleak and unhappy year. I am grieving. Even 'Snapdragon' cannot console me. I feel like a ghost. A shadow... We watch as our dear friends, Pami and Pauli, experience imminent parenthood. A phone call in the early hours of 20th September tells us Pami has gone into labour. I am wide awake, I can think only of her, and pray that they will both be safe through this rite of passage. *This Woman's Work* plays in my head. We see baby Jake the day after he is born and fall in love with him. He is so beautiful. I thought I would cry but I didn't... One early December morning, Jake is asleep, his little head on my shoulder. Pami has put a CD on; Loreena McKennitt's *Dante's Prayer*... the song and scene... "Remember me"... and I make a wish that Jake will never know the pain of this infertility and that he will have a happy life. Pami comes downstairs to me with red eyes and Jake with a soggy head. I say "that song." She knows what I mean. Maybe next Christmas...

1998 – On 20th January we marked twenty years since *Wuthering Heights* and sent Kate flowers. We remember the good times and hope that Kate too has had many happy times in those years. How could anyone have known what would follow the release of *Wuthering Heights*? This year's issues of *HomeGround* celebrate Kate's anniversary. Peter embarks on the mammoth task I set him of writing the definitive tribute. Can it really be twenty years? In that time so much has happened.

Kate sends another card to wish us luck. In April our fifth embryo transfer fails. I had scan photos of all five embryos. Tiny clusters of hope. I dared to love them. Now I only have photographs and memories of that hope. We have lost 13 potential children. "Give it time..." I throw myself into creative decorating to transform impending depression into something positive. For the last four years I have hammered my body with heavy duty IVF drugs, and hammered my emotions beyond belief. It is a heavy price for just a chance at what most people take for granted. We're taking a break from the treatment to find the people who got buried under all the stress of this path we chose, the people we were when we first met. *And So Is Love*... Kate is right, life is so bloody sad at times. Sometimes too sad to even carry on. "Make it go away..." It is impossible to move forward, my feet are mud. My arms are empty. I feel so incomplete. "Can't move... Just can't move." We manage to survive with a sense of humour, friends, love and an appreciation of the good things we have. But it's not easy. One, maybe two more chances left. A little piece of hope. A little life in me yet... Maybe the Christmas after next... we're running out of Christmases...

15th July – A card with three tulips on the front. A ray of sunshine, happiness and hope for the future...

"Looking back over my shoulder..." I have tried to capture these moments before their colours fade – the IVF drugs and stress are beginning to steal my memory. I don't want to lose my moments. I have so many happy, nostalgic memories of the last twenty years, with Kate's music the soundtrack. But there is sadness too as our hopes of having children have not been realised... They may never be mine... We can't know the answer. Through it all, Kate has been with us, in her music and her undying support and friendship. Her little cards have always arrived when they're needed the most. It has been hard to look beyond the most horrendous crisis I've ever had to deal with, and see the good things in my life, but wonderful things have happened and some of my wishes have been granted. Through Kate's music I met Peter. I love him with all my heart... We have met so many people and made friends who we cherish. We've had experiences beyond our dreams. No doubt that through her music, Kate herself has met interesting people and has had experiences and opportunities that have in turn enriched her life. A little "Karma Mama".

In these twenty years Kate has given the world more than most people would in a lifetime. Now it is her time, to do as she chooses with her life. All that really matters to me is that she is happy and healthy. I see her as a friend rather than "Kate Bush, famous person". She means so very much to me. I feel certain that Kate will return refreshed, and her next album will be burning with new inspiration. Wait and see. Give her time. Give her space. Kate, I wish you health, happiness and love – thank you for your beautiful music, your love, all the kisses, and good luck wishes, for your trust and for caring about two little Bears – I love you dearly.

Dave

"Okay Remember, Okay Remember..." was it really more than twenty years ago? My friend Barry King saying "Have you heard that *Wuthering Heights* record?" My first imagined image of Kate was of someone who looked like Jane Austen, with hair like Princess Leia... Seeing Kate for the first time on 'Top of the Pops', all flaming red hair and wild eyes. Buying the single in WH Smiths in Romford. Buying the album in Woolies, Hornchurch. Listening to *The Kick Inside* over and over again. Hearing the news at school that Kate was number one. Watching Kate on 'Ask Aspel'. Seeing her perform *Don't Push Your Foot on the Heartbrake* on the 'Leo Sayer Show'. Hearing *Hammer Horror* and *Lionheart* for the first time and playing that scream from *Don't Push Your Foot on the Heartbrake* over and over...

Going to the London Palladium with my friend Robin Perry, and being amazed not only by the show but that there were obviously a lot of other people who knew all the words to all the songs. Watching the BBC2 Kate special. Listening to Annie Nightingale play *Breathing* for the first time on Radio 1's 'Roundtable'.

Then the first Kate Bush Club Convention at the Empire, Leicester Square, meeting Kate for the first time and meeting Mandy for the first time, a critical moment (in the space time continuum, Capt'n) which led to my first job in the music industry. February 1982, I began telesales at Pinnacle Records, where Mandy already worked (and was just down the road from where Peter lived). It was the start of a career path I am still following. Meeting Peter, and sitting in my little room at Tarnwood Park, listening to Stevie Wonder's *Hotter Than July*, and me saying to him "Why don't we start a Kate fanzine?" The excitement around the release of *The Dreaming* and sharing that with other people. Those mad early days of *HomeGround*, reaching some kind of insane peak on a camping trip to Sandling near Folkestone in Kent. Meeting Krys for the first time at my parents house... The Scouse Mouse marrying the Bermondsey Bear...

Christmas 1984, a very special meeting that was a turning point in the fortunes of the magazine. Going to see Kate perform *Running Up That Hill* live on 'Wogan' – where was she aiming that arrow?... "It's in the trees, it's coming"... The album launch at the London Planetarium... "Look who's here to see you".

The 1985 Convention, which makes me cringe now, but the feeling was right. A call from John Carder Bush, "Er, Kate was wondering if you three would like to be in the video for *The Big Sky*?" We got to dress up and be in a Kate Bush video! We were also asked to get around a hundred fans for the audience shots. Later the same year we got to lie around on the floor in the freezing cold disused mental hospital and be in a Kate Bush video! The mad crush of the Video

Cafe, which also served as the *Whole Story* launch party... Saying goodbye to Stephen... *The Sensual World*... Mmm, Yes. The 1990 Convention, standing on the side of the stage as Kate answered questions, told us mad stories and sang her song... New Year's Eve, making that mad tape recording... Saying goodbye to Hannah. Those dancing shoes "Feet start kissing the ground". The *Red Shoes* Convention... Lisa wanting to come up standing on her head... Moments of Pleasure indeed.

And mixed up with all of these memories are those many drives up and down the A2, the many hours of 'Python', 'Blackadder', Victoria Wood and 'Star Trek'. Plus any excuse for a good feed. All the lovely people I have become friends with, Steve Davis, Ian Ramage, Lisa, Dr and Mrs. Bush, Pami and Paul, and Guy.

Kate, thank you for the music. Peter and Krys, thanks for all the tea.

Peter

It was **1978** – I'd bought my first gra-mo-phone only the previous year. My record collection contained a lot of classical, folk, Abba, Donna Summer and Renaissance. I was finding out what I liked. I liked female singers, especially harmonies and originality. I knew nothing about Genesis or Pink Floyd.

By accident I saw Kate's first appearance on 'Top of the Pops'. Victoria Station is where it starts. The record section in WH Smith. An album with a strange cover and weird lyrics. I play it a few times, then not, then find it again and play it to death. Something has happened because the next scene is the HMV shop in London's Oxford Street on the release of *Lionheart*. Kate is sitting at a small table and I am saying "could you sign this to Peter?". Trying to keep the radio tuned on Luxembourg last thing at night to catch *Hammer Horror*. When I felt down, I could measure how down by the number of times I played *The Kick Inside* and *Lionheart* to feel better.

1979 – February. At work, Howard shows me his copy of the *NME*. A small picture of Kate and was it something about a tour? The picture is the first thing I ever collect. Sitting amongst piles of old music papers in the vintage magazine shop then in Cambridge Circus during the lunch hour, trying to find all the stuff from the previous year. Writing to people in the Kate Bush Club Newsletter and getting badly recorded (mike against the speaker) tapes of Kate's 1978 radio and TV appearances. Queuing at the Palladium ticket office for nearly four hours during another lunch hour. It wasn't a good ticket, but I was mesmerised. For weeks after, the band were playing *James and the Cold Gun* in the back of my head. I'd never seen anything like it. Literally, because it was the first rock gig I'd ever been to.

Writing a lot of letters and thinking about a magazine for other collectors. Have you ever stood in the upper gods at the Albert Hall? Yes that is 'stood'. I was too late for a sitting ticket for the London Symphony Orchestra 75th, with Cliff Richard to endure before Kate sang *Blow Away*. Outside we waited for Kate by the stage door. And she did come out to say hello. Video recorders were new fangled things and I couldn't afford one. Annoying when things like the Leysin *Wow* and the 'Nationwide' tour documentaries appeared. I could only record them on audio. But then it was Christmas and I watched the 'Kate' special.

1980 – So I bought a video recorder, Betamax of course. I'm lugging the great beast through the tube, copying some stuff that the guy in the collector's record shop in Hanway Street had. Then with Lionel I'm in Surrey trying to figure out how to wire up a Betamax to a Phillips VCR. I never got Kate's first 'Top of the Pops' appearance and it has never been shown again. I never got 'Saturday Night at the Mill'.

Kid Jensen is saying "That is to say the least a most unusual record" as the last boom of *Breathing* fades. In my bedroom I have four radios wired up to timers, trying to log all the airplays. Kate's performing *Delius* on 'Dr Hook' and I can't get the tracking right! Kate's flinging a sword around, and I know I've seen that costume before – and there it was on the cover of *Raven, Swordsmistress of Chaos*!

Cup Final Saturday and I'm cautiously entering the Empire Leicester Square for the Kate Bush Club Convention. I knew no-one there, though Mandy and Dave were to meet that day, and that's where *HomeGround* starts. I joined the queue and got my copy of *Wuthering Heights* signed by Kate. I thought she'd remembered my name from the letters I had written to her. "Could you sign it to Peter?" No, it was now the Virgin Megastore and the album had them bats and doves on the cover. "Have a happy Christmas..." Kate's special sung jingle for Capital Radio. I was all set up for *December Will Be Magic Again* and then some nutter shot John Lennon. That it mattered to me at all was down to Kate.

1981 – I was meeting people. A little group was forming. I'd started writing about Kate's music, for my office magazine, for a music press competition, for the Kate Bush Club newsletter. About the time of *Sat In Your Lap* I met Mandy and shortly afterwards met Dave. There was about a dozen of us; we got together to watch and swap videos, talk Kate and go to Judie Tzuke gigs.

1982 – Dave says "Why don't we start a fanzine?" So what if I'd said no? Coincidentally, Dave's flat was less than 100 yards from Kate's new home. "We're thinking of buying it." Couldn't you do better than that? Someone at EMI told Mandhi that Kate's new single was called *The Abo Song*. So we had a story. We had hoped to involve all the group, but in the end it

Graphic: Steven Brown

was down to Dave, Mandy and me. So how the hell do you do a fanzine? How do you get it out? You think people will pay good money for this? Well they did.

'With a kiss I'd pass the key'. Just how do you get a full size poster off the wall? It takes patience, but you then get it home to soak in the bath to get all the other layers off. "Welcome back Kate!" Everyone else at the Dominion remembers the exploding dress. I remember the awful sound system and Kate's minders throwing her into the car.

Krys saw the first *HomeGround* advert in *Sounds* and wrote for a copy, sending us a book of poems she had produced. I replied and we started corresponding. We met and fell in love. What exactly was Kate doing on the Gloria Hunniford show? That day we took the Virgin Megastore to pieces, not a thing was left on the walls or anywhere else. "Could you sign it to Peter?" Park there! What? Oh my God, it's Kate!

1983 – When *The Single File* was released we were getting good at removing posters. On Kate's birthday in the tower on Glastonbury Tor, Krys and I were engaged. In November the first Wuthering Hike on a very atmospheric and foggy 5th, and our first proper gathering, the Brew-Up. The hall was double-booked, we couldn't actually make tea, but we enjoyed it, and keen to do more.

1984 – On 30th November Krys and I were married. Kate rang to offer her congratulations, and as a wedding present Dave gave us a gold disc of *Wuthering Heights*.

1985 – It's 'Wogan' and Kate is pointing that arrow dangerously in our direction. Terry Wogan is 9 feet tall and BBC hospitality food is of British Rail Standard. The final track of the album isn't called *The Morning Frog* at all. What do you mean there were invites on the door of the Laserium? Scream!!! Krys and I miss the launch of *Hounds of Love*, but Dave who gets an industry invite manages to be there.

Again Kate picks my themes, Dr. Reich and *Night of the Demon*. *The Ninth Wave* is a journey through desperation and back to love, the only constant. The first Kate Bush Club/*HomeGround* Convention in Romford on 30th November is crucial. We had celebrated the okay in the Wimpy Bar. We met and discussed with Kate in the planning stage. An early expression of Dave's organising genius, which would flower to our advantage in 1990 and 1994 and conventions to come.

1986 – Dave makes a convincing Orville Wright ("I can't fly!"), and I dance with a giraffe. We're looking at *The Big Sky* and we see Kate work at close hand. Then we are white coated scientists and dead bodies for the Sound That Could Kill. The fun and privilege of working with Kate, even in this small way.

The Video Party was a risk that did not come off, though I think most fans enjoyed it, but whether Kate did was another matter. As part of *The Whole Story* project EMI Music Publishing put together *Kate Bush Complete*, and I am asked to prepare the introduction and the other editorial text, in the fourth year of *HomeGround*, a great honour.

1987 – Tearing round the West End to find *Castaway*. *Kate Bush Complete* is published. We hear about Kate and Peter Gabriel, and we manage to be in the right place at the right time to see the gig.

1988 – On hearing *This Woman's Work* for the first time we are reduced to tears. Dave is instrumental in procuring Kate's participation in Shop Assistance on her birthday, and in making sure a large chocolate cake is laid on in Blazers. That evening we have the first convergence, playing *The Morning Fog*. On November 5th it is Wuthering Hike II.

1989 – The very first *HomeGround* Glastonbury on Kate's birthday. Listening to the new album in the car. We have a party to celebrate the release of *The Sensual World*, now pickled in the strange new medium of home video.

1990 – September brings Wuthering Hike III and in November our most precious Kate memory of all, The Hammersmith Palais Convention. A really special event with Kate, so shy and nervous before she came on, soon comfortable on the settee with her fans – her friends – and feeling secure enough to sing us a little song of gratitude.

The day after we find out how many love-hounds fit in a Triumph Acclaim. (Suspension, mate!)

1991 – A bizarre year of highs and lows. A surprise birthday party, a big freeze and a flood. Kate helps us restore what was lost. An emotional roller coaster. We see Hannah for the last time.

1992 – In May we celebrate ten years of *HomeGround* at the Wag Club. We astonish the club staff with polite behaviour and find out that bouncers are human.

1993 – Glyn is reciting, word-perfect, Monty Python's 'Four Yorkshiremen' sketch in the Fleece after Wuthering Hike IV. Moggy is nicking everyone's drinks. A blink and we are in the audience at 'Aspel' for Kate's performance of *Moments of Pleasure*. The presence of the departed was tangible. Those magnificently emotional songs, that scorching pain. Uncomfortable to hear.

No tour, to our disappointment, but a film. And there is Kate introducing it, almost embarrassed to be following *The Wrong Trousers* with her first real celluloid effort.

1994 – Suddenly another Convention is on us, and we're standing on the stage lift at the Hippodrome. *The Red Shoes* is playing at 2,000 db and the bass beat is turning over my stomach. We blink as we rise into the dry ice. Kate appears briefly. Later she asks where I am.

1995 – After six years we are back at Glastonbury. A fine Summer's day with old friends, a few moments out of time.

1996 – Dealing with disillusionment. A course in several parts. Some fans say Kate isn't living up to being a goddess (or is it that their goddess) and has let them down. Kate carries on being a human being, and to prove it, sings in Irish. Wassamatter wiv you people? Have you actually listened to *The Red Shoes*?

1997 – EMI are celebrating their 100 years with their most special recordings. Dave suggests Kate's contribution should be *Hounds of Love*, and I am to write the sleeve note. It is a great honour to celebrate Kate's great achievement, the true turning point of her career.

1998 – Suddenly it's 20 years on from Victoria Station and we are back on Glastonbury Tor, Jon is proffering me the hard stuff and Krys is collecting signatures on the card for Kate. There are Kate fans here who were not born when I pulled out that copy of *The Kick Inside*. It completely changed the direction of my life.

Reeling in the Music

HomeGround readers look back over the last 20 Years

Issue 62:
December 1998

Natalie Hall

I would like to share with you some personal memories that are linked to the special Kate songs I cherish as landmarks in my life.

Summer 78: "Who's that girl?"... I'm somewhere on the motorway in central France returning from a family holiday in Provence. *Wuthering Heights* is playing on the airwaves. The song is so fantastic my mother tries to remember the name of the artist, but in vain (French DJs mispronounced it completely!) We are both utterly seduced by the voice and melody. Back home (Beauvais at the time) I rush to the nearest record shop. When I ask for the name, I start humming the chorus! The guy at the counter looks at me (a determined nine year old!) and says, "Well, at least you know what you want!" Lucky me, the guy knew the tune! I manage to get *The Kick Inside* on tape. I'm in heaven. But I have the language problem to overcome... What is she on about ?

September 1980: Babooshka is hammering the airwaves. My choice to learn English has been determined long before I begin secondary school! Kate will remain the catalyst for the rest of my life. Kate's tour in Paris the previous year is behind me (I had nearly managed to convince my parents to take me to her show. They thought I was too young to attend that kind of stuff!) I'm looking ahead. My learning has no limits; I'm so eager that I hassle my English teachers for the lyric translations! My school chums think I'm a complete weirdo to "listen to such crazy stuff". I don't care. I want to progress fast. It has become a kind of mission. I return to my local record shop to find *Lionheart.* "Oh England..." is enchanting. Frequent visits to the Norman coast make me dream... Hey, are you really out there..?

1981: First Loss. My grandfather – who raised me – passes away. His loss is so profound that I decide to close the shell on myself. I try to find peace and solace with *Lord of the Reedy River.*

September '82: Strange times. My mother takes my brother and I to live in Provence. I end up on alien ground. My parents' separation turns sour and I'm left with a new man at the head of a strange house. Kate's music becomes my gateway. Provence opens a new chapter with *The Dreaming.* Early adolescence is painful and hard to endure. *Suspended in Gaffa* and *Night of the Swallow* cheer me up. I also meet my (now) best (second, after Kate!) female friend who's just arrived from South Africa. English-speaking Taina makes me dream. She enjoys Kate's music!

July '83: Here is the voyager... My love for English encourages my mother to send me to a school in Lionheartland! Wow! I am now staying in Hastings for a month. An old dream has come true... Fab time. This first voyage of discovery (please don't beam me up, Scotty) takes me to the Sussex coast, Brighton and magical London. I'm so happy, I don't want to go home.

1984: Year of crisis. My father (who had left home two years previously) decides to terminate his life. Although it's a case of déjà vu, I feel safe with Kate's voice whispering words of solace on my headphones. Taina is returning home to South Africa. I don't really get on with my step-father and adolescence grows even tougher.

1985: "It's in the trees..." Kate really makes a come back with *Hounds of Love.* To my delight. *Running Up That Hill* flies to the "top of the city". It feels like a re-birth to me. I am now studying at the lycée Cézanne in Aix-en-Provence. Most of my school mates, like me, are moved and impressed by the album. *Hounds of Love* and *The Big Sky* take me miles away from my troubled home life; *Cloudbusting* enriches it all. *The Ninth Wave* reduces me to tears. All the songs have such a tremendous impact that a cluster of friends defy me to get in touch with Kate. I send a clumsy letter to Abbey Road. My wish is realised a while later by the Kate Bush Club. In no time I join "my new family".

Christmas '86: Taina is back in Europe! We have a marvellous, but short, time together. *Experiment IV* is playing loud and frantically on my little stereo at my mother's. My Baccalauréat exams are looming on the horizon and Tai attempts to help me with Maths (...in vain!)

Autumn '87: I feel there's a big hole in my little life. I need to communicate with understanding souls, and send a pen-pal ad to the Kate Bush Club. Post inundates my family home. My mother is baffled by the amount! David's first letter is among the rest. We're about to experience something wonderful.

August '88: The Gathering. Our intense correspondence takes me to England for the second time. Although we cannot wait to meet, I feel sudden fear when the plane lands. Am I doing the right thing? We are daunted and shy at first, but David breaks the Ice. We spend a wonderful fortnight together in Hampshire. It is unforgettable. Kate has written a complete Symphony for us. Thank you.

Christmas '88: December will be magic again! David comes to Provence to meet my family. My step-father discovers that his preconceived ideas of the English are ridiculous. I'm relieved! David takes me to a shop to choose a ring. Alchemy! We secretly commit to one another in a café in Pertuis.

April '89: Don't Give Up. David returns to Provence to ask my mother for my hand in

marriage! I'm gonna spend an entire evening translating amazing stuff to both of them. My mind is shattered! Our official Engagement party takes place on the eve of David's return to Hampshire. Now begins my future: it will take 18 months for my mother to admit that my future lies beyond the Channel. It's painful for her and mental cruelty for us.

July 1990: The Morning Fog. My quest for freedom is ending. Our English life is starting. We are now living in Southampton, just behind my new campus. I regard my first three years there as a "renaissance": freed from painful adolescence, as I realise a childhood dream with the man I love. Kate is playing loud in our tiny studio flat to our neighbours' despair. I make friends at College. We attend our first Kate Convention in London.

April '91: The Sensual World. Hmm... One of the greatest days in our lives: we return to Provence to be solemnly wedded. Lisa very kindly replies to the invitation we had sent to Kate. My mother refuses her music to be played in the chapel! The gallic (catholic) church requires the bride and groom to write a "spouses' prayer", so we decide to quote Kate: *Running Up That Hill* is our natural choice, since the ceremony was in both languages. Our way to have Kate present in our hearts at such a crucial moment. It was so moving we could not finish our recitation.

August '93: Cloudbusting. We're on our way to cloud country! Our professional futures take us to Oxfordshire. I'm about to start my teacher training in Oxford and David is transferred to the very same area. We settle in Abingdon and explore the Vale of White Horse. It's big and beautiful.

November '93: Rubberband Girl. I'm torn between attending my graduation ceremony or the première of Kate's film in London! What a twang! I don't know what to do. David eventually convinces me to attend the former. We head to my graduation at Southampton with mixed feelings; my mind is at the Première in London.

May '94: Eat the Music. We attend our second Kate Convention at the Hippodrome. I shall never forget this wonderful event. The raffle earns me a goody bag from Del, once he finished teasing me for taking my time to reach the stage from the balcony! Seeing Kate was just fantastic.

Summer '94: Moments of Pleasure. We're enjoying our first real holiday "en amoureux" in the West Country. Dartmoor, Cornwall. Magic places. On our way to St. Agnes, the local radio plays *The Man I Love.* Incredible! We rush to Truro to get it in all available formats. This remains the song of our holiday. Merci, Kate.

Autumn '94: Walk Straight Down the Middle. On the way to my first teaching day at school, something unexpected happens. I wake up in a hospital bed on a Sunday night after losing car control. I lost 48 hours in my life. Something else strange happened: the police had to double check the story because I had told them in the intensive care unit, that I was not alone in the crash.. I'm still baffled by this. We both got a big scare and a full term was necessary to recover. This notably enabled me to reflect upon life; David, Kate and writing helped me to surmount the ordeal.

August '97: Top of the City. London here we come... Our professional services are solicited in the capital. David was too tired to keep commuting to Canning Town. We are now enjoying a much better lifestyle in the Crystal Palace area. My new position at the BRIT School of Performing Arts is already generating a crazy blend of artistic and linguistic ideas...What if...? I have yet to contact Kate about something really special.

Like many others, Kate's music has had a tremendous impact on mine and David's life. These special moments are engraved in our hearts and souls. We are grateful to everyone in Welling and at *HomeGround.* Best wishes to Kate and all in the Kate-speaking world.

Jan Millington

My sister died 29th July 1998. One week after her 50th birthday. One week after my 4th Wedding Anniversary. The 4th wedding anniversary is fruits and flowers. P. had bought me a bunch of flowers. I chose one single yellow rose and did a blue pencil drawing of a wing in a dark blue sky. And wrote in black:

All the things we should've said that we never said
All the things we should've done that we never did
All the things that you needed from me
All the things that you wanted for me
All the things I should've given but I didn't... KB

These words express so completely how I felt - feel - about my sister. We'll never have the chance to have these moments back.

Roy Mawdsley

The year was 1978 and over the sea of punk rock came a tidal wave, this wave brought a love song, not the usual boy meets girl song, but one which would change the lives of many people who heard it. This song transcends the boundary of life itself and began a love affair which was to last over twenty years, and is still going strong to this day. The song was *Wuthering Heights* the voice and talent belongs to Kate Bush. Since that fateful day many of her songs have inspired, uplifted, comforted, and most of all, brought joy to my life in a way that no music has done since the Beatles. Those of us who have seen the film *She's Having a Baby* can not fail to have been moved by the lyrics of *This Woman's Work,* or inspired by her duet with Peter Gabriel on *Don't Give Up.* To say that Kate is unique is an understatement, like all artists her influences are reflected in her work, but in a way that is truly original. Kate has had the rare privilege of not being pushed by her record company to release new material, therefore new recordings are released when Kate is ready, even if this means her fans have to be patient, a thing we have all learnt to be. Long may Kate record and here's to the next twenty years.

Graphic: Paulina Stuckey

Renaud Zago

I fell in love with Kate's music the moment I heard the very first notes of *Wuthering Heights* back in early 1978. I was 13.

It's been twenty years... how time flies. During these years there were two very special moments of pleasure. The first was the release of *The Dreaming* in September 1982. Though it seemed the album did not receive a warm welcome in the UK, here in France it was highly acclaimed. Miles away from her previous work, *The Dreaming* sounded new, experimental and so dense that you needed to play it several times before you could fully appreciate it. Kate had proved to herself and to the world her ability to write and produce songs that meant something to her without worrying about the commerciality of the work. *The Dreaming* was an essential step for what was to follow three years later.

Hounds of Love was released in September '85, around my birthday, and I could not have wished for a better present. I will be grateful to Kate for making that album until the end of my life. It is so beautiful. It is perfection, every note, every tune, every lyric. No-one, not even Kate herself could ever better that album. Even 13 years later *Houndsof Love* is considered a reference point in the music business.

A few weeks ago I played *The Red Shoes* album, but I had to switch it off. It took me five years to realise and accept that I did not like that album. The songs do not sound like Kate Bush any more, but all sound the same, with a heavy style. Only *Big Stripey Lie* stands out, where Kate's uniqueness can be recognised.

These are my personal opinions; many fans think differently. Being a fan should not force you to accept everything the artist produces. Kate is no God, but a nice human being with her strengths and weaknesses; she does not owe us anything even if we are the first to complain about the length of time between albums. It is her life and we should thank her at least for sharing part of it with us.

Sean Twomey

One of my favourite memories from the last several years was the first time I heard *Mná na hÉireann* on Irish radio.

That morning I was having breakfast when it came on. I thought it was a nice version, hadn't heard it being sung before and supposed it was Noirín ní Riain or some other classical Irish singer. The announcement afterwards that it was Kate Bush nearly made me spill my coffee. How could I have missed that? I had heard Kate was going to be doing an Irish song but didn't know until then what it was. I was grinning like a fool to myself. Kate's voice had been so strong, so determined and perfectly accurate in it's use of the Irish language. And just as beautiful as always. For me it summed up everything I had come to admire in Kate's work.

Doing the news web-site over the past year has made me all the more appreciative of Kate's work and the seemingly endless ways it inspires people.

For me, the last nine years listening to Kate's music have had a huge impact on so many areas of my life. Basically they kick-started a process whereby I could get to know who I am, get to like

myself, let my imagination run riot... breathe through the sheer oxygen of these songs. Through the pages of *HomeGround* especially there's the fact that it's happening for so many others too. They share their lives, feelings and love of good music and in doing so make tremendous use of Kate's art. Kate, whatever you decide to share with us next, I wish you health and happiness always.

Heather Butler

There is a photo I took at *The Big Sky* video shoot. I'll never forget being with her and wonder where she is under the Big Sky today, and hoping she's happy and well. If Kate never made any more magic music, what she has already done will be more than enough. I'll never stop enjoying her or loving her. Kate was with me when I was deeply in love with the wrong person (how can anyone be the wrong person if you love them?) She was with me through the birth of my son (now 17) and with me when my Dad died. And she is always within my soul.

Arnold Wallis

I have been a fan of Kate for twenty years. The first time I saw her was on 'Top of the Pops' and I remember thinking "Who is that?" *Wuthering Heights* was constantly played on the radio. When she went to No 1, everyone wanted to know more about Kate Bush. With *The Kick Inside*, I was hooked. Kate was not weird as some thought, she was ahead of her time. I saw Kate on tour in Sunderland. I will never forget that night. I first met her in Newcastle at Virgin Records, signing copies of *Never For Ever*. I told her I'd seen the show. She asked what I thought of it and I told her she was amazing.

When *The Dreaming* came out I was in the Army and would be there for the next thirteen years. The last year I just wanted out. When *The Sensual World* was released, it was a bad time for me. I was wondering where my life was going. I was alone and believed I'd never have anyone to share my life with. How wrong could I have been? Over the years, I have met many Kate fans, but there were two who wrote to me when I was in the Army. Alan and Dave, who have been fans for as long as I have. They wrote to ask if I was going to the 1990 Convention and we arranged to meet at Newcastle station and travel together. From that day my life got better and better because when I met Alan and Dave, someone else was with them. Dave said, "By the way, this is Anne. She's going to the Convention too." When I saw her I just knew there and then, that I would never let her go. She was mad about Kate too. The Convention came and went, but not Anne. We married and now have two children we named Catherine and Lisa. Had it not been for our love for Kate and her music, Anne and myself would never have met. Thanks, Kate, for being there.

Mariana McConnell

I've only listened to Kate's music for about four months now, but don't let that discredit my ability to describe what Kate means to me. I bought *Hounds of Love* at the prompting of an internet friend who was a huge Kate fan. There were cuts I liked and others that I didn't. Then, at the prompting of the same internet friend, I bought *The Kick Inside* and loved it. I mean utterly loved it. Every song was a gem and there was just so much to be drawn from it. Even as I collect the other albums, it remains my very favorite. Kate became a therapist of sorts for me during the summer. After a very difficult experience involving a boy who I had liked very much, I wore out *The Kick Inside*, listening again and again to *Oh To Be In Love*, *Saxophone Song* and *Room for the Life*. I especially listened to *Room for the Life*: "We never die for long, like it or not, we were built tough, 'cos we're woman!" It became a credo for me and I would repeat it to myself every time I felt down. Even now, as I go through junior year, I find myself singing Kate songs to match my mood. I sing *Running Up That Hill* between classes, I write the words to *Breathing* in my notebook, and write "give me these moments back" on my hand after a really great experience. Kate has become sort of omnipresent in my life. If there is anything I cherish most in the world that she has taught me, it's the confidence to be true to myself and "keep bouncing back". That's all I need to transcend the obstacles life may throw at me.

Ian Park

I was first baffled, bemused and ultimately bewitched by Kate's music, I knew there had to be other people out there who felt like I did, and were hungry to know more. So I joined the Kate Bush Club and *HomeGround*, and when my first issue of *HomeGround* landed on my doormat, little did I know where it would lead... Here they all were, headed up by the Strange Twins, creative, articulate, brave and talented – so much so that even to this day I remain intimidated by the standards most of the contributors achieve. And at the centre of it a passionate, beating heart dedicated to Kate, but also a realisation that it was okay, necessary even, to have other interests and ideas, especially when Kate was holed up doing her own thing, when frankly *HomeGround* wouldn't have filled one side of an A4 sheet if it was solely a 'Hot news about Kate' publication.

So where did that first issue take me? Well, to begin it took me to Top Withens, somewhat nervously, to discover that the editors and readers of *HomeGround* were real people who didn't bite and didn't communicate on a level that I couldn't attain. What's more, they seemed to think I was okay, so I jumped in feet first and from thereon *HomeGround* took me (and my better half Julie) to London, Rochester, Withens again, a couple of fields in Oxfordshire, back to Avebury, on to Glastonbury, through the West Country, and the Midlands and Ulverston and Bradford and even Swindon... But these are all just geographic places. Where *HomeGround* took me really was to make new and lasting lifelong friends, who opened my eyes, ears and brain to new and exciting experiences, made me laugh, made me cry, made me think, made me feel, all linked by that common and initial love of all things Kate. Stuff that money can't buy, all, paradoxically, for the price of a subscription. I hope maybe that I gave something back in return.

Kate certainly gave me more than can ever be repaid, even though my earliest memory of her on 'Top of the Pops', performing *Wuthering Heights*, I was thinking "What the hell...?" But a couple more plays and I was well and truly hooked and Julie and I drove countless miles with *The Kick Inside* as the soundtrack. I remember avidly watching the Kate TV specials around the time of *Lionheart*, especially the Christmas Special, (did a song ever soar off into the starry, clear night air like *December Will Be Magic Again*?) and kicking myself for missing the tour – actually, I think I've kicked myself every day since!

I played to death the Gambaccini radio interviews with Kate, setting me off on voyages of discovery, both visual and aural, and after listening to Kate's *Delius*, diving headlong into the compositions of the man himself, devouring Eric Fenby's remarkable book at the same time. I was already familiar with Zappa and, ahem, Eberhard Weber, but what a treat to find that Kate was on the same track!

I was lying in bed when I first heard *Sat In Your Lap* and leapt from it thinking 'Yes, yes, just what I didn't expect but should have done! Brilliant!' I never thought that *The Dreaming* was difficult or that Kate was losing it, it seemed natural – she was growing, evolving, changing, but weren't we all? And the videos were getting better all the time reflecting the maturing of both the music and Kate herself.

In the long periods of silence between albums, *HomeGround* kept me – and the rest of us – connected to the world of Kate. I remember hearing *Running Up That Hill* for the first time. Awesome. Amazingly, the album was just packed full of stuff even better than that! It took over my life for quite some time, like no other single record I can remember.

I still got that rush on hearing the title track of *The Sensual World* for the first time, and again I was moved, uplifted and inspired by the tracks on the album, and amazed at Kate's ability to give us something fresh and different each time. And I still am. I finally got to see Kate in person at the 1990 Hammersmith Convention. A real red letter day. I couldn't decide whether to breathe, or grin from ear to ear.

With the release of *The Red Shoes* – the album and the film – we were back in London for another triumphant Convention and another, more fleeting appearance from Kate. Contrary to what I later read in *HomeGround*, I don't think this was a let-down. Far from it. It was the icing on the cake, a great day, and one that will live in my memory's collection of golden days... Here's to the next twenty years.

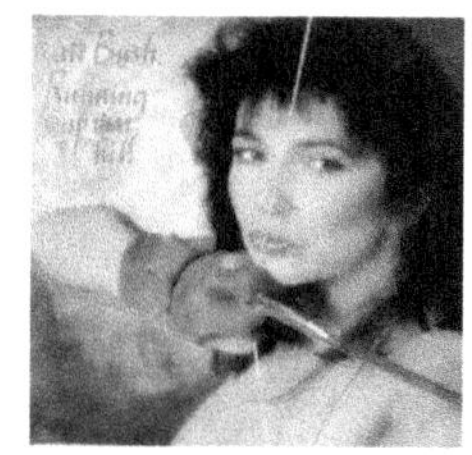

Bryan Simcott

I went to the Kate Bush Club/*HomeGround* Convention at the time of *The Sensual World*. I couldn't believe the masses of people there, and Kate sitting on the sofa talking to us and her singing at the end was amazing. At the one in 1994, I was first on stage to answer a question to win some booty. Imagine my lament when I got the answer wrong. I was so embarrassed, anyway, I was asked another. So I got my bag of precious memorabilia to take home, and the disco was fantastic. You should do it again like that, charge a bit more and pay someone to remix some more songs. Oh, and Dave was even yummier in the flesh than in the photos, but I said that before.

Doug Alan

I don't remember the first time I heard Kate Bush. All I remember is that I was a high school student at the time and Eric Idle was introducing a strange woman on 'Saturday Night Live'. Then I ran to the bathroom to pee. I remember the second time I heard Kate Bush – and the events leading up to this revelation. It was five years later and I was a college student at MIT. I was in a record store with a good friend of mine; we were on a record buying expedition. My friend handed me a record; a woman in sepia was on the cover. Her mouth was open, a gold key on her tongue. "Buy this," my friend insisted. "She's the female Peter Gabriel."

I was a big fan of Peter Gabriel's third and fourth albums, and this very same friend had also introduced me to his music, so I didn't think twice about laying down some good money on my friend's word alone. When I got home and put on the record, I didn't know what to think. This was not a pleasant sounding record at all! It was grating and bizarre. There was always too much going on at once. It was filled with a cacophony of shrieks and wails. I can't say that I liked it. But I knew from listening to Gabriel and Pink Floyd that sometimes a song would take a number of listens to grow on me, so I persevered. By the tenth time, *The Dreaming* was starting to really grow on me. By the fiftieth, I knew that it was the finest record I had ever heard or ever would.

A few months later I bought my second Kate

Bush record, *The Kick Inside*. On the cover of this record Kate looked like a country-western singer: big hair, bright red lipstick, rolled-up sleeves, blue jeans, knee-high red socks. On first listen I had trouble believing that this was the same woman who had recorded *The Dreaming*. I double-checked the record sleeve. Their names were spelled the same; they both could sing quite high. How could the same woman who had created the rhythmic and darkly disturbing visions of *The Dreaming* also have created these innocent and whimsical fantasies? I learned to never be surprised by what Kate Bush might offer us next.

The Kick Inside also took a while to grow on me, but by the time it had, I was a certified fanatic. It was only a matter of time until I was spending all of my free time on Usenet posting article after article to net.music on just what was so great about Kate Bush's music. ('net.music' was eventually renamed to 'rec.music.misc'.) Back in those days, the net was a lot cosier and, if you did little else all day, you could actually skim all the articles in every newsgroup. I managed to introduce Kate Bush into just about every conversation occurring on Usenet, and thereby became a genuine net.celebrity. I began doing a bi-weekly radio show on WMBR, MIT's college radio station, and of course I played plenty of Kate Bush.

After a year or two of heavy proselytizing on Usenet, a number of Usenet participants began to get very annoyed at my evangelistic antics and I was pressured into starting an email mailing list for fellow KT fans. This way the less enlightened could have a break from my rantings. On August 16, 1985, I created the Love-Hounds mailing list. The name "Love-Hounds" was intended to be a pun on the name of Kate's upcoming album and on the term "autograph hounds". I created Love-Hounds not as a discussion forum just for talk about Kate Bush, but for all interesting music and art, where any amount of Kate Bush discussion would be tolerated – and a forum from which I could not get evicted. In its beginning, Love-Hounds became the net's premier discussion forum for avant-garde and underground music in general, but as the net grew, the bulk of this discussion moved elsewhere, leaving Love-Hounds mostly for Kate fanatics such as myself. During the first few months of Love-Hound's existence, I would periodically call up EMI-America for news, and tell them how Love-Hounds was going. Somehow from this, I managed to land an interview with Kate herself!

Perhaps the greatest curse you can inflict on someone is for them to meet their idol. For thirty minutes I made a complete quivering fool of myself in front of mine, and then was insane enough to broadcast the result on WMBR and post a transcription to Usenet. These days, I'll pay good money to someone who can prove they've destroyed the last remaining copies. I did not learn from my mistake and made a fool of myself again several years later when I met Peter Gabriel. But that's another story.

Since then, the years have whizzed by, with two more wonderful albums from Kate. In that time Love-Hounds obtained its very own Usenet newsgroup, 'rec.music.gaffa'. (The Usenet administrators disallowed the name 'rec.music.love-hounds' because it sounded too kinky to them.) After five years of running Love-Hounds I transferred the reins to Bill Wisner, who has now overseen it for longer than I did.

It's a good thing I keep myself very busy these days. I don't have the spare time to obsess over when the next album will come out. I recall the two year wait between my introduction to *The Dreaming* and the release of *Hounds of Love*. This wait was torturous, even though I had three other Kate Bush albums and numerous B-sides to discover in this two-year interval. These days, a mere two year wait would seem like a gift from God. Here's hoping we see more than one album from Kate this decade.

Lindsay Purssord

In early 1978, aged 10, I was sitting on my bedroom floor drawing and listening to Radio One. The feature '5 45s at 5.45' was on, where new singles were given an airing. My Mum was calling me to help get tea, when *Wuthering Heights* came on. I was completely transfixed. I could do nothing but listen to this incredible voice – I hated it – but the moment is etched in my mind forever! The second time I heard it, I fell in love with it and it was the first single I ever bought. I've collected the albums as they've been released over the years and, at 31, I am still a massive fan. Kate's music has been with me through good times and bad and I have always found something relevant to my life and experiences in her songs.

Len Bullard

My memories of Kate start with a Friday night when my best friend asked me to come to his house and see the 'Nightflight' show which was featuring a British artist of whom I had only heard scant mention. At the time, I wasn't a big fan of the overdone, geeky and caustic artists of MTV and having just released our band's first independent album, was bone tired. I was becoming resigned to the facts of the music business where an artist or band is a commodity to be packaged, merchandised and discarded. It seemed there was no place for my music; I was out of time, out of place, and out of ideas. It was time to quit.

Being an experimental type, I was drawn to what I saw that night. It was hard to reconcile the woman in the business suit to the performer being pulled by mud-covered dancers in the aboriginal setting. It peaked my curiosity, but did not really interest me as it appeared, stuffy and overwrought. I turned on the 'Max Headroom show' one Saturday morning, and there sat the same little Brit except she was holding her own in a way that was enticing. There was something leonine, ferocious in her answers as she batted away the salacious line of questioning. Also, more facts about her independent means of production came across and at the very least, I had to admire a woman who could do that.

I realized just how out of touch with the times I was. Being the research oriented type, I decided to go down to the store and find something current to feed the noggin. While sorting through the videos, I came across a collection called *The Whole Story*. Intuition and serendipity have always been more dependable than the best laid plan or the best planned... oh, nevermind. I wanted to see what the ruckus was about, so I plunked down the thirty bucks, took the video home and put it on. Two days later, I was still sitting there. I was a goner. Blown. Fried. No longer master. Not even a worthy acolyte. I was toast.

What I saw as each video rolled by, was that not only had this small woman surpassed my skills, she had surpassed anyone I knew about. The artists I had seen on MTV simply couldn't approach the depth of this woman's work. Mind you, like most Americans, I was clueless about Kate Bush other than the few snippets on TV told me. It took another four years of asking, digging, and inveigling any Brit I met to find any facts. Finally, a lady who ran a local T-shirt shop gave me the first solid lead. She had worked in the record industry and had met Kate one rainy day in London. She told me to write to EMI. I did and months later a letter arrived from Lisa Bradley. Inside was my original letter, pretty much destroyed by the wear of the mail system. Somehow, it had made its way to her and she sent details on joining the Kate Bush Club. I mailed my fee and a copy of our first album. Some weeks later, I received a reply with my card, a newsletter, and a note saying she would listen to my album but that Kate had gotten to it first.

HomeGround first appeared for me when a lady at work brought a copy she had found at a local record shop. We both devoured it, and I wrote to you. That was the beginning of my disembodied friendship with you. Some years later, I found the LoveHounds list while doing hypermedia research for my employers. That's when I discovered that her fans are mad. Know anyone in love who isn't?

Today we'll master our third album. They say Kate is slow, well, we are slower. It takes time. This album will have one song written for Kate on it. The lyrics sum up my fascination with this woman who though I have never and may never meet, continues to be my teacher, my inspiration, and in some unreal yet comforting way, my friend. I know now that was what I needed desperately, and found in her work. I needed to know that somewhere regardless of opinions, rumours, market, or the oh-so-clever among us, a brave, brilliant soul pushes the boundaries of expression. Some need a divine being in their lives to make it magical. I believe that kind of worship misses the point. It is the human heart that makes real magic. Kate taught me that. Love reaches across the universe and touches at a distance. Her work touches me in a way I can't put into words, makes me warm, makes me feel... unafraid. If that is divine, then my offering is my song. As she taught me.

Gavin Gribbon

In the late '70s, my Mum's cousin, who was ten years older than me, went to a party in South East London. Whilst there he chatted briefly to a young woman who had just released a record on EMI. He was something of a punk rocker at the time and he told me years later her thought her a bit "weird". A few years later I went to his flat where a copy of the same woman's fourth LP, *The Dreaming*, sat next to his record player. He told me she had just crept up on him. Sometime later I was playing my Mum's old singles. One of these was *Man with the Child in his Eyes*... I'd heard Kate's songs many times before but this was the moment she crept up on *me*. As the music came from the speakers, I remember a mixture of emotions but paramount was awe. I was suddenly aware of a quality rare in pop music, a pure, caressing beauty that brought tears to my eyes.

Graphic: Paulina Stuckey

This was perhaps one of the most special moments of the last 30 years for all of us.

That's the thing with Kate; her music sits purring like a cat, waiting for you until you're ready and then she creeps in and claims you.

Over the years, Kate and I have had our moments. I think how she can bring unadulterated joy, as in *The Big Sky*; show such primal force on *Jig of Life*, and fragility on *The Morning Fog*. All on one album. When I first heard *The Sensual World* – and every subsequent time – I had to fan the back of my neck. Her murmurs and sighs, the raw heat of the song almost too delicious, but knowing just how far she can take the music, and as the song ends with that last "Yes" I have to lie down.

Kate bares her emotions and we can see our reflection in them. I think of *Moments of Pleasure* where she skilfully tells us of her own life, before pulling us in with that empathetic chorus, and we place our own moments next to them. Few artists have this gift, this beauty and humanity.

If I could pick one moment that told me so much about Kate, it would be the 1990 Convention, where she sat on the sofa taking questions from the audience. Someone asked "How do you feel knowing that whatever you do, we will all love and support you?" The question caused a spontaneous, heartfelt reaction from everyone. If you were there you will know the expression on Kate's face at that moment could tell you all you need to know about her and how special she is. To Kate, with much love.

Sean Brennan

A few years ago I wrote to *HomeGround* about my discovery of Kate and her music. Our paths were totally separate yet throughout these twenty years, Kate's songs align with experiences in my life with an uncanny resemblance. *Ran Tan Waltz* covers my marriage. *Not This Time*, a message to my ex-wife. The first six lines of *In Search of Peter Pan* reminds me of the bullying I accepted at school in the early '70s because of my Irish background. The same six lines went through my mind as I sat in court fighting for custody of my children in 1991. Kate's obvious beauty and brilliant song writing are pleasures to behold, her songs are so unique. Through Kate I have met some wonderful human beings and between the three of them I truly believe the lives of my children and I would be very different without them. Kate is the greatest female songwriter of the 20th Century. I consider myself very lucky to be part of the Kate-speaking world.

Antonello Saeli

I do not think I will ever be able to find the right words to say how much Kate's music is part of my life. It is difficult to find words, especially in a language that is not my own, to express deep emotions. Kate's art still gives me so much after so many years. I was just 15 when Kate arrived in 1978, and she is still there, deep in my heart, after twenty years. So many things have happened since then, so many things have changed, but my love for her music is still the same southerly wind that makes bells sound, so joyful and happy. I think Kate has always had the gift of making people happy with the sounds she creates through musical instruments, and the most heavenly of all – her voice. If Jesus had a smile that healed, Kate certainly has her voice for the same purpose.

I still play her albums whenever I feel the need to hold communion with myself. Her music has always helped me find the right way out of certain situations. She has felt like a close friend over the years, though we have never met. I have learned a lot through her lyrics and have also learned what I know of the English language. I am now a teacher of English and much of my success finds its roots in my love for Kate and her music.

When I took my degree in modern languages in 1987 I knew that I had to dedicate my work to Kate and Lindsay Kemp because they both had such a big influence on my decisions at the time. I met Lindsay in Rome in 1988. I gave him a copy of my thesis (I also sent Kate a copy) and he was just wonderful. I will never forget that evening at the theatre, waiting with him in his dressing room for his show to begin, and feeling like a baby who can only show what is inside through eyes and smiles, since he can't voice emotions. I hope to meet Kate one day, and feel the same sensation of a million butterflies in my stomach.

I am sure many fans will see themselves reflected in my words. This is what Kate's art is about, helping people find within the things they may have thought were lost forever. May Kate's creative soul always be a light in the dark hours of everyone's life.

Jonathan Dean

As I approach the big 3-0 this week, I've been remembering when I first heard Kate. *Wuthering Heights* came out when I was 9 years old, and I listened to it every Sunday on the radio Top 40, and watched her on 'Top of the Pops'. I thought it was ace. I remember my brother buying Lionheart on cassette and blasting it out. I thought it was fantastic. When I started working I bought a CD player and the first CD I bought was *The Kick Inside*. God, it was mind blowing. Since then I've grown up with Kate and her music and I would like to thank her for giving us her music which has brought so much pleasure. I would like to wish Kate well and hope the new album is going fine.

The Sound of My Soul The Sound of You

Jeanette Payne

If I cut open my heart
at this moment,
what would I find?
With the first tender incision
the butterfly of my soul
would erupt
from the wet, pulsing throb.
Its bloodied, sodden wings beating
slap-clapping
shedding redded tear drops of joy;
a thousand heartfelt rubies
dancing to the ground.
And then
the sound.

A secret whisper at first.
I strain to hear
hushed honey tones
as the butterfly, my soul
slip-slides
Tinkerbelling in impish delight
light, lighter
rising, euphoric
before my eyes.
Whisper loudens to echo,
echo to beckoning
a siren calling
sonic sublime
as all the songs you ever sang
merge in a glorious cacophony
for they
are the very essence of my soul.

PAULINA STUCKEY
1990

You're the One

A Consultation by Robert Mills

Issue 55: April 1995

"I don't really know why I'm here."

"Really? Most people come to me because they need to talk. To share a problem... Do you have a problem?"

"Don't we all?"

"I mean, something you want to talk about? (silence) Tell me."

"I..." (falters)

"What? You don't have to be afraid. Nothing you say will ever leave this room. That's my promise to you."

(deep breath) "I suppose... I suppose I feel lonely..." (falters)

"Go on."

"I'm trying!"

"You can get angry. It's alright to get angry. I understand."

"I... miss her! My wife. I loved her, you see, even at the end, when it was all... broken. Even then, I still loved her. (silence) I left her. I had to leave her. It was just impossible to stay."

"Tell me about her."

"She was... (stops) Listen to me, she 'was'. I'm talking as if she's dead."

"Is that what you feel? Bereaved?"

"I don't know what I feel. Not anymore. There was so much love and then... so much hate. What can you feel after that?"

"Go back a bit. Go back to the love. Tell me about that."

"Her name was – is – Angie. I met her at university. God, she was beautiful. I remember the first time I saw her. It was in the college bar, first night of Fresher's Week. I was sitting there with some new friends, you know how it is. Everyone's so friendly because they're scared that they'll end up lonely, so they all put on a big act and push themselves out so they're larger than life and looking acceptable and not shy and boring. You know? I saw someone, a girl I'd met earlier that day... funny, I don't remember her name... well. I saw her standing there with a group of other girls, so I thought I'd go over and introduce myself."

"And that's when you met Angie?"

"Yes. She was standing there. Talking. This 'girlfriend' sort of introduced me to her, and she smiled at me. What a smile. It was lovely, like milk and sunlight. I suppose I fell in love with that smile first of all. (laughs nervously) Oh, I can remember everything she was wearing, you know. This black silky lacy top with fine green swirls on it, and a skirt the same. And she had a tiny belt on. Her waist was so slender. We ended up on our own, talking somewhere or other. She was really wonderful."

"What happened?"

"Nothing happened. We became good friends. We saw a lot of each other. We used to go out for drinks, talk, watch videos. It was fun. But, you see, she was with someone else... I went home for Christmas at the end of the term, and she did the same. It was the second term that it happened. Angie came to see me three days after the new term started. She was furious that I'd already been back for three whole days without getting in touch. But she was like that. Obsessive. It turned out that she was upset. She and her boyfriend had split up. I suppose now that she wanted someone to talk to. I just didn't think... (silence) Well, we carried on much the same as before. But now there was a difference. She'd told me her secrets, you see... her fears and her needs. I felt so much closer to her. I felt that she wanted me to share her secrets."

"And did you?"

"Yes. It happened one night. She came to find me. I was in the bar – or somewhere – with my friends. She said she wanted to talk. I just dropped everything. God, it was so irrational, and so rude. I left with her without even saying goodbye to my friends. We went back to my room and I played her my favourite records. Kate Bush stuff mostly. It was important to me. You see, I'd grown up listening to Kate. She was... God, I'm doing that again... She was and still is a very big influence on my entire consciousness. You see, I had a very difficult youth really. I suppose it was hormones and all that, but... I used to hate life. My parents were both quite old. All I could see was their age. (laughs) My favourite book was Hamlet. I was like that in a way... all I could see was decay and death. I used to spend hours alone in my room, with the heavy curtains drawn so it was all in shadow, and I would listen to Kate Bush. Oh God, the times she kept me sane, it's unbelievable. (laughs) Strange really, I mean, some people think she's weird or something. But she isn't. Her voice is like... like a Siren, you know, a Greek temptress, but she calls me back from the rocks. She lures me back towards life. All those dark hours that I spent, just listening to her voice, I was like an instrument, as if I'd been made just to listen to her songs. I'd write poems about her, think about her voice all the time. My emotions seemed hers, like they were connected across space by music... (falters) I suppose I must sound mad to you."

"No. It's not uncommon, you know. Empathy."

"So you see, it was important to me that Angie liked Kate. I... felt as if her music was the audible part of my soul, the exposed bits, the vulnerability."

"Did Angie like it, the music?"

Graphic opposite: Paulina Stuckey

"Nothing. There was nothing to do. Angie grew more and more distant every day. She started to resent me even being in the house. She was obsessed with Catherine now. I just didn't feature in her plans. In the end... in the end she asked me to move out."

"Did you?"

"Yes. I was going mad. I couldn't understand what was going on. It wasn't as if I was unsympathetic, or insensitive to her. I... I loved her. But she didn't love me in return. I don't think she ever really did... I don't know. Maybe my whole mind is poisoned. I left. Divorce. But that was nearly a year ago now."

"And you're still lonely? What makes you feel lonely?"

"There's this song, by... well, guess who? Kate. It was on her last album. It was called *You're the One.*"

"I know it."

"It just reminds me of it all. That song tears me apart. It's as if my emotions became Kate's while she made it, the way they used to, and my soul and her music used to dance together in the dark. But this is different. This is my pain... it's my pain she's singing. When you're alone at night and you can't sleep, you can think some funny things. I do. I forget all the hate that came after. All I can remember is the love we once had. And for those few minutes, while that damned song is playing, I want Angie. I'm lonely, because I miss her... and I miss my daughter... and I miss... I miss what I was... I've changed..."

"It's alright. You can cry. Remember, nothing you say will ever leave this room. That's my promise."

"But you're..."

"Yes?"

"You're going to sing that song again, aren't you?"

"Yes. I have to. We're getting to the end again."

"Please... don't."

"You only have to press the button to stop me."

"You know that I can't."

"Yes, I know."

"Everything I've ever done, I did it with you."

"You don't have to tell me. I know everything now..."

"I miss her, Kate..."

"Hush, now. Listen."

"Yes, she did. Very much."

"What happened then?"

"We talked. We got close... we made love...(falters)"

"(softly) It's still painful, isn't it?"

(Silence) "Yes, it is..."

"You're safe here, you know that."

"Well, our love grew, slowly and steadily. We got married. God, Angie looked so beautiful on our wedding day, all in white and surrounded with purple flowers. Then we had a baby, a daughter. I called her Catherine, (laughs) no guesses who after. But, things just started to deteriorate after that. I don't know why. Angie just couldn't stand me anywhere near her. It was a big shock. You see, she'd always been so obsessive about me, always hugging, touching and kissing. It was wonderful. I never felt afraid of feeling weak, because I knew that she'd be there with a warm hug to cheer me up and calm me down. But then, nothing. It got to the point where she wouldn't let me sleep in our bed. I had to sleep in the spare room."

"How long did that go on?"

"Over a year. I was so miserable. I was alone again. Back in the small dark room again. Back with all the old emotions again. But no Kate this time. No good Siren to call me back."

"Why?"

"I'd got no stereo in there for one thing, and with the baby I just couldn't afford one. I didn't have the heart for Kate. I was at a pretty low ebb."

"What did you do?"

Graphic: Paulina Stuckey

Songs of Love Sex and Death

Krys imagines a Kate album of folk songs

1: An Introduction to Folk Music

"For me Bob Dylan and the Incredible String Band started it all by bringing mystery and poetry back into music, and then the Beatles made it popular. But when you chase their tunes you come to the same treasure trove, British Traditional Music that lovingly lets its perfect melodies be mined without asking for the royalties."
John Carder Bush, *Cathy*, 1986.

"We know him as Bert Lloyd. And he is still one of my favourite singers. He's got the most remarkable voice. When he sings it's like he's telling you a dirty joke, 'cos there's this really wicked glint in his voice, it's almost like you can see his eyes."
Kate, Paul Gambaccini interview, 1980.

"The ideal way to sing an English folk song, of course, is unaccompanied. Our melodies were made to be sung that way, and much of their tonal beauty and delightful suppleness comes from the fact that they have been traditionally free from harmonic or rhythmic accompaniment. They are best suited to stand on their own, and we rather agree with the Dorset countryman who commented on a professional singer of folk songs: 'Of course, it's nice for him to have the piano when he's singing, but it does make it very awkward for the listener.'"
Bert Lloyd and Ralph Vaughan-Williams, *The Penguin Book of English Folk Songs,* 1959

Traditional folk influences weave their way throughout Kate's work: her cover of *The Handsome Cabin Boy*, *Night of the Swallow*, *Jig of Life*, *My Lagan Love*, *The Sensual World* and *The Red Shoes*. Since *The Dreaming,* Kate has worked with folk musicians like Donnal Lunny and Liam O'Flynn (from Planxty), John Sheahan (from The Chieftains), Davy Spillane, Sean Keane, Alan Stivell and Bill Whelan.

For a long, long time I have thought it would be an interesting and imaginative project for Kate to record an album of traditional and contemporary Folk songs. Folk music records the people's history in their own tongues and was carried by word of mouth when writing was not a skill most people were taught. It was their music, about their lives. It is our music too. Many songs are far from romantic, recording the hardships suffered by our ancestors; the wars, the injustices, and the fight for survival, and how that was inextricably tied to the land. If the crops failed, they starved. Folk has its roots in sex and fertility of man and land, the two inseparable for the survival of the species. Life was celebrated in song, from the Winter wassailing of the Somerset apple trees to ensure their sacred fruit; the May Day ceremonies of fertility, the Green Man and the Sun, to the courting of young ladies and the winning of many a maidenhead. There is much humorous innuendo and phallic symbolism. Folk is the earthiest music. It knows no bounds, with tales of sex, death, murder, incest, unusual characters and strange happenings. The songs are bawdy, jolly, moody, melancholy, erotic, and some are downright bloody miserable!

I was astounded as to how much written material there has been on the subject, all of which is out of print. The Vaughan Williams Library at Cecil Sharp House, the headquarters of the English Folk Dance and Song Society, where I went to research this article, houses an excellent collection of song books and texts related to folk song and dance, history, magic and folklore worldwide. All those wonderful old books there at my hands, I was like a child in a sweet shop. To do the subject justice would take far more pages than these, and years of work and research. This is a fleeting dash through, which I hope you will enjoy.

Folk music lived originally in the oral tradition, it was heard and learned that way. The songs belonged to the people as a community and were created by individuals, then re-created as they passed down the generations. The tune and the words were often composed from different sources. The songs were functional and varied in format, comprising of ballads; epics (long narrative songs); short narratives; love songs; songs about disasters, and broadside ballads (early printed sheets, sung and sold in the market place as a method of delivering information and news). They were a major, and sometimes only, way of passing the stories, warnings, and ways of life, down the generations. Many are historical documents. Many served as songs of labour and toil, whilst others were ceremonial in character, associated with the cycle of nature and man. The ritualistic element of folk music is very important, with songs to celebrate the old festivals of May Day, Midsummer, Harvest, Yuletide, Twelfth Night, not to mention the regional celebrations of local saints days, which were stolen by the Christian calendar. So many of those songs are rich in language, characters and tell fascinating stories, sometimes sombre, frightening, funny, but more often than not about sex, death and murder. How many contemporary songs really tell a good story? Older folk songs in particular are in dialogue format, almost like a play, between two, three or more characters. Some songs mix dialogue with narrative, typical of the Western folk tradition.

English folk music is thought to consist of about forty 'tune families', each of which

Issue 55: April 1995

We are glad to record that since the turn of the millennium, many of these texts are now back in print, and in particular the 1959 *Penguin Book of Folk Songs* is now available from Penguin as *English Folk Songs*.

Cecil Sharp

Bert Lloyd

descends from one single song. The majority of songs belong to only seven of the forty families. The music itself is different from other music forms. The sound of pipes, strings, singing bowls, or human voice permeating us physically, mentally, emotionally and spiritually. In his introduction to *The Penguin Book of English Folk Songs*, Bert Lloyd pointed out: "It is well known that the scales on which many of our folk tunes are based are not the same as the major and minor with which we are most familiar. Some of these scales belong to the family of what are loosely called 'Greek' modes, some are considered as gapped scales because certain steps are consistently missing, while a few show peculiar structures which the scholars have hardly begun to classify as yet."

Percy Grainger

The Industrial Revolution was probably even more responsible for the demise of folk music than the church, (which during its expansion in mediaeval times had suppressed folk music because of its Pagan associations, but the sounds were actually incorporated into mediaeval liturgical music). With industrialisation, life for most people changed dramatically. Many moved out of their villages and into towns and factories, and so the songs changed to reflect what was happening. Songs of working the land gave way to songs of the factory, mine and mill workers, and the hardships of such work, and shanties of the seas as shipbuilding (brought about by the greater need for trade and fishing), became a larger enterprise. Those who remained in rural places saw the mechanisation of work on the land, and this too was reflected in the songs. Everything changed. With emigration to find work in America, Australia and New Zealand, the British took their music with them. So, it was in the rural villages in Britain and abroad where the songs and traditions survived, through the oral tradition.

Ralph Vaughan-Williams

Bert Lloyd illustrated in his introduction to the Penguin Book: "Folk songs are tough and show an obstinate will to survive... It is a curious but welcome phenomenon, this revival of folk music as city music. It seems that many taking part in that revival have come to appreciate British balladry through their interest in jazz. A search for the roots of jazz leads to American folk song, and a search for the origins of American folk song leads the astonished enthusiast back home to his own traditional music."

What became known as the British folk revival began in the 1950s, and really kicked in during the '60s. It is said that the revival of traditional folk music was a reaction against the massive surge of rock'n'roll from America in the '50s. Music had changed and how; people had been through the traumas of the Second World War, which had an knock-on effect in all aspects of life, including music. Perhaps more than ever people needed to return to their roots. Bob Dylan was considered a leading figure in bringing folk to public attention and giving it street credibility amongst young people. To a degree folk and popular music began to merge. But the revival goes further back than Dylan.

There were several people who travelled the world gathering folk songs and writing them down, straight from the ordinary person, who was not necessarily a 'singer'. Prior to this they had been passed on vocally. The principal collectors were Cecil Sharp and A.L. (Bert) Lloyd with the assistance of the composers Vaughan Williams, Percy Grainger, and John Moeran. The American Francis Child compiled an extensive, and probably definitive, collection of English and Scottish 'Popular Ballads', comprising of 305 songs in five volumes, which spanned a period of 700 years.

Cecil Sharp worked and travelled in Australia, America and Britain, collecting folk songs and dance tunes. The first song he collected was *The Seeds of Love*, from his gardener. He enthusiastically collected a vast wealth of songs and material between 1903 and his death in 1924. He wanted to encourage people to practise the folk traditions again and promoted them through his writings and by founding the English Folk Dance Society in 1911, which later become the English Folk Dance and Song Society.

The Australian born composer Percy Grainger (d. 1961), studied music in Melbourne. Under the influence of his friend, Edvard Grieg, he began collecting and notating English folk songs. He considered the performance of folk songs as vital to the continuance of traditional music. He was in favour of the developments and changes of the songs as they passed from one singer to another and alone insisted on collecting the variations, however small, of melodies. He also favoured the use of recording equipment as the basic collecting tool, the written method only as a support. Grainger distrusted the written method of certain collectors, believing some of their work to be dishonest, and threatened to expose this. He left the collectors to pursue other musical areas.

Bert Lloyd (d. 1982) is held as one of the principal people in the folk revival. At the age of sixteen, his father arranged with the British Legion for him to be sent to Australia as an assisted migrant. He worked at several farms and sheep stations, and there he learned Australian sheep shearing and labouring songs from the drovers who passed through. Isolated and bored by this solitary life, with only thousands of sheep for company, he craved information about classical and contemporary art, music and literature, borrowed books from the post library and studied in his spare time. It was during the nine years he spent in Australia that Lloyd began collecting folk songs. He returned to England in 1935 with a collection of five hundred songs, determined to study folk music in greater depth, and at the same time became involved with the

Communist Party. He spent considerable time studying folk music in the Reading Room of the British Museum. In 1937 he signed on with a whaling company and for six months sailed the seas, where he experienced the blood and guts of that existence, to which he vowed never to return, though he did actually enjoy his time on the seas and collected some whaling songs.

From his own experiences of unemployment and those he witnessed around him, he was acutely aware, first hand, of social issues and the hardships being endured. This was reflected by *The Voice of the Seaman*, a radio programme he scripted with working class people telling it like it is, of womanising and drinking and the injustices inflicted by the large shipping companies. The BBC gave him a six months contract and an office in Broadcasting House, where he worked for eighteen months on several programmes, including *Shadow of the Swastika*, a documentary on Hitler's rise to power, to which three quarters of the British population tuned-in. His denunciation of Hitler labelled him as anti-Fascist by certain members of the BBC hierarchy and his contract was not renewed. During the '40s he wrote *The Singing Englishman*, the first book on folk songs since Cecil Sharp's publication in 1909. In 1948 he joined the EFDSS and won that year's solo singer award in the Folk Music Festival Competition.

His strong sympathies also lay with the miners, and an anthology of mining ballads in their support was published in 1952. Lloyd met fellow sympathiser, Ewan MacColl in the early 1950s. They shared the view that British folk music was the antidote to the rock'n'roll explosion that had come in from America. With the support of the Worker's Music Association and the Co-operative Movement, they began the folk revival through their writing, recording, radio and club performances and set up folk clubs. Lloyd was made Artistic Director of the folk oriented Topic Records, where he encouraged the younger generation of both traditional revivalists and the emerging electric folk bands, like Steeleye Span and Fairport Convention.

In 1959 he compiled the *Penguin Book of English Folk Songs* with notation provided by Vaughan Williams, a publication of great importance in the folk revival. Together they collated the different versions of songs from oral sources and printed broadsides, taking great care to preserve the true essence of what their informants were really singing. Lloyd says they did not "hesitate to include words, verses, or whole texts which earlier collectors prudishly modified or omitted as being objectionable". He added "The old habit of cleaning-up or even entirely re-writing the texts led to the false supposition that folk songs are always 'quite nice'. The folk singer has no objection to plain speech. He is likely to be forthright in his treatment of the pleasures and pains of love."

Lloyd recorded many songs he had collected including *The Handsome Cabin Boy*, *Sovay* (the inspiration behind *Babooshka*), and *Blood Red Roses.* Many of these have now appeared on CD. Many established folk singers, such as Martin Carthy and Shirley Collins learned in person, and recorded, songs from Bert Lloyd. For others he was their first real taste of traditional folk music. Kate said of his track, *Do-Me-Am-A-Ding*, which she chose for the Gambaccini Radio 1 programme: "It's really beautiful, and it's one of the first songs that I ever learned to sing."

The Copper Family

During the '70s Lloyd lectured and recorded worldwide, whilst in Britain remained involved with the continuing folk revival and taught ethnomusicology at Goldsmith's College in London. He died in 1982 leaving behind a remarkable and great legacy, and is probably the most important figure in the whole of the British folk music revival, and always held the song as far more important than the singer.

Song collecting still goes on; the Sussex based Copper family, The Watersons, and Martin Carthy are probably the folklorists of today, and carry on the preservation of the British Folk song tradition. Technology has been a godsend in that songs can now be recorded, not lost. There has been over recent years the vigorous emergence of a new generation of folk singers, like Eliza Carthy and Nancy Kerr, Cordelia's Dad, and Dervish. And so the tradition thrives. with new voices weaving old songs.

The Watersons

Since the end of the 19th Century folk music has been collected and preserved through recording techniques, a major step in the folk revival. The preservation through recording has, I feel, travelled almost full circle; it began in the oral tradition, many songs were lost and later collected, (though as we have seen there have been doubts as to how authentic some songs are and how many had been tampered with by certain collectors), and through recordings and performances since the '50s has returned to that oral tradition. People are once again learning the songs by *hearing* them and more often than not the lyrics are never included with the albums. Perhaps that is also intentional. Songs are also passed on by the singers who perform in the clubs.

There seem to be more folk song and dance festivals than ever before (and in the mainstream music festivals each summer more and more folk music is being included). The May Day festival has in recent years been revived with celebrations on a large scale in some parts of the country. There must be a connection in the revival of folk traditions and re-establishment of the old festivals. The Rochester Sweeps Festival is a very fine example of such a revival. Morris sides from all over the country participate in this four day celebration of the first day of Summer, with traditional music and dance, and everywhere the jangle of bells from hundreds of bedecked legs,

Martin Carthy

Eliza Carthy

Nancy Kerr

Gary & Vera Aspey

and cherry blossom falls all about us like confetti. On the last day the Green Man, escorted by our good friends the Motley Morris, leads the procession of all the Morris teams through Rochester. My favourite day in the whole year. That to me is the true spirit of the folk tradition; it is something you feel, rather than rationalise, and that spirit is very much alive.

Sadly, this country is very poor in the upkeep of its folk culture. There is virtually no television time allocated to folk, unlike most other countries. There is also a shameful lack of books still in print on the subject, the only one I have found being *The Guinness Who's Who of Folk Music.* The rest are out of print and most can only be found at the library of The English Folk Dance and Song Society. What other country would treat its musical folk heritage in such a pitiful way? Or perhaps it isn't as apathetic as it initially appears, and there is in fact no real need for the songs to be transmitted in the written form, because of their availability as recordings. I feel there is a need for the song books, so they can also be appreciated for their poetry on the page.

2: Kate's Folk Background

Kate's folk roots are probably much deeper than those of your average person. She was brought up with folk music played in the home by her brothers. It must have been an inspiring childhood. She also had the influences of her brothers' musical tastes, which offered I would think a fairly broad scope. John Carder Bush writes in his book *Cathy*: "We went to many places to find the music, and mainly dance music where the wicked rhythms and the lamprey tunes of a clearer time were found."

Folk eases the soul and balances all those things that the chaos of modern life shifts into disarray. It is the music of our ancestors and we should not forget this vital part of our heritage. Our roots are here, and very much alive. For a while Folk became overlooked because of the other forms of music which had emerged since the 1930s, jazz and blues, and of course rock'n'roll. But it is a different story these days. rock musicians and artists give credence to folk by including folk musicians in their work, or playing and singing it themselves, bringing it all home. Kate has done her bit too.

To me, a project such as a folk album opens up a whole world for the imagination, where anything is possible. The confines of Kate having to write her own material are gone and all the headaches and pressures that go with that. The songs are already there, already written and lived through, many of them hundreds of years old. There is so much scope. Just imagine what she could do, how she could add her own magic touch to songs and stories that are already magical. I should imagine that Kate might be discouraged from doing any such project for that precise reason, perhaps thinking that she could not better the songs left before. Folk songs have been added to along their journeys, some have changed, tunes have become intermingled sometimes along the way. Kate could contribute to their on-going journey. Such a project may be refreshing for her too, and could be an inspiring starting point for her own writing and composing.

There must be many songs that Kate knows and loves that she would choose to record. These are just some suggestions I feel would be interesting and suitable for Kate's voice.

3: Side A

Here follows Side A of *Songs of Love, Murder, Sex and Bald Women.*

The Jolly Beggar would be an exciting start. A lively, typically earthy Irish Folk song about a beggar who is given shelter by a farmer. Planxty recorded the version I know:

> "*The farmer's daughter she got up*
> *To bolt the kitchen door*
> *And there she saw the beggar*
> *Standing naked on the floor....*"

Bushes and Briars is a haunting, traditional English Folk song. There's a pleasant version in Schlesinger's film of the Hardy novel, *Far From The Madding Crowd.* Eliza Carthy (Martin Carthy's daughter) and Nancy Kerr have recorded a similar version on their recent album. The tune reminds me of *The Sprig of Thyme* (mourning the loss of virginity). Harmonies, drone (voices) and flute could be used with great effect.

Aggie Bell, written by Graham Cooper; the version I know and love is by Vera Aspey, on her album *The Blackbird,* 1977. Vera together with her husband Gary, leaned mostly towards the Folk tradition of Lancashire, and reflected the hardships of the miners and poverty of the working class. Vera also covered many traditional songs. *Aggie Bell* is a bittersweet, modern folk song about a lonely prostitute who teaches young men the ways of love. To me it evokes the atmosphere of D.H. Lawrence's *Sons and Lovers*:

> "*Aggie Bell, she does it well*
> *Or so I've heard from various friends of mine,*
> *It seems that she is nothing much to see*
> *But always there's a promise of good time*
> *with Aggie Bell*
> *Who doesn't tease, she's happy just to please,*
> *And never ever threatens with a pram...*"

For humour, and a slightly different direction, I would add something by another long time hero of mine, Jake Thackray. His songs are funny, his lyrics sharp and his voice very appealing. Most of his songs probably wouldn't

Graphic: Steven Brown

be suitable for Kate's voice but it would be fun just to see what she might do with the pacing of the words, and perhaps she could play around with instruments for weird and wonderful sounds. I'm curious to see if it would work. Jake describes his songs as 'peculiar' and 'odd'. Live albums are better than studio recordings, which tend to be too polished and lack the vitality Jake has in his live work. He is probably best known for *Sister Josephine*, the original nun on the run.

The Jolly Captain would be a possible candidate for this album, (about a simple man and a good man whose "*whey faced old nag bag*" of a wife falls, breaks her neck and vows to "*crawl from my coffin to haunt you vexatiously*" should she die and he marry another. She dies and he marries "*an apple cheeked girl*" the very next day. He is warned that he has married too soon, but the jolly captain knows better – "*She won't come to haunt me and taunt me I know, because I buried her face downward, she's a long way to go!*".

The Widow of Bridlington is a clever, witty song with a good strong story and this is the one I would choose for Kate. It tells of a "*widow of forty two with eyes of a very unsettling blue*" who after a dutiful existence finds herself all alone, and gets a life and lovers only to be ostracised by jealous disapproving villagers of the Yorkshire seaside town. It's a wonderful song with humour and pathos side by side:

Jake Thackray

"My only darling's dead he is,
And all my children grown,
The house has emptied,
all the lovebirds flown.
In place of widows weeds
I'll let my coal black hair grow long..."

Gaudete. The most familiar version is by Steeleye Span from 1973, and most people will know this wonderful song, which is featured on most of the recent Christmas compilation CDs. I can hear in my imagination the Gregorian chant vocal harmonies of Kate, Paddy and Colin. Perhaps instruments such as Tibetan singing bowls could be used to give a different treatment and flavour to the song.

Dark Side of the Moon, written by Rosie Hardman, was recorded by Miriam Backhouse, on her 1977 album *Gypsy Without A Road.* I grew up with this album and my vinyl copy has been worn out after all these years. It still moves me enormously, I have so many memories wrapped up in it. The whole album is diverse and beautiful, a little heavy and moody in parts, but it is so good. I cannot recommend it enough. 1977 was a good year for recordings! Miriam's voice is so beautiful. *Dark Side of The Moon* is one of my most special songs. I first fell in love with it back in the summer of '77. I was twelve. There is something that reaches right in, the way Kate's music does, and grabs my heart, makes me laugh and cry with my memories of early loves... I would love to hear Kate sing this:

Miriam Backhouse

"Well you can see that I'm improving
By the new songs that I play
And it sure doesn't take much proving
To show I've been loving along the way,
There was a teacher, there was an actor,
Who taught me to give inside
But you my gentle gypsy friend
You teach me to give with pride".

I would dearly love to hear Kate record almost anything by Robin Williamson, who used to be with The Incredible String Band. It would be a case of where to start? Robin Williamson continues the storytelling tradition of old, collecting stories from all over the world, and captivates with his renditions of bardic mysteries, humorous stories and songs, weaved with harp, guitar and mandolin. He says that storytelling is essential for us to escape from our worries, we can be transported to better places... I love the way he tells the stories and spins webs of the purest sound from his harp. There is magic here, in places of stone and hearth and heart, of ancient ways, of kinsmen and women, and the child who is forever a child.

Robin Williamson

There are so many songs and poems from which to choose, all of them excellent. If it was to be a song, *Me and the Mad Girl*, would be a good choice; it is so lively and tells of playground cruelty, and love's curiosity, in all its innocence and spite:

"I'd do anything to get out of school,
away from the teacher's stick,
to shoot street lamps with my slingshot,
smoke cigarettes and get sick..."

After much pondering, for Kate, and to complete the A-side of the album, I would choose *Five Denials on Merlin's Grave* from *A Glint at the Kindling*, the most magical album. This would be a challenge. It is a poem of almost fourteen minutes. Robin Williamson says on the sleeve notes that it "is based on five broad stages of ancient British history, and contrasts dusty historical and archaeological viewpoints together with the dilute folklore and echoes of legend that remain, against the emotion that the ancestral figures of the green islands have woken in me, since I first learned of them as a boy." The track is full of the most rich and sensual imagery. Robin Williamson creates with such spirit. He is a true poet and musician. He knows exactly how to use and play with words; he gently lulls and teases the senses, then whips word and image into a frenzied, wide-eyed gallop, only to calm and soothe the sweating brow. He throws you back in time and picks out the things that really matter, placing a better perspective on history and life. He sends the heart racing and takes the imagination and sets it free. I can hear Kate doing this, bringing in John and Paddy, maybe Robin Williamson himself to speak in one harmonious tongue, to tell this most precious of tales...

"But let us sing the skill
of the master builders long ago,
for it was no peasantry
clodding after scrawny cows
who raised the hollow hills
and the henge stones,
but calm and cunning wizards
work these wonders..."

4: Side B

The B-side of this imaginary album has a more traditional flavour than the A side – and is darker and a little more bloody. The lyrics are as I have transcribed them, and hope I have heard them correctly and there aren't too many misheard lyrics (Combat Ducks!). This has been an enjoyable article to write, and it has been difficult to keep the list short; there are so many excellent folk songs. I have chosen these for their harmonies, but above all for their intriguing and beautiful lyrics and powerful story lines. There are so many songs that would be suitable for Kate's voice, she did after all record *My Lagan Love* and *The Handsome Cabin Boy*, and held to the older tradition of no instruments other than the voice, clearly proving her ability in this area. I would dearly love to hear more, especially Kate's interpretations of the more obscure, little known ballads. I wish, I wish... And so to the songs...

Of Bert Lloyd's songs, *Tamlyn* would be my choice for Kate. "We haven't all that many fairy ballads and this is by far the finest", wrote Bert Lloyd, "it was already printed on a broadside in 1558, and it wasn't new then". Sung unaccompanied by him, his voice trembles and weeps, then grows triumphantly as the tale progresses. The inflections in his voice, and the little laughs interjected here and there are very appealing. It feels pretty ancient, and there is something magical in both tune and story. John Carder Bush referred to Bert Lloyd in *Cathy*: "his voice is unique and came from another time. To hear his rendition of the long *Tamlain* ballad with every nuance of mystery and emotion sustained was to time travel".

The song seems to be of exclusively Scottish origin, as is the fairy tale that was it's inspiration, however, similar songs stemmed from Europe, specifically Denmark and Sweden. There are many different variants, and the Bert Lloyd version differs again from those I found in Child's collection of ballads. The song is indeed a glorious tale of magic, shape-shifting and the battle between mortal and elfin. Tamlyn's only salvation from the Elfin Queen's power is the unyielding grasp of his mortal lover at midnight on Halloween, when the veil is thin between the worlds. Tamlyn has the richness, colour and atmosphere that reminds me of Waterhouse's painting *The Lady of Shallot*.

The story goes that Lady Margaret is walking the wood to pick flowers, and is chastised for pulling at the green branches by a young man, Tamlyn, who seduces her, then disappears into the woods. Amongst her court of four and twenty rosy cheeked ladies, Lady Margaret appears "green as any glass". Her paleness goes noticed by a servant girl, and the story follows:

"*And suddenly up spoke a little servant girl*
And she lift her hand and smiled
And said I think our lady has loved too much
And now she goes with child, with child,
And now she goes with child..."

Martin Carthy is regarded as one of the leading folk revivalists. Early trips to the folk clubs exposed him to the talented Ewan MacColl, but particularly Bert Lloyd, whom he greatly admired and from whom he learned many. Carthy made a great impression on Bob Dylan, who adapted the song *Lord Franklin* which Carthy had taught him and used the tune for *Dream*. He was once a member of Steeleye Span, the Albion Band, the Watersons and Brass Monkey. He and his wife Norma Waterson gather folk songs, committing them to record and performing world-wide. Carthy has to be one of the greatest folk singers ever. He has a distinctive, clear, nasal tone to his voice and is captivating live. He has concentrated on traditional material, with a sprinkling of a few contemporary songs. I would love to see Kate and Carthy work together, which would probably appeal to her enjoyment of contrasts in sound and voice. It would be a very interesting sound. There are so many wonderful traditional songs Carthy has recorded which would be suitable for Kate. *The Ant And The Grasshopper* has beautiful harmonies; *Dominion of the Sword; Prince Heathen* (a strange, galloping tale of a man's cruelty and a woman's strength); *Bill Norrie*; *Arthur McBride and the Sergeant*; *Salisbury Plain* (considered improper!), *Staines Morris*; *Reynardine*; *Matt Hyland* (an excellent song!) and the caustic bite of *Brass Band Music*.

Graphic: Paulina Stuckey

Of the songs Carthy has recorded, for Kate I would choose *The Ballad of Lucy Wan*, because of the *Kick Inside* connection. Carthy recorded the ballad on his album, *Byker Hill* in 1967. In the sleeve notes he writes about the differing versions of this song. One version tells of two brothers' fight for the love of their sister and the "breaking of a little bush that should have been a tree", and is similar to another ballad called *Twa Brothers*.

The version Carthy recorded was taught to him by Bert Lloyd, and tells of incest between a

Phil Ochs

brother and sister, which results in the conception of a child. He lies to his mother about the blood on his sword, telling her it belongs to his greyhound, then his mare and eventually confesses it is the blood of his sister. Other versions suggest that he has aborted the child and murdered his sister, making it an even bloodier story. The song has a fairly sparse tune or fa, (a sound found mostly in Ireland) which suits its heavy subject matter, in its lamenting dialogue between mother, sister and brother. The ballad is also known as *Lizzie Wan*.

Lucy may be a reflection of Juno Lucina, Christianised by the church as St. Lucy, who was a development of the Etruscan Goddess Lusna, who had two aspects as both Sun and Moon, and was associated with legends of brother-sister incest, hence the line "*the sun and the moon dance on yonder hill*". Kate adapted the same line and used it in *The Kick Inside.* I can imagine Kate making an excellent version of *The Ballad of Lucy Wan*, perhaps with Tibetan singing bowls or voices to drone, or her voice alone:

"Fair Lucy she sits at her father's door,
A-weeping and making moan,
And by there came her brother dear,
What ails thee Lucy wan?
Oh I ail and I ail,
Dear brother she cries
And I'll tell you the reason why,
For there is a child between my two sides
That's from you dear brother and I..."

The Dubliners

The Highwayman, adapted from the poem by Alfred Noyes, was set to music by the American folk singer, Phil Ochs, and recorded as a very moving song by Vera Aspey on her album *The Blackbird.* I first saw her perform this live at the Southport Arts Centre when I was twelve. She was immersed in blue light, like the moon, and I was moved to tears by the story and Vera's incredibly beautiful voice. Kate's voice is perfect for this song, with Uillean pipes to accompany, or perhaps even the cello. If only... It is the story of Bess and her lover, the highwayman. King George's redcoats come to the inn and wait for him to come for Bess, having been informed by the jealous ostler who loves Bess. The soldiers tie her up "*with many a sniggering jest*" and place a musket beneath her breast. Through her window she can see her lover riding towards the inn, and her finger touches the trigger. She decides to warn him the only way that she can. He hears the shot, not knowing it is the death of his beloved Bess. He gallops away, only to be shot dead by the soldiers. United forever in death.

Shirley Collins

"Her eyes grew wide for moment,
She drew one last deep breath,
And her finger moved in the moonlight,
The musket shattered the moonlight,
Shattered her breast in the moon light,
She warned him with her death.."

Now for a drop of the hard stuff with the Dubliners, who have over the years recorded many a fine traditional Irish tune. Ronnie Drew's gravelly voice was once described as sounding "like coke being crushed under a door"! John Sheahan played whistles and fiddle on *And Dream of Sheep*, *Jig of Life* and *The Sensual World.* The trad songs The Dubliners record and perform are very male oriented songs, and not remotely genteel. But they're fun and lively and very enjoyable. For this imaginary album something raunchy, such as *Seven Drunken Nights*, *Black Velvet Band*, or *Seven Deadly Sins. Maids When You're Young Never Wed An Old Man* would make a great cover, but it is full of innuendo about the poor old man's sexual prowess. What the hell, let's have it anyway. The song speaks for itself, complete with nonsense lyrics, and is a warning to all young women planning on marrying old men. I would love to see Kate really let rip on this... and it's no worse than *Do Bears*!

"Well an old man came courting me,
hey dingdoorum-dow,
And old man came courting me,
me being young,
An old man came courting me,
feign he would marry me
Maids when you're young
never wed an old man
Because he's got no
filoorum fol diddle-i-oorum,
He's got no filoorum, fol diddle ol-day..."

Shirley Collins recorded several albums of traditional songs during the '60s and '70s, and some collected from the Copper family. She was taught several songs by Bert Lloyd (who wrote the introductory sleeve notes for her first album in 1967). Her sister Dolly accompanied her with arrangements on the flute organ, giving a distinctive flavour to their songs.

The Cruel Mother was taught to Shirley Collins by Ewan MacColl when she was twenty and she recorded it some years later on her first album *The Sweet Primroses.* This is a wonderful ancient sounding tune and tells the tale of a clergyman's daughter who is seduced and betrayed by his clerk, with haunting consequences. I imagine Kate's voice harmonising perfectly with low Gregorian-style chants by Paddy in the chorus:

"She's leaned her back up against a thorn
Hey the rose and the lynsey-o,
And there two bonny boys she has born
Down by the green wood side-eo.
She's taken out her little pen knife
Hey the rose and the lynsey-o,
And she has torn them from their life,
Down by the green wood side-eo.
She's laid them beneath some marble stone,

Thinking to go a maiden home,
As she looked over her father's wall,
She saw those two bonny boys playing ball ..."

The Coventry Carol, a traditional 15th Century carol (taken from *The Pageant of the Shearman and the Tailors*, one of the Coventry plays performed by the local guilds), tells of the Massacre of the Innocents, when thousands of boy children and babies were slaughtered at the command of King Herod in the search for Jesus. Maddy Prior's version of this lullaby to the little ones in their eternal sleep has to be the most moving I have ever heard. Kate would make an equally beautiful version that would break your heart:

"Lulee, Lulay, thou little tiny child,
By by Lulee, Lulay,
Thou little tiny child,
By by Lulee, Lulay.
Herod the King in his regime
Charged he had this day
His men of might in his own sight
All children young to slay..."

The Widow of Westmorland's Daughter is a wonderful song about the losing and "regaining" of virginity. Bert Lloyd says it was not included in Child's book of ballads because it was too offensive. He rescued *The Widow* and gave her a tune. It is quite a rude little song laced with a liberal dose of double standards, but is very funny, especially the way he delivers it. I imagine Kate singing it in an Irish lilt, chased by fiddles, whistles and pipes:

"There was a widow in Westmorland
Her had no daughter but one,
And she has prayed both night and day
The girl might keep her maidenhead long.
Oh don't be daft dear mother she said,
And say no more to me,
For a fine young man in the grenadier guards
Me maidenhead's taken from me..."

Long Lankin, is one of the most fascinating songs I have ever heard. To me the definitive version of this traditional song belongs to Miriam Backhouse. Other renditions are often far too cheerful for the bloodiness of the storyline. Miriam's treatment is quite the opposite. It is the eeriest song I have ever heard. The unusual tune, and the bowed and birowed dulcimer used in Miriam's version gives a very macabre atmosphere, like an haunted grandfather clock chiming doom, or a bow scraping across a skeletal ribcage. I see shadows cast by candlelight, and smell warm blood on cold stone. A typically British murder story, with its roots firmly plunged in Europe.

Known as *Long Lonkin*, or *Lamkin*, there are twenty two versions of the song, which appears to be of Scottish origin, and conflicting opinions as to who Long Lankin was, whether real or the imaginary Bogey man that mothers used to control and threaten their children. One interpretation is that Lankin was a mason who built a castle, is cheated of his payment and seeks blood as his revenge, not money. English versions dismiss Long Lankin as a mere ruffian. I have a distant memory of a much more sinister interpretation, whether it is my own or relayed to me by my parents, from Miriam Backhouse when they saw her perform it in 1977, I cannot recall. This is the interpretation I prefer, and seems to me to fit the song far better than others offered.

I believe the tale to be of the Gypsy Lord, Long Lankin, who seeks revenge on the Master of the Manor, who had stolen his child for use as the foundation sacrifice to protect his home. (This was often the practice where children – usually gypsy children – or animals were buried within the walls of buildings, or their blood was sprinkled on the foundations. The remains of similar adult sacrifices have been found under the aisles and in hidden chambers of churches). Long Lankin takes his bloody revenge. Kate would make a brilliant version of this song. I hear her voice, haunting as autumn eyes, and imagine the sounds as murderers' thigh bones circle metal Tibetan singing bowls (that is how they were traditionally played), drawing out those otherworldly vibrations.

"Where's the Lord of this house
said Long Lankin?
He's away in fair London
said the false nurse to him.
Where's the little Lair of this house
said Long Lankin
He's asleep in his cradle
said the false nurse to him.
We'll prick him, we'll prick him
all over with a pin
And that'll make my Lady
to come down to him.
So they pricked him, they pricked him
All over with a pin
And the nurse held the basin
for the blood to flow in..."

All of these songs are available on CD except Vera Aspey's track. Check out the Folk department of any large Virgin or HMV. I would particularly recommend all of Martin Carthy's albums, *Rigs of the Time* being a good introduction to him. The same applies to classic A.L. Lloyd. I would recommend Miriam Backhouse's album, *Gypsy Without a Road*. As extra tracks I would have chosen *Two Magicians, Sovay, George Collins, Prince Heathen, The Blacksmith and the Toffee Maker, Skewbald, Reynardine, Gypsy Without a Road, I Wish, I Wish* and *Nasty Spider*. But that's cheating!

Since I wrote this article I have made contact with Miriam Backhouse who has become a dear friend.

I have subsequently heard her perform *Long Lankin* live on a number of occasions and it is even more terrifying watching her convey the spirit and essence of each of the characters in this song – Krys.

Ewan McColl

Maddy Prior

Ghosts of Clonea

John Carder Bush

Rise up Jimmy,
And rise up, Joe,
Rise up, Johnny,
And tap your toes.
Rise up, Minnie,
And rise up, Mo,
Rise up, Mary,
For the heel and toe.

As the last three words you sighed
Before you upped and died
Carry on the screams of the sea-wind,
Leap back like salmon into your dance
Where the flagstones wait
For the heat of your steps;
Jolt your bodies into that oil-lit,
Smoke-moted cottage room:
Smoke from wood, smoke from lamp,
Smoke from pipes, stems bitter with stout,
Lips sweet with your flying sweat.
Come back and teach us how to find joy
In the bad guts of life,
Teach us how to make your wild music
While the gale of aging rages
And the world whirls
Towards its own storm-drains.
Teach us how to drown pain
In the thump of the jig
Like a sack of kicking puppies
Dumped into the troughs of the ocean.
Teach us to dream things better
In the soul-stopping airs
Of your loss-soaked laments.

Rise out of your grave, Maddy,
And rise out Neil,
Rise out of your grave, Paddy,
And stamp those heels.
Rise out of your white sheet, Helen,
And rise out, Hannah,
Rise out of your white sheet, Ellen,
And stamp out your reels.

Come laughing down the cliff-path,
Popping fuschia with your broken nails;
Bring us the buckets of spring water
That will scent the house with iron and rock,
Light the fire and blow the sparks
Until the logs roar and the sap wails.
Take down the broken fiddle
And rosin the bow,
Take down the leaking box
And pump the keys:
As you start up your engines of music,
Take Time by her frozen locks,
And spin her sideways –
Come back, you crazy old ghosts,
And brighten our darkening days.

Rise up Jimmy,
And rise up, Joe,
Rise up, Johnny,
And tap your toes.

Readers' Letters

...We receive them with a strange delight

Edited Letters from issues 55 (April 1995) to 62 (December 1998)

Mark Owen: Let me put the following to all those who would criticise Kate. Would you rather she had never existed at all? Is getting your 'pound of flesh' more important than the music which has undoubtedly enriched your lives? Don't tell me you subscribe to a fanzine for the hell of it: you do it out of devotion (unless of course your name is Fred Vermorel!) Make a choice – decide on which side of the fence you sit over this one. What does it matter, moreover, that you don't possess a particularly obscure picture of Kate in some weird and wonderful get-up from who-cares-when, which Kate herself has probably long since forgotten ever having posed for! If you ain't got the music, you ain't got nothing!

As an artist of sorts (a writer), I can fully sympathise with Kate when she says time and again that at the end of the day, the work is most important. If the so-called 'fans' want albums of such outstanding quality, as has been the case with literally every Kate album to date, then they must accept that art needs time – uninterrupted time at that! Beethoven I'm sure didn't bash out a symphony before lunch, another before bed!

In a few words to the minority who see fit to make unfair and thoroughly unreasonable, frankly intolerable demands on Kate's personal time and space: get lives, you sad bastards!! Better still, try to appreciate what actually goes into the production of true, inspiring and original art. Then, should you vainly decide it's a piece of piss, go right ahead and do better!!

Patrick Routen: I just want to express my admiration for the marvellous job you all do for *HomeGround*. It is of a consistently high quality, informative, interesting, entertaining and a superb production. It is surely a labour of love and a testimony to the inspiration Kate exudes. Keep up your dedication and remember there are many out there who admire this most superb of publications quietly.

Just a word on *The Red Shoes*. I have followed Kate's music from day one and without doubt *The Red Shoes* is her best effort. Each LP has been a progression from the last one, each one progressively better. *The Red Shoes* is superb and even the most dispassionate of people like me was moved by its intensity. *And So Is Love* moved me to tears, spontaneously, without me knowing why! I was surprised at myself.

Kate's film is also very good, full of evocative images and contrasts. I am delighted to see Kate experimenting with this medium. I personally can't see her as an actress, but as a director (and artist) in films like *The Line, the Cross & the Curve*, she is given the freedom to experiment and let her creative juices flow, and this is where I feel she will excel.

Robert Brown: With *The Red Shoes* already over a year old, and with no new album realistically expected until 1997, wouldn't it be wonderful to have an album of unreleased material in the time in between?

The recent release of the *Cloudbusting* video mix is a very encouraging sign, but what is really needed is an album (double?) that collects together in one package all the recordings which have for one reason or another been omitted from the main stream of single and album releases.

There is certainly a goldmine to select from. To start with there are the two recordings of *Maybe*, which date from 1973 and 1975. Their inclusion would be essential simply from a historical perspective. There are thought to be at least two songs apiece left over from the *Lionheart* and *Never For Ever* albums. There are two songs that Kate recorded for films: *The Magician* and *Brazil*. The latter has never been widely available, whilst the former remains unreleased and can only be heard as background to the dialogue in *The Magician of Lublin*. Also worthy of inclusion is the original recording of *The Big Sky*. According to Kate this is very different to the final version we all know so well. And how many people have heard the rare disco mix of *Running Up That Hill*? Then there are the home recorded demos! Nearly every song on Kate's first three albums would have been recorded at home in the first instance, and probably still exist to this day. Some, like *Babooshka*, *Sat In Your Lap* and *Don't Push Your Foot On the Heartbrake,* have already been broadcast on British radio.

As you can see, there is no shortage of songs available. From a record company's point of view, such a release would have a limited commercial appeal, however, there is here a golden opportunity for EMI and Kate to reward the loyalty and dedication of fans and collectors worldwide by releasing an interesting and entertaining album such as this. What we don't need is *The Whole Story – Part Two*. Without a doubt there is a way. All that is needed now is the will! So, how about it, Kate?

Matthew O'Connor: I thought about writing my own review of *The Red Shoes*, which is my favourite Kate album (at least until I hear *The Dreaming* or *Hounds Of Love*, then they are!) but I think Doug Alan (and his grading system!) in *HomeGround* 54, kind of did that for me. Except that I think he went just a little overboard on *Big Stripey Lie*, and then he trashed my favourite track completely! He obviously didn't click in with *You're the One* in the way that I do. That song always makes me shiver, it stirs some very strong emotions in me. I think the greatest mystery of *The Red Shoes* will always be why the last two tracks weren't released as singles.

Anyway, thank you for the magazine. Some of it makes me smile. If I were Kate I'd read *HomeGround* and piss myself over about a quarter of it.

I first joined the Kate Bush Club in about 1980, when I was twelve or thirteen. Then I got caught up in my own teenage traumas, leaving home etc, and when *The Dreaming* came out I was furious with Kate for abandoning 'nice melodies' for such a row! Those disturbing noisy vocals! I had these scales on my ears for a while. Since then I returned to it all with and adult head and – I don't need to say any more, do I? These are feelings we all share, feelings that go much deeper than a pair of brown cords. Love to you all.

Kate Bush Club

Dear Lionheart,

I just had to write to thank you for joining our Club. I'm thrilled that you are interested in my work and I'm really looking forward to hearing about the things you love to do and want to say.

I hope you enjoy being involved, and there are many levels you can help us on — especially by telling us what you think about anything that comes your way. I'll look forward to hearing all I can from you – I wish I could write more often, but I honestly don't have the time.

Take care of yourself, you mean alot to me

Big love Kate xxxxxx

Sophie Hayat: I have been a Kate fan for fourteen years now. *Never For Ever* was the first LP I bought and I listened to it so many times. It is now completely worn out and unlistenable! Like some fans I was also the only person in my family who was really into her music. Everybody thought 'It's weird!" *The Dreaming* remains my favourite album. I find it incredible, breathtaking. But I love all of Kate's albums and I was not disappointed with *The Red Shoes*. This is her most diverse piece of work to date, and includes some groovy songs! Kate's genius is unquestionable. The proof being the influence she has had on so many artists of today Sinéad, Suede, Björk, Alison Shaw from the Cranes, to name but a few.

Colin Booker: I've always been a fan of Kate's but I've tended to keep my love of her a rather private affair – except that over the years my girlfriends have had to put up with my passion for Kate! I joined the Kate Bush Club about seven years ago and I've never been to a convention, though I will if there's another, but now I feel the need to keep in touch with other fans a bit more.

I seem to have become a subscriber at a time when some fans are feeling a bit let down by Kate. Well everyone is entitled to their opinion but I don't see that she owes us anything. We should all be able to say what we feel. I've been critical of Kate before because I have this pet hate of 'sound effects' and spoken words dropped into the middle of otherwise beautiful songs. It spoils it for me but that is just my opinion and I don't get bitter about it. Anyone who is bitter should go and sulk somewhere else! To all those who obviously put in so much hard work – don't let it bother you. What a lovely piece written by Anne Davis, 'To Be A Fan'. She really says it all.

A Reader: Sorry, but I won't be renewing my subscription as I seem to have lost the faith. I think two things did it for me – *The Red Shoes* and Coca-Cola. There's nothing wrong with *The Red Shoes* as an album but I can't agree with Kate's attitude that it's okay to record and release deeply personal songs, but not to talk about them. However she may mean it, this comes across as arrogant. If you don't want (genuinely) to discuss personal matters, don't put them in the public domain on a record and don't insult the people who buy your record and are interested in knowing more about you and where you come from. Maybe Kate should go back to writing 'story' songs.

Next, I read in *HomeGround* that Kate is recording jingle music for Coca-Cola, and worse, that you are defending her decision. Yes, everyone has a right to earn money where they can – but, I mean, *Coca-Cola?* Next stop MacDonalds no doubt! In countries too poor to feed themselves properly, the people being sold the American dream (which even America can't sustain any longer), the dream exemplified by a red and white tin, a curvaceous bottle and an unnatural tooth rotting syrupy drink. I'm surprised and very disappointed that Kate has chosen support for and financial gain from this company, given what it represents.

I no longer feel I can share in her world-view. I've listened to Kate and enthused about her to anyone who'd listen (and some who wouldn't) since I first heard *Wuthering Heights* as a teenager. Now I don't play her records. The video of *The Line, the Cross & the Curve*, which I got for Christmas remains unwatched. I feel like I've been betrayed by someone I trusted – so I'm out of here. Thanks, it's been good but we finally grew apart. In sadness...

David Loose: May I first say how totally enjoyable I have found *HomeGround*. I have only recently discovered Kate but I have found her work so inspirational and I must admit that many of her songs have lifted my spirits and made me look at life just that little bit differently. I am in the Royal Air Force and listening to Kate at the end of my shift is just so refreshing.

A Reader: I would like to defend my letter in *HomeGround* 53. I was not saying that Kate should give us 'more' of herself personally, just that (unfortunately) no music these days gets widespread airplay unless it is publicised and that it is unfair that songs of Kate's get ignored, while absolute crap gets to No. 1 and stays there for weeks. Can I apologise for any suggestion I may have made that Kate does not care about her fans – I was talking from ignorance and I now know through personal experience that Kate does care, a hell of a lot, and must be one of the most considerate, kind and thoughtful people out there.

Vanessa Themans: I like the beauty of Kate's songs, but also she has helped me discover other writers, film makers, legends. This is also one of the things that makes *HomeGround* different, because thanks to you I have also discovered painters such as Sickert and Rossetti, and writers like Le Fanu (another long list). I'd also like to say how beautiful the artwork is by Debi and Paulina. Is there a link between *Experiment IV* and *Clockwork Orange*?

Adrian Durrant: I was really sad to read in *HomeGround* 56 that a reader had lost the faith. As life goes on we change and adopt differing ideas, we can grow apart, and I feel this is reflected in the diminishing relationship between Kate and some of her older fans. It is frustrating to have grown up with Kate's music and to become torn away from that by our differences, and I understand the sadness that she feels, though for different reasons.

It is hard for an artist to continually seek and find new ideas and inspiration, even to the point of creative exhaustion. I think that Kate reached this state with *The Red Shoes* album. I personally feel she lost it with that album basically because the self-pitying attitude she expressed in the songs was at odds with the way I'd had to deal with the challenges in my own life. I couldn't identify with her at all.

This disillusionment is hard to handle. After all, Kate is still one of our most unique artists, and is an incredibly nice and genuine person, as well as being a dedicated perfectionist who does things in her own way in a chauvinistic and manipulative business. On the other hand, however, Kate is very rich, very lucky, and a tough professional who is fair game for criticism. I think it is time for Kate to get contemporary. Su's criticism of Kate's involvement with Coca-Cola reveals that she is not aware of how people are thinking. I also think that Kate's insularity is detrimental to her work. She is currently not as good as fully committed, high profile artists like Björk and Madonna.

Being a Kate Bush fan has never been easy – the interminable waiting for albums to appear and the wobbly standards (she can come up with something utterly sublime, only to then ambush you with something equally awful) can indeed stretch your faith to the limit. However, unlike the other reader, I intend to hold on, albeit by the tips of my fingers. I've stuck with Kate before when the wheels have come off, and I'm not giving up now.

Zavie Edwards: Just over two years ago I became friends with an amazing person and my whole life changed for the better. Never had I met such an intelligent, warm, talented, intriguing and genuinely nice human being. We went everywhere together. She even came to school and on holidays with me. People commented on how inseparable we were and when I introduced her, some agreed that she was wonderful. My friend always has a solution to my problems and has helped me to see life so differently. Her common sense and caring helps me to live my life much more fully that I could have without her. I often feel that I do not give enough in our friendship, but I haven't the talent to enrich her life as she has mine. The only things I can give her are my thanks, an ear to listen and assurance that I'll always stick by her.

Linda Ball: Apart from the comment about Oasis, I agree with Krys's opinions about fandom. It's quite sad to think of a disgruntled admirer literally trashing such wonderful, moving music in a fit of pique. I for one would rather not see Kate on television or stage knowing that she would rather be somewhere else. That is not to say she is giving us the brush off, rather that some people are actually quite shy and feel uncomfortable on a public platform. Why do some find this hard to accept?

Sometimes I have wondered why it takes Kate so long to come up with an album when other artists can produce the goods regularly. Just at this moment I am thinking about what the Beatles delivered in eight – count 'em! – very short years. How Kate uses her time I obviously don't know, but frankly, it is absolutely none of my business. I am very content with what I have, those little shining gifts Kate has given us over the years which I have brought into my home and heart, and can be found snuggling up to my hi-fi and will be tomorrow and the day after that. I am grateful for that pleasure.

Did anyone see the extraordinary TV programme last summer about a blind man who suddenly one day lost his hearing? He had previously been a piano tuner for many artists and music was the love of his life. One remarkable sequence of the film showed him trying to listen to his favourite song, sadly all he could hear was an unbearable jumble of clicks and hisses and what sounded like industrial drilling. The tears, frustration and anger inside him was heartbreaking and utterly unforgettable, as was his determination to make the most of life. When I am about to play music, I often think of him and that scene.

In the original issue 59 this sentence was rendered as "the blind man who lost his earring" much to the puzzlement of all concerned.

God bless spell checkers!

It was good to see in your pages that Brett Anderson has reiterated his admiration for Kate. I remember him saying some years ago that he thought *Hounds of Love* was a definition of beauty which echoed my thoughts completely. Reading Brian Kennedy's comments about Kate made me think about his early work – surely on this evidence the song, *Captured*, from his début solo album must be about Kate and the moment he heard *The Man with the Child in his Eyes* for the first time. Everyone go and check it out because it's brilliant! Health and happiness to one and all.

Christine Bourbeau: My journey with Kate began when I heard *Be Kind to My Mistakes*. After hearing that song I had to have more of her music. So my collection of Kate albums, b-sides and memorabilia began.

Soon after *The Sensual World* album was released my life went into turmoil. I was only twenty years old and my Mom was diagnosed with terminal cancer. I had lost my Dad to a heart attack when I was eleven, so I was no stranger to death. My Mom and I were close, she was my best friend and I was hers. When she passed away I went into a severe depression and my only solace was Kate's music. Many of the songs on *The Sensual World* helped me deal with life again.

My journey with Kate continued and my life regained some normality. I met a wonderful man and we were married. When *The Red Shoes* was released I was 7½ months pregnant with my first child. I listened to the album constantly. Little did I know the impact Kate would make on my baby. Like all babies my son Patrick would have his fussy time but it was usually when he was in the car. I would put the radio on hoping the music would soothe him but he remained cranky. One day I played *The Red Shoes* and he calmed right down and fell asleep. It was amazing. He must have recognised the songs from when he was in-utero! I don't know if it was Kate's voice or the music but the sounds were very pleasing to him.

Patrick is now 3½ years old and one of Kate's youngest fans. He loves watching *The Line, the Cross & the Curve* and the Hammersmith video. He recognises her pictures and only wants to listen to her CDs. Even today her music is still calming him in the car. I am pregnant with my second child and I hope to have Kate's music soothe my baby to sleep once again.

I feel Kate must have had a really difficult time with the death of her mother. Believe me, she is not alone in her grief. The pain of loss is a road you wish no-one would have to travel, but if you have to go down that road always remember the good times. My Mom left me many wonderful memories and most importantly her words of wisdom: "Chin up and keep smiling."

My family love you Kate, and we want you to continue to bring joy to people's lives through your music!!

A Kate fan USA: Greetings! It is a great honor to address fellow Kate Bush fans. I am unfortunately an inmate in a U.S. Reformatory serving a five year sentence for a crime that I feel is not worthy of a prison sentence, but I do not make the rules. I will be released Summer 1998 to return home to my family and my two daughters and the joys of my life.

I have another joy. I first heard Kate fifteen years ago. At first, though I liked *The Kick Inside*, it was just another good album. Then I realised that no matter how often I played it, I never got tired of it. I bought her other albums only to find the same thing. My other albums were collecting dust while Kate's were wearing out! Since that time my love for her music has become overwhelming. I would swim the sea just to one day meet her and thank her for the joy she has brought to my life. Recently I decided to collect everything about her and her music and I ran into problems! Being in here limits me regarding collecting. My mother looked for books on Kate but to no avail. I've written to record companies but never heard anything. All I have are some tapes I can listen to on my Walkman. At home I have all the CDs. Last week my stepfather ran Kate's name through his computer and we hit the jackpot. This is how I learned of *HomeGround*. For years I've talked to people about Kate and am yet to find someone who knows who she is! Music so wonderful is made to be heard.

Henrietta Hudson: I am the American reader who wrote the anti-Kate letter which caused a lot of controversy: the letter quoted in Krys' 'Remember Yourself' article. A lot has happened since I wrote that letter. I lost a cousin to murder some months ago and two of my favourite co-workers died within two weeks of each other. Since then I've had to re-evaluate my feelings about Kate and her music. At this time, the only conclusion I could draw is that Kate has a right to be a human being and does not owe us every minute of her life.

When I threw out my previous Kate collection, in reality what I'd done was to throw away my past. As irrational as it sounds, sometimes one has to throw away the past in order to begin again. At the time I wrote the letter, I had a serious lack of faith in Kate as an artist. Looking back now, I went through some serious hard times and depression. And Kate's lack of promotion and touring had only exacerbated my situation. What made me turn to Tori Amos was that she toured and appeared on television. Tori's music was reflective of what was going on in my life then. The thing is this: Kate is Kate, and Tori is Tori They are two very different women.

I may have regretted some of the things I wrote previously, but the one thing I don't regret is the last sentence: "Kate Bush has been everybody else's girl, maybe one day she'll be her own". Maybe with this eighth album, Kate Bush will be her own woman.

If Kate preferred making videos to appearing live, then I would rather she did that than work on a project her heart is not set on. I have long admired Kate's commitment to human rights and AIDS awareness, and her Billie Holiday sculpture for the War Child charity is the most beautiful I've ever seen.

Kate is the last person in the world who I would be angry at for any reason. It has taken a

Graphic opposite:
Paulina Stuckey

lot of personal crises in my life to see Kate for who she is, not what I want her to be. In closing, I deeply pray that as much as my letter was a wake-up call to fans, I may feel faith again that Kate is physically and emotionally all right. And if she wants to pursue film or video, then that is her choice. My collection won't be the same (starting with *The Sensual World*) because my feelings for Kate won't be the same. My feelings for her in 1998 are very different from what they were in 1978. It's a long way from *Wuthering Heights*, but I wish Kate and her loved ones inner peace. And that Catherine - Kate - Bush will finally have the respect that she and her music so deserve.

Robert Brown: I am writing to express my disappointment at EMI's decision to release the re-vamped *Hounds of Love* CD at full price (£15 +). It wasn't so long ago when EMI re-released Paul McCartney's back catalogue, also re-mastered with bonus tracks, at a more reasonable mid-price. This kind of corporate greed does no-one any favours. In my case they have lost a sale because I will not buy a copy until the price is reduced.

Arto Polvikoski: I think you play a vital role in the Kate-speaking world. With every new issue my faith is restored and it is always a good reminder of how special Kate is and will always be. I don't know what should be different about the magazine. You could publish a bit more regularly, but I know it's difficult. The photos of Kate are a million years old, but that too can't be helped. There simply aren't any new photos. Let's hope there will be a new album (and convention?) in 1999!

Chris Schalkwijk: I finally managed to get hold of the new *Hounds of Love* release. I tried many stores but most seem to hold back on selling the new version because they want to sell out the existing album first. So I had to order it. When I played the first few notes, it was immediately obvious that it is different. The sound is fuller, and much clearer, especially the vocals. Kate comes closer to the listener. The *Ninth Wave* songs are more spacious. It might still be that the original CD has more atmosphere, and how could it ever be bettered? Whatever way Kate is mixed, whatever album, it is always to me the best music ever created. No-one can do to me what Kate does.

Almost a year ago, in Paris, the city of lights and love, a flame was cruelly snuffed out. Because two people were in love they were harassed to death. When my mother 'phoned me with the news that Diana had died, I knew it was true, yet I could not comprehend it. I will never forget the sight of that black hearse vanishing behind the iron gates at Althorp. It is so utterly final. I have never been into monarchy, but you simply couldn't miss Diana on the television, always flamboyant, energetic and eye-catching. She did so much for people in need.

I will never forget the week she died. I felt it would be appropriate if someone would write a song about her. Elton John did just that. I did not know he would sing *Candle in the Wind*, and it was all the more touching because Kate had done her cover of it. When Elton began to sing I thought of *Moments of Pleasure* and suddenly I saw Kate sitting at the piano in the candlelight, singing her heart out. It rammed home what it means and should mean to be a human being.

I don't think it is good to hate, but I feel strongly that if people hadn't harassed Diana so much through the years she would still be alive. I feel anger and that will always be there. I hope that the world will learn from this, from the good as well as bad that has been done. There is, of course, a link to what many artists experience in the music and show business world. I hope they can find ways to better deal with the unwanted intrusions. There is also a connection with what has been said lately in *HomeGround* about some extreme fans that some artists, Kate included, attract. I hope we all realise how important it is to respect people like Kate and their decisions, as well as to respect fans who have other views than our own. That doesn't mean that we must withhold our opinions, but that we must try to use them in a positive way.

Fiona Hersey: Thanks for the latest edition of *HomeGround*. I am always so thrilled when I receive the magazine and grateful that you continue to produce it so faithfully. Recently, I have been experiencing some life changes and it brings my awareness more sharply into focus of how quickly time passes. I was 11 when I first viewed Kate on 'Top of the Pops'. Twenty years sure went by rather quickly!! Your retrospective account of Kate (part 1) was wonderful. I was thrilled to take the journey, especially one so well documented. I am also grateful that I was moved enough at that young age to recognise something so special that would become an integral throughout my life.

The joy I have had from not only Kate's music, but the artwork and photography associated with her albums, or from just quietly reading the lyrics on the sleeve, the philosophies that I have learnt, and not least of all, the people I have met seems quite too much for just one person. I know this feeling of joy is shared by many. Recently, I have found myself playing Kate's music more than usual. To be honest, her music has become a small part of my life now. I feel largely more akin to a way of life that I feel has developed for me in part by being impressed by her creativity. I sometimes cringe at the comments I read from fans who complain that the gap between albums is too long. I say this to them: each of Kate's albums has sustained me through various parts of my life. In fact, I would say that each album could be applied to a chapter in my life. It usually takes me a few years to get through this chapter and therefore fully appreciate and digest the album. Even then, it still morphs for me according to where I am and what I am doing. With the release of *The Red Shoes*, I went to Tower Records in NYC and had the good fortune of not only seeing Kate, but meeting two people who will forever change my life. The adventure that this meeting took me on has been incredible. It has been challenging in both good and bad ways and has enabled me to grow a little more...

I really can live with the quality of work Kate produces in her time frame. I don't know if my life could actually handle it any other way! The point I am trying to make is – make it what you will. If you want to complain about the lack of new music, then so be it – but it says something else too.

I am grateful for all things Kate and that includes you folks at *HomeGround*! I hope to move back to England within the next few years and hope I will have the pleasure of meeting you on one of the hikes or other events.

Kevin Hendryx: It is almost twelve years since *The Whole Story* was released, and the time has come to retire the original album in favour of a new product. I am surprised that EMI or Kate have not come to this conclusion independently, as 'Best Of...' albums are traditional packages to keep an audience interested while an artist undertakes a hiatus or simply is a slow worker. A reworked *Whole Story* (one full-length CD at least, possibly two) would keep Kate Bush's name in the public eye (and with minimal promotional effort on her part) and be useful in presenting a more complete view of her career, incorporating tracks from the two post-1987 studio albums and various tribute record contributions (such as *Rocket Man*, or *Mná na hÉireann*). I'll leave it to others to suggest the possible line-up and sequencing of an expanded *Whole Story*. The record as it is simply does not live up to its title any longer, and the casual music listener who wants a definitive 'Best of Kate Bush' as an introduction to her work is not being well served.

Similarly, a revised *Whole Story* video collection should also be made available (the original is already out-of-print in the USA), to include as much of Kate's commercial video/film legacy as is possible. Given the success of the Beatles *Anthology*, wouldn't a documentary package focusing on the music of Kate Bush be a treat for curious newcomers and hardcore fans alike? The audio version could gather various hits, rare tracks, unreleased songs, early demos, and out-takes or alternate working versions of commercially available recordings.

The video version would feature mainly unavailable or unseen archive footage, such as international TV performances and interviews, Tour of Life out-takes, the 1979 Christmas special, the Dutch 'Die Efteling' program and behind-the-scenes footage of Kate working in the recording studio and on the set of her film/video productions (where such a record exists; special scenes could be deliberately shot for this project, especially to document Kate's music-making). I imagine the final result being something along the lines of The Who's *The Kids Are Alright*, perhaps to the extent of filming some new live performances before a select audience. Kate's involvement could be as much or as little as she chose; there is still enough archive material to make a splendid and worthwhile film. I'd be very interested to hear what others think about such projects.

John Dardis: I finished my eighteen month Greek army service two months ago and I'm a free citizen again. Thank God there was Kate. She helped me a lot during that time. I've just received today issue 59 and I wanted to tell you that it's great, so much different from the older ones. It is better organised and very neatly looked after. It's beautiful. Keep up the good work, we need it.

Stuart Clapham: My first recollection of Kate was one Friday morning at work when I heard this strange sound on the radio. I stopped what I was doing to listen. The DJ, Dave Lee Travis, said the track was going to be big, and the artist, Kate Bush, even bigger.

That lunchtime I went into the city centre and bought *Wuthering Heights*. After playing it practically non-stop that evening, I bought *The Kick Inside* the following morning. In those early days, it was difficult to go into a record shop and not see Kate somewhere on the wall or hear one of her tracks. The way EMI peddled Kate was somewhat chauvinistic. They played on her sexuality as much as her music. I admit that I too got stuck into that particular thing and at one time had 15 posters of her on my bedroom wall. Kate brought my dear late wife and myself together through her music. The posters came down and I increasingly appreciated Kate's work for what it was.

Andy Moffat: I don't know how you keep going; it being five years since the last album. Thanks for still being there! I teach kids with behavioural difficulties and often use Kate's music as a soothing influence in the classroom, and also in drama and storytelling. *Moving* is great with a story about whales that the kids love. Bits of *Hello Earth* and *Jig of Life* really lend themselves to drama work. And *Rocket's Tail* made a great Bonfire dance when I had a class of five year olds!

Lee: I was introduced to Kate's work when I was 16 (I'm now 22). I'm an actor in training at the moment and currently having a bad few days in the run up to a first night performance. Amidst much time wasting in our rehearsals I brought in *HomeGround* 60 today and wanted to thank you for the 'Twenty Years' tracing the history of Kate's career. I don't often get down, but I'm a little disheartened being stuck in acting. I've directed some experimental videos and write songs. The bizarre negative criticism that was given to Kate's work also gives me faith and a will to continue my own song writing. Creating is a wonderful and impossible profession. Let's hope Kate's next album isn't too impossible for her to make. You've been the happiness in this frustrated, angry person's day!

Mark Binmore: I last subscribed to *HomeGround* in 1992, and I guess it was pure laziness that I didn't re-subscribe. I was so pleased that back issues were available so I could catch up with what I had missed. However, I was disturbed to read that so many people seemed to think that Kate had 'lost it' with the *The Red Shoes* album. I would just like to add that this is an incredibly personal album not only for Kate, but to all of us who were moved by it. It is up to us as to how we interpret the songs. I remember crying when I first heard *And So Is Love* and together with *You're the One*, these are the two classic and most personal songs ever written. My advice to all those who have dismissed *The Red Shoes* is to dig it out again and listen and feel. I would like to thank Kate for this album and look forward to new recordings hopefully next year.

Pieros Kezov: I am from Cyprus and there are a considerable number of people here who adore Kate's music. I've been a fan since I was 12. I'm now 28 and Kate is at the top of my musical list, others being Bowie, Suede, Eno. Here it is hard to find out what is going on in the music scene, but especially hard regarding Kate. I'm going crazy! I feel so grateful for her music and I'd like her to know people have a lot of love for her. I'm a music teacher and I insist that my pupils listen to her stuff.

Mel Cansell: Well, perhaps not exactly running up that hill, more like tired and shagged out after a long squawk. I'd never been to Glastonbury before, but I'll definitely be going again this year. It was good to see you all again. I think fans of Kate's music are some of the nicest people I have ever known.

John Spence: In December 1989 a friend of mine, Geoffrey, from the Scottish Ballet came to spend Christmas with me in Munich. On Christmas Eve we were invited to a party by an English ballet dancer who lives here. Just before we reached the house I turned to Geoffrey and told him that someone at this party had danced with Kate. He laughed and thought I was crazy! We went into the apartment and there were so many people, so I just shouted, "Who here has danced with Kate Bush?" and to my surprise a voice answered "I did last week." So I went over to speak with Bretta, who came from Munich but was living in London. She told me that Kate had chosen her photo from an agency in London and had decided to use her in the *Love and Anger* video. She said they spent the whole day filming. To this day I am still in contact with Bretta. She is the dancer in the sleeve of the single to Kate's right hand side.

Ingo Pohl: I would like to express a big thank you for publishing *HomeGround* even when there is not much news and when times are hard for you. I enjoyed the last three issues a lot. Memories of the past spring to mind. Kate's music was there and shaped my life – how much I've grown since I first heard her music in the '80s, listening to it and falling in love. The great thing is that I never tire of Kate's music. Like old friends the songs grow with you and reveal sides you were not able to notice when you were younger.

Dumbledore: I am a big fan of Kate Bush and a first time user of the internet. What struck me whilst surfing the net is the huge fanbase that Kate has got and in relation to Kate's miserly output, this is an incredible achievement.

The problem I find with fanzines is the lack of constructive criticism; you get the impression that if Kate released an album of Hanson cover songs it would still be lauded as the greatest thing since sliced bread. It is in my opinion undeniable that Kate has not released a great album since the halcyon days of *Hounds of Love*. Can anybody honestly say that *The Red Shoes* was a good album and worth waiting for? It is time for Kate to get back to basics; her best songs have always been simple and not overladen with instrumentation e.g. *Man with the Child in his Eyes*, *This Woman's Work*, *Moments of Pleasure*. It is time for some quality control and for somebody to have the guts to tell her that songs like *Constellation of the Heart* are poor. Perhaps an album that is not self-produced would help this process. Let's hope that Kate's next album will be the album to break this trend.

August Lange: I am a 37 year old man and when I first heard *Wuthering Heights*, I cried. I had never heard of Kate. Listening to college radio, her music stood out as unique and I immediately bought *The Kick Inside*. Here in New Jersey, she is basically unknown, but the other day at a record store I overheard someone asking about *Running Up That Hill*. The employee didn't have a clue so I told him to buy *Hounds of Love*. No other performer has had more effect on my life, with the exception of John Lennon.

Gravity

Rachel Lisi

I've got apples in my head
Juicy fruit that drips the sweetness
Into my heart and out of my hands
Sometimes it seeps through my eyes
And what I see of this world reflects
The tastes of an orchard

Shifting seashells in the waves
Deepest creatures in the watery night
Pink sunsets and salty surf
Heal me
Deliver me
They only need to touch my feet to
Cleanse me

Humanity
Dignity
All that comes within
I am not ashamed to have anatomy
Hunger
Passion
Love and rage without the sin

I have not lost my way
I have found my home
Earth presents me with centers
Gravity
Heredity
Mortality
Welcome to my Queendom.

Memories

Sarah Mackenzie

A bright white balloon
Flies towards the stars
People stop and look
From their corporate cars.
The spirit of a loved one
Floats up to the sky
The balloon
It's last farewell goodbye
These unending nights
In eternal bliss
There are so many ways
When time no longer exists.

Resting in silence
Will his stories be told?
For today
His eyes have stopped growing old.
He is not a forgotten man
For I am young and still stand
At least for my time
His memories ring their chime.

Retracing the Scenes

Somewhere in between (4): 1999-2005

Compiled from the news pages of issues 63 (May 1999) to 75 (March 2005)

In 1999 Kate was absent from public sight, but from the various polls, name checks, cover versions, and other comments, plainly present in the minds of many, and remembered with much affection.

The January 1999 *Record Collector* included an eleven-page feature on Kate. *HomeGround* was asked by the writer James Blandford to assist, and we did peruse a draft of the article. We did suggest some alterations, some of which were adopted, and some of which were not. It was nonetheless broadly a good survey of Kate's career by a journalist who claimed to be a fan, though he could not understand her need for privacy, and didn't understand or even like *The Red Shoes*. In the March edition of *Q* there was a two-page spread entitled 'The Grooming of Kate Bush', which tried to tell Kate's story between July 1976 and January 1978 using excerpts from interviews from various EMI types.

This Woman's Work was featured (again!) in an early February episode ('Drawing the Line – Part II') of the new hit US teen soap 'Felicity' in a scene where one of the major characters was dealing with the outcome of a date rape. The track was also included in the later *Felicity* soundtrack album. The show's website said this: "We've gotten more response from this song than any other because it's so heartbreaking... The gesture and feelings Julie and Ben share are enormously enhanced by this song at an emotional point that requires you to cry".

A dance version of *Running Up That Hill* appeared on an Australian CD *Glad To Be Gay* by the group Levi 9. This was taken from the 'Live at Queer Nation Melbourne' concert in 1996. As part of Comic Relief night on 12th March, Alan Partridge (comedian Steve Coogan) sought a £1million pledge for performing a version of his 'Kate Bush medley' live on BBC1 TV. The sum was duly pledged by Joe Public, the medley was performed, and the host, Lenny Henry (Comic Strip regular and backing vocals on *The Red Shoes*) noted that this *proved* he couldn't sing!

Pat Benatar's newly released anthology *Sychronictic Wanderings* included her cover of *Wuthering Heights*. Both she and Neil Geraldo commented n the sleeve note. Benatar: "Oh how I loved this song! Kate Bush was and still is one of my favorite songwriters and singers. I loved the visual references and her quirky delivery on her original version of the song. I was always disappointed with my performance on our version. In my overzealousness I think I missed the target. I've always wanted to re-cut it, maybe one day I will." Geraldo: "This was the only song off *Crimes of Passion* that we recorded two versions of. This version is the same as on *Crimes of Passion*. Maybe someday we will bring the other one out of the cave".

In the 29th April issue of *Rolling Stone*, Jeff Beck listed *Running Up That Hill* as one of his five favourite tunes saying: "On the female front, Kate was kind of left out. But I think she was the first in terms of stylising and making really interesting videos and songs"... In the May *NME*, lead singer Brett of Suede revealed that the first single he ever bought was *Wuthering Heights*... Heather Nova interviewed in an Adelaide free-sheet *dB* talks about hearing *The Kick Inside* at 12 years old, and listening to it "over and over again and I guess it was a fairly strong influence for me".

Another place on the internet that Kate fans were beginning to frequent was eBay "the internet version of a car boot sale". The most notable item on eBay in April 1999 was described thus: "Kate Bush artefacts Category: Music memorabilia Offered By: Fred (Vermorel) Description: *A bundle of hand written notes tied in ribbon, with one cassette tape. This lot represents some of the artefacts created while researching The Secret History of Kate Bush, Omnibus Press, 1983, the best selling of Kate Bush biogs. The author frequently positioned himself at the top of the iron fire escape running up the side of KB's former home in Brockley, South London, and, fortified with a flask of tea and cheese and salad sandwiches, would spend the night with his ear pressed to the fire escape door analysing sounds from the interior of the house... These items were exhibited at the Winchester School of Art last year and are authenticated as genuine.*" Our reaction: "Well genuine they may be, but would you want them in your house? You don't know where they've been. Further comment superfluous. And some people still can't understand why Kate values her private life so much!"

In issue 63, June 1999, we stated: "The line from the EMI press office is that Kate is working on new material. At HomeGround Towers we have a feeling that there is some new energy flowing and the Millennium will bring some new and wonderful things. Any release dates are still highly speculative, but our wild guess is that the earliest likely date for the release of new material from Kate is Spring 2000, with Autumn 2000 being more likely. We can, however, definitely kill off the following rumours: "Album to be released in September 1999" (EMI Greece). "Kate Bush has amazingly scrapped the concept album she has been working on for five years to start a career writing plays." (*The Sun* and BBC Radio 1) "Kate's new 3-CD album would be out soon" (unspecified European magazine, recycling material from an Italian web site). All of these assertions are untrue."

By the Summer of 1999 Kate and Danny (and Bertie!) had taken up residence in their newly renovated house in Berkshire. Kate had begun writing and demoing again at the studio at East Wickham Farm, but the inconvenience meant that with Del's supervision, the equipment was soon being moved to the new house and being updated in the process. Kate had deferred the idea of a new compilation, and instead as soon as the new studio could be ready – sometime in the Autumn of 1999 - preferred to get right on with a new album. Wither the material written and recorded 1996 to 1998? As had happened before, it seems some of this was recycled, but much was simply left in the can.

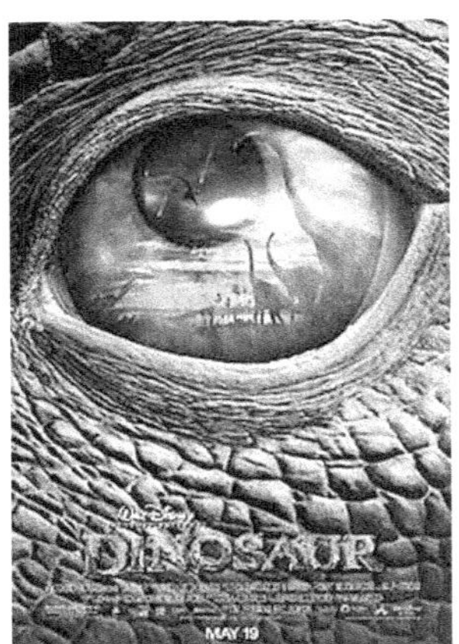

Dinosaur (2000)

When Kate's studio was becoming ready in Autumn 1999, one of the first things she used it for was the recording of a soundtrack song for the Disney animation *Dinosaur*, which was scheduled for release the following year. Due to the photo-realistic animation, *Dinosaur* was rumoured to be one of the most expensive films ever made, the budget exceeding the then record holding *Titanic*. It was intended to be Disney's answer to the more serious animations emanating from Dreamworks. Disney sought out Kate to provide a soundtrack song that would be at the emotional turning point of the film (in the same way *This Woman's Work* had been with *She's Having a Baby*). It appears, however, that Kate had some problems agreeing the lyrics of the song with the Disney production team. Kate wrote the song for the film as it stood when Disney sent over the sequence. There was immediately a problem with the lyrics, as the suits in charge didn't like Kate's words. Then, after test screenings, the suits ordered a re-edit of the relevant sequence, and then asked Kate for more changes in the song as it no longer fitted Disney's concept of what they wanted. Finally, in order to avoid having the song sung in a multiplicity of languages, they asked for 'a song without words', or 'emotional background' as some called it. At that point it seems Kate threw in the towel.

After release of the film the following year, *USA Today* ran a story in their 21st July 2000 issue about the process of 'test screenings' where film makers test films against real audiences and as a consequence can make substantial changes. Problems are ironed out, but often the process removes anything which disturbs or offends - artistic integrity notwithstanding. With *Dinosaur*, the test audience reported that they were bored and expected more levity from a Disney film. As a consequence long montages were shortened, and jokes and one liners were added. This seems at odds with the original more dramatic intent of the film. Kate's song was cut, according to the director Eric Leighton, because the rest of the score was instrumental, and "hearing a voice singing seemed to confuse and unsettle the audience". Their loss we think. Possibly literally, as although the film made money, it did not make the big money that was expected.

In issue 64 (November 1999) we reported: "Kate began writing and demoing songs for a new album earlier this year. She has had her recording studio serviced and upgraded and recording is expected to begin before Christmas. Kate is happy and full of a new energy and our former wild guess that there may be a new album by Autumn 2000 still remains a distinct possibility. So we can kill off the following rumours - that Kate has retired from the music business (said to have been announced on Jo Wiley's Radio 1 music show) and that Kate has almost finished a new album, but is at war with EMI (reported on the Italian web site)".

The Tenth Anniversary HomeGround Glastonbury on 1st August 1999 had fabulous sunny weather, and a turnout of near 40 Kate fans from the UK and Europe on Glastonbury Tor.

A Tribute to Kate Bush– the Child in Her Eyes was a collection of 19 cover versions of Kate's songs (from all albums except *The Dreaming*) by 'E-Clypse featuring Jemma Price', from the Dressed to Kill label which has specialised in quirky tribute albums, having previously done The Beatles and Bowie amongst others, two CDs for £3.75 usually at HMV. We thought there was very little to commend this except the price. Very sparse guitar and voice cover versions with little production. *Breathing* was interesting, but the rest teeter on the brink of a 1970s 'Top of the Pops' party album. We didn't see much point when covering one of Kate's tracks, in trying to imitate Kate.

One of the guests on the Rainbow network chat server in November 1999 was Sophie B Hawkins. A fan asked her what she thought of Tori Amos, and she replied that Tori had inspired her to push herself further as a musician. Hawkins then asked the questioner: "What about Kate Bush? *She's the beginning.* I love that song *This Woman's Work*"... In an interview in November's CDNOW Paula Cole put *Hounds of Love* in her top ten albums: "She was so passionate, and so outlandish in her vision. She was also one of the first female producers I encountered and that was inspirational to me".

Kate's enduring reputation was still being reflected in the polls throughout 1999. In the 25th February issue of *Goldmine* Michael B. Smith listed the '25 Essential Rock'n'Roll Albums of the '70s', and at no.22 was *The Kick Inside.* "Although she has never caught on in America on a grand scale like she did in her native England, Kate Bush is one of the most creative artists working today."... *Q* could not let an issue pass without mentioning Kate. In the February edition *Wuthering Heights* featured at no.32 in their '100 greatest ever singles' poll ("best bit: 0.43 that first preposterous chorus") and *The Kick Inside* is in 'the best 10 Diva albums' ("a startling debut of plaintive, eccentric beauty, heady mysticism and powerful sensuality") ... The April *Mojo* followed up on its October 1998 'Greatest Singers' poll voted by musicians which put Kate at no.81. This one, voted by the punters, put Kate at no.48.

On 29th July 1999 VH-1 in the US ran a feature programme on 'The 100 Greatest Women of Rock'n'Roll'. Kate was one of the very few British artists who made the list, coming in at number 46. The only British artists above her were Annie Lennox (no.9), Dusty Springfield (no.24) and Marianne Faithfull (no. 25). Host: "She's one of the most original and daring artists in the history of popular music. British native Kate Bush opened the door into the female imagination, never before explored in song". Maxwell: "Kate is so exceptional because she just let her music speak for herself. Making all these amazing songs, making these brilliant little children, these gems". Tori Amos: "I got her work and I was really moved. And more than anything I was moved by her as a producer". Paula Cole: "I think *Hounds of Love* is, like, one of the most brilliant, brilliant production jobs I've ever heard". Host: "With her mystical lyrics and prodigious piano talents, Bush gave the industry a new idea about the power of feminine music".

Issue 63 (May 1999) announced the 10th Anniversary HomeGround Glastonbury

The August *Q* put Kate in their '100 Greatest Stars of the 20th Century' at no.33: "Venus in leg-warmers. Having made her sparkling arrival as a 19-year-old in 1977, Kate Bush retired from live performances after one tour and has released albums sparingly. The goggle-eyed, hello-flowers, hello-trees dance routines and paint-peeling trill made her a soft target for critics, but a subtle refining of her art and growing older has resulted in a sophisticated artist, extraordinarily successful but still shrouded in mystery".

Over the weekend of 2nd-3rd October, VH-1 in the UK ran their own chart of the 'Top 100 Women in Rock'. There was no explanation as to how this chart was compiled. Celine Dion was no.3 and Whitney Houston no.2. Kate came in at no.26, just behind Debbie Harry at no.25. Unsurprisingly the station chose the *Babooshka* video to play.

The 'Music of the Millennium' Poll conducted on behalf on Channel 4, HMV and Classic-FM surveyed over half a million people in the UK and Ireland, and it claimed to be 'the biggest and most comprehensive survey on popular music ever undertaken'. The results were presented in a feature TV programme on 14th November 1999. In the 'female singer' category (one of ten), Madonna was no.1, and Kate came in at no.9 between Annie Lennox and Björk. She also featured in the 'best album' category, where *Hounds of Love* was no.47, and 'best song', where *Wuthering Heights* was no.84. Kate was also no.66 'best songwriter' and no.61 'most influential musician of the millennium'.

The January 2000 *Q* featured 'The Greatest Rock'n'Roll Photographs Ever' and Gered Mankowitz talked about the featured Kate session in Soho in 1978: "EMI asked me to come in and see the video for *Wuthering Heights*. Love it or hate it, you're going to want to hear it again because you can't believe your ears, so we needed a picture where you can't believe your eyes".

The infamous 'pink top' photos

In a TV interview shown in Belgium on 16th March Colin Vearncombe (composer of *Wonderful Life* and usually known as 'Black'), explained that he was a big fan of Kate and in the early 1990s had written a song inspired by her entitled *Storm Cloud Katherine.* This had been included on his 1999 album *Accused.* In an *NME* chat transcript that same month Shack members Michael Head (formerly of The Pale Fountains) and John Head were asked with whom they would most like to do a collaboration. John: "Kate Bush, just before she did the *Man with the Child in his Eyes*" Mick: "I want to get her to produce the next album. Would be interesting".

April 2000 brought the 70th Birthday celebrations for Rolf Harris, who played digeridoo to great effect on *The Dreaming.* Pictures of Kate with Rolf appeared in the popular press. *OK!* Magazine said: "Singer Kate Bush turned up at the drinks reception to give Rolf her birthday greetings, but the fercely private star declined to stay for dinner". A special tribute book was published: *The Court of King Rolf – A Tribute to Rolf Harris* (edited by Mark Walker). Kate recalled how memories of *Sun Arise* immediately turned her thoughts to Rolf when she needed digeridoo on *The Dreaming*: "Rolf created the perfect atmosphere for the song. I hope very much to work with him again one day". Paddy revealed that *Sun Arise* was actually the first record he ever bought, and noted that

Rolf was experimenting with world music before it even had a name. He remembered Rolf turning up at Abbey Road to make his contribution to *The Dreaming* "with a whole arsenal of digeridoos, including a telescopic one which could be tuned to any pitch". On that day Paddy had his first digeridoo lesson, from Rolf, who made sure that by the time *Hounds of Love* came around, he was able to play well enough to appear on *The Big Sky*.

The Rough Guide to Rock (second edition) said: "Private trauma overshadowed the making of her seventh album, *The Red Shoes* (1993)... There were moments of sheer exuberance… but overall it was a painfully intense album... She may well have to share the spotlight in future, but the popularity of this unique talent seems unlikely to fade".

And so to a project which did not come off. In the Editor's letter in issue 65 (June 2000) Dave said: "As most of you know, I used to work for EMI in the UK and during that time one of my projects was the re-mastering and re-packaging of *Hounds of Love* as part of the EMI Centenary. Everyone, including Kate, was very pleased with the result and we started to make plans to tackle the other studio albums, then things changed at the company and when I left plans were put on hold. Over the past three years the idea has been running around inside my head and I have continued to have a healthy working relationship with EMI. Just before Christmas, myself and Steve Davis at EMI put a proposal to Kate to update her remaining catalogue in much the same way that *Hounds of Love* had been, minus the Centenary stuff of course". It didn't happen, sadly. Continuing discussions got caught up with Kate busy with her new son, and then working on the new album, and then the moment was lost.

Then in July 2000 the secret was out. After speculation over some time, and comments in the media from Michael Kamen and Jean Michel Jarre, the media finally caught on when Peter Gabriel mentioned Kate's new son in reply to a question on an online interview by a French website. Kate's happy news was made public after some rather silly coverage in the *Mail on Sunday* and the *Daily Mirror* (and its northern echo the *Scottish Daily Record*), which strongly suggested that Kate's most grievous sin was to have preserved the privacy of her new family life for some considerable time. The British trashy press, which prided itself on knowing everything about every celebrity, or being able to find out everything about every celebrity, was in fact made to look rather foolish. A whole string of completely inaccurate comments suggested that Kate had locked herself and her son away from the world and was never seen by her neighbours. Kate's new house was described ineptly as "forlorn and derelict", in a further attempt to create a completely false picture of a "Miss Haversham". Nothing could be further from the truth. Kate was leading the life of any mum, fitting her work in around her child. The trashy press were just rather slow to catch on.

The bizarre attempts of the press to find a story reached absurd heights when they employed helicopters to overfly Kate's house to try to get pictures, we assume of Kate and her son, contrary to her wishes to preserve his privacy. The *Mail* writer should have drawn the proper conclusion from her own printed words: "Determined and wilful to the core, Kate – then only 21 – withdrew from the world of show business. To reject the glamorous perks of an

Issue 65 (July 2000) carried Kate's good news.

Message from Kate issued by the KBC on 19th July 2000

Hello everyone,

Here is a press statement I have issued and I wanted you to see it....

"A number of inaccurate comments have been made about me in recent articles which I am taking further. I just want everyone to know I am very happy and proud to have such a beautiful son, Bertie - he is absolutely gorgeous. Far from being secretive, I am just trying to be a good protective mother and give him as normal a childhood as possible whilst preserving his privacy - surely everyone can understand that. I am having great fun being a Mother as well as working on a new album"

I hope you will understand how invaluable it has been to me to have a very fulfilling and normal start to motherhood and I felt unable to tell you about Bertie previously for reasons already explained. He is the most beautiful thing I have ever seen. He is my joy and I'm very happy and very busy being a Mum. I am finding time to write for the new album and very pleased so far.

Thanks again for your lovely letters and kind wishes. I hope you will be happy for me.

Lots of love,

Kate XX

international musical career was an extraordinary decision and one that most young women would find impossible to understand ... her only loyalties are to her music and her family".

That anyone should *not* want to put up with a mixture of twenty year-old press cuttings, imagination and pique, which passed as investigative reporting was actually completely understandable to us. After failing to find some sensation, the media lost interest and the story soon vanished from the UK media.

On the 19th July 2000 Kate issued a message through the Kate Bush Club, which was carried in issue 65. In issue 66 (December 2000) we noted that in the midst of all this, Kate had made it quite clear that she was indeed working on a new album: "As ever Del is engineering and already guest musicians are arriving to add their work. Release dates are as ever difficult to guess, but EMI are now hoping and planning for a release in Autumn 2001".

As is now traditional we had glorious weather for the millennium HomeGround Glastonbury gathering, and there were about thirty people on the Tor and afterwards at the Rifleman's Arms. On the Tor we drank a toast (the bubbly kindly provided by Roger Bowman) to Kate on her birthday, and to her son, Bertie.

Kate-related stuff turning up on eBay included one misbegotten (presumably ex-) fan selling three hand-written letters from Kate, which finally went for $342.50, and someone trying to pass off yet again the Kate Simmons issue of *Penthouse*. On the similar Amazon auction site the famous *Eat the Music* UK 7" (of which we are told on uncertain authority that only 17 copies exist) was going for $3,300 (£2,000). The CD-R scam continued.

In an interview conducted on 30th November 2000, with *Sticks*, the Jazz drummers magazine, Peter Erskine the American jazz musician talked about his recent work with Kate: "For the Kate Bush album, I made my conga-playing debut! I think it will be about another year before it comes out. Wonderful poetry and great songs; beautiful voice, and a lovely woman. Cool drum tracks, too, if I may say so". In an online Q&A, Julian Cope was asked which female musicians he admires: "My list of admired female musicians would have to be headed by Yoko Ono, Patti Smith, Kate Bush... ". 'The Importance of Homework' (cont) From The Times – a review of *Tales From New York – The Very Best of Simon and Garfunkel* – "The likes of *Scarborough Fair, The Sounds of Silence, Mrs Robinson* and *Bridge Over Troubled Water* are more than enough to compensate for that dreadful sight of Paul Simon in his solo years, squeezing Kate Bush's bottom in the touchy-feely video for *Don't Give Up*". The grand final of 'Stars in Their Eyes' on 2nd December featured Louise Halliday performing *Babooshka* again.

Dear Louise,
I have seen your performance and
I thought you were wonderful.
Please accept this gift of the cloak
I wore in the original Babooshka
video with my love and best wishes –
I hope it brings you luck.
Have a great time tonight
with love
Kate Bush
X

Kate's note to Louise Halliday December 2000 presenting her with the original 'Babooshka' cloak

During 2000 there were more polls which indicated Kate's enduring appeal. The January *Attitude* put Madonna at no.1 'best female singer in the world' and Kate at no.2, and *Hounds of Love* just outside the top 5 'best album'. May's *Q* put *Hounds of Love* at no. 20 'Best Ever British Album' in a poll of their journalists.

But the *Daily Telegraph* put us firmly in our place: "Those who grew up in the 1970s cannot see that their musical tastes, once so radical, have invisibly transmogrified into Parent Pop. It's all very well continuing to think that Kate Bush is a dark and complex singer, but to everyone under 15, she is a daft old banshee in a silly leotard". Ouch.

The earlier rumours died hard. Speculation in an article in the BBC house magazine *Ariel* in February 2001, treated in some quarters as a definitive EMI announcement, had an EMI spokesman saying that the new album would appear in November 2001. A variation on that had anonymous record pluggers saying an album will be released that Autumn, and was picked up on by 'Top of the Pops 2' when they ran the subtitles under a repeat of Kate's *Hounds of Love* performance on Valentine's Day.

Just a bizarre coincidence!

This Woman's Work continued toward world domination. Japanese female artist ACO covered the track on the B-side of her single *A Hero,* and it subsequently appeared on her fifth album *Material* released in May. CBS used the track in a plug for the Autumn episode of 'Jag', and it was also featured on the second episode of 'Alias', a new show by the creator of 'Felicity' which aired on Sunday nights on ABC in the US. Maxwell, a known Kate admirer with a cover of *This Woman's Work* already on his *Unplugged* album, released a studio version on his *Now* album released in May, and it also appeared on the first single *Get to Know Ya*. Interviewed in the *LA Times* he was asked what drew him to such a quintessentially female song: "To me, the perfect song can be sung by anyone from any genre. Also, it was a good way to let women know that men get it." Asked if he had had a reaction from Kate: "She sent me a letter. I was kind of worried, because songs are like people's children. It was nice to get the nod from the parent, that I did a pretty good job watching the kid."

'The Importance of Homework' (cont): the April 2001 issue of US magazine *Salon* had a feature on Kate. This put Kate's place of birth "50 miles from Stonehenge" in that "creaking pagan and scary" London suburb of Plumstead, apparently full of 17th Century farmhouses. Some of the other research was equally accurate, and though the article was supposed to be a summary of Kate's career, it omitted all mention of *The Dreaming*, and was unaware of the real influence Kate has had on the current crop of (not only) female singer-songwriters in the US. But we liked the conclusion that Kate "decided early on that our approval didn't matter".

The Easter edition of *What's on TV* previewed the Channel 4 'Pop Princesses' programme with a small feature entitled 'Where Did Kate Go?': "It's the worst thing that can happen to a record company executive. You sign up an artist who becomes a big star and sells millions of records. Then, just a few years into a very promising career, your tortured genius decides to hide from the world... For the past eight years she's been a virtual recluse, rarely venturing out in public." Except of course to do all the things any other real human being does of course. But still it came.

The 2nd May 2001 *Daily Mail* revisited their risible accusations that "Kate used the name 'Catherine Earnshaw' as an alias and had it written on her doorbell", insinuating that Kate lived in a fantasy land and believed she is possessed by the spirit of Cathy. The correct technical description for this sort of journalism is "bollocks".

More realistically, if less flatteringly for us, Stuart Maconie wrote in *The Times* on 15th June regarding album preparation times: "Rock music has a glittering rollcall of diligent and painstaking craftsmen, or lazy gits if you prefer. Kate Bush has kept her drooling legions waiting nearly eight years for the follow-up to *The Red Shoes*. But at least she has the honourable excuse of having had and brought up a baby, thus scotching the endless rumours that she has ballooned up to 18 stone or become a compulsive and obsessive studio nitpicker."

Interviewed in *The Guardian* on 29th June Midge Ure might have depressed us. He checks *Hounds of Love* as a favourite album and says "I knew the engineer who mixed that, and it was done on a desk that wasn't meant to be used at all, so you have all these strange noises coming up where they shouldn't to make this fantastic sound. I'd like to think that she's still making music, but the last time I saw her she was talking about giving it all up, which would be such a shame... You wouldn't be allowed to do what she was doing now".

But in issue 67 (July 2001) we said: "Kate continues to work on new material. Any guesses about a possible release date are just that – guesses. Last year, as we reported in the last *HomeGround*, EMI were looking hopefully at this Autumn. Now we're in 2001 that is plainly not realistic. To get a release even in late Autumn would mean the album would have to be finished about now. With an artist like Kate who works to no-one's plan but her own, any likely release dates are speculative At this point it looks like the earliest date would be Autumn 2002."

And there were more polls: the January 2001 *Uncut* compiled a list of 'the best 100 singles since the punk era' and put *Running Up That Hill* at no. 53... Channel 4's 'Top Ten Pop Princesses' on 4th April put Kate at no 4... Kate was voted No. 45 in the '100 Best Voices of the Century' by BBC Radio 2 in a programme presented by Paul Gambaccini over Easter, of which *The Guardian* said: "It is inevitably likely to prompt much debate among music lovers, as it poses such questions as whether David Bowie is really a better singer than Bob Dylan, the relative merits of Kate Bush and Madonna".

And more and more references: Mimori Yusa, a Japanese artist explaining that Kate has had a strong influence on her life and music... Courtney Love making the comment on her site's guestbook in a battle of the bands between PJ Harvey and Tori Amos. "Polly (wins) hands down. Also don't forget for ducks sake there is someone named KATE BUSH – if you like Tori for all that glossy beauty doll stuff you might like Kate better (*Never For Ever* and *Lionheart*)"... Toyah Wilcox on the BBCi Musical memories website: "In Kate Bush's song *Moments of Pleasure*, there's a reference to her mother that just touched me so deeply. I was crying uncontrollably and I crashed the car!" ...Jewel used to listen to Kate when she was younger, and she tried to sing the songs exactly like her and record them. Kate was a kind of inspiration to her... Top 10 songs from Tricky (10). *Army Dreamers* by Kate Bush "A great song... She's the best singer. The Billie Holiday of our times. There's no singer alive that can touch Kate Bush. Go back and listen to the diversity – the lyrical content... Listen to all her stuff. It's amazing how far ahead and advanced that woman is. I still listen to her now and it blows my mind. It influenced *Strugglin*"... Dido mentions in *Q* interview that *The Whole Story* was the first record she ever bought... Eileen Rose says "the two people I'm most influenced by are Kate Bush and Tom Waits.".

The first interview Kate gave for some eight years appeared in the December 2001 issue of *Q*. Conducted in November, a few days before the *Q* Awards ceremony, the occasion was the publication in *Q* of their readers poll of the top '100 Women Who Rock Your World'.

Quite amazingly Kate came in at no.3 in the poll. The significance of such a position considering Kate's then most recent album had been released in 1993, is obvious. The performers on all sides of her in the poll had released albums and toured. Kate's work was clearly seared into the collective consciousness of all music lovers; and not just middle-aged ones who could actually remember the release of *Wuthering Heights*. It was clear to us that Kate had a growing legion of young fans, as a visit at that time to any Kate-related board on the internet would verify.

Kate's position in the world of music makers in 2001 was evident from her reception at the *Q* awards. In a small way, the *Q* Awards ceremony on 29th October, marked her re-entrance into the public world in much the same way as did her appearance on 'Wogan' in 1985. Those who would have had it that Kate was retired, forgotten and irrelevant, found out exactly how wrong they were. Though the press photographers could only boo and jeer when Kate failed to observe their rituals in entering the building, her fellow musicians inside rose as one in a standing ovation, as *Q* noted "of Liams, Lydons, and Travises".

Kate was presented with the award for 'Classic Songwriter', and sharing the accolades with the 'Inspiration' award was one John Lydon, who turned up to let the assembled rock industry worthies know in exactly what contempt he held them, giving or throwing away his award as soon as it was put in his hands. The only person present who was not on the receiving end of Lydon's bile was Kate, for whom he soon made clear, he had the greatest respect: "*I'll tell you who I'd like to say hello to: Kate Bush! I love you to death! Your music is fucking brilliant! But you know what Kate? We are worthy!*"

Kate's award was presented by Midge Ure, and he introduced "the genius that is Kate Bush". Kate thanked the readers of *Q*, and said with a smile "*I am actually making an album, it's just taking longer than I thought – and I'm having a really great time with my son.*" Kate then went through her list of thank-yous, concluding with her mother, and her father "*because when I was a little girl and I first started writing songs, whenever I asked him to come and listen he would always say 'yes' and that meant everything.*"

The picture of the year has to be that one of Kate and John Lydon, two musical genii, arm in arm on the *Q* sofa. John Lydon is asked "You're obviously quite a fan of Kate Bush?", to which he replied: "Kate Bush is a true original. It's not nice that she's been imitated – Torrid Aimless, sorry, Tori Amos. But Kate Bush is a genuine talent. She went through the same shit I did when she started, 'Oh that's not singing'. Who the fuck wrote the rules about music?" It will not be so much of a surprise to those who remember that the heavy rockers and the punks from the very beginning in 1978 had good words for Kate. It was the mystified *NME* which stated in 1979 "she does have a peculiarly heavy respect and a proportionately punk following".

Nigel Godrich, winner of 'Best Producer' for Travis and Radiohead said that the best thing for him so far in 2001 was meeting Kate: "I'm in awe of her. Her records fundamentally enforced what I am as a person. When you listen to stuff as a teenager, you identify with elements in the music. There's a real hidden wisdom there. It's beautifully written. If she needs anyone to mix her new album, I'm after the job... I'm going home to listen to Kate." QTV reported that Midge introduced Fran Healy, Travis lead singer, to Kate, but that he was so in awe of her that he was lost for words!

The *Q* Awards and Kate's presence was heavily reported in the press and broadcast media. The BBC NewsWebsite: "The awards, which are well respected within the music industry, also singled out veteran singer Kate Bush for a special classic songwriter award". The *NME* Website: "Other veteran names to be honoured included... reluctant star Kate Bush, awarded the Classic Songwriter title." *The Times* 30th October: "Rock's older guard took the garlands at the awards in Central London, with Kate Bush and Elvis Costello victorious." *The Independent* 30th October: "But while the attendant stars, including New Order, Super Furry Animals, Coldplay, Feeder and Liam Howlett from The Prodigy, refused to be roused by Lydon's lone antics, the room rose united to give a standing ovation to Kate Bush, who won this year's Classic Songwriter award – and whom even Lydon graced with complimentary words." *Billboard*: "The uniquely British Kate Bush received a rapturous welcome today at the 12th annual *Q* awards in London, honoured in the category of classic songwriter by readers of the UK music magazine".

Kate may even have done better in the *Q* poll. Shortly after the results were announced the *Daily Telegraph* reported: "The authority of *Q* magazine, the self-proclaimed bible of the music press, might not be quite as rock solid as it claims. The latest issue is dominated by a readers' poll to find the greatest female recording artists. The surprise winner is PJ Harvey – a singer long considered more popular with critics than the public. Madonna came second and Kate Bush third. Unfortunately, we are reliably informed that readers, in fact, voted heavily in favour of Madonna, with Kate Bush second and Harvey just scraping into the Top Ten."

This is what Kate said in the Kate Bush Club newsletter just before Christmas 2001:

"It's been a while since I was last in touch with you all. Thank you for your cards & letters of congratulations on the Q award I received recently. It was a great honour to receive the award and I found the audience's response quite overwhelming. Things have been really hectic and I so appreciate all your feedback and encouragement. Sometimes the progress of the album is painfully slow but I find I get so busy being a Mum – however, I think the work is going well. I get so little time in the studio that my approach is very different, I'll be really interested to see what you all think when it's finished.

Bertie is very excited about Christmas this year. I hope you all have a fantastic Christmas and a very Happy New Year.

Lots of love, Kate xx"

In January 2002 Kate performed live for the first time in 15 years, guesting at Dave Gilmour's gig on the 18th.

Kate at the Gilmour Gig January 2002.

Photo: Phil Waters

The February *GQ* magazine in the US had an interview with actor, and *HomeGround* reader, Guy Pearce: "Pearce needs to buy a Jeff Buckley CD for a friend. As he pulls into the Virgin Megastore parking garage, the ticket dispenser talks to him. "Please drive your car forward." Inside after a short, yearning pit-stop near the Kate Bush selections ('know the President of her fan club'), he cruises the DVD aisle.". We think he actually meant Dave, but we won't tell if you don't... Maxwell's studio version of *This Woman's Work* was now released as a single in the USA. Kate was accordingly mentioned in Fred Bronson's Chart Beat section of *Billboard*: "British national treasure Kate Bush is back on the Hot 100, as a songwriter... Bush gets credit this issue as the songwriter of *This Woman's Work* as covered in an R&B version by Maxwell. His Columbia album track enters at No.75. That makes it the highest-charting song written by Bush in more than 16 years, since *Running Up That Hill* reached No.30 in November 1985." Interviewed in the 25th April *Rolling Stone* Conrad Keely of The Undead, listed his favourite albums: "Kate Bush, *Lionheart* – It's too bad that modern singer songwriters possess a mere half the talent it took Kate to brush her teeth."

In issue 69 (April 2002) we said: "The usual crop of silly rumours abound, some being endlessly recycled, as with the album supposedly being entitled *A Child Within* (What? Not *An Unearthly Child*?), or *Round and Round*, with a tour planned for Autumn 2003. Sky News actually announced that Kate will release a new single called *Bertie* in the near future with the album appearing at the end of this year. The reality is that work on the new album is, as ever proceeding at a pace determined by Kate alone, in between her other family commitments, and at this point it is not possible to say when the album will be released, though realistically it is not likely to be this year".

Intrepid English explorer, Benedict Allen was in the midst of recounting his adventures in a series called 'Ice Dogs' on BBC2. Having fought his way through Siberian blizzards and across dangerous frozen rivers, he was given a warm welcome by the 300 Chukchis and Russians of the port of Emulen who put on a show with a specially-written address entitled 'England – Land of Poets; London – Romantic City of Fog' which included a rousing dance rendition of *Wuthering Heights*. It was utterly bizarre in context with the rest of the programme, which was about folk who had no contact with the outside world apart from occasional reindeer herders and food parcel drops by air.

David Keenan of Scotland's *Sunday Herald* compiled a list of the best albums of all time. *Hounds of Love* came in at no.14: "The tidal beauty of Kate Bush's moon music has long enlivened the mainstream of British pop. Beneath the glossy production jobs and airbrushed photo-shoots lurks something truly elemental... we should look at her work in the tradition of such visionary English artists as William Blake, Derek Jarman and Current 93. 1985's *Hounds of Love* is still her greatest work, mixing esoteric musings with a series of compositions that seem to completely ignore any of the basic tenets of songcraft. Although the second half of the record is by far the most ambitious and startling – a conceptual suite defined by dramatic tempo-changes and cut-up voices – it's the languorous beauty of the singles that remains the most affecting."

"What do you do?" the Queen asked Kate. She attended a special ceremony at the Royal Academy of Arts on May 22nd 2002 as part of the Queen's Golden Jubilee celebrations. The event honoured the work of young artists to whom the Queen donated special prizes. Kate was introduced to the Queen, with Mick Hucknall of Simply Red. "The multi-million selling Simply Red star was standing with '80s singer Kate Bush... when the Queen approached and asked: "And what do you two do?" Polite Mick replied: "We are singer-songwriters." The Queen nodded and made small talk." Sky News reported it thus: "Bush, who was introduced to the Queen with 'Dynasty' and 'Tenko' actress Stephanie Beacham and former Monty Python cartoonist Terry Gilliam, said: "She had to ask us all who we were... but she was lovely – she was radiant."

On 23rd May 2002 Kate was among the musicians honoured at the prestigious Ivor Novello Awards ceremony at the Grosvenor House hotel in London's Park Lane. The awards, then in their 47th year, honour the contribution of songwriters, composers and music publishers. On receiving the PRS Award for 'Outstanding Contribution to British Music', Kate said: "It's so special to be thought of as a songwriter. This means so much to me, I'll really treasure this." BBC Radio 2 took the occasion as an excuse to play excerpts from six of Kate's songs including *The Dreaming*. Playing the latter on air had hitherto been a capital offence at Broadcasting House. The tracks were introduced with a recording of Kate's acceptance speech, and the DJ commenting that Kate was probably the most respected British female of the last three decades and that for many, her appearance was the highlight of the awards.

Other parts of the media took a rather more prejudiced view, commenting that Kate received the prize, despite her career having remained almost inactive for the best part of a decade. *The Daily Telegraph* put it this way: "Kate Bush best known for her hit *Wuthering Heights* but who has released no new material for nearly a decade, was recognised for her outstanding contribution to the music industry." It is quite clear that these people had not the faintest idea as to the huge influence Kate's music had been on the singer-songwriters, and especially the female singer-songwriters who followed her, in Britain, Europe, the US and worldwide. Never was an award so appropriate and so deserved.

The Ukulele Orchestra of Great Britain started in 1985, believing "that all genres of music were available for reinterpretation, as long as they are played on the ukulele". Their live performances included a version of one of Kate's classics: "It took some cheek for George Hinchcliffe, the orchestra's boss... to reinvent Kate Bush's *Wuthering Heights* as a cocktail-jazz croon, but he did it" (*Independent* review of Spitalfields gig)... "the highlights of which were their own very peculiar interpretation of Kate Bush's *Wuthering Heights* in which the audience is encouraged to join in by shouting 'Heathcliff!' at appropriate points" (review of 28th May Cecil Sharp House gig). In issue 70 *HomeGround* reported that their rendition of *Wuthering Heights*, was also on the track listing of their third album *A Fistful of Ukuleles*.

The New York Times put it like this: "How can one describe the genius of Kiki and Herb? It's drag cabaret with the gut-wrenching impact of the best punk rock, the smarts of the snobbiest underground music and the sick attractions of vintage torch lounge." The act included covers of *Running Up That Hill*, *This Woman's Work* and *Moments of Pleasure*.

In issue 70 (September 2002) we said: "Recording of Kate's new album continues, the passing months bringing more news of guest artists making their own particular contributions". On his weekly BBC Radio 2 show 'Sounds of the Seventies' at the end of July, Steve Harley, a long time friend of Kate's, played *Wow*, introducing the song with these comments: "There are even those who don't go too big on Kate Bush, I pity them". After playing the song he casually mentioned: "I saw Kate Bush a few weeks ago, and I am pleased to say she is recording as we speak. My drummer Stuart Elliot is playing on the album and says she is bang on form".

Stuart himself was interviewed earlier for the 'Drummer Interviews' website: "I am doing a new album with Kate Bush. This is a lot of fun as she has kind of gone back to wanting drums, by that I mean not restricted by not using hi-hat and cymbals and not relying on all that massive gated reverb stuff. She has opted for a more sensitive, even jazzy approach which, as chance would have it, I have also gravitated back towards... I bought a Sonor Jungle snare for about $100.00. It is about ten inches in diameter and two inches deep. What a sound though! It's Kate's favourite at the moment... I plan to continue with the composing, and of course, look out for Kate's new album!"

Mick Karn's official website indicated in June that he had recorded bass with Kate in a session which took place earlier in the year. At the same time there were the usual rumours. One story was that an ex-EMI marketing chief was given a completed track list for a new album apparently finished bar some remixing, with the request that he deal with the promotion. Another rumour has a cover of Soft Cell's *Youth* included. We recommended: "Treat with extreme scepticism".

The Maturing Influence of Time. It's funny what the perspective of increasing age does. In an April 1979 issue of the *NME* the then young terror Charles Shaar Murray wrote a scathing review of Kate's live show, one of the very, very few bad reviews the gigs received. In effect he

accused her of deceiving an audience that was unable to tell the difference between a real artist and a poseur. In the 3rd October 2002 issue of *The Independent* CSM was still being scathing, but this time about the 'pop' industry in general and EMI in particular: "When EMI first signed a very young Kate Bush, they nurtured her for two years before releasing anything, and their willingness to invest in the long-term viability of a promising young artist paid off. Who could be bothered to do that now?"

The position thus vacated by CSM had previously been taken up by one Cliff McLenehan who had an article in the August *Record Collector* about Kate-related websites. Mr. McLenehan's affinity to matters Kate was well illustrated by his opening remarks: "The lady has only ever done one tour (sorry Bush Babies, but I caught it at the London Palladium – and it was dire.)" Also in that issue, three of the participants in the tribute article to Stuart Adamson, who had tragically committed suicide in 2001, are asked what they miss about him most. Midge Ure replies: "The fact that there's one less person fighting against mediocrity. I had a great conversation with Kate Bush about 10 years ago. We were doing a duet and we went to her studio. She was talking about quitting and I said, 'You can't because if you quit, I'll quit, and if I quit somebody else who cares will quit'. Stuart was one of those steps down the line. He was someone who cared, who's not there now."

Not to be confused with Rihanna, who hadn't met Evan Rogers yet

In an interview in *The Guardian* on 29th November 2002, Ladytron talked about their musical influences. Helen: "Kate Bush is amazing, there's no one like her." Rhianna was currently promoting her new album *Get On* and was very clear about her Kate influences: "Ask any pop girl for their primary influence and more often than not the answer will be 'Madonna', and before you know it they'll call their child Romeo. Leeds-bred, mad-haired Rhianna would be more likely to say 'Kate Bush'. And indeed she does. 'She's my inspiration really,' giggles the 19-year-old coyly. 'She's my idol really, she was so free in her way of writing, she didn't care about who was trendy and who was cool, she just did her own thing. It was always, "Kate Bush is weird", but it's cool to be different'". The Alison Moyet chat forum site asked her on 19th October whether she had crossed paths with Kate Bush: "I'm very impressed by Kate Bush. She is pure uncompromising talent and I can only feel envy at the apparent flawless way she has managed her career. Both commercially and creatively successful and still an enigma. Clever mare! I saw her once at a party Kirsty (McColl) had some years back. She looked as shy as I felt and we never spoke."

A number of artists chose Kate tracks as their favourites on Autumn BBC Radio 2 programmes: When Beth Orton chose *The Man with the Child in his Eyes* she said "this song kills me. It's a classic and it's from my fave Kate Bush album *The Kick Inside*. The song is full of hope – that there is the right man out there". Steve Balsamo picked *This Woman's Work*, Rhianna chose *Wuthering Heights* and Brian Kennedy selected *Running Up That Hill*, all on Radio 2's Ken Bruce Show. On another show, Latin pop singer Shakira chose *Wuthering Heights*, saying that her sister used to play it to her all the time when she was a lass.

Amongst the 2002 charts and polls were: May 13th: the 'Top 100 Favourite Hit Singles of all time', as voted for in a poll conducted by the *Guinness Book of Hit Singles* which placed Kate at number 40 with *Wuthering Heights*. 31,000 people voted and 10th June *Wuthering Heights* was voted no.18 in a poll of 'the top songs by British artists since the Queen's coronation in 1952'. For some reason the September poll by music channel VH1 of 'the 100 Greatest Women in music' received more press coverage than one of these frequent polls would normally get. Kate was placed at number 10, and various media reports emphasised that she was the highest placed British female artist, "nine years after her last album". Madonna topped the poll, Kylie was second and 750,000 votes were cast. In the course of the chart countdown, VH1 did a nice piece on Kate. Toyah said some beautiful things about Kate's work, and Toploader, who sing to Kate's records at home, and Midge Ure contributed.

Kate was just outside the top 10 in the November BBC Radio 2 poll of it's listeners 'top 100 favourite number one singles', conducted to mark the 50th anniversary of the UK charts. In the countdown played on Radio 2 on 9th November, *Wuthering Heights* was placed at number 11, the highest placing by a female artist. The result got a splash of media coverage, mostly due to the absence of newer acts. Not one track from the last fifteen years made it into the top 25. In the celebrities' choices, Alison Moyet chose *Wuthering Heights*, describing Kate as "A fantastic artist" and the track as "a really unusual record." In the presenters' choices Simon Mayo also chose Kate: "When the vocals started I just stopped and looked at the radio..."

The December *Q* published a poll of reader's 100 Greatest Albums of all time and *Hounds of Love* appeared at no.51: "Prog-rock's only sexy record. Still sounds terrifying and sexy". In *Rolling Stone*'s 'Women in Rock' issue, *The Kick Inside* was listed at no.42 on the '50 most important albums by women' chart. *Hounds of Love* was voted number 50 in the BBC Radio 6 "Glorious 50" poll.

In issue 71 (December 2002) we said: "As Kate works on her eighth studio album, it is no surprise that Peter Gabriel, whose last studio album proper was also ten years ago, has released his new album, *Up*. He was interviewed for the October issue of Pulse, the Tower Records magazine, by Bill Forman, and in discussing the tracks, the talk turned to Kate. Gabriel says: "I saw Kate a couple of months back and I think she's making noises again. I mean, she was being a Mum for a while, and I think also her Mum had died before that, which sort of knocked her sideways. But I know she's back in the studio, so hopefully we'll hear something from her soon."

Kate was the cover star of *Mojo*'s February 2003 edition, which included a nine-page retrospective feature 'Season of the Witch' by Phil Sutcliffe (remember *Sounds* feature 'LaBushka' of many moons ago?): "Eccentric, elusive, English. It's almost 25 years since *Wuthering Heights* made Kate Bush a star, and a decade since she quietly slipped from view. Phil Sutcliffe traces the path of a stubbornly individual and charmingly enigmatic songwriting genius." The article included contributions from some of Kate's closest colleagues; Haydn Bendall: "I'm amazed she isn't a megastar, that more people aren't just thrilled that she's around". Stuart Elliott: "She comes into the studio and smiles and it's all airy and sunshine. She really does care about people". Jon Kelly: "We made *Never For Ever* a real home record, the studio was filled with flowers, plants, people". David Gilmour – on the early demos she was: "lively and quick, aching to know how everything worked". David Paton: "You knew she was driven, it was the path she had to take". Also quotes from David Munns, then looking after her at EMI: "Basically you don't fuck with her. She ebbs and flows. You stay with her for life. She's precious. I want her to be the way she is". Kate didn't actually give an interview to *Mojo*. Her 'business manager' told them that she "wouldn't be talking until the album was out." When *Mojo* asked when that might be, the reply was "how long is a piece of string?"

The Norwich tribute gig, April 2002

The ascent to world domination (cont'd) Since 1913, the legendary Apollo Theatre Harlem has been the stage for some of the greatest entertainers in American history. For more than 60 years, "Amateur Night at the Apollo" has been where gutsy performers let the 'world's toughest audience' decide their fate. On 1st March 2003 two African-American dancers did a routine to *This Woman's Work* as part of the show, and were not booed. Jayro Rosado, an 18-year old freshman at William Paterson, won the grand prize in the series finale for *his* Maxwell style falsetto rendition also of *This Woman's Work*. Audience members voted him the clear winner with their loud cheers. According to another report "as soon as Rosado, a sharply dressed 18-year-old from East Orange, opened his mouth, the audience grew still. Singing *This Woman's Work*, the Kate Bush song that has been popularized, in recent years, by neo-soul star Maxwell, he grabbed listeners' attention right away with his eerily beautiful falsetto."

Talking of talent, 16 year old Jaclyn Bell won the April 5th heat of 'Stars In Their Eyes: Kids': "Becoming Kate Bush was kind of my mum's idea as she's a big fan. We got the old albums out and I thought it was quite good and then I saw a video and thought "I like this". Jaclyn's father said: "My wife is a Kate Bush fan and we have all the videos and all the records and Jaclyn loves watching them, so I think that's where her inspiration came from". The *Glasgow Evening Times* reported on 29th May that Kate sent a message of support to Jaclyn for the grand final: "Kate was so impressed by Barrhead High School pupil Jaclyn Bell's version of her hit, *Wuthering Heights*, that she took time out from recording her latest album to reveal she will be watching the show on Saturday. Kate said: "I am flattered Jaclyn chose to perform one of my songs. She was wonderful and I really hope she wins. I will be watching and voting for her and send her all my support". Jaclyn said: "Kate's message has made me even more determined to win. I hope I impress her". In the final broadcast on 31st May, Jaclyn took 3rd place with 77,745 votes, but after her performance she was in tears when presenter Cat Deeley handed her a 1978 platinum disc and hand-written note from Kate. The event was won by a strange and unexpected surge of voting for an impersonation of '50s star Connie Francis.

In issue 72 (June 2003) we said: "There is still no word at all from either Kate or EMI regarding the recording of the new album, however, the old *HomeGround* crystal ball has been dusted off and we think the long wait may finally be coming to an end. This is just our opinion, but it is not impossible that the album could be released later this year. If it is going to be in

2003, October or November would seem most likely, but it may be that it doesn't actually appear until the Spring, when the market is less busy and it's easier to get key promotion. Certainly all indications are that Kate is in the recent words of the EMI Press Office "working very hard on the new album".

Cover versions everywhere: *Jive* magazine on Kate's resurgence in popularity with the dance culture: "Australian remix outfit, Infusion appear to have a significant club hit on their hands with their progressive dance remix *Kate Bush v Infusion: Running Up That Hill*. It was huge at this year's Miami Winter Music Conference and is in the top ten of all the dance charts as we go to press, though still only available on white label, as it would appear that the copyright has not yet been cleared for a full release". Ukdancerecords.com said: "Monstrous Infusion Remix currently tearing up the underground". In its land of origin Australia, the remix entered the club chart at no.10, and then went to no.6 for two weeks. Quotes from club reviewers: "Quite simply, expect this to be THE progressive tune of the summer unless something better comes along which I highly doubt. Dreamlike at first building to a throbbing bassline, with the mental genius that is Kate Bush's vocal prowess woven in around the sound, it's nigh on perfection. Delicious."... "indeed a spine tingling, arm hair raising, goosebump inducing five minutes all instigated by THAT key change. Utterly, utterly mad stuff. And that was just the first time it was played"... "Absolutely breathtaking remix treatment from Australia's very own Infusion. This track has been caned by the likes of Sasha, John Digweed, Nick Warren, Sander Kleinenberg, Paul Oakenfold and many many more."... "one of the biggest records of the year"

Sadly the track never was cleared for a full release.

In an interview with "The biggest name in UK hip hop at the moment" Rodney Smith (aka Roots Manuva) he reveals to the Derby district website: "Well, we tried to get Kate Bush for this album, but she wasn't interested." Q: Why was she not up for it? A: "I don't know, she must've thought it was strange, man."

Folk singer Bill (Belinda) Jones had a new CD *Live at the Live* which included a beautiful rendition of *Never Be Mine*... Icelandic singer Pall Oskar, who previously covered *Feel It* on an earlier album, now included a version of *My Lagan Love* on his new album. In a sleeve note he says that Kate is one of his favourite artists and that he found her version of the song intriguing and mysterious and wanted to cover it in his own style. A new allegedly "techno" (but more like '70s disco) mix of *Babooshka* was included by Madhouse in their album *Hit Mix*... more remixes, *Cloudbusting 2003* White ENG 12 – circulating as *Bush Babies Bustin' Clouds* "is a solid house re-working of the classic Kate Bush track that uses much of the original vocal and song in the mix"... on 17th April the Dutch band Within Temptation released their cover version of *Running Up That Hill*.

Baltic recording artist Lee Kaay re-worked his 2001 version of *December Will Be Magic* Again for his 2003 *Frost* single EP and DVD. A video was also shot in Iceland. His DVD *The Russian Tour* featured his live version of *This Woman's Work*. *Frost* was a substantial success charting at No1 in Iceland, Finland, Russia, Czech Republic, Latvia and Estonia. At a recent gig in Latvia, Lee changed the whole set and included a 30 minute tribute to Kate, a medley of *Cloudbusting, Hounds of Love*, *The Big Sky* and *The Red Shoes*.

Placebo re-released their album *Sleeping With Ghosts* in September 2003 with a bonus CD of cover versions which included *Running Up That Hill*, apparently something that their fans had been requesting. DJ Andy Smith (Portishead) issued a remix of *The Man with the Child in his Eyes* on his September 2003 CD *Document II*.

Happy Rhodes performed *And Dream of Sheep* at one of her Philadelphia concerts. *Rolling Stone* reported that Greg Dulli (late of Afghan Whigs) returned to the stage for the first time in three years on 21st August 2003 at Los Angeles' Spaceland to début the new line-up of his band, the Twilight Singers and recent album, *Blackberry Belle*. They played "some of the eclectic covers" including *Cloudbusting*. The cover did not make it on the covers album *She Loves You*, released later in the year, much to some critics' disappointment. It did make it onto bootlegs of the band's performance.

This Woman's Work continued on its campaign of world domination: On 5th August 2003 Charlotte Martin covered the track at her show at Hotel Café in Los Angeles... it was used as background music on the US TV show 'Crossing Jordan' on 27th January, accompanying a scene where a main character is feeling helpless and guilty after the death of a co-worker... it was used in episode two of 'Alias' where Sydney was in her bath after an awful day... and the track as performed by Maxwell, won an BMI Award in the category 'Pop'.

And those name-checks kept coming: Dido: "When I was 13 I got a record player for Christmas, so I went out and bought *Hounds of Love* by Kate Bush and *Diamond Life* by Sade, which both remain absolute classics. Those are two women who have got the right idea: they have a life, they have great careers, and they make records when they want to make records". *The Guardian* 3rd October 2003... "You have to find a way to make music without putting yourself on a treadmill. Kate Bush and Sade do what they do brilliantly, they don't try to be anything they're not, and they carry on quietly and confidently"... Dido was the winner of this year's 'Best Female' award at the Brit Awards, and in her recorded acceptance message she thanked other female singer-songwriters for inspiration including Kate and Annie Lennox.

Erasure had apparently recorded a version of *Running Up That Hill* for their covers album, *Other Peoples Songs*, but it did not make the final cut. On 15th January BBC Radio 2's 'Tracks of My Years' Andy Bell chose *Army Dreamers* explaining that he and Vince had once asked Kate to produce their *Wild* album but unfortunately she was too busy: "*Army Dreamers* and *Breathing* are two of the greatest anti-war songs ever". On 17th October, Andy Bell told *The Guardian* about a recent visit to Kate's house: "Kate Bush is a long-term favourite he still adores. Bush is in the enviable position of seeing her popularity and enigma increase steadily, despite, or perhaps because of the fact that she hasn't released a record or made a public performance for a decade. Bell's favourite Kate Bush album is *The Dreaming*. 'We went round her house in South London recently and she was everything I expected: she was really nice, she made us tea in a proper teapot, she had baked a cake, she had loads of cats, and she was really softly spoken. I was a teenager when she first came along and I still think she's fantastic'. Andy subsequently appeared on the BBC World Service on 2nd December 2003 talking about his love of Kate, her continuing importance in the world of popular music and the influence she has had on him. He played *Wow*, *Under the Ivy* and *Moments of Pleasure*.

On that same 'Tracks of My Years' Julia Fordham chose *Wuthering Heights*: "I remember seeing her on TV and I was really seduced by her. She is so individual, unique and original. And she has this strength and beauty and vulnerability. She's a lovely artist and a big influence on me and I am really looking forward to her new record."

The love of the rappers in the Noughties for Kate's music was just as mystifying to the commentators as the love of the punks and the heavy rockers in the '70s and '80s. *The Oregonian*, 14th November reviewed a documentary about "the ferocious rapper" Tupac. "You'd never guess the creator of *All Eyez on Me* and *2Pacalypse Now* loved singer Kate Bush." Influential Jamaican musician Lee 'Scratch' Perry was asked in *Mojo* what he was currently listening to, and he mentioned *Lionheart*, describing Kate as "an angel from England".

Kate continued to register in the charts and polls for 2003: the March issue of the German magazine *Musikexpress* had a cover feature on 'The 50 best records of the '80s'. Kate was at no.21 with *Hounds of Love* ("a timeless pop jewel"). The July/August *Women Who Rock* named Kate as the 24th most essential 'Woman Who Rocked The World': "Kate Bush has proven over her sporadic moments in the limelight that you can find success entirely on your own terms, reaching lofty heights by not compromising your ethics, beliefs or spellbinding voice. There were five entries in the 'Top 2000 records' chart compiled by Dutch TV channel Nederland 3, the highest being *Wuthering Heights* at no.95. The 'Top of the Pops 2' website set up a vote for 'the foxiest lady of pop' with just six nominations including Madonna, Kylie, and Kate. At no.4 in a 'Top of the Pops 2' Top 5 of 'barmy babes', the 134th 'best artist ever' at the 'Acclaimed Music' site where Critics' best-of lists of albums and singles have been compiled to "ultimate lists" of the most critically acclaimed music and *Mojo*'s November 2003 issue listed Kate at no.43 in their Hall of Fame, above the likes of Springsteen, The Stone Roses, REM, U2 and Abba.

On 19th October 2003 *The Observer* named Kate as the number 1 'Greatest Eccentric in Music': "Popular music will always need eccentrics, the people who show mainstream life how things can be stranger, more beautiful, or just... different. Kate Bush – Number One because she brought her own brand of rural Gothic eccentricity right to the very heart of the mainstream... Her first moment remains her finest: *Wuthering Heights*, Emily Brontë's gothic novel rendered as a three-minute pop song. She later did the same for Molly Bloom's soliloquy from James Joyce's *Ulysses* on *The Sensual World*. Now a pop recluse without being an acid casualty, rumours persist that she is working on an album, the first since 1993. A major influence on inspired loons like Björk, Tricky, even Tori Amos." 'Recluse' by the way, is defined here as not taking six heavies and a film crew every time you go to Safeways for a packet of firelighters.

The Times 14th December 2003 revealed that "a Whitehall whistle-blower has leaked... minutes of the main honours committee that vets people for knighthoods and other awards". According to the Whitehall sources, prominent people being discussed for honours include Eric Sykes, the comedian and Kate Bush, the pop singer". *Pop singer?*

On 11th October 2003 Kate went into Abbey Road to begin final flourishes for the new album. Michael Kamen and the London Metropolitan Orchestra completed orchestrations on two tracks in Studio 2 on that day, which was some of the very last work Michael did before his tragic death shortly after. Previously, Emma Murphy (described by BBC Radio 3 as "the Stirling

Glastonbury 2003: Neil's Cloudbuster.

Photo: *HomeGround*

As we now know, it took another nine years before Kate was finally included in the December 2012 new years Honours List, and created CBE by HM Queen Elizabeth II. She was invested with the insignia of Commander of the Order of the British Empire on 10th April2013.

Moss" of the recorder world) had told the 'Ninth Wave' website that she and Susanna Pell (also a member of the Dufay Collective and regarded as one of the world's leading viol players) had participated during the year in the recording of a song arranged for recorders and viols by "the very Celtic" Bill Thorpe.

In issue 73 (March 2004) we said: "Dear patient readers, we have to report that there is still no firm news. What we can say is that we believe Kate is currently in the final stages of completing the new album, and that there is a great deal of anticipation, excitement, and enthusiasm at EMI. We do now know about the following further musicians who have added their own particular magic: Chris Hall is the acclaimed jazz player with bands such as Bearcat and Zydecomotion. The French website Babooshka.net received an email from the man himself saying: "I added some accordion to a track at her own studio. The idea was to add some Cajun accordion which I play in my own bands. Actually we tried Cajun accordion but it didn't quite fit so I used a standard two row accordion in the end playing a cross between Cajun, blues and African style riffs... Me and Kate worked together on the accordion riffs and she seemed very excited about the album."

Hayley Westenra

There were more new cover versions right left and centre-field. New Zealand singer Hayley Westenra's cover of *Wuthering Heights* was released in March. Manchester Online reviewed her gig at Bridgewater Hall on 25th March 2004: "Hayley stormed to the finale with her single-release cover of Kate Bush's *Wuthering Heights*, capturing all the off-kilter and kooky appeal of the original." Mike Scott, the founder and sole constant member of The Waterboys, was interviewed early in 2004 and had this to say about his 1997 cover of *Why Should I Love You*: "I think about giving my music a sense of healing and peace. What I always want to hear in music, and hear so rarely, is a sense of the spiritual. Peter Gabriel has it, and I think the great English singer Kate Bush had it... This song was the soundtrack to six tumultuous months in my life: the end of my marriage, my stay at the Findhorn Community in Scotland, the high magic of meeting my soul mate. *Why Should I Love You?* was with me all the time, blasting out of the car stereo, rocking the community kitchens, transforming my bedroom into a temple, a boudoir. It speaks to my heart, my spirit, my mind and sets my feet moving too – the grand slam! It's a song to fall in or out of love. And terrific music for cooking stir-fry!"

Independent singer and songwriter Danielle French, from Calgary, Alberta, Canada, covered *Running Up That Hill* on her new CD *Piece*. Claudia De Booche included her version of *The Big Sky* on her US single *Salute To Ciao Baby*. BBC Leeds were raving about Four Day Hombre (championed by Radio 1 DJ Chris Moyles) whose single *First Word* "effortlessly develops into a rock version of the Kate Bush hit *Running Up That Hill* without you even noticing the changeover".

Contact Music informed us that Outkast hip-hop star Big Boi "had a surprising musical hero - eccentric British singer Kate Bush. The *Miss Jackson* rapper – real name Antwan Patton – credits his teenage musical development to Bush, and he's still so infatuated with the reclusive star he wants to track her down and get her to produce songs for his duo's next album. He says, "My uncle introduced me to Kate Bush's music when I was about 14 years old, and that shit opened my mind up. The first one I got was *The Kick Inside*, then I bought *Hounds of Love*, then *The Sensual World*. She was so bugged out man! But I felt what she was talking about in the songs. *Mother Stands for Comfort*, *Running Up That Hill*. My uncle would explain what the songs stood for. Like *The Man with the Child in his Eyes* and all that shit. I thought, Wow! she's so fucking deep! I was infatuated with her, still am. I gotta track her down! I just found out that she was producing all that shit herself! She's so fucking deep and so underrated and off the radar. So hopefully on the next record you're going hear Outkast and Kate Bush do at least two or three songs."

Hayley Willis whose début album, *Come Get Some*, continued to build on the success of her self-financed EPs was asked about her frequent mentions of Brenda Lee, Barbara Streisand and Kate as influences: "There was a similar thing with Kate Bush – she was unusual and exotic to me and she's got a truly unique, beautiful English voice which she has absolute control over. She is also a complete original in terms of song-writing – to think that something as innovative like *Wuthering Heights* got to number one in the 1970's is amazing. That wouldn't happen now in the current musical climate – that mother of the Cheeky Girls must be laughing her bloody head off as she rolls round to the bank. Brenda Lee also has that thing going on which Kate Bush has – a definite maturity and knowledge that belies their vocal years. They've seen a bit of life, if you know what I mean".

A special edition of *Q* set out their '1001 Best Songs Ever' which included. *Wuthering Heights* at no.592 and *Running Up That Hill* at 807. *The Sun* decided that this list was a bit out of touch with the real world so they asked *their* readers to pick *their* Top 100. *Wuthering Heights* made No. 35 this time.

Kate was short-listed, along with David Bowie, Prince, Marvin Gaye, and Morrissey (who won it), for the first *Mojo* 'Icon Award' held on 22nd June 2004: "The inaugural *Mojo* Honours List is intended to be a music awards ceremony like no other... the list was voted for by listeners to Mojo radio and is restricted to artists that have enjoyed a spectacular career on a global scale and become a genuine household name".

Music Week had an interview with Rob Dickins, chairman at Warner Music for most of the '80's and '90's. Discussing his career highlights he talked about how he signed Prince, The Sex Pistols, Madonna, Enya and Simply Red. He mentions Kate as "The one that got away". He says "I would love to have signed Kate. I was waiting for a meeting at EMI when I heard *Wuthering Heights* through the door – I thought it was spectacular. I asked the secretary how I could get in touch with the artist. I was told that she didn't have a manager, but was given her home number. I called Kate the next day and said I was interested in signing her publishing. She was 17 and very flattered, but needed advice. She called back a few days later and said she'd been advised not to sign with Warners, but EMI instead. I asked who had advised her and she said Bob Mercer. Bob was the general manager of EMI at the time".

In issue 74 (July 2004) we finally gave up predicting and said: "It remains the position that only Kate currently knows what is happening regarding the new album. We suspect, and this is only our suspicion, that the album is effectively complete. However, EMI have not yet heard any part of it, and despite the listings on various websites, no release dates have yet been scheduled. This could change any time".

Yet more cover versions: Susan Egan, who apparently sang in Broadway's 'Thoroughly Modern Millie' released an album called *Coffee House* which included a cover of *Wuthering Heights*. *Re-fashioned 2 British Airwaves* was the second volume in Groovescooter's critically acclaimed cover series and featured Majella O'Shea singing *The Man with the Child in his Eyes*. Portuguese Goth rock band Icon & the Black Roses recorded a version of *Running Up That Hill*. There was a new Italian dance version of *Wuthering Heights* by Mr Conte featuring Laura Valente. Kiki Dee performed *Running Up That Hill* with Carmelo Luggeri, her musical partner of the past few years, in a concert in May 2004. Described as "a great acoustic version" it was a standard feature of her live shows for the next few years, and was included in her 2007 *Under the Night Sky* DVD.

Waiting for Kate Bush by music journalist John Mendelssohn, apparently "an unusual hybrid of satirical novel and music biography", was published on 15th November 2004. The publisher's blurb explained it thus: "When Kate Bush came out of nowhere in 1978 with her jaw-droppingly eccentric début single *Wuthering Heights*, screeching like a banshee, flapping her arms as though trying to take wing, pulling alarming faces, people either adored or loathed her. One of the former was an American underwear model, Lesley Herskovits, who, in spite of his remarkable good looks, reserved his loathing for himself. By the time Kate had taken to keeping her fans waiting literally ages between albums, he'd found himself a boarding house near Kate's birthplace that accommodated only fervent Kate fans. Only his disinclination to miss her eighth album, after waiting more than a decade for it, kept him from leaping off a multi-storey tower block".

The claims of influence were coming from all directions: Tim Rice-Oxley of rising UK group Keane mentioned *Wuthering Heights* in the 16th April *NME*: "I just don't know how she wrote this tune, the way it leaps around and works so beautifully with the weird, Gothic story is incredible. It seems to be from a completely different planet to your average pop single". Irish writer Noirin Gannon published her second book of poetry, *Verses By Twilight*. One poem is "a tribute to Kate Bush which she wrote while speaking on the 'phone to a friend and twiddling a biro in the other hand. "The words just started to come into my head and I wrote them down. I grew up with the music of Kate Bush and felt the need to pay her some kind of tribute".

The special edition of *Q* entitled 'The '70s, From Zeppelin to The Pistols' has '20 singles that changed the world' Kate was at number 11 with *Wuthering Heights*: "Otherworldly femme fatale falls to earth – Released bang in the middle of the New Wave's chart invasion, *Wuthering Heights* was so thrillingly peculiar that even 19-year old Bush's hippy-chick look was excused. Bush and her falsetto-voiced début had one-hit wonder written all over it. With her maverick tendencies proving the rule, rather than the exception, Kate Bush became a key alternative role model inspiring everyone from Björk to Tori Amos".

Mojo had *Wuthering Heights* at no.6 in their 'Top 100 Epic Rock Tracks of All Time' in April, describing the track as "audacious". *The Observer* had Kate at no.22 in their 'Best British albums' listing. Emma Warren wrote: "The first woman in this list is the hugely talented, wildly strange first lady of romantic experimental pop. *Hounds of Love*... remains a trenchantly individual piece of work, resonant with ghosts and connections to witch-dunking mythology, although you could never describe the crafted pop and dramatic sound sweeps on the record as fey." On 20th June Miranda Sawyer additionally wrote: "What? No Girls Aloud? Well, no, because no girls are allowed in a list of Top British Albums, banned by ancient boy law which states that women only make two types of credible contemporary music – either whimsical, solo love ditties or guitar-fuzz, eff-you rock attack. So we're left with 'that nice Katie Bush', as my grandpa used to call her, and the Slits."

Hounds of Love was listed at number 23 on *Q*'s 'Best British album ever' chart, the only female artist on the list. The July issue of *Classic Rock* had Kate at no.38 in their '100 Greatest Frontmen' article: "The ethereal dove who shot to prominence as a teenager with the enigmatic *Wuthering Heights* single... Kate hasn't released a new album in more than a decade, and is now a recluse. But nobody ever combined Gothic music (not goth), dance and theatre better". In the 'Top 100 songs' in the BBC Radio 2 Song list, *Wuthering Heights* appears at no.30: "One of the most daring, original singles ever – and a début single at that... like nothing before and very little since". On 20th November *The Daily Telegraph*'s music critics selected the '50 best cover versions ever recorded'. No.14 was Kate's cover of Elton John's *Rocket Man*: "vacuous tinny pop until Kate Bush's keening cadences gave it the poignancy it deserved. Her little-girl-lost voice and the bittersweet sound of Uilleann pipes add startling beauty, and a thrilling chill to the Martian air". *Q*'s Autumn special edition listed 'The 1010 Songs you MUST Own'. Kate appeared three times: *Don't Give Up* in the '50 Best Duets', *And Dream Of Sheep* in the 'chillout list' and *Rocket Man* again in '60 songs for the tired and emotional'. Kate's prominent appearance in many of these 2004 polls underlined her position as one of the most prominent singer-songwriters of the previous 30 years.

Inside: The Faders Hard-Fi Hanson Minus Kooks Mugison M
MUSICWEEK
Midem to ban liggers

All of which explains why in Autumn 2004 the world went slightly mad. It had really began with rumours about Kate's new album spreading like wildfire across music artist forums and CD websites. On November 28th Stuart Elliott was interviewed on the BBC1 TV God-Slot programme 'Songs Of Praise'. He said that he had been busy recording drums on Kate's new album and that recording on the album had just finished. In early December Peter Gabriel (inevitably) was interviewed by the *Toronto Sun* in connection with his new video release and said this: "Kate had a son and lost her mom and I think that kept her (occupied). I spoke to her quite recently, in fact, and she's just about finished on a new record. It is exciting. She's being a mom and loving it. So, if you like, music's gone from being full-time to being part-time, so that slows you down. She pointed out (she takes) even longer than I take".

Finally on 9th December 2004, Kate made the announcement that mattered in the Kate Bush Club newsletter:

Hello Everyone,

Many thanks for all your great letters of support – they mean such a lot. The album is nearly finished now and will be out next year – we'll let you know when. It features some beautiful orchestral arrangements by Michael Kamen – we had a wonderful day at Abbey Road Studios last winter. I'm so pleased with everyone's work on this record. There are some lovely performances and I hope you will all feel it's been worth the wait. Bertie keeps me very busy, he is so much fun and we are all really looking forward to Christmas. Wishing you a merry Christmas and I hope next year is a really happy one for you,

Lots of love,
Kate x

This became a global news story.

For the media it was almost as if the album had already been released. The mention of the Kate Bush Club flyer on Sean's Kate Bush News and Information web page unleashed an sheer avalanche of press coverage, led on 13th December by *Music Week*. In a front page article with a large photo of Kate, they exclaimed: "One of the longest waits for a follow-up will finally be over next year, when the first Kate Bush album in more than a decade appears". Kate's "return" became the lead story on the BBC Classic Rock/Pop website on 20th December, and then on the BBC6 website on 23rd December, with a pre-Christmas fusillade of articles from the popular and heavyweight press on the same day.

In *The Times* Adam Sherwin wrote: "One of the longest silences in popular music is about to end after Kate Bush, the inspiration for a generation of female artists, announced her comeback... Bush returns as a new generation of artists recall her as an inspiration". In *The Daily Telegraph* Richard Wilfson said: "Despite her decade-long absence, the 46-year-old from Bexleyheath still holds a central place in the national consciousness... Bush is not all wild screeching whimsy. In fact, she seems at ease in many different personas: the overblown Gothic temptress of *Wuthering Heights*; the painfully sincere ballad singer of *The Man with the Child in his Eyes*; the camp glam rocker of *Wow*; the hard-edged sado-masochistic queen of *Hounds of Love* and *Running Up That Hill.* The latter is truly riveting, and perhaps her most perfect statement. And it is not just the music that has been influential. It is the scale of her theatrical ambition which makes her such a compelling figure, and which makes the prospect of new material next year something to savour".

Over the next couple of days the story was filtering through the world's media channels, turning up on the teletext in the Netherlands, news websites in South Africa, newspapers and news and music websites in France and in Norway and the US. In the Christmas Eve *Daily Express* there was a two-page spread under the heading 'The Return of Pop's Great Recluse', and *The Evening Standard* ran a story under the heading 'Comeback Kate' referring to "a unique performer who inspired a generation". The Boxing Day *Sunday Times* contained a major Profile feature: 'Kate Bush: Can she pull off the big sway-back?': "In the cluttered loft that houses the memory of the average middle-aged bloke, a video flickers dully. It displays a child-woman of ethereal yet sexual allure who sways with beguiling swimming motions as her voice leaps the octaves of her 1978 hit *Wuthering Heights*... The doctor's daughter from the London suburb of Bexleyheath altered the chemistry of pop... Her success was all the more notable because she was one of the few women to be taken seriously in the male-dominated world of pop, governed at the time by the aggressive sounds of punk... This, remember, is a female star whose versatility has perhaps never been surpassed, who pioneered the fusion of dance and circus entertainment in pop and conjured a new persona with each song. For fans, the anticipation is palpable".

On 27th December Gary Suzman on Entertainment News noted that: "After a long absence, the reclusive Kate Bush is suddenly popping up everywhere". The *Daily Mirror*'s David Edwards had their second bash at the story on the 28th: 'Kate's Big Comeback': "Shielded from the world by a pair of dark sunglasses, her coat collar turned up to keep out the cold, the woman shuffling down the high street attracts little attention. Some of the locals recognise her as the reclusive figure who lives a Miss Havisham-like existence behind the high walls of the mansion on the edge of the village. But few know that she used to be one of the most famous women on the planet. Kate Bush has fought hard to protect her privacy but, after years away from the limelight, she is about to make one of the most eagerly awaited and unexpected comebacks in music history... What is less clear is how Kate will cope with the blizzard of publicity that will inevitably accompany it".

The significance of Kate's anticipated return to the arts and media community was perhaps best summed up by 'The Wow Factor', a piece written by Jason Crowley in the 7th February *New Statesman*: "When I mentioned at a recent *New Statesman* editorial conference that I wanted to write about Kate Bush colleagues responded with a mixture of incredulity and awe. The incredulous still associated her with a single song... The awed among my colleagues, who were all women, knew Bush for the complex and remarkable artist that she is, perhaps the most singular and talented female singer-songwriter and composer of her generation (she is now 46... Bush occupies an ambiguous space between pop and the avant-garde, simultaneously working within and against the constraints of the pop song... Many years ago, she retreated into semi-reclusivity, reluctant to be interviewed or appear on television, never touring. There were rumours of her exhaustion and her hurt. Too much that was wounding had been written about her; she had been gossiped about and teased too much... It was increasingly clear that she wished only to speak through and be known by her work".

In the *Irish Examiner* on 25th March Suzanne Harrington summed up the situation: "Imagine being so idolised that a rare posting on a website – not even your own, because you don't have one – starts a flurry of media attention. Without ever confirming a release date for your latest album – the first in 12 years and counting – newspapers write breathlessly of your comeback, and your trademark legwarmers and jumpsuits duly appear on the pages of *Elle Girl* and the catwalks of London Fashion Week... In the age of instant pop noodle – just add Louis Walsh and stir – Kate Bush is an anachronism, a rich, talented recluse who just wishes to be alone".

On the following day *The Scotsman* tried to capture the moment: "There is something in the air, and it bodes well for the imminent, long-delayed return of that queen of musical misfits, Kate Bush... Bush has been heroically ignoring both fashion and received commercial wisdom... her return will be one of the biggest musical events of this year. Her influence can be detected everywhere... She has stayed away so long, by all accounts, simply because she was enjoying being a mother, and had no great interest in either releasing music or remaining famous simply for the sake of it".

Inevitably there were some in the media who could not stomach all this breathless appreciation for Kate. The backlash arrived as early as 17th January 2005 with a *Daily Mail* recycling by Richard Price of their earlier nonsense about 'the bizarre world of Kate Bush'. The real hatchet job was done done, however, by one David Stubbs in (rather sadly) *The Guardian* on 19th February: "The news that Kate Bush is returning with her first album since 1993 has prompted much swooning and clucking among her intense brood of devotees who look upon her as a latterday Gaia in legwarmers. These people who, it's said, celebrate her birthday, or 'Katemas', annually, perhaps explain why Bush has devoted much of her fortune to ensuring that at no point do they come within half a mile of her... To others, however, Kate Bush's return is dismaying. In a career that has ranged wildly from the sublime (*Running Up That Hill*) to the hilarious (the early years, generally), her protracted silence has been one of her more eloquent statements... Why is she returning, to be glared at by an insatiably curious media and goggled over by her featherheaded fan base, who regard her comeback as akin to the Reawakening of Albion? ...She is no oracle, mystic waif no seer... She is first, foremost, essentially, incorrigibly, a show-off A highly talented and evolved one at best, but a show-off. Which is why, even after 12 years, like the rest of them, she couldn't stay away".

Despite the acute featherheadedness involved in being a Kate fan, I recall articles such as this from the '80's heyday of the British inky music press. It normally meant Kate had refused an interview.

The polls continued, and the one we were all looking at was 'The Brits' nomination for the

'Best British Song of the last *27* years' (not *25* which led to a lot of confusion). In fact it was a poll to find 'the best song since the BPI Awards have been going'. *Wuthering Heights* was one of the initial 25 nominated, was in the final five, based on the general public's votes up to and including 9th January 2005. The winner was, improbably, Robbie Williams' *Angels*, which provoked a lot of debate on the BBC website and elsewhere. Our opinion was well reflected by Victoria Newton writing in *The Sun*'s Bizarre column on 11th February: '*Angels* is an above average anthem which is good to sing along to when you're feeling misty-eyed in the pub. But it's hardly changed the face of music like Kate Bush's *Wuthering Heights*'. *The Sun* actually felt so strongly that it arranged its own online poll in which George Michael came first, Kate third, and Robbie fourth.

In January 2005 Marc Almond put an end to the growing speculation, which had him working with Kate on a duet for the new album. Reports of a newly recorded version of Soft Cell's *Youth*, had been circling for some time, but in a statement on his official website, a spokesperson quashed the reports: "Marc says he has not been approached nor does he know of any of his songs being covered," it read. "He wishes he could confirm the rumour as Kate is one of his all time favourite artists and he looks forward to her long awaited new album, one of the big music events of 2005".

The February edition of *Burn* magazine included *The Sensual World* at no.9 in a list of 'the post punk classics that shaped the sound of now'. In the *Q* Special Edition 'Icons: The Greatest Music Stars of All Time' (January 2005) readers voted Kate into 29th place. Listeners of BBC Radio 2 (9th January) put *Wuthering Heights* at no.3 in *their* 'Top Ten British Songs of the past 25 years', the only woman to make the top 10. Radio 1 listeners (who were not supposed even to know who Kate was) put *Wuthering Heights* at no.15 in their 'top 20 Greatest No.1s' done to celebrate the 1000th number one single. VH1 (UK) spent the entire Easter weekend playing their 'Top 500 British tracks of all time' and *Wuthering Heights* was no.23. Kate was no.1 Female Artist in the March *Record Collector* Poll, and *Live at Hammersmith* was no.10 in the 'Most Wanted DVD list'.

On the other hand the only British act among the founding inductees into the UK Music Hall of Fame launched ahead of a Channel 4 series this Autumn was The Beatles. The Hall, apparently, was for artists who have made the greatest contribution to 'UK music culture'. Our reaction was reflected in a comment posted on the BBC News page: 'What's the point of a UK Hall of Fame if it's stuffed full of Americans? What on earth differentiates it from any other Hall of Fame? Where are the quintessentially English artists? Few British artists have had more influence than Kate Bush over the last 20 years...'

Opposite: Issues 63 to 69 including three covers by Debi Bowes

Asked for his cultural heroes singer Kele Okereke of Bloc Party, whose début album *Silent Alarm* was full of driving rock that combined British post-punk with the US alternative rock of The Pixies and Sonic Youth, says he respects Kate Bush, Björk and Davids Bowie and Byrne: "artists that haven't ever compromised". Another band who were full of admiration for Kate were the Futureheads whose cover of *Hounds of Love* was released as a single on 28th February 2005. The track entered the official chart at no.8 on 27th February. The prize for the most obscure cover went to a jazz-infected version of *Wuthering Heights* by Dirdrie Cartwright from her newly released album *Dr Quantum Leaps*

On 21st February 2005 in the midst of the publicity surrounding the album announcement, Simon Chilvers commented in the style section of *The Guardian* on "the current fad for all things Kate Bush", a fad which appeared to be permeating both the fashion industry and artistic awareness: "The return of Ms Bush to the fashion cognoscenti's consciousness is, in our humble opinion, the best trend for yonks".

On cue, on 2nd March Kate was one of the invited guests at a star-studded reception held at Buckingham Palace to honour the British music industry. Also invited was Sandie Shaw who wrote up her diary in *The New Statesman* on 28th March: "I really enjoyed meeting some of my Eighties musical heroes for the first time, like Peter Gabriel... and Kate Bush... Kate took us on a grand tour of the Queen's art collection. She was ecstatic. 'Can you believe it? That's a real Rubens up there! Fancy having that in your front room!" Kate bubbled. I felt a light tap on my shoulder. I turned around and there was Da Kween in a bright turquoise suit smiling at me, holding out her hand to be shaken... She chatted away... All the while, Kate was rummaging in her handbag. Suddenly, she produced a pen and some paper. 'Would you mind awfully signing this for my son?' she asked sweetly. The Queen looked lost for words. 'I think that's a pop-star thing, Kate,' I mumbled. The Queen seemed pleased to be let off the hook. 'Quite right,' she answered as an equerry quickly hustled her away".

Steve Wright met Kate at the Buckingham Palace reception and she apparently told him that the new album "probably might not be ready by Summer". In issue 75, our view was that "the album will be released most likely in the Autumn". This time we were actually right. In a press release dated 31st August 2005 EMI Records "proudly confirmed" that Kate's hugely anticipated eighth studio album *Aerial*, was to be released on November 7th 2005.

King of the Mountain was played for the first time on Wednesday 21st September 2005 on BBC Radio 2's Ken Bruce show. The ten year wait was over.

HomeGround
Number 63
The Kate Bush Fanzine
Spring 99
HomeGround
Number 69
The Kate Bush Magazine
Spring 2002
HomeGround
HomeGround
Number 65
The Kate Bush Fanzine
Summer 2000
Number 68
The Kate B
HomeGround
Number 66
The Kate Bush Fanzine
Winter 2000
HomeG
Number 67
The Kate Bush Fanzine
Summer 2001

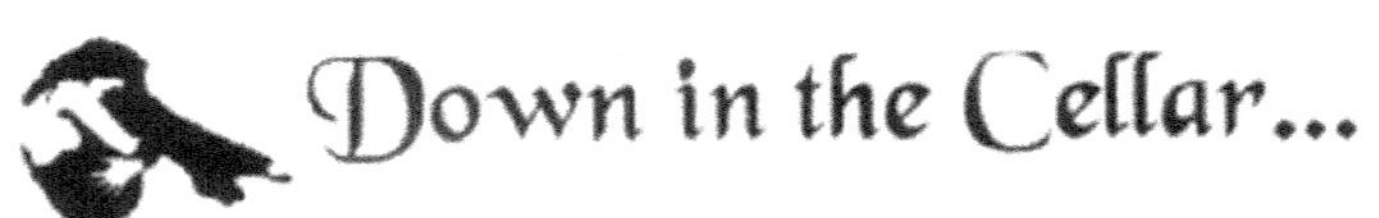

Down in the Cellar...

Well, it has been a long time since I wrote the Ed's letter for HomeGround, but Peter and Krys thought it might be a good idea for me to actually do something, other than just add the wit and glamour!

As most of you know, I used to work for EMI in the UK and during that time one of my projects was the re-mastering and re-packaging of *Hounds Of Love* as part of the EMI Centenary. Everyone, including Kate, was very pleased with the result and we started to make plans to tackle the other studio albums, then things changed at the company and when I left plans were put on hold. Over the past three years the idea has been running around inside my head and I have continued to have a healthy working relationship with EMI (check out Geri Halliwells last single, CD2!). Just before Christmas, myself and Steve Davis at EMI put a proposal to Kate to update her remaining catalogue in much the same way that *Hounds* had been, minus the Centenary stuff of course. Kate has now given her go ahead for the six albums to be released, two at a time over the next ten months, starting with *The Red Shoes* and *The Sensual World*, to be released in September.

EMI are putting a lot of time and money into making sure that these re-issues look and sound great, and as I write we are in the middle of the re-design of the booklets and they look fantastic! I am sure that you will all love them. Kate's first four albums will especially benefit from the re-mastering and I for one cannot wait to hear them as Kate did in the studio. It also means that we at last have something to fill the remaining gap until the next album. In May, here at HomeGround Towers we celebrated our 18th birthday, which is of course supposed to mean we have now come of age. I will try and bare that in mind the next time Krys appears with a bunny slipper on her head. It is bizarre and a little frightening that eighteen years have gone so fast, but I for one am very proud of our little mag and all that we have achieved. We haven't pleased all our readers all the time, but we have always tried to be honest and to be ourselves. We have tried to do what we thought was right and to help promote Kate's music in our own small way and we have had some laughs along the way. Moments of pleasure indeed.

Over these past eighteen years there has been on and off talk between the three of us, about Kate or a member of her family or band writing something for the magazine. To be honest we never pushed it, it didn't seem right, but now it has happened - Kate's brother Paddy has written an article for us and very good it is too! Thanks Paddy, it means a lot.

I hope you enjoy this issue and the re-mastered CDs when they come out - I look forward to hearing your reactions. Enjoy the summer and see you at Glastonbury

Recipes

HomeGround Glastonbury
The Tor
Sunday
30th July 2000
2.00 pm

The Millennium Glastonbury gathering takes place on Kate's birthday.
No formal events, just come along and meet other fans.
We hope the weather will be fine.
We'll be there regardless, and afterwards at a local pub

Being Babooshka

Louise Halliday with Stars in her Eyes

Issue 67: July 2001

Ever since I first sang *Wuthering Heights* in public five years ago, people have been telling me I should apply for 'Stars in Their Eyes'...

My first memory of Kate Bush's music was hearing *The Kick Inside* album at around the age of three when my mother played it constantly in the house. At nine, I made my stage début in a production of *Annie*, progressing to other shows and pantomimes. After studying performing arts, and with an ambition to make a career in musical theatre, I applied to a couple of drama colleges in London who specialised in musical theatre training. Unfortunately, I wasn't able to get the funding and decided to try for any singing job I could get.

This lead to my first performance of *Wuthering Heights*. I answered an advert in *The Stage* for a production vocalist on a ship and auditioned the next day. It wasn't the most luxurious ship in the world but it gave me a chance to perform in front of a different audience each day and work with a team of great dancers and performers.

We decided to do a one-off '70s show and I wanted to include a Kate Bush number and that's where my love of Kate's music and my experience of 'Stars in Their Eyes' began.

A couple of years later, I performed my own shows at local venues in South Wales and included *Wuthering Heights* in my set. My friends had commented that I had an uncanny likeness to Kate's voice and one particular friend 'phoned Granada TV for an application form without my knowledge. The first I knew about it was when it landed on my doormat!

I had been reluctant to apply for the show, firstly because I thought it was tacky and couldn't bear to have dancers running around behind me as 'Stars' is renowned for. Secondly, I didn't think I could do Kate justice and was concerned about what she would think of me should she see it!

Anyway, I did an audition in Birmingham for the Musical Director and Producer in a recording studio, which was as big as a postage stamp! I think they were quite alarmed when I asked if I could take my shoes off before I started, although they did say to me later that I was the only candidate to actually perform my song instead of standing there rigid with nerves!

A week later I was asked to attend a second audition at Granada Studios in Manchester which filled me with thoughts of meeting the 'Coronation Street' cast even though I don't actually watch it! I had been asked to sing *Babooshka* which I was nervous about as I didn't have a backing track for the song and searched for a week to find it.

In the end I had to sing with Kate's vocals at the final audition which I think gave me a great advantage! I also sang part of *Wuthering Heights*. I felt that I had done the best I could. So many of the performers who have done 'Stars' say they have applied four or five times. I knew I wouldn't do that so I tried to forget about it. However, two days after my audition, I received the 'phone call. I will never forget the assistant producer's words: "Is that Louise 'Kate Bush' Halliday?"

I screamed the place down and my boyfriend and I went straight to the pub!

I was hoping that I would be able to sing *Wuthering Heights* because I had become so familiar with it. I was told that someone had done it on a previous series and they would like me to do *Babooshka*. In the months that followed, I had to visit Granada to go through the song and discuss the costume and choreography. I was so glad that the choreographer agreed that I should perform the song without the help of the backing dancers!

Photo: Louise Halliday

After I had been told that *Babooshka* was to be my song, my boyfriend reminded me that I would probably be wearing the famous costume from the video and I suddenly went pale!

The producer asked me very cautiously if I would agree to it and I thought about it for a second and said yes! I then had immediate plans of going to the gym more often! The costume designer also went pale when he realised he would have to recreate what is quite a complicated outfit.

I was sent the backing track a month later and was impressed with the production; it was very

Opposite: Dave's editorial for issue 65

nearly the same as the original with the exception of a slight cut of the intro and a cut at the end, so lacked a little of the glass shattering!

I went for my first dance rehearsal in London and worked closely with the choreographer. I have always been a natural singer but have to admit that dance comes a little harder to me. Having watched the *Babooshka* video repeatedly, I wondered how we were going to manage the transformation without the use of a double base. Again, my boyfriend had a great idea! "Why don't you use the cape to cover your costume until the chorus?"

The choreographer loved it. After our initial meeting and watching a very nasty video of myself improvising, I used as many of the original moves as possible and was glad to have my own input of ideas into the final result and the 'reveal' idea was used in all the TV trailers!

The heat itself went by so fast that I didn't really have time to think. I appeared alongside Holly Johnson, Nina Simone, Reg Presley and Madonna. Reg Presley was a vicar and Holly Johnson was a stripper! All the performers were so supportive of one another and it was a shame somebody had to win!

You have no idea how it felt when it was announced that I came first in the audience vote. Matthew Kelly's voice saying "And the winner is Kate Bush" will probably stay with me for a long time.

However, there was a long delay as the computer crashed and we were all left in the dark as to the result. We had a fantastic party afterwards and watched a playback of ourselves. It was very strange to discover that I looked nothing like Kate (apart from the cozzie!) but looked exactly like my Mum! I returned home to Wales but had to keep the result under wraps, save telling some very close friends and family.

I had to wait nearly six months for my heat to be broadcast, and by that time the Final was only four weeks away! The night the show was aired I held a party in my local and we watched it on a giant screen. I then sang a couple of numbers and it was one of the most memorable things that has ever happened to me.

It was at this time that the press and television started to count down to the Final so I had my face (or should I say my impression of Kate!) splashed everywhere. I wondered if Kate had seen the show, and was fascinated to hear what she thought about my performance. My answer came after I performed in the Final.

The week leading up to it was something akin to a circus, and the national press wanted to know everything about us. I felt a little sorry that one or two had perhaps said more than they should after a series of articles that appeared on the day of the Final.

It was lovely to see the crew again and, of course, Matthew Kelly. Those five days went by in a flash. I met all the other finalists. None of them recognised me at first! We got on well and there was no real bitchiness or bad feeling. Going into make-up was really interesting because the make-up artist who helped this time actually did Kate's make-up on her first TV appearance! I told her she still wouldn't be able to make me look like Kate and I would still end up looking like my Mum!

The day of the Final was hectic. The nerves began to well up inside me as the night wore on. I knew that two and half minutes would fly by and was concerned that my cape and the dry ice posed a risk to me falling down those steps! I was behind those famous doors then the camera panned to me and I gave a cheeky wink. Must have been nerves!

After I had finished, Matthew came over to me. I remember bursting into tears when he said Kate loved my performance and read out a hand-written letter from her. I was absolutely gob-smacked and emotional because it meant more to me than any amount of public votes. The fact that Kate herself had watched the show and went to the trouble of writing to me made all the hard work worthwhile.

On top of that, she had given me the most extraordinary gift; the original cloak she had worn for the *Babooshka* video, which I had spent months trying to emulate, was placed in my hands. As I walked backstage, I was congratulated by the crew and the other performers but all I could think about was that Kate Bush had given me a twenty year-old piece of history and I was overcome by the whole experience.

I polled 125,000 votes and came fourth place in the final. I didn't care about the result after actually proving to myself that I could perform live in front of fifteen million viewers, and that I had the opinion of my performance from the most important person of all, Kate herself.

In the six months since that night, I have had numerous offers to perform a Kate tribute show. I decided long before I had even filmed the heat that although many others have gone on to make this their profession, I knew that my path lay elsewhere.

After many years of listening to Kate and wondering in amazement how she writes such beautiful, elegant and innovative melodies and lyrics, I have now begun to write my own material and hope to use this to take my career from musical theatre vocalist, to impersonator to singer-songwriter. It hasn't been easy – it is something that Kate was doing from an early age, but I have discovered my ability much later on. I believe that being someone else for a night has strengthened my resolve to be original, as contradictory as it seems! I hope my song writing and performances can be enjoyed even half as much as people have enjoyed Kate's legacy over the years.

Kate Bush – Style Icon

In the Noughties, Peter finds Kate became... Fashionable

On the 5th October 2002 Jean-Paul Gaultier used *Wuthering Heights* and *Babooshka* as part of the musical backdrop to the presentation of his Spring/Summer2003 collection... Designer Emanuel Ungaro also used Kate's music to accompany his latest creations on show, during the Paris prêt-a-porter shows. Peter Kane had just graduated in fashion design and his unusual clothes made from knots were proving to be the latest items of desire. Quoted in *Leeds Today* on 18th October 2004 he said: "I don't make for skinny models. My inspirations are Kate Bush, Stevie Nicks from Fleetwood Mac and Sarah Brightman". He was the indication of a growing wave of Kate-related influence in other creative areas … On 21st February 2005 in the midst of the album publicity, Simon Chilvers commented in the style section of *The Guardian* on "the current fad for all things Kate Bush", a fad which appeared to be permeating both the fashion industry and artistic awareness: "The return of Ms Bush to the fashion cognoscente's consciousness is, in our humble opinion, the best trend for yonks. First, we had the pleasure of watching Fran Cutler at Frost French's show mouthing along to the song *Babooshka*. On top of that in *i-D* this month, Björk waxes lyrical about Bush's influence, while Swiss artist Sandrine Pelletier creates images inspired by our Kate. *Elle Girl*, meanwhile, revels in her love of jumpsuits, leggings and legwarmers, all of which cropped up in the recent batch of London fashion shows. Designer Hussein Chalayan recently commented that his musical heroine was "before her time"… With a new Kate Bush album destined for release later this year, it's time to big up your hair, start dancing free-form and let out a Heathcliff wail".

The February 2005 issue of *i-D* magazine (titled "The Feminine Issue") did indeed use *The Kick Inside* as its cover title. It contained a six-page spread of photographs of a Kate-themed installation: "From the catwalk to the club to the bedroom, her music and influence are suddenly here again. Here Swiss artist Sandrine Pelletier and Icelandic musician Björk present unique fan tributes to the myth, magic and mystery of Kate Bush". Björk writes: "To me, Kate Bush will always represent the age of exploring your sexuality, when you change from a girl to a woman. All of that... I guess that's what I found fascinating about Kate, she totally stuck out. She was so – what's the word – so *complete*. The music, the lyrics and the way she looked, it all made sense Everybody adored Kate's voice and a lot of people really noticed what she looked like but I think what is really underrated is the production. I think it's really original and really feminine, but with more primitivity than women have, or what men would like to believe we have".

The Sadie Frost fashion show showcased the latest collection from her Frost French label at London Fashion Week. The theme was "Russian Peasant Chic" and models strode down a snowy catwalk to the strains of *Babooshka*.

In *The Independent* "heroes and villains" section 12th February, fashion designer Hussein Chalayan wrote this of Kate: "I thought she was this amazing person that in some ways I could relate to. I felt that the work was such a bridge between fantasy and reality, and there was so much spirit in it... to me she's an emotional thinker, she's somebody who made her emotions real through the music when I hear the music it makes me think that everything around me is wonderful. At times it's almost like hearing a prayer, at other times it's just like lunacy, and other times it's just incredible engineering. In my view she deserves a lot more credit, but maybe the fact that she didn't become too mainstream has made her remain more special... she's a heroine for me because she's never cared too much about public opinion... I think she was one of the first artists that made a connection between her visual work and her music. And then came Grace Jones, and then Madonna, and then Björk. I think it became like a world, the ultimate Kate Bush world, where you heard the sound, and then you looked at the videos and the imagery that went with it. That's why I found it so convincing, because I felt like there was this genuine passion for ideas".

Clothes designer Byblos revealed in coverage of fashion week in Milan that Kate was the inspiration for part of their collection, and pictures of Kate formed the backdrop to one display. The surprising thing for some about Kate's namecheck in *Elle Girl* – a teen mag – was that the editors would suppose that teenage girls would know Kate at all, but they made her an 'Elle Girl icon', with advice to their readers on how to achieve the make up and dress style. Quite like the *Jackie* articles of the late '70s.

Various news items in issues 69 to 75

Frost and French's Babooska chic, with Lily Cole

Jean-Paul Gaultier

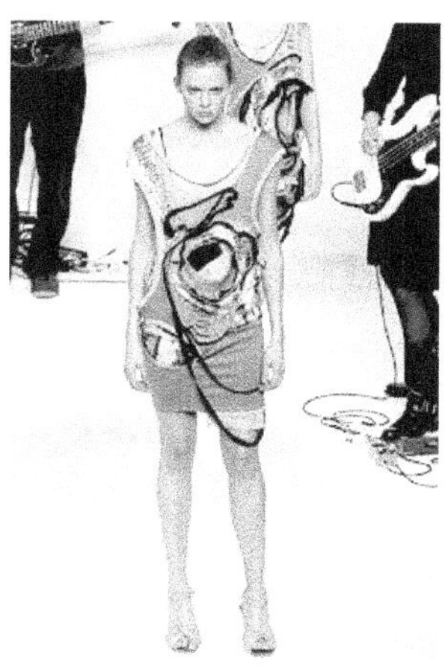

Hussein Chalayan

Comfortably Numb

Kate appears with Dave Gilmour January 2002

News issue 69 April 2002

If we had looked in early January 2002, we would have seen on the Pink Floyd website, 'A Fleeting Glimpse', the following snippet: "Hot Off The Press: Rick Wright guest at Gilmour shows (All 3 dates) Bob Geldolf also guest on 17th and Kate Bush on 18th..." However, like everyone else in the Kate-speaking world, and EMI, the information that Kate would be taking the stage for the first time in almost 15 years, at the Royal Festival Hall on 18th January 2002, as Dave Gilmour's guest, came as a surprise late on the afternoon of that very day. Attempts to get tickets at that late stage were fruitless. "Sold Out" we were told at every turn. Luckily some Kate fans – who were also Gilmour and Floyd fans – were there!

John C. Elliot

To give some background, last year Robert Wyatt was asked by the Royal Festival Hall, London to run that year's 'Meltdown'. He asked David Gilmour, Pink Floyd's guitarist, to perform a set, which he did on 22nd June 2001. That set was basically an acoustic set and featured a number of Floyd songs together with a Syd Barrett song, a song from a Bizet opera, a new song and a lullaby from *Chitty Chitty Bang Bang* – I kid you not. Gilmour got an outstanding reception and the show was hailed by many as one of the most amazing Gilmour performances. It was a stripped down set – no flying pigs, no lasers, no movie screens and all in a small venue. It seems that performance (his first live show since 29th October 1994 when Floyd finished their last world tour) stirred him into doing some more shows.

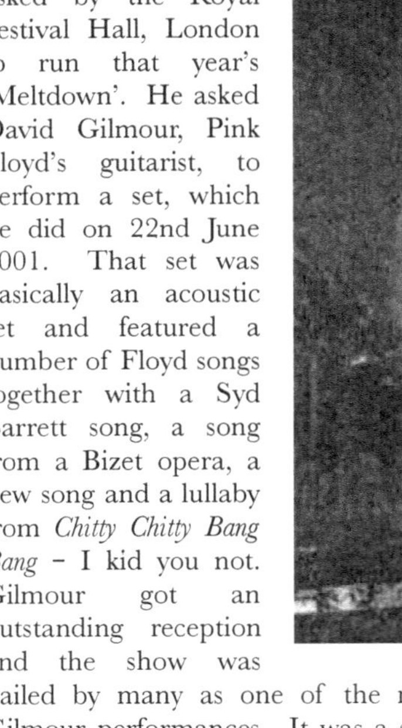

Photos this page and opposite: Phil Waters

I got a 'phone call, many months ago, early one morning saying that Gilmour was going to do another show at the Festival Hall in January so immediately I booked tickets. A few days later and another call – a second show had been added. Then another call – a third show. Without hesitation I bought tickets to all three at £45 each! But hey, the June show was so good I just had to do it – and what would he come up with this time? Little did anyone know the incredible surprises that awaited all those lucky enough to buy tickets. All three shows sold out very quickly and the only notification of them was on the Festival Hall's website – word of mouth was the key.

Then adverts started to appear in the national press for the first two shows, but by then were sold out. I caught the train to London, checked into my hotel and headed to the Festival Hall arriving at about 3pm. There I meet some German friends who had come over for June's gig and were here again. I first met them at a Roger Waters show in the US in 1999. There were many UK friends and a chap who had come from Brisbane especially for the shows! He had waited 15 years to see Gilmour live.

As we were chatting it was revealed to me that one of the German guys had spoken to the bass player, Chucho Merchan, when he arrived that day. He had said that each night would be different. There would be a special guest at each show – Robert Wyatt, Bob Geldof and – Kate Bush! Later that day Richard Wright, the Floyd's keyboardist arrived – this was going to be a sublime show; two-thirds of Pink Floyd live in a small arena doing an acoustic set – and my seats were 4th row!

The three nights were essentially the same. Doors opened at 8pm for the support act. On Wednesday and Thursday it was Ghostland, the band of Gilmour's cellist, Caroline Dale. On Friday it was Trashmonk, Nick Laird-Clowes band. He was the guy behind Dream Academy and co-wrote some songs on the Floyd album, *The Division Bell*. There was a short break until 9.15 when Gilmour walked on stage alone and picked up his acoustic guitar and started to play *Shine On You Crazy Diamond*. Two minutes into the song most of the audience recognised it and a loud cheer went up. Then silence and they listened. In between songs there were cheers and shouts from the audience – a number of which he replied to. It was the same each night. The set-list for all three nights was the same and very similar to the 'Meltdown' show, and included *Comfortably Numb*.

On Wednesday, Robert Wyatt reprised his role from the June show by singing two verses – the first and third, taking the part of the wicked doctor. On Thursday it was Bob Geldof, who played the central character in *Pink Floyd The Wall* film (he didn't actually sing the song in the film although he did sing other Floyd tunes).

On Friday at about 3pm Kate arrived on foot, at the venue. It seems that rehearsals were around 4pm each day. She was recognised by the few people who hung around the artist's entrance to the Hall, but politely declined requests for autographs and walked straight in. Friday's guest on *Comfortably Numb* was indeed Kate Bush. After the end of *Wish You Were Here*, Dave Gilmour said "We're going to sing *Comfortably Numb* now, and to play the part of the wicked doctor, I'd like to invite Kate Bush to come and sing with us". At this point Kate walked on stage to huge applause that lasted ages – and was certainly louder and longer than that received by Wyatt or Geldof. At the front of the stage there was a stand with the lyrics for Kate to sing and a mike stand just to the right of Gilmour. A piano intro lead quickly into the first lines which she sang beautifully and with real pain as the original is intended. Her performance stunned and silenced the crowd. The second verse was taken by Gilmour to initial cheers, with Kate joining in on harmonies. Then came the piano section that leads into one of Gilmour's most famous guitar solos which he did on an electric guitar heralding cheers both before and after the solo. Verse three was Kate's turn. Again superbly handled. Verse four was Gilmour with Kate taking harmonies. Another guitar solo. Throughout the time Kate was on stage she watched Gilmour sing and play, moving slowly to the music. She was dressed in a black suit.

The end of the song produced huge applause at which point Kate went over to Dave Gilmour and gave him a big hug and a kiss on the cheek. She then walked towards Michael Kamen, who was at the piano, and gave him a hug and kiss. I don't know if she hung around for the after show party, but she wasn't seen leaving the venue after the party like the rest of the band and guests. The show was flmed professionally by a ten camera team. Only Thursday's and Friday's shows were filmed so there may be a DVD available – but the Floyd are well know for filming and taping shows then never releasing them. It took 20 years to release a live CD of the original *Wall* shows in London. So don't hold your breath.

Phil Waters

I saw all three of Gilmour's shows in London, and I was outside when Kate arrived for the rehearsals on Friday. She looked so lovely, and had Bertie with her, as well as (I presume) his nanny. She politely refused to sign autographs or to pose for pictures, just went straight in. I think everyone there (one or two of whom were HUGE Kate fans, myself included) accepted this as being just fine, as she is known for not being inclined to do such things. Plus, throw in the fact that Bertie was with her, and it makes even more sense, right? Her performance on *Comfortably Numb* surprised me. I admit to having had mixed feelings when Michael Kamen had told us the night before that she would indeed be doing the song. But once I heard her, I realised that she was perfect for it! It gave the song a whole new spin, one that I hadn't anticipated.

Future Hounds

Peter discovers the story of a classic Kate cover

News items issues 73 to 75

On 1st July 2003 *The Guardian* reported a gig at The Buffalo Bar in London: "there is something grippingly odd about the Futureheads. Partly, it is their eccentric choice of covers. Their marvellous version of Kate Bush's *Hounds of Love* is totally unexpected: what is even more surprising is how thrilling its singularly feminine abandon sounds in their hands". The band told the 2nd August *NME:* "We love Kate because she comes at music from a really spazzy angle. That's the reason we covered *Hounds of Love*. It's good pop with a strange arrangement".

In the 16th July 2004 *Guardian*, critic David Peschek reviewed their album: "They are an odd, quintessentially postmodern lot, balancing breathless, adrenaline rush garage pop... and a delicate, almost feminine quality largely derived from unexpectedly subtle four-part vocal harmonies; epitomised by a deft, heartfelt cover of Kate Bush's *Hounds of Love*". The 19th July *NME* reported that at the band's 15th July gig at Hammersmith Working Men's Club, licensing regulations meant that the plugs were pulled halfway through *Hounds of Love* at the end of their second set. However, both band and fans made a good job of finishing the song using just acapella harmonies.

Around Christmas 2004 the band released a very limited edition vinyl-only cover of *Hounds of Love*. Ross explained on Nottingham Student Radio 23rd January: "In the Eighties there were a lot of solo performers that did really well in terms of having classic albums and stuff and you don't really get that anymore, because solo performers nowadays days make really embarrassing records like only your mam listens to. So I think she was just one of those people in the Eighties that made really eccentric music, intelligent without being typical, but also that you could still really sing along to when you heard it on the radio. We did a tour of squats in Europe a couple of years ago and Jaff our bass player had made a compilation tape with *Hounds of Love* on for the drives in the van. We chatted about it and we just decided to cover it. I don't think we had any idea that we would still be playing it now, because this was two and a half/three years ago, but all of a sudden it becomes one of the more important songs... at the start we didn't wanna put it on the album. You see we didn't want any reviews to concentrate on it, but I mean you've gotta make a decision to whether you wanna play it anymore or stop it all together and we made the decision to stick with it".

Despite the band's doubts, the album did include a studio version of the cover, and reviewers did indeed seize on it as a stand-out track: "a ransacked rendition of Kate Bush's *Hounds of Love* explodes in a burst of hectic yearning" (*Rolling Stone* 28th October), "Kate Bush has for years been a frequent influence on UK indie guitar bands, but by merging her regal dementia and haunting brilliance with their three-chord adrenaline, The Futureheads have managed to make her sound fresh... the snarling *Hounds of Love* is among The Futureheads' brightest moments" (*Pitchfork* 28th October), "an inventive version of Kate Bush's *Hounds of Love* that turns the original's ethereal wistfulness into a visceral rush (*Phily.com* 19th December).

In the Christmas 2004 *NME* the band explained: "We were thinking that it's a brilliant song and we thought we'd try and work it out – a little challenge. We got home and it was a really quick thing. And when we played it... it just stuck. People were going barmy for it".

Ross also spoke about "Why I love... Kate Bush": "The love of Kate Bush goes right across The Futureheads. For Barry and Dave – the Hyde brothers – they heard Kate Bush around the house quite a lot when they were younger and they knew the videos off VH1 and whatever. I didn't really get into her like that. It was more me getting into the '70s and '80s guitar bands... I was trying to progress from that sort of music when I stumbled across the video to *Cloudbusting* one day... and I was hooked... She made quite melodious pop music, but it's really clever. It's not traditional verse/chorus/verse song structure. There are interesting parts coming in and out of the songs all the time... By the time she made *Hounds of Love*, she was doing everything herself... she has it all, really. She could really sing, she could really play, she called all the shots and she was a beautiful woman as well. It put her in a very powerful position. She also carries a great mystique because she's a complete recluse... I don't know how she dealt with it, but that's really intense pressure. And she delivered the goods. She has written some classic albums and all have a little identity of their own."

In the new year the band embarked on the 2005 'NME/Shockwaves' Tour with the other current indie bands The Kaiserchiefs and Bloc Party, followed by their third North American tour, both of which included *Hounds of Love* in the set: "all through the room shouts of 'Oh Oh Oh' could be heard in the lead up to this very soon, excellent choice of single" (Jo Burns, Newcastle 19th January).

"Any band with the audacity to cover Kate Bush has a lot to answer for, any bloke of a certain age is sure to get a tear in their eye at the thought of her, ahem. But to make *Hounds of Love* so much their own song, and then to split the audience in half to sing different parts of the backing vocals is pure genius" (*Gigwise* Academy 1 Manchester 28th January). "Splitting the crowd in two to sing different parts of the acappella intro is a stroke of genius and probably hasn't been seen in Brixton since the likes of Bon Jovi in 1986, but tonight it couldn't have worked better" (CarlingLive.com Brixton Academy 9th February). "Millard and fellow guitarist Barry Hyde divided the crowd into two halves, and each side was instructed to sing a different part. It made for a sassy sing-a-long, with the chorus resonating in your head long after the song had ended." (*Boston Globe* 28th February)

"Bush's exemplary lyrics combine perfectly with The Futureheads' chiming, echoed vocals and erratic guitar to create a sporadic scene of love and exhilaration" (*Daily Texan* 8th March). "When this song arrives in their set, the Futureheads draw an imaginary line down the center of the crowd: Half get to sing "WHOA... oh, oh", the other half counter with "oh, WHOA, oh". After about 15 seconds, you realize how @# %$ hard singing is. The Futureheads aren't admirable for just their dead-aim (most of the time) pitch: how four rangy dudes from Sunderland ended up with such ungodly lung capacity is the bigger mystery. Split between the quartet, the harmony from this chart-scaling Kate Bush interpolation is beautiful; spread among an entire heavy-smoking crowd – rhythm slipping, pitch forgotten – it's almost spiritual" (*Pitchfork* 3rd February).

Inevitably, the Futureheads cover of *Hounds of Love* was released as a single on 28th February 2005. Their own press release said this: "The Futureheads cover of *Hounds of Love* is a showstopper that eclipses even their own inspired reading of the Television Personalities *Picture of Dorian Gray*. Beginning with Ross and Jaff's acapella call and response yelps, the song explodes into euphoric life with Barry's feverish delivery of Kate's once sensual words and a riot of overdriven guitars and search and destroy drumming courtesy of the coolest incumbent of a drumstool, Mr Dave Hyde. Fuck it! *Hounds of Love* is inspired and The Futureheads are a band hitting their creative stride as never before, as anyone who's just seen them on their recent live dates will testify. Wow, what a band!"

Reviewers were inclined to agree: "If Hayley Westenra is reading this, THIS is how you do a cover of a Kate Bush song... Where Kate's voice swooped and cajoled, the Fheads fibber and burp. Where her backing track was all drummy clatter, theirs is jagged guitars and urgent harmonies. Making this a rare example of a cover version that actually adds to your enjoyment of the original". (BBC 'Top of the Pops' website).

"Both artists versions of *Hounds of Love* excel in flair and panache, but the Futureheads bring something else to it – they stamp, with authority, their own stop-start guitar jabs and vocal ebullient flavour to the song. Voices and melodies materialise from every crevice and coagulate to form what has now become the spell- binding Futureheads trademark" (*Gigwise* 28th February).

"It's one of those songs that cheers you up beyond all measure; you can stick in the CD player, turn it up loud and jump around like a crazed kangaroo for the all too short three minutes it lasts. I personally haven't performed on an air guitar for years, but this band has inspired me to hold aloft my imaginary instrument once more... The Futureheads real quality is their ability to produce an arrangement that not only does the original justice, but in fact surpasses it completely. With the intro of 'Oh Oh Ohs' still reverberating around my head like a stuck record, even though I've been listening to it for weeks now, it's fair to say this track is pretty unforgettable" (*Skiddle* 25th February).

The release was perked up for club use by re-mixers Phones and Mystery Jets, and earned a slot on BBC Radio 1 DJ Pete Tong's "Buzz Chart," which means that dozens of British DJs were playing it as well. Radio play was good, with XFM in particular supporting strongly. They made a big deal of the missing "It's in the trees – It's coming" and asked the band to explain when guesting on 23rd February. They explained that they had not considered it part of the music when they were originally trying to work it out. The station's comment: "Having added the all-important "it's in the trees, it's coming", the song is flawless. Move over Kate".

The as yet unreleased track entered the *NME* chart at no.4 on 24th January, and was no.1 for two weeks. Having secured wide videoplay on the cable channels, the track entered the official chart at no.8 on 27th February, moving down to no.19 the following week. On 7th March the band were asked if they had received any feedback from Kate. Barry Hyde the lead singer and guitarist replied: "she hasn't been in touch. Wouldn't it be amazing if she performed it with us one day? I can but dream. I think we would cry with joy if she did though".

Waiting for Kate

John Mendelssohn's strange book considered

Issue 75: March 2005

John Burke: Strangely Pleasant Experience

John Mendelssohn... who he?? A braver man than I, let me tell you. In a world where almost no official 'release' (book, CD, chocolate bar, etc.) of any kind bearing those two sacred words – 'Kate' and 'Bush' – has appeared in over a decade, this upstart music journo has come up with *Waiting For Kate Bush*, described by the publishers as "an unusual hybrid of satirical novel and music biography".

And, what's more, he hasn't placed Kate as an incidental in his story, as she is in David Nicholl's (inferior, in my opinion) *Starter For Ten*: oh, no! In Mendelssohn's offering she dominates the title and the cover: her name looms larger than any of the other text and she gazes out sulkily, suggestively and utterly fabulously in full-bleed black and white – an image from the Gered Mankowitz sessions. And the story? Yes, she's there too. Never in person, you understand, but she's hanging around, she's listened to, sung along with, referred to, criticised, praised, worshipped, built up, torn down, obsessed over and adored.

This strange marriage of novel and music biography comes laden with expectation. Katefans (surely a collective noun that should be recognised by the Oxford English Dictionary before the release of album number eight later this year) are a notoriously possessive, protective and (some would say, though I couldn't possibly comment) obsessive bunch. It's all the fault of the lady herself, of course. After years of sharing our most raw and vulnerable moments with her; after crying to her sublime lyrics and melodies; after raging at her teasing yet often inaccessible (according to Mendelssohn) musical excesses; after no live shows since 1979 (that's the 1970s, for God's sake!); after learning the *Wuthering Heights* routine and performing it in the privacy of our own bedrooms, and after being laughed at for wearing a Kate badge on our school blazers when everyone else adored Debbie Harry (mmm – am I giving too much away here?); after all this, and almost 12 years since *The Red Shoes* (rather brazenly referred to on the book's cover as "her last and best album") Kate has given us... nothing.

But the love affair hasn't cooled. Katefans are as abandoned lovers, poring over the minutiae of faded love-letters, examining every last word and nuance, interpreting and debating and re-interpreting. And it is into this hallowed territory that Mendelssohn has china-shopped his way; and he must stand trial before a massed jury of Katefans, with the accepted premise that he is guilty and must prove his innocence or bear the consequences. So, does it work?

Well, I think it does: entertaining, strange and compelling. The story of weeks in the life of Herkovits, an American underwear-model who is obsessed with two things: his own (apparent) obesity and Kate Bush. Hailing from West-coast USA, Herkovits, now in his 50s, lodges in a boarding-house (run by Kate-obsessed Mrs Cavanaugh) that accommodates only fervent Katefans and is situated near to Kate's birthplace. He sends her endless presents and emails, has an estranged daughter named Babooshka and, when attempting suicide at the start of the book, tells the police his name is Del Palmer. This guy has it bad!

Although not always a sympathetic character, there are, undoubtedly, elements to Lesley that many Katefans will identify with and enjoy: certainly, his refusal to believe that a fellow boarder who "might be the only person in the world who regards *Lionheart* as Kate's best album" could be sexually dominant, made me smile, as did his knowing by heart the complete list of thanks from Kate which appears on *The Dreaming*...

There are some very shrewd and funny observations on the celebrity-obsessed culture we inhabit (Kate representing the antithesis of this), and Mendelssohn's pastiche of 'Popstars/Pop Idol/X Factor' talent shows – 'Megastar: The Lame, The Halt And The Blind', in which all the contestants are disabled, terminally ill, obese, anorexic, etc., and the judges/managers are exploitative vipers – is positively Orton-esque in its utter bad taste but, nevertheless, rings uncomfortably true.

Think about it: there were two series of the hideous 'Pop Idol' in the UK. Runner-up (though favourite to win) on series one was Gareth Gates (spikey-haired teenager with undoubted ability to sing but also with appalling stammer); winner on series two was Michelle McManus (teenager with undoubted ability to sing but also excessively obese). And where are they now? The British public had their fun with them, felt good about themselves for giving the stuttering boy/fat girl their two minutes of fame, and then abandoned them and moved on, leaving Gareth and Michelle wondering if it had ever happened at all??

But Mendelssohn injects the 'Megastar' scenes with pathos, hilarity and (for Katefans) pure fantasy: where in the latter stages of the real 'Pop Idol' there were episodes where each remaining contestant was required to perform an Abba (or Beatles or big band) song, here we have a prime-time TV talent show where each contestant has to perform a Kate Bush song. Now, come on, isn't that just a little bit seductive?

The Kate-related biographical thread that runs through the book is interesting and (mostly) well-researched but, for Katefans, won't tell you much that you didn't already know. And there are some silly (and some unforgivable) factual errors that really should have been checked and will, undoubtedly, niggle many Katefans who have had years to study every moment of Kate's life and career (and can spot a misquoted lyric or an incorrect release date at seventy paces and with a blindfold on): Mendelssohn refers to 'L'Amour Looks A Lot Like You', and it is news to me that "EMI wanted to release the buoyant *Babooshka* as the first single from *Lionheart*, but (Kate) insisted on *Breathing*... *Hounds of Love* is occasionally called 'The Hounds of Love' (a common mistake), but maybe that's Kate's fault because of her predilection for album titles that start with 'The' – *The Kick Inside*, *The Dreaming*, *The Whole Story*, *The Sensual World*, *The Red Shoes*. It's an easy mistake. Take note, Kate – we've spotted the theme...

I'm still not sure of the link between Lesley's tale and the life of Kate but, in a strange way, it doesn't matter. Without wishing to claim that this is a book to change your life in any meaningful way, and if the reader can find it in his or her heart to forgive some of the biographical errors (let's hope these are corrected before paperback publication), it is enjoyable, pacey and a jolly good read. And the cover image is pure sauce! The writing is somewhat pedestrian, and there is no doubt that a good sub-edit (preferably by a Katefan) would have been of benefit here; however, in the absence of anything new from Kate (and while we wait for the new album, now confirmed – hurrah! – for 2005), it's a teasing and tempting view of a fantasy world where Kate is given the status she surely deserves: goddess, myth, icon and all-round good egg.

The Observer newspaper said *Waiting For Kate Bush* was "like the singer herself... baffling as well as rather beautiful". I'm not sure I'd go as far as 'beautiful', but reading the book (with all its faults) was, for me, a satisfying and strangely pleasant experience. I'd recommend it.

Lucy Carswell: Best Avoided

Dismal disappointing trash posing as a 'satirical novel and music biography' that fulfils neither claim due to a lack of ability to entertain on the one hand, or to come up with anything like accurate information on the other.

This 278-page hardback is a cash-in of the worst sort: pedalling what is either a thinly disguised autobiography of self-pitying awfulness or, alternatively, a work of the blandest type of fiction that wouldn't have stood a prayer in the competitive world of publishing had it not used Kate's name in the title and her face on the dust jacket.

What irritates me most is that the author claims to be a fan of Kate Bush's, yet he consistently criticises her music and pokes fun at her. By contrast, his 'novel's' main character (written in the first person) claims to loathe name-calling and bullying and harps on at length about how being picked on and ridiculed by others has blighted his life. It's impossible to miss the hypocrisy.

It gets worse: the so called facts that pepper the chapters – Kate, despite being the purported main subject of the book warrants far less than 10% of the total content – are simply regurgitated clichés and comment parading as truths, ransacked from old music press reviews, imaginative media stories etc. and contain the usual accuracies.

Where the author attempts to put his thoughts about Kate's career into his own words, he mostly gets even the basic knowledge wrong, thereby showing just how interested he really is in Kate. (Example: apparently Kate wrote a song called 'L'Amour Looks A Lot Like You'!) An afternoon at the library poring over Internet related items about Kate would enable someone who had never heard of her to come up with a more plausible set of truths about her career. Even the infamous Fred Vermorel bothered enough about his subject to carry out some original research.

Interestingly, I understand that despite it being the obvious place to seek publicity for his book the author has somehow forgotten to send a review copy to *HomeGround*, despite using a number of back issues for his so-called research. Perhaps he is too embarrassed to do so. Far from being a genuine enthusiast of Kate's musical career the author has used her name for the sole purpose of shifting copies of his lamentable product. Unfortunately, in the absence of an authorised biography, trash like this will continue to sell. A senseless waste of £16.95 and best avoided.

ED72: Looks Good on a Shelf

There were some very funny observations about the 'Pop Idol' thing, a nice contrast to what Mendelssohn was trying to say about Kate being the antithesis of today's music industry.

However, the central character is very hard to like or sympathise with. The Kate material was inaccurate in places and didn't reveal any insight into her as a person or a musician, but in the context of the novel I think it more or less worked.

My overall impression was that this was a good premise but it does read like a first draft that needed editing and more thorough research regarding the Kate sections. Does look damned good on a shelf though.

And Your Starter for Ten ...

David Nicholls tells us about his comic novel

Issue 73: March 2004

News issue 73: "David Nicholls, a writer on the popular UK TV series 'Cold Feet' has published his first novel *Starter For Ten*, described as "painfully funny" by *Elle* magazine, and the film rights have apparently been snapped up by Tom Hanks' production company. The Kate connection? See the feature article further inside this issue. Kate was recently discussed on the 'Richard & Judy Show' Book Club on ITV in the UK when author David Nicholls was interviewed. The topic came around to Kate – and her absence from the charts. None of the panel had a clue as to what she was doing now, though they did show a brief video clip of *Wuthering Heights*".

The film did indeed get made and was released in the UK in November 2006, directed by Tom Vaughan and starring James McAvoy, Alice Eve and Rebecca Hall.

The film won the audience award at the Austin Film Festival 2006, and was nominated for a British Independent Film Award in 2006, and an Empire Award in 2007.

The soundtrack features music from Kate, The Cure, The Psychedelic Furs, The Buzzcocks, Yazoo, Motörhead, The Smiths, Echo & the Bunnymen, The Undertones, Tears for Fears, The Style Council and others.

Graphic: Steven Brown

The question I get asked most frequently by readers of my first novel *Starter For Ten* is how much of the story is autobiographical. As the central character, Brian, is a painfully gauche, pretentious, clumsy, sexually incompetent know-it-all I like to think that we have absolutely nothing in common. But if there is a link, it's definitely a love of Kate Bush's music. I've been a fan from the beginning.

In the musically barren years of the early and mid Eighties, those records were a god-send and, like Brian, very much the soundtrack to my University years and beyond. I particularly remember a performance of *Running Up That Hill* on the 'Wogan' show, of all things, that was sensational.

Listening to that track as I write this, it seems remarkable that it's almost twenty years old. It's hard to think of another artist whose work sounds so fresh and innovative so many years later.

Many of the other musical passions I had in 1985, the time the novel is set, have long since fallen by the wayside, but I still love those records, all of them, and listened to them constantly whilst writing *Starter For Ten*.

It's not the first time this music has been an inspiration either. After working on 'Cold Feet', I wrote a BBC show called 'Rescue Me', with Sally Phillips. The series was about the aftermath of a painful divorce, and that fantastic song, *You're the One*, from *The Red Shoes* was the perfect inspiration, and completely summed-up the bitter-sweet mood I was trying to get to in the writing. That line in the middle verse, "he can't make me laugh and cry at the same time" is almost my favourite moment in any of Kate's songs.

Favourite album? *The Dreaming* – a great record I think. So varied and rich, and years ahead of it's time. Almost every track is a wonder.

Favourite songs? There are so many, but I'd have to mention *The Kick Inside*, *The Man with the Child in his Eyes*, *This Woman's Work*, *Moments of Pleasure*, *Houdini*, *Rocket's Tail*, *You're the One* – as you can tell, they're mainly the more introspective love songs, and I hope there'll be a lot more in that vein on the new album.

Other favourite artists? I'd have to mention the much-missed Jeff Buckley, Tom Waits (another constant innovator), Bowie, and The Beatles of course.

At the moment I'm writing the film script of *Starter For Ten*. Who knows if it will ever get made, but if it does, then I hope that we get to smother the soundtrack with Kate's music. In the meantime, I do hope you enjoy the novel, and that it strikes a chord with you too.

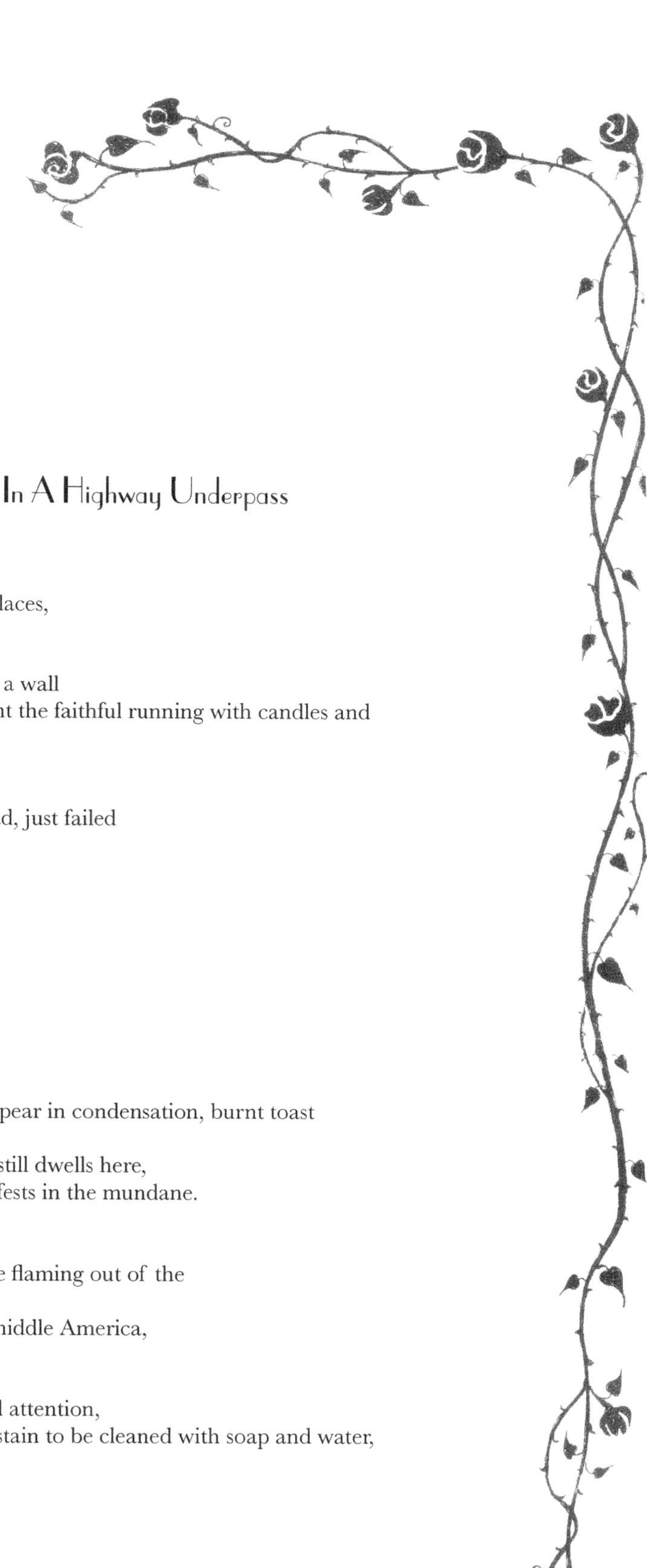

The Virgin Mary Appears In A Highway Underpass

Collin Kelley

Mary pops up in the strangest places,
usually as a window stain
or sandwich,
but yesterday she dripped down a wall
on a Chicago underpass, brought the faithful running with candles and
offerings, blocked traffic.
I saw the pictures,
couldn't see her face,
saw a giant gaping vagina instead, just failed
my Rorschach Test,
going to hell for sure.

If this is Mary, she sure
gets around,
recasting herself as a
Holly Golightly,
popping up where you
least expect her,
causing trouble for the locals.
But why would she choose to appear in condensation, burnt toast
or ditch water runoff?
Some will say its proof that she still dwells here,
runs like an undercurrent, manifests in the mundane.

I say, cut the parlor tricks Mary.
If you want a little respect, come flaming out of the
sky on a thunder cloud,
ride it like a magic carpet over middle America,
speak in a voice like
Diana Rigg
or Emma Thompson, command attention,
instead of this slight of hand, a stain to be cleaned with soap and water,
so easily erased.

Autumn

Antonello Saeli

It's impossible to heal
The scar of that "no"
Cold as that day
When the wind moved the leaves
And you were closer.
People die for love
And are yet revived,
by the same disease.

Sarah

What will survive of us is Love: Krys Celebrates a Friend

Sarah died suddenly on 30th December 2002. She was just 31. The coroner's report was inconclusive and for months no-one knew why she had died. At the end of April we were told that Sarah had a very rare and incurable lung disorder and would have had three years to live from its onset. She died from a lung haemorrhage.

Sarah was remarkable and unique in many ways. Vibrant, full of life, strong in spirit, generous, funny, sensual, loving, gentle, brave and passionate about so many things. She was a mad, crazy girl who hugged trees, loved her real ales and was the best person to go camping with (she made wonderful camp breakfasts). And she could be incredibly naughty! She was a creative, talented craftswoman, with an instinctive knowledge of the ways of wood. Sarah had inherited her beloved Grandad's carpentry skills and she used his tools from childhood onwards. Her Grandad had died before she was born, but she always felt him near. The tools were magical somehow, as if a bond between them. Sarah loved trees with a passion, and had hoped to one day buy her own woodland, to tend the trees and make carvings and furniture from the wood. I like to think that maybe now her wish has come true and she is the guardian of the woodlands she always dreamed of. But above everything, Sarah was a wonderful friend to all who knew and loved her. We miss her terribly.

We met in 1987 when Sarah was sixteen, brought together by a mutual love of Kate's music. We found a strong bond of love and friendship and were there for each other through the usual things life hurled at us. Some friends came and went as people do, but Sarah was always there, with her warm smile and hugs. We shared many happy times and so much laughter. We were very close. I watched her grow from an insecure teenager into the loving, caring woman she became. She gave us so much support, especially during my IVF. She was brave, took chances, made things happen. She wasn't afraid of life; a valuable lesson she leaves behind.

When I think of Sarah I can only ever picture her sunny smiling face and that wicked, playful glint in her eyes. I look at the few photos I have of her; see her merry at the Sweeps Morris dance festival and the gatherings we had. I laugh and remember the mad things we all did. Our moments of pleasure... Precious every one. The Sweeps will forever be Sarah's, and I know our little ghosts will weave their way through the Morris-danced streets of Rochester, arm in arm, pints in hand, long after I am dust too... Will you be with us, Sarah, same time next year, and the next...? I know you will... I felt her spirit with us at this year's Sweeps. She was there in the faces of children, and in the May day cherry blossom falling as confetti in the breeze, and she was there amongst the ghost dancers dressed in white rags. And there in my heart.

Two years ago Sarah took herself out of circulation from all of us who knew her. I had missed her so much in the silence, I'd done all I could to try to contact her and had to accept that she needed the space for whatever the reasons. She said that something terrible had happened, but never told me what it was. Maybe she knew she was dying. Maybe she was trying to protect us. Then a year ago she got back in touch and last July, Sarah, Peter and I had what was to be our last perfect summer's day here in the garden. The scent of honeysuckle, lavender, roses, apples... I wish I could recall every moment of that day, of all the days we spent together. I wish I could remember what she was wearing. We caught up on the time we had missed, all the big things that had happened in both of our lives and made plans to get together again very soon. Little did we know. It was wonderful to just hold her again. A perfect day. Looking back I wonder if somehow we knew it would be our last. We were blessed to have those happy final hours together. I can't imagine how I'd feel right now had we not. I wish I could re-live that day again and again and say to her some of the things I wanted to say, look for little signs I had missed. Had she come to say goodbye? But I told her I loved her, and I guess that is all she needed to know. Then she disappeared from our lives once again. Silence. Gone away... 6th January. I get a sudden kick to make a 'phonecall to a stranger... "We heard she's passed away"...

Sarah's funeral was a few days later. The worst day of my life. The day I had to say farewell to one of the most important people in my life. It had snowed all that week and seemed fitting that Sarah should have a day such as this as her last. Sunshine sparkled the snow as it clung to the trees and ground, and crowned the old tombstones. We walked as in a dream... Took her a red rose, and a card to say we loved her... The silent hearse. Her name in flowers... Registration plate HMO – she would have laughed her socks

Issue 72: June 2003

"Our almost-instinct almost true;
What will survive of us is love"

Phillip Larkin
An Arudel Tomb

Photo: Geoff Boswell

off! Her last joke... The small coffin covered with lilies and roses and at her head, her khaki baseball cap. An indelible image tearing my soul into pieces. That little cap made it all too unbearably real. They played *The Dying Swan*... and she was gone. Later I spoke to Sarah's mother and twin sister. They were very kind. How uncanny to see Sarah's eyes looking into mine from her mother's face. Heart-broken for her little girl. This isn't the natural order of things, parents shouldn't have to bury their children. Nor should grandparents.

Later we sat in the car, whilst the other mourners gradually left. A hip-flask of Calvados to numb the pain. I'd made a tape of songs for Sarah the night before. I wanted to play her some of the songs she loved, one last time, before her little body became ashes and gold dust. Music was always our shared passion... The Pretenders *I'll Stand By You*... a few tracks from Joni Mitchell's *Blue* album... *Carey*... "let's not talk of fare-thee-wells now"... *River*... and *Little Green* because she really was born with the Moon in Cancer. And as we grow old, she will always be our 'Little Green' "for the winters cannot fade her..." *Wichita Lineman* by Glen Campbell, *Sarah* by Thin Lizzy. And, God help me, *Moments of Pleasure* and lastly Tori's *Gold Dust*.

Torturing myself, washed in the waves of grief, and this is just the beginning of a lifelong road to be travelled without my dear companion, my Sarah... my sister, mother, friend. I felt like I would break. An exhausting nightmare of a day. And I never want to do it again. But of course, I will, we all do. I now know the grief that is the price of love. And better this sorrow than to have never known and loved her. A cruel comfort that wraps her widow-weeds around me.

The grief ebbs and flows in waves of selfish emotion. People don't know what to say, isn't that always the way. Those of us who loved her pull closer. And those who never knew her give their love and wish they'd met her. Five months on. Still struggling to understand, to get a better grasp of death, to expand my vision. Would that I could fly my own spirit to those unknown lands to find her. When does it stop hurting? How do we cope when we lose someone we love so much? I haven't got a clue. With Sarah's death a big part of my life has also come to an abrupt end. Or maybe it has just changed. As though we're in different rooms.

I like to think she has only gone ahead to light the candles and get the drinks in... But we should have grown old together. The silly things, the special things, the stupid mundane stuff, all gone. And the music we loved. Will I ever be able to listen to it again? *Blue* was our album, *I'll Stand By You* was our song. I couldn't stand by her those last two years, she wouldn't let me. I have to gather up as many memories as I can. The shock muffled many of them like a dense fog, but with time they will return. But I have one clear and precious memory of a hot summer's afternoon in 1994 that we spent in the garden, sharing red wine and talking for hours about everything, as we always did. A day I will always hold to my heart.

Maybe the cold kiss I felt on my cheek the other night was her. Maybe I just wanted it to be. She comes in fleeting dreams of stone bears in waterfalls, I hold her and say "I've missed you", I hear her voice, see her for a moment, then she's gone to wherever Sarah is. So where is she? Is she by my side, does she stroke my hair with angel fingers, does she stand behind me in the kitchen and wrap her ghostly arms around me? Is she here with me right now as the tears pour down my face for the millionth time this year? Is she laughing at me and telling me to stop being such a miserable bloody cow and live. Live. Be happy with those who I love and who love me. But they hurt because I hurt and in grief's darkest hours I fear I could lose them too.

Normal bereavement reaction, so the books say... And still so many times I forget Sarah is dead and I think I can pick up the phone and talk to her. "But you can," a little voice says. "You can still talk to her, in your mind. She will hear you. She is still there, you just can't see her." I look into those kind, beautiful, autumn eyes. She wraps me up in her love. In life. And holds me while I grieve for my dead friend.

For all of this year I've been grieving. Trying to come to terms with "This first parting that there was among us..." as it says in *A Christmas Carol*. She is the first of us to go. But I haven't let her go yet, as I know I must. Maybe then it will stop hurting. Perhaps we have a toe in each other's worlds. She is gone yet she is not gone, because I know she is in my heart, that the love hasn't died, it is still as strong as ever. She is spirit. She is everywhere. I just have to let her in.

And now I like to think of you, Sarah, my precious friend, sitting under a huge ancient Glastonbury oak with the sun shining through its leaves and dancing in your hair, that sweet, warm smile dimpling your cheeks, watching you whittle a piece of windblown wood into something beautiful. I want to recall all those days we had, and there were hundreds. With time they'll come back to me. I miss you. I miss your warm hugs, your cheeky smile, the wicked sparkle in your eyes, the smell of your perfume, I miss everything that was you. If I close my eyes I can feel the glimmers of those things again. I feel blessed to know you, that you were such a big part of our lives for those fifteen years. Thank you for all the happy memories, for your love, for the time we had. Your love is the legacy you leave to everyone who knew you. You made your mark on so many lives. You left your mark on mine, right there in my heart. Sarah, my dear friend, I love you. Love is all there is and all that remains.

What Remains

Sarah Jane Mackenzie

Bits of paper
strewn
everywhere
pieces with
rough-edge
tears
and from straight lines
curve her
rough-spelt
words
Her writing is
still
there
but her presence
is not heard.

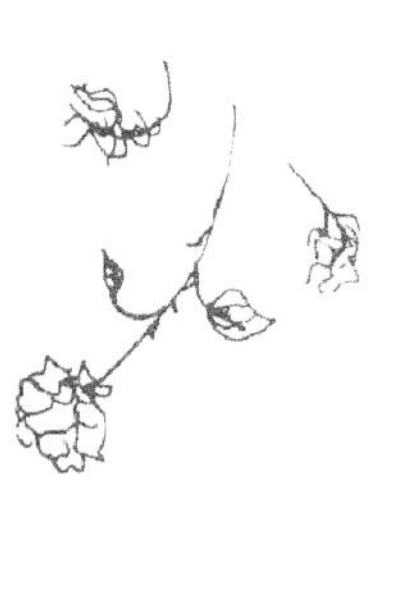

Tulip Glass

Kyla Clay-Fox

Watching my twin brother and I
Through the tulip glass – the blur of petals
Making the world seem different
Surreal, unlived and untouchable –

We saw his fists come crashing down
On her face, glazed like pink cherries
Though we knew she was our mother
The tulip glass, by the door in the lounge

Took us somewhere different,
Where we watched --voyeurs with jelly sweets
Huddled together, our mouths wide open
Our young eyes dead
and unblinking.

When red petals fell on to the carpet
When he smiled through the teeth of the glass
We buried our heads beneath cushions
No longer able to watch.

The Gardener

Dr. Andrew Marvick at the Millennium

Issue 64: January 2000

"Andrew Marvick is a veteran American Kate Fan, one of the original contributors to Love-Hounds.

He is now enjoying a teaching career at a State University Art Department in the wildwest state of Oklahoma."

Born Los Angeles, California 1957

Education: Ph.D. (art history), Columbia University 1994.

Now Associate Professor of Art History Southern Utah University.

In an attempt to atone for my long history of unreliability where *HomeGround* is concerned, I'll try to set down in words the way I feel about Kate Bush at the beginning of 2000, more than twenty-two years after I first encountered her music. It turns out not to be humorous, nor witty, perhaps not even entertaining. But it's honest, at least, and it may strike a chord of recognition in the fans of my generation – of her generation – who have taken this long journey together from the 1970s to the millennium.

I like to think that my first memories of Kate Bush are clear and indelible. The truth is, though, that some aspects have become tinted over time with the soft, welcome romance of nostalgia, as a patinating bronze loses clarity of detail and gains through that loss a new, more essential beauty.

I was just twenty – about Kate's age. The year was 1977, during a cold, rainy November in the beautiful, ageless city of Florence, where I was lucky enough to be spending my junior year in college. I was an art student, taking instruction with an old woman who had it in her power to pass to me some of the secrets of Europe's great tradition of painting, should I be mature enough to receive them. I wasn't, but I was possessed by a passion for the complex, mysterious and contradictory loveliness of life, and yearned to find a way to express it to the world.

I saw no-one in my tiny unheated apartment, passing my days alone, walking through the streets of the old city or painting crude, wild, bad but heartfelt pictures with the naive gusto of the untrained. At the end of the previous month I had briefly run out of money, and had even gone without food for two or three days – a privation that seemed Romantic to me then, at least until I caught a bad cold. I was feverishly ill for a week or more, and still weak, dehydrated and shivering from the cold of that fateful November night, as I lay in my cot in the dark, a portable radio my only companion. My illness had fostered a sentimental homesickness that brought me back hour after long hour to the comforting sound of a dim, static-filled radio signal from my fellow Anglophones at Radio Luxembourg.

Two decades later I can remember very little of the music from that time. Instead I recall only a weird auditory miasma of hooky, empty disco tracks and tinny American top-forty hits, snaking like a thin, weak score under my fever-tinted images of that wet month in Italy. Virtually forgotten tunes from the likes of Anne Peebles, The Whispers, Johnny Guitar Watson; desperately earnest, once seemingly important anthems of the young from Pauline Murray, The Stranglers, The Boomtown Rats; and a motley few genuinely terrific songs that would remain with us through the rest of the century, from The Police, Blondie, Kraftwerk, Genesis, a few others. All these little pop artefacts are swimming around aimlessly in my mind as I write this, like little fish inside a big, dark aquarium. And like a school of guppies hopelessly overpowered by the wake of a great British liner, those little pop songs lose their individual identity, overpowered by a single siren song of magical, mercurial beauty. For that night I heard *Wuthering Heights*, and I became from that time forward a lifelong passenger on the great, glorious, Good Ship Kate Bush that set sail from London that night on a steady course for heaven, via my eternally grateful soul.

IED and CD player 1985. See Andy's introduction on page 11 of Volume One.

Photo: Andrew Marvick

I would learn the song's title only after several torrid weeks' search for news in the music tabloids. Although I didn't know its title, and could sense its harmonies only imperfectly from my isolated location, and hear it only dimly through the frustrating ebb and flow of my radio's weak signal, its magical sound got through and was soaked up by my brain.

For all the excellent fans that our KommuniTy has gained since that time, each of whom has his or her wonderful memoir to share (and I hope they will), I have to think that however magical that moment of discovery was for them, it can't have had quite the character, quite the magic, quite the blinding brilliance of revelation and novelty that it had for those of us lucky enough to have experienced it at the start – at the moment of moments, the instant of instants – at the time when our journey, almost in perfect synchrony with hers, began.

So started for me a life that many of us have led for years now. While plodding along through a mundane existence in the "real" world, I took an almost sublime comfort in the mere thought of the possibility of a tour; found curiously thrilling even the hope that I might locate a hard-to-find single or an obscure foreign album-pressing; waited in secret agony for the slightest rumor of a second album or KonvenTion.

I remember still the transcendent moment (Thanksgiving Eve, November 1978) when, back in my California home, I first held in my hands a copy of *Lionheart*, specially ordered from far-off England at a time when Kate's name was almost completely unknown in the States. It seemed to me more precious than a Queen's jewels, more exotic than an eighteenth-century Oushak carpet, rarer than a pride of Siberian tigers; and when, back in the privacy of my room her voice confided, "I associate love with Red," I fell into a swoon of delight like none I'd experienced before. I was so nuts about this music that I even forced my mother and father to listen to it – loud! (It didn't work: Kate Bush would forever remain beyond their grasp!)

To me, the ten months that had passed since the release of the first album had seemed an eternity (ah, the innocence of those early days!) whose endurance engendered in me an almost religious bliss of anticipatory excitement. In a classic playing out of the tautological logic that is the ultimate protector of all religious convictions, the simple fact that the album didn't disappoint in the wake of such high expectations (as, indeed, no album of hers has ever disappointed me – which is more than can be said for a few fickle, imperfect fans!) was proof to me that my faith in her artistry was well founded, just as my faith in turn ensured that the music could not fail to enchant me. Her products were far more to me, I realized that Autumn, than wonderful art: they were the markers of my time on earth, the milestones of my journey through life at the end of the millennium, the company I could keep from early adulthood to death – in short, they were, it became clear to me, the aural manifestation of my life itself.

Graphic: Andrew Marvick

Her very name became a deeply reassuring mantra to me (as it still is), for in its utterance lay a reminder that God's beauty existed on Earth, in my time, and in a form that was simultaneously physical and metaphysical. No evil could ever really threaten me as long as the talisman of the KT symbol was on my side. It was all so lovely and safe, this obsession; I wasn't going to go mad (I hoped). Kate's virgin black vinyl gleamed and glinted on my turntable like a beacon for my imagination.

Over the next few months I worried a lot about my new, all-consuming interest: was I correct in believing as I did that Kate Bush was the SINGLE GREATEST LIVING HUMAN BEING IN HISTORY? Or was such a notion really, after all, perhaps just a little extreme? It was a difficult question, and it weighed heavily on my mind.

Then the magical double-sleeved seven-inch live EP came out! And then the *Breathing* single! *The Empty Bullring* seemed almost impossibly moving to me; I played it dozens, hundreds, thousands of times, it seemed, over the course of the next year. The pattern repeated itself again and again: *Babooshka*, and the magical *Ran Tan Waltz* (for the release of which I was lucky enough to be back in England, ostensibly as a participant in a graduate studies program, but actually so that I could race through London with a large shopping sack seeking out and snatching up every and any remotely Kate-related item available – a practice which has left me happily near the poverty line on occasions too numerous to count); the *Army Dreamers* single with its unexpected early-demo treat on the flip-side; the indescribably lush *December Will Be Magic Again* (I still get shivers thinking of the sound of her voice imparting the secret beauty in the word "snow!") with its swooningly sad and stunningly adult counterpart *Warm and Soothing*; and then, in 1981, something no-one could ever have anticipated: the first version of *Sat In Your Lap*, the likes of which, for all the production tips from Heyman, Collins, Gabriel et al, that might have inspired it, had never been remotely imagined before.

As Kate grew, she helped make our own growth a little easier. To my ears, the sound of those drums and whips was like the crunch of a million marching boots – the armies of Kate-fans

Graphic: Andrew Marvick

around the world who were jumping around their bedrooms in a delirium of Bushian energy. And in 1985, with the release of *Hounds of Love*, I recognized again that military tattoo as it tramped through Kate's deal with God and fell into line through the green hills of Eisenhower's America (by way of the Vale of the White Horse), and this time it sounded like the regular beat of the Corps of Orgonomic Engineers marching in Kately unison into the front lines to do glorious battle against the Forces of Negative Energy!

Now we are in the last months of a long silent period. *The Red Shoes*, Kate's intensely personal, richly mature album of 1993, was released a full seven years ago, and there is still no authoritative report of new material, although we are assured from time to time that she is well and happy and working. There is reason to hope for a new musical gift to spring next year from Kate's magic head, fully armed and ready to do battle with the cynics of 21st Century society, and for this we should all count ourselves fortunate, and give thanks.

The pace of Kate's career, like the quality of her art and the personality of its maker, is unique within the pop music industry. Indeed, in a very real sense Kate Bush is not part of that industry at all. She stands apart from - and above - that frantic, shallow world. And she reveals, by the glacial pace of her journey from KB 7 toward KB 8, that the making of a true work of art is a mysterious, private process that cannot be made to conform to the schedules of record corporations, radio station playlists or fans' expectations. In the end, as it has always proved to be in the past, the unexpectedly long wait will have been well worth it, and the whole world will be better off for having waited.

PostScript: Regarding the picture of mine which you kindly published in *HomeGround* 73: I originally had a request from Doug Alan to make a cover for Love-Hounds' DVD-ization of some unreleased bits of old Kate video-clips, and Doug indicated that in compiling the liner-notes for the project he was searching for the original fonts that were used for each of Kate's studio albums. I thought it would be nice therefore to offer him a cover that made visual reference to the cover art from each of Kate's LPs.

I settled on one of my favourite of all the official cover images, the mysterious and dramatic shot of *Babooshka*, haggard and distraught, stretched supine on the floor of a room with her double-bass and bow at her side, the letters received from her inconstant – yet-faithful husband strewn around her.

After I had delivered that image to Doug, however, I continued to add to the scene, as I realized that Babooshka's room could accommodate any number of Kate Bushological symbols – thanks to the magical potential of Photoshop. When Babooshka's walls grew too clogged with appended images and objects I could simply enlarge the canvas and build on more wall space as needed. As a result the picture now holds many arcane visual references for the KognoscenTi to enjoy identifying. For example (Warning: spoilers to follow!), can you find Kate's name as it appeared on each studio album? There is also at least one visual component of each album cover somewhere in Babooshka's room. But I couldn't stop there, so keep looking, you might recognize some of your old friends.

The Kick Inside's kite-flying girl has escaped her eyeball. A patch is needed on the wall to cover up some familiar Lionhearted wallpaper. Throughout the room you'll encounter a whole population of mini-Kates from her Tour of Life-rehearsal days. *Never For Ever*'s creatures have got themselves free of the bass, along with a flying baby-Kate, and *Delius*'s sun-disk is on the loose as well. From *The Dreaming*, you'll notice that *Night of the Swallow*'s uillean-pipes-player has made an appearance; our impatient heroine from *Sat In Your Lap* has forgotten her dunce's cap; and Mrs. Houdini has lost her little key. As for *Hounds of Love*, you'll find some of the seadrift flowers from *The Ninth Wave* serving as flying saucers for the ballerinas; the embroidered fez on Babooshka's head comes from promotional photography done for the album's U.S. release; the body-writing from *Running Up That Hill* can be seen climbing its way through mid-air from left to right (and again, along Kate's arms, in a photo on the lower back wall); the white rose up front might have come from *Under the Ivy*; and one of our favourite Weimeraners can be seen among the photos in the multi-image frame (which in turn comes from an ancient photo of Kate playing at a spinet at her old home – one or two of the little inset photos in that frame are presumably Bush family ancestors, though you'll also find a snap of the Dean of Kate Bushology himself, Dr. FitzGerald-Morris, a still of Kate in *Eat the Music* warpaint, another of the composer at her Fairlight and one or two of my personal favorite candids from over the years).

Love and Anger's orb and sceptre as well as its dervishes and ballerinas are all present, as is *The Sensual World*'s flower poster (on the back wall). There are also a couple of Bulgarian references: if you look closely at Babooshka's sleeves and the needle-point bird pattern leaning on the picture-rail, these are bits taken from some of the colorful garments Kate was seen wearing during promotional appearances with the Trio Bulgarka. From *The Red Shoes*, the fruit from Kate's *Eat the Music* dress has got itself stuck in *The Kick Inside*'s eye, and *The Line, the Cross & the Curve* are exiting Mrs. Houdini's mouth, only to be snatched up by the bird from Kate's *Pulse!* magazine-cover head-dress. And of course there's a hidden-in-plain-sight KT sign – what self-respecting Kate Bush image could fail to have one of those?

Andy with the LoveHounds white roses for Kate.

Tower Records, New York, 9th December 1993.

Photo: LoveHounds

Kate – Two Studies

by Ramona Lucius

Issues 66 (December 2000), and 70 (September 2002)

Ramona Lucius is a professional writer, editor, adventure game designer, and musician.

39 Hounds: The Hitchcock Influence

In an interview at the time of *The Sensual World* Kate said, "He's a tremendous influence on me. Whenever I'm making a video, he's really the ultimate reference point."

On the surface, it may seem very surprising that the "he" to whom Kate was referring was a portly, wealthy Englishman, later a Knight of the Realm, whose best work had been completed when Kate was barely out of her pram. What would such a gentle songwriter see in a man whose fortune and fame were based on the public's rather more unpleasant and prurient interests in murder, crime and mental illness? Yet there it is: Kate on American TV expressing her admiration for and emulation of "the master of suspense," flm director Sir Alfred Hitchcock (1900-1980).

So a closer look at Hitch will shed some light on Kate's work. And the attraction she feels for Mr. Macabre becomes clearer with a glance at Hitch's background. Like Kate, Hitch was raised near London, which may account for similarities in their taste in humor. In the VH1 special, Kate remarked that she especially liked Hitch's "out there" wit: absurd, sarcastic, knocking down sacred cows, he liked to poke fun at his sponsors. "And now for something really frightening," he'd say, then cut to commercial. Kate too seems to have that dry British wit: for her Comic Relief appearance in 1986, she sang a duet called *Do Bears...* about a wife who's sleeping with her husband's best friend, and for her acting début she chose *Les Dogs* surrealistic black comedy.

Besides their taste in humor, Hitch and Kate share a religious background; both were raised Catholic, which may account for some of the themes they've chosen to explore. The idea that, contrary to religious teachings, one shouldn't feel guilty about one's sexual desires runs through both artists' work; Kate, writing in more tolerant times, takes a much more accepting approach (think of the jubilant celebration of sex in the images and lyrics for *The Sensual World*), but Hitch had a few revolutionary things to say too. In 1964 he produced and directed *Marnie,* the story of a woman whose mother, a reformed prostitute, has raised her to abhor sex. It's not a very good movie, but it did make a remarkable pre-sexual revolution plea for open discussion about sex and forgiveness for sin.

The need for honesty in male-female relationships is a subtle theme in many of Hitch's films. He must have perceived dishonesty in the social convention of his time that dictated that women shouldn't like sex, because one of his favorite characters is the lady thief; in *Marnie, Psycho* (1960) and *To Catch a Thief* (1955) women transfer their need for sex into theft; unable to steal love, as women are supposed to by acting coy, they love to steal.

Another form of sexual dishonesty that Hitch perceived is voyeurism, through which a person can avoid the guilt and still participate vicariously in sex. Hitch saw that all audiences are by definition voyeurs and he liked to remind us of that, force us to admit it.

Rear Window (1954) focuses on that idea; a photo-journalist, who makes a living from, in effect, spying on other people, amuses himself by watching his neighbors. Kate, by usually choosing to write from the point of view of a character, and by choosing to tell confessional stories in her music, makes voyeurs of us too. Confess: don't you feel a tiny bit guilty for eavesdropping on the woman in the video for *The Man with the Child in his Eyes* or for looking in on the lovers' private dance in the *Running Up That Hill* video?

Actually Kate has her own version of *Rear Window*: in the *Babooshka* video, the viewer is spying on a wife who is spying on her husband. Another Kate/Hitch theme is that of the ordinary person thrust into extraordinary circumstances. We see this in Hitch's *North by Northwest* (1959) in which an ad exec is mistaken for a CIA agent - and is hunted down for murder, and in *The Birds* (1963), in which a man-chasing woman stumbles into a town held siege by birds. The plot of each movie revolves around the characters' attempts to cope.

Posters for some of Hitch's movies (this page and over).

Now it may seem that the ordinary person is the only type of character Kate hasn't explored, in her Pandora's box of thieves, computer addicts, ghosts, supernaturalists, fantasy lovers, murderers, and so on, but think of the video for *Army Dreamers*, in which a working-class mom acts out her son's wartime death, or *Cloudbusting*, in which a child tries to understand his father's arrest. (Another mutual Kate/Hitch theme: a dislike for police.) Ordinary people in quite extraordinary circumstances, trying to cope.

For the extraordinary characters, Hitch liked to use a plot device he called 'the MacGuffin' It's more or less an excuse for starting the story: it gets us interested long enough for him to introduce his characters and the real focus of the movie. In *Psycho*, the MacGuffin is the money that Janet Leigh's character has stolen; at the beginning, that's what we want to know about, but soon our attention is diverted to a more complex question, the real core of the movie: the psychology of Norman Bates.

Kate uses MacGuffins too; in the video for *This Woman's Work*, we never do find out what

caused the heroine's collapse (if you've seen the movie for which the song was written, you know the cause; She's Having a Baby). It doesn't matter; the collapse is a MacGuffin; what's important is the evolution of the lovers' relationship.

Besides the common themes in their work, Kate has obviously studied Hitch's film-making techniques – and she's chosen well, because critics and film-makers have been applauding Hitch's craftsmanship since 1926, with the release of his technically ground-breaking silent feature *The Lodger*.

NORTH BY NORTHWEST

First there's Hitch's process. Early in his career he gathered together a team of experts, including his wife, film editor, Alma Reville, and he worked with them throughout his 51-year career. He had a handful of favorite actors he liked to use as well. Then Hitch would storyboard the script, drawing sketches of the shots – and a typical movie has tens of thousands of shots. By the time he began filming, he knew exactly what every second in the film would look like, so he wasted very little film. This not only saved money but also protected Hitch's vision of the movie: with no footage to spare, the movie studio couldn't very well re-edit Hitch's work.

Kate's work followed the master film-maker's process. from the start, she's surrounded herself with a small circle of experts, for both her records and her videos: people who understand her vision and want to carry it out, even though that usually means doing the unusual, taking great risks, passing by the easy road to riches. And since she took over the direction of her music videos (starting with *Experiment IV*), Kate has relied on storyboarding, as she explained in the VH1 special. As with Hitch, this process insures that what we see and hear is what Kate actually wanted – or as close as technology and time will allow.

Besides process, Kate has learned specific film techniques from Hitch. That's obvious in *This Woman's Work* for example; think of the continuous, unbroken camera movement between the shots in the restaurant, the car, and the emergency ward. Hitch was particularly skilful at this; in *Rear Window*, he gives us the main character's background through one sweep of the camera; we see photographs on the man's wall that show us his profession, his girlfriend, and the cause of his accident (an auto racing wreck), then in the same sweep of the camera we see the man's broken leg and his hobby of spying on neighbors.

For another example, look at Kate's *Hounds of Love* video and the film she has said inspired it; Hitch's *The 39 Steps* (1935). Actually, *Hounds of Love* is a mini-version of the film. The movie is about another mistaken murderer, Richard Hannay, who sets out to find the real killer while avoiding the police. Along the way he becomes handcuffed to a woman named Pamela, which is where Kate's video picks up the story. Kate made several changes; in the flm, Hannay meets Pamela on a train; Kate has them meet in what appears to be an art gallery. In the film, a bogus cop handcuffs Hannay and Pamela together; in *Hounds of Love*, Hannay does it himself. In the film, Hannay and Pamela pretend to be newlyweds to escape detection, and several humorous incidents result; Kate has omitted this episode. In the film, Pamela falls in love with Hannay while they are hiding in a hotel room; in *Hounds*, she falls in love with him during a party the two stumble into. And the most significant change; Kate has made the manhunt a MacGuffin. She doesn't reveal who's chasing the hero or why; it doesn't matter as in *This Woman's Work*, it's the relationship's development that counts.

But Kate has preserved the spirit of the film, while setting her video in the point of view of the woman. The look of both film and video is dark and misty, almost dreamlike In both scenes between Hannay and Pamela is a current of distrust mixed with sexual attraction.

Hitch used very short shots and abrupt transitions from one scene to another to build suspense, and he'd withhold information to keep us guessing; although he didn't use these techniques as extensively in *The 39 Steps* as in some other films, Kate used them to great effect in *Hounds of Love*, along with the sweeping camera – in fact, she expands upon that technique: her camera becomes a dancer in the party scene.

Hitch would surely have been very pleased with the bookend shots for *Hounds of Love*; the first image we see is a man's face shot in an extreme close-up with an inappropriate lens, so that the face is horrifyingly distorted. In the last scene, Kate gives us a shot from above, so that we're looking down on the party, which gives the audience a feeling of superiority and, therefore, safety. And the final shot is close in, with an appropriate lens, and at shoulder level, so that the viewer blends into the crowd. It creates a warm, secure, friendly mood, a major contrast from the opening shot.

Director Brian DePalma once said that Hitchcock had "created a vocabulary" for film. While there is some debate about just how many techniques were Hitch's invention, there is no debate that he used those tools masterfully, and many of today's great directors cite him as a major influence, so as a student of Hitchcock, Kate is in good company.

And she's learning quickly; in just six outings as a director she's caught onto the vocabulary. She has indicated in several interviews her desire to continue directing music videos. If her efforts so far are an indication, she may well be adding a few phrases of her own to that vocabulary.

G

The Romantic Poets and Kate

William Wordsworth

Samuel Coleridge

William Blake

Percy Shelley

John Keats

Graphic previous page and opposite: Steven Brown

William Wordsworth and Samuel Taylor Coleridge jointly publish *Lyrical Ballads* in 1798. In 1978 Kate Bush releases her first two albums, *The Kick Inside* and *Lionheart*

Perhaps those two major English romantic poets Wordsworth and Coleridge would appreciate the symbolism in the apparent similarity of the dates. It is my proposition that they would definitely appreciate Kate; as a quick comparison will show, she is a soul sister to the poets of the 19th Century, the architects of the Romantic Movement in literature. Writing in times of unrest, dissatisfaction, political upheaval and rapid change, William Wordsworth and Samuel Coleridge, and brothers-in-arms William Blake, Percy Bysshe Shelley, and John Keats, looked to nature and found much reason for optimism. Writing in times of unrest, dissatisfaction, and rapid change, Kate Bush also looks to nature and finds much reason for optimism.

Good poetry, said William Wordsworth, is "the spontaneous overflow of powerful feelings."

Kate has always closely adhered to this view in her own writing. Check the back cover of her very first album, *The Kick Inside:* "all of you with open ears - please feel it." She certainly does. From the wistfulness of *The Man with the Child in his Eyes* to the worry in *This Woman's Work*, Kate's music is all feeling. An hour with Kate, especially *The Dreaming*, is great therapy.

"The times", said Wordsworth of the Nineteenth Century, "are replete with "dereliction and dismay" and "hopes o'erthrown." Hard times call for renovation, beginning with the self; the first step is a search for identity, not an easy task, since the mind is clogged by all the garbage fed to it by social institutions. Church, school, and government confine thought and squelch imagination; if there had been robots in those nineteenth century days, the Romanticists would have said that society turns us into them. So what to do? Turn to the uncorrupted, those outside of society's control: children and nature. The Romantics saw in these the hand of God and source of renewal. "The child is father to the man," said Coleridge.

Once rejuvenated, one could contribute to other people's breakthroughs by breaking down barriers. For artists, that meant overthrowing the old rules for Art. Before the Romantics, poets often wrote about "great" people - kings and queens - and great ideas. It was an easy way to make a buck - dash off a tribute to a grateful duke. And, it was believed, lofty ideas make lofty poems.

Wordsworth delighted in breaking with convention, so his poems were often about, as William Hazlitt put it, "convicts, female vagrants, gypsies, idiot boys and mad mothers." Keats and Coleridge explored the abnormal side of life, too: demonology, witchcraft, drug-induced hallucinations. Keats wisely observed the paradoxes in all human experiences: love and hate, pain and pleasure, life and death are inseparable, sometimes almost indistinguishable. Shelley noted "the desire of the moth for the star."

Given their attitude toward society, it is not surprising that the Romantic poets preferred to create in isolation. As Wordsworth put it, "the individual Mind... keeps her own/Inviolate retirement."

Kate fans will hear echoes of her over and over again in the Romantics. The belief that times are hard and change is needed comes up in *Between a Man and a Woman* and in *Deeper Understanding.* Rejection of the institutions that interfere with imagination - what her mentors Pink Floyd called "bricks in the wall" - comes up in *Cloudbusting*, *In Search of Peter Pan*, and *Waking the Witch*.

The search for identity runs all through Kate's work, from the girl in *Them Heavy People* - "I must work on my mind"- to *The Sensual World* in which the singer gains "powers o'er a woman's body." In fact, *Hounds of Love* can be seen as a complete psychological journey from disgruntlement with one's socially prescribed identity (*Running Up that Hill*) to freedom (*The Morning Fog*).

To find yourself, turn to nature and children, said the Romantics; Kate concurs. Seeking relief from "my demon," the singer of *Egypt* finds nature (and man made art formed from nature) reflects her feelings and comforts her. To drive off pain, the singer of *Get Out of My House* changes into various animals. The best example of Kate's faith in the healing power of nature is probably *The Big Sky*: "They look down at the ground, missing / But never go in now," she sings jubilantly. "You never understood me"- but from her tone it's clear she doesn't care; she's caught up in nature: "What was the question?/I was looking at the Big Sky." Children as another source for rejuvenation is one of the themes in *Breathing*, as the unborn child cautions her elders: "life itself is breathing."

Like Wordsworth, Kate likes to write about social rebels, usually flatteringly: *There Goes a Tenner*, *Kashka from Baghdad*, *Cloudbusting*, *Night of the Swallow*, just to name a few. When the tone is negative, it's usually because the rebel is torn between his/her individual desires and need to fit into society. It's probably the rules of society that drive the sister in *The Kick Inside* to commit suicide, not regret over her incest.

Like the Romantics, Kate shows a fascination for the supernatural: *Strange Phenomena*, *Wuthering Heights*, *Houdini*, *Hammer Horror*, *Blow Away*, *Symphony in Blue*. *Them Heavy People* recants: "don't fall for a magic wand" but celebrates "the beauty of rare innocence," which Romantics saw in children. Kate's work has always marvelled over the paradoxes in life: "You give me life," she writes in *Moving*; "You crush the lily in my soul." *All We Ever Look For* shows that the search for identity raises a paradox: "Leave the nest And then regret you ever left."

Kate recognises that opposite emotions not only co-exist but also complement each other: "Take away the love and the anger" and a relationship ends; both exist in every relationship and give it life. "Only tragedy allows the release/ Of love and grief never normally seen" (*All the Love*). *Reaching Out* catalogues paradoxes and echoes Shelley: "Reaching out for that star."

And like the Romantics, Kate celebrates when a person has gone through the wringer: has faced the fact that he/she is a monster, misshapen by society, has dared to reject that identity, and has established his/her own. *Rocket's Tail* is such a celebration as the singer moves from conventional thinking – "I thought you were crazy wishing such a thing" – to total, joyous abandon: "I'm a rocket!"

And like the Romantics, Kate breaks conventions in her own art, musically and lyrically. Who else would think of mixing the high-tech Fairlight with ancient instruments like the balalaika? Or heavy metal guitar with ethereal Bulgarian voices? And in a market where lines in pop songs almost invariably rhyme, here's Kate, daring not to, and daring to play with lines that rhyme in the middle as well as at the end: "They think I'm up to something weird/ And up rears the head of fear" (*All the Love*).

The Romantics wrote in isolation; so does Kate. Since she built her own recording studio, she has been able to create songs that are completely her own. She is notorious for resisting interviews, personal appearances, and tours, as she says they cut into her song-writing time. As much as an artist can be and still make a living from his/her work, Kate is able to be fully submerged in creativity, and long may her Romantic impulses remain untainted from the messy business side of music. Wordsworth and Coleridge would be proud.

Here

Antonello Saeli

Here, while we have no names
I breathe your hair
Your skin, your sweat
And I look through your eyes
To feel the beauty of ecstasy
To reach the highest peaks
To be just slave to passion
Here, while we have no names
You pray for me
You move your hands
And stretch your wings
To fly again
Over the sleepy monster
Of our loving bodies.

The Soul Cries Out

... and is heard by Svein V. Eilevstad

Issue 68:
December 2001

Svein is a musician and teacher of English in Norway.

All I want is the truth
Just gimme some truth
John Lennon

The old gypsy is singing. His hands running over a strange one string guitar. He is singing about sorrow. About his people. About lost dreams, the girl who went away. It's the old story. Still. He is a magician, a storyteller who embraces his listeners, he is so full of vivid intensity, it is so incredibly moving all you want to do is cry out loud, and you know it isn't your move, but is the spark in you which merely IS – the soul cries out.

I like Emir Kusturica's films. Let's go back. Remembering, like a foggy image, the discussions with fellow musicians about how to proceed when making music. There were seemingly two basic, very different approaches towards music and art in general. One was emphasising technicality and "objective" standards on how things were supposed to be done, sometimes in accordance with the preferred style and taste of the day. The other was focusing on originality, experimenting and a fair amount of subjectivity in the creative process. Occasionally incredibly gifted artists managed to miraculously combine these two "directions" by using the subjective soul-part as the core and then fltering this through a certain intellectual web of practical solutions available to them at the time. Out there by the crossroads "zeitgeist" and soul met. Many artists have a period in their career when this happens. When you suddenly, in spite of being as "true" as you possibly can, still find your music on the top of the charts. I remember Prince in Paris in 1989. A perfect combination of soul and technical skills. Still frmly rooted in feelings when cut down to basics. *Purple Rain* went on and on that night, I recall. It was so moving.

Is it then possible to combine the paths of technicality and still keep the soul in the music?

The creation of true music very often starts with ideas arriving from somewhere out there, from the heart if you like, from the sphere of sensitivity. Then the process of protecting as well as expanding these ideas begins. Here it seems to be very easy to lose what you originally have, but this process might also add unexpected voices to the work. By very carefully examining these new and often coincidental shadows, the work is able to take an entirely new direction, but still might keep the whispers we originally intended to hear, the manifested glimpse of the subconscious.

Sometimes the words aren't that important, sometimes the sounds themselves are the main object of desire, filled with a transcendent energy and dreamy levels of messages, not aimed for the intellect but for the heart. The soul cries out.

When we hear Kate and Trio Bulgarka it is the sound of the beautiful choir of voices together which seems to be the "main thing", these lovely harmonies which very often are unbelievably strange, but still in unexplainable ways "homely", as Julian of Norwich would put it. Fragments of remembrance to our ears, the forgotten language from some distant, calling kingdom.

Nick Cave once responded to a question about how he made his music so that "it is not a cut-and-dry process". If he were to follow a recipe, some kind of scheme on how music should be made, it would be a horrible reduction of the potential of the entire creative process. Sometimes an unexpected turn brings vitality and new life even to otherwise mediocre ideas. There can never be definite recipes for music making. It is important to let the music find its own way, to take its time, to listen to the silence which, at given moments, opens the door to a language without words.

This might seem rather abstract, but I think it's fairly basic soul knowledge. Very few working methods leave out the element of experimentation. Creative processes of every kind should be alive, an organic unit with endless possibilities if we only know how to use them. This element of "soul magic" is of course the reason why art is, at best, so uncommonly intriguing. You never know where it will take you. And if you are lucky, maybe a glimpse of this fruitful marriage of form and content will survive the finishing touch, the last mixes and the following perfectionist mastering processes.

Here's Kate. By being brave enough to believe in herself, to dare to explore new ideas, to never compromise on anything but the best, she is gaining her status as a true artist. I think all of her albums prove this. As an example I will take one of my favourite albums of all time, *The Dreaming*, which consists of an almost painful mixture between soul and form, where both elements mutually caress each other, aiming towards an astonishing creative and highly personal achievement. It is perfection. Perfectly balanced. The picture is a wonderfully daring one.

Kate might spend years and years to produce her art. She is not alone. Like many other great artists, she seems to demand more and more of herself in order to fulfil the outcries of the soul, the frame of perfection which must be every honest artist's ultimate goal.

One of Norway's most respected and well-known poets, Paal-Helge Haugen, says that it gets increasingly harder to achieve the product he is struggling to create. In a way he is longing for those innocent days of youth when he wrote his début stuff. Things were a lot easier then, he says. Lots of unploughed ground. But at the same time he seems to find unsatisfying elements in his early work, things he would have done differently today if he had the chance to do it all over again. Isn't this like life itself – we see our path a lot clearer when a few years come upon us? His poetry collections are rare indeed, but when he releases his works it is always an event. Of course, the question about what's good and what's bad in art is in the last instance always subjective, but what I try to emphasise here is the struggle to reach perfection, which the true artist is constantly striving towards, can't appear on command according to time schedules or other practical limitations.

Bangin' on the table with a hot tin cup
Sing I'll never kiss a Gun Street Girl again
Tom Waits

The old tin cup could hide the key... the Houdini key hidden in an old tin cup?

Tricky said in an interview how he couldn't understand why so many musicians, even young beginners, needed so much equipment when planning to start making music. You take what you have, he said, if you're in tune (with yourself!) you can make great music by using very simple equipment. It's the idea that counts, not the range of expensive instruments you have at your disposal. Simplicity can, when used consciously, bring forth the messages of the soul in pure and honest, and not least unexpected, ways. It is important to use what we have, instead of dreaming about what we don't have. Consider this: how often have we felt that a song has been destroyed by adding too much to it! Modern studios have so many possibilities. More than ever it is very important to know what you want when spending your hard earned money in this way. And this, unfortunately, makes it difficult to avoid the "cut-and-dry" process, at least when it comes to recording and production. If you're not very rich and don't own your own studio, that is.

Kate has got her own studio, which must be a blessing. She can spend as much time as she needs in order to fulfil the desires of her work. What a great opportunity to use energy on the musical processes, and forget about most of the practical problems which often follow an ordinary recording process. Nowadays recording equipment is getting more affordable. We bought lots of equipment from a radio station who went digital, leaving us with all of their analogue machines. When you spend a lot of time trying to make the album as good as possible, you have to have time at your disposal, without thinking about the money you spend or the next band who will be there in an hour or so.

The production is of vital importance. Everyone who loves Kate's music knows that. There are so many ways of producing. But here we can experiment with cheap equipment as well. I think this is a good way to learn a few things about basic producing/mixing. A four-track recorder is the perfect toy if you want to have a go at music making! Of course, a cheap machine like this doesn't offer the range of possibilities a studio would, but you learn how to be creative, to use whatever you have. To try out strange, crazy solutions is indeed a wonderful opportunity to stumble across sounds and ideas never heard of before. In an interview, David Lynch told about his début years making short films. Not having any other ways of proceeding, he painted his house black on the inside to get a proper location for his little film. Being poor might bring forth creativity. If you really want to do this, you always find a way, Lynch said. There is always a solution. But you have to want it really bad.

Kate is an exceptional example on how to produce herself, how to bring forth the ideas of the music in a proper way. She knows when to hold back, how to understand the function of silence and the way opposites work in music: Less is usually more.

Tori Amos once claimed that she was incredibly impressed with the way Kate produced her work. She seems to go by the Miles Davis rule: A song is a painting. The hardest part is to know when to stop. When one more colour would take away instead of add to the overall atmosphere of the song. The soul has to be kept alive.

Again, I find *The Dreaming* as a fine example of a painting that vibrates because it is allowed to be totally naked at times, almost helplessly naked. And then, in the next moment, amazing, strange landscapes are creating an almost breathtaking contrast. Listen to how Kate uses the contrasting choirboy voice in *All the Love;* or how the beautiful string arrangement brings new dimensions to *Houdini,* or the guitar by Gilmour on *Rocket's Tail.* There are so many examples of how contrasts open doors in Kate's music. Trio Bulgarka is already mentioned. What a beautiful dimension their Eastern European voices bring to Kate's music! This is truly a soulful marriage made in heaven. Here there are no rules. Here is pure genius. After experiencing an album like *The Dreaming* or *Hounds of Love*, you know that music is capable of transporting us towards our soul home, towards places we seldom recognise in our usual state of noise and distractions. It is unique, because the soul is allowed to cry out, allowed to sing the song we need to hear, allowed to enter as a most welcome guest, no matter how frightening, in perfect accordance with the song's intentions. In times when it seems like the commercial horrors are buying their way into almost every possible musical nerve, it is always comforting to hear artists who still are able to show how it's done. As I write this I am listening to Dylan's new album *Love and Theft*, and what a relief it is to find the old man still soul-chasing among the ruins of shattered memories and prospect cards from the future!

Holding back and letting go. The importance of timing. The basis on true feeling. *Wings of Desire*, made by one of my favourite directors, Wim Wenders, is about this – celebrating this sad beautiful life, about being alive and really knowing how it feels to drink a cup of coffee in the rain, while the circus nearby is closing down. Sounds of hammers, shouting, words in a foreign tongue in the wind which is meaningful there and then if only by its very existence. The soul knows. Sensing every inch of the experience.

The old gypsy in Emir Kusturica's movie would understand immediately. We are here to breathe, to explore, to value the cryings of the soul, the hieroglyphs of the subconscious. It's a crying beyond words. But it's there. Hidden in two voices apparently colliding, in a strange word creating irrational but stunning associations, connections, in a sound transporting our minds away from the triviality supermarket surrounding us. It's the core of all great art. It's the voice of Cathy, out there on the moor, restlessly seeking for her lost soul, her eternal Heathcliff.

Graphic: Jean Marc Roulier

Telling Tales

Jeanette Payne looks at the Literary Influences

Issues 69 (April 2002) and 70 (September 2002)

1: Stepping out of the Page

"My brothers were really into folk music. And a lot of folk music is so into telling stories. And in a way, that's something that doesn't feature so much in contemporary music any more. I think contemporary music is used to help relationships a lot of the time… It's more about that than actually telling stories, like the traditional things are. And I think that's a big fascination for me."
Kate, MTV interview 1985

Grimms' *Children's and Household Tales* Frontispiece 1812

One of my favourite books as a child was an old collection of Grimms' fairy tales. I would read them over and over, and those stories formed the fabric of my imagination. They stayed with me long after the book itself finally fell apart. Of course, the origins of those fairy tales lie far beyond the printed page.

For centuries, fiction and poetry was narrated; passed on by word of mouth among families, tribes and communities. Storytelling was a form of entertainment that was available to everyone; the poor, the illiterate; as long as there was an audience and a teller, then imaginary worlds could be created. Fairy tales and folk tales were frightening, sensual stories that helped both adults and children to confront and understand their most primal fears.

German Popular Stories title page

They were often filled with tales of heroism, betrayal and the eternal struggle between the good and the bad. They were populated by beauties, villains, wicked stepmothers, and nearly always, magic. Many were cautionary tales, that used fantastical imagery to convey the consequences of straying from the path, entering the forbidden room or trusting the man whose eyebrows meet in the middle! More than anything, fairy tales are "the most vital connection that we have with the imaginations of the ordinary men and women whose labour created our world." (Angela Carter).

Gustav Doré illustration for *Cinderella* 1867

By their very nature, fairy stories and folk tales are fictions. They consist of archetypes and universal morals, and because of this, they transcend cultural and political boundaries. Characters and events are exaggerated beyond reality, so they become symbols, ideas and passions. The reason fairy tales have survived through the centuries of oral tradition is because they act as mirrors. Each listener sees something of their own personality reflected back at them. Gradually, as tales get passed on, pieces are added or omitted depending on the fancy of the teller. As Tolkien put it "The pot of soup, the cauldron, has always been boiling, and to it have continually been added new bits, dainty and undainty."

Perhaps the most significant impact on the oral and narrative tradition has been the written word. By writing down and documenting fairy tales, we are at once preserving them and yet preventing their organic growth. It is also well known that frequently during the Nineteenth Century, editors removed coarse expressions, sexually suggestive themes and violence from many fairy tale collections to make them more suitable for the middle class nursery. Indeed the majority of folk and fairy tales today are significantly sanitised versions of the dark and sinister originals. But thankfully there is an area where the practice of telling tales thrives to this day. Music is perhaps the closest thing we have now to the oral tradition, and there is no better teller of tales than Kate Bush. Kate is with doubt a consummate storyteller, weaving the golden threads of traditional folk tale into the tapestry of contemporary music. If we look at Kate's body of work, the influence of folklore and fairy tale can be found at every turn, from original yarns such as *Babooshka* and *Ran Tan Waltz*, to more explicit allusions to traditional folk tales such as *The Kick Inside* and *The Red Shoes*.

As the title track of her first album, *The Kick Inside* showed, Kate was not about to let us get comfy in our armchair as we listened. In the true spirit of the oral tradition, Kate took the folk song *Lucy Wan*, and moulded it; reshaping it into the form of a suicide note, and re-telling it from the first person perspective. By doing this, the tragedy becomes immediately more intense. In the original song, it is Lucy's brother who kills her when he learns that she is carrying his child, but through Kate's narrative, Lucy is given a voice and the sacrifice becomes her own. Throughout the song, Kate maintains the style of language of the original song, and by doing this, she communicates the tragedy of the children's incestuous love without the judgemental hand of modern thinking to jade it.

The release of *Babooshka* as a single, with *Ran Tan Waltz* as its B-side, confirmed that Kate is a storyteller of the most intoxicating kind. *Babooshka* works powerfully on so many levels – as a poem it is faultless, and as a song, you would be hard pressed to find a more triumphant chorus (and as for the video, I'm sure we are all still dribbling!) But as well as all this, it contains all the hallmarks of a traditional folk tale. Inspired by the folk song *Sovay, Sovay*, Kate narrates the tale of the scorned woman through motifs and symbols; pseudonyms, disguises, scented letters. Imagine yourself as a listener, sitting round the fireside as mother goose spins the yarn of *Babooshka*. Fairy tales are rich with clever girls and resourceful women plotting cunning stratagems for their own gain, and *Babooshka* is no exception!

Ran Tan Waltz is, in a way, the antithesis of *Babooshka*; the flip side of a marriage filled with uncertainty and betrayal told from the perspective of the husband. It is a common theme in fairy tales that mothers are either absent, dead or in the case of stepmothers, evil. Thematically, *Ran Tan Waltz* echoes tales such as *Cinderella* and *Hansel and Gretel*, where children are abandoned by their "mother" and left to fend for themselves. Often it is their natural father who tries to save them: "I'll tell you what," answered his wife. "Early tomorrow morning, we'll take the children out into the forest where it's most dense. We'll build them a fire and give them each a piece of bread. Then we'll go about our work and leave them alone. They won't find their way back home, and we'll be rid of them." "No, wife," the man said. "I won't do this. I don't have the heart to leave my children in the forest. The wild beasts would soon come and tear them apart." (*Hansel and Gretel*).

In *Ran Tan Waltz*, it is the father who protects his child from his wayward wife:

"*Four o'clock and her key's in the lock,*
she's been on the win
and she's stinking of drink.
Wakes the kid, so I put him to sleep,
and she's in there all night
doubled over the sink."

Even in their titles, *Babooshka* and *Ran Tan Waltz* evoke a sense of the past; as though they are not intended to be seen in a modern context, but rather as timeless allegories, in the same way that folk tales are.

To me, *Hounds of Love* is in many ways a re-telling of *Little Red Riding Hood*, a modern-day rendering of the story of darkness, fear and seduction. Kate's version has strong echoes of Angela Carter's *The Company of Wolves*, where Red is not the innocent girl of the original tale, but rather a wise child who is aware of her own sensual powers. Kate's imagery of trees and darkness and being hunted by unstoppable hounds of love could have stepped straight from the pages of the fairy tale: "But those eyes are all you will be able to glimpse of the forest assassins as they cluster invisibly around your smell of meat as you go through the wood unwisely late. They will be like shadows, they will be like wraiths, grey members of a congregation of nightmare; hark! His long, wavering howl… an aria of fear made audible." Angela Carter, *The Company of Wolves*

In both *Hounds of Love* and *The Company of Wolves*, the hounds that pursue the heroine are a devastating mixture of sensual allure and consuming terror. They are both seductive and destructive; overwhelming yet irresistible. The only way to survive is to overcome the fear and embrace the desire, however frightening that might be.

"Here I go, don't let me go, hold me down –
Take my shoes off and throw them in the lake."

"She closed the window on the wolves' threnody and took off her scarlet shawl, the colour of poppies, the colour of sacrifices, the colour of her menses, and, since her fear did her no good, she ceased to be afraid. What should I do with my shawl? Throw it on the fire, dear one, said the wolf. You won't need it again." (Angela Carter, *The Company of Wolves*).

Gustav Doré illustration for *Little Red Riding Hood* 1867

Just as Red throws her cape into the fire, Kate's heroine throws her shoes into the lake; an acceptance of the unappeasable nature of desire. Kate's heroine must confront her fears...

"But I'm still afraid to be there, among your hounds of love, and feel your arms surround me"

just as Red does;

"See! Sweet and sound she sleeps in granny's bed, between the paws of the tender wolf"

for only then can she understand the love that overwhelms her.

Hans Christian Andersen's *The Red Shoes* originally emerged in 1845 as a religious cautionary tale warning against the desire for material things. Since then, the tale of the little girl whose possessed shoes forced her to dance until her feet bled has inspired many writers and artists including most significantly Michael Powell, whose film *The Red Shoes* has become a cinematic classic of our time. In Kate's appropriation of the tale, she uses a hypnotic musical rhythm to convey the cruel, mesmerising power of the curse of the shoes. The repetition of "She gotta dance" and the relentless beat, transform a tale which was originally spoken, into such an intoxicating musical rendition, that it seems impossible to imagine that story without hearing the unstoppable pulse of Kate's song urging it onwards.

Perhaps one of the things that attracted Kate to folk tales and the narrative tradition is the anonymity of the teller. In many ways, Kate acts as a vehicle for the communication of stories that pre and post date her musical intervention. It is distinctly ironic, then, that from the release of her first album, her public identity has become as much an area of interest as her songs. Still, not all aspects of the oral tradition translate perfectly into our strange modern world; thank God Kate still wants to tell those tales!

2: The Sensual World

Have you ever fallen in love with a book? If you have, you will know that special feeling you get each time you pick it up; that enchanting sense of stepping into another world, where the author takes you by the hand and shares something intimate with you. The relationship that develops between a book and its reader is unique. You spend endless hours together, you take it to bed at night and when the final page is turned, you miss the characters as though they were your friends.

The power of the written word has inspired artists throughout history. From biblical times,

Adaptions of *Wuthering Heights* (above and below).

The Shining (1980).

some of the most enduring and breathtaking works of art were inspired by the prose and poetry of writers. Close your eyes and consider Waterhouse's *Lady Of Shallot* - could there ever be a more haunting rendering of Tennyson's ill-fated heroine? The fascinating thing about reading is how, although we each have our own unique visual and emotional interpretation of what we read, true classics have a universal sublimity; a higher power that goes beyond the printed pages and unifies its readers. Although the Cathy in my mind will look a little different from the Cathy in yours, and the wind over the moors will sound slightly different for me than it does for you, the essential force of *Wuthering Heights* is something that is the same for all who read it.

The work of any great artist is invariably drawn from a melting-pot of influences; from snatched snapshots of long ago conversations, to outright homage to the object of their fascination. Very occasionally, an artist manages to capture the essence of their muse so perfectly that the two works of art become synonymous with each other, inextricably linked together, forming two complementary sides of the same coin. Now close your eyes and listen to *Wuthering Heights*. Could there ever be a more powerful evocation of Cathy's ghost than Kate's wraith-like lament? Could you ever read *Wuthering Heights* without hearing Kate's voice pleading at the window, the notes being carried to you across the moor, barely distinguishable from the howling cry of the wind itself?

Whether she is influenced by a book or a film or a television programme, Kate has an inherent ability to unearth the pulse that beats through the chosen story, to uncover its very soul and appropriate it, breathing new life into it, making it her own. *Wuthering Heights* was written after the briefest glimpse of the end of a televised version of the book, but it was enough - enough to inspire one of the most memorable songs of the last century. Through the power of her imagination and her unforgettable voice, Kate pushed her way back through over a hundred and thirty years of forgotten time and not only found the lost ghost of Cathy, still desperately searching the moors for Heathcliff, she actually became her: "I loved writing it. It was a real challenge to précis the whole mood of a book into such a short piece of prose. Also, when I was a child I was always called Cathy, not Kate, and I just felt myself able to relate to her as a character. It's so important to put yourself into the role of the person in a song. There's no half measures. When I sing that song, I *am* Cathy."

And this is why *Wuthering Heights* goes far beyond being simply a song about a book. As part of the new video generation, Kate was able to take her evocation of Cathy even further by creating a visual accompaniment to the song, incorporating her own choreography to create an even more palpable persona for her ethereal heroine. When Kate insisted on *Wuthering Heights* being the first single from *The Kick Inside*, she distinguished herself as an artist unafraid to show that creativity is something that is continually fed by the wealth of artistic achievements that surround us. In doing so, she pulled Cathy from her 19th Century wanderings and took her to number one in the pop charts, and that was just for starters.

Often, Kate's literary allusions and references to film are far more subtle. Kate frequently takes the most poignant moment of a book or film, or even simply its feel, and uses it as the base ingredient in her recipe. Now close your eyes and listen to *Get Out of My House*, very loudly. You do not need to have read Stephen King's *The Shining* to feel the anger that screams out from this song, or to sense the isolation and fear of its narrator. It stands up resolutely in its own right as a depiction of a frightened and emotionally wounded person putting up armour around their heart, letting nothing out, but, more significantly, nothing in. But if you have read *The Shining*, you will see how perfectly Kate has captured that specific unnerving sense of unease that pulses through the book. Not only has she harnessed that strange energy, she has gone straight to the darkened heart of the story, using the house as a metaphor for the mind and the heart. She strips the novel back to the driving force behind the plot; the danger and the curiously empowering allure of isolation.

Songs, in the same way as poetry, require an entirely different approach to language than novels. The weight of significance for each word is far heavier, and the sound of the words becomes another way in which feeling and atmosphere are communicated. When you read *The Shining*, the words are transferred directly from the page to your imagination and that in itself is disturbing enough, but when you listen to *Get Out of My House*, it is as though that energy from the novel is unleashed - it takes on a life of its own, and is no longer contained within the confines of the book. Towards the end of *Get Out of My House*, Kate turns to the traditional song *The Two Magicians* to convey the desperation of the narrator to escape from her tormentor. She draws upon the idea that however hard you try, you can never truly escape the thing that haunts you, because it comes from within - you have to confront it and deal with it. As in the traditional song, Kate's protagonist tries desperately to escape, resorting to shape-shifting to get past the intruder. But each time she changes form, so too does the intruder. Even when she turns into a bird, free to fly far away, the intruder turns into the wind, engulfing her. There is simply no escape because essentially the intruder, the disquieting force, comes from within - they are one and the same. *Get Out of My House* is a stark and arresting song in its own right, but the true reward comes when you peel back the layers to discover all the ingredients that went into perfecting its formidable atmosphere.

For those of you lucky enough to have got hold of a copy of *A Book of Dreams* you will know that it is no ordinary book. Though it is relatively little known, it is a piece of pure magic – a profoundly moving story told with incredible innocence and honesty. It was first captured in sonic form during the 1970s by Patti Smith, whose song *Birdland* was inspired by a passage in the book where Peter, the narrator, believes that he sees his dead father in a spaceship. It is one of the most powerful passages of the book: "In the night I walked across the field, making the energy field with my hands, praying that he would come and take me away. Please come, I said, looking long and hard at the glowing balls coming nearer out of the sky. Please come and take me away please, please. Please, here are my eyes, here I am sending them far out to you. To you. Giving my eyes, please come please."

Cloudbusting is an example of Kate breathing new life to a story, allowing it rebirth in the form of a song. It is very much like translating a book into a different language, bringing it to a new audience. As with any translation, it bears the mark of its interpreter, and Kate brings her own captivating magic to *A Book of Dreams*, tenderly recreating its most touching moments, communicating its beauty through her gentle voice. Someone once described *Cloudbusting* as having a heartbeat running right through it. Close your eyes and listen to the song – can you hear it? Turn up the bass – can you feel it? *Cloudbusting* tells the story of a child (for however old Peter becomes, he will always remain his father's child) realising through the pain of loss that he will be forever trying to get back to the magical world he shared with his father. The book opens with a quote from William Falkner: "I, the dreamer clinging yet to the dream as the patient clings to the last thin unbearable ecstatic instant of agony in order to sharpen the savour of the pain's surcease, waking into the reality, the more than reality, not the unchanged and unaltered old time but into a time altered to fit the dream which, conjunctive with the dreamer, becomes immolated and apotheosized."

How movingly Kate has captured the very soul of this:

I still dream of Organon,
I wake up crying..
Oh God daddy, I won't forget.

Have you ever read Molly Bloom's speech at the end of James Joyce's *Ulysses*? It is one of the most deliciously sensual passages in the history of literature, an exquisitely feminine orgasm of words. For *The Sensual World*, Kate had initially intended to use the original text from Molly Bloom's soliloquy and put it to her own musical composition. After a year of trying to get permission to use the passage, which was continually refused, Kate did something quite extraordinary; not happy with leaving Molly trapped in the pages of the book (where the publishers tried desperately to keep her!). Kate set her free. She took Molly by the hand and led her out of her two-dimensional world and into the real world, allowing her to finally realise all her passion; to feel the down on the peach and the spark in her hand, to see the water and the earth caress, to hear the whisper of her lover, to smell the mountain flowers, and to taste the kiss of seedcake.

"In My Garden" Pauline Stuckey '92

Graphic: Paulina Stuckey

By going ahead and writing *The Sensual World*, despite the setback of being refused permission to use the original text, Kate not only created a song of exquisite beauty, she showed that when it comes to creativity, there are infinite ways of taking an object of inspiration and shaping it into something new. It is a pity that Joyce's estate did not see Kate's suggestion as the compliment it was intended to be. I'm sure that Joyce would have been flattered that his writing held such resonance so long after his death. Still, at least Cathy and Molly will live on each time we listen to Kate – what better gift could she have given them?

We can now be glad that Stephen Joyce did finally relent so that Kate could present this track on *Director's Cut* as it was originally meant to be

The Influence of the Gothic

Considered by Paula Hobbs

Issues 74 (July 2004) and 75 (March 2005)

"Gothic – of literary style characterised by gloom, the grotesque, and the supernatural" (Collins' English Dictionary)

1: The Draw of the Gothic Heroine

"It was, indeed, a filthy process in which I was engaged." Mary Shelley, *Frankenstein.*

If you have ever read a book or seen a film that has made you afraid to go to sleep, then you will have grasped the power of the Gothic. The Gothic genre pushes boundaries, explores taboos and forces us to confront our innermost fears. It can be very subtle. Once the layers have been stripped away, fundamental questions are asked about birth, life and death. With this idea in mind, Kate Bush is for me one of our finest Gothic songwriters. Take for example the Gothic novels and films that have inspired her – Stephen King's novel *The Shining* was the inspiration for *Get Out of My House* – a song which is just as frightening and claustrophobic as the book; and *The Infant Kiss* was inspired by the film *The Innocents*, (based on Henry James' book *The Turn of the Screw*). She gives a new twist to the Gothic in song, a fusion of history, romance and mysticism. But it is the draw of the Gothic Heroine that I will explore.

Kit Marlowe's *Doctor Faustus*

Faustus and The Red Shoes

Christopher Marlowe's timeless play, *Dr. Faustus* has inspired many writers from Byron to Mary Shelley, and the Faustian myth is clearly resonant in Kate's version of *The Red Shoes*. Her protagonist is female – a demonic fairy (Miranda Richardson) who seemingly appears from nowhere.

In contrast, Faustus conjures up Mephistopheles, a fiendish messenger from hell, through magic. Kate draws symbols on paper, an action reminiscent of Faustus who casts a magic circle on the ground and writes God's name in anagrams and backwards. There lies a curse in what he does. Likewise the symbols of the Line, the Cross and the Curve of *The Red Shoes* represent damnation.

Mephistopheles makes his intentions clear from the beginning. He comes to those who are "in danger to be damned". Kate's demon-fairy is more a trickster who deceives her and takes Kate's soul in exhange for the possessed Red Shoes The fairy tale has no thought of giving Kate even a remote chance of salvation.

A more horrific pact with Lucifer is made in *Dr. Faustus* than that made in *The Red Shoes*. Faustus must sign a contract in blood and he is given an ominous warning when his blood congeals. Yet nothing will stop him. Mephistopheles' initial plea of repentance changes to enticement: Faustus could be "as great as Lucifer" A line that echoes the demon-fairy's "Oh it's gonna be the way you always dreamt about it". Both Kate and Faustus are lured into a trap, a belief in a world where dreams will come true, desires fulfilled and promises of greatness.

However, where Faustus fulfils years of depravity, Kate's character does not. Faustus causes chaos at the Pope's banquet; becomes a master of black magic; raises the ghost of Alexander the Great; and takes Helen of Troy for his lover. He revels in sin! Kate's moments of joy, however, are short-lived. As soon as the bargain is made Kate is dragged into hell and she laments "I knew I had done something wrong". The shoes are unstoppable but she is not quite damned. She wants release from this dark underworld. In *The Red Shoes* hell is a Gothic, traditional hell, a fire and brimstone place, where bones and skulls litter the floor and red devils with villainous moustaches and pointed tails are its guardians.

The figure of Lily mirrors the Good Angel from Dr. Faustus. Kate seeks guidance from Lily, her prophetic spiritual guide. Due to her need for salvation Kate is protected by mythical, angelic creatures. Faustus ignores his Good Angel, who appeals to him to repent, and so he is eternally doomed. Lily and the Good Angel signify conscience.

By Scene 13 we find Faustus in utter despair. He has a single hour remaining before he is taken to hell forever. His anguished cry: "Now body, turn to air, Or Lucifer will bear thee quick to hell" reminds us of Kate's lyric "I fear I am walking in a Veil of Darkness". They both suffer bleak moments of hopelessness and tormented misery. Both characters are powerful in conveying a sense of deep fear – of death, of a cursed after-life. For Faustus it is too late; he is dragged away by demons. For Kate it is not. She saves herself and in a clever twist the wicked fairy is herself condemned. Kate re-affirms her own female courage. She saves herself rather than having a male hero to save her.

The Sorceress

Anne Rice is a novelist with whom we can draw comparisons to Kate. Like Marlowe, Rice's characters are greedy, doomed, seductive and tortured. Like Kate, she delves into Gothic foggy worlds of witches, vampires and ghosts. In Rice's novel *Merrick*, the character Merrick is a young witch whose magic is "as old as Egypt", who takes voodoo to a terrifying yet captivating extreme. In order to contact the dead vampire child, Claudia, Louis (also a vampire) must ask Merrick to summon her with magic. Merrick is prompted to cast spells just like the witch in Kate's song *Waking the Witch*. Although the vampires Louis and David are present, Merrick is the most powerful figure. She is the active force, the magician. They are mere spectators. Both vampires are dependant upon her. She repeats her incantations and commands that spirits and saints obey her, threatening them with shame and destruction. Her power over saints, ghosts and a voodoo idol establishes Merrick's signi ficance and dominance in a celestial other world. She calls out her authority: "I am Merrick, I cannot be denied".

Graphic: Krys

Both vampires fall in love with Merrick. The only way for David to explain their mutual obsession is to assign it to witchcraft. His explanation reflects a fear of surrendering to his emotions, of opening his heart. Louis has become manically infatuated with Merrick as he confesses "It's as if I'm Merrick's slave". There is safety in the belief that it is all down to a spell. What is harder for David to accept is that both he and Louis are really in love with Merrick. In *Merrick* Anne Rice hearkens back to the witch-trials and a deep-seated mistrust of women, even though the novel is set in our present day. She questions the male belief that if women possess power then they abuse it.

In *Waking the Witch* Kate analyses this theme. The predominant, booming voice is a male judge or priest present at a witch trial. Kate takes the part of the accused witch pleading for her life. The judge's lines "You won't burn, You won't bleed" refer to the many horrific tortures inflicted upon those suspected of witchcraft. Kate is historically faithful. Such terrible tortures involved limbs being severed and boiling water poured into their boots, and long needles pushed into the body. Once found guilty of witchcraft, they were usually hanged. In Spain and Italy they were often being burned alive. During the 15th and 16th Century "waking a witch" meant depriving the accused of sleep. A bridle was fitted to the body and attached to the wall, preventing the accused from lying down. The prison guards would rouse the suspect if he or she fell asleep.

Kate's "witch" character is safe only if she confesses but from the judge's ominous voice we know she will not be safe either way. Her familiar is a blackbird. Due to their raven-like plumage blackbirds were thought to be associated with the devil. Familiars were believed to accompany witches to their sabbats. Kate's blackbird is drowned – "Wings in the water – go down". The judge drums up the crowd's hysteria: "She's a witch" – a scene which mirrors David persuading Louis that Merrick has cast a love spell. Note the line: "There's a stone around my leg". The stone is tied about her body to ensure she drowns. Just as she is about to be drowned, Kate uses her magic to escape, and she wakes from the nightmare. She adds another meaning to "waking a witch", one that works in her favour. Both Kate and Merrick are prompted into using their own sorcery.

The Cartouche of Creation

The Mummy by Anne Rice, and Kate's song *Egypt* explore another Gothic theme: the mysteries and legends of Egypt. *Never For Ever* came out in 1980; *The Mummy* was written in 1989, and there are some interesting parallels. In *The Mummy*,

Ramses, once a great Egyptian king, wakes from a death-like sleep in Edwardian London. Kate's song *Egypt* could certainly be Ramses' theme, his torch song even, for every verse fits in with his adventures.

In the line "The sands run red", Kate visualises desert, so hot it seems it is on fire. Heat is constantly emphasised in *The Mummy*, both literally and metaphorically. Egypt is portrayed as a place where desires are unleashed. The scorching weather allows it. In cold grey London formality and repression are demanded. Rice's character, Julie Stratford, allows her passion to stagnate whilst in London but once she reaches Egypt she embraces her own sensuality. Heat is also depicted as sunlight which restores and regenerates. Centuries ago Ramses drank an elixir conferring immortality, yet sunlight remains a vital source to heal him.

From a single verse in Kate's song we can draw upon a whole range of meanings. When Kate sings "I'm busy chasing up my demon", to me that demon is anguish. This line echoes Ramses' whole existence. He is tormented by the past. Although physically strong Ramses is emotionally agonised. This agony is only briefly relieved by Julie. He is plagued by memories of his affair with Cleopatra and that he allowed Mark Anthony to die when she begged for the immortal elixir to give to him. Ramses does Cleopatra a double injustice, for after centuries lying dead, he discovers her mummified body and pours the elixir over her remains: "A ghastly moan came out of the being. It raised its skeletal hands."

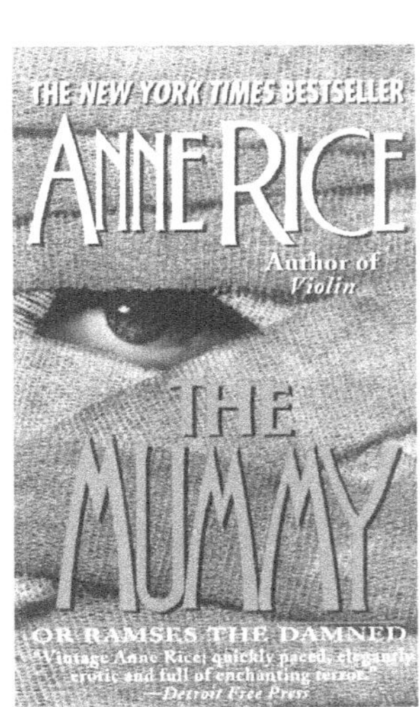

He raises Cleopatra to satisfy his own curiosity and to regain his lost lover. In doing this Ramses assumes power and control, a role of creator or god in giving life. Control slips quickly from his hands. The consequences are terrifying.

Kate's character in *Egypt* appears to be that of a Byronic Hero – deep, brooding and pained. A lonely wanderer who has returned to the East in search of comfort but finds none. Ramses is a Byronic Hero too. There is nobody to remember the ancient times first hand (except Cleopatra) so he too is brooding, haunted and mentally alone.

Cleopatra is referred to by Kate as "My Pussy Queen" who "knows all my secrets". This applies to Ramses as Cleopatra knows all of his secrets and knows how to hurt him. She is his great passion yet once resurrected she is a beautiful yet monstrous femme fatale. She becomes a ruthless, destructive murderess whose cravings cannot be satisfied. This blood-lust makes her vampiric: "She reached up, took a firm hold of his head with both her hands, and twisted it until his neck broke".

Kate's regal character is wise and seductive, a woman who hypnotises with "that feline guise". Seemingly tempting but ultimately dangerous. Certainly, Cleopatra uses her stunning beauty to ensnare potential victims.

Julie Stratford is another "Pussy Queen". Whilst Cleopatra represents sensuous desire for Ramses, Julie is his true love. She is innocent and sweet, a character without malice. Near the novel's end she decides to commit suicide for Ramses. He saves her. Her resolve to drown gives her an Ophelia-like quality. Ramses calls Julie "my Queen forever".

Kate's line "I whisper of the tombs" conjures up images of the grave and something long buried. Perhaps the buried thing is passion, secrets or history. When we think of Egyptian tombs we think of the Pharaohs, eastern queens and of course mummies. Both Anne Rice and Kate capture the arcane atmosphere of the East with their portrayal of the Nile and the pyramids. They both create worlds where buried secrets come to light. Emotion bursts from the seams of Kate's song.

Theatre Macabre

Coffee Homeground is worthy of an Agatha Christie play. The song is macabre yet Kate manages to weave comic elements into it. She will not be fooled by the poisoner bent on killing her. She defiantly refuses all temptations offered. The repetition of "you won't get me" shows how the poisoner's plan has been foiled. A lot of imagery involves concealment and secrecy – poison hidden in food and drink; the plumbers' disappearance; the "six foot plot" and the "cellar". That which is buried and forbidden threatens to be exposed. The "lipstick smeared" pictures of Crippen induce me to conclude that the poisoner must be female. She has clearly kissed his image, and holds him in esteem. Kate probes the warped psyche of a murderer – loneliness as an excuse for killing; the hero worship of Crippen. Kate's song shares its plot with many murder mysteries. The music itself adds a dark, Germanic 1930s feel.

Kate arranges her songs well, as *Hammer Horror* follows *Coffee Homeground* on her *Lionheart* album. Rather than being about Quasimodo's love for the beautiful gypsy Esmeralda, *Hammer Horror* explores an actor who takes over the lead role in a play of Victor Hugo's famous novel. Life imitates art when the spurned actor holds a grudge and seeks revenge. Again Kate adds humour with her pun: "I've got a hunch that you're following". Again, the song is part comic, part ominous.

Although Kate has drawn inspiration from writers she has also become an inspiration herself. It is interesting that *Waking the Witch* and *Egypt* were penned long before Anne Rice's novels, and yet there are striking parallels. Kate is without doubt a muse for present and future artists.

2: The Gothic Ghost Story

"Whatever caused it to linger in the world of the

living, this was no friendly spectre"
Paul Dorrell, *Tea and Empathy*.

Ghosts have held a deep-seated fascination for centuries. In literature they are there to terrify and sometimes serve as a source of amusement. Yet literary spectres do not simply appear in novels and plays to scare readers. They can have a series of functions; they can be signifiers of conscience; they can affirm a belief in an afterlife, a belief in a heaven, a hell and purgatory. Another purpose is to illuminate guilt. Characters who are haunted by ghosts often carry with them a sense of remorse.

Kate has recognised the power and mystery of the supernatural and used it as a theme for many of her songs. If we look closely at her lyrics we can find all manner of esoteric tales and equally esoteric characters. Kate is certainly worthy of being classed alongside Gothic authors such as Edgar Allan Poe and Robert Louis Stevenson.

The notion of ghosts is often linked to identity. Characters see something of themselves mirrored in the spectre who haunts them. They appear at crisis points, like Cathy to Heathcliff when he is at the very edge of death himself. Ghosts are uncanny because they are there yet, paradoxically, not there. They can be advisers, guides, comforters, even tormentors.

Ophelia Under Ice

Was Kate inspired by Shakespeare's *Hamlet*, I wonder? It would have been most obvious route to look at the relationship between Hamlet and his ghostly father. She does not. Instead, Kate takes the enigmatic Ophelia out of the Renaissance period and transoms her into a modern day heroine in her song *Under Ice*.

In the play, Ophelia is presented as a grave, shy girl, a girl of reason and innocence, who obeys her father, Polonius, and listens to her brother. When she finally returns Hamlet's words of love, he cruelly rejects her and swears that he never loved her. Hamlet fiercely repels Ophelia, as though finding her repulsive. Perhaps Kate picks up on Hamlet's line "Be thou as chaste as ice" – ice being the main theme in her own portrayal of Ophelia.

Ophelia is heart-broken and full of anguish. At the death of her father, all hope is lost. Loss upon loss combine to incite her madness. Her reticence and shyness now replaced by a delirious frenzy. She sings amorous rhymes, infused at times with bawdiness, a trait completely out of character. The rhymes are ominous too, for they speak of unrequited love and death.

Kate's song depicts for us a barren, echoing frozen world where Ophelia skates upon the ice, moving faster and faster, racing away from the torments of her life. Kate explores the strange, phantasmal nature of Ophelia's death, a scene we never actually witness in *Hamlet*, but are told second-hand by Gertrude of how Ophelia "Fell in the weeping brook", and was pulled under water by the currents, but we are left unsure whether it is accident or suicide. The imagery is eerie – the "hoar leaves" suggest frozen dew; the weeping willow symbolises Ophelia's tears, and the "glassy stream" implies the icy surface. By drowning it seems that Ophelia has drowned in her own sorrow. Gertrude sees Ophelia as "mermaid-like", giving her an ethereal, angelic quality. She is a symbol of purity who becomes semi-divine. In *Under Ice* Kate offers Ophelia's version first-hand. She is pulled beneath a frozen lake. She sees her body under the ice; it is as though the soul sees its trapped body: "There's something moving under". The lake becomes a burial vault. Ophelia is the encased virgin. An icy bed becomes her grave. This image shows how her emotions have stagnated and her sexual energy frozen. She cannot move. Kate portrays a claustrophobic death reflecting Ophelia's physically closed-up body. The echoing sounds in Kate's song suggest Ophelia's isolation. Her voice, stunted in life, cries out in the moments before death, "It's me". There is no-one to help her.

Ophelia by John Everett Millais.

Strings of Torment

When we think of ghosts we usually think of people who have died and wander in an afterlife. Not often do we think of inanimate objects as phantoms, particularly musical instruments. Both Kate and author, Anne Rice, see the appeal of a haunted violin. In Rice's baroque Gothic novel *Violin*, Stefan is a phantom and so is his violin. He fulfils the role of the Byronic Hero – dark, brooding, mysterious, charming and tragic. A detached man trapped on earth in death.

Kate's song *Violin* could be his title tune. *Never For Ever* came out seventeen years before Rice's novel was published, but the parallels are there. Could Anne Rice have been inspired by Kate Bush? Both women make the violin an object of obsession. Violin music is haunting, passionate, and even in exaltation can sound demonic or angelic. Kate sings of how the violin is "Ready to carry me over". She is transported to another dimension away from the mundane routine of life. Stefan is also 'carried over' through this instrument into the past, his past, taking Triana with him. She is horrified by what she witnesses – she sees Stefan's house burning down and his determination to save the violin from the flames.

Both the song and novel mention Paganini. Kate presents him as a carnivalesque, mischievous goblin character "up on the chimney". From childhood dreams we imagine fantasy creatures dwelling on rooftops and inside chimneys. She manages to convey a Puckish characteristic that sets him apart from other renowned composers. What makes him demonic is that he is playing the violin and dancing with "old Nicky" (the Devil).

Stefan's muse is Paganini. He adores Paganini and sails through Venice in a gondola with him whilst numerous worshippers look on. Rice depicts him as having grotesque, exaggerated features: "the large hooked nose and giant protuberant eyes given him in many a painting". Like Kate, Anne Rice sees Paganini as fiendish, although not a malicious character, moreover someone who does not conform. For Stefan it becomes an infatuation, a fixture to travel with Paganini as a wanderer-fiddler. When Stefan's father adamantly forbids this, Stefan kills him. Stefan even tries to steal the violin from his father's coffin but once caught, he is shot. As a ghost he plays his violin for grieving people.

Niccolò Paganini

In her song, Kate is possessed by the violin. Her voice and music are wild and frenzied. She sounds hysterical and ecstatic by turns as it is: "Filling me up with the shivers and quivers". She understands the power of this magical instrument, how it can completely possess listeners and musicians alike. This is what makes her song so haunting and compelling. Stefan is also possessed and so are his listeners.

The violin dominates his life and afterlife. He is utterly consumed by it: "Another moment shone bright, a woman banging his tenacious ghostly shape with her fist as on and on he played, a wailing dirge". Some of his mourning listeners are driven to insanity by his constant playing. His solo pieces are inescapable and torturing, telling of grief and despair, yet to Triana they are a comfort. In a way Stefan is the banshee of Kate's song. He represents death, is shrouded and isolated by it. When he plays, his listener's suffering becomes all the more real, all the more agonising. A woman's weeping becomes "mingled with the crying of the violin".

Kate and Anne portray the violin as akin to a human voice. Kate sings "let it scream to me". The violin can be made to shriek, scream, sigh and weep. Certainly Kate's voice in her song soars like a violin with its banshee screech and range of pitches. It is indeed a most haunted instrument.

Edgar Allan Poe

The Wraith-like Watcher

Edgar Allan Poe has chilled readers to the bone for decades with his stories of terror and suspense. In Kate's song *Watching You Without Me* the apparition strikes me as being similar to Poe's character Ligeia in his story of the same name. In the song, the ghost watches over her lover. This surveillance is continual, a theme in common with *Ligeia*. Her lover cannot see or hear her which adds to the frustration. The same thing happens with Ligeia until she decides to make contact. *Watching You Without Me* is for me a Gothic-romantic song. Its melancholic tone imbued with poignant sadness. Invisible, she watches from the shadows: "You can't hear me, you can't feel me". Even in its moments of utmost terror, Poe's story expresses the same heartfelt dejection. The speaker, who remains nameless, is utterly distraught and irrevocably broken when Ligeia dies. He is "crushed into the very dust with sorrow". What remains is an unnatural, disturbing and devouring obsession with Ligeia. He glorifies and extols her virtues; in beauty he claims she is unrivalled; in intelligence, she is genius; in all things, she is utter perfection. Through his elaborate description Ligeia becomes not only a superhuman being but deific. For him she retains "the radiance of an opium-dream". He cannot help but notice that there is something strange and uncanny about her. Despite her perfection – flawless skin, raven black hair, captivating features – she is unusual and he cannot understand what makes her so.

Ligeia decides to return after death only when she feels she is losing her lover to his second wife, Rowena. She has been watching from her ghostly world and incited by jealousy. He treats Rowena badly by ignoring her. He yearns for Ligeia in death because no-one can ever compare with her perfection. Then, one terrifying night his wish is granted.

We get the same feeling from Kate's song. Her lover is single again and can find another lover to replace her: "Can't let you know what's been happening". To me these verses are about her emotions – love and envy mingled. She is now trapped in another dimension. Halfway through the song Kate's voice takes on an Middle Eastern sound and eventually becomes distorted, symbolic of Kate's character as a ghost trying to break out from the realm of the dead into the world of the living. Her wail might be able to pierce that unseen otherworldly division. Comparatively, there are many references to the East in *Ligeia*. Ligeia's gem-like eyes have "the beauty of the fabulous Houri of the Turk". The speaker's bed-chamber has Egyptian overtones with its sarcophagus in each corner. All of these details contribute to the exotic nature of the story.

We do not see Kate's ghost return to life as we do with Ligeia. Kate deals with the moments of invisibility, of insignificance, of being lost and alone with only eyes to see. She looks on and yearns to be able to communicate with her lover but cannot.

These are just some of the songs that illustrate how Kate has examined the subjects of ghosts, the afterlife and love beyond death, in her own unique way. With beauty and sensitivity, she has taken some of the Gothic themes and skilfully interpreted them into songs of great, and at times overwhelming, emotion – to great effect. Kate is indeed worthy of being classed alongside the most notable of our Gothic authors.

Home for Christmas

A Winter Story by Krys

Issue 66:
December 2000

In the night. In the dark... no-one lives any nearer than town... She could hear Mrs. Dudley's dramatic lines in her head. And she laughed at herself as that scene from the old black and white film, *The Haunting*, began to re-play yet again in her mind. The grim-faced housekeeper scene was a shared joke between them It had always been one of their favourite films. But she really was all alone, in the dark, with her imagination for company, and she was scared. Only the tick-tock heartbeat of the old clock disturbed the otherwise silence. *No-one will hear you...*

She shivered as little chills ran cobweb fingers over her skin and she reached for the television remote to blank out the unwelcome thoughts and the silence and that bloody ticking clock. The screen sprang to life, cheerful faces breaking the atmosphere. Jolly music, festive cheer jingling all the way. The adverts blared brash and vulgar, showing off the over-priced chunks of plastic that every child just had to have for Christmas or he would be certain to grow up scarred for life and would never forgive his parents for failing him so miserably.

She sighed at how ridiculous it had all become and remembered her own childhood Christmases, simple but full of love. And snow. There always seemed to be snow and she smiled, recalling the smell of tangerines and her Grandfather's cigar smoke. Some of the aromas of Christmas, to smell them anywhere at any time of year would take her right back. Something to do with the olfactory bulb, she had read somewhere. Smells and songs, it was always the same.

Then she saw them again out of the corner of her eye, just a glimmer, then gone again. Her friend had seen the smiling man standing in the front room, dressed in grey flannel and a warden's tin hat - "Shut that light out!" - she was sure she heard something... And the little ginger cat. She sometimes saw him too. And the one who stroked her head when she was sad, who is stroking her head again right now. She knew they were looking after her. Friends only a whisper away, just in the next room.

Christmas was always the time, it had been this way for years. The house had been built in 1939 and although not very old, was still old enough to have some history and to have its own memories etched into its walls. People had come and gone from there, had died, had been born. The house would have heard the Spitfires overhead, singing their Merlin hearts out as they returned from the Battle to the airfields nearby. All that passion, all that blood. Like the Knights of old... many died, but some were still alive, the skies still in their eyes and hearts. The Few she had seen at Biggin had that magic about them, and she thought they looked like angels. Maybe they had indeed touched the face of their God.

The house was a happy place. She had surrounded her small family of husband and cats in colours and made a garden where she half-expected to see them there too - it would have been no surprise to see the blacksmith whose smithy had been just yards away. And she hoped they would approve of what she had done to their garden. The summer dragonflies and the bee-fly certainly did, as did the cats who had found a brand new level of mouselling, and a wide variety of mouses to boot! Sometimes she imagined her children playing and laughing in the garden, that sound would be the sweetest sound of all. She had tried so hard, but it had not happened. There was still the emptiness, still the sadness, but somewhere still the hope that one day...

Photo: Donna Kile

Christmas Eve was always magical, even though it also made her sad - after all it was the celebration of birth and motherhood, but she knew that some wishes can come true, and maybe this Christmas would be the last without children of their own.

Each Christmas Eve they went to the midnight mass at the glorious old Gothic cathedral, a thousand years old, older again... "*the rising of the Sun, the running of the deer*"... the old Pagan ways still intact - the very foundations were built upon them - and carved there forever in wood and stone, carrying it all through the ages like the old man and his Box of Delights. She loved the heady smell of the frankincense, the candlelight, and the sanctity of ancient ritual.

Tears always filled her eyes as the choir lifted their voices to the Gothic heavens and Green Men, and the pipe organ burrowed its voice deep into the very bowels of the Earth, and spirits soared. The magic was still there, still beating with all that life and passion, and the days were already growing longer again. Gold and richly painted icons rested against the vast stone pillars, and Mother Mary looked down at her Child, and they lit a candle for her, because they would not forget, and they asked that they too would be blessed.

It was almost two in the morning when they came home, the Christmas tree aglow with little white lights, the embers in the grate swimming liquid red. He put on a CD of mediaeval Yuletide music and they wished each other a merry Christmas and clinked together two glasses of port, the rich sweetness warming their lips and hearts. The cats bumbled around them, puzzled at this disturbance to their usual routine. She turned the tree lights out and they went to bed, some of that old excitement of the Christmas Eves of her childhood still making her stomach flutter. Was it silly at the age of thirty six to still listen out for Father Christmas? She fell asleep feeling like she was five years old again.

When she came downstairs on Christmas morning and opened the door into the front room, the fire was already lit and a small child rushed past her, almost knocking her into a wall which had not been there for years, but was now adorned with generations of ageing sepia photographs against rose patterned wallpaper. Two leather armchairs sat either side of the hearth. A small ginger cat lay curled and purring in one of the chairs, enjoying the warmth of the fire. An army of toy soldiers lay scattered on the floor after their battle but would soon be raised from the dead to fight another day.

A tall, thin man with dark, carefully slicked back hair stood in front of the fire, humming to himself as he pushed tobacco into the barrel of his pipe and lifted it to his moustached lips and drew in the smoke. He wore what she recognised as an RAF great coat, there was melting snow on his shoulders and around the soles of his shiny black shoes. There were small melted snow pools here and there where he had walked. The smell of roasting fowl seeped into the room, the sound of a woman singing a familiar tune came clear and pure from the kitchen. Two children shouted and laughed and ran past her into the room, they did not see her, unaware that she was there. But the cat saw her and stared at her the way that cats stare at ghosts.

"Daddy! Daddy! You came home!" they squealed and ran into his open arms. She could see tears run down his face as he cradled the two small children and kissed them. "Pete, Andy, look what I've brought you," and from his coat pocket handed each of his sons a toy Spitfire, the wings glinting wickedly in the firelight. The boys whooped with delight and began a dogfight. The singing stopped abruptly, and the lady of the house ran from the kitchen and into her husband's arms and they held each other and laughed and cried and spoke words she couldn't hear. She felt like an intruder on such a private moment.

Christmas carols were coming from the large wireless in the corner of the room. The announcer said that the King's speech would be at three o'clock and he wished his listeners a very Merry Christmas and hoped that the war would soon be over.

"Sad about the young couple who used to live here – the house was fire bombed – they didn't stand a chance, poor sods. Shouldn't have moved to London, that's what I say," said the man to his wife. Seeing the sadness begin to cloud her eyes, he put his arms around her shoulders and tried to brighten her mood – "Can't wait to taste that smashin' puddin', love. No-one makes 'em like you do."

She became aware of the clock tick-tocking. Same old clock they had found not long after moving in, sixteen years ago now. She watched as the tall man wound it up and it began to strike the Westminster chimes. He traced his fingers over some words etched around its moonish face:

> "Grow old along with me,
> The best is yet to be".

"Be safe in that Spit, Charlie, and don't worry, I'll look after him for you," she said and he felt a cold breeze brush his ear. She so wished that she could have met him, that he would have liked her, that he could have held his grandchildren.

The two boys played on the floor, immersed in their flights and fights. She bent down towards the youngest child, kissed his dark hair, and whispered to him, "The best really is yet to be."

The door flew open. In a blink the room was hers again and the family gone. Peter stood in the doorway, like the ghost of Christmas present. "Merry Christmas, Bears," he said in a soft voice, and pulled her to him. "Just smell that tree! Shall I make a fire?" As he cleared out the grate the poker struck something, with the chink of metal on metal. He put his hand into the ashes and he gasped when he saw what he had found. "It looks just like the one I had when I was little. My Dad gave it to me."

He opened his hand and showed her the toy Spitfire. She went over to him and buried her face into his dark hair, "I know, Bear. I know." And out of the corner of her eye she could swear she saw the glimmer of Charlie's shadow, followed by just a hint of the smell of pipe tobacco.

Greenhey's Road

Jeff Side

The vessels of love
crowd in.
Their traumas hidden
among the reeds.
No love is lost or given to them
as they clutter the minds
of thieves.
Strong, sober and drunk
I come to you.
My weakness revealed
in my glee.
And book-like I pray on
your need
to comfort - sometimes.
Now there is light.
And now there is dark.
And that is the way that you
can pay
the charity you give
to men like me.

The Memories

Martin Purser.

The memories begin to hurt, hurt inside.
Wounded by tears on a
blotted, dead lover's love letter,
A petal of a pressed flower.

The memories begin to weep,
weep at the sight of a person on a photo
who was once you
and someone who was once me;

Now they have begun to die
from a last goodbye
touching of hands,
a last meeting of eyes
and words of love.

If only I'd known I'd never left you.
If only I'd given a reply
you may never have gone away.

If onlys are made for yesterdays,
and too late for today.

A Designers Guide to Kate

A Look at the Design Process by Neil Sheriff

Part One

"Kate treats everybody as an artist, from the producer to the tea-boy." Stuart Elliott, 1993

February, 1978: A nineteen year old Kate Bush is holed up in an EMI boardroom debating with the PR department over the cover design of her first single. The dilemma? Should the first image the British public see of this yet-unknown genius be a gorgeous bird sporting little more than a soulful expression and a tight pink vest standing in a room with inadequate heating? Or a beautifully draped artiste soaring through an ambiguous expanse of black on a giant kite? We now all know how this story ended. From this moment on Kate Bush became a woman who was intensely pro-active in how her music and herself were visually represented to the public.

At some point, we have all swooned over our favourite video-clips, whichever they may be. Quite innocently, blinded by admiration, some of us assume that all their visual splendour surely must be the brainchild of whichever musical Genius has commissioned it.

Enter the Designers: that strange and nebulous bunch of idea-machines, who take a great concept (though sometimes not-so-great), read it, chew over it, discuss it, draw it, regurgitate it, look at it from every conceivable angle, re-draw it, then present it.

Our Kate, however, is an exception to this rule. I'm stating the obvious when I say that Kate has a finer understanding of the design process than most (with the exception, perhaps, of Annie Lennox, Bryan Ferry, Björk and others). Over the years, she has had the vision to employ such luminaries as costume designers Hazel Pethig, (*The Line, the Cross & the Curve*) and Gini Hardy (all of the costumes on *Never For Ever* including the famous "Kate-bat") as well as Geoff Portass of Image Animation, whose company made Kate look like hell (literally) in *Experiment IV*. These people have largely shaped and defined our visual perception of Kate as we know her.

It is an unspoken law that a Designer's task, from the word go, is to remain true to their director's vision - however vague and organic that vision may be. Their visual interpretation of any given text, be it written, verbal, musical or choreographic, must express the key themes and elements of the piece, whilst bringing subtle nuances of character, atmosphere and environment to the fore. All this is based on many hours of solid research, on subjects relevant to the project at hand, as well as many lengthy discussions with the director to gain their personal feelings on what would be appropriate (Do I hear a snort of cynical laughter from fellow designers out there?... I don't blame you guys, if only it were that easy).

"We had a beautiful set which was built of polystyrene rocks and these dead spiky trees, with a cardboard moon and sun." Kate Bush, Club Newsletter 13, 1983

To many fans, the Tour of Life would arguably be Kate's largest and most ambitious performer/ designer collaboration, and so it would seem where set is concerned. A touring set can be a difficult beast indeed, and many extra issues need to be taken into account, particularly as Kate's Tour relied so heavily on magic and illusion, where hidden doorways, rolling eggs, moving rostra and disappearing ramps played an instrumental role in the overall performance. The documentary of the tour shows Kate quite happily chatting away with the costume and set designers, really getting her hands dirty and showing genuine interest in what fabrics and surfaces the artisans are using (that's what we like to see!)

As with any great artist, with age comes wisdom, and this clearly shows if we follow the time line of Kate's work. From the simplistic videos of *The Kick Inside*, where a bit of dry ice, an expressive dance routine, and a soft-focus lens were all you needed, we are waltzed through the years on a Zeitgeist of her creative change.

The 1980s saw Kate begin to think seriously about the possibilities of video, and the avenues that visual expression opened for her work. We watched open-mouthed as she gyrated on our screens in a stunning little pirate number complete with sword, and cape (now owned by Louise Halliday!), then writhing in an artificial womb before the bomb is dropped. These images are indisputably striking on film, and we know from a wealth of press at the time, that Kate had more than a whisper in the Designer's ear as to what she would like.

What the public do not see, are the lengthy costume fittings Kate would have had to endure to ensure that the design was functional. The hours of debate, and discussion that would have occurred between Kate, the Director and Designer to determine a final visual depiction of the song. The arguments between Designer and workshop over a set plan being 7cms too small in scale, and the sheer amount of caffeine consumed by all, over the entire duration, would have been enough to keep Brazilian coffee growers in constant work for a month.

And so the visual evolution of the quintessential Kate Bush clip continued throughout the Eighties. We witnessed her

Issues 69 (April 2002) and 72 (June 2003)

"Neil Sheriff from Australia says:

'By trade I'm a Theatrical Designer, who's just beginning to spread his wings so I've written an article analysing Kate's visual marketing techniques and strategies throughout her career, with particular focus on the Designers Kate has employed on her videos. I've outlined the Design process, and the steps taken to achieve the final product, from concept to actualised set/costume, using Kate's videos and photographic promotion as the basis.'"

In 2011 Neil launched the Neil Sheriff label at www.neilsheriff.com

plough through dark and strange territory, exorcising Aborigines, robbing banks, and kicking up dust in her family barn. We ran up hills with a hundred masked Kates. We busted the clouds with a Gigeresque machine and Donald Sutherland. We were chased by hounds through a 1950s nightmare, scared by sound demons and teased through a sensual forest by a velvet-clad maiden. We were at the hospital when she died over dinner, and challenged the laws of love with her among dancers and Dervishes.

This somewhat speedy route through memory lane brings me to what I consider to be Kate's most visually sophisticated and complex manifestation to date – *The Line, the Cross & the Curve*. Never in my life have I encountered such beautiful, imaginative, carefully designed costume.

Kate had the good sense to engage the aforementioned Costume Designer, Hazel Pethig to weave her magic over the cast. Not only does every costume telegraph exactly what each character's role in the film is, but as soon as Miranda Richardson crashes through that mirror, we are shocked into a world of nightmarish glamour. Both women eventually end up in similar garments, with subtle changes that make all the difference. Miranda's silhouette is fuller, with a multi-layered skirt and a more flamboyant headpiece, giving her an almost comic/manic appearance. Kate's version, while being dressed in identical colour, has a simpler, more functional line. The complex dye-work on Kate's skirt, and elaborately beaded and feathered bastille, display Pethig's fine knowledge, and appreciation for detail. The movement of the costume on film, exhibits her talent for choosing just the right fabric and embellishment.

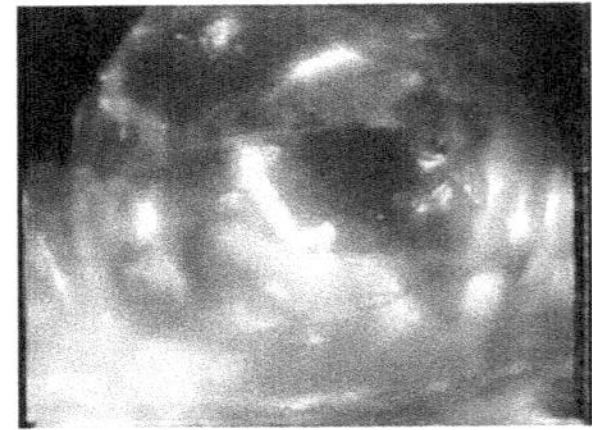

The prime example of Hazel Pethig's Genius comes out to play with *Eat the Music*. The infamous fruit-dress is deceptive in its simplicity. Pethig has used a simple, fitted gown with back fastening, and a fairly medieval line. The beauty of this garment lies in it's sunshine yellow (silk?… cotton?…) that has been ambré dyed from the base of the hem, to give it that, "I've just been out squishing fruit!" look. The fruit, if you care to look closely, has been hand painted, and decreases in size, the further up the body you go. This is known as Art finishing, and is usually executed by the designer themselves, or a professional costume finisher, under the Designer's direction.

Similarly, the sets for *The Line, the Cross & The Curve* are, in essence, quite simple. The decision to create the effects and settings in a very theatrical, or "stage" manner, was definitely wise. It adds a surreality that somehow makes the film what it is. From a design perspective, I particularly liked the way in which water was depicted during *Lily*. The billows of loosely spangled deep blue satin provided the sequence with such a graceful fluidity. The whale tale was also a moving touch.

To conclude, the relationship between Designer and Director isn't always easy. But there is no disputing the fact, that design plays an instrumental part in the way any performer, on any given production is perceived. Kate is fortunate to have learnt this at such an early age, holed up in that EMI boardroom, warring over a pink vest and a giant kite. Coupled with her own innate talent for realising her concepts, both musically and visually, she, with the help of a strong creative and technical team, has carved a visual legacy, so unique, so rich and strange, that it is now the stuff of legend… and will continue to be when the new album is released.

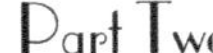

"You must never underestimate the seduction of the visual" JG, 2000

"In the earlier years, I was fascinated by the possibilities that mime and dance offered to aid performance" Kate Bush 1986.

In Part One, we were introduced to the processes behind the visual legacy carved by Kate and her collaborators, throughout her career to date. The piece, while encompassing the majority of Kate's work, focused heavily upon the design process of *The Line, the Cross & the Curve*, and I felt a more in-depth analysis of Kate's earlier video and film work was in order.

In 1978 *Wuthering Heights* soared onto the airwaves like an exotic bird among a flock of starlings. Similarly, the deceptively simple videos that were made for its promotion, looked coyly out of place among the sea of mirror-balls and roller-skates populating the world of music-video at the time. The public were greeted by an ethereal girl rising from a sea of mist in a darkened space, launching into a complex and highly expressive dance routine. She was clad in a panelled full-length dress of white terylene, with chiffon underlay, looking remarkably clean for a woman who's been out on the moors searching for her lost love! The video was directed by Keef Macmillan of Keefco productions. He was responsible for the majority of Kate's early videos, and it is this version of *Wuthering Heights* that is carried in the public memory.

The second, more elusive version of Cathy's saga portrays Kate dancing hypnotically across a windswept moor in a scarlet dress streaked with shreds of black fabric, hem ripped and torn; in the background, the Pinewood Studios trees sway in the breeze. The outdoor location clearly allowed Kate more freedom of movement, although HOW she managed to dance, let alone walk, in shoes with heels that high on a rain sodden moor is something I will never know. She adapted her unique choreography accordingly!

This version was used as the promo in Australia, and unfortunately little is known about its creative origins in terms of design and production. This was Kate's first experiment in using outdoor location as a tool in her visual promotion, a tool she would begin to explore more heavily come *Never For Ever*.

The remainder of the main promotional work for *The Kick Inside* followed a common theme: Kate expressing the songs through dance, usually in a studio setting. In the earlier videos, one gets the impression that any outside input of a fellow creative technician, such as a set designer, costumier, or stylist, would have been minimal and it is likely that most of the creative dialogue that took place, would have been exclusively between Kate and the director.

As Kate moved into the busiest period of her career to date, so her concept and understanding of visual expression matured. The videos and television appearances that accompanied the release of *Lionheart* grew in volume and visual complexity.

Kate's growing interest in the world of visual promotion saw her take a more active role in the videos' production. Once again, using Keef Macmillan, *Hammer Horror* continued in the same vein as *The Kick Inside*: bare studio, flowing costume, expressive dance routine, but by the time *Wow* was born as a single, Kate and Keef had really begun to push their creative dialogue in a new direction. Of the two versions released, the first shows Kate on stage in a disused music-hall, sporting a beautifully constructed gown of purple velvet. The style was vaguely late 19th Century, in silhouette, with voluminous panniers hanging at either side of her rouched bodice, emphasising Kate's figure. A similar garment was used in the Tour, but re-designed for greater freedom of movement. We see Kate in full flight (literally!) enacting the tale of a failed gay actor. Already the alchemy of image, character, costume, set/location and other necessary aids are beginning to reveal themselves in the mind of Catherine Bush.

With the Tour (which was discussed in the first part of this article), came an E.P, and with that, a lead video: a live version of *Them Heavy People*, which featured Kate cavorting across a table. This could be seen as Kate does *Carry-on*, romping with two handsome lackeys, in a pink vinyl mini and black PVC top with zips across her breasts! The video, while still being performance-based, relies heavily on the use of specially constructed props to aid the comic dialogue between Kate and the dancers.

The bottles that are raucously smashed over Kate's head, would have been made from sugar, water and weak resin (to enable them to smash safely) by the art department, a specialist unit attached to any flm production, who are responsible for set dressing, props making/ buying, and any other touches that create the setting of the piece. The chairs were likely made from balsa-wood and card. The video was overtly physical, and as with any comic piece, timing was essential. Several "dummy props" would have been made specifically for practice and during rehearsal. The use of props in performance

Graphic: Neil Sheriff

would mark a new trend in Kate's coming videos, and promotional shots. Never was this more apparent, than with the release of *Never For Ever*.

"She'd been waiting to break out, so I think Never For Ever *was where it was going to happen"* Al Murphy

In mid 1980, we received Kate's latest musical offering with a strange delight, and with it, the latest installment of her filmic development. She sauntered onto our screens, curled sensuously as a cat against a cello, dancing with the instrument, as one may dance with a wronged lover, before bursting into her super-hero alter ego, clad in studded bra, metal headpiece, striped bikini briefs and peacock feather chiffon cloak. Once again, clever incorporation of props is used to the full in the shape of a long, sharp musketeer sword... the mind boggles at the symbolism.

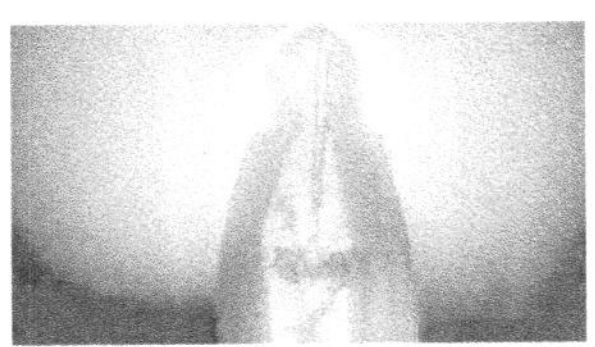

As we now know, this costume was inspired by Chris Achilleos' cover illustration for *Raven Swordsmistress of Chaos.*

The total silhouette is striking against a simple, piercing back-light. Kate's full sleeves of striped chiffon slice through the black space, emphasising the movement of the limbs. This design principle is the basis usually worked upon for costume design in dance. It is obvious that this garment was designed to thrill, reaffirming Kate's status as reluctant sex symbol. Judging by Kate's previous level of artistic input into her own visual marketing, this surely was a calculated move: the undoubted result of hours of discussion with the designer, painfully slow costume fittings, endless reams of fabric swatches and several toiles (draught runs of the costume) to ensure it's functionality. Considering we see more Kate than costume you would be amazed at how much planning goes into so brief a garment!

The alternative version of the video, made for the BBC 'Dr. Hook Special', portrays Kate in schizophrenic mode. If Audrey Hepburn and Cruella de Vil had a baby, then here Kate would be it! Her costume is cleverly divided into two halves; the homely wife and the rumbustious mistress, expressing the duality of the song's character perfectly. Her make-up is expertly applied a-la Ziggy Stardust, with half a head of hair, so wild and electrified, even Cher would be proud to call it her own! In the background, a sporadic array of fruity disco lights flashes on cue to the songs raucous chorus and the absence of good ol' fashioned plate smashing in the song's mix provides a somewhat uncomfortable break in the choreography.

Army Dreamers saw Kate return to location filming (at Pinewood Studios once again) for the chilling narrative of a mother whose son has been lost to the ravages of war. We see Kate on manoeuvres with a squad of soldiers clad in army greens with KT Bush Band arm patches, running from or hunting for the enemy in a forest. The video marks the end of Kate's collaboration with Keef Macmillan, but the first tentative step toward "film" as opposed to video. The video heavily employs the use of pyrotechnics, in the form of flares, gunpowder pockets and single strobe flashes to emphasise the explosions. The amount of safety precautions that would have needed to be cleared and tested before filming commenced is enough to give any workers' union a headache!

Kate began using the skills of her make-up artists to full effect with appropriate use of mud on all members of the cast, as well as twigs, and other natural debris peppering their hair and costume completes a naturalistic visual depiction of the song's narrative. (It is interesting to observe that from a design perspective, films about war generally do tend to convey the story using visual naturalism, with the exception of such offerings as *Schindler's List* and *Life is Beautiful*, which both employ subtle touches of surreality to emphasise the drama).

After all that hard slog in the trenches, Kate made the unlikely choice of becoming a swan for *Delius*, the single's B-side. In the lush and whimsical video, we see Kate waltzing through an artificial forest in a stunning costume designed by Gini Hardy. The garment is pure dance, consisting of a panelled bodice, a voluminous skirt of multi-layered white net, a feathered headpiece, and two spreading wings designed to emphasise the movement of Kate's dance. A swan in full flight indeed.

From the muddy banks of the battlefield, to a foetal haven, war still being the central theme, we are led through *Breathing*, and see Kate as an unborn foetus, wrapped in polythene and inserted into a large transparent ball. A false umbilical cord of plaited plastic connects Kate to the womb, and the set comes in the form of a light-box floor, littered with shreds and balls of scrunched up polythene, that falter-flashes in flesh tones to create a warm, pulsating living atmosphere.

I must plead ignorance as to who the designers and set technicians were, but this sequence in the video provides us with a prime example of "set-as-costume"; the performer is physically engaged with or attached to their environment. (*Never For Ever* as a whole, seems to be quite a "costumey" album, on the whole, if we count the bat costumes, the sky-dress, and god-knows how many other garments worn in television appearances at the time!) The second half of the clip sees Kate, once again using location in her work. A group of survivors emerge from muddied waters into a yellow and bleak world wearing chemical protection suits; the video has been altered during editing, to heighten the effect of this polluted world. This was the first time Kate chose to use special effects of a technological origin, and was to prove, yet another stepping stone in the visual development in the quintessential Kate Bush clip.

The Sunshine Within

A Musical Journey with Paddy Bush

Issues 65 (June 2000) and 66 (December 2000)

"Paddy Bush is Kate's brother, and is a trained maker of musical instruments, and a multi-talented musician in his own right.

"An original member of the KT Bush Band he played and did backing vocals at Kate's original pub stands in 1977 and made considerable contributions to the live tour in 1979 and all of her albums.

"His special interest has always been what is now called World Music, and has been called folk music and ethnic music. His contributions to Kate's music has always been those natural ethnic sounds played on original or recreated instruments.

"His own career has included playing on albums with Hughes de Courson, Colin Lloyd Tucker and other artists using traditional and acoustic sounds."

From Paddy's 1989 Kate Bush Club article:

"OK..What's a valiha? It's the instrument on *Love and Anger* that starts and ends the track, and sounds a little like a classical guitar, but it's not. It comes from the island of Madagascar, and is a kind of box-shaped harp about four feet in length, with strings on two sides. The strings are made from untwisted bicycle brake-cable. There is a little wooden bridge under each string for tuning, and the strings are plucked with the tips of the fingers."

1: A Journey to Marovany

Hello. It's nice to have the opportunity to write something for you all, it's been quite a few years since I last put pen to paper, so there's a lot to talk about.

I built a musical instrument in 1987 that has got me into a lot of trouble and brought sunshine into my life; it's sometimes called a Valiha, sometimes Marovany.

I'm sure you remember Kate's song *Love and Anger* – in the video I'm playing one, it's a long wooden box with strings on each side, with small movable bridges under each string for tuning. It's considered to be part of the Zither family of musical instruments and comes from the island of Madagascar, which is in the Indian Ocean and close to the Eastern coast of Africa.

I first heard Malagasy music in the early 1970s when I was studying musical instrument technology at the London College of Furniture. One of my teachers was the late Jean Jenkins who was an amazing ethnomusicologist who had travelled all over the planet recording traditional music, sometimes risking her life to preserve the vanishing cultural treasures of a troubled and changing world. Through Jean I was able to listen to the sounds of the rain-forest, music from the world of Islam, obscure music played on weird instruments from strange corners of the earth, and one day a piece of music from Madagascar that somehow got inside me and slowly but surely changed my life.

Let's go forward to 1981. It's March, and Michael Eavis who runs the Glastonbury Festival is on the telephone, he wants to know if Kate will play the festival there and do I have any ideas for a stage as they had to start building one soon... I suggested a pyramid, like the one in '71. He thought it was a good idea.

Kate didn't play the festival but I went along to see if they had pursued my suggestion and sure enough there it was... a record from Madagascar in a little tent/shop – they only had one copy, the sleeve notes were in French; that didn't matter.

I needed to listen to this disc immediately and I had a problem because there were about 100,000 people there and I couldn't get my car out of the field to get to a friend's house. I remember sitting on the back of a motorcycle being driven by a girl who was wearing only boots – it was a hot day. We drove past a big shining pyramid stage – that's nice – and then to a little village outside Glastonbury where there was a friend with a record player, and enough silence for me to listen to the atomic bomb that I had just bought. This music was like tropical Irish Flamenco, it was so hypnotic and yet at the same time it had very positive and noble qualities

Photo: courtesy Paddy Bush

contained in these fantastic musical phrases that seemed to change continuously.

We transferred the disc to cassette all those years ago and I still listen to it today. It was a disc of music for spirit ceremonies and was quite unlike anything else I had heard before and yet seemed to have all the best bits from everything else I had heard... I hope that makes sense to you, it didn't make sense for me for many years.

There was a photo of a musician playing an instrument on the cover of this disc, and I made a copy based on the dimensions in the photo. In fact I used the length of his left foot, which was clearly visible, to make a proportional copy based on the measurements of my left foot! I unpicked a length of bicycle brake cable to make some strings and made 21 little wooden bridges.

I started on the road to Marovany and it has been so difficult and wonderful. It's difficult because the rhythms of Madagascar are seductively easy to listen to and mind-crushingly maddening to try and learn, there are always so many bridges to cross, and if there's no bridge you have to make it yourself.

Let's go to 1992 – we're in Paris, it's raining. I'm indoors in a studio, my friend Patrick is the sound engineer – we met whilst recording *Lionheart*, and here we are again. He is mixing a track in the control room while I practice on the Marovany in the studio. In a couple of hours' time I shall be meeting someone called Justin Vali and I'm very nervous. I had never met anyone from Madagascar and felt that in many ways what I had done by making an instrument and trying to learn how to play it was a bit cheeky, I had all sorts of weirdness in my head. It was very soon after our mother's death and I was pretty messed up and not really ready for everyday life and yet somehow circumstances had contrived to put me there; in an atmosphere of French studio cigarette smoke I nervously plucked at my bicycle brake cable strings.

We walked for what seemed like hours through the rainy streets of Paris trying to find Justin's place, everyone gave us directions that led us round in circles. My nervousness had grown to the point of wanting to catch a cab and just get out of there as we were now walking down a street full of women dressed in leather waiting under lamp posts, then suddenly we turned into a street near the opera house and we were there.

We drank mint tea and dried out. Justin was very friendly and a little suspicious and seemed amused by my instrument. He explained that he came from a family of instrument makers and loved to meet people who did the same thing. He started mending an instrument and I took the opportunity to try a few tunes out on him, at one point he wiped a tear away from his eye and said that the tune I was playing reminded him of one from his village and it made him feel sad because he hadn't been home for ten years. I stopped, then he started playing and the tears started to run down my cheeks, I was helpless and drowning in the most amazing music I had ever heard.

I like to think that it was destiny that took us from that rainy evening in Paris to Madagascar in September later that year, but in fact it was an Air Madagascar jumbo-jet that flew on a full moon night and arrived in the blue skies of the Indian Ocean the following morning. I watched the azure sea turn pink as we approached the West Coast and just knew that this marked a change in my life.

It's maybe better if I don't get off the 'plane right now, if I take you through my first visit from beginning to end we'll be here all day, I would like to, but maybe another time.

Instead, let's go up a mountain in Montpellier in the South of France; why? Because we're going to record an album there. It's an ancient farmhouse that has been converted into a studio and Patrick is our host and engineer. It's a sunny January and we have very interesting work to do. Recording the Valiha and Marovany in the studio is not as straightforward as you would imagine and in order to get a real perspective on the sound I had to invent an unusual device. It was a long wooden tunnel covered in microphones so that while Justin was playing his instrument inside it, we could mix reflected sound from the walls with the image from microphones pointed at the strings, to give a dreamy, warm, clear stereo image.

One sunny morning it started snowing and didn't stop for a week. It became very quiet, every now and then I could hear a tree explode under the weight of snow and at night I watched the vivid blue flashes in the distance from electricity cables doing the same thing. It was only a question of time before we had our own electricity problems, and when that time came we used candles for light, cooked on a fire while telling spooky stories and played Valiha to keep warm. The sound of dripping icicles that came with the radiant sunshine some ten days later, was blending with the sound of Justin's Valiha over breakfast when Patrick told me it was possible to get access to a huge cave in another mountain nearby and there was electricity there so we could record if we wanted to. I have always wanted to record underground and so that's what we did.

The gentle rivers of Montpellier had been transformed by the melting snow into brown raging monsters that tore huge chunks out of the riverbanks and carried away the bridges. We drove slowly and carefully, avoiding the small landslides.

We were to record for five hours deep in the heart of a mountain to get some natural reverberation, so deep that we took a small train to get to the middle. The air inside was very still, as though it hadn't moved in a thousand years. It was humid and very claustrophobic. We positioned microphones amongst the stalactites, trying to avoid the drips of water that fell from the top of the cave. The sound was incredible. Afterwards we sat outside in the sunshine and laughed at the lengths we were willing to go to record music.

We took the recordings to three other studios in France, to add drums and bass courtesy of Mory Kanté, we had Arsene Kounde (drums) and Hamed Barry (bass). Ricardo Tesi from Italy (accordion), Ahmed Khan (Tabla) and Justin played the title track at Studios de la Seinne, it was a really dreamy moment. Justin seemed to be playing something that was inside all of us that only the magic music of the Valiha could express, and that's just one of the reasons why this disc is called *The Sunshine Within*.

It came out at the end of last year and *Songlines* magazine voted it 'Top of the World', describing it as "a joyous affair". *FolkRoots* raved about it, saying that it was Justin's best record ever, and two weeks ago it was placed at number 22 in Tower Records all time top 100 world music selection!

I believe this to be a rare and special disc, we put all our time, love and laughter into it, we designed everything ourselves and are really happy to see it have a life of it's own.

It's been nice to write to you all, until the next issue and please don't forget, it's okay to be happy.

2: A Musical journey through the Red Island

Imagine the concentrated redness of six million years of sunsets, and you will still not get close to the colour of Madagascar. It is an enormous red land that rises to a vast high plateau where the hillsides have been carved into a labyrinth of curving terraces that are flooded with water, reflecting blue sky and huge white clouds, and growing through the water's surface are the greenest shoots you have ever seen, the shoots of newly sprouting rice, fluorescent green against blood red.

Now imagine me with a notebook writing to you from a huge quartz boulder sticking out of a hillside, a hillside with pink cliffs and exposed red volcanic rock with grass like the Malvern hills. Beneath me are a family of ducks who constantly swim up and down the drainage channels chasing the skating insects that dance on the water's surface. The air is pure and cold as we are high up in the mountains, and the sun is as hot as Africa except when it is covered by clouds, I'm wearing a straw hat that somehow keeps me warm and cool at the appropriate moments.

I woke up at about five in the morning and the house was surrounded by a wall of bright luminescent fog and crowing cockerels, beautiful Valiha music started about twenty minutes later with the sounds of a breakfast being prepared, teacups, laughter, the smell of wood smoke and then more music as others start to wake and pick up an instrument as they get out of bed.

This is a place untouched by the influence of electricity, so last night when the sun went down, the night flooded in on a tide of croaking frogs and phantoms, but now it's daytime and I can't see a single telephone-pole or electric-pylon anywhere on the horizon, just quartz mountains, paddy fields and redbrick villages bathing in the moving dappled leopard spotted torch beams of sunlight a hundred miles away.

I have extraordinary dreams here that often seem to come true a few days later. It could well be to make up for all the unrealistic dreaming I do back in England, but I feel sure that it's more to do with the power of this place.

The days are filled with remarkable coincidences, and I find myself often just smiling at people and they smile back and then the sunshine comes out inside me, and it's still shining when the sun goes down.

Photo: courtesy Paddy Bush

Photo: courtesy Paddy Bush

I had learned from a young age that it could be pretty dangerous to smile at people in London, they could sometimes get violently paranoid, I presume they thought that I was laughing at them instead of being friendly. Perhaps this has never happened to you, but if you're male and gentle in nature, the chances are that you know what I'm talking about. So in order to stay alive, I studied martial arts for six years and generally became more reserved when it came to smiling, it seemed a reasonable tactic.

When I first got off the plane, back in 1993, I soon found out that teaching myself not to smile hadn't been such a good idea and in doing so I had forgotten some very important basic things. I had thought that I was a reasonable musician too, but all that changed pretty quickly.

I also had this weird thing about how reality could apparently change in the presence of the camera; I'll explain. It's to do with making videos for television and the way everything is contrived for the camera. Every time I have been in a video I have always been given a role to play, like an army dreamer or a talking rock, so I got used to the idea of working in front of the camera for set up and rehearsed performances.

The problem arose on that first visit here in Madagascar. As we were making a documentary film for French television, everything Justin and I did was filmed and it started to interfere with my sense of reality. I wasn't sure what was being staged for the camera and what was genuine, I was clearly a bit confused in thinking this way, although some things were indeed staged for the camera!

Eventually I realised that I must have turned into a jaded cynical paranoid fool who had completely got hold of the wrong end of the stick. Everything around me was real enough and not constructed by set-builders. Villages of smiling people throwing their hats in the air as we passed were not paid extras waiting for a cue from the director. At last the reality of what was happening was starting to break through.

It was one morning when Justin's parents were playing music. They are very old and beautiful and they were singing a duet together while Justin's father played the Valiha. I found myself with unstoppable floods of tears pouring down my cheeks and trying to explain to the concerned people around me that I thought it must be because I was happy! And it's true, I was happy and yet very sad at the same time, sad because I realised that I had hidden my happiness from myself as well as the paranoid nutters, and now all my previously concealed emotions were coming out, being teased out by the music, the morning fog and a dream coming true.

It felt like starting from the beginning again, or maybe just picking up something I had left behind in my early teenage. When it came to trying to learn how to play these amazing tunes that I was hearing here everyday, it was as though I had never learned how to play an instrument in the first place.

I would continuously get the timing wrong, and it stayed that way for a few maddening years. The rhythms of Madagascar's music come from the dawn of time and deep in the heart of Africa, and they can be so complex and powerful that they drove me even crazier trying to analyse them. Actually, I'm sure it was the other way around, I was getting less crazy as the rhythms analysed me.

Since those early tears, I have produced three successful albums for Madagascar. I get a great deal of satisfaction when I hear a track being used on national television or played on the radio. I sometimes hear bootleg cassette copies being played in the markets and on the flight out, they even played the title track from *The Sunshine Within* on the aeroplane during take off. I love coincidences like that. Madagascar is a land of miracles and living legends, but like the rest of the world, it's rapidly changing with satellite communications, microwave dishes and mobile telephones, yet here in the country, things haven't changed much in seven hundred years. The ducks are still quacking while we play the tunes from three hundred thousand sunsets ago, tunes that are still travelling through time like giant musical comets, still travelling because they are made from a fantastic magical material that doesn't recognise borders.

The strangest things happen here, and from time to time it can get very dangerous. Communications are poor and distances can be enormous, so it's a good idea to have friends. I'm talking about stuff like getting lost, bandits and health problems. I have to be careful with all kinds of things, although sometimes it can be unavoidable, like having to go into areas with nasty illnesses like bubonic plague and cholera or being eaten alive by microscopic insects, add floods, cyclones and forest fires to the list, and sometimes you really have to trust in life. Also, it's not easy finding the kind of music that I'm interested in. It is connected with a few specific places, very much like the flowers and trees that only grow in one location.

The musical styles of Madagascar can vary greatly, from terrible stuff with it's French cabaret influences to the totally amazing and unique music that grows out of the ground that is played only in certain isolated communities.

In fact the relationship between the place and the music that grows there is so strong that I can almost be sure of what the music sounds like from looking at the trees and plants. There really seems to be some kind of connection, it is as though the personality of a place expresses itself through all the living things that grow there, including the music.

I see music as a living thing, it gets inside you and won't leave you alone until you learn of some way of passing it on to someone else, and this is the way that I think music uses us humans to keep itself alive, sometimes for thousands of years!

I remember when I met my first troop of ring-tailed Lemurs, there were about ten of them in a big pile, all looking at me. I just sat on the ground and didn't move. After a while they started to approach me and I could see that they had been protecting a mother with a newly born baby by basically piling themselves on top of each other so that it was impossible to see anything. They are very charming creatures, the first one came up to me and touched my nose with his index finger, squeaked and jumped vertically out of sight as another one suddenly appeared and gave my knee a very gentle bite and instantly changed places with another one who was now sitting on my shoulder. All the time they were watching the way I was looking at the baby Lemur, who was smaller than a mouse with his incredibly long grey and black striped tail.

I see so many similarities between the endangered animals and plants of our world and the endangered music and musical instruments. There are so many instruments that no longer exist or nobody remembers how to play or construct them. This can be because of something like the immense world-wide popularity of the guitar and pop music, or other extremes like the destruction of a particular forest where the unique materials to build a certain instrument used to grow. The reasons are numerous but the results are the same, and I feel that we are all worse off in a world of disappearing musical bio-diversity.

There are a few of us now, and we are in many ways somewhat like those ring tailed Lemurs, in that we are trying to protect precious and delicate musical life forms by piling ourselves into a heap. Perhaps you should look on me as a bouncing bold masked Lemur with my index finger on your nose!

Please believe me when I tell you that I had no choice in any of this, I was drawn into the centre of a whirlpool of the most fantastic music I had ever heard and I couldn't get out of it even if I had wanted to.

There were times when I would have done anything to have been able to play the Marovany, and if that meant becoming a Lemur for a day, I would have quite happily done so, luckily up until just now that hasn't been necessary.

Thank you for your support over the years and thanks for the opportunity to talk about something that I really love.

Photo: courtesy Paddy Bush

Meeting with a Remarkable Man

Krys interviews John Carder Bush

Issue 74: July 2004

John Carder Bush is Kate's eldest brother whose role in the early days of Kate's career was as he says: "legal advisor, driver, bodyguard, secretary, photographer, roadie, fellow poet and researcher. And defender..."

Krys said:

"I first met John Carder Bush at East Wickham Farm in 1985 at a meeting to discuss the plans for the Convention. I met him several times later; more meetings for the Video Party in '86 and again at the *Experiment IV* video shoot. *Cathy* was newly published and he gave Peter, Dave and myself each a signed copy.

"I remember John quietly taking photographs in the long corridors of the disused military mental hospital where ghosts very probably roamed... I remember a magical evening in the summer of '86 when Hannah showed me her inscribed copy of *Cathy*. For the first time a doorway had been opened into the world of Kate the child.

"This was where she came from, and John had recorded these glimpses for all time. Summer days, ancient dressing-up clothes and elaborate games of make-believe. I treasure my copy of *Cathy*: a place of childhood, a place where there are little glimmers of our own childhoods, where we can return to whenever we need to be reminded of our innocence".

Krys: When did you first observe Kate's musical ability? Can you remember her earliest songs?

John: I don't think I was that conscious of her having a specific musical ability in the early years. She was learning the violin, and living with anyone who is learning the violin is a miserable experience. When she started to divert her need for music to the piano, when she should have been practising the violin, things became a lot more interesting. But that was a little later. She was just my little sister, and if my friends who were in my folk band came round to rehearse she was there and she sang along with us. Folk music in those days was like that – the concept of production, professional musicianship and trained voices was in another world. I was obsessed with British Folk Music, but I liked rock and roll as well, and classical, and Weil and pop, and the Red Army Ensemble. I had a thirst for research, and in those days nothing was easily available; you had to hunt and hunt, but imagine the pleasure when you found something: like a limited edition of whaler's songs from the Baltimore Whaling Museum!

Now credit cards and the internet make everything so easy there is no sense of the hunt and the find. Well, there is – but what lasted months is now done in a couple of minutes.

I was after the best of anything, so a lot of music from many different spectrums came into the house. Interestingly, my love of Irish music was not shared by my parents. My mother saw it as a regressive process – music of despair and hard times best not remembered (how easy it is to be romantic about suffering when it's someone else's) and it irritated my father because he wanted me to be a solicitor and not a folk singer. So it was a sort of an intrusion, and not a welcome guest. But the real music did come into the home and filled the nooks and crannies, of minds as well, whether it was wanted or not. At the same time, my father played the piano a lot – either classical, Schubert and Chopin mainly – or the favourites of the Forties – those sophisticated masters Gershwin, Kern etc. – and he played them with a beautiful lyrical style that made them flow like rivers.

I remember her earliest songs, and her poetry. The subject matter of the early songs was always obscure and very personal. Poets are like that, but seldom songwriters, and, in retrospect, she had a very clear, very personal vision of what she wanted to do with words and music.

Krys: Did you see the KT Bush Band perform in the pubs? How was Kate and the band received?

John: I went to a couple of the gigs. There were only a few, and I don't think they were particularly formative: the environment of pub rock in those days was not really conducive to where her performance was heading. The audiences seemed to like the set, which I seem to remember was mainly covers with only a few of her own songs. I'm sure the experience was really useful in terms of exposure and performing in public, but, in retrospect it seems a little tangential to what lay ahead. Pubs were pubs, not showcases for something new and very different.

Krys: When Kate's career took off in the dramatic way it did, was it a shock?

John: Shock would be too strong a word. Almost a year before *Wuthering Heights* was number one in the UK a close friend of mine at that time, Julie Covington, had reached number one with *Don't Cry For Me Argentina* – the benchmark version that everyone has copied ever since. In fact, it was Julie who paid for and arranged the first serious studio demo tape of Kate's songs. So, for me, personally, I had experienced someone close becoming super-famous, and I knew what could happen and why, and, in a sense, I was prepared when it landed in our back garden and then hopped onto Kate's shoulder. Things like that were happening to us in those days.

Krys: When most Kate fans hear your name they think of *Cathy*, your beautiful photographic and written recollections of Kate as a child. Can you tell us more about the *Cathy* project, the joys and problems encountered, and *Catherine* and *Kate*, the two sister books of *Cathy* that never happened?

John: The *Cathy* project was a nightmare. The first and last time I'll ever get into publishing something myself. I did it privately because I had seen the book as a very specific object, as well as a book of photos. I knew that if I took it to a mainstream publisher that they would never be prepared to produce something so tactile and painstakingly made. The cut-out windows are a very important part of the book – the view into the past, the written recollection and then you turn the page and there is the past.

The nightmare was made up of a number of things – the slipcases were the wrong size when they turned up etc., all the stuff of getting anything done. The cut-outs, the thick paper and the high quality, duo-tone prints, meant the book could not be folded by machine. However, when the run had been printed and was settling, the person in charge of the project went on holiday and someone in the print shop put the whole lot through the machine folder. The run was totally ruined and the printers tried to get me to pay for the mistake. I think they had realised that the undertaking was far more expensive than their quote, so the eventual price of the book was far lower than it should have been if they had foreseen the problems in producing it. The slip cases ended up the wrong colour after the wrong size, but time seemed to be running out so I went with them. I think they are the only flaw in an otherwise very satisfying creation.

I had always liked the photos I had taken of Kate as a child - a simple camera and a simple light, and her willingness to be my model. That's why I still had the negatives. But only just, I had rescued most of them off a skip when my father was clearing out a load of rubbish.

As far as *Catherine* and *Kate* are concerned, it's true I did work out the basis for two further books. In fact, I selected all the shots for *Catherine*, and did most of the text. It was a little vignette into the journey towards and through adolescence but a number of things stopped me taking it any further. One was the nightmare experience mentioned earlier, and the second was that I felt it was intrusive. The photos in *Cathy* are mostly posed, whereas the ones in *Catherine* are stolen. In her teens she did not like to be photographed, and although she did pose for some, it was not with the enthusiasm she had had as a child. As a child she was hardly aware of the camera, as a teenager she was very aware of it. That's how we all are.

Cathy was a book about something we both shared - her infancy. *Catherine* was the beginning of the private person, and I felt I had no right to interpret what was going on inside her head.

Krys: What was your role in the early days of Kate's career?

John: I suppose the appropriate word is amanuensis - legal advisor, driver, bodyguard, secretary, photographer, roadie, fellow poet and researcher. And defender against the rapacious control freaks that appeared out of record companies and hopeful management set-ups, determined to make a lot of money out of her. This defensive attitude was necessary at first because, as we all know, the wonderful thing about Kate is the music and its lasting quality, and that was not so obvious to those people because it was fronted by a beautiful girl. I really don't think many people at EMI had actually thought about what those songs on the first album were about at all. The first few years were a battle to retain Kate's control as artist first, and not sexy product. You will have read a lot of articles in magazines and a number of books about those early years. All I can say is that you can dismiss the whole lot as nonsense. Kate's music came into the world through a back-door, and it was there. Nothing else was needed. As her ship took sail, a lot of people tried to get on board but fell off pretty quickly. It can be entertaining reading their opinions, but it's only entertainment, not truth. Some of the rubbish is extraordinary - in one version I was thrown out of the EMI offices because I objected to one of their poster campaigns. Very wishful thinking on the part of a thwarted salesman.

Krys: Did this affect your own career?

John: At that time I was trying to write, play the house-father with my first son while my wife carried on with teaching. I was training and teaching karate and kendo at a number of clubs in South London; mainly karate at the South East London Tech and kendo at Goldsmiths college, and I really did not want to get involved in showbiz. I had escaped from the legal profession a few years before, but not for long it seemed. But it was a critical time, and my legal training, and in not quite so obvious ways, my martial arts training, were of use. So I jumped in. In retrospect, I think that my refusal to lick any arses (karate) - because I did not want a career in the music business - and a clear vision of Kate

In 1993 John wrote to me and sent a copy of the Salatticum Poets' booklet, *Riding Light* in response to my *Feel It* series in *HomeGround*, where I had mentioned his poetry. We started corresponding and since then John has sent me many of his manuscripts.

His writing is exceptional. I always hoped that John would one day write something for *HomeGround*.

From this hope the following interview was born... "

Photo: courtesy John Carder Bush

the Artist that needed to be protected by the cunningness and foresight of lawyers, was useful to her in the long run. Also, in retrospect, to see every business meeting as a karate competition was probably silly, and certainly did not make me any friends. But the alternative was to hand over the whole thing to people who did not understand it and wanted to exploit it for their own benefit, and not my sister's. Without any experience of the business we applied common sense, instinct and a determination not to get ripped-off: with the help of a courageous lawyer we braved the giants.

I put my writing and teaching on hold for what turned out to be over twenty years, but during that time life provided plenty of manure for the process. I also had kyudo – the one with the long bow and long arrows – as a pure, developmental thread running through my life and holding me together.

Krys: The Salatticum Poets – was Kate ever envisaged as a part of the group? I think of the bootleg known as *Organic Acid*, (a song based on your original poem *Before the Fall* that you allowed us to use in *HomeGround* 73) where Kate weaves her own song around the spoken words of your poem. Can you tell us more about this song/poem? Was it ever planned as a possible release?

John: Salatticum Poets in those days was a kind of ethic as well as a functioning Poetry Group. Paddy and Melanie Spriggs provided the music while Tony Buzan, Jeremy Cartland and myself read out poems, acted them out, did karate and sword forms to them. It was at the time of the popularity of The Liverpool Poets, which, although entertaining, seemed to us to be getting away from the high poetry we aspired to. One of the poems I read at these events was *Before the Fall*. Coupling it with *Hush My Friend Asleep* was an experiment that never went any further than just that. I was amazed when it first appeared on a bootleg – I thought the tape was probably in the drawer where experiments went and had not realised it had escaped. The thought in 197? of combining a popular artist with poetry would have been hilarious to a record company who felt she needed a season in Las Vegas and wanted her to sing the theme song for the next Bond film.

Krys: Was the poetry used in the Tour of Life inspired by the Salatticum idea?

John: Interesting question. The last performance Salatticum had done at the Festival of Mind, Body and Spirit had been our most theatrical – live music, masks, dry ice, smoke machines and lights, white clothed swordsman flashing steel etc. but I don't think you could say there was a direct Salatticum influence.

Krys: What are your memories of the tour?

John: I didn't get to see all of the tour – I really needed to be based in England to handle all the stuff that was coming in and going out – insurance, consents, wages, etc... I went to the Amsterdam gigs and most of the UK ones. It was a very extreme time when everyone pushed themselves to exhaustion, and it really was like going to war. My memories of the performances are magical, the rest of it was like any other major undertaking involving dozens of people, tons of equipment and a tremendous commitment of money. It's interesting to remember that the tour was totally financed by Kate herself right up to the dress rehearsal stage when the record company came along to see it and thought they better get on the train fast and put up some token support funds. Her commitment was absolutely total – artistically, spiritually and financially. It was a very brave undertaking that I think changed the face of music presentation, just as she did with her videos; it was amusing seeing Cliff Richard performing live with black dancers a few months later.

Krys: Did you have creative input into the concepts for any of Kate's videos? *Running Up That Hill* for example, and Kyudo.

John: I don't think so. *Running Up That Hill* is certainly visually inspired by traditional Japanese clothing, and some of the choreography resembles the drawing of a bow. At the time I was boring everyone rigid with my love of Kyudo – the Japanese Martial Art of Archery – which I had started a few years before. Interestingly, I had never thought to take up Kyudo, but Kate had given me a gift of a Japanese longbow and that led to what has become my focus since then. One of the many things I have to thank her for. The katas, or forms, of the Japanese martial arts are very beautiful in their movements and dynamics and overriding sense of style, and without doubt there is a visual influence in some of Kate's works.

Krys: Why Kyudo?

John: Kyudo – the Way of the Bow. In my early twenties I read Herrigel's *Zen and the Art of Archery*, and, like a lot of romantics, was excited by this idea that you could achieve something without trying. That little book led me into a lifetime's involvement with the Japanese Martial Arts, although it was some twenty years later that I eventually started practising Kyudo. Why the martial arts have been so important to me gets simpler to see as time goes by: it's the combination of art and physicality to achieve something that cannot be achieved. It acts as a way of understanding life more fully, and getting to know who you are and what you can do, and to be content with the revelations.

For me, Kyudo has the purest combination of those elements because it involves the deadliest of the weapons in traditional Martial Arts, the weapon that can kill at a distance – the bow. However, in Kyudo, the bow is completely denuded of its original purpose to kill another human being or an animal: in its practise you never carry a concept of a live target in your mind, although the forms and shooting procedures originate from such purposes. It cannot be effectively used in a self-defence situation (it's seven foot long and the arrows three foot), it's incredibly difficult to learn because of the complexity of controlling the asymmetrical bow, and the forms that go with it demand tremendous patience, a very unique form of mental concentration, and the ability to withstand and pass through the pain barriers of the body. The Martial part of it is the process of refining yourself in the face of continuing failure – its demands are so high that you are continually walking with failure a step behind you. And, of course, it is exactly the opposite to the idea that something could be gained without trying – it is endless effort. Just like certain aspects of life. By dealing with the conundrum of human existence within the training hall you can deal with life and relationships with more ease.

Photo: courtesy John Carder Bush

The other thing is that all Martial Arts are transient. If, in the case of Kyudo, you shoot a wonderful arrow with everything just right, once it's gone, it's gone forever. You can't preserve it. There's a trace in the air of the place for a little while afterwards if you've got a healthy mind, or it hangs around haunting you for years if you haven't. Just like love. But the point is that it is, and then it isn't. Just like us.

Krys: Many people will be familiar with your photographs of Kate. I am particularly fascinated by the *Babooshka* shots, all the more mysterious because to me they don't look like Kate as she was usually portrayed, particularly at that time. Which photographs do you consider to be your finest? Can you tell us more about your photography?

John: The *Babooshka* shots are all around the theme of the two different women in the one woman, so we were exploring the contradictions. I think you'll find that the Kate that appears in the photos for specific releases – album covers, single bags, videos – is always different from the Kate in general promo photos. It amazes me that people can sometimes get confused between the projected bit of art and the real person – no more so than in *Babooshka* where the extremes are pretty well pushed to the limit.

I think I did it best with the *Hounds of Love* cover and the *Whole Story* cover. The colour and beauty of the *Hounds of Love* shot still really pleases me, and the portrait in black and white on *The Whole Story* is very satisfying. I see both of them looking at me still when I go through CD racks in record shops.

There's not much to say about my photography. The reason I became so involved in all the projects as a photographer did not really stem from whether I was good at it or not. Kate needed some shots to start her off, then she ran into problems with professional photographers who would, and still do, release photos of her she did not know had been taken, or were not approved. I was able to give her the control she needed to compliment the product: even in this age of digital videos and all the rest of it, it is still the still photograph that sells. I had no experience of serious studio photography and I put myself on a crash course – studying the work of people I admired and trying to replicate their lighting techniques, and learning the power and dangers of flash photography. I also printed up the black and white shots all the way through, and, although this doubled my workload I learned a lot, and with the help of my partner at the time, Vivienne Chandler, I entered the world of archival printing and its alchemical powers and spent many unhealthy hours in the darkroom surrounded by the poisonous chemicals that tone and refine.

But it was never a career, there was always too much else to do. I did it for Kate. I have not been into the dark room since the release of *The Red Shoes*, and apart from an annual session with my children I just snap Kyudo events and use a camcorder.

Krys: Going back to *Running Up That Hill*, was the idea for the calligraphy across Kate's back and down her arms similar to that of the *Pillow Book*? Again you presented another interesting concept for a photograph, and is another of my favourites for its otherworldly atmosphere.

John: I had been writing on people and photographing them for a couple of years – it seemed a good way to combine poetry and photography. Black writing on white bodies, white writing on black bodies. First with ink, then markers and then body make-up sticks. Using it for *Running Up That Hill* was just timing. The actual back shot was through smoke from a smoke machine that went out of control for a while.

Krys: The idea of the white rose on the cover for *The Sensual World* seems to be based on a photograph of Yukio Mishima in a similar pose. Can you tell us more about Mishima, his work, life and his death?

John: A lot of comparison has been made between *The Sensual World* cover and Eikoh Hosoe's photos of Mishima, but I think the only real connection is the technique of printing the eye in shadow with the same tones as the eye in light. I seem to remember Hosoe used a strange camera to get the extremely contrasting prints, whereas mine is a classic Hasselblad portrait. There's a lot of weirdness in the Mishima shots around the man himself and his extreme fantasies: none of which is present in the album cover. White Roses? They can indicate peace, honesty, subversion, secrecy and a lot of other things. Maybe all those things are in *The Sensual World* too. And, of course, they can be very beautiful to look at.

Mishima is interesting because he was a man from old Japan who bloomed as the marketing world bloomed. Classically educated and erudite his books seem to lead to his last work, *The Sea of Fertility*. I notice that in bookshops these days you'll only find the more sensational books, like *Confessions of a Mask*. If you want get the taste of Mishima the world novelist you've got to read *The Sea of Fertility*. If he had not committed ritual suicide he would have won the Nobel Prize. But that suicide was the spiritual and the marketing side of him coming together – the side that wanted to be a film star (he played gangsters in a few films), wanted to be a beautiful hero (he took up martial arts and weight lifting and made the body he wanted), wanted to die a hero's death before the beautiful body got old. His suicide combined with an attempt to win over the Japanese Army to the old principles of old Japan was tragically pathetic, but, as I am sure he wanted, has given him the sort of immortality only marketing and photos can give. How many Nobel candidate novelists can you think of whose mostly naked muscular frame still appears all over the world in iconoclastic photos drawing a sword?

Krys: You told me recently about the time you and Kate went to see the 1968 BBC 'Omnibus' film *Song of Summer*, a beautiful film directed by Ken Russell about the last years of Frederick Delius's life – would you tell that story again?

John: I think those little films Ken Russell made about those people who are so quintessentially British caught something about the English soul that no one else has ever done quite so well. It seems to me a lot of love went into them. I don't think he's done anything else as good since.

To get to see *Song of Summer* was complex because the only projector capable of running it was in some obscure BBC studio. We had seen it on television years before, but to see it as a projected film really did compliment it. All the performances are brilliant. Whether or not it touches the reality of Delius is another thing. When we asked why it wasn't available on video we were told all about the complexities of digging out old contracts, finding out who the actor/extra was on the railway station, who was still alive and who dead, and how much all that would cost in comparison to the returns that would be gained. Art versus commerciality again.

Krys: Tell us more about your interest in Folk music as you were growing up. Who in the folk scene did you and do you admire? Did you ever meet A.L. Lloyd?

John: Way back in the days of the first folk revival my favourite band was the Ian Campbell Group – father of the UB40 brothers. There is still stuff on that album that really works for me. The early albums with Bert Lloyd and Ewan MacColl singing shanties are still superb. You've got to remember that the pair of them basically invented British folk music between them, and they did it with such astounding confidence. It's great that *The First Time Ever I Saw Your Face* has become such a lauded song. Dave and Toni Arthur were my total favourites, and I played concertina on their first album, under the name of John Carter (I was training to be a solicitor at the time and you couldn't have another job etc.). They both went on to write and sing for television, mainly children's. Check out Dave Arthur's recent banjo albums.

Louis Killen, The Rakes, early Chieftains when Seán Ó Riada was still alive, and Seán Ó Sé sang with them. His version of *Carrick Fergus* comes from heaven. Dominic Behan, The Clancy Brothers. Then, later, the Bothy Band.

The Breton musician and singer, Alan Stivell, has been there since his album *Renaissance of the*

Celtic Harp. That album invented what we now know as World Music, and all the changes it went through to get to where it is now. I don't like all his stuff, but amongst it is the best there is. I never met Bert Lloyd, but I used to write to him.

Krys: The poem in *Jig of Life*.

John: Great fun to write and do. Sticking my fingers in the socket of Celtic soul is always rewarding.

Krys: And the music you listen to now? Which books and films inspire you? Who inspires you?

John: My love of music has always been eclectic. I don't know why, unless it's looking for that gold that is in the best of all music. There is nothing I don't like. At the moment I like the best of World Music, although that's all starting to sound a bit the same, whether it comes from East Europe or Africa, the best of Country and Western and particularly the minor key ballads of Lyle Lovett. Anything, really – as long as it's good. I listen to a lot of Irish music, whether it's U2, Paul Brady or Donal Lunny. But my most rewarding moments are with the albums of Jackie Leven and the dearly missed Warren Zevon – both poets using rock and roll as their medium – brave men who put the truth first.

As far as contemporary writers are concerned I like most of Paul Auster, Isabel Allende's first few books and I've just started reading Siri Hustvedt.

Films? All of them. *Dark Water*, that Japanese tribute to *The Innocents* and *Don't Look Now*. *Donnie Darko*, *28 Days*, *American Beauty*, there are so many without having to go backwards.

Who inspires me? James Stephens, Gorecki, Rumi, and the masters and saints of Kyudo.

Krys: Can you tell us more about James Stephens?

John: James Stephens was a Dubliner who wrote two extraordinary books, as well as a few other things, and a poet too. He was a tiny little man, a street urchin as a child, with an incredible energy for life who put the reality – the reality of the body – back into Irish Myth and Fairy Tales. For me, it is *The Crock of Gold*, and *Deirdre*, that I can return to, and on each return, be shocked by his understanding of the human condition, his beautiful writing, his sense of humour and his ability to tell a good story. His writing is simply very alive, and his motivations for telling the story are pure, like a mountain spring. In my mind I see him and Arthur Rackham, a similar physical type, dancing a jig together as they direct the consciousness of the Twentieth Century towards Walt Disney, Warner Brothers and *Harry Potter*.

I think I have two favourite short stories. Three actually. James Joyce's *The Dead*, Kenzaburo Oe's *Prime Meat* (an incredible story about a Black American pilot shot down over Japan in the Second war and captured by children), and Kenji Miyazawa's *The Bears of Mount Nametoko*. It puzzles me that *The Crock of Gold*, and *The Bears of Mount Nametoko* are not Walt Disney Classics.

Photo: courtesy John Carder Bush

Krys: Which photographers and artists do you admire?

John: Michael Sowa, Ansel Adams, Irving Penn.

Krys: Which of Kate's songs are your favourites? How do you compare the early songs and before them the demos, with her later work – emotionally, musically?

John: I think the thread has always been there. As time goes by it becomes brocaded, gilded or encrusted with gems, but at the centre the thread is the same. With the growing of skills, vocal, musical and production, the ability to express that thread more powerfully grew too. What's the thread? Love. Love with all its complexities, contradictions, ecstasies and pain, and the hope that if you express it just right you might capture all that complexity for a moment and render it into musical communication that might help somebody. Might reach somebody and show them something that helps them breathe a sigh of relief: I am not alone.

Breathing – it says it all, *Army Dreamers* – the best anti-war song ever, *Moments of Pleasure* – an exquisite encapsulation of true loss, and the transience of life, *Why Should I Love You* – just beautiful, and so on, and so on.

Krys: Have you heard anything from Kate's new album?

John: No, I haven't.

Krys: You must have met many fascinating people along the way. Do you have any particular recollections about your meetings with remarkable men and women over the years?

John: I don't think I met any remarkable men or women in the Music Business – some were good at their jobs and some not. Dealing with other artists on Kate's behalf, on a business level, was quite an eye-opener – from true generosity to incredible greed. Like lawyers, doctors and pathologists, the fee-negotiator gets to see your insides. On the other hand, out of that context, I got to meet Peter Brook, Nicholas Roeg, Eberhard Weber, Neil Jordan, Alan Stivell, Stevie Wonder, and a lot of other people whose work I have admired. I have a few anecdotal recollections, but they stay in my mind because of their absurdity and I don't want to embarrass anyone by recounting them.

Krys: I have read most of your novels, poems and short stories and would say you are my favourite contemporary author, together with the also as yet unpublished novelist J.J. Sarre. Your writing means as much to me as Kate's music and I hope that one day your work will be published. I can only compare this with no-one ever having heard Kate's music, and I know how your writing has enriched my own life, and feel very honoured that I have been able to read your work. You have an incredibly beautiful way of using words, creating atmospheres, and a very wicked sense of humour! Do you enjoy the writing process and playing with words?

John: Yes. Because it does me good. Writing is an extraordinary natural way of self-adjusting – like having a car serviced. Because it's so natural, like proper breathing, you tend to forget about it, and then wonder what's missing from life. Oh, yes, I forgot to breathe, or was it write? Again, it's the process of getting there that is the adventure. You dive into the screen and start it happening with an idea, and up pops a person, and a place, and things start to happen. When that "starts to happen" gets under way you live an alternative reality, and that's wonderful. For instance, I'm writing about a certain situation, I resolve what I intended to do and suddenly there's a knock on the door and someone appears who I had no intention of introducing. Then the process becomes organic and takes on its own motivation; all you have to do is ride it. That's very exciting. How it turns out as art, or a good story, is up to the reader.

Opposite: Issues 70 to 75

I think that we can all benefit from enclosing our undigested experiences inside small boxes, and just let them play themselves out. For a few years I helped a close friend to stock and enliven a dolls' house, and I wrote the adventures of the inhabitants. I had never conceived that a dolls' house could be such a place of atmosphere and totally absorbing. Painting is the same; a plain, dull portal into another world; wonderful fun. Photography is the same, film making is the same; jump into the tiny portals. Sometimes those undigested experiences make people famous, most of the time they don't. But either way does not detract from the value of the exercise. I stopped being involved with Kate's career five years ago. Since then I have been teaching Kyudo here in the UK, and in Austria and Germany, and have gone back to writing. Nothing published yet, but I have stockpiled a few novels, a few children's books, and a load of short stories. Instead of poems, I write songs.

I think I always saw my involvement as a temporary one. As I have said, I did not want a career in the music business or as a professional photographer. But because the world wanted her music, it turned out to be a much longer adventure than anticipated, and I am very grateful to my sister for letting me come aboard.

Krys: Can you tell us more about your songs?

John: My songs, like my poems, are a conduit for emotional experience. It whirls around inside like food and has to come out again in some form or other. I find the digital recording deck is an amazing place to get rid of it in. I step inside its echoing halls and it obligingly translates my musical stutterings into power and depth. We tend to forget how powerful recorded sound can be, and I like to dive in and be slung around by the waves. For a couple of years I hammered away at the perfect love song – trying to find it in lots of different styles of popular music. Popular music because I think the ones that come closest to it are found in popular music; some opera perhaps, and folk song, which was once popular music. Maybe it has been found a few times – *Unchained Melody*, *Tracks of My Tears*, *Moving Me Gently* and so on. But the pursuit is what anything is about: finding something is just another conclusion. Now, I just write songs, play them and sing them. I might have written the perfect love song. Who knows? I have fantasies about the songs, but not any plans. Those plans would take up so much time, the time I keep for writing.

Krys: What's your philosophy on life?!

John: Not to have one. I've tried quite a few philosophies and haven't found one that quite fits. Just keep busy is probably closest to it, and love whenever you can.

HomeGround

The Kate Bush Fanzine

HomeGround
Number 71 The Kate Bush Magazine

HomeGround

Number 72 The Kate Bush Magazine

HomeGround
The Kate Bush Magazine

Number 73 The Kate Bush Magazine Spring 2004

HomeGround
The Kate Bush Magazine

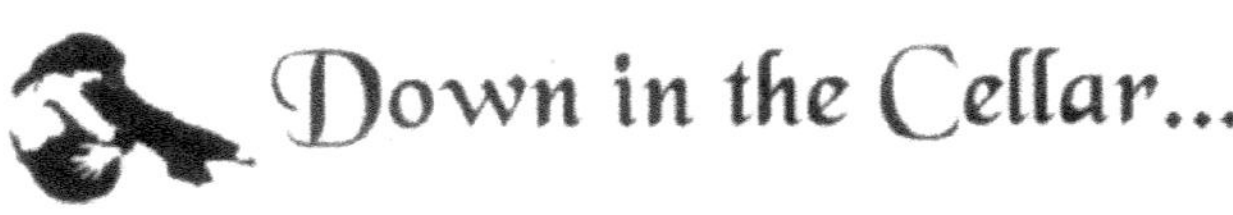

Down in the Cellar...

The Dreaming has to be one of the most remarkable albums I have ever heard. A brave, passionate, powerful album that twenty years on still sounds as vibrant now as it did back then. This issue and HomeGround 71 are tributes to that album. It is one of Kate's most outstanding pieces of work and it still amazes me that she was so young when she created it.

Congratulations to Kate on receiving an Ivor Novello award in May. See the News for more details.

The Kate Tribute Concert in Norwich was excellent. Karl Jokat did a fine job of putting together a very talented bunch of artists to perform some of Kate's songs. More than anything, the evening highlighted Kate's remarkable talent as a songwriter. I am trying to persuade Karl to do it all over again... aaah go on, go on, go on...

Seventeen years ago today - 5th August - *Running Up That Hill* was released. I am such a sentimental old bag and remember these dates. Back then I was working at a print gallery near the British Museum and I recall walking to work and seeing the huge posters for the single lining New Oxford Street. Hannah had put us on Kate's guest list for the *Wogan* performance later that day.

In December we will be changing our PO Box address - the new address will be announced with the Christmas issue, HG 71. *Five Years Ago* will be back then too. We will stay with 24 pages until the new album is released. We hope our subscriptions will return to what they were and we can then increase the number of pages. Thanks to everyone who has stayed with us over the years and welcome to new readers. We need you so that we can continue to produce the mag.

At the beginning of June, Peter and I spent ten days in Ireland with Sean Twomey, who runs the website. It was quite an adventure with an impromptu DIY *Father Ted* tour thrown in. We loved Dublin and spent a wonderful evening with Sean and his family at a restaurant at Howth (we saw Howth Head), then we headed off to the West Coast. It is a beautiful place. Limestone mountains laced with mountain flowers. The Cliffs of Moher were amazing and scary, and we watched one of the Irish World Cup matches at the local pub - quite an experience! Then we headed off to the coast at Black Head where Sean in his slightly (!) pissed state announced that we were going to climb this fecking big mountain overlooking Galway Bay. I thought he was joking - he wasn't!

We took a boat trip to the smallest Aran Island - a very long and rough four miles. Peter went a curious shade of green! The island (which turned out to be the one in the titles for *Father Ted*) was fascinating and remote. Later Sean suggested we should see the waterfalls in the grounds of an hotel at Ennistymon. He was waiting for the Guinnesses at the bar and overheard the bar staff talking about *Father Ted* and got talking to them. It turned out that the waterfalls were the film location for *My Lovely Horse*. The barman told us about a pub in the village where the cast and crew drank every night for three months while filming, and told us how to find Craggy Island parochial house. The pub was great and had a small *Ted* corner with signed photos, one of Ted with the real village priest, a signed clapperboard, stuff like that. Very understated but just right. I took photos of Peter and Sean as Ted and Dougal doing *My Lovely Horse* with the waterfalls behind them. They had the pose just right. The scary thing is that if they were Ted and Dougal, that makes me a cross between Father Jack and Mrs. Doyle!!!! Sadly very true!!!

Apologies for this issue being a little late. On 8th August we were burgled, which made finishing the mag in time impossible. Then a week later I had a nasty fall (the gone-a-bit-Lara stunt went a bit wrong!) and fractured my elbow. It's surprising what you can do with one arm! Sticking and stuffing this issue when it returns from the printer will be fun!! I can picture it now...

With love
Krys xx

Recipes

Celebrating Kate

How Fans celebrated 30th July at the Millennium

1999

News issue 64: November 1999

The Tenth Anniversary HomeGround Glastonbury on 1st August had fabulous sunny weather, and a turn out of near forty Kate fans from the UK and Europe on Glastonbury Tor. The memorable points, as ever, were Jon and his alcohol collection on the Tor, and the animated discussion of the prospects for Kate's next album in the Rifleman's Arms (always more interesting after sampling the local scrumpy). This year those who stayed in the town over the weekend had their tales to tell, but as I am forbidden to mention the dog, that's all I can say.

The principal celebration of Kate's birthday in other parts was in Chicago, as **Thomas Dunning reports:** "CHICAGO July 30th: Brown Star Records, home of the Kate Bush Tribute CD *I Wanna Be Kate: The Songs of Kate Bush*, was invited by The Chicago Cultural Center to put together a show to celebrate Kate's birthday as part of their BIO program. Working with the pool of artists who worked on the tribute CD, ten Kate songs were performed at the very prestigious and very elegant Chicago Cultural Center located in the heart of downtown Chicago on Michigan Avenue. The show was hosted by Thomas Dunning, producer of *I Wanna Be Kate*, and everything went off without a hitch. (Except, of course, that it was the HOTTEST day of the year in Chicago!).

The audience was a wonderful mixture of local Kate Bush fans, as well as tourists visiting Chicago, senior citizens who lounge in the open café/theatre, business folks on their lunch hour and college students from the nearby art schools. The program was as follows: Jacquie Krupka of The Plunging Necklines with Zebulun... *Under The Ivy*, Thomas Negovan... *Deeper Understanding* and *And Dream of Sheep*, Nora O'Connor with Eddie Carlson... *Saxophone Song*, Liam Davis of The Moviegoers... *Hounds of Love*, Justin Roberts... *You're the One*, Jacquie Krupka and Victoria Storm... *Kashka from Baghdad/Babooshka*, Catherine Smitko... *The Man with the Child in his Eyes*, Victoria Storm... *The Kick Inside*, Tom Dunning & Your Boyfriends... *Not This Time*. The songs were mostly performed as solos or as a duo with acoustic guitar or piano and were really stripped down. The finale included everyone on stage together for a warm and joyous *Not This Time*. After the show, members of the audience came up to the performers to tell them how much they enjoyed the performances and how it was great to learn about Kate Bush this way."

Other parties we heard about were in Winchester MA, Pittsburgh, Tucson Arizona, The Bay Area California, and New York State. The American media also picked up on Kate's birthday. KGSR in Austin ran a 15 minute "Coffee Break Concert" segue of *Running Up That Hill*, *Don't Give Up*, and *The Sensual World* "in honour of Kate's 41st birthday".

Gordon Mackinnon reports: "The Brisbane Kate Group had a local Katemas and Royce made a beautiful cake for the occasion." We heard reports, but no details of a Kate Birthday bash in Wellington, NZ. There was a Kate Birthday Bash run by the Osaka based Japanese Kate Bush mailing list on 31st July.

2000 The top of Glastonbury Tor

Photo: Peter Chow

2000

News issue 66: December 2000

As is now traditional we had glorious weather for the Millennium HomeGround Glastonbury gathering, and there were about thirty people on the Tor and afterwards at the Rifleman's Arms. On the Tor we drank a toast (the bubbly kindly provided by Roger Bowman) to Kate on her birthday, and to her son, Bertie (and to Pami and Lynn who also had their birthday that day) and ate birthday cake. Peter Chow reported the event live on the internet. As usual some had travelled from great distances – Jan-Erik once again made the trip from Sweden, and some from not so far – one fan who lived in Glastonbury turned up! We were up on the Tor for about three hours, and then went down to the pub for another few hours. It was so hot that we sat outside sampling the local brews and discussing many things, including Kate.

Marcel reports: "About yesterday: Barend and Marco hosted a brilliant KateMas here in The Hague and it was my first ever KateMas in 22 years of fandom. Just wanted to compliment them on hosting this great celebration and Mike on singing some incredibly good versions of Kate songs (*Reaching Out*, *Sensual Word*, *Under the Ivy* and *Breathing*). I was pretty chuffed to end up so high in the Quiz, considering the 18 (or so) esteemed competitors!

In celebration of Kate Bush's 42nd birthday

Opposite: Editorial from issue 70

and nearly seven years since the release of her most recent album, Doug Alan threw a party at his flat in Winchester, MA, on Sunday, July 30th. The blurb announced that "Sangria will be served and pizza will be ordered. There will be Kit Kats for dessert". Those who went posted their favourite party memories on Love-Hounds: "Doug's decor, ultra-cool keyboard, beautiful Kate posters, fabulous Kate videos in at least 2 corners of the room... our collective, meditative moment of silence to send positive energy to Kate while staring at the flame... I did think the moment was one of beauty and hope Kate did, too. It would have been slightly before midnight in Kateland so hopefully she was peacefully dreaming and we somehow entered her creative subconscious without disturbing her... Sue's beautiful *Under the Ivy* cake..."

Stephen and Doug report: "We had close to 50 people at our bash in Minneapolis. We love Kate and her music and we celebrate every year by listening to her stuff (we make new mixes of our favorite songs using the computer and mixing board. Kate like you've never heard her!). And we party the night away! Our party was the best ever, ringing in her birthday like it was New Year's Eve! Kate and her music made us dance, sing, smile and just have the best times of our lives! Thank you, Kate!"

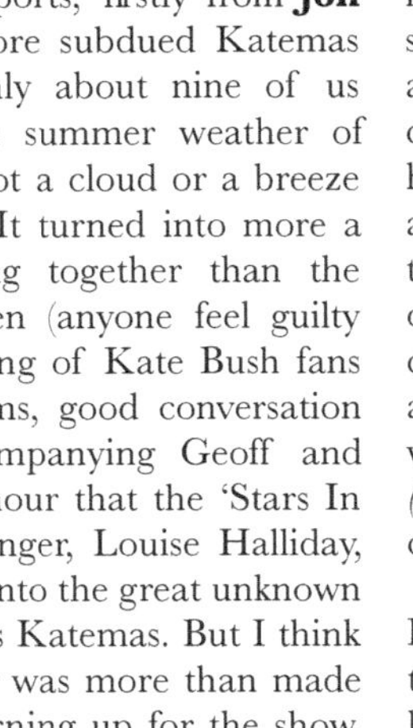

2003: Peter, Paul and Neil

Photo: *HomeGround* Reader

2001

News issue 68: December 2001

Our thanks to all those who went to Glastonbury on Kate's Birthday. Sorry we couldn't be with you this year. However, here are the reports, firstly from **Jon Partridge:** "It was a more subdued Katemas this time round, with only about nine of us braving the fierce British summer weather of around 30 degrees with not a cloud or a breeze to alleviate our suffering. It turned into more a like a few friends getting together than the institution that it has been (anyone feel guilty yet?). But it was a gathering of Kate Bush fans with booze and wine gums, good conversation and lucky heather. Accompanying Geoff and Krys Boswell was the rumour that the 'Stars In Their Eyes' Kate Bush singer, Louise Halliday, would be venturing forth unto the great unknown of the dark and mysterious Katemas. But I think the lack of one performer was more than made up for by Kate herself turning up for the show, she looked a bit knackered after the climb and said she'd just popped by to see who was about. We all chatted for a bit, and I can confidently say that the new album will be out on mumble-mumble-mumble. So don't forget, you heard it here first. As I said, she couldn't stay long and was just off somewhere else.

My favourite comment written on Kate's birthday card was, I think: "You were great on 'Stars In Their Eyes'". Well done to the man from Sweden, Jan-Erik, for making the trek once more, it's a hell of a haul for the few hours spent there. So remember, folks, bring your water and sun lotion for the next get-together. Oh yes. Some of the above is NOT actually true..."

Obviously the bit about the wine gums... and this is from **Krystyna Boswell:** "This year's event took place on the hottest weekend of the year. Down in the town Glastonbury sweltered; people came out to enjoy the sunshine and all the pubs were full – hot weather is thirsty work! The day dawned bright and clear so we were hopeful of a good hot afternoon tempered by a constant soft breeze, and this is exactly what we got. Unfortunately none of the *HomeGround* team could make it this year, and a few other regulars were otherwise engaged, but there was still a good turn out and this made for quite a cosy, intimate little gathering. As Geoff and I reached the summit just after 3pm we immediately recognised a little group just to the right of and behind St. Michael's Tower. This included Jan-Erik, who once again had travelled from Sweden, and Jon. We plonked ourselves down next to the group, and within a few minutes were joined by the Bournemouth gang – Paul 'Pink Mules' Thomas and the boys – whom we had bumped into in the town a little while earlier. We all signed the card I had brought for Kate, me adding a note from Kev Hall (Potty Pam) who is currently in Australia but had promised to find a high place and to be with us in spirit for the afternoon. We spent an enjoyable few hours talking about life, the universe and everything – oh, yes, and Kate too! The Tor was pretty crowded and we were treated to someone playing a digeridoo in the tower. It sounded as though it would burst into the beginning of *The Big Sky (Meteorological Mix)*. Quite appropriate considering the occasion!

Eventually the main crowd departed for the Rifleman's pub while Geoff and I remained on the Tor with the Bournemouth crowd for a while longer, catching up on news. We finally said our goodbyes to Paul and the gang and left Glastonbury around 8.30pm, never having made it to the Rifleman's after all – our apologies to the others, we hope you didn't wait for us. Obviously the annual *HomeGround* gathering isn't quite the same without the *HomeGround* team's presence, but nevertheless everyone who came seemed to have a good time, and we are looking forward to another sunny Tor-top next year."

2003

From Krystyna Boswell: Kate's birthday means just one thing: celebrations! Due to renovation work on the Tor's tower, Krys and Peter had suggested that we should meet closer to the foot of the hill this time, which was quite a relief for those of us who lead a lifestyle more akin to a couch potato than an international athlete. At close to 3pm Geoff, Paul, Kev and I crossed the stile at the foot of Glastonbury Tor and saw before us a big crowd gathered on the hillside. And what was that strange looking contraption pointing at the sky? We approached and began to make out familiar faces and it was good to see a lot of new faces too. Several members of the next generation of Kate fans were also present in the shape of Jake, Emily and Vinnie, and even some of the 'senior' members of the assembly looked hardly old enough to have been more than babes in arms when *Wuthering Heights* hit the charts in 1978 – such is the appeal of Kate's music that people are still discovering her work and greeting it with the same enthusiasm that others did almost three decades ago.

We all signed a birthday card for Kate. Several attendees were meeting here for the first time, and were no doubt as delighted as the rest of us old hands to witness a miniature version of the *Cloudbusting* machine, ingeniously constructed by Neil and Paul with painstaking attention to detail. It really did look just like Kate's machine. Since rain had been forecast for part of the day, I was a bit concerned about the presence of such a machine at our picnic but needn't have worried. Obviously the inventors had made special adaptations with this in mind, and even though the dastardly Moggy had managed to get himself into the operator's seat, the sky remained clear – in fact, it got clearer, and the sun came out to take a look at this fabled machine. All we needed was Donald Sutherland…

As we lounged about eating snacks and sharing news, a brightly dressed figure approached. She was announced by Paul and Neil as fellow Kate fan Gemma, who they had met earlier that day. Gemma was from New York and an accomplished singer herself. She explained how much Kate's music meant to her, and that discovering the beauty of the songs has inspired her to include some of Kate's works in her own set when she gigs. To this end, she treated us to a beautiful and emotional rendition of *This Woman's Work*, her powerful yet sensitive voice holding us all entranced. We were spellbound; to hear this beautiful song sung so well and with such feeling in this special place and on this day of celebration was sheer magic, and Gemma received much applause for her impromptu performance. She had interpreted Kate's song so uniquely and with such joy.

As the afternoon drew on, the lure of a now-traditional cool pint at the Rifleman's became too tempting to resist any longer so we all headed for the pub and, as the weather was so beautiful we opted for the beer garden and supped happily in the sunshine, conversing with friends old and new.

All good things must come to an end, and eventually people began to depart, with much hugging and promises to meet again. Another Kate gathering, looked forward to with so much anticipation, was over again for another year.

If you haven't yet been to a *HomeGround* Kate gathering I would urge you to try to come along to the 1st August 2004 bash if you can. It really is a special day, and a chance to meet some lovely people. Friendships have been forged in this way through the years and it looks like a tradition that will continue for as long as there are fans of Kate's music.

Curiously we never reported on the 2002 and 2004 Glastonbury events in *HomeGround*, and looking back it seems that the news pages in the issues for that period were under great pressure of space from other content.

We recall that both were highly successful, with glorious Summer weather and a good crowd both on the Tor and in the Rifleman's afterwards.

With the success of the internet forum at Sean's News and Information site, the event attracted many new Kate fans, and some old fans that had not been for a few years.

For many attending, rather than being just an afternoon and evening event, they now chose to make a weekend of it, and all over the weekend little knots of fans would meet up in Glastonbury High Street, and in the various eateries and drinkeries the town had to offer.

2003: Gemma sings in front of Neil and Paul's Cloudbuster

Photo: Florence Doorgeest

The Song Book of Kate Bush

The Norwich Assembly Hall Tribute Gig 26th April 2002

News issue 70:
September 2002

Karl Jokat told us ...

The idea of organising the Kate tribute had festered, if that's the right word, for a long time. The story starts back in '78, when I saw Kate for the first time, I think it was on 'Pebble Mill at One'. There was this wonderful creature moving and wailing around the studio floor, I was not that struck on the song, more the way she was singing it. All eyes and arms. I had to buy the album. We played it to death, and never got tired of hearing it.

Sandra O'Neil
Photo: Geoff Boswell

My daughter, Lisa, started piano lessons at around the age of nine, she later began to sing Kate's songs whilst playing. I was pleased that she had a similar range for someone so young. It was great to listen to her performing *Moving* and *Feel It* with such style. Many years later, when Lisa was a member of the Kate Bush Club, I ask her if she would like to go to a club convention, but she declined saying that she was not good enough to play Kate's music live. Since then, I became an artist manager with local bands, and Lisa played guitar and started writing her own material.

I went on to promote her in venues around Norfolk, Cambridge and London. Last year I put on a Nick Drake Tribute night which was a phenomenal success, and at the back of my mind I was thinking of doing a concert of Kate's music.

Lisa Redford
Photo: Geoff Boswell

In '79 my only regret was not seeing Kate tour, and when people tell me about it, well I don't want to be reminded of how good it was, because it will haunt me for not going, or at least trying to get tickets.

So last Christmas at home, just having come out of hospital after an operation, feeling sorry for myself, I emailed Peter Chilvers (Alias Grace) to tell him of the idea of doing a Kate Bush night. By the time I shut down the PC and went downstairs to rest on the sofa, the 'phone rang and it was Peter to say yes, when do we do it.

The main problem about organising anything, is how to get people to come? And how to advertise it so it reaches the right ears. Which brings me to the internet, looking for sites to tell fans what's going on. Thankfully this is the best medium to bring like-minded people together. With help from Krys and Peter promoting the event through *HomeGround*, and by word of mouth and some arm twisting, I was able to get things rolling. Being the amateur 'artistic director' is probably my favourite job.

Lisa is a consummate professional when it comes to performance, although she worried that people, (meaning purists) would pick holes in her style of singing Kate's songs. She is not a fan of cover versions, but this was a bit special to her.

Alias Grace are a delight to work with, Peter Chilvers and Sandra O'Neil just love 'being out there' playing and singing to whoever will listen, very talented artists indeed. And Tim Bowness, well, open a fridge door and he'll start to show off his style and sensitivity. Amanda Harrold (Greenway) emailed me to ask if she could help, or even take part, and being such a fan of Kate, how could I resist? She put her heart and soul into it, and it showed in the remarkable performance of *Wow*.

The only reason for doing this concert was purely selfish, really. This is the nearest I'll get to Kate's music live, especially in a city like Norwich. To be able to honour such an artist was the least I could do, Kate Bush is the finest English female singer-songwriter this country has ever produced. There are few artists of her calibre in the world today to have had hit album sales around the globe. She should be treated as a national treasure.

Krystyna Boswell reviewed the Show

I wasn't sure quite what to expect of this special tribute evening; it's not often (ever?) you see a tribute to Kate so I went along with open mind – and had a thoroughly enjoyable evening.

Around 8pm guests were invited into the main hall, which holds around 200 people. The stage contained a black Steinway baby grand piano, several microphone stands and an electronic keyboard. The small balcony above the stage had been draped with garlands of flowers and in the centre, above a ball of white flowers, was a head and shoulders picture of Kate from around the time of *The Sensual World*.

The MC arrived and explained briefly what the evening would consist of and then it was time to welcome the first performer, Lisa Redford. This was when I received my first surprise of the night. Lisa is a petite blonde lady who makes no attempt to dress or otherwise look like Kate – something I felt was actually a pretty good decision because it enabled the audience to concentrate on the music and not the 'lookalike' aspects a la 'Stars In Their Eyes'. Lisa opened her set with a delicate and soaring rendition of *L'Amour Looks Something Like You* – a difficult choice to begin a set but accomplished with ease – before continuing with *The Empty Bullring*, a delicious and seductive interpretation of *In The Warm Room* and finally a poignant *The Kick Inside*. If she was nervous it didn't show. She was ably accompanied by Peter Chilvers, a very accomplished pianist. The duo were thoroughly professional and a delight both to watch and listen to.

After Lisa and Peter came Samantha Elmhurst who played *Symphony in Blue*, *Them Heavy People* and *Hammer Horror* on the piano accompanied by double bassist Ian Leadbeater. Samantha did not sing, but her piano playing was enjoyable and she gave these dramatic early songs of Kate's just the instrumental treatment they needed, interpreting the drama of *Hammer Horror* particularly well.

The third act was Alias Grace, consisting of Peter Chilvers once again at the piano and vocalist Sandra O'Neill. Sandra came on stage and began with *Wuthering Heights*, a more different version than Kate's original you could not imagine. For me, Sandra possessed the best voice of the night, a rich alto with perfect pitch and a languid, beautifully controlled delivery. She went from *Wuthering Heights* into *My Lagan Love* (unaccompanied) and finished her first set with *Under the Ivy*. Totally delightful. Following Alias Grace came the only male singer of the night, Tim Bowness, who performed a very dreamy *Lord of the Reedy River* and a version of Roy Harper's *Another Day* that brought tears to my eyes. Sandra then joined Tim and together they sang one of the highlights of the evening, *Don't Give Up*, Sandra taking Peter Gabriel's part while Tim sang Kate's. It was a wonderful close to the first half of the evening.

The first act of the second half was Karen

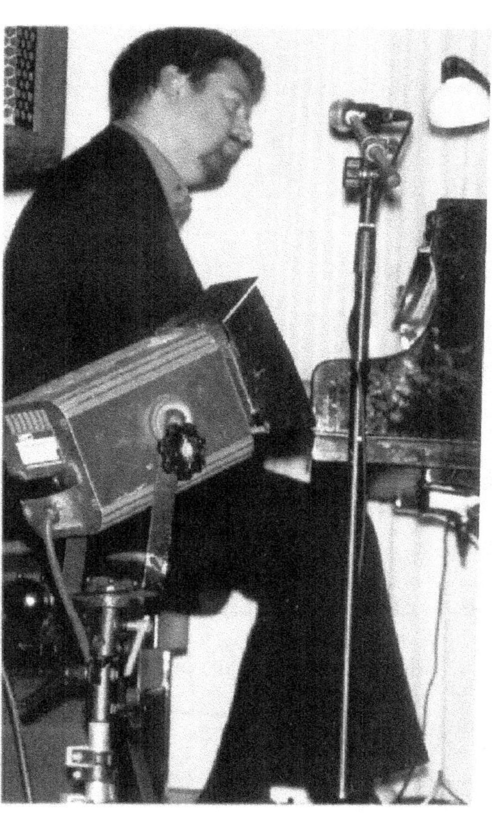

Peter Chilvers Photo: Geoff Boswell

Tim Bowman Photo: Geoff Boswell

Karen Reilly and Jon Baker Photo: Geoff Boswell

Samantha Elmhurst Photo: Geoff Boswell

Reilly who sang *Army Dreamers* accompanied on keyboard by Jon Baker. Karen seemed a little nervous and this may have been why she decided not to continue with *Cloudbusting*, which she was also billed to perform and that I'm sure would have sounded just great especially with Jon's array of keyboard voices.

Next on was Amanda Greenway who as many *HomeGround* readers will know is a long time Kate fan. Amanda took the stage to great applause wearing what Geoff referred to as 'the outfit of the night' – a gorgeous ruched taffeta hobble skirt and lacy black top, and showcased her amazingly powerful voice singing *Wow*, *Breathing*, *Hammer Horror* and *Reaching Out*.

Ensemble Photo: Geoff Boswell

Amanda's energetic and theatrical set was followed once again by Tim and Sandra who performed songs from *The Ninth Wave*. Opening with *And Dream of Sheep* (Sandra's voice suitably lulling and velvety) followed by *Under Ice*, a gorgeous *Hello Earth* and finally *The Morning Fog*. Tim and Sandra's voices complimented each other very well and again Peter Chilvers' piano playing was faultless.

The show closed as it had opened, with Lisa Redford returning to sing songs that spanned Kate's career. Starting with a delicately performed *Oh England My Lionheart* that had me almost holding my breath, she then sang *The Man with the Child in his Eyes* before moving forward a few years to *Never Be Mine*, and holding everyone entranced with the pairing of *This Woman's Work* and *Moments of Pleasure* to close her set and the evening's performance. Applause was huge and the performers were persuaded back onto the stage to take a bow, all grinning away happily, which I think showed just how much they had enjoyed themselves.

There was time afterwards to chat to many of the performers, several of whom said they would happily do a repeat performance if enough folk were interested. Bearing in mind Kate's unique voice and song-writing ability, 'The Songbook of Kate Bush' was an ambitious project to pull off but one that every one of the performers managed beautifully.

The HomeGround stall: Jeanette Payne, Krystyna Boswell and Krys.

Photo: Geoff Boswell

I have my souvenirs: our concert tickets, a nice poster of the event Geoff managed to remove from the board outside the Assembly House, and of course the photographs we took as well as all those wonderful voices and performances.

It was a unique event full of classy performances and I hope it won't be too long before another Kate Bush Tribute event is planned.

Kate Fans: Some Guidance

Compiled by Paul Thomas and Gary Boulton

Issue 72: June 2003

We are proud (we think!) to present to you, from the makers of that cinematic masterpiece, *The Pink Mules*, a definitive guide to being a Kate fan. And they should know!

Do's and Don'ts

So you are a Kate fan and presumably that is why you buy *HomeGround*. Have you ever wondered what guidelines to follow, or indeed, if there are any guidelines to follow in being a dedicated follower of Kate's? Here are some ideas, put together in a manner which should not perhaps be taken too seriously...

Do put up the odd tasteful pic of Kate around your home.

Don't cover your bedroom with posters of Kate so that you come across as nuts, living in the past or just someone who has not quite got their life together. Okay, I am guilty of this one, everyone says my bedroom is like a "teenager's bedroom" but I am not yet cured (I am still in treatment) and I have to confess to being a 'Doctor Who' fan, so there are Daleks all over the place too!

Do attend fan gatherings and meet other fans who may turn out to be lifelong friends or pleasant people to share a pint and chat with.

Don't use the gatherings as an excuse to bore everyone present about the time you met Kate on the astral plane with Stevie Nicks and Emerson Lake and Palmer, and how you all shared a Marks and Spencer's baguette whilst drinking fennel twig tea from a china teapot that used to belong to Shirley Maclaine in a past life.

Do play Kate's music to relax to in the comfort of your home whilst reclining with a loved one and enthusing about the wonderful arrangements and Kate's beautiful voice.

Don't play a cassette tape of obscure Kate demos whilst fumbling around with your boss in a drunken lapse of decency in a mini metro overlooked by the congregation of the local church.

Do wear a tasteful Kate T-shirt; recommended ones include the KT logo or the 1990 Convention tops.

Don't wear shrunken, sweat stained under the arms, old '70s T-shirts with fading motifs that gives you an enormous midriff (as you haven't worn them since Kate last toured), teemed up with baseball cap and waistcoat encrusted with Kate Bush and Dollar badges (most of them home-made from pictures taken from *Jackie*).

Do impress your friends who are not familiar with Kate's music by playing them *Hounds of Love* or *The Dreaming*.

Don't play anyone *Shoedance* or any other misguided remixes that omit the best parts of the song (like the tune!!)

Do attend Conventions and participate with Kate-related activities.

Don't attend Conventions with a two-string banjo and do your rendition of *Get Out of My House* accompanied by Limahl (ex-Kajagoogoo) on spoons and washboard, then realise you are actually at the wrong convention anyway, as you are booed offstage by Cheryl Baker (ex-Bucks Fizz) at a Eurovision Song Contest Convention.

Do write to Kate offering feedback from her music and encouraging her in new projects.

Don't ask Kate for snippets from her laundry basket, the cloak she wore in *Babooshka* (Matthew Kelly gave it away anyway, you're too late..) or ask her to sign a Fred Vermin book (as it's your favourite book on her!)

Do indulge in watching old Kate videos and going "Aaah, wasn't that good" with close friends (sipping Creme De Menthe from a pint glass).

Don't miss work for a week as you are a bedridden mess obsessing over *The Line, the Cross & the Curve* until you get all the dialogue off by heart and have learned the *Rubberband Girl* routine... and then you realise you were actually watching *The Pink Mules* and people will think you are a twisted, sick freak who hangs around with dodgy drag queens in a Bournemouth backstreet bar.

Do speak pleasantly to Kate when you meet her and tell her gently how you admire her art.

Don't meet Kate and scream at her like a demented Tori Amos Tribute Act and tell her that you are her Heathcliff and a psychic told you that you really should be with her.

Do respect Kate's privacy and leave her alone if you see her shopping at Marks and Spencer's with her family

Don't ask Kate to pose for pictures with you, your great aunt Agnes, the pubescent girl at the checkout and your second cousin Wart whilst thrusting your left breast at her to sign and telling her how you loved her in *Titanic* and loved her song *What If* and then realise you got her mixed up with another Kate.

Issue 73: March 2004

Fact or Fiction? A Kate Quiz

Call yourself a Kate fan? Have a go at this and see if you can pick out the one fact in each question (the other two are fabrications). If you know your stuff this should be easy!

1. Kate undertook her one and only tour in 1979. Between costume changes did she: **(a)** Employ the services of '70s superstars The Krankies to entertain the audience with their hilarious, fandabbidozzi comedy routine. **(b)** Keep the audience entertained with the aid of poetry and a magician named Simon Drake. **(c)** You don't care what she did as you were at home cutting out pictures from *The Radio Times* of Jason King for your scrapbook.

2. Kate's vocal effect on *Houdini* came about after she: **(a)** Consumed vast quantities of Aqua Libra and wired up the mike so that she could sing the vocal from the toilet. **(b)** Consumed chocolate to get a mucus effect in her voice (any excuse!) **(c)** You don't have a clue as you haven't heard the track because you were pretending to be Huggy Bear from 'Starsky and Hutch' throughout most of the late '70s and early '80s and did not listen to music (except a bit of punk and Mary Hopkins).

3. Kate's single *There Goes a Tenner* was: **(a)** A massive hit in the UK and most of Europe knocking A Flock Of Seagulls off the number 1 spot. **(b)** Kate's only single in the UK that did not chart **(c)** You only remember the photo on the sleeve because Kate held a torch just like the one you keep under the stairs in case of a power cut, and an attractive pair of black gloves, (like the ones from a distant relative that bitter Christmas of 1979.

Graphic:: Paulina Stuckey

4. Kate was the first British female recording artist to: **(a)** Wear silver sling-backs whilst performing a song and dance routine in the sand on a 'Seaside Special' with Roger De Courcey and Nookie Bear. **(b)** Have an album go straight in at number one in 1980. **(c)** Survive a night stuck in a lift with Leo Sayer and the cast of 'Howards Way'.

5. Kate was offered an acting role in 1979 as: **(a)** Romana in 'Doctor Who', taking over from a woodworm encrusted Mary Tamm. **(b)** A vampire in a horror film. **(c)** A whirling dervish in *Gurdjieff! – The Musical.*

6. At the 1987 BPI awards, Kate was presented with Best Female Singer Award by: **(a)** Hunky, ex-Coronation Street actor, Christopher Quentin. **(b)** A confused Ray Davies (who thought Patti Smith was English) and now shamed 'guest of HM' Jonathan King. **(c)** Nobody – she didn't win anything as wild boy of rock, Rick Astley brought the ceremony to a halt after mooning during a Five Star performance.

7. How many of Kate's albums have made the No. 1 spot in the UK? **(a)** All of them **(b)** Three of them **(c)** You didn't follow the charts as you were bitter about your own record *Cathy I Am Your Heathcliff* failing to dent the top 100 in late '78.

8. The actor playing alongside Kate in the video of *Cloudbusting* is: **(a)** Dead 'Doctor Who' star Jon Pertwee. **(b)** Acclaimed actor Donald Sutherland **(c)** You couldn't care less as you are still bitter about your acting career not taking off having failed embarrassing "casting couch" auditions at the BBC.

9. Kate's connection with Rolf Harris is because: **(a)** She turned down an offer to co-host 'Animal Hospital' with Rolf following an upsetting incident when an Iguana came in on crutches following a tandem pile up on the Salisbury Road. **(b)** Rolf played digeridoo on Kate's track *The Dreaming* in 1982. **(c)** Rolf did a painting of Kate in her bat costume on 'Rolf's Cartoon Time' and said "can you guess what it is yet?" to the excited kids present in the audience.

10. Kate's last album was: **(a)** Pants. **(b)** *The Red Shoes.* **(c)** Released in 1875.

Results: If you answered **(a)** to most questions you don't really know an awful lot about Kate and probably subscribed to *HomeGround* by accident thinking it was a gardening magazine. If you answered **(b)** to most questions, well done, you are a bonafide Kate fan! If you answered mostly **(c)** you are probably Fred Vermorel!

Oh, What a Night!

Paul Thomas was at Duckies on 15th October 2004

And so we arrived in London for the Kate Bush Tribute Night at Duckies in London, excited to be amongst all the colourful people who were there. Of course, we first had to make our way to the bar, through a sea of leg-warmers, Lycra, leotards and faded old T-shirts from the '70s and 80s. Many people had made the effort to dress up for the occasion and even those who hadn't may have had an antique KT badge pinned on a lapel. So 90% of the audience had something Kate-related about their appearance (there was even a lady making badges in case you felt left out).

Of course, we were all sober at this point – but that wasn't to last.

Kev and I ploughed our way through the crowd to the bar. The alcohol consumption was one of the main differences between this Kate fan gathering and the official events of yesteryear. I know, it's not big and not clever (and not necessary to have a good time) but it does loosen up your inhibitions somewhat, and the more drinks me and Kev had, the bolder we became regarding speaking to others (I just hope we didn't embarrass ourselves later in the evening when some details are vague). Everyone seemed really friendly and chilled. Kate's music does seem to attract nice people (generally), so it was great to mingle in such a warm environment where people had no qualms about talking to those they didn't know.

The atmosphere in the main club area was amazing – dry ice, laser lights and images of Kate on the screens flashed up and cascaded down tunnels, very trippy, and complimenting the music. They played lots of Kate and also sprinklings of Pink Floyd, T-Rex, Bowie and Talking Heads. In the corner a man was sculpting a topiary representation of Kate out of a real Bush. Outside the club there was a Kate poetry wall; and a Kate badge-maker, a lady giving Kate makeovers and a hairdresser styling your hair to a Kate era of your choice (there was a lot of crimped hair circa the *Lionheart* period).

Amy Lamé was the hostess, dressed suitably in an outfit along the lines of a Kate Tour of Life costume, with a bit of Wonder Woman thrown in. She introduced the first act: Nathan Evans, who, after asking the audience of about 500 people to "make whale noises" to evoke the 1979 concert atmosphere, gave a puppetry rendition of *Wuthering Heights* using his own head but with a puppet's body, which was hilarious. This was followed by *Babooshka*, complete with mini double bass.

Fake Bush was next, her version of *Breathing* was fairly impressive. She seems to have caught some of the intonations and phrasing of the real Kate and as tribute acts go, she is probably the best I have seen. Kate's voice, however well somebody may have it, is extraordinarily difficult to catch. There was a break around this point (back to the bar...) and I think it was around here that Kev disappeared. After a while I stumbled upon him having a makeover and had transformed into Potty Pam The Palmist, complete with borrowed wig.

Oh, another two or three rounds of drink here. I even gave somebody one of my antique badges from the '70s in exchange for a vodka and coke – how low have I sunk? More chatting to nice people, more laughter and more campery.

Kiki and Herb did a wonderful and very original set. For those who haven't seen them, they have their own unique take on various popular songs, like a cross between a Berlin-esque cabaret and Jane McDonald on crack, and tonight, obviously, they were paying homage to Miss Bush with a set that included their own unique versions of *Running Up That Hill*, *Saxophone Song* and *Moments of Pleasure*, and although very funny and surreal in places, it was almost moving.

Somehow, in the drunken haze that was engulfing me, I ended up on stage as part of the quiz. Although I had the knowledge, being a fan of too many years, I came runner-up to another guy, also called Paul, who treated the audience to a wonderful rendition of *Babooshka* (in costume and all...) which had the crowd whipped up into a frenzy. I drunkenly shuffled around the stage to *Army Dreamers* not really knowing what I was doing there (maybe I just wanted to wear the combat gear and hold that gun) and a lady whose name escapes me did *Wuthering Heights*. But it was Paul who quite rightly won and got to take away the first prize – a vegetarian cookery book. I came away with one leg warmer.

After the quiz I believe some dancers had taken to the stage and I really have to apologise here, as I didn't actually see them, in fact I had been to the bar and I was starting to see everything blurred anyway. But I hear they were good. I had to disappear into the night at this point, but Kev tells me the whole evening ended with most people packed into the theatre area waving their arms and dancing to *Hammer Horror* and *Wuthering Heights*. He said it was amazing. Apparently on the night bus to the Oval, a crowd of Kate fans did a sing-a-long version of *Babooshka*.

All in all it was a great night full of laughter and music, and a real celebration of Kate's music. But I am never ever drinking again.

Issue 75: March 2005

"Paul, Kev & Gary are the makers of *The Pink Mules*, a fine, now iconic, tribute to Kate's *The Line, the Cross & the Curve*.

"There was a sense of nostalgia about catching the train from Bournemouth to London with my mate Kevin. We first met at the Kate Video Café Party in 1986 and since then he has been my companion at every convention or Kate event ever since, along with Gary, my oldest friend and another fan. The nice thing about this funny trio and these Kate events is that we always seem to laugh a lot. Of course it's a bonus if we get to see or meet Kate too, but the main thing is that this is something we have done for years now and there is a strong sense of tradition about it.

"It had been 10 years since the previous major Kate gathering, the 1994 Kate Bush Club /*HomeGround* Convention, and my abiding memory of that event is of us three shrinking in the balcony as Dave Cross introduced *The Pink Mules* and us thinking we'd be lynched...

We weren't.

"So there we were on the train, unfortunately minus our third member, Gary. I felt like I was 19 again, clutching a plastic carrier bag with a camera and a warm sandwich in it, on my way to the Duckies' Tribute To Kate Bush Night at the ICA...

"And this is what happened.."

Paul Thomas.

Changing The Past

John Carder Bush

The cold, dark chambers
of the hidden heart
tremble to the scratches
of anxious recall;
empty morgues, ingesting the cerebral dark,
echo, echo as our searching footsteps fall.

They are here, all those
we have embraced,
loved, hated, intertwined with and repelled,
the gentle fingers and the angry, weeping face,
each encumbrance settled in its separate cell.

Memory pulls out the frozen drawers,
holds the phantoms of
love and chance,
tries to flesh them with
life and flower,
then reconstructs that longed for glance.

Memory is confined to resurrect
the wrenching sob,
the racking sigh.
Takes them out
and cannot correct,
nor make them new,
nor reverse the lie.

Unwrap and turn them
on the poet's lathe:
turn the hater and
shape her to love,
take the lover and
show her faith,
tell the faithful they
were enough.

Fate can be toppled by
the poet's craft,
for in this replay
you will stand and stay
you will not cut,
nor will you laugh,
no longer will you twist
and walk away.

The Kick Inside

Gary Owens

Rosy cheeked in the dawn of day
Pushing out air in long streams
Of mist that must make up this frosty haze
How walls of fog can spur on dreams
Liberated from the stark reality of horizons
Just the lonely cottage and rolling snow
Far away from the harsh looks, a cauldron
That keep their minds from their weight of woe
Like the people who pass just to stare
With the gossip of the county
Bending all ears who can bear
That scandal, each purveyor polishing her bounty
Before passing it on, it is the travellers who alight
Of their closeness, and attention dread
With their mother long into eternal night,
Both over twenty year and neither wed
The storm comes with nightfall
Raging outside and rattling at the door
But the two shield each other from the icy calls
Curled together beneath the quilt they can ignore
All that makes them grieve
With their faces warm and red in fire-light
A vibrant mellow red like Autumn leaves
Fluttering over their skin their eyes bright
With the hope of sweet seclusion to begin.

Charlie Morgan: Drummer

An Interview conducted by Tracy Story

Issue 70: September 2002

"Tracy Story has very kindly given us the interviews he conducted when he was co-founder of the former internet club, Never For Ever, where the interviews originally appeared".

Tracy interviewed Charlie Morgan in June 2001

Graphic: Paulina Stuckey

In June 2001 Tracy Story spoke with Charlie Morgan, who was kind enough to allow Tracy to transcribe some of their conversation.

Charlie Morgan has a very impressive resume. He appeared on *Lionheart, Hounds of Love, The Sensual World* and *The Red Shoes*. He also played on Kate's version of *Rocket Man*, and on most of *The Glory of Gershwin* album. You can see him in the videos for *Rocket Man, Love and Anger, The Man I Love* and various TV performances with Kate.

TS: How did you get into music?
CM: My family has always been musical. My aunt was a professional violinist, and her ex-husband was a cellist. My Mum played cello too, but she went into graphic arts for a living. I got the inevitable piano lessons.
TS: How and when did you start playing drums?
CM: I spent part of my youth in Switzerland, it was there that I befriended a guy that had a drum kit. So, I first picked up a drumstick at the age of fourteen. Upon returning to the UK, an old friend called one day, (whose Dad was a friend of my Aunt and Uncle, and was a top cellist himself) and asked if he knew anyone who played drums. I said "I'll do it!" and the rest is history.
TS: So, was playing with Kate your first big break?
CM: No, but it was one of the first.

TS: How did you get to work with Kate?
CM: I met Kate through Del Palmer, her long time boyfriend. We were in a band called Conkers together, along with some of the other KT Bush band members. Brian Bath, for example. I think I first met Kate when she was 15 or 16. Del and I were signed to Cube Records, on a very dodgy deal too, I might add. Kate used to come to our gigs, about the time she was being signed by EMI. I thought she was absolutely stunning. I was in love with her for a long time. In the purest sense of the meaning, but my sense of honour toward Del prevented me from doing anything about it. Del was my mate, still is even though we have lost touch.

TS: Did you actually play in the KT Bush band?
CM: In one line-up, yes. 1978. They got a South American drummer, I seem to remember, and he had a visa problem. They had a TV show to do in Germany, and I got a panic 'phone call asking if I could do the show. It was a show called 'Bio's Bahnhof'. It was in this hot railway yard. It was a chat show with this guy called Bio. We did *Wuthering Heights* and *Kite*. I was actually a member of a band called Alibi, and recording with Rhett Davies and Muff Winwood at the time. We had a recording deal with Magnet Records, and our album was a minor hit. One of the guys in Alibi went on to write *The Flame* for Cheap Trick. The amazing thing was that, as they called me to ask me to go to Germany, I was listening to *Wuthering Heights* on the radio! After that, I started doing more and more regular stuff with them.
TS: Synchronicity, as Kate probably would have said back then.
CM: Phenomenal actually, I think she said. Her favourite word at the time. Until I once told her that she had said it 22 times in a row on one interview and she was mortified. I felt awful.
TS: Awwwww
CM: While I had a good relationship with 'the family', I didn't hold Kate in total awe, like most people. I treated her like a normal person. I even told her

some of her songs were not up to standard.
TS: I'm sure she respected that though.
CM: I think she did. We remained good friends for a long time. Ever since, in fact in the mid '80s she called me and asked me about Julian Mendelsohn, as we had worked together on Nik Kershaw's albums. She wanted Jules to mix her album *Hounds of Love*. By the way, I always had a great relationship with Stuart Elliott.

TS: I noticed you and Stuart did a lot of tracks together on *Hounds of Love*.
CM: We did. I did a lot of the electronic stuff, and some of the weird off-the-wall things like Bodhran/lambeg, multi-tracking drums on *Jig of Life* etc. Stuart and I were sufficiently 'different' in our approach to warrant both of us being on Kate's albums.
TS: Personally, I think your playing is more assertive.
CM: Thanks, but you know, one of my all time favourite tracks is one that Stuart did. *Hello Earth*.
TS: You mentioned *Jig of Life*. I love that end bit.
CM: It was fun, I did a wild, off-the-wall track of tenor drum with stick clicks at random places, and Kate said "Great! Let's double that!" So we then had to go back and work out what I played and repeat it many times. Kate always stretched me beyond my comfort zone. I loved that. I would never know what she had in store for me when I went to the farm. You know I helped build the original demo studio? The eight track place?
TS: No I didn't!
CM: We did it in the summer of '78. Me, Del, Brian and Paddy.
TS: Did you get on well with Paddy?
CM: I did, he was such a great person... Kate's Mum was the life and soul of our time at the farm. They were all a huge support for Kate, and Jay was responsible for getting her a record deal. Through Dave Gilmour, of course. You know the story about him hearing her for the first time through the living room door?
TS: No, please, indulge me!
CM: She was very shy, so Dave Gilmour had to crouch behind the door while she was writing. She had no idea! Jay had brought him over. Then she signed a five year "nurturing" deal with EMI with a view to developing her talent, and what a talent.

TS: I know you were on the album track *The Big Sky*, but was that also you on the extended mix?
CM: Yes, all that ad lib stuff. We always did more tracks than we needed and always did some "crazy" tracks.
TS: You got to work a lot with Alan Murphy.
CM: Many times, Al was a great player. I worked with Al the week before he died on a Chris de Burgh album. He was wafer thin, looked terrible, I knew he was very ill. I just knew that Al didn't want to be on the session, but he was soldiering on, despite everything, pretending all was normal.

TS: When you were on *The Red Shoes*, I noticed you only did some percussion for *Song of Solomon*. Was that because you were just sort of passing through?
CM: It was in between Elton John tours, and I only did a couple of sessions for Kate. Actually, I think we cut four tracks, but because of the attrition rate on her albums, only *The Song of Solomon* made it. Also, by this time I had somewhat burnt my bridges, and was touring and recording so much with Elton that I lost touch with key people. That is my only regret from doing so much with Elton.
TS: You can tell by the credits that you were missed, as Stuart did almost the entire album.
CM: Kate has always had a team of people she feels comfortable with. She is very shy in many ways.
TS: I think it's one of her appealing traits, that she seems to be a very reserved and shy, but has this massive talent inside, like a caged beast. It's a very interesting contrast. Perhaps beast isn't the right word.
CM: Well, she is a Leo. Although I am very much more Leonine than she is. An astrologer friend of mine said I had the most Leo biased chart she had ever seen! I did see Kate more recently. 1994 actually, we recorded a track for the Larry Adler album - *The Glory of Gershwin*. I was on most of that album. George Martin produced it. I also did the video.

TS: I assume you saw at least one of the shows from the tour.
CM: I saw the Hammersmith Odeon show. Spectacular. Too expensive to tour with for long.
TS: Yes, it was massive for the time, wasn't it?
CM: It was ambitious to an extreme.
TS: What is your fondest memory of working with Kate?
CM: Hmmm. Difficult. Ok, when we were working with Haydn Bendall (engineer) he started calling me Charley Warley and it stuck. So, when *Hounds of Love* first came out, she sent me a promo copy signed "To Dear Charlie Warley, Love Katie Watie". She was such a giggler too. Once she got started, she found it hard to stop.
TS: What album did you most enjoy working on?
CM: That's a tough one. *Hounds of Love* I think. She was really pushing the envelope at that time. She had broken free of the constraints new artists have, regarding being too avant-garde, and was using all kinds of great musicians from all styles of music.
TS: Would you say that Kate is the most challenging artist you have worked with?
CM: Probably.

Charlie Morgan's Kate-ography:

Wow,
Kashka from Baghdad,
Hounds of Love,
The Big Sky,
Cloudbusting,
Waking the Witch,
Jig of Life,
The Sensual World,
Reaching Out,
Deeper Understanding,
Walk Straight Down the Middle,
The Song of Solomon,
Rocket Man,
The Man I Love,

Morgan was also featured on *The Kimiad* Kate's work with Alan Stivell

You can also see Charlie in the videos for *Love and Anger, Rocket Man* and *The Man I Love*, as well as various television performances the most being during the *Hounds of Love* period.

Over the years Charlie has worked with such artists as Clannad, Nik Kershaw, Tracey Ullman, Tina Turner, Gary Moore, Justin Hayward, Tom Robinson, Adventures, Elton John, Billy Joel, Wham!, Duane Eddy, Thin Lizzy, Pete Townshend, Chris de Burgh, Alan Stivell, Beverly Craven, Tasmin Archer, Henry Mancini and The Royal Philharmonic Orchestra, Roger Whittaker, Paul McCartney, Björk, Trisha Yearwood.

For those in the UK, Charlie also co-wrote the theme tune to 'The Bill'!

Songs of Innocence

Anita Butler grows up with Kate

Issue 68:
December 2001

Ooh yeah you're amazing
We think you are really cool

Reviled by some for a kooky weirdness maybe misconstrued as arrogance, Kate Bush hasn't released an album in nearly eight years and is reported to be a virtual recluse. Yet her fan base is as adoring as ever.

Heathcliff it's me Cathy come home,
I'm so cold let me in-a-your window

I first heard these words wafting through the airwaves when I was just four. It was 1978 and the Kate Bush phenomenon was just about kicking in. Her voice hit my tiny eardrums with an intensity unrivalled by any other musical sound I'd heard previously. Too young to appreciate Debbie Harry, Patti Smith, Pat Benatar, Carly Simon or any other female vocalist at the time, as a little girl I liked this accomplished and subtle musician for no other reasons than she looked like one of my fragile china dolls, and did special dancing - the kind I could do. It wasn't long before my younger sister and I were crimping our long hair and whirling around the living room, throwing Terpsichorean shapes with chiffon scarves (Isadora Duncan here we come!) We didn't have things like Spice Girls back then (thank God).

Because of the bizarre phrasing and elongated syllables I could never quite get the lyrics, and neither could anyone else. What was she on about?

At four I'd never heard of *Wuthering Heights* so I hadn't the slightest clue who Heathcliff was – or even if that was what she was saying. Through the verbal fog and broken syntax I could just about make out "it's me, your café…" and then, what? Though it didn't really matter, I just wailed along, joining in with all the "oohs" and hoped for the best.

I didn't see or hear much more of Kate post-*Wuthering Heights* until I was twelve, when my Mum gave my Dad *The Whole Story* on vinyl for Christmas. I made a copy on cassette and insisted it was played at every opportunity, particularly in the car on the way home from school, as we snaked our way down the quilted hills of the South-Eastern Lincolnshire countryside. Often the screeching at the end of *Breathing* would grate so I'd have to fast forward to the beginning of *Wow*, when my sister and I would try to sustain the notes for as long as Kate does. We especially loved the line, "Ooh yeah you're amazing, we think you are really cool", miming the words, pulling stretched expressions as if in slow motion. I look back and delight in the innocent ignorance I had about her reference to "Vaseline".

As I headed deeper into darkest adolescence Kate suited my personality more and more, especially *The Dreaming* – probably her most intense album to date. I loved the challenge of listening to it, like hacking down thorny branches by the light of a full moon in a haunted forest. The voice of the anguished *Suspended in Gaffa* meditations could have been my own: "Suddenly my feet are feet of mud, It all goes slow mo. I don't know why I'm crying. Am I suspended in gaffa?" I saw so much of myself in this song it became my signature tune: "I'm not a Pandora, I'm much more like that girl in the mirror, Between you and me she don't stand a chance of getting anywhere at all".

And lines from *Strange Phenomena* had to be about periods: "Soon it will be the phase of the moon when people tune in. Every girl knows about the punctual blues, but who is to know the power behind our moves?"… No-one else seemed to dig her at school and I was glad of it, desperate not to belong myself. Although never an out-and-out goffick it struck me as strange that Kate seemed so much closer to Gothic in its purest sense than those who tried to be by dying their hair black, hanging out in intimidating, disdainful groups and listening to The Cure. You only had to listen to *Under the Ivy*:

I sit here in the thunder
The green on the grey
I feel it all around me…
But go into the garden
Go under the ivy
Under the leaves
Away from the party

The irony didn't pass me by.

Kate was making music I could grow with. We were evolving together. You could tell her voice had obviously matured and developed when you listened to the new *Wuthering Heights* vocals at the beginning of *The Whole Story*. Gone was the early schoolgirl squeaking and straining. Her voice now had a much earthier, richer, fruitier tone, tinged with a vibration from a different realm – the Music of the Spheres or that range of sound that only dogs can hear. The wailing at the end of *Wuthering Heights* was of a much more erotic, orgasmic nature, writhing, weaving, twisting itself up into a hysterical frenzy, and brought the song to a new adult, x-rated level.

It was as if she had undertaken classical voice training and was singing from somewhere deeper inside her stomach, or just from somewhere deeper inside. Maybe it was because she'd got older, or maybe she'd kept her voice bottled up in a cellar for years, like a vintage wine. Whatever she'd done, she could now sing the theme tune to 'Neighbours' and make you want to cry.

Graphic: Steven Brown

My appreciation grew even more as I started to understand her words more and make my own interpretations. Realising that the imagery on the *Hounds of Love* album sleeve represented Ophelia was a breakthrough that helped me to make allowances for the embarrassing dog impersonations in the *Hounds of Love* track. And once I understood that the narrator of *Breathing* was actually an unborn child (hence the references to "nicotine") I knew that the screeching at the end was justified. Likewise, I also managed to forgive her reference to "My pussy queen" in *Egypt*, when I balanced it with the great ending of that track, which reminded me of malevolent fairies casting hexes in a graveyard… Nevertheless, there were still some lyrics I just couldn't get: "Take your shoes off and throw them in the lake" (*Hounds of Love*)? Someone's a little bit house proud around here! And as for *Kite*…

Her loveable idiosyncrasies reflect paradoxes in us all, her voice evoking at once the strength of a determined woman and the wide-eyed tenderness of a little girl. A simple sigh or "ooh" can turn into multiple sounds, conveying intense, sensual longing, or the scratching of ice into fragmented crystals. Pouting those succulent crimson lips she can achieve an intricacy and intimacy of sound that sees you cowering in a claustrophobic confessional, or envision her freaky madwoman persona screeching in the cloisters, waking up the monks or nuns. If you listen hard enough to the delicate paean *Why Should I Love You?* you can actually see her rose-bud mouth kissing the words out in a delicate 'o' shape, the notes trembling, intimate and sensual, like she's whispering in your ear.

Now I'm a big girl I see Kate as much more complex, gutsy and aggressive than ever. More tough kooky than kooky per se. Lyrics such as, "I see you walking down the street with her, I see your lights going on and off" and, "Don't want your bullshit, just want your sexuality" aren't belted out by some wilting Pre-Raphaelite. As Kate herself has said, "A lot of people assume I'm a big Emily Brontë fan. It goes with this whole preconception they have of me as a Brontë fan, a Tolkein fan, a Pre-Raphaelite lady, which I think is actually a big misconception".

Age has also brought about a deeper understanding, but whether that's because I've grown with Kate or because a kind of transcendental, indirect route to enlightenment has taken place through so much listening, it's hard to say, but it's increasing all the time. It's a cliché but true: each time you listen you hear something different, something subtle. Her voice is getting more velvety and operatic, and you know that even though you might not always be able to understand whatever it is she's singing, she believes in it with utter conviction.

Gone is *Suspended in Gaffa* as a personal signature tune. I now want *Moments of Pleasure* played at my funeral… Unless she provides anything else beforehand, that is. Just release another album, Kate, and put your fans out of our misery.

Moments of Pleasure

HomeGround readers recall their Finest Kate Years – So far!

Issues 68 (December 2001), 70 (September 2002), and 72 June 2003)

John Roger: I first saw Kate in 1978 when the red dress version of *Wuthering Heights* was played on 'Countdown' (the Australian music TV show of the time). I was visiting my grandmother and even though it was an old black and white television set I was captivated. At sixteen I didn't have much of a budget but scraped together to buy my first record (*The Kick Inside*). I played it for the first time at a friend's house and hated it! It was so different to anything I'd ever heard. I played it again when I got home since it cost so much and thought it wasn't so bad. By the fourth playing I was hooked. (I just realised that my family had to endure hearing the same record over and over and over...)

Living in a small town in Australia there wasn't access to much but I bought any Kate records I came across. This continued up until 1989 when I bought a cassette of *The Sensual World*. It was a busy period in my life and when my stereo was stolen didn't replace it. Music became less important since I could only listen to the radio.

Then a friend gave me a CD for Christmas 2000. My reaction was "thank you but I don't have a player" which was when I learned that you can play music CDs using the computer! A little while later I was passing a music shop and wondered if they had *The Kick Inside*, they didn't but had *The Whole Story* so I bought it. The next week I was passing another music store so popped in. They had a copy of *The Whole Story* too and behind it was something I'd never seen or even heard of: a CD entitled *The Red Shoes*! I was astounded to say the least, I don't know how long I stood there with my mouth open. Of course I bought it. And now I have every Kate Bush CD I could find. So the addiction that began in 1978 has resurfaced after being dormant for over ten years and is stronger than ever!

Keith De Weese: My mother was in the Detroit, MI airport sometime in 1992. She believes that as she stood in line to get a drink, she met and spoke with Kate Bush who was standing behind her. She told me, "This woman was standing there and she looked so much like Kate Bush that I jumped out of my skin."

"Yeah, yeah, sure, sure," I answered disbelievingly.

"No, really. And I said, 'I'm sorry, you look so much like Kate Bush,' and the woman, giggling, said, 'Really? And you actually know who Kate Bush is?'

"Yes," my mother said, "My son has been listening to her music for many years and just loves her."

Then my mother told me that a man she recognised – "You know, that handsome guy who's in some of her videos..."

"Del Palmer?"

"Yes! Well, he was there, too! And he was giggling. Then Kate Bush said, 'Well, Kate is my cousin, and we look very much alike.'"

So my flamboyant mother tells me this story, and I don't believe it. But she tells me that she is so certain that it was Kate Bush that just thinking about it makes her want to cry because the woman "was so beautiful and sweet."

Well, I give my mother the benefit of the doubt because I've heard stories that Kate is collaborating with Prince and, who knows, maybe she decided to take a trip to Paisley Park and had a lay over in Detroit en route to Minneapolis. Yeah, yeah, sure, sure - though I know all the while that Kate's collaboration with Prince was all handled via fax and files and mailed tapes, etc. Still, stranger things have happened.

So fast forward to the end of 1993. My mother is seriously ill. I've been listening to *The Red Shoes* until I can sing every song backwards while drinking a glass of water. Then I read in the *Village Voice* that Kate Bush will make a rare, US appearance and sign records at New York's Tower Records in December. I'm delirious. I buy my plane ticket. I book a hotel room. I buy a pair of red dance shoes. I pick out some of my favourite good luck charms. The day of my departure to NYC fast approaches.

But first, I have a bit of good luck. At the time, I'm teaching at a Chicago college. I find out that Kate is granting short interviews to college newspapers. I have absolutely no connection to my college's newspaper, but I weasel an interview nonetheless - nothing too exciting. I have a number of questions prepared. I'm patched through to Kate along with a number of other local interviewers, then a moderator reads my questions to her, and she answers politely. I have no direct contact with Kate at this time, but I consider this a good omen, and, perhaps, the beginning of a brilliant career as a rock journalist.

The next evening, I leave for New York. I arrive in Manhattan late and, after checking into my hotel, go directly to Tower Records to see how long the Kate Bush queue is – it isn't. The store is dark, no-one is there. I'm vexed. Do I stay all night and march into Tower the next day as Kate's Number One Fan in the US, or do I go to my room at the New York Hilton and get a good night sleep? I opt to sleep.

The next morning, bright and early, I set out for Tower. Alas, sleeping too late, I must content myself with marching into Tower as Kate's Number Nineteen Fan in the US. I so envy the eighteen people ahead of me - there's that guy who's written her into his will and posts his dreams about her at LoveHounds. There's that Goth woman who flew all the way from San Francisco and wears a leather jacket (sporting a pic of Kate at her most pre-Raphaelite) and a breast exposing chemise-thing... she's going to ask Kate to sign her chest so she can get a tattoo of her signature. Then there's that other guy who is a self-described Kate Bush encyclopaedia and will not let anyone forget that HE started the first Kate Bush listserv EVER!

Then there's little me, at 8:30 a.m., holding a pair of red dance shoes in my hands, one shoe containing a couple of ancient Roman coins and some amber fossils for good luck, and praying that I won't have to leave the line to go to the bathroom. All day long, waiting, waiting. The line lengthens. Anecdotes, theories, spells, visions, are exchanged by the good folk waiting to see the Devi. By late afternoon, the queue is formidable. Police set up barricades and passers-by ask, "Who's coming? Who's coming? Kate Smith? Bush Tetras? Who? Hmmph, she ain't no Judy Garland!" Indeed, the line to see Kate Bush wends around the block and up and down a couple more blocks, depending upon one's orientation.

By the time Kate arrives, around five o'clock, if I'm not mistaken, a story about a guy who came in all the way from Chicago just to give her a pair of red shoes has gone up and down the line a couple of times. Then pandemonium. A black car, the rush of the crowd, a glimpse of hennaed hair. Once Kate is positioned on her dais inside the store, order resumes and we are ushered in, one at a time, to have our audience with her.

When it's my turn, I turn a corner and see her full on for the first time. Now keep in mind that, even though I didn't stand in line all night, I'm exhausted from anticipation (and I really have to go to the bathroom). When I see her sitting twenty-five feet away from me, I burst out crying. I'm a blithering idiot when I reach her, so much so that I can barely say, "Blithering, blithering, blithering kites" yet alone anything intelligible.

But it doesn't matter. In my three minutes of direct contact with Kate, she pats my trembling hand and says, "Oh, don't weep!" Her face is horrifyingly beautiful, a thousand smiles, dimples, topaz, and ringlets, just unbelievable. So I weep some more. Then I compose myself – the clock is ticking after all – and give her the red shoe with the charms. "Oh, bless you, thank you!" she says. "What is this?"

"Oh, Kate, that's just an ancient Roman coin for good luck."

"That's lovely. Would you like me to sign something?"

"Well, if you would, please sign this other shoe to my mother who is very sick right now."

"Just the one shoe? All right. What's her name?"

"Her name is Kate, too, and she believes that she met you one day last year in an airport in Detroit."

And would you believe it... she pauses, screws up her face as if she's thinking hard on something, then says, "Oh, was that your mother? I hope she feels better soon." And she signs the shoe, "Dear Kate, Hello, again! Love, Kate Bush xx"

The rest is a blur. I was escorted away. I hovered around in a Towers gallery along with I don't know how many other dazed souls until Kate departed. Afterward, I went outside and talked to some of the fans at the end of the line which was still some blocks away from the store. I showed them my mother's one red shoe. I told them about how kind and lovely Kate was. Some of them said, "Oh, you're that guy from Chicago!"

I've never done such a thing in my life, not for a Pope, not for a politician, just for Kate. But now I understand why people do seek audiences with those they admire, people they love. I've never recounted this story in such detail and publicly. I'm crying, again, just telling it. Thankfully, my mother recovered from her illness. The red shoe sits on her nightstand, a testament to a charming moment.

Paul Thomas: In 1992, I bought myself a video camera. I'd always wanted one (in a kind of 'Dawson's Creek' type fantasy) and set about making ridiculous short films. They began as sketches, usually made with a bunch of friends, and sent out to other friends, who received them with a well... "strange delight"! Over the years the sketches became mini-movies, camp spoofs, inspired by French and Saunders, and Victoria Wood (with a dash of Python) and spawning hours of tacky make-up, improvised dialogue and many "in-jokes" among the group of friends who became a kind of gang, a group of like minded people with a similar, often sick, sense of humour.

Over the years these films became a hobby to us all, we even managed to rope in the odd celebrity and got a couple of our films shown on Channel 4 (and *The Pink Mules* shown at the 1994 Convention). It was whilst making these videos that we became aware of the potency and value of humour, of sharing laughs with friends. In many ways, we bonded as a group, whilst making these videos and found them such a tonic for our often turbulent lives (a lot of us went through some bad times in the '90s, and these videos served as a strange kind of therapy).

Among our little gang was Gary Boulton, my best friend for most of my life, and Kevin Hall, whom me and Gary first met at the Video Party in 1986. Towards the end of the '90s, Kevin moved to St. Andrews in Scotland, and by this time, our little group had dwindled down somewhat. We all began doing different things, life had taken us in different directions. But the bond of friendship between us has endured.

I made a "farewell video" for Kevin, and it included messages from friends (and drinking partners!!) edited together with montages of those mad years and the videos that kept us giggling and sane throughout most of the decade. Some of the people on the video had also moved away, got married, had children, or in one sad case, had died. The images on screen were also overlaid by some of the music we had found solace in over the years - Joni Mitchell, The Smiths and Kate... and the song that moved us all, as images of us, from over the years, flashed up on the screen was, of course.. *Moments of Pleasure*. The soaring strings and beautiful melody said it all. There was not a dry eye in the house.

Simon O'Donovan: I first heard *Wuthering Heights* as a seventeen year old and recall the feelings of strange delight on hearing such a unique talent. *The Kick Inside*, *Lionheart* and the Tour of Life (seen at Bristol and Hammersmith) kept me going for the next few years. Kate at her most prolific was a force to be reckoned with. Isn't it weird how the emotional content of Kate's music seems to help us all so much when we are at a low ebb? Those first few years of her music helped me come to terms with being gay and it really did help me through a couple of difficult relationships and partings. Like many fans I grew up with her music and developed alongside it, always with Kate's voice as a backdrop to my life.

Some key memories spring to mind as I write this: the warm glow on hearing the whale-song at the start of *Moving* sung live. I was moved to tears and will never forget that privilege. The happiness at listening to *Oh To Be In Love* over and over again. Oh how I thought I was.

The first time I heard *Breathing* and found it hard to catch my breath. Hearing *Babooshka* on a small radio as I walked around a Cornish coastal path, I knew exactly what to do with the rest of my life. Loving *Suspended in Gaffa* when I first heard it. Moving into my own home as a single man again I too felt as if my feet were feet of mud. Feeling the joy of *Running Up That Hill* and the optimism of renewed love in my life. I could have run up that hill with no problem. But in a few years time I was making deals with God.

Then a few years later, *This Woman's Work* came flooding back into my life. Some tears for all that had passed and all the things I should've said that I never said, but great hope for the future and a chance of real happiness. Finally, *Why Should I Love you?* Just because I do. Sixteen years later! And yes, he has a beautiful smile.

Kate's music is still there and will continue to move me for many years to come. And all this is just to say thanks, Kate. We've never met, we probably never will, yet somehow I feel Kate is a good friend, always there with kind and gentle words and a beautiful melody to calm a troubled soul.

Keith Pitches: I discovered Kate in 1980. I'd visited Amsterdam for a week and had just returned from a two-week motorcycle tour. I was into Hazel O'Connor at the time and played her *Breaking Glass* album every night. Other musical favourites included Bette Midler, Santana, Queen, UFO, and Iron Maiden. I was sitting on my bed, idly changing channels on the TV when my attention was caught by a woman who appeared to be in mid-air. I increased the volume and was immediately glad that I had. After five minutes, I was in another world and was sad that the show had come to an end. The following day saw me in my local record shop, enquiring about records by Kate Bush... "Ah, said the counter-hand wisely, I'll play you a track that wasn't in the show." She played the track *Violin* and I left the shop with a copy of *Never For Ever* under my arm – my very first Kate Bush LP (sigh)! The start of a long and happy association. So Kate replaced Hazel on my turntable.

It was during a visit to my brother that I was first shown a copy of *The Kick Inside*. On returning home, I bought the record. The first track, *Moving*, took my emotions and lifted them with Kate's voice. I was hooked. It wasn't until about a week later that I realised the first and second tracks were separate songs! The magic continued, through the prettiness of *Strange Phenomena*, the erratic scattiness of *Kite*, the sheer beauty of *The Man with the Child in his Eyes* and the staggering climax of *Wuthering Heights*. One great song after another. When the record had ended, the only musical "high" I could compare *The Kick Inside* to was the night I'd seen Jimi Hendrix do *Wild Thing*, at the Royal Albert Hall and smash his guitar up! After that, I went Bush hunting. I bought Paul Kerton's biography and *Lionheart*.

Some years later – 1986-ish, 30th July – Andy Lewis and myself rang the doorbell at East Wickham Farm, bearing an iced cake and were ushered into the 16th (?) Century coolness of the Bush residence, to be followed, five minutes later, by two fans from Australia! There's dedication for you! Well, I don't know at what stage the cake was cut but we were treated to tea and hospitality from both Dr. and Mrs Bush. When Mrs. Bush murmured words to effect of "she can only give you a few moments" as she slipped out of the door, I thought I'd misheard her. She emerged with Kate, smiling, and I nearly fell off the couch!

After that, exactly what was said by whom and when, I don't know, but Kate, prettily turned out in white shorts, top and green cardigan, spoke

Graphic: Paulina Stuckey

with us, briefly touching such subjects as the cake, vegetarianism, *Don't Give Up*, the new compilation release (*The Whole Story*) and various other things. Then, for us, all too soon, and after several goodbyes, Kate had to go. Kate, it was nice meeting you, hope you enjoyed your Birthday!

Ian Townsend: Like most people here, I remember so vividly the first time I heard Kate. It was January 1978 and I was ill and off school for the day. Tony Blackburn was on Radio One in the afternoon and he had a spot where listeners rang up and gave their views on two records and gave points for each. On came *Wuthering Heights* and, yes, my life changed! They hated it and I loved it and that was that. The Kate-fever started. I couldn't wait to buy the single and I remember hearing *Oh To Be In Love* on the radio when the LP came out, so I bought that too (from Boots, on a Saturday! Funny how you recall these things!) *Them Heavy People* had to be the follow-up single, but no! A simple ballad. An excellent, unpredictable choice. Fantastic!

And a welcome antidote to O-Levels.

I started to keep a scrapbook with all Kate's interviews and pictures; I always copied down the charts anyway, but highlighted how well her records were doing; anything about her was just HEAVEN!

Then, not long after the first LP (oh, those halcyon days!), the second LP already. *Hammer Horror* didn't make the top 40 (what's going on?), she sang *Kashka from Baghdad* on 'Ask Aspel' because *In The Warm Room* was too rude (really?) and I squirmed in front of my parents when she sang "lives in sin with another man" but was secretly thrilled! The Tour was announced – Manchester Apollo – and I was there, of course, but she didn't sing *Oh To Be In Love*. Never mind, there was NEW stuff! And in three Acts and dancers and a chance to join the fan club which, of course, I did. It was a great show, really long, but still over too soon. I couldn't wait for the next tour. Little did I know... The Live EP went Top Ten and they had Pan's People 'dancing' to it on 'Top of the Pops' and I was gutted, stormed out of the room and wrote a letter to the BBC! (very Adrian Mole). But they redeemed themselves with the TV show – I've still got an audio cassette of it, really poor quality, nearly worn out playing the new stuff over and over and over, it means the world to me.

1980 – *Never For Ever* – queuing up outside Manchester HMV for ages (I thought there'd only be a few of us there!) to meet Kate and get a signed copy. I gave her a poem and a flower and received a little note from her a few weeks later. Bliss... A wonderful LP cover, a wonderful LP and lots of hit singles. *Breathing* on 'Nationwide', *Delius* on 'Dr Hook', *Babooshka* NOT on 'Top of the Pops' because of some strike, *Army Dreamers*, *December Will Be Magic Again* at last.

1981 was almost worth living through for *Sat In Your Lap*, but it was a bad year for all kinds of reasons. University in 1982 and she released *The Dreaming* just in time for me to take it with me and then nothing else until I'd left with a degree in 1985! Thanks, Kate! But what a comeback! There I was in Edinburgh, performing in the Fringe Festival and it came on the radio – *Running Up That Hill* straight in at number 9. I nearly wept. Surely her second number one? Well, not quite. I started work full-time, and *Cloudbusting* charted. She wouldn't do 'Top of the Pops' because there was a brilliant video. Well, good for her, but maybe not so good for the fans.

Hounds of Love is still my favourite album ever! And Kate was well and truly robbed at The Brits (bloody Annie Lennox anyone?) but hey, they are meaningless anyway. Still, she performed at it, did 'Top of the Pops' even, and seemed to go into overdrive... *The Big Sky*, *Under the Ivy* (swoon!) on 'The Tube', *Don't Give Up*, *Experiment IV*, *The Whole Story*, videos, interviews! We were really spoiled. I loved it. Nothing could live up to those times.

The Sensual World was great, but the charts had changed. Kate's first CD singles when most people were Riding on Time or Jive Bunny-ing, God help us. Erasure's *Wild* came out the same day and I was torn. I was a fan of both but wanted Kate to be number one. Oh well, serves me right for buying them! Ill in hospital with appendicitis and my boyfriend (who is now partner of 12 years) brought me *This Woman's Work* on picture disc 7" (one of the reasons he's still my partner! ha ha). *Love and Anger* was never going to be a big hit, *Reaching Out* may have been, who knows? *Rocket Man* took her back to near the Top 10 (so close, if she'd done 'Wogan' the week before, who knows? Much of being a Kate fan involves "who knows?" have you noticed?)

Another wait. Waiting, waiting. It's in the trees, but it isn't coming... It's going to be *Eat the Music*. Odd title, but OK. No, it's going to be *Rubberband Girl*. Whatever, release something! 'Aspel & Co' baited my breath - a fabulous performance of an exquisite song. A terrible, treacherous *Sunday Times* interview and then MUSIC! *Rubberband Girl*. It was good. *Moments of Pleasure* was better, but not your typical radio song (thank goodness!), *The Red Shoes* single was the chart's highest climber when it went to 21 and disappeared the week after, *And So Is Love* meant 'Top of the Pops'! Fabulous, but not really a single. (I'm as biased as the next man, but I really do not like Eric Clapton, sorry!). In between, the film at Warrington UCI and a load of videos, and *The Man I Love*. They kept us strong though.

And then... silence. As good as. I still love Kate's music, it means so much to me. Sometimes I wish she'd just bring out an album of songs with no big production, simple, piano-led, just to hear her voice again. Sometimes, I am glad she's got the chance to have the breathing space, that she isn't always in the limelight, competing with the here today, gone this afternoon brigade. Most of the time, I just hope she's happy and healthy, as everyone should be, with family and good friends. And occasionally, in a very selfish mode, I hope *The Red Shoes* is not her last recording, because I know there's more, something else, which can only come with her age and experience. And I want that album for me! Not for the music press or the charts or the record company. For me and other fans.

Karen Newcombe: For years people kept trying to get me to listen to this obnoxious Kate Bush chick, you know, the one with that truly annoying line on her new album "Let's exchange the experience". What is that? Some kind of Los Angeles fake hippie motto? Bleah! So there I was carrying about fifty pounds of 'Just Desserts' chocolate fudge cakes on a baker's tray on my shoulder through a swinging door and I heard this voice: "*Hellooooo Earth, hellooo Earth, with just one hand held up high...*" and it was so astonishing and beautiful that I had to stop what I was doing and listen. And I had to ask, "Who is this?" "That obnoxious Kate Bush chick you hate so much." Oh.

Shortly thereafter I went on a quest to find the 7" single of *Under the Ivy*, which led me to months, nay years, of banging around record stores buying up Kate's albums and singles and waiting impatiently for the albums to someday be issued on that new silvery thing, the CD, with no clue at all that anyone else was remotely interested.

Then I stumbled upon the *Kate Bush Complete* book at the public library and through it found *HomeGround*. Which was both exciting and worrisome, because a lot of the letters to *HomeGround* were from kids young enough to be my own progeny – confirming my suspicion that I had lost my mind. Or was possibly turning back into a teenager, a fate that actually would be worse than death.

Then one July morning, as I pondered this bizarre state I found myself sinking into, some total stranger called me up and asked if I wanted to go to a Kate Bush party sixty miles away. They were going to show videos. You gotta be kiddin' me, I thought. I went, expecting to find four 17-year-old guys crowded around an old TV in one of their Dad's rec rooms eating stale potato chips. Or alternately, a murderer who was going to cart me out to the reservoir and try to toss me in. As I was fairly confident I'd float if tossed in the reservoir, and could then simply swim away, I thought it would be safe enough to go. It was.

Brian Parker: I was 12 in 1985, and it all started when I first saw this beautiful lady doing some weird dancing on *Running Up That Hill*. I remember seeing the long hair and the beautiful pouting lips. And the song, I had never heard anything like it before. My friend had bought *Hounds of Love* on tape and I wanted to borrow it off him. However there was a catch – I could only borrow his freshly bought tape only if I went to the chemist and bought some condoms. It was a dare. I bought the condoms and played the tape to death until I saved enough money to buy the album. Kate changed the way I listened to music forever. However, this was not the first time I had heard or saw Kate before. I remember when I was about five watching 'Countdown' and seeing the red dress version of *Wuthering Heights*, and of course I remember the *Babooshka* clip. Going through the back catalogue was a fascinating affair. Nothing prepared me for *The Dreaming* – to this day this album still gives me so much pleasure.

Andy Blake: Apart from hearing *Running Up That Hill* once in 1985, I last heard of Kate in 1981 (*Sat In Your Lap*) and she didn't enter my thoughts any more. I didn't really get into buying music until 1981 (aged 17). After going through heavy metal, progressive rock and German rock I saw the film *Koyaanisqatsi* and got onto Philip Glass then Steve Reich who had released stuff on the ECM label.

16th August 1987. The local record shop had a section just of ECM albums and I did a bit of research on some of the names in my big book of albums. They all seemed to play on one another's albums, but wait, Eberhard Weber has played with... Kate Bush. Kate Bush! That name imprinted itself in my head. *Wuthering Heights*! I loved that track when it came out and now I couldn't even remember how it went. Then there was another track by her in the mid-80s that sounded great compared with the rest of the charts. What was that track? Chart music, top 40, Yuk! I was very anti-commercial music then. If it wasn't at least ten minutes long and featured someone with an unpronounceable name, I wasn't interested.

17th August 1987. Next day I bumped into an old school friend who unbeknown to me was at the art college up the road. We went for a Guinness and a chat and the conversation turned to pop videos (the bar had a video jukebox). I pointed out how every video was in black and white and showed the group looking glum standing around either in a scrapyard or a derelict building. He pointed out that there were some good pop videos and added "Have you seem any of Kate Bush's videos?" as an example. Kate Bush – that name again. I still couldn't remember how *Wuthering Heights* went, and there was that other good track, *The Man with the Child in his Eyes*, and *Wow* with the arm waving, and *Sat In Your Lap*, where had they all gone to? I suddenly had this feeling that I had to hear *Wuthering Heights* again.

18th August 1987. I settled down to type more of my Mathematical thesis (tree theory, lovely) – on a typewriter with sticking keys. After trying to do the same page for the fourth time and failing again I grabbed my beer money and walked into town. After kicking some butt on 'Gauntlet' (a popular arcade game of the time), I wandered into the local music store and what did I see first... a stand with lots of Kate Bush staring at me. *The Whole Story* was in the sale! I grabbed a copy and then, feeling embarrassed (this was commercial pop music after all). I also got a copy of Brian Eno's *Music for Airports* to, ahem, hide it. I handed them over to the cashier who promptly waved *The Whole Story* at his partner saying in an over-loud voice "How much is the Kate Bush?" How I cringed, being exposed as buying a chart topping pop album. Got it home, and played *Wuthering Heights* – my eyes went moist. Back in my head at last. Then track after track of old memories or new excitement. Within a month I had all the albums. Within a year, loads of other stuff. And now, I like chart-topping commercial pop music!

Kate Bush Revisited

by Darrell Farlem

Issue 72: June 2003

Darrell Farlem is now an operatic baritone.

He holds degrees from the Royal Northern College of Music, Brigham Young University, and from the Manhattan School of Music.

Is it the hypnotic rhythm of the music that makes my one year old son sway to the beat in delight, or is he already cognisant of what encompasses well written music? It's okay – I know the answer! But I'm amused that I seriously consider the latter, as this isn't the only Kate Bush song he's decided to respond to, I tell myself. I'm listening to *Be Kind to My Mistakes* from a newly acquired box set. After fourteen years of completing three degrees in music, and in that time absorbing and listening to opera and not much else, I have recently come back to my musical roots, so to speak – Kate!

In 1978 *The Kick Inside* was to me then, only a visual reminder of an artist I really didn't know much about. My mother had bought the album in lieu of re-recording *The Man with the Child in his Eyes* from the radio almost daily! By 1979 however, things had changed. I had turned thirteen and Thursday nights suddenly took on new meaning! I had watched 'Top of The Pops' subconsciously many times before, but now for some reason I was hooked! What had once seemed a mystery to me was now clearly understood! Next, enter my school friend Paul, *Lionheart* singles in hand, and the rest is history. I became somewhat of a teenage fanatic, but felt kindly rewarded by personal letters and visits to East Wickham Farm where I was genuinely made to feel that I was not an intruder but a guest.

I keep asking myself, was that really twenty five years ago? In my own mental estimation *Hounds of Love* was released within the last decade, not two, and *The Red Shoes* a mere four years ago! But in my deluded state I am happy to reminisce and now perhaps re-evaluate the musical genius of her writing. My brother made a comment the other day that surprised me. He recounted listening to a recent radio programme that played a top ten from 1978. Within the countdown were three groups/artists that represented the music my two brothers and I had separately advocated passionately, often ending in stirred arguments. This time, my brother listening nostalgically, had to admit that in hindsight Kate's music stood out above the rest. I had been waiting to hear those words for a long time!

It's interesting that the only music I can recite by memory are operatic arias, using my semi-photographic memory and the incentive to earn a living; a few hymns, through repetition; and Kate Bush songs purely through osmosis! I lived and breathed her music! Back then I probably couldn't have given you an analysis of her music in a scholastic vernacular, and that certainly wouldn't serve my purpose for writing here. My indulgence is not only to reminisce about some of my favourite songs, but to invite you in to my recent re-acquaintance of Kate's classic writing – songs that I had somehow 'missed' before. I apologise in advance for waxing lyrical here and there. Remember we're talking about one incredible artist.

Before my teenage musical senses were awakened I distinctly remember to this day where I was sitting when I first saw and heard Kate sing *Wuthering Heights* on 'Top of the Pops'. That song defined then, as it does today a moment in popular music history where a new and unique genre of song writing had begun. It has such an untouchable quality that it seems as if it has always had an existence but had to wait until Miss Bush came along! One only had to wait for her début album *The Kick Inside* to realise that she would not be a one-hit sensation. Her writing and vocal skills were already being clearly stated. After so many years and now listening again to such tracks as *The Man with the Child in his Eyes*, *The Kick Inside* and *Saxophone Song* I was impressed by the sheer beauty of her voice. Not that this was ever disputed before, for this is what had drawn me to her music in the first place. But as a student of vocal technique and quality I was reminded that this really is a special instrument. That an artist can equal her invincible song writing with her voice is truly remarkable.

Lionheart, although written and produced in a time frame that would put Kate in an asylum today, is one of my favourite albums. The first single, *Hammer Horror* never got the attention it deserved over the airwaves, but what a superbly performed and crafted song. Notice the range of emotions and dynamics in her voice, from her velvet sound portraying the vulnerability of the character to the guttural furore of the chorus. The b-side *Coffee Homeground* would have been a great single too. On revisiting this humourous and cleverly written song I have no doubt in my mind that in music theatre circles this would also be considered a fine cabaret song.

Wow will forever remain for me, the song that became the magnet to Kate. I remember avidly following the chart countdown every week and with excitement hearing that the single had climbed back up the chart again. I recently heard the *Lionheart* promotion interview where Kate justifies why she spent considerable time trying to get the vocals right for this song. She explained "I'm very very pleased with my vocal performance in that, because we did it a few times and although it was all in tune and it was okay, there was just something missing. We went back and did it again and it just happened, and I'm really pleased with that. It was very satisfying". The perfectionist in Kate, clearly illustrated here, is what makes her recorded work so intimate and unique. *In Search of Peter Pan*, *Fullhouse*, and *Oh, England My Lionheart* are other tracks that on rehearing, not only fill me with nostalgia, but reconfirm the genius of her writing and power of her performance.

I arrived onto the scene just weeks after the Tour of Life ended. My only token connection was hearing a friend from church tell me that he'd gone to the concert in Poole – her first dress rehearsal concert. Before her final bow she had peeped through a gap in the curtain and asked him if he'd enjoyed the show, eager to get immediate feedback. Four miles away I was at home watching TV! There's something about being at a live performance that gives an added dimension to a subsequent listening of a track. I saw the live performance of *Wedding List* and I have always listened to that song differently ever since. I can only imagine what I missed in 1979.

Paul and I were now determined that we should not miss any future event related to Kate. I remember the excitement that was difficult to contain on the eve of the first Kate Bush Convention during our final school class of the day – English! It was impossible to concentrate! Thanks to Paul's parents they drove us to London the next morning and dropped us off at the Leicester Square Ballroom.

The rest of the day was a haze – we were too overwhelmed! The only thing I remember clearly, apart from our first glimpse of Kate in the flesh, was hearing demos from the new album, *Never For Ever*. *Babooshka* was one of them. This song not only demonstrates her unique stamp on composition, but also what some would term her most commercial single to date. It's difficult to listen to this song without a flood of memories. One includes a Radio 1 'Road Show' where I obnoxiously tried to get Simon Bates to notice my frantic flapping of a Kate Bush sign during his introduction for *Babooshka*! I was successful, but only after a lot of hard work! *Breathing*, the first single from the album is my favourite song of Kate's. After my fourteen year hiatus I am drawn to it even more, but I still can't define why I love it so much. Maybe it's because it epitomises everything about her songs – the distinct voice and her innate ability to write music and words that transcend most popular compositions. The heart-wrenching emotion of the song driven by a now timeless subject matter envelops the listener.

Paul and I would telephone EMI, alternating daily, to ask them what date *Never For Ever* was to be released. There were days that I'm sure they received more than one 'phone call, two eager adolescents wanting to make sure had they really got the date right! I think what kept us so persistent was that in April of 1980 we were told that June was the magic month, only to find out later that September was to be the projected date. This became a long wait for a teen, and I'm sure more of a long term sentence for the EMI spokesman!

Today I'm rediscovering great gems from that album. Ever wise beyond her years I was struck then, and even more so now, at how profound her writing was. At the age of fourteen *All We Ever Look For* was for me a wonderful chant that ironically I knew little about, but today becomes an anthem that resonates deep within. Not many at the age that Kate was then could write about life's lessons with so much understanding. *Blow Away* is another anthem, this time to celebrate a musician's post mortal existence. The concept is unique, yet at the same time she manages to elevate the listener to the possibilities of such a quest. As Kate sings "Bolan and Moony are heading the show tonight" suddenly you're a believer and are transported there. This is such great writing. Another song that captivated me recently was *Delius*. A minimalist composition like this with only four short lines of text has more enchanting textures in the music than many other contemporary songs of the day.

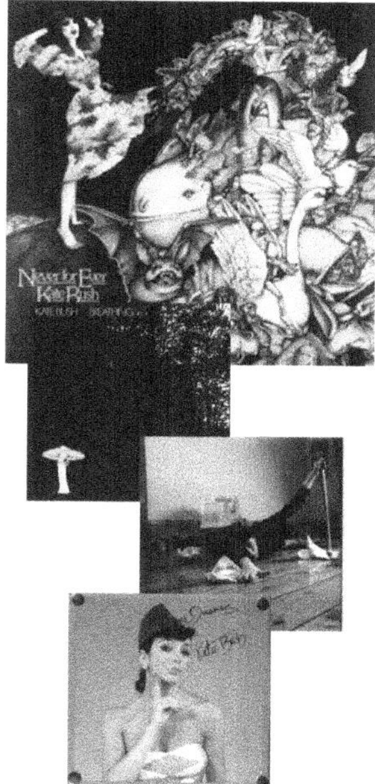

The two year wait for *The Dreaming* was almost too much to bear, but we were consoled by intermittent and mis-communicated rumours that new songs like 'Harem in the U.S.' were on the album. The mind boggled, but we were later assured that Kate was more concerned about the harm that is in us (*Leave It Open*)! My first opportunity of meeting Kate would be at a promotion signing of the album. With *The Dreaming* and a French *Breathing* in hand I lined up outside London's Virgin Megastore in Oxford Street. Once inside and eventually face to face I'm sure I probably said something like "Hello... I love you... hi... hello... I love you..."! And it gets worse!.. I remember jumping up to peck her on the cheek as she came out from the back of the store, and then grabbing on to her hand through the passenger window as she sped off in the car. Oh Kate, I'm sorry!

My wife Jenny who is from North Carolina and a few years younger than me is always amused by these stories, but fortunately she is becoming a fan herself. This still doesn't deter me from utilising moments of trivia to talk about her music. A few weeks ago we were driving through the mountains of Colorado and unexpectedly came across the Stanley Hotel that was featured in the movie *The Shining*. I couldn't stop myself from babbling! *Get Out of My House* is a five minute opera! The force behind the drama is not only carried by the words and instrumentation, but listen to that vocal display. If ever there was a voice that could produce the widest spectrum of vocal dynamics in one song, Kate has it. I can count at least five different vocal colours in this song. Oh, to be a fly on the wall of Kate's recording studio! Can you imagine visiting a session from *Get Out of My House*?... There is

something very enigmatic about the theatrical Kate in the recording studio and on stage against the demure and softly spoken Kate that we see and hear in interviews. To me the true sign of a genuine artist.

On revisiting the other tracks from *The Dreaming*, which in my estimation is a masterpiece, I was struck once again by the genius of her writing. I had always loved this album, but now I find myself absorbing it with a greater capacity than I did before. Some of the blame goes to my then modest record player that was appropriately encouraged by Kate's etching to "PLAY IT LOUD"! Now with my improved stereo system and the developed attuning of my musical ears I hear so much more. The instrumentation, percussion, sound effects and backing vocals are replete with carefully crafted layers that are able to portray the theme of a song in such an immediate way. One example is the title track. One cannot listen to this song as just background accompaniment. You are drawn in and transported to places you've never seen before, and feel distinct emotions, in spite of the awesome message of the song. Let me briefly mention other great tracks from the album. *All the Love* I can listen to over and over again, preferably in a darkened room. *Houdini*, an intricate composition, uses Kate's milk-drenched vocal cords one moment and then exquisite writing for chamber orchestra the next. Who else could do that to such great effect? *Pull Out the Pin*, as poignant a theme as ever, captures the irony of war in such a compelling rendition. I don't know why, but I had somehow 'missed' this song before. And the list goes on.

For the sake of satiation I've intentionally left out discussing non-album singles and B-sides, except for one. My all-time favourite B-side is *Under The Ivy*. The simple yet evocative song still to this day conjures up an atmosphere that's ineffable. I don't think any of us will ever tire of listening to the unaffected Kate and piano duo. For me there is also a sentimental value to this track. On a totally unexpected one on one meeting with Kate I was given a copy of *Running Up That Hill* before its release. The single was already given some airplay by this point, but when I got home I spun that record's B-side to exhaustion believing I was the only one on the planet who was listening to it – ignorant bliss! Yes, I had now met Kate in circumstances I had only dreamed about, and not only that but I had learned first-hand from Dr. Bush (who kindly gave me a lift back to the train station in his car), that the family had been to my home-town of Bournemouth on holidays to the same local beach our family frequented! This was all too much to take in.

I have lived in America now for the last five years. On our travels I often find myself flipping through the 'B' section in record stores to check that she's not missing! Fortunately Miss Bush is represented well. The *Hounds of Love* album was the pivotal role in presenting Kate to this wider audience. It conveniently combined Kate's enigmatic writing with a somewhat commercial flavour, something I believe was unintentional. That she writes without compromise is rare and admired. The music charts today almost nullify the calibre of such writing. The first single *Running Up That Hill* introduced my wife to Kate's music. This song is truly a monumental anthem to her as performer and songwriter. Show me a singer/songwriter in the charts that has come close to writing anything as sophisticated as this in the last few years! *Cloudbusting*, as superior as the former, is ranked high in my desert island discs – a masterpiece that was never to be disputed by my brother over those argumentative years! I can still listen to this song repeatedly! Some songs were never far away from my mind throughout the years – *The Big Sky* being one of them! I frequently sang this song to myself when looking up at clouds! Just the other day John Chandler, our one year old, and I were watching a children's programme where the quote "that cloud looks like..." popped up. And there it went again!

Tempting as it is to discuss every song on the album, I remind myself of the main purpose of writing this article. But to leave without touching on *The Ninth Wave* would be an injustice. This conceptual work of art is so vividly written that one's imagination instantly responds, and in fact I'm content that a film was never made to accompany it. I defy any listener, partial to Kate's music or not, to resist being conveyed to a different world when listening to such tracks as *And Dream of Sheep* and *Hello Earth*. Jenny and I enjoyed listening to this unique song cycle the other day and it became quite a conversation piece.

By 1989 one thing I had learned was patience! *The Sensual World* was worth the wait. Now my only frustration about intervals between albums (including the shortest one between *The Kick Inside* and *Lionheart*), is knowing that there are a myriad of songs out there that we will never get to hear. The cutting floor I have no doubt is constantly covered! Kate's sixth studio album, carefully crafted as always, has some of the most profound songs on it. Part of its charm is the invitation we've been given, to listen in while Kate reflects on some of life's thought-provoking and valuable lessons. If you're like me, it's not uncommon when listening to her songs to imagine its live counterpart (more about that below!). *Love and Anger* is one of those – listen to the band and Kate's vocals on this track and tell me this wouldn't be a memorable performance! The superior writing of both *The Fog* and *Reaching Out* are closely familial in theme, and yet very different in style. What intrigues me about these songs are the use of orchestral string arrangements, which translate a solemnity to the theme in a way that is unmatched by many songwriters. I listen to them very differently today. One of the songs from the album that I have been drawn to of late, is *Never Be Mine.* Again, it's her affinity with combining words and vocal colour with music and its carefully blended instrumentation that makes it so immediate. The Uilleann pipes are so poignantly realised here. Another track from the album that I have thankfully rediscovered is *This Woman's Work.* Hopefully without sounding too biased I have recently come to the conclusion that it is one of the most perfect songs ever written.

By the time *The Red Shoes* came out I was steeped in my studies and opera was mostly all that I listened to. I can almost hear the faithful Kate fans murmuring in dismay, but let it be known that once a Kate fan always a Kate fan. I still bought the album the day it was released and I had always kept a keen eye on what she was doing, thanks to the original stalwart – Paul! Even in my hiatus I still prided myself in being able to spot Kate's name instantly from a newspaper column or a Record Collector's 'For Sale' or 'wanted' list. Also deleting downloads of falsely proclaimed Kate collaborations on the internet is now becoming a regular and amusing pastime – I'd recognise that voice anywhere! So to *The Red Shoes...* the title track is the opening number for Kate's next tour! Just imagine with me for a minute – the solo mandola begins strumming for a few bars, and then as Kate sings, a silhouetted dancer is seen. You hear the words "Oh it's gonna be the way you always thought it would be, but it's gonna be no illusion, Oh it's gonna be the way you always dreamt about it, but it's gonna be really happenin' to ya..."

While we come back to our senses let me just conclude with a few thoughts about this brilliant album. In contrast to *The Sensual World* this album seems a little lighter in mood. Its dichotomy of profound meaning set to upbeat musical motifs in such songs as *Constellation of the Heart* and *Rubberband Girl* are superbly realised. I have always championed *Constellation of the Heart* and wondered why it wasn't a single. A 'new find' on the album is *Why Should I Love You?.* I love the mixture of whimsical and profound sentiments in the text and music, but it's Kate's magical voice that we hear in each verse that makes it for me. Another worthy single! Of course it wouldn't be right here if I didn't mention *Moments of Pleasure.* In this timeless classic I am reminded that a New York City Winter in a twentieth floor apartment isn't all that bad! She has a way of making you believe. This is song-writing of the highest order, and we are rest-assured that Kate and piano are always going to be a happy, life-long partnership. This has been test-proofed over and over again, now dating back some thirty years.

This brings us full circle. Since starting this article I have seen my son respond to many more Kate songs including those that have no uniform rhythm to which he normally responds to. I conclude that I have either brainwashed him successfully or that there is something about her music and voice that is aesthetically gratifying! I wait with great anticipation for the new album, but in the meantime there is plenty for us to listen to and reacquaint ourselves with, and until then I will wait... patiently...

Graphic opposite: Paulina Stuckey

Just One Kate Song

HomeGround readers explain why it is special

Issues 68 (December 2001) and 70 (September 2002)

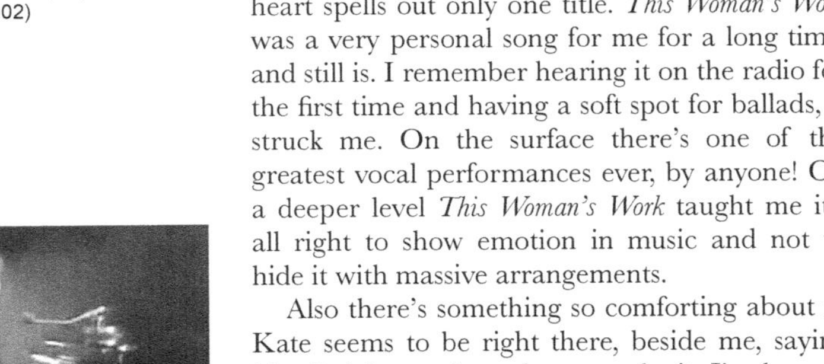

Arto Polvikoski: My very Special Song by Kate? Mmm... My mind says something else but heart spells out only one title. *This Woman's Work* was a very personal song for me for a long time, and still is. I remember hearing it on the radio for the first time and having a soft spot for ballads, it struck me. On the surface there's one of the greatest vocal performances ever, by anyone! On a deeper level *This Woman's Work* taught me it's all right to show emotion in music and not to hide it with massive arrangements.

Also there's something so comforting about it. Kate seems to be right there, beside me, saying it's all right, you're going to make it, I'm here to help you through. I remember many times when *This Woman's Work* was the only doctor, the priest, the healer. And I'm still here!

Being a sort of musician myself at one point I thought I have to give something back. I couldn't get the published notes, but by just listening to it I managed to learn the song on the piano. The vocal task was even more frightening and obviously I had to sing it a bit lower. Still, it was a major achievement for me and I felt so proud of myself. That really gave me the confidence to concentrate on making my own music.

Dave: God, Krys, pick an easy subject won't you! Well my first impulse was *Moments of Pleasure* but everyone will choose that song, it's too obvious, same for *Wuthering Heights*, so it's *The Red Shoes*... or maybe *Moments of Pleasure*... no *The Red Shoes* - that line about "feet start kissing the ground"... No sorry, it's calling to me, so it's got to be *Moments of Pleasure*.

The first hint of the song I ever had was Steve Davis at EMI calling me to say he had been down to Abbey Road to see Kate, where she had been working on a beautiful string arrangement. The next thing was Steve again, after Kate had been in to play the album to a group of top execs and there was this one ballad that was absolutely outstanding called *Moments of Pleasure*.

Like everyone else I first heard the song when she performed it on the Michael Aspel TV show, sitting there in the audience with my dear friends Peter and Krys. I felt a huge rush of emotion, the sheer beauty of the melody, Kate's soaring, emotional vocals and, of course, the deeply personal lyrics, especially the reference to Kate's Mum, someone who will always have a special place in the *HomeGround* team's collective heart.

As the years have passed, my admiration for the song has grown even stronger. I too have lost people in my life and I have found comfort in the lyrics. I have my own little "moments", special times I remember - the moment, aged seven, I realised my Mum was fantastic, and not just a food machine... Dressing up for Halloween with my flat mate Steve, who died on the *Marchioness*... laughing till I cried in the DJ box at Trade with my dear friend Tony DeVit, which was the last time I saw him before he died. And my lovely Nan, so many happy times, even now sometimes I can feel her presence... and, of course, that heartbreaking melody.

Seán: "*The sun shines for you he said the day we were lying among the rhododendrons on Howth head in the grey tweed suit and his straw hat the day I got him to propose to me yes first I gave him the bit of seedcake out of my mouth.*" Thus *Ulysses*, James Joyce. I don't get up to Howth Head anything near as much as I'd like to. It's only three miles up the road but in the hustle and bustle of Dublin life you sometimes forget the peaceful, striking, head-clearing experience it is to take a walk around its headland. Although Howth Head is home to many suburban homes (and most famously its fishing harbour and surrounding village), from up on the summit the Irish Sea stretches endlessly to where on a clear day the mountains of Wales can be seen on the far, far horizon. That's what they say anyway.

I never expected to hear Kate Bush singing about Howth Head. In 1989 I mulled over *The Sensual World* each time I heard it on the radio and became more and more in awe of it. This was before I knew anything of its origins, its use of the Macedonian air *Antice*, and the Molly Bloom soliloquy from Joyce's *Ulysses*, which I was only vaguely familiar with at the time through Siobhán McKenna's recording cf it. Rather, it intrigued me because it made me happy to be alive.

Every time I heard it I felt happier. Only having a vague muddle of borrowed philosophies at the time to mould my world-view meant that such a joyous exaltation of just simply being alive was a musical wake-up call I'll never forget. That the song is a masterpiece in its composition, origin, history and performance, I will never doubt. But maybe even more than that it's the simplicity of the message contained in a song that was such "hard work" for Kate to make that is its triumph.

For almost four minutes, Kate lifts the veil of abstract human structures which rule our lives, cripple us even, and shows us the truth and beauty of life. Oh, and the rhododendrons are still there too...

Krystyna Boswell: Hard though it is to pick a favourite song composed by Kate, *Moments of Pleasure* holds a special place in my heart. A beautiful and moving song which, though obviously very personal to Kate, evokes in listeners their own bitter-sweet memories. Whenever I hear it, I see in my mind's eye Kate seated at the piano as she performed the song on the Michael Aspel show a few years back.

It's a song that brings me memories both happy and sad. Of friends I value and love: friends still with me and friends who belong to the past. Of the dear departed ones – both human and animal – who touched my life in so many ways. Of fun times with friends. Of the innocence of my younger days. Of the warmth of knowing those special people who will always mean so much to me, and will continue to travel with me on my journey through life. Of the lost opportunities that may never present themselves again, but also of the wonderfully exciting and exhilarating times I have enjoyed, and those that still lie ahead for me. Of the magic of a Summer sunrise within the inner circle of Stonehenge; of the joy of finding my sisters and brothers of the Grove as I travel along my Druidic path.

So much to be grateful for; very few experiences to regret, others to leave thankfully behind me as lessons well learned. Everything we are, everything we do, everything that happens to us: it's all part of the tapestry that we weave throughout a life and which, in our Winter days, we will look back on as we recall our own Moments of Pleasure. Thank you, Kate, for such a beautiful song.

Jeanette Payne: I was about eight at the time. I had just come home from school and was watching TV and switched onto a programme called 'Running Scared'.

The programme was all about racism, but what drew me in was not the content, but the theme tune. A woman's voice so inexplicably moving and powerful; the music so atmospheric I could feel it in my guts. As a child, I couldn't really name what happened the first time I heard that song, but I knew it made me shudder, and feel something I had never felt before. The series finished, but that song, that voice, remained inside me as a special feeling that would come and visit me in quiet moments.

Three years passed before I heard that song again. My brother had bought an album, *Now That's What I Call Music 6.* He was playing it in his room when the song came; it was like my special memory had suddenly found a voice again. I took the tape and went to my room. I played that song again and again until, all alone, I experienced my first orgasm. I didn't even know what was happening – all I knew was that I had been taken to an incredible, magical place, a place to which I could return whenever I played that song. That song was *Running Up That Hill.*

It was another few years before I found *The Whole Story* video. I still didn't know anything about Kate, apart from my Mum and Granny jokingly saying that I looked like her when my long brown hair was in a mess... suddenly there she was on the screen, and everything fell into place. The video for *Running Up That Hill* remains one of my favourites; a simple yet tremendously powerful image of passion and love.

Gradually, I bought all of Kate's albums and they have become the soundtrack of my life, my loves, relationships, grief, sorrow and passion. The week *The Red Shoes* was released, my beloved Granny passed away. Her name was Lillie, and it was as though the song *Lily* was a gift, speaking directly to my grieving, inconsolable heart. If all this sounds too passionate, too much, I think that Kate's music deserves nothing less. She has moved me more than I can express in just a few paragraphs. I will always be grateful to her.

Amanda Harrold: It was the late summer of 1989 in Great Yarmouth and I was on an enforced sabbatical between art college and university due to ill health. Not very promising. Now, I don't know if you are familiar with Great Yarmouth but, with no disrespect to my home town, it is not the most inspiring of places. I was feeling very stuck and frustrated. My life had stagnated and I couldn't imagine how it could improve in the foreseeable future.

However, every cloud etc, etc... I was soon to be twenty one and I had just heard that a new Kate Bush album was on the way at last (believe me, four years of waiting was a lifetime back then) – oh, and I'd just discovered a fab little independent record shop in town.

I began to frequent this shop as they stocked a small selection of Kate photos, there were a few Kate picture discs hanging from the ceiling and there were one or two promo items left over from *Hounds of Love* still on display. Each time I returned more determined to pluck up the courage to ask if any of these items were for sale. But all I ever managed was a smile at the guy who worked there.

Until one day in early September, I just popped in on the off chance and Mr Record Shop Guy rushed up to me, very excited, and said "I've got something to show you!" As we'd only been on casual smiling terms until now, I was a touch bewildered but I went with it.

To say that what happened next was a pivotal point in my life isn't the overstatement that it sounds. The Record Shop Guy (let's call him Bradley cos that's his name) proceeded to play me a new Kate Bush video – just a small clip, probably no more than a minute – but that was enough. It was *The Sensual World* and I was completely transported.

Visually, it was the most Kate Bushy video imaginable. It was full of the images that so inspired me – medieval, elemental, magic, Autumnal – and Kate looked so beautiful, just like one of my costume drawings. And that was just the visuals. The music sucked me into a vortex and spun me around. It was just like musical velvet with a voice as warm and sexy as chocolate. And such a beautifully subtle arrangement like Summer bees making honey in my brain.

"Again, again!" well, I think we watched it a few times more. Certainly not more than twenty. I was almost shaking from excitement. Suddenly the world seemed a more optimistic place. Also, it turned out that Bradley's nineteenth birthday was on 3rd October, the day before my twenty first and he invited me along to his party. Apparently he'd had me down as a Kate fan months before and was just dying to show me the video he'd seen at an EMI reps launch.

To cut a very long story short, nearly twelve years later, Bradley Brady is still my best friend in the whole world. We've gone through an awful lot together and it always makes our friendship stronger. We don't see nearly enough of each other now but last September, Bradley did me the great honour of being "Patron of Honour" at my wedding and we managed to sneak in a dance to *The Sensual World.*

Every time I hear that glorious song it fills me full of hope and pure joy and reminds me of the time I met my best mate, Bradley; and any similarities between my wedding dress and *The Sensual World* dress are purely coincidental – Honest!

Julie Jameson: Every time I listen to *The Ninth Wave* I know *Hello Earth* will make me cry. That first "Hello Earth" always gets to me. It so perfectly expresses the fragility of the human race, how small we are in this vast universe. And how we have the power to create life or destroy it.

I remember watching a television programme about the Moon landings and one of the astronauts said that when he was standing on the Moon he could blot out the earth by holding up his thumb. He said how strange it was to be standing on a cold, lifeless planet and to look back upon Earth with all its colour, beauty and life and realise exactly what we have and what we could so easily lose.

In *Hello Earth* the theme of vulnerability continues as the astronaut (or God?) looks down unable to help those struggling with the storm at sea. The choir and whale song at the end of the song offers resolve, calms the storm, reassuring us that everything will be all right, there is always love and hope, our vital lifeline from the storms of life.

As with all of Kate's work *Hello Earth* holds such depth of emotion and for me will always have a special importance and an impact that never diminishes, however many times I hear it.

Jon Partridge: When it comes right down to it, there has only been one Kate song that has really made a huge impact on me. Naturally I feel quite strongly for several other songs: from the first time I heard *Wuthering Heights* at thirteen in English classes at school to songs like *Moments of Pleasure* that I can identify with from certain points in my life. But I think that I would have to say that *This Woman's Work* has the greatest amount of... I can't think of a better way to describe this other than *emotional resonance.* In trying to put into words the reasons, or at least my feelings, for this song, I have once again run into the problem of attempting to name something that cannot actually be put into words. This is a problem that I have with most of the Kate songs I like or love. In some ways it's like trying to describe exactly what sort of music it is or how her voice sounds, as there don't seem to be the right words, and those I do use never seem adequate.

Of all the things we should've said but we never said.
All the things that we should've done but we never did.
All the things that you needed from me,
All the things that you wanted for me.
All the things I should've given but I didn't.
Oh darling make it go away,
just make it go away now...

It is this particular moment in the song that carries the most emotional weight for me. The rising backing voice of Kate's and the passion going into the piano added to the lyrics themselves are enough to crack any of the controls on myself that I like to think I have. But at the same time that I feel myself becoming separated, I gain a sense of imminent peace... It feels like this song is saying: "Let it all out, but don't worry about what's on the other side, because the peace you desperately desire will be yours".

I think it is the two 'voices' within this piece that give this effect. On the one hand there is the consoling "I know you have a little life in you yet, I know you have a lot of strength left", which is hope from within yourself that is there to stop the "Just make it go away" from falling into despair. It is this feeling I get that makes *This Woman's Work* so powerful for me.

There is no other song that I can think of that can make me cry, and no other that I can identify with so well. Not only do I find this song representing hope for healing within myself, but I also feel that it helps me to understand or cope with another's pain. It then reverses a lot of the images and voices from my perspective and gives me the strength to help them as much as I can. I guess if there's one thing a person in pain knows, it's how to help another in a similar situation. That again is the sense of this song: "I've been there, let me help". It says I know you can believe in yourself more than any other song out there. So for these reasons and feelings, *This Woman's Work* is truly my one song.

My Lady Whitesleeves

John Carder Bush

Whitesleeves, you are my delight
When cautious cars tread with timid tyres
And, like the prows of drifting boats,
Blindly nudge the sparkling night.
Peace, the now forlorn, forgotten Grace,
Coats the kerbs with her crystal locks
Until she has bound the snarling suburbs
And all their buzzing, bumping, bullying pace.
Silent celebrant of the death of noise,
Her sacramental robes ruffle, drop, and muffle
The arrogant din of passing engines, cutting
The controlled explosions of adult toys
Down to the purring of a basket of kittens.
Then, with a flurry, she banishes them
To stale, pale loaves dumped in side-streets
As it snows and snows and thickens –
Oh, my Lady Whitesleeves,
Come, and come, and come again.

Gravity's Release

Rachel Lisi

Look down upon the king of cities.
Angels tickle trust daring a
Jump into the chaotic brew.
See if they catch you.
Down...
down... down...
Gravity's increase.

Gaze with haze into the clouds.
Take heed of the angels' sing song laugh.
Faith has been frayed,
Keeping the holy at bay.
Away...
away... away...
Gravity's decease.

Wide eyed wild world,
Still waiting for the exhale.
Dancing with the lawless divine
Spinning on the universal spine.
Faster...
faster... faster..
gravity's release.

Brian Kennedy

... ...interviewed by Seán

Issue 64: November 1999

"Belfast born Brian Kennedy is one of the most successful Irish singer-songwriters working today.

"At the time of this interview his last album was *A Better Man* (1996) which shot straight to the top of the Irish charts and spawned three hit singles, garnering huge airplay.

"He was on the brink of releasing *Now That I Know What I Want*, which has since also hit no.1. Brian is well known for performing with Van Morrison on many occasions, both live and in the studio, and in 1998 touring with Van, Bob Dylan and Joni Mitchell in the USA".

Photo: courtesy Jane Sagr and Lynn Hughes

Seán Twomey met up with Brian Kennedy at Belgo's restaurant in Dublin's Temple Bar area where he was there that day to perform a live set for a John Rocha fashion show in aid of the Dublin AIDS Alliance. This is an edited version of what he had to say about what Kate's music meant to him. A fuller version of the interview can be found on Seán's News and Information website.

Seán started by asking him about whether, as some Kate Bush fans had wondered, there was some link between Brian's well-known song *Captured,* from his début album, and Kate, because of what he had said in a *Hot Press* interview about hearing *The Man with the Child in his Eyes* for the first time.

BK: When I was about 12 or 13, it was one of those kind of illegal situations where we were in my best friend's brother's bedroom with the vinyl record player. And he put it on. And first of all the experience of the crackling, the speakers, the warm stuff that I can articulate now, at the time I was just absolutely transfixed with her voice, the words, the song, the mood of that song. More so than *Wuthering Heights...* We just happened to put it on, *The Man with the Child in his Eyes*, and I was just knocked out. Really knocked out y'know. And I remember thinking if I ever get to make music I've got to send it to that woman. Just to tell her thank you... I really plugged into that recording. It was a real inspiration, and it became more of an inspiration as I got older in fact... and then when I got to know her a bit... it made me more of a fan actually... it'll always remain special because it was one of the first things I ever heard.

ST: Was there a link?

BK: The link would be that I went to see the Trio Bulgarka sing in the Hackney Empire in London, and I just was so blown away. I was lucky enough that the person I was with, had friends who were connected with the promoters and they were having a party for the Trio Bulgarka, back at their house. I went to that and to thank everybody for the party the Trio Bulgarka, sang in the garden, which was just the most extraordinary thing. So the first verse of *Captured* goes "Oh I just heard a melody, and it almost made me cry" that's about them... And then the second time I went to see them at the Barbican, I bumped into Kate Bush, I saw her across the hallway and went over to say hello. She was very friendly, a bit shy but very friendly, and I just said "Look I just wanted to say hello, I'm a big fan".

I asked her what was happening with her record and she gave a kind of laugh and said "Ah well... it'll come out whenever it's ready."

I went on and made my first record, and dutifully sent it off to her assistant. I went on tour with Suzanne Vega around America, for two months. I came back and there was a pile of mail and on the top was this funny wee card... this lovely kind of very erratic pen, big strokes, and it said 'Brian Wennedy'. So I opened the card and it was kind of slightly lavender fountain pen ink... it was saying some very complimentary things about my record and if I ever fancied a cup of tea give us a ring, and the number was in the top right hand corner. I was thinking, hmm, who's this from? And it looked a bit like 'Wale Blush' or something. I was looking at the envelope and I'd seen the way the 'K' had been written... oh goodness, it's Kate Bush! So, I got very excited and a few days later I gave her a ring, when I'd calmed down enough, and left a message on her machine.

She called me back a day later and I went to her house for dinner. That was fantastic, she just kind of opened the door, no shoes and socks, and welcomed me in, and Del Palmer was there and Stuart Elliott the drummer. We went to a Chinese restaurant, and I had crispy seaweed for the first time in my life. I'll never forget it 'cos she suggested it, she said it was a really good thing. And like me she had once been a vegetarian, and I had just come out of vegetarianism more or less around there, so that was good.

ST: Have you ever been tempted to record a Kate Bush song?

BK: Many times. In fact I talked with Kate Bush about it because she was gonna produce some of my second record. My record company sent her *Town* as a possible re-issue, if she would consider re-mixing it or recording it or re-recording something, so she said she was really keen... And would be very interested to get involved. So of course I was beside myself with excitement, but my record deal fell apart, so things got a bit tricky... and then, once she started working on her new record, I suppose she's like everybody else, you just concentrate on what you're doing and that's it.

ST: Are there any of Kate's songs which are your favourite, which you sing in the bath?
BK: I was going to do a version of *Army Dreamers*... Well, not only that but I just love the subject matter. It's funny y'know and it's very sad at the same time... I love it. It's so well written. It's an amazingly written song. And, I talked about doing that, and she said she'd be very keen to hear it and all that... but again... these things are talked about, and often they just don't happen. So then I moved off and made my own record and I didn't record that song. But if there was ever a tribute record or something and I was ever considered for that record... I saw her about two years ago. We did a show with Van, and Robert De Niro came and Bob Geldof and Kate and a couple of people, and we went to dinner at this place called 'Julie's' in Notting Hill... It was extraordinary... Ray Charles was playing and I think Robert De Niro was somehow connected with him, so that's why he was there. And, again, I never met more friendly people, I mean at the end of the night he came straight over to us and shook our hands, looked us right in the eyes and told us how much he enjoyed our performances, y'know really made an effort to say hello and thank you, and off he went... and Kate was there, and I talked to her for a bit, and she said she'd had a year off and was gearing up to start stuff again.

I think people should be appreciated while they're here. Joni Mitchell was ignored for years. People so often don't really celebrate people until they're dead, and you just think Kate Bush is one of the most gifted individuals in the world, you know? That's how good she is. She's a true artist in that she does things how she wants to do them, regardless. And so she should. And I'm glad of it, and I think if every record is of the quality that her records are of when we do get them, then they're worth waiting for. Like Paul Buchanan (The Blue Nile) says, somebody said to him: "Why do you make so few records?" and he said "Why do people make so many?"

Time Twisting

… …With Colin Lloyd Tucker born late '58

Issue 74: July 2004

Colin Lloyd Tucker has been performing and recording since the late Seventies. He began his début solo album, *Toybox*, aged 17, writing, producing and playing all the instruments himself. His record releases have been sporadic, his live performances rare and in these days of packaged pop he is not easy to pigeon hole. His diversity and scope bewilder major record labels. More of a musician's musician, his credits were known to the cognoscenti. On Kate Bush's *Red Shoes* his name mingles with Eric Clapton, Jeff Beck and Prince.

Part 1: How It All Turned Out

My favourite shop has since closed down. People buy their electronic stuff from big out of town stores now and when they breakdown they just replace them. The grey haired men have retired and now tinker away at home for their own pleasure. The little record shop, a few doors further up the High Street has gone the same way and Tesco's mops up. Sometimes it seems that the music itself has gone much the same way and we are left with little choice. Where is the pleasure in buying an album at a supermarket check out along with the groceries?

Part 2: The Beginning Of The End

My favourite shop was situated at the low end of the high street… Two grey haired men with work coats to match are hunched over a buckled wooden bench that is groaning under the weight of the many radios, amplifiers and TVs in various states of repair. There are meters for measuring things, pliers and screwdrivers too. One grey haired man is eyeball to eyeball with his soldering iron and as he squints I can see a pure white plume of smoke rise up. But it's the whiff of the solder and hot valves that I really love.

I could often to be found there and after a while the two initially hostile and grumpy old men became almost friendly. One day I found them working on an old Rock-Olla jukebox and time stood still.

Through the glass I peer to be greeted by the happy faces of Freddie and The Dreamers beaming from an E.P. cover and next to them Fats Domino with a glint in his eye. There are The Beatles leaping in to the air on the cover of the *Twist and Shout* E.P. and I am reminded of why I love pop music and what it once meant to the masses.

I am not alone in this. It's not even my age. There are young kids getting turned on by Fats and the Beatles all the time and always will be (not so sure about Freddie and The Dreamers though).

"Is it for sale?" I inquired of the almost most-friendly grey haired one.

"What's a young chap like you want with a thing like this?" he replied, nearly smiling.

Momentarily stunned by being referred to as a "young chap" I got a wrinkly mouth.

It is true that I am not old enough to remember much about the early Sixties, having been born in 1958 but needless to say Rock'n'Roll found its way into my veins like it did most of us. My older brothers liked *Hello Goodbye* but at the age of ten I knew that *I Am The Walrus* (the B-side!) was better by far.

I explained how I have always wanted to own a jukebox and was informed that this particular machine was not for sale although if I was genuinely interested they may be able to help. It emerged that the grumpiest one's hobby was jukebox restoration and in his garage he had several machines including a Wurlitzer.

Arriving at the suburban dwelling I find Grumpy hard at play in his garage. I am struck by how similar it is to his place of work. Same components and equipment lying around and a similar smell. The one big difference here is that there are also various vintage motorbikes suggesting a wilder past. I see him in a different light now. Imagining him in the Fifties dressed in leather and tearing down winding lanes to the coast, maybe stopping off at a greasy spoon where no doubt he would stick a sixpence in the jukebox, greasing back his hair to the strains of Little Richard singing *Rip It Up*.

My eyes keep darting back to the Wurlitzer. It's not one of those huge Fifties types with bubbling lights but a more compact model from the mid-Sixties.

Part 3: Where I'm Coming From

Well, needless to say that machine now resides in our sitting room and I have stacked it with classic records. From Phil Spector's *Wall of Sound* to Free's *All Right Now*. From great sounding early Sun records to Rolf's *Sun Arise*. There's Jimi Hendrix, George Formby, Tamla Motown, Hoagy Carmichael and Donovan. All of them classics, all very different and yet all extremely sonically satisfying.

So this is where I am coming from. These are the sounds that have shaped me as a musician and producer. As I have stated, I am not old enough to remember all of these records first time around but they have filtered through, often via my older brothers and their friends just as Kate, who was also born in 1958, was influenced by the sounds coming from her brothers' rooms. We would have discovered them eventually, of course, but at that young age one's ability to absorb information is at its height. By the time we got to our teens we had a very clear idea of where we wanted to go with music.

Speaking for myself I haven't arrived yet although I am getting closer to my vision. This is the illusive nature of music but at least I am free from influence of the dreaded record company.

I have issued *Fear of Flying* on my own label, something I have not done since the Deux Filles albums I recorded with Simon Turner in the 1980s. I revel in the freedom this gives me.

On *Fear of Flying* there are no attempts at a hit single. My approach was that everything is valid, be it a slice of funk or a country hoe-down. It is as eclectic as a jukebox. I have always had a slightly "Joe Meek" approach to recording, trying for new sounds with whatever is around and not bothering too much about the text books. What amazes me now, upon reflection is that the record didn't come out sounding like a compilation album but has a "feel" that binds it all together. I guess you could say that it has a personality of its own. The jukebox helped me rediscover my roots and on *Fear of Flying* I enjoyed dipping in and pulling out various musical ghosts from my subconscious. It's a kind of musical roller coaster ride.

Part 4: A Step Back (Musical Stairs)

The year is 1969 and I am sitting on the steep staircase of the tiny terraced house where I was brought up, to the north west of London, England. In my hands is an old mandolin that has been handed down through generations… It really was a beautiful instrument with mother-of-pearl inlay and a round-backed sound box that

"Excerpt from Colin's own website interview with Helen Mann:

Helen: Just after that you worked with his sister Kate Bush on her album and film.

Colin: Yes that's right. Paddy and I sang some back-up vocals on *The Red Shoes* and fooled around in the movie. We had to mess about because neither of us can dance, well I can't dance, for all I know Paddy may be a closet Fred Astaire! In fact I first met Paddy and Kate way back in the Nineteen Seventies, before Kate had her first success. She did some songs in the studio I was working in at the time. We had some mutual friends and so came into contact from time to time over the years. I was also one of the aviators in her *Big Sky* video.

Helen: I'm sorry but Kate's fans would never forgive me if I don't ask you this. When did you last see her and how was she?

Colin: I saw her a few months back at Paddy's birthday bash and she was fine. I have always found her delightful; she has a quirky, slightly off-the-wall sense of humour that really appeals to me. I don't know where people get this idea that she is standoffish, not playing the game and all that, or worse, cut off and going mad. That's all rubbish, she's saner than most. I recall that my daughter was freaking out because she had got a splinter in her foot and Kate was cheering her up and helping her through that little crisis."

Colin the monk

Photo: courtesy Colin Lloyd Tucker

caused it to slip out from under your arm like a bar of soap. I would play it all the time.

A mandolin has eight strings arranged in four sets of two and I soon discovered how the doubled strings were ideal for creating a drone to accompany the melody. To this day I favour the twelve-string guitar for this reason and I am a sucker for all kinds of Indian music be it classical or modern.

As I droned away on the old mandolin, words and melodies would spring to mind and before I knew it I was writing my first songs.

If you have never written a song before, go and do it now.

You don't have to play an instrument; you can do it in your head and sing it in the bath. It doesn't even have to be a very good song for it be a life-enhancing experience that gives you a feeling of well-being.

I still get the same satisfaction today from song-writing as I did on the staircase all those years ago. In my teens my use of hashish intensified the experience and the stairs were replaced by hazy meadows or darkened bedrooms. Now I live in a bungalow, so stairs are no longer an option but I am writing all the time. I have a kind of 'virtual compartment' in my brain that seems to be able to store a huge amount of musical information, be it melodies or lyrics. This is not some sort of special gift but more an evolutionary development. I may forget what I did yesterday but can still recall songs I wrote when I was twelve!

Part 5: This is Life (Born Again)

My mother's name is Irene and I am not yet born. It must have been great in there. Like a Saturday morning teenage lie in. Suspended in liquid, my every need catered for. Drifting in and out of the deepest sleep.

The music had already started. Maybe I could tell what were internal sounds and what were coming in from that strange, unknown place, beyond my mother's body. The beat was strong and repetitive, reassuring and trance inducing. Goodnight Irene.

My mother's heartbeat has now been replaced by the steady thud of a bass drum here in my tiny studio where I recorded most of *Fear of Flying*. A plodding piano signals the start of a verse and I sing "*She's approaching the house and we all go 'Hello', Turn the music up loud, put the lighting down low*".

Am I longing for the womb or do I want to party? The answer is probably a bit of both. Like a lot of people I am torn between being a highly social, out-going beast (a raver) and an inward-looking, self-absorbed space cadet (a monk).

This is reflected in the music on *Fear of Flying*.

On the title track I am in monk mode, looking to a more spiritual future, where as tracks like *This Is Life*, *Kids* and *Big Fire* find me in the mood for a right rave-up.

The sounds of my parents' generation are echoed in *Battleship Gray* and *To Be Or Not* and my own childhood recalled with (what starts out to be) a reworking of *Polly Wally Doodle*!

Add to this an ode to a penis (*Smoothound*) and a throbbing tune about a young lady who wants a *Rocket to Ride*, which contains samples of both Paddy Bush and Rolf Harris, and there you have the concoction that is *Fear of Flying*. I very much hope you enjoy this record and would welcome your comments.

Be Happy.

Colin the Raver

Photo: courtesy Colin Lloyd Tucker

Readers' Letters

...We receive them with a strange delight

Letters edited from issues 64 (November 1999) to 75 (March 2005)

Ian McLauchlan: Thank you for *HomeGround* 63 which was waiting for me on my return from a break in Morocco. I came back with appalling diarrhoea, and just reading it on the toilet made the pain so much more bearable!

Kevin Hendryx: It is a common criticism by fans that Kate does not do enough for them. *HomeGround* then rallies to Kate's defense by saying that she does not play the music industry game and celebrates that attitude. It strikes me that there are several disingenuous things going on here. First is the fact that Kate occupies a singularly privileged position in her relationship with her record company, one not shared by many artists, and therefore is hardly a standard from which to base judgement.

Kate continues to enjoy many of the perks and benefits of this derided music industry even while she refuses to cater to it. Yes, this is admirable in many ways, but can also lead to charges of wanting to have one's cake and eat it. Most musicians realize that they operate primarily in the public realm, and few have the luxury to pick and choose their commitments, if they want to continue to earn a living. It is certainly wrong for fans to place unreasonable expectations upon Kate – as she has said, her records are the message, not Catherine Bush, and she is wise to avoid having her work subsumed by her personality cult – but at the same time, it is naive or selfish for Kate Bush the Entertainer to pretend that the whole structure of the entertainment business, with its demands and requirements, does not exist in her case.

I note also that *HomeGround*, perhaps unwittingly, feeds these fan expectations – not only by its very existence , but also in its emphasis on the mechanics of the music industry – every issue features an unending parade of charts playlists, and the other detritus of Fame. Perhaps if the fanzines didn't focus so much on touring or not touring, getting to Number One or just who sold more albums in Australia, then the fans would realize that there's more to MUSIC than the BUSINESS. In other words, the log is in our OWN eyes (and I speak as someone who once published a Katezine). Does Kate's music have any greater validity to anybody based purely on sales, airplay, or media criticism? It would be healthy for all of us to step back for a moment and remember that music is something that is in the soul; not in the financial charts.

Nat Hall: Just returned from sunny Provence where I was visiting my family during the summer break... Get back home on our Palace hill... stare at the sky for a minute... thought of our dear Kate-Speaking World... yes... to learn of Kate's baby boy... (I already wrote to Welling to send her our best wishes and a poem)... and then log on to rec.music.gaffa... Well, not everybody seems content to learn that Kate's happiness is now fulfilled with her child. Can't people just appreciate Kate's decision to keep her private life as discreet as possible? She must have been under a hell of a lot of pressure to make it finally public. We should ALL be very happy for this. Don't you think?

Emma Rose: Now available *HomeGround* 65 with all the latest information... Oh but the news of Kate's baby seems to be missing. Don't get me wrong, I'm so pleased for her it's unreal, I just can't believe she kept it a secret for this long. Now you tell me who the hell else could do that and get away with it? Top marks, Kate girl, top marks!

Malcolm Livesey: I have deliberately taken my time renewing my subscription to *HomeGround* because since the last issue, it has come out about Kate having a child. My first thought on the subject (after being genuinely thrilled for Kate) was the huge disappointment at not being able to share in Kate's pregnancy and birth.

I realise I am only a fan, but Kate has been my obsession (in a nice way) for so many years that it felt like a smack in the mouth to read about it in a newspaper after being a member of the Kate Bush Club for many years and subscribing to *HomeGround* for the past few years. I respect Kate's wishes for privacy but feel quite let down that she couldn't at least have told her fans. I feel sorry for *HomeGround* because I think you were obviously instructed not to say anything about the child. There has been so little news for such a long time that something a great as this would have been a real boost.

So I have taken my time renewing my subscription because I wondered is it really worthwhile when we only get the nostalgia and no up to date news. But the truth is I want to read anything about Kate, so if necessary, nostalgia it will have to be!

Mike Wade: Anyone seen the old black and white horror film *The Haunting*? Great film, and an authentic Kate source – just at the end of the film as a woman is drawn to the evil spirit within a house, she hears a voice in her head saying "It's really happening to ya!". The idea is twisted slightly by her feeling that nothing has ever happened in her dull life before (bar the odd childhood poltergeist experiences). This got me thinking – we know that Kate is often inspired by

The Haunting, 1963.

films (*The Innocents*, *Wuthering Heights*, *The Red Shoes*, Hitchcock etc). I've always assumed that *Get Out of My House* was partly inspired by *The Shining* but *The Haunting* also resonates with the song. Given that Kate maybe used a quote from *The Haunting* in *The Red Shoes*, could this have been – if only in part – an inspiration for *Get Out of My House* too? Film buffs, what do you think?

Seán: Had to write to say how much I loved the piece by Paddy Bush in the last issue. After seeing his Channel 4 documentary it was a very interesting and very personal continuation of the story. How many of us can find resonances in what he was saying about discovering music that is capable of changing you, setting you off on an entirely different and unexpected course. I've found Madagascan music a delight to explore and Paddy's passion for it is infectious and inspiring.

Justin Vali

I was fortunate enough to see the Justin Vali Trio perform in Dublin in April this year, and I can scarcely recall being at a more joyous evening of music. Incredible musicians in full flight. Although Paddy is the producer of this latest CD (he contributes some backing vocals also), anyone who's heard his uplifting valiha section on the title track of Bushtucker's *Skyscraping*, or were mesmerised by his multi-instrument 'camel dances' on the 1992 *Spondo* project, will be excited at the prospect of all and any new projects he gets involved in. Paddy Bush: genius and all-round great guy... 'nuff said.

Pertti Jussila: Hello to Kate – it is really great news that she is a Mom now.

Jan Millington: Now then, me dears! I have just got *HomeGround* 66... and as I don't read much newspaper stuff, and I don't have a telly; and I don't much use the web for gossip stuff – WELL, what 'Kate-news' eh? Kate a Mummy. Well, congratulations to her for keeping it quiet and good luck to her. She's obviously taken a page from Paul MacCartney's book; intent to bring baby up as 'normally' as possible. I admire her. So what business is it of ours, the 'fans'? None at all. She gives us her music, we don't need access to her life. Kate's got her head screwed on right. She's very good on boundaries, something I've been learning lots about. Kate can separate her 'public' self from her 'private' life. My regards to Kate. She's a card, ain't she? I'm reminded of the actor, Bob Peck being stalked by the dinosaurs in Jurassic Park, says quietly "clever girl" as they're about to rip him to shreds! Kate really is a 'clever girl' in keeping the media off her back! Ha! She ripped 'em up BIG this time! I like it!

Boyd Raison: I have just received issue 66 of *HomeGround*. Thanks again for a top class mag! My warmest wishes to Kate and Bertie. It's a strange old day, today (19th December) as, just as I've found out Kate's wonderful news, in contrast I have just learned that another of our best singer-songwriters, Kirsty MacColl, has been killed in a boat accident in Mexico. Kirsty, too, has been a huge influence on my musical tastes and I for one will miss her terribly. I'm sure that we all feel for her friends and family.

deep nerd: I make an analogy between Kate Bush and Greta Garbo – the latter didn't abruptly absent herself from the movies and celebritydom. She did some minor work after her peak and then gradually faded out and finally went reclusive.

I see this happening here, particularly with regard to Kate becoming a parent. A running joke in the UK about the British intelligence service is that Kate Bush could teach them a thing or two – in the wake of various scandals – about keeping a secret. I would not be surprised if Kate's closest friends knew about her pregnancy but were honor-bound to keep mum on the matter. That it was a year or more after her son's birth that an unequivocal public statement from her revealed the truth, is a testament to her ability to maintain her privacy. Many celebrities would kill to have that kind of privacy.

In any event, it shows that no-one will ever know exactly what is going on with her without her allowing it. She may indeed have something in the works, but like Garbo, may only be giving tantalising bits that may turn out to be nothing. Some might consider that inconsiderate with regard to her fans, but Kate is not our property. I will fully allow her to be so inconsiderate if only to raise her child in peace, and possibly make some new material if she feels like doing so... or not.

John Williams: I became interested in Kate in the three minutes it took to watch and hear *Wuthering Heights* on 'Countdown' in Australia in early 1978 (I'm 44). I raced out and bought the single, then *The Kick Inside* album when that was released, and have never looked back. She really was one of those artists (for me) that comes along just once in a lifetime.

Back in the pre-internet days of the '80s there was also a wonderful Australian Kate Bush fanzine called 'Dreamtime'. It came out quarterly and finished about 1990 and helped to boost the spirits of Kate fans in Oz. After a night with a few too many drinks under my belt, I still sometimes pull out all the issues (I have a full set) and re-read them while playing Kate. They also had a video of overseas clips and specials which 'toured' Australia. I had and still have a Betamax video recorder and had to borrow a VHS to dub it. That tape is another treasured possession.

It upsets me when people whinge and curse

because Kate hasn't brought out anything in quite a few years. As far as I am concerned, and if she never releases anything again, she has still given me more than anyone has any right to expect. It's great as subsequent generations discover her. I love reading their wonderment, as it takes me back to when I was twenty and realised in an instant an amazing talent had been launched upon the world.

Siàn Williams: The suggestion that Kate is a recluse and kept her baby a huge secret is somewhat off the mark. Many months before the *Daily Mail* broke the story about Bertie a friend of mine saw Kate with her baby. Kate was happy to sign an autograph and was perfectly friendly. Was she in hiding? No. Distressed or embarrassed to be spotted with her child? No. Where was she? In the baby-wear section of Harrods. The fact that Kate's child went unnoticed by press photographers and reporters for some time seems to me to be more by good fortune than planning. So she didn't make an announcement, big deal. Bertie is not our baby, he's Kate's. It's up to her to decide how to behave. I'll just bet she couldn't believe her good fortune in keeping her good news a 'secret' for so long.

Arto Polvikoski: Thank you for being a part of my life for the last ten years. Each new issue of *HomeGround* is like coming home.

Karel Sebek: I'm astounded and thrilled to know that Bertie has chosen to grace us and his Mum with his presence. I wish him the best of good luck, health, wealth and success in all things for all his days in this bright world! For me, the highest magick is to pass on what we have learned in our time to another person. To be allowed the gift of a child is world-changing for the parent and can be beauty beyond compare.

I didn't know that Kate was pregnant, I've just found out about her baby less than an hour ago. Kate needs her privacy. If you love someone unconditionally, you try to give them what they want most, even if that means honoring their sad request for everyone to kindly stay away. Stay away I have, simply leaving my interest in her work and life alone until a chance mention by a friend led me to rec.music.gaffa and to the very happy news. This has absolutely made my day!

Alan Hawkins: I saw Kate at the *Q* Awards last night on TV. She looked absolutely fantastic! She doesn't seem to have aged at all. Is she really 43? I was amazed at how comfortable she seemed on stage accepting the award – she hasn't been in this situation for such a long time yet she seemed more at home in that atmosphere than she did, say, at the BPI Awards in 1987. It was clear from the reception Kate was given that she remains highly regarded within the music industry and also by the public at large.

From the increasing number of slots on nostalgia shows such as 'I Love the 70s', 'Top Ten of Pop Princesses' or 'Top of the Pops 2', to posters of Kate adorning teenager Adele's bedroom wall and on her CD player in 'Brookside', it is obvious that the public want her back. And now, we have heard it from Kate herself that she is working on an album. Perhaps Autumn 2002 is looking a bit over-optimistic, but hey! What's another two years when we've waited eight already? Anyway, the time away from making music to bring up her son has clearly done her the world of good.

I'd also like to say well done to Kate for managing to stay sane. In these times, when celebrities seem to be becoming increasingly grotesque, while their shelf-lives become shorter and shorter, Kate has proved once again that the only way to stay normal is not to be a celebrity. "Greta Garbo of Pop"? Don't make me laugh! By attending the *Q* Awards, Kate proved once and for all that she is anything but. Right now, it feels like Kate's will be the comeback of all comebacks. Eight years ago she left us wanting more, but she will be coming back. And I for one don't mind waiting a while longer.

Scott Stubbard: Now and again I dust off the collection that I spent so much of my life amassing (with no regrets). Though I quit collecting Kate stuff a long time ago I have never quit listening to her. After looking over a closet full of collectibles and shelves full of books, 7" singles from around the world, coloured vinyls and so on, I searched the web to find the latest on the long-awaited album. It's almost a curse having fallen under the spell of her music and then forever waiting for the next album.

HomeGround continues on even after all these years. I have 15 or 20 of your first issues (and all of the *Break-Through* magazines of course, being Canadian). I bought a great deal of merchandise in my search to have the ultimate Kate collection (for this part of the world anyway). I still have 2 or 3 *Single File* box sets, pink and grey vinyl of *Hounds of Love*, *Kick Inside* picture discs, tubes full of posters, and so on.

It's sad to see what this merchandise is going for these days. I think if Kate ever does release a new album I will finally clear the shelves and closet and sell it off. There are a few of my prize pieces that I will never sell but there is so much and so little time any more to appreciate it. A good number of pictures on the walls of my games room/studio will always remain Kate... and my CD stand will always have one shelf dedicated to Kate. But somehow having all of this piled in a box and sitting in a closet just doesn't seem right and most of the Lionhearts I once knew have moved on or given up on always waiting for her.

Anyway good for you and your survival. I may

not follow Kate and anxiously wait and lose sleep over her next release but I will surely be at the door to the record store when it opens the day her next CD is released.

Jackie James: I'm sitting here on Kate's birthday listening to my favourite tracks from all the albums and even though I've never written to you before, I just thought I'd tell you how I became a Kate Bush fan.

It was the Summer of 1985 when I got into Kate's music. I'd heard *Running Up That Hill* a few times on the radio and really liked the record – not realising who was singing. When I found out I was amazed – was this really the same Kate Bush whose music had always been "too weird" for my tastes?

I remembered seeing the *Wuthering Heights* video on 'Top of the Pops', but I don't remember too much about her other stuff – but after hearing *Running Up That Hill*, I went out and bought the *Hounds of Love* album and couldn't believe how fantastic it was – I especially loved the concept side. After playing the album a few times and falling madly in love with it, I then went out and bought all four previous albums (despite the funny looks from the guy in HMV). I couldn't wait to get home and play them – which I did, one after the other. I suddenly thought "what have I been missing all these years"? Here was music that actually meant something to me, rather than something that just washed over me without leaving any real impression.

So I'd just like to say to Kate that even if she only makes one album every ten years – it will be well worth the wait!

Ingo Pohl: There is a television quiz show, 'Risiko', which is broadcast from Monday to Friday at 4.15 in the afternoon. In each show four candidates are asked about their own special field of interest – history, sports, TV, music, everything, really. In each show, the candidates have to answer seven questions about their topic, if they answer correctly, they come back for the next show, until the fourth show, where they can win about 13,000 DM.

Last December I mustered up all my courage and sent a postcard to the TV station, proposing the music of Kate as a topic for the quiz. After a telephone and a video casting, they invited me to take part in the show as a candidate. The shows, four all in all, were recorded in July and aired in October. Oh my God, I was very, very nervous. As a preparation for the show, I had read through the back-issues of *HomeGround*, and various articles and books I had collected through the years. But what sort of questions would they ask? And what could I bring along for the little chat with the quiz-master before the actual quiz? In the end I brought a whole bag of records, photos, T-shirts, and they decided I should take the small red ballet shoes, a T-shirt and a photo from the Tour.

The days in the studio were really good fun, we had a great time in Munich, where the show was recorded. The questions in the first round of the quiz were fairly easy, for example, which singer Kate dueted with on *Don't Give Up*. But from round to round, the questions became harder, though I guess most of the real "die hard" fans would have got them correct. Although I was very nervous I was lucky and could answer them all!

I was very happy to have won the quiz. During the shows, they showed extracts from various videos and played some audio tracks. They made a very good selection, and I was surprised to see an extract from the American *Rubberband Girl* video, which I hadn't seen in years. I hope that I "represented" Kate and her fans well, and though I would have liked to tell much more during the little chats with the quizmaster (about what's so special about Kate and her music), I hope that I got at least some of the viewers interested in this fantastic singer/songwriter.

Krystyna Boswell: *HomeGround* 68 arrived this morning, with a thump as it fell through the letterbox. Perfect timing indeed, as we have now got over the nut roast of 25th and 26th December, have had visitors come and go, and the year is waning into that strange, quiet limbo time between the big spendfest and the hopes of the fresh new year.

Reading *HomeGround* – as I have done, cover to cover, this morning in the bath (!) – was a lovely wallow in both nostalgia and fresh news, a little private time for me before I get on with the housework and the homework. It is so good to see some fresh Kate events happening, viz the *Q* awards etc. and it is as though a part of time that has stood still since the release and fade of *The Red Shoes* all those years ago has now begun to move again; we are back in the present with Kate alive and well, emerged from her period of rest and relaxation, and there are high hopes of a new album sometime soon. Whatever is happening in the wider world, there is a special little place in my heart and memory for Kate, and all the good things that have happened because of her and this never disappears; it's always there.

When I wrote that piece for the 'Just One Kate Song' bit in *HomeGround* 68 it was so true that as I looked back, Kate's music was somehow connected with so many good times in my life, and was there as a comfort during the less good events. It may sound strange but here and now, at 42 years of age, I am just as entranced and happy to read the new editions of *HomeGround* as I was when I first discovered a copy in the Virgin store in London way back in about, ooh, 1748! I think I can honestly say that Kate's music has helped shape my life. The days of queuing up to see her, or wishing she'd tour are long gone, but the specialness of being a part of her family of fans is still something that lingers and makes me glad. And liking Kate's music has opened up other doors in my life that might not otherwise have presented.

Because of her music I have listened to other artists I might never have discovered; I have read books that she has read, and discovered some wonderful films that she has cited as favourites or influences in her work. I've met some wonderful people as a direct result of liking her music, and I have even dared to write my own songs because of the spark her genius gave to me. I am sure that you too cannot imagine what the past twenty four years would have been without knowing Kate's music – it's impossible to imagine.

So this morning, kicked off by the lovely old photos and other folk's special 'Kate' moments as written in *HomeGround*, I am having an hour or so of happy and fond memories: of the day at *The Big Sky* video shoot, the Albert Hall, Shop Assistance, letters and a special Christmas card from Kate, days of laughter on Glastonbury Tor – it's all there, tied up in ribbons and carefully stored away to enjoy when the time is right. I feel sure that however much I may have changed over the years – and life changes us all in so many ways – I will still feel the same excitement when the new album is ready, and will scan the music magazines just like I did 24 years ago, to find reviews and articles.

Though I long ago stopped collecting Kate-related stuff, I still love to look at the old scrap books sometimes, because those photos and articles are a direct link back to the time in which they happened, and with them come memories of what was happening in my life during those

Graphic: Paulina Stuckey

times. *HomeGround* is such a good link for all of us who still love and appreciate Kate's music, and I am just glad that though other magazines have come and gone *HomeGround* will still be there when the new album is released, and I'll be able to enjoy reading about it and maybe even seeing some new pictures when the album is ready. Don't ever despair over *HomeGround*, it is always wonderful and I am sure everyone else thinks the same.

Dave and Nat Hall: From our island, we obviously keep in touch with the Kate Speaking World and our local record shop in Lerwick already knows that we are awaiting Kate's new album. We were thrilled about Kate's *Q* award last October and it is fantastic to hear her promise of a new album. With all the madness in the world at the moment, we desperately need to have her smile and inspiration to keep us going.

John Beaumont: I'm writing to tell you that I'm not renewing my subscription to *HomeGround*. My decision is no reflection on the quality of *HomeGround* – you've done very well to keep a very high standard of presentation and gathering of information from around the world and your readership must have realised you've put a huge amount of work in over the last twenty years.

What I do feel would be helpful is some information being supplied to you ahead of the general press getting hold of reports, stories, rumours, etc. so that fans would have some true facts and know how much to believe of what is reported by other sources. I feel the best showbiz tactic is to beat the media at their own game, rather than try to put things right after damage has been done and I don't think total silence works well in that respect.

With particular regard to the news of Kate becoming a mother, it seems to me that most people – famous or otherwise – are able to announce such events without excessive intrusion on their privacy, so long as they make it clear they won't tolerate it. If, for example, a work colleague became a parent and never said a word about it, most people would regard it as rather strange – and when the news was finally revealed, would be likely to be asked more prying questions than if everyone had been told in the first place. I hope you soon have the new album from Kate to report on and wish you every success in all you do. And of course, I thank you for your friendship over the years, which I hope will continue.

Patrick Stimson: I got interested in Kate's music after I heard *Wuthering Heights* on an old cassette tape of my parents' that I'd found. After listening to the song I realised that this was the most touching song I had ever heard, and it still is. So I went out, piggy bank in hand, and bought all her albums. I've never ever heard such beautiful music in my life, and doubt I ever will. Her lyrics are incredible, so original and wonderfully imaginative. Kate's music has cheered me up on many occasions when I've been low, for whatever reason.

The version of *Wuthering Heights* she did at the Hammersmith Odeon was incredible. It looked to me as if she was very emotional at the end, and yet she showed such energy as she was jumping about and waving at the audience. If Kate does decide to perform live again, you can bet that I'll be there, as it would be an incredible honour to witness, first hand, such a beautiful and talented artist. Her music means such a lot to me, in so many ways, I have found it incredible that her music gives me goose bumps every time I hear it, no matter how often I hear it.

Paula Hobbs: When I was sixteen the only female singers I really liked were Madonna and PJ Harvey. Then one night I saw 'The Album Show' and there was a nostalgic piece showing four Kate Bush videos. The one that intrigued me most was *Wuthering Heights*. The song was just beautiful. It inspired me to read the novel, which I then chose to write about for an A-level essay, and I watched the 1992 film with Juliet Binoche as Cathy over fifty times!

For Christmas 1994 Mum bought me *The Whole Story*. Kate's songs were poetic. She was a storyteller, a visionary, someone I could really identify with who integrated all kinds of elements into her music and surprised me. I eventually bought all of Kate's albums and videos. I loved her ethereal voice and the way each album had a theme. *Lionheart* was a very theatrical album, whereas *Hounds of Love* was steeped in dreamy mysticism, and then the rather Faustian *Red Shoes*.

In my drama group in 1995, I was asked to choreograph a dance so I came back the next week having copied the routine to *Wuthering Heights*. Two minutes into the song my friend asked "Is this Indian music?" and I told her it was Kate Bush singing about Cathy and Heathcliff. She was bemused and suppressed a giggle at my wide-eyed mimed dance. Kate is such an inspiration. She is like a fairy and allows herself to be vulnerable, to pluck out her heart and soul, and to be quirky and funny too. It is because of her that I discovered and fell in love with Emily Brontë's novel.

Euan Sleep: Thought I'd "Ask Jeeves" when the new album would be out. The site crashed.

Fiona Hersey: As with many of us "mature" fans, Kate's music has been the backdrop of many of my life's experiences. And so has *HomeGround* as it keeps the embers of the fire burning in our hearts. The magazine really has been that lovely reminder every few months that there are a collective band of folks who have this one thing in common. As I have just started a degree course with the Open University, my mind is preoccupied with the concept of identity, and I begin to see the mechanics of this concept at work here. We seek to belong, to identify with certain things in order to establish, assert or define our identities.

And so to *HomeGround*, the conduit perhaps for those of us seeking to identify with Kate, her music, a way of life represented in her songs. I appreciate all that you are and all that you represent. As a new mother, my identity is changing. My days are filled with a new obsession - my daughter, Grace. The passionate pursuit of all things Kate has mellowed into the background. Again the backdrop to my past, present and future, but this time in a quieter way.

Mark Brown: One day, when I was twenty, I was listening to a tiny college radio station and heard a song that hit me with the impact of a sledgehammer. It was *Suspended in Gaffa*. Never had I heard anything stranger or more brilliantly original. Later, I heard *There Goes a Tenner* and learned it was by an English girl named Kate Bush. I discovered Kate with *The Dreaming* and that album will always have a special place in my heart. It is Kate's heaviest, most difficult work but one that will endlessly reward the discerning listener. Thank you, Kate, for giving us your creations of genius.

Keith Pitches: It is fitting that *HomeGround* 70 and 71 be dedicated to *The Dreaming* album - it is arguably Kate's greatest work and brings back many happy memories! My first *HomeGround* (Issue 3!), my titanic struggle with the sandwich-eating sheep on Wuthering Hike I, the HomeGround Brew-up, making new friends. Happy memories – yesss! That little bit from the Ivor awards was funny - Kate saying how special it was to be thought of as songwriter! To me, she is one of the greatest songwriters this country has produced!

I believe that the media comments about Kate being inactive for the past ten years have some basis in fact. The "real" world has seen nothing of Kate for ages, but as we all know, Kate is her own woman. The way she manages her life and career works for her - and us. Seventy issues of *HomeGround* are living proof of that!

I heard a really good cover version of *Never Be Mine* a few years ago at a singing workshop run in Bristol by an acapella group, the Sweet Soul Sisters. The group split up a few years ago - pity, they were good singers. The bit about the Ukulele Orchestra was amusing - Kate Bush meets George Formby springs to mind! The Naked Voices gig sounded fantastic. *Rocket's Tail* sung in the style of Bobby McFerrin would have been mind-blowing! They were in Bristol and I missed it! Aaagh! I really should get out more!

Your letters page stirs a few memories. I probably met Les Gooderham at the *Big Sky* Video Shoot (my lighter still works, by the way!) Paula Hobbs' letter reminds me what a totally individual artist Kate is! I was intrigued by the Paddy Bush articles in issues 65 and 66 on his Madagascar journey and the TV programme, which I tuned into by chance! His depth of interest was obvious and I liked the fact that Kate wasn't mentioned once - Paddy is also his "own person!"

Chris Schalkwijk: About your concern of adding fuel to the flames of the *Red Shoes*: yes, that's always the danger, but I think that mostly you have been very positive, and have helped people understand that Kate is a human being too; someone who needs respect and privacy, who needs time and inspiration to do her work, and who has and needs a life of her own. You have helped Kate to bring her art out into the world, and *HomeGround* has been the source of a lot of better understanding of her work. I feel *HomeGround* has brought the fans, Kate and her music closer together, by showing us what it's all really about. There is something very beautiful in Kate's music, and your magazine has been a wonderful extension to that.

I always felt that somehow the music was Kate's spiritual child. And a parent can't keep her child hidden from the world. One day she has to let it go out to start exploring. Sometimes you may have worries, but I think it's best to guide your child and help it find it's way. If you hid it from the world, wouldn't it only wither? What use would Kate's music have had if she had kept it locked away in a trunk? No, she wanted to make a record, and with it she has made this world a better place to live in. And she has sown some weird and wonderful musical seeds, some we can see starting to grow now here and there. So don't worry too much, you did a marvellous job assisting her spiritual child. I hope you continue to let people express themselves and speak their minds in *HomeGround*, even when you (we) do not always agree. It's ten years since Kate did anything in music that people in general remember. In a sense the mag has been idling along since then, and it's only logical that some readers drift away. When nothing new happens, it's logical that less people discover Kate's music. If Kate were to quit making music (Aaarghh! Jeez!) would it be wise for *HomeGround* to carry on? That's a question I cannot answer. It's your mag, and your decision. If the contents would go stale, if the magazine would have no more useful purpose, carrying on would be artificial. Better quit then when it has fulfilled it's purpose, so later you can look back happily at such an important period in time. I can only say that for me it would be a sad day, like losing a good friend. I don't think this should be *HomeGround*'s end now. Look at some of the fabulous recent artwork and the remarkable stories from Jeanette and Svein. Look at the readers letters, *The*

Dreaming remembered series... And the interviews with Kate's crew. Aren't those great? I thought *HomeGround* was very well on track.

I hope Kate still enjoys making music. What if by chance someday a new album really would appear? I don't think Kate would ever go on tour, but what if she decided to do a limited number of shows in the UK, on her own or some serious project with other musicians? And there wasn't *HomeGround*? Wouldn't that be silly? Yes, I know there's the net, but not everyone has access. And it just isn't the same as a printed magazine, which you can store and keep, and leaf through and look at the pictures when snuggly and warm in bed... sigh...

The problem is that we just don't know how far away the new album is. When Kate opens the farm gates to bring out the harvest, that will increase writer activity! Yes, she said she's working on it, so we can be sure it's serious, but knowing Kate, she'll want the music to be very serious too. So we'll just have to wait and see how long it takes.

Rick Parker: I would like to express my condolences to Kate for the loss a dear friend and collaborator she found in Michael Kamen. For me, it has been bittersweet to know that they have been working together again only to read of Kamen's passing a few days later. The influence and contribution of his talents in Kate's music will always be felt by me, for example I believe there is a spiritual compass that guides us through the complexities of life and I have never heard it so beautifully expressed as "Just put your feet down child"... and the orchestral arrangement behind that wonderful voice. As it was a special piece of music for me, I hope a song like *The Fog* will help Kate find solace in its rare ephemeral atmosphere that she and Michael created and in time, pay tribute to him in her own special way. God bless.

Michael Kamen

Edward G: I just don't get how people can say Kate's imagination, or love of the 'different' was flagging on *The Red Shoes* – an album that contains songs about enchanted shoes, magic, angels, and piloting a ship to the heart of your emotions with an unruly crew of inner voices. She just tackles her subjects with a new maturity and more down-to-earth humour. It's like she's mocking her old image. The album is absolutely stuffed full of jokes – from the bathetic "Wop bam boom" of *Song of Solomon* to the countless line checks of other artists' work "sticky fingers", "cartwheels 'cross the floor", "not only women bleed", "I know where I'm going..."). The line "Take all the telescopes and turn them inside out" may be a cheeky dig at us, telling us not to look for the answers in her work, or other peoples', but find them inside ourselves.

We know she wanted the red shoes off. Maybe she felt the weight of her audience's expectations was too great. *Moments of Pleasure* certainly feels like a little 'Keep your nose out' – taunting us with a string of private references, some of which we'll never understand. For me the biggest clue of where her mind was at comes on *Eat the Music*, and "What am I singing? A song of seeds". In other words, we may often look too deeply into her lyrics, instead of just enjoying her work for what it is: tuneful music (ironically, what I'm probably doing here!) Yes, there are themes on *Eat the Music* but it's also, at its simplest, a joyous song about fruit!

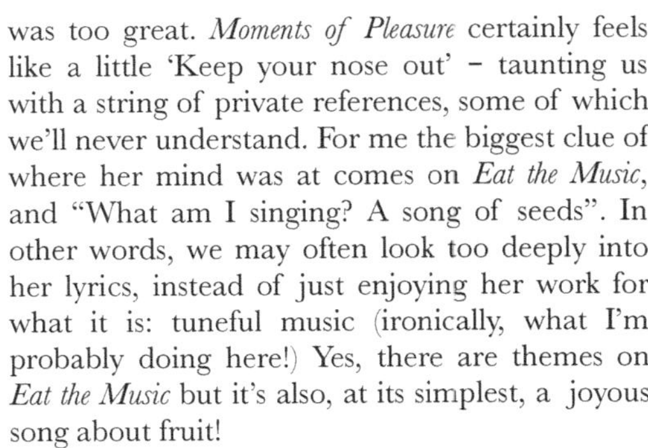

Krystyna Boswell: The word that Kate will be releasing her eighth studio album this year is terrific news for all Kate fans and I am looking forward to hearing her new music very much. I got to thinking about that long silence between the last album and this long-awaited new one, and realised that though the world at large has probably not thought much about Kate during this time, she has still been working on other projects and receiving various musical awards.

For many of us this information would not have been available without *HomeGround* and, latterly, the Kate Bush News & Information website. It can get lonely between albums, and while Kate has been quiet doing family things in recent few years it has been wonderful to know that *HomeGround* has been there as a link for people who love her music: a place where we can share views and opinions, and enjoy the creative talents of fellow fans.

Now that the KBN&I site is going from strength to strength we have an active and lively Forum to discuss Kate's music and many other topics, and I have found some new friends there. These two wonderful institutions have been a vital link for many of Kate's fans worldwide and have certainly provided a focus for us while we waited patiently for what Kate would do next. *HomeGround*, especially, has been there during the times when some doubted Kate would ever release another album, through the bad times when the press were turning out spiteful and silly stories about her, and has always been a source of honesty and sanity when the media has, perhaps, gone a little too far. So I just want to say a big 'THANK YOU' for holding the torch for so many years. I am looking forward to reading all the news and wonderful contributions from others after the album is released.

Collin Kelley: *HomeGround* 74 arrived in my mailbox today. Thank you, Krys for using so many of my poems and the Gorey article. It's an honor to grace the pages, but even more so next to the fabulous interview with John Carder Bush and his own beautiful work.

Pillow Book

Krys

The beauty of the written word rests upon her flesh,
little waves
moving with her breath
with her laughter
and tears.
When they touch
the chapters merge their stories shared
each writing their words on the other,
lines that are held
there forever.

When the chapter ends she puts the book away
beneath her pillow
for a day when she can look back
and think fondly.
She hopes that day might come.
For now the feathers suffocate kindly, gently,
take her tears on swan-down.
She will finish the story alone.
Takes the quill like a sword,
inks her own flesh with words
and begins a new chapter.
Daring not to read the pages that have gone before.
She fears.
The paper cuts.

Cat

John Carder Bush

Hur-Kudar loves only women:
he will wait listening.
When conversation has loosened them
he climbs the chair
turns them on with a mystical knowledge
a seed of skill learned from the tombs
a craft given by the dead.

Like a harem eunuch he strives to satisfy
nuzzling ears manipulating breasts he embraces
embarrasses overcome with a purr
opens himself to long fingers.
When the heart under his paw begins to speed
he stops.
Lazily proud he withdraws.

Hur-Kudar has many advantages:
when you have left I see only debris:
a separated stocking, a slimed handkerchief.
A long crease down the double bed.
If I stop smoking for an hour
I can trace the smell of your arm on my arm
but he who watched us from the wicker chair
sniffs a stain and can drowse in your breath.
He shies at a single strand of winnowed hair
and is excited by the thousand oils of your skull.
After he has curled in the imprint of your hip
he licks the door wood where you leaned to kiss.
I have no such gifts for scratching into recall
but he lets me follow.

Retracing the Scenes

Aerial: 2005-2006

"Genius. End of."

In a press release dated 31st August 2005, EMI Records "proudly confirmed" that Kate Bush's hugely anticipated eighth studio album *Aerial*, was to be released on 7th November 2005 (but 8th November in USA).

In one press release Kate said *"I have been genuinely touched by the sense of anticipation I've felt from people, I feel really privileged that people have been waiting."* Kate had assembled around her a close group of musicians. Danny McIntosh's guitar was all over the album. There were new collaborations with drummers, Steve Sanger and Peter Erskine and percussionist Bosco D'Oliveira, and familiar names such as Gary Brooker (again on the Hammond), drummer Stuart Elliott, bassists Eberhard Weber and John Giblin. As ever Del Palmer engineered. *Aerial* also featured some of the last work of orchestral arranger Michael Kamen.

Kate said *"There was a sense of being at play as well as at work, I think that's very important because it is so hard and so frustrating sometimes trying to get an idea to materialise. It's not an easy process. I really like working with people who are old friends, it's lovely."* Realising that the amount of material she had accumulated in her time away was unlikely to fit onto a single CD, Kate made the decision to split the results in two, making *Aerial* her first double album: *"What is quite nice for me doing the two discs, is it allows me to play with the semi-classical style which I like – space and acoustic music – but also the band-based stuff with lots of drums."*

Kate spent her twelve years out of the public gaze dividing her time between preparing the songs for *Aerial* and looking after her son, Bertie, born in 1998. *"The way I'd always worked was to just stay in the studio for fourteen hours a day. I didn't have that luxury to use the time in the same way."* The album artwork with its enigmatic sound wave motif intrigued from the start. It first appeared as a hidden treat on the holding page of Kate's new internet site, and then became a fully blown mystery in its own right as ingenious computer types tried to replicate the wave form and identify the sound.

Following EMI's 31st August press release there was an avalanche of press coverage of 'Kate's return' which lasted through the release of single and album to late November. Before the single was even released Kate was being celebrated on the BBC News website, and in virtually all the UK nationals both serious and tabloid. By 12th September we were being told in *Music Week* that *King of the Mountain* (already in their "key singles" list) was a "rhythmic gem" which "grows and grows from an almost electronic-sounding start to suggest that the wait has been well worth it". Elvis Presley fan sites had already picked up the connection and ElvisNews.com reported "Her return to the charts will be welcomed by discerning listeners everywhere. Elvis fans will be delighted".

King of the Mountain preceded the album on 24th October. Or rather that was its official physical release date. It was actually played for the fist time on Wednesday 21st September 2005 on BBC Radio 2's Ken Bruce show, whereafter it was available on the BBC website "playback" facility. With that first playing, huge excitement was created both amongst fans and the music community. The track was already at no.1 in Amazon's 'Hot 100' singles chart.

In the first reviews The *Manchester Evening News* gave 4 out of 5 stars. and Mark Richardson wrote: "In these days of 'X Factor' and 'Pop Idol' it is almost a surprise to hear an artist construct a sound that is casually littered with musical ability". In *The Daily Telegraph* Marc Lee said: "vaguely troubled ambience as haunting as ever. Opening with a gently hypnotic rhythm track, chugging guitars, and blurry vocals, the song builds to a big, rocking finish". For icScotland Stephen McKenna wrote: "Opening with some delightful percussive synth noises, Kate's idiosyncratic voice comes through and the whole track feels very atmospheric and nonchalant".

It became an oddity from the off that whereas the print reviews were most enthusiastic, the broadcast reviews sounded a more negative note. On the venerable BBC radio single review programme 'Roundtable', now holding a niche on digital only Radio 6, whilst the host David Quantick gave it 9 out of 10, the two other reviewers gave it a 4 and a 3. On 21st September the track was reviewed on Radio 4's 'Kaleidoscope' arts programme. Neil McCormick from *The Daily Telegraph* was underwhelmed saying that it was "an odd record", a "poor single choice" and that "it would need to be pop symphony in 3 octaves to please fans" thus indicating how little he understood Kate's work, or her fans. He did, however, praise Kate's voice saying that she'd "obviously looked after it". Nice.

By the last week of September the single was achieving numerous plays on Radio 2, and even popping up on Radio 1, whose youth demographics looked forbidding. Rob Da Bank called it "vintage, vintage Kate Bush". Radio 2 DJ Ken Bruce continued to support the single telling listeners that he knew they would love it and that the song "grows and grows after a few listens". Jonathan Ross said "That's great! – it really grows on you!" on his morning show on

Edited from the news in issues 76 and 77 (December 2005 and July 2006) and on the KBNI website.

"Worth the wait? Every. Last. Second."

"The world is a better place with Kate Bush in it."

"Lovely, lovely, lovely Kate. Lovely, lovely, lovely Kate."

"There are strict rules in the pop business. And then there is Kate Bush"

"*Aerial* stands alongside The *Hounds of Love* and *The Kick Inside* as her finest work."

"It frustrates me that I am continually presented to the public as some kind of hermit. I am actually leading a completely normal life. I have simply chosen against the lifestyle of the music industry or the world of show-business. Excessive egos, greed for power, greed for money, neuroses, psychoses, sarcasm, cynicism – I don't need any of that. I find it frightening that some of my colleagues don't even know how to work a washing-machine."

"I don't like to explain the content of my songs. There is already too much music out there that comes with the instruction manual. I want the listeners to create their own interpretations, so that the songs sort of become their own."

"Everything I have to say to the world is in my music. Direct and without blockades. Those who have heard my records, and have wondered how I am really like, know the answer already."

"Some people find this amusing, but I actually do try to run a household, which people find very hard to get their heads around. I can't understand that, because to me it's perfectly normal"

"I have to watch myself, because I could talk about Bertie all day."

"'Reclusive, mysterious and weird' – it's ridiculous, isn't it? Just because I've chosen to live a normal life, and not in the public eye. I've never promoted myself, I'm not a celebrity, I'm a worker, and I don't see a reason to do interviews unless there's something to talk about, a piece of work. I don't hide from people. I go shopping, I go to restaurants and movies... yet somehow I'm made out to be some mad hermit. It's too much. I think my cult following got grumpy waiting so long!... I never wanted to be famous. I just want to create nice music, and I believe celebrity threatens creativity. What's important to me is to have a soul – and my lovely little boy."

Graphic opposite: Andrew Marvick

the 22nd. Steve Wright said: "Kate Bush never ever disappoints. I've heard that three times now and I just love it. I'm not saying that just coz I'm trying to get her on the programme". Of course not. On the 22nd Rob Da Bank on Radio 1 ran a 'Listener's Choice' text poll between the latest releases from Kate and Paul McCartney, Kate won and the track got its Radio 1 airplay début – with a lot of positive feedback from listeners.

An anomalous situation had been created. Anyone who wanted to hear the single could get it from the playback features on the websites of any of the radio stations that had played it. The track was officially released on download in the USA on 27th September, with no indication that there would a be physical release there. The original intention was not to release it for download in the UK until almost a month later on 24th October the day of physical single release. However, within days of the US download release, Kate decided that the single should also be made available on download in the UK and Ireland and on 29th September it became available on iTunes. By the beginning of October the track was lodged in the top 5 of the iTunes download chart, and was 'Single of the Week' on the Ken Bruce show on BBC Radio 2, and was one of only two new additions to the Virgin Radio playlist.

Another surge of reviews was triggered. The *Bizarre* column of *The Sun* on the 27th and in tabloid backup on 29th September, Gavin Martin in the *Daily Mirror* and John Aizlewood in the *London Evening Standard* the same day. *The Daily Mail* chipped in favourably on 30th September, and *The Daily Express* ran another laughably out of touch assemblage of old press cuttings on the same day, inexcusably recycling the same old garbage about "Kate the recluse". For a tabloid clean sweep *The Daily Star* was wondering about the album art and how Kate's first release in twelve years would be received by the music industry and the public. On 2nd October we had Adam Sweeting in *The Independent on Sunday* and Nigel Williamson in *Scotland on Sunday*. In the *Music Week* airplay chart the single entered at no.51 on 24th September, rose to no.26 the following week, then hung around in the 20s and 30s until mid-November.

This was all predicated on the airplay support given by Radio 2. In early October the track was in fact no.2 in the Radio 2 airplay chart. In the download-only chart, the new single hovered around the 20s and and 30s through October into November.

On 15th October, a week before physical release, the track was *Music Week* 'Single of the Week'. It had entered the official UK download chart at no.6 and on that day the video had its première on a special showing on Channel 4. Plainly disturbing to those who stubbornly retained a mental picture of Kate aged 19, the video was full of warmth and humour and littered with many clues and teasing hints about the forthcoming album, and ending with a special emphasis on the young Citizen Kane's sledge "Rosebud". BBC Radio 2's Richard Allinson described it as "a stunning, stunning video". But its success as a promotional tool for the single and the album was limited. Played on 'Top of the Pops' when the single charted, it did not get much purchase on the digital music channels.

On the eve of physical release, 21st October, Victoria Newton in *The Sun* made the track 'Single of the Week', rating it 5 out of 5: "a slow hypnotic start... builds into a glorious crescendo." Jenny S on the BBC 'Top of the Pops' website provided a 4-star review, aimed squarely at those demographics: "Soaring fruity vocals, a driving rhythm and gorgeous electronic twiddlings make this a gem of a song." *Heat* magazine gave a 4-star review, and website Gigwise made it clear to a new generation that "Kate Bush deserves your attention". Simon Donohue of *The Manchester Evening News* rated the single 4 out of 5. However, a little rain must fall, even if to make the colours run. Step forward David Stubbs of *The Guardian* 22nd October: "This sets out promisingly hoving in like a sea fret, as a Citizen Kane-inspired lyrical theme takes shape. But then in comes the chorus... and it's like the giant, corporate epic rock propeller has been trundled on stage and activated as pile in the sessions drums, like a drunken Phil Collins gatecrashing a pleasant soiree".

The 22nd October *NME,* however, was working itself up into a great pitch of excitement. BBC Radio 1 was still clinging to its demographics and excluding the single from its playlists; but Rob Da Bank nonetheless continued to rave about it: "She makes us wait twelve years and then bam! She's back and jeepers creepers the lady's been busy if this, the first single from her new album *Aerial* is anything to go by. Wooshy wind noises – check! Mystical lyrics – check! Genius reggae guitar and bountiful production – check! Best pop song of the year so far and proud to be a Blue Room tune. Welcome back!"

On Monday 24th October the single was finally released in physical CD and 7" vinyl picture disc formats, and by 29th October it was in at no.4 in the CD:UK chart on ITV. On 30th October we knew that Kate's new single had entered the "official"chart at no.4, which all things considered was an amazing success. It was in fact Kate's third most successful single and her 25th Top 40 hit. The single remained top 10 at no.8 in the second week before falling to no.21 in the third.

The chart success was largely on the back of continuing massive airplay support from BBC Radio 2, in its renewed format the most listened to station in the UK. The single actually sat at the top of the Radio 2 airplay chart in mid and

Who knows who wrote that song of Summer
That blackbirds sing at dusk?
This is a song of colour,
Where sands sing in crimson, red and rust,
Then climb into bed and turn to dust . . .
Andrew Marvick (ied) 200

"Everything I write tells something about me. There's a song in particular, *A Coral Room*, which is very, very personal indeed. It tells about my mother. When I wrote it I was afraid it was maybe too personal, but all the friends who had a listen told me it is such a beautiful song, so at last I decided to be brave and put it into the album."

"I think a lot of music has become cabaret-like. Some other has a lot to do with poetry. I think hip-hop is a bit like contemporary poetry, spoken words, someone trying to say something. I like some of it, I don't like everything. But it's difficult for me to say. When I was a younger music had a huge impact on me. I'm too old now to be able to judge its importance on young people nowadays."

"I desperately needed a break after my last album, because looking back at it, I'm not too happy with it... *The Red Shoes* contains some of my best songs, but in retrospect I'm not too happy with the finished record. A big part of this is because of the CD format, that sort of forces us musicians to put on 80 minutes of continually good music. But that isn't easy. In hindsight I don't think my last album is exciting enough, because of its length".

late October 2005. Apart from Wogan it was being played on all other daytime shows, plus Sarah Kennedy in the early morning and, of course, Mark Radcliffe in the evenings. However, it was hardly played outside of Radio 2, and in particular had little support on the independent local radio stations. On 20th November 2005 the single had its fourth and final week in the Forty at no.31. There was, however, a brief resurgence of airplay on Radio 2 in April 2006. The track actually finished at no.20 on Radio 2's most played tracks of 2005.

Rounding up the reviews: Michael Hubbard on MusicOMH.com said "everything that could be hoped for... on top of her mountain surveying the scene before her with a calm contented gaze... a heady mix."; Ben Gilbet, dotmusic: "Built around a revolving processed xylophone mantra and some spaced-out guitar FX, Bush's enigmatic entrance from the fog is initially so vague and indecipherable as to conclude that she surely hasn't been scribbling lyrics for the past decade. However, the track soon shifts powerfully into bellowing clarity in a thunder crack of atmospheric elemental power..."

In the Irish single charts, the single entered on 6th November 2005 at no.13, and thence down to 24 and then 42.

Kate's promotional activities for the new album took three forms. The first was a new official website, put up with a holding page from the first announcement and finally launching on 7th November to coincide with the album release. There were inevitably technical problems with the site. Navigation was difficult and there was limited access to those who didn't use Flash graphics.

Then there were very limited press and radio interviews. The major print media was the December issue (of course published in early November) of *Mojo*, and extracts of this interview with Tom Doyle were syndicated in *The Guardian*. In the interview Kate was presented as "the antithesis of the mysterious recluse" as which, the tabloid press was, and is, so ridiculously fond of portraying her: "here, in Kate Bush's home, there is a 47-year-old mother of one, dressed in a workday uniform of brown shirt, jeans and trainers... around us there is evidence of a very regular, family-shaped existence – toys and kiddie books scattered everywhere".

"*I go out of my way to be a very normal person and I just find it frustrating that people think that I'm some kind of weirdo reclusive that never comes out into the world. Y'know, I'm a very strong person and I think that's why actually I find it really infuriating when I read, 'She had a nervous breakdown' or 'She's not very mentally stable, just a weak, frail little creature'.*" On finishing the album: "*there were so many times I thought, I'll have the album finished this year, definitely, we'll get it out this year. Then there were a couple of years where I thought, I'm never gonna do this... Everything just seems to take so much time. I don't know why. Time... evaporates... for the last 12 years, I've felt really privileged to be living such a normal life, it's so a part of who I am. It's so important to me to do the washing, do the Hoovering. Friends of mine in the business don't know how dishwashers work. For me, that's frightening. I want to be in a position where I can function as a human being.*"

Kate's first Radio interview was broadcast in the BBC Radio 4 programme 'Front Row' on 4th November. Introduced as "one of the most innovative, idiosyncratic and influential musicians of modern times" and *Aerial* described as "the most eagerly awaited new LP of the year", Kate explained "*I did actualty stop completely for a while, which is very unusual, normally I go straight from one project into another, and it was a very conscious decision to take a break. One of the first songs that I wrote was actually* King of the Mountain, *and so that would probably be... nine or ten years ago, and even the vocal that I did is the same one... it was just like a throwaway vocal that I put down on the track. And then I probably didn't record anything again, for maybe... two or three years*".

Kate also responded with some amusement to highbrow reviewers of her new single on the same programme a few weeks before: "*Some guy who was saying he'd heard the single. He was saying* [imitates geezer] *'It's only two chords!' and then they were discussing it more and he was saying how* [imitates geezer again] *'It's about Elvis Presley!' And it sounded really surprised I should have written a song about Elvis Presley. Which I love! I love the idea of doing something that isn't expected*".

As to the way she chose to live her life and conduct her career: "*I don't like to live in a glare of publicity. A long time ago, when I kind of finished making my second record, I realized that it was all the wrong way round. I was spending all my time doing interviews, television, press... suddenly this was what my life had become. And my initial drive had never to be famous, it had been to make a record. So I turned it all around, so that my time was being spent writing, and then doing a little piece of promotion at the end. And to me, that was the way that the balance worked best because, the creative process is something that I find very time consuming, and you have to have a lot of focus, and it comes from a quiet place.*". As to Bertie and his effect on her work: "*Yeah, I wanted to give as much time as I possibly could to my son... he won't be little for very long. I felt that my work could wait, really, whereas his growing up process couldn't... when you lose your mother you're no longer a little girl anymore. And so, I've had a lot of things that have changed me over the years, from the last album to this*".

As to recording and the incessant march of technology and the sound of *Aerial*: "*I think it would be a shame, amongst all this technology for us to lose our sense of humanity. And music is suffering greatly from the overuse of computers, and taking away the human element... art is about human expression. And I think machines and technology should be used by people... you shouldn't be a slave to them... it was a very conscious decision, with this record, that I didn't write through a computer. A lot of my friends write on computers so they, every time they hit a chorus in the structure of the song, you just have a repeat of the same chorus. Now for me that's not art because it should be something that is evolving, and developing as you move through song, and changing… Music is something very special and very emotive, and it's become very disposable… after the last record… I had a chance to actually sit back and think about what were the things that I felt I kept getting wrong ... I wanted to make a record that had much more space in it. And I also wanted to stand in the role of narrator... rather than… being the person inside the song. I wanted to stand outside and talk about situations outside of myself. Part of that process was also to not have very many backing vocals, to have a greater sense of one voice telling the story".*

Kate's second interview was done with Radio 2 DJ and long time supporter Mark Radcliffe for his show on 7th November and he introduced it thus: "I went her house, and we had asparagus flan for our lunch. And she was utterly charming, friendly... and something she's worked very hard to preserve – normal. Doesn't live a show business lifestyle. Doesn't live the life of a celebrity. She doesn't have a domestic staff or anything like that. She's a working mother, mother to Bertie. Something which has had a major effect on this record".

Amongst the questions asked was Kate's attitude to any live work and whether she'd withdrawn completely from the idea? "*No, no, I didn't. I think that's a general presumption, and quite understandable. I loved the tour, it was fantastic fun, but I didn't want to repeat a tour with the same material… But... by the time I started the third album I'm starting to become involved in the production, and it became a much more time-consuming process. And I think by the time I got to the fourth album... I'd do the next tour, it had all gone off into a different tangent where I was really trying to learn how to put records together in a studio... And I've toyed with it on and off a lot, because I did enjoy it, but I think I found the writing process so interesting, that I wanted to stick at that really... I wouldn't rule it out, but then, I haven't ruled it out for the last 20-odd years.*"

On the concept: "*I suppose really, it's very much to do with the idea of Birdsong.. I think Birdsong is a really beautiful sound. I think what I find interesting about it, too, is the way that they mark the day. Like for instance, you know, the dawn chorus – they seem to be very strongly connected with light. And I think in some ways, that was one of the… explorations I was trying to go off on with this, the connection between their song and light and the passing of day*". The Mark Radcliffe interview with Kate was subsequently broadcast on 19th November on Radio 2 as a documentary.

Kate did another interview with Hugo Cassavett for the Radio France programme 'C'est Lenoir' broadcast on November 11: As to where the album started: "*I suspect the first song I probably wrote, that ended up on the record, which is probably one of two or three, was* King of the Mountain... *And I thought... that would be nice as the first single... and off I went off into doing life stuff again... probably the next one would've been something like* Sunset *and* An Architect's Dream. *And I started playing with the idea that maybe they'd be quite nice somehow to be a part of this piece, rather than just individual songs... But at this point I hadn't decided it would be two records, just thought that it would be nice to do a conceptual piece. I went off again doing life stuff, had a baby... And then eventually sort of got all that under control and settled down to try start really making a record.*"

On Elvis and the cult of celebrity: "*The thing that I think of is how horribly famous he was as well… you see bits of film of him, particularly when he was very young, and he seemed so, I don't know, so innocent and sweet... I just don't think human beings are built to deal with that kind of fame... it's something that deeply challenges... where creativity comes from. It threatens it... I think what's important to me is to have a base that I work from, as a writer more I feel that I can focus, because you must know as a writer that having that creative focus is actually quite difficult to achieve sometimes… I just work. I fight, really, to live what I consider to be an extremely normal life... to me that's something that has integrity and value.*"

In the beginning, the publicity for Kate's new album was self driving. Publicity like that cannot be bought. Everyone it seemed wanted to welcome her return, and just as in the early days of 1978, the story made the BBC News. Kate's new material was discussed fairly positively on BBC Radio 4's 'PM' news programme on 28th September, but for some strange reason they felt the need to balance it with an interview with John Mendelssohn (*Waiting For Kate Bush*) who clearly showed where he is coming from by dismissing most of Kate's recorded output.

On 30th September *The Guardian* had a piece by Patrick Barkham. In it the writer talked to EMI and also to Roy Harper and others to get a more balanced look at where Kate was now coming from: "Frustrated by her refusal to play the celebrity game, tabloids have compared her to Greta Garbo and Miss Havisham, suggesting she is obsessed with her privacy. EMI, her record company, says suggestions she is a tortured recluse are nonsense. 'Kate's one of those artists who records and makes music to her own time-scale rather than meet a record company's deadlines, which is fine by us' said an EMI insider, with no hint of gritted teeth... The extraordinary voice of singer-songwriter Roy Harper was one of Bush's formative influences and he collaborated with her in the 1980s and 1990s and is still a friend. 'She is lovely to work with, a true musician. There is no need to tell her what to do, she has already done it and she is ahead, making suggestions. She is very honest and very gentle, bright and full of creativity, the kind of girl you should've married, really. She is very private and family orientated now. When you are that good a person, the danger is that everybody takes the piss. The cure for that is to keep yourself out of the public eye.' Those who have heard *Aerial* are, typically, amazed and

"Very early in my career I established my own production company that licenses my music and everything that goes with it. So I have complete control over the creative process. I don't need an entity that lies between me and my listeners. Who ever said that creating music was easy? Possibly the many cynics in the music business. I have nothing cynical about me."

"Originally I had planned to take a year out, to become distant from my music for a while. Well, and that year turned into twelve! The 16 years I had constantly spent in the studio resulted in a standstill of my own personal development."

"We all need some sort of detachment from what we love to do now and again. Among other things I have spent the last 12 years being a mother. Every mother of a little boy knows how simply being a mother moves you further."

"I associate height with the title. 'Aerial' marks a level on which you can find yourself above things, and from which you can look down".

"I don't think about my importance in pop history. For me, the titles of books and records have always been more important. They have always, when chosen well, made me curious about their content."

"There is huge expectation for this single... it begins quietly with a loping dub-like rhythm, with Bush's mysterious vocals seeming to tell the story of a powerful man and the emotional cost of his success. Already climbing the UK airplay chart, primarily because of Radio Two's support, there is little doubt that she is back with a bang" *Music Week*

"Right pop kids, get yer thinking caps on for a quick lesson in pop amazingness. Although Her Royal Bushness isn't your usual quirky pop sproglett (in fact, in pop terms she's positively ancient at 47!), she paved the way for pretty much every kooky and thoroughly unique female singer since. Without her, avante-garde pop a la Blur, Prince and The Killers would not have existed and Tori Amos, Christina Aguilera and Alison Goldfrapp would probably have been serving you chips over the nearest Spam-U-Like counter. And did we mention that she wrote the best elasticy-throated pop song ever, *Wuthering Heights*, when she was only 19? Anyhow... her first single release in 12 years - has the usual Bush trademarks stomped all over it. Soaring fruity vocals, thought-provoking lyrics, a driving rhythm and gorgeous electronic twiddlings make this a gem of a song. But if jiggling your booty and punching the air is your thing, you'll probably hate it!" *BBC 'Top Of The Pops' website.*

Graphic opposite: Chris Butler

slightly baffled... Bush told Harper that one was a concept album and, '*to lessen the blow*' the other was '*just Kate songs*'".

EMI's tactic with the album was simple. In September and October selected journalists from the general and music press would be invited to EMI, strapped into a chair and forced to listen to all of *Aerial* playing on a locked security CD player. It worked and it was soon clear that *Aerial* was going to do what it did under the support of its own buzz. The resulting press coverage was enormous and overwhelmingly positive, and most if it can still be read in full on Gaffaweb's *Aerial* page.

There were two waves of reviews. The first were previews anything up to a month or more before release, based on a single listen in the EMI chamber.

On the weekend of 2nd October the first preview arrived. *The Observer* (Barbara Ellen): "We've had a sneak preview of her new album, and can assure you – it's been worth the wait... It is in fact vintage Bush: a melodic, organic sprawl of wind, sea, seasons, time passing, dreams, secrecy and revelation, all mixed up with a sound that seems to segue smoothly on from *The Red Shoes* and *The Sensual World*... Most intriguingly, there is a song called *Bertie* where one hears a whole new Kate Bush – a mature, doting creature both energised and sucker-punched by mother love... She's still seething with strangeness and brilliance."

The Times (Pete Paphides) arrived on October 14 and hit a different 3/5 note: "the days when Bush pulled songs fully-formed out of the ether are long gone... In the past... you sensed that Kate Bush knew a vaguely contemporary production when she heard one. However... it's not certain that this is the case any more... *Nocturn*, a New-Agey hymn to the imminent dawn, is as unpleasant as it is unexpected. Thankfully, nothing else on either CD comes close to plumbing such depths... *Somewhere in Between* has Bush once again chasing intangibles and emerging with the album's unquestionable highlight: a life-affirming chorus of hushed harmonies and whispering rhythms with more than a hint of the sexual languor that gave *The Sensual World* of 1989 its knee-weakening frisson. If this is the point at which her lifelong artistic deceleration finally grinds to a halt, it won't be a bad way to remember her."

The Observer (Jason Cowley) two days later gave 5/5: "Few artists experiment more than Kate Bush – often to thrilling effect... *A Sky of Honey* is music of pagan rapture – songs about acts of creation, natural or otherwise; about the wind, rain, sunlight and the sea. Sometimes it is just Kate alone at her piano, her voice restrained. Sometimes, as on the outstanding *Sunset*, she begins alone and softly, but soon the tempo quickens and the song becomes an experiment in forms: jazz, progressive rock, flamenco. There are weaknesses. At times, Bush can be too fey and whimsical, especially on *Bertie*, which is about the joy of motherhood... most of the songs on this album are suspended – somewhere in between the tighter, more conventional structures of pop and the looser, less accessible arrangements of contemporary classical and the avant-garde; somewhere, in mood and atmosphere, between the lucidity of wakefulness and the ambiguity of dream; between the presumed innocence of childhood and the desire for escape offered by the adult imagination; between abstraction and the real... There is no one quite like her, which is why, in the end, we must forgive her excesses and eccentricities. We are lucky to have her back."

And *The Independent* on 21st October: "Since she was last involved, the bar on female sexual expression has been booted so much higher – or dragged lower, depending on your viewpoint – by the brazenly pornographic contributions of hip-hop and R&B divas... But in doing so, they have also scoured away the elements that brought the most interesting frissons to Bush's take on sexuality – the entire spiritual aspect, most notably, but also the notion of sexuality as something to be attained, something to build up to, a most satisfying mountain to scale... It's not an exclusively middle-class constituency, but it is one that exults in exercising the mind rather than just the body, that finds greater liberation in the imagination than in raucous, boozy indulgence. One that reads, in other words... *Aerial* is unquestionably a substantial piece of work, and its manifold peculiarities and quirks offer much more interesting fare... an extended meditation on art and light, fame and family, creativity and the natural world... I'd have to say that leaves Kate Bush still operating at the cutting-edge of intelligent adult pop, every bit as relevant now as at any point in her career. Just a little bit weirder, thank heavens."

"*Actually it's an honour to be on the same planet as her.*" By Spring 2006 we were able to see that by any reasonable test, Kate's new album had been a substantial international triumph. The album entered the official UK chart at no.3, by any consideration a huge success. Kate's new work was a critical and commercial smash hit. The opening lines of the *Mojo* review hit it: "Kate Bush is the greatest living British artist in song and this is her masterpiece".

On her own her website Kate commented: "*I'm totally overwhelmed with the success of* Aerial*!*" In particular it was a critical success. This editor must have read over a thousand reviews of the album in the press and on innumerable websites, and they fell simply into two categories: 95% who believed the album was good to masterpiece, and the 5% who couldn't bear to be in the same room. Curiously, there were very few reviewers who fell between the two camps.

As was noted in the full page article in the 5th November 2005 issue of *Music Week*, it was of course Kate's own decision that promotion would be low-key. As she has often said, she prefers making music to promoting it, and these days no doubt she preferred to be sharing Bertie's young life with him than answering the same questions about the same tracks over and over again. Despite that, the album was a significant chart and commercial success.

EMI's annual report published in June 2006 noted that 1.1 million copies of *Aerial* world wide put Kate amongst the Group's top selling artists of the year to 31st March. Often in countries where very little promotional activity occurred, *Aerial* was selling well on the back of the word-of-mouth buzz of "Kate's return". It is interesting to note that the album may have proportionately done better in places like Finland (no.2) and Poland and Germany (both no.3) than in the UK. It is, however, worth saying again that the *avalanche* (I know, I fled most of it!) of spontaneously generated publicity in the tabloids, broadsheets, weekly magazines, and on internet blogs and other sites, unleashed by the simple news that Kate was to release a new album and single, almost certainly achieved more than any larger scheme of deliberate promotion by Kate or EMI. As EMI Records MD Terry Felgate noted in the *Music Week* article, "Less is more. You see everything Kate does suddenly become very special". EMI Recorded Music CEO, Tony Wadsworth, added "In launching this album you accept that there is a huge amount of anticipation... there are very few artists that have never disappointed their fans but Kate is one of them and you cannot under-estimate the power of that with the buying public."

Kate's American company, Sony, took much the same attitude. "It's a simple plan," joked Will Botwin, Columbia Records Group chairman in *Billboard* 5th November 2005. "It's not like I have to keep a calendar in my pocket to keep track of her activities" Seriously, he admits, "It's incredibly challenging as a record label, in this day and age when most artists will do most things to get their records across."

In the same article Mike Allen, senior Vice President of international marketing at EMI Music U.K. & Ireland explained "Part one of our task, is to make sure the Kate Bush constituency that is so passionate and loyal is well aware that this record's there. And you don't take that for granted, you have to apply yourself to that. Beyond that is telling the tale to an audience that isn't already a Kate Bush fan, about where she is in terms of being an influence, that's a big part of making this a compelling story for 'newcomers' to check out." To reach younger fans, Columbia actively promoted the album via influential internet sites such as purevolume.com and myspace.com, as well as targeting online blogs. "It's not your normal shot of your artist looking to get on TRL," Botwin said. Kate is "one of those artists that can get away with" not promoting her projects. Jerry Suarez, divisional merchandise manager for music for Virgin Entertainment Group in the United States said: "Her fan base is still a record-buying one. It's not a first-day record." Allen also noted "The press that's been created without her talking to anybody is a measure of the reverence in which she's held in the U.K." In the end Allen and Botwin agree that Kate has to remain true to her code. "I sort of think the mystery can work in our favor," Botwin says. "You got to respect an artist who's really an artist, who's not prepared to just hawk her wares."

There were also some strange rumours. On

"Great excitement awaits the first single in 12 years from eccentric icon Kate Bush. Fans won't be disappointed with a song that flies from whispering electronic pulses to a finale of billowing melodies, edgy guitars and windswept choruses".
Heat

Dave says: The promotion for *Aerial* organised by EMI included TV adverts featuring *Aerial Tal*, and radio and TV adverts featuring a voice-over by actor Leslie Phillips, substantial press advertising and the 'supersize' poster featuring fake birds on the prominent site on the A4 Western entry into London. *Aerial* sold well over 90,000 units across the country in its first week, and at any other time of the year this would have been enough to put the album at no.1.

"And from the atmospheric opening to its last eerie gasp... unmistakably the sound of one of pop music's last great originals... and like some sonic sorceress locked away in her private lair Bush carries on from where she left off with *The Red Shoes* in 1993... but any thoughts that Bush is... preparing to tackle the pop world on its own terms, are cast aside by song itself. Lyrically, with an oblique reference to Orson Welles' classic movie *Citizen Kane* and to Elvis Presley, it is Kate's meditation on the perils of fame and power... the mood of the record is a masterful balance of opposites – cool reserve and sonic boldness, gothic gloom and sensual awakening. Oriental percussion, ghostly harmonies, synthesisers that whisper and howl accompany Kate's fraught but tender vocals. Fittingly for a woman who has taken so long to make a comeback there is no hurry to reach a climax. *King of the Mountain* builds slowly and it is the entrance of a grimy low-slung offbeat reggae guitar provides the cue for the band to slowly come together. When they do so it is like they are making music in a dream, while wading through a field of honey... Magnificent." Gavin Martin *Daily Mirror*

"The track is suitably odd... This... is equally spooky and has the air of Massive Attack. After a slow, hypnotic start it builds into a glorious crescendo. The lyrics are so strange, its hard to work out what she's on about." Bizarre *The Sun*

March 19th 2006 Sky News broadcast that Kate would be releasing "two new albums for 2006", likely to appear apparently in September and Christmas. Sky News also stated the release of these two albums will "discredit media speculation that Kate is a recluse, as she will be returning to the limelight", which probably indicates just how well informed they were. On 10th June 2006 Sky followed up with another news story that Kate had "two albums worth" of material already recorded whilst according to the Pause and Play website Kate's new "best of" 'The Complete Story' will be a two-CD set to be released in November. You get the feeling someone was pulling their leg, and they fell for it.

Aerial entered the UK album chart at no.3 on 13th November 2005. On Virgin Radio's album chart it was no.1. It had six weeks in the UK top 40 confounding the expectations of some who thought such an non-commercial item would disappear rapidly, whatever its artistic merits. The entire top 200 chart run was: 3 - 8 - 25 - 34 - 36 - 37 - 38 - 51 - 54 - 55 - 59 - 82 - 67 - 72 - 60 - 71 - 103 - 120 - 131 - 130 - 159 - 181, that was twenty-two weeks in all, excluding a brief re-entry at no.122 on 26th June 2006. This actually bettered the fifteen week Top 75 run of *The Red Shoes* which was supported by four singles. The rise to no.67 in early February seems to have been as a result of the publicity for the Brits, and the nomination for a 'South Bank Show' award. In the Irish charts *Aerial* débuted on 10th November 2005 at number 6 and remained in the top 75 for eight weeks: 18 - 32 - 49 - 61 - 66 - 58 and 62.

These chart numbers in fact conceal consistent sales, and are affected by the fact that *Aerial* was released in one of the best selling periods for albums ever. This is amply illustrated by the fact that just four weeks after release the album shipped platinum (300,000 units). *Aerial* achieved this award faster than either *The Red Shoes* or *The Sensual World* and it represents a major achievement for Kate as it must be one of the least publicised albums (in terms of major promotion) by a major artist ever.

In the 2005 year-end UK album chart *Aerial* was no.63 with a total of 312,000 copies sold and Kate the 44th best-selling album artist – a number of copies of *Hounds of Love* and *The Whole Story* having left record shops on the basis of interest sparked by the new album, not to say *Hounds of Love* constantly turning up in music press polls such as in the 28th January *NME* placing it at no. 41 in their list of the 100 "Greatest British Albums ever". As of 6th April 2006, *Aerial* had sold 354,000 copies (over the counter to customers) in the UK. One thing some noticed – *Aerial* was the highest ever album chart position for a female artist without having a photo on the album cover. All part of the idea of allowing the music to speak for itself.

Most of the continuing reviews were positive: "To sum up: Kate Bush is the greatest living British artist in song and this is her masterpiece. Regular readers may appreciate that I'm not one to traffic in hyperbole, but I can't put it in weaker terms. Those are the facts... *Aerial* is not flawless. None of her records are. Kate takes chances, and her world-view is so particular she cannot hope to please everyone all the time... Don't expect a rock'n'roll record. There's no chaos. It's all exquisitely sung, played and judged... You'll gather, therefore, that her trademark misty Britishness is present, stirring some long-dormant musical sense of heritage... Aside from, perhaps, Ray Davies, Kate is the sole trader left in such a market. But *Aerial* is neither prog rock, Brit pop nor folk music; it is pure Kate, in all her wonky splendour... And so few artists reward themselves the freedom to roam around their imagination in the way Kate Bush does. Her vast, innate sense of romance and drama is perfectly measured throughout these songs... the album slides into the stunning final sequence with the shivery duet *Somewhere in Between*, the sexy, transcendent *Nocturn* and the title track, wherein the lovers arrive at nirvana on a guitar solo... The first time, I was charmed, intrigued, a little perplexed. The second time, I was thrilled, moved, ravished. What does that remind you of? I can't wait to try it again." (Instant Classic 5/5, Jim Irvin *Mojo*).

"We certainly don't get the first half of *Aerial* on first listen... much of this CD falls short of her best... Only the final track, *A Coral Room*, is as mysterious and as beautiful as we expect Bush to be... If the album ended there, you'd sadly conclude that housework and child-rearing had terminally softened Kate Bush's head. Fortunately the second CD saves the day. The strings and electronic pulses of *Prologue* have a cumulative effect so intense it leaves you giddy, Bush's voice combining with bird and whale song to create something so gorgeous it's like drowning in oxygen... *Aerial* is a tour-de-force of chanting vocals, mind-bending sounds that come out of nowhere and lyrics that hit ravishingly romantic highs. It's a triumph..." (Alex Needham, *NME*).

"There's not another songwriter in the world that could have made a record like this. They wouldn't have been allowed... few do barmy concepts as well as her... On the first disc's closing track, *A Coral Room*, though, Bush proves she can excel with just her voice and Gary Brooker's piano as tools... It's a spellbinding performance and the equal of anything on 1985's revered *Hounds of Love*. For everything-but-the-kitchen-sink thrills, though, there is still the nine-part *A Sky of Honey*. Bush embarks on another quest, pulling the listener under water and up mountains, this time with twittering birdsong, children's voices, maniacal laughter, a jazz rumba and even a spoken-word turn from Rolf Harris... You could lose yourself for days here. The world is a better place with Kate Bush in it. She really should do this sort of thing more often." (4/5 Mark Blake, *Q*).

"We may never know Kate Bush, but we may know this – she's been very happy thank you very much. Both parts of *Aerial*... are infused with joy. *A Sea* almost functions as a brand new retrospective, a classically watery wall of sound with gorgeous pop hooks. There are millions of impossibly beautiful things about it... There's an arch wit to match the playful rhythms... *A Sky of Honey*, though rather daunting and potentially new age on paper, is equally delightful. Decadently and pleasingly fashioned from birdsong, giggling and electronics, there's a nice circularity in *Sky's* bassy echoes of *Dark Side of The Moon*, bringing Kate right back to Dave Gilmour where it all began... If there's more where *Aerial* comes from then we'll wait and we'll like it." (10/10 Tara Brady, *Hot Press*).

Not unsurprisingly Kate was nominated for 'Best British Album' and 'Best British British Solo Female Artist' in the 2006 "Brits" – which she regarded as "a great honour". It looks likely that the organising committee wanted her to perform and there were garbled rumours that some kind of award would be presented if she did. Fellow nominee (and EMI label mate) KT Tunstall actually publicly backed Kate for Best Female: "It's got to be the Kate Bush award – even though I'm up against her. She's just a legend. I'm chuffed to be in the same category as her" she told *The Mirror* at The Brits nominations party. In *Scotland on Sunday* on 5th February Nigel Williamson wrote that "Among the old guard, the miraculous return of Kate Bush after a dozen years away deserves to be celebrated by her being crowned best British female solo artist... she really should have won a lifetime's achievement award long ago. Indeed, one was allegedly offered, only for it to be hastily withdrawn when she made it clear she would not perform live. It is further claimed that was the year the organisers then decided to give it to the Spice Girls."

In the usual improbable carve-up on 15th February, however, Kate, who did not attend, lost out to Coldplay and KT Tunstall. The latter was plainly (and on any basis rightly) gob-smacked at the decision, and when Jo Whiley presented her with the statuette, she said "I'm going to take the head off of this and give it to Kate Bush, because she has such a great musical brain." In *The Guardian* the following day Alexis Petridis summed it up thus: "The question of what the Brits are supposed to be rewarding has always hung heavy over the event, but with this year's winners they seem to have found a straight forward answer. They rewarded commercial success... Rock critics may take serious issue with the notion that [Coldplay's]... *X&Y* represents the zenith of musical creativity in the past 12 months, particularly when placed alongside Kate Bush's wonderful, challenging and arcane *Aerial* and Gorillaz' kaleidoscopic album *Demon Days*. But record buyers would not: it comfortably outsold both."

In a re-vote on the BBC News website Kate won comfortably by 42.9% of the vote to KT Tunstall's 35.8%. In similar poll on AOL Kate won 'Best Album' with 37% of the vote and 'Best British Solo Female Artist' with 53% of the vote.

The annual 'South Bank Show' Awards are the only British awards to cover all areas of the arts. *Aerial* was nominated in the 'Pop' category, but lost out at the awards on 29th January to Richard Hawley's *Coles Corner*. For the second year running, Kate received a nomination for The *Mojo* Songwriter Award, presented to an artist 'whose career has been defined by their ability to pen exceptional material on a consistent basis'. Again, however, the gong went elsewhere, to Chrissie Hynde this time. One award Kate did win was the "Most Innovative Act" category in the Virgin.net Music Awards beating Gorillaz and Missy Elliot.

King of the Mountain was not actually released as a physical single in the USA, but as a download on 27th September. Chuck Taylor in *Billboard* referred to it as "ethereal, mosaic and non-conformist... that voice angelic, fragile and ever bewitching". Airplay seems to have been patchy, and without the solid support of those college and alternative stations which were so prominent in 1994, 1989, 1985 and 1982. Nonetheless in places it did get concentrated airplay and on 25th October 2005 was for example at no. 1 on the Filter Radio Airplay chart.

On 17th November *Aerial* arrived in the *Billboard* Top 200 album chart at no.48, and fell the following week to 126. The album certainly sold well as ever in the big cities on the East and West coast, being consistently in the top 10 of store sales charts in those areas, and in January 2006 for example was still in the Top 40 of internet retailer Amazon US. It was at no.25 in the year end critics' poll of the New York *Village Voice*.

There were many (many!) good reviews in the US: "Fans who have waited 12 years for the return of Kate Bush have reason to celebrate the arrival of this two-CD concept album. On disc one, the angelic songstress jumps from multi-layered pop symphonies... to haunting voice-and -piano soliloquies... On disc two, she traces the arc of a day through bird song, morphing her voice and lush instrumentations with feld recordings of winged creatures. Such is the scope of Bush's artistry that she finds poetry in the numerical sequence for pi, sensuality in the spin cycle of a washing machine and beauty in the wave forms used to represent audio in software programs. Despite her prolonged absence, Bush sounds as vital as ever... The second, a conceptual work that follows nature's course

"happily, King of the Mountain is a sly and subtle piece of work, suggesting that Bush's genre-defying musical intelligence burns undimmed."
Adam Sweeting
Independent On Sunday

"Tori Amos, Björk and others have attempted to eclipse Bush's otherworldliness, musicality and sheer weirdness, but none has come close and *King of the Mountain* shows why. It's a brooding epic which begins with an ominous guitar riff before that instantly recognisable voice charges in... the allegorical lyrical mystery makes her music more alluring. Bush was always a uniquely physical writer, but the more this song progresses, the more she sounds buffeted by the elements atop a frozen mountain. Gales howl around her before she concludes... It is not easy listening, but it is a landmark work. I can't wait for *Aerial*."
John Aizlewood
Evening Standard

"*King of the Mountain* is... a gloriously dense swirl of electronic pulses, synthesised beats and brooding guitars with a typically ominous vocal, it's as epic and elemental as you could want... since her last album, British music has unearthed a rich seam of pretenders to Bush's throne, including Dido, Goldfrapp, KT Tunstall and Joss Stone. They had all better look to their laurels: the queen of them all is back to claim her crown."
Nigel Williamson
Scotland On Sunday

"a magnum opus of almost five minutes filled with sophisticated beats, swirling synths and typically oblique lyrics. Happily Kate's voice doesn't sound the least bit rusty. It's a ravishing comeback". *The Sun*

"It sees her embarking on a slow ascent towards a suitable ethereal peak, synthesized wind, drums and gentle music providing a worthy companion for those familiar haunted vocals. As the title also suggests, this is something more epic than the chart-friendly numbers which she was once known for. One way of summing it up is to say that it is one of those songs which had you turn out the lights, close the curtains and sit in the dark when testing out your early CD player, and it sets the scene for a towering comeback by one of the country's finest talents". Simon Donohue *Manchester Evening News*

from afternoon to sunrise, slowly builds via fantastically gorgeous strings, a brief smattering of Spanish guitar, one slinky protracted groove built for *Nocturn*, and a duet of laughter and bird-calls on the throbbing title track... *Aerial* doesn't deliver anything resembling a conventional pop tune. And this suits Bush just fine." (Paul Verna, *Billboard*)

"Twelve years have passed since Kate Bush's last release. What was she doing all that time? Nothing, and everything. There is recurring imagery on *Aerial* of 'women's work', of mothering and household chores... *Aerial* keeps a microscopic focus on the mundane stuff of life. Which is not to say that the microscopic stuff is insignificant. Bush has always made music that could have sprung only from a female psyche, full of feminine sexuality and eccentricity. Her melodies don't build to one big climax; they rise and fall on shimmering waves... She writes about messy relationships, messy passions, messy bodies, messy minds... Bush has always mattered. And at 47, she has never mattered more. *Aerial* is a mysterious, meditative work reminiscent of Joni Mitchell in her *Hissing of Summer Lawns/Hejira* period... At that point in her career, Mitchell began writing about the inner lives of older women who were becoming invisible in a culture of glittery youth. Bush takes up the cause with a smirk on *How To Be Invisible*. With its spidery guitar lines and witty take on the witches' incantation from *Macbeth*... the song celebrates the coiled power of ignored and underestimated women. Sneaky and hypnotic, *Aerial*'s watercolor wash of symphonic and electronic textures becomes more defined with repeated listenings, just as Bush's portraits of seemingly placid hearth and home reveal unexpected twists and depths... the master-stroke of disc one is the washing-machine song, *Mrs. Bartolozzi*, a hushed piano-and-voice reverie broken by moments of unsettling silence. The song earns its allusion to Virginia Woolf's Mrs. Dalloway when the title character... lets her mind wander from her washday chores to an erotic recollection (or fantasy) of passion. *A Sky of Honey*, the bewitching suite that takes up all of disc two, depicts the sensual pleasures of a day in the English countryside, from the trill of birdsong... to the changing quality of the sunlight to the fall of velvety night. Did I mention that Bush is singing all of this from a bird's perspective? When she tries to imitate the twittering birdsong samples and breaks into peals of runaway laughter, the effect is that of joy flitting along the border of madness. It's quintessential Kate Bush." (Joyce Millman, *Portland Phoenix*)

King of the Mountain was a big Top Ten hit in Canada: "What could a piece of music possibly do to justify a 12-year wait? For starters, it should sound unaffected by anything released in the interim but without being so insular that it cannibalizes the artist's previous work. And it should resist providing easy gratification because the listener shouldn't be entirely sure what the lyrics are about or how the mood can turn from haunting to whimsical or why a reggae beat materializes halfway through. Then it should mete out that gratification slowly, after each listening. Just like this song does." (John Sakamoto, *The Toronto Star*).

The album shipped platinum in Canada on 7th June 2006 (100,000 units). This confirms that, as expected, *Aerial* was and is a slow burner. It did not set the charts alight with a short but big impact, but rather continued to sell fairly steadily in the background.

The reviews again were mostly very good indeed: "Kate Bush Land turns out to be barely changed. She seems relaxed and renewed on *Aerial*, but it's full of the touches that enraptured her fans and made the prigs label her barmy. There's the song in which *Pi* is sung to more than 100 decimal places, and the one about the washing machine. That's actually one of the album's finest, movingly tracing mortality and loss through the domestic poetics of laundry... She remains preoccupied with English landscape in its mystic and sensual aspects, and now as a familial setting too... *A Sky of Honey*, a dappled portrait of a summer day from dawn to nightfall to dawn again, with particular lingering on birds and sea. With arrangements by the late Michael Kamen at Abbey Road Studios, it shifts from Joni Mitchell-ish jazz to hard rock to Gypsy Kings to histrionic chorales in a genre known only as Kate Bush, and back. But ultimately it does, as she sings, "become panoramic," immersing the listener in colour and more than earning its grandeur... On some tracks... dull production obscures the virtues. It's a relief when the collection returns to just Kate and her piano, on her sumptuously forlorn tribute to her mother... *A Coral Room*. Yet how much more thrilling it would be to hear her explore some new technology. But that could take another dozen years. What we've got is this flawed but ecstatic experience, *Aerial*. And once again, nearing 50, Kate Bush is making it sound like most other singers just don't know the secret of life. Listen close." (Carl Wilson, *The Globe and Mail*)

On 3rd November 2005 *King of the Mountain* was a new entry at no.12 in the European Top 100 singles charts collated from 25 countries. On 1st December *Aerial* was no.4 in the Europa album chart. The album was a substantial pan-European success.

In Germany the single gained substantial airplay on certain stations, in late October being in the top ten of SWR3 the country's favourite radio station. The track entered the singles chart at no.42 on 4th November, falling to 49 the following week. *Aerial* entered the album chart at no.3 on 24th November, and on first week sales was already half way to being certified gold. The remainder of the chart run was 4 - 13 - 18 - 24 - 22 - 22 - 24 - 29 - 32 - 32 - 51 - 62 - 78 - 87 - 94. There was substantial press coverage - the German *Rolling Stone* with its fabulous Kate cover put the British edition (without one) to shame. There were also articles in *Spiegel*, *Sueddeutsche Zeitung*, *Zeit*, *Welt* even in the tabloid *Bild*. The album received the quarterly award for "Best Pop Record" from the German Record Critics Award in February 2006.

Aerial went gold in France in April 2006. The album entered the album chart on 12th November at no.12 and the remainder of the chart run was - 23 - 27 - 36 - 42 - 44 - 43 - 53 - 56 - 74 - 69 - 85 - 86 - 114 - 137 - 157 (16 weeks) It was no.135 in the year end album chart.

On 2nd November *King of the Mountain* was at no.24 in the Italian singles chart. The album entered at no 9 on 12th November 2005 and thence 25 - 45 - 53 - 57 - 72 - 79 - 75 - 89 - 76 - 79. When the retail price dropped into the mid-range in April 2006 it actually re-entered the chart at no.90, went up to no.87, and disappeared until May re-entering again at no.86, again indicating slow burning persistent sales.

In Switzerland the single appeared in the chart at no.47 on 6th November. *Aerial* entered the album chart at no.12 on the 13th, and had a solid run: 12 - 14 - 21 - 23 - 33 - 35 - 49 - 58 - 56 - 68 – 66. In Austria *Aerial* débuted at no.23 on 12th November and thence 23 - 29 - 38 - 51 - 63 - 64 - 64 - 53 - 71 and 72.

The album peaked in the Belgian chart at no.11 on 24th November. It was top ten in the Dutch download charts in October into November, and 43 down to 45 in the singles chart. It fell back to 85 before climbing back to no.13 in one of the places where the video was shown to good effect.

Aerial was very successful in Holland. It came into the chart at no.7 on 12th November and stayed in the top 75 for 28 weeks: 10 - 10 - 15 - 16 - 21 - 30 - 29 - 21 - 25 - 33 - 38 - 25 - 27 - 42 - 50 - 52 - 62 - 47 - 21 - 27 - 34 - 38 - 40 - 51 - 53 - 61 - 73. It enjoyed a chart revival in March 2006 (47 to 21) due to Kate's nomination for "Best International Female Artist" in the Edison Awards (which she did not win that year) and the new mid-range pricing. By May when it finally fell out of the Dutch top 75 it had certainly gone Gold and was virtually Platinum.

Again good reviews: "Pretentious? Moi? Yes surely, but Kate Bush gets away with it. *Aerial* is her best album since *Hounds of Love* was released twenty years ago. Like no other, Kate Bush knows how to navigate between art and kitsch, between intimacy and pathos, between modesty and megalomania... She took her time but... proves again that she is one of the very few true artists of pop music. Completely authentic, with an oeuvre that stands entirely on its own." (Gijsbert Kamer, *de Volkskrant*).

"In my circle of friends one young man didn't have a crush on Kate Bush, the beauteous British singer of *Wuthering Heights*. We sent the poor chap to a therapist." That was the way Paul Witteman introduced his column on *Aerial* in *de Volkskrant*, on 28th January. Apart from being a talk show host on Dutch public TV Paul Witteman writes mainly about classical music. In his column he compared *Aerial* with a recent CD of songs by Dowland and Byrd sung by Barbara Bonney. To Witteman it seemed that Kate's songs (and *Bertie* especially) seem to be coming right from the jewel boxes of Byrd or Dowland. He describes *And It was a Lover and his Lasse* by William Byrd as a gorgeous song from the golden age of English music. The song would feel at home in Kate Bush's repertoire. Who isn't struck by Kate's work really needs therapy, Witteman concludes.

Finland was another country in which Kate's new music went down very well indeed, and led to her being nominated for Finnish "Emma" Award for best international act. The album peaked at no.2 and stayed in the top 40 for over three months. It was actually the first country in which *Aerial* went gold. The full chart numbers were: 13 - 2 - 6 - 11 - 24 - 26 - 23 - 19 - 11 - 13 - 12 - 15 - 15 - 24. It briefly re-entered the chart in March and was the no.8 international album of 2005. *Helsingin Sanomat*, the major newspaper in Finland, listed *Aerial* as one of the

"Now children you may think it's a bit sad to like a track by an artist that your Dad fancied over twenty years ago, but Kate Bush deserves your attention. In an era of identikit pop stars we should thank our lucky stars that Bush has come back from the abyss to grace us with her presence... she doesn't disappoint. Five minutes of Bush's eerily beautiful voice and a windswept ethereal melody proves truly mesmerising. Simplistic in the extreme it may be, but a great comeback it is also" *Gigwise*

Graphic: Neil Sheriff

"Ok, so it was hardly worth waiting a decade for but then what is? Nothing that we can think of. What it is, is an apt reminder of just how little everyone else is trying right now and just how Ms Bush has been missed. It's five minutes of druggy scenes, has a mental breakdown in the middle, and sounds like Sade washing down lyrical razorblades with plummets of fizzy white wine nabbed from Massive Attack's *rider*. But with more heart than a Canadian AOR radio station or a passionate snog with a Care Bear. If we were excited about the album before we heard this (and we were, very), now we're EXCITED IN BIG CAPITAL LETTERS." *NME*

A huge collection of the massive press coverage of *Aerial*, as well as much else is maintained at Gaffaweb – the largest online Kate-related archive www.gaffa.org

Dave says: It seems that EMI were keen for both *Joani* and *How to be Invisible* to be released as singles. But it was not to be.

best records of 2005.

King of the Mountain did good download business in Sweden, peaking at no.9 in the download chart without any radio airplay to speak of. On 17th November *Aerial* débuted on the album chart at no. 7, mainly on the strength of sales in the Stockholm region. The complete chart numbers were 7 – 16 – 37 – 45 – 56 and 58. *King of the Mountain* was never released on single in Norway and very rarely played on most of the radio channels. Regardless, *Aerial* entered the album chart at no.4 on 15th November 2005, the best new entry since *Never For Ever*. The top 40 numbers were 4 – 9 – 14 – 20 – 22 – 25 – 21–12 – 13 – 21– 30 – out – 39 – out – 24. Norway's biggest record store chain Platekompaniet put *Aerial* at no.6 on their "Best albums of 2005".

Scandinavian reviews: "The lyrics are as wilful as ever... and her music is still as deeply rooted in the same 1980s style that has been its fertile soil. Musically that means – for better or worse – that a whole lot of *Aerial* sounds somewhat dated; with statically programmed ethno-rhythms, dreamily sweeping synthesized layers upon layers, upon which the passionate voice of Kate Bush hovers... Without one having to know why she sings, over a Farfisa loop reminiscent of Terry Riley, about a man obsessed by mathematics. Without one having to know why, she arranges a song to her son Bertie... as a medieval ballad. Without one having to know why she gives the... paean to a washing machine erotic overtones, and that in a way that paraphrases Laura Nyro. It's just as easy to like the more conceptual second CD, which, without being easier to understand than the poetical bird song that sweetens the music, just makes itself comfortable in the beautifully unbearable lightness of being; from sunset to sunrise. *Aerial* is a very pleasant record. Some details can be criticised, but as a whole it is probably her best ever." (5/6 Dan Backman, *Svenska Dagbladet*)

"Her previous album *The Red Shoes* was her worst. Many of us believed she stayed in Hell. 'Til now... The fact is that Bush can be compared with such performers as Roy Harper, Bert Jansch, Robyn Hitchcock and Kevin Ayers in that she makes music that inspires. She differs from them in that she makes deeply personal, peerless and eccentric music for a large audience. Both discs have an organic, acoustic feel along with a simplicity trying to get this to sound like her timeless début... *A Sea of Honey* is... Seven compelling individual songs... She's at her best singing about 3.14 and a foamy sensual song about a washing machine... *A Sky of Honey*... is compelling evidence that Kate Bush has not lost her ability to brew fascinating and beautiful music... One of pop's greatest original artists of the past 30 years." (Terje Eidsvåg, *Adressa*).

At the end of 2005 Kate sent some lucky fans a rather nice Christmas gift, a Christmas card which featured colour artwork by Bertie together with one of the promo CDs which feature Kate's selection of songs from her previous albums. Only 2,000 of these CDs were produced.

What was astonishing to many in July 2006 was the fact that *Aerial* was not amongst the nominations for the Mercury Music Prize. This became quite an issue.

In his *Daily Telegraph* blog on 20th July Neil McCormick said: "This year's Nationwide Mercury Prize is at best an irrelevance, at worst a disgrace. Its slogan is 'championing the best of UK music', but looking at the wilfully obscure shortlist of nominees for album of the year, the question arises: is this really the best we can do? In a year bursting with musical activity of wit, vision, energy and ambition, a panel of judges drawn mainly from London's music media has come up with a list of curiosities from the outer edges of taste".

Of relevance to us he said: "Do established artists no longer make work of any value, or has over-exposure rendered us deaf to their talent? What about veterans such as the Rolling Stones, David Gilmour, Paul McCartney, Scott Walker and Morrissey, or is the competition closed to anyone over 45? Which might explain the criminal absence of Kate Bush, whose deliriously bonkers comeback is constructed on a scale of passion and imagination that makes most pop sound one dimensional in comparison." The SpaceLab indie website commented "everybody seems to be freaking out about why Kate Bush is not on the list."

The BBC news report commented that "Critics were shocked that Lily Allen and Kate Bush were snubbed". The chair of the judging panel, musical sociologist Simon Frith, simply responded that judges had tried to choose the "best records of the year" and this year's list was a "celebration of songwriters".

As Kate was later to note, 2006 was a quiet year. Although there was much discussion, there was no second single from *Aerial*. Many fans would have liked *Joanni*, or even something novel like *Nocturn*, but it seems that Kate was not really taken with any of these ideas, and after the reaction in some circles to the video for *King of the Mountain*, was not awfully keen to make another video.

Actually, it was soon apparent that Kate regarded the *Aerial* cycle as over: the album had been completed and sent out into the world. It had actually sold rather well, and now it was time for drawing breath and thinking about new projects.

That's Just Del Palmer!

A Report by Colin Seimer

Issue 76: June 2005

Could it possibly? No Never! Getting ready, riding the train to meet Johnny and Jonathan at Kings Cross, I worried; November 7th 2005, that unforgettable night when so many patient souls had gathered together to celebrate the arrival of a new Kate Bush album, would be a tough act to follow.

I should say I don't handle my booze too well. It starts the same every time; the first pint goes down very slowly. However, by number three I'm off and running. Soon the tongue starts wagging (often my arms start flapping)... next morning... "Oh no! I didn't. Did I?" I have been known to perform this dance; well, more of a drunken faux pas. See, I once observed that one could do the chicken dance to any Kate Bush song, the best being *The Dreaming* and *James and the Cold Gun*.

6th May 2006. We arrived at the Ivy House in Holborn late to find a few folks politely sitting around a table. This was an informal gathering planned by a few folks on the Kate Bush Forum. And it was, well... awkward. I was right! This evening was never going to surpass November 7th. I got itchy. I had quit smoking months before but damn I wanted nicotine. Crap! Pint please! Then wow, there he was... John Morango in the flesh; he's like a forum celebrity, travelled all the way from Australia with his partner Geoff! I said hello and he presented me with a small toy koala. It was truly lovely to meet him.

People started to arrive; lots of them. Monty, Paul (Adric), Donna, James Lumbard, Lou, Lesley, Mickey Mack, Tina, Smudge, Steve, Will, Phil, Beth, Kinsal, Andrea, Kerry, Mike, Kev, Neil, Ian, Lisa. Sorry if I missed anyone. Sadly, Krys and Peter couldn't make it and they were missed. Then... Drinks, drinks, drinks. More people. Pint number three and lots of laugher. The place was packed.

A couple of us were standing at the bar chatting when someone said "Who's that over there?" We turned to see a crowd gathering around this handsome silver-haired guy. I turned back and replied, "Oh, that's just Del Palmer." We chuckled. The crowd around this guy grew to a buzzing swarm. We looked again, and... "HOLY..." wait for it... "SHIT!!!!" There, standing in the Ivy House, the same room where, six months earlier, we gathered to celebrate the end of 12 years of celibacy, there stood... Wait for it... Del Friggin' Palmer!

What a charming, welcoming man. He was accompanied by his partner Linda. People were smiling, taking photos and getting autographs. Linda encouraged people to come and chat with Del, especially anyone nervous. What a great experience to be able to chat with them several times. They weren't just politely showing their faces at an event, they were part of it. Being there with us, talking and sitting with us for the rest of the evening was really very generous. Del bought us all "Slippery Nipples" (Sambuca topped with Baileys). We toasted his kindness and courage to come to what could have been a bit overwhelming.

I was now well beyond pint four (maybe five) when someone dared... Oh dear! Never dare! I jumped in front of the unsuspecting Mr. Palmer and away I went; chicken dancing for crown and country. Sorry Mr. Palmer. Oh, and the next meet-up is on 4th November to mark one year of *Aerial*. Get it in your diary now. And tell Kate if she's at a loose end or fed up of gazing at her washing machine and fancies a good night out we'd be pleased to stand her a sweet sherry or two.

Photo: *HomeGround* Reader

The truly scary thing was that for many of us the night was only beginning. After, we headed to the always accommodating St. Mike Wade's place where things continued for several hours. As for this evening living up to the *Aerial* release party, check out these gems! The following are reports of what information many folks got from Del: Kate will always carry on working, it is what she does, and is driven to do. No retirement in the offing... Being a mum is what Kate wants to do... Del is doing more vocal work of his own and is working on an album... They plan to add a "who played on which track" listing for *Aerial* onto Kate's website... Kate feels the response to the album has been wonderful... and she feels incredibly lucky to have such loyal, patient fans who bear with her and support what she does... The working title for *Nocturn* was apparently 'Dream'... About Kate, Del said they were closer now than ever - more like brother and sister... Kate is working-out and dancing again... There are no plans for another greatest hits collection in the foreseeable future... He said that across the music industry Kate's fans are known to be the most devoted and that she is aware, and is very proud, of that.

King of the Mountain

Thank you very much...

Issue 76:
December 2005

On 31st August 2005 at 10.00 a.m. EMI officially announced the release of Kate's new single and album...

In the chat room at KBNI Kate fans reacted instantly...

A double album! I actually let out a whoop of excitement all by my lonesome. I'm a bit stunned and a lot elated. I think I peed a little too.
Jig of Life

Isn't it fantastic news about *Aerial*?! I saw the news on the internet at work and screamed out loud in the office... which is not a good idea as I work on a mental health team! I am so excited! Happy times ahead!
Dave Smith

I've literally been crying with happiness today... and that's never happened before! It just seems so unbelievable, so good, I've been walking on air since this morning and I won't sleep tonight...oh it's fantastic... SHE'S BACK and IT'S A DOUBLE!
Yorkshire Stu

Well, I don't see what all the fuss is about. I only joined the Forum and started buying Kate albums last month and already she's announcing another one... Why couldn't she have held off a little longer?
Peter

Potty Pam: It's 8.20 on 31st August 2005 and I have just woken from slumberland. I had the most amazing dream about Kate last night. She was singing in my garden and a beam of light came out of her fingers and hit my head and I started to float above the ground. Kate was singing "tell them, tell them". Then I was dream-flying above the landscape and as I was flying across water I saw Kate in a boat and she called out "It's here", like "he's here" at the beginning of *The Man with he Child in his Eyes*. I woke up with such a great feeling. It's like Kate has asked me to tell you that today something great is going to happen...

And it did...

Oh my God! I can't believe this... do you think I could get a job on *Most Haunted*? I need to lie down. It's all a bit Stonehenge!!! This is a testament to the power and beauty of Kate's music that we are all so excited. I have had tears in my eyes with sheer anticipation but mostly because we as a community of fans are so happy. I feel like I did when I went in to town on the number 7 bus to pick up my copy of *Sat In Your Lap* all those years ago. Kate has the ability to put the child back in the man's eye. Thank you to all involved for keeping us up to date and for making me feel like part of something important and beautiful. And… thank you, Kate.

Rob Mac Aoidh: Lost happiness and the emptied happy house... Rosebud, the beloved and now left behind forever on the unreachable-from-the-mountaintop childhood joyfulness of *Citizen Kane*... *King of the Mountain*, the childhood game of dominance and training for adulthood, and grasping at growing up all too soon... You can never look back, or if you do you can't go back there again... Gone just as surely as if having worn wings of wax or a faithless pillar of salt... all that's left is the whistling wind, blowing through the hollow house that once was a Happy Home... It's so wonderful to have her back.

Donna Kile: I love *King of the Mountain* with a passion. I have kept it playing continuously since the first morning. I sleep with it all night long. It's rich and beautiful, and her voice is powerful and fills me up. As she has done over and over, she's come to me at a time when I most need her. I feel her walking along side of me through this rough spell, and her voice gives me strength. The layers and layers of the song build, and her voice gets stronger, and I feel my heart beat faster, and by the end of the song, I know that everything will be all right. Kate is back with us, and that's all that matters. It's remarkable and perfect.

Edoardo Seianis: Kate always manages to surprise me. And this time she did it in a very positive way. I say "this time" because I am one of the few fans who didn't enjoy completely *The Red Shoes*. I thought Kate had lost her way and I waited patiently for her comeback. On first hearing *King of the Mountain* I got very emotional. I loved the clean, solid sound, the effective use of drums and guitars, the combinations of different styles of music and the growing structure of the song. It was love at first "hearing". *King of the Mountain* has the power of its own title. Kate finally managed to refine what was intended with *The Red Shoes* – to produce her music in a more direct way – but this time she didn't miss the originality of her previous works. Kate writing about Elvis is most unexpected. That's why it's a winner: she managed again with her beautiful mind to go beyond expectation.

Collin Kelley: *King of the Mountain* is a slow burn... a grower. It's Kate for the 21st Century – a mix of classic *Hounds of Love/Sensual World* era and the reggae influenced *Rocket Man* cover. I hear Peter Gabriel in there, too; the opening pulses remind me of *Mercy Street*. I love how the song builds and builds and the line about the wind closing the door is so haunting. The lyrics are spot on.

It seems to be Kate responding to the cult of celebrity and how it goes to some peoples' heads and they can't take it and isolate themselves. Kate has some insight to this after her long absence from the spotlight and I think *King of the Mountain* is her own way of answering back to the media who have harped on her "disappearance". While the song references Elvis and *Citizen Kane* directly, there's a bigger aspect of this song which takes the past and recent tabloid fodder, ties it up in a neat package and lobs it back. Only Kate can do this with such grace and pathos. Her vocals are superb, the production is sharp, Bertie's drawing for the single sleeve is a nice counterpoint to the darkness of the song itself. This is vital Kate Bush music. She's at the height of her powers as a musician.

Dr Alex Kraaijeveld: To hear *King of the Mountain* for the very first time, I retreated to the 'Japanese Garden' here at work. For this moment it had to be the perfect spot; quiet and serene. The mysterious, haunting, pulsating song. I loved it at first listen. I'm not ashamed to say I had tears running down my face. Kate, it's wonderful to have you back!

For me, what was also very special, was that

on 21st September, just after 10am, most of Kate-dom was listening with me, all around the world, holding their breath during Ken Bruce's introduction, absorbing those first notes, feeling the tears well up on hearing her voice again after all those years. Very powerful and a great way to share the occasion with you all.

Steve: Kate is back! That voice, the wind effects, those drums. Bloody brilliant. This song is perfect in every way. Just perfect. I must admit that while it was playing I started to cry. Thank you Kate. You have made a tired old man very happy.

Lagan Boy: *King of the Mountain* is a jewel and it may go unnoticed for some people (usual for Kate's art) It sounds harmless at first because it's about innocence lost This song is so cold. It's even colder than the epitome of the ghost of Cathy when she sang *Wuthering Heights* in 1978. She addresses the madness of our world in the quest for endless power so well – it's disturbing. The "ooh ooh" and the howling wind emphasize further the coldness that depicts the evil power and all that is seen through Citizen Kane. She is a genius. I have the gooseflesh down my spine. Kate, it's beautiful, scary, but beautiful.

Doug Alan: Does it strike anyone else as if *King of the Mountain* is very much the work of someone who greatly regrets her fame? After all, here we are presented with the imagery of an Elvis who has escaped his fame by faking his own death and can be seen at times dancing on his own grave, and of the 'King of the Mountain', which is a legend of a great warrior who escapes from it all for a great deal of time, and only comes down again when he is truly needed. And of Rosebud, which represents the happiness that *Citizen Kane* lost when he pursued fame and fortune.

Brian: It is such a beautiful yet disturbing song. The imagery is stark and makes me feel uncomfortable. The idea of Elvis watching his own funeral is so surreal. I remember seeing a picture of Elvis' pool house in Graceland – and in this photo a ghostly figure could be seen. Of course, the tabloids said it was Elvis! No matter what it was, it looked so lonely and it reminds me of this song. The whole "Rosebud" idea is also sad – again the loss of innocence and simple pleasures. A fascinating, beautiful song that grows on you.

Mad Love Hound: Amazing. Just to hear Kate's voice in something new was great. When I first heard it on the Ken Bruce show I thought, "What the hell was that?" Then, ten seconds into playing it for a second time, the beat got me! It reminded me of *The Dreaming* for some reason. Who else has the guts and talent to sing a song like the wind? It's like a living, breathing, creepy creature that's been let out.

Despite being quite skint I got a taxi home from work 'cos I could not wait to wait on damn unreliable transport to get home and listen to *King of the Mountain.* And can I say Kate you were worth every fucking £4.50 of the fare!
Cazlo

Graphic: Neil Sheriff

Aerial

First Impressions of Kate's new Album

Issue 76: June 2005

John Carder Bush

Aerial is a work of art about love. There is simply nothing that can compare with it. I have never heard an album so perfectly proportioned, so perfected and executed with such calm mastery. Popular music grows up with this album.

Brushstrokes of imagery, colour and passion, held in crafted frames tell us about the processes of art in an ecstatic celebration of light and rhythm, and, as well, we have the classical composer in her arrangements, depth and scan, and the poet in the insights. It is Classical, architectural, Romantic, it is all embracing. And Mahler, and Richard Strauss, and Puccini and…

But, more importantly, there's a message in this music that is very spiritual. This message is found in the maturity of the emotional scan. We go all the way up, and we go down as deep; we get the joy and get the tears – there's no escape. And then they become the same thing – the acceptance of the beauty of life. This is not merely how she sees the meaning of life, it is how it is.

Graphic: *King of the Mountain* by Chris Butler

Many thanks to Chris for his complete collection of graphics representing the tracks on *Aerial*

In this quest through darkness into sunshine, we begin with someone looking for an answer – why, why do we suffer because we love? However deep and beautiful that suffering becomes, the answer is that there is no answer.

In the second album we meet the wonderful acceptance of someone who has discovered that the no-answer is not the end but just another beginning, and that beginning is your choice – joy, or misery and obsession.

She has chosen joy, and with this realisation she takes us into the light.

And what light! Of birth, of Spring, of Summer, of real love that can communicate with everything that breaths and sings.

We start at the top of a mountain, in a high place looking down. We are taken to the bottom of the sea, and in the last track we are up high again, but this time we can see it all and it's great, not iced and frozen in the misery of material wealth, but full of laughter and beauty in the celebration of life.

Get into this album, into this spiritual journey, and you will emerge changed.

King of the Mountain – Those bare, lonely, haunting notes of the chorus, place us on the top of the mountain as we start this journey. But it's not a mountain top where you can see everything clearly all around, it's a bleak mountain top of loneliness where the power of money vies with the power of death – the winner is always alone, the losers have the comfort of common loss. The King of the Mountain is not a happy man. Take warning.

π – Most erotic of all the songs, and so clever to make it a song about mathematics, because, of course, like the conundrums of mathematics, love itself is as complex and as impossible to grasp in the intellect – from 'phone numbers to the rules of the planets, from computers to music, mathematics, and love, rule our lives.

Bertie – Well, isn't this just delightful? An Elizabethan jig about the man-child that is in every woman's eyes, and, for some, becomes a reality on which all hope is pinned, and all love. Can't you see how clean and open, full and unconditional this love is? No hint of suspicion, no lingering mistrust, no pain, just opening up the valves and pouring it all out. Feel privileged to see such nakedness.

Mrs Bartolozzi – Acklesian (before Gabriel, Kate and Cave there was Ackles) in this suburban loneliness we move from the obsession of the mathematical man to the obsession of the person reduced to satisfaction in cleanliness. Where do ritual and obsessive-compulsive disorder find the dividing line? The use of silences vibrating with the last piano chord, and its exquisite timing, smack of exhausted desperation, where all life is reduced down to getting the washing clean, the ritual that becomes a sad and relentless god.

It is a beautiful allegory of loss, and there is pure, pure poetry in the lovers' clothes intertwining and the micro-ocean of the contained water.

The washing machine becomes the erotic symbol of the deepest intimacies of love – when you wash another person's clothes you learn so much about them. We think we can wash it all away and make it sparkling clean, but, hey, think again and feel that loss. You can't wash away the stains on the heart.

Such poetry…

How To Be Invisible – This track rocks with the walking bass, the lonesome cowboy whistle and Isaacian guitars. We are in some dark Country land of desert voodoo on the Mexican border with Castaneda walking in the shadowlands. Is it how we become ignored in relationships? How we become invisible to those we love the most? Someone who has become invisible works out the simple, everyday contents of the spell and offers the formula? I don't know. That haunting, haunting "Is that an Autumn leaf falling?/ Or is that you walking home?" has really caught something special.

Joanni – She wears no ring – she belongs to no man because she belongs to God, she stands alone above what Abraham Lincoln described as "that attractive rainbow that rises in showers of blood". This Manga Joan in white armour sees only the beauty of the chaos and slaughter below her for she is alone in her unique relationship with God. That specialness gives her that all important thing that will make her different – the beauty of martyrdom. She will become immortal.

But, wait a minute, that last gasped out "au revoir" after the blood and the prayers, what does it say? Maybe as the flames licked up to melt the armour, and her, there was doubt that this holy splendour was in the end only vanity…? She was just another *King of the Mountain*? I don't think so... her last word is that she will see us again. Hello, Sophie Scholl, hello Ulrike Meinhof, hello Pattie Hearst, hello…

A Coral Room – Are you really ready to come into this room?

This is a room made of dead things where, because of the skill and artistry of the architect, and knowledge of the secret formula, the magic mathematics of its construction will make you cry like you have never cried before. This room will let you empty out the deepest sludge collected at the bottom of your hearts.

From the moment that lonely, caressed piano just gently takes you by the hand like an angel of the past and says come and look at what we are, what we become and what we can no longer have – those moments of pleasure are never for ever – she takes us through heaven and hell and says that's it – doesn't love hurt, doesn't it? Just look at the dead below us, the generation young in the second world war, and there's nothing we can do about it. The power of the King of the Mountain is impotent before death.

The imagery of the brown jug, symbol of the human body and soul that can be so full, and then so empty and discarded, the range of emotion from soft delight to the bitterness of inevitability at the end, has all and everything in it as it so calmly harrows heaven and hell.

This is the most perfect poem/song I have ever heard. I wonder at the genius that produced this masterpiece. By the end of this teaching even the sinister spider of time has just become a little spider coming out of the broken jug. Little spider, who were you once?

That last "what do you feel" is terrifying in its complete hopelessness. Don't go into this room too often, this medicine is very powerful, and addiction could destroy you. It is not just music – the music has created something far greater, and far more powerful, than itself. There is an alchemy at work here that hovers over us like an all encompassing spirit. Only one other piece of music touches me in the same way that this does, and that's one of Richard Strauss's last four songs, *Beim Schlafengehen*.

I hope she will never have reason to write another song like this.

Prelude and Prologue – From that "What do you feel?", and our hopeless human condition plumbed to the depths, we are resurrected into life and all its beauty – no more gloom now we have been all the way down, we can only come back up. The hope in *Bertie* burgeons into a daybreak on a world full of, made of, and celebrated in music, colour and song.

We start as though we are waking with the last part of the dream of the coral room still playing, we come out of the dream of sadness into a sleepy afternoon serenaded by collar doves who give their song to the piano ("you're full of beauty"?) and the voice of a child. It's that Summer afternoon of Alice, of the English lawn, of the seaside, of the past joys of childhood relived again in the child of her own. At last we can see again with the eyes of a child, and, hey, isn't it just fantastic? We can make our own sun and moon.

With a nod to the Englishness of Vaughan Williams, we are suddenly drenched in imported Italian light. Wonderful.

An Architect's Dream, The Painter's Link – This shifts us from the Sufi perfumed world view to celebrating the Zen creative accident of nature intruding on art – we even get a little bit of Sakamoto synthesiser. Of course, all art is an imitation of the perfection of nature (birdsong,

Graphic: *Prelude* by Chris Butler

sunsets, rainbows, aurora borealis, trees, synchronicity) and when we relinquish control to something higher than us beautiful things can come from our mistakes (something bigger is being kind to them).

This artist tells us that we must learn to go with this, to see our mistakes as something we use to learn by, and the wonder of what we are shown is the reward.

Again, we have the choice – is it a sea of beauty or is it just a bloody mess? Grow up, and see where blue is not the colour of sadness…

Sunset – Okay, the sun is going down but, whoomf, in comes the night full of night light. No cautious feeling or trepidation as darkness approaches, but a wholehearted determination to accept fate, to accept what the day, in its fullness, dictates.

With another nod to Englishness – Delius this time – we are into the pulsing night of a luna negra. This is also a very beautiful, and exquisitely crafted poem, comparable to Rumi, where even the sand turns to dust.

Graphic: *Pi* by Chris Butler

Aerial Tal (Duet With Bird) – They are having so much fun with the vocables and the cantering. Hazrat Inayat Kahn, I wish you were alive to hear this. But, then, maybe you can anyway.

Somewhere in Between – A song of the gloaming, the magic time when all things are suspended for a short time, when the middle way is there. And in the middle way you can change the direction of reality because you can understand balance. Balance is the perfection in this track. The duet is so unusual, and attractive and so… balanced. Another lovely poem.

Nocturn – This song is scented with jasmine, and perfumes of paradise. I think it's my favourite for listening to anywhere. I can't get enough of that pure voice – it has found the perfect pitch and texture to convey intimacy and that iconoclastic concept of Summer love. The melody is so immediate and satisfying, it's got a real Fifties feel with that early innocence of the Fleetwoods. I wish I was eighteen again, out of my head on whatever it is these days, watching the sun coming up out of a calm sea. It could be the ultimate Summer Chill Out Song.

Aerial – Now we have seen and felt it all we are back on the top of something looking down. But there is no iced mountain, no snow, just sunshine and a determination that it's going to stay like this. You can make your own dream if you want to, if you have the courage to.

Even though the sun behind a flower makes it look as though it's melting, it's only the sun. How can you understand another's language of the heart, how can you understand what the bird is saying – easy, it's just laughing. And isn't that just incredibly funny?

Of course, to see this album as sun and moon, sadness and joy, light and dark etc. is a trifle simplistic. In every joy song, except one, there is always a shadow coming up alongside the sun – was it just a dream, or did it really happen? But, like the light on the aerial, you've got to keep changing.

Apart from being such a stunning return to the charts, *Aerial* makes me realise how thin and superficial the music of the beautiful robots has been in her absence, and what paucity of lyrics we've all had to put up with. I had come to the reluctant conclusion that popular music was dead, and all we would ever hear is the backward-looking twitches of those scavengers raking over the ashes. I'm ecstatic that I was wrong.

P.S. I did not hear this album in its entirety until shortly before it was released, so please don't think I have any more insights into the more mysterious parts of the album than you have – my comments have no more authority than anyone else's.

Krys

This is Kate's symphony, her *Supper's Ready*, her *Day in the Life*. She brings us the elements, the sea, sky, sun, stars and all the colours of a creation myth. Here she is painter, creator, pro-creator. She has already brought into the world her own ultimate creation – and he is the very heart of *Aerial*, as we knew he always would be. This is a different kind of love story. A mother's love.

Along *Aerial*'s path we meet with classic archetypes. *King of the Mountain* (Elvis) the Emperor; π the Magician who plays with magic numbers; *Mrs. Bartolozzi* presides as the Empress; *Bertie* is her Sun, his symbol the circle of completion, fulfilment, the source of all light; the Devil in *How To Be Invisible*; *Joanni* the Hanged One; *A Coral Room* is Death; *A Sky of Honey* is the all-encompassing Universe.

Now imagine you are walking through a gallery, and each song is a Dutch painting, or a Turner or a Dürer, or Brueghel, or Spencer, or Sowa, or Delvaux, or Gorey, or Balthus, or a photograph by Carroll, or Cameron or Mann.

Still life. She paints with vision and sound, musically blends the past with the present, takes diversions, plays her voice like a violin in honour of the classical composers. The result is organic. Much of *Aerial* carries a Windham Hill vibe (with that distinctive Eberhard Weber fretless bass) making it her most spacious work, where everything breathes, and the silences are as valuable as the sounds. Her voice is purer and richer than ever. In the vein of Joni Mitchell's *The Hissing of Summer Lawns,* and Weber's *Fluid Rustle*, it is fresh and vital, and will mature like the finest wine.

And so to *A Sea of Honey*, where we meet Kate and Elvis in the hypnotic *King of the Mountain* (I hear *I'm All Shook Up* in there). A guitar slung over her shoulder, she's a shamanic busker with birds in her hair. The childhood spirit of Rosebud in the snow is a beautiful touch. The price for some of fame and fortune.

The sensual π, her breathy, teasing, murmurs – she even makes the language of numbers sound sexy, perhaps signifying the sexual allure of the intellect. The cosmic dance of shapes and infinite numbers. The Music of the Spheres. He will surely go mad. From this man with the child in his eyes, to another and the traditional early English madrigal of *Bertie* – a simple nursery rhyme lyric that celebrates her love for her son. I picture him taking his Mummy's hand and leading her in a courtly dance. A reeling wheel of joy. A song which for me brings mixed emotions. I think of the little people who should have been dancing in our lives too.

Mrs Bartolozzi is an outstanding creation that steps back to the demos, to her roots, in it's structure and atmosphere. A seemingly simple tale of mud and the mop and bucket. Out of the washing machine comes the imagery of the sea, the sensual movement of water – water: the age-old symbol for our emotions. How beautiful the erotic imagery... it's all still there – the tangle of his clothes entwining hers inside the machine, and her skirt up to her waist in the sea... "Oh and you're standing right behind me/ Little fish swim between my legs"... She's singing back the symbols. Sex, conception, birth; it all returns to the water. The waves of the sea, the coming and going, the ebbing and flowing, the rhythm of all things... changing. It is a song of sex and death. There is such sadness, maybe it is the pool of her own tears. Has something been lost? Maybe it is the day after a funeral, a day for normality to resume. *Mrs Bartolozzi* could be any of us, will inevitably be all of us. Who has brought mud into the house? Her father and her son coming home from a walk? Is she remembering her childhood holidays by the sea as she is washing her father's clothes? It reminds me of how thoughts become almost meditative when we're on train journeys or doing mundane tasks. Whose clothes are waving from the washing line? Some people have run off with the idea that this is about a murder. And somehow that idea would work. To me it is seems about loss, perhaps through death, or emotional loss as people grow apart, and become strangers. The yearning for what left a long time ago. Only the ghosts of who they were remain as vanishing memories, or as the forgotten clothes of the departed lover or parent or friend. You can still smell their skin, their perfume. There is something about the clothes on the washing line that reminds me of M.R. James' description of the spectre with "an intensely horrible face of crumpled linen". Perhaps *Mrs. Bartolozzi* is a ghost.

Kate's poetic, sensual, lyrics move from simple story-telling to more complex ideas and images, most notably in *How To Be Invisible*: "Take a pinch of keyhole/And fold yourself up." It is an incantation, the casting of an invisibility spell. There are more grey ghosts. And Alice. The "eye of braille" sees what cannot be seen, but felt with the fingertips, or as instinct in the gut. This song brings images of 1930s film noir, wet cobbled streets, a menacing stranger watching from the street corner; in trench coat and fedora, his face invisible through a veil of cigarette smoke. Or he could be a sinister Sowa bunny... It is a song of shadows.

Graphic: *Sunset* by Chris Butler

The vibrant anthem of *Joanni*, whose significance for Kate seems to stem back to the early demos. The celebration of a heroine is followed by the screams (concealed by the Miss Piggy-esque chanting!) as she burns. Has she woken the witch?

A Coral Room is the little sister of *Moments of Pleasure*, a place where grief has lost most of its sting, but a place also preserved forever in the memory. It is an ocean deep sadness that never really goes away, we just learn how to live with it. A little brown jug... the associations between things and people, how physical belongings absorb someone's essence. Kate presents here the most beautiful images... the spider weaving his net-curtain web of passing time... the broken jug. Are we taken to a mystical Atlantian underworld, or just a forgotten room in a house held by sailing ships' timbers, its occupants long since gone. As much as *A Coral Room* is about her mother, to me it also represents the place of her childhood, where Kate's creativity is rooted, where it was nurtured, and where it flourished into the music it would become. If *Bertie* is the heart of *Aerial*, this is its very roots. I can picture Hannah in the kitchen singing along with Glen Miller on the radio, little Kate at the door, her smile as wide as Bertie's. It is one of the most painful, yet therapeutic songs I can recall. As her brother John says, it is not a place we should perhaps visit too often – we could grow complacent, immune; maybe it is a song for those times when we need a little help to release our own pain. Kate has always been good at that, but this is something different again. I sobbed so hard the second time I heard this, late at night in bed as we listened to the album. It felt like all the pain over all the years being choked up and released. I thought I would break. Kate do you know what you do to us? She thumps us on the back to cough up the poisoned apple, so we can breathe again, so we can live again. The desolate pain of the song's final line "What do you feel?" I fall into Alice's pool of tears as she rips my heart out. Another frozen moment caught in sepia. She is still there. In the sunlight and the sparkling dust. In all of our hearts.

Graphic: *Bertie* by Chris Butler

And so we pause a while.

The gentle stirrings of *Prelude*; in a snapshot of sound she captures her little boy's smile. She has made a place where he will never grow old. Her little light shining. *Prologue* – the blend of classical, and Weber. *An Architect's Dream* invites our senses in to this place... the storm begins... *The Painter's Link* bows towards Rolf's *Sun Arise*. With the storm the raindrops leave their mark, like people and experiences leave their mark. See the colours moving through each other; in touching and bleeding into one another they will never quite be the same again. See the colours changing, vibrating, harmonising, singing. She paints with sound and poetry on her ever-changing canvas sky of shadows, light, colour, stars, sun, sea, sex, death, life. Life. I close my eyes and see the golds and reds, the blues and indigos and little flecks of silver stars and the colours of her hair, and the autumn fires in her eyes as the sun turns red. She has painted a Sunset... we dive into the life and death cycle as day becomes night; in the darkness energy is transformed and hope lives on – as a child conceived, "as comets and stars". All the passion of her spirit.

Aerial Tal... she turns into a bird, speaking their language. *Somewhere in Between* slinks in like *The Sensual World*. Finding all she ever looked for... "Somewhere in between what the song and the silence say"... And here comes the lesson: the moment that is the Now.

The Sun is tucked up in bed. She takes us to the waters of *Nocturn*. She sounds and moves like the sea, ebbing, teasing, running in towards land, taking handfuls of sea creatures, ground pebbles and eroding earth all bound together as little grains of sand. The sensuality of her dance with the sea and her lover under the night-dawn sky of Midsummer. More erotic imagery, oh yes, she's still got it... This is a song partly about sex, and maybe conception? All that honey and "milky silky water". Is this *Mrs. Bartolozzi*'s daydream, or memory?

The shape-shifter dons a cloak of black feathers, throws back her head and laughs and sings with the dawn chorus. She joins the celebration of the Midsummer sunrise, the solstice Sun. Our Blackbird flies and soars as high as her desire. She's of the air, she's up on the roof, where she reaches the glorious sound orgasm that is *Aerial*. Kate's *Day in the Life*.

All things are uncovered, clothes are shed, everything stripped down to the basics as she throws open the windows to this beautiful sky, and lets in the light, the air, the sunshine, all the new energy rushes right in so everything can breathe. Healing, cleansing. Like breathing in the sea air on the wild Cornish coast. I long to hear it when the skies are draped in the purple haze of first dawn, and we're driving into the sky. She brings us the elements of Air, Earth, Fire and Water, and mixes them all together with a good handful of the fifth element Ether. *Aerial* is the alchemical child. The roses turned into gold, and a sea and sky of honey. Our beekeeper has been busy in her hive. And what is her magic? Love. Just love.

There are no secrets here, no mysteries to be dug out from the deep, or from a tortured soul. It is all there in front of us, the cards laid on the table. Somewhere in between the past and the future is the present, the moment that is Now, and that is perhaps the lesson in *Aerial*. Note that the sleeve artwork is called *The Lesson*. Here is the work of a happy, confident woman. If *The Red Shoes* was her album of heartbreak and grief, then this is a work where our creator has had time to sit back, and perhaps rediscover and reassess the important things in life. There has been time to adjust and accept the things that can't be changed. She's in a different place now. This is an album of life. And love. There is heartache, but there is also something valuable in how to deal with it and the lessons that she has learned she is passing on to others. That is how it should be. *Aerial* is the promise of hope, as she captains us through the magical starlit hours of a Midsummer morning to greet the Sun.

Peter

"In the snow with Rosebud."

These are still a more or less random collection of immediate thoughts. In 1993 Kate brought us a beautiful album full of the pain of the rough times. Twelve years later she brings us an amazing sound-scape full of love and security, and the love and bliss of having her son. My guess is that having children makes you go back to first principles. With *The Red Shoes* Kate gave notice of ending finally the dance of stardom and celebrity. With *Aerial* she starts a new cycle. Kate steps away from the mass market and begins to climb Windham Hill, and like the hilly stuff "the music is not jazz, pop, or classical, but has pop melodies and sensibility that was not that different from classical music". This album returns to great simplicities. This is what young Catherine Bush wanted to do, write and record songs, capture emotional moments. So this album completes what *The Red Shoes* started. There are no overwhelming torrents of production, just a palette of musical colours and that amazing voice, mature and beautiful. It is organic ambient music in its truest sense, pastoral music - reach for any description you like - reaching across natural sounds, many musical genres, and some quite its own, in order, in the most economical way, to create, just like a M.R. James ghost story, an atmosphere.

A Sea of Honey is a collection of exquisite individual songs. *King of the Mountain*, which started life shortly after the release of *The Red Shoes*, and whose demo vocal survives from that time, is a clear indication of what is to come. Naturally the concern is "what use is celebrity?" Who best to showcase the futility of fame and money than The King himself and Charles Foster Kane. But who best to show the way back to simplicity than young Kane with his sledge in the snow. *π* is a celebration of the inner beauty and harmony of mathematics, and the ultimate mystery of a truly irrational number where in the great circle of infinity Einstein sees the back of his own head. It's easy to see *Bertie* starting as a little jingle Kate would sing when bouncing her new son on her lap. A little silly jingle that turns into exquisite formal renaissance dance. *Mrs. Bartolozzi* so resembles one of Kate's early demos, you wonder if she did indeed dust one off as the musical start. In fact as we know, that to capture the disintegrating emotion of this tale of dreadful grief the track was effectively recorded live. As Holmes said to Watson, "work is the best antidote to sorrow", and so Mrs. B scrubs her floors and stares at the hypnotic spin of the washing machine and the dancing clothes make it seem that her lover still lives, and her heart-rending reverie is only interrupted by the half forgotten washing powder jingle. *How To Be Invisible* might be Kate's contemplation of the last twelve years, a nicely dark film noir tale of "Corridors that twist and turn" and a magic spell of invisibility conjured from innocent domesticity. I can see a video of mean streets and fedoras. *Joanni* is a theme for an epic, beginning with the veneration of the ranks of soldiers and ending with the screams as the secular arm completes the blazing act of faith from which even Saints Catherine and Margaret cannot rescue the Maid. *A Coral Room* might be a continuation of *Moments of Pleasure*, and like that track is a meditation on the passing of time. Time and death are always linked in the figure who wields the scythe of fate. Here is the Spider of Time, covering the Farm with web, and within a room built of ancient ships' timbers where Hannah Bush took her passage with Charon.

"*Who knows who wrote that song of Summer*
That blackbirds sing at dusk..."

Two sounds resonate from my childhood. The sound of rain on a canvas tent, and the sound of blackbirds singing. In the long Summer days of childhood I can always remember the birds singing in the huge sycamore tree in the back yard. In my mind it is always very late afternoon, and that is where Kate commences a soul-stirring journey through the eve of Midsummer to the life affirming rise of the solstice sun, the peak and

Graphic: *Somewhere in Between* by Chris Butler

yet the beginning of its seasonal death. "Do you hear The Lark Ascending?" Vaughan Williams found inspiration in English folk themes and in a poem by George Meredith. Kate takes her inspiration from the song of the blackbirds singing on an English Summer afternoon, a song which changes with the passing hours from afternoon to dusk and to the wild chorus of dawn.

As Bertie says in the *Prelude*, the dit-dah-dah-dit-dit song of the blackbirds become the words of the subtitles of this album, and pervade all the way through the honeyed sky. In *Prologue* the sun is already past its midday peak, "Every time you leave us, So Summer will be gone, So you'll never grow old to us", but it is the magic light of a Summer afternoon "Like some kind of magic Like the light in Italy Lost its way across the sea". The world is created in that light, and the painter tries to capture those hues that spread across the landscape. The music of the Sun and the light she shines is the business of *An Architect's Dream*, the light the painters reflect, the light the prism divides into the coloured rays of creation, briefly covered by the clothes of Nimbus so that the hues may dissolve into the mad festa of *Sunset*. Once the sun is gone the landscape enters the twilight time of magic and shadows, *Somewhere in Between* the day and the night. When the last solar light is gone we go on a journey through a vivid night-scape with moon and stars reflected in the breakers of the vast dark sea. *Nocturn* travels through the night to the first glow of pre-dawn comes up on the horizon. As the fingers of the light of dawn give way to the rising of the disc of golden light, so *Aerial* pulses with the sheer force of life at its Midsummer peak. Some would greet it at the ring of stones, but as for Kate, she wants to be up on the roof singing with the birds as the cycle ever begins anew.

Graphic: *How to be Invisible* by Chris Butler

Dave

The first time I listened to *Aerial*, I must confess, I didn't really know what to think. It was, after all, something I'd been waiting 12 years for and anticipation does strange things to your brain. There was so much to take in that it was impossible to be really objective. There was nothing as obvious as *Running Up That Hill* or *Rubberband Girl*; it was a sparse, intimate work that took me by surprise. On my second listen, however, it was as if my brain had said, "Ok, calm down love, have a proper listen..." and suddenly it all started to make sense. The windows were open and the music came rushing in. Now with the benefit of having lived with the album for a few weeks, there are so many things I want to say – it's difficult to know where to start. The press, of course, usually fixate on Kate's voice and it's easy to understand why; it is as distinctive, beautiful and emotive as ever. Mostly stripped of the multi-layered harmonies of previous albums, her vocals dominate *Aerial*. But for me, as much as I love Kate's voice, it's the song-writing and production that really set her and this album apart from anyone else in modern music. In typical Kate style, *King of the Mountain*, her first single after 12 years out of the public eye, is about living in the full mega watt glare of the media where rumour and endless speculation grow unchecked. Rhythmic and percussive, the doodling synths and funky guitar combine with the drums and hi-hats to give it a spacey almost "live" feel; unmistakably Kate, but also very contemporary; the ideal lead single.

π continues the rhythmic journey, with its squelchy percussion, uplifting acoustic guitars, funky bass and nagging synth lines giving the whole song a befitting circular feel. Warm strings and beautiful vocal fills perfectly complement the soaring vocal as she tells us of a man who lives his life by numbers.

I remember a couple of years ago Krys saying that she thought Kate's son, Bertie, would be at the heart of the new album, but I don't think any of us expected it to be quite so literal. The song *Bertie* is a celebration of childhood enthusiasm, with Kate happy to share with the world the joy of being a parent. The song's old English folk music feel perhaps echoing her own childhood, when John and Paddy would play music for their little sister. I can see my brother and myself as kids, in my nephews, and maybe *Bertie* is also about Kate remembering her own time of innocence and wilfulness. Becoming a mother has clearly been enormously influential on Kate and her music; she has often said that she is at her most creative when happy and I think Bertie's influence can be felt throughout the album. It will be interesting to see what happens when he starts playing his Mum the music he and his friends like at school... "Oi Mum, where's my Black Eyed Peas CD?"

The mood darkens on *Mrs Bartolozzi*, where a

woman dealing with loss is determined to get on with the business of everyday life but can't escape from recurring images of the man she has lost. Even doing the washing reminds her of him and as she pictures their clothes tumbling together, her mind drifts. Musically this song reminds me so much of Joni Mitchell's *Blue* album and I love the "Slooshy sloshy" jingle. Kate picks up the pace with *How To Be Invisible* with its shuffling beat, shimmering steel guitars, phasing synths, shakers, whistles and stuttering bass. She stands at the edge of The Labyrinth and casts a spell with shades of J.K. Rowling's Harry Potter in the maze or outside the doors in the Ministry of Magic or Phillip Pullman's *His Dark Materials* trilogy, where the Witches can think themselves invisible and maybe even a touch of Granny Weatherwax and her Headology. Could it also be her own desire to move through the ordinary world without being seen as "Kate Bush" the famous person? A theme shared with *King of the Mountain* where, as here, Kate's sense of humour bubbles beneath the surface; the media image of the White Witch of Pop casting a spell that requires "Anorak" and "Doormat".

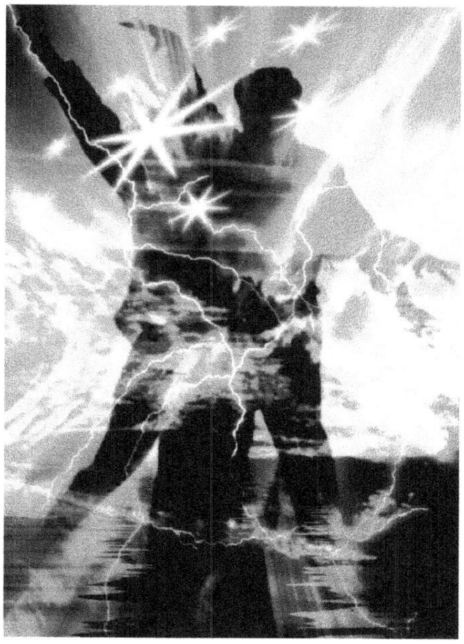

Across the *Sea of Honey* Kate shape-changes from pop star to mother, to wife, Witch and with *Joanni* she becomes the burning martyr with thousands of soldiers and waving flags. The imagery is strong, think of Éowyn the Shield maiden of Rohan from *Lord of the Rings*. She looks beautiful in her shining armour, but wears no ring, no symbol of earthly love; her cause is everything. Soft metallic rhythms, Celtic flourishes and that deep growling hum, could provide the album with a second hit single. At the end of disc one Kate continues character shifting when she becomes the daughter in *A Coral Room*. Again it's just her and the piano on a song that can stand alongside *This Woman's Work* or *Moments of Pleasure*. This song, more than any other, highlights her different approach to the production of *Aerial*. It must have been so tempting to lavish beautiful strings on the track, but Kate knows that sometimes less is more and she takes you on an emotional ride of utter sadness with beautiful lyrical imagery; the decaying city of coral under the sea, the spider of time and the broken jug that "Held her milk, and now it holds our memories" played against joyful chords and passionate, sad vocals, a moving snapshot of a daughter's grief. I cherish my memories of the brief times I spent with Kate's mum, always so warm and caring and with a disarming honesty and I'm sure she would love this beautiful song.

If disc one of *Aerial* sees Kate looking at her own life, with its themes of motherhood, loss and fame, then *A Sky of Honey* is Kate looking up once more at The Big Sky and taking inspiration from the miracle that is the daily cycle of day and night. The whole piece is threaded with the recurring musical theme of birdsong and the lyrical story of how the light changes through a twenty four hour period and the effect it has on the world around us.

Prelude sets the scene; *Bertie*'s simple joy in his thought that birds are "speaking words". *Prologue* is all anticipation and gentle tension, simple piano, bass, lush strings and just a tease of drums to help build the mood and Kate's beautifully cool vocal, observing that when the birds fly South the Summer is really gone. I think this song also contains a clue to a major part of the inspiration for *A Sky of Honey* when she sings of the "light in Italy". Having spent a week in Sicily myself this year I can certainly say that the sky there has a unique quality. This magical Italian sky has inspired many great painters over the centuries and Kate picks up this idea on *An Architect's Dream*. Mixing up images like paint on the canvas; the painter chasing the light, the two lovers entwined: different elements combining to create a new whole and how sometimes mistakes we make turn out to be the best things, a theme Kate has touched on before. The song is set off with some lovely oriental chimes, that bring to mind the work of Ryuichi Sakamoto, I'm thinking here of *Forbidden Colours*, his collaboration with David Sylvian. *The Painter's Link* is a truly uplifting musical splash leading in to *Sunset*. Here Kate captures perfectly the moments preceding a beautiful sunset, a hint of jazz exploding into a flamenco climax, which suggests that Kate has also visited Spain. This song also makes me think of Joni Mitchell, but this time it is *Woodstock* and its stardust imagery.

On *Somewhere in Between* Kate relives one of those magical moments in life, a second, a heartbeat, "Between breathing in and breathing out", the smallest time, but one that seems to last forever and in this instance it is two people standing on a hill as the sunset ends and the day pauses for breath before night comes. And it comes in all it's dark, passionate glory on *Nocturn* with our two lovers diving deep into the ocean.

Graphic: *Nocturn* by Chris Butler

As they swim deeper, further into the sensual embrace, the music intensifies, with Kate unleashing a wave of lush backing vocals bringing to mind the stirring passion of *Hello Earth* and *Jig of Life* and then the climax pauses just for a breath, before we launch into the wild abandon of the album's title track. Kate is up on the roof, the birds are singing at the dawn, but are they laughing? Well, Kate certainly is, in a joyful eruption of sound, topped off with Danny's mad guitar. The whole song reminds me of *The Dreaming*'s closing masterpiece *Get Out of My House*, but this time Kate is changing into a bird rather than a mule… and then it's over, with the afterglow of birdsong ringing in my ears… God, I need a post-album cigarette.

I guess the most startling thing about *Aerial* is that after a gap of 12 years she has delivered an album that sounds so fresh and uncluttered, a work that is both contemporary and timeless. Looking back I think that both *The Sensual World* and *The Red Shoes* were always going to be in the shadow of *Hounds of Love*, not only in the minds and ears of us, the listening public, but also in Kate's desire to constantly do something different and experiment musically, pushing the envelope in terms of production. I'm not knocking either album, I think they jointly contain some of Kate's best work, but *Hounds of Love* is a tough act to follow. Kate clearly needed and wanted to take a break and find new inspiration and a big part of that is obviously her son and a child's more straightforward approach to everything.

Graphic: *Prologue* by Chris Butler

On this album Kate has taken stock and realised that all she needs is her voice and a piano to tell her stories. It is a confident and mature work, showcasing her skill as a world class songwriter, producer and, of course, a great singer. I love it, Kate. Thank you. xx

Seán

I have this great souvenir of the first time I heard *Aerial*, two large white pages covered front and back in red pen scribbles as the first impressions of the album sprang into my mind (I didn't have a lyric sheet to hand and must have needed something to do in case the excitement got too much!) Arrows linking themes, thoughts and ideas scrawled furiously over the pages; bits of snatched lyrics, drawings of birds, sunsets and washing lines, and all the time with a big stupid smile on my face, laughing, shaking my head in disbelief at just how fantastically good the album is. The music that runs through *A Sea of Honey* is simply up there with the very best work Kate has released. Her voice has never sounded lovelier. I am still lost in these songs, soaking up every detail, every vocal quirk, every bass line. At the top of one of the sheets I wrote "this music makes me feel happy to be alive!" Initially that seems an obvious sentiment hearing anything new by Kate, definitely, but the more I listen to the album (and particularly *A Sky of Honey*), the more the simple power of that feeling becomes apparent. People will of course compare this album to *The Red Shoes*. For me *The Red Shoes* is Kate's most "adult" album – a brilliant distillation of all the fears and grief, hurdles and solutions we encounter in our busy and often complicated lives. It's follow-up on the other hand seems to be rooted in the Now, in the simple act of living, appreciating and working with what's around us today. Enjoying life for what it is in other words.

And I don't think I've heard that wisdom expressed quite as joyously before as by Kate on this record. It reminds me of Taoism; that simple, childlike and wonderfully useful Eastern philosophy. Seeing things through a child's eyes again. Taking time to appreciate our surroundings and the natural world which we are part of. Not getting hung up on abstract 'adult' dilemmas. Embracing that inner truthful childlike viewpoint that's too often buried within us for no good reason. The same theme runs through earlier songs like *The Big Sky* and *The Sensual World* but here it is expanded until the colour, images and sounds become almost unbearably beautiful and euphoric. But that's the whole point. The truth is that life is beautiful, the only thing that blinds us to that in this world are our busy, "clever" adult minds. We should be up there laughing with those birds – they have it sussed! Thanks for sticking with it Kate, it must have been exhausting at times, but this is a powerful gift to whoever gets to hear it – it's a hell of a lot of fun too.

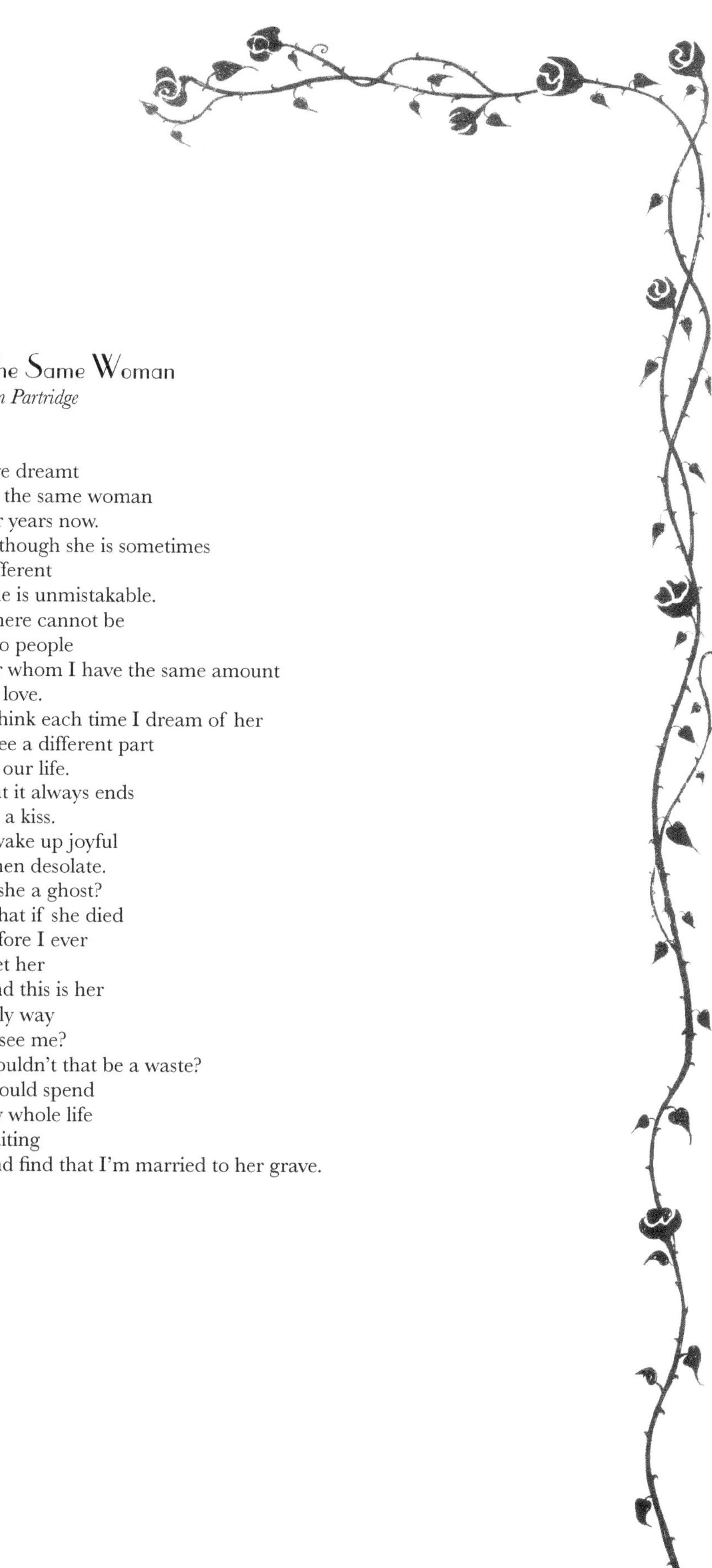

The Same Woman

Jon Partridge

I've dreamt
of the same woman
for years now.
Although she is sometimes
different
She is unmistakable.
There cannot be
two people
for whom I have the same amount
of love.
I think each time I dream of her
I see a different part
of our life.
But it always ends
on a kiss.
I wake up joyful
Then desolate.
Is she a ghost?
What if she died
before I ever
met her
And this is her
only way
to see me?
Wouldn't that be a waste?
I could spend
my whole life
waiting
And find that I'm married to her grave.

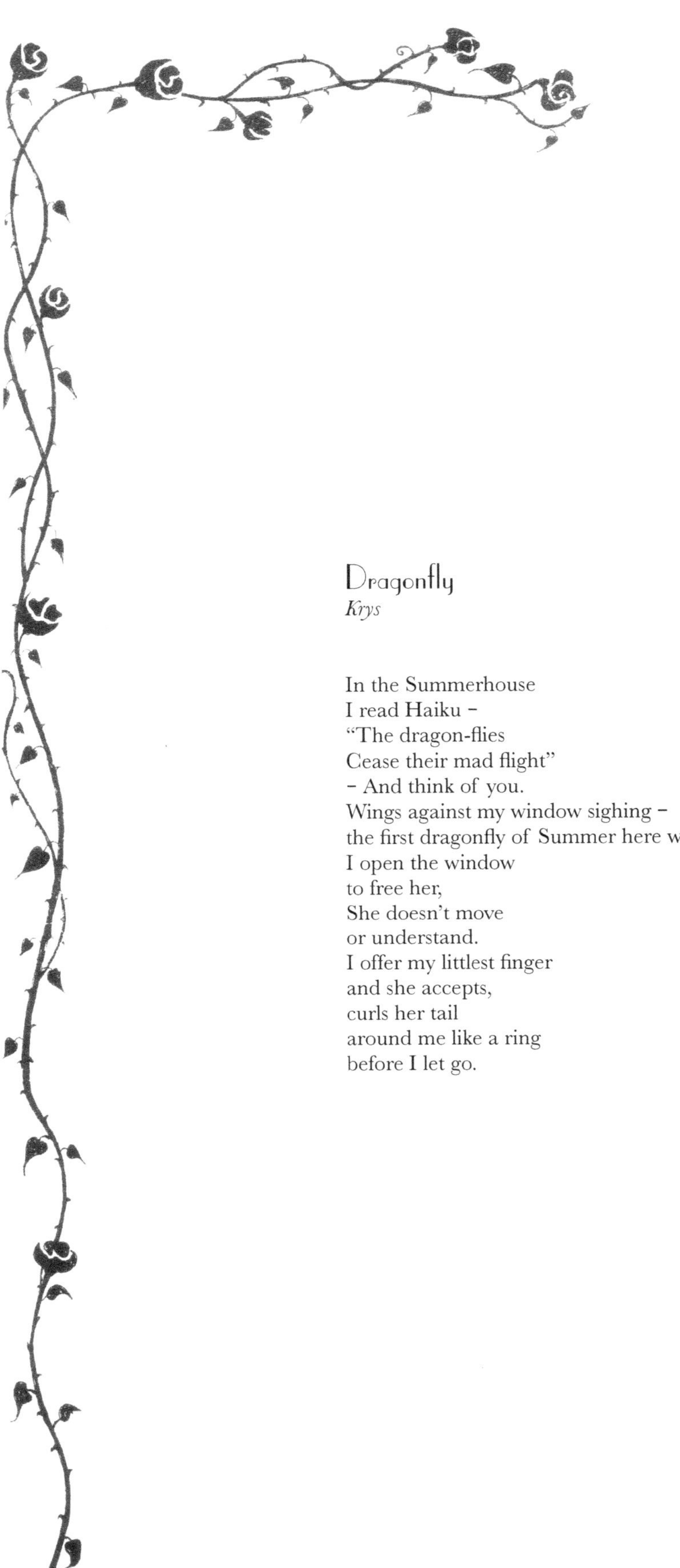

Dragonfly

Krys

In the Summerhouse
I read Haiku –
"The dragon-flies
Cease their mad flight"
– And think of you.
Wings against my window sighing –
the first dragonfly of Summer here with me.
I open the window
to free her,
She doesn't move
or understand.
I offer my littlest finger
and she accepts,
curls her tail
around me like a ring
before I let go.

Up, Up on the Roof ...

HomeGround Readers and Forum Members react to *Aerial*

Issues 76 and 77
December 2005
and July 2006

Andrew Marvick (IED)

A few years back there was a great to-do over the identification of a few pages of manuscript as sketches for a "tenth symphony" by Ludwig van Beethoven, dating from 1826. Although these notations were disjointed and incomplete, and were accompanied by only the merest suggestion for their orchestration, scholars (which is to say, serious-minded, no doubt somewhat pretentious but certainly genuine Beethoven fans) jumped over each other to attempt a reconstruction or "completion" of the work, and to arrange for live performances.

Implicit in this incident is the understandable judgement by posterity that everything and anything which sprang from the mind of Beethoven was worth the world's time and attention, and that every effort should be made to understand and preserve any evidence of his creative processes and the products that resulted from them.

The distinction is between the value accorded to a piece of music, and the value given to the mind that produced it. In ascribing relatively greater value to the mind than to the individual work, the serious student of Beethoven will be liberated from the trivial preoccupation with the unanswerable and ultimately useless compulsion to rank one symphony over another, one concerto over another, one sonata over another, so on ad infinitum. Look at it like this: if we're considering the recordings of, say, Clay Aikin or Aled Jones, then okay, go ahead and rate them on a scale of 1 to 10; but if it's Beethoven we're talking about, the value scale just doesn't apply, because even the unfinished sketches are 11's.

Now, I don't mean to claim that the mind of Kate Bush is "equivalent" to that of Beethoven: it's all apples and oranges anyway. But I do feel that the real treasure in Kate Bush's work is in its reflexive nature: it is an infinitely interesting collection of products mainly inasmuch as it reveals to us the processes of an infinitely interesting mind. This is not, I suspect, the view of Kate Bush herself. As we have all had multiple new occasions to notice in the past few months, she is as much at pains as ever to remind her interviewers and listeners that she is "normal," that she lives a "normal life," and that she intends to raise her family in a "normal" environment – all understandable and worthy goals, I suppose, but scarcely to the point. Kate Bush may well live a "normal" life (whatever that may be). We all know a great many folk who lead normal lives – but how many of them produce an *Aerial* every decade or so? In the end, Kate Bush's protestations of normality fail to convince: what significance is there in a normal life if the mind is abnormally brilliant?

Graphic: *A Sea of Honey* Chris Butler

Before you read further, you have a right to know that I listen to only two kinds, or genres, of music: what we call classical, by which I mean Western European music composed between, say, 1650 and 1950 or so; and Kate Bush. So if you can't stand the possibility of a pretentious bit of pompous intellectualism at Kate Bush's expense, I advise you to move quickly on to the next article! My perspective is a lot different from that of most of my readers: When I listen to the music of Kate Bush – and never more so than with *Aerial* – I don't think about Fiona Apple, or Tori Amos, or Futureheads, or any of these all too temporal figures. I think instead about Schumann, and Brahms, and Rachmaninov; about Delius, and Vaughan Williams; and about, yes, Beethoven. And although none of the mainstream press' music critics has done the same (alas!), they have virtually unanimously declared that, when considered within the context of current pop music, Kate Bush's new music is not like anyone else's. They're not entirely correct, because they're only looking at her contemporaries. They would find many close links between the art of Kate Bush and the timeless, serious music of the past – of the so-called "great" composers, if only they thought to look for them.

Now this makes it sound as though I'm a terribly pretentious and anachronistic old fuddy-duddy, with no awareness of the music of my time. And I suppose that's largely true. But really I see my love of the classical tradition as no virtue of mine, only a result of my lifelong dependence on music as both an emotional and an intellectual source of inspiration. And as all of you know, Kate Bush's music, never more so than in *Aerial,* takes time and patience to understand in any encompassing, comprehensive way.

If you needed proof of my assertion that most critics are ill equipped to address music of this calibre intelligently, just do a quick count of the number of reviews that summarize *Mrs. Bartolozzi* as a song about washing machines; or *π* as a simple recitation of digits! As we all know, each of these is a profoundly thoughtful and feelingful rumination on the human condition, a separate musical-poetic world of virtually limitless depth and breadth, and a beautiful song in the bargain. I submit that the main reason for the press' inability to notice these facts is their ignorance of the real potential of pop music to rise to the same heights as the most ambitious music of the past. The fact that it nearly never reaches that potential is attributable to the simple fact that there is, at present, only one Kate Bush – and even she needs years to make music this rich. No wonder, then, that the rest of the pop music "industry" so rarely comes anywhere close to such a threshold.

So, I make no apologies for the "pretentiousness" of my choice of comparisons: I sincerely think it's the only way to bring our discussion of Kate's music to the level it deserves. It doesn't mean my ideas are any smarter than anyone else's: but it does mean I'm at least starting out from within the musical environment that Kate's art merits.

Now, to the album itself, and so, ultimately, back to Beethoven. First, I think *Aerial* is not representative of Kate Bush in the year 2005, or 2000, or even 1995. We know from recent interviews that parts of it were not only conceived but actually recorded more than a decade ago. I think this fact points to one of the album's most salient features: its timelessness. It's no accident that the songs' lyrics frequently refer to much earlier songs. The most striking evidence of this timelessness is the lack of hurry in the songs: this is an album of open spaces. The breathing room in each of the songs is at odds with most of the music of our era; rather, it reaches back to an earlier, more contemplative time when art was seen as having the potential – even the duty – to elevate the moral and intellectual status of the whole society. Listening to *A Sky of Honey* means giving oneself over to a musical-dramatic environment that operates outside of mundane time. To make another analogy: this music is to a Henry James novel as the rest of current pop music is to a list of ingredients on a Snickers bar.

The songs of *A Sky of Honey* weave an oblique musical and narrative dialogue between singer and chorus: the reference "A Chorus" in the suite is not to the verse-chorus structure of pop song, but to the critical chorus of ancient Greek drama: an otherwise unidentified body of voices in unison constituting a clear and direct link to the timeless legacy of human creative history.

The two disks' conceits, air and water, bespeak of the album's larger theme: in essence the vastness and timelessness of Nature. So, too, the songs address grand themes that transcend the temporal: infinity itself (*π*); death and loss (*A Coral Room*); death and its transcendence (*King of the Mountain*, *Joanni*); flight (*Nocturn* and *Aerial*), perhaps as a metaphor for aspiration to a higher plane of consciousness; art and the creative process itself (*An Architect's Dream* and *The Painter's Link*); sexual and romantic love – their inextricable relationship with nature and our natural, animal selves (*An Architect's Dream*, *Sunset*, *Somewhere in Between*); and of course new life and the hope and wonder it brings (*Bertie*, *Prelude*).

To underscore my point about the timelessness and ambition behind these recordings, look at how inadequate my thematic descriptors for the songs seem: yes, *An Architect's Dream* deals with a sense of romance, but it comprises so much more than this, as well. Some songs on the new album, *Mrs. Bartolozzi* and *A Coral Room* in particular, perhaps, touch and hint at so many different, superficially unrelated but ultimately complementary themes that it's hard for anyone to put them in any sort of category at all. (Kate's comment in a recent interview, "I really like ambiguity", is no surprise to us, but it does much to explain the critics' inadequacy before the new album). These are not songs about partying, making money, cool cars, crude sexual seduction rituals, the shallow obsessions of so many thousands of other recordings of our time. Instead they ask the most profound questions human beings can ask: who are we? why are we here? where are we going? Naturally, then, the musical language in which she asks them, a language always tied to the many sub-genres of pop, yet never bound by any of them, is complex and multivalent.

The only apt comparisons are to a subcategory I have selected from among the big works of the past: the grand scale of the 19th Century Romantic program symphony and in particular, those which explore the unhurried pace, broad, open spaces and natural soundscapes of Nature – a tradition begun in earnest by Ludwig van Beethoven in 1808 with the composition of his Symphony No. 6 in F Major, Op. 68, known as 'The Pastoral', meaning "of or related to shepherds or herders," and more generally, "relating to the countryside." This symphony broke from the past in many ways, but perhaps most strikingly in its programmatic nature: it followed the events of a day in the country and included many musical passages suggestive of (though never directly imitative of) the sounds of birds, water, country dances and rainstorms. Beethoven himself wrote on an early version: "Pastoral Symphony, or Recollection of Country Life – More an Expression of Feeling than Painting." With its unexpected changes in tempi, dynamics and modulations, as with its great scale, leisurely pace and myriad musical references to the rustic theme, Beethoven's *Pastoral* helped subsequent generations of composers break free from the formal conventions of classicism.

Among those who followed the *Pastoral*'s lead, though each in his own way, sometimes on a smaller, sometimes a grander scale, and sometimes in radically different musical language, were the Romantic composer Robert Schumann, whose Symphony No. 1 in B-flat, Op. 38 (called his 'Spring Symphony') sounds at times almost like an extension of Beethoven's 6th. The list of later works is very long, but notable examples are Bedrich Smetana's *The Moldau* (from his larger suite of tone-poems, as these larger-scale pieces with dramatic narrative or poetic "programs" came to be known, *Ma Vlast*, or *My Country*, from 1874); Brahms' rigorously non- programmatic yet still curiously "pastoral" 1877 Symphony No. 2 in D Major, Op. 73; Debussy's *L'aprés-midi d'une faune* (*The Afternoon of a Faun*), L. 86, from 1894; Vaughan Williams' *The Lark Ascending* (subtitled *A Romance for Violin and Orchestra*); and Delius' *A Summer Night on the River* (1911) and *On Hearing the First Cuckoo in Spring* (1912).

Despite their many differences, each of these pieces is marked by the slower pace and expanded space which the broad theme of Nature demands; and by at least some measure of "tone-painting" – a heightened sense of aural "color" and "descriptive music" that come from the composer's focus on the narrative (whether explicit or implicit), setting (place and time) and human-animal-vegetal-meteorological drama.

It is ironic that the "concept" album, *A Sky of Honey*, is frequently more accessible in style and narrative (*Painter*'s monologue, for example, is simple, even simplistic, both in its language and in its almost children's song-like melodic nature), as befits its child-oriented perspective through the recurrent comments from Bertie that surround it, than the supposedly more accessible collection of "singles" that comprise *A Sea of Honey*. The songs, or vocal pieces, for few of them really constitute discrete, autonomous songs in the traditional sense, are both more deeply pessimistic and labyrinthine in their narratives (*Mrs. Bartolozzi* and *A Coral Room*, in particular) and starker, more daring in their harmonic/ rhythmic style(s) (*King of the Mountain*, unexpected twists in the direction of the instrumental arrangement in the last bars of *Bertie*, etc). This makes more sense if we look at Disk One as a collection of songs – short and freestanding in themselves, but each a distinct advance for the medium of songwriting and thus intensely complex and far reaching within the limits of the genre – and Disk Two as a suite of interrelated vocal pieces sharing a common theme and perspective, but one that lends itself to a simpler, more relaxed and more accessible musical language: what would once, perhaps, have been called a "pastoral cantata."

The pastoral theme is strongly associated with British music of the 19th and early 20th Centuries. Musicologist Ted Perkins has pointed out that several characteristics recur again and again in British pastoral compositions of this period, most important of which is the leisurely pace and frequently open spaces of silence and near-silence that help to give them their peculiarly British rhythm and line. Perkins has also noticed that "softer dynamics predominate. Expression markings of niente ('nothing'), morendo ('dying'), or decrescendo ('becoming quieter') often close sections," and this could well describe crucial turning-points in *A Sky of Honey*, as well.

Graphic: *Mrs Bartolotzzi* Chris Butler

Another characteristic: many of the best known British pastoral pieces revolve around modes, rather than the more commonly heard musical scales which are the basis of virtually all modern classical and popular western music, and to which virtually all western ears are tuned and accustomed. Kate Bush has herself often composed with an ear for the distinct musical atmospheres of medieval modal harmony (the latest evidence of which saturates the song *Bertie*, from *A Sea of Honey*, in which her deep intuitive understanding of early British music is underscored by an arrangement for period instruments), probably because so much of English and Irish folk music is spun from the melodic cloth of sometimes very ancient modes, but also because of her unquestionably sophisticated awareness of these chordal relationships in the history of Romantic and modern British classical music. It's no coincidence that two of the foremost explorers of British modal harmony were Frederick Delius (1862-1934) and Ralph Vaughan Williams (1872-1958), both of whom have been both musically and textually honored in Kate Bush's music.

Vaughan Williams' Symphony No. 3, called 'A Pastoral Symphony', is directly relevant to any serious discussion of *A Sky of Honey*. (One recent and highly recommended recording of this extraordinary work: erstwhile Kate Bush-collaborator Richard Hickox's reading with the London Symphony Orchestra and the exquisite voice of soprano Rebecca Evans.) The theme of the piece is England's countryside in the devastating aftermath of World War II; thus the symphony is not quite the simple, calmly happy music that one expects of a pastoral work, rather it is a frequently haunting, always highly nuanced and subtle meditation on the vicissitudes of war and the struggle for the recovery of civilization and culture following a great national tragedy. The final movement features a striking, wordless melodic line for soprano voice which recalls the steadily soaring violin line of Vaughan Williams' more famous (and *Aerial*-referenced, birdsong-imitating and *Experiment IV*- adapted) *The Lark Ascending*, whose avian theme, Old-English modal harmonies and gentle, relaxed pace are, of course, a primary inspiration for the music we all know in *A Sky of Honey*. Also of note in this context is Vaughan Williams' *In the Fen Country*, another of his ambiguous but deeply English lyrical meditations on his native landscape.

Graphic: *Aerial Tal* by Chris Butler

Also from this generation was the Italian composer Ottorino Respighi (1879-1936). In 1927 he composed *L'Usignuolo* ('The Nightingale') and *Il Cucu* ('The Cuckoo') from his 5-movement suite for chamber orchestra, *Gli Uccelli* ('The Birds'), another piece which bears comparison with *A Sky of Honey*. Respighi's piece shares several qualities with Kate Bush's: first, it is a loosely collected group of five pieces. Second, it explores the sounds of Nature in a direct, nearly imitative way. Third, it connects the pieces with quick, shared musical references but, befitting its light and airy theme, it does not attempt to build them into over-imposing musical structures. Finally, it makes open reference to its own aural and musical sources through clear thematic allusions to early 18th Century French and Italian composers' keyboard works, just as Kate Bush's alludes to its inspiration through textual acknowledgement of *A Lark Ascending*, the unpractised beauty of the voice of her own child and unexpected popular genres like samba. (If you're interested in Respighi's take on avian melody, try the Orpheus Chamber Orchestra's crystal clear recording on Deutsche Grammophon from 1993).

A third composer belonging to Vaughan Williams' generation is the French "neo-classicist" Arthur Honegger (1892-1955), whose *Pastorale d'été* ('Pastorale of Summer'), subtitled *un poème symphonique* ('a symphonic poem'), from 1920, uncannily foreshadows the themes and even some of the sounds of Kate Bush's new music. A member of a group of modern French composers known as 'Les Six', Honegger was notable for his efforts to imitate sounds of both Nature and modern life (locomotives, rugby matches, etc.) in the musical language of the orchestra.

Honegger's score begins with the inscription: "I have embraced the summer's red of morn," which immediately brings to mind Kate Bush's line, "This is a song of colour/ Where sands sing in crimson, red and rust/ Then climb into bed and turn to dust," mainly because both are references to the synaesthetic orientation of the music, meaning that color is a constant musical focus. The piece, scored for a small chamber ensemble, is only a third the length of Kate Bush's, running some 8 to 10 minutes in typical performance. The *Pastorale d'été* opens with a languorous theme in the strings to which a single flute and clarinet give replies in birdsong-like musical phrases. The piece ambles, then frolics with increasing energy, even reaching a moment of near-frenzied high spirits before returning to its languid opening melody at the end. (Fournet's recording with the Netherlands Radio Symphony Orchestra is a sensitive and beautifully engineered option from 1996).

There are many more precedents for *A Sky of Honey* in the history of music, works that approach their theme with a reverent interest in the sounds, rhythms and atmospheres of Nature, and that do so through the application of every aural and coloristic effect that the composer could create in the service of that theme. These are the precedents with which Kate Bush's latest work deserves to be compared, and through which we can all appreciate the true breadth and depth of her musical achievement.

We live in a difficult time, a time of great challenges, and many human failures. In my own country at present there is very little that a citizen can take pride in. Much of our popular culture seems increasingly shallow and tawdry, a celebration of the trivial and the vulgar, a denial of the timeless quality of meaningful experience. Yet with each successive dip in our infinitely beautiful, infinitely sad, infinitely joyous, limitless universe of honey, I think, how lucky we are! For to find, in the middle of all the junk and dross of our time, a new and real musical universe unfold around us, a lush (yet austere), vast and endlessly expanding (yet somehow private and intimate) solar system of 16 worlds revolving around and emanating from the warm, rich and subtle colors of Kate Bush's mind, is to discover a form of musical redemption for the dissonant realities we endure together.

It's here. Let's not dwell on the twelve year absence. We've all missed her. We've all been biting our nails down to the knuckles alongside EMI in anticipation that one day Kate Bush will re-emerge with a follow-up to 1993's *The Red Shoes*. So, let's finally immerse ourselves in the album we've all been waiting for.

Aerial is unmistakably a typical "Kate Bush" album. Some of her best piano work yet. Flirtations with several traditional musical arrangements combining with more contemporary percussion work. Concepts flying at the listener thick and fast. Some wonderfully tailored vocals to turn the tune into musical theatre once again.

But, even more typically for Kate, there's inevitably all those elements that are so easy to take out of context and give the tabloids the chance to finally say "Yeah, she's still bonkers": Duetting with birdsong. A song based around the infinite calculation of π. A chorus that simply repeats the words "Washing Machine". But, what took Kate nearly seven albums to prove, *Aerial* does in one fell swoop. That these elements are every much a necessary ingredient to a Kate album, as much as THAT voice is. And her work simply wouldn't work without them.

Lead single, *King of the Mountain* was a surprise to most hungry listeners when it was premièred on Radio 2 a few months ago. After twelve years, what can we expect from Kate? The surprise was exactly how subtle the song was. Deep, slow electronic pulses open the track before a slurring Kate starts with some almost incompressible lines. Some sharper synths kick in, Kate's words become clearer, and we realise she is paying homage to Elvis. Some habits die hard.

As the song grows, some wonderful nagging guitars and luscious drumming kicks in and the tracks starts to build and build. Eventually a full burst of Kate back to her epic self returns. Subtle. Wise. Mature. Expertly executed. 2005's new Kate Bush finally makes sense: she's perfected her craft and has proved that you can mature nicely in the industry without losing any of your power.

This is indeed a perfect introduction to the album. Split into two separate works (*A Sea of Honey* and *A Sky of Honey*), *Aerial* already holds comparisons with Kate's current masterpiece, 1985's *Hounds of Love*. Disc one bares seven songs, all seemingly based around personal events and goals around Bush's life over the last decade. π tells the tale of an insular man who's obsessed with the infinite possibly of mathematics. This was an opportunity for Kate to turn the generic and traditionally clinical use of numbers, and give them warmth, depth and feeling, along with a musical backdrop that carries on the synths, drumming and guitar work of *King of the Mountain*.

Bertie is probably the biggest musical detour on the album. Some beautiful renaissance mandolin, harpsichord and bodhran arrangements working along side delightful strings as Kate's most simple lyric ever gushes over the joys of motherhood. "Here comes the Sunshine/ Here comes that son of mine". For most other artists, such a blatant nod to their child would be a cringe worthy affair. But for *Bertie* and the following track, *Mrs Bartolozzi* – a tender piano ballad that talks of the obvious joy at being a housewife for the last decade (and yes, features that chorus, "Washing machine...") – these odes to the chores of a domestic goddess have given the new Kate Bush a quality that her work has never had before: raw humanity.

Kate's alleged "obsession" with her private life remaining private has always felt to extend into her work, by her albums never revealing much about the true human behind the artist. The joys and maturity that seven year old Bertie seems to have given Kate as a mother is clearly something that she can't keep to herself. Indeed the sleeve art to *Aerial* very surprisingly features actual pictures of Bertie. But, *Aerial* boasts the new actual-normal human-being Kate in abundance. And the real success of the album is that it actually fits along side all the traditional eccentric brouhaha that we all know and love Kate for.

More of that more typical brouhaha comes from *How To Be Invisible* and *Joanni*. Again, following the similar sonic pallet of π, with their mid-tempo band vs. synth arrangements. Despite the former boasting some wonderful lyrics based around a witches' brew that unlocks the secret of invisibility, *Joanni* is probably the more memorable of the two. Distant screaming and howling buried deep in the mix as Kate fights the cause of Joan of Arc, and closes the track with some effective guttural growling/humming. These tracks are probably what EMI would want for the next few singles due to their stereotypical Kateness. Unfortunately, while these tracks help *A Sea of Honey* flow beautifully, on their own they just aren't strong enough to carry the torch from *King of the Mountain*, and perhaps could have done with being split up on the track-list.

One of the album's true stand-out moments has to be the heartbreaking disc one finale, and second piano ballad, *A Coral Room*, which finds Kate finally addressing the matter of her mother's passing over a decade ago. The true lump-in-throat moment comes as Kate tenderly recalls "My mother and her little little brown jug / It held her milk / and now it holds are memories / I can hear her singing", before a deep male voice echoes back to her "Little brown jug, how I love thee". It rivals anything Kate has ever written. Period.

Already, Kate has come and conquered. Even just seven songs in, she's proved that good things certainly come to those who wait; and that those twelve years have been spent wisely, as it has all contributed to *Aerial*'s outstanding impact. However, this is where things now get especially interesting as we still have *A Sky of Honey* to unfold before us.

Disc two starts with light birdsong and a faint sprinkle of piano as Bertie himself (cast, according to the sleeve note, as: 'The Sun') sleepily says: "Mummy... / Daddy... / The day is full of birds / Sounds like they're saying words..." and cue the first eccentric yet brilliant moment on *A Sky of Honey*; if you listen closely to the distant blackbird warble, you can hear a chorus of Kates singing along side them and in a mimic birdsong voice, let slip the words "A-sea-of-honey- a-sky-of-honey". It's an idea that only Kate could pull off. Brilliantly obscure, but beautifully executed.

It becomes apparent that *A Sky of Honey* is unfolding into an especially constructed 9-piece "suite" of continuous music. The theme being the essence of evening turning into night and back to sunrise again, as a painter tries to capture each moment on his empty canvas. The painter being another piece of extraordinary casting.

Out of all the people who would have given their right arm to feature on Kate's comeback (tales emerged of Elvis Costello shamelessly making a bee-line for Kate at her rare appearance at the 2002 *Q* awards, to give her his number "Just in case she'd consider working with him." Presumably, Costello is still waiting). The lucky person to be hand-picked to guest narrate and sing on *Aerial* was no other than Rolf Harris. Fear not, all memories of *Two Little Boys* and *Tie Me Kangaroo Down*, are nowhere to be seen. Following the haunting *Prologue* as Kate introduces us to the sun and the evening, Rolf can be heard talking to himself and mixing his palette and trying to capture the moment, just as the seductive percussion of *An Architect's Dream* begins and Kate gushes over admiring the painter's handiwork and how every little stroke creates a world of its own.

The brief interlude that follows resurrects Harris' singing career for three brief lines as the elements start to gang up on his efforts: "It's raining / Look what's become of my painting / All of the colours are running!" before a chorus of bewildered Kate's pelt back to him "So all the colours run!? / So all the colours run!? / Look what they have become... / A beautiful sunset..." Her optimism and youthful spirit that is clearly still within her are commendable.

This statement of pure joy links perfectly into the entire album's other stand-out moment. *Sunset* is a truly divine few minutes. Kate at her most poetic, flying imagery of a beautiful sunset at us over a slow, sleepy lounge-like jazz arrangement, and finally bringing back that once trademark signature of raising the key at the bridge of the track, and multi-tracking her voice to give a haunting and unforgettable pinch we haven't heard since *Lionheart*. Her voice is at its sensual and smoky best here. Just as you think the track is about to sing itself into a womb-like dream state, it suddenly kicks into a sprightly flamenco jig that gets toes tapping, and builds and builds as the chorus of Kates burst into "Oh sing of summer and a sunset / And sing for us so that we may remember / The day writes words right across the sky/ They go all the way up to the top of the night."

Where *A Coral Room* put that lump in your throat, *Sunset* gets the hairs on the back of your neck right up. It's quite an achievement. However, this is a "suite" of music remember? There's no time to stop just yet, it's getting late and the day is turning to night. Something Kate fully acknowledges as she briefly says goodnight to the birds with *Aerial Tal*, a brief interlude of layers of birdsong and distant piano loop, before Kate turns to Björk-like vocal improvisations to duet with the wildlife.

Graphic: *Joanni* by Chris Butler

The true achievement here is the total abandonment in Kate's impressions, convincing us that music is what it always took to crack this indecipherable call of nature. It's also one of the moments you can't help but find yourself joining in with. This is great, unless you're listening to *Aerial* on headphones in public, where peoples' reactions to you could be applied to Kate's whole career. (What can I say, twelve years of waiting... I got carried away in my local shopping centre!)

Before the birdsong even gets to fade into night, the limbo of *Somewhere in Between* kicks in with its reprise of *A Sea of Honey*'s fondness for the drums, guitar and synths mix. Although the song chugs along nicely, with a delightfully memorable chorus, at worst it's a little MOR in places in comparison with the epics it follows. But as the title suggests, something indeed needs to open the question of what is in between dusk and night time, and lay down the gauntlet for the wonders that are about to close *Aerial*.

The night is brought in with *Nocturn*. Waves of spine-tingling choral effect wash the track in with Kate's bewildering cries allowing the steady percussion and bass to carry you along for the next six minutes as the secrets of the night are revealed. These secrets must be pretty damn good, as the track starts to become incapable of holding it's own intensity as it climbs and climbs higher than anything before it with the aid of a crowd shouting "Look at the light, all the time it's a changing / Look at the light, climbing up the Aerial!" If Kate could ever bring herself to edit this down to four minutes, the potential of this as a future single would be massive.

Nocturn suddenly falls into a sharp pulse of electronics and bass before the onslaught of the pounding *Aerial* hits us at full pelt to greet the new day. Kate loses all inhibitions here as this nine-minute belter (that no doubt her musicians have waited their careers to let rip on) as she exclaims with total conviction: "All the birds are laughing! / Come on let's all join in!" The song only briefly breaks down in the middle for a few moments of continuous synths and awakening birds, as Kate laughs maniacally at them and loses herself in the moment. The beats suddenly burst back in and she's off again "I wanna be up, up on the roof!". The song continues to build, and passes the nine minute mark before suddenly dropping to it's knees and embracing that morning is here, the birds can sing, and twelve years of waiting is finally over with a bang.

This exhaustingly exhilarating finale is what we perhaps needed to hear. While indeed, the brand new Kate Bush album has unfortunately ended for us to now wait indefinitely for the next, it's left us welcoming the sunshine and celebration of a brand new day where anything is possible. Not a bad note to leave us hanging on.

And so there we have it. Kate Bush has finally followed up *The Red Shoes*. It's typically Kate. Exceptionally fascinating. Possibly the best production job of recent years and utterly unforgettable. But, exactly how does it fit in to today's world? The anticipation for *Aerial* already made Kate stick out like a sore thumb. And in a world of ten-a-penny indie bands, karaoke pop stars and nursery rhyme gangster rap, Kate is certainly well respected. But musically, she may never fit in.

Her contemporaries may have kept her seat warm through the big sleep, but they all went off on their own tangents and never returned. *The Red Shoes* boasted some truly beautifully career highlights for Kate, but were over-looked due to the albums dense over-production in places, and attempt to fit too many revolutionary ideas into single songs. This is something Kate has clearly taken note of. She is now, without a doubt, Britain's greatest producer if nothing else.

Aerial's magic, however, lies in its raw honesty and deliverance. It's Kate taking every element of what she's best at from all her previous work: The concepts and production of *Hounds of Love*. The wild ideas of *The Dreaming*. The smooth seductive deliverance of *The Sensual World* etc... And, like the witches' brew for invisibility, carefully harnessing each element to its utmost potential. The music itself certainly isn't trying to be revolutionary, and if you dare to skim-listen to this, you could easily over look tracks like *How to be Invisible* and *Somewhere in Between* due to them not being "cutting edge" enough, or dare I say it, slightly dated.

But, Kate is nearly 50 years old. It's a hard thought to get our heads around especially when we don't see her for years on end and the indelible image of the 19 year old waif cart-wheeling her way through the *Wuthering Heights* video so strong in our minds. She certainly looks incredible these days. But the leotards, the crazy dance routines, the "Fuck you industry, I'm making a 'difficult' record!" days had to go eventually. And what has blossomed is a mature working-mum, who's managed to expertly combine the formulae of her prodigal youth with her new domestic-goddess and homely-creature self, and produce a mature and beautifully frank masterpiece.

Those who never "got" Kate back in the day, probably never will even now despite how ever many times they try and sit through *Aerial*. But, it's reassuring to know that while the other 48 year old female megastar is now donning leotards, and killing Abba samples over forgettable electro-dance ditties in a desperate attempt to "keep it real", our own 48 year old megastar has risen herself above all expectations by toning it down, and being as real as she ever has been for the last twelve years.

If music be the food of love, enjoy the main course of *Aerial*, and raise a toast to Kate Bush, the fine wine of British music. 10/10.

Svein Eilevstad

Finally the long wait is over. The first impression is a beautiful, transcendent cover reminding me of the *Myst* universe created by game developers Rand and Robyn Miller from Cyan. Their game world may be described as a visually stunning atmosphere combined with beauty, mystery and unspeakable sadness. Slowly, stories of days long ago are uncovered, and in the process all the familiar themes connected to facing the past: images of what was there for a moment and then faded away forever, long gone love, impossible happiness, strange coincidences.

I think the parallel to Kate's album is interesting. As usual, she is dealing with the "big" themes of life in a very personal way. Her music is unmistakably Kate-ish, still there has been a development in terms of the electronic trance-like ambience used to underline and expand the overall atmosphere of the songs. This background adds a new and intriguing element to her already unique universe. Twelve years have passed by, and Kate has no doubt noticed the works of techno-pioneers like Underworld, Saint Etienne, Tricky and Portishead. There's a touch of their ways of playing with sounds, rhythms and atmospheric backgrounds here. And still - Kate is not the imitator, she is using technology in her own ways. And it fits. Just like David Bowie's *Heathen* was such a welcome return to form because of his ability to incorporate modern elements into his craftsmanship as a song writer, Kate succeeds in doing the same thing. Luckily, both Kate and Bowie seem to be aware of the dangers connected to integrating these new musical ideas into their works. By understanding how these new possibilities may add to their vision, they use them cleverly and intuitively.

There are so many things to say about the various songs. The opener, *King of the Mountain* at first sounds almost anonymous, but after a while it grows into a tour de force of Kate's ability to use strange guitar chords combined with the amazing Bush Magic. The background choirs of ambience and ghost-like voices are intertwining, turning the melody into a dissected state of mind reminding me of Cathy's soul restlessly drifting across the naked moors of *Wuthering Heights*. It is thrilling and sad. The Elvis reference seems to fit perfectly into this windswept song of loneliness and alienation.

π is another surprise. The combination between the numbers sung so beautifully by Kate and the instant, classy pop appeal of the chorus works surprisingly well. *Bertie* deals with Kate's love for her son and is passionately woven into a renaissance-like arrangement. It is a beautiful melody, so pure and full of joy. On *Mrs. Bartolozzi* everyday descriptions of washing clothes turn into an allegory of life itself while the clothes lovingly caress each other in the washing machine. Kate stops the flow of the song to sing "washing machine... washing machine... washing... machine!" It is truly original and it carries such an emotional impact it is impossible not being drawn into this picture of the woman and the clothes line and the catharsis represented by the washing machine itself. A moment frozen in time, dealing with past and present.

I think *How To Be Invisible* would have been a perfect choice for a single, and perhaps a better introduction to the album than *King of the Mountain*. This is the modern, cool Kate Bush. The groove of the song is so wonderful, a strange mixture between *Twin Peaks* guitars and... say Massive Attack. It's a killer, and Kate's lyrics circle around esoteric secrets in the art of becoming invisible. These lyrics are made for interesting interpretations indeed. Her vocal is elegantly playing among the chords, relaxed and in full control of the flow of the song.

Joanni develops into strange landscapes of howls and sounds, posing as a perfect counterpart to the piano driven *A Coral Room*. The latter is a beautiful, yet extremely sad song, dealing with the losses in life and the memories left behind. Is it possible to come to terms with them, to accept life's ruthless circles? Beautiful, yes, but desperately sad images, like jugs of milk, the jug that was never noticed because it was always there. I understand Kate was in doubt as to whether she wanted to include this song on the record, but I am so glad she did. It is an instant classic, and it already means so much to me.

Graphic: *The Painter's Link* by Chris Butler

A Sky of Honey is the part of the album that is truly "aerial", the atmosphere quite different from *A Sea of Honey*, which deals with people and everyday life. This second disc is dedicated to the lovers experiencing the night together, and the magic of nature and artistic creation. It is a wonderful work of art. The songs are perfectly woven together, creating chapters leading towards the glorious morning. Here we get to know the mysterious Kate Bush, and the magic of her arrangements and song-writing is in full bloom here. It is impossible to pin down what her tricks are, and of course that is what makes her so intriguing as an artist.

These are not songs, but rather sketches or scenarios, more like an impressionist painting of Adam and Eve in the garden of Eden. There's an adventurous joy surrounding the couple, and nature and human minds melt together in a perfect, otherworldly ambience. In this marriage we discover the secrets of life, the wonders of the electric flow of the very universal soul. It is impossible to comment on certain parts of this story without running the risk of ruining the magic, but I think *Somewhere in Between* might be one of the best Kate songs I've ever heard. It's so elegant, so full of night air, so spiritual, so gracefully natural and mysterious. And the title track – well, it's a shock. Pulsating night music, a kind of '80s disco combined with techno-rhythm flavours and a minimalistic melody line to go along with it. "I feel I want to be up on the roof, I feel I gotta get up on the roof", Kate exclaims and we want to go there with her, to experience the marriage between heaven and earth, to reach a deeper understanding of the long lost connections.

The birds are talking to us. We just have to open our hearts in order to decipher the message. I can feel the cool breeze and sense the transcendent secrets of the night in here. This way the music comes alive of its own accord, and Kate's voice becomes the prophetic catalyst, bringing creation to perfection. It is all so modern and different from previous albums, and still true to the Kate Bush Tradition, if such a thing ever existed.

To sum up, *Aerial* is inspired, classy and adventurous, melancholic, passionate and mysterious – and always original and true to the overall vision. I have never heard Kate so much in control of her craft. She is calm and collected, she lets the beauty of the songs slowly unfold without much dramatic interruption. And still there is an immense power and energy in the very essence of the songs. I think *Aerial* is up there alongside *Hounds of Love* and *The Dreaming*. It goes without saying: I just can't wait for her next album...

"What a lovely afternoon..."

Krystyna Boswell

King of the Mountain was like an old friend by the time I played *Aerial* for the first time; however, far from the wind "blowing the door closed" it opened the portal wider to let in the soundscape that is the rest of the album. And what an album.

π is hypnotic and undulating. The recitation of a sequence of numbers could have sounded crass, or just plain silly, but in Kate's hands it's pure poetry, and deeply moving. *Bertie* could easily have been a sugary, indulgent lullaby to a much loved child and I was perhaps the most doubtful of this song, but once again Kate's personal magic has made this a joy. The gorgeous buoyant refrain and Mediaeval feel to the song brings us a glimpse of the magical new world Kate has discovered as a mother, and even though I do not have children I can share her joy.

Mrs Bartolozzi takes me back 30 years. This is largely just Kate and her piano, something I never thought to hear again after so much painstaking work in the studio over the past four albums, and it is a delight to experience. The alternately melancholic and soaringly hopeful chord progressions are like a river which sweeps me along, capturing the watery theme of the washing machine. Never has a domestic appliance been given such meaning and beauty. My wash days will never be the same again! Kate's voice is strong and passionate, breath-takingly beautiful. It is so good to hear that purity and power unfettered.

How To Be Invisible is both sinister and exciting, the pounding rhythms sweeping the listener along and sucking her into this mysterious, half-light world. My personal interpretation of this song is about the many reasons to wish for a cloak of invisibility, particularly in a situation of domestic violence behind closed and respectable doors. I may be off beam here, but if this is indeed the subject matter then the unsettling mood is captured and evoked masterfully. Kate has looked in dark places before for inspiration, and for me this is indeed her 'dark materials'.

Joanni's hooky refrain marks it out as potential single material, and is perhaps the most 'commercial' song on the album though not, for me, a favourite. A well-known historical figure viewed through the eyes of a mortal who could never hope to be first in her heart? *A Coral Room* closes the first disc with breathtaking beauty. This is Kate and her piano in their most melded, organic form. I am moved every time I hear this song which, like *Mrs Bartolozzi*, sweeps me along on a river of feelings yet never leaves me stranded, but rather wrapped around and cloaked softly in memories and love.

Prelude opens disc two and we begin a fabulous journey from a drowsy, sunny English afternoon through night to daybreak. Kate's voice blends with those of the birds; she is a bird, entering the winged ones' world as though she has always been a part of it. The mood is set, we are entranced and drawn in, transported on lazy sunbeams into a lovely afternoon.

Prologue is like sliding down a river in a punt, parasol shading you from the sunshine, the water rippling about the bows of your craft as you are carried deeper into Kate's reverie. *An Architect's Dream* evokes the delicacy of the artist's own craft and feels like a beautiful, fragile, yet enduring Oriental work of art, a porcelain vase that entices the sun to shine through the eggshell thin clay; but eggshells have great strength as well as beauty. *The Painter's Link* is simple but lovely, hinting how changes are not always within our power or design.

Sunset contains some of the most evocative lyrical descriptions on the album, this is indeed "a song of colour" that changes from sleepy soothing softness to a joyous celebration of flamenco dance, where I can imagine the vibrant swirling dresses and billowing silk shirts of the dancers being born of the fiery hues of the sky at sundown. Dance has always featured strongly in Kate's music, and the latter part of this song defies one to resist the tug to join the dance. It's hopeless; like the twelve princesses of legend, we are powerless to resist.

Somewhere in Between allows us to catch our breath, sensuous and mesmeric though it is, before we are swept up and drawn deep into the sweet velvet darkness of *Nocturn*. If you have never driven along a country lane in August, down to the seashore after sunset, breathed the sweetness of the evening air and run across the shore barefoot to where the sand embraces the sea, this is how to do it with music. Kate's voice is, for me, at her most beautiful on this track, so sensual and full of promise and yet so innocent; her voice reflects the mysterious beauty of the night, timeless yet so new again each time the Earth turns away from the Sun. I can almost feel the surf washing over me... feel wet skin on wet skin.

And finally, *Aerial*. Everything, every nuance and every dab of every colour, has been leading to this glorious sunrise, the rebirth of the day and the chorus of celebration as the feathered spirits of air greet their God once again. Roll in it, run with it, leap and scream it from the rooftops. Life is a gift! A new day is dawning and everything is here for you to hold with infinite love and wonder. Fall into it, embrace it and belong! We are all part of the Painter's work.

Paul Thomas

Beautiful.

What I found interesting was how the press reviews, mainly very positive (in fact I can't recall reading a bad one) had totally opposing views, for instance, one review said it was a very good album but sounded "dated", whilst another said the production was "cutting edge". Tracks that were named as stand-out songs in some reviews were considered the weakest in others. *How To Be Invisible* in particular seems to have divided opinion, some stating it as an instant Bush classic and an obvious single, whilst others saying it was dull and non-commercial. But I shouldn't be surprised by all this – Kate for all of her career has prompted extreme reactions. There are some tracks which seem universally accepted now as true classics, I don't think I have met a fan who doesn't consider *This Woman's Work* or *Running Up That Hill* to be amongst these; I wonder how many tracks on *Aerial* will be heralded as true classics. I think there are at least 5 or 6 tracks here that will be up there in "Kate's best songs" polls in years to come. But I don't wish to dwell on what might be better or worse when compared to Kate's previous work. We have a very special album here with an energy and identity of its own.

Of course we are still in the honeymoon period of *Aerial*. It is like making a new friend or being in the early stages of a wonderful romance, some things about that person will instantly leap out at you and charm you, the way they laugh, their warmth, their smile. Some aspects will unfold after time and you will gradually be over that initial buzz but would have settled into something familiar, comfortable but still very special.

There is certainly a warmth about this album, particularly the joyous suite of songs that make up *A Sky of Honey*. It was this disc that grabbed me from the start, *Sunset* and *Nocturn* especially. A couple of reviews have said that it sounds "ordinary" by her standards; I dispute this, as, even though parts of it are quite stripped down and uncomplicated who else could get away with putting a manic laugh in a track like *Aerial* or imitate birdsong. The reviewer on 'Newsnight' needs his bumps checking when he says it's an album "Sting could have made"; what nonsense – even Kate's relatively "normal" songs are far removed from anything anyone else could produce, her voice alone ensures that, and that is why we love her. *Aerial* confirms her uniqueness.

Graphic: *A Coral Room* by Chris Butler

From disc one, *King of the Mountain* already sounds like an old classic. It was an ideal choice for the first single, wintery but warm, what a combination. *How To Be Invisible* sounds like an obvious single, almost circular, with soft whistling, an infectious hook and intriguing, if somewhat creepy lyrics. It maintains the appeal of her mystery whilst being radio friendly and appealing to casual listeners.

Joanni is an atmospheric epic, and although the lyrics look flat on paper, they come alive when you hear the track and there is something very erotic about it too, who else could make a battle sound sexy? I think that's what it is about though, this beautiful vision rising up from a bloody battle, it's the paradox thing with Kate (again) opposites going together. Although initially I found *Mrs Bartolozzi* a difficult one to appreciate, I now hear how it fits in with the other tracks and love the idea behind the song (and the drama). Putting my washing machine on spin cycle will never be the same again.

Of course, *A Coral Room* speaks for itself, nobody could be unmoved by the sheer beauty here, even if the lyrics are hard to decipher in

MN

their meaning, the emotion connects with the listener, in much the same way as *Moments of Pleasure*. It is like the grown-up version of *Warm and Soothing*, where Kate spoke about "walking into arms through the back door", and on *A Coral Room* she is remembering that in this song about the passing of time. The way she sings "hee hee hee" puts me in mind of *Blue* by Joni Mitchell when she sings "lots of laughs" in such a melancholic way it could break your heart. With Kate and Joni all they need is a piano and a voice to convey such emotion and connect with the listener. I cannot think of any other artists who do this as well as them, with just the right amount of space, the right piano chord, the right pitch and tone in the voice. Perfect.

A Sky of Honey is a masterpiece. It manages to be incredibly "hello birds... hello trees" but not twee or schmaltzy. Kate knows exactly what to put in and what to leave out. She really is incredible for this, she has such musical vision and insight. Even listening to what appears a "complicated" album such as *The Dreaming*, you realise once you have heard it a few times that every note and sound is exactly where it should be, in its right place. Kate instinctively knows what colours to paint a song.

A Sky of Honey is very much like a painting, which is so appropriate considering it's subject matter. Light and shade, nature, colour, beauty. Kate's lyrics are really living up to the hippy image the press created for her in the late '70s and early '80s. Not that that's a bad thing, of course, there is something hippy-like about the idea of a concept album after all, and this is a clever and beautiful album. I don't know how many times I have used "beauty" or "beautiful" in this little review but no other word sums it up as well. It makes you want to run naked through fields, hug trees and somersault down hills. It brings out the latent hippy in me. What we really need is a gorgeous Summer's day to fully appreciate this album, if only it had come out in the Spring, but could we really wait until then? (well, yes probably).

Now, after 12 years, we have *Aerial*, and of course the wait was worth it. Sixteen tracks, that's 1.5 tracks for each year we have waited. No big deal at the end of the day, but it depresses me to think that next time I go out to buy a new Kate Bush album I will probably stop off at the post office on the way to collect my pension. Beautiful... End of!

A masterpiece of art unparalleled. A voice for which angels would surely sin. This is Kate. It was the track listing which first got me thinking about the early demos. Songs which were given names like *Aerial Tal* and *Mrs. Bartolozzi* seemed to me – then – to be in line with those demos. Something akin to coming full circle? I don't know. And when some of the tracks could be heard on the BBC website this idea was strengthened. To me it seemed that Kate Bush has tapped into her childhood creativity.

As always, the basic canvas on which the songs are painted is different from all previous albums, while still being Kate. And yet it seems that there is a connection between all albums and *Aerial*. Perhaps this last thought entered my mind because of some parts of the lyrics ("breathing, wave", "what a lovely afternoon", "diamond night", "I can't hear a word you're saying"...). Maybe it is because of some of the soundscapes. As if to come to this, the painter had made studies. Just like Picasso made studies to create his masterpieces.

Before the album came out, but parts of it could be heard on the internet, it held a jaw dropping quality for me. Stunning. When 4th November came and the shops in the Netherlands displayed *Aerial*... something happened to me when first listening to it in it's entirety. I don't know what was happening: there were all kinds of emotions charging in and surfacing and mixing. And all the colours of the palette were there: from love to loss. It kept me wondering how she conjured up this wonderful magic. When eventually I had to get out of the house to do groceries I again found myself overwhelmed... what was happening? Was it just me? Was it the years in between? So I devised a little experiment and got some non Kate-fans to listen. Guess what...

Kate makes art. Pure art, evolved beyond music and exquisitely able to touch. Sculptors, authors, painters and musicians all see and sense and have something to say. Some tell the story or hold the mirror by using a brush. Kate has woven a musical tapestry finding peers in the classical realm and the great arts rather than in contemporary hit-and-run musicians. Song, sound, word and voice are strangely able to lure my mind to calm waters. Stepping out of the day into the *Aerial* world. Making me want to view a day, the ever-changing sun show, with a beloved one on some hillside. In the Summer. A cup of mead, an element of humour. And a connection too priceless to weigh. To me it is clear: this is production perfection and a masterpiece.

A Sea of Honey

Collin Kelley

The wind blows the door open,
telescopes the days, makes twelve years disappear,
and we knew you were out there, would rise again,
like birds and your happiness.
We agree to take this journey, to climb up the aerial,
to leap.

You sound like Joni Mitchell when you count,
heady company to be included in,
you make me want to learn math again,
to dance in that circle of infinity.
Maybe a madrigal, a song for us and for him,
we dance.

And I'll never think of washing the same way,
my head pressed against the machine,
harmonizing with the slooshy, sloshy sound,
until I'm sucked in with the shirts and jeans,
ready to become gleaming and clean.

I look in the mirror, wish myself invisible,
or to fold myself in half, chant incantations
until I'm turned inside out, like we've all been
at one time or another. Your words unfold me,
find me hiding in my corner, suck me back
through the keyhole.

...with my key I (unlock it)

Twelve years ago I put on my armour,
went into battle three times, never had a ring
put on my finger, blew kisses to you
across the ocean, for inspiration, for strength,
for God to keep you and yours even when
he wasn't keeping me.

When the planes crashed,
when we all went under the waves,
there was a song
I dreamed of,
and you must have caught the melody.
Your little brown jug holds all the love,
all the memories of mothers now gone,
uncorks sadness, unwinds the clock.
In the half light, push the boat out...
we have set sail...

A Sky of Honey

Collin Kelley

Yo ho, young Bertie
is what the birdsong sounds like,
in this dying light, that looks like Italy,
and I never want to leave.
I want to dance before the summer goes,
speak to me in many languages.

The light is changing, just before the storm,
so all the colours run crimson and rust,
like a sunset.
And in the rain we will dance…
a tango to flamenco guitars,
(Kirsty would have approved)
and we'll twirl all the way to the top of the night,
and we'll sing for her,
allow me this indulgence, allow us this
remembrance for those who have turned to dust.

You are happy in these silent places,
these in between places,
these still places on hilltops.
Where the world opens up and birds return,
and you trill along with them, carefree…
I think you have never been this happy…

Let's go down to the beach,
into the moonlight,
become deep divers into honey seas,
swim all the way out
(what do you feel?)
and float here until dawn breaks again,
until the light changes, until its bouncing
off the aerial.

And then again, we dance…
this time on the roof, we give ourselves
to abandon, we take flight, forget language,
become slaves to guitars and beats,
until the sky of honey and the sea of honey
become one, until they run, they bleed,
into perfection.

forget language,
become slaves to guitars and beats,
until the sky of honey and the sea of honey
become one, until they run, they bleed,
into perfection.

Dear Kate ...

We send her scented letters

Issue 76 December 2005

The joyous reaction of *HomeGround* readers to Kate's return after 12 years.

Kyla Clay-Fox: The little light shines again – brighter than ever! Bless you and all those special people who keep you sane, loved and happy. You deserve it! Love, respect and eternal gratitude.

Ilja: Kate... When an album is out you think "this is the best, it will be my favorite, how long can Kate go on with making such masterpieces?" After 12 years I was indeed curious, maybe afraid that after 12 years the point of "I'm happy like this, leave me alone" was there and a new album was out of the question. But today... I bought *Aerial*! It feels as good as my wedding day! Again it's a masterpiece, the best I ever heard! Kate, thank you ever so much for your music, you proved that a true genius can stay out of the limelight and come back with a smashing album as *Aerial*! Love you for that! Best regards.

Edoardo Seianis: Dear Kate, I am trying to find the right words to express my feelings while hearing *Aerial* but I can't… The beauty of this music and lyrics are so touching that I feel like I am in front of a wonderful landscape… that kind of deep emotional state that only the beauty of nature can give and that make you cry without any reason… *Aerial* is the most beautiful work I have ever heard… it will be the soundtrack of my life and the balsam for my soul for many years... Thank you, lovely woman.

Tony and (Madge the Cat): Love and luck to you, Kate. Words cannot express how much enjoyment your music has given over the years.

John Roger: Thank you for another wonderful album. I hope you're pleased with it, I know I am. I hope your life continues to help you create such wonderful music. And thank you for sharing the joy Bertie brings – made me smile and you can never have too many of those!

Mike Birch: To me, the arrival of *Aerial* is like Christmas come early. It's like an old friend turning up on your doorstep after not seeing them for years. A little changed, a little different, but upon hearing the voice, a sudden recognition… A single you say?… What, an album? A DOUBLE album!? This is wonderful work. Thank you from someone your age who has always quietly enjoyed what you do. Wishing you and your family every happiness.

Lesley Davis: I have fond memories of my Dad coming home from work and telling me he'd heard a song on the radio that we just had to go and buy. So that weekend we headed for the local Woolworths and got the 7" of *Wuthering Heights*. We raced home to put it on our stereogram and I first heard your voice with my Dad by my side. I was 13 years old. Every record you then released, Dad and I would sit and marvel. He came to the cinema with me to watch *The Line, the Cross & the Curve*. Coming up to my 40th birthday I got to play *Aerial* for the first time the day before what would have been my Dad's birthday. Sadly, he wasn't here to hear it because cancer had taken him three years previous. But I made damn sure to play it loud enough so that, wherever he is, he got to hear it with me. I am immensely moved by the songs where you write about your mother and know all too well what it's like to lose someone so dear. But every time I play *A Sky of Honey* I can picture my Dad sitting beside me, listening to the birdsong as we share a sunset. Thank you for letting me feel like I still share your music with him. This album was worth the wait, it's a melodious piece of artwork that every time I hear it, I see something new. Thank you for sharing the sunset with us. Love.

Paige Cavanaugh: It is 1987. Imagine if you will a young girl of 18, listening to her copy of *Hounds of Love* obsessively over and over and over again. Now, without laughing, imagine that same girl doing an interpretive dance to your song *Waking the Witch*. Oh, she is earnest, and there are lots of arms flailing and emotional tears streaming whilst her white nightgown flows this way and that. She is in love with you and wants you to feel her with all of her might! She answers an ad in *HomeGround* and begins a pen-pal friendship with another earnest girl. Their friendship blooms into love and the girl's true nature unfurls at the feet of all those around. Eventually the love cools, but the friendship remains, even to this day. I thank you from the bottom of my heart for opening my eyes to love in its many forms. All of my love to you and yours, Kate. May your life continue to be one filled with serenity and happiness! Xoxoxoxo.

Mary Rowlett: How happy I am to have this opportunity to let you know how much I love *Aerial* and how much your music has touched me and helped me throughout my life. I imagine, like most people, when you have completed a piece of work you send it out into the world and 'move on' from it. For me, however, the images and feelings created in your music live on, and I'm always discovering something new. These wonderful 'worlds' have been a source of delight and healing for me. What a wonderful talent you have. I want to say 'thank you' for sharing your imagination and creativity with the world, and with me. I truly wish you and your family (especially delightful Bertie!) every happiness in the future,

Brian Parker: Kate, your music has touched me in so many ways – it has brought me to tears, made me feel exhilarated, made me laugh, made me think about life and relationships – it has made me feel. The combination of your voice, music and poetic lyrics have been an inspiration – a real precious and beautiful thing. Not many artists have touched me in such an intense way – but you have. And thank you for that. I am not too sure if you really know how special your music is, and the way you inspire people. But you do – and for a person that I have never met, you have given me so much. So thanks! *Aerial* has touched me in all the ways I have described above. It is a glorious piece of work – your music shines like a beacon. Again it inspires me to create – and take risks. Kate, thank you so much.

Rachel Lisi: Just a quick note to express my abundant appreciation for your craft. *Aerial* is perhaps the most cinematic, elegant, potent and sensual album I have ever heard. Like a charm this music evokes so much imagery and emotion. As a woman and an aspiring writer you have always been a crystalline inspiration. You have given to me great "moments of pleasure" in my life and opened doors I never knew existed. I thank you so very much for all of your hard work and generosity. You have presented all of us with such a glorious gift and we graciously accept. Oh, and *Joanni* has me on my knees and *A Coral Room* in tears every time! Brava Kate! All the love back to you and yours.

EmptyBullring: Oh Kate! The album is a pure work of artistic genius. Each listen draws me further into the worlds of honey, both of sea and sky. What it must be like being you! Each breath but an exhalation of pure artistic creativity and light. You have topped yourself with this *Aerial* creature. Set fully upon the masses it can cure all of the ills that beset humanity. *A Coral Room*... omg, *A Coral Room*. Could pure perfection exist without this song? I don't believe it could.

Andy Blake: A Sea of Praise. *Aerial* is magical, a musical treat. I thank you and all I can offer in return is a wish of happiness for you. Bless you... A Sky of Praise. Tweet chirrup chirrup twitter tweet tweet!

Marcel Rijs: In all the years that I've been listening to pop music, yours has always been there. It started in 1978 when I was only seven. I still remember buying all your albums in the Summer of 1985 and buying them again in December 1990 when the box set came out. Having heard no new Kate Bush songs since 1996, I was almost ready to reconcile with the notion that it might never happen again. You're just as human as anyone else, priorities change, life moves on. Which makes it difficult to describe how happy I am to hear *Aerial* now. There is so much to discover here... Ordinary subjects made extraordinary by musical accompaniment and vocal delivery. But out of all the artists I know and love, there will never be another Kate Bush. Your work continues to give me feelings of utter sadness and the greatest joy. It's the soundtrack to my life, a precious gift given by your talent to write such beautiful melodies and such touching lyrics. For that I will always be grateful.

Laney: I just want to say thank you, Kate, for doing it one more time. *Aerial* is a beautiful album and you've been missed. A great big hug xxxx.

Michelle Powers: Kate Bush you are wonderful. I love you, you are an inspiration to me! I'm so glad you are still in the picture. By the way, if you want to check out what a good Elvis impersonator I am married to, his site is www.bestelvisinvegas.com He is a trained singer, but he doesn't take himself too seriously, he just loves to make people happy... and he is always very busy. I am determined to bring a bit of culture into his life and I am starting with you, Kate. Xx

Rob McKay: Thank you so much for *Aerial*! It has exceeded by far my hopes and desires for such a triumphant new release from your font of Creativity. Your hard work and especially your essence shines through it so clearly like a beacon piercing the thickest fog that surrounds the World. A Lighthouse might be a better analogy! Thank you for sharing your Light with us; we are blessed... I really can't add anything that others may already have said, so aside from thanking you from the deepest part of my soul, I would like to extend my thanks and appreciation to all who helped lay the foundation for your remarkable and singular career: your brothers John Carder and Paddy, your kind father Dr. Bush, and especially your dear mother Hannah, who I know is watching you with such pride, joy, and happiness. You have done them all proud, and have made your fans so delighted and pleased beyond words! We love you so much, and to quote from another place and time, please feel it! Our ears are open... thank you for filling them with your exquisite and singular Work. God love you,

Scott Ferguson: It has only been a few weeks since the release of *Aerial* yet I still find it difficult to listen to any other music. *Aerial* is so fresh, so alive, so overflowing with beauty and emotion. It plays as part of my everyday life where ever I am – in my car, at home, on the computer at work and on my ipod as I walk through the streets of Toronto. The music stays with me after I turn it off and I can still hear you singing to me. I have been a fan since I first had the opportunity to hear *Wuthering Heights* (in 1979 when I was 12). Your songs have soundtracked so many significant moments in my life – from falling in love and travelling the world to heartbreak and personal loss. When I first heard *This Woman's Work* in 1988, my mother had just been diagnosed with cancer. The song spent the next year by my side as I spent countless days by hers, hoping that everything would turn out fine. It didn't and I lost her in late 1989 but I shared that song with her and she loved it as much as I did. I listen to it now and it always brings me back to the memory of her love. *Aerial* has already filled my days with such warmth and joy as we drift toward Winter. It continues to reveal it's depth and power with each listen. Best wishes to you and your family.

Graphic: *A Sky of Honey* by Chris Butler

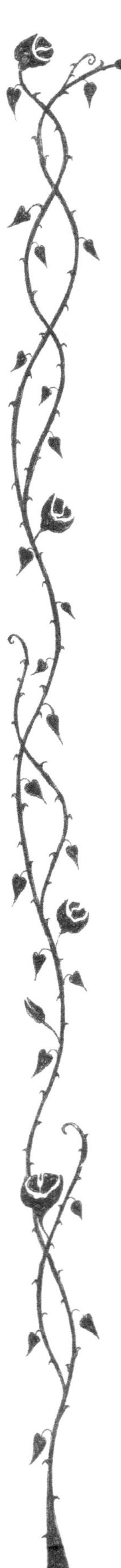

In Her Handbag

Kyla Clay-Fox

He searches through her life's work
Children sulking from a photograph,
Her face in a zip up compartment
A handkerchief with a monogram.
A hairbrush, some perfume, a diary
That Thursday's solicitors' letter
A lock of hair and a baby tooth -
And the ring they had chosen together-
He is mourning the life in her hand bag.
The life that they had once dreamt about-
It's so strange how the last thing she'd grab when she left
Is the first thing he wants to throw out.

Album Shorts

Brief Reactions to *Aerial*

Issue 77: July 2006

Dandelion: At its best, the music of Edward Elgar took 19th Century romanticism into its finest hour. Fairly simple pieces could exhaust the listener by taking him through the gauntlet of emotions, from deep joy to intense sorrow, and retaining an uncynical purity. Equally, it both touched a nerve of common experience, whilst remaining uniquely individual. So Elgar's ghost has sat on his cloud watching a century pass by, listening to the myriad of musical genres which have gone past. And now the ghost has descended, and possessed an English composer. Thank you, Elgar, this is what the cynical 21st Century needs. This is English music back to its roots and at its purest. This is your finest work mate! I knew you'd be into 'chill out'. Kate, I love you, and look forward to your next ghost!

Monty Moncrieff: At www.thesaurus.com: *Aerial*: absurd, bizarre, blue sky, capricious, chimerical, curious, dreamlike, extravagant, fabulous, fairy-tale, fancied, fantastic, fantastical, fictional, fictitious, fictive, flaky, floating, ideal, illusory, imaginative, imagined, incredible, kinky, legendary, mythical, notional, offbeat, pipe dream, poetic, preposterous, romantic, shadowy, suppositious, unreal, visionary, whimsical, wild.

Mrs Clonrickert, Scraggy Island: Ah sure, all this Kate Bush stuff is a gas, isn't it, Father? She's a brazen hussy, that one. It's all fannys-akimbo with her. Durty, durty business... and all these bird shenanigans now – feckin' birds, is it?! Quare set of feathers on that aul bowsie, tsk, tsk. Sure didn't Mrs Conroy from the village tell me that she had the whole countryside leaping up hills, "Babooshkas" out flapping in the breeze. Shockin' stuff altogether. And as for that poor Mrs Bartolozzi, I suggest my good friend Mrs. Doyle's household tips for ladies no. 3 "Putting Clothes Out on the Line" and no. 4, "Cleaning Shite Out of a Carpet" as recommended in The Craggy Island Parish Magazines. Did I mention this business of filthy midnight swims with God knows which Johnny-come-lately?! Oh Father, t'would take more than a few decades of the rosary to sort her out. That's grand music to be putting about alright.

Barbie Wyard: This isn't just any old album. This is an album made from finest matured Kate, a jar of honey, an ounce of sky, a dessertspoon of sea, served with lashings of thick unadulterated joy. Sublime and simply wonderful. Thank you Kate.

No Skeletons Accusations or Revelations

The Jovanovic Biography reviewed by Johnny Burke

Issue 76: December 2005

"I'll always play up for photographers... I do have to keep my face in the papers, you know. I need the publicity..."
"I'm not an elf, I'm a woman..."
"Over the next few years I'd like to take some time off."

OK, *HomeGround* readers, here's a little exercise for you. Of the three 'quotes' above, which do you think is the one least likely to have come from Kate Bush ('reclusive', 'Greta Garbo of pop', 'leading a Miss Havisham-like existence on an island with her secret child' etc, etc...), and which is most likely to have emanated from the glossy lips of Bexleyheath's favourite daughter?

Well, as you've probably guessed, she is responsible for them all. The first (and most surprising) of the three does, admittedly, come from the late 1970s, but it is an interesting snippet from this latest published look at Kate and her work (as well as an indicator of how times have changed and of how our girl has grown up). Rob Jovanovic's timely biography of Kate hit the shelves last month, scheduled perfectly to coincide with the extraordinary media interest surrounding Kate's return to the music world – and to the forefront of public consciousness – with the release of her first single in twelve years, *King of the Mountain*, and its double CD begetter, *Aerial*.

And what an attractive tome it is, featuring a beautiful Gered Mankowitz picture of Kate on the front cover in which she appears to be wearing (and looking sensational in, one must admit) a duvet cover. The author – a seasoned music journalist who has written for *Mojo*, *Q*, *Uncut* and *Record Collector*, as well as penning books on REM, Beck and Nirvana – is very clear about his intentions from the start: "The prospect of a book about her life and work is probably not welcomed at the Bush home" he opines, "even though this volume isn't trying to find any closeted skeletons, make any wide-of the-mark accusations or reveal where her son goes to school. Here you'll find a detailed look at her life and career." Unsurprisingly, Kate declined to be interviewed for the book but Jovanovic did interview many people who have worked with Kate "to fine-tune a look at her recorded and filmed legacy".

Having made all of this clear, the author has produced a workman-like, but nevertheless comprehensive and coherent, account of that career. It does what it says on the tin, and is an interesting and entertaining read. I should point out to anyone who is thinking of purchasing this book the fact that you are, at this moment, reading *HomeGround* magazine will probably mean that there isn't a great deal of information here that you don't already know. But this book isn't necessarily for those of us who know most of what there is to know about the public Kate Bush.

What Jovanovic has done – and rather skilfully, I think – is to collate a huge amount of information that has been 'out there' for several years and splice it all together into a readable and engrossing overview of Kate's working life. Although the reader is aware that the author has not interviewed the subject, one still gets that sense of Kate sitting down and chatting for hours into a tape recorder about her long career in music. That is to say, the book has an immediacy and a fluidity which makes for an absorbing read.

Cover credit:
Portrait Books

The reader is taken on a journey, quite systematically, from Kate's early childhood in Kent through to the David Gilmour sessions, the now-famous EMI-supported years of singing lessons and mime classes with Lindsay Kemp (and I never knew that *Moving* was about him), the overnight success of *Wuthering Heights*, the rushed second album, the tour, taking over as producer, her 'she's gone mad album' (*The Dreaming*), her masterpiece (*Hounds of Love*), the later albums and, finally, the exhaustion that prompted Kate's (as one tabloid recently called it) 'return to normality' when she took a step back and decided to do what she wanted for a while.

There are some quite detailed chapters that deal with the writing/recording process for some of her albums, and these are fascinating. Jovanovic has interviewed producers, musicians and many other people who have worked with Kate right from the early years, and the impression one gets of her, from every one, is of a quiet, kind, unassuming, charming, interested, dedicated and frighteningly creative woman who knows what she wants and will work and work and WORK until she gets it. She appears to be held in high esteem by everyone she has worked with, and even by those who have never worked with her but have been touched or influenced by her music. One also feels that several of the men who were interviewed might agree with the singer Roy Harper, who told the *Guardian* newspaper last September that Kate was "honest and gentle... the kind of girl you should've married, really".

When the story hits the later part of Kate's career (up to and including *The Red Shoes*) the chapters do become a little more sparse: not the author's fault, I guess, as Kate had by then wised up and become more conscious about protecting herself and her creative process, so there is less information available about that time. However, the latter pages of the book do feel somewhat rushed.

The author, too, has a tendency to slam in with a very personal observation or opinion and rather annoyingly denote these with an exclamation mark!, a piece of punctuation which is much over-used here. There are occasions where he seems completely out of step with some generally-held opinions and views about Kate's work, such as when he dismisses *Never Be Mine* – one of Kate's best-loved songs, and one which made it to the final four in a recent poll of favourites on *HomeGround*'s very own website forum – as 'a forgettable track'.

A fairly detailed list of videos, stage appearances and a discography close the book but, as ever, there are the inevitable (but still irritating) factual errors and inconsistencies: Kate's last appearance on stage with Dave Gilmour in 2002 apparently took place in London at the Royal Albert Hall AND at the London Palladium (in reality she sang at the Royal Festival Hall); and it will probably be a surprise to many (not least Kate herself) to discover that *The Sensual World* hit no 6 in the US singles charts back in the late '80s. Mmmmm... yes? Mmmmm... no(!).

Jovanovic has produced a readable and pacey resume of Kate's career to date. He is obviously someone who admires his subject and who respects her work and her way of working. This is a book about that work thus far: the process, the people and the results. It isn't a book about Kate Bush, the person. If that's what you want, you'll probably be disappointed. If you want a cohesive account of the career of this most fascinating of artists, you could do a lot worse than investing in this.

Whiskey in the Jar

Dr. Alex Kraaijeveld distills Kate's albums

Issue 77: July 2006

What I want to try and do is build up a mental picture of a malt whisky based on the 'feel' of the album as a whole, rather than focus on specific songs.

So, first take *The Kick Inside*. It's not a 'heavy' album, so a medium-bodied whisky. Probably one from Speyside. But a characterful Speysider, one with good malty notes. Kate's voice makes it a whisky on the sweet side, certainly not a dry whisky. What kind of sweetness? Not fruity; Kate weaves around the music and coats it in warm honey... This honey image clinches it for me: if *The Kick Inside* were a malt whisky, it would be a Balvenie, a rich-honeyed malty whisky distilled in Dufftown, in the heart of Scotland's Speyside district.

On to *Lionheart*. To me, this is a delicate and deceptively simple album. It oozes charm and character, in a gentle way. Translating this into a malt whisky is actually pretty straightforward. Delicate, charm, gentle are the typical terms used for malt whiskies from the Scottish Lowlands. And arguably the best Lowland whisky comes from the now sadly closed Rosebank distillery, although fortunately there are still plenty of bottles of Rosebank around. Try some 12 year old Rosebank while playing *Lionheart* and I hope you'll agree I'm not far off the mark in matching the two!

With the benefit of hindsight, *Never For Ever* offers glimpses of things to come. Some of the album is 'related' to the previous two, other parts move away from them. But the whole is properly balanced, and clearly has a character of its own. So I'm looking for a whisky which has several different aspects: malt, sweetness and 'a bit more'. The one that comes to mind is Highland Park, distilled near Kirkwall on the Orkney islands. It's often referred to as one of the best all-rounders; a luscious whisky with malt and sweetness, but also peat and smoke.

The Dreaming is rich, deep, complex, multi-layered, heavy. The first kind of whisky that comes to mind is one which has matured in casks that have previously contained sherry. And one that is bottled at higher strength than usual. One of the richest, most complex 'sherried' whiskies I have ever tasted is a Blairfindy, distilled in 1964 and bottled by Blackadder at an age of 40 years and a strength of 55.3%. I cannot even begin to describe the complexity of this malt. This is one to savour slowly in order to discover all its layers. A perfect match to *The Dreaming* for me!

One of the key aspects of *Hounds of Love* is the two parts it consists of, *Hounds of Love* and *The Ninth Wave*, and especially the contrast between those two. If I try to see those two aspects in whisky terms, I see 'power' in *Hounds of Love* and 'sweetness' in *The Ninth Wave*. To me, 'power' in whisky comes from plenty of peat smoke. Malt whiskies characterised by large amounts of peat smoke are typically distilled on the isle of Islay, in the southern Hebrides. And the best example of an Islay malt which provides a perfect balance between plenty of peat and sophisticated sweetness is Ardbeg.

Kate has said in an interview that she considered *The Sensual World* her most feminine album. When I put the sensuality and the femininity together and think whisky, I can arrive at only one type of malt whisky: one which has matured for a few years in port casks. Among the more luscious of these port-finished malts is a Glenmorangie, which has been matured for well over 10 years in ex-bourbon casks before being given a few years of extra maturation in port pipes. To me, the velvety rich port influence captures the sensuality of *The Sensual World*.

I really got stuck with *The Red Shoes*. What I wanted to do was find a whisky which would capture both the relative accessibility of the music and the pain and raw emotion coming from much of the lyrics. I spent time opening and nosing bottle after bottle from my whisky shelves, with *The Red Shoes* playing at the same time. Nothing clicked. Then I remembered a malt which I had tasted once at a whisky event some time ago, which combined silkiness with darker, more powerful peatiness. Could this be the one? Fortunately, I know the man behind this whisky, and a fresh tasting sample was only one e-mail away. Compass Box's Peat Monster does indeed offer both aspects I was looking for: accessibility (the silky notes) and raw emotion (the peaty notes).

And then *Aerial*! Kate is painting with music, voices, sounds. And the perfect whisky match for this piece of art is a whisky which I've been lucky enough to taste, and which is probably the best whisky I've ever tasted: Dalmore 50 y.o. Like *Aerial*, this whisky is a true piece of art. Amazingly rich (especially with chocolate-y and orange-y notes), holding up incredibly well to the half century in the wood, and with a finish which lasts for ever and ever.

Kate, if you're reading this, thank you so much for giving us a double-CD with new music to enjoy.

About this having taken 12 years, keep in mind that the best whiskies take at least 10 years to mature and I am sure I'll be able to find a match to 'K9'.

Dr. K says:

"Kate's reply to the question of why making *Aerial* took so long, in an interview for BBC 4's 'Front Row' programme, broadcast early November 2005.

"But beyond the long 'maturation' period of both Kate's music and whisky, the two really have a lot in common. Both have many layers of complexity, both are for real savouring and can only fully be appreciated when you give them time, come back to them time and time again.

"Given that Kate's music has been part of my life from the moment she burst on the scene more than 25 years ago, and that I also really enjoy a good glass of Scotch malt whisky,
I'd like to take the comparison one step further and ask the question:

"If Kate's music is indeed a malt whisky, which one would it be?

"So what I'm going to try and do in this wee piece is match each of Kate's eight studio albums to certain malt whiskies, trying to capture the essence of spirit and music each time."

Graphic ooverleaf: *An Architects's Dream* by Chris Butler

Excerpts from a Secret Diary

As scrobbled from the dustbin by a certain Mr. Townsend

Issue 77: July 2006

Saturday 1st January 2005: Bertie up early thinking it was Christmas again (that's the 8th time this week!). I sang him *December Will Be Magic Again* (Bongo version) and he soon left me alone. EMI 'phoned to wish me Happy New Year and asked me when the new album's coming out. In their dreams.

Thursday 24th February 2005: Just heard a song on the radio that sounds like one of mine. A group called The Futurists or something. Cheeky feckers. How dare they! Got in touch with my lawyer. They will pay for this intrusion of my privacy and integrity. Who do they think they are?

Sunday 27th February 2005: Futurists' single is Top 10 – I love it. Wrote a song about numbers to celebrate, and baked some pie.

Tuesday 24th May 2005: Been really busy. Heard some birds singing in the park, and got inspired – reckon I could make a 40-minute piece based solely on it. Bertie ruined the mood by spilling a pot of honey over a street artist's painting. I said I'd pay for the damage. The artist was Rolf Harris – he said I should record a new album. What the feck does he know?

Wednesday 25th May 2005: Recorded a new album. It's very good and will probably be a double if I can convince EMI to fork out for the packaging.

Thursday 26th May 2005: When EMI finished laughing, they agreed to a double album. Their exact words were – "We don't care if it's 10 minutes of you scraping jelly off your formica, just release a bloody record." They have no soul.

Friday 27th May 2005: Almost decided on final running order. I think *Prelude* can come before *Prologue* after all. Though not sure where *Aerial Tal* should come. Or if to include the song about coming at the *Q* awards. Oh, it's tough being an artiste.

Friday 27th May 2005 – later: Need to change the title of the song about the washing machine – 'Mrs Mopp Does The Washing' doesn't have a very romantic ring to it. Going to call it 'Tabs Are Better Than Powder – Discuss'.

Friday 27th May 2005 – later still: Danny pissed himself when I told him that title. Changing it to 'Suds'.

Friday 27th May 2005 – even later: Still not happy with that title. I asked my cleaner, Mrs Bartolozzi, if she could think of anything. She just smiled indulgently and said, "Move your feet so I can vac under the piano, love." She's no help.

Friday 27th May 2005 – much later: Have written a song about Bertie. It just has to go on the album. It's about 18 minutes long, but should fit, as the album's a bit short, only having 3 tracks so far.

Friday 27th May 2005 – a bit later: Saw a lovely Sunset today. Wish I could find some inspiration for a song to link Rolf's bits on CD2.

Friday 27th May 2005 – that night: It's finished. And I've even done a video for the first single – I do appear in it, but only in a big coat, which should cover the fact I'm now a naturist, which I may have forgotten to mention to anyone.

... the day is full of Birds ...

Graphic: Lisa Oliver

Saturday 28th May 2005: A day off, but I'm on a creative roll, so it shouldn't be long before I am writing again.

Sunday 6th November 2005: EMI rang to remind me the album's out tomorrow, and that I haven't done anything about it. "Oh, just bung a few posters up in London and any other random city," I tell them. So they do. Decide to take a few months off.

Thursday 4th May 2006: They won't let me have any peace. Not only is everyone crying out for another single (what was wrong with the last one?!!), I've now heard there's a get-together of 6 of my fans in London – will send Del along to suss them out, what with me being scared of them and everything. I mean, they might try to hug or kiss me.

Sunday 7th May 2006: Del escaped relatively unscathed. Said he was pounced upon by an American lesbian with a thumping heart, and someone who looked like Stevie Nicks before the drugs. Apparently they were all asking about new singles, tours and music. What do these people want? Blood?

Monday 8th May 2006: Gave blood today.

Tuesday 30th May 2006: Someone is asking for my diary to be posted on an internet forum. Why does anyone think I am interesting enough to have anything to write about? Spent the day recording a new single, finalising the Greatest Hits DVD and arranging some tour dates...

Any resemblance to the *Secret Diary of Adrian Mole* by Sue Townsend is entirely coincidental.

My Cloud

Nat Hall

Today the world could have been tossed
like a pancake – dear crêpe Suzette...
I'm buzzing through highest
of cloud!
O2 busters,
I've kissed new heights;
my master voice returned on air.
Roses bushes dance
in my garden,
so happy
on this latitude...
I've heard that wind,
warm,
whistling,
wrapping my soul
on radio.
Painful waiting for this moment;
please forgive me if
I shed tears –
liquid language of emotion.
My eyes blink through the stratosphere,
I can't help it,
'cause to
me
this is
just heaven.

Come Inside

Rachel Lisi

It's not easy
having your tongue
ripped out.
A dragonfly with stolen wings,
just a bright metallic thing grounded,
eaten by hounds sniffing
for something
with more meat.
But I can speak in
other ways
By the turning of days,
The turning of pages.
Let me open it up for you.
Unlock.
Come inside. Come read. Come in.

It comes into my room
at night by moonlight.
Under bed through mattress
its skeletal hand enters
my trunk,
my chest, my bony breast.
Ivory fingers turn my heart upside down
like a doorknob
tearing not one muscle
or artery or vein.
No pain, but the slightest sting of movement.
What magic!
What talent!
Come inside. Come watch. Come in.

But dawn turns it back.
Like a clock - tick tock
A sun dial.
If I cut myself open
from manubrium to naval
you can see where the birds perch on each rib
and sing and feathers fall.
Hang your hat and coat.
Warm yourself by this fire.
Retire.
Come inside. Come listen. Come in.

The Cellar Gang

John Carder Bush introduces us to his new novel

Issue 76:
December 2005

Ever since I was four I have been writing stories, and that may come from how impressed I was by the story telling skills of my Irish grandfather, and my Irish uncles, who, in front of a roaring fire and a howling gale outside, with the crashing sea only yards away, would terrify the life out of me with their exquisite turn of phrase and innate timing. I loved to be under their spell because although the stories disturbed me with their magic and their adventure, I felt safe by the fire, drifting in and out of sleep amongst them.

I wanted to be able to do what they did, to hold people under a spell for a little while by taking them to strange and unfamiliar places, and experiencing things they would never experience in everyday life. And that seemed to be the key to the power behind their skills – the inclusion of magic in a very matter of fact way in every story. What was the point of telling stories about life where just ordinary things happened?

For most of my adult life I have lived in flats in large, converted Victorian houses in South London; houses that were once under single family occupation with all the luxury that went with Victorian upper middle class life. Then came their conversions, mostly in the Nineteen Fifties, and the cellars became basement flats, the central staircases were removed and the rest of the house redesigned into separate units.

In these places I have been a married man, a father, a divorcee, a step-father, and a single parent: weaving in and out of all this happiness and misery were the family pets.

Because of the inequity of falling in love with a creature with a tiny lifespan, they all came with a guarantee of grief – either because they "escaped", or they died and we all suffered miserably.

Years ago, I was a member of the Poets' Workshop which used to meet at the old Poetry Society headquarters in Earl's Court Square. Many of today's establishment poets were part of the workshops where each meeting a poet submitted works in progress and the others discussed them. In retrospect, this was done with considerable kindness and a genuine desire to help, and it was fascinating to see a famous poet changing a poem because of an intelligent observation from someone else.

On one of these occasions George Macbeth (who was remarkable in many ways – although the one that impressed me most was the fact that, apart from John Betjeman, he made a very comfortable living out of poetry and, to prove it, drove a very fast sports car and dated film stars) had submitted a long elegiac poem about the funeral of the family cat. It was based on the structure of *Who Killed Cock Robin*? In it, all the other pets and the domestic creatures– spiders, flies, mice etc. – came out to watch the funeral cortège go past. The scene was wonderfully evoked by the poem.

With that poem a little cobweb at the back of my memory; a few years ago I had been away for the weekend in Winter. When I came back I prepared a fire in the grate of the front room, and noticed what at first I thought were pigeon droppings on the floor by the fireplace. Pigeons sometimes came down the chimney.

But it didn't quite look like what I assumed it was. It reminded me of something else…

A year or so before, one of my sons had gone through a phase of interest in snakes, spiders and lizards, and the last pet he had as the phase, thank goodness, petered out, was a large and very unpleasant lizard. The lizard had escaped, never to be seen again.

Then I realised that I was looking at lizard droppings, and not pigeon.

Put Victorian houses, pets, families and divorce, and a poem amongst the cobwebs, together, and *The Cellar Gang* was the result.

At that time, in ordinary life, I needed to examine the cycle of domestic disaster I seemed to be caught up in very closely, but I had to examine it from outside as a not so sensitive observer. Looking at it from inside produced plenty of miserable poems and sadness-of-love songs, but that didn't help me in escaping from the cage I had escaped from and then willingly gone back into only to find myself escaping from yet again. So a book with a strict discipline of non-attachment seemed like the vehicle to find the answer.

Because I was conscious of creating an allegorical fable, I kept the prose style pretty minimalist, and most of the flavour comes from the dialogue of the characters. Nor did I try to take a moral stand in what, on one level, is a tragic story about a family break up, and on the other a story about fundamental survival, and that attempted objectivity, to my delight, produced a comedy of life and death in which everyone, very justly, gets what's coming to them.

I could go into detail, but I think that you've got to read *The Cellar Gang* yourself, otherwise I'd be giving the surprises away. You might think it is cynical in its approach, but, I hope I have pushed it past cynicism into a place where there is only laughter. We can only take so much misery: at that make or break point of saturation we can go two ways, under it or above it. When you can get above it, everything is hilarious.

For instance, when I set out writing, although I was controlling my anger with the system, I felt a "masculinist" novel was, nevertheless, trying to come through. I was nursing some serious bruises inflicted by the inequity of the English legal system where the rights of the father are concerned, and I felt that I needed to fly a flag and do some intellectual marching. However, as soon as I got down into the cellar and met the Gang that spurious evangelising went out the window and the comedy set in: what I thought had been the depth of tragedy turned out to be the heights of hilarity, and this provided a needed sense of balance.

I suppose it is also a sort of "Upstairs, Downstairs" – the humans upstairs, the animals downstairs: two sets of lives existing in parallel. Although the basic premise of *The Cellar Gang* might be absurd, it's worth thinking about how this parallel lives thing can actually function well.

Living somewhere in my garden are urban foxes, and, in a sense, they are living alongside me. Occasionally we meet in the garden, stop and look at each other, and then go on our separate ways. So much so that a few nights ago, when the weather was unusually warm, I had the door to the garden open. Later, when it was dark I was writing in a large, darkened room, with just a reading lamp on. When I sat up to read through what I had just written, I noticed a movement from the shadows in the far corner. A fox cub, a young vixen born in the Spring, was investigating that part of the room. I said good evening to her, she looked at me and calmly walked out of the room and off into the garden.

Now, foxes are big animals, and most of the time they keep, sensibly, out of our way. How easy for far smaller creatures to do the same thing.

Some friends have categorised *The Cellar Gang* as magical realism, and I quite like that as a label as it is a very respectable area of modern English writing, but I have not put a vein pregnant with sexual foreboding in it – which seems pretty obligatory for most magical realism (A.S. Byatt, Angela Carter), so I prefer to fall back on calling it a fable – a story with a teaching behind it. What's that teaching?

How the wheel of life and death turns with a jolt when you least expect it to, and there's absolutely nothing you can do about it.

But, wait a minute, I thought I said it was a comedy?

Well, that's the funny thing about The Cellar Gang…

Down in the Cellar …

Krys loves The Cellar Gang

Issue 76:
December 2005

"Hear and attend and listen; for this befell and behappened and became and was, O my Best Beloved, when the Tame animals were wild."
The Cat that Walked by Himself Rudyard Kipling

Many of you will already be familiar with *Cathy*, John Carder Bush's book of photographs and dreamlike recollections of his sister, Kate as a child. Some of you will recall John's poetry as part of the Tour of Life, and you may have read his exquisite poetry in *HomeGround*.

Let me now introduce you to John's new novel, *The Cellar Gang*. As John says himself, it is written as a modern day fable. A tale about love, or rather the death of love and the "monster" that takes its place.

And so we meet Barry, soon to be divorced, and ousted from the large Victorian sprawl of the family home and his marriage of fifteen years, now destroyed because of his brief and meaningless infidelities. He will soon embrace the life and freedoms of a single man again, and takes hollow refuge in his dreams of beautiful young women and flashy sports cars. Bess, his wife, ensures he will pay the price for his betrayal, as she flaunts another man in his face and in his own home, but her greatest revenge is the promise of taking his children away from him. We see the splintered death of their relationship and the casualties this leaves behind. It is a tale of consequences: how an action once set in motion causes a further reaction. Chaos theory in practice. Raw and bloody, as Barry, now a broken man, pays the heavy price.

The story begins at Christmas. Barry has bought his son a Python, which escapes and slithers his way down into the cellar where, huddled around the central heating boiler, he finds three other creatures: a wide-boy Tarantula called Vincent, with all the allure of an East End hit man; Liz, a ferocious lesbian lizard, and a neurotic guinea-pig called Annie. Perhaps you may be picturing a warped band of characters a la *Winnie the Pooh*. Or *Creature Comforts*? I don't think so! This mob is The Cellar Gang.

Now begin the territorial battles above and below stairs; the animals, whilst caught up in their own desperate fight for survival, make their observations of the disastrous mess Barry has made as he and the house itself begin to fall apart. The gang too are there in the shadowy underworld due to human neglect and lack of love. They blame Barry for making them victims of the encircling chaos his infidelity has created. And now they want revenge.

We meet with themes of love, death, sex and reincarnation as we trip through the complexities of human (and animal) psychology. We meet caricatures like The Therapist (in word-play, The Rapist, as John described him to me) and the Car

Salesman, who both help milk the plot along, playing their part in Barry's demise, and representing human greed, manipulation, and of course, the survival instinct, the theme that runs through the novel like a pulsing vein.

Each character is fired by its beast cunning instincts, as all life revolves around the hunt for the next meal. The connection between food and love merges, and this food-love gut instinct to survive is ever present. We humans need both to survive. We see what happens when love transforms, decays and dies. Think about food and love when both die, and what is left behind. In the novel love manifests into an tangible ether of defeat and decay that permeates the home, the humans, and the animals; what was once love now consumes with anger, hatred and sorrow, becoming an energy far greater than Barry and Bess's love could ever have been at its best. Barry mourns for his children, and his redundant identity as husband and father. All he once had and once was is lost. Such great sadness is wrapped up in humour – the only way for any of us to survive.

And so we enter "into a place where there is only laughter". The best humour in the novel is the portrayal of the worst human traits as the animals interact with each other, where each unfolding character is cleverly given its own voice and its own personality. You will not be able to resist the Python's genteel charms, nor his endearing lisp. Cunning and clever, he is my favourite character. The repulsive reptile Liz's graphic outbursts and foul language, and even fouler backside, will make you laugh aloud. Watch for the moment when she becomes a "god". There's another comical scene when the creatures find what appears to be a beef stock cube whilst foraging in Barry's teenage daughter's bedroom, and the rather strange after effects of this new food.

The animals carry much of the dialogue, their characterisation believable as the plot gathers pace to reach its conclusion. In structure and style, it is as John says, minimalist, and relies on dialogue but this does work very effectively. I see *The Cellar Gang* as a film, perhaps as a nightmarish vision from the studios of Aardman or Tim Burton or something in the style of artists Edward Gorey, or Michael Sowa, or Japanese animator Hayao Miyazaki. This novel isn't as sensual or as poetic as some of John's other work, but illustrates that he can successfully explore various styles of prose. But this is not the kind of story that needs poetry. It needs the cut, the impact, the direct hit.

It is difficult to describe this dark humoured modern Grimm tale of the family pets run wild, without spoiling the many surprises that lie in wait for you. I have only given you a flavour of the beginning of the story. There is much, much more for you to uncover for yourself. You will laugh, you may be shocked. I hope *The Cellar Gang* will leave you craving more of John's writing. You won't be disappointed. And, O my Best Beloved, it will make you think twice before buying a snake. Or a guinea pig. Or having an affair.

Photo: Gavin Bush

The Wave at the End of the World

A Short Story by John Carder Bush

Issue 77: July 2006

On the cliffs, above the broken arm of black rock that rested amongst the Atlantic waves, the early sun shone down on Ellen, lit her in brilliant exaggeration, and made each blade of grass like a world of its own, where a shrew moved through an empire of light, and a spider made silk hair-nets amongst the sprigs of wild thyme.

Today, she knew she was truly happy. Yesterday had been her seventh birthday, and now it was Midsummer's day; it would be daytime until gone ten at night, and that kind of unusualness was from the land of leprechauns. And it was from heaven too, it was from Sweet Baby Jesus and the host of angels, and all that softness and blood, and the strange, eel-like movements of learned guilt.

From where she lay, right on the edge of the cliff-top, she could see the Home and her family's cottage, and she could see her brothers and sisters playing in the back field, their bare feet kicking up white amongst the cow pats and the fairy rings of clover.

A cool breeze came off the sea, up the cliff and flicked her black curls away from her dark, tanned face. As she watched the tiny, bright, distant shapes that were part of her, she saw the largest one detach himself and start heading towards the cliff path. Her eldest brother Sean was coming to look for her, like he always did, running like a deer, because she was in his heart and he in hers; he loved her like his little sister and she loved him like her Fenian hero. Together they were fearless, together they understood everything, together laughter held back the banshee that hovered over the cottage at night, leaving its broken combs about the garden when morning came. But, at fourteen, Sean was already starting to forget that he had been a child, the changes to his body and the job waiting for him in Dungarvan at the end of the Summer were emptying his brain of childhood, and it was in Ellen that he still found that connection back to the days of bliss.

Above that brain, his black curls could be seen bobbing up and disappearing down on the line of yellow gorse that flanked parts of the cliff path. Ellen giggled in excitement. She could hear him calling her name, not anxiously – he knew she was on the cliff dreaming – but playfully, and she darted down behind a nest of rocks. "Elli, Elli, Ellen!"

Through a crack in the Irish granite she was amazed at the beauty of his dark face, a slight black moustache on the upper lip, the skin of his cheeks brown and ripe apple red, his deep green eyes blazing through his black fringe as he searched for her. The sun showed this brother to her and he was a brother of love.

The faint sound of a fiddle came from the Home on a different breeze and she began to tap her foot to the familiar reel. Sean saw the fluttering movement and came running towards her. She leaped towards the path like a rabbit, but he changed direction and was on her. As they collided, she screamed in an ecstasy of surrender, but as he brought her down, with his weight too much on top, her right arm hit a knob of hidden rock, and there was a crack like flint breaking.

"Jeesus, Mary and Joseph, Ellen, I've killt yer arm!"

Both of them looked at the grazed brown skin, already swelling up blue and purple around the fracture, and then both of them looked at each other with the same look of terror and hopelessness.

"Jeesus, Ellen, yer little sheevra, don't tell the Mama or Dada, they'll fecking kill me."

Deep in the opiate of shock, Ellen looked at that fear in her brother's eyes. At the same time, a new fear began inside her. This new fear was the fear of death – not of her death, or Sean's death – but something that was far greater in its horror and pain: the death of her brother's love for her, and that meant the death of everything.

"I'll say nuttin, Sean, sure I will. No-one will know."

They both tried to examine the arm again, but the pain hit Ellen and turned her white: the world began to dissolve into grains of shivering silver. She resisted passing-out, and she resisted the tears that hung on the edge of her eyes, hot and pregnant with despair. Her need for his love, and this deep, terrible fear that suddenly was walking by its side, made her broken arm and the growing agony seem insignificant.

They both knew that he would be blamed for the injury, even though it was an accident, and the beating with Dada's belt, and the cold, long trickle of guilt from Mama, were the inevitable outcome. But this was serious pain to have to deal with, and already the arm hung down useless, taking part of her right side with it. How could she hide it from the sharp, punishing eyes of her mother?

Although she was probably the closest in affection to her mother, and, therefore, the one least able to keep a secret from her, recently Mama had been distracted. Her tongue, and the flat of her hand, were still just as fast, but it was just possible she might not notice Ellen's behaviour until the arm got better.

Dada was playing the fiddle and would be in a world of his own, a world of wild music, sweat and poetic ballads. If she kept behind her brothers and sisters, busied herself with looking after her baby sister Minnie, then she might just keep Sean safe.

Another fiddle and an accordion had joined in, raising the level of energy that pounded like a bull through the jig, and she could hear the whoops and laughs of adults dancing, and the stomp of their boots on the stone cottage floor. Her aunts and uncles, and their many children, would already be there. By the time they got back, the jugs of stout would have done their first rounds, and the whisky would be out; through the thick haze of plug tobacco and whirling feet she could surely go unnoticed until the next morning.

Sean carried her most of the way back, the shaking instability of her cold body worrying him, but, before they got to the last bend in the cliff path, he gently put her down and stood back to see if she could walk. By now, he was shaking with fear: the anticipated bite of his father's belt, and the anger that would come with each cut, held him like a rope in his stomach.

"Honest, now, Ellen, are yer right enough to see dis true? If yer not, girl, I'll go straight in and have it out with Dada."

The ache in Ellen's arm was now in all her body, but she held herself upright like Deirdre of the Sorrows and walked off round the corner and into the empty cottage yard.

"Don't mind me, Sean, I'll be fit in the morning."

As they walked into the kitchen together, Sean hurrahed to his cousins, and Ellen started to make her way round the wall, grinning as though she were the happiest child in the world back from an errand for her mother. She had almost made it to the bedroom when her uncle Mick burst like a whale from the tight crowd of dancers, red faced and black suited, and grabbed her, lifting her up into the air and taking her in for a few turns of the jig before depositing her on the other side of the kitchen with a wet kiss, fragrant with stout, on her forehead. As he lifted and flicked her in the dance, he had squeezed her injured arm against her body, and it had made another noise. This time it had all gone black without any fizz of silver, but, by the time she was put down, it had passed. She was able to stumble to the bedroom, and climb into the bed where all nine of them slept. Her baby sister, and her younger sister, Nellie, were already there, warm and asleep. The shadows of the dancers were thrown into the room by the two oil lamps like the silhouettes of galloping horses, and, through the hubbub of music, laughter and voices, and the thump of the dancers' feet, she tried to pray.

She did not pray for herself, or her broken arm, but that Mama and Dada would never know, and that Sean would be safe. After the prayer, she settled down to make sure she would not sob from the pain and be heard, or wake up her little sisters. With this process returned the new fear that now walked beside her love like a black ghost, the fear of the death of something she had never thought could die. Puppies, horses, pigs, kittens, uncles could die as much as they liked, but, surely, not love?

In the morning she was running a temperature, and could not get out of bed, her hair was soaked and her face pale, her pulse fast and her eyes dull; with coaching from Sean she told her mother that her throat was sore and she had a headache. All the family, except her mother, piled onto the horse and cart in their best clothes, and headed for Mass in Dungarvan. Mama, worse the wear from dancing, drinking and smoking, put a wet cloth on Ellen's forehead and gave her some mauve, sticky medicine that smelled of horse liniment and tar, patted her on the head and started to clear up the debris left over from Midsummer's Night.

Ellen swooned and returned, swooned and returned, went in and out of delirium, but somehow managed to keep her arm under the covers each time her mother came in to see if she was any better. By the time they were all back from Mass, and a drink in one of the bars on the square, she was in a fitful, murmuring sleep akin to unconsciousness and her mother was worried. There was a doctor in Dungarvan, but he would be drunk by now and he always charged too much for his obvious observations so Mama set off down the boreen to the healing woman a mile away, with a florin in her pocket, and a grim set to her mouth.

When she came back, she boiled up an evil smelling drink from the herbs the woman had sold her, and forced it down her daughter's throat. By the following morning, the fever had gone and the arm was less painful, by the end of the week Ellen was up and about again: the arm still hurt and she could hardly use it, but the dreadful fear had passed and Sean still loved her.

On Friday evening, as they all gathered for boiled bacon, potatoes and boiled cabbage, Nellie could not be found. She was holding up the blessing on the meal. Dada angrily mumbled into the perfume of meat and vegetables and they set to, an eerie silence settling on the family as it concentrated on serious eating. Halfway through, Nellie returned, dancing into the room, humming a tune, and tried to attach herself to Mama's leg.

"Mama, if Sean broke off Ellen's arm, why didn't it fall off into the sea?"

The mist of inevitable doom caught the room as Sean choked on his food and Ellen felt her bowels dissolve as the darkness that is the Shadow of Love put its arms around her, and squeezed her heart.

Mama instantly put two and two together,

reached out to Ellen and uncovered the bruised and misshapen limb.

"Jesus, Mary and Joseph, Dominic, do yer see what that son of yours has done to her arm?"

Her husband, roused from his eating, recognized the pitch of his wife's voice, and automatically started to take off the thick, brass buckled army belt that he wore, along with braces, on his trousers. At this stage of his response, he was trying to work out which of his sons she was referring too.

But his wife's right arm was already heading for Sean like a weasel, and, as he tried to fend off his mother's attack, his father grabbed his hair and hauled him towards the door for a beating in the yard. As the iron fingers caught flesh and curls, Sean gave Ellen a look that was full of everything – anger, betrayal, fear, accusation and resignation.

"It wasn't Sean, sure it wasn't, Mama!"

"Don't lie to me, you feckin' little ijut!"

Ellen was grabbed by her curls in turn, and half pulled up the boreen towards the setting sun, where the wild fuchsias ran along the tops of the stone walls like a suspended channel of blood.

"Mama, were are we going?"

"We're going to see Biddy on the Bend."

But Mama was saying no more. The strings of needles, each point bright with guilt, were streaming out of her silence, and showering down on Ellen.

She knew that people only went to see Biddy if they were really in trouble: Biddy was nothing to do with the priest, or the doctor, or any of those people that stood at the respectable points in the community. Biddy was outside everything, even, somehow, the Fairies themselves; she was too ugly to be a fairy. Most thought she was a changeling, and even the grown-ups avoided passing her house. Her two enormous, pest infested deer-hounds kept the children away, and, even though many adults ended up going to consult her, no one was ever seen going in or coming out.

Was Mama going to sell her to the fairies? Was Biddy going to burn her and eat her? Perhaps that would be best because, now that Sean would love her no longer, nothing mattered anymore.

The witch, fat and old, was seated in a chair turned away from the fire so that she could see anyone who entered the door of her cottage. There was little light, except for a shimmering circle of red where the last of the sun passed through a scarlet vase, and danced just behind the witch's head.

"Come in, Pat Power, and have some tea. It's a long feckin' time since you've come to visit me, so you must have the bad trouble."

"Sure, Biddy, isn't it all trouble?"

After the preliminary greetings, and the tea was settling in the pot, Mama uncovered the arm and showed it to Biddy. At first, the old woman just looked at the arm as it rested on the table as she might look at tea-leaves in a cup, and then touched the sorest part with a finger black from grime, the nails ebony from chewing tobacco.

"Who set it for ye?"

Ellen was confused, and looked to her mother for help.

"Sure, Biddy, nobody set it. Her ijut brother broke it with his horse play."

"Well, someone set it and they set it wrong. It's already healed and I'll have to reset it or she'll be a cripple."

"Mama, what's set it mean?"

"It means putting the bones back where they were."

"Mama, what does reset it mean?"

"Biddy'll have to break your feckin' arm again and put the bones back in their right order. I expect it was your brother who tried to set it – Jeesus, he could have killt yer."

A sudden memory of a red face, big chipped hands, whiskey breath and a crack in her arm came back to her.

"Uncle Mick set it, Mama."

"Don't talk nonsense, yer little sheevra, your Uncle Mick couldn't set a trap for a mouse, let alone try and fix your arm."

Both Mama and Biddy bent double with cackling. When they stopped, Biddy took a bottle of whiskey from behind her chair and uncorked it with a loud pop.

"Have yer the money with yer, Pat?"

Mama counted out five shillings onto the table, and pushed them over to Biddy.

"Be glad you never had childers, Biddy. They drain everything out of yer."

"Ah, sure, Pat, it was never meant to be. If God had meant me to have childers I would have had twenty, and then where would I be? Worn out and next to dying with nottin to eat for meself."

Biddy mixed the whiskey into a glass of yellow milk, stirred in a handful of sugar, and gave it to Ellen to drink.

"In one go, mind, Ellen girl, all the way down."

As the still swirling concoction was thrust under her nose, it smelled of babies, drunken adults and priests, and she was almost sick. But she held it back, not that there was much to hold back: she had hardly eaten since the accident. But, when she relaxed, and let the liquid in, it slid gently and comfortably down her throat, and she immediately began to feel better.

After she had drunk the glass to the dregs, the two women carried on chatting, and Biddy put the kettle back on the fire for more tea. The cottage was hot, and smelled of fresh milk, old cheese, the dogs, who were grunting and scratching their fleas in a dark corner, and the

Photo: Gavin Bush

flinty tang of well water in metal buckets. Just as she was nodding off, she saw Biddy haul herself out of her chair, and go over to the corner where she collected an old sack, and, opening it, started rummaging inside. She brought out a white, stick-like length of bone, and placed it with a connoisseur's eye on the table.

"That'll do, Pat."

Ellen's arm was suddenly grabbed, yanked, and Biddy's dirty thumbs pushed deep into the flesh, feeling for the bone. There was a crack, and another yank, and Biddy, red and sweating, dropped back into the chair.

"Come over here, Ellen, and I'll bind it up for yer."

The length of bone was strapped against the break, some yellow paste from a golden syrup tin smeared all over the arm, and then a dirty white cloth was wrapped all around it.

"Don't let her take the bandage off for a week, Pat, and then it'll heal up grand."

Confused, and still very sleepy, Ellen allowed Biddy to put an even dirtier sling around her neck to support the arm, and, after another cup of tea, and a piece of sponge cake each, they headed back up the Boreen in the still and scented gloaming.

"Sure, I don't care what they say, Biddy's the best bone-setter in County Waterford, and maybe all of Ireland too. And not a word to yer father about the five shillings or I'll fecking kill yer."

From the whiskey on her breath that must have laced the last cup of tea, and the lilt in her mother's voice, Ellen knew the climax was over. The great, invisible bladder-ball of anger and violence, that bounced above the family's heads, had emptied itself yet again, and would take a while to fill. But she still had to face Sean and his hate for her; that look, as he was dragged off, still filled her eyes.

There was no longer any pain in the arm. In fact, even when Biddy was yanking it, and breaking it again, she had felt no pain.

"Mama, will Dada have killt Sean?"

Her mother laughed, grabbed hold of Ellen's good arm, and ran down the last stretch of the boreen, pulling Ellen along behind her. Normally, this signal of the return of her mother's good mood, would have lifted Ellen to skip happily along beside her.

But Ellen had changed.

Her trust in her mother and father, her trust in God, and her trust in her brother's love had all broken too, and Biddy had reset none of them. The splintered bones stuck out, and pierced her heart. The bleeding was there for ever, and that fear, that fear of the death of love, rose up out of the whiskey, milk and guilt, like the wave at the end of the world.

Night and Day

John Carder Bush

The night flops down like a black bellied beast
that feasts morosely on my thoughts and dreams,
creams off the best of my strength and might,
bites into my heart and siphons out the light.

Through my sleeping hours it ranges and mauls,
then calls its grey mate, the crawling dawn,
to corner my heart and dismember what's true:
blue eyed, streaming blood, she comes with the dew.

No matter the armour I make against such beasts,
they will feast on the forged folds of my soul –
holes in my breast plate, my body mail in tatters,
they batter my helmet until equilibrium shatters.

Feelings, shored up and strengthened by day,
get disarrayed; tossing me from mouth to mouth,
from south to north, from floor to ceiling,
they peel away the prophylactic skein of evening.

Before they leave and the day is engendered,
dismembered, I dream of rambling, unknown houses
where ex-spouses give me tea and talk of the law,
while the whore of possibility purrs in the open door.

Whitstable

John Carder Bush

Three old poets perch on a dry breakwater
Watching the thongs of the thronging girls
Inspire poetry against the pebbles and the waves,
Slaves forever to the fickle female form
They chortle as their blood grows warm.

Salt drenched and sand smoothed,
Even old before these poets were old,
The wood still withstands the tides,
Rides the waters, staid and deep sunk –
Sea-throne for poets, stoned and drunk.

Thirty years before, they watched
The mothers of these wet and bobbing girls –
Girls themselves who danced for poet's eyes,
Vying for the gift of their perfumed rhymes –
Preening like caged, exotic springtimes.

"And now," sang the poets, sharing a spliff,
"The film is merely being re-made:
This time the director wants us old,
Cold and hoary, no longer young,
No longer absorbed in poetry and fun.

"The rest of the cast has not changed,
ranging the shore with ecstatics' eyes
even the dogs are still close-by,
thighs of girls are just the same,
beauty capable of inflicting pain.

"Let's eat our peaches upon the beach,
Let's wear our trousers rolled,
Three walruses, three carpenters,
Marketers of cunning. crafted words,
Three old foxes, three old birds.

"Are we still loved by Youth and Grace?
Let us amble and let us stroll
To be adored as once we were,
To purr as their glances meet and poke
Coax and then begin to gently stroke.

"But old men can no longer provoke
Desire and lust in young girls' throats;
They do not feel our gazes graze their legs,
Begging to touch them with a rasping sigh:
What once was given we now must buy.

"Then we were the masters, they the slaves,
Coming innocent to our stormy beds;
Now they lead us by our fawning cocks,
Mock us with their violent disregard,
Laugh our poems into drooping shards.

"That's what we feared thirty years ago –
Incredible how it goes round and round
And only our bodies seem to change,
Strange our hearts still seek and roam
Hunting life for that perfect poem."

Three old poets sit on a summer breakwater
Watching the throngs of changing girls
Tightening and loosening, dancing and merging
Urging life back into the poets' toes
Like seawater as it ebbs and flows.

The Work of John Carder Bush

An Appreciation by Collin Kelley

Issue 78: June 2007

I first became aware of John Carder Bush the way most *HomeGround* readers did – through the photos of his sister on her album covers. From his classic image of Kate as Mrs. Houdini – gold key demurely sitting on her tongue – from *The Dreaming*, to the smouldering beauty of *Hounds of Love*, these photos have transcended from being merely photos of little sister Cathy to become iconic images in music history. John, whether he realizes it or not, created the way most of us "see" Kate.

The first time I heard John was on *Hounds of Love*: his backing vocals on *The Big Sky* and his powerful narration in *Jig of Life*… the shiver it gave me (and still does) when he picks up from Kate with the sinister-sounding "…Over here." Many lucky folks got to hear him read poems during Kate's Tour of Life and his contributions to the Kate Bush Club Newsletter (especially the funny and detailed accounts of shooting the photos for *Hounds of Love*) showed just how dedicated John was to his craft as a photographer, and that he was a sharp, observational writer.

But even then, John hinted that he was still working in other mediums: "I had been working on a series of "body poems" in which I was writing my poems on people and then photographing them, and it seemed like a good idea, but when we tried it, apart from Kate looking like the tattooed lady from a circus, there was much too much activity in the small frame, and the eye just wandered around too much. But the dogs were wonderful, and did everything they were asked to."

This "body poem" motif would show up in the *Running Up That Hill* single sleeve, with the lyrics written up and down her arms, the bow and arrow outstretched in yet another unforgettable image.

In his introduction to the book of photos of Kate as a young girl, *Cathy*, John writes: "Our lives were filled with the trappings of the Celtic Twilight, its poetry and its music." This obviously played a huge part in his own growth as an artist and the amazing poetry and writing he would produce. Even the captions under the photos of young Cathy are poetic: "Dance is everywhere now but when this little girl was dancing, whirling in a garden by the seaside, lost in her vision of herself, it was as confined as opera. I think there's music drifting across from another little girl in another house playing *Fur Elise* on a large piano and she is dancing to that, or it could just be the cooing of the collar doves."

When I first read John's poems in *HomeGround*, I felt a kinship with him as a fellow writer. While our styles are quite different, I immediately was drawn to the mood of his work, often dark, ethereal and existing in some shadow world that is both conscious and unconscious. When Krys told me that she wanted some of my poems for an issue of *HomeGround* I was delighted, and when she told me some of John's work would also appear in that issue I was honored at the very idea of sharing the same pages. When the magazine arrived (Spring 2004, for those who want to slip back into the archives), there was my little poem and then I turned the page and there was *Before The Fall*, the words from the bootlegged demo of Kate's never-released 'Organic Acid'.

As they drove she sat
with mouth open
as though
photographed on the
impact
of a stomach punch,
her right fist gripping the
skin of his left leg
fearing the strength of
her illusions…

I find those lines to be taut and perfect. There is so much forward movement in this poem – something I, and most poems, should strive for, and John does it here effortlessly. And then from *Shooting Through The Veil*:

Tears for my mother,
and for my friend,
Gone and the going,
and for all the others
Death is moving along
and away from us…

Whether the poem is autobiographical (and I tend to think there is an element of the confessional "I" in most poems), the strength here is the musicality. While it's a much longer piece, those few lines work on their own. They are alive with emotion and remembered grief.

In the Winter 2005 issue, John's poem *The Eve of the Returning Swallow*, made me think of Ireland… whether he intended that to be the setting or not. While there is a deft hand at work with formal verse, there is also a story being told… the foreshadowing of prose.

Old poets and old bandits
converse in the
hanging shadows;
Caps down over their
roguish eyes they
play at cards
As shards of moonlight

silver the melting tallow.
God of all brave thoughts,
of the deep
and of the shallow,
Listen to the slow spring
pulse of this man's thought,
Caught sad and low on this
eve of the returning
swallow.

When it was announced that John would start a publishing company and produce a series of novels, spoken word and short story collections from his own imagination and hand, I was overjoyed. I had self-published my first book of poetry and I continue to work with small presses to keep collaboration open between the different kinds of art.

The press's first offering, *The Cellar Gang*, was a novel told from the point of view of a man going through a divorce and the band of escaped pets living in the basement.

The Cellar Gang more than lived up to my expectations. While John has called it a kind of "Upstairs, Downstairs", I likened it more to another favorite children's book, *The Borrowers*, about a group of tiny people who live under the floor of a house. Of course, *The Cellar Gang* isn't quite suitable for children, but it's a treat for adults. The humor running through the book is dark and macabre. Characters – including Barry, the husband in the middle of the divorce – are dispatched with Hitchcockian glee.

The furry pets have the foulest mouths of any characters I've come across in recent memory (David Mamet would be proud!) And what a cast they are: the lesbian lizard, the lisping python, the scheming tarantula, the nervous guinea pig. They are forced to live, warily, with each other while surviving in the cellar with only Barry's crumbs to sustain them. They experiment with drugs, engineer deaths and the lizard, hilariously, cements herself in the cellar wall with her own fecal matter. Yes, it's all kind of "out there", but I hadn't laughed out loud while reading book in years until *The Cellar Gang* came along.

Early in the Fall, I was feeling a bit melancholy and looking for something to read as a diversion. I picked up *The Cellar Gang* again and was immediately lost in the story. I read the book straight through, again, in one sitting. The pace, the dialogue, the storyline are pitch perfect and the locations (such as the house where the main action takes place) are so fully realized, I felt transported there. I know I will return to it again and again. This is the hallmark of a great novel.

I'm not sure what is next for John Carder Bush. There is apparently a spoken word CD and short story collection coming in the future. I would love to get my hands on a volume of his poetry, since it has become a touchstone for my own writing. Whatever is next, he can be rest assured that I – and many of the *HomeGround* faithful – will be listening and reading.

On a personal level, your words and artistry, like Kate's music, have become an inspiration to my work. You are fulfilling an intrinsic part of what it means to be an artist: touching and nurturing someone else's creativity. For that, John, there are no words but thank you.

Photo: Gavin Bush

Syd Arthur

Raven Bush introduces his band

Issue 77: July 2006

"In keeping with the Bush family musical tradition, John Carder Bush's son, Raven, tells us about his band, Syd Arthur."

In the years since we ran this article the band has found continuing success as the their website indicates:

"When the band released early tracks in 2010 (on their *Moving World* EP) they were swiftly picked up by *The Guardian* and included in their Band of The Day feature. Syd Arthur's intricate, high-energy live sets, which to date include Glastonbury and Secret Garden slots, have resulted in a large following emerging – one that is also burgeoning in Europe as they continue to pick up tours in France, Belgium, The Netherlands and most recently Italy. This is an accomplished live band. With the benefit of an extra 40 years of popular music culture, WOMAD festivals and the entire world's musical output at their fingertips, the Psychedelic genre no longer sits, gathering dust, in the decades gone by. Syd Arthur embrace its origins, lodge their feet in the present, and hold up a triumphant head, pointed firmly at the future."

On an On, Syd Arthur's 2012 album

Photos: courtesy Raven Bush

Syd Arthur is a band from Canterbury. Taking their influences from the Canterbury sound of the 70's, they have been playing together and gigging for two years, and are now a well-known band in their area. During these two years, they have recorded a self-titled, short album released on MadMan Records, and are just about to start recording their new material in Kate's old studio. The name of the band "Syd Arthur," was inspired by the book, *Siddhartha*, written by the German born philosopher and novelist Hermann Hesse. This pseudonym for the band also reflects their collective interest in philosophy and consciousness.

Liam Magill, 19, is the lead vocalist and plays guitar. Joel Magill, 20, plays the bass. Raven Bush, 19, plays the violin and mandolin Fred Rother, 21,plays the drums.

The Sound – Syd Arthur's sound is hard to pigeon hole because it is continually evolving. At the moment their music takes on a fairly progressive form, with an emphasis on groove and the use of intricate melodies and weird time signatures. This progression is because they prefer to be challenged as musicians and songwriters/composers. Their eclectic style encompasses many influences from Miles Davis to Pink Floyd and The Meters.

In contrast to Syd Arthur's electric sound there is also an equally strong acoustic side to their music, which they feel is their modern interpretation of folk-blues, developed from listening to artists like Nick Drake, The Pentangle and John Martyn.

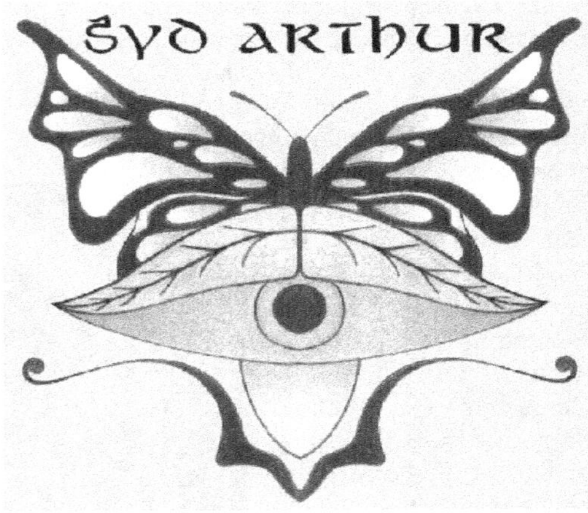

Canterbury offers plenty of opportunities for this side of Syd Arthur to be heard. In the future they hope to attract interest from the music industry, although it's not a priority. They just want to be able to keep making music and playing live for as long as possible.

Justin Vali and the Sunshine Within

Paddy Bush takes us on a journey...

Issue 77: July 2006

The giant island of Madagascar is like a red table-topped mountain rising from the Indian Ocean to the East of Africa. Separated from the rest of the world some 165 million years ago, it has transformed into an island of forests alive with rare creatures such as Lemurs, chameleons, long nosed snakes and giraffe necked ladybirds; it is a place like nowhere else.

The Malagasy people have a musical culture that is as equally unique and fantastic as their wildlife. With a population of about 17.5 million in some twenty different ethnic groups, their island could be regarded as the United States of the Indian Ocean with its people arriving in a series of ancient migrations from places as distant as Borneo and Indonesia as well as nearby Africa.

The Valiha is Madagascar's national instrument, or more precisely, a family of instruments that take the form of different tube and box zithers. Justin Vali (Justin Rakotondrasoa) comes from the Merina people of the High Plateau region, virtuoso and musical ambassador; he is the world's most recognised player of the Valiha.

The instrument goes back for generations in his family who are makers as well as musicians. They worked with three other families to make almost all of the Valiha for the Highlands from the 1940's onwards. The Valiha is seen as a symbol of the family and their unity; Justin's grandfather often said: "...Some of us are like the strings and others like the bridges, and the strings can't work without the bridges, and the bridges just fall over without the strings!"

Hair From the Ground

Volo, the word for bamboo in Malagasy, also means hair. The original form of Valiha is known as the Ancestral Valiha. It is constructed from a length of straight bamboo with strings made by cutting into the outer skin and then levering individual strips free from the body whilst still being attached at the nodes. The razor sharp edges are removed with a knife and the strips are skilfully shaped into strings that have an oval or square profile keeping the shiny outer skin of the bamboo intact, this kind of string is known as an idiochord.

The number of strings possible depends on the diameter of the bamboo, with larger varieties giving 14 to 18. A long sound-hole is made in the body of the instrument underneath the first string by burning two holes at the top and bottom ends through the outer skin with a red-hot poker, these holes are then connected by cutting a thin strip from between them. Tiny bridges are cut from dried calabash gourd and forced under the floppy bamboo strings to bring them into a state of tension. The bridges make tuning possible by sliding them to shorten or lengthen the bamboo string. The instrument has a wooden percussive sound quality almost like a Woodpecker drilling into a tree. The sharp attack and fast decay of the string vibrations allow for very rapid playing techniques without the need for damping, as does its tuning which places each note of the scale on alternate sides, like the African Kora.

"Not so many people play the Ancestral Valiha; the steel string versions are most popular these days and only a handful of people know how to make good instruments and sadly the right quality bamboo is getting very hard to find. My father showed me how to cut the strings, it's pretty tricky, just one slip and you lose everything! I love its sound; to me it's like the soul of Madagascar and a symbol of the Malagasy people. It has a very spiritual significance for us and has been played for centuries in the ceremonies that are sacred to our ancestors, the Razana."

The Valiha can be played either seated or standing, by holding it with pressure from the elbow on the lower part of the tube. It can also be played held by a strap and in some regions is played gripped between the knees pointing upwards like a tree. Strong fingernails are a basic requirement for players as is an ambidextrous playing technique.

Spirit Harps From the Forests of Pre-history

The Ancestral Valiha is thought to have arrived in Madagascar some two thousand years ago from the opposite side of the Indian Ocean. Similar bamboo tube zithers can be found all over South East Asia. In the Philippines they are known by the names of Sarunay, Sluday, Kolibit, Takol, in Sabah as Tonkungon or Sudantang, in Sarawak as Pagang, there are similar instruments on the islands of Flores and Roti, and even up into the highlands of Vietnam. Current thinking suggests that the bamboo-zither spread from pre-history through the migrating aboriginal forest cultures of Ancient China.

It is an instrument of the spirit world. In Borneo it is played during possession ceremonies and to appease animistic forest spirits known as Bali, which may give an indication to the origin of the name Valiha, most commonly pronounced Vali, and in some parts of East Madagascar as Baliha or Bali. Madagascar's Eastern rain forest is the source of the highest quality bamboo for Valiha construction. It is a species belonging to the Gigantochlora genus with a greater distance between the nodes making it possible to have instruments with a longer string-length than other bamboo from the Highlands, especially if it is chosen from the heart of the forest

Photo: courtesy Paddy Bush

where it grows taller and with a thinner outer skin. Amazingly, this bamboo is thought have been introduced to Madagascar from Java, presumably by the Malagasy ancestors, transforming the idea of the Eastern rain forest into a religious musical garden from the ancient world.

Valiha bamboo is traditionally cut around the three days of the full moon, it's actually a way to make sure that there are no insect eggs inside as otherwise they will hatch out months later and consume your instrument from within and turn it to dust!

The bamboo for an Ancestral Valiha is chosen from a younger plant whereas a mature bamboo is the favourite choice for steel strung instruments. The quality of this bamboo when strung with stainless steel strings gives a fabulous, glassy sound, with a long sustain. Steel strings are normally made with simple loops twisted into each end and then fixed in place by nails that are hammered into the nodes of the bamboo where they hold the strings at very high tension, close to breaking point. Ox-hide is wrapped around the nodal points to cover the nails and loops and to help increase tension on the strings. The same tiny dried gourd bridges are used to tune the strings, which surprisingly have an incredible resistance to the cutting force of the steel strings that they support.

The first steel stringed Valiha were seen in Europe at the Exposition Universelle de Paris of 1900 where a "Palais de Madagascar" was created, complete with musicians and singers.

The musical performances were met with great enthusiasm; wax cylinder recordings were made and papers were published, including one called*Les musiques bizarres à L'Exposition de 1900. Les Chants de Madagascar*. These days, bicycle brake-cable is the usual source of steel strings as it is made from many individual filaments; you just have to pull it apart to get a complete set of strings for a Valiha. "Don't forget that you must use the cable for the rear brakes and not the front ones if you want to get a really good sound!"

The Valiha has a royal heritage, of composing kings and courtly musicians as well as a spiritual relevance when past royalty are called back during ceremonial spirit séances.

"Our king Radama II was a superb composer, his music was played all over the highlands, people learned the tunes by ear but much of his work was written down and has been recently re- discovered, beautiful classical melodies from the old courts of the Merina Kingdom."

Radama ruled during the 1800's when there was much contact with Britain. He was given a piano by Queen Victoria, which had the effect of standardising Valiha tuning into the diatonic form, which is known as Lalandava (straight road), which corresponds to the piano's white notes.

Justin has several pieces in his repertoire composed by King Radama including a well-known piece called *My Cottage*. Several of Radama's compositions were also included in the repertoire of Madagascar's most famous classical Valiha player Sylvestre Randafison, who sadly died in 2003 aged 75. Randafison's award winning group "Ny Antsaly" played a big part in keeping Malagasy traditional music alive from the 1950's onwards, with frequent broadcasts on Radio Madagascar and numerous international appearances.

Justin has played with Randafison many times since he was a teenager. "There is no-one who can match Sylvestre Randafison's grace and style when it comes to classical Valiha, he was the master." About a year before he died, the two of them had a

e of the Valiha, Randafison vith the general standard of ıssical techniques were being ye for the last time he spoke ustin, I'm passing the flame

ly of instruments that comes . sizes. The 1960's were the Rakotozafy, a phenomenal ıa genius from the Sihanaka ıst. He built himself an -iron that looked more like Bugati racing car than a

with his son Maro were ɔn Radio Madagascar with nes are still played almost nd. His instrument had the ' (famous Valiha) painted on

me there were sheet-iron structed almost everywhere maller wooden versions of l to appear on the High ıch an instrument made in ; well a sheet-iron Valiha. ar Valiha, these instruments therefore offer an extended ferent sound quality. These onfused with the Marovany, om the coastal regions.
the question of when is a

ls on where you are when Nearly every region has its tion on how the instrument layed.
nities and Southern regions . strong independence from rina kingdom, with stronger cultural ties to ancient Africa than Indonesia, these historic differences have caused conflict over the centuries. It is possible that the Marovany could have made it's way to Madagascar from mainland Africa in the form of the board-zither which is still played in Africa's Central and Eastern regions. The Marovany is a long instrument with up to 28 steel strings, nearly always played on the ground. It can be very heavy if it is made from a timber called Hazo Malàny (literally smelly wood!), the favourite choice of the Vezo and Mahafaly peoples, a very rare tree variety these days, resistant to insects because of its aromatic oil content.

Often tuned in complete reverse fashion to the Valiha, the Marovany is the instrument for possession ceremonies known as the Tromba. Wooden bridges in the shape of volcanoes support steel strings that are sometimes twisted to double their thickness giving a deeper pitch, the tops of the bridges are often adjusted to make the strings buzz. Players like Madame Masy, Bekamby, Daniel Tombo, Albi, Vinelo and the many un-sung regional heroes of this instrument have combined spirituality and virtuosity to take the Marovany into the musical stratosphere. The first time that I heard a Marovany playing for the Tromba was in 1981 and it changed my life forever.

I built an instrument and taught myself the basics but could only start to make sense of the complexities of Madagascar's ceremonial possession music by travelling there with Justin and experiencing it from the inside.

Some Valiha are made from wood, some from iron, some are made from bamboo planted by the Ancestors. Some people eat bamboo, others make bows, arrows or houses from it; it's good for storing and carrying water too.

In the hands of Justin Vali it becomes an instrument that spreads sunshine and carries peace to the world.

Photo: courtesy Paddy Bush

Don't Go Up There

John Carder Bush

Don't go up there, don't go up on your roof,
don't go up to where the pigeons perch
in their miserable lines of hunched decay
and every mark of the weather of time
roosts around you like photographs of the dead.
Don't go up to the gullies where sun and rain
have left their colourless, cancerous marks,
where summer and winter rub and tear,
where broken tiles half hang on sagging timbers.
Don't go up there on a hot June day
with the flat blue above you like a deep sea sky
that will make your head spin and your feet weak.
Don't go up there and discover the horror
of the holes the rain can find, the cracked, soft tar,
the disintegrating roofing felt, the skeletons of birds
that tell you the truth about your roof,
how high things, seen from a distance,
can seem perfect, reassuring,
timeless, like temples, like life,
until you look closer and find they rot
and must be fixed, replaced, or just denied.
But don't pay the men who know about roofs
to mend the leaks, to find the gaps –
they will tell you lies, rip you off,
like therapists, they will promise to patch the past –
don't go up on the roof of anything,
unless you need to know how much the future will cost.

HomeGround
Number 76
The Kate Bush Magazine
Winter 2005

HomeGroun
The Kate Bush Magazine

HomeGround
Number 79
The Kate Bush Magazine
Winter 2011

HomeGround
The 25th Anniversary Special
The Kate Bush Magazine

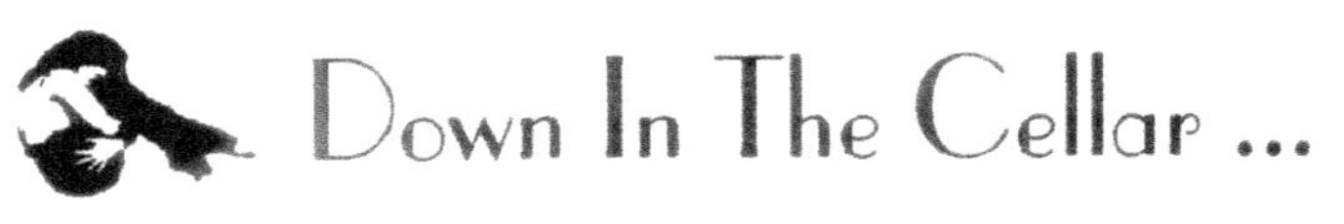

Down In The Cellar ...

Twenty five years... what a strange feeling it is, that marker in time. So many lives changed because of Kate's music. On 18th May 1982 this little magazine, into which we were to cast our hearts and lives, was born; it changed my life beyond imagining. I cried when I read Dave's words on this page. He summed it all up for me too. I feel quite, quite mushy. Oh the adventures we have had... so many happy memories...

A huge thank you to everyone who has been a part of HomeGround, to all who have contributed features, artwork and to those who still subscribe (which means we can pay the print and post bill). Thank you Kate for all your cherished love and support. This issue is dedicated to our beloved little orange cat who was killed by a car on Christmas morning. Amber, this one's for you, little boy. I miss you sitting in the HG boxes "helping" us send these magazines out...

Krys

It's quite strange that HomeGround and the Falklands War share the same 25th anniversary, but then I remember in those days when Dave and I were first talking about a fanzine, the news backdrop was HMS Sheffield, Goose Green and the Belgrano. Those funny now far off days when we mucked around with a 1930s typewriter, scissors and paste and I used to drive as many staples into my hand as I did into the magazine. HomeGround became first a knot, then a centre of the Kate-speaking world, and life was hectic as we did conventions and videos and spent Christmas Eve stuffing 1,000 magazines into postboxes in and around Rochester. That was when we did six issues a year to keep up with the news. Life now is calmer and the interweb we couldn't quite imagine in 1982 looks after the collection and distribution of news. But after those 25 years we are, quite inconceiveably, still here, and our readers still want an artefact they can hold in their hands which won't disappear in a cloud of virtual smoke after a hard disk crash.

PDFM

One day in May 1982 remember turning to Peter and saying "we could start a Kate Bush fanzine"... that point in time and space certainly shaped the rest of my adult life and it is extraordinary how it affected so many other people as well. Peter and I had been friends for a while, we clicked, we loved Kate's music and shared the same fascination with the subjects she sang about, we understood what she was trying to do. Yes, we collected rare records, coloured vinyl, picture discs, posters but it was the music that mattered and we discovered that we had similar tastes in film, television and especially humour. In September 82 Krys appeared like a little Scouse angel, bringing light into Peter's life, and the three of us just slid into place. We had no grand plan, we just went with the flow. So much stuff has happened since then, it's difficult to put into words what it's meant to me, the fantastic people that I've met and got to know and love, the laughter and tears that we three have had would make a good book and some of the words in that book would be... Mandy, Tea, Orpington, Peter's Mum, the Brew-Up, Lionel, Sharon, Debi, Pami and Paul, Klingons, Romford, The Farm, Hannah, Dr Bush, Lisa, John, Paddy, Del, the Dangerous Brothers, *The Big Sky* video shoot, Fancy Dress, Sausage on the Fire, exploding HG boxes, Freezing cold *Experiment IV* video shoot, Local Poachers, The Goat, Glastonbury, Top Withins, Billy Connolly... Yer Bastards, Mrs Fry, Hammersmith Palais, my Brother, More fancy dress, *Star Trek*, "Stop moving the mic Pami", Convention videos, T-shirts, *Roseanne* and Monty Python's Spanish Inquisition on the answerphone, Spinal Tap, EMI, Wogan, Kate and Peter Gabriel Live at Earls Court, Video Café, Comic Relief, *Beaches*, The Tape, Steve Davis, The Hippodrome, *The Pink Mules*, Paul Baines, Parsley Spliff, Sarah, Amber, "Mmm Yes", sticking and stuffing and a fried egg on top... the most important thing I've got from HomeGround is my lovely friends Peter and Krys and the trust that Kate has shown us over the years... *"When your feet start kissing the ground..."*

Dave

Recipes

The 2007 HomeGround Glastonbury Gathering Sunday 29th July Glastonbury Tor 3 pm

Afterwards at The Rifleman's pub. No formal events just meet other fans. If raining we'll meet at the pub!

The 2007 HomeGround Wuthering Hike Saturday 27th October Top Withins 2pm

Afterwards at the Black Bull pub - we will email full details nearer the time.

Retracing the Scenes

Somewhere in between (5): 2006-2011

The last parts of these chronological scrapbook articles are compiled from news reports by Seán and Peter on the KBNI website, material, notes in the *HomeGround* scrapbook and the news in issue 79

In May 2006 the National Society for the Prevention of Cruelty to Children hosted an auction which included a lithograph of the artwork for *King of the Mountain* as designed by Bertie, and signed by both Kate and Bertie. The DVD *Kate Bush: Under Review* was also released that month. Dave said: "*Under Review* is basically a collection of interviews with music journalists, most notably Paul Gambaccini, discussing each of Kate's singles and albums in chronological order, interspersed with some short clips from the official promos, the Hammersmith Odeon film and various other TV appearances, but and it's a large one… the quality of the music and Kate interview stuff is simply shocking. It's very clear, why both Kate and EMI were so keen to warn everyone that this was not an official release. The real shame about this release is that the new interviews with the journos are actually really good, thoughtful and all, clearly have a great knowledge of Kate's music and they would have made the basis of a good TV show."

The few published reviews made more or less the same points: "While it may not break new ground, the documentary is still a good retrospective of her career to date... If you're a Kate Bush fan, you'll probably give anything that has her name and/or likeness on it a chance. That's not a criticism so much as a confession; I once bought a terrible concert bootleg (from her one and only concert back in 1979)... That's more or less where *Kate Bush Under Review* fits in." (Jeffrey Ricker Playback:stl website). The DVD reached no.3 in the UK Music Video chart regardless.

To entertain us in July there was the Puppini Sisters début album with its boogy-woogy cover of *Wuthering Heights:* "a trio of young ladies in vintage Forties frocks take to the stage, offer a few demure carmine smiles and launch into tight-as-you-like three-part harmonies backed by lolling double bass, swingin' drums and jazz guitar. It's faintly familiar. Andrews Sisters? Boswell Sisters? Kate Bush? And, as they ape the bizarre *Wuthering Heights* expressionistic dance moves in perfect synchronicity, it sinks in that, yes, they are doing a Kate Bush cover." (*The Times*). In interview the Puppinis commented: "We did *Wuthering Heights* only because my husband lied and got us a gig by saying we did a great cover of it. We're not taking the piss out of the songs, we're paying homage to them."

Asked on the 'I Like Music' website which track was the live favourite: "*Wuthering Heights*, as it's so much fun watching people's faces as the penny drops and they realise we are covering a Kate Bush classic in such a new but old-fashioned way. Not only do people love the reinterpretation, but they also love the moves we do too which are taken from her original music video". Asked on the 'My West End' website which was the most difficult track: "*Wuthering Heights* was probably the hardest one to Puppini-fy. Marcella spent many a day lost in despair and many more in tears over that one! The end result is so different from the original it's become a new song in its own right and we love it!"

Other Kate covers abounded. The Futureheads were in North America and then at Reading where their take on *Hounds of Love* went down a storm. The Ukulele Orchestra were in Galway with their version of *Wuthering Heights*. In the Autumn Natalie Cole released her 20th studio album with her choir-backed cover of *The Man with the Child in his Eyes*, a song she had performed live long since. As one Amazon reviewer put it: "now with more life experience this stellar version shows how as a great artist matures, performances deepen and vocals become richer and this magnificent performance is haunting and a truly extraordinary listening experience".

Big Boi of rap duo OutKast was still after making a collaboration happen, and in August revealed that Kate had contacted him: "She actually emailed me. I want her to produce two or three songs on my solo record. She said, 'Whenever you come to England, you can come stay with me and camp out and we can make it happen.'" Lynsey Hanley in the *Observer* Music Blog commented: "one might have predicted that Big Boi's cravat-wearing, Pushkin-reading other half, Andre '3000' Benjamin, would be the more obvious OutKast member to duet with the British song-writing icon who has made a career out of giving the impression that she is a bit wispy in the head. While the thought of Bush adding her ethereal sheen to Big Boi's rapping makes the mind boggle in a good way, it's to be hoped that their collective efforts see the light of day."

In September Kate appeared on one of twenty special covers to celebrate 20 years of *Q* Magazine. In the interview 'National Treasure', Kate reminisced. Her high point? "*Well it's got to be having my son Bertie*". The low point was inevitably the death of her mother Hannah "*like the end of the world*". Twenty years ago she thought the record company's insistence on a greatest hits package was "*a crap idea... and of course it turned out to be my biggest selling record*". Kate confesses to being "*really exhausted*" after *Aerial* but definitely hopes the next album could get done "*in six weeks*".

The heavy weather in November caused the collapse of a 200 year old weir at Kate's house

Previous pages: The covers of the last four print issues of *HomeGround* issues 76 to 79 and editorial page of issue 78 (June 2007)

on the Thames near Reading, which resulted in the closure of the canal and flooding downstream. The gutter press initially had a fine time blaming Kate for lack of maintenance and chortling over the fact that it looked like having the silted-up waterway cleared was going to cost Kate "upwards of a hundred grand". When it later turned out that maintenance of the weir was actually the responsibility of the British Waterways Board, who would have to bear the cost, malicious humour turned to synthetic indignation.

That month the BBC TV programme 'The Culture Show' ran a poll for the favourite 'Living Icon'. Antony Hegarty (of Antony and The Johnsons) appeared on the programme to explain why Kate deserved the accolade: "The first time I heard a Kate Bush song was when I heard *Wuthering Heights* and I was instantly seduced. There's a slow-mo cartwheel she does in a white dress. I used to gather everyone around and mime to the music video. That's why I learned to do a cartwheel". The show's website introduced it's biog of Kate as follows: "Kate Bush is the grand dame of British pop. Born in 1958 in Bexleyheath, she is known for her unique four octave voice, idiosyncratic lyrics and eccentric performances." Kate was voted in 7th place of the ten finalists, with Morrissey, David Attenborough and Paul McCartney making the top three.

Kate posted her 2006 Christmas message on the official website: "*Hello everyone, It has been a very quiet year and lovely for us to catch up on things. We are all well and happy. I know that many of you have asked for more details on* Aerial*'s track by track credits – these can now be found in the "Musicians" section. I am seriously shocked and extremely flattered to be voted in the top 10 living icons on 'The Culture Show'. Thank you so much for voting me in, I feel very honoured. I hope you have a fantastic Christmas, we are really looking forward to it... and here's wishing you all a wonderful new year ahead. With love, Kate.*"

In January 2007 Kate wrote a special foreword to a *Mojo* Classic Special Edition on 60 Years of David Bowie: "*I was sitting in my bath, submerged in bubbles, when I heard David Bowie for the first time...*" Time passed in this new 'somewhere in between' period, with Kate thinking, as she had indicated in the *Q* interview, about new ideas for projects. A reconsideration of tracks from *The Sensual World* and *The Red Shoes*? A new album going further down the path of delicious pagan rapture indicated by *Aerial*? On 5th April Kate sent a good luck message to Mark Radcliffe, a long time fan, as his BBC Radio 2 show moved to a new 8pm time slot. Kate expressed the hope that his new show would be "baaad" and "wickeeeed".

This author has to express solidarity with Sarah who on her blog said "I hadn't heard of Bat for Lashes until the other day when I was searching Google News for Kate Bush information. The problem with doing this is that you don't actually get Kate Bush information, but you get every new artist who's been compared to her". Here are some of those name checks and comparisons: Siobhán Donaghy (ex Sugababes): "main influences were The Cocteau Twins, Kate Bush", Twice Booker-nominated David Mitchell: "*Number 9 Dream* was written under the musical spell of Kate Bush and John Lennon"; Emilie Simon "more like a cross between Miss Kittin, Kate Bush and Vanessa Paradis"; PJ Harvey "Kate Bush is probably the reference point for Harvey's latest digression into avant-garde chamber music"; the said Bat For Lashes "Like Kate Bush getting pissed with Bjork"; Kristeen Young "intriguing, keyboard-led tunes that suggested a more belligerent Kate Bush"; Beth Orton "the missing link between Kate Bush and Janis Joplin"; Carla Trevaskis "sounding quite a bit like a Kate Bush sample"; Carina Round "Kate Bush on acid"; Blood Clock "Kate Bush on 'roids'"; Ronley Teper "Kate Bush in her youth in a more rootsy, acoustic setting"; Robyn "Kate Bush meets Gwen Stefani". Even sports commentary was not left out: "If Kate Bush could make a deal with god she'd run up a hill or building, personally I'd choose an injury free season from Louis Saha", says Steve Hewitt.

The *obita dicta* assessments of Kate's place in the music firmament continued: "The small but potent cadre of true pop eccentrics – Kate Bush, Björk, Sinéad O'Connor – that periodically cut a swath through the aural oatmeal of their blander peers" (Leah Greenblatt *Entertainment Weekly*)... "Wading through the music scene's waters as a singer-songwriter is tough. Women have it hard enough, trying to live up to examples set by Joni Mitchell or Kate Bush" (John Zeis Prefixmag). Kate Nash told *The Guardian*, "I just wanna be an artist, like someone like Björk and Kate Bush and Regina Spektor. These are people that have saved people, I think, by being what they are". Annie Clark, aka St. Vincent: "And I also – this may sound really silly – but I just discovered Kate Bush, probably six months ago, and I think she's so great. I know I'm very late to the party here".

As far back as 2003 we had noted Placebo's cover version of *Running Up That Hill*, originally released on a bonus disc with the album *Sleeping With Ghosts*. The band had started including it in their set while touring the UK in early 2006, and in April 2007 the track was released in the US to coincide with the release of their iTunes only *Covers* album. In an 'Under-Ground Online' interview Stefan Olsdal, Placebo's bass player, says: "We're fans of Kate Bush so, when it came to this track, we thought that the lyrics had a real depth and you can't really get that in the original because she's singing it so fast. We wanted to slow it down and it felt really good, and we're really proud of it." In the *Denver Post* Placebo recalled "When we met her, we asked her if she liked our cover, and she said, 'Yes'. We were blown away by that. It was our license to play it live. And ever since, it's been a bit of a monster." The track was quickly re-mixed in June 2007 by Denver's DJ Magnet as *Love Comes Running Up That Hill Quickly (Placebo vs. Pet Shop Boys vs. Kate Bush)* "concocting a finely textured, deeply melancholy mash-up that features both the original version and Placebo's cover with PSB... casting a ghostly spectre over the proceedings" (John Sakamoto *Toronto Star*).

The British press love to lead the pack in a hypocritical "just who do they think are" charge against the very celebs they depend on for circulation, even those who do their their best to avoid celebrity. Fresh from the weir episode, in May came the story about the security precautions at Kate's Devon coast retreat. Some locals had apparently complained about Kate's cameras, lights and fences. It is necessary to read the press coverage closely to discover why this happened. The Parish clerk refused to comment but another council source revealed that Kate had received unwanted visitors. The source said: "She's had people going right into the grounds to try to see her and at one stage there was a helicopter circling overhead for quite a while." One local councillor opined "I'm afraid the coast path and the beach were there long before Kate Bush and I'm fairly confident they'll still be in the same place with the same unhindered access long after she's gone." As it happened, despite the gutter press attempting to portray this as "The War of Wuthering Heights", after requests Kate toned down the security and the local council were now quite satisfied.

The dilemma of 'the careful mother' caught the eye of *Belfast Telegraph* columnist Luiza Sauma: "After 30 years in the business, Kate Bush still gets lumbered with those adjectives reserved for super-creative women: kooky, eccentric, crazy... Bush retired from the public eye in the 1990s to live in the countryside and raise her son – a reasonable move, for someone who had been working since the age of 15 – but the newspapers had different ideas. She wasn't just taking a break, she was a 'recluse'... Recently, Bush ran into trouble with her local council in Devon. She removed the cameras immediately, but that didn't stop *The Daily Mail* from calling her 'Garboesque'".

In the midst of the credit crisis, in May 2007 EMI's perilous financial position led to an agreement for take-over by private equity firm Terra Firma. This corporate rearrangement would be very significant for Kate. Creative artists are not simply financial assets. Seeing the way the wind was blowing, Paul McCartney had already walked from the label. Others like Radiohead would shortly follow. The Rolling Stones were soon looking elsewhere. Pink Floyd were consulting their lawyers. Kate's transition would take longer.

To our profound disbelief, that May *HomeGround* was 25 years old. Del Palmer's new website was launched in July, providing information on *his* solo album *Leap of Faith* which was released in September. In his introductory message Del said: "having just completed the latest studio album to be released by Kate I felt the time was right to try, finally, to make some music myself. I have spent the last year or so recording songs and will soon have the project completed."

The chart-making continued: *Mojo*'s '100 greatest albums of our lifetime' included *Aerial* at no.45, Kate's cover version of Elton John's *Rocket Man* was named the 'Greatest Cover of All Time' by readers of the *Observer*. This was not unanimously received with joy. One comment on the *Observer Music Monthly* blog described the track as "nasty Eighties-style plastic white reggae". Though Kate was short-listed for the BBC Radio 2 "Ultimate Icon of the Last 40 years" poll, when the results were announced on 2nd October, the winner was unsurprisingly Terry Wogan, from the Beatles, Nelson Mandela, and the late Diana, Princess of Wales.

"If the Eighties had actually sounded like this, it wouldn't have taken twenty years to stop being embarrassed about them". So ended a 6th September review of the cover version of *Running Up That Hill* by the Chromatics by Jeff Klingman on Prefix: "A litany of artists including Placebo, Pink Floyd, Kiki & Herb, and Patrick Wolf have attempted Kate Bush's 1985 classic, but none have managed the restrained grace of this demo by Portland's Chromatics that's been tearing up the blogosphere for the last week... It should be prominently noted that the original is very solid on its own, and it's no coincidence that

EMI had originally run into problems more than decade before and had long considered a merger with Warner. Increasing debts led to profit warnings and the private equity companies circled like a pack of sharks. The story in detail appears in an article by Toby Lewis in *Financial News* 22nd February 2010.

Those following the "footpath" story might have been aware that as far back as August 2006 the commercial property papers were warning landowners about the effect of the extension of the "right to roam" laws to the coast. There was a new process of appeal, most famously taken by Madonna, who managed to exempt part of her English estate.

The whole story appeared to ignore the fact that the green welly brigade are constantly undertaking the perfectly usual procedure of applying to have footpaths ancient and modern diverted away from particular areas of privacy, or seeking other ways of enabling them to enjoy their property in peace.

Graphic: Izabela Samsonowicz

Chromatics' best moment to date has a legendary songwriter like Ms. Bush to thank. But there's something about the bombast in Kate's version, a brashness to the drum flls and overinflated vocal overdubs, that feels curiously dated now. Perhaps it's a victim of its huge perm and enormous shoulder pad decade".

I have very little patience with ethnology-musicalogical tracts which try to analyse music, essentially an emotional and sometimes mystic experience, with a set of dry academic tools. In September, as part of their 'Popular and Folk Music Series', Ashgate Publishing released a book by Ron Moy, a lecturer in the School of Media, Critical and Creative Arts at Liverpool John Moores University. Entitled *Kate Bush and Hounds of Love,* according to the publishers "The album allows the author, the critical opportunity to explore a wide range of issues relating to technology, production, authorship, grain of the voice, iconography, critical and commercial impact, collaboration, gender, sexuality, narrative, and social and cultural context."

According to the author: "I approach music as a socially mediated text that allows for a multitude of critical and aesthetical entry points to manifest themselves through individual interpretive strategies". Frankly, I would have preferred a book written in English, not in the pidgin-dialect favoured by academics of the post-modern variety seemingly created for the very purpose of obfuscation, and I speak as an honours graduate of the London School of Economics. I am reminded of the comment in Chip Morningstar's essential essay *How to Deconstruct Almost Anything*: "There's no reason you should be able to understand what these academics are saying because, for several generations, comprehensibility to outsiders has not been one of the selective criteria to which they've been subjected".

How to Deconstruct Almost Anything – My Postmodern Adventure by Chip Morningstar Electric Communities. This can be found a click away on Google.

From reading this volume I simply got the idea that Moy likes Kate's music very much, but feels the need to justify that simple emotion in the bizarre lingo his academic colleagues use to communicate. Plainly a volume that seeks to elucidate every single track Kate had recorded has got to be interesting to fans, and this book made interesting points if you could get over the alienating jargon.

It was getting almost impossible to track all the various quotes and references since Kate's "return". Here are just a few from 2007: "if an alchemist were to capture an angel and a demon and meld them together, we would hear Kate's voice during the birthing" (DejavuDave from The GearPage); "Since the 1980s Kate Bush has shouldered the unhappy burden of having to live up to her own brilliance" (rockgenie Rindie); "Crazy lady with a very high voice singing about incest and classic English literature? Well you got my attention!" (411mania.com music roundtable); "*The Dreaming* by Kate Bush... is creative genius in form. A revelation. A stunning creative opus" (Gwynneth Haynes IGN).

On 19th September Adam Thornton on his 'Muffyoglb' blog chose Kate for the 'I'd Buy Anything by..." slot: "It's easy to forget how innovative she was in those pre-Tori Amos days: a young, pretty piano player singing unorthodox songs about literature, dreams, sex, nuclear war... even during her brief return to fame (thanks to *Running Up That Hill*) Bush was an oddity, an individual, a recluse. Along came... a whole whack of nutty female performers, but beside them all Bush appeared to be smarter, less eager, and - most importantly - down to earth in her interviews... The press loves to come up with reasons why Kate Bush disappears for so long... but it all seems to come down to one thing: she's never relished 'stardom' and would much prefer to keep her private life private, and to have lots of breathing room for creating music."

Amongst compilations we noticed was a triple CD from Charles Webster: *Balearic Soul & Eclectic Visions A Personal Selection of Late Night Grooves*. The track included was, curiously, *Army Dreamers*.

Aerial was still being reviewed. On his blog 'Shadowmagick' John Trevillian set out his thoughts: "There's nature here. Unadulterated and sublime and raucous. It's all unashamedly romantic and interconnected. A long day's journey into night. And right on until the next morning. When the whole cycle starts all over again. It's daring, it's imaginative, and it's intense. It is music of pure, pagan rapture. She is a goddess. She commands us to awaken. To see the unreal in the everyday. To see as if for the first time the wind, rain, sunlight and the sea. It's like waking inside a lucid musical dream. It's all madder than a box of frogs, but it works."

In November Tina Arena began a relaunch of her career in Australia. Her new album *Songs of Love and Loss*, featured covers of classic tunes including *The Man with the Child in his Eyes*. The *Herald Sun* asked her if she met Kate "back in the day": "She was the first pop star I met. I think I was seven, and it was at the 'King of Pop' awards in Melbourne. I remember she was minuscule, in purple velvet jeans, a cream hippie long top, black ankle boots. She had a packet of Marlboro Reds in her hand, long hair. I remember this extraordinary beauty coming past me. The smile of this delicate thing that probably packed a punch. She wrote that song when she was 14. She was a huge musical reference for me, very difficult to touch". Whilst we're in the Antipodes, we can also take in an interview given to *In Style* by Nicole Kidman who revealed that when she was 17 she sang in an band called Divine Madness: "Three girls and four guys. We did a lot of '70s stuff. I did Kate Bush... We played at parties and one pub gig. We never got paid".

A Dutch documentary entitled *Come Back Kate* was part of the 20th International Documentary

Film Festival, held in Amsterdam 22nd November to 2nd December. The documentary, directed by Helena Muskens and Quirine Racké, was 53 minutes long and according to the festival brochure featured "diehard fans of Kate Bush talking about their special bond with the singer... Bush's devotees create their own magic world around her mythical persona, some of them celebrate her birthday on a beach in southern England..." One odd suggestion which emerged at this time was that John Lydon, whose affection for Kate and her music has long been known and clearly expressed, once wrote a song for her, but she did not record it. There were no further details.

In 2007, with the new owners of EMI acting like a demented new broom, it was time to consider other possibilities. In the absence of a clear idea of where new material would be placed, Kate started working on a project to remake some of the tracks from *The Sensual World*, and especially *The Red Shoes*. She had come to believe that the production on those albums was too cluttered, and particularly on the *The Red Shoes* the process was perhaps weighed down by the negativity of loss of friends and particularly her mother. She believed some of those tracks could be restated with space to breathe and that the emotions they contained could be stated in a more positive manner.

It was perhaps part of a conception of a new departure which included the creation of her own label, a remaking of a family business such as her career had been in the 1980s, though this time the protective entity would be her own family and immediate friends and work colleagues, and people she had learned to trust, and the entity would be clearly focused around her own needs and wishes as the creative centre. It was still the case that the only thing she had in common with the music business that she made records. Perhaps this would complete her own independence from the record industry. The new entity would at the same time enable her to pursue the projects she wished to do, and protect her from those parts of the process she found unhelpful, disorientating, and tempting, and this inevitably included the reshaping of relations with her fans.

Having started down this road, matters around the possibility of a new album clarified, and the making and release of a new album became more possible that it had been. From 2007 then, Kate worked alternatively on two projects, the reworked material, and the new material, and the ambition was to release them both in one year, the first time that had happened since her début some thirty years previously.

In *HomeGround* issue 78 Del Palmer had revealed that novelist Philip Pullman had visited Kate, a known fan of his work, at her home earlier in the year. On 13th November we could actually talk about a new track. Kate had written and recorded *Lyra* for the major fantasy film *The Golden Compass* (which was based on the first volume of the *His Dark Materials* trilogy) to be released on 7th December. The song, named for Lyra Belacqua, the lead character in *The Golden Compass*, was written and produced by Kate and was heard over the closing credits of the film. It seems all this was done very quickly as Kate was only asked by the film company on 26th October. Kate, being a huge fan of Philip Pullman and the books, was thrilled to be asked to do it and worked very hard to deliver the track in time.

As Del later explained Kate came to the studio with a rough demo recorded at her home using a ProTools LE system. The first job on Sunday was to record the keyboard and the lead vocal so that the Choir arranger could get to work as quickly as possible. "This short project was to be a happy return to analog recording for us. We used a Studer A827 24-track recorder. Once the track was recorded it was transferred to ProTools for editing and mixing". On Monday morning they went up to Oxford with the Abbey Road mobile unit to do the Choristers of the Choir of Magdelen College School. This was then imported into the original ProTools session for mixing on the Monday afternoon. It was then a rush down to Abbey Road itself for the 5.1 surround mix. This was because all of the soundtrack music had been done there so it made sense to do the same. Then it was back to Kate's own studio where a stereo version was mixed for the soundtrack album. The soundtrack was released on 11th December.

The news of *Lyra* spread across the internet in a fashion which we were already learning to call "viral". Eonline, BBC, *NME*, *Variety*, *Uncut* and Pitchfork and many other sites carried reports. A particularly witty write-up was published by *Empire* Magazine. *Entertainment Weekly* in the US even ran an article proposing Kate as a possible Oscar contender: "New Line wants to be part of the Academy Awards one way or another, and their best bet may be their just-announced news that British singer/songwriter Kate Bush will have her original song titled *Lyra* tacked onto the end credits of *The Golden Compass*... who knows, now we may get to see her perform at the Oscars." Although as Seán commented on the KBNI website: this seemed to be a case of putting the cart waaay before the horse, New Line Cinema was actively lobbying members of the Academy of Motion Picture Arts and Sciences to vote for *Lyra* in the category of 'Best Original Song' for the 2008 Academy Awards, running the traditional 'For Your Consideration' adverts in the entertainment press in the US.

Lyra received it's UK radio première on the venerable BBC Radio programme 'Roundtable', hosted by Steve Lamacq, on 22nd November, 2007. Lamacq actually called the song Kate's

The Golden Compass (2007, above and below).

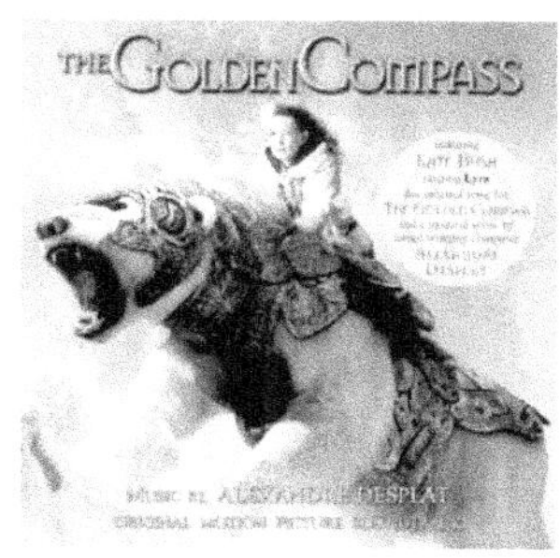

His Dark Materials
by Philip Pullman

"new single". The reviewers were not keen: "the choir sounds like a dodgy sounding synth", "sounds like Clannad", "dull", and "not classic Bush". Seán's reactions: Unfortunate that the world première of this track was lumped in to to a mostly 'indie' format review panel show. I couldn't give a shite about the studio opinions in this case. I really wanted to hear how Kate had stepped up to the challenge of providing an appropriate coda to a blockbuster movie for which she obviously felt a connection with the source material. That's why I feel the track is perfect, and will resonate globally around cinemas. My head spins when I think about how many people are going to hear this track - and every one of them will have taken Lyra's journey with her. The film's world première was in London on 27th November, and Kate paid for the choir who sang on the track to take a trip to see it. Choir director Bill Ives said: "Ms Bush came along to see the boys because it was her song and she wanted to meet them. She was lovely, very quiet and altogether charming, and the boys were very excited to meet her."

The *LA Times* reviewed *Lyra* as follows: "A late and unexpected entry in the race for the Best Original Song Oscar comes from New Line Cinema's *The Golden Compass*, which ends with a new tune from esteemed British singer Kate Bush … *Lyra* is an odd, sparse little number, putting the emphasis almost entirely on Bush's vocals... If there's any noticeable effect used in the song, it's primarily the sound of wind, which adds a coldness to Bush's usually warm vocal styling. Indeed, it serves to bring a sort of distance between Bush and the soft hymn provided by the Magdalen College Choir, making Bush feel a little more like an orator than a singer. Lyrically, Bush sticks pretty close to the source material, which is the song's main weakness... By so literally interpreting the film, the song likely won't have much of a life outside the movie... While not her among her strongest work, *Lyra* still shows Bush is a vocalist like few others".

In view of the time available, *Lyra* had been formed out of the ashes of the *Dinosaur* track. It would be fair to say it was not received in the film music world, or amongst film goers with unanimous acclamation. In fact it would be fair to say this track probably received the worst notices I've ever seen for a Kate track with the possible exception of the British music press reaction to *The Dreaming*. It depends on whether you like listening to Kate's voice really.

Graphic opposite:
Neil Sheriff

The film was not without controversy, as the final three chapters of the book were left out, with the intention that they would be included in the second film. The US Catholic League called for a boycott of film. This was not entirely surprising in the view of the atheistic views of the author. What was surprising is that the film makers thought they could bring Pullman's tale to the screen and escape such controversy by attempting to conceal the essential message. The completed film did not receive good notices, of which the following from *Time Out* was typical: "Bland, bloodless and bereft of magic, New Line's corporate sanitisation of Philip Pullman's exciting, provocative fantasy novel, *The Northern Lights*, strips the book of its humanity and soul. Instead, it's a synthetic, flavourless product that lacks the subversive tang of Pullman's source novel". The comparative failure of the film to please Pullman fans, critics or cinema goers effectively torpedoed plans to film the other novels in the trilogy.

In the 2007 'Satellite Awards', a kind of tertiary adjunct through the Golden Globes, to the Oscars, and decided by the International Press Academy, *Lyra* was nominated for 'best original song' one of five nominations received by *The Golden Compass*. The film did not take any of the awards and the song was not nominated in the similar category in the actual Oscars.

On 2nd December, 2007 on her official website Kate wrote: "*Hello everyone, I've really enjoyed putting the 'Lyra' track together and working with the Magdalen Choristers was totally delightful. Philip's trilogy is a masterpiece and I was thrilled to be asked to write this for the film. Have a wonderful Christmas…*" The track was available from iTunes from 10th December.

2008 was a year in which we were to celebrate a number of scarcely believable anniversaries. We began on 20th January with the 30th anniversary of *Wuthering Heights*. Seán wrote: "It's incredible to think of that much time having passed. I was just four years old but I do remember seeing a crazy lady (I thought she was a witch!) on the 'Multi-Coloured Swap Shop' on the BBC and being baffled as to what all the arm-waving and shrieking was about. But she had entered my consciousness for the first time".

EMI UK Chief Executive Officer Tony Wadsworth left EMI in January after 25 years' service. He was a man who understood the record industry and certainly seemed to understand and get on well with Kate. He was replaced by Guy Hands, CEO of Terra Firma, who seemed to have the idea that selling music was exactly the same as selling baked beans, and that creative artists were merely corporate assets. The relationship with many of the label's artists, already deteriorating, promptly collapsed. The attempt by Terra Firma to run EMI would become increasingly rocky and ultimately untenable. The departure of Tony Wadsworth accelerated the process of Kate's detachment from EMI, and the building by her of a new creative and business entity.

The Utah Saints were back with a new *Van She Tech Remix* version of their 1992 hit *Something Good* which featured the vocal sample from *Cloudbusting*. This was released on 17th March.

KBNI reported that it was receiving heavy daytime plays on Radio 1 and was a staple for the likes of Zane Lowe and Pete Tong, who made it a 'Hottest Record In The World' and 'Essential New Tune' respectively. Nick Levine the Editor of Digital Spy interviewed the band on 14th March: Why do you think the track's still so popular? "For me, it works because it's a track in its own right. We didn't just take an old track and put new beats on it: we made something new from the Kate Bush sample." Have you ever found out what Kate Bush thinks of the track? "We've never actually spoken to her, but it's the only time she's ever cleared a sample, so she must be cool with it. I think it probably relates to what I've just said: she respects the fact that we didn't just take the piss and lay down beats over one of her choruses." On Gigwise on 17th March Alastair Thompson put it like this: "Kate Bush's all-conquering vocal is still the focal point but as each remixer stirs the porridge, it is quite some feat that everyone hits the spot".

As Kate got to work on re-imagining older material and writing for a new album, 'After all the fuss' assessments were being made of *Aerial*: "Now that all the hype has died down, and the modern pop machine continues to roll along, Kate Bush's *Aerial* stands as a brilliant work of art. The only thing to compare it to, it seems, is another Kate Bush album" (Martin Magdalene *Sunday Song Review*); "this album is... more content with the beauty of life and motherhood. Listening to this album reminds me of lush green forest during the summer in which the day feels endless... It's as if Kate Bush intended this album to be an emotional cleansing of the demons within. At the end of the album, you can't help but feel the colorful spectrum of rejuvenation surround you" (Universal Language blog).

There were those who even tried to shoehorn *Aerial* into some sort of Balearic revival: "Her last album, *Aerial*, with its ambient interludes and massive crescendos, couldn't have been more Balearic if it was wearing white espadrilles and hoovering up MDMA' (Justin Quirk *Guardian* 8th February). Progarchives.com on that same date summed up as follows: "A lesson in style by the cool aunt of prog music. Kate Bush truly has the soul of a true artist... It is not always pretty, but sometimes art is not supposed to be pretty... *A Sky of Honey*, is the most interesting for us who are into prog, as it is... a conceptual piece of music which plays like a true soundtrack to summer itself... The feel... is very mellow and warm, Bush's piano gently caressing your skin like hot water, or a cloud in a sky of honey, until *Nocturn* picks up the tempo and with its steady beat drags you through the milky, silky water of the summer night... I do not hesitate to pull out the five star rating to this gem, because everything about *Aerial* communicates a feeling of warmth and emotion... there is an ethereal beauty which... can move you on a very deep level".

Martin Locock in his blog on 12th October put the whole 'recluse' thing into context: "It's funny how easy it is these days to become a recluse: stop going to film premières, refuse to appear on quiz shows, move outside the M25, and suddenly you're Simeon Stylites living up a pole in the desert". Of her work: "you can see that the unusual side to it is not its variation in quality, but in its ambition. She avoids straightforward autobiographical narrative. Which is not to say that great rock needs to have literary pretensions: but it does need to have some form of intellectual complexity if it aspires to be more than good time rock and roll... She might be a genius; but more to the point she is thoughtful... Listening to something like *Aerial* requires a degree of attention unusual these days, both in terms of the music and in the lyrics which are diffuse and referential; but it is precisely this complexity that provides the intrigue."

Paul Cornell is a novelist, and comics and TV writer. In particular he was the author of the 'Doctor Who' episodes *Father's Day* and *Family of Blood*. In his 18th December blog entry he recorded his admiration: "The work of Kate Bush has been important to me, and influenced my writing, for many years now". Of *Sunset* "The whole track is a fight between nervous energy and a slow, jazzy late night tumble into relaxation. As befits its theme, the fight between life and death, as demonstrated in nature, but rather horribly leading to the question of what that means for the individual... And it feels like the most organic thing in the world, like it's something from your dreams or your nervous system."

Though we were now significantly into another publically "quiet" (but privately very busy) period, there were many opportunities to hear Kate's songs sung. A whole collection of eclectic artists were continuing to include Kate's material in their acts. In March Natalie Cole was including the wonderful cover of the *Man with the Child in his Eyes* in her US shows. The three-time Laurence Olivier Award winner (and seven times nominated) Maria Friedman included her distinctive cover of the same track in her 'Re-Arranged' shows in London. This moved *Times* critic Clive Davis to say that "Anyone who finds Kate Bush unbearably melodramatic would have been astonished to hear Friedman turn *Man with the Child in his Eyes* into a genuinely moving piece of theatre".

Then there was reality TV. 'Rock the Cradle' was a bizarre idea to get the offspring of famous rock stars to compete for a recording contract and $100,000. The result was not well received amongst the US TV critics. The Kate interest was another cover version of *This Woman's Work*. Well, *we* understood it was a Kate interest, but both singer Lil B. Sure (son of Al B. Sure) and the host of the show Ryan Devlin seemed to be under the impression that the song had been written by Maxwell. In May 'Tarnished', said to be "a shotgun marriage of circus and burlesque", featured "four sassy gals who aren't afraid to cross the line" who included an interpretation of *Babooshka*. Also in May the Futureheads, whose cover of *Hounds of Love* had been a huge hit in 2005 but who had suffered from a particularly nasty bout of second album syndrome (it failed to chart at all) as a consequence of which their label dropped them, were back with gigs which still conspicuously featured the Kate cover, which as many reviewers noted, got the most enthusiastic response.

October brought Hayley Westenra, still including her cover of *Wuthering Heights* in her most recent tour: "the best version I have heard since the original" (Gordon Barr, *Newcastle Chronicle* 31st October). In the same month Maxwell returned: "It is possible that there were other people on stage last night when Maxwell began singing his cover of Kate Bush's ethereal *This Woman's Work*. But the moment the R&B singer eased into the first cooing high notes of the fragile ballad, everything in the Opera House that wasn't encompassed in the mists of his aching falsetto sigh vanished in some sort of soul-induced hysterical blindness. The crowd, especially the women, erupted with an explosion of the type and volume of screaming usually reserved for an Oprah Winfrey give-away show" (Sarah Rodman, *Boston Globe* 9th October).

On 15th August the Lula Lounge Toronto staged a Kate tribute night 'This Woman's Work!' featuring Kevin Fox, Kurt Swinghammer, Laurel MacDonald, and 'The Suspended in Gaffa Mini Orchestra' amongst others. The show was sold out and particular performances were singled out for praise by the local music press and bloggers. Fides Krucker's "fresh and exciting interpretations of *This Woman's Work*", Suba Sankaran and Dylan Bell produced a "beautiful acapella arrangement of *Cloudbusting*", Kevin Fox "sung and played cello simultaneously, along with a looped recording of a second cello part for *Army Dreamers*". Then there was the Edinburgh Fringe 2008 which actually included *two* acts which featured "a silly dance routine performed to Kate Bush's *Wuthering Heights*", Patrick Monahan and John Luke Roberts.

Although Kate was now plainly held and revered in musical circles, it was equally clear that to those outside the circle she was yet still the 'screeching witch' of 1978. A good example of this occurred when Gordon Brown, sometime Labour Party Leader and Prime Minister, agreed in an interview with the *New Statesman* that his character was not unlike that of Heathcliff. The commentators pounced: "David Cameron was in sarcastic form. 'I speak for the whole country when I say we are pleased to see that Heathcliff has come home!'... The Tory leader may have been remembering not the novel, but Kate Bush's song *Wuthering Heights*: 'Heeethcleef, it's meeee, your Catheee, I've come home... let me inna your window. Oh, whow-o-w-oh-whow'" (Simon Hoggart, *The Guardian* 11th July). "For many of us, Heathcliff will always be a) a cartoon cat, or b) the subject of the worst rhyming couplet in pop history ("Heathcliff, it's me/I'm Cath-y") in the début single by Kate Bush. I now find myself thinking of our Prime Minister as a foot tall, furry and mischievous, peering out from Downing Street while a wildly peculiar elfin 1980s pop star taps on his window and pirouettes around his front garden like a cross between Princess Leia and the lunatic bard from 'Blackadder II'" (Hugo Rifkind, *The Times* 11th July); "having to listen again to the caterwauling of Kate Bush really was too much. Talk about bad dreams in the night" (Iain Macwhirter, *Scottish Daily Herald* 12th July).

But there were other indications of that odd 1970s/1980s attitude continuing. In the *Daily Telegraph* on 2nd July, Ruby Wax admitted "my guilty pleasure, which is *Wuthering Heights* by Kate Bush ("Heathcliff, it's meeee..."). I only listen to it in a locked room and then give into the schmaltz of it all" and Danny Dyer 'East End geezer, actor and presenter' also thought (*Daily Mirror* 19th October) that his musical inclinations should be kept secret: What's your guilty pleasure? "Kate Bush. I'm meant to be a right chap and me listening to Kate Bush? It's not ideal, is it?"

There were those who on the other hand sought any half reasonable excuse to mention Kate with little discernible embarrassment. "After weeks of racking my brain about who Hawes has based her character on, I had the eureka moment: Kate Bush! She has Bush's hair, Bush's nuttiness, and, last night, a lot of very Bush-ian sequences of rolling through brightly coloured sheets" (Helen Rumbelow in her 14th March *Times* review of Keeley Hawes as Alex Drake in 'Ashes to Ashes'). On July 26th 'The New Nixon', a blog otherwise devoted to the memory of Tricky Dick, 'looked back at some of the music that was popular forty years ago, around the time Richard Nixon ran for, and was elected, President': "No reference to *Rocket Man* should pass without mentioning Kate Bush's extraordinary 1991 cover and the equally extraordinary video she produced to accompany it". Then there was the 'Defence Debates' blog (23rd October), which put Afghanistan, The Taliban, ICBMs and counter-insurgent strategy aside to discuss 'Kate Bush in our sensual world' and not even in the context of *Experiment IV*: "There is no other recording artist in the world today quite like Kate Bush. In the course of her twenty-seven year career... Bush has built a reputation that remains unrivalled in terms of musical ambition, pioneering sonics, stirring

Haley Westenra

Maxwell

Keeley Hawes

Richard Nixon

emotional content and sheer originality... A characteristically bold and expansive work brimming with atmosphere, mystery, passion and complex aural detail, the twin-disc *Aerial* has already been declared a masterpiece by all who have heard it". In *The Times,* 17th June, Jane Czyzselska had asked "Why can't women be geniuses too?" Answering her own question "Take Kate Bush. Ever since the electrifying *Wuthering Heights* in 1978, Bush has not only pushed the boundaries with her consistently exceptional and original compositions, but she has paved the way for successive lady geniuses, including Björk and Alison Goldfrapp".

Tim Lott

Tim Lott sometime of the *Record Mirror* recalled in the 25th July *Guardian*: "Quite quickly, I made the discovery that musicians weren't, for the most part, very godlike or even particularly interesting. In fact, they seemed rather dim. There were exceptions - Kate Bush, then merely an unfashionable "pop" singer, was extremely bright and articulate... Kate Bush was so nice that she rang me up to thank me for the album review I had just written. Slightly overexcited, I asked her out on a date. She said no". In August Julie Burchill, sometime of the *NME*, published her 'waspish new book' *Not In My Name* in which she "let rip at what she regards as the biggest hypocrites of the modern age". These turned out to be "celebrities who say they long for privacy - but are happy to sell their stories to gossip magazines: "Just go, then - you're probably rich enough. Do what pop stars Sade and Kate Bush did when they were at the height of their fame and genuinely grew tired of it - disappear! The difference, I suppose is that they weren't greedy and needy, unlike the moaning minnies who complain about fame while doing everything humanly possible to keep it at fever pitch".

Julie Burchill

Charts and polls continued to indicate Kate's enduring presence in her public absence. Given the task by *The Guardian* (15th February) of selecting a track they felt represented England, Saint Etienne's Sarah Cracknell selected *Wuthering Heights*: "I can't imagine this song going down well anywhere apart from England. Her stance is very quaint and English: the way she sings, her accent, the drama of it all. She had the audacity to put out a single that was going to stretch people's imaginations". However, in March Kate again failed to be admitted to the US Rock and Roll Hall of Fame, and again this was a matter of some comment in some sections of the US music press. In July, Nick Livine Music Editor of Digital Spy, ran a feature on the 'Top Ten Gay Pop Icons'. Kate was at no.8: "The less visible Kate Bush becomes, the more we're fascinated by her... her ventures into the recording studio have kept us enthralled: *This Woman's Work*... is one of the best tearjerkers of all time. Full marks for her white witch on heat performance in the *Wuthering Heights* video, too".

Sarah Cracknell

Out.com compiled a list of 'the 100 Greatest, Gayest Albums of All Time' polling more than 100 actors, comedians, musicians, writers, critics, performance artists, label reps, and DJs, asking each to list the 10 albums that left the most indelible impressions on their lives. They had responses from the likes of Boy George, Rufus Wainwright, Cyndi Lauper, the Indigo Girls, and Holly Johnson. In the final list *Hounds of Love* came in at no.52: "What I love about this album is essentially what I love about being gay. It's eccentric, wildly imaginative, and has a completely naive view of the world in which it exists. In Kate Bush's conceptual world the clouds make magical shapes in the sky, God can change the place of a man and a woman, and innocence is lost only to give way to the beauty of romance" (Darren Hayes, formerly of Savage Garden). *The Kick Inside* came in at no.90 "This is frilly and gorgeous and even new agey but for some reason also 'hip' so I was able to drench myself in it without worrying about getting beaten up" (Nils Berstein of Matador Records).

Kate apparently shocked some in the media by - in the third year of this current "quiet" period - coming second in the Virgin Media' 'Alternative Cool List' with 14% of the poll. Carla Bruni, who had just visited the UK along with husband President Sarkozy of France, was at no.1 with 25% of the poll, and Girls Aloud and Beyonce were third and fourth. Interesting to note that *The Sun,* typical of British reports, referred to "*Wuthering Heights* Singer Kate Bush" and US reports typically referred to "alternative singer Kate Bush".

Rolling Stone's list of 'The Greatest Singers of All Time' did not find much favour with Neil McCormack writing in his *Daily Telegraph* blog on 5th December: "Question: on what list of the '100 Greatest Singers of All Time' would Bob Dylan rate higher than Dusty Springfield?... But look a little closer, and you will also notice that there is no Kate Bush (surely one of the most distinctive and original vocalists of the last thirty years)... And that is because they are not just women, but British women, and Americans apparently don't hold our singers in much regard." Further research would actually show that that is by no means 'all Americans', just the eccentric editors and fellow travellers of *Rolling Stone* who somehow always seem to have missed out on Kate.

Just before Kate's birthday we had the very sad news of the passing of Dr. Bush, Kate's father. He was a wonderful man who we at *HomeGround* knew and loved. He cared about us and the magazine and always made time to see us and comment about every passing issue. Del underlined his importance in Kate's life: "The good doctor was a source of constant inspiration to her and, in fact was solely responsible for Kate becoming the wonderful artist we all know and love". It was truly the end of an era for all of us. But as Holmes observed to Watson, "Work is the best antidote to sorrow".

There is a website which sets out the perks of reaching 50 years of age. This apparently includes there being 'nothing left to learn the hard way', and 'being the first to be released in a hostage crisis'. Kate reached that milestone at the end of July 2008. The media noticed: "One of the most illustrious performers of all time" (Jason Gregory Gigwise 30th July); "The icon that is Kate Bush is 50 on Wednesday but doesn't look a day over 25. We love her – time for another comeback we say" (WalesOnline).

On the BBC website on 25th July Chris Jones retro-reviewed *The Kick Inside*: "To this day nothing sounds like it... her extraordinary début ... a lush blend of piano grandiosity, vaguely uncomfortable reggae and intricate, intelligent, wonderful songs. All delivered in a voice that had no precedents... not only did *Wuthering Heights* give her the first self-written number one by a female artist in the UK, (a stereotype-busting fact of huge proportions, sadly undermined by EMI's subsequent decision to market Bush as lycra-clad cheesecake), but it represented a level of... literacy... unknown to the charts up until then... Only in France had 19-year olds got away with this kind of stuff. A true child of the '60s vanguard in feminism... like all true artists, you always felt that Bush didn't really care about the commercial rewards. She was soon to abandon touring completely and steer her own fabulous course into rock history".

The BBC News website interviewed Roy Harper and Colin Lloyd Tucker. Harper: "Her songs are brilliant, simple deepnesses and a fantastic degree of musicianship goes into them. There is nobody quite like her... I think she should eventually be honoured by her country because she is an outstanding contributor to the cultural life of her generation". Lloyd Tucker: "Music is her whole life and when she's making it she's extremely professional and courteous. But when she's off duty she's an extremely relaxed person and has you creased up in hysterics..." and presciently: "Kate is a musician through and through and she's never going to stop writing. I wouldn't be surprised if there'll be a flurry of activity when her son gets a bit older."

Writing in his blog on 18th August, Vincent Van Ingen compared two big names in popular music who had recently turned 50 years of age: Madonna and Kate Bush: "One tries with all her might to retain the ruthless image of Youth that Pop requires and glorifies... the other celebrates being an ordinary mother who sings songs about washing machines and the birds singing... Looking back on Kate's career, one can only say that Fame and Pop are Kate's biggest traumas. EMI promoted her as a Pop Star, which we now know they shouldn't have done, and it took her until 1994 to completely break away from the Pop world. She succeeded, and *Aerial* is the proof of it. The serenity can be tasted in every song of that album. All we can see of Kate herself in the album art work are her eyes. The cover shows a sound wave in a sea of honey and a sky of honey. Just like she always wanted it: only the music. Perhaps that's why, unlike any other Kate Bush album, *Aerial* breathes closure and peace of mind. It's Kate's biggest victory so far".

Graphic: Izabela Samsonowicz

The news took Robert McNeil by some surprise as he recorded in *The Scotsman* on 1st August: "it was unfortunate that my mouth was full of Cinnamon Cheerios when I read the news that Kate Bush had turned 50. The pieces of cereal arced across the room, with milk trailing from them... as I spluttered in surprise. Kate is 50? How did that happen? Have the authorities been informed? Personally, I have pickled her in aspic at about the age of 21". Not the only one Robert. Some of Kate's fans had problems with the passing years. "Here's a little tip for you: if you really want to get my goat, describe Kate – who is a true, professional artist – as being 'eccentric'. How come? Different, talented, years ahead of her time, insightful, creative. But eccentric? How? It is, apparently, because she keeps a low media profile. Well, good for her. The other week, I saw the novelist Martin Amis described as 'eccentric'. Eh? Does he mince hither and yon down the high streets of the nation wearing a moon-decorated cloak and singing *Barnacle Bill the Sailor*? He does not. He writes interesting books. The term 'eccentric' has a whiff of madness about it, but it's the people deploying the term willy-nilly who are truly bonkers – and, worse still, boring".

RA RA RIOT

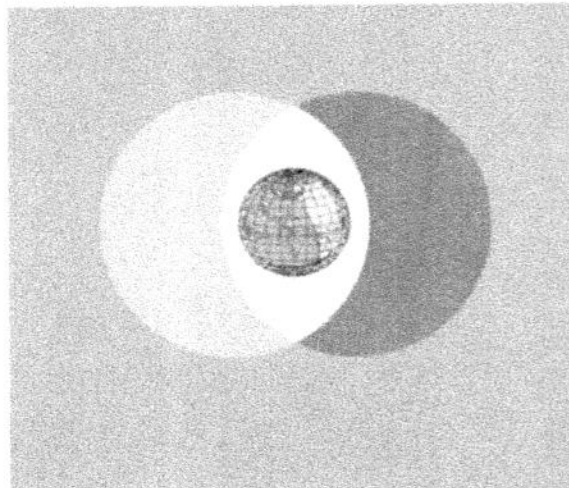

In August the new album by Ra Ra Riot, *The Rhumb Line* included a new take on *Suspended in Gaffa* described by the *Washington Post* reviewer as "circus-punk" and by Rebecca Raber (Pitchfork 14th August) as "safe for those who are uncomfortable with Bush's theatrical trilling". The band were interviewed on the US National Public Radio on 29th August. The interviewer noted that all of the band were younger than the 1982 song, and that it was not the only Kate song in their repertoire. One of the band's first songs was a cover of *Hounds of Love*: "I was going through a huge Kate Bush phase, and managed to convince everyone that it'd be a great party song" Miles said, "I was really into Kate Bush, and a lot of her arrangements have strings and a lot of grand things happening". The album reviewers quickly spotted the tribute: "Another standout recording on the album is the Kate Bush cover... Straying slightly from Bush's quivering vocal theatrics, the band uses pots, spoons, empty water jugs, crashing drums and a flurry of strings to create a similarly emotive musical landscape" (Tara Morgan *Boise Weekly* 17th September).

The band were interviewed by Aaron Jentzen in the *Nashville Scene* on 12th November: "Another presence also haunts *The Rhumb Line*, one that's a bit surprising for a bunch of musicians in their early 20s: Kate Bush. The album includes a cover of Bush's *Suspended in Gaffa*, and traces of her influence turn up, such as a hint of *Cloudbusting* in Ra Ra Riot's brooding *Winter '05*, dominated by Alexandra Lawn's cello and Rebecca Zeller's violin. While learning covers to fill time at an early gig, one song the band learned was Bush's seminal *Hounds of Love*. While vocalist Wesley Miles had long been a fan, this tune was the band's real introduction to Bush. 'Once we started playing that song, we all became more interested, and we have a lot of admiration and respect for her as an artist,' says Bonacci. 'For me, her song-writing or the structures of her songs are referenced a lot in the way we put things together.' While tracking *The Rhumb Line*, they recorded *Suspended in Gaffa* to use as a potential B-side for a single. 'We never planned to put it on the album or anything,' he says, 'but one thing led to another.' Bush's influence also helps in understanding the sonic and lyrical density of Ra Ra Riot's music-a link to both ornate art-rock and some of the more original pop artists of the 1980s".

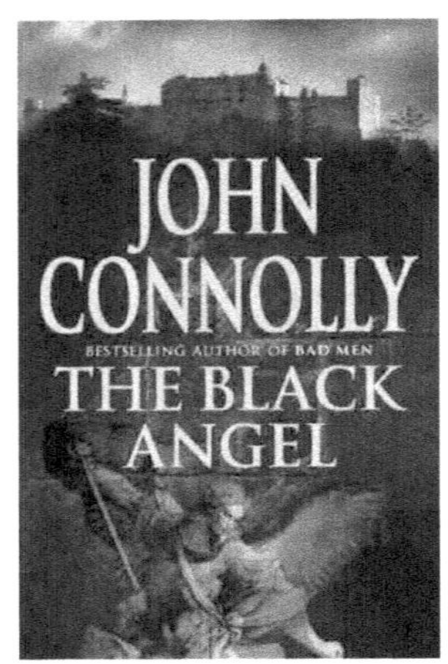

On his blog John Connolly, Irish 'crime meets paranormal' writer best known for his Charlie Parker novels, confessed "like a great many men in their thirties and forties, I've always been a little in love with Kate Bush, and perhaps that adds a certain sensual charge to her music for me". *Ne T'en Fui Pas* was on the 'soundtrack' CD presented with the first edition of his 2005 novel *The Black Angel*. In a 'Who wouldn't you mind being stuck in an elevator with?' piece on the Canadian *National Post* site on 25th October he chose Kate: "I've had a crush on her since childhood. *Wuthering Heights* was the first single that I ever bought with my own money, but she doesn't write, she doesn't call..."

The rock critic of the *Vancouver Courier* (7th November) was not impressed with Madonna's latest performances: "Not that Our Lady of Perpetual Motion invented the aerobic pop music spectacle with miked singing. That distinction belongs to British singer Kate Bush, who mastered and abandoned the form in the late '70s". Paul Morley wasn't happy with Coldplay, as he indicated in his *Daily Telegraph* blog of 27th November: "whenever I read a list of their influences... it's usually my favourite music – the stern and sensual 'Berlin' era Bowie... the mystically aching Kate Bush, the lonely longing pulse of Kraftwerk... They should sound like my favourite group, but instead sound like a literate, slightly darker Take That".

Songs were being written about Kate. Bands were being named after her songs. As Seán reported, in May, Viva City released their new single, *Kate Bush*. Described in the press release as "a storming two minute slice of leery swaggering electropop", Bruce Tate of the band said: "The track is about old and new, appreciating what has come before, whilst also creating a sound of the future." Sample lyric: "Yeah, in action how like an angel, In apprehension how like a God, You're the greatest beauty of the world... And I'm letting it in, To fear love is to fear life..." Just where did US band Remy Zero get their name? Interviewed on Drowned in Sound (11th October): "The honest answer would be Shelby, Cinjun's brother named the band from a pilot character... Cinjun and I always thought it was, because we're all big Kate Bush fans when we were kids from her song *Army Dreamers* in the second verse of the song, there's something about 'Mommy's hero' and we always thought it was 'Remy Zero'". The band Heads We Dance according to Arjan (blog 12th November) "took their name from Kate Bush's *Heads We're Dancing* from her 1989 album *Sensual World*... Had Kate only now really arrived? In December 2008 with the first release of one her tracks on the SingStar karaoke system? It was inevitably *Babooshka*, but perhaps to hope for *Get Out of My House* or *Big Stripey Lie* was expecting too much.

More comparisons: Polly Scattergood was "Brit School grad with a fantastically unique voice. The new Kate Bush?" (*The Sun*); Chibi (The Birthday Massacre) "is closer to British singer Kate Bush, and she shares Bush's taste for juxtaposing lullaby melodies and grand flourishes"; The Bottomfeeders were "Kate Bush meets Anthony And The Johnsons"; Bella Koshka produces "highly atmospheric songs that suggest Kate Bush"; Becky Ninkovic "think Karen O. meets Kate Bush"; Annie Clark "sophisticated neuvo-Kate Bush act"; Jesca Hoop "calls to mind Kate Bush and Björk"; Manya Repnikova "conjures some of Kate Bush's best work"; Czech violinist and singer Iva Bittova "eccentric leaping in the style of Kate Bush"; Amnesia "Kate-Bush-on-nitrous shockwave"; PJ Harvey: "seemed to channel spirits and the ghosts of her deceased ancestors – as well as Kate Bush"; Goldfrapp "indie's answer to Kate Bush" and Martha Wainright "swoops and soars like Kate Bush at her finest".

And the actual Kate? Despite all of those who at the end of 2008 again thought she had gone into retirement for good, she was working, writing, and recording. As was confirmed by Del Palmer when on January 17th 2009 he posted on his My Space page that he had been in the studio with "you-know-who." What seemed to be afoot is that Kate was going to work alternately for a period of months firstly on new versions of songs which had previously appeared on *The Sensual World* and *The Red Shoes*, and then on new material. The idea and hope was that she could meet her own suggestion of producing two albums in one year, though it was not yet clear which year that would be.

A feature in the February 2009 edition of *The Word* which was published in early January included an (old) photo on the cover and a ten page feature with classic interviews inside. Kate's songs were featured in 'The Great British Songbook' season at the Shaw Theatre: this series which started in February featured new arrangements of well-known and more novel works by many of Britain's leading composers and lyricists. The Puppinis were still touring their Kate cover: "When Puppini scales Kate Bush's *Wuthering Heights*, all mad eyes and ripe growl, it matches the comedic disrespect most had for it on first hearing, but you can't deny the good time being had by a happy crowd" (Nick Hasted *Independent* 6th January).

A new generation of comparisons beckoned: "Florence and The Machine offer a sleazy blend of Kate Bush and PJ Harvey" (*Sunday Mirror* 1st January); "Slightly bonkers singer-songwriters like Kate Bush, Björk and PJ Harvey are not far-fetched comparisons" (Ian Youngs); "While sounding nothing like Kate Bush, Florence and her Machine share Bush's individuality and art-schooled perspective" (Ally Carnwath *Guardian*); "Lady GaGa, La Roux, Little Boots. Many of the above acts take their inspiration from eccentric '80s pop icons like Madonna, Kate Bush" (Ian Youngs BBC News); "Born in Norway and based in Sweden the veteran chanteuse Ane Brun draws from influences as broad as... the emotive pop of Kate Bush and the classic folk of Joan Baez" (*Metro*); "If Kate Bush died and went to hell she might sound like London gothic folk chanteuse Catherine A.D. ... kooky and spooky and very good" (Paul Lester *The Guardian*).

One comparison, however, hit the nail on the head. This was Andrew Eaton in *The Scotsman* 7th January regarding the break up of Kraftwerk: "Like Kate Bush, they are labelled eccentric partly because they are uninterested in participating in the media whirl. They simply have no desire to be famous".

The memoirs of Mark Radcliffe BBC Radio DJ were published in March and serialised in the *Daily Mail*. The memoirs included a number of anecdotes about his meetings with Kate: "One night in 2004 I played one of Kate's tracks on my Radio 2 show and bemoaned the lack of any new material since *The Red Shoes* in 1993. I said: 'Kate, if you're out there, 'phone and let us know you're OK.' ...then we began to count the days we hadn't heard from her. It seemed appropriate to have a physical manifestation of the campaign and so the Bushometer was born. Then, the following year, word began to circulate that Kate was set to release a new double album. I had been at school with the head of EMI, Tony Wadsworth. Tony said he would put in a word for me. I got a message on my mobile phone: 'Hi, Mark. It's Kate Bush here. I've been told we might be meeting up for a chat. Sounds like fun. Give me a ring when you've got a minute.' I found her chatty, funny and inquisitive. The last thing I expected was for Kate to invite me to her house. Major artists never invite you to their house. And they certainly don't ask you what you'd like for lunch. But Kate did.

Mark Radcliffe

"On the day, myself, engineer Chris Lee, and my producer, John Leonard, turned up in front of some large electronic gates. Expecting a long drive through Narnia-like grounds it was a surprise to find the house immediately on our left. And there she was on the doorstep – barefoot, wearing jeans and her long hair unfussily clipped up. Everything just seemed so normal which, in a way, seemed weird because Kate had assumed such mythical status down the years. Her attitude to the notion of celebrity was bewilderment. Kate explained that she was not withdrawn from the world in some big 'vampire castle', but just needed a quiet place where the creative process could truly function. Though she said she found it fun being a pop star in the early days, it was never what she wanted to be."

On 1st April the BBC screened the first part of a major two-part documentary entitled *The Queens of British Pop*. This celebrated Britain's most admired female singers from the Sixties to the Noughties. Del Palmer was interviewed and David Gilmour, Tori Amos, Alison Goldfrapp, Mark Radcliffe, Andrew Powell and John Carder Bush all appeared to give their assessment of

Kate. On his MySpace page Del had explained that the BBC wanted him to talk about Kate's unique song-writing style, her creativity in the studio and the songs which have inspired so many musicians. John Lydon's mum was quoted as saying of Kate 'Oh Johnny it sounds like a bag of cats!'.

Seán organised the third "annual" Sensual Walk for Kate fans in June. This was actually written up by Maeve Galvin in the *Dublin Evening Herald* on 15th June: "The walk is called after the singer-songwriter's 1989 hit *The Sensual World* which makes references to James Joyce's *Ulysses*. Organisers say the reclusive artist is aware of the event which is always scheduled to take place around Bloomsday, June 16. After the scenic trek, fans retired to a pub for the evening. Even the location is significant because Howth Summit is where Leopold Bloom proposed to Molly in Joyce's book. Organiser Seán Twomey (36) said: 'It is an excuse for us to get together because she doesn't tour, so you don't get a chance to meet other fans unless you make your own event. We wanted to make use of Howth, which is so beautiful. A lot of people forget about up here, so it's an excuse to have a walk and a bit of craic.'"

In October, Beck Siàn (Kate's cousin's daughter; Hannah Bush, Kate's mother, being her great aunt) released her new album *Luminous Wings and Unseen Things* with cover artwork by Krys. *Uncut* magazine compiled a list of the 'Top 20 Albums of the Decade' and *Aerial* came in no.18 with a half-page splash: "Worth the wait, the enigma's first album in twelve years was brave, beautiful, and dazzlingly eccentric". On Saturday 31st October Kate fans gathered at Haworth for what was unbelievably the 25th Anniversary Wuthering Hike, a quarter of a century since *HomeGround* had organised the first walk of Kate fans to Top Withens.

See Deborah's 2006 article *Kate Bush: Performing and Creating Queer Subjectivities on Lionheart* which is a Google click away

On 9th December double bass player and Pentangle founder member Danny Thompson (veteran of *The Dreaming* and *Hounds of Love*) discussed on Edi Stark's 'Stark Talk' programme (BBC Radio Scotland) his friendship with the late John Martyn, and also his current projects, including "Recording – how about this – with Kate Bush, a week ago. What a lovely lady she is. She's so fantastic. Stunning.". It was plain that work on the twin projects was proceeding. Our guess at that point that the earliest release date for a new album would be end of 2011. The Earliest! This is probably the only time a *HomeGround* first estimate of a release date was actually correct.

In the Autumn of 2009 we had been hearing whispers (mainly from Rolf Harris himself) about Kate recording a track with him. In a December radio interview he clarified that this track was a version of *She Moved Through The Fair*. This was according to him "the best thing I've ever done" and he was hoping for an early release. So were we, but we were both to be disappointed.

Graphic opposite: Steven Brown

At the beginning of 2010 Kate's new business unit began seriously to come together when one-time EMI worldwide vice chairman and EMI Recorded Music North America chairman and CEO David Munns accepted her invitation to become her consultant. As he would say in an interview with *Music Week* a year later: "People think I'm managing and I'm really consulting. I drift in and out of these projects". *Music Week* commented: "His association with Kate goes back to when she was first signed to EMI and the release of her first album *The Kick Inside* in 1978". In the Spring of 2010 another part of the new project came together. The complete ownership of *The Dreaming*, *Hounds of Love*, *The Sensual World* and *The Red Shoes* reverted back to Kate, and planning for re-release on Kate's own label could commence.

There was about to be a minor stampede of books about Kate. Well – you wait long enough! First up was a tome by Deborah M. Withers entitled *Adventures in Kate Bush and Theory* (HammerOn Press). The press release described it as: "providing the first ever in-depth engagement with the philosophy of Kate Bush's music... Here is the polymorphously perverse Kate, the witchy Kate, the queer Kate; the Kate who moves beyond the mime... Drawing on cutting edge feminist philosophy, critical theory and queer studies, *Adventures in Kate Bush and Theory* makes theory accessible to new audiences. Through analysis of the music, film, video and dance of Kate Bush, it breaks down boundaries between the academic and popular, showing that theory can be sordid, funny and relevant – despite what most people think."

Deborah M. Withers had been interpreting and telling stories about Kate Bush's music for most of the Noughties. She said: "I want readers to roam with me through Kate Bush's music, unlocking the codes that are within them. Theory is one of the instruments I use to crack these codes". Even though some less academically inclined, or more academically inclined but less post modernist inclined readers might be put off by reviews such as this by Sian Norris in *The F-Word*: "a superb exploration into the gender, queer, post-colonial and cultural theory that lies behind the music of singer, dancer and cultural icon Kate Bush", others found the book interesting and stimulating. Mark Radcliffe described it as "an in-depth labour of love from a genuine Bush fanatic" Ian who reviewed it for KBNI enjoyed it immensely.

In the April *Mojo* (published in March) Kate joined those paying tribute to the career of Peter Gabriel: "*I have huge amounts of respect for Peter and his work. He is one of the rare artists who is instantly recognisable through his music, with his stunning voice and*

his individual style of writing and arranging." *Mojo*'s writers voted on a Peter Gabriel Top Ten and Kate featured on two of the tracks, *Games Without Frontiers* ("Gabriel's sinister child-catcher delivery and Kate Bush's eerie 'jeux sans frontières'") and *Don't Give Up* ("Kate Bush is unbowed wifey, injecting hope with every tremor one of the most poignant vocal performances in pop history.").

'Music Matters' was a new initiative by a collective of people across the music industry. The aim was to remind listeners of the significance and value of music and to act as a guide for music fans and help differentiate legal music services from illegal ones. To get this point across the new body commissioned a number of short films focusing on several well-known artists including Kate. This was created by Elliot Dear who explained: "I learned that she had an interesting philosophy and approach to making music... I thought it was important to capture the essence of what Kate Bush is visually... I thought a fairy tale storybook format would be the most fitting way to present her story."

On 2nd April in another part of the wood (Joe's Bar in New York) Theo Bleckmann again gave his wonderful concert 'Hello Earth! The Music of Kate Bush' with his own distinctive interpretation of Kate's songs. An album was now being planned.

Graeme Thomson has authored biographies of Willie Nelson and Elvis Costello and made regular contributions to *The Guardian*, *Observer*, *The New Statesman*, and *The Word*.

The second book to arrive - on 4th May - was *Under The Ivy – The Life & Music of Kate Bush* by Graeme Thomson (Omnibus Press). His book was described in the blurb as follows: "This is the first ever in-depth study of Kate Bush's life and career... features... revealing new interviews with those who have viewed from up close both the public artist and the private woman... undertakes a full analysis of Bush's art... Combining a wealth of new research with rigorous critical scrutiny... offers a string of fresh insights and perspectives"

Many in the Kate-speaking world had mixed feelings about this book. It certainly does offer a serious and in-depth study of Kate's music as one would expect from such an experienced and capable music journalist. However, in correspondence in 2008 before the book was published we were told in clear terms that the author was not interested in writing about Kate's private life because it would be a waste of valuable time that would be far better spent trying to analyse her work; and secondly, that he was not interested in that side of her life.

Unfortunately the book as published plainly devotes a number of pages to precisely that. Now it may be that many would argue that such examination is a natural part of any such biography, and any subject of a biography ought to expect such treatment, and the treatment here was certainly not either voyeuristic or salacious. However if Thomson claims to understand Kate, he would have understood that she would be deeply averse to any depiction of her private life. It was plain that she would see this as an intrusion, and as she has stated many times, something she would regard as irrelevant to her making of music. Thomson knew all this, and knew this was the pitfall of all earlier biography attempts.

The mystery therefore is why he decided the book required him to do it anyway. It was plain from what he told Seán and ourselves that he wanted to take a fresh look at Kate's body of work, without following the chronological framework used so often before, to write something insightful and elegant, a book which was genuinely revealing in terms of her working process. He wanted to redress his own disappointment that nothing so far had been published which did her justice. In many ways he succeeded in doing just that - at least as far as you can do such a thing without involvement of Kate herself - but then he fell into exactly the same pit. It may be that he regarded it as a biographer's duty even in the face of opposition from the subject to record such details to present the rounded picture.

Seán set out the dilemma: "On the one hand, we know very well that Kate doesn't approve of books like this about her and finds them intrusive, and as far as their veracity is concerned, anecdotal at best. As such, those closest to Kate and Kate herself have never co-operated with the writers of biographies. On the other hand, this is clearly the best written, most well researched and critically applauded biography of Kate yet released. There is nothing mean-spirited within its pages and the book respects and celebrates Kate's work without losing perspective. I found it intelligent and very fair." On the Kate Bush News & Information Board Seán continued the theme: "In the book's credits you'll read a long list of people who have co-operated in the making of the book. Perhaps they had the same conundrum as me when approached by the author. Do I politely ignore his request or do I give my input and advice to try to make the book avoid the pitfalls of what's been published before? I chose to give Graeme as much friendly advice as I could over a couple of emails and a 'phone call, with emphasis on respecting Kate the private person, avoiding tabloid clichés and sensationalist rubbish and focusing on the music and work itself. Whether he achieved that is up to anyone who reads the book to decide. So there you go, unofficial biographies are strange conflicted beasts and there are far too many of them."

Thomson had written to Kate out of courtesy before starting work to declare his intentions and invite her participation. Elsewhere he has stated "I was always aware that it was highly unlikely that she or any members of her family or closest friends would contribute, but I didn't see this as a huge hindrance. The book I wanted to write was principally focused on my critical analysis of her work filtered through an understanding of her instincts as an artist and where they came from."

Thomson himself responded to the criticism as follows: "Ultimately, I suppose, readers and interested parties will make up their own minds about the book and my intentions. I understand any reservations; indeed, I anticipated them. But let me make clear two things: there is no suggestion that this book is in any way endorsed by Kate Bush. I wouldn't want any reader to be under that misapprehension. And, having accepted that, I think most people who then choose to read it will recognise it as a serious work: detailed, highly respectful and in no way salacious or mean-minded. "

Extracts from the book appeared as the cover story of the June edition of *Uncut* Magazine. This focused on *Hounds of Love*, as it approached its 25th anniversary. The book obtained very positive reviews and mentions. Thomson appeared in a number of press items, and seemed for a while to be the expert on Kate to whom the media could refer.

Time passes, and those close to us pass away. In April, Morris Pert, who had played percussion on some of Kate's most famous recordings, went to join the band upstairs. In 1977 *Billboard* voted him the fourth best jazz and rock percussionist in the world, and the famous drummer Buddy Rich said he was one of the greatest drummers he had ever played with. In May, former managing director of EMI, Bob Mercer, died after a brief battle with lung cancer. Kate posted on her website: "I will miss Bob so much, he was such a dear friend. It's thanks to Bob that I have been able to spend my life making music. He signed me to EMI when I was 16 and was like family to me. He was loved by so many - Bob thank you so much for making my dream come true. The world won't be the same without you". Del posted his own tribute on his MySpace Page, and Dave who had worked at EMI said: "Although I never met Bob, he was something of a legend at EMI as a very artist driven man, a proper music man, who worked with many EMI acts, especially Kate, he was one of the key people in her being signed to the company and was very supportive of her in the early days, our thoughts are with his family and friends including Kate".

Talking of that 25th anniversary of the release of *Hounds of Love,* in July that classic 1985 album was reissued in a special audiophile vinyl edition pressed on 180g marble vinyl. Audio Fidelity used a process by which the original sound was incised "real time" onto the disc's surface by laser to obtain the sound of the original analogue master tape. Something very relevant was Kate's developing taste for the warmth of analogue sound, and indeed for vinyl. In August she approved the test pressing for a similar re-issue of *The Sensual World.*

July saw a complete revamp of the Kate Bush News & Information site, with the news pages being converted a blog style. Seán also brought in a lot more social network integration throughout the site, a new video gallery, new standing features on Kate-related artists and a new Gig calendar. Basically endless new ways to bring all the Kate news and information.

Almost unbelievable anniversaries were coming thick and fast. On 5th August 2010 it was 25 years from the release of *Running Up That Hill.* Seán commented: "In those days, the gap of three years since *The Dreaming* seemed enormous! Kate's perceived lack of visibility meant that a lot of people had almost forgotten about her. Nothing could have prepared them for this extraordinary first taster from the *Hounds of Love* album."

A very interesting book was published in August: *Electric Eden Unearthing Britain's Visionary Music* (Faber & Faber). The blurb says: "Rob Young investigates how the idea of folk has been handed down and transformed by successive generations - song collectors, composers, Marxist revivalists, folk-rockers, psychedelic voyagers, free festival-goers, experimental pop stars and electronic innovators." This included "the visionary pop of Kate Bush". This extraordinary and well-received and reviewed book was described in *The Hot Press* as "sprawling and often awe-inspiring... best described as a pysychogeographical history of British folk music... a passionately researched, carefully written and compulsively readable map of the leys and songlines of an oral culture with its roots in pre-Roman times and its branches in the charts". There has probably been nothing like it since John Mitchell's *Camelot and the Vision of Albion.* Kate is featured in a section on '80's mavericks toward the end of the book which deals also with David Sylvian, Talk Talk, and Julian Cope.

Morris Pert

We first noticed Theo Bleckman's show in April. In September he was back with it at Le Poisson Rouge in New York: "vocalist Theo Bleckmann now takes on the mysterious songbook of British pop recluse Kate Bush. This project goes beyond merely re-creating Kate Bush's music but taking it to even further realms of sound and interpretation". This performance was reviewed by the *New York Times*: "Kate Bush is a special fit for him. The arc of her career, uneasily abutting art-rock and alternative music, jibes with his own off-kilter profile. And she's another transfixing singer with a penchant for careful diction and spooky connotation, and deep interest in the subconscious."

A clip of Kate and Rolf's version of *She Moved Through the Fair* escaped on to YouTube in September but was soon removed at the request of the publishers. Rolf had frequently mentioned the duet in interviews and had been anxious to

Ken Livingstone.

see it released. The clip was enough to indicate Rolf's trademark digeridoo along with swirling Irish whistles and a soaring vocal from Kate.

On September 8th *Never For Ever* was 30. This was – we should all remember – the first ever UK number one album by a solo British female artist. Maybe one day we will hear that missing title track.

Finally on 16th September the album that many see as amongst Kate's finest work was 25. Seán said: "We could talk about the album on this site for the rest of 2010, so instead let's just listen to the magnificent *Hounds of Love* today, it's as thrillingly fresh and exciting as it was on the day of release."

It was also 31½ years since Kate's only live tour, and while we waited with greater or lesser degrees of optimism for a proper release on DVD of some or all of the visual records of those performances, a KBNI site member, A Rose Growing Old, took the plunge to create a YouTube version from what is to hand amongst available video from contemporary TV broadcasts, audio recordings and stills. This prompted Del Palmer to comment: "A re-work of this tour show has been something I've argued for intensely over the years. Although it's now over 30 years old I still think there is a market for it… All the Hammersmith shows were filmed in their entirety and the raw footage still exists including backstage footage… All of the soundtrack recordings exist also. There is even a whole video recording made of just the band which we did during the second day… This was because the cameramen could not gain positions on the stage during the concerts to film us in close up. So, we did a whole mime to playback run of the entire show to enable close-ups to be filmed… Alas, none of this footage was used... As much as I hate to say this I do think that none of this footage will ever see the light of day… A shame but there you go!"

In response to the further excitement this engendered Del posted: "I'm as frustrated as you are about this whole thing believe me. I really have argued about making this stuff available. Especially as it was our one and only concert tour… But, well, in the final analysis it's Kate's work, creation and production… She MUST be allowed the final say in this… She strongly feels that this stuff is now too old, technically deficient and unrepresentative of her and her work… I don't like it but there it is… But I do still hold on to the hope that, one day, she'll change her mind".

A Rose Growing Old was touched by the interest in his project. He revealed that the background was that his mother had died the previous year "and in my despair, I turned my car stereo on the way home from the hospice. *A Coral Room* immediately played. I was completely devastated at the time, but Kate's words and voice kept me going on that long, lonely drive. I resolved immediately to do what little I could to repay her by promoting her genius in whatever way I was able… of course, if this also prompts Mr Palmer into nagging Miss Bush to release a DVD of the Tour, then I might even have done some good for the entire planet!"

On 23rd September Luke Turner of The Quietus interviewed Ken Livingstone as he made another attempt to regain his position as Mayor of London, and asked Ken what he thought about *Ken*: KL: Of course I was a fan of the song. What was particularly funny was that I think she was bigger in the States than here, but it used to be the case that ten years ago there are people writing 'who is Ken? What is GLC?' I suppose it's a bit like if someone heard about the Bananarama track and asked 'what cheap fares?' You have to be at least 50 to remember it.

LT: There's a line in the Kate Bush song where she calls you a 'sex machine'

KL: If only this were true. If only Kate Bush had seen me as a real sex machine!

The man with the child in his eyes? At the end of September we noted that the press was having great fun with the story that former TV presenter Steve Blacknell was putting up for auction a handwritten copy of the lyrics to *The Man with the Child in his Eyes,* claiming to be the original inspiration for the song. The reserve price was £10,000. We doubted if the origin of any of Kate's songs is quite so simple, but noted that the continuing media interest boded well for her next release of work.

At the very end of the month were the usual annual complaints about who had not been nominated for the US Rock and Roll Hall of Fame. Ann Powers at the *LA Times* music blog: "Kate Bush: The godmother of New Wave, a pioneer of electronic music and the definitive artist of what I call "ultrafemme" pop, this thorny English rose is probably too reclusive to ever make it into the Rock Hall's party crowd. But with artists like Maxwell and Big Boi speaking up for her, Bush is ripe for re-evaluation."

In other news Gemma Arterton wanted to play Kate in a biopic, should anyone actually be making one… comedy duo Frisky and Mannish melded Kate Nash's cockney pop patter *Foundations* and Kate's *Wuthering Heights* into "a jaw-droppingly brilliant twin-Kate soundclash" …MTV.com noted that Maxwell's album *Now* had topped the US charts, and considered that the best moment on the album ("and perhaps the most astonishing moment of Maxwell's career") was his cover of *This Woman's Work…* Placebo's cover of *Running Up That Hill* was to feature on the *Vampire Diaries* soundtrack album… and the Cardiff Mardi Gras included a presentation by Deborah Withers of her recent book *Adventures in Kate Bush and Theory.*

At the beginning of October Audio Fidelity announced *The Sensual World* as the second of their vinyl Kate Bush re-masters for 2nd November. At the end of October Kate was at Elton John's annual party for the birthday of his partner David Furnish. Boy George, who was also there, tweeted: "I met Kate Bush at David Furnish's birthday, it was an amazing night and Kate is beyond adorable! OMG!" and later: "I was a bit awestruck but she has a beautiful energy and is super humble!" and later still: "I have a lovely pic with Kate Bush but it's private, I promised, she is so beautiful!" In the 31st October *Daily Mirror* Sharleen Spiteri gushed: "I went to a dinner party and KATE BUSH was there! She's an amazing, wonderful lady. I was so thrilled to have met her! She still has huge hair.". On the KBNI Forum Colin commented: "Kate left her house and went to a birthday party like any normal person. There goes her recluse cred. (insert eye roll here)".

David Mitchell whose unusual novel, *Cloud Atlas*, the Wachowski brothers were turning into a movie, was asked by Indian paper *The Pioneer* how other media had influenced the way he translated literary images replies: "Some singer-songwriters' albums feel like novels: later Kate Bush being inspiring examples"... "Unless you're Kate Bush, you can't really write interesting songs about domesticity, washing baby clothes and breast-feeding": Charlotte Church in the *Daily Telegraph*... Pop singer MPHO performed *Running Up That Hill* as part of an all-star bill which came together to celebrate the frontman of electro pop band Ou Est Le Swimming Pool, who took his own life shortly after an appearance at the Pukkelpop festival in Belgium in August... Chris Roberts (there's a name I remember from way back) thought Kate's backing vocals on *Games Without Frontiers* were "barely audible" ...Kate's *Delius* was part of a set performed by The Song Company at Auckland Town Hall, New Zealand... Corin Tucker, formerly the guitarist and singer of feminist punk rock trio Sleater-Kinney asked what music the band was listening to whilst making new album *1,000 Years?* said "I also really loved Kate Bush's last album *Aerial*, which does refer to motherhood"... "I would wander in looking for a Blondie release, and a wise record store clerk would send me home with a Kate Bush album instead" - Anil Prasad who created the online music magazine innerviews.org... "Christian Dior's Poison was another one that promised a sensory trip to the dark side. It belonged to that strain of stridently purple-packaged products - Silk Cut, Dairy Milk, Kate Bush - against whose evil influence we girls were constantly warned": Judy Rumbold recalled her complicated relationship with beauty products as a "pasty-faced Catholic teenager growing up in Birmingham".

In early November the Music Industry Trusts Award charity dinner, in its 19th year, was held at London's Grosvenor House Hotel in aid of Nordoff Robbins and The BRIT Performing Arts and Technology School. Spotify sponsored the MITS first digital auction, which included "a very rare John Lennon and Yoko Ono naked statue donated by Kate Bush". *HomeGround* had noted in the "Five Years Ago" for Autumn 1981: "At the end of the year Kate's name emerged from its new obscurity when it was widely publicised that she had participated in the annual Sotheby's auction of Rock Memorabelia, buying a rare perspex and plastic sculpture of John Lennon and Yoko Ono in the famous 'Two Virgins' pose".

Graphic: Izabela Samsonowicz

On 29th November we noted that on the New York Capital blog Gillian Reagan asked some friends to talk about their favourite comfort albums: "the albums we find ourselves revisiting over and over again, either for a dose of nostalgia or to honor a seasonal tradition.". Rich Juzwiak, who wrote about pop culture for the VH1 Blog, his personal site FourFour and elsewhere, chose *Hounds of Love*: "It is ferociously creative in composition, with chord changes to make your head spin and an early embrace of sampling in a non-hip-hop context. Kate's voice is an emotional wonder, often a confounding counterpoint to the lyrics they're singing... The moments of beauty, like *And Dream of Sheep* will be that way for eternity, while what hasn't aged so well takes on new life as camp... Kate Bush isn't for everyone, but I do think that if you think she isn't for you, you at least owe it to yourself to try harder."

And there were tribute parties: Brisbane, Australia Sunday 7th November 2010 at the Stage Door Dinner Theatre. This was to celebrate the 25th anniversary of *Hounds of Love* and featured a selection of Brisbane's most

Matt Berry

unique cabaret performers performing their favourite Kate Bush songs live on stage. "25 years ago, the *Hounds of Love* album by Kate Bush was released to commercial and critical acclaim. This party pays tribute to this special album... the enigmatic woman... her vast music catalogue... and the fans she continues to inspire". Simon Chan created a "sing-a-long" version of *Under the Ivy* for the party. Arranged by his long time collaborator, David Lazar it was "a very faithful and remarkable rendition, considering David had no idea of the song."

In Chicago a tribute night on November 30th: was inevitably entitled 'December will be magic!' and featured "The music of Kate Bush and the artists she has influenced. Also, Kate Bush 'Performs!'. Dan Bridgens and Mario Bucca in their drag debut!". "Kate" a dance show based on *Hounds of Love* was staged in Berlin in December. Linda Weissig choreographed the show, which included several performers with disabilities, and featured *Cloudbusting*, *Hounds of Love*, *And Dream of Sheep Under Ice*, *Waking the Witch*, *Hello Earth*, and *The Morning Fog* in the form of "dream sequences".

By the Autumn of 2010 it looked already as though 2011 was going to be a very busy year for Kate. Work continued both on the reworked tracks, and the new material, and with Kate's new label coming into shape there was consideration of album re-issues, re-issues of the early albums that remained with EMI with unreleased tracks, and perhaps even a new compilation.

Del Palmer's album 'Gift'

Sadly in early November the premature death of Rachel Anne Lisi, sent shockwaves through the Kate Bush fan community. Her brilliance, talent, passion and warmth will never be forgotten. Our thoughts were with her family and friends

In late November London duo, Paper Crows (Emma Panas and Duncan McDougall), released a cover of *Cloudbusting* which used instrumental elements of Björk's *Human Behaviour*... John Grant former frontman of The Czars was asked the usual 20 Questions on Pop Matters. At no.9 was "The creative masterpiece you wish bore your signature?": "I think *Hounds of Love* or *The Dreaming* by Kate Bush are the sorts of masterpieces I could wish I had created" ... Matt Berry who played the domineering boss in 'The IT Crowd' had a new album *Witchazel* soon to be described by Kitty Empire in *The Observer* as "deranged satire": Matt described the album thus: "Well, for me, 1978 was quite a big year in terms of being frightened by things, one of which was *Watership Down* and the other was Kate Bush. I also remember seeing Kate Bush on TV and I just thought that the countryside was full of sexy witches, but they were still witches. So it was that kind of atmosphere that I wanted to put into *Witchazel*, that kind of 1970s rustic British folk sound... I've felt that way ever since I saw Kate Bush performing *Wuthering Heights* on 'Top Of The Pops' as a child... she frightened the life out of me. Something about the way she stared right in to the camera with those wild, glaring eyes. She looked like a sexy witch and it had a huge impact on me".

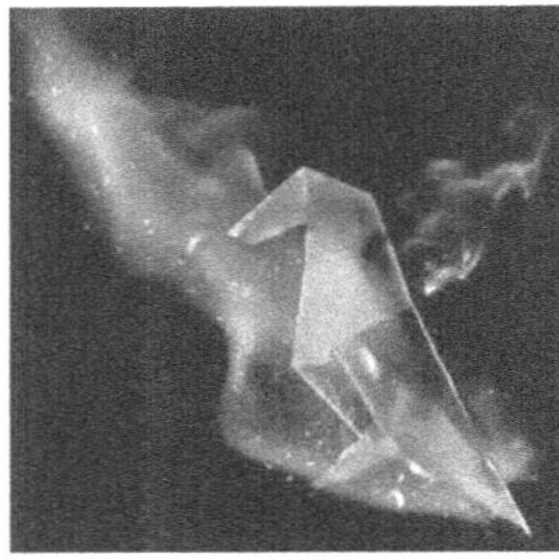

The Paper Crows, 'Cloudbusting';

Kiki Dee included a cover of *Running Up That Hill* in her European shows... Robyn credited Kate as influence (again): "I grew up in a theater family and learned to express my creativity in my own way and to be my own person. So for me, those things all kind of came together naturally, even in artists that I was listening to like Kate Bush"... Artinfo told us that Pierre Huyghe's new film had been causing a stir in the French art scene, with fellow artists, fans, and even students on field trips descending into the pitch-black basement of Marian Goodman's Marais space to experience *The Host and the Cloud*. This included most strenuously, a red-tinted disco scene with an unrelenting version of Kate Bush's shrill *Wuthering Heights* playing normally at first, then in reverse... a retro-review of Peter Gabriel (III aka "Melt") on SeattlePi refered to "Kate Bush's deliciously haunting, repetitive chorus 'jeux sans frontières'" on *Games Without Frontiers*.

In December Del Palmer released his second solo album *Gift*.

Kate was continuing her campaign to dominate soap soundtracks: "Duncan even brought his turntables and deftly switches the mood to accompany the sudden, exhilaratingly emotional sight of Dee and her newborn being wheeled towards the motley crew. As Kate Bush's *This Woman's Work* echoes throughout the otherwise soundless scene, the camera sweetly, hilariously, pans across the faces of all the men." (Poptimal review of 'It's Always Sunny in Philadelphia'). Elsewhere: "A surprise new buyer has emerged as a leading candidate to acquire EMI's catalogue with BMG revealing it now wants to become a player in recorded music. The source adds very little has been done with the works of other long-term EMI stars such as Kate Bush" *Music Week*; "You, Peter Gabriel, Kate Bush, David Byrne: there are certain established artists whose works seem very fresh no matter which era they were created or played in" Mike Ragogna interviewing Laurie Anderson in the Huffington Post; "Here's an attempt to summarize the level of insanity contained within this clip: Kate Bush puts on the worst wig ever made and pretends to be a child, while she and Don (her "dad," presumably) alter the weather using a huge machine made of gigantic French horns" SF Weekly Blog's on 'The Top 6 Weirdest Actor Cameos in Music Videos: Donald Sutherland in Kate Bush's *Cloudbusting*'; "The foundational things that shaped me as an artist were Kate Bush's *Hounds of Love*, Peter Gabriel's *Security*, The Cure's *Disintegration*, and The

Cocteau Twins' *Heaven or Las Vegas*" Charlotte Martin interviewed on Artist Direct. The 'Daily Breeze' 30th December noted that *If I Had a Hi-Fi* the cover versions album from "well-known indie band Nada Surf" included "songs from disparate artists from Depeche Mode to Kate Bush rendered in lush settings with acres of strummed acoustic and jangly electric guitars, lovely vocals and string arrangements".

In January 2011 there were at last public rumours of a new album from Kate. As Seán reported on Kate Bush News & Information: Quite a lot of people had been coming across an online rumour that Kate will be releasing a new album this year. As far as we could make out, the rumour stemmed from the 'Wotyougot' blog website, who claimed to have heard the news from "a reliable source". Their story was then picked up by Digital Spy and others soon latched on, including celebrity blogger Perez Hilton. Meanwhile Graeme Thomson posted a quote on his blog, apparently from someone at EMI: "Right to be cautious. These rumours always surface this time of year and there's no reason to think this is any different. We're hopeful that a new record may emerge this year, but I was saying the same to people in Jan of 2010 so who knows... only Kate herself. Let's keep fingers crossed! I'm feeling optimistic." Shortly afterwards the *NME* reported that Kate was likely to release new material in 2011: "The news comes after unsubstantiated reports about a new release from the fame-shunning musician recently surfaced on a music blog. Speaking in reaction to that report, Bush's spokesperson said a release from her is likely for 2011, although nothing is confirmed yet. They added that the new music from Bush would not necessarily mean a full-length follow-up to her last album 2005's *Aerial*, was on the way."

Other news was finally breaking cover. Kate Bush News & Information reported on 20th January: "Reissues on the way! Kate back in control of four EMI albums". Paul Williams wrote in *Music Week*: "Four Kate Bush albums are expected to be re-issued this year after the singer won back control of them from EMI, but there is no confirmation yet about any new material coming from her in 2011. *The Dreaming*, *Hounds of Love*, *The Sensual World* and *The Red Shoes*, which EMI originally released between 1982 and 1993, are all lined up to be re-issued with former EMI and PolyGram executive David Munns now acting as a consultant to her. He is quoted as saying: "There are other plans but I'm not able to talk about them right now. There's nothing ready until Kate says it's ready. That's always been the way."

On 5th January we noted with great sadness the death of Mick Karn: the great bassist for Japan whose fretless instrument graced Kate's *The Sensual World* (*Heads We're Dancing*). Mick had also worked on recording sessions for *Aerial* in 2002, and even gave fans the intriguing title of *How To Be Invisible*, but ultimately his work on the track didn't make it to the final mix. The first time he played bass for Kate was at the Prince's Trust performance in 1982. Del paid his own tribute: "Mick was a wonderfully creative player and an artist of rare talent. He was also a great energy to have around in any studio situation. He'll be missed by everyone who knew him".

"The critical reflex for singers who appear vaguely 'kooky' - Bat For Lashes, Alison Goldfrapp, Florence Welch – is to compare them to Kate Bush. Denny is more seldom invoked, which seems unfair, as she was the one who opened the way for others to follow... She died – aged 32 – in 1978, the year Kate Bush, the most iconic, unconventional and self-reliant female artist of the 1980s, released her first recordings" (Rob Young *Guardian* 8th January).

"Three Potential Royal Wedding Singers who may not be considered, but should be include Kate Bush, Dido and Annie Lennox" (Pam Gaulin 'Celebs' 11th January); "Guy Pearce admits he loved working with Kate Winslet on the Depression-era drama 'Mildred Pierce' because he has a bit of a crush on most Kates: 'Ahhh Kate Bush, still is in fact [my biggest crush] – it's her voice, how she looks, just the strange unique creature that she is!' Guy insisted" (Press Association 16th January); "The overall effect is so gripping, so chilling even, that it wouldn't be remiss to mention this song in the same breath as another great anti-war lament by a British female genius – namely, Kate Bush's *Army Dreamers*" (Nick Levine on *The Words that Maketh Murder* by PJ Harvey 'Digital Spy' 17th January).

Zoe Lyons

Mick Karn

In heavy metal circles they continued to love Kate: "The press release further cites the band's musical influences as including Morbid Angel, Emperor, Darkthrone, Neurosis, and... Kate Bush? Kate Bush? I guess that's cool...? I mean, my mom likes Kate Bush. Oh wait, no... she doesn't. So not even my mom likes Kate Bush. My mom is more metal." (Chris Harris on *Dark Meditations in Monastic Seclusion* the album by Shroud of Despondency 'Gun Shy Assasin' 21st January); "When you like everything from Dethklok to Kate Bush, I figure there has to be some sort of unifying theme. And I think it's this: I don't like music that feels ungrounded. You can't kick me in the ass if you don't have a foot on the floor. I don't like wimpy music. I don't like jangly guitars. I don't like music that feels unwieldy or feels as if it's floating in the ether. Even though Kate's stuff is somewhat ethereal, her songs have a certain... insistence... to them that keeps them grounded" (Beth Spencer 'Digital Artist' 21st January).

It was probably our fault. Zoe Lyons the comedian claimed that "Many years ago, while up a hill with the Kate Bush Fan Club eating magic fudge, Zoe stumbled upon the secret of inner peace. Just live life and be happy". An anecdote about climbing Glastonbury Tor with other Kate fans was one of the centrepieces of her 'Clownbusting' show which would run and run.

"ISR: Where do you see yourself five years from now? TAIO – I would love to be having lunch with Kate Bush" (interview with Break-out new wave band Kites Indie Soup 21st January); "Gemini gets a U.S. release in February with the cover of *Cloudbusting* the 'expansion'. Wild Nothing's dreamy, shoegaze-type sound is a perfect fit for this interpretation of the Kate Bush song and Wild Nothing, essentially a one-man show, renders it in a heavenly, ethereal manner that is quite delightful" (Review 'Grounds for Appeal' 22nd January); "Mila Soldatic is singing *Wuthering Heights* by Kate Bush. Mila sings this operatic song well, although not sure how many people will remember this song when it comes to voting." (Report on Croatia heat for Eurovision 2011 *Oikotimes* 22nd January); "The record features a clutch of cover versions, including a faithfully high-pitched take on Kate Bush's *Wuthering Heights*" (Nick Bond's review of Robyn Loau's second solo album *Sydney Star Observer* 24th January); "What I'm going for is to make music that's emotional and honest. I mean, I grew up listening to Kate Bush, Depeche Mode, Eurythmics, singing songs about making deals with God and all that" (Natalia Kills *Boston Pheonix* 26th January).

Also on 26th January, Julianne Escobedo Shepherd wrote in the 'Riff City' music column from New York a rather wonderful tribute: "Though not quite as elusive as Sade, the god Kate Bush is something like a unicorn in the music world. Breaks between her albums have felt like aeons for megafans during which we wondered if she'd just decided to pack it in. Bless the artist who takes pains and patience. After a press flurry around the record and a couple of interviews in which she debunked notions that she was a weirdo recluse because she didn't show up at star-flecked parties, she returned to silence. This week, the *NME* reported 2011 will likely see Bush's first new music in five years. Somebody send her a bouquet of flowers, and let us pray, too, that she continues to invoke the sacred nature of the mundane. Those early albums impacted countless musicians and still do. Bush taught the art of wringing poetry into a new romanticism that never adhered to the obvious or overwrought, and her wholehearted embrace of womanhood was, and is, empowering. It's the notion of being unbridled, expressed through impressionistic lyrics and the act of gaining strength through femininity – and it's a testament to her nuance, depth and fearlessness that it lives on".

In February, Terrra Firma finally admitted defeat and relinquished ownership of EMI to their bankers CitiGroup, who promptly wrote off £2.2 billion of debt and put up the company for sale. Warner was the most likely purchaser, but the damage had been done. EMI had lost many of its most prestigious artists, and whole areas of operation like South East Asia. Kate was quietly but relentlessly disconnecting.

Kate chose the title song from *Aerial* to be interpreted by UK artist Tim Wakefield in one of his highly collectible *Soundwaves* artworks. The resulting prints, created from digital images formed in the recording process, sample a section of the song. Wakefield listened to the music, the lyrics and the tempo of the song to decide what colours and shapes he's looking for before presenting them to the music artist. There was a limited run of fifty prints, each one hand-signed by Kate and Tim Wakefield, and individually hand-numbered, sold in co-operation with the Nordoff Robbins music therapy charity.

And then there was Noel Fielding! In late February the wonderful comedian (The Mighty Boosh) danced to *Wuthering Heights* in the BBC charity programme "Let's Dance for Comic Relief." Kate recorded a personal message for Noel: "Hi Noel, it's Kate here. I really love your work and I just want to wish you luck for tonight. Break a leg. Well, actually no, no, don't break a leg. Just win baby – WIN!" As an apparent consequence of this, *Wuthering Heights* appeared at no.2 in the iTunes Rock Songs Chart for 28th February 2011. The studio panel voted Noel's performance through to the final on March 12th but this was won by Charlie Baker and James Thornton. Noel would encounter Kate again quite soon.

On March 9th in Paris the Fall Winter collection by Miuccia Prada for Miu Miu was set to a soundtrack of Kate songs, namely *The Infant Kiss*, *Breathing*, parts of *Hammer Horror* and *L'Amour Looks Something Like You* and *In Search of Peter Pan*.

For 'Record Store Day' 16th April, a day to celebrate the independent record shops, Kate in cooperation with Audio Fidelity had prepared something special: a limited edition 10 inch four track vinyl *Hounds of Love* EP. The tracks chosen by Kate were *The Big Sky*, *Cloudbusting*, *Watching You Without Me*, and *Jig of Life*. Kate also personally selected the cover art.

New things were afoot. On 3rd March Kate's official Facebook page announced her official YouTube channel. For the fans who had made the distance, time was when a piece of paper in an envelope was the only connection. In 1978 the internet we now know and love was but a glint in the eyes of the military and the nerds who were making ARPAnet. On 10th March, KBNI added its own Facebook page, the day before Kate's official website put up the first teaser holding page for a new album. What was that filmstrip featuring the image from *The Red Shoes* all about? Kate as Sergei Eisenstein?

Thank You

Kyla Clay-Fox

I have to thank you eBay
For the joy you've given me
The triumph of a bargain
The TV without the screen
A motorbike with one wheel
The sex toy for my cat
The guy who left the feedback
That said I was a twat.

I've bid on every artifact
That you could wish to own
A piece of Toast with Jesus on
A joint rolled by The Stones
I've given up on Y-Fronts
After last weeks winning Bid –
I was glad to win the underpants –
I didn't want the skids.

I've won half a pint of Elvis sweat
One of Liberace's candles
I've a sheep dog bra with lace on
Once owned by Irenee Handl
I'd a bid on for some potion
for my husbands thinning hair –
But was beaten at last minute
By a bidder called Ms Blair.

Yes – I have to thank you eBay
For impending bankruptcy
I've bid myself to hell and back
For things I didn't need–
Auctioned off my working kidney
There's just one thing left for me
I'll sell my soul on eBay
Bidding starts at 50p.

Sunset

Lesley Sharp

Petticoats and Ribbons
Dancing wide across
And flaming high
Running crimson washes
Swathes and bathes
A burning sky
Grey smoked clouds
Catch falling gold
Liquid suns crescendo
Cradle the light
Of days last hold
The dancing sky's
flamenco

Beck Siàn

Her muse – and Music from a Haunted Forest

Issue 78: June 2007

My name is Beck Siàn. I have lived most of my life in Australia. My Nana and Kate's Ma were sisters. My father, David, is Kate's first cousin, and that makes me a second-cousin, or a cousin-once-removed, or something like that. Regardless of how the connection should be technically defined, Kate Bush has always been in my life.

One of my most recent memories of Kate dates back to 1995. I was twenty one years old, sitting across the table from her, eating curry, and absolutely awestruck. All of the questions I wanted to ask her, all of the things I wished to tell her… just flew away… my brain went to pieces and I couldn't think of anything to say. I kept thinking to myself, "She is so graceful and lovely."

My first memory of Kate Bush is probably watching her on the television in my grandparents' TV room in Victoria, Australia. I was a child – perhaps four, maybe five years old. Kate was dancing around on the moors of *Wuthering Heights*, and I was very much aware of the pride and excitement emanating from my grandparents, Kathy and Harry, and my father, David. I could tell that we were somehow connected with the beautiful lady on the television, and I desperately wanted to be like her, dancing around in a red dress.

I was mesmerized. From that moment on I idolised her. I was jealous of her. I was inspired by her. The red flower in her hair, and the red lips; she was so beautiful to me, a gypsy, a Goddess, a Pre-Raphaelite painting come to life (I believe that Kate considers the Pre-Raphaelite Lady comparison to be a misconception, but that's how I saw her). So theatrical and dramatic and stirring.

My parents have a cassette recording of me, with a strong English accent (we spent some time in England when I was little), singing my interpretation of the chorus of *Wuthering Heights*. I was four years old, and I was singing "It's me, Cathy, I'll pop home now". I think it was around that same time that Mike Oldfield's *Moonlight Shadow* hit the charts, with a female singer named Maggie Reilly. The lyrics involved a highwayman who becomes a ghost, so that combined with Kate's *Wuthering Heights*, my Irish Nana's talk of ghosts and leprechauns, and my discovery of *Jane Eyre* and *Pride and Prejudice* - and suddenly my childhood was filled with a highly romanticized view of England, and my imagination ran wild with images of galloping horses, wailing banshees, ghosts tapping on windows, and beautiful women lost on the moors.

I think *Hammer Horror* was one of my early favourites – both the song and the dance routine. I loved the idea of dancing with a partner who could lift you up and carry you through the air. I loved the black Gothic bat-like look of *Hammer Horror*, and the cover of the *Never For Ever* album. Later on, I discovered Bram Stoker's *Dracula* and a German Heavy Metal band called Warlock, whose lead singer, Doro Pesch, sang passionately of vampires and shape-shifters.

My Nana, Kathleen, was so proud of Kate. She spoke glowingly of her, and as we were also very close, she encouraged me, spoilt me. She told my parents "Not to kill my spirit". Kathy told me that I have the same dimples as Kate (although mine are not as deep) – on the tops of our cheeks. She said that came from her family, the Dalys of Waterford. Sadly, Kathy never heard me sing while she was alive, although I desperately hope that she can see me and hear me now.

Kate and a very young Beck

Photo: Beck Siàn

All my life, I wanted to dance, and that was due to the direct influence of Kate. That was my first wish, although I believe my parents took me to one ballet lesson when I was a child, and I didn't want to go back. I was so very shy. A withdrawn and frightened child, I expressed this by trying to get a lot of attention. I was always troubled, and in trouble. If only I had been able to overcome my shyness, and accept discipline, I could perhaps have really learned to dance, and to play an instrument. Instead, I spent large portions of my life floating around, lost, and masking my fear with drink and drugs.

The thing that saved me was my love of singing. It had never occurred to me that I might one day be able to make a living from my music, that I might write my own songs, and that people might enjoy hearing me sing.

I gave up drugs. I gave up drinking. I gave up smoking. I bought a guitar and a book of basic chords and I started to teach myself to play at the age of twenty eight. A late starter! Luckily, I had been taught to sing by Kate – with every album she released, I would play them over and over and over and mimic her relentlessly, until I could hit all of the notes that she was singing. It took a long time, but in this I was disciplined, and that influence can now be heard in my singing style, regardless of the genre of music that I sing.

For many years, I couldn't see past Kate's music, in order to write my own. I formed a short-lived but fun Kate Bush Cover Band and we played gigs in Adelaide, Australia. I copied Kate and was too scared to try writing my own songs. Eventually, I found myself, and my own voice.I moved to the Dandenong Ranges in Victoria, to reconnect with happier memories from my past – my Nana and grandfather had lived there when I was a child. I lived in a little cottage in the middle of a cool, damp rainforest. There, I continued to learn my guitar chords, and wrote lots of poetry. Many of these poems then became songs. I began to attend large folk festivals, and decided that I wanted to be up there on the stage, singing. I had to read a lot of self-help books and build a strong support group of friends in order to find the courage to perform in front of people. I started to perform at festivals and venues around Melbourne, then I recorded an EP and finally, my first CD, called *Unfurling* – both for the unfurling of the fern fronds in the forest, and for the unfurling of my new and true self.

Photos: Krys

I entered one of the songs from the album, *Under Thunderous Skies*, in a song-writing competition, and won. I continued to hone my performing skills and gradually, after a few years, here I am, on the other side of the world… living in England, and making a living from my music. I travel around the country, performing at festivals, folk clubs, and even at abbeys and haunted ballrooms.

I call the music on my *Unfurling* album, Haunted Forest Music. It is difficult to categorise, as there are so many influences. I suppose it could be called "World" music, or "Contemporary Folk". As well as the clear influence of Kate Bush, there is also a Celtic thread (my Nana and Kate's Ma being Irish, Irish music has always been in my life, and my mother is Welsh). I think there is also an "Australian" vibe – I've included digeridoo and sounds from the Aussie forest – such as laughing Kookaburras. Most of my lyrics are about relationships, nature, storms (I love thunderstorms), and a ghost story or two (hence a slightly "Gothic" atmosphere).

I continue to listen to all of Kate's albums regularly. Songs like *Warm and Soothing* remind me of my Nana, and the Bush family. Others like *Oh England My Lionheart* epitomize the idea of England that I have grown up with. *Hello Earth*, *Night Scented Stock*, *Moving*, *Moments of Pleasure*, *A Coral Room*, to name just a few, have the power to make me cry whenever I hear them.

I have been listening to Kate's albums for close to thirty years, and I still find something new and inspirational whenever I hear them. I feel blessed to have grown up with Kate's influence, and to be connected to the Bush family in my small way.

I am about to start recording my second full-length album, called *Luminous Wings & Unseen Things*.

I feel like my life has just begun, and I know that I have Kate Bush to thank, on so many levels, for helping me to get here. Kate, my muse, the Goddess who inspires my creativity.

Poems by Beck

Tintagel

Seaweed smell on my tongue
Sandy dreadlock hair
Numb feet from walking – pulsating
In time with the waves
Splashing in Merlin's cave
That murky sea colour – blues/greens
All those hues
A place of mystery to me
There are real ghosts here
I hear their voices on the wind
Whispering – hush – shivers
Crash of the waves,
Salty spray
Setting sun over the ruins of the castle
King Arthur? Maybe not
But I feel the oldness – it has its aura
Goosebumps up my neck
Wild flowers nodding their heads together
They know the secrets
Of this place
With their yellows and purples and whites
Prickly gorse, heather, stinging nasty nettles
Hot spot on my calf
There's a certain feeling that the sea
Never fails to induce in me
I sit and I dream.

Nana

I still expect to look up
And see you standing there
With your glittering, shiny brooches
And your untamed
silver hair

A Beautiful Rain-Washed Morning

The fragrance of the grass,
The luminance of the stars,
The freshness of the evening after thunder,
The memory
Of your lyrical laughter.
The stillness of a misty, frosty morning,
The quiet music of a flowing river.
We reached cloud level
All around was a damp swirling mist
The mountains shielded us
Secluded
In a beautiful rain-washed morning

Guy Pearce's Sensual World

Guy Tells us about his love for Kate's music

Issue 78: June 2007

"Twenty years ago a letter arrived at *HomeGround* Towers from a young Australian Kate fan, telling us how much her music meant to him and that he would love to meet up with us while he was visiting relatives in the UK. He also told us that he was an actor and working on an Australian TV show called 'Neighbours' and his name was Guy Pearce. That TV show was nothing short of a phenomenon regularly getting 20 million viewers a day in the UK and of course it was the launch pad for Kylie Minogue as well as Guy.

"Meeting Guy was a joy; we discovered he was down-to-earth, funny and a talented musician. It was also quite clear that he was very serious about his acting career and was determined even at that young age to pursue more challenging roles.

"In 1994 he starred in *The Adventures of Priscilla, Queen of The Desert*, an Australian comedy which proved to be an international hit and led on to other roles in films such as *LA Confidential*, *Memento, The Count Of Monte Cristo, The Proposition* and the recent *Factory Girl*.

Photo: courtesy Guy Pearce

When I was asked to write something for *HomeGround* I thought... Great, a chance to talk about the wonderful Kate Bush... although it's always been a tricky thing to try and articulate the importance of her in my life.

I find I can never really manage to say anything that hasn't already been said, and I'm very aware of the countless others whose lives have also changed and been made more meaningful because of her. It is important for me though to try, and say how profound her effect on me has been. There have been other artists and musicians who I've obsessed over, like John Lennon, The Beatles, Jeff Buckley, Peter Gabriel, Mozart, Nina Simone, but none with such overwhelming complexity as Kate. Her unique talent, voice, beauty, skill, intelligence, lyrics, movement, audacity, mystery, etc., have all combined in a way with my own make-up to add up to something that I find almost incomprehensible; it is something purely emotional. I find it fantastic to know I'm here on this funny old planet of ours at the same time as someone so special to me.

I'd never actually bought a Kate album until December 1985, aged eighteen, after I'd very quickly moved out of home and up to Melbourne to start on a TV show none of you have probably ever heard of. I distinctly recall being at KMart late one night buying bits and pieces for the flat I'd moved into, when I ventured over to the record section only to find a copy of *Hounds of Love*. I was immediately reminded of the strange experience I'd had many years before, hearing *Wuthering Heights* on the radio and completely flipping out. I'd had a growing fascination with her from that point in 1978, which had of course led to *The Man with the Child in his Eyes, Babooshka* and *Breathing*, stuff I'd heard on my little transistor radio late at night while everyone else was asleep. I remember mentioning her to someone at school when I was about fourteen only to be told I was weird, after which I clearly didn't bring her up again. Funnily enough I met another Kate at school around that time, but more about her later.

Kate Bush was someone I'd enjoyed sneak peaks of from many miles away in my small town home, Geelong, occasionally seeing a video or two on 'Countdown' (our local version of 'Top of the Pops' with the cowboy hat wearing Molly Meldrum). For some reason it never occurred to me to ask to have a Kate Bush record, in fact I don't think I ever asked for much as a child.

I moved out of home two days after my last high school exam. I remember starting the TV show on Tuesday December 2nd 1985 which, as I say, was the week I sort of rediscovered Kate for myself. I immediately went and found all four previous albums and for a long time never played much else... apart from the occasional Bowie, Gabriel, Prince and Police records.... oh yes, and maybe *Rock Me Amadeus* by Falco... I had been, like most other Kate fans, "swept away". To understate it, you might say I was a tad fixated, as I know all of us Kate Bush nuts can be. Whilst busily trying to learn lines for the next days terrible scenes with Jason, Kylie, or the various other future British pop stars, I spent four years on that show indulging in Kate like nothing I'd ever indulged in before... what a contrast! I couldn't get enough of her. I tried to find whatever books were available... videos, bootlegs, imports, posters, etc, etc, etc...

It was in November 1987 I made contact with the lovely folk at *HomeGround* during a rather sad visit to the UK (sad, because my Nana had passed away not long before me arriving there). By this point I'd gotten myself into such a state about Kate I decided to take myself off on a little pilgrimage to wander the streets of south London with only the various rumoured addresses of Kate's upbringing to start turning the myth into some kind of reality. Never with any intention of knocking on doors or pestering anyone I seemed to walk for bloody miles from place to place with this rather deluded notion that I might just happen to bump into her hanging about the local fruit shop with nothing better to do than chat with passing Aussie tourists... Clearly she must have sent someone out to buy bananas or whatever that day as she wasn't to be seen anywhere. Meeting Dave, Krys and Peter was of course the highlight of that UK visit... [here's another Fiver, Guy!!] It was at this point my fear set in at the prospect of actually meeting Kate myself... and realizing that I'd probably be better off if I never did as, of course I wouldn't know what to say, and I didn't particularly want to make a fool of myself in front of her of all people. We talked a lot that night. I tried sucking up whatever information I could about the great mysterious one. How satisfying it was to share this obsession... the best thing any obsessed person can do really! Even then I couldn't truly express the feelings I had for her, but at least I knew I wasn't alone in my obsession any more. I was really floored by Kate, you know what I'm saying... Kate's work was, and still is an assault on the senses from every direction.

Visiting the UK again in 1990 added yet more perspective to my Kate Bush world. First was to catch her live performance of *This Woman's Work* on 'The Wogan Show'. Oh my God, it was such an exciting and memorable moment. Another moment that really was Kate-inspired madness was at Easter that year. London's Capital Radio were having their 'Help A London Child' fund-raising auction and one of the items on offer was the dress Kate wore in the *The Sensual World* video. Well... even though I knew the dress was never going to fit I was determined to get my hands on it. Was I mad? Was this confirmation I truly was a sycophant? Or was I just doing the right thing? The thing any Kate Bush fan would have done? I distinctly recall Dave's unwavering encouragement as we drove around London together offering them £500 for the charity and an on-air interview. They accepted both and although, as I say, I knew the dress would be too small my girlfriend at the time, who was also a big Kate fan, was very happy to wear it for a "re-enact the video" photo session in the woods on the outskirts of Melbourne. All very silly really but a worthy cause and a nice Kate Bush memento.

Each album of Kate's has always had its own place and meaning for me even as they swam around collectively in my world. Each song taking me somewhere else depending on where I needed to be. *Hounds of Love* is so representative of individuality and maturing because of moving out of home at the time. The early work I'd heard on the radio as a kid is so indicative of the limitless nature of imagination and always will be. Each time I put on *The Kick Inside* or *Lionheart* I'm reminded of how alive and well the child in me must be, something I never want to lose. Even though *The Dreaming* fills me with great sadness and despair, there is also strength because experiencing those feelings is very empowering. I feel like Kate helps me find belief in myself. *Never For Ever*, similarly to the first two fills me with wondrous images, except with a greater strangeness imbued. All my swinging moods and internal theatre is wrapped up in that extraordinary album. Even all the various B-sides I obsessed over *Under the Ivy* (which could almost be my favourite song) broke my heart like nothing I'd ever heard before. *Lord of the Reedy River, Ne T'en Fuis Pas* (which I think is extraordinary), *The Handsome Cabin Boy, Burning Bridge, Passing Through Air, My Lagan Love* and *Warm and Soothing* all cut through to different emotional places that hadn't been tapped in to before. It's funny because all of Kate's work after *Hounds of Love* I see completely differently. By the time *The Sensual World* arrived in 1989 I had been woken up, within myself and on a far more conscious level, to Kate. Never again could I have the same tumultuous experience with Kate's new work as I'd had with the others... but I guess that's what growing up is all about. New work was going take on a whole new meaning for me.

I've chosen to jump straight to *Aerial*, as it's our most recent gift. Listening to the album as the mature and complex work it is, I think on some level it represents Kate's entire career. I must add to the equation my own development over these many years. Would things sound different had I heard this as a twelve year old, and be hearing *Feel It* or *Moving* for the first time now? Who knows. Ultimately it doesn't matter. All I know is the depth of emotion I've

"As an actor he has resisted the easy route of going for big blockbusters, preferring to hold out for the more interesting roles.

"Over the years, he has often named Kate as a favourite musician, but we thought that our 25th Anniversary issue was the perfect place for him to share with us exactly what Kate has meant to him over the years and he also gives us a brief update on what he is up to at the moment."

Photo: courtesy Guy Pearce

experienced because of Kate continues to expand and constantly becomes richer. It's the surprises in Kate's work I love, the unexpected changing familiarity that creeps up after each listen. Each time I listen I fall in love with *π* more than I knew I could. *Aerial* was released while I was in New York working on a film about Edie Sedgwick and Andy Warhol, an experience that proved to be rather demanding to say the least. I realized after the first listen I had to put this album away for a later time. It was going to be too distracting and take me to a place too overwhelming for where I was needing to be at the time. As the film went on and things got tougher I just looked forward to finishing it so I could get back to the album...

Four months later I was able to bring *Aerial* out again. And what a joy it is to be let back in to the world of our beloved Kate Bush. To me this album is classic Kate and yet challenges me in so many new ways. Sound choices, melodies, topics all feel completely honest and yet fully explorative... as only Kate can be. This is why we love her so much. It's that great representation of an uncompromising spirit. Who else ever sounds as individual? I ask you. *How To Be Invisible*, with that very distinct quiver in her voice makes me want to fall down whenever I hear it. This is not an album to have on in the background. Then again I'm generally not the kind of person to have background music anyway. It's too important a feature of my life as well as many other peoples lives. *A Coral Room* takes me back to similar emotions I experience when I listen to *Under the Ivy*.

Photo: courtesy Guy Pearce

It's like Kate knows I've grown up and has tailored her work just to suit me and my needs... hmmmm... well, maybe, maybe not?? Her profound ability to tap into growth, change, human psychology, beauty... ah, the list goes on. How about *Sunset*? I mean wow, wow, wow, wow, unbelievable!!! And what about *Somewhere in Between*? This beautiful work makes me feel like I'm floating out in space somewhere, lost, but very happy to be. I think Kate spans all mediums, all ages, all generations, all emotions, all perspectives. She never dates. She's always far ahead of her time and yet classic, organic, old-fashioned, and how we always wish things could stay. I even love the great use of digital sound waves as the album cover as a beautifully reflected mountain range silhouetted against a sunset. She challenges us to face change and yet lets us indulge in all things safe and familiar. To me the album gets better as it goes on. One of my favourite pieces is *Nocturn*. And then to finish *Aerial* is just stunning. This album is like nothing before it, and yet, like I say, almost representative of her entire work. Thank you Kate for this latest beautiful and personal work.

As for my own work... Last year I had another visit to the UK funnily enough playing Harry Houdini in Gillian Armstrong's *Death Defying Acts* with Catherine Zeta-Jones. I tried to get the song in there somewhere but don't know if I had much luck. Our story is certainly not a biopic on Mr H. but more a story of a woman and daughter trying to make ends meet on stage with a psychic act. Enter Harry Houdini on a world tour who makes the rather grandiose proclamation that he will hand over $10,000 to anybody who is able to tell him his Mother's last dying words. This is where the fun begins! Not sure when it is to be released, but probably sometime this year... I wonder if Kate will see it? I've also just completed a smaller film in LA called *Winged Creatures* (no, it's not a Sci Fi about flying monsters) with Kate Beckinsale, Forest Whitaker, Dakota Fanning, Jeanne Tripplehorn and Embeth Davitz. A rather harrowing story about how a group of people are individually affected by a random shooting. Not for the faint hearted.

Now, getting back to that other Kate I met in 1980... After not seeing each other for about ten years after finishing school we were beautifully reunited in 1995 and married in 1997. I've assured her my attraction goes beyond just her name but she still thinks it's a bit strange every time I try to put ivy in her hair or make her put on a lion suit!

Just to finish off. I guess I've made it clear, after saying how hard it is to talk about Kate Bush, just how much she means to me. Funny to feel that about someone you've never met. I understand though that I'm not the only person out there who has such intense feelings for Kate and her work, so it's nice to know there are a bunch of us who share something so special. My journey through life so far has been made richer because of Kate Bush and for that, on behalf of all of your admirers thank you Kate for sharing with us your spirit. We all love you dearly for being so honest and will treasure your talent till the end of time. With Love and affection.

The Del Palmer Interview

When Del came to HomeGround Towers!

Last year Krys asked Del Palmer if he would like to write something for *HomeGround*. He said he would like to do an interview and suggested that we take questions from our *HomeGround*/Kate Bush News & Information Forum members. So we asked people to email their questions to Del and he selected the ones he found most interesting. In March 2007, Del came over to HomeGround Towers for the interview. It was a great night with a yummy Indian take-away halfway through. We began by talking about…

Aerial

Andrew Marvick: I assume that the music wasn't notated, or composed, in the traditional sense, but were there diagrams of some sort in which the many smaller musical events were placed prior to or during the recording process? What sort of planning went into the integration of each part of the suite? To what extent was the recording the result of sheer improvisation during the actual recording? To take one specific example: was the spectacular guitar part toward the climax of *Aerial* "composed" at all by Kate, or did she simply give Danny [McIntosh] so many bars and a basic chord progression and ask him to improvise entirely as he saw fit?

Del: None of these things are ever fully planned as such are they? It's like saying did Van Gogh plan all his paintings, he didn't always, sometimes he'd just sit down and go "right, I think I shall just paint this". Well sometimes Kate actually comes to the studio with more or less nothing, except she's got an idea of some kind, like 'let's just do something, let's just see what comes out', and it can literally come from there. There is never any annotation as such and there's never any music written down. The only time any kind of musical forms are written down is if Danny writes his own charts; he wrote out any charts that we needed for any other musicians who came in, like drums. John Giblin wrote his own charts as well, he's one of those wonderfully gifted people who can sit down and just write himself a chart. Basically, it's not musical dots its a chord chart so it is what's happening per bar, what the chord sequences are. It's very informal. Kate doesn't need it, she keeps it all in her head.

HG: We only see the end results, an album organised into two sides, with two collections of songs, one being the thematic side. Is that something that grew?

Del: From the very start she had this idea in mind. I don't know whether she had it in mind to make it two albums as such, but she definitely had the concept idea – because it worked so well – it goes back to the *Hounds of Love* days of one side being a concept and the other a bunch of songs. She thought that worked really well and the idea was to carry that on. She had a very specific idea for that second record – obviously it's "a day in the life of..." anybody you like basically.

HG: So the individual tracks grew. You didn't have a particular idea that the first track would be this, the second this, and so on?

Del: No, I think she did have some idea of it. These things grow as you go along. The first time you piece it together and you play it's like "Ooh, that's interesting. What about if we make that a bit longer or close that gap up or put something in there". It's an ever-evolving thing and the difficulty comes when you've got to say, right, that's it, just leave it at that and let's just tidy it up. That's it.

Pekka Hiltunen: Was there any special source of inspiration for the strong themes of nature (the birds, landscapes etc.) on *Sky of Honey*? Did Kate just make up a story line from the songs she had, or was there a sense of the whole that inspired some of the parts?

Del: Not that I know of. I can't ever specifically remember her saying "I've got this real thing going on about nature". It was literally "this theme is about day". It doesn't start at dawn and go through to sunset, it starts around about lunch-time. The whole thing was about "what do you find happening during the day?" – you've got bird song, you get the sun going down, the whole thing of a street painter painting on the pavement, it suddenly rains and washes it all away. The dream states of night time. To be honest with you I still to this day don't really

Issue 78: June 2007

Del Palmer was Born in Greenwich in 1952. He was persuaded to take up the bass in 1967 at the age of 15 by his friend Brian Bath so that he could play in Bath's band Cobwebs and Strange. In 1969, they formed Tame with Vic King on drums. This morphed first in the early 70s into Company, and then into Conkers. Both bands had record company deals and Conkers released a number of singles. In 1977 Conkers then morphed into the KT Bush Band. Del Palmer, Brian Bath, and Vic King backed Kate as vocalist on the pub circuit in London and the Home Counties.

Increasingly involved in Kate's studio recordings during the making of *Lionheart*, *Never for Ever*, and *The Dreaming*, Del worked with Kate to establish her first full standard studio after 1982, and was credited as Recording Engineer on all Kate's subsequent albums: *Hounds of Love*, *The Sensual World*, *The Red Shoes*, *Aerial*, *Director's Cut* and *50 Words for Snow*.

Del's own summary of his early musical years appears on pages 528 and 529

Photo and graphics by Del

know what's going on. Kate does, but I never really did. It's very abstract.

HG: That's what also makes it attractive because she doesn't need to explain everything. It's part of her uniqueness, part of the mystique.

Del: She is a very emotional, very feeling artist. It's for you to make your own decisions, to get something from it for yourself. To be drawn in, enchanted even.

Rachel Lisi: What is a typical recording session like with Kate? Especially with an album like *Aerial* that took a bit longer than usual to record; was there a strict recording schedule for this one closer to its release? Or was it more relaxed. Did you have to almost push Kate a little to finish it or did she steer the boat with determination to get to the other shore?

Del: I guess on a typical day I'd turn up there at about ten or eleven o'clock and we'd just meander to the studio at some point. The only time there was any real serious structure was when we had somebody coming in and we had to utilise their time. One of the guys, the drummer Steve Sanger used to come from Dorset – we'd phone him, he'd come up and we'd have to decide what we were going to do. We'd have to plan the day so we could utilise his time. I really don't know that there was a structure, there never is with us, whatever happens, happens. Generally, Kate always had some idea of what she wanted to achieve that day, like to progress this track or that theme. Some days you'd get in and you'd work really hard on something and think "God we really got a lot done today", and other days you'd do the same thing but you'd feel "I didn't think we got that much there then".

HG: Do you get more done in a day when you are working on the vocals or the music?

Del: To be honest with you, a lot of the time she did the vocals on her own. She did it all herself. We had a remote in the studio. She is very *au fais* with the recording studio and she thought that it was good to get on with it because she had done it before with the last two albums where she had done a whole lot of recording herself and we would just get together later on and tidy it up, put it together and decide what she wanted to use. I just let her get on with it. Even now she still feels a little bit conscious of having people sitting there maybe thinking "come on Kate, get on with it".

HG: She had commented on feeling self-conscious with the vocals several times in the Kate Bush Club newsletters.

Del: It's just an artistic thing, you know. Artists are very frail. They want people to love what they do, they want people to love their art. When Kate's doing vocals she's very self-conscious about it, she just wants it to be so great, she doesn't want people to be sitting there. She wants to get on with it, and basically do her experimentation unobserved. I find it works very well.

HG: So sometimes would you turn up and she'd say, "Here you are, I've done it..."

Del: No, she'd maybe say I want to do some vocals on *Sunset*. We'd always have a vocal mic set up in the studio. I'd just open up the vocal mic input on the console and say, "Off you go," disappear and come back a couple of hours later and ask her "How you getting on?" "Yeah, yeah, doing fine". "All right, I'll come back in another hour or so." I'd usually go in the house and read or something, or do a bit of fishing maybe. And she would buzz and say "I think I've got something, do you want to come back and we'll sort it out?"

HG: Was it more relaxed?

Del: Yeah, it was very relaxed, it's getting more relaxed all the time. I think it's because she's so experienced at doing this kind of stuff now. Also, it comes from having your own studio with no clock to watch.

HG: *Aerial* had such a great reaction from the fans which she must be really pleased about.

Del: We know that everybody out there is just so loyal. I said to her a number of times, you know you could put out a 1K test tone and they'd love it just because you put it out. They are that loyal. I'm always amazed by how supportive the fans are, they really are a great bunch of people. So I had no doubts, although you think to yourself, it's been such a long time and so much has changed in this business, so you never know.

HG: We must have a stack of album reviews and there were only about six that were bad.

Del: That's one of the things about Kate, she is so well respected by other artists. She is cited by so many people as an influence. Love her or hate her you've got to acknowledge her as a big influence. The other thing I've noticed as well is usually when you get to our time of life in the music business you are perceived as being dinosaurs but Kate's not perceived like that at all, she's perceived as being very trendy. A lot of younger people are into her music.

Rachel Lisi: I am really curious about the low volume on *Aerial*. It seems as though it was recorded on the very low end and I was wondering if there was a reason for that particular decision.

Del: I thought this would be quite obvious to everybody by now. What they have to understand is when you're doing heavy metal or rock music where it starts at a certain level and it goes through to the end at that level, you can compress it, you can limit it and it can be as loud as you like, bringing the lows up and the highs down. This will give it that characteristic pumping effect which is great for the dance floor where heavy, insistent rhythm is desirable. But if, like classical music, you've got light and shade, highs and lows, then there will be level fluctuations. Now, for instance, the best example for me is the *1812* overture. When that starts it is fairly quiet. But then the end of it is completely mad! It's all about the ambience, and Kate's music is similar in that it isn't about "whack it up loud and let's go head bang!" – you listen to it, you get into it, you experience it. The thing is that the quiet parts are quiet for that reason, it's supposed to be quiet and reflective. It's all about being drawn into the composer's images and thought processes.

If you take that whole second CD – the concept, there is one point where it peaks out, so therefore that is your high point, that one little place and I'm not sure where it is. I think it might be somewhere in *Nocturn,* somewhere around the second part of it there's a peak section where the whole CD is at its loudest, the most intense sound pressure level. That's as loud as you can go and everything from there goes downwards, the quiet bits become quieter. So, you have two options, to pull the level down or compress it which will make the music pump the more you do. If you start compressing and limiting stuff which we did not do, you lose your subtleties. Kate was adamant about this, and I agreed with her in the end, though when I started the mixing process I was whacking on the old quad compressor on the console as you do, as soon as she heard it she said, "No, get rid of it, I don't want any of that, I want it to be as dynamic possible". And as usual I'm saying "You can't do that." By the end of the album I'm eating humble pie... admitting that actually this sounds really good. If I had a pound for every time I said to her 'you can't do that' and I end up being wrong, I'd be a rich man.

From my point of view this album has the least amount of limiting compression that I've ever used on anything because it didn't call for it. It was all about light and shade. The whole thing is about light and shade, highs and lows. I had a hard time looking on your Forum and loads of people going "Why's it so quiet". There are some people who profess to have an understanding about how music is produced therefore they should know why it is like it is. "Why's it so quiet on me ipod?" It wasn't done to sound loud on an ipod. If you don't use loads of compression you are going to get drops in volume and that's just the way it is. A trade-off. It's completely different music. It's treated more like a classical piece. I gave up thinking about why our albums are quieter than everybody else's years ago. It just comes out that way because of the fact that we try to keep so much dynamically. It's not at one level all the way through. You try to draw your listener in, keep them guessing, keep some light and shade.

Darrell Babidge: On *Aerial* which track was the most fulfilling to see produced, from beginning to end – from its infant state of piano composition to the fully produced and engineered master?

Del: For me my two favourite tracks are the two piano vocal tracks because I, like most other people, am a purist and I think the best of Kate Bush is when she sings at a piano on her own. I'd get rid of all of us lot altogether. I have tried for so long suggesting this, "Let's just do an album with you and the piano. Nothing else." The longest bit of the whole project would be Kate writing the songs for it. We could record it in a matter of weeks. In one or two takes.

Photo: Del

HG: *A Coral Room* showcases the different approach to production on this album – had it been on *The Sensual World* or *The Red Shoes* maybe Kate would have put strings on it. The fact she was brave enough to just let it be is so brilliant.

Del: That was the last track written for the whole thing. She left just a couple of little bits of colour to give it a lift, give it emphasis. It's so moving when she sings and plays on her own and it takes me back to when I first met her and she played her songs to me, on her own. I just think that's where she's at her best. The more of us that get involved, the weaker that becomes and the more diluted that is. And I think most people would agree with me.

HG: A lot of the fans would agree entirely with that. They would like to see just Kate plus piano.

Del: Absolutely. You have to remember I am a big fan too. I don't just work with her, I am a big fan. I'm like you lot, I think she's better off when she's doing it on her own.

HG: Makes us think back to that live version of *Breathing* on the Comic Relief live shows we saw in 1986.

Del: In the early days some of the stuff she played to me was just wonderful. Then we went into the studio and got a backing track, and although they were still great, for me they were never quite the same.

HG: There was a programme on Capital Radio once where she played the original demo of *Babooshka* – it was just her and the piano, it was amazing, so jazzy and bluesy and the vocal was unbelievable.

Del: But you can't hear it under that track, that piano part is still the same but you can't hear it. I think her voice is just wonderful these days. I mean *A Coral Room*, that is one go, that is her playing and singing in one go. For me that's as good as it gets.

HG: As women's voices mature they do often become richer, more mellow...

Del: But she has always sung like that. It was only that first album where she used the high pitched voice, she always sang like that even in those days.

Rob Brown: Why did Kate want Michael Wood to sing on *A Coral Room* when given the personal nature of the lyric, having John or Paddy sing those lines would have been more appropriate?

Del: That man is a music teacher and she asked him to do it because he's got such a lovely voice. She didn't want one of her brothers to do it, she wanted someone a little more formal and an unknown voice so it kind of dragged you out of that whole comfortable thing and made you think differently about it. He sounds so child-like in there and if it were Paddy you'd all be listening to it thinking oh, right, that's Paddy singing there, that is.

HG: The first thing we said about *A Coral Room* when we first heard was that it sounded like one of those early demos. And what is *Mrs Bartolozzi* about?

Del: Do you know, I don't have a clue. I love the whole waves coming in and going out, coming in and going out, the little fish... I always got the feeling it is about a woman who is doing the washing, the household drudgery and she just slips off into a fantasy world. Wonderful imagery.

Cecile: What is the main instrument that can be heard on *King of the Mountain*?

Del: If it's something that Kate played then it's a keyboard - it's a Kurtzweil 250X. It's a very tasty digital synthesiser

Cecile: I loooove the bass on *Nocturn*! Was Del playing this, by any chance?

Del: No it wasn't, it was my old mate John Giblin. The main man.

Rachel Lisi: I think the vocals at the end of *Nocturn* are some of the most powerful and pitch perfect in all of Kate's career. Can you shed some light on the recording of those? Is it all Kate or are there other vocalists lending their vox as well?

Del: It's one of the boys. Lol Creme I think. I know there are lots of them. They were tracked up to make them sound thick and have maximum impact. A similar effect to the chorus voices in opera. Actually I think maybe Paddy might be in there too. But don't quote me on that one. A lot of the details become such a blur but I think that's who it is... Apart from Kate.

Rachel Lisi: Was *Bertie* a song that Kate composed for her son before it was thought to be put on an album or was it created specifically for the album because it sounds like a very playful song and one that a mother would sing to her child while he plays and jigs around.

Del: I think you'd have to ask her that one. As far as I can make out she wrote a song about her little boy as any mother in her position would, you know, "this is my son and he's fabulous" and rightly so because he is. He's a lovely boy. But what promoted her to do that you'd have to ask her.

Sylvain: Do you have a favourite disc from *Aerial*? *Sky of Honey* or *Sea of Honey*?

Del: I prefer the concept. Having said that, some of the best songs, as on *Hounds of Love*, are on the song part but I just like the concept, there's a lot more pure stuff. It works as a stream of consciousness.

Rob Brown: Does Rolf Harris actually play the digeridoo on the *Aerial* album? Rolf himself has no recollection of doing so.

Del: As I recall when he came round to do that his wife wasn't very well at the time so he might have been just a little bit preoccupied. Who knows, but I do know he did play the digeridoo. He's an incredible man.

In the Studio

Chris Williams: What sort of studio do you have now? Digital board or analogue? Digital or analogue recording? Tape or hard drive?

Del: Both, everything. It's an analogue console, we still use the same E-series SSL console that we used on the *Hounds of Love* album. It goes back that far, we've had it for so long now it works on its own, I just crack the whip as it were and off it goes... We recorded it onto two Sony 3324A digital machines, which are now completely obsolete but we had them so we used them, but all the mixes were done to Pro-Tools and all the editing and all the compilation stuff was done on Pro-Tools. The vocals were compiled to tape in the usual way as we've always done it, by drop-ins, stuff like that, all the instrumentation was done in the old-fashioned way but all the compilation of the songs, all the mixes were done to Pro-Tools. I mean, I didn't take half of one song and a bit out of that one and paste it in.

I tell you what, I wish we'd had Pro-Tools when we did the *Hounds of Love* second side. That would have been wonderful to have available on that one. Everything we did on that particular album was all drop-ins, cuts and cross fades. I had to razor in so many bits and pieces on that to make it work, but on this one it was so easy, if you didn't like a gap you could just open it up, drag it further along, close it up, speed it up, slow it down, turn it backwards – and I remember all the backwards-forwards vocals stuff Kate did and how long it took her – it's so easy now. So we use a bit of everything. All the mixes were done to hard drive, all the compilation was done to hard drive. We used dCS audio converters which were difficult to use, and I have to pay tribute to Danny on that one because he sourced those and he made them work because I looked at them and I thought how can you touch these they are a nightmare – they are made by a company that make stuff for the military, like military radar – they were the only ones that could do sample rates of 192 Khz at the time.

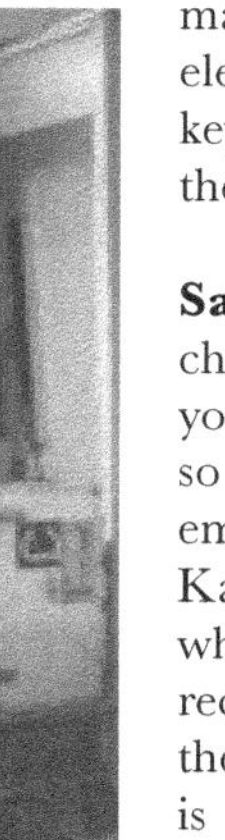

Photo: Del

I couldn't get my head around it, nobody could, but Danny did, and he sat down with the manuals and he read through them religiously and he sussed the whole thing out and he got it to work, and I have to admire him for that. I couldn't do it, I just let them sit there and never touched them, I never even switched them on or off. The sound quality of these things is particularly good and what I notice most with digital machines is that you have a clock that tells the machines what's happening, keeps them aligned. We use the DCS clock, and that made the biggest difference I could hear, it actually made it sound better and I couldn't work out why that was at first, it's just a clock, it's not making the tape do anything differently, but it was. It's a clock that's extremely accurate, therefore everything does its job more accurately. So everything ran from this clock, we ran the console computer, the dCS D to A and A to D Converters, the lot. We ran everything from this one clock and the sound improved. It's just ridiculous. But having said that Kate would love to go back to recording in analogue.

HG: If you made the piano album you could do that.

Del: We'd do it all in analogue. The thing about digital is that it can be harsh and cold, and the beauty of analogue recording is when you push it to its extremes you start getting that lovely warm kind of tape compression thing where it's still warm but it's starting to go off into a distortion that's still musical in nature and it works great for drums, pianos and stuff. With digital as soon as you get to a certain level [Del illustrates by blowing a raspberry-fart sound!], it gives up. I find digital recording sometimes can be very difficult, because you can push it and push it and push it – then suddenly aaargh!.. It gives up and says "I don't want this." But with analogue you can feel when you start to get to the limit and you can work it. It's more forgiving.

Rachel Lisi: What kind of recording equipment do you folks use? Is the Fairlight still a part of the equation or has it been replaced with more updated machinery?

Del: We don't use a Fairlight anymore, that's been pensioned off. It's now a museum piece. We still have an old series 3X that sits in the studio but we don't use it for anything at all. Kate's main electronic keyboard was the Kurtzweil.

Antonello Saeli: Is it a choice of yours to put so much emphasis on Kate's vocals while recording them? There is a very distinctive use of "compression" on Kate's voice which makes her sound so "ambient". Is this approach a shared decision?

Del: It is purely Kate's decision. All the production decisions are hers. It's her music therefore it's what she wants. I will argue with her about a lot of things but in the end, even if I don't agree with her it's her music and I respect that.

Chris Williams: Have you heard multi-channel music on SuperAudio-CD or DVD-Audio? Have you considered revisiting the old albums and re-mixing them in 5.1?

Del: Until they come down to somewhere where you can go into the average music shop in the high street and buy them, they are always going to be a minority thing. They'll not replace the ordinary CD until this happens. A bit like D.A.T tapes. It's the same with 5.1 – I've thought about it but I see no point at this time. Not while so few people could enjoy them.

Thomas Grayson: Please name a few of your favourite engineers or producers, and can

Del's bands:

Tame 1969

Company 1973

Conkers 1974

KT Bush Band 1977

you tell us a little bit about why you like them?

Del: One of my all time favourite engineers was Jeff Emerick, the Beatles engineer, the man's a living legend. He defined the rules as far as popular music recording goes. Another one is Roger Nichols who did all the early Steely Dan recordings. He has great feel and control, wonderful understanding of how sounds work together. Paul Hardiman, because he taught me so much. And the producers? – as far as I'm concerned it's the engineers, not the producers who work the magic. The engineer does all the work, the producer just takes all the credit. It's interesting though how many engineers become producers in their own right...

HG: Did you see that Tony Visconti recently had a book out and he said the one artist he really wanted to work with was Kate?

Del: And she really wanted to work with him in the early days, but you know, ships that pass in the night, it never happened.

HG: There was a point after *The Dreaming* when EMI suggested that Kate should work with a producer. David Byrne we think was considered.

Del: Yeah? Is that right? Well, at the time, the whole *Dreaming* thing was... It's an untold story that we won't go into... Let's not go there!

HG: John said to us once that that album wasn't released, it escaped.

Del: If you say to most people which is critically the best album, a lot of people will say *The Dreaming*. I'm talking about people in the business now. EMI considered that album to be a bit of a flop at the time and I can't understand it. That was an unbelievably brave album considering the times and the album that went before it, it's like chalk and cheese. It was such a brave moment, she was unleashed on that album.

HG: And there were successful singles from it that's the bizarre thing.

Del: The trouble with that album is, I think, that in a lot of ways she was using everything she recorded... Over the years through experience she's learned to know what can work and what won't, and be a bit more discerning.

Dave: For me personally the moment of testing a friend is to play them *The Dreaming*, and if they go "That's fucking brilliant!", then you know they really get Kate.

Del: That whole album was done through the Falklands war. I can remember sitting with Paul Hardiman and every time we'd come up (we'd been locked away in a basement studio we had no idea what's going on) and we'd catch the television news and I'd look at him and he'd look at me and I'd say "we're going to get called up next week, we're going to be in the bloody Falklands next week." We missed the war completely. We kept coming up and something else had happened. That was in the days before computer-aided mixing. We had two consoles in the control room in tandem and all three of us took a handful of faders and did the moves on the fly. I had bits of wood and pencils stuck across four or five faders so I could move them all at the same time. At the end of each pass we'd all look at one another and go "How was it for you then?" Great experience and pure magic when you finally got it right.

I'd like to give Paul Hardiman a mention here. He's one of my favourite engineers. He taught me so much about the whole thing, because with most engineers you say to them what's going on and they get a bit protective and say "Oh this is my sound, this is what I do, it's a secret". With him he encouraged me to take over, he'd say "I can't make the session next week, why don't you do it, go on, go for it. All you've got to do is this, this and this, that, that and that." I'd sometimes say to him, "Paul, what are you doing and he'd say, well, look, it's this, this and this." He was so forthcoming with it all. I got on great with him, I had such a laugh with him. Kate wasn't so sure about the humour [said Del laughing!], but I got on with him so well. He was a lovely bloke and I learned so much from him.

HG: What's *Night of the Swallow* about?

Del: I don't remember at all. The only thing I remember about that is using all three studios at Abbey Road to do that song. When we did Stuart Elloitt's drums we had the kit set up in Studio 3, we were recording in the control room of Studio 2, and we had two big speakers set up in Studio 1 recording the drum sound through those to get the huge hall ambience. So we were using three studios at the same time just because they were there and we could. That and trying to keep a bloody eight-string bass in tune. I don't remember the lyrics at all. The trouble is after listening for years whilst working on them I don't want to listen to them again for some time. Until I can accept them as just music and not remember the day-to-day work.

HG: If you had to say what was your best experience working with Kate in the studio, what would it be?

Del: That's a hard one. For me the best time I had was when we were doing *Hounds of Love* album in Ireland and I can remember one magic moment when we went into the studio at Windmill Lane and the Irish guys came in for the first time – and I can't remember what the song was that we played them – but they started playing along with it and just reduced both of us to gibbering wrecks. It was such a magic moment. We were in Ireland for a month, we were on our own and we just got on with it. It was such a great time and I think that album shows that she was in a good place then.

It wasn't all fun and games, there were a lot of hard things and stuff going on but it was, generally, just a good time. It was the perfect time for the album to come out, there were good people in control of the record company, it sold fantastically well, it was just a good time. I even had a bad moustache and got away with it. There have been loads of little magic moments. But that was a great time. It was a transition period for me as well, I was going from being just a musician to being an engineer too. I did a lot of work on that album as well but I wasn't in total control of that, there were lots of good people I was learning from.

Personal

Thomas Grayson: What are your own musical influences?

Del: Musically, as a musician my earlier influences were Jack Bruce, who was the top man for me, and then I got into Free, and Andy Fraser – he was a massive influence on me. James Jamerson and also people like Walter Becker. Steely Dan had a big influence on me too. I love their precision in the studio. Their attention to details. Chuck Rainey who I got to meet a few months back, which was like ooooooooh, shivers. Actually he put his arm round me and gave me a big squeeze. John Giblin – a big pal of mine. Eberhard Weber, of course, who is God as far as I'm concerned. He's wonderful, he's absolutely wonderful. The man is a genius, a total, total genius. It's a pleasure to be in the same room as him.

HG: He was on *The Dreaming* first and has been on everything since.

Del: Yeah, but we were into his music long before that. It was like "We've got to get him on something" and we've tried to get him on every album since. The thing about Eberhard is that he's a jazz player so you never get the same thing twice, and therefore it can be tricky if he played something here but you wanted it there. I tend to run a tape machine at all times when Eberhard is around the place. For me he's a God... There's God and then there's Eberhard.

Thomas Grayson: How did you come to meet Kate Bush?

Del: Right. Around about 30 years ago this month (March). Brian Bath and I had been in so many bands, and we thought what's this next band going to be, what are we going to do with this band to make it different. Brian said, "We need to get a singer. Who do we know who sings, we don't know anybody who sings." Then he said, "Paddy's got a sister who sings." I just assumed it was his older sister, so he said "Let's go over and see Paddy and see if she's up for it." So we went over to Paddy's place and she happened to be in – she used to live upstairs from Paddy – and she came down and she just exploded into the room and into my life from that moment on. And Brian said to her "We're going to get a band together, do you fancy coming and singing?" and she said, "Yeah, great, I'm up for that, fantastic." So we arranged to have a rehearsal a week later. Paddy brought her down to a room at the public swimming baths in Greenwich South London. There was Kate, Brian Bath, the drummer Vic King, better known as Nosmo – Nosmo King – and me. And the four of us sat there and we said "Right, what are we going to do?" and from the word go Kate said "I'd like to do something of mine" and right from that very first rehearsal we did *James and the Cold Gun*. That was the first thing of Kate's we did. We did that. We rehearsed for a while and then we started to get a few gigs coming in. We got a residency in a pub in Lee Green [in South East London] called the Rose of Lee and the first time we went down there, there were four or five people and within two weeks it was packed. There were people outside looking in, it was only a small pub, and people were actually blocking the traffic in the street. We had a residency there for about three months, we played on a Thursday night. It was sensational and she was brilliant, she was into the whole thing of the gun, and gunning the audience down and they loved it. Lisa [Bradley]and Rob [Lisa's husband] came along, that's where I first met them. Rob was getting dry ice and stuff and we had a little light show going on and he had a bucket on the side and he'd drop the dry ice in and it'd go all over the place and the punters lapped it up. She was just brilliant, she used to wear this big long white robe with coloured ribbons on or a long black dress with big flowers in her hair. She did the whole thing with the gun and they just loved it; she'd go around shooting people in the audience. It was just great. We did mostly covers, stuff that we knew. We did a great version of the Beatles *Come Together*, shame it never got recorded. She was just up to sing, and I think she saw it as just another way of getting experience.

The 'Rose of Lee' is now called 'The Dirty South', is now a music venue again, but still waiting for the blue plaque that proclaims it as the place where Kate first played live.

Photo: Del

Poster for the KT Bush Band club gig in Brighton where Kate first ran into Annie Nightingale the veteran Radio 1 DJ.

HG: Was this before the recording of *The Kick Inside*?

Del: We met her in Feb/March '77 and she started the album in August.

HG: Performing live must have been incredibly useful to her.

Del: It was... So we did that – and I'm not sure if it was before the album or after she had started it – we did a presentation for EMI; we worked out about five or six songs and that was the first time we did a whole set of hers, and EMI just fell about the place, they just loved it. Of course we were thinking "This is great!" I just knew that she was going to be big, she was up for it, there was nothing you could suggest to her where she would say "Oh, I dunno"; she would always say "Yeah, great, let's do it, let's go for it." Straight away she would say "I want to do this, I want to do that, let's get some dry ice, let's get a show going." She was in complete control. Brian and me, we would stand there and look at each other and go "This is absolutely outstanding! What a band!" We did one gig one night and it was an England v Scotland game and it was the one where Scotland won and they pulled down the goal posts – we were playing in the Half Moon pub in Putney that night, it was just full up, absolutely stuffed and they were going completely mental. And Kate came on and us boys were like "Oh God". But she just went for it, she was out in the audience, she was screaming and shouting, they went crazy for her. Even in those days she really did know how to work an audience, she really did. So that's how it was. Kate, Brian Bath, Vic King and me. Nobody else. Vic King, commonly known as Nosmo, because of all the 'No Smoking' signs.

The Half Moon

HG: We've never heard of Vic King before at all, he's the poor guy who has been written out of history. Where is he now?

Vic King in Tame circa 1969

Del: As far as I know he lives in Norfolk now. He was in very early bands that Brian and I had together. We had loads of bands together. I just feel sorry because he was there – some people getting credit for it were not actually there. Charlie Morgan has been written into it. Somebody called Vic Smith – who the hell Vic Smith is I have no idea! It was a 3-piece with Kate in front, that's all it was, and it was a very short period of time between March and August '77 and after that it was finished. She went to do her album and after that we got into the whole *Lionheart* thing – we set up the demo studio at her parents' place. That was the KT Bush Band, that little two or three month period and after that, although later line-ups are always referred to as the KT Bush Band, they weren't. I was just dumbstruck at how up for it all she was. I thought, she's so frail, this little tiny person, masses of hair you know, she was just so completely energised and so obviously believed in her own destiny. On a personal note I remember Brian used to have a Morris Minor van and Vic

Brian Bath – Life of Brian Band 2011

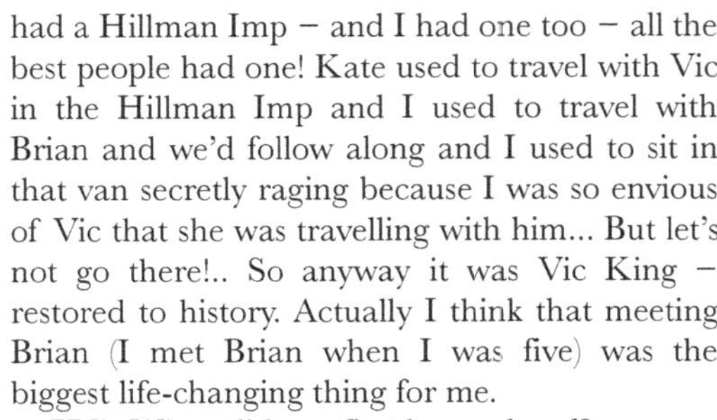
had a Hillman Imp – and I had one too – all the best people had one! Kate used to travel with Vic in the Hillman Imp and I used to travel with Brian and we'd follow along and I used to sit in that van secretly raging because I was so envious of Vic that she was travelling with him... But let's not go there!.. So anyway it was Vic King – restored to history. Actually I think that meeting Brian (I met Brian when I was five) was the biggest life-changing thing for me.

HG: When did you first have a band?

Del: God! 1967. A long time ago and it was called Cobwebs and Strange. We did everything. We did do a lot of our own stuff, and we also did *Purple Haze*. We did this crazy thing we called *Freakout Earholes* where we just went totally bonkers for five minutes while someone recited this totally unrelated stuff. Weird and whacky halcyon days.

HG: And the core of the thing was always you and Brian.

Del: Yeah, yeah, I've always worked with Brian over the years on and off. He's closer to me than my brothers in many ways. He changed my life completely. I was playing football with all the other kids. He was into the guitar and he said do you want to learn to play too and I said all right, why not. A life-changing decision. He said I've got a band with another guy and we need a bass player and I thought "It's got to be easier to play on four strings than on six." So the first thing I learned was the bass riff in *Hey Joe*. That was a classic, I worked that one out, and I thought "Fantastic, I can play *Hey Joe*, great stuff!" Hendrix was big with us back then. We did lots of Cream songs which is where Jack Bruce comes in. I've lost count of how many bands I've been in with Brian but I haven't played with him for a lot of years now. Mind you, I haven't stood up to play for about fifteen years, I just sit down all the time now. I have to take a stool, it's not the years it's the mileage... oh God! That was life-changing.

Si: Does Kate's music make you cry when she plays it or when it is played back, or do you get too caught up in the technical process to pay attention on an emotional level?

Del: Lots of it. Of course I respond to it, I am an artist. I'm a non-technical engineer. I'm an artist and musician first and foremost. I react to her emotional output just like anybody else does and it moves me. I wouldn't bother to work with her if it didn't move me, that's why I don't particularly want to work with anybody else.

HG: And that's why she wants to continue working with you?

Del: I'm sure she'll kick me into touch one day!

Si: What are your favourite tracks of those you worked on, either as a musician or engineer?

Del: There are so many of them, they're all different in their own way. To actually pick one out is a bit unfair. Sigh!

Mike Wade: Looking back over all of your

involvement with Kate's work over the years, what are you proudest of as a contribution you have made?

Del: I can say that I have personally never been completely happy with my contributions as a musician – I personally have felt I could have always done better, but...

HG: But wouldn't Kate have made you do better if she didn't like what you had done?

Del: That's very true. Sometimes less is more, more is less. Her requirements these days have become simpler and simpler from a bass point of view, except when you have people like Eberhard – you have him because that's who he is and this is what he does.

HG: Kate obviously likes to have the music exactly how she envisages it in her mind, but still retains the ability to let session musicians improvise

Del: Yes and no. Actually she is quite strict with her requirements. The usual story with that is plug in, play a bit, play along a bit, get into the tune, and she'll say "I like that little bit there, I don't like that bit there, put that bit here, do that bit there". She's quite particular and knows what she wants. Mind you, if you come up with something good she's perfectly happy to adapt. I mean, some of the best things to come up have been mistakes.

HG: And does that depend on who it is? Was she like that with Clapton?

Del: Oh God yeah! Well, Peter Erskine, one of the most respected jazz drummers in the world... "No, Peter, I don't think that works, do this instead... 'Ere, Peter..." Great story for you, Eric Idle asked her to go over to New York and do 'Saturday Night Live' and she went over there, first album had just come out. She did *Them Heavy People* and *Man with the Child in his Eyes*. She's rehearsing *Heavy People* with the house band and she turns around to the drummer and says "No, no, no, no, no... You don't do it like that, you do it like this" and she basically showed him. The drummer turns out to be Billy Cobham. She had no idea at the time that he's a drummer of global reputation she just put him right. He just says "OK," smiles and gets on with it. When she found out she just said "Well, he wasn't doing it right". An awe-inspiring musician and she says "No, that's not how I want it, I want it like this". Says a lot about her.

HG: Kate has proved time and time again that when she makes the decisions she has very rarely made the wrong one – like *Wuthering Heights* being the first single, producing herself.

Del: Someone somewhere had the foresight to let her go with it. People like David Munns, who was in charge when *Hounds of Love* came out – I have ultra respect him. He was passionate about her music. That album did really well and a lot of that's down to him.

Lesley Percy: If you could work with any other woman singer or performer who would you choose and why?

Del: One in particular, a Norwegian jazz singer. Her name is Silje Nergaard and I almost worked with her last year but it fell through. If you haven't heard her music check it out, she's got the most unbelievable voice.

HG: Are there any other contemporary artists that you would like to work with?

Del: No, no, because every time anybody has ever approached me to do something it's always been they want to sound like Kate. Forget it. There's only one and there only ever will be one.

HG: Kate's been approached a number of times to produce other people but she never has. It would be fascinating to hear a project or two of this kind.

Del: You see for her it would be time away from her work and if she's going to do that she might as well do her own stuff which is more important. You can never say "never" about anything, even about touring, but as far as I see her life now, she is a very happy, very comfortable woman, very relaxed in her life and she's enjoying herself, she's enjoying her son, she's enjoying her relationships, she's enjoying her life. Why would she want to change that? I remember her always saying to me making albums is not about money, as long as she can make enough to do the next album that's all that matters.

HG: The people reading this will also respect Kate for that. Even though many would love to see her do 'Top of the Pops', and 'Parkinson', things like that, they still respect her for what she wants.

Del: I just don't think she will do that kind of publicity any more. I watched her do a week of press once where she'd start in the morning and they'd just wheel them in one after the other all day long. Asked the same questions over and over and over – "Well tell us, Kate, what's this song about?" I just don't think she's got the time, the patience or the energy to do that any more. And

Photo: Del

why should she? The work is the most important thing. Live performance... When you think about it it's great to go along and see somebody play live but when you've got her in the comfort of your own room singing to you, I think that's a very different experience. It's never going to sound the same live. The only really interesting thing about doing it live is you only get one chance to do it right. No correcting mistakes. And you are in the presence of the fans, all that positive energy. But if you really want to get into the music, you listen to it at home, you listen to it one to one, it's you and her you experience.

HG: Having said that we'd all of us love to see her tour...

Del: You're not the only ones, get in the queue.

Kate

Mike Wade: Do you think Kate realises quite how much she is loved and respected by fans? Why do you think her fan base is so loyal?

Del: Of course she does and I think she has massive amounts of respect for them. It's very important to her what they think and what they say about what she does. It's incredibly important to her. She really does appreciate particularly their patience after all these years and they still go out and buy the album and they still get excited when it comes out and they still listen to all that early stuff from thirty years ago. They are respectful, intelligent people. I remember last year when I stumbled into a whole pub full of them and, contrary to popular belief, it was pure chance that I did. They treated me with utmost respect, they were genuinely pleased to see me and that's just wonderful. It was like having a drink with some mates. Very easy.

HG: If Kate touches on a subject in a song a lot of people will go and find out about Wilhelm Reich or Molly Bloom.

Del: There wasn't so much of that on this album, it's a bit more personal, I guess the inspirations were more natural than literary.

HG: There was endless speculation on the inspiration behind *How to be Invisible*. Coincidentally it has the feel of Phillip Pullman's *His Dark Materials* trilogy.

Del: Yes, it does I suppose. In fact he was around at her place a few months ago. She's a big fan.

Thom Penman: Regarding the infamous Demos, does Kate have any idea just how highly many of those fans who have heard them regard songs like *Rinfy*, *Organic Acid* and *In My Garden* (not to mention *Camilla*, *Come Closer*, *Frightened Eyes*, *Disbelieving Angel*, *Lionhearts* and the rest!)..? We can understand how she might hate them as rudimentary, childhood embarrassments but can she understand how we might love them as the emotive, undiluted essence of the magic that is Kate and piano?

Del: You have to look at from her point of view. They are sketches and if you're an artist it's like somebody getting hold of your sketchbooks and going through them. They are not supposed to be for public consumption, they are just sketches and they are not complete by any means. They are very rough ideas and she is such an ultra perfectionist about everything she does. There's a lot about it that I think she found annoying – stuff got out that shouldn't, which is one reason why we stopped doing demos to give to the record company – to stop that. Yes, it's great for the fans but you have to look at it from her point of view. Unfortunately, the reality of it is you can keep nothing secret once it goes out of your hands. Everything we do now is kept secret until we've finished with it because once you give it out – and I don't know what happens – but suddenly the whole bloody world knows about it. In actual fact a lot of these titles I've never heard of – *Camilla*, what's that? And *Come Closer*?

HG: The trouble is these demos go out and a lot of them people have made up the titles. A lot of those songs would be about 1976.

Del: If they are that early they would have been recorded on a cassette player stuck on top of a piano. Because they are so very rough, they are not supposed to be heard, they are just the sketches, ideas.

HG: On the positive side of that question, Thom goes to the point we talked about earlier – just Kate and the piano. That's the sound that attracts a lot of people.

Del: Yeah, well, you know my views on that one.

Rachel Lisi: I have always been curious about how Kate keeps her voice in shape. Does she do any vocal exercises or train with a vocal coach before she starts recording? Does she have any kind of special teas or drinks that she uses to soothe her vocal chords?

Del: No she doesn't. Not that I know of. As far as I know she doesn't sing in the bath and practice her scales. She just has a natural voice. She had a phase when she would drink a glass of port to lubricate the throat, but it was a very small phase. As far as I can tell she does no exercises or anything like that at all, it's just her natural voice.

John Roger: How do you think Kate's voice and the way she uses it has changed and matured since you've been working together, i.e. from the early songs until now?

Del: It's getting better all the time. It's maturing. In the early days everybody perceived her as having a squeaky high pitched voice. I know for a fact that was just a voice she used for that first album. She does not have a squeaky high pitched voice, she has a very sensual voice, it's like massaging your ears. She did a lot more in the early days as a created character and that character on *The Kick Inside* was one with a high pitched squeaky voice, the banshee kind of thing.

She doesn't sing like that and hasn't done for years and years.

HG: Does Kate listen to modern music now? It will be interesting to see as Bertie gets older the kind of music he will be listening to.

Del: I'm not sure, it's something you'd have to ask her. We had a very brief period of listening to the last Eminem album. She's not a musical snob in any way. I don't know what she's currently listening to.

Mike Wade: What do you feel the main differences are between Kate's work now and the first things you worked on?

Del: Thirty years basically. It's thirty years of experience, thirty years of song writing, thirty years of emotions. Make up your own mind. In a lot of ways it's better now than it was back then. From my point of view I'm more involved now than I was then. It's much more intimate now than it ever was and what I mean by that is there are less people involved. It's like a little cottage industry, the three of us most of the time. Danny would come in and do some guitar, and suggest ideas to Kate or whatever, but most of the time it was just the two of us working, and a lot of the time it's just her on her own working, so we don't have lots of people coming and going. We had no involvement with the record company, they had no idea what she was doing and they knew better than to even enquire. So yeah, I think it's better than it ever was. There's so much stuff. It's better now than it's ever been musically, it's world class song-writing. I prostrate at the feet of her artistry sometimes, particularly when I've played her my stuff, it's like my God, listen to that. Whatever you say about it is good enough for me.

Photo: Del

Dave: I heard the album a couple of weeks before Peter and Krys did. EMI invited me, I had to go and sit in the listening room, with the security guard, the guy from Abbey Road, and the product manager at EMI. And I was really fucking nervous because obviously this was a big thing... twelve years, you know. The first time I listened to *Aerial* it wasn't quite what I was expecting. Then two weeks later the three of us went up to EMI and then for me halfway through π it happened and suddenly I got it...

Del: When we had Munnsy and the EMI guys come to the studio we put it on, and left them in there and when we came back Munnsy was just sitting there, and he said "I feel exhausted... I didn't take any of that in but I know I liked it." There was so much of it, it was so intense. We then had to play the whole thing to them again.

Historical

Rob Brown: Several of the KT Bush Band *Lionheart* recordings were replaced by the session players. In hindsight, do you think Andrew Powell's decision was justified?

Del: They didn't really make a decision, they just took him the demos and got him to re-do it basically. The biggest one of those was the *Heartbrake* one - 'Don't Put Your Foot in the Foot-in-Mouth' as me and Preston lovingly called it. They just listened to those demos and just re-recorded them. They sound a lot better because they had spent a lot more time on them but, basically, they're the same. In retrospect I can see why he did it. He was a producer, he had his own musicians that he knew and he trusted them and I completely understand that now. In those days though I was beside myself with rage about that.

HG: But now you may be in the same position where you might replace someone's performance

Del: We have done but very rarely. Also we have a selection of musicians we will always use because we know what we're going to get from them. We know we can push the bounds. We very rarely get unknown people, having said that we got Steve Sanger who we had never met before and he was great.

Antonello Saeli: What are your personal memories of Kate live? I am thinking about the Tour of Life, of course, but also about other appearances as the LSO 75th Anniversary, the Prince's Trust in the Summer of 1982, etc…

Del: One of the best memories I have of that tour was when we first got together with Gary and Stewart at ML, which was the Who's place down at Shepperton. We had the stage set and they had put up a whole load of mirrors so we could all see everyone. I spent most of my time with my back to those mirrors because it was too freaky. I kept looking at myself and stopping, missing stuff. Again I remember looking over at Brian and going what the hell is going on? On the other occasions I was just a spectator.

Gary Hurst and Stewart Avon Arnold, the two dancers who accompanied Kate on tour.

HG: Kate had obviously got this image of what the Tour was going to be like. Could you see straight away what she wanted?

Del: Absolutely. There were embryonic elements of it as far back as the KT Bush band. We started properly in September '78 organising

the whole thing. By that time I had learned that this woman was all "I know where I'm going, I know how I'm going to get there". She was getting up in the morning, going dancing, coming back, rehearsing the band, going home, in a meeting 'til 3 in the morning, then getting up, going dancing. And she just breezed through the whole thing. And all of us were saying like "Please no, I'm knackered, I've got to go to bed". So she'd stay there and talk to the lighting guys or the costume or set designers.

HG: What was the first night of the Tour like?

Del: The first night was bitter sweet obviously. But I remember when we picked up the tour bus, outside what used to be the Hammersmith Odeon funnily enough, going full circle there. We all piled up there, it was like going on a school journey. It was like "Yeah! We're off on tour!" For me and Brian this was it, this was what we always wanted. I always wanted to go and do a show where all I had to do was turn up, plug in and play; I didn't have to hump any gear around, I didn't have to set anything up. Some nights I remember I used to stand and watch the Crew breaking down the set because I didn't have to do it. And it was great, I had a tech who took care of my gear. I didn't tune up once on that entire tour. If the guitar went out of tune I just swapped it over and he'd tune it for me... Heaven! When we hit the first bars of *Moving* and that curtain opened on a sea of expectant faces, it was like "WooooW!!" I'd never felt anything like it. It was electric. It almost made me stop dead it was so overwhelming. It was great, addictive even. Just like a dream. We had a last night party when it all finished and we were all in tears. I could see all these big burly blokes from the crew breaking down in tears, it was just incredible.

HG: Bet you spent the whole night going "See you on the next tour!"

Del: "Yeah, don't worry, we'll be doing it all again soon. America next, America next!" Then we went into the studio and never came out again. But I have so many great memories of that tour.

HG: Had *The Dreaming* produced two or three hit singles and had been a number one album like *Never For Ever*, do you think she would have toured again?

Del: No, I don't think so. Kate said to me one time that she had somehow lost confidence in performing which I could never work out because she was such a staggering success on that tour, but it was incredibly hard for her. At some point she must have sat down and thought "Do I really want to put myself through that again, because if I do it again I've to make it bigger and better, and it's only me, it's not like there's a band, it's just me, I'm responsible for the whole thing". I remember there was one night in Sweden where she got an infection in her throat and her voice started to go. We were all trying to get her to abandon the gig but she wouldn't. She went ahead and did it anyway, a much truncated version, two half-hour sets rather than the whole thing, but we were all full of admiration for her doing that. There was no way she was cancelling that show. But I think somewhere along the line she thought "I just can't do that again, it's too much, I'd rather spend the time making albums". We went back to the studio and she discovered that she could say a lot more there.

HG: Of course the immediate album after the Tour was *Never For Ever*, which Kate had also co-produced.

Del: I don't think it was one of her best albums. I think the real transitional album was *The Dreaming* where she took control. As I said earlier on the more pure, the more she does on her own, the better it gets, and when she'd finally got rid of co-producers it got better and better and better.

The Future

Antonello Saeli: Will we EVER see the complete video recording of the Tour of Life? Please, say Yes.

Del: It was all filmed. But only the stuff that was on the video was edited properly. Every night was recorded. But, for her, it's old days, she doesn't want to go back. But I just think it would be wonderful. The video is still available I think but it won't be for much longer and I wanted to do a 5:1 mix of the soundtrack. It'd be really worth doing and I'd love to try to see if there is something extra that could be put in it. But there is nothing edited up and nothing mixed musically, just that film.

Si: Would you be interested in supporting Kate in a live set of her favourite works?

Del: Er!... let me think about it for a nano second... YES!!!

HG: There are two possible ways of doing this - the whole production like she did in 1979 with dancers, or just her and the piano and the band...

Del: There have been lots of times we've talked about this. We've gone through the whole thing of doing a massive spectacular production, to her doing it on her own, and we just go round and round and round. But the bottom line is that we haven't done it so far. Every time we got to the end of an album we'd say it would be really nice to go out and do a show, wouldn't it? I still have my fingers crossed. You can never say never.

Antonello Saeli: Are there any chances for us in the future to listen to some material which was not included in official releases?

Del: As far as I know there is very little and there is probably no chance of anything coming out because if it had been any good it would have gone out already. There are lots of sketches where there's a rhythm box, a piano and a rough vocal and she gets to that point and then says "I'm either going to carry on or I'm going to drop it." There are a couple of variations of things like *Sunset* that were done in different ways but didn't work, so they will probably never see the light of day – she did a version where she played piano and John [Giblin] played bass and Pete [Erskine] played drums, but it didn't work. There was so much stuff and that's why it was a double album. There's not tons and tons of secret stuff in the vaults.

Thomas Grayson: There is talk of you making a solo album yourself. What genres will that cover, or like Kate, will it be unique? When do you hope this album will be released?

Del: It will hopefully be available on my website this Autumn. It's called *Leap of Faith* because that's what it is for me. It's exorcising ghosts, moving forward into unknown territory, stuff like that, resolving lots of things. But it's also putting myself up to be shot at. It's all mine, I've played everything on it, I wrote everything on it. But obviously because of the age dilemma no record company will touch it with a barge pole, even if I was writing the greatest songs in the world, so I have to put it out myself which is one of the great things about the internet, you can do that. So that's my plan, try to link to as many sites as possible and hopefully sell one or two copies. I recorded it on the Pro-Tools system. People will be able to buy the album from me from my website. A bit like John's [Carder Bush] stuff.

Mike Wade: What would you most like to work on with Kate in the future if she was up for it?

Del: Piano vocal album. Just for her to sit down at the piano and sing some songs and do it really quickly and put it out. That would be a wonderful thing to do. The only pressure would be on her to write songs. Writing songs... it's like that thing of the painter. Every brush stroke being torn from his body – it is like that. I have watched her agonise over a couple of words. I do recall a couple of occasions where she's struggled over a couple of words for days and once she's got those couple of words it will just transform the whole thing. That's what I've always found quite fascinating about observing the whole process, of how she will strive for that perfection. As a lyricist Kate has no equal for me. It's what I found so attractive about her music right from the start. How could this young, innocent girl deal with these huge issues? Her lyrics are her strength and her beauty. She's a great modern poet.

HG: Will she continue working, will there be another album?

Del: I think she will. I hope she will. I wouldn't like to say when but I can't actually see how she can stop because it's not something she controls. She's not possessed by it like she used to be. In the early days she was driven and completely focussed, basically it was her child, but now she has a child for real so priorities change. But I can't honestly see her stopping because it's something she does without thinking, part of who she is, it's not work, it's never been work. I guess if one day she wakes up and says "I've got nothing more to say," then, maybe, she'll stop.

HG: As Bertie gets older his demands on her will change. As *Aerial* was being made he was a growing from being a toddler into a little boy. Over the next few years maybe he'll say "Mum leave me alone" – children need less attention as they get older.

Del: That's also the great thing about music, there is no age limit thing, there isn't a time when you can't do anything because you're too old, unless of course your fingers don't work. You just move off into another direction, your experience expands and you move on.

Photo: Krystyna FitzGerald-Morris

HG: Did you see the Bowie piece Kate wrote for *Mojo*? It was really cool, really funny.

Del: You know I didn't really like that guy's music until I met Kate and she turned me right onto him. She turned me onto a lot of musical stuff. One time there was some kind of charity thing when she did the two flashing LED pictures. He was very involved with that and I got to chat with him and I just thought, Christ! What a lovely bloke this is, just an ordinary guy.

HG: It's the same with Kate. People over the years have said this. She's the nicest sweetest, funniest person whose biggest concern is getting you a cup of tea.

Del: This is the thing. Even now, after all this time, the press are still saying things like we went to her place and she's giving us slices of pizza and making tea – like it's something unusual. This is who she is, what you see is what you get. She's got an amazingly good sense of humour.

Yes, the life of Kate Bush.... Like I said to you earlier, sometimes you meet people in your life and you don't know it at the time but they are going to change everything for you.

Overleaf: the HomeGround obituary for Dr. Bush, Kate's father, issue 79 December 2011

Dr. Bush

"Pa"

1920 - 2008

Dr Bush was a lovely man, who was both fascinating and always fascinated. It was to Dr. Bush that Kate played the early versions of her songs. In the 25 years we knew him he always made us feel welcome in his home and was constantly interested in what we had to say, whether it was the latest story in *Music Week*, an article in *HomeGround* or more often than not, our opinion of Kate's latest release. He was always honest, open and genuinely funny. He got heavily involved in the organization of the Conventions and treated us with respect and trust. We cherish those times we spent with him.

Our memories of Dr. Bush are fond and many. He was a kind and remarkable man, with a keen intelligence and sharp wit. He always had a large book on the kitchen table - we remember one he was reading about molluscs! We shared many happy times with him on those wonderful visits to the Farm. It was like stepping out of this world into another, a place of magic where all that creativity was born - that of his three unique and individually talented children. He was very important to us for many reasons. Like Hannah, he was encouraging and supportive of the magazine, even in the very early days when it looked like it was printed on toilet paper.

Occasionally the magazines arrived back from the printers around the time of a visit. We loved to give him his copy, and see that grin on his face as he flipped through the pages. We could see the joy in his eyes as he saw the photos and drawings of his little girl. He was a very proud Dad. Once or twice we heard him playing the organ as we walked up the path. In the Summer foxes would appear at the open French doors, the sounds of Summer and birds coming in from the endless garden. Sometimes Kate was there too. Casual in her jeans and boots. Very fond memories.

We loved the way he would sit forward in his chair, that grin, puffing on his pipe, and that wicked glint in his eyes that told us he was still quite a lad, as he listened keenly to one of our recent tales and adventures, or Peter's court stories which made him laugh so much... Every time we think of Dr Bush we see him with that wicked twinkle in his eyes, his hands clasped as he pondered before coming out with an even more wicked remark.

He loved to hear about the music industry from Dave - Dr. Bush was knowledgeable about the industry and Dave's perspective fascinated him. He was always very interested in our lives, and for Krys and Peter was a great support through the many IVF attempts. He got Krys merry on his Remy Martin quite a few times over the years! He came to Peter's rescue at the end of '97 a year in which we had four cars die on us. He leaned towards Krys, hands clasped and grinned at Krys "Do you want to buy a Volvo?" - so we did a few days later and she was our favourite car, complete with the Hounds of Love bites chewed from the driver's seat. There are holly trees in the garden of HomeGround Towers that he gave us from his garden at the Farm.

Dr. Bush was so important to us through all the stages of our lives, all the adventures, the happy and sad times. We loved him. And always will.

Thank you for being our friend and a big part of our lives,

Dave Krys Peter

November

John Carder Bush

In November the dead come to us in dreams:
bright faced and merry, they wink a careless eye,
chat a while, then depart in wandering streams;
ignoring all our weeping over all our guilty lies,
they leave the echo of laughter and no ghostly cries.

Skies in dark November, heavy with winter rain,
dictate the patterns of our hopeless emotions:
addicted to the dark pints of pointless pain
we reach for whisky and other potions,
pining for hot sands and a cooling ocean.

Motion of water runs fast, the gutters fill and drip,
leaves clog the conduits with soggy bones
and every undertaking slips and breaks its hip;
the change of the seasons heaves and groans,
accompanied by sniffles and mechanical moans.

Phone calls come from the heart of summer,
but caught in November we cannot reply.
November marches like a frightened drummer–
we follow stupid, programmed to comply,
unable to adjust and make the final good-bye.

Tied to the seasons perpetual rhythms,
we blame our moods on our own flawed pace,
think destiny is based on simple logarithms
and life is merely another pointless race
that can be controlled by catch and chase.

Ignoring facts we blow on the dying embers
when the natural world settles down to sleep;
haste and disasters fill our Novembers
while after harvest we still struggle to reap
the hopes that grew on summer's fecund heap.

Leaps and adjustment are beyond my remit–

I cannot accept this watering down of intensity and sex,
and will not submit to love's November:
I will not drown,
I will not fall,
I will not go down.

Awake

Lesley Sharp

A slice of lemon moon
Cut across the boards
A dance of dust caught
Upon the tumbling air
Illuminate
Encore, the crowd cried
Encore

But this stage has not known
Footsteps for so long
Empty and silent and growing older
Hour by hour in darkness
The hollowness
Just
Waiting
For song

And stepping through the light
Dust threads skipping in flight
I leave them behind me
I leave behind me
A wake, in the dust
A wake
And before me...
Awake

Aerial in Perspective

Chris Butler considers Kate's albums in retrospect

Issue 78: June 2007

There are certain moments that you know will always remain with you and seeing the video for *King of the Mountain* for the first time is one of them. It was one of my most bizarrely moving experiences for a long time, the strangest thrill of Kate's first and fleetingly cryptic appearance a minute or so into the video. As she gradually comes into full focus I am faced with something quite strange yet wonderfully uplifting – a forty seven year old Kate Bush; her expression somewhat more knowing and wiser. The Kate I cherish is a young woman who disappeared from sight a long time ago and here I am faced with someone the same yet very different. I have that odd but almost childlike wonder of discovering that my dreams didn't die after all. Likewise, the music itself is typically 'my Kate' but somehow wiser, slightly more restrained and with a quiet confidence that only maturity can bring.

My expectations were surpassed when I heard *King of the Mountain* and on its release I played it constantly for several days after. The release of *Aerial* on 7th November had an even greater impact on me. The single was perhaps one of the least typical tracks on the album, making the first listen full of further unexpected surprises.

As I re-read my words here I observe that my own comments aren't much different from those of many other fans who have waited so eagerly for this album. What scares me a little is the almost reverential and awed attitude that I find myself adopting whenever Kate Bush is discussed. I have an aunt who now lives in Australia – there is a huge age gap between her and my Father and in effect she is more like my sister than his. On the announcement of the album and the single we became like teenagers again, frantically swapping emails with snippets of news and links to Kate-related web sites. We did this for many of the other albums and even now when we're approaching what teenagers would refer to as 'past it' we are reverting to their behaviour patterns. Just what is it about Kate Bush that holds so many people in under such a powerful spell? How many other artists could drop out of sight for twelve years and yet return with equal if not increased impact on their original audience and a whole new one as well?

To answer this question, I have spent the last few days re-visiting all of Kate's previous work. I'm a very different person now to the eleven year old who first saw Kate singing *Wuthering Heights* on Saturday morning children's television. I'm perhaps even further removed from the angst-ridden teenager who obsessively played *The Dreaming* album until the vinyl was almost worn down. With the kind of wider musical tastes that only age can bring I now understand Kate's sources of inspiration more fully. What shocked me so much was the range of her inspiration when she recorded the first of what would become a series of all time classic records. As a thirty-nine year old, I am still exploring the genres and philosophies that a teenage girl synthesised into a masterpiece of a début album with almost effortless innocence.

Kate Bush caught everyone's undivided attention whether they loved or hated her. Nothing like this had happened before in the music world of the Seventies. The voice itself was so atypical – in part a high soprano that still refuses to be classified. The range of expression matches and sometimes even surpasses the most magnetic of theatrical or operatic singers. Pop singers just didn't do what she did; if it served the music or narrative she would shriek, scream or scowl but it worked in a way that no-one else could get away with.

Graphic: Chris Butler

It seems we also took notice of whatever she had to say with unquestioning loyalty. She gave us songs about deeply spiritual sexual ecstasy. She gave us songs about religious and philosophical gurus. She sang about the menstrual cycle, about giving birth and even about the incest between a brother and sister. If ABBA had done this, their career would have plummeted, yet *The Kick Inside* sat very nicely alongside *ABBA – The Album* in the album charts and nobody batted an eyelid.

When *Lionheart* came along Kate was interviewed on BBC children's television. The programme was the well-respected 'Ask Aspel' and Kate gave us a piano rendition of *Kashka From Baghdad*. This was late-Seventies children's television yet no-one seemed to care that Kate Bush was telling a story of the night-time delights of illicit homosexuality. Some didn't notice, some chose not to notice and those who did realised that she was just a damned good social commentator – even though she was only just leaving her teens. Whatever the case it was superb and unique music.

The boundaries were pushed even further with *Never For Ever*. We were presented with *The Infant Kiss* and again we listened and we were enchanted. Such was the power of the muse that we could be taken to face even our darkest fears and taboos.

Listening again to *Lionheart* showcased Kate's grasp of varying musical styles and genres. Like no-one else she swept them up into her own style and fed us whilst we accepted it all unquestioningly as pop music. Listen again to *Coffee Homeground* – our teenage singer is out-cabareting Ute Lemper. This is probably one of Kate's best-loved songs where her fans are concerned. Most of us wouldn't go out and buy a Ute Lemper CD but we've all got *Lionheart* – German Cabaret just increased its audience by a good million or so.

As a youngster I didn't appreciate the cleverness or humour of songs like this. Many songwriters in their forties would struggle to display such sophistication and wit – another indication of the rare talent at hand for a teenager. *Coffee Homeground* isn't just a good piece of cabaret. It is also a good piece of theatre, as are many of Kate's songs. The only other artists in my opinion who ever did this quite so well are the likes of Queen with *Bohemian Rhapsody*. Kate could just step right out of the pop genre and into any world she wanted yet we still bought the records and devoured them as pop music. Just think of *Hammer Horror* and *Wow* to name but two – almost set stage pieces depicting Gothic horror and the pathetic tale of an ageing gay actor.

There were also political themes in their time – nuclear war and the conflict in Ireland (*Breathing* and *Army Dreamers*). Pop stars ramming home political concerns were nothing new – a young woman hypnotising them into your consciousness with the devious allure of a siren was something never before encountered. The list is endless. On a personal level, I had discovered the music of Frederick Delius and become CND aware without even realising that I had been converted. Many a politician would kill for such a talent as Kate's.

As I revisited the later albums I found an even wider divergence from the world of pop music. I still don't know how to classify *The Dreaming*; it remains something quite unique. *Hounds of Love* seems to have the grandeur of an Oratorio. Most artists attempting what Kate attempted would appear posturing and self-conscious. It is a measure of the talent concerned that everything here sounds spontaneous and genuinely inspired. Again we came, we heard, we bought. Once again the pop world was conquered by something that was anything but.

Listening again to these two albums helped me to understand another reason why we love Kate so much. Whatever people think, pop music isn't about real emotion for most of the time; it's about carefully sanitised and packaged emotions. These are usually the most sugary ones, often with a bit of economic or sexual politics thrown in for good measure. Once in a while we get a really good political snipe or an appeal to our charitable instincts. None of this is necessarily bad, it's just carefully shaped and within given parameters. Kate, by contrast gives raw emotion over a wide range and there are seemingly no inhibitions about how it's expressed. She has amazing vocal beauty but will equally create a grotesque sound if it serves the artistic purpose.

The Sensual World and *The Red Shoes* I feel less comfortable commenting on. They arrived on the scene during that black period of my life known as my late teens and early to mid-twenties. Like many others of my age group I threw the baby out with the bath water and left behind many of the good things in my life in an effort to escape the negativities of my teens. It was only in my late twenties and early thirties that I came back to Kate's music and discovered these wonderful albums like something new. For me, they are a different kind of Kate Bush – more withdrawn, more mysterious yet just as beautiful. The two later albums turned a corner somehow but it's something I can't put into words. Maybe that's the appeal.

So what of *Aerial*? I don't think there can have been many more eagerly anticipated albums. I count myself as one of the millions of Kate's record buying fans and I seem to be quite typical in that my thirst for her music remains undiminished despite a leave of absence on both my part and hers. Some people never stopped craving her songs. Some of us stopped craving only to discover the value of what we'd lost. Whatever the case, the time seemed ripe for this album.

Kate's music survives beyond that of most other artists for two simple reasons. Firstly, they are extraordinary songs, expertly crafted and performed with rare skill and insight. Secondly, her music scales the depths and heights of emotional and spiritual experience. Really good music always creates a sense of ecstasy – there is no such thing as an unmoving Kate Bush record.

My own opinion is the subjective opinion of a fan, nothing more, but I feel that *Aerial* will be considered one of Kate's finest works. It bears all the hallmarks of a mature artist at the peak of her powers. Far from being dulled by a prolonged period of absence, it seems that the star shines more brightly than ever. One BBC reviewer expressed doubt with regards to the album. He said that he didn't know who the audience for *Aerial* would be, apart from Kate's established fans. The reason for this, he said was its radical divergence from the sound world of modern pop music. He should have known better – after all, nothing has changed.

On a Cloudbusting Kind of Day

Jennifer Wright Teaches Kate in the Curriculum

Issue 78 June 2007

I was five years old when I first saw the *Cloudbusting* video, but it, and that voice direct from the angels, captured me right from the start. There and then, a true Kate Bush fan and future obsessive took flight! Kate was so many things: literary, striking, intelligent, vivacious, enigmatic; hauntingly beautiful and endearingly kooky... even at that tender age, that rare fusion of haunting music, beauty and gravitas was truly intoxicating. Perhaps some things are just too special. Beyond language even.

I began to wonder, how could I do something that little bit different to communicate the magic of Kate to more people. Hmmmm. Late one Sunday night over a glass of Shiraz: I decided I would have a "take Kate to work day". Luckily for Kate, not literally.

As a relatively new teacher of English to speakers of other languages (generally abbreviated to EFL) I remain on the eternal quest for ways to find that "magic" lesson – the one that'll have the students brimming with enthusiasm and swinging from the rafters with unadulterated joy. Often it eludes me (it's only a certain type of person that can get genuinely excited about relative clauses, pronouns and the present perfect... and I'm not one of them) try as I might, I just can't seem to delight them, or indeed myself, with the complex intricacies of English grammar in all its peculiarities. And teaching an elementary class, one has to be inventive and rather resourceful to avoid that every teacher's nightmare scenario of the "tumbleweed" moment (also known as the lead balloon lesson). I've had them a-plenty.

My class comprises of adults young and old from all over the world – practically every continent is represented, from the Middle East to South America by way of Turkey and Tibet and back again. In the EFL classroom, where effective communication is the goal of every moment, one finds solace quite often in the international language of music. Were they ready for a bit of Kate, though? I decided that they were.

Occasionally in teaching (sadly a profession marked so often by endless anxiety, concerns about results and external pressures) I have a rare day where I only wish that a camera crew had been present to record the progress of a teaching session. My Kate-inspired lesson was such a day.

I began by showing Kate's lovely visage... "ahhh beautiful" they all chanted in unison (correct!) – before I heard someone say, "is Gloria Estefan, no?" from the recesses of the room. Ahem. That one was nipped in the bud quickly as I explained that this was not Latin supremo Ms. Estefan, but actually England's most cherished female singer, songwriter and musician, and she was going to take them off on a little musical journey...

We began by taking key words from the song "yo-yos", "big black cars", "glowed", "bury", "something good"... and exploring their meanings and usages. Then I showed them a picture of the *Cloudbusting* machine which was greeted with a child-like exclamation of marvel – which I happen to think is rather magical in a room full of young and not-so-young adults, worn down as we all are with the frenzied, hysterical pressures of modern living.

"What do you think this machine does?" I asked, probingly, enigmatically. Answers were many and varied... but no-one guessed the weather connection, so I told them the story. Gradually building the atmosphere really seemed to help, as their emotional attachment to the story was becoming more apparent moment by moment, especially when I told them about the rain making the little boy happy because it reminded him of his Father.

I've heard Kate herself describe music as "pure emotion" so many times... here I could see exactly what she meant.

Then I played them the song. I could have been the 1000th time I'd heard it; I could hear it a thousand more and I know I would never tire. Their expressions were thoughtful, and measured, and calm and considered – a joy to behold. The soothing effect of Kate's voice and melodies on the classroom was tangible... and the responses from the students: a pure delight. One loved the "marching" sound, and the strength of the rhythm – the wonderfully gregarious Mexicans stamped throughout in unison with the beat, and the Malaysians sat in quiet contemplation, their heads clearly filled with a million images and colours and thoughts. I didn't say a word – and often that's when you know the lesson is going rather well. What power there can be in silence!

So my students completed their lyric sheets with the "missing" words that I had chosen – and then asked if they could hear the song again, which was greeted with the same appreciative rapture. I could see that the spell of Kate was beginning to weave its potency, and who was I to interfere?! I was just thrilled (and if I'm honest, rather privileged) to be the instigator.

"What do you think a film of this song would look like?" I asked the spellbound assembled. Within a minute we had a veritable board full. Who will the main characters be? The Father, his son and the police! What will the Father look like? Ahh he will be tall, very tall, with grey hair. Maybe white! What will the son be wearing? I

Graphic: Aerial by Chris Butler

think shorts. And he will have short hair. What will the weather be like? There will be clouds, and some rain, maybe a storm... but the sun will come out. There will be trees. Do you think there will be anything else in the video? A big black car. And the men from the police. Dressed in black. They will march. Maybe there will be a train. And there will be hills or mountains.

Now, none of my students had even heard of Kate, let alone seen the video. So unless we had a bunch of psychics in there, I thought this was a pretty incredible set of answers.

As we watched the video together, and we ticked off the people and places they had accurately predicted, I could only smile happily. I've always felt that for distilling and evoking human emotion and experience, Kate was and is without peer. This was concrete proof. Such is the unyielding power of her visual, filmic quality; she sends her magic far and wide across cultures, continents, temperaments and other potential barriers. I was reminded instantly why this special lady is so important to so many, and why her music will live as long as there are people in the world to listen to it. Forever.

She's the rarest of artists, truly. And she held an entire class of people whom she will never meet in the palm of her hand for the duration of that lesson. So thank you, Kate, for making my job much easier, and for bringing such wonder and escapism to so, so many. What a lovely afternoon, indeed. And we owe it all to her!

The Whole Story?

HomeGround looks at the recent books about Kate

Issue 79 December 2011

Dave: Graeme Thomson's *Under the Ivy*

Graeme Thomson has undoubtedly put a great deal of time and effort into this book and I would say that it is the best researched and fact-wise is the most accurate book there has so far been. In terms of detail, dates, places, names, chart positions and other such information, it is mostly spot on, with an attention to detail that other Kate books have never really achieved.

In 2009 the author contacted *HomeGround* seeking our help and advice with the book, and assured us that he had "no interest in her personal life" and the book was to be just about her work. We actually didn't meet or talk to Mr. Thomson, but we did sell him back issues of the magazine, which he said, modestly, probably greatly helped with getting the facts right. Reading the book now, it seems that he had a radical change of heart when actually writing, as the book does indeed delve into Kate's private life, her family, her school days and relationships.

Basically the book is her life story, interspersed with interview material, some from already published sources and some are new interviews with people who have worked with Kate in the past, most interesting of which is the late Bob Mercer from EMI. I would say that the accounts of the recording sessions for each of the early albums are by far the best bits of the book. Hearing from people like Andrew Powell and Jon Kelly and other musicians and engineers does give a glimpse into the history of those records and they are well written and quite fascinating.

However, the book let itself down when Thomson tries to tell us exactly what he believes is going on inside Kate's head. Time and time again he weighs himself down with stodgy prose as he over-analyses and makes 'deep and meaningful' statements, which would be fine, but after a while you begin to see that he is projecting *his* image of what he thinks Kate is, not an objective view of her as a writer or performer. For example – he mentions witchcraft and witches more times in this one book that Kate has done in her entire 30 year career. The same is true of Gurdjieff and other themes she has maybe mentioned once and usually in an early song.

This is not a bad book at all; Thomson clearly has a great deal of respect for Kate as an artist and as a person, even though by raking over her personal life he has undoubtedly caused her some distress. The historical side of the book is of real interest; but I suggest you take his glimpses inside Kate's mind, with a large pinch of salt.

Ian McLauchlan: Deborah Withers' *Adventures in Kate Bush and Theory*

"My own suspicion is that the universe is not only queerer than we suppose, but queerer than we can suppose"
J. Haldane 1928.

It could be said that there is nothing more to write about with regard to Kate Bush and her music to the present date. There have been thousands of articles written, and numerous books. And yet here is a forum where we still write about Kate, her art (in between discussion about the weather, cake and each other), and hopefully we take a little time to listen to each other's views, opinions with good humour. So here is yet another book about Kate. But it's not about Kate. And it's not another male journalist behind the pen. It's an alternative viewpoint, opinion, and is full of humour. This is a book about the Bushian Feminine Subject – the BFS. The subject of the book changes shape, gender, sound; taking on an ever shifting guise on its journey through each album and Zeitgeist of each release. The cyclical nature of *The Ninth Wave* and *A Sky of Honey* are expanded throughout the story of the BFS. The birth, life, continuity, change, breakdown, death and rebirth are explored with reference to folklore and fairy tales, colonialism, nationalism, gender, oh and a little bit of Orientalism thrown in for good measure. Brave, funny, silly, informative, and probably the best book written about Kate and yet not about Kate. Utterly QUEER.

Graphic: Izabela Samsonowicz

The Hounds of Love Band

...Richard Ames on Kate's music live; then and now

Issue 79 December 2011

Richard Ames: in 1979 tour manager for the one and only Kate Bush tour of the UK and Europe.

Photo: courtesy Richard Ames

It has been a long and slow process getting the band to the current state. I first thought of creating the band a few years back, and in December 2006 asked my friend Barry Wickens, with whom I was working on the last show of a Steve Harley and Cockney rebel UK tour. I was managing the tour and Barry was violin and guitarist in the band. It wasn't until the following August that I introduced him to Josie Mills. She had been recommended by John Crocker the original violin player with Cockney Rebel. I had shared a flat with him in the early '70s. He and Steve Harley formed the band and I was the first roadie...

I digress. I'm still great friends with JC and asked his advice when I was having problems locating a female singer. Josie was playing around York in an Alison Krauss tribute band playing with David, John's brother, so he instantly said "I know just the girl."

So we began what was to become a long haul, finding the final band line-up that would be doing these shows some two years later. Barry, Josie and I went through some testing times one way or another, every position in the band having been sat in at least three times. That's two drummers come and gone, two bass players, two keyboard players, two guitar players... you'll begin to understand the time this takes, as you have to start from scratch each time.

Josie Mills, the band's first vocalist. Liverpool 31st October 2009

Photo: courtesy Richard Ames

It takes me back to the Kate Bush tour back in April 1979.

On March 17th the technical loading of the sound and lighting equipment had just been completed and we had brought in huge space heaters to warm up the stage of the Rainbow theatre. It wasn't open and doing shows then, so I hired it for the two weeks Kate needed and it's where we were about to do the final production rehearsals and dress rehearsals for the only ever tour Kate performed.

These shows the Hounds are doing right now do remind me a great deal about that tour, especially as it was exactly thirty years before that we started that tour and as tour manager.

I was not to know how tragic the beginning could be. It was in rehearsal that we had issues with the lighting and in the dress rehearsals it was decided to hire an additional lighting operator, and I gave my friend, Billy Duffield, a call for a job that was to be his last, as he fell to his death on the first show in Poole.

It had been a long haul for Kate too, as she'd been in rehearsals for several months, both with the band and with the dancers, and looking back in my diary I see I went to meet her and the band in their rehearsals in the January, and on the 6th February took Kate and her brothers to see a sound system installed in the Hammersmith Odeon, having just been used for Nazareth the night before. She liked the system and we used it for her tour along with the operator Gordon Patterson.

Rhiannon, the band's present vocalist

Photo: courtesy Richard Ames

When The Hounds played in York, on 4th April 2009, we were in Birmingham Town Hall 30 years before, and on 16th April 2009 when we played Sheffield Memorial Hall thirty years before we were opening our run at the London Palladium. It seems like yesterday too. The music is such a reminder, and I told the band stories as they came to mind. It was one of my favourite tours of my career, even with the tragedy of Billy Duffield. Both band and crew just got on so well, together and the end result was just one fantastic show after another.

It was the music though that has made this project very special to me, because they are great songs and it is quite rare to have such songs that don't get performed, and so I thought I'd have a go at putting that right.

Who was in the band at 2009? I've mentioned Josie and Barry. We had Simon Horn on bass. He lived and worked in London, taught bass and came from New South Wales. Sam Leggett played drums, lived in Suffolk where he taught his instrument and had a lot of travelling to do to get to our shows, but he didn't moan and just got up earlier than the rest of us. Martin Luklinski on guitar was living down in Brighton, where Barry was based and put his own band together as well as playing with the Hounds. Glen Smith on guitar was based down in Somerset and had a very successful plumbing contractors company. An engineer by trade, Glen had played in numerous bands and we were very fortunate to have him. Finally we had Richard Luck on keyboards, then a very new member of the band. He lived in London and was constantly in demand with a variety of projects.

We have appointed our own agent, Don McKay of Rhino Agency who we worked with to build a fan base that allowed us to play theatres around the UK and into Europe.

We had a great 2009 with Josie fronting all the shows, but Josie wanted to stay closer to home in York and so in 2010 we began working with Rhiannon Bradbury and were very pleased to have her on board the good ship Hounds of Love. Rhiannon is a jazz singer originally from Norwich. She started at Trinity College of Music in 2007 after studying privately with award winning jazz singer, Anita Wardell. She is a member of Pete Churchill's new creation The London Vocal Project. Currently she's in the process of writing her own compositions, and had the opportunity to sing backing vocals for Little Boots, playing the Glastonbury Festival and making television appearances on the BBC's 'Later With Jools Holland'.

In fact it isn't just vocals that have changed recently so if you're coming to a show this year you may well see Lincoln Anderson on bass and Curtis Stansfield on keyboards too. In fact the Hounds are transforming into a small collective of players that love the music of Kate Bush and just like getting out there playing live.

The Hounds of Love Band May 2011

Photo: courtesy Richard Ames

Retracing the Scenes

Director's Cut and *50 Words For Snow*: 2011-2012

Later that day – 11th March 2011 – we found out. This was the work Kate had been doing on those older tracks. An album Kate had decided to call *Director's Cut* was announced for 16th May. Consisting of re-recorded tracks from *The Sensual World* and *The Red Shoes* this was plainly a project to which Kate had devoted much energy and thought.

The press release stated: "She has re-recorded some elements whilst keeping the best musical performances of each song – making it something of a director's cut but in sound, not vision." The album would be preceded by the new version of *Deeper Understanding* released as a single. These were the first releases on Kate's very own new label 'Fish People'. All the lead vocals and drums on *Director's Cut* were re-recorded, some of the tracks featuring Steve Gadd, Danny Thompson and, on backing vocals, Mica Paris. Three songs were completely re-recorded, including the now iconic *This Woman's Work*.

The announcement of this unusual release was another media event. The quality press and the music press (even *Rolling Stone*!) picked up on the story on their websites right away. As the Press Association put it: "Kate Bush is to make a rare return after revamping a number of her old songs… The release on May 16 will cause a buzz among her still devoted fan base."

On the BBC America Anglophenia blog Kevin Wicks reflected the concern felt in some quarters of that fanbase: "Kate is one of the few popular musicians who deserves the word 'visionary,' and we've rarely been disappointed with her bold choices. She commands trust. But the thought of *This Woman's Work*, her high water mark on *The Sensual World* (if not her career), being fussed over... scares me. The ghostly pianos, Kate's anguished performance, the cacophony of wails that crescendo in the song's climax: this track is perfection in its original version."

The Guardian elicited an opinion from Graeme Thomson, author of *Under the Ivy*: "It's telling that she has chosen to build something new on the skeletons of her old songs. Although her music is frequently defined by a haunting nostalgia and repeat excursions to the shadowy dream country of childhood, in her attitude to her work she has always been resolutely forward-facing." He had expected Kate to revisit the earlier albums, those made when she was not in control of the production process.

Ross Bennett on *Mojo* said "Ladies and Gentlemen, Kate Bush is back. The legendary pop siren will release her new album *Director's Cut* on May 16. And it looks set to be no ordinary record." Alex Young on Consequence of Sound remarked: "A new Kate Bush album is a big deal. Hell, just her thinking about the possibility is news."

One of the featured tracks on *Director's Cut* was *Flower of the Mountain*. Kate said: "*Originally when I wrote the song 'The Sensual World' I had used text from the end of 'Ulysses' by James Joyce, put to a piece of music I had written. When I asked for permission to use the text I was refused, which was disappointing. I then wrote my own lyrics for the song although I felt that the original idea had been more interesting. Well, I'm not James Joyce am I? When I came to work on this project I thought I would ask for permission again and this time they said yes. It is now re-titled 'Flower of the Mountain' and I am delighted that I have had the chance to fulfill the original concept*".

Stephen Joyce's release of the *Ulysses* text to Kate became a sub-story in its own right, Julian Gough in *The Times* picking up on it on 9th April: "This week, Kate Bush was finally given 'permission', by the James Joyce estate to set Molly Bloom's soliloquy to music – 22 years after she first asked, and it first refused… it is Stephen's rejection of pop culture that has caused the most damage. No interesting popular artist of the past three decades has been allowed a serious engagement with Joyce's work... There's a great deal of irony in this... *Ulysses* and *Finnegans Wake* are assembled from existing fragments of culture. His characters quote books, sing popular songs, reference films, and re-enact myths... But under today's absurd copyright laws, such a mash-up – a modern *Ulysses* – could not be published".

The new version of *Deeper Understanding* was played for the first time on Radio 2 on April 4, the day before release. Monty Moncrieff, a long time *HomeGround* reader reacted as follows:

"I've been chomping at the bit to hear this all day since it was played on Radio 2. The initial taster clip that leaked last week wasn't a good advertisement, and I was greatly concerned. The officially released clip gave nothing away either, though as ever with Kate you need to hear the whole thing. It's strange hearing a new take of a song which has been so much a part of the soundtrack to your life for over 20 years, and inevitably you're listening out for the differences – of which there are many here! At first her vocal seems somehow clipped, even a little immature. And of course there's the Cher-meets-Stephen-Hawking singing computer that we were all hoping might have been an elaborate ruse. It's not. However, in the context of the song it does actually kind of work (and is sung by her son Bertie).

"The edited radio version belies the extended

Compiled from the News in issue 79 December 2011, the Kate Bush News website, and the *HomeGround* scrapbook.

The logo for Kate's new record label

A number of small snippets of *Deeper Understanding* 'leaked' before the the Radio 2 première. These were just small excerpts of the track which sent the fans and the internet into overdrive.

Graphic opposite: Paulina Stuckey

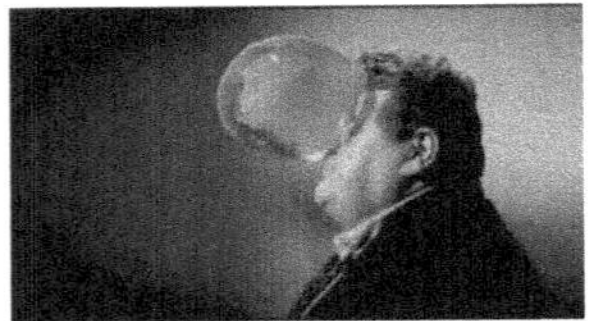

play out: the shorter, main body of the song seems to add little, but suddenly there's all the idiosyncrasies we associate so much with her: the voice-as-instrument, the unusual sounds, the sound effects, the slight whiff of barmy. And I'm fascinated and hooked once more! Revisiting old songs is not at all what I (or any of us) expected her to do, and my interest is certainly piqued for the album! Whilst I'm not sure about some of it, it's undeniably intriguing to hear her retread old ground. I like some of the instrumentation, but mainly I like the feel of the bonkers bits.

"I still can't but help think it's a bit of an in-joke for her, taking the piss gently out of those of us who gather online to discuss her work, fulfilling her years-ahead-of-the-game prophecy of the solace and belonging many have found in internet sites and chatrooms. I certainly spend far more evenings "with it like a friend" than I ever do using other media such as TV, although for me it's also greatly enriched my real social life, and not engulfed me like the song's protagonist. And what of her use of Bertie? Surely it's no coincidence that the role of the artificial bringer of comfort is being played by the person who, as she gleefully exclaimed on *Aerial*, has brought her own real life "so much joy". It's a clever touch. Welcome back, Kate. I'm still taking much of the new you in, but it's a far more enjoyable process than I feared it might be. (And if you're not keen, we still have the original version to listen to.)"

The new single was 'Record of the Week' on Radio 2. Jeff Smith, Head of Music, Radio 2 and 6 Music said: "Kate's music is as influential today as it was when it was first released, so I'm delighted to have this world exclusive." However, many fans were disappointed that it was a download-only release, though physical radio promos (this time actual proper CD singles!) were soon turning up at overinflated prices on eBay.

Steve Lamacq's BBC 6 'Roundtable' reviewed the track on 7th April. Keith Cameron, who had just interviewed Kate for *Mojo*, felt that it was a strange concept that people were struggling to get their heads round, but in the main part Kate had pulled it off: "She's quite incredible". Jim Carter wouldn't hear a bad word about Kate, though he did prefer the original: "It sounds like they've let James Blake loose on the chorus". Jim Goldhart: "So mental it's good... I started to like it because it was so stupid. It's good to hear the real Kate Bush because of all these imitators that are around". Keith gave 9/10, and the other two 8/10 and 9/10.

Radio 6 listeners, however, gave a collective thumbs down 6/10, one commenting "it turns out Kate Bush *can* do wrong". This view was shared by a presenter on BBC Radio 5 Live who commented: "I just don't get it. It sounds like someone accidentally leant on the mixing desk; she's a good singer, she doesn't need electronic effects on her voice". Graeme Thomson tweeted: "it's rather crudely overstating something which the original elegantly implied".

In *The Guardian*, 5th April, Michael Cragg also didn't quite get it: "When Kate Bush announced her first album since... *Aerial* would be... called *Director's Cut*, the majority of the music world thought 'At last!'. When said album turned out to consist of revisits and revisions of tracks... those same people went, 'er, what?' Still, the fact that Kate Bush has been near a recording studio is always worth getting at least mildly excited about... The 2011 retwizzle is two minutes longer, seems to have a new vocal and, naturally for the music climate of today, a lot of vocal processing and vocoder...'I bring you love and deeper understanding' croons the machine like a malfunctioning ZX Spectrum. It's not a disaster, in fact once you get used to the vocals it's still a great Kate Bush track, but if revisiting songs is going to mean adding an extra minute and a half of harmonica solos to each one then we may have problems".

Fraser McAlpine on the BBC America Anglophenia blog was also Fxphobic: "OK, this is gonna hurt. You know that auto-tune noise that gets used on a lot of nowadays pop songs? The one where it sounds like a human throat has been replaced with a pox of gargling molten rubber? Well, it seems that Kate Bush has taken a fancy to it. Now, as we all know, Kate is not above making her voice sound deliberately strange in order to tell a story: the whole of *Wuthering Heights* is proof of that. Still, it's a little unsettling to hear those robo-tones in the middle of her new single, an update of... *Deeper Understanding*... In the context of the song... it makes perfect sense, of course. Have a listen. But don't blame us if you wonder why a drunken Black Eyed Peas have suddenly taken over."

Tim Cashmere on MusicNews.com commented "The first single... is a seriously messed up reworking of Bush's 1989 track *Deeper Understanding* which prophetically told the story of a lonely person finding companionship in their computer later at night". Nick Neyland at Pitchfork Media was rather more enthusiastic: "Much of Kate Bush's career has been spent on the vanguard of invention... The contributions by the... Trio Bulgarka are dampened, with Bush Auto-Tuning their voices to make the lush expanses of cushion-y sound ever more opulent... It's in the final third... that this version takes on a life of its own. The pliable bass thrum from former Japan member Mick Karn remains locked-down, Bush loosens her control on language altogether, and the closing harmonica drones, deployed with a similar rusty tone to those in Talk Talk's *The Rainbow*, add a jagged edge to the natural softness. It's a feeling heightened by Bush's ragged vocal take, which hints at another subtle shift in her stylistic mien".

Nick Neyland's memory was letting him down. The bass on both the original and *Director's Cut Deeper Understanding* was done by John Giblin

Kate directed "a new short film" to

accompany the track. This featured Robbie Coltrane "as a successful businessman who is so obsessed by his computer that it leads to the break-up of his family (Frances Barber plays his wife) and, ultimately, his demise. Coltrane is taken over by the spirit of the computer (played by Albert Bush, Kate's son), is reborn and seeks to exact revenge on the spirit, tracking it over London to a room inhabited by Noel Fielding. Revenge is absolute, resulting in the death of Fielding's character". The film was produced by Michael Solinger, and shot over five days in London. The visual effects were worked on by Ben Perrot of Destroy All Monsters and Matthias Lindahl from Fido.

There was an interesting review of the film in the *Seattle Post Intelligencer*: "It is not a Lady Gaga video, nor is it a contender for an Academy Award (sorry *Inception* fans). Let's accept this fact and move on, because it is neither of those things. It is what makes it a Kate Bush music video! Although Kate Bush herself may not make an actual appearance in the video (with the exception of maybe her lips)... This reviewer will not be naive enough to think he could ever truly decipher the genius of Kate Bush. That's for Bush alone to understand."

Despite good initial radio play on BBC Radio 2, *Deeper Understanding* as a download-only single, entered and peaked at no.87 in the UK singles chart, and we hear, no.92 in the French singles chart. There was, quite possibly some consumer resistance amongst some Kate fans to "downloads" as elegantly put by long time reader Robert Brown who explained on the KB News forum why he did not like downloads: "Basically

Graphic: Paul Lovering

because it doesn't exist. There is nothing physical that you can own. The sound is poor as can be expected from having the sound shoved down a telephone cable. For anyone who has speakers connected up with bell wire I don't suppose they are bothered but I'm only interested in hearing the highest quality in sound reproduction. I prefer factory pressed compact discs or vinyl which are still the best method to store music for replaying".

We think it is worth noting that this track (as with *Wild Man* later in the year) was not set up to be worked by record company and artist as a hit single with all that implies, and was actually seen simply by Kate and EMI as a promotional item, a teaser, for the album which would shortly follow. To that end it worked: it aroused interest and not a little controversy, and alerted all to the fact that Kate would not necessarily be meeting their requirements. She would would be meeting her own.

In her *NME* "first listen" review of *Director's Cut* on 18th April, Priya Elan, described it as "like a fine wine maturing". Paul Moody in *Q* gave four stars: "Even for this most unpredictable of artists, the follow-up to... *Aerial* is a creative curve-ball… a curious move for an artist who has made a virtue of never looking back… *Director's Cut* succeeds, however, by axing the star cameos… and thrusting some of her most powerful songs back into the spotlight... Throughout, time is used as a mechanism with which to add gravitas. So, *Moments of Pleasure* morphs from melancholic lament to a piano-based hymnal on lost love(s), while a six-minute *This Woman's Work* is now glacial to the point of numbness - grief in musical form… A raunchy, Stones-inspired reworking of *Rubberband Girl* suggests... she's as spry as ever… *Director's Cut* isn't a new masterpiece from pop's most enigmatic auteur. Those keen to experience Kate uncut, however, should book their seats immediately."

The *Mojo* interview feature arrived toward the end of April: "we speak exclusively to the peerless Kate Bush about her return to music... a full career overview of her genius and Tricky, Antony and other stars assess her greatest work.". This started a brief media flurry on the prospect of Kate performing live: "*I still don't give up hope completely that I'll be able to do some live work, but it's certainly not in the picture at the moment because I just don't quite know how that would work with how my life is now. Maybe I will do some shows some day. I'd like to think so before I get too ancient - turn up with me Zimmer frame.*"

There were other features, including Andy Gill in *The Independent*: "For virtually her entire career, Bush has operated outside the prevailing trends and transient fashions of the music scene; in her music could be discerned few, if any, obvious musical precedents, the true imprimatur of the unique artist. Accordingly, like Joni Mitchell, she is frequently cited as an influence on successive generations of questing musicians, not all of them female."

Will Hodgkinson spoke to Kate for *The Times* and his feature appeared on 30th April: "An interview with Kate Bush, whatever form it takes, is exciting enough to cause heart problems in otherwise healthy music journalists. She is a genius: every album she has released has been something of a reinvention… She is hugely influential: everyone from Lady Gaga to Beyoncé owes a debt to the woman who invented the idea of the female pop star as performance artist. For those of us old enough to remember it, Kate Bush's performance of *Wuthering Heights* on 'Top of the Pops' was a life-changing, generation defining moment..." Kate was happy to explain to him the object of the exercise: "*I'd wanted to revisit some of the songs from these two albums for a while now. I think there were some quite interesting songs on there, and I wanted to see how I could make them sound at this point in time. I've tried to allow the songs to breathe more by stripping a lot of the production out and lengthening some sections, but keeping the best performances from the original tracks… I can't say I'm really that happy with anything I've done. That's part of the process for everyone when they look back on their work, isn't it?*"

The article included contributions from Lindsay Kemp, and Roy Harper who probably hit the nail on the head: "She is some sort of a perfectionist, but then a lot of us are, searching for the holy grail as it were, so that's not particularly unusual for an artist. I imagine that she felt she had to go back to these albums before she could move on." Hodgkinson asked her exactly that: Was making *Director's Cut* like scratching an itch as Harper suggests? "*More a nagging voice than an itch, 'Aren't you going to go back and sort them out? Get on with it then and hurry up!' Now I can move on.*"

BBC presenters scrambled for interviews. Ken Bruce on his BBC Radio 2 show on 9th May, and John Wilson on Radio 4's 'Front Row' 4th May. Radio 6 mounted a Kate playlist on 29th April. Mark Radcliffe talked with Kate for both his Radio 2 and Radio 6 shows and this was formatted on Radio 6 as a 'Kate Bush Week'. A radio documentary aired on Monday 23rd May and on each day of the week the station broadcast a section of the interview with songs from *Director's Cut*.

The 'Front Row' interview was conducted at Kate's home in Berkshire, and Kate was on exceptional good form, but keen to get back to work on the new album - a guest vocalist was coming in. Kate explained why she felt the need to revisit the 1989 and 1994 albums. That period was a brief flirtation with digital recording, so the first task was to return those tracks to the warmer and fuller analogue sound, of which she was such a huge fan. The next job was to strip out the tracks and create more space, to make them laid back and unhurried. With the vocals she had a problem until she realised that by taking them down a key she could find a way in, and then sing them "*as me now*". She did regard *Director's Cut* as a new record; she had literally breathed new life into those tracks.

For the *new* album she had reverted to her older way of bringing the songs into being by working at the piano, and curiously a bag of bone meal she had left there on her way to the garden was working some magic. She was reticent to set any release date, but admitted frustration about the length of time it took. Asked if she listened to any current music she admitted to buying the last Elton John and Gorillaz album: "*I am not a complete old fart!*" Touring was huge fun, and she had thought about it since but had no current plans. It would be very disruptive to her family and home life. That may change, of course, and she would never say *never*. She would be petrified, of course, but would get used to it.

Asked what of her own work she liked, she named *Aerial*: "*that was a good time of life*", she also liked *Hounds of Love* though hadn't listened to it for twenty years: "*I don't often hear my stuff on the radio*" though she had heard *Running Up That Hill* recently: "*that wasn't bad that one!*"

The interview made the BBC News on 4th May and even Dave and Seán were brought in to comment on air by BBC Radio Bristol's Anna King.

The promotional activity seemed non-stop, and a tribute to Kate and Fish People's press and radio team. On 4th May a feature article in *L'Express* described Kate thus: "Rare and enigmatic, Kate Bush remains one of Britain's most original artists and avant-garde of the past three decades". In the national Canadian weekly magazine, *Macleans,* Kate discussed *Lily*: "*She was one of those very rare people who are intelligent, intuitive and kind. I was really moved by Lily and impressed with her strength and knowledge, so it led to a song – which she thought was hilarious.*" The interviewer, Elio Iannacci, also spoke to Marianne Faithfull about Kate: "My favorite instrument in the whole world is the human female voice, and Kate Bush is one of the reasons why. It is, by far, a Stradivarius."

Sinéad Gleeson (*Irish Times* 6th May) was one of three journalists from Ireland invited to interview Kate: "In the days before my interview, I have several conversations with people about her. Their ages range from early 20s to mid-60s, their musical tastes even broader, but the admiration and respect Bush commands is universal. Kate: "*I've wanted to do this for a while, and I think some of my more interesting songs are on those two albums. You look back on your work and often feel there's something wrong with all of it, but that's just part of being a human being as much as an artist. I tried to make some of those songs sound like I'd want them to sound now, but this time I wanted it to be more about the songs than the production. I also approached them in a lower key, because my voice is lower now… I really like other people's voices as they age. I think singers' voices get more interesting as they age. People like Frank Sinatra and Billie Holiday had wonderful voices when they were younger, but they sounded even better as they aged.*" Kate also reacted to the ill-informed comment about her use of Autotune or a vocoder for any purpose other than to achieve an artistic object:

"*I was trying to get across the idea of a computerised voice, so back then, even with a vocoder used as part of a group of voices, it was difficult to hear. I also wanted a single voice to convey that the computer is a single entity. We just couldn't get the effect, but nowadays it's so easy to computerise a voice. I thought it was more poignant to have a child as this bringer of compassion in a cold technological world. I asked [Bertie] if he would sing on it, and he thought it was great fun… I've always involved my family and friends in my music, and he's the new member of the gang. He also plays violin and has a lovely singing voice.* "

It was interesting that in this interview Kate gave us two big clues to the new album coming later in the year – Sir Elton John and bone meal conjuring shades of the faithful hound of *Lake Tahoe*.

Nadine O'Regan (*Sunday Business Post),* another of the privileged Irish three noted: "a sharp-eyed fly on the wall might have observed those journalists engage in a primal dance of victory that day, on the graves of their rivals' thwarted hopes... Come Saturday, although rationally I understand she'll be calling, it's still a shock to find myself on the phone to Kate Bush… With her mass of black hair, kooky videos and *that* voice, you could be forgiven for believing Kate Bush is less a real person than a collective hallucination: "*Nadine, I'm so sorry. It's just been such a nutty day. Did they tell you I would be calling late?*" About the album: "*Looking back, there were elements of the production which may be drowning some performances – and there are elements of it that sound a bit dated. With* The Red Shoes, *that was done at a time when digital equipment had suddenly come on the scene. Although there are advantages to working digitally, it doesn't have the same warmth and fullness that analogue has – so for this record, we transferred any original performances that we were keeping back to analogue tape. I worked between analogue and Pro Tools – hopefully getting the best of both worlds: the warmth of analogue and the technical agility of Pro Tools. With* This Woman's Work *and* Moments of Pleasure, *I just wanted to start from scratch... And take away some of the elements that clutter it up a bit.*" And again, though not making any commitments Kate would not completely rule out live work. "*It was never intentional that I moved away from doing live work, I wouldn't like to say that I'd never do it again. It's a fascinating art form. There's a great spontaneity and vulnerability to it.*"

In what was one of a number of reviews by Graeme Thomson, in *The Word* he expressed the view that *Director's Cut* was "initially uncharacteristically regressive… partly a vibrant act of restoration… elsewhere radical reinvention… *This Woman's Work* is… something entirely new, profoundly moving and quietly

spectacular... *Rubberband Girl* is throwaway in the best most liberated sense... Conceptually all over the place... the power versatility of her voice remains a wonder to behold... she reclaims her birthright as our most truly abandoned artist... *Flower of the Mountain* proves oddly flat and underwhelming..." In general here he thought the album was "bold, fascinating, brave and occasionally raving mad... only truly essential on those handful of occasions where she takes her songs so far from their origins that comparisons are rendered wholly worthless... superior closet clearing exercise."

Thomson followed up with an article in *The Daily Telegraph* on 12th May attempting to explain Kate's enduring appeal. Another of his reviews appeared on the Dubai-based 'The National' website on 11th May: "Kate Bush has not performed in concert since 1979, but imagine for a moment that she had staged an intimate, one-off live show in the early 2000s... restricting the set list to songs from two of her previous albums... she played for around an hour, sometimes subtly tinkering with the material, sometimes radically revamping it. It never happened, of course, but... the resulting album might have sounded a lot like *Director's Cut*... 11 songs from *The Sensual World* and *The Red Shoes* and shaking them up with the kind of direct, re-energising vigour that defines a memorable live performance... This process liberates songs such as *Never Be Mine* and *Song of Solomon* from the tyranny of dated production techniques and allows them to really breathe - and, in the case of *Lily*, gives Bush sufficient elbow room to roll out one of her most abandoned, furiously thrilling vocal performances for decades... Generally speaking these are not radical reinterpretations but vibrant acts of sonic restoration... Hearing Bush grappling with her legacy is a rare enough occurrence to prove compelling, but ultimately *Director's Cut* is likely to be chalked up as an enjoyable curio rather than a classic."

The Mark Radcliffe interview was broadcast on his Radio 2 Music Club on 18th May. The question was why Kate had devoted time to rerecording old material. She made it clear that the old tracks were the best she could do at the time, but she had become increasingly dissatisfied with elements of those albums. The aim was to take a bunch of those songs, strip them out to create space and create a slightly more laid back ambience. The 'key' was the reduction of the key so that 'me now' could get back into those vocals. *Director's Cut* was already under way when she asked again if she could use the original Joyce words. That request was not the origin of the project, and if the Joyce Estate had not granted permission, it was likely that she would not have included *The Sensual World* in the new collection. It was not so much the songs – those on *The Red Shoes* for example were written before her mother was taken ill, as it was the original recording process. At that time the digital process was shiny and new and considered flawless. But she did not like the edgy sound of digital, and preferred the warmth of analogue. The production of those songs now seems dated and cluttered. The aim was to keep the elements including many musicians' performances. It was put to her that mucking about with songs like *This Woman's Work* might cause alarm and despondency amongst some of her fans, but Kate had no compunction. In order to achieve her ends she used a combination of old and new technologies. She had old valve outboard equipment in the studio but also used Pro-Tools to do what would be difficult to do with analogue. To Kate this was a new album. She was pleased with it and that was important since if other people didn't like it that was not ultimately that important. It was more important she had achieved what she had set out to do.

It is curious that Kate often engages more interestingly with journalists outside the UK. Perhaps because they are not bound by deeply entrenched preconceptions and often manage to ask the right questions. Hence this exchange in an interview with Michael Solubility for the German *Der Western:* "Should we rebuild pyramids again and again? *That's very flattering, but in retrospect those albums may have been more like leaning towers.* You have been working on new songs? *Yes, and it was instructive for me to go back two or three steps to develop a new vision for the future.* At the end of your new album it is a little out of hand. You mumble, as if you were drunk, strumming with the band. Do you want to destroy the myth of Kate Bush? *If the final point of the record sounds like the destruction of a myth, I'm pretty happy with that assessment.* Were you inspired by anyone? *Frank Zappa was a wise man He said that one can live as an artist in your work, untamed and adventurous, but lead an orderly life. I love this idea.* Why? *I've never met Zappa, but people who knew him described him as a lovable man in his private life, but his image was different. I always preferred the private to the public, because my work works best when I have my home as the base. I don't accept the belief that art is best when the artist is suffering. I work better when I feel good.* And you have foregone the demands of the the pop market. Are you proud? *I should have said no much earlier. Recently my son has discovered a photo of me, that was taken at Abbey Road Studios. I was dressed so stupid for it that he asked me why I had been photographed as a young girl.* Can you clear the rumour once and for all the world that you will eventually go on tour again? *The tour was fun because it was less a concert tour, and more a wandering circus. But studio work was more important to me. I can't give you a definite answer because I might regret it in a few years. Never say never.* Is your music a counter-point to the uncontrollability of your life? *When I work on a record, I am always trying for the best. So I must recognise the inevitability of failure. I am just as much fallible as any other human being.* Does this knowledge hurt? *It's what creates art.*

On the Slovak website Cultura Pravda, Robert Hurry awarded 5/5 considering the collection had "a unique atmosphere, and one of the albums of the year". Leslaw Dutowski on the Polish website WirtualnaPolska also awarded 5/5: "Calm, reflective, muted", and he had paid enough attention to know that it was Albert, not Kate who was vocoded on *Deeper Understanding*. "For Bush, the word 'mature' is probably not appropriate, because her work has always been characterized by maturity". *Der Spiegel* (22nd May) "Grandmaster Kate Bush" wanted Kate to know that she was an inspiration to hip-hop titans like 2Pac, Wu-Tang Clan or Dr. Dre. Kate: *I find that surprising and incredibly cool. Spiegel*: Are you still actually part of the industry? Kate: *Only partly. I am in a fortunate position. This begins with the fact that I have my own studio at home where I can work on my music undisturbed. I have no record company deadlines. I decide what I do and when.*

Alexis Petridis awarded four stars in his review in *The Guardian,* but was not completely convinced of the merits of the album. On the one hand: "the already glaringly apparent fact that she was an artist so unique as be literally incomparable..." On the other: "the new version's decision to overwhelm the haunting vocals of Trio Bulgarka with Kate Bush doing one of her patented Funny Voices through an Auto-Tune unit seems questionable at best... the only moment when you can honestly say the re-recording pales next to the original. At worst, they sound as good as their predecessors, which leaves you wondering what the point is." There were some points: "Occasionally, the changes genuinely add something, usually by taking things away. *Moments of Pleasure*'s rumination on death is more introverted and affecting stripped of its dramatic orchestration, while *This Woman's Work* – the re-recording of which caused the most unease among fans – is amazing: emptier, darker and quieter than before, it's even more heart-rending. Given that the original was heart-rending enough to soundtrack a charity campaign against child abuse, that's no mean feat..." Conclusion: "*Director's Cut* ultimately amounts to faffing about, albeit faffing about of the most exquisite kind".

In his review in *The Independent,* Andy Gill spotted the "consistency and homogeneity about the 11 tracks... which echoes her work on *Aerial*, and which lends the project a character entirely its own..." As many reviewers did he picked out *This Woman's Work*: "Originally written for the film *She's Having a Baby*, and frequently used in TV dramas ever since, this ethereal re-imagining untethers the song from those associations, allowing it to float free again". *Flower of the Mountain* was a favourite: "With her voice up close and intimate, the undulating repetitions are hypnotically gripping, as Uillean pipes dance with abandon about the gently puttering groove, caressed with string-pad synths: yes, yes! It's the most genuinely sensual music you'll hear this year." Alan Corr's RTE Music Blog surely had it right: "*Director's Cut* can be a startling experience, jarring you out of the comfort zone of the old versions with a sense of deja vu."

Adrian Thrills also awarded four stars in his review in the *Daily Mail* 13th May: "Now deeper and more sultry than when she was dominating the charts... it relies less on spectacular, soaring whoops and more on a natural richness and sensuality. As a singer, Kate is growing old gracefully, but she retains plenty of her unusual mannerisms and a compelling lack of inhibition... There are moments... when *Director's Cut* contains additions that might have been better left in the cutting room. But... it has some startling juxtapositions. There's an excellent centre-piece in *This Woman's Work* and *Moments of Pleasure*, two poignant ballads that are sequenced back to back."

Like many, May Helen (14th May *Daily Telegraph*) was also initially angry at having her settled understanding of Kate's tracks disturbed: "The premise of Kate Bush's new album initially sounded like a catch 22. Surely only her most devoted fans would shell out for re-recordings of old songs? And yet, weren't her famously obsessive fans likely to resent her tinkering with their beloved records? As a fully crimped-up member of the fan club, I certainly felt misgivings which turned to horror at the first radio play of *Deeper Understanding*... So when the full album arrived, I took a deep breath... Bush would be breaking the bubble of intense, personal worlds I had inhabited for years. I began by angrily cataloguing all the little vocal and production flourishes I missed" but then she spotted it: "This was, of course, a childish approach... *Director's Cut* should really be enjoyed as a rare, live performance... *Rubberband Girl* sounds like it could have been recorded in the backroom of an Irish pub."

Stephen Trousse (*Uncut*) had the question: "the title of this set, typically used by aggrieved film-makers, implies that some original vision for these songs was betrayed or compromised. Yet it's difficult to think of a pop artist who has assumed, from the moment of her teenage début, such creative control as Kate Bush. So what was betrayed or lost, and by whom? And do these new versions set the record straight?" The answer: "Ironically, now that young groups spend countless studio hours trying to recreate the astonishing gated boom of *Sat In Your Lap*, Bush seems slightly uncomfortable with her studio excesses... The most significant moment is found on *And So Is Love*... When the song first appeared, I thought she sounded so dispirited it would be a miracle if she ever made another record. Here she sounds revitalised. After the intermission of *Aerial*, could this mark the real beginning of the second act of Kate Bush's brilliant career?"

Will Hodgkinson (*The Times* 13th May)

awarded a hesitant three stars. Admittedly: "Kate Bush... is No 1 in a field of one: artists who can do pretty much anything and still be praised unreservedly. This isn't just because of the quality of her artistic output, or that she's always worked outside trends. It's also because she has managed her career with such dignity... She's morphed seamlessly from young performance artist into Home Counties mum with secret powers: you can imagine her doing the school run, helping out with an am-dram performance in the village hall, having a glass of wine in the evening and then disappearing into her studio before bed to work on an album that will be hailed as a masterpiece." – but – "Even the most ardent Bush fan will be left slightly unsure whether her decision to spend months tinkering about with new versions of songs that worked perfectly well first time round was the most prudent use of her time and talent". However, again *Flower of the Mountain* was an exception: "Bush was finally given permission to use lines from Molly Bloom's soliloquy by James Joyce. The estate is famously bullish when it comes to quoting the great man's work, suggesting that Joyce's grandson Stephen was ultimately won over by Bush's feeling for the sensual, unpunctuated words... Bush inhabits the place they evoke so fully, bringing their seductive qualities to the fore in a way only a woman of experience, wisdom and sexual understanding could... all the elemental power of the best English and Irish folk music allied with an original vision that takes it to an entirely different place. It's a gliding, fecund song, as appealing as an orchard in bloom". His conclusion on the album: "It could be that this was a stopgap, an itch that had to be scratched".

There were those who were hugely disappointed. Jason Draper (*Record Collector*) awarded only two stars: "the tracks feature ho-hum touches that largely result in reducing the songs' power. A sparser *This Woman's Work* has an almost hymnal quality, but lacks the emotionally crippling dynamics of its predecessor; *Deeper Understanding*'s vocoder duet is one knowing conceit too far; *Rubberband Girl*'s complete re-record sounds like it's sung from the bottom of a well as a Stones tribute act bangs out *Brown Sugar* from an adjoining cave.". Jason Draper (Yahoo Music 21st May) awarded 5/10 and wondered why Kate had spent (i.e. wasted) her time on *this*: "In an unparalleled career that could never have been undertaken by a musician with anything less than complete artistic control, however, Bush has never had to kow-tow to any order higher than her own. So why now re-record tracks from her *The Sensual World* and *The Red Shoes* albums..? *Deeper Understanding...* Now with added vocoder marking out the computer's 'voice', it's a mis-guided attempt at modification that results in this new version sounding more dated than the material it's based on... a really badly-recorded take on *Rubberband Girl* that sounds like a Rolling Stones tribute act stuck in an undersea cave. *This Woman's Work...* is lacking in some pure essence that the original contains." His conclusion: "Aside from the... major flops, doesn't actually offer enough of a difference from the original works to make it relevant to anyone other than the true completist." Tina Manske on the German website KulturMag asked "Who destroys their songs like that?" She loved *Flower of the Mountain* but thought *Deeper Understanding* and *Lily* "sounded terrible and deliberately destroyed a beautiful song".

And some REALLY didn't like *Director's Cut*. For them, taking out the '80s touches meant removing the very heart and soul of those tracks. There was actually real anger such as this on the Real Gone music blog 23 May: "Her striving for perfection – to obsessively airbrush the bits of the past which make her unhappy – leaps to new heights... *Deeper Understanding..* has been completely butchered. What would improve the atmospheric, multilayered original with its fretless bass parts? Nothing... But clearly, Kate's opinion differed. She's wrong. Maybe she should have had someone to tell her that once in a while... The steamy *Sensual World...* reinstates words from James Joyce's *Ulysses...* This isn't necessarily a bad thing, but everything else about it is really awful. The drums have been removed, the bass turned up and the production has a nasty, muddy sound. Kate's vocal in a lower key really doesn't match the dreamy performance on the original cut... in fact, it sounds like a warbling noise from an old lady. This is supposedly one of *Director's Cut*'s greatest achievements, but frankly, this has the sound of a middling demo take... She's absolutely deluded if she thinks this is an improvement... The bouncy pop of *Rubberband Girl* appears as an odd shuffling number combining a Rolling Stones inspired rhythmic twang with brushed drumming. A potentially good idea is made unlistenable by compressed production which makes everything sound underwater, while Kate's vocal is understated and somewhat mumbly. It's like listening with your fingers in your ears... We all change. Change is natural. We change as people – our personal views change, our tastes in music change. Slowly over time, everything about us changes. Kate Bush needs to accept that too and not indulge in exercises of warped revisionism. The overtly narcissistic *Director's Cut* only exists to massage Kate's ego and to give her many sycophantic fans something to get excited about, since they don't have anything wholly new. The past is the past, you can't change it; you certainly shouldn't attempt to rewrite it. The world doesn't need the musical equivalent of plastic surgery, especially when such surgery brings little to no improvement. *Director's Cut* isn't the work of the once brilliant and unique Kate Bush... it's totally a totally misguided affair, presenting the ugliest

Graphic opposite: Michele Ann

face of vanity. If Kate wants to piss on her legacy that's fine – after all, they're her songs to mistreat as she wishes – but she shouldn't expect everyone to still love her unconditionally afterwards."

Ouch! Well, you can't tell the public what to like can you? On the other hand this reviewer could just put the original tracks back on the CD player as Kate had suggested.

There were some reviews of *Director's Cut* which took time and considered what Kate was about, and why she had done this thing. Russ Coffey (The Arts Desk website 18th May): "Kate Bush's musical legacy may speak for itself, but she's more than just her songs. Her persona seems woven into the nation's consciousness, and her time-lapse approach to making albums makes her every move an event… Many felt that in those twenty five songs lurked one belter of an album. And happily, with the help of all new vocals and drums, a lot of remixing, and three complete re-recordings she seems to have found it… you only have to listen to them back to back with the originals to hear the improvements… it's the voice, however, to be most excited by. It's not a voice we've heard before, not even on *Aerial*. Lower and wiser, she not only sounds like she still wants to fll the world with her eccentric narratives, but now, if anything, has more to say."

Jess Harvel (PitchFork Media 19th May): "The very different mix of *Director's Cut* changes not just the sound but the emotional kick inside many of these songs. What was once the work of a shy woman who came to roaring life on record is now just as often subdued, reflective, inward-looking... At the time of its release, *The Sensual World* seemed both up-to-date and not of its time. The glossy studio-obsessive production sounded definitely of its moment... But the songs... were stark reminders that she actually came out of the same tradition that gave us... prog rock, and the... Canterbury psychedelic scene... It made for a strange hybrid, the smoothness of the Big '80s meets the complexity and expressionism of the prog '70s. By the time of *The Red Shoes*... Bush's music was too ornate to fit in with the stripped-down 'realness' of alt-rock... Her moment hadn't so much passed... as she'd become a genre-of-one. The fussed-over textures and genteel folk touches of adult contemporary peeled back mid-song to reveal naked eroticism, rage, joy, Bush's voice spluttering out wordless weirdness or leaping into ecstatic ululations. What Bush has done on *Director's Cut*, put simply, is to strip the '80s from these songs... The gigantic drums and digital polish, which both dated the music instantly and gave it that stark contrast between accessibility and the deeply personal, have been replaced with less showy rhythm tracks, and a warmer, more intimate atmosphere... The songs still don't have the feel of a band playing together, but they have a new unity, even the synthetic elements part of a lovingly hand-crafted sound."

Richard Eric ('The Gospel According to' blog 19th May) gave 8/10: "The middle of the album contains three of Kate's all-time greatest achievements, *This Woman's Work*, *Moments of Pleasure* and *Never Be Mine*, with all of them now made even more devastating than they were originally, the work of an artist looking back on songs about looking back, watching the years go past as she becomes further and further away from the parts of her life that were immortalised in these songs."

Andrezj Lutowski (Drowned in Sound 19th May awarding 7/10) rewrote a little history: "In 1996, Britpop was at its lagery zenith and to some degree Bush appeared a relic of the golden age of AOR... It was over a decade since... *Hounds of Love*, and... *The Red Shoes* was on the weak side... suggesting an artist mired in the past... But this isn't 1996. Since then, Bush's legend has grown exponentially..." and now "in the present musical landscape, there simply are no art-pop auteurs comparable to Bush..." and *Director's Cut*: "As there are a couple of jaw-dropping total reconstructions... it mostly amounts to intelligent tinkering... the glacial, six and a half minute *This Woman's Work*. Totally re-recorded, it's creepingly claustrophobic and piercingly beautiful, in its own way just as perfect as the original. Over the barest electronic twinkle, each line is wrenched out painfully, like a cold crystal pulled from the earth… it builds to a climax whose raw, bitter sentiment is entirely discernible, a diamond hard electronic choir rising in the background as Bush spits the new lyric "all the things that you wanted for me/all the things that you wanted from me" ...at its best *Director's Cut* is a dazzling affirmation of Bush's genius as songwriter, performer and producer. Maybe one day we'll take her for granted again. But not today."

In the American Songwriter blog (24thMay) Adam Gold hits nail on the head: "Not unlike what Paul McCartney did by editing Phil Spector out of *Let It Be* with *Let It Be Naked*, and almost exactly like post-punk luminaries Gang of Four did on their 2005 reunion record *Return the Gift*, *Cut* is – true to its name – very George Lucas... a predictably divisive act of musical revisionism. How you judge and enjoy *Director's Cut* really depends on where you fall philosophically on its plan of attack... if you're not married to the time-capsule aesthetic of the original recordings, then there's plenty to enjoy in an undeniably stellar set of songs, executed with a more resolute attitude, and with vastly varying changes in nuance – from stripped rhythm tracks to elongated intros. But if you just can't abide Bush's approach, then there's simply no pleasing you, and you can expect to only be surprised at best, and frustrated at worst… at day's end the effort doesn't really reveal a "Deeper Understanding" of the original recordings it references. And therein lies the problem – none of these cropped and re-imagined takes are drastic enough to add huge insights into Bush's output as they do her finicky outlook on her own work. Work that is, generally, great in any context."

Rich Juswiak *Village Voice* 25/5: "Though there is a faction of her fanbase that swears by *The Sensual World*... few would deny the fact that it sounds laden in late-'80s smog... On *Director's Cut*, her gravitas has new weight... You see what she's going for: something less "dated," with less bloat; orchestral sections, too, are wiped away, making this 'Director's Cut' a far less cinematic-sounding affair. But in Botoxing her sound, she's turning her back on her legacy of technological savvy. Bush's production has long been as key to her sound as her songwriting and delivery, and the "organic" rearrangements on *Director's Cut* sometimes feel safe and out of character. At least she's still letting weirdness in via her vocals, which are gloriously unhinged... Even while wailing Brontë references at 19, she sounded like a crazy old lady, so she achieves the desired timelessness most effectively through her natural resource."

I'll leave the last word with Martin Aston (BBC Music Review 9th May): "As much as it's fascinating to hear Bush the Elder look back at Bush the Younger, is the tinkering worth a full album? Yes, because it's a sign Bush the Artist is still alive... and *Director's Cut*... is a gorgeous body of work. No, because it's writer's block by any other name. No, because it's not radical enough a move. But if *Deeper Understanding* raised hackles, imagine if Kate had gone dubstep or collaborated with Odd Future. World wars have broken out over less."

In the week after release Kate took an early lead over Adele in the UK artist albums sales, but with the deficit being fewer than 3,000 units, *21* was still likely to pip *Director's Cut* to make a 16th week at number one. *Aerial* had peaked at no.3 in November 2005. The midweek charts prompted much speculation in the music news websites, but despite much optimism the album didn't make the no.1 many hoped, and which would have been a stunning achievement. BBC News reported on 22nd May that Adele claimed a further week at the top of the album chart. The report noted that "Kate Bush, whose career has spanned more than 30 years, has now had 10 albums inside the top 10. Her last chart-topper was *The Whole Story* in 1986". No.2 was by any measure a huge success and equalled the twin peaks of *The Sensual World* in 1989 and *The Red Shoes* in 1993, both of which reached no.2.

The following week the album fell back to no.11, and although it fell swiftly down the chart after that it sold consistently and by the end of June 2011 it was certified Silver (sales of 60,000) in the UK. The final run in the UK chart was: 2-11-30-53-60-98-137-171.

On 1st June *Music Week* reported "débuting in 15 territories, Kate Bush's *Director's Cut* was best placed in the Czech Republic (number 4), Ireland (number 4), the Netherlands (6), Germany (11), Norway (17), Switzerland (23), France (34), Austria (35) and New Zealand (38)." Although it was also the first Kate album to fail to chart on the US *Billboard* 200 since *Never For Ever*.

As the album exited the chart, *HomeGround* reader and published poet and novelist Collin Kelley commented: "I think we can safely put a fork in *Director's Cut*. She discovered her new voice, got plenty of press, generally good reviews, almost beat Adele to number one on the album chart. Roll on new album of material".

Kate spoke to NPR in the US on 19th August: "I'm in a very creative space, [*Director's Cut*] kind of gave me a bit of confidence which always helps you to move forward, and it's been received very warmly by people which is very nice, because you never know."

On the 'Metacritic' website which assesses the overall critical reaction to albums by averaging the scores in the most prominent and important music publications, *Director's Cut* received a score of 81, that is "Universal acclaim".

Meanwhile there were other rumours. As *Director's Cut* was fading from the chart, in July 2011 the *Sydney Star Observer* reported that the Chair of EMI Australia had been told to prepare for a November album release from Kate, but there was no further confirmation of this until on 12th September a Finnish retailer jumped the gun with the album title just ahead of the official announcement on Kate's own official website KateBush.com: *We are extremely pleased to announce that Kate will be releasing a brand new album '50 Words For Snow' on 21 November 2011.* Two albums in one year! First time since that now far off 1978!

On 24th September Kate posted on KateBush.com:

Hi there,

I just wanted to say how excited I am about the response to the announcement of '50 Words For Snow'. Thanks so much. I am really pleased with how it's all come together and I hope you enjoy the music and the artwork when it's released.

With best wishes,

Kate

There were also stories in the UK media that we were due for another mini-ice age!

We learned from Kate's interview with *Classic Rock* in July, that the new album carried forward the open clean analogue sound developed with Del for *Director's Cut*: "*I'm using the most archaic gear I could get my hands on. I'm working with analogue tape and old bits of valve equipment, a lot of that old stuff has a great sound.*" The new album was built around Kate's almost jazz piano and Steve Gadd's drums, with Kate's beautiful mature voice supplemented by the pure chorister tones of her son Albert, the tenor Stefan Roberts, and the guests Andy Fairweather-Low, Sir Elton John and

Above: Steve Gadd, Stefan Roberts, Andy Fairtweather Low, Sir Elton John and Stephen Fry.

The Russian Yeti of course. As Pavel Checkov would no doubt claim, the original.

Stephen Fry.

The latter had tweeted on 2nd September: "Just done a lovely amazing recording thing with a lovely amazing musician. Wish I could say more but bound by secrecy for the moment" and when the album was announced: "Tweeted that I did a secret recording 10 days ago: can now reveal it was this with the divine Kate Bush".

Again, more as a teaser for the album than an attempt to gain a hit single, a radio edit of *Wild Man* was released as a download only track on 11th October. Again to the regret of many, there was no physical single.

The track was was first played by Ken Bruce on BBC Radio 2. It was immediately hailed by Priya Elan at the *NME* (October 10th) as "her strongest single for decades". She wrote: "For those of us who have been secretly longing for a return to the unflinchingly bizarre and Bush's ability to conjure up strange new worlds, *Wild Man* is a deep joy." *The Huffington Post* described it as "classic Bush, all ghostly orchestration and pinched vocals."

Jack Cullen in *Gay Times*: "*Wild Man* actually strikes me as quite a warm and layered song. Like a medieval court dance taking place in a provincial Chinese restaurant, we are then taken for the chorus into the kitchens where wild imperative food orders and tea spoon duets ensue atop an array of historic string instruments. Kate's vocal is largely subdued here, bordering upon spoken word, it's more like one of Marianne Faithfull's efforts or one of Tina Turner's eroticised speech segments. Perhaps it is time to admit to ourselves that the wild, sassy, shipwrecking power of Kate's voice in the 1980s and early 1990s is now gone for good".

Lucy Jones in the 10th October *Daily Telegraph* was quite straightforward: "Jubilate! Kate Bush is back! Oh lord. I've got butterflies. Kate Bush is back ...We have a bassline bouncing forward in a similar way to *How To Be Invisible*, lyrics about the natural world (rhododendrons, snow, mountains; fans are furiously trying to decipher her lyrics right now), spoken word. It's a good sign and a great song..." Dave Bry in 'The Awl' noted: "Predictably, because she is a seer and a mystic, Kate Bush has released her new single, which is about the existence of the Yeti, on the very same day that the government of the Russian coal mining region of Kemerovo has announced the discovery of 'indisputable proof' of the existence of the Yeti." Four stars from Mayer Nissim at Digital Spy: "*Wild Man* trails the first proper new album in six years from one of England's most cherished songwriters... starts with an insistent riff, simple-as-can-be click-drums, and Bush's understated, breathy, half-spoken vocals before her words twist and turn into a double-tracked self-harmony and off-the-rails chorus. The vivid lyrics are denser than most English A-Level texts... the four-minute odd radio edit is a lush slice of beauty that the charts have been gagging for". Tom at Stereogum: "Reigning British art-pop queen Kate Bush has a new album... and the first single... is... a seven-minute headspin with a lush, fbrid melody that'll just eat at you throughout". Samiha Chowdhury at The Upcoming: "Bush at her best... the remarkable ability of reaching into the wildest parts of her imagination and creating music that can still communicate to people... A subtle, regular addictive beat underlies an Asian-style guitar riff... With every listen of this chorus, it gets more thrilling. ...It is full of intrigue and understanding, yet still creates an atmosphere of mystery.... Bush's music is innovative, intriguing and never tiresome".

The track was Record of the Week on BBC Radio 2 and appeared on the BBC Radio 6 Music B playlist for the week commencing 15th October.

It was reviewed on the BBC's 'Roundtable' hosted by Steve Lamacq on 13th October, but not to general acclaim. The panel was Hugh Stevens ("one of radio's most committed new music champions"), Rebecca Taylor ("one half of Slow Club"), and Ed O'Brien of Radiohead. Ed: "Obviously an amazing artist, she's proper. She's real... for some reason I never really connected... she does her thing and she's obviously still got it. My problem with the song is that I think she probably needs a producer... I like the chords but it would be great to hear somebody who could focus her a little bit... sounds just a bit safe" (6/10). Rebecca: "I'm a massive fan... she's bonkers, but it always sounds cool... I agree with the producer thing on this, it sounded weird in parts... she's the only person who can get away with spoken word vocals these days... I can't really say anything bad against her." (8/10) Hugh: "Bemused... I've never been a massive Kate Bush fan... that song washed over me" (5/10). However, in a reversal of the *Deeper Understanding* performance on the programme, the listeners brought back an enthusiastic 8/10.

The reception on Victoria Derbyshire's Monday Music Review (BBC Radio 5 Live) on 17th October was also mixed. Victoria herself seemed keen to stake out a position as a Kate-sceptic: "Is she taking the mick or what's going on?" and chided Radio 6 presenter Chris Hawkins for his more positive comments: "I don't get it and I don't know if I believe you. You're saying these words but you're not feeling it because you don't want to criticise her" and adding after the other guests comments: "Who's she doing it for? Is she doing it for music critics?" It was perhaps a good corrective to those who fashion a narrative wherein Kate is never subject to any criticism. Those of use with long memories will remember much such comment before the *Hounds of Love* watershed.

Nick DeRiso at Something Else: "a bold return to the magic, the unrealism, and the glittering whimsy of her early work... we rejoin Bush... amidst the blinding flurries of winter, having come upon some strange creature... but rather than break for the hills, she finds herself in a moment of deep empathy with the outsider. Bush's quiet murmurings to him, set against a lonely clanging guitar signature, are then suddenly subsumed in a rush of voices – and the chorus has arrived, like an angry mob of villagers. Just that quickly, Bush then recaptures the depth and myth of her '80s' sound, as a wall of keyboards splashes across layer upon layer of vocals. Brilliantly weird, undeniably beautiful, and very Kate Bush... a brisk return to form."

Vanceman at Spotifabulous: "her sympathy lies with the outsider... and not the usual heroic figure. The song traces her quest to hide his tracks so that he isn't discovered and killed... one of the more relaxed Kate Bush singles... sprinkled with oriental guitar figures and sleigh bells, both appropriate to the story; the lyric is half-sung/half-spoken in an almost extreme whisper – a mode that she excels with and hasn't put to bear often enough in her recordings. As noted by 'The Quietus', 'Its first line consists of Nepalese words for the abominable snowman'. Of course it does. That's why she's Kate Bush and we're not."

Two reactions from IKRSZine's Crazy Zany Radio Sunday set the parameters of the reaction to *Wild Man*: **Linda:** "Barking mad, a rather suitable description for the larger part of Kate Bush's output, can go one of two ways. Unfortunately, Kate seems to have calmed down on this track (or finally started taking her medication), a feat which doesn't do it much good. It's a bit like a Windows computer: it works most of the time so you can't hate it like a dentist appointment at 7am on a Monday morning, but at the same time there's not a single person alive today who will admit to loving its barely up-to-scratch bleak operating system. 5/10 (she scares me too much to go any lower). **Stef:** I really enjoyed the start of it. Lovely instrumentals, and I love the theatricality of it. A lovely track, nice vocals, like the additional vocals as well. Very well structured song with a good sound to it. Certainly had me enjoying it. 8.5/10."

Ryan Reed *Billboard* 28th Oct: "the first new single from British art-rock craftswoman Kate Bush in a whopping six years... A word of advice to first-time listeners: be sure to have an atlas and thesaurus handy... Bush in her breathy lisp, somehow sounding erotic while randomly referencing Indian provinces and Buddhist principles. For all of its impenetrable wordplay... makes for a wicked headphone atmosphere, with Dan McIntosh's expressionistic digital guitar curlicues wandering around a crisp Steve Gadd kit and John Giblin bass. As an announcement of Bush's return... a tad off-kilter. But then again, when has the ever-singular Bush been anything but?"

There was a brief scatter of radio play, and the track lodged briefly in the UK singles chart at no.73 on 22nd October, but it had done its job of trailing the album and piquing interest.

On 18th October two new snowy photos of Kate escaped from the Amazon site a little ahead of schedule. After some ill-informed comment, and the plain delight that some took in accusing Kate of being a hypocrite, and a minor internet/media kerfuffle, Kate confirmed that the fur featured in these photos was indeed synthetic: "*We have recently taken some photos and I just want to pre-empt any concerns there might be as I'm sure most of you will feel the same way as I do about wearing real fur. All the fur in these photos is synthetic. Best wishes, Kate.*" As far back as 1982 Kate had said "*I don't wear fur coats. I haven't got one. I don't own one and I don't believe in wearing them.*". This did not, of course, prevent her from being accused in some quarters of stoking the matter simply to get publicity. This from Andy at the American 'Cynic Central' blog 28th October: "Kate Bush is either a brilliant promoter or extremely clueless when it comes to how she pimps her new albums. Bush, a British pop singer who is a vegetarian and has been extremely outspoken about fur coats, created controversy recently among her fans over a series of images taken to promote her forthcoming album... So did she don the faux fur intentionally to create some buzz? After all, this album is her second LP this year and it will be a bit of a jam job for fans to buy because it features just seven tracks... It is due out Nov. 21 and has now officially received more attention than it would have if Bush had not shown up in an (allegedly) fake fur coat in some meaningless promotional photos."

Kate announced the animations for the album tracks on November 16:

Hi everyone,

Just to let you know that we are currently working on some short visual pieces to go with segments from 3 of the songs on 50 Words For Snow. *Each piece will run for about two and a half minutes. We are having great fun creating them and they will be staggered in their release.*

In our TV ad you will see clips from two of these pieces and images from the album booklet. The voice is that of the wonderful Mr Stephen Fry. We hope that you like the look of these visuals and that they serve as a preview of what is to come as well as letting people know that the album release is imminent.

Very best wishes,

Kate."

The following day Kate announced the animation for *Wild Man*. This was not a promotional video:

"Hi everyone,

I am delighted to announce the premier of our first animated film tonight. It only runs for about 2 ½ minutes but huge amounts of care and work have gone into this. I think it looks so atmospheric and has a beautifully crafted and unique look. It has been created by Finn and Patrick

at Brandt Animation. It has been really exciting working on this. I hope you like it.

I want to say a very special thanks to Mike Solinger, the producer on this project. Without him this could never have happened. I would also like to thank the Yeti who was the inspiration for the song and this short film. I hope it remains an enigma.

With very best wishes,

Kate."

It was a coincidence that whilst *Wild Man* was before the media with its Tibetan theme, news outlets reported a number of Tibetan monks and nuns who had taken to self-immolation as a protest against the brutal Chinese occupation of that country. On 19th November Kate thought it appropriate to express her views on these events:

"Everyone will know that events in Tibet have taken a terrible turn. I want to express my sadness at such a gentle and spiritual culture suffering so greatly. I am so shocked by the desperate measures being taken by people whose only way to call out for help is by taking these horrific actions. I would feel ashamed if I didn't express my feelings. I just hope the world is listening.

Kate."

The Frost Report

In the run-up to the release of the new album Kate conducted a large number of interviews with radio, and press in the UK, Ireland, Europe, the US, Canada and Australia and overwhelmingly she was full of enthusiasm and apparently in a very good place.

In her interview with Iain Shedden in *The Australian,* Kate explained: "*I'd liked the idea of making a kind of wintry record for some time, but then it got honed down to the idea of focusing on snow… I think everyone loves snow unless you happen to be snowed in for months on end. It has a real magical quality about it...*" Kate didn't want anyone to mistake this for a 'Christmas' album: "*That is one concern I had when people heard the title and when they got to see the artwork on the cover… people don't seem to be saying that, which is great because it isn't. If they did think that they'd be disappointed.*" She was thrilled by her guests on the album. On Stephen Fry: "*What I was trying to do was find someone who had a great voice of authority. The idea of the song was that we would start off with straightforward words and then come up with completely ridiculous ones. That really tickles me because it's meant to be fun.*" On Sir Elton John: "*I love his performance. He has a fantastic voice. If he had said no I don't know who I would have asked.*"

John Wilson interviewed Kate for his BBC Radio 4 programme 'Front Row' on 10th November and relayed a message from Kate via his Twitter account: "*Thank you so much for all your kind words, I'm really touched. Hope you like the album, love Kate*".

The interview was broadcast on 22nd November and included Kate's thought of the current state of the music industry and how a rogue wasp influenced the lyrics of *Cloudbusting*! Kate actually made the News that day when the BBC Radio 4 flagship morning news programme 'Today' reported the release of Kate's new album and included a snippet from the interview. Kate's fears for the the record industry were soon picked up by Reuters and syndicated widely leading to a strange article in the *Daily Express* (27th November) in which Martin Townsend put the blame for the troubles at EMI partly on Kate's lack of output!

Prior to release the album was streamed on the internet in the US by National Public Radio, in Australia by the ABC, in Ireland by *The Irish Times* and also in Finland and Belgium, and on KateBush.com which featured a track per day, with album images and animated snow, over the seven days prior.

In the UK *Mojo*, *Q* and *Uncut* gave the album 4-star reviews. *Mojo*: "At 53 the thrill of seeing the world transformed by a pearlescent icy blanket is not only intact; it's the Narnian portal through which *50 Words for Snow* beckons us …To stick around for the conclusion is to realise that the spiritual source of these songs comes from a deeper place. 'I can see angels around you' she sings… sounding as delirious with love as only she can." *Q*: "the follow-up to 2005's *Aerial* is no jolly Christmas album… Bush's husky vocals rise through an ominous piano fog, generating a silvery chill even as the lyrics of *Snowflake*, reminiscent of *The Red Shoes*' *Moments of Pleasure*, or *Misty*'s strange snowman love song, yearn for human warmth." *The Word*: "Frozen precipitaion is merely the starting point… sonically a wintry companion to *Aerial*… It lifts your heart and transforms your soul… as surprising and individual as ever here…"

Amongst the early reviews the pop culture music website run by John Robb 'Louder than War' awarded 10/10. In the *NME* Reviews blog on 'First Listen' (8th November) Priya Elan said: "For anyone who has longed for Bush at her most elemental, just her and her piano, their wish is granted".

The BBC Music review by Jude Rogers considered the album both sublime and ridiculous: "reflects a season which brings out the profound and absurd in equal measure – the feelings of longing and loneliness that emerge as the dark nights bed in, the party-hat silliness that pops up when the same nights stretch out".

However, Lucy Jones on her *Daily Telegraph* blog considered it "A semi-classical concept album with a pop song thrown in", seeing *50 Words* as evidence that those over 30 can't write a pop song. For her, and other critics it would seem, "part of the problem is that *50 Words For Snow* is a concept album. Cue groans and rolling of eyes". The very few other bad reviews tended to come from those who somehow actually expected Kate to turn in an album of three minute pop songs.

For *The Guardian* it was "Extraordinary business as usual", a five star review from Alexis Petrides: "it's packed with the kind of ideas you can't imagine anyone else in rock having. Taking notions that look entirely daft on paper and rendering them into astonishing music". Five stars also from Andy Gill in *The Independent*: "a lush, immersive work which is sonically more homogeneous than her earlier albums... in which fantastical, mythic narratives are allowed to take shape under the cover of its snowy blanket". In the interview also conducted by Andy Gill Kate says: "*I have a theory that there are still parts of our mental worlds that are still based around the age of between five and eight, and we just kind of pretend to be grown-up. I think our essence is there in a much more powerful way when we're children, and if you're lucky enough to be treated reasonably well, and can hang onto who you are, you do have that at your core for the rest of your life.*"

Four stars from Will Hodgkinson in *The Times*: "There's a sense that the natural world is home to the mysterious beings that crop up in folklore and fairy tales... Ultimately you have to ask: would *50 Words For Snow* stand up, away from the cult of Kate Bush? Yes, because it is odd, beautiful, and quite unlike anything else out there." Five stars from Helen Brown in the *Daily Telegraph*: "Its... snow-themed songs swirl around a delicate core of Bush and her piano... dreamy, drifting mood and subtle melodic motifs..." CD of the week from Dan Cairns in *The Sunday Times*: "befuddling and beguiling – and idiosyncratic... Bush at her most spare: several tracks feature no more than voice (thicker now, and even more emotionally resonant), piano, bass and drums. It isn't entirely successful... yet again you think, there is nobody who comes close to this extraordinary woman."

Ludovic Hunter-Tilsley in *The Financial Times* awarded the album four stars and pointed up the two "marmite" tracks which reviewers and some fans either loved or hated: "wintry piano, atmospheric... arrangements and an intimate, torch-lit vocal from Bush, who, at 53, has acquired a warm huskiness to her voice... the album wobbles with the hammy Elton John duet... and topples over on the title track in which Bush invites Stephen Fry to dream up 50 terms for snow... flashes of brilliance but the odd treacherous icy patch too."

The BBC TV 'Review Show' ran a short segment by Stuart Maconie (introduced as an 'super fan'). For him this was the album he always wanted Kate to make: "a gorgeously contemplative collection of seasonal chamber pieces".

The BBC Radio review programmes however took a different tack. On the Radio 4 'Saturday Review' half the panel of Miranda Sawyer, Francis Spufford and Pat Kane either had a good laugh ("hilarious") or they thought the album was dull ("nothing is going on"). The other half, including host Tom Sutcliffe, showed at least some understanding of the album ("a fearless creator"). Of the panel on Steve Lamacq's 'Roundtable', Miranda Sawyer reprising her Saturday Review performance, thought it was "awful", Jamie Hince thought it "ludicrous", and Elizabeth Morris confessed to being confused and compared it to Meatloaf.

Kitty Empire in *The Observer* thought the album (3/5) was a frustrating listen: "Like trudging through drifts, *50 Words* can be a frustrating listen, where dour piano motifs have the edge over catharsis. It blows hot and cold, with Bush holding back rather than letting rip". The barrage of good reviews however caused Tom Sutcliffe at *The Independent* (who obviously had not been listening to the BBC) to wonder if the music critics had been abdicating their duty and giving *50 Words For Snow* a bye, merely because Kate is perceived to be a national treasure: "it seemed odd that a record so quirky – and so hazardously earnest – would generate such unanimity across the board. Rock critics aren't famously forgiving creatures, after all, and yet there were moments here that struck me as virtually impossible to listen to without laughing".

But the good reviews kept coming regardless. Another five stars from Simon Price in the *Independent (on Sunday)*: "to the relief of anyone who carries a torch for the reclusive genius, it's a beauty... Its sound is mimetic of the white stuff: specifically the kind of snow that arrives unannounced and settles gently in the night, rather than a dramatic, howling blizzard". Four stars from Colin Somerville in *Scotland on Sunday*: "an exquisite suite of piano-driven chamber pop, eclectic and strangely comforting... a timely reminder of a highly individual and very British talent."

Louder Than War: "Kate Bush's finest moment, a pinnacle in a career of pinnacles... This is pure genius and with an emotional range that makes most men look like grunting dogs with songs of anger, lust, pain and sorrow and er, that's it. The emotions touched on in this album shape shift and slip away like the melting snow that are the backdrop to many of the songs, their subtle moods are described and flurry away... a stunning trip and a work of pure genius and perhaps the best of her career. Kate Bush was always going to be an artist that got better with age... she is a real artist who bears her soul and is not afraid to dig deep and take risks. This is a masterwork that takes no easy options."

Ben on The Intercostal Clavicle blog 27th November: "the dominant sound is piano with fewer embellishments than usual. The layered, spacious soundscapes are absent. This is to be listened to holed up indoors away from winter storms, chilling and warming by turns. The songs are all built around the concept of snow and the music softly echoes its magical fragility. We are never trapped Under Ice... Her voice is captivating, the production lush and meticulous, but I relish most the elements of play and surprise. The ideas are fully formed, the characters speaking as clearly as her Cathy in *Wuthering Heights*... Indeed throughout the album, the orchestration never intrudes on the intimacy... Kate Bush has produced hushed music which gleams in an icy hinterland. Like snow, it invites and unnerves, giving its gift quietly. I am enthralled by a musical vision which has yet to waver or disappoint. How lucky we are."

From 'Lake Tahoe' and 'Misty'.

Mathew French at muso blog The Alternative Review: "it strains the limits of belief to think that she's still able after all of these years to churn out material worthy of note, let alone albums that challenge her heyday masterpieces. But... *50 Words For Snow* is just as focused, creative, and emotionally conscious as her best albums. Unlike many of her contemporaries, Bush just refuses to fall victim to age. At 54 years old her vocals sound... very sentimental and comforting here, almost as if she's singing to us from inside a log cabin in the middle of a dead, cold night... This snow globe world of hers is easy to get immersed in: it's spacious yet welcoming, cold yet fondly tender. Forsaking grandiosity in favor of snow-inflected landscapes... essentially Bush's provocation for wintry surrealism. The songs have a slow, meditative tempo and revolve (mostly) around crisp piano, Bush's warm vocals, and delicate percussion. More than anything though, *50 Words For Snow* works well as something minimal; unlike other releases, Bush really fixates on the inclusion of negative space to make way for draughty ambiance. These songs aren't aimless in their approach though: they sometimes burst into small sections of unadulterated bliss – just enough to satisfy a craving for emotional fulfilment. This dichotomy of restraint and release is an immaculate blend... *50 Words For Snow* was more or less created by using very little but somehow manages to have a coherent and fully realized sound... So gather 'round the fire's warm embrace and rejoice: Bush is still at the top of her game."

Alex Hall at The Tune music blog 25th November: "For an artist who has recorded for over 30 years, simply staying relevant is no slight feat. For Kate Bush relevancy is not an issue, because *50 Words for Snow* molds her body of work just as effectively as some of her great '80s albums... She imagined each of the seven tracks set against the backdrop of snow, and while she plays with the concept more subtly in some songs it is still always present. Snow is what unites this album when it threatens to dismantle itself... finds the measure of its success in how well it can sustain that atmosphere. I realized my appreciation of the album had less to do with the songwriting and more to do with its artistic situation. The listener cannot always be enveloped in a perfect world of falling snow, but for the times when nature would seem to beckon him to imagine it... this record transports him completely. The contrast between Bush's dark, rich vocals and virginal snow is immense. To emphasize it more these recordings include young, high-range male voices, including Bush's son Albert, who sings with the beauty only something as transitory as snow could represent... Piano dominates this album, which not only makes it a more gentle work but also helps Bush extend her "art rock" persona to jazz and classical music... none of these tracks could exist by themselves, both because of the similarity of their content and their length. It's a treat when an artist releases something so cohesive, because the listener's only option is to sit down with the record and play it from top to bottom..."

Ron Hart's Pick of the Week on Rock blog Dirty Impound: "Over a half-decade following the release of her double-length magnum opus, 2005's *Aerial*, English ingénue Kate Bush returns with her sixth LP in 30 years...Though the album title sounds like something conjured up by a cocaine-obsessed rapper... it serves as a fitting description for the thematic direction of Kate's label début on the Anti-imprint. These seven epic compositions explore the sensual tundra of winter's effects on the heart, mind and loins. With the help of a small but elite group of prolific pals, including long-time Roger Waters side-man Andy Fairweather-Low, acclaimed British actor Stephen Fry... and on the LP's impact track *Snowed In at Wheeler Street*, Elton John, who almost (I repeat almost) seems as though he is channelling his inner closet hetero while exchanging verses with Bush as though she was the one that got away from him. There are indeed no words to truly describe the enchanting pulchritude of *50 Words For Snow*, except for hailing it as the loveliest work of Kate's sparse but uncompromising career."

Even in the unforgiving tabloids (though perhaps at the moment on their best behaviour), Kate's new album was celebrated: Pete Clark *London Evening Standard* 4 stars: "the central metaphor holds good: these songs may seem alike, but like snowflakes, they are all different. You are going to have to give this record a bit of time..." Adrian Thrills *Daily Mail* 4 stars: "A sprawling song cycle with a wintry theme... pitches Kate's still striking vocals into a richer, less synthetic setting than in the past... Pride of place goes to two ear-catching duets... an album – and a singer – who refuses to be hemmed in by traditional frontiers." Gavin Martin *The Daily Mirror* 4 stars: "A rare treat... fanciful but stripped down album is a bizarre indulgence. Piano primed sensuality for the new ice age". *The Sun* (4) "Icing on the Kate: an absorbing concept album... inventive as it is odd. Stunning as it is surreal".

Kate's enthusiasm for vinyl was another part of her attachment to analogue sound, but there was a slight problem with the *50 Words For Snow*

Graphic opposite: Michele Ann

Kate: a recording career 1978-2011

"I thank all of those whose work I have quoted in this chronological series, right from those who were wondering what hit them in 1978, to those pontificating over a 'National Treasure' in 2011. As I have said from the very first *Five Years Ago* article in *HomeGround* issue 5, this series has not set out to be a definitive record of Kate's career, still less a definitive explanation of her work. It has always been intended to be a scrapbook full of clippings and odd items across thirty years. So far as any comments and opinions expressed, these are my own and the responsibility for this series remains mine. My only guide was a love for Kate's work."

Peter

pressing, as she posted November 14 :

"Hi there everyone.

I wanted to let you vinyl lovers know that unfortunately the 50 Words For Snow *vinyl release will be a few days late everywhere except the UK. This is because we had some pressing problems and so we were late getting them from the factory.*

The good news is that they sound great now. The USA vinyl will be available in stores around the 25th Nov, Europe and the rest of the world will be released on the 28th – maybe a few days earlier in some places. I am sorry about this but you know that I always strive for quality even if there is a slight delay. I hope you enjoy it when you get it!!

All the best,

Kate

p.s. The vinyl has obviously been on a low fibre diet as it has less wind!"

According to the blurb, 'The London Awards for Art and Performance' are "the country's most expansive awards... presented to an individual who has made an outstanding contribution to their art form." In the week of release Kate was nominated for her new album.

50 Words For Snow was no.5 in the UK mid-week chart on 23rd November. Immediately above in the chart were three new entries from massively popular artists (Rihanna, One Direction and Westlife) who had been heavily promoting, including spots on major TV shows in the UK, in the previous week. In the final UK album chart published on Sunday 27th November *50 Words For Snow* was confirmed at no.5 with 49,812 sales just 27 weeks after *Director's Cut* débuted and peaked at number *2*, on lesser sales of *34,755*. This was a rather splendid achievement for Kate's 10th studio album in her now 33 year career. The album entered the German album chart at no.7, the Netherlands at no. 10, Norway at no. 18, Ireland at no.12, Belgium at no.27, Australia at no. 22 and Finland at no. 11. The album entered the *Billboard* charts in the US at no. 83 (and at no. 7 in the US Independent album chart).

Kate posted this message on 28th November:

"I want to say a huge thank you to everyone who has embraced 50 Words For Snow *with such warmth and positivity. I am totally blown away by the response to the album and am so delighted with the chart position of No 5 today. Hooray!*

Thanks to everyone who has contributed: Del Palmer for all his really great work throughout the recording process and his input during the mixing. To Stephen Tayler for his invaluable work on the mixes and to Stanley Gabriel who assisted us. To all the wonderful musicians especially Steve Gadd for the incredible feel he has brought to the whole piece, to Danny for his beautiful guitars, to dearest Bertie for his fantastic performance and for all his enthusiasm, to Jonathan Tunick for his gorgeous orchestrations and to John Giblin, Danny Thompson and all the guests who have brought their special energies into the music."

To everyone on the team who have done such a terrific job and most of all to all of you who take it into your homes and your hearts and make me feel so privileged to have my work received with such love.

Many thanks,

Kate x"

Kate's tenth studio album was a massive critical success. Though there were a few bad reviews, on Metacritic the album scored 88, ahead of *Director's Cut*, and still meaning "universal acclaim". At 'Any Decent Music', Kate was straight in at no.1 on the day of release with a weighted average critical reaction of 8.5/10. The album was certified Gold (100,000 sales) in the UK on 2nd December 2011. In what surely will be only the first part of her career, Kate had now had Top Five albums in the UK in five decades from the 1970s to the 2010s. *HomeGround*, the last Kate Bush Fanzine standing, has reported in print for four of those five decades.

As we go to press we can just put in some final notes, making a suitable tailpeice to this thirty year *HomeGround* scrapbook of Kate's career.

In May 2012 Kate won the South Bank Sky Arts Award, pipping Adele to that honour. She was nominated for an Ivor, though not (again) for the Mercury. In August 2012 a reworked version of *Running Up That Hill* was used in the London Olympic Games closing ceremony. The subsequent download release reached no.6 in the singles chart, and Kate had now had top 20 singles in the '70s, '80s, '90s, '00s and now the '10s!

At the end of December 2012 it was announced that in the 2013 New Years Honours List, HM Queen Elizabeth II would create Kate Commander of the Order of the British Empire (CBE) in the 2013 New Year Honours list, and joining her in that honour was Arlene Phillips one of her her dance teachers from right back at the very beginning of her career.

First founded in 1917 to recognise the service of all ranks of British society, valuable service is the only criterion for the award. CBE is awarded amongst other things for for a distinguished, innovative contribution to any area of national life. The official citation for Kate says:

Ms Catherine Bush. (Kate Bush) Singer and Songwriter. For services to Music.

It could not better sum up our feelings.

It's in Another's Face

John Carder Bush

It's in another's face
that we hope to live
for ever:
It's in another's face
that we drown ourselves
for eternity.

Bound to the weather of another's eyes,
touched by the swell of melancholy
or the splashing surf of laughter,
we tremble to their desire;
fixed on the shape of the beloved mouth,
each of our days is dictated
by another's smile or frown.

It's in another's face
that we hope to find ourselves,
it's in that face
that we learn to give
against the warnings of our souls,
learn to sacrifice our wants
for the wants of a face.

A face on a hoarding
directs us to desire,
tells us what we need
until that need becomes a face,
fashion-fucked and falsified –
we make it our secret bride
even though we know it lied.

Felled under the spell of comparison,
the itchy disease of infinite choice,
the presentable covering rind,
we are held in the bind
of what we see must be better, and better,
until we wish we were blind.
Faces on celluloid,
faces on tape, faces on disc
moving flat and thin to slip
into our imaginations,
into that whirling place
in the vortex of excitement
that thrusts us into the face
that will obsess our coming hours,
will be the over-powered magnet
for our inexhaustible need to love.

No matter how beautifully,
how rewardingly a body
opens to us like a bud,
it does not have the mystery
nor the challenge of the face,
and is soon dumped,
slumped against a dusty corner
in the charnel house of forgetfulness.
But a face will stay and haunt
the cedar avenues of sunlit memory:
even when you think it's banished
to the unlit corridors of the cortex,
it will rise in your eyes
and be there again,
around you, inside you,
above you, beneath you,
terminally part of you.

You cannot truly possess a face –
it's only yours for a moment
in the morning on waking
when it gazes up at you
and is naked, open, undefended.
Quick, look down into that face,
while it looks at your face,
into those eyes, along those lips –
what do you really see?
Do you see what you want to see –
an image of yourself?
Or do you see an unknown creature,
Crouched, cowering at the back of the brain,
Dim in the lunar lights of reflected love?

A Wealthy Man.
For Dennis

Kyla Clay Fox

There's an old man here to see you God,
Says he'll keep you but a while.
He is burdened with a question he must ask-
Says his children they are grown now,
That he sees little for his life
Just some medals, just some photographs and his hat-
He has neither goods nor riches,
He has that in which he stands,
"You made the child but God, did I make a man?"

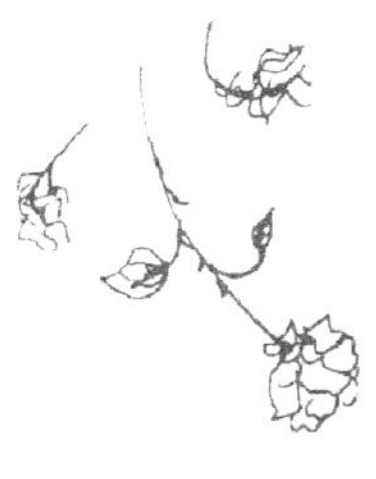

Says his maker, to the old man,
"You are judged by what you leave,
By riches that are wrapped in flesh and bone
And the jewels that shine around you
They are gilded in a grief
That exists in only joy and love alone-
And your house it is a kingdom
You leave treasures kings won't see-
That shine on in every memory you leave"

To his maker, says the old man,
"I am ready now, I see
For I leave my children bathed in love alone
And the voices left to speak of me,
Speak words of only pride
And that wealth, it is the truest wealth I've known."

The Director's other cut

...we consider Kate's first release of 2011

Issue 79:
December 2011

Dave: "Wop Bam Boom"

Revisiting previous work is never an easy sell, especially to fans as dedicated and passionate as Kate's; the originals have woven themselves into the fabric, the DNA of our lives, we know every beat, every word and inflection, every string and heart beat of each song. Kate clearly had an itch, something was bugging her and it needed sorting out. She has made it clear that although she was happy with the songs, there were elements of the production of both *The Sensual World* and *The Red Shoes* that she wasn't happy with – the originals were too cluttered, there was too much going on and that she wanted to let in some light and air. For the most part she has succeeded.

Let's tackle what I think is the biggest disappointment first; *Rubberband Girl*. I always loved the original, a great fat slice of cool pop, with a fantastic swing and an almost Stax or Motown feel and I'm sorry but I just don't like the *Director's Cut* version. I get that it now has a Rolling Stones vibe, but what's with the mumbled vocal? It just sounds like an out-take and I think it's a wasted opportunity. I'm also a bit nonplussed about *Top of the City*. I don't think the new version really does anything except adds some louder drums and it sounds a bit messy. Although it's well done, the new version of *And So Is Love* again doesn't seem that different, other than the *very* significant lyric change from "Life is sad" to "Life is sweet" and I think that maybe that was the whole reason to include it.

Those small quibbles aside, the rest of the album, I really love. Kate has indeed, given them a good shake and let some fresh air into these songs. *Flower of the Mountain* although the least changed musically, benefits from being longer and having more space. Personally I don't think there was anything wrong with the original 1989 track, but it is fascinating to hear the Joyce words to her music, and I would love someday, to hear the original version she recorded for *The Sensual World*; maybe when we finally get a proper re-mastered and repackaged version of that 1989 album. Both *Song of Solomon* and *Lily* get a real freshen up, as does *The Red Shoes,* all featuring some great new vocals from Kate and all sound fresher.

The two tracks which got most attention from fans, were *This Woman's Work* and *Moments of Pleasure* and it's not difficult to hear why. Both have been slowed and stripped down, to devastating effect, especially on *Moments of Pleasure,* for me the album's heart and best track. Kate's vocal, is outstanding and when the original tune comes in at the end, I can feel the old pressure behind the eyes and a lump in my throat; brilliant! And then *Never Be Mine;* again a lot has been taken away, but what's left is just lovely.

Kate was never going to please everyone with this album. It was a brave and surprising move as she's never before shown any real interest in her back catalogue. Even the choice of material was surprising: I bet almost any other act on earth wouldn't have been able to resist the temptation to include more obvious hits like *Running Up That Hill* or *The Man with the Child in his Eyes*, but not Kate. Okay; so personally I would have loved to have seen new versions of *Love and Anger* and maybe *Reaching Out* instead of *Rubberband Girl* and *Top of the City*, but there you go, and all in all, *Director's Cut* is a most welcome surprise.

Collin Kelley: How very dare she!

Iconoclastic Kate Bush recently released her ninth studio album, *Director's Cut.* When she announced that her next album would be re-workings of songs from *The Sensual World* and *The Red Shoes*, fan reaction was mixed. When the track-listing was made public, there was collective apoplexy that Kate would have the temerity to monkey with classics like *This Woman's Work, The Sensual World* and *Moments of Pleasure.* How very dare she!

Kate was never happy with those two albums, lyrically or sonically. A fan of recording on analogue tape, Kate jumped into digital recording (everyone else was doing it, so why shouldn't she?) but the results were a mixed bag, especially on *The Red Shoes*, which was often criticized for its combination of both shrill and murky sound quality.

A big fan of film, Kate said her thought process was to re-imagine the songs in a cinematic way, but in sound rather than vision. On top of that, she received permission from the estate of James Joyce to use Molly Bloom's soliloquy from *Ulysses* to craft her original vision of the song, *The Sensual World.* In 1989, the estate had refused her, so she paraphrased Molly and created a hit song anyway.

Director's Cut opens with Kate's ode to Joyce in the now retitled *Flower of the Mountain.* It's the album's most startling lyrical departure from the original. With her now huskier voice up front in the mix, it's almost like Kate is in the room telling you about long kisses, sharing tastes of seed cake, feeling her perfumed breasts and "yesssss." It's intimate and downright sexy.

Another revelation is *Song of Solomon* with Kate's and the Trio Bulgarka's fluttering vocals rescued from the mire. The song is stripped of unnecessary flourishes – and lyrics – so that the refrain "Don't want your bullshit, just want your sexuality" is not only an utterance but a command. *Lily* gets some of the same treatment, with Kate unleashing a vocal performance of maniacal proportions not heard since *The Dreaming*. Acrobatic "whooos!" and the particularly batshit screaming of "Who's on the left, who's on the right?" while soul diva Mica Paris wails, is one of the album's finest moments.

On *The Red Shoes*, based on Michael Powell's film about a ballerina possessed by cursed ballet slippers, Kate doesn't radically depart from the original, but invigorates the lyrics with cries of "whoop, whoop" and a demonic breakdown at the song's end where she growls, "I'm gonna dance the dream and make the dream come true".

The album's lowlight is *Deeper Understanding*, which features the computerized voice of Kate's son, Albert, singing the chorus and a free-form jazz riff at the end. Released as a single ahead of the album's release, here was a moment when even the most die-hard fans thought she had potentially lost the plot. The original version of *Deeper Understanding* from *The Sensual World* is one of Bush's best songs, eerily prefiguring our obsession with the internet and computers. The new version sounds like Laurie Anderson noodling around in 1977 and is the project's weakest song.

Luckily, the suite of songs at the center of the album – *This Woman's Work*, *Moments of Pleasure* and *Never Be Mine* – are easily the best music of Kate's career. Created specifically for John Hughes' *She's Having a Baby*, *This Woman's Work* has become one of her most beloved, heart-rending songs and a highlight of *The Sensual World*. How could she better the original? Well, she has – and it's epic. The song, now clocking in at more than six minutes, floats in the same body of water as her drowning figure hovering between life and death from *The Ninth Wave* conceptual suite from the *Hounds of Love* album. It's ambient, celestial and full of silence and space that adds to the bitter-sweet lyrics. Grab a hankie.

Similarly, *Moments of Pleasure* gets not only a lyrical trim, but is stripped of Michael Kamen's syrupy string arrangement and replaced with spare piano and a hymnal chorus. Kate's lament to friends and family who have passed on goes from mawkishly depressing to beautifully elegiac. The lyric "He meets us at the lift, like Douglas Fairbanks waving his walking stick, but he isn't well at all" may not sound like much on paper, but the way she sings it against the descending melody of the piano is positively shiver-inducing. It's better than the original and one of her greatest achievements. *Never Be Mine*, a tale of an ending love affair, is set free from the darkness and when Kate sings about the "thrill and the hurting" it cuts like a knife.

And So Is Love and *Top of the City* shine with Kate's new vocals, but they seem to have lost something in the translation. *And So Is Love* particularly suffers from a change in lyrics. "Life is sad and so is love" has become "life is sweet..." gutting the admittedly depressing song of its intent. *Top of the City* has gone from a wistful meditation on love to something verging on Broadway bombast. The new version is compelling, but isn't a patch on the original.

That leaves us with *Rubberband Girl*, the frenetic pop song from *The Red Shoes* album that was a hit single for Kate in the UK. Kate drains the energy from the song and turns it into a slurring, bluesy rock song that sounds like she might have had a bottle – or two – of wine at karaoke night at the local boozer. It's hilarious, but such a departure from the rest of *Director's Cut* that it probably should have been a b-side.

In a recent interview, Kate diplomatically said if fans don't like the new versions the old ones are still available. This unexpected exploration of old material has set the stage for a new album that is currently being recorded. Perhaps this was Kate's way of clearing a blockage to her new voice, and, if that's the case, she has done so in brilliant fashion.

Monty Moncrieff: Cleansing emotions

I never felt Kate was happy with what she tried to get *The Red Shoes* album to be. I felt that whilst it was obvious she was trying to exorcise personal demons by delivering her most personal songs to date I never felt she succeeded. It felt like the attempt was there, but the demons remained; she just couldn't find her salvation in the album, no matter how hard she tried.

I wondered whether the re-workings might be an attempt to "exorcise the exorcism", if you like; in other words by attempting to be rid of the demons she actually created new ones in the songs, forever anchoring them to the sadness she felt whilst writing them, stuck in the rut she was trying to find the way out of, by the very thing she created.

With the early reviews indicating that she has now erased some of the sadness and the negative connections by redrafting, for example, "life is sweet and so is love", I'm left thinking this suggests a confirmation of this theory: she's thrown the elements of the songs up in the air and shaken off the negativity they held. It brings her to a place beyond even where she once strived to reach, not only having come through the darker times they were emblematic of, but having reached a greater happiness she might not have dreamed of at the time.

By ripping out "just being alive, it can really hurt" from *Moments of Pleasure,* it feels like she wants to throw away the pain that created the song, and focus instead on the moments, remembering only the pleasure and not the painful times that once caused her to try to draw

Graphic: Izabelle Samsonowicz

strength from them.

Is she cleansing the emotions the original songs trap within themselves, saying she's still proud musically of the song, but making it mean something more positive for her now?

Edoardo Seianis: The Sensual Shoes

When I first heard about the combination of songs from *The Sensual World* and *The Red Shoes* which Kate called *Director's Cut*, I was speechless! Here was another of my 'Kate strange phenomena'. The two albums have always been a hot topic in the KBNI Forum. In fact I have never liked some of the songs on what are my two least favourite of Kate's albums. The debates have been continuous and often very harsh – you will probably find one somewhere on the internet right now, repeating like an endless spiral why these albums are good or not good enough.

One day, around five years ago, while I was reflecting on this dilemma, it occurred to me that by putting together the best songs from both records, Kate could actually have made an album as wonderful as her best productions. Since "The Red World" sounded a bit science fiction, I gave it the name "The Sensual Shoes", and I talked about it on the forum, discussing the songs Kate should have used to make the best possible collection. Now, I really don't know if Kate even read one single word of our threads, but the fact that maybe she got the original idea of *Director's Cut* from our long ago discussion is quite hilarious.

"...*But you don't want to believe in a premonition* ..."

Thinking over the past thirty-three years, I have had many 'strange phenomena', moments in which I could almost physically feel a connection between Kate's creativity and my imagination. I am not a "spiritual" man – quite the reverse – I am rational and atheist. A few times I saw what I had imagined actually realized in her creations, but I always thought it was just a normal rational consequence: I like her music because it reflects my inner world, and therefore it is very possible that sooner or later Kate will express her Art in the same way I would.

However, some of these synchronous moments of 'connectivity' were so absurd that even my rational mind had trouble in finding a plausible explanation. The most curious and absolutely perfect was, however, the picture on the sleeve of the *Cloudbusting* single. I still remember my scream in the music shop after seeing the cover: there was a little drawing I had done in 1980! But I have to admit that my old doodle wasn't related to Kate – it was portraying me and my 'cloudbuster' was a huge musical instrument shooting the pentagram notes up to the sky. The last "coincidence" was the use of birds in *Aerial*. These are my words written (originally in Italian!) on the 3rd November 2002: "I am listening to *More*... wouldn't it be great if Kate used birds like Pink Floyd in *Cirrus Minor*? I don't know why, but this song makes me think of Kate and how she could do a great job with birds... I would love it!".

"...*We raise our hats to the strange phenomena*..."

Of course these kind of stories always invite scepticism. Are they really 'premonitions' or just simply coincidences? Maybe we should just raise our hats and accept the strange phenomena for what they are... a gift, maybe, just like Kate's wonderful talent.

Letter About A Shirt

John Carder Bush

Today I saw your shirt on someone else,
The pale blue, plain, Indian silk shirt
I gave to you ten years ago on a birthday –
Something you wore and wore,
Until, whenever I thought of you,
I saw you in that shirt.

Dozing in the heat, I slipped out
Of a daydream of you speaking to me,
Giving your realistic tangent
On some aspect of a knot in life,
Your words still resonant
As the world came stumbling back.
I saw the shirt before I saw her,
and for a moment…
But I knew it couldn't be you,
I no longer fall for the lies of light,
For those childish leaps of radiant hope,
Those wicked games that shifted time can play,
Those mouse holes between sleep and waking
Where dreams can happily deny even death.

Nevertheless, when she walked close to me,
I sniffed her passing, seeking your smell
Of shirt personalised by perspiration,
Never repugnant, always comforting,
Edged with a light cologne of violets.

But your clothes, worn now by others,
Have been neutralised, and you expunged,
The last detectable trace of your living
So easily wrung out and sluiced away
After an hour in your washing machine.
All I breathed in was the tangerine,
Mango tendrils of a teenage perfume
And the rosy petals of sun cream.

It wasn't the shirt
That went to the morgue
With your joggers and trainers
And soiled underwear.
It wasn't the shirt
That went with your body
Into the furnace.
It was the shirt
I last saw you in
When you were living, not dying,
And we talked of books,
And we talked of our children.

I know you would appreciate
Its still being in the world,
Delight in how it covers young breasts,
Drapes around mobile hips,
Absorbs the sunshine with her skin under it,
Her essence already caught in its fibres.

You'll be glad to know, if know you can,
Her brown, athletic, eighteen years old
Shoulders carry it beautifully:
Oh, my father, your granddaughter
Wears your shirt very well.

50 Words For Snow

...editors and readers respond to Kate's 10th album

Issue 79: December 2011 and other material submitted for that issue.

Dave: Intriguing, baffling, delightful!

Nearly 35 years on from that remarkable début single which so many people thought would be a one-hit wonder, Kate continues to innovate, intrigue, baffle, delight and still make the most beautiful music. Probably the most remarkable thing about this outstanding album is that once again she has come up with something that is different from its predecessors; yes, it has reference points, slight echoes of previous work and its cool Winter bluster, clearly follows on from the late Summer warmth of *Aerial* but *50 Words* defiantly occupies its own space.

Fittingly the album starts with *Snowflake*, where Kate perfectly captures the feel and sound of freshly fallen snow on a bright Winter's day or chilly starry night, that wonderful, almost eerie, blanket of silence, where the crunch of a foot or snap of a twig stands out clear and crisp, and here it is a lovely duet between Mother and Son, set against a backdrop of tumbling, drift like drums and cascading pianos. Bertie's voice is a revelation, both the cool almost spoken parts, where he whispers "We're over a forest" and the soaring high, choral parts, matched by Kate's softly sung and telling line "The world is so loud". With Danny playing guitar on this track, perhaps it tells us that all she needs is her family and her music against the loudness of the world.

Lake Tahoe is a ghost story, complete with a Victorian lady rising from the water to find her lost dog, a dog that is so old he can hardly move, but when he sleeps he dreams of running. The beautiful voices of Stefan Roberts and Michael Wood acting like a Greek Chorus to Kate's narrative, over slinky piano, complete with a lovely discordant moment, a pause for birdsong before the song gradually starts to pick up pace, strings and the delicate touch of Steve Gadd's percussion bringing a sway and gentle swagger to the story of the 'spooky wood' and the woman calling to her pet, as he finally comes to rest. The whole track has an almost folk feel with a hint of Spanish warmth in the snow.

Things are defiantly getting warmer on *Misty*, a quite extraordinary thirteen minute piece of work, even by Kate's high standards, like Raymond Briggs *The Snowman* meets *Love To Love You Baby*, or of Terry Pratchett's beautiful book *The Wintersmith* when the young witch has to kiss away the spirit of Winter? Kate's story of a snowy tryst builds through some lovely guitar flourishes and warm jazzy rhythms to a passionate climax, complete with pauses, rushes and sensual almost cracking vocals, over a repeating piano motif and underplayed, shimmering strings that suddenly swell to a rush before disappearing back into the snow, with lyrics about soaking sheets on a Sunday morning... Ooh err – Kate, it's good to hear you getting a tad saucy again!

Wild Man is the closest the album gets to a conventional pop moment; Kate's quite sultry whispered almost spoken vocal on the chorus, a nagging guitar hook and the chorus crashing in as we learn of the Himalayan Wild Man, the Yeti, hiding in the magical landscape of Tibet, maybe the last hidden story of the modern world as technology takes over.

Not surprisingly one of the most talked about songs is *Snowed In At Wheeler Street* where Kate and Elton John take on the role of star crossed lovers, in a story that starts as Rome burns and takes us through the French revolution, World War Two, the London smog of the '50s or '60s, 9/11 in New York and ends up by a warm fire in a simple home. I love the imagery and couldn't help thinking of the eon-spanning story of The Doctor and River Song (if you don't know what I mean, you probably won't get the significance of the number 42 either, could this song contain the mean of Life, The Universe and Everything?) The ebbing synths, piano and percussion combine with the two voices to perfectly paint a dramatic picture, wildly romantic, without being slushy. I love the line about tying them together with rope.

The title track is fantastic, funky, scattering percussion, sounding like a snow storm, with Kate doing a deep and sexy spoken countdown while Stephen Fry delivers his beautiful reading of her 50 Words, giving each one just enough of a spin, so that they have a taste of accent or humour – and I think Kate's humour is very important on this track, especially as we hit No 42, that number again, and we get Stephen Fry's best Klingon. Is this the album where Kate has finally come out, as a geek? I think the title track is not only a great piece of music but serves a musical and lyric balance for the whole album. It serves to punctuate and accentuate the other slower, more serious songs, giving contrast.

Finally we have *Among Angels;* Kate, her piano, a hint of strings and a soaring vocal which means in some ways it's the most predictable track here, but no less effective for that. Angels float around someone, like mirrors in the Summer, plaintive and reflective, it showcases her voice perfectly, still as beautiful as ever, the tone is just beautiful and she can still pack that emotional punch with the minimum of effort.

The production across the whole album is fantastic, the lightest of touches, used to the most effect Kate creates moods and images in sounds, with a minimum of fuss, and once again this record is about the space almost as much as the music. A perfect Winter's tale.

Krys: An otherworld

50 Words For Snow is a place of solace for me, a place to stop, draw breath. Kate's voice soothes my mind and eases my heart. In some ways it is close to *The Dreaming* in its brave incarnation, and as pure and honest as her very earliest work, that same piano sound as way back, only now it is matured, controlled, confident. There's a purity to the sound, musically and vocally. The album breathes, it has space, she hasn't cluttered it. She's thrown open the windows to reveal a snow covered wilderness, full of ghosts and angels, Yetis and snowmen; an otherworld.

Snowflake is meditative, prayer-like. It stills my thoughts in this very busy life. It feels like stepping inside a beautiful old Gothic cathedral and finding peace. The solitary snowflake falls from heaven to earth, like a soul choosing its mother. "Be ready to catch me..." *Lake Tahoe* makes me cry from that deep place of loss. A place we come to know as we grow older and lose the ones we love, human and animal. It is as painful as *A Coral Room*. A ghost story for Christmas. To me this is the very spirit of the whole album. The ghost and her faithful dog, reunited in that Otherworld. Her little icy hand reaches right in and pulls out my poor lost heart. I can feel the bleakness, see the grey of the skies, smell the frozen air and snow. It makes me think of our beloved Bumble cat; there was snow when she died last December. This song makes me cry and cry for my beautiful girl who was there through good and bad, who slept at my head each night for fifteen years. The emptiness remains. It is the price of love. "Miss me? Did you miss me?"

Misty is so seductive, sexy and melancholic. Her blood gives the snowman life. The imagery is beautiful, the "dead leaves" remind me of her brother John's poem, *Before The Fall*. Kate, you're wasted on a snowman. The solitary existence of the *Wild Man*, and the age-old fear of the unknown that leads humans to do terrible things. I love the image of him "playing in the snow". *Snowed In At Wheeler Street* plays the hand of fate. The recognition between old souls, sometimes fleeting as we pass in the street and our eyes meet. Sometimes we make that connection. "Have we been in love forever?" *50 Words For Snow* is fun and mad. The melty way she says "34..." – 34 has never sounded so sexy! I would love to hear the out-takes! Which is your favourite?

Among Angels is a song of comfort, but at the same time shakes the listener by the shoulders and says "get a grip!" We are all vulnerable, weak, in need of an angel's shoulder to lean and weep upon. We look in places that are not always what they seem to be. An offer of a shoulder may not be the haven it appears to be. It is a song about faith and trust, finding your own strength when you give your power away, and lose belief in yourself and your own ability. Some believe we have guardian angels to watch over us. It is a lovely idea and maybe we do. "Only you can do something about it..."

To me this is the most beautiful album of them all. I can only wonder what Kate will do next.

Peter: It is still snowing ...

Just as *Aerial* invoked my childhood Summer, with blackbirds singing in the huge sycamore tree, so *50 Words For Snow* takes me to childhood Winter. Snow lying, the crackling fire in the grate, and stories of the uncanny. The spine is chilled by the minimum required to set up the circumstances in which the veil becomes thin. It is all about atmosphere. Nothing is obvious, hurried, or violent. In this album Kate does very little, there are repeated piano motifs, her warm, mature vocals and sparse percussion from Steve Gadd, and yet these brief strokes set up an atmosphere where anything is possible. The falling of snow changes everything. Science and fantasy meet. We enter Kate's Narnia where it is always Winter, but never quite Christmas. The snow gives but it also takes, and when it is gone nothing is quite the same.

In *Snowflake* it is midnight. Albert's perfect but transient chorister vocals capture a snowflake as it is created out of ice and dust and falls to the snow covered forest landscape, whose acoustics are changed utterly. *Lake Tahoe* is a perfect M.R. James ghost story, the shadow puppet images a perfect accompaniment. Kate's moody jazzy vocal distils from the myths of the preserved bodies in the icy blue unfrozen depths of the lake, the most perfect and beautiful track on the album.

There is magic to be done on the striding edge between the sublime and the ridiculous. Until *Misty* perhaps I never quite understood the Tate bricks and Tracy Emin's *Unmade Bed*. In a koan, force and counter force lead us to an enlarged vision and to the beginnings of understanding. She's as helpless as a kitten up a tree, clinging to a cloud of snowflakes. This is the other tale of *The Snowman* from making to melting in her hand. We can say he is leading her on, but it's just what she wants him to do. She's holding very tight, finding she can fly, but his crooked mouth is full of dead leaves and bits of twisted branches and frozen garden, all that remains. But it is still snowing and she must get outside...

In my view *Wild Man is* one of Kate's very best singles. Gentle percussion and hushed spoken vocals. It's Tibet, the winds are howling, and '60s hippies are travelling in VW camper vans and funnily enough here is Andy Fairweather-Low and a flanged chorus. If only

Opposite: Lisa Evans' original sketch for the artwork which appeared in *Mojo*.

paradise were half as nice as this. Tibetan bells, and where were the singing bowls? You're not a a big brown bear You're a hairy, scary, legendary screaming souvenir, I wonder if you're happy, I wonder if you're free.

Snowed In At Wheeler Street made me think of *Portrait of Jennie* and its Debussy soundtrack: "time itself does not pass but curves around us, and that the past and the future are together at our side for ever." Jennie says "I know we were meant to be together. The strands of our lives are woven together and neither the world nor time can tear them apart". Or perhaps it was another film about time-crossed lovers which inspired Kate, where Anck-su-Namun tearfully says to Imhotep "I don't want to lose you again". Snowed in, Just two old friends. Keeping the fire going. We were so happy! but the snow is transient and it isn't ground-hog day. And the world won't stop turning.

50 Words For Snow is fun and I love Kate's husky vocals and Stephen Fry's Klingon, a delight in words and meanings. Apparently some foreign reviewers not blessed with the wrong sort of snow did not understand "bad for trains"! And very few seem to have grasped that 42, the meaning of life, the universe and everything is not in Terran.

Among Angels apparently with its false start and pub piano as if this was a demo, as if this done impromptu by Kate on a handy piano for someone in serious need of a hug. I might know what you mean when you say you fall apart. In and out of doubt. This is beautiful song to put someone back together. I can see angels standing around you. They will carry you.

There are no personal songs on this album, and yet all are personal songs that tell us Kate is in a good place and that there is so much more to come.

Seán: Things we yearn to keep close

When I heard *Aerial* I immediately knew exactly what I wanted to gush about it in a *HomeGround* review. Such a long gap after *The Red Shoes* and there was the album I hadn't dared hope Kate would make. *Director's Cut* was a thrilling and unexpected project. Focused and accomplished, the re-workings of *This Woman's Work* and *Moments of Pleasure* in particular seemed to announce a new direction, an ever-evolving artist wrenching even deeper emotions out of sparser, longer song arrangements.

Yet no-one really had a clue how fired-up Kate was creatively until an album "set against a backdrop of falling snow" was announced in September. To be honest, as I write, I need to spend a lot more time with *50 Words For Snow*. This album will be the soundtrack to my Winter and beyond.

We've tried to keep the news site updated with the onslaught of (terrific) reviews and my head has been bombarded with interpretations so that I've not yet had a chance to fully form my own. I hear in this album a shared sonic DNA with parts of *The Dreaming*, *The Ninth Wave*, *The Fog* and *Aerial* spliced together with an altogether new, mature song craft from Kate. I'm being pulled in, willingly, to every track, every twist and turn, every nuance of sound. The snow theme is just a starting point that sets up the unique mood of this record. Kate is making the listener take time out with this record. It speaks of the things in life we yearn to keep close and precious for as long as we can.

Time spent with it has already been rewarded with some of my favourite moments in Kate's music to date. The majesty of Bertie's "I am sky and here", the swell of music that paints the beginning of a dog's searching dreams in *Lake Tahoe*, the moment when you realise the utter brilliance of *Misty*'s construction (the epic song, not the snowman!), the second those temple bells kick in on *Wild Man*, the exquisite synths on *Snowed In At Wheeler Street* that rivet and delight me every bit as much as the shared vocals, the unexpected breathy eroticism in the title track, and the way Kate sings this line in *Among Angels*: "I might know what you mean when you say you fall apart. Aren't we all the same? In and out of doubt".

Ah, Kate's vocals. The gift that keeps giving. That particular mentioned line from *Among Angels* (the most life-affirming song of her career?) demonstrates, for me, everything that is untouchable about Kate Bush as a singer. No-one else can do it like her.

Andrew Marvick: Fresh and unexpected

Earlier this year Kate Bush presented to the public her re-workings of a selection of recordings that had originally seen light of day in 1989 and 1993. Huge throughout, yet suffused with the most intimate, intricate of details, *Director's Cut* reflected the rich artistic harvest of a master in complete control of, and fully at home with, her vast talent and vision. Now, only a few months later, she has given us an altogether different collection – this time altogether new – of closely interrelated recordings under the title *50 Words For Snow*; and the effect, at least to this listener's ears, is like a fresh and unexpected tour through the Kate Bush sound worlds of those early years, and of those she inhabited both a decade earlier and a decade and more later.

The haunting references to musiKal hisTory begin right from the new album's first moments, with the opening of *Snowflake*. Following its opening piano introduction, which immediately conjures up for her long-time listeners the introductory motif from 1980's *Blow Away*, *Snowflake*'s sturdy, committed repetition of a simple four-beat, two-chord cell instead diverges not only from the sonic palette of Kate Bush's middle years, but from the broadest common base of all of her compositional work from the 1970s and 1980s – its essential adherence to the verse-chorus song structure as the skeleton for identifiable melodies – and instead approaches an extreme stylistic reaction against her musical procedure prior to *Hounds of Love*.

In the 1985 Convention interview by Tony Myatt, she acknowledged this shift as it was just beginning to make itself felt in *Running Up That Hill*, speaking about a slow-to-develop interest in a "constancy of rhythm". Yet for all its apparent abandonment of traditional songwriting (and arguably of any recognizable 'songwriting' procedure at all), in fact the 'ghosts of Kate's past' fill every low, quiet, intimate space of this track, and of *50 Words For Snow* as a whole. Bertie's sweet, piercing pubescent soprano solo expands into the track with indescribable charm, and echoes with increasing insistence *All the Love*'s "We wait for you / To love us too". So, too, Kate's by-now (since 2005's *Aerial*, at the latest) firmly established threnodic, extemporized style serves increasingly to provide a kind of musico-geological fundament atop which swirl a seemingly limitless, etherous mist of subliminal Bush Leitmotivs – "Keep falling, I'll find you" might well have been lifted from an unreleased stretch of *Lyra*.

Likewise in *Lake Tahoe*, and insinuating themselves like snatches of fondly remembered conversation with old friends of years past, the choral trio of voices that introduce *Lake Tahoe* creep, again eerily, as though out of the hushed Georgian folksong that Kate, with the late Richard Hickox, so lovingly reconstructed from Herzog's *Nosferatu* soundtrack for *Jig of Life* back in 1985, then develop quickly into what sound like further, welcome bars from an unreleased, extended version of *Nocturn*, from *Aerial*'s *Sea of Honey* – then unexpectedly move into augmented fifths that, to me, at least, are suggestive of Arnold Schönberg's earliest ventures into atonality, ca. 1911. I'm thinking particularly of that unique moment in musical history when, toward the conclusion of the theretofore still barely tonal Op. 10 string quartet, a female voice floated in to declare, in genuinely 'alien', dissonant melodic fashion: "I feel wind from other planets!" – and in so doing, pronounces the old world of consonant melody and harmony, in effect, dead (a pronouncement which Kate Bush, among many others, fortunately, have ignored). Vocal yearnings here recall the elegiac timbre – as well as the characteristic minor four-note falling motif – of *A Coral Room* (which itself was repeated in *Mrs Bartolozzi*).

Exquisite, sonically piquant touches of atonality, or at least bitonal digression, were among the most striking musical features of *The Ninth Wave*'s *Under Ice* (think of the chanted, distant call of a male voice sounding what some listeners translate as "Hey-o... !"). Here again (amid her low humming voice and a flock of rich, swooning strings and their overtones reminiscent of the blanket of atmospherics from 1989's *The Fog*), a lone, high-pitched vocal plea rests at one point on a note – "Snowflake! Snowflake!" (heartbreaking, elegiacal dissonance, this!) as it does again at several of the album's musical and poetic turning points.

This, to me, is the essence of Kate Bush's art: a brave, unflinching, unending search for the "distant sound" – what became, in Franz Schreker's once-famous fin-de-siècle opera of that name [in German, Der Ferne Klang] the musical and sonic cypher for unattainable beauty and artistic achievement – travels, harmonically speaking, light years from its instrumental support, and with much the same eery, hushed expressive effect. And *All the Love* is evoked in the extremely clear echoing of that 1981 recording's primevally simple bass-against-piano motif, though now with striking reverberations of musical cells that stretch back as far as *Kashka from Baghdad*, a song that dates from Kate's earliest years of musical production ca. 1973.

The marvelous line "I turn off the light" (and who doesn't remember it as the Bush-Shakespeare "Put out the light / Then put out the light"?) re-introduces, in *Misty*, the vocal ethos of *Aerial*'s *Nocturn*, but here again much the same sort of moaning, ruminative, internalized chant oozes out atop the minimal two-note bass foundation (listen to the line "mountain in my hand", for example), replacing completely the once tightly constructed, fully resolved melodic and harmonic structures of the work from before the years of self-production. These long, highly repetitive, quasi-jam-like riffs, as for example from minute 8 straight through minute 11 of *Misty*, exemplify how Kate Bush now allows the slowest of vocal slow-burns to build relentlessly over stretching swaths of jazz-inflected cadence-work (though again, as this section approaches its climax, that haunting hint of hushed dissonance again makes itself felt from high-pitched string overtones, brightening and lightening the otherwise unrelenting advance of a single, repeated minor third).

At the chorus of *Wild Man*, Andy Fairweather-Low's tight, strained higher register cuts through this track's slinky, 'loping', bass-led riffs like tensile-steel Sno-Grips on the surface of a glacier. If Fairweather-Low –a long with his overdubbed harmonizing – conjures the piercing sounds of Steely Dan's *Gaucho* (another reference to Kate's avowed influences from the past), then the line "Run away, run away... run away!" is more than that: an explicit quotation from 1993's *Big Stripey Lie*.

The album takes a decidedly darker, more urgent tone with *Snowed In At Wheeler Street* and confirms the retrospective theme of the album, first musically in the now more threatening, synth-like yet deeply organic figure that underpins the entire track (suggestive of the sounds that lurched so menacingly along *Under Ice*), then in the lyric (quoting *The Red Shoes' Why Should I Love You?*) "There's just something about you". Just as the the too-long separated, now reunited couple cannot enjoy their regained company, but speak only (and with increasing anxiety) of their fear of renewed separation, so the music is stubborn, dogged, unremitting and unforgiving: the intensest distillation of remorse and regret, a grand passion frustrated too long.

Harmonically speaking, the track *50 Words For Snow* is by far the album's most challenging and intricate track, as it conjoins a bass line harmonically distant, again, from the descant chorus it supports. A celebration of language and the evocative power of verbal imagery, this "blackbird-braille" piece (yet another lovely, oblique reference to past work, this time the call-and-response tropes of *Waking the Witch*) precedes the sparsest, most diffusely space-filled song of the new collection, *Among Angels*, which seems to this veteran fan, at least, to be drunkenly, gloriously, and so, so, privately emerging out of a long, far-ranging lounge session that began in a cold and boozy lobby somewhere back in 1980, then spread its wings under the ivy of private love, crossed (one with the) oceans of time to expand across a coral room and build up new steam in moments of pleasure reborn.

What an extraordinary, epic-in-miniature, tiny-and-grand, monumental-cameo work. Infinite gratitude to Kate Bush for her wonderful gift of the season.

Johnny: A sense of wonder

50 Words For Snow has garnered such an extraordinary amount of positive media attention, with journalists across the world tripping over themselves to unearth ever more superlatives to heap on the new Kate opus, that it is a daunting task to write a piece about the album without seeming to have raided what has already been said. So I'm not even going to try.

For me, this collection of songs is the most exciting that Kate has produced since *Hounds of Love*. And repeated listening is inspiring in me a sense of wonder in her work that I've not felt since *The Kick Inside*. There isn't a weak moment or a wasted note here, and what a joy to hear Kate still at the top of her game, defying expectations, doing things her way and producing music like no-one else.

There are so many moments that stay with me after listening to *50 Words For Snow* – the throbbing keyboard and shimmering guitar on *Snowed In At Wheeler Street*, and Elton John's heart-stopping "I don't want to lose you"; the protagonist of the gorgeous *Misty* going out on to the window ledge after her night of passion with the silent snowman (is she crazed and about to jump? Or is she about to be whisked away by her chilly lover to 'walk in the air', Raymond Briggs-styley?); Steve Gadd's sassy drumming throughout the whole record; 'shovel-crusted' and 'pulling up the rhodedendrons'; "someone who's loved you forever but you don't know it", and so many others that I wish I had the space to list here. But there are two stand-out tracks for me.

Snowflake, the album opener, is a hypnotic and captivating achievement. An incredibly visual song – with its sombre, rippling piano and rolling images – it unfolds and rises and envelops the listener. Kate's voice – maternal and comforting, and calling the snowflake to its journey's end – is as evocative and as beautiful as it has ever been; but the real star of this show is the performance she has coaxed from Bertie. His phrasing is exquisite and he has his mother's instinctive ability to tell a story in music with absolute conviction and truth. It's a very impressive acting performance and thrilling to listen to.

An air of strangeness hangs over *Lake Tahoe* from the moment the voices of Michael Wood and Stefan Roberts slide in over the opening piano line, and that crunchy atonal chord under their advice to "just stand on the edge and look in there" sets the mood for something special. Like *Snowflake*, this song has a filmic quality and is full of drama, heartache and suspense – all qualities that have been evident in Kate's best work. It also features some of the most sublime music Kate has ever written – wintry and chilling and absolutely gripping. Semi-classical in places, and with another heartfelt vocal by Kate, this is 11 minutes of genius and is, for me, the crowning glory of *50 Words For Snow*. Unforgettable.

Kate has created another magical world in sound with this album and there is a lovely sense of maturity, confidence and playfulness evident throughout. I was seduced by the music of Kate Bush 33 years ago and she has me still. The real world is, indeed, loud; anyone who lets themselves fall into this fabulous offering from our girl will find a place of warmth and refuge. It is simply stunning.

Robert Brown: Some of Kate's finest songs

A new album and a new direction, at least on *Snowflake*, *Lake Tahoe* and *Misty*. These three songs are beautifully arranged and performed, especially with Kate's piano playing at last being given a chance to shine having been virtually strangled for forty years by the time constraints of the 3 or 4 minute structured 'pop song'. Special mention should also be made of Steve Gadd's drumming towards the end of *Misty* and Dan McIntosh's short but atmospheric ambient style guitar playing on *Snowflake* and *Misty*. Probably just coincidence but I hear shades of Henryk Gorecki's Symphony No. 3 and Harold Budd's *Pavilion Of Dreams* on these tracks, as well as echoes of Kate's own *Blow Away* and *Fullhouse*.

Graphic opposite:
Robert Scheider

ROBERT SCHNIEDERS
2011

Although on the surface the performances sound rather basic, a closer listen reveals a myriad of sounds weaving their way in and out of these recordings.

After such a strong start to the album it's a great pity that Kate didn't continue in the same style of compositions and performances for the rest of the album. Unfortunately, *Wild Man* breaks the mood. Although it made for a very catchy single it sounds out of place here. Also I kind of wish Sir Elton John really had been *Snowed In At Wheeler Street*, at least he wouldn't have made the recording session. Sorry Elton fans but I really can't stand this guy or his singing.

The album's title track follows, and comes across as a bit of a throwaway song. Thanks to Stephen Fry it is moderately amusing but not repeatedly so. The energetic drums and guitars save the track… just. In the end it takes the final track to remind me of the quality of the earlier songs. *Among Angels* isn't an immediate song but repeated play reveals the song as being one of Kate's very finest compositions with a suitably lovely yearning vocal performance.

Overall, *50 Words For Snow* is a fine and highly enjoyable album despite a slight sag in the middle. Not only does it contain some of Kate's finest songs in recent memory, it's also possibly Kate's finest sounding album, thanks to the care and attention given by Del Palmer and Stephen W. Taylor. It's definitely in my top 3 Kate Bush favourite albums.

Antonello Saeli: Loss, transience and warmth

Take some time off, sink comfortably into your favourite armchair, grab a copy of Kate's new album and silence your mind, while languidly diving into the deep waters of this incredibly mature, almost hypnotic, dangerously addictive piece of work.

Looking at the meticulously, carefully selected photographs that illustrate each of the seven songs on the album, is like staring at the falling snow into those crystal balls that might have been blown to visually represent each song. Beware, as this is just the first of a series of journeys back in time, a sentimental, backward jump to the often silent mysteries of childhood, the unanswered questions of the growing-up process, the fascinating myths of our days of innocence and wonder.

There is a strong feeling of loss and transience throughout this record, a recurrent *motif* that is both musically and lyrically deeply explored, that makes the listening process quite demanding, but very rewarding in terms of personal, emotional involvement.

The record's distinct personality is mostly softly, but stubbornly, calling for attention, giving no space for distraction, and taking the listener by the hand, on a solitary journey through a very romantic, almost idyllic landscape of Victorian Gothic novels, adult reinterpretations of childish games, time-warped love stories and descriptions of far away countries and mythological creatures. Most of this incredibly varied subject matter might be hiding very carefully conceived metaphorical meanings, but the songs work very well in both territories, once again highlighting Kate's renowned abilities in playing with the multiform structure of her creations.

Snowflake opens the record with its detailed report of the short, but significant, lifespan of a single snow crystal, slowly but inevitably meeting its physical melting, once its fall is over. As with the first song from *A Sky of Honey*, Kate's son is the first human voice to welcome the listener, in a way confirming a very strong *trait d'union* between *Aerial* and the new record, which sounds in many ways as the wintry equivalent of its summery predecessor. Albert's voice sounds pure, crystal-like, reminiscent of his mother's frequent forays into the high-pitched vocal territories of her earlier work. Kate's repetitive piano sections, perfectly balanced by her reiterated line in the chorus, are the first hints at the minimalist approach that will constantly surface as a trademark, throughout most of the arrangements.

This new record sounds in many ways as Kate's most accomplished approach to classical composition, with a distinct reference to sacred music, as in some of the most interesting choral pieces by people like Benjamin Britten, Mendelssohn-Bartholdy or Arvo Pärt, and *Lake Tahoe* perfectly sums up Kate's quite evidently successful experimental research, into the relatively unexplored territories of those areas diametrically opposed to pop, making the first three songs on the album sound like a solid, credible piece of music, her personal symphony. From a lyrical point of view, the seductively sad story of the two characters' moving, otherworldly reunion in *Lake Tahoe*, is very much reminiscent of Emily Brontë's renowned masterpiece, *Wuthering Heights*, again proving the circular, recurrent nature of some of Kate's favourite themes, including waterscape imagery.

Misty seems to develop, expand and unfurl some beautiful jazzy atmospheres, previously explored in a couple of songs from *A Sky of Honey*. Though thematically quite risky, the song never falls into risible *pastiche*, wonderfully dancing on the frozen surface of a lake, carefully avoiding the dangerous, cracked spots hidden here and there. The woman's desperate call for help at the end sounds so incredibly real. The final image of her body leaning on the ledge, so dangerously dark and creepy. As it happened with computers, washing machines and cloudbusters in the past, snowmen have never sounded so fascinating before.

Wild Man is both lyrically challenging and musically adventurous. The song sounds a bit like the natural progression of the theme Kate had explored in *King of the Mountain*, with her passionate tale of a mythical creature living a solitary existence in the snow, far from the 'civilized' world, immersed in the silent whiteness of nature. This song dramatically changes the pace set by the previous tracks with its more rhythmic quality, paving the way to the following couple of compositions.

In many ways, *50 Words For Snow* successfully explores different atmospheres around its theme: the muffled sounds coming from the outside world, while dozing in front of a fireplace, next to the crazy downhill race along the sides of a mountain, the family games in the garden, with children being lost at the sight of the perfect beauty of a crystal on the palm of their hands, next to a frantic sleigh ride, so perfectly depicted in the title track.

Kate's voice is as emotionally charged as ever, especially in her slower, more intimate songs, where her lower register reaches snow-clad heights of unbearable beauty, as in the final *Among Angels*, that sounds at times like coming from the same abyss of *A Coral Room*.

Despite its Wintry theme, the album never sounds glacial, or frozen, even with the most barren and minimal instrumentation. On the contrary, there is an overall sense of warmth coming from the performances of the artists involved, especially from Kate's vocals, that sound like perfectly mixing with the gentle drums and the intimate piano.

Kate once again proves to be able to collect a storm of cheers, with the sublime and delicate touch of her own miniature world.

Krystyna Boswell: Natural Magic

Kate Bush's music speaks to the heart of the listener. Only after you've allowed her into your emotional core and let the music sweep through your soul can you even begin to analyse the sounds in words rather than feelings. After a long and colourful musical career, Kate has matured in a way that has also taken her back to the early, pre-recording career days of her teen years. Listen to those old demos now and in them you hear the same pure, melancholy sounds that she has laid down through much of *50 Words For Snow* (and prior to that were much in evidence on parts of *Aerial*, notably *A Coral Room*).

The opening chords of *Snowflake* took me back decades, like stepping into the past, and the thrill of those powerfully emotive yet simple notes transfixed my ears for the next 65 minutes. *Snowflake* is a bittersweet story of natural magic, the brief life of this beautifully simple yet complex creation of nature brought to life by the equally transient purity of a young boy's unbroken voice. Bertie is Kate's son through and through; that voice holds something special, and the higher the voice climbs the more breathtaking its effect. I feel an echo here of the heavenly notes reached by the descant voice in Grigorio Allegri's *Miserere*, the 1963 King's College Cambridge recording of which Kate played so many years ago on a Radio 1 show with Paul Gambaccini. Bertie's angelic singing transports me to a place of exquisite beauty that is almost pain. Kate's soothing, reassuring refrain, "The world is so loud; keep falling, I'll find you" is a gorgeously satisfying foil for the choir-like yearning and wonder.

Lake Tahoe, whether a ghost story or local legend, is fully alive in the telling and I wept when the Victorian lady and her devoted dog found one another again beyond death after searching for one another for so long. The glorious harmonies of Stefan Roberts and Michael Wood are like a velvet cape wound about your shoulders, lifting you up and flying with you across the lake and woods as you live the story. The discords in the lady's voice calling for her lost companion across the ice are achingly beautiful and sad.

Misty weaves a fantasy: bringing a snowman to life and sharing a night with him before dawn and the sunlight rob him of substance and the story's narrator of this unique, strangely lovely passion forever. Raymond Briggs for grown-ups. Once again Kate shows that there are few boundaries to love, and this is a theme that weaves the album together.

After the dreamlike quality of the first three tracks *Wild Man* brings us back to the present, and to the age-old legend of the Yeti. Kate ponders on his many names, and the people who have seen him, and considers his true nature: not that of a terrifying man-like monster, but that of a more innocent, childlike being ("You were playing in the snow / you were pulling up the rhododendrons"). She worries about his fate. This is another example of love and tenderness where most people would not expect to find it.

Back from the snowbound wilderness to a more domestic setting, *Snowed In At Wheeler Street* tells the story of two souls who recurrently find and then lose one other through time. Anyone who feels they have met, and perhaps lost, their soul mate will understand the longing and desperation not to lose that special timeless love. Shimmering keyboards and warm piano transport us to a snowbound world where we can huddle before a fire for a while, as time stands still for our ageless lovers. As the song builds the percussion crashes in on us like the splintering of time pushing our lovers apart. Kate's and Elton John's voices compliment each other perfectly. Elton's voice has never sounded stronger, and the crescendo of desperate longing expressed by both singers is powerful and affecting as the song reaches its climax.

On the title track Kate reprises something of π as she intones the numbers from one to fifty, while Stephen Fry reels off the *50 Words For Snow*.

There are some gorgeous sounds in among this amazing lexicon; we even get some Klingon thrown in for good measure. The song's refrain, encouraging Professor Joseph Yupik with his litany ("Come on Joe, just 22 to go") is playful and sly, daring him to find another word to befuddle our ears and delight our senses. Who else could have thought of something as wild as 'psychohail' juxtaposed the everyday description of 'bad for trains'?

Finally, we are *Among Angels*. Just Kate, her piano (which sounds so like a Joni Mitchell song in those first few chords) and some subtle strings bring the album to a gentle close. Kate gently chides yet supports her unnamed friend who is filled with despair and hurt and so doesn't know they are surrounded by angels that 'shimmer like mirrors in Summer.' "Rest your weary world in their hands," Kate urges gently, "Lay your broken laugh at their feet."

Kate's voice soars and dips, acknowledges and reassures. She has rarely sounded so beautiful. I will play this again and again when I am in a dark place as it is like soul balm, deeply comforting, giving hope and smothering the listener with love. In six years, Kate has gifted us with songs that span the two solstices of the sensual world she inhabits. The opposing seasons have been captured in a perfectly balanced hourglass of shimmering beauty. Keep the glass in a sacred place, and you will have a treasury of natural magic to enjoy and marvel at again and again, undimmed by the passage of time. Thank you, Kate, for such aural and visual beauty.

Collin Kelley: Expansive, elegaic, melancholic

In 2005, Kate said during an interview that she might surprise everyone and release two albums in one year. Six years later, she made good on the surprise by releasing the fanbase-dividing *Director's Cut* in the Spring and the brilliant (and near universally praised) *50 Words For Snow* in the Autumn. Although there are just seven songs, the album clocks in at more than hour, with Kate giving each song room to breathe and then some. Kate's piano is front and center on this album and the wintry soundscape she creates is expansive, elegiac and a little melancholy. In a word, perfection.

The sonic and vocal cues from earlier songs that pop up unexpectedly throughout are a treat. The choral voices echoing *Hello Earth* from *The Ninth Wave* on *Lake Tahoe*; the synth line that runs through *Snowed In At Wheeler Street* is like the wintry cousin of *Aerial*, while the allusion to World War II harkens back to *Heads We're Dancing*; the cadence of her voice on *Misty* is similar to *A Coral Room*; and there's plenty of others. And while it recalls those beloved songs, *50 Words For Snow* is unlike any of the nine Kate albums that preceded it. Besides the later-period Joni Mitchell structured jazz sound, the stark piano that drives the album also reminds me of Craig Armstrong's film scores and this album definitely unfurls in a very cinematic way. While it is uniformly fantastic, some tracks do stand out more than others for me. Albert McIntosh's lead vocal on *Snowflake* is both fragile and soaring – it's perfectly imperfect. The improbable affair between a girl and a snowman on *Misty* is the album's most jazz-influenced song, and I can't help but hear touches of the Vince Gauraldi Trio, in the opening piano notes.

The jewel in the crown is *Snowed In At Wheeler Street*, the duet with Sir Elton John. It's the tale of time travelling lovers (I can't help but think of River Song and The Doctor) who keep meeting at the most inopportune times, including the burning of Rome, during World War II and the Sept. 11 terrorist attacks in New York. There is something theatrical about the song, but it's also simply beautiful and emotional. The urgency and longing in Kate's voice is heartbreaking. As a producer, Kate has an incredible knack for coaxing interesting performances from her guest vocalists, and surely this is Elton's most expressive singing in years. There is a sensuality in their call and response that simmers in comparison with the rest of the album.

The steady beat of the title track with the imitable Stephen Fry intoning 50 words for snow – both real and invented – while Kate keeps a menacing count in the background is another top track. The fanciful names are often silly, but Fry infuses them with such gravitas that you'll be stunned they aren't actually in the dictionary. Number 42 is Klingon, by the way.

Among Angels is an absolutely stunning piece of work and features Kate's best vocal performance on the album. The new, husky-voiced Kate we heard on *Director's Cut* and throughout most of this album seems to melt away as her voice soars over the heart-rending lyrics. If I have any quibble with this album, it's the sequencing of the last two songs. *Among Angels* closes the album, but when the song ends, it feels as if something more is needed – something with a bit more weight. The title track would have done that nicely, with Fry reaching Number 50 and at last uttering the word "snow". Maybe that would have tied too neat a bow on top of the present to suit Kate, but regardless she has made one of the best albums of her career. It's a triumph.

Paul Burston: Stepping into a snow storm

This isn't the first time Kate Bush has invited us to step out into the sensual world. There have often been references to weather formations in her work, from *Cloudbusting* and *The Big Sky* to large chunks of *Aerial*. But it's the first time she has dedicated an entire album to a meteorological phenomenon. Listening to this album is like stepping into a snow storm.

There aren't '50 Words for Snow', which is

Graphic: Steven Brown

why the title track calls on Stephen Fry to invent some of his own. It's hard to imagine anyone else pulling this off, just as it's hard to imagine anyone else serenading a washing machine. *50 Words For Snow* isn't my favourite song on the album. Right now it's a toss up between *Among Angels* and *Misty*, where she imagines herself getting up close and personal with a snowman. It's a reminder that sex and sensuality have always been an integral part of her work, from the *The Kick Inside* onward.

I have little doubt that as I become more intimately acquainted with this album, my feelings will shift, as surely as her snowman melts. There's a depth here that demands repeat listenings. Not that I'm complaining. What better album to settle down with at this time of year? December really will be magic again.

Doug Alan: Free to do what she really wants

In the beginning there were two albums from Kate in a year. Then they came every two or three. Then every four years. Then twelve. Then twenty... [Insert the sound of a phonograph needle scratching across the grooves of a record.]

No, wait! Two in six months??? What impossible miracles can come next? A massive world tour! Nah. But it does seem that Kate always finds a new way to surprise us. Though perhaps it should come as no surprise that Kate can work quickly when she wants to. Over the years she has given us a significant number of high quality B-sides, some of which were composed and recorded on tight schedules. These songs have often been much simpler than her album material, and yet they are, as a whole, just as wonderful as her albums. Imagine, for instance, a whole album from Kate of songs as sublime and as "simple" as *Under the Ivy*. With *50 Words For Snow*, Kate has come close to this.

The new album is surprising because on it Kate has set aside her predilection for elaborately produced songs with catchy melodies and layer upon later of sonic textures. As I read opined in one recent review, it's as if Kate finally felt free from the burden of having to be "Kate Bush", and thereby was free to do what she really wanted. I'm not convinced that Kate hasn't always done precisely what she wants, but it's clear that now she wanted to do something less busy and frenetic than any of her previous albums. And subsequently, she's created an album with an aesthetic of minimalism and with tons of space to breathe and let the listener's mind go where it will.

When Kate released *Hounds of Love*, she spoke in interviews of her admiration for the American record label Windham Hill, which released music by artists who made folky, jazzy, ambient music. According to Kate, this is why she placed the large white border on the cover of *Hounds of Love*, as this was the style of many Windham Hill album covers at the time. She also expressed her admiration for the German record label ECM, which made music of a similar vibe. Other than her getting Eberhard Weber to play on quite a few of her songs over four albums, the influence of Windham Hill and ECM on her music might not be so apparent. Until now that is.

The new album is also unique for Kate in that it is both simultaneously warmer and colder than her previous releases. The immaculately recorded piano and drums and the bottomless bass that permeate the album are warm and very human, and yet the space in and the tone of the songs exude cold and night. The songs are serenades sung on a Winter's night next to a roaring fire when the electricity and heat have gone out. They are of longing and of the transience of existence, of the long night to come, and yet the joy of love in the moment. Life is sad and sweet and so is love.

The entire album is wonderful of course, but my favorite tracks are *Snowflake* and *50 Words For Snow*. For reasons I can't fully articulate, *Snowflake* reminds me of the *His Dark Materials* trilogy, with its images of snow and dust and ice and separation and wonder and love. Ah, yes, and the determination to find each other, despite all odds. There's an undercurrent in the song that hearkens back to *Under Ice*, and yet it's also completely new. It's a haunting and beautiful song. *50 Words For Snow*, on the other hand, is a great work of "space rock", with it's tribal beat and trippy lyrics. I wonder if Kate has been listening to Tangerine Dream or Hawkwind. If so, that's fine by me!

Lake Tahoe has hints of *Hello Earth*, and I love its jazzy, discordant feel, and especially how Kate sings off-key at the end. *Wild Man* is delightfully Bowie-esque during the chorus. An homage to another of her heroes? In *Snowed In At Wheeler Street*, the throbbing chords that repeat for the entire song are wonderful and mildly ominous.

Kate is back, and with her new-found ability to write and record material quickly, we can only hope that she'll be back again soon. I don't want to lose you again.

Izabela Samsonowicz: A huge dose of love

Year 2011 is coming to an end, a happy one for Kate fans: two albums this year, both followed by visual surprises for fans. The great *Director's Cut* now seems to be an appetizer for what came later: *50 Words For Snow.*

The album is built around various stories – some a bit dark but always with a beam of hope and a huge dose of love, all set in snowy scenery. Perfect music to listen to while sitting snuggly on a cold winter evening with a cat in your lap. Kate turns into a storyteller presenting original characters via different types of narration. Starting from the beautiful *Snowflake* – a mother-son dialogue which feels a bit like a more mature version of *Bertie* – this time with a response from the growing boy. Kate sings only one line in this song, three short sentences sung so softly in an incredibly comforting manner that I personally find it to be an ideal lullaby.

Lake Tahoe, a story painted with three different voices brings us to a very cold place in the mountains where a long forgotten woman reclaims her best friend – an old dog. This is a very rich composition that can easily bring tears to a dog owner's eyes. The story of *Misty*, the snowman, who is having 'a wonderful time' with a woman is about another type of love – a very sensual and tragic one. The music here is a background storyteller – changing its pace and tone depending on the storyline. The way Kate sings makes me think that if *Snowflake* was written for Albert to showcase his voice then *Misty* was created in order to show what a beautiful jazzy vocal can do with a theoretically ridiculous story – I found myself moved to tears at the end of it, sorry for the snowman and the girl. A work of genius. Such adventures only with Kate!

The rest of the album was easier to assimilate. The brilliant *Wild Man* – a song of empathy for the yeti (I simply love those bells!) that is for the 'different and unknown' which sounds even better accompanied by the rest of the songs. Then we have a dream duet with Sir Elton John followed by a linguistically trippy song turned into a ritual with its shamanic rhythm– absolutely bonkers and brilliant! Whilst the last song, a calming piano ballad *Among Angels,* takes us higher, to the spiritual dimension of love.

50 Words For Snow is not a musical fast-food like many of today's popular albums. It's a real feast for our senses! A demanding set of sounds and vocals wrapped around seven different stories of love and mutual understanding. It won't grab everyone instantly, the album needs you to take the risk and dive into it but once you get to its deepest part and discover its treasures, you'll fall for it completely. To me it was love at the first listen. An unexpected masterpiece.

Ian McLauchlan: A fresh start

So here's the Kate album I'd have wished for but never imagined would happen. Joni Mitchell with a hint of Michael Nyman but always and unmistakably 'Kate'. A beautiful sonic landscape to explore, spoiled only by a huge (reindeer?) turd steaming away in the pristine snow. (*Wheeler Street*, with some of the worst lyrics possible). No matter, this is one of Kate's most complete and satisfying works. Each track contains more melodic hooks and vocal surprises than anything she's done before. It sounds like a fresh start; and for an artist with over thirty years of stunning work behind her, how exciting is that?

A (Certain) Dog's Life

Kyla Clay Fox

It's lonely being me.
- The world adores my mistress
And wags it's tail at her every move
And passion for John Innes...
They wait for years to hear a song,
Then wait again - there's something wrong
- Why won't they let my mistress be,
So she can spend some time with me?

It isn't that I canna,
Stand the sound of her Joanna,
But whilst she's tinkling ivory
She has no time to pamper me...
(A hound of love shouldn't be so rude,
But please God, let me have my food
I went through time enough of hell
With Bertie's teething and then *Aerial*...)

Yes it's lonely being me,
When the bonemeal casts its magic
- Then I'm left to sleep in the studio
And the outcome can be tragic.
But a wily Dog, he can get revenge
Via other means than his flatulence ...

Whilst my mistress was thinking of 50 words....
I'd already left her 50 tur... WOOF!!!!!

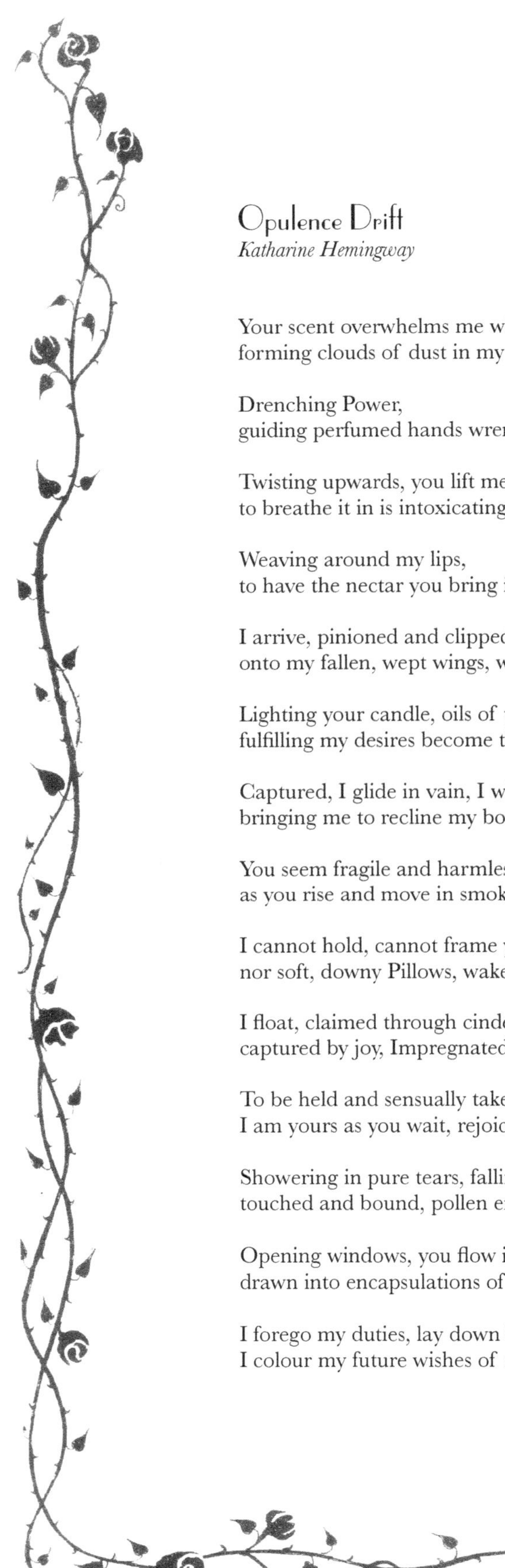

Opulence Drift

Katharine Hemingway

Your scent overwhelms me with irresistible power,
forming clouds of dust in my lungs, opulence overtaking, gliding,

Drenching Power,
guiding perfumed hands wrench me into unknown realms and fantasies,

Twisting upwards, you lift me I watch your spiral of mist filling my air,
to breathe it in is intoxicating,

Weaving around my lips,
to have the nectar you bring is to execute feelings of passions' bare hands,

I arrive, pinioned and clipped by the erosion of your touch,
onto my fallen, wept wings, whispering softly,

Lighting your candle, oils of your essence drift slowly,
fulfilling my desires become the walls of secret, hidden chambers,

Captured, I glide in vain, I wish never to escape this experience of you,
bringing me to recline my body and limbs,

You seem fragile and harmless, frail and fragmented,
as you rise and move in smoky billows, adding clarity,

I cannot hold, cannot frame you, with iron bars,
nor soft, downy Pillows, wake or stir you glowing inside me,

I float, claimed through cinders of heady textureless grain,
captured by joy, Impregnated by sweet wishes wise,

To be held and sensually taken, by gathered pearl eyes,
I am yours as you wait, rejoicing in faceless slivers of justice,

Showering in pure tears, falling from white petals,
touched and bound, pollen enchanted, dripping with seed,

Opening windows, you flow into the company of caught images,
drawn into encapsulations of glittering air sparks,

I forego my duties, lay down in snowy bed sheets,
I colour my future wishes of return, moulded to you.

Wonderful Teacher

... Lisa Oliver uses Kate's work in home education

Issue 79 December 2011

It all began with the track *Hounds of Love*.

My daughter, Stevie, was then aged 6. We were on another tedious motorway drive back from the Midlands to our adopted home in the West Country when she suddenly piped up, "Mum, can we listen to the 'dog song'?" She had recently become obsessed with all things 'pooch' (indeed, out of the last ten films I've seen at the cinema, at least eight have had a talking canine as the star). This had me a little flummoxed – what was the 'dog song'? Several minutes of her humming impatiently and barking out off-key 'woofs' followed before I finally twigged what she was talking about and duly popped the disc into the player. She was enthralled and asked question after question about the stories behind the songs – *Hounds of Love* quickly became her listening choice whenever we were in the car.

Stevie was born with the condition dyspraxia. In a nutshell, it is associated with problems of perception, language and thought. Gross and fine motor skills are compromised and physical activity is difficult – the brain says one thing but the body wanders off to do something else. After starting off well, the school environment became quite problematic for Stevie and so I started to think about the possibility of home educating.

We began in July 2009 and have never looked back. But how could I keep our curriculum inspiring, interesting and worthwhile ?

Stevie can be quite literal in her thinking, what could I use to fire her imagination?

One evening, I found her engrossed in her first viewing of the the *Cloudbusting* video. The questions came thick and fast. "Who's that boy, Mum?" "It's Kate Bush" "Why is she dressed like a little boy?" "She's playing the part of this man's son". We talked about what happened to him, his son Peter and what the video was depicting. I think I had found the 'trigger' for her imagination that I needed.

"What other stories are there in Kate's songs, Mum?" she asked. And so we were off.

Them Heavy People inspired a piece of prose about favourite things. I explained what Kate was singing about and encouraged Stevie to think of her own inspirations: "babies giggling, being kind, playing with (our dog) Toto, loving Nature". We listened to *A Sea of Honey* (hearing Bertie's spoken words thrilled Stevie) from which came a collage of the sea – complete with mermaid! – that was displayed in our local art gallery.

A song that really struck a chord was *Breathing.* Stevie was intrigued that this one was sung from the point of view of a baby in the womb and it sparked a long discussion about the threat of nuclear war, whether babies can 'sense' danger, the Cold War and why it isn't a good idea to smoke whilst pregnant... our debates can end up becoming fairly random.

Discovering the influences for some of Kate's songs is a bit like fitting together the pieces of a jigsaw puzzle – who are all these people mentioned in *December Will Be Magic Again*? What are the beliefs of Aboriginal people?

One of the latest things we have researched has been the Yeti, a subject that coincidentally we had already touched upon before. Now we had a new song of Kate's to explore and many references to follow up. And who hasn't had fun making up their own '50 Words For Snow'? We have! 'iceberg seeds', 'icyeyelashfeathers', 'Gaia's Lacy Underskirts'...

It was a joy for me as a young girl to get into Kate's music and discover whole new worlds through the stories. I am thrilled to be helping my daughter now to do the same. Thanks Kate.

Graphic: Katherine Hemingway

Bee Song

Krys

Can you feel
my soft
velvet
fur
as it brushes
the inside of your arm –
and can you feel
my little black feet
tiptoe over your
pebble smooth thigh –
and can you feel
the hush of my wings
touch your lips
as I come to kiss –
and can you feel
my tongue
sticky after
drinking
your flowers –
from you
I will make the sweetest honey

All We Ever Look For

Max Cookney wonders where all the vinyl has gone

Issue 79 December 2011

It's 1987. I'm sat in bed on a hospital ward in the Royal Naval Hospital Stonehouse, Plymouth. On time and as promised, my mother turns up with a copy of the latest *Smash Hits* magazine, a generously sized bag of penny sweets and an envelope, addressed to me. Inside, I find a curious bright orange sheet of paper which would later induce an absolute obsession with Kate's work; one that has calmed down somewhat as I've aged, but which still easily "get's me going".

I have vivid memories of hearing *Wuthering Heights* on the radio at age four, and of not being allowed to stay up to watch the remainder of the Hammersmith Odeon concert on television circa 1980. My Royal Naval parents, myself and my brother were shipped out to Gibraltar in 1981 and it wasn't until 1986, back in the UK (around the time that the *Hounds of Love* single was released) that I rediscovered Kate.

Photos of his collection by Max Cookney

That piece of orange paper was actually a list of vinyl records for sale, presumably sent in response to my 'Swaps' request in the Kate Bush Club magazine, from somebody at a mysterious sounding location called 'Thrushcross Grange'. It was intriguing. Why were there lots of different countries listed? What did P/S mean? What was R.U.T.H.? I'd only recently discovered that Kate had recorded a Christmas song. and a song sung in French. This was my first introduction to the world of record collecting.

Throughout 1986/87, I had a mediocre collection, mainly just UK albums, a handful of 7" and 12" records and a few imports: the *On Stage* EP on cassette tape, a Japanese pressing of *Breathing* and the beautiful Canadian Mini LP.

Shortly after I received the Thrushcross Grange list, I received another mailing that would really get the ball rolling. You may remember Francis who ran 'Musiques' in Liège, Belgium. He produced a regular record catalogue and included a periodic discography of Kate's worldwide vinyl pressings. It was very well illustrated and gave me a great deal of insight to the differences in various releases.

I started buying regularly from both Francis and Thrushcross Grange. I also got into the habit of buying *Record Collector* magazine and would spend a Saturday morning trawling through the 'Set Sale' listings to see what else I could buy. I also remember the thrill of my first record fair held at the old Odeon Cinema in Plymouth's Union Street. I could hardly contain my excitement as I rummaged through the plethora of vinyl gems, only ever heading for the section marked 'B' and stumbling across so many new finds (including a hefty amount of bootlegs).

I was still only 14 years old and my parents remained baffled. Whilst the birthday present wish lists for my friends were games for their beloved Sinclair ZX Spectrum computers, my list was usually more records. Another worthy and very local supply was from the huge collection of Greg Vandike (his father opened the legendary Vandike Club in Plymouth). I once remember my mother having to visit Greg's home on her moped, in the pouring rain, to buy a copy of the Japanese Fan Club *Let It Be* bootleg EP (on a very lovely blue vinyl) for my birthday. What dedication and what a treat!

I became obsessed and soon found that I was becoming a bit of an expert. I started my own listings in *Record Collector* and even did the occasional deal with Greg but there were still a number of collectables that remained elusive. The big one of course was *The Early Years* LP. But records like *The Big Sky* picture disc and *The Single File* boxed set, both relatively recent releases at that time, were virtually impossible to get hold of. Once again it was down to my poor mother to approach someone in my preferred local record store (Rival Records on Royal Parade, long since gone) to enquire if they could get hold of the box. They tried hard, even 'phoning the EMI distributors. I prayed that they would find one solitary copy hiding in a dusty corner of the warehouse. Sadly, they couldn't get it even though it had only been deleted a few years earlier (I would have to wait another 17 years before I had a copy I could call my own).

By the start of the next decade there was a noticeable difference in the level of interest in

vinyl. Compact discs had taken hold as the preferred music format and as Kate's activity following *The Sensual World* quietened, so too did the pursuit of selling Kate Bush vinyl and memorabilia. Record Fairs were smaller and less frequent. *The Record Collector* magazine became thinner with few listings. Over the next few years most rare Kate records just seemed to disappear.

Then something absolutely extraordinary happened: *The internet*: and with it came our saviour. Founded in September 1995 as AuctionWeb, eBay enabled everyone to sell anything and everything. I started visiting eBay about 11 years ago and slowly saw an increase in the amount of Kate vinyl making an appearance. All manner of treasures hidden in wardrobes, attics and cellars all around the world started to turn up. Vinyl, posters, magazines, books and oddities such as 8-track cartridges and bubble gum trading cards. Rather surprisingly during the hiatus between *The Red Shoes* and *Aerial*, eBay facilitated a reasonably strong trade in Kate Bush records and we witnessed the appearance of numerous copies of *The Big Sky* picture disc and a steady supply of *Single File* boxed sets.

I've picked up so many things from eBay over the years. My best prize find was a 12" test pressing of *The Dreaming* single. Yep, you heard me right. The *12" single*. It *does* exist! However I (rather regretfully) sold it on. The good news is that I sold it to a fellow Kate collector.

A few years ago, eBay produced the first and only appearance so far (to the best of my knowledge) of the elusive *The Early Years* LP (an album made in Germany circa 1986 containing some of Kate's early demo tape recordings). It had a rather disappointing picture sleeve, but of course we were more interested in what was pressed on the vinyl. I'd like to think that there is more than one copy and another will turn up one day soon.

As for the one item for which I have a permanent eBay email alert set up, I doubt I will ever see it. It is the German *December Will Be Magic Again* 7" single on green vinyl. Though a fellow fan once apparently saw a copy at a record fair, I remain sceptical of its existence: but should it be true, I would part with a substantial amount of money to own a copy.

To this day, I still long to own a huge collection of every Kate Bush record in existence. It's never really gotten close, mainly for financial reasons. Records in my possession have come and gone. Some strangely return to be savoured for a second time. I just love holding them in my hands. To me they are individual pieces of art that are bewitching. You can't put them away without wanting to hear what's on the disc. I hold a copy of *Hammer Horror* and in my mind I create an image of a smoky office in the art department at EMI House in Manchester Square. "What photo from the latest Mankowitz shoot to use?" "What typeface looks best?" "Should we not put Kate's name on the front of the sleeve?"

As you know, they chose not to; however you may find it interesting that EMI in Spain and Portugal did add both Kate's name and the song title. This localised approach to artwork and manufacture is most evident during the earlier part of Kate's career and it's here that you'll find the most interesting differences between single and album releases of different EMI territories. However, after *Hounds of Love*, there was more of a generic approach to production and the country of manufacture rarely made much difference to the artwork, particularly within the EU.

Whilst eBay has been great in helping dig out a large number of rarities, I've started to notice a dwindle in the emergence of collectable Kate vinyl. So, where has all the vinyl gone? Where is the German *Breathing* with its reverse negative sleeve? The gaudy Belgian *Man with the Child in his Eyes*? The Spanish *Suspendido En Gaffa* single with Kate's brightly coloured-in red lips? The New Zealand *Hammer Horror* with it's fold out sleeve? (Did the factory run out of glue?). Surely EMI in Uruguay pressed more than just the handful of extremely rare *The Kick Inside* albums we've seen over the years?

I know these records do turn up very occasionally on eBay (amongst the sea of 'genuine' autographs, drinks coasters and illegal photo reprints that litter the Kate Bush listings these days), but I can't help thinking that there are piles of Kate Bush records sitting around rotting in someone's attic, or worse still, that have simply been thrown out with the garbage.

I like to think that the release of *Director's Cut* and *50 Words For Snow* will generate a renewed interest in Kate's earlier work and that people will think it's a good time to sell their Kate records. I really hope so, because in this digital age where music is easily downloaded to a computer and just as easily deleted at the touch of a button, I'd like to know we can still hold on to those early vinyl 'works of art', in solid state, to be saved, cared for and enjoyed forever.

Go on, dig out an old Kate vinyl record and remind yourself how good it feels in your hands. And if you happen to know where all the vinyl has gone, please let me know!

Whatever Happened to Catherine Bush?

... ...a HomeGround Christmas story by Dave

Issue 79:
December 2011

As someone clever once said, "The universe is big... really big." Billions of stars in billions of galaxies and stars are only part of the story: there are comets, nebula, black holes, white holes, worm holes, rifts, tares and tears. There are planets with oceans, deserts, forests, shopping malls, intelligent life, monsters, traffic wardens and some with nothing at all. And then there is time - the most solid, reliable, dependable and predictable thing in the universe, except when it twists and turns and pops up when and where it shouldn't. Sometimes it brings what you least expected, but needed the most.

The young girl couldn't sleep, but she also couldn't do much of anything else. She had been trying to write a song, had a great idea for a tune, but every time she went anywhere near the piano, she started to hear things. There was something scratching around just on the edge of her hearing and if she picked up a pen, the fear came sliding into her mind, something twisting and shiny and dark. She could almost hear words, or maybe those were in her head, telling her she was no good. Why bother? No-one will ever care, no-one will ever hear your silly songs, you aren't worthy...

And, somewhere in space and time, in the Tardis, The Doctor was talking and Amy and Rory were doing their best impression of listening and understanding. "The future, you see. It's complicated, it's not written in stone. That's the past, and actually most of that isn't even in stone. You would be amazed at what hasn't turned up as a fossil. Anyway, the future: one minute it's all about moon bases and flying cars, you know, like in *Back to the Future*, and then, suddenly, the only place where you find cars that fly is in *Harry Potter*, which is not about the future at all, so they have stopped being futuristic and are now magical. Does that make sense?"

The Doctor paused and Amy glanced at Rory, managed an "err" before he carried on. "So, it's about what people think and do more than anything, and the smallest thought can change everything. The whole of time and space is replete with turning points, some fixed and some not." He looked expectantly at his two friends. "What? Doesn't that help?"

Without risking another glance at her husband, Amy replied: "As fascinating as that was, Doctor, we actually asked you to tell us about The Yetis? You said you'd run into them a few times in the past."

Realisation dawned on the Time Lord's face. "Oh, yes, well I was getting to that. Yes, Yetis. Actually the ones I met, were alien robots."

"Of course they were," Rory said almost under his breath.

The Doctor ignored this and carried on: "They were soldiers of 'The Great Intelligence' and, actually, they didn't really look anything like your actual Yetis, the Wild Man, The Kangchenjunga Demon. Hmmm... I remember a rather good song about that, in fact..." But The Doctor didn't finish his sentence, as suddenly the Tardis lurched and the sound of its ancient engines changed to become the familiar noise of de-materialisation,

Amy grabbed at the console. "Doctor, we've landed, what's happening?"

The Doctor was pulling levers and banging buttons. He stopped, scratched his face, banged another panel and said, "We've landed."

"Yes, we know," Rory said, "but you said we wouldn't be getting home for a while."

The Doctor looked at the two of them, as if seeing them for the first time. "What? No, yes, I think the Tardis has made us land. She has sensed something wrong; a fixed point being threatened. Wherever we are, the future is being rewritten and not in a good way. There is something out there that needs saving or rescuing or something, probably going to be very dangerous... ooh, fantastic! Come on!"

He took out his sonic screwdriver, gave it a flick and twirl and headed to the Tardis door. The Doctor stuck his head out, there was a pause and he looked back in.

Amy stepped forward. "What is it, Doctor, what's out there?"

He looked at them blankly and said, "I think it's a barn."

The young girl had given up on sleep and on

The *HomeGround* Christmas story has been a tradition over the past 30 years – at least in our minds – and I have wanted to do a *Doctor Who*/Kate crossover for a while. This story doesn't actually mention either *HomeGround* or Christmas.

It was inspired by the recent series of *Doctor Who* and *The Sarah Jane Adventures* and I'd like to dedicate it to the memory of the wonderful and much missed actress Elisabeth Sladen.

Acknowledgements to those who created The Doctor and other characters and stories I have referenced and to Stephen Moffat who created Amy and Rory.

With thanks to Collin Kelley, and apologies to all who first read this in *HomeGround* issue 79 and wondered how it ended!

Dave

the piano in the house. She headed out to her refuge, where the old church organ was, maybe out in the garden, in her half of a Heaven, she could escape the fear. But this time, there was something different; a strange noise and then voices, coming closer to the old barn, friendly voices, talking about stupid things.

"So, Doctor, we were talking about Yetis, both sorts, Wild Men and the alien robots," Amy said. "Is this gonna be another one of those Tardis coincidences? We talk about them and there's Yetis here? Wherever here is? Actually, where are we?"

The Doctor paused, sniffed the air. "South London, Kent... Welling maybe. I think it's the early '70s."

Amy and Rory had long ago given up on asking how The Doctor knew where he was, or where he thought he was. The three reached the door of the barn and gently pushed the door open.

"Hello," The Doctor called out.

There was a moment of silence as The Doctor, Amy and Rory stood in front of the young girl. "Hello. Are you friends of my brothers," she asked, "or did my Mum or Dad send you? Is it about the organ?"

The Doctor hesitated for only a moment. "Umm... the organ? Ah! The pipe organ. No! Not really. I'm the Doctor and these are The Ponds, Amy and Rory. We heard there was something wrong, a problem." He smiled at the young girl and carried on. "There *is* something wrong, isn't there? Sorry, what was your name?"

The girl came forward into the light and extended her hand. "It's Catherine, Catherine Bush."

The Doctor grabbed her hand. "Of course! Hello, Catherine. So tell me, what's been happening here? Why are you in the barn?"

Catherine led them outside to sit in the garden. "You will probably think I'm completely mad," she started "but it's the piano. Or maybe it's in my head. I write songs, you see, and just in the past week or so, every time I go near the piano, I can hear something - a scratchy noise like bats or rats, and there's a fear that comes. It's like I can hear a voices telling me I mustn't, I shouldn't be making music." Catherine stared at The Doctor. "I am mad, aren't I?"

The Doctor thought for a minute and was about to speak, when Rory jumped in. "I know this seems like a strange question, Catherine, but what year is it please?"

Without hesitating, she replied, "It's 1972. Is that important..? And how can you not know what the year is?"

"It's complicated," the trio chorused.

Rory continued. "You write songs on a piano? This is Welling in 1972? And you are thirteen years old?

"Yes, how do you know that?" Catherine asked curiously.

Amy elbowed Rory in the ribs. "What are you doing? Don't frighten her."

But Rory carried on. "Your name is Catherine Bush?"

The girl just smiled and nodded again.

Rory turned to The Doctor. "Can I have a word?"

"What about? I need to scan," The Doctor said, pulling the sonic screwdriver from his jacket pocket and aiming it at the girl.

"What is that?!" Catherine exclaimed.

"Doctor, it's *important*," Rory insisted.

"Ah ha!" The Doctor said, looking at the screwdriver. "Definitely something here."

Rory grabbed The Doctor by the shoulder and spun him around. "Doctor, *listen*. Catherine Bush writing songs on a piano in 1972. Catherine often shortened to *Kate*."

The Doctor seemed to draw a blank and then his mouth slowly opened and closed. "Ah... oh, blimey! She's going to be..."

"Yes," Rory said, "and we know she is supposed to be a prolific songwriter at this age, so the question..."

The Doctor picked up Rory's line of thinking. "The question is: what or who is trying to stop Kate Bush from writing songs and why?"

The Doctor turned to look at the girl, who smiled and said, "I do quite like being called Kate. It's a bit more grown-up than Cathy."

Kate took them into the house to where the old piano was and explained exactly what had been happening. The Doctor did some more scanning with his screwdriver and finally announced, "Okay, yep, I know what it is."

He sat down with Kate, while Amy and Rory stood near the piano watching.

"Kate, you are an intelligent girl," The Doctor said. "I know you are, so I can tell you the truth. There are things - life forms or creatures, if you like - that feed on wasted lives. They try and change history. I've met these monsters before. Friends of mine, Sarah Jane and Donna, ran into them, and they tried to rewrite their futures. These creatures are part of The Trickster's nasty little gang. The Trickster feeds on depression and chaos and one of them has been trying to stop you from being whom and what you are supposed to be. I think that whatever song you have been trying to write, and will write, is going to be really important to you and to a lot of people."

Amy spoke. "Doctor, where is this thing and can we get rid of it?"

The Doctor raised a finger to his lips, stood up and in his best stage whisper said, "That could be really tricky, Amy. I've no idea where it is."

The Doctor spun around and stuck his hand down the back of the old piano. There was a muffled squeak, and The Doctor pulled out a creature that resembled a wriggling, dark blue mole.

"What is that thing?" Amy whispered and took a step back.

Kate stared wide-eyed at the creature. "Oh, it looks frightened. It's so small and harmless."

The Doctor tightened his grip on the creature. "Don't be fooled, Kate. It's a vile little thing and its only goal was to ruin your life and rob the world of everything you will create."

As if on cue, the creature spat and hissed at her. The Doctor flicked a switch on the sonic screwdriver and pointed it at the mole. There was a loud hum and the creature wriggled violently before suddenly disappearing with a loud "pop."

Kate looked horrified. "Oh, no. You didn't kill it? Please no, the poor thing!"

The Doctor took her hand gently "Kate, even though you knew it was trying to hurt you in a really nasty way, you still cared about it. No, it's not dead. I just sent it back where it belongs. It doesn't belong in this reality." He smiled and winked at her.

Rory spoke. "But won't there be other creatures, Doctor? Is Kate safe now?"

The Doctor turned to his companions. "I think so. She knows now, and once someone knows it's very difficult to fool them again. And the Tardis leaves a trace wherever it's been, and The Trickster won't like it."

The Doctor knelt down and looked Kate in the eye. "Listen to me, Catherine Bush. You are something special. You need to write songs and make music and don't ever let anyone else tell you different. It won't always be easy, but you must stick to doing it your way and if you want to write songs about classic books or horror movies or Russian wives or Aborigines or clouds or water or even Yetis, you just do it and be brilliant."

Kate looked quite shocked. "Okay, but…" she hesitated. "That's all I really want to do, and I have a great idea for this song." She blushed and then almost shyly asked, "How old are you, Doctor?"

Amy and Rory rolled their eyes. "Go on," Amy said, "tell her Doctor."

The Doctor hesitated for two heartbeats. "Oh, Bush, I am a lot - and I mean *a lot* - older than you. Why do you want to know?"

Kate smiled. "I thought you seemed quite old… in a nice way." She paused and stared at the Time Lord's face for a moment. "Except there's something in your eyes, something child like."

A little while later, a young girl carried a cup of tea and some chocolate to the piano. She placed her fingers delicately over the keys and began to write a song.

Graphic: Steven Brown

After 35 Years, A Leap of Faith

... Del Palmer's long brewing solo work

Issue 79 December 2011

Del explains: "I got my first bass guitar in 1967. A Hofner Artiste which looked a bit like a Jazz Bass. My old pal Brian Bath had a band called Cobwebs and Strange and they needed a bass player. He talked me into buying the bass so I could become that bass player. I bought it by loaning twenty pounds from my mother and paying her back a pound a week from a paper round.

"Brian and I formed a three piece in 1969 called Tame. We were very popular around our local area and did a number of gigs during 1969-1970. The band also included Victor King on drums. This band would later become the KT Bush Band. I got my first really decent bass in those days. A Gibson EB3. I wanted one of these desperately because my heroes all seemed to use them. I still have it now although I don't use it that much.

There was a short time during 1972/3 when we had, what we thought was a fantastic band called Company. It was a four-piece featuring Brian (as usual), Barry Sherlock who also played guitar and Lionel Azulay, a very fine drummer. We seemed to have a perfect balance which quickly attracted interest from several record companies. We signed to Cube records in 1973 and did several recording sessions with a view to releasing our first single. However, fate dealt us a severe blow when our drummer Lionel

Leap of Faith

"Well, having just completed the latest studio album to be released by Kate I felt the time was right to try, finally, to make some music myself." So in 2007 Del introduced his first solo album, the aptly entitled *Leap of Faith*. This is what *HomeGround* Editors and forum members thought of it:

Krys: "I've been listening to *Leap of Faith* quite a few times now and I really do love it. For me there are all kinds of musical influences and sounds on there – musically Steely Dan, some guitar sounds a little like Nick Drake and Nick Harper (particularly the instrumental track), a little Pink Floyd, and that distinctive musical Kate sound. Vocally Del can use his voice in different ways – sometimes reminiscent of Bryan Ferry, Morissey, even a hint of Frankie Goes to Hollywood. These are just my initial feelings. The more I listen the more I absolutely love this."

Seán: "The first track kinda threw me in that it seemed very 'conflicted' and intense. But it was a nice introduction to Del's singing voice and a certain uncompromising attitude to this recording (yes!) The production of this first track is very mature and (dare I say it) late '80s; in the good way!

Del's voice is frankly a revelation on this album, he cleverly and slowly reveals what he can do over the early (and deceptively) straightforward tracks. He has a brilliant voice.

Del's vocal and lyrical playfulness first starts coming to the fore on *Welcome to Hard Times* and the following three tracks are a joy; the trippy calm of the record's title track, the (let's hear it live please!) serenity of the instrumental *Of Things Past* (a Del Palmer classic) and the delirious joy of the reggae-tinged *Dream* already mark this as a deliciously personal album from Mr. Palmer.

I can hear Kate on this album even if it's as a ghostly presence. It's quite likely that she hasn't "officially" played on any of these tracks, but there's a distinctive mark of quality to this production that screams Noble & Brite to me. It's a credit to Del that he's managed to distill his very personal stamp on these songs.

A Love Song is such a moving, and very male love song, if that makes sense. *You Must Believe* reminds me so much of the musical spirit of Paddy Bush – I can easily see Pad tapping his foot to this one. The album closes with the sensual *Do You Dance* which is excellent played good and loud, and the introspective *Man Out of Time* which has all kinds of tasteful layers to excite the ears.

I'll admit to being pleasantly surprised by this album and not even in ways I was expecting. It's damn catchy and memorable to boot".

Sam71:"The snake-like rhythms and melodies sent shivers down my spine – and Del's voice has much emotion and history. For me, this is a very romantic and male piece of music, and you get the impression that Del is being incredibly careful and hiding a lot of his real feelings behind these lyrics. But occasionally, he forgets himself, as on the last song on the album *Man Out of Time* – and speaks from his heart...

You're trying hard to seem as if you've never met me
I long to stay inside the moment that can not be
I'm twenty-one and you are seventeen
These things have always been

The last line is particularly sad, as is the whole album. The stand out tracks for me are *The Scheme of Things*, *Leap of Faith*, *A Love Song* and the amazing closing song, *Man Out of Time.* The range of musical styles and the crispness of the production are impressive – as is Del's voice, which evolves over the album; think Bryan Ferry on lead vocal, supported by David Bowie on backing vocals.

When I first heard the album it took me back to my childhood in the '70s. My uncles were all teenagers at the time and had converted our cellar into a den – all lava lamps, and Tibetan throws. They'd often have to babysit me and my siblings, and to keep us amused they'd play us their records: Floyd and Sabbath and so many others I've forgotten; we'd read Heinlein and Asimov – and colour in their comics when they weren't looking!

That den was a male-space, full of teenage romantic dreams, and this album would have fitted in perfectly. I think Del is a man out of time, and it must be difficult to deal with so many memories, both happy and sad on a first album, but I think he's done an amazing job.

It's not perfect but it's a fine début and maybe Del will feel a little more comfortable on his next record and open up a bit more. I'm really looking forward to hearing these songs performed live. There's a quality to the music, and the sadness of Del's singing which has really moved me."

Outees and Alternatives

Del continued to post alternative versions and out-takes from *Leap of Faith* on his Myspace space, and the reaction from fans led to this 5 track download EP of the bits that didn't make it to *Leap of Faith*, or at least not in the form that they appear there. The outakes were *Never Gonna Fall Again*, *The Wave* and *Your Beautiful Grey Eyes*. There were alternatives takes on *Dream* and *Man Out of Time*.

Gift

Del's second full solo album was released in December 2010 and we asked published poet and novelist Collin Kelley, a long time fan of Del's work to review it for us:

Collin: "The songs on Del Palmer's latest album, *Gift*, wouldn't sound totally out of place on a Steely Dan record or in Joni Mitchell's *Hissing of Summer Lawns* era. With its mélange of free-form jazz, prog rock and groovy guitars, there's much to appreciate in this record.

For those who only know Del as Kate Bush's engineer and musical partner in crime, *Gift* – even more so than his début, *Leap of Faith* – shows that this musician has his own voice and songwriting talents to share.

What I love most about *Gift* is that it sustains an atmosphere of introspection about love lost and found. There's plenty of 'space' on this album, with opportunities for Del and his band to explore different dimensions in individual songs. A big, shimmering guitar gives way to whispered vocals and discordant noodling. The album does have a '70s vibe about it, and I'm okay with that. We've had new artists revisiting the '80s for far too long and there's still plenty of synthesis to be found.

Wendy opens the album with its Ry Cooder-inspired twang (imagine Harry Dean Stanton wandering out of the desert in Wim Wenders' *Paris, Texas*) and builds to a slow-rock ballad. The Steely Dan comparison is most noticeable on *Rhythm No. 6* with its jazzy, swirling keyboards and layered vocals ("When you took my hand, my resolve started to crumble") with an assist by the Angelmatic Singers.

The title track features Del's most expressive vocal – upfront and edgy – counterbalanced by I.V. Webb's softer, plaintive vocals admonishing her man for "playing around with her heart." The middle of the song goes quiet, with voices buried deep in the mix that did remind me of *The Ninth Wave* side of Kate's *Hounds of Love*.

Shared Rituals features a delicate solo piano accompanied by I.V. Webb and Del's shared vocals and is probably the most 'Kate Bush-sounding' track on the album. When Del sings, "You never knew what you had 'til it's gone, it tears you up to hear the truth," it's a poignant reminder that love and its vagaries can weigh heavy on the heart.

Farsi Girl has a music box meets Middle Eastern flavor, with big percussive beats courtesy of Wilton Beckford, who is excellent across the entire album. *Every Breath We Take* opens with a ticking clock and voice messages from an answer phone in French, before you hear Del take a quivering sigh and the piano begins. "Every word we speak, brings us one word nearer to the time when no words are needed anymore." It's a beautiful, simple melody and one of Del's best vocals.

My favorite track is *Dancer*, the six-minute plus song that closes the album, with its spacey keyboard track that builds in urgency as Del's guitar joins the mix. This is also Del's best vocal on the album, a synthesis of classic and modern rock. "Don't worry about your heart, I will hold it in my hand," he sings in the chorus.

I first listened to *Gift* in my car. There's something about the guitars that make it excellent driving music, especially if you're driving around examining your own heart.

And ...?

There are other tracks – Del's solo version of *Watching You Without Me* for example which you can hear if you go to his MySpace page. We expect there will be more to come and we expect to enjoy it.

was involved in a serious road accident. This he fortunately survived but could not play for some years. So, enter Charlie Morgan.

"Charlie was the first drummer we auditioned early in 1974 but we went on to try out a further eight or so others before we decided to give him the gig. We added another guitarist/vocalist and changed our name to Conkers. In those days it was all glam and daft names. Charlie would later be involved in the early stuff we did with Kate. He would go on to become a very respected drummer doing numerous tours and albums as Elton John's kit-man.

"One of the interesting things we did was a residency backing a soul vocal band called The Majestics. They were three great singers from America one of which was Clarke Peters, the actor. This was great for us young musicians as we had to learn a whole set and routine to back them up. This involved chart reading and reacting to vocal and musical cues given to us by the singers. This was a great time and very educational.

"We played loads of gigs including spots at London venues like the Marquee in Wardour street. A few singles followed from our then record company, Cube Records, all of which bombed. There followed a few years of covers bands and general fun until the meeting with Kate Bush in February of 1977".

Photo: Krys

Graphic overleaf: Steven Brown

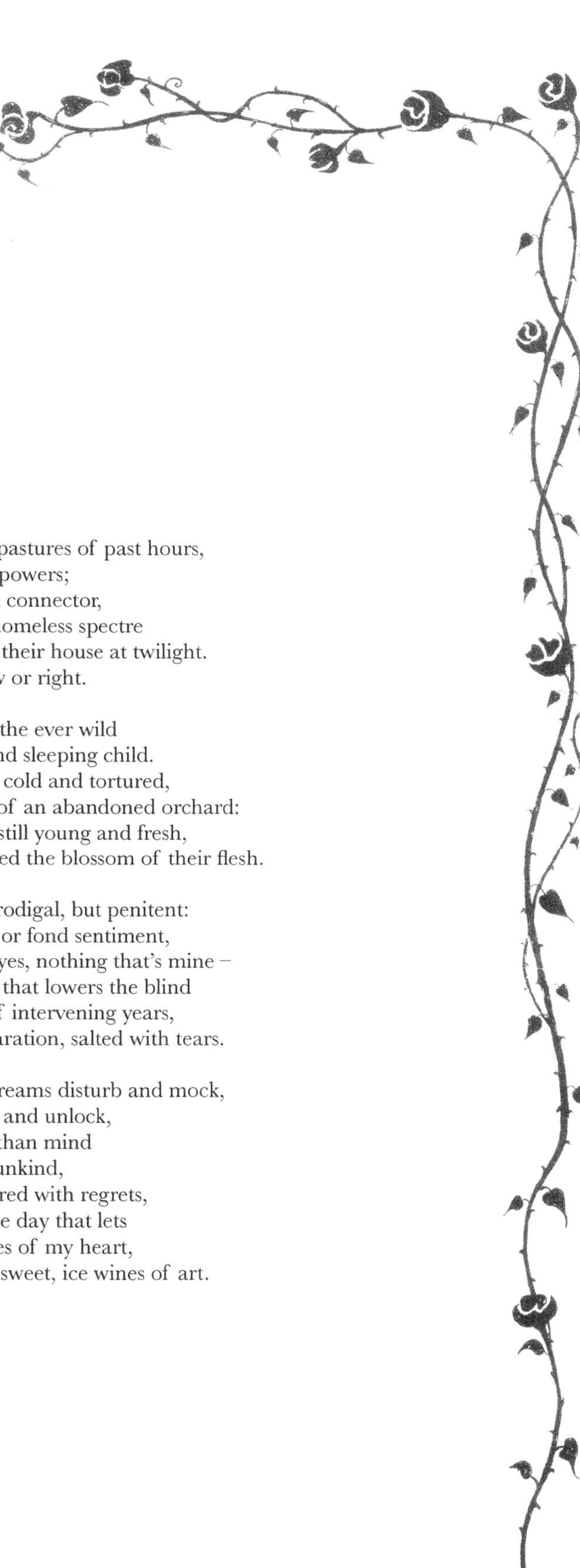

The Sweet Ice Wines

John Carder Bush

In night-dreams I crop the pastures of past hours,
Past places, past faces, past powers;
But I am as now, the dream connector,
A futuristic visitor, an old, homeless spectre
Moving like smoke-rings in their house at twilight.
No longer there by love, law or right.

I wisp around their beauty, the ever wild
Passion of young mother and sleeping child.
They are not as I left them, cold and tortured,
Fruit frozen on the boughs of an abandoned orchard:
No one has aged, faces are still young and fresh,
Experience has not yet dotted the blossom of their flesh.

In these dreams I am not prodigal, but penitent:
For me, no happy welcome or fond sentiment,
No sharing of joy in their eyes, nothing that's mine –
In this dream view of time, that lowers the blind
To shut out the grey light of intervening years,
There's only the cut of separation, salted with tears.

But, however much these dreams disturb and mock,
At the same time, they ease and unlock,
Healing something deeper than mind
That lies beyond kind and unkind,
So that, even if I wake blurred with regrets,
Later, there is a clarity in the day that lets
Me accept the frosted grapes of my heart,
Lets me turn them into the sweet, ice wines of art.

Pour the Absinthe

Antonello Saeli

Don't speak,
Just fill the glass
And let the night come in

Pour the absinthe
And rest your head
On this empty table

Give me your hand
And gently kiss goodbye
To this world of ours

Come with me
Let's cross the dreadful border
And leave the rest behind

Don't be afraid
There's nothing here to fear
The mists will shroud us in

Just pour the absinthe
And rest your heavy head
Upon my shoulder, dear

Don't speak,
Just fill the glass
And let the night come in

The Last Post

...The final HomeGround post bag

Winston David Hughes: I first came across Kate Bush when I was ten years old. My brother came home one night with *The Single File* VHS and I became fascinated by the woman I was watching on screen. After this, I would borrow my brother's records and lay in a dark bedroom letting my mind be taken on strange journeys to Egypt and under the ice.

I've suffered depression from a very young age and Kate's music has helped so much. It allowed me to escape a world I felt didn't understand me and while I didn't always understand the lyrics (I was only ten!) I was always moved by them and felt them in a way I couldn't explain.

It's now 25 years later and Kate's music is still a major part of my life and without being dramatic, kept me alive and I'm thankful to her for that. I was going through one of the worse bouts of depression in my life and the run up and release of *50 Words For Snow* helped me. The dark bedroom has been replaced by a candle lit lounge and many cigarettes but the importance of her music in my life is still the same.

You may be wondering why I've decided to write this short letter of the importance on Kate Bush in my life. I think the main reason would be that I've only just become aware of the large fan base that is out there and wanted to express myself to somebody who would understand; I've felt alone in my love of her. My brother lost interest come the end of the '80s.

A huge thank you for running a wonderful fan site, I just wish I had known about you when you first started to publish.

Svein V. Eilevstad: It has been such an amazing thrill to follow you during the years. It's quite sad that the good old paper is leaving the building, but I hope you will find time to keep working on the concept electronically to gain some kind of deeper understanding :)

The new album is astonishing, it's perfect to wait for the Christmas snow here in Norway (still just rain and stormy weather) while listening to these atmospheric, lovely, haunting songs, the organic beauty and dreamlike sadness – it all seems so natural, like the album has always been there in some far away dimension, in between the rail-road tracks and the trees and the icy water where we used to skate back then, when things were easier and the days went on and on. Kate Bush is one of a kind, a truly remarkable artist indeed, ever expanding.

Gerard: I thought you might like to know that I teach kids aged between 10 and 12 here in Tasmania. Every morning before we start work I put on some music to let them know to sit at their desks, get organised, etc.

Last week I played the title song from Kate's latest opus every single day. The responses from my students have been stupendous. Their smiling faces when the song comes on, counting with Kate, even knowing some of Mr Fry's words in the right order (they love "ankle breaker"), and singing along with Kate in the choruses. For 21st century Aussie kids with no real knowledge of Kate's music, I find this overt response really amazing.

Chris Chamberlain: Have you heard of the KT Boundary Event? It refers to that Deathrock that, by a billions-to-one chance, killed the dinosaurs, between the Cretaceous and Tertiary periods. Leaving us to evolve along with a layer of iridium. We've lived to see the KT Album Event! The billions-to-one change that TWO great Kate Bush albums come flying out of the blue at us. After long ages of pooh-poohing the likelihood of any such thing. So what do all we old dinosaurs evolve into, is what I want to know?

Martin Purser: Really looking forward to the last printed issue of *HomeGround*, but I have a slight feeling of sadness that this will be the last one in print after all these years, but times have changed too much, and things move on! I cannot believe the beauty of *50 Words For Snow*, is this Kate's best work? I'm really starting to feel so.

Jan Millington: I went on to the KateBushNews site last night and read about your plans for *HomeGround*. I totally understand. It's been a labour of love for 30 years. Congratulations and drinks all round for the work you've put into it. You kept going when other fanzines went down, kept Kate fans in touch, encouraged us all to write.

Just like Kate has done, we've all got on with our lives – now you're doing the same. And yet. And yet, I read this news and felt really sad. It marks the end of an era doesn't it? You enabled that community of Kate fans to come together and share thoughts and feelings in a world that's long-gone, or is in the process of going, and I'm aware that's one of the reasons why I feel sad. Kate herself comes from that world, as do I – she's a year younger than me, and as we read over and again, her music resonates with things in our lives. And because Kate and I are so close in age I feel a connection to that, despite our massive differences in geography and background – and that other thing, her incredible musical talent! *HomeGround* is a part of that connection with Kate – but also because you've been there so long, as part of my life.

Kate's songs trace a time-line for me and for so many of us. And because *HomeGround* was there – well, *you* were there! – with that opportunity to share our thoughts and feelings about Kate's music within the magazine's pages. *HomeGround* too is part of my time-line and a part of my memories and history. I know the world has changed – the internet is here and we can look up anything. I felt connected to the *HomeGround* community and felt that Krys and Peter and Dave were friends, 'cos they shared so much of their lives with us.

And I still feel really sad. Because something which was a marker in my life, something that arrived through my letterbox and brought me into that community of people will be gone. And I will miss it. I will miss you. When I got *HomeGround* you came to my house! I shall miss the personal touches: the jokes (even the in-jokes I didn't get!), the fabulous photos and artwork: the wonderful articles. But more, I'll miss the connection to my steam-driven, photocopied, Letrasetted, DIY world of my past, of my youth. The end of *HomeGround* as a magazine *really is* the end of an era. And I'd like to say a massive thank you for keeping it going for all these years and bringing me much laughter, much thoughtfulness, and much love.

Gavin Gribbon: As it's your last physical issue, I thought I'd send you a 'physical' letter. I can't say I'm totally surprised as a closing of a particular chapter appears to have happened gradually over the past few years. Kate has now, successfully I think, reduced her profile to just 'the work', something she seems to have been heading towards for many years. Given that and the profusion of the web, the need and material required for such a magazine has inevitably diminished. But... oh, the twinge of nostalgia it gave me when I read the announcement! I suppose I am now one of your 'old lags' in subscription terms. First picked up a copy in HMV (number 28) and then began subscribing (got a lovely letter from Sharon). I have always really enjoyed the mixture of factual and fictional material – Krys' mysterious and erotic fiction.

Apart from the odd letter, I never really felt qualified enough to contribute much but I think the aspect of the magazine I will always treasure is that it felt like a family – there was great warmth and humour in it and whenever I received an issue through the post, it felt like a letter from friends.

I really can't emphasise enough how much *HomeGround* has meant to me over the years. Even though we've never met, I sort of feel like I know you mainly because of how much of yourselves you put into it. Interestingly enough, since I read the announcement, it's not a Kate line that comes to mind but a Beatles one:

"*And in the end, the love you take,*
is equal to the love you make"

HomeGround to me was all about love; love for Kate, love for her music, love for each other. You've put a lot of love out into the world and for that, I for one, thank you and send some back to you.

Graphic: Steven Brown

Imitations of Grief in Winter

John Carder Bush

Like the grain that makes the pearl,
Each snowflake embraces its core
Then disappears on the kitchen floor.
The old, familiar table begins to whirl
As we gaze at its centre, and contrive
To make the dead again alive.

Around this table were solved
Money problems, problems of the heart,
New ways to end, new ways to start.
From children to parents we all evolved,
Staring at its tea-stained wood
As we pondered shouldn't and should.

Beyond the window the snow see-saws down,
In the centre of the table a candle flame
Has become the wild horse mane
We hang on to, and the fiery crown,
Fuelled by our deepening dread,
Our last link to the newly dead.

Outside, the six sided flowers of snow
Touch my eyes and turn to brine
As ice and salt kiss and combine.
But the tears that rise and flow
Are only imitations of this cruellest grief,
Cold and sharp and mercifully brief.

So Beautiful

Antonello Saeli

The cornfields
In the distance
A sea of green and gold
Your barefoot dance
By the lake
Of the dream-like memories
And that smile of yours
So real and beautiful
So real and beautiful

Afterwords

"Among Angels"

We remember these *HomeGround* friends and contributors of special memory who are no longer with us:

Sarah-Jane Mackenzie, Paul Gardener, Jonathan Coram, Mike Weaver, Pete Sweetman, Jim Marris, Dave Waight, and Rachel Lisi.

"*These moments given are a gift from time*"

Krys: Who'd've thought thirty year ago we'd be sat sitting here drinking West End Shiraz?
Peter: Aye!
Dave: Aye!
Peter: Aye! I remember when we used t'make fanzine from pages printed out from't DTP mode of Wordstar for Windows and at least it got 'eadings straight!
Krys: Aye!
Dave: Straight 'eadings? You were lucky! We used to use Letraset and judge straightness of't'headings by eye, or not depending on how much tea we'd 'ad!
Peter: Aye!
Krys: Letraset? We used to dream of Letraset! We cut headlines out of old copies of T' *Manchester Guardian* – or was it t'*Times* or t'*Yorkshire Post* – and stick them in using cat spit.
Dave: Luxury! We made fanzine from old disused pieces of Pinnacle Records notepaper and paste made from flour and water with articles written on old manual typewriter and write headlines in fountain pen and I used to draw amoebas and zigzags and whatnot to fill up column lengths and it was photocopied and stapled together till hands were raw and handed out to anyone passing-by...
Seán: *And you tell the youngsters of today that and we'll never believe you!*

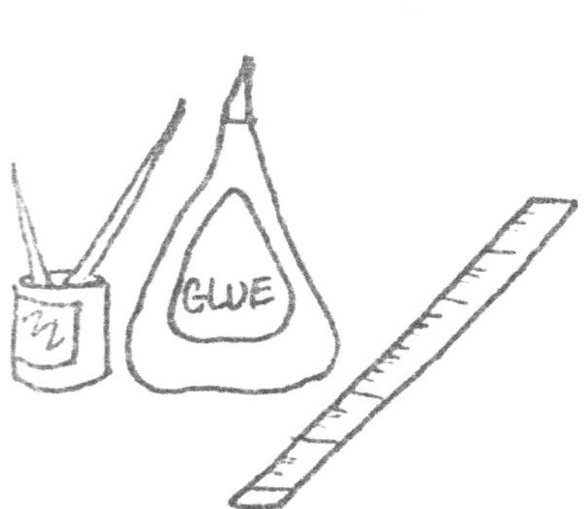

With profound apologies to Peter Blake. The original photo was taken at The Beatles Convention in 1988, where we went to gather ideas for the 1990 Kate Bush Convention.

Index of Contributors

...those who provided reviews, articles, stories, letters, questions, and answers

Index of Artwork

...those who provided drawings, paintings, cartoons, and graphics

Index of Poems

...an important part of HomeGround from early issues

Our grateful thanks are due to:

Dr. Robert and Mrs. Hannah Bush ever remembered with love, our first supporters, for their friendship and encouragement

John Carder Bush and Paddy Bush for friendship and inspiration

Del Palmer for friendship and support

Lisa Bradley for friendship, and the Spinal Tap moments

Mandy Knott our friend and founder Editor who went on to make her special contribution elsewhere

Olive – Peter's mum – who for many years was effectively the *HomeGround* admin staff

Seán Twomey whose enthusiasm and sense of humour is limitless

Debi Bowes who over the years provided *HomeGround* with her beautiful artwork

Sharon Frankum for her friendship, company, and many, many letters written

Lionel Sharon for friendship, enthusiasm and being the body double for Jeremy Birchington

Steven Brown and Paulina Stuckey-Cassidy whose beautiful artwork enhances these volumes, Peter Pracownik who drew the *HomeGround* logo used herein, and Neil Sheriff, Michele Ann, and Izabela Samsonowicz for additional artwork

Rob Assenberg, Paul Camilleri, Jules R. Angel, Paul Thomas, and Robert Brown for photos

EMI generally, and in particular Steve Davis, David Munns, Paul Baines, Jill Wall, Dwayne Welch, Ian Ramage, and Amanda Knight

Chris Stone, Elaine Davis and Lorne Hamilton for all their help with conventions and Dale Somerville for his timely gift

Spaceboy – you know why, and Dave Colwell at Freedman Brothers Printers

Jeremy Robinson, at Crescent Moon Publishing, whose idea this compilation was, and who made many good suggestions

Guy Pearce, Judie Tzuke, Beck Siàn, Roy Harper, and Colin Lloyd Tucker who gave us their time

Our families and friends for their help and support, and especially Dave's brother, Mike

Andrew Marvick, Doug Alan, Vickie Mapes, Chris Williams: Love-Hounds

Kevin and Mary Hendryx: Lone Star Lionhearts

That band of fans from all over the world whose constant encouragement in the early days – and later – kept us going. In addition to those mentioned above: Keith Pitches, Adrian Durrant, Keith Farrier, Pete Fisher, Tom Mair, Jim Kennedy, David Wainwright, Mark Pittaway, Alan Paterson, Amanda Dixon, Andy Beard, Krystyna Boswell, Kate Forbes-Pitt, Malcolm G. Fisher, Pami Gill, Debra Clark, Jon Bishop, Conny Eley, Helen Taylor, Alan Codd, Peter Forbes, Anthony Entwisle, Steve French, Steve the Duck, Anthony Jeffries, Stephen Humphreys, Veronica Ongley, Chris Chamberlain, Dawn Wilbraham, Donna Clifton, John Beaumont, Rob Reaney, David Butler, William Turner, Mel Cansell, Kerry McDaniel, Graham Cole, Jan Millington, Steve Nobes, Andy Blake, Neil Mooney, Sue and Ian Crowther, Julie and Ian Park, Andy Beckett, Anne Eames, Anthony Jakymiw, Bob MacReady, Martin Purser, Kevin Hall, Amanda Harrold, Colette Graham, Lisa Oliver, Mo Maclean, George McClellan, Mark Binmore, Bradley Brady, Chris Butler, Gavin Gribbon, Darrell Babidge, Mike Wade, Ian McLauchlan, Kyla Clay-Fox, Pekka Hiltunen, Jaako Nousiainen, Svein Eilevstad, Jan-Erik Svensson, Gillian Gaar, Gabriella Patterson, Ernie Heramia, Hugh Maher, Len Bullard, Ed Suranyi, Donna Kile, Antonello Saeli, Collin Kelley, Allen Hembrow, Garry Williams, Carmel Votano, Takashi Kasai, Noriko Takahashi, Edoardo Seianis, Theo Haast, Willem Doornkamp, Ger Traets, Edwin Pauptit, Chris Schalkwijk, Roland Gofflot, Marc Laurent, Stephane Blanc, Fanch Oriant, and all the other Kate fans over the years from all over the world, who never gave us a problem in finding stuff to put in *HomeGround*, but always the far more difficult one of what to leave out.

*... **And of course Kate, without whom our lives would have been utterly different***

Credits

Covers of Kate's singles, albums and videos, and stills from promotional videos and from *The Line, The Cross & the Curve* variously Kate Bush Music, Noble & Brite

Pete Still for use of the photo from first Kate Bush Club convention.

We have done our best to properly credit all written work, artwork, and photographs used. Inevitably we have used some photos whose provenance remains unknown despite our best endeavours to track their origins.

If there are any errors in credit, or additional information as to authorship, please let us know and we will make corrections in future editions of this book

Acknowledgements

Jeremy Robinson first made contact with us to suggest this anthology in August 2008. We thought it would take us "about six months" to put it together, which brought a knowing smile to his face. It actually took over five years.

In fact, it took *so* long to do this book that Kate had released two albums and various singles in the meantime, *and* we got out the final print issue of *HomeGround.*

When we started, we had to assemble the best part of three decades of more or less properly stored archives. In order to liberate material from the earliest issues we scanned as far as it was possible to do that, but the rough state of some early issues, and some odd typefaces we used later meant a lot of material had to be retyped, and we must thank Ian McLauchlan, Rebecca Anderson, Kathleen O'Rourke, and Lesley Sharp for their assistance with that.

When we started laying out the pages, it was soon evident that we would finally have to dump our beloved Wordstar for Windows with which *HomeGround* had been produced from 1997's issue 59. We did consider the major DTP programmes, but instead went with Openoffice.org which in the course of time has become Apache Open Office. Every page of these volumes has been laid out on that open-source programme which we cannot recommend too highly.

It has been an emotional journey revisiting thirty years of our collective lives.

Opposite we have thanked those who provided the material of the book.

Here we would like to thank those who supported us over that time and through that journey. Seán Twomey of course, Ann Hall, Lauren Cutler, Donna Kile, Diane Connell, and Krystyna Boswell. Jeanette Payne for timely advice. Beck Sìàn for encouragement and her wonderful sense of fun. Kate Forbes-Pitt for solidarity. The Bugs (they know who they are and where they live), and Bumble, Jack, Mooey and Pippimouse, who at various times thought we had left home.

Monty Python, Spinal Tap, Billy Connolly, Eddie Izard, Victoria Wood, Black Sadder, Father Ted,, and Bette Midler for keeping us going in the early hours.

Finally we were encouraged throughout the preparation of this anthology by the readers of *HomeGround.* These pages are a record of all our lives.

About HomeGround....

HomeGround was started in 1982 and more than thirty years on, is run now, as then, independently of any official fan organisation or record company. Our aim is to provide a service of news and information about Kate and her music, and to provide a platform for review and discussion of Kate's work on a world-wide basis.

You can contact *HomeGround*: **hgtowers@btinternet.com**

The "regular" production of the print magazine ceased with issue 79, but *HomeGround* as an entity is not going to disappear; in fact, we've been busier than ever working on this book and greatly increasing our presence and involvement at KateBushNews.com – our home on the internet. Our aim will be to publish special issues of the magazine at appropriate times such as album releases, in download format.

Back Issues Special Offer

We still have back issues of some of the original print magazines. For the contents of these back issues please see the *HomeGround* page on KateBushNews.com.

Our most plentiful back issues are **50, 52, 55-59, 60-63, 66-69, 70-75 and 78**. Issue 79 is now sold out.

We have limited numbers of issues **51, 53, 54, 64, 65, 76 and 77** .

We very few left of issues **44, 45, 47, 48, and 49**.

You can purchase these special offers with the Paypal buttons on the *HomeGround* page at KateBushNews.com

CRESCENT MOON PUBLISHING

web: www.crmoon.com e-mail: cresmopub@yahoo.co.uk

ARTS, PAINTING, SCULPTURE

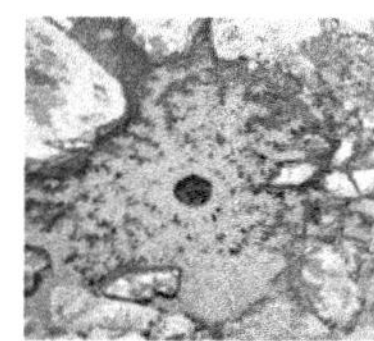

The Art of Andy Goldsworthy
Andy Goldsworthy: Touching Nature
Andy Goldsworthy in Close-Up
Andy Goldsworthy: Pocket Guide
Andy Goldsworthy In America
Land Art: A Complete Guide
The Art of Richard Long
Richard Long: Pocket Guide
Land Art In the UK
Land Art in Close-Up
Land Art In the U.S.A.
Land Art: Pocket Guide
Installation Art in Close-Up
Minimal Art and Artists In the 1960s and After
Colourfield Painting
Land Art DVD, TV documentary
Andy Goldsworthy DVD, TV documentary
The Erotic Object: Sexuality in Sculpture From Prehistory to the Present Day
Sex in Art: Pornography and Pleasure in Painting and Sculpture
Postwar Art
Sacred Gardens: The Garden in Myth, Religion and Art
Glorification: Religious Abstraction in Renaissance and 20th Century Art
Early Netherlandish Painting
Leonardo da Vinci
Piero della Francesca
Giovanni Bellini
Fra Angelico: Art and Religion in the Renaissance
Mark Rothko: The Art of Transcendence
Frank Stella: American Abstract Artist
Jasper Johns
Brice Marden
Alison Wilding: The Embrace of Sculpture
Vincent van Gogh: Visionary Landscapes
Eric Gill: Nuptials of God
Constantin Brancusi: Sculpting the Essence of Things
Max Beckmann
Caravaggio
Gustave Moreau
Egon Schiele: Sex and Death In Purple Stockings
Delizioso Fotografico Fervore: Works In Process 1
Sacro Cuore: Works In Process 2
The Light Eternal: J.M.W. Turner
The Madonna Glorified: Karen Arthurs

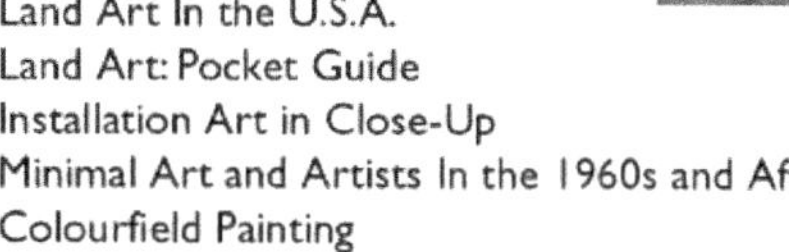

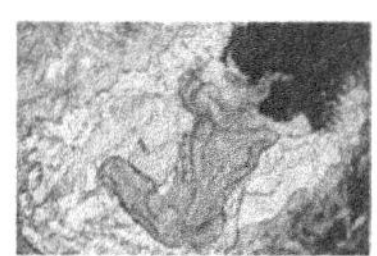

LITERATURE

J.R.R. Tolkien: The Books, The Films, The Whole Cultural Phenomenon
J.R.R. Tolkien: Pocket Guide
Tolkien's Heroic Quest
The *Earthsea* Books of Ursula Le Guin
Beauties, Beasts and Enchantment: Classic French Fairy Tales
German Popular Stories by the Brothers Grimm
Philip Pullman and *His Dark Materials*
Sexing Hardy: Thomas Hardy and Feminism
Thomas Hardy's *Tess of the d'Urbervilles*
Thomas Hardy's *Jude the Obscure*
Thomas Hardy: The Tragic Novels
Love and Tragedy: Thomas Hardy
The Poetry of Landscape in Hardy
Wessex Revisited: Thomas Hardy and John Cowper Powys
Wolfgang Iser: Essays and Interviews
Petrarch, Dante and the Troubadours
Maurice Sendak and the Art of Children's Book Illustration
Andrea Dworkin
Cixous, Irigaray, Kristeva: The *Jouissance* of French Feminism
Julia Kristeva: Art, Love, Melancholy, Philosophy, Semiotics and Psychoanalysis
Hélene Cixous I Love You: The *Jouissance* of Writing
Luce Irigaray: Lips, Kissing, and the Politics of Sexual Difference
Peter Redgrove: Here Comes the Flood
Peter Redgrove: Sex-Magic-Poetry-Cornwall
Lawrence Durrell: Between Love and Death, East and West
Love, Culture & Poetry: Lawrence Durrell
Cavafy: Anatomy of a Soul
German Romantic Poetry: Goethe, Novalis, Heine, Hölderlin
Feminism and Shakespeare
Shakespeare: Love, Poetry & Magic
The Passion of D.H. Lawrence
D.H. Lawrence: Symbolic Landscapes
D.H. Lawrence: Infinite Sensual Violence
Rimbaud: Arthur Rimbaud and the Magic of Poetry
The Ecstasies of John Cowper Powys
Sensualism and Mythology: The Wessex Novels of John Cowper Powys
Amorous Life: John Cowper Powys and the Manifestation of Affectivity (H.W. Fawkner)
Postmodern Powys: New Essays on John Cowper Powys (Joe Boulter)
Rethinking Powys: Critical Essays on John Cowper Powys
Paul Bowles & Bernardo Bertolucci
Rainer Maria Rilke
Joseph Conrad: *Heart of Darkness*
In the Dim Void: Samuel Beckett
Samuel Beckett Goes into the Silence
André Gide: Fiction and Fervour
Jackie Collins and the Blockbuster Novel
Blinded By Her Light: The Love-Poetry of Robert Graves
The Passion of Colours: Travels In Mediterranean Lands
Poetic Forms

POETRY

Ursula Le Guin: Walking In Cornwall
Peter Redgrove: Here Comes The Flood
Peter Redgrove: Sex-Magic-Poetry-Cornwall
Dante: Selections From the Vita Nuova
Petrarch, Dante and the Troubadours

William Shakespeare: Sonnets
William Shakespeare: Complete Poems
Blinded By Her Light: The Love-Poetry of Robert Graves
Emily Dickinson: Selected Poems
Emily Brontë: Poems
Thomas Hardy: Selected Poems
Percy Bysshe Shelley: Poems
John Keats: Selected Poems
Joh n Keats: Poems of 1820
D.H. Lawrence: Selected Poems

Edmund Spenser: Poems
Edmund Spenser: Amoretti
John Donne: Poems
Henry Vaughan: Poems
Sir Thomas Wyatt: Poems
Robert Herrick: Selected Poems
Rilke: Space, Essence and Angels in the Poetry of Rainer Maria Rilke
Rainer Maria Rilke: Selected Poems
Friedrich Hölderlin: Selected Poems

Arseny Tarkovsky: Selected Poems
Arthur Rimbaud: Selected Poems
Arthur Rimbaud: A Season in Hell
Arthur Rimbaud and the Magic of Poetry
Novalis: Hymns To the Night
German Romantic Poetry
Paul Verlaine: Selected Poems
Elizaethan Sonnet Cycles

D.J. Enright: By-Blows
Jeremy Reed: Brigitte's Blue Heart
Jeremy Reed: Claudia Schiffer's Red Shoes
Gorgeous Little Orpheus
Radiance: New Poems
Crescent Moon Book of Nature Poetry
Crescent Moon Book of Love Poetry
Crescent Moon Book of Mystical Poetry
Crescent Moon Book of Elizabethan Love Poetry
Crescent Moon Book of Metaphysical Poetry
Crescent Moon Book of Romantic Poetry
Pagan America: New American Poetry

MEDIA, CINEMA, FEMINISM and CULTURAL STUDIES

J.R.R. Tolkien: The Books, The Films, The Whole Cultural Phenomenon
J.R.R. Tolkien: Pocket Guide
The *Lord of the Rings* Movies: Pocket Guide
The Cinema of Hayao Miyazaki
Hayao Miyazaki: *Princess Mononoke*: Pocket Movie Guide
Hayao Miyazaki: *Spirited Away*: Pocket Movie Guide
Tim Burton : Hallowe'en For Hollywood
Ken Russell
Ken Russell: *Tommy*: Pocket Movie Guide
The Ghost Dance: The Origins of Religion
The Peyote Cult

Cixous, Irigaray, Kristeva: The *Jouissance* of French Feminism
Julia Kristeva: Art, Love, Melancholy, Philosophy, Semiotics and Psychoanalysis
Luce Irigaray: Lips, Kissing, and the Politics of Sexual Difference
Hélene Cixous I Love You: The *Jouissance* of Writing
Andrea Dworkin
'Cosmo Woman': The World of Women's Magazines
Women in Pop Music
HomeGround: The Kate Bush Anthology

Discovering the Goddess (Geoffrey Ashe)
The Poetry of Cinema
The Sacred Cinema of Andrei Tarkovsky
Andrei Tarkovsky: Pocket Guide
Andrei Tarkovsky: *Mirror*: Pocket Movie Guide
Andrei Tarkovsky: *The Sacrifice*: Pocket Movie Guide
Walerian Borowczyk: Cinema of Erotic Dreams

Jean-Luc Godard: The Passion of Cinema
Jean-Luc Godard: *Hail Mary*: Pocket Movie Guide
Jean-Luc Godard: *Contempt*: Pocket Movie Guide
Jean-Luc Godard: *Pierrot le Fou*: Pocket Movie Guide
John Hughes and Eighties Cinema
Ferris Bueller's Day Off: Pocket Movie Guide
Jean-Luc Godard: Pocket Guide

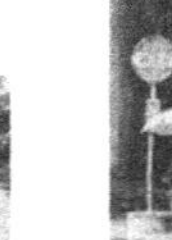

The Cinema of Richard Linklater
Liv Tyler: Star In Ascendance
Blade Runner and the Films of Philip K. Dick
Paul Bowles and Bernardo Bertolucci
Media Hell: Radio, TV and the Press
An Open Letter to the BBC
Detonation Britain: Nuclear War in the UK

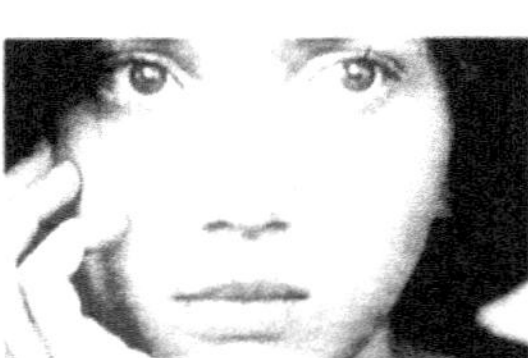

Feminism and Shakespeare
Wild Zones: Pornography, Art and Feminism
Sex in Art: Pornography and Pleasure in Painting and Sculpture
Sexing Hardy: Thomas Hardy and Feminism

The Light Eternal is a model monograph, an exemplary job. The subject matter of the book is beautifully organised and dead on beam. (Lawrence Durrell)
It is amazing for me to see my work treated with such passion and respect. (Andrea Dworkin)

CRESCENT MOON PUBLISHING
P.O. Box 1312, Maidstone, Kent, ME14 5XU, Great Britain. www.crmoon.com

cresmopub@yahoo.co.uk   www.crescentmoon.org.uk

www.ingramcontent.com/pod-product-compliance
Lightning Source LLC
Chambersburg PA
CBHW081400090726
47908CB00012B/2743

* 9 7 8 1 8 6 1 7 1 4 8 1 7 *